Lecture Notes
in Business Information Processing   437

More information about this series at https://link.springer.com/bookseries/7911

Marinos Themistocleous ·
Maria Papadaki (Eds.)

Information Systems

18th European, Mediterranean
and Middle Eastern Conference, EMCIS 2021
Virtual Event, December 8–9, 2021
Proceedings

Springer

Editors
Marinos Themistocleous (iD)
University of Nicosia
Nicosia, Cyprus

Maria Papadaki
British University in Dubai
Dubai, United Arab Emirates

ISSN 1865-1348   ISSN 1865-1356 (electronic)
Lecture Notes in Business Information Processing
ISBN 978-3-030-95946-3   ISBN 978-3-030-95947-0   (eBook)
https://doi.org/10.1007/978-3-030-95947-0

This Springer imprint is published by the registered company Springer Nature Switzerland AG
The registered company address is: Gewerbestrasse 11, 6330 Cham, Switzerland

Preface

The European, Mediterranean, and Middle Eastern Conference on Information Systems (EMCIS) is an annual research event addressing the discipline of information systems (IS) from a regional as well as a global perspective. During the last 18 years, EMCIS has successfully helped bring together researchers from around the world in a friendly atmosphere conducive to the free exchange of innovative ideas. EMCIS covers technical, organizational, business, and social issues in the application of information technology, and it is dedicated to the definition and establishment of IS as a discipline of high impact for IS professionals and practitioners. The conference focuses on innovative research of significant relevance to the IS discipline following sound research methodologies that lead to results of measurable impact.

The COVID-19 pandemic along with the travel bans, movement, and gathering restrictions issued by many governments, as well as the restrictions on individual mobility by many universities and organizations, led EMCIS 2021 to be held as an online event, which took place during December 8–9, 2021.

This year, we received 155 papers from authors in 36 countries from all continents. Poland led the table with the most submitted papers followed by Germany, South Africa, Cyprus, Greece, France, Portugal, UK, Australia, Tunisia, Italy, USA, UAE, Saudi Arabia, and others. All papers were submitted through the easyacademia.org online review system. Track chairs assigned reviewers and the papers were sent for double-blind review. The papers were reviewed by members of the international Program Committee and/or external reviewers. Track chairs submitted six papers and each of these papers was reviewed by a member of the EMCIS Executive Committee and a member of the Program Committee. The conference chairs submitted one paper in total which was reviewed by two senior external reviewers. Overall, 54 full papers were accepted for EMCIS 2021 (a 35% acceptance rate) in the following tracks:

- Big Data and Analytics (six papers)
- Blockchain Technology and Applications (eight papers)
- Cloud Computing (two papers)
- Digital Services and Social Media (seven papers)
- Digital Governance (four papers)
- Emerging Computing Technologies and Trends for Business Process Management (three papers)
- Enterprise Systems (one paper)
- Information Systems Security and Information Privacy Protection (five papers)
- Healthcare Information Systems (five papers)
- Management and Organizational Issues in Information Systems (ten papers)
- IT Governance and Alignment (one paper)
- Innovative Research Projects (two papers)

The papers were accepted for their theoretical and practical excellence and for the promising results they present. We hope that the readers will find the papers interesting and enjoy productive discussion that will improve the body of knowledge on the field of information systems.

December 2021   Marinos Themistocleous
                                                        Maria Papadaki

Organization

Conference Chairs

Maria Papadaki   The British University in Dubai, UAE
Marinos Themistocleous   University of Nicosia, Cyprus

Conference Executive Committee

Vincenzo Morabito   Bocconi University, Italy
(Program Chair)
Paulo da Cunha   Coimbra University, Portugal
(Program Chair)
Gianluigi Viscusi   Imperial College Business School, UK
(Publications Chair)
Nikolay Mehandjiev   University of Manchester, UK
(Public Relations Chair)

International Program Committee

Aggeliki Tsohou   Ionian University, Greece
Alan Serrano   Brunel University, UK
Andriana Prentza   University of Piraeus, Greece
Angeliki Kokkinaki   University of Nicosia, Cyprus
António Trigo   Coimbra Business School, Portugal
Carsten Brockmann   Capgemini, Germany
Catarina Ferreira da Silva   University Institute of Lisbon, Portugal
Celina M. Olszak   University of Economics in Katowice, Poland
Charalampos Alexopoulos   University of Aegean, Greece
Chinello Francesco   Aarhus University, Denmark
Demosthenis Kyriazis   University of Piraeus, Greece
Elias Iosif   University of Nicosia, Cyprus
Ella Kolkowska   Örebro University, Sweden
Euripidis N. Loukis   University of the Aegean, Greece
Federico Pigni   Grenoble Ecole de Management, France
Fletcher Glancy   Miami University, USA
Flora Malamateniou   University of Athens, Greece
Gail Corbitt   California State University, USA
Gianluigi Viscusi   Imperial College Business School, UK
Grażyna Paliwoda-Pękosz   Cracow University of Economics, Poland
Paweł Wołoszyn   Cracow University of Economics, Poland
Heidi Gautschi   IMD Lausanne, Switzerland
Heinz Roland Weistroffer   Virginia Commonwealth University, USA

Hemin Jiang	University of Science and Technology of China, China
Horst Treiblmaier	Modul University Vienna, Austria
Ibrahim Osman	American University of Beirut, Lebanon
Inas Ezz	Sadat Academy for Management Sciences, Egypt
Janusz Stal	Cracow University of Economics, Poland
Kamel Ghorab	Alhosn University, UAE
Karim Al-Yafi	Qatar University, Qatar
Klitos Christodoulou	University of Nicosia, Cyprus
Koumaditis Konstantinos	Aarhus University, Denmark
Lasse Berntzen	University of South-Eastern Norway, Norway
Leonidas Katelaris	University of Nicosia, Cyprus
Luning Liu	Harbin Institute of Technology, China
Małgorzata Pańkowska	University of Economics in Katowice, Poland
Manar Abu Talib	Zayed University, UAE
Marijn Janssen	Delft University of Technology, The Netherlands
Mariusz Grabowski	Cracow University of Economics, Poland
May Seitanidi	University of Kent, UK
Miguel Mira da Silva	University of Lisbon, Portugal
Milena Krumova	Technical University of Sofia, Bulgaria
Mohamed Sellami	Telecom SudParis, France
Muhammad Kamal	Coventry University, UK
Pacchierotti Claudio	University of Rennes, France
Paulo Henrique de Souza Bermejo	Universidade Federal de Lavras, Brazil
Paulo Melo	University of Coimbra, Portugal
Paulo Rupino Cunha	University of Coimbra, Portugal
Peter Love	Curtin University, Australia
Piotr Soja	Cracow University of Economics, Poland
Przemysław Lech	University of Gdańsk, Poland
Ricardo Jimenes Peris	Universidad Politécnica de Madrid, Spain
Sevgi Özkan	Middle East Technical University, Turkey
Slim Kallel	University of Sfax, Tunisia
Sofiane Tebboune	Manchester Metropolitan University, UK
Soulla Louca	University of Nicosia, Cyprus
Stanisław Wrycza	University of Gdansk, Poland
Steve Jones	Conwy County Borough Council, UK
Tillal Eldabi	Ahlia University, Bahrain
Vishanth Weerakkody	University of Bradford, UK
Wafi Al-Karaghouli	Brunel University London, UK
Walid Gaaloul	Telecom SudParis, France
Yannis Charalabidis	University of Aegean, Greece

Contents

Cloud Computing

Digital Governance

Digital Services and Social Media

Emerging Computing Technologies and Trends for Business Process Management

Healthcare Information Systems

Information Systems Security and Information Privacy Protection

Big Data and Analytics

Phi: A Generic Microservices-Based Big Data Architecture

Amine Maamouri[1]([⊠]) [ID], Lilia Sfaxi[2] [ID], and Riadh Robbana[2] [ID]

[1] Faculty of Mathematical, Physical and Natural Sciences of Tunis, University of Tunis El Manar, Tunis, Tunisia
amine.maamouri@fst.utm.tn
[2] National Institute of Applied Sciences and Technology, University of Carthage, Tunis, Tunisia
{lilia.sfaxi,riadh.robbana}@insat.ucar.tn

Abstract. We present in this paper Phi, a generic microservices-based Big Data architecture dedicated to complex multi-layered systems, that rallies multiple machine learning jobs, stream and batch processing. We show how to apply our architecture to an adaptive e-learning application that adjusts its recommendation to the emotions of the learner on the spot. We deploy our application on the cloud using AWS services, and perform some performance tests to show its feasibility in a realistic environment.

Keywords: Microservices · Big Data architecture · Cloud-native applications · DevOps practices · Performance evaluation

1 Introduction

The need for Big Data platforms and solutions is increasing for companies looking to get the best out of their data [15], but also for researchers [18]. These solutions tend however to be difficult to implement and to put into place due to their complexity and various needs, which is mainly due to the 4Vs characterizing the data: Volume, Velocity, Variety and Veracity [9]. Each one of these characteristics comes with a set of constraints that should be applied on the resulting platform, that are sometimes challenging to put in place. **Scalability** is one of the most pressing issues that should be addressed in a Big Data system, as the target platform needs to be able to adjust to the increasing volume of incoming data, as well as the increasing number of requests. The high velocity of the data creates a need for **Availability** of the platform, so that no precious data is lost due to bottlenecks or breakdowns. The variety of the data sources and the changing type of the data requires **Flexibility** in the storage systems. And finally, to insure the veracity of the processed data, the platform should insure **Data Quality**, as expected by the end users.

This project is carried out under the MOBIDOC scheme, funded by The Ministry of Higher Education and Scientific Research through the PromEssE project and managed by the ANPR.

M. Themistocleous and M. Papadaki (Eds.): EMCIS 2021, LNBIP 437, pp. 3–16, 2022.
https://doi.org/10.1007/978-3-030-95947-0_1

For a long time, Big Data applications were relying on monolithic systems for their stream layers [10], which tends to make their debugging and deploying a real hardship, especially if the requirements are evolving with time [17]. It is then crucial to choose the right architecture for these complex operations, that will help applying the previously mentioned Big Data constraints, while enabling an agile development process, as well as a smooth distribution of responsibilities between the members of the team. And the microservices architecture may turn out to be one the most appropriate styles that can insure all these properties.

A microservice is "a *small application that can be deployed independently, scaled independently, and tested independently and that has a single responsibility*" [19]. Microservices rely heavily on the notion of separation of concerns, where every service is an independently deployed process, where services are loosely coupled and where they exchange messages using lightweight communication channels. These particularities are well-suited with the Big Data constraints. In fact, using microservices enhances scalability, as each separate component or service can run on a separate server, and can therefore be independently scaled up or down, without interfering with the others [3]. They also insure availability, as separate services run in parallel, exploiting the available resources of each server, which increases the performance of the system. This separation can also insure that, even though one part of the system fails, the rest of the system can continue to run smoothly. The use of microservices can improve the data quality, as the system is easy to maintain thanks to the loose coupling and strong cohesion of the services, as well as the single responsibility principle, that makes tests easier to perform [7]. Two principles used in both microservices and Big Data are the *Polyglot Programming* [14] and the *Polyglot Persistence* [16], that encourage the use of multiple programming languages and several storage systems in the same application, in order to benefit from the advantages of each one of them. The separate processes in the microservices architecture helps apply these principles, as it is mostly recommended that each microservice keeps its data separate from the others, which helps when the need arises to choose separate storage types. This liberty insures the so-needed flexibility of the Big Data systems.

Based on this observation, we chose to rely on microservices as a basis for our Big Data architecture. We aim to design an architecture destined to complex real-time systems, that combines several types of processing to gain insight from heterogeneous data sources. Our architecture should be generic, applicable to any business domain, and configurable according to the needs of the end users. Even though several existing big data solutions based on microservices were defined in the literature [1, 5, 10, 13, 17, 25], most of these solutions target specific domains, and do not propose a generic solution for recurring problems. In fact, genericity is an important criteria, especially to enable the automation of the infrastructure and the definition of patterns [23]. Companies which set up Big Data applications in several business domains need to adopt a familiar approach, so that they are not bothered with needless specificities, and that the development and deployment of complex solutions becomes faster with time. On the other hand, the microservices architecture is part of the DevOps mindset, that relies heavily on key principles such as automation, containerization and cloud computing [20]. We aim in our solution to make the most out of these technologies.

We present in this work Phi, a Microservices-based Big Data architecture that is technology- and application-agnostic. The choice of the name Phi was made to continue with the tradition of using Greek letters for Big Data architectures. Aside from the fact that our architecture looks aesthetically like the letter φ, this letter also represents the golden ratio, known to "*have inspired thinkers of all disciplines like no other number in the history of mathematics*" [11], which represents nicely the concept of genericity we aim to address. Our contributions in this article are mainly:

- The design of a generic architecture that supports multiple machine learning algorithms, their training and real-time execution.
- The application of this architecture on a realistic use-case of an adaptive e-learning platform.
- A performance evaluation of the main components of the developed system.

2 Related Work

Nathan Marz [12] defined a big data processing architecture called Lambda. It was designed to take advantage of both batch and stream processing in order to handle a huge amount of data. Lambda is composed of three layers: a speed layer that ingests data sources, processes them and updates the speed views in the serving layer; a batch layer that runs a periodic processing over all the data and saves the views in the serving layer; and the latter, which is available to applications to query the results.

J. Kreps [8] invented the Kappa architecture to overcome the complexity of Lambda. It is based on the principle of merging the real-time and batch layer, which makes it less complex than the Lambda architecture. However, it does not allow permanent storage, making this architecture mainly suitable for online data processing.

These standard solutions were great inspirations for our work, especially when it comes to integrating multiple layers in the same application to handle its complexity and help with dividing the work among a heterogeneous team in a smooth way. However, we especially focus our literature review on the articles presenting Big Data platforms that rely on the Microservices architecture.

Miao et al. [13] present Qunxian, an online Big Data analysis platform for educational services that focuses on the integration of the Big Data and Data Science environments, as well as on the importance of teamwork and shared resources. It relies heavily on the use of collaborative solutions, such as Docker compose, Jupiter Hub and Spring Boot.

Singh et al. [17] propose a microservices-based reference model dedicated to knowledge discovery in Big Data. In this work, microservices are mainly used in data collection, and the solution provides a pipeline for machine learning model generation and visualization, but no streaming layer for real-time processing; as opposed to the work of Tserpes [21], who proposes *stream-MSA*, a model that proposes a microservices-based application pipeline that processes high frequency data streams.

Asaithambi et al. [1] created MOBDA, a service-driven approach which aim is to build an effective Big Data architecture for a smart-land transportation system using a hybrid model.

Zheng et al. [10] defined a microservices-oriented platform dedicated for internet of things big data applications that focuses on decoupling the data processing logic from computing resource management. They apply their solution in the specific cases of Monte Carlo Analytics and Convergence Analytics, thus failing to define a general architecture that can be applied to any use case.

Zhelev and Roseva [25] insist on the advantages of using microservices and event-driven architectures in a Big Data stream processing platform. They present very briefly an example of such a platform in the case of autonomous vehicles, without giving general-use recommendations or patterns that can be applied to other cases.

All of these solutions integrate microservices in their design in order to increase the scalability and extensibility of the Big Data application. However, most of them are very strongly related to a specific use case or a set of specific technologies, lacking therefore the needed genericity we are looking for. Besides, very few solutions combine a stream processing layer with a training and model generation layer.

3 Phi Architecture

Developing arbitrary functions to process an arbitrary data set in real time is not a trivial problem. To compute such functions, you have to use a variety of techniques and tools to create a complete Big Data system.

Phi Architecture is a multi-layered Big Data architecture designed to put together several complex processing procedures using microservices in order to solve a multi-paradigm problem. It helps organizing the developers' code into a set of decoupled modules, having each a specific objective, design and implementation, but which, coupled together, compose a rich application. Using a set of independent microservices has many advantages:

- *Enables a heterogeneous team to work together*. In fact, in a Big Data application, we are confronted with polyglot systems, which need many distinct expertise level: programming, database management, security, design, web and mobile development, system and network, etc. Our solution favours the separation of concerns for a better integration. In fact, the layers are loosely coupled and highly cohesive, which makes their development faster and their integration easier.
- *Makes the maintenance and problem detection easier*. Separation of concerns is the best way to help have a faster localization of failures.
- *Makes it possible to scale parts of the system, instead of all of it*. In fact, in a Big Data system, composed of different storage and processing systems, we do not always need to scale the whole system every time we have a performance problem. Dividing the system into modules enables scaling parts of the system independently from the other at production.
- *It is easy to reuse and replace modules*. Any development team should focus on making their system reusable and easily manageable. We can think of several applications that can use parts of our solution, and using a layered design helps easily reuse and replace any module we like.
- *Each module can be deployed in a different system*. In fact, the modules do not have the same needs in terms of hardware requirements. Some modules need a scalable storage, while others favor power processors or larger RAMs. Independent modules

can be deployed on different servers, which helps improve the overall behavior without needing to buy very expansive hardware.

- *Performance is enhanced*: Thanks to the power of parallelization, many heavy processing operations can take place at the same time and on separate physical infrastructures, which helps fully exploit the available resources.

Phi defines five layers that communicate with each other, as shown in Fig. 1[1].

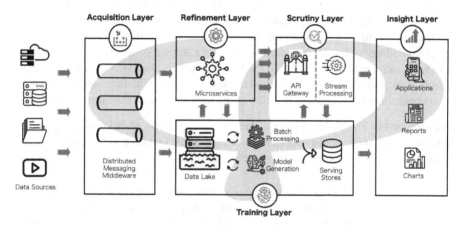

Fig. 1. Phi architecture

Acquisition Layer. The acquisition layer's objective is to collect data from the heterogeneous data sources, and to temporarily store them, in order to prevent any data loss, but also to direct them to their target storage or processing layers.

This layer can use a real-time streaming data pipeline or a full-fledged event streaming platform. During data transmission, the system stores each record in a data pipeline, consumed by the other components of the application. This method helps prevent the system from any data loss by playing the role of a buffer in case the application stops working or has a temporary lag.

Refinement Layer. The refinement layer takes as input raw data from the acquisition layer and transforms it into usable information to be transmitted to the following layers. These transformations can be as simple as data cleaning and mapping or as complex as extracting information using deep leaning models or heavy image processing jobs. The refinement layer is composed of several microservices working in parallel, each one of them responsible for the processing of part of the data coming from a defined source stream, ensuring in this case the scalability of this layer (as the number of components running in parallel can be increased on demand), but also its performance (as this layer insure co-locality of computation and data). Each component in the refinement layer will use its own storage system in order to locally save the results for faster processing.

---

[1] Icons made by https://www.flaticon.com/authors/pixel-perfect.

The same data are sent to the data lake in the Training layer to be used in the global processing. This technique will increase the performance of the system thanks to the principle of co-locality [4], while creating replicates for the data, thus improving its fault-tolerance.

Scrutiny Layer. Each one of the microservices in the Refinement Layer will generate results that need to be merged in real-time, in order to be aggregated and to produce a unified result. This is the main objective of the scrutiny layer: to consume the upcoming results from the refinement layer, and proceed with the processing of these data by coupling them with historical results if needed, or by using models generated by the Training layer. This is a real-time layer, used for jobs like prediction, recommendation or plain old filtering. Its results should be saved in a storage system to be reused later if necessary, and also sent in parallel to the Insight layer for display. An API Gateway is present at the entrance of this layer, which role is to abstract the functions provided by the microservices [24], group them, filter them, then send them to be processed.

Training Layer. The Training layer's objective is to perform global processing operations, including machine learning and model generation, that need to be provided to the stream layers. It mainly contains two types of storage:

- *Data Lake*: Used as a raw data storage, it contains all historic data, in their original form, before any processing. Keeping data as they were initially generated can be useful in case we need to add new functionalities to the system, but also to make sure that, even after the processing is made, we do not risk to lose any information we may need later. It is a scalable storage, that enables parallel processing algorithms to run directly on the data.
- *Serving Stores*: These are mainly databases containing processed data that can be used by other layers' jobs as input, or directly accessed for visualization.

These two types of storage enable data duplication, useful to perform analysis without disturbing the serving stores, thus providing a high availability level. All sorts of global high-latency tasks that require a visibility over the whole dataset can be performed, such as training algorithms or statistics extraction jobs. The batch processing jobs can either be performed periodically or on demand.

Insight Layer. The insight layer provides a user-friendly interface to be displayed to the users in order to show the results of the real-time processing coming from the Scrutiny layer, but also the globalized results found in the serving stores. It can be composed of a web application, an integrated dashboard, or even a sophisticated data visualization tool. It should be interactive, and highly dynamic to show in real-time the extracted knowledge.

We present in the following section how to apply Phi to a case study, in the form of an adaptive e-Learning application. This application is just a proof of-concept on how to apply Phi on a complex application composed of many processing layers. We will present in future works how to apply Phi on applications of completely different domains and technological stacks.

4 Case Study: Phi for an Adaptive e-Learning Application

4.1 Description of the Use Case

Due to the pandemic, learning has fundamentally changed. Most schools are adopting online learning all over the world. This new trend is proving to be efficient for information retention, which means that it may very well still be applied even after the disease is over [22]. This is why investing into intelligent e-Learning platforms is worth the effort, especially in this period.

Our target application is an Emotionally Intelligent Tutorial System, that simulates a human tutor with an emotional intelligence. This intelligence aims to improve the learning experience of a learner, by optimizing their cognitive capacities. Our system needs thus to be able to detect the emotions of the learner, and adapt its behaviour to reach the optimal emotional state.

In order to do this, our application needs to react, in real-time, to any change in the behaviour of the learner while he/she is taking the course, instead of just giving him/her a report or waiting for quiz results to react. To ensure this, we use facial recognition to analyze his/her emotions, thanks to videos taken by a webcam for example. This analysis is then coupled not only with information about the learner's activities on the platform (courses he/she's taking, quizzes he/she passed or failed, tutorials he/she started but did not finish, etc.), but also his/her personal information (age, place of birth, diploma, etc.). A recommendation algorithm is then run, to adapt the learning path to the preferences of the learner, depicted by his/her past behaviour as well as his/her emotions. For example, if the system detects that the learner is confused at some point in the course, it can suggest to direct him/her to another chapter or course explaining in more details the notions that were presented when this emotion is detected.

The system is then composed of the following components:

- A web application presenting a list of video tutorials organized by category. This is the main system that interacts with the end user, both to collect his information and interactions, and to give him/her back a response, in the form of a recommendation, a transcript, etc...
- A face and emotion recognition system, that reads the facial expressions of the learning while he/she is following the video, and extracts his/her emotions.
- A transcript generator, that will transform the sentences said in the video into text. This operation is useful in our process, as it helps easily detecting the subject presented in the course when the learner was confused.
- A real-time recommendation system, which represents the main component of our application. This system focuses on detecting changes in the facial expression of the learner (confusion, anger, boredom...), associating it to his/her information and previous history on the platform, and suggesting right away (in a non-intrusive way) another course or tutorial to consult.
- A static recommendation system, which works in the background, on a periodic basis, to look for adequate courses in the catalogue to present to the learner in his/her main page.

4.2 Data Stream

In order to adapt the learning path of a learner with his/her history and emotions, we rely on two main data streams, that can later be enriched with any data related to the learner's choices or preferences:

– *Learner metadata*: the metadata generated by the e-learning platform, which contains all the learner's data related to his/her previous and current courses.
– *Camera recordings*: After the agreement of the learner, the platform will start collecting camera recordings while he/she is following an online course.
– *Video tutorials*: These are the main video courses. These courses are stored in a separate extensible file system, and loaded as a video stream to be displayed and processed on the fly.

4.3 Architecture

The obtained architecture is represented in the Fig. 2[2]. All the deployment is done on the cloud using Amazon Web Services components.

Acquisition Layer. The acquisition layer captures the data flow such as user metadata and webcam recording using Amazon Kinesis, then saves the raw data in the Data Lake presented in the Training Layer. Simultaneously, it sends the same data to the refinement layer for pre-processing.

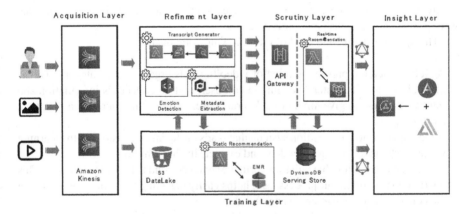

Fig. 2. The adaptive E-learning application

Refinement Layer. The refinement layer contains multiple components that refines and processes the data acquired from the acquisition layer. In our application, this layer has three main functions:

---

[2] Icons made by: https://aws.amazon.com/architecture/icons/.

- *Facial Emotion detection:* This component consumes real-time videos in order to detect the facial emotions of the learner while he/she is consulting the video tutorial on the platform. We use Amazon Rekognition Image for facial expression analysis.
- *Learner's metadata extraction:* This component captures all the activity of the learner, along with data about his/her profile. It transforms the collected data into a readable form in order to extract the necessary information. We use Amazon Cognito as an identity provider alongside a Lambda function to save our users metadata in the serving store, a DynamoDB table.
- *Transcript extraction:* For each video tutorial, we trigger two lambda functions. The first one is used to create a Transcribe Job that gets as input the video and processes it to extract the transcript. The second one is triggered by CloudWatch (the monitoring and observability service) to get the results and store them in an S3 bucket, our datalake.

Scrutiny Layer. The Scrutiny Layer implements the real-time recommendation algorithm, which is a content-based recommendation, that takes as input the detected emotion, the user metadata and the detected transcript, processes the data in order to make a decision about whether we should keep the pre-defined learning sequence, or change it. For example, if we detect that the learner is confused at some point in the lecture, the system is going to propose, instead of continuing with the following notion, to add more exercises, or to redirect him to another course or chapter that further explains that notion. Depending on the choice of the learner, the course can either be automatically adapted to his/her needs, or a suggestion is sent to him/her to jump to another section. In this part of the architecture, our main component is a lambda function that will generate recommendations to each specific learner based on his/her emotion. The lambda function is integrated to an API Gateway route, which is the rendez-vous point of the captured emotion, the transcript sentence in that instant and the course's ID. The recommendation results are stored in a DynamoDB database, accessible for future calls with GraphQL to get the recommendations history for a specific course's video.

Training Layer. This layer is composed of many distributed storage systems and databases. As a data lake, we choose Amazon S3, as it is designed to be highly fault-tolerant. It also provides a high-speed access to the data and is suitable for applications dealing with large and increasing datasets such as ours. As a serving store, we opt for DynamoDB, a key-value and document NOSQL database, known for its great scalability and elasticity.

The Training layer also groups all types of high-latency, periodic and globalized jobs. In our system, we implement two types of tasks: the course recommendation training algorithm (based on a pretrained model by google called *googlenews word2vec model*[3]) and any type of statistics job we want to perform on the collected raw data, such as the most successful courses, the rate of course completion, the variety of learners' profiles, etc. The training algorithms are pre-run with test data, but keep perfecting their results with the new data the system collects every day from the learners, as well as their inputs about their emotions and chosen path. In this layer we choose to use Amazon EMR as it can process a high volume of data in a distributed manner for a better performance and a fairer resource sharing.

---

[3] https://code.google.com/archive/p/word2vec/.

Insight Layer. The Insight Layer contains the main web application where the courses are displayed, and where the user interacts with the recommendation the system proposes. To implement the front-end, we use Angular. AWS Amplify is integrated into our application as a library, in order to provision some resources to the cloud and to let us access these resources using typescript code. We also use Amazon CloudFront, which is a fast content delivery network (CDN) service that provides data and APIs to clients with minimal latency. As an API, we chose to use GraphQL because of to its flexibility and ease of integration with multi-endpoint applications. In order to get the best out of our GraphQL web services, we use AWS AppSync, a fully managed service that helps develop GraphQL APIs while scaling the GraphQL engine up and down to meet the API request volumes.

4.4 DevOps Principles

As part of the DevOps practices, we integrated a continuous integration and deployment (CI/CD) pipeline that helps us develop and easily integrate new services and jobs. The use of Microservices helps implementing DevOps techniques thanks to their fine granularity and loose coupling [2]. The AWS Amplify Console allows us to deploy and host full-stack serverless web apps using a Gitbased process. Our Github repository is linked to Amplify Console, and every code commit triggers a single workflow that deploys updates to the application.

5   Evaluation

Performance tests were run on several components in our application in order to estimate the required execution time and the quality of results obtained. Our goal in this performance evaluation is to measure:

– The performance of the static and real-time recommendation systems.
– The read/write performance of the serving store.
– The scalability of the facial recognition module.
– The performance of GraphQL APIs.

Figure 3a presents the performance of the EMR cluster while handling the data of an increasing number of users. For this test, we vary the number of users between 3000 and 30000 and calculate the execution time which includes the time needed for starting, bootstrapping and terminating the cluster, and the time taken to train the Word2Vec Model. Currently, the used cluster is composed of one master node and two worker nodes. We notice that the time needed for the whole operation increases sharply beyond 9000 users, but remains below 2 h even with 30000 users. These values are reasonable, especially considering that the static recommendation is a periodic operation that takes place once a day (at 4am) on the background. The EMR cluster is also configurable, and we can increase the number of nodes on demand, thus improving considerably the execution time when needed.

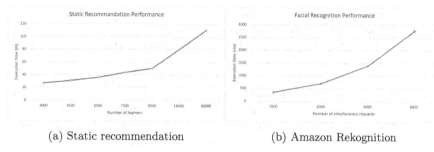

(a) Static recommendation   (b) Amazon Rekognition

Fig. 3. Performance evaluation

To test the performance of the real time recommendations, we used a tool called Artillery[4] which allows us to carry out load tests for HTTP APIs and web services. The duration of the test was 150 s, we launched 4144 scenarios and 12432 requests in total and we obtained the results shown in the Table 1.

Table 1. Real-time recommendation performance evaluation

Scenarios	Launched (nb)	4144
	Completed (nb)	4144
Requests	Completed (nb)	12432
	Mean Response/second	80,81
Response time (ms)	Min	789
	Max	29113
	Median	922
	p95	1391
	p99	29008
Response codes (nb)	200	12269
	504	163

We had a great and mostly stable performance with a minimum execution time of 789 ms and a median value of 922 ms with more than 95% of our launched requests finishing their execution in a time under 1391 ms. These results are very satisfying, as 2 s is considered to be the threshold for a website acceptability [6].

In the real-time recommendation pipeline, the facial emotion detection, using Amazon Rekognition, is the job that consumes the highest amount of time and resources. In order to estimate its performance, we run a test in which we vary the number of simultaneous requests and note the response times as shown in Fig. 3b. We notice that the obtained numbers are very acceptable, with less then one minute for up to 3000 simultaneous connections.

---

[4] https://artillery.io/.

We also run a performance test to estimate the read/write time of our serving store when the system is under stress. We simulated the use of the platform by 30000 simultaneous users for 24 h. DynamoDB could handle up to 80000 read/write requests at the same time without any loss, as shown in Fig. 4.

As for the performance of our GraphQL API, and thanks to AppSync, the API can receive up to 1000 queries per second before throttling, and the execution timeout is fixed to 30 s. In the case of our system, the API provides a median request execution time of 135 ms out of 4000 sent requests in total. On average, the end-to-end response time of AppSync GraphQL endpoints ranges from 100 ms, to 200 ms.

The performance evaluation made on our application shows that, for the right technologies and deployment choices, our architecture is able to support a complex application with acceptable execution times and a great scalability, thanks to its flexibility, configurability, and the separation of concerns of the layers and microservices.

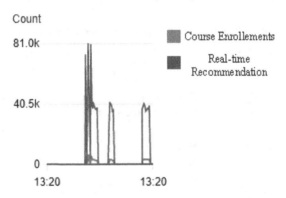

Fig. 4. DynamoDB performance evaluation over 24 h

6 Conclusion

In this research work, we designed a Big Data architecture called Phi that palliates some of the existing Big Data architectures' shortcomings by providing a flexible and scalable set of layers designed to run complex machine learning algorithms on huge data sets while providing real-time insights and recommendations. We applied this architecture to an adaptive e-learning use case, which aims to detect the emotions of the learner by analyzing his/her facial expressions in real-time and providing recommendations to adapt his/her learning path dynamically to his/her needs. We implemented this system using AWS components and deployed it on the cloud. We showed that our architecture helps obtaining very reasonable performance values for its main components, thanks to its flexible structure.

This application was developed in the context of a research project[5], which aims to help improve the online learning experience. We developed a first prototype in collaboration with other teams, responsible for the improvement of the machine learning algorithms' performance. We are currently applying our architecture on other use cases, particularly for a national research project we are currently working on, that aims to provide a solution to detect potential terrorist attacks in crowded public places.

Acknowledgements. This research was partially supported by AUF (Agence universitaire de la Francophonie) and Telnet Innovation Labs. We want to express our deep gratitude to our colleagues (Ms. Faten Chaieb, Ms. Meriem Chater and Ms. Aroua Hedhili) and students (M. Zakaria Naaija, M. Wael Rabah and M. Houssemeddine Kacemi) from INSAT who provided insight and expertise that greatly assisted the research.

References

1. Asaithambi, S.P.R., Venkatraman, R., Venkatraman, S.: MOBDA: microservice-oriented big data architecture for smart city transport systems. Big Data Cogn. Comput. **4**, 1–27 (2020). https://doi.org/10.3390/bdcc4030017
2. Balalaie, A., Heydarnoori, A., Jamshidi, P.: Microservices architecture enables devops: Migration to a cloud-native architecture. IEEE Softw. **33**(3), 42–52 (2016)
3. Furda, A., Fidge, C., Zimmermann, O., Kelly, W., Barros, A.: Migrating enterprise legacy source code to microservices: on multitenancy, statefulness, and data consistency. IEEE Softw. **35**(3), 63–72 (2018). https://doi.org/10.1109/MS.2017.440134612
4. Guo, Z., Fox, G., Zhou, M.: Investigation of data locality in MapReduce. In: 2012 12th IEEE/ACM International Symposium on Cluster, Cloud and Grid Computing (CCGRID 2012), pp. 419–426 (2012). https://doi.org/10.1109/CCGrid.2012.42
5. Gurtzick, T., Al-Sefou, S.: How we implemented (and secured) a big data microservices infrastructure - insideBIGDATA (2018). https://insidebigdata.com/2018/04/16/implemented-secured-big-datamicroservices-infrastructure/
6. Jordan, D.: Website response time standards (2018). https://www.websitepulse.com/blog/response-time-standards
7. Kiss, T., et al.: Micado—microservice-based cloud application-level dynamic orchestrator. Future Gener. Comput. Syst. **94**, 937– 946 (2019). https://doi.org/10.1016/j.future.2017.09.050, https://www.sciencedirect.com/science/article/pii/S0167739X17310506
8. Kreps, J.: Questioning the lambda architecture (2014). https://www.oreilly.com/ideas/questioning-the-lambda-architecture
9. Li, X., Zhang, F., Wang, Y.: Research on big data architecture, key technologies and its measures. In: Proceedings - 2013 IEEE 11th International Conference on Dependable, Autonomic and Secure Computing, DASC 2013, pp. 1–4. IEEE (2013). https://doi.org/10.1109/DASC.2013.28
10. Li, Z., Seco, D., Rodríguez, A.E.S.: Microservice-oriented platform for internet of big data analytics: a proof of concept. Sensors (Basel, Switzerland) **19**(5) (2019). https://doi.org/10.3390/S19051134, https://www.ncbi.nlm.nih.gov/pmc/articles/PMC6427148/
11. Livio, M.: The golden ratio: the story of PHI, the world's most AstonishingNumber. Crown (2008). https://books.google.tn/books?id=bUARfgWRH14C

---

[5] We will provide the details of the project if the paper is accepted, in order to respect the anonymity requirement of the conference.

12. Marz, N.: Big Data Principles and Best Practices of Scalable Real-Time Data Systems, vol. 53 (2013). https://doi.org/10.1017/CBO9781107415324.004
13. Miao, K., Li, J., Hong, W., Chen, M.: A microservice-based big data analysis platform for online educational applications. Sci. Program. **2020** (2020). https://doi.org/10.1155/2020/692 9750
14. Arun, M.: Polyglot programming. Int. J. Eng. Res. Technol. **3**(2) (2014). https://www.ijert. org/research/polyglotprogramming-IJERTV3IS20972.pdf
15. Papadopoulos, T., Singh, S.P., Spanaki, K., Gunasekaran, A., Dubey, R.: Towardsthe next generation of manufacturing: implications of big data and digitalization in the context of industry 4.0 (2021)
16. Schaarschmidt, M., Gessert, F., Ritter, N.: Towards automated polyglot persistence. In: Seidl, T., et al. (eds.) Datenbanksysteme für Business, Technologie und Web (BTW 2015), pp. 73–82. Gesellschaft für Informatik e.V., Bonn (2015)
17. Singh, N., Singh, D.P., Pant, B., Tiwari, U.K.: μBIGMSA-microservice-based model for big data knowledge discovery: thinking beyond the monoliths. Wirel. Pers. Commun. **116**(4), 2819–2833 (2020). https://doi.org/10.1007/s11277-020-07822-0
18. Sun, Z., Huo, Y.: The spectrum of big data analytics. J. Comput. Inf. Syst. **61**(2), 154–162 (2021). https://doi.org/10.1080/08874417.2019.1571456
19. Thönes, J.: Microservices. IEEE Softw. **32**(1), 116 (2015). https://doi.org/10.1109/MS.201 5.11
20. Trihinas, D., Tryfonos, A., Dikaiakos, M.D., Pallis, G.: Devops as a service: pushing the boundaries of microservice adoption. IEEE Internet Comput. **22**(3), 65–71 (2018). https://doi.org/10.1109/MIC.2018.032501519
21. Tserpes, K.: stream-MSA: A microservices' methodology for the creation of short, fast-paced, stream processing pipelines. ICT Express **5**(2), 146–149 (2019). https://doi.org/10.1016/j.icte.2019.04.001
22. World Economic Forum: The rise of online learning during the COVID-19 pandemic (2021). https://www.weforum.org/agenda/2020/04/coronavirus-education-globalcovid19-online-digital-learning/
23. Zepeda, S., Estrada, J., Estrada, D.: Generic software architecture for semantic and visual queries. In: 2019 6th International Conference on Systems and Informatics (ICSAI). pp. 1553–1558 (2019). https://doi.org/10.1109/ICSAI48974.2019.9010342
24. Zhao, J.T., Jing, S.Y., Jiang, L.Z.: Management of API gateway based on microservice architecture. J. Phys.: Conf. Ser. **1087**, 032032 (2018). https://doi.org/10.1088/1742-6596/1087/3/032032
25. Zhelev, S., Rozeva, A.: Using microservices and event driven architecture for bigdata stream processing. In: AIP Conference Proceedings, vol. 2172, November 2019. https://doi.org/10.1063/1.5133587

Designing Monitoring Systems for Complex Event Processing in Big Data Contexts

Carina Andrade$^{(\boxtimes)}$ ⓘ, Maria Cardoso ⓘ, Carlos Costa ⓘ,
and Maribel Yasmina Santos ⓘ

ALGORITMI Research Centre, University of Minho, Guimarães, Portugal
{carina.andrade,carlos.costa,maribel}@dsi.uminho.pt,
a78439@alunos.uminho.pt

Abstract. Nowadays, the amount of data that is constantly being generated presents new challenges for the technical and scientific community, such as the challenge of ensuring Complex Event Processing (CEP) in Big Data contexts, which arises to meet current advanced analytical needs. Therefore, some works are dedicated to the design and implementation of integrated CEP systems in the context of Big Data, as it is an example the Intelligent Event Broker (IEB) on which this work is based on. The IEB is a collection of several components that are integrated and validated to create a homogeneous system that will process events in real time in Big Data contexts, focusing on a rule-based approach. Considering the complexity of the IEB in constantly running contexts, it is important to have the ability of monitoring the evolution of the system, to avoid its uncontrolled growth. To accomplish that, we have previously proposed a component named "Mapping and Drill-down System" for the IEB, composed of a Web visualization Platform and a graph database. The main goal of the work presented in this paper is propose an architecture for the Mapping and Drill-down System component to monitor, in real time, the IEB's execution data, by collecting, processing, and efficiently storing it in a graph database for later visualization through the Web Visualization Platform. The graph database and the Web Visualization platform are the key components of the Mapping and Drill-down System. With this work, it will be easier to understand the behavior of the IEB in constantly running contexts, ensuring its controlled growth and helping the community in the design and development of CEP systems for Big Data contexts, especially in the monitoring component of such complex systems.

Keywords: Intelligent event broker · Complex event processing · Big data · Monitoring · Log analysis

1 Introduction

Currently, there is a vast amount of data that is constantly being produced. For example, communications between different machines generate data at high velocity and there is a need for automated decision-making processes. The Complex Event Processing (CEP)

© Springer Nature Switzerland AG 2022
M. Themistocleous and M. Papadaki (Eds.): EMCIS 2021, LNBIP 437, pp. 17–30, 2022.
https://doi.org/10.1007/978-3-030-95947-0_2

concept allows applications to extract, understand and transmit valuable information to recognize potentially relevant situations.

In this sense, the huge amount of heterogeneous data constantly generated by a world of interconnected things and the need for more advanced decision-making processes have significantly increased the need to explore and use Big Data, demanding that these decisions should be made in real time, as one of the main challenges is to obtain value from real-time (streaming) data. Thus, it is essential to integrate CEP in the era of Big Data to create innovative architectures capable of processing a large volume of events in a simple, scalable, and integrated way.

To address this gap identified in the literature, we have proposed the Intelligent Event Broker (IEB) architecture (Andrade et al. 2019). The IEB is a collection of several components that are integrated and validated to create a homogeneous streaming-oriented CEP system for Big Data contexts. Due to the complexity of the IEB (that can have several business areas integrated into the system with a vast amount of data and rules being processed), it was necessary to create a component that runs in parallel to the main components of the system, ensuring the constant monitoring of the IEB's daily operations. That specific component is called Mapping and Drill-down System and has as key components a graph database, proposed by us in (Andrade et al. 2020), and a Web Visualization Platform, proposed by us in (Rebelo et al. 2019).

To clarify the incremental valuable contribution of this work to the scientific and technical community, it is relevant to highlight that although the Mapping and Drill-down System is briefly mentioned in (Andrade et al. 2019), the same was not detailed nor developed in that paper, being now necessary to propose a detailed architecture and demonstration case for this specific component, due to the complexity of ensuring a logging/monitoring system for a CEP system in Big Data contexts, in this case, specifically for the IEB, but with enough generalization to make it applicable to other CEP systems in Big Data contexts. This is seen as the main contribution of this work, allowing researchers and practitioners to take advantage of all the logs generated by the IEB (or apply the same ideas to any similar system they intend to propose or implement) and to exploit all the resulting information, in order to make more assertive decisions about the daily operations of a CEP system in Big Data contexts. Therefore, the main problem that this work is aiming to tackle is the adequate monitoring of CEP systems in Big Data environments, by proposing a monitoring system that works in parallel with the IEB presented in (Andrade et al. 2019), ensuring its justifiable and controlled growth. The data collected should indicate what happened, and when it happened, and should support an analysis of the system's performance.

In this context, we can consider a production line having various production machines, working every day. Each production machine has a specific function in the final product assembly process and after finishing the steps of a specific machine, the product flows to the next one. If we guarantee that the IEB system receives the data from each machine in a real-time context and we have rules defining what is a good result for a parameter of the product assembly, we can track the product for the next machine or block it for quality control. With that, we are preventing more components from being spent unnecessarily once some parameter does not have the expected value (and was detected prematurely).

Regarding our research process, the Design Science Research Methodology for Information System (Peffers et al. 2007) was followed since our main goal is to produce an IT artefact, namely a model (with its architecture and the supporting data model) for a logging and monitoring system for CEP in Big Data contexts. In this paper, we also present a demonstration case to access the efficacy of the proposed solution. This is very important to validate this work and to show that we can effectively use the proposed model to monitor the IEB and hopefully contribute with an approach that other practitioners and researchers can use to propose similar systems.

This paper is structured as follows: Sect. 1 presents an introduction to the topic; Sect. 2 gives a brief overview about the related work identified in the literature; Sect. 3 proposes the system architecture for the Mapping and Drill-down System; Sect. 4 describes a demonstration case focused on a prototype of the system; and Sect. 5 presents the conclusions and future work.

2   Related Work

Ensuring adequate logging mechanisms in a system allows us to have an overview of the system behavior in production. Logs can be seen as messages collected from a specific point of the system that can have different formats and purposes, as mentioned by (Oliner et al. 2012): i) performance – to optimize the system performance; ii) security – to detect security problems; iii) forecast – including logs in the forecasting models; and, iv) reports – to provide details about the users' profiles, for example.

In the Big Data era, systems tend to use more complex and dynamic components, some of them including distributed processing, communication between different networks or different data sources, among others. Logging Big Data Systems can help to ensure that each interaction between components will be monitored, to prevent or track failures (Miranskyy et al. 2016).

Regarding the integration of the CEP concept with the Big Data era, some works are aiming to move forward in this research field by proposing system architectures that integrate these two topics. The work of (Hadar 2016) and the work of (Flouris et al. 2016) propose two distinct architectures that achieve this purpose but lacks considerations such as the one focused on this paper: a monitoring system to prevent the uncontrolled growth of the main system (IEB), which can be caused by the inclusion of several business processes to be actively followed, checking business requirements and acting over the results of their verification. Besides the fact that this type of need is not considered in the few proposed architectures for CEP in Big Data, to the best of our knowledge, there is no available system architecture such as the one proposed in this work.

According to the literature, there seems to be a lack of contributions focusing on the logging and monitoring of CEP systems in Big Data environments, which is understandable since the merge of these two topics is also a novel area. However, there is existing literature that focuses on logging/monitoring strategies for traditional CEP systems: Lan et al. (2019) present a logging/monitoring system for CEP, focusing on IoT devices, in which the authors discuss the monitoring of the arrival and processing of events. The authors mention the need to process huge amounts of data with low latency. Jayan and Rajan (2014) also discuss a logging system for CEP that focuses on network security logs, which include operating system logs, network logs and security devices logs. Similar to Lan et al. (2019), the authors focus on the volume of the logs, mentioning the problem of having a huge amount of logs, which may affect the performance of the CEP system, reason why we believe that works studying the combination of Big Data technologies with CEP systems, and the adequate logging and monitoring strategies of those, result in significantly valuable contributions to the community.

Considering that the work presented in this paper is proposing new components and capabilities that are related to previous works proposed by us (Andrade et al. 2019), and considering the complexity of the IEB System proposed and discussed in those previous works, an introduction of its several components is needed, which can be seen in Fig. 1. Given the variety of data sources (*Source Systems*) and formats available in many organizational contexts, it can become difficult to collect and process all this data from the IEB. With this, Kafka (a distributed streaming platform) is used to collect, disseminate, and standardize events (*Producers* component).

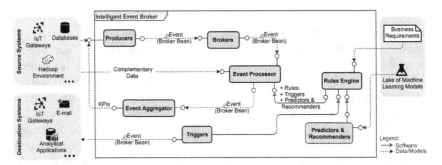

Fig. 1. Summary of IEB system architecture

The events are collected from its source system using Kafka Producers developed for this purpose. The *Producers*, after collecting the data, serialize them in the form of Broker Beans (simple classes that represent the business information) and produce the events by publishing them in a Kafka cluster (*Brokers* component). These topics containing the published events are subscribed by the *Event Processor* component (Kafka Consumers) which is continuously processing new events. The *Event Processor* is therefore one of the most relevant components of the IEB and it acts in collaboration with the *Rules Engine* component, which is responsible for executing several business rules defined within the organizational context. The Rules Engine component establishes communication with three other components: i) *Rules* - business requirements are converted into strategic, tactical, and operational rules; ii) *Triggers* - represent the connections to the various *Destination Systems*, i.e., after the condition of a rule is evaluated as true, these *Triggers* can, for example, perform some action in IoT Gateways, send an e-mail or just send data for an analytical application; iii) *Predictors and Recommenders* - ensure the ability to interpret previously trained Machine Learning models and use them to predict occurrences and recommend actions. Moreover, the *Event Processor* output can also be submitted to the *Event Aggregator*, which is responsible for receiving the data, performing aggregations, and storing them to calculate the relevant Key Performance Indicators (KPIs).

At this point, due to the complexity of the IEB, (Andrade et al. 2019) also mentioned a component dedicated to the IEB monitoring, perceived to run in parallel to the main components of the system, logging the daily operations of the IEB. This system was named Mapping and Drill-down System and it is composed of a graph database whose data model was proposed in (Andrade et al. 2020) and a Web Visualization Platform that was proposed in (Rebelo et al. 2019). However, as discussed in the previous section, those works are not detailed enough so that researchers and practitioners can explicitly understand how to implement a logging/monitoring solution for a CEP system in Big Data contexts. For this reason, the work presented here focus exclusively on proposing a logging/monitoring solution so that we can apply it to the IEB (or other similar system) and ensure that such CEP system can be adequately monitored and analyzed at scale. The next section details the proposed architecture.

3   IEB Logging System Architecture

To create a concise monitoring system, capable of monitoring a complex CEP system like the IEB, it is relevant to design an architecture that reflects a set of technical concerns and details (Fig. 2). Although this work focuses on extending the IEB, it must be highlighted that the architecture proposed here aims to structure the main components to achieve an effective monitoring system for CEP systems in the Big Data context, from the collection to the visualization of the data.

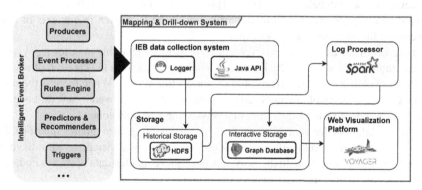

Fig. 2. IEB logging system architecture.

Consequently, it is our intention that the community can extract general knowledge from the proposed solution, as the constructs and technologies here proposed can be adapted to work with other CEP systems in Big Data contexts developed in the future. The architecture presented in Fig. 2, proposes the use of some technologies that were considered the most appropriate for the monitoring system, based on the data that can be extracted from the execution of the IEB, which is comprehensibly considered the data source for this monitoring system.

The date and time are the crucial information of the system, representing when something happened in it. To collect the monitoring data, Log4j is typically used in some of the IEB components[1] (e.g., the Producers). This technology was selected because it is a widely used (Dickey et al. 2011) open-source and flexible tool, making it an adequate choice for implementing a log system to monitor the IEB's components.

However, some components do not make feasible the use of Log4j to extract the monitoring data, because they are developed using distributed frameworks (e.g., Event Processor developed in Spark), which requires a way of centralizing the logs generated by the several nodes in the cluster. In these cases, it is used a Java API.

Once the information is collected, the data needs to be stored. One of the most suitable storage systems for the historical and scalable storage of this data is the Hadoop Distributed File System (HDFS). When using Log4j for data collection, Talend Open Studio for Big Data was used as an intermediate tool to send the produced logs to HDFS. When collecting the data through the Java API, it is stored directly in HDFS.

Being the data stored in HDFS, it is relevant to emphasize the use of Spark, where the appropriate transformations are made to the raw logs in a scalable way, as Spark distributes the load throughout a cluster of processing nodes. However, since, at this point, the IEB's data is already collected and stored according to the needs of the monitoring system, there is no need for significant changes to the data contained in the logs. Thus, Spark is mainly responsible for organizing the data to be exported to Neo4j, the technology that supports the graph database of the Mapping & Drill-Down System.

After performing these steps in Spark, it is possible to visualize a graph in Neo4j with the data related to the IEB monitoring. For a clearer visualization, this graph database will feed the Web Visualization Platform (named Voyager), already developed and proposed in previous work (Rebelo et al. 2019). This visualization platform is seen as highly dynamic and immersive, to follow the evolution of the IEB, even in contexts of high dimensionality, volume, and complexity.

In terms of infrastructure, a server can be used to execute this monitoring system. To accomplish this, we used Docker as a technology that allows the creation of several containers holding each technology that composes this system. When there is the need for high scalability, all of the proposed components can be deployed in several nodes of a cluster, in order to ensure the needs of a production Big Data context.

This architecture has as a principle the constant and long-term monitoring of a CEP system's operations, and therefore, the collection, storage, and visualization of the data carried out in near real-time. In this way, it is guaranteed that the data is always updated, being possible to draw real and timely conclusions.

4   Demonstration Case in the Context of Industry 4.0

Considering the system architecture proposed in Sect. 3, a demonstration case was carried out to validate it in the IEB context. Previously, (Andrade et al. 2020) has demonstrated the IEB system in the context of Industry 4.0, namely in Bosch Braga, Portugal, hence the demonstration case presented here follows up on this previous one, using Active Lot

---

[1] More information available in page 3 of (Andrade et al. 2019).

Release (ALR) data. ALR is a system responsible for supporting quality control during manufacturing and packaging processes in the factory, aiming to classify lots of products as valid or invalid, for them to be adequately delivered to the customer.

To better understand the demonstration case for this work, contextualization of the proposed data models is required. In this context and considering that two storage systems were proposed to store the logs in different phases of the system's monitoring (HDFS and Neo4J), the two data models will be explained below. In addition, some prototype specificities will be discussed, as well as the results that were obtained in this demonstration case. Furthermore, the outcomes achieved with this monitoring system are already properly integrated into the IEB Web Visualization Platform previously highlighted in this paper.

4.1 Data Models

HDFS is a file storage system and it fits into the scope of historical storage that is available for analytical purposes when ad-hoc queries are required. Since this work focuses on data generated at high speed, as the IEB is a streaming-oriented system, this storage system must respond to this fast production of data, and later, it must ensure fast data search.

The proposed approach for data organization intends to create a table for each IEB component, containing the data related to its monitoring. However, as the data collection process was developed in different ways (i.e., Log4j and Java API), the placement of the data in this storage system will also be different. Since the IEB Producer component code allows the use of logging mechanisms using Log4j, the data is forwarded to a single log file in HDFS, using Talend Open Studio for Big Data. Each line in the file corresponds to a new event that occurred in the IEB, containing the information of the produced event and when it was produced.

Other components make it difficult to use logging mechanisms via Log4j, as they are developed using different frameworks, sometimes distributed (e.g., Spark for the development of IEB Consumers and Drools for specification and interpretation of Business Rules in the IEB). To overcome this problem, an API was then designed to collect the data, storing it directly on the HDFS. Thus, the monitoring data of a given IEB component will go in small files to an HDFS folder (as can be seen in Fig. 3), reserved to receive the data from the Consumer, and then these small files will be grouped in a single file. However, this HDFS organization strategy may change in the future, if considered relevant, as the monitoring system evolves and becomes more complete. The graph database is used as a storage system for the IEB monitoring data and falls into the category of interactive storage. Figure 4 shows a representation of the graph-oriented storage system supported by Neo4j, representative of the data collected and transformed for the IEB monitoring system, at the time of the IEB execution. For a better understanding of the graph depicted in Fig. 4, it is essential to highlight that the nodes of the graph are represented by circles and the relationships are the links between those circles. Each circle will have a different colour, representative of the IEB component (e.g., Producer or Consumer) and the name of the nodes will be the name of the file found in the IEB codebase. Time attributes are the key point of this monitoring system since time will be the core property in the relationships between the graph nodes, representing when something happened in the system.

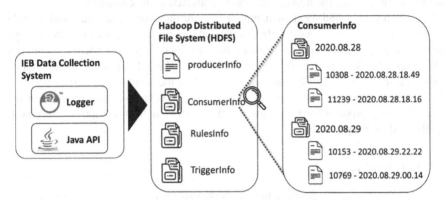

Fig. 3. HDFS storage system data model.

In this data model, as can be seen in Fig. 3, there are three types of Broker Beans (objects representing a piece of IEB data, such as a specific event, a business KPI, a business entity, among others): i) ALR Broker Beans that represent ALR events that reached the IEB system; ii) Broker Beans representing the calculated ALR KPIs; and iii) Broker Beans created during the verification of the Rules and that are intended to be used later by the Triggers. Thus, the system starts in the *ALRProducer*, the component that produces the ALR events, and, therefore, it is important to store the data containing its behaviour in the system. This component instantiates the Broker Beans that arrive at the system through the ALR events. The same happens in the *AlrOperationalConsumer*, which also instantiates these Broker Beans, and the storage of its behavioural data will also occur, containing the information of the event that has just been consumed.

Operational or analytical Consumers (*AlrOperationalConsumer* and *AlrAnalyticalKpisConsumer*) are constantly waiting for new events and they execute a *RulesEngine* that is responsible for executing Business Rules that have as input the consumed events. The *RulesEngine* class instantiates a *RulesStatelessSession*, which represents a set of all the rules that will be verified by a Consumer. These Consumers instantiate the Triggers (in this case the *CassandraTrigger* to store data in Cassandra[2]), which can be triggered after the Rules are verified. Regarding the storage of the verified Rules, the name of the Rule and the activated Trigger must be collected, as well as the Broker Bean used for the verification of the Rule, which can be a *MultiValueKpi* Broker Bean or an ALR Broker Bean.

Considering the Triggers, a relationship must be created between the Trigger node (*CassandraTrigger*) and the Broker Bean used to take any action, being the Broker Bean in this case called *LineEvent*. This component implements the Trigger interface and propagates the data to the Destination System (namely the NoSQL database Cassandra).

For further information, the complete data model proposed for the graph can be seen in (Andrade et al. 2020).

---

[2] https://cassandra.apache.org/.

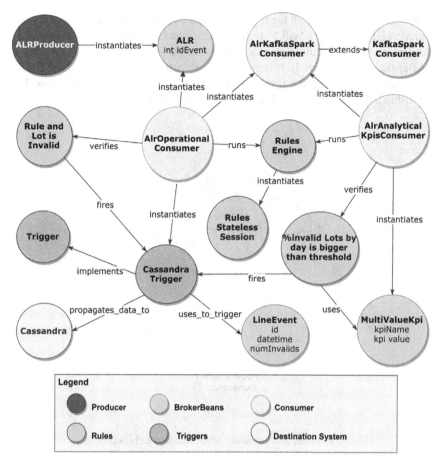

Fig. 4. Neo4j storage system data model.

4.2 Producers and Consumers Monitoring Process

Regarding monitoring, data collection is the stage that differs the most among the IEB components, and it needs proper attention. Considering the Producer's functionality, it is essential to collect some information that makes its monitoring feasible. The Producer's *name* and *id* and the *date* and *time* of the event are essential data for monitoring this component. For this purpose, it is necessary to place the logs in parts of the IEB codebase that are considered strategic, extending the IEB codebase to collect the information whenever a new event is produced.

After the log data is collected, the same must be stored in a system with the capacity to store large amounts of data, providing high performance in sequential reads and writes, as is the case of HDFS. To store this data in HDFS, Talend Open Studio for Big Data was used, where a job was developed to look for the log file on the server and to store its information in a file in HDFS. This job is executed automatically minute by minute, so that the data that is produced via streaming in the IEB, is updated in near real-time in HDFS as well. This way, all the log data generated during the production of an event is stored in HDFS, where it will be further transformed via Spark, being later stored in a more interactive and intuitive storage system like Neo4j.

After the data is in Neo4j, it is possible to visualize it in a graph (Fig. 5), which includes the link between the Producer and the generated ALR Broker Beans. Each relationship indicates the date and time of the Broker Beans production.

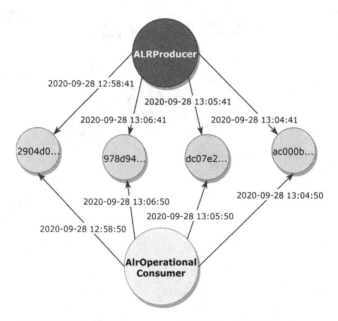

Fig. 5. Producer and consumer relationships with broker beans.

To start the collection of the monitoring data in the Consumer (which uses the Spark framework, as previously described), it was considered that the development of a Java API would be an appropriate approach. This Java API allows for the collection of data needed for monitoring the IEB, and establishes direct communication with HDFS since when the Consumer component consumes an event, this data is stored on it.

After that, the focus will be the transformations in Spark and the storage of the transformed data in Neo4j. At this point, the graph also contains the link between the events (related to the ALR Broker Beans) and the Consumer, containing the information of the date and time when a certain event was consumed by the Consumer.

After the collection, transformation, and storage of data on Neo4j, both from the Producer and Consumer, it is relevant to analyze how these two systems fit into a single graph. The expectation is that an ALR Broker Bean is produced by the *ALRProducer* and later consumed by the *AlrOperationalConsumer*, resulting in an event with two connections: one related to the production time and the other one related to the consumption time. The graph produced by the two components is represented in Fig. 5 where it is concluded that the result was the one expected. This data is in constant growth since it is collected and stored in a streaming context.

4.3   Data Representation in the IEB Web Visualization Platform

Since the data is adequately stored in Neo4j, this graph is the data source for the Web Visualization Platform proposed in (Rebelo et al. 2019). When accessing the platform, a connection to the Neo4j database and validation of the data can be made, and after that, the user can freely explore the graph.

The first exploration on the platform presents a statistical summary of the data presented in the accessed database. In this exploration, information about the attributes of the Neo4j database is presented, both information about the nodes and information about the existing relations between them. In this same component, the user can develop queries to collect the needed information regarding the monitored data.

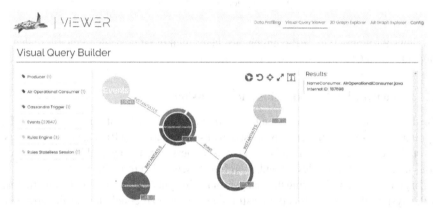

Fig. 6. Voyager visual query viewer presenting the monitoring data.

As can be seen in Fig. 6, in the "Visual Query Viewer" component, it is possible to visualize, in a generic way, the quantity of the data available in the graph (on the left). In this specific case, 1 Producer and 1 Consumer were logged, as well as 22.047 events. In the centre of the screen, the organization of that data is available by an interactive graph that evolves as the nodes are clicked, providing a more immediate interpretation when navigating through the data. The *AlrOperationalConsumer* focused on the centre of the graph (the purple circle rounded by red, green, and orange) instantiates 22.043 events. Only with this information can be concluded that, if exists 22.047 events in the database and only 22.043 were consumed there are 4 events that, at this point, already were produced by the *Producer* but were not yet consumed by the *AlrOperationalConsumer*.

Besides the representations mentioned so far, there are more components developed in the platform which allows visualizing the graph developed in Neo4j with other techniques. For example, Fig. 7 show us all the ALR Broker Beans (yellow nodes), the *ALRProducer* (red node) and the *AlrOperationalConsumer* (purple node) using the 3D concept. Other techniques such as Augmented Reality are used in other components of the Web Visualization Platform (Rebelo et al. 2019).

As seen, the visualization component of this work is focused on several graph visualizations demonstrated so far, including significantly enriching analyses on the data

Fig. 7. Voyager 3D graph explorer.

that flows throughout the IEB components, hence making it possible to monitor what is happening in a CEP system in Big Data contexts.

4.4   Demonstration Case Insights and Discussion

The demonstration case explored in this section is used as proof-of-concept for the CEP logging/monitoring architecture proposed in this work, targeting Big Data environments. Through the exploration and analysis of the usefulness and efficacy of this demonstration case, some insights are relevant and, therefore, discussed here in this subsection.

In general, and considering the analysis of the insights retrieved from the functioning of the system throughout this demonstration case, we can conclude that the proposed architecture can be considered significantly adequate to ensure its main purpose, i.e., adequately log and monitor the daily operations of a CEP system in Big Data contexts. The demonstration case has shown that the system could adequately collect and process a vast amount of log data without a significant increase in the processing time or even a decrease in the overall performance of the system.

Although there are no signs of an increase in the processing time of the step that collects and stores data in HDFS, once we increase the amount of data, the same doesn't happen in regard to the Spark processing and Neo4J storage. In this specific step of the process, the processing time increases as the amount of data also increases. In such cases, we have noticed an increase of 13 s in the processing time, a value that may not be considered relevant when we take into account that, in this specific scenario depicted in this example, we have made the data increase around 5000 times. Moreover, since we are using Big Data technologies in our architecture, to achieve lower processing times, we can simply scale-out our Spark and Neo4j clusters, reason why combining CEP concepts with Big Data technologies and paradigms is so relevant.

Regarding the visualization platform, and when comparing it directly with the Neo4J option for the visualization of the graph database, we can conclude that their behavior is similar, presenting the data for analysis almost immediately, without any noticeable delays. When considering the visualization of the whole graph and when it exists a huge amount of data, the visualization platform needs more time to organize the graph, which is understandable. The increase we have registered in those cases was around 10 additional seconds, highlighting again that in such scenario we had 5000 times more data, which may rule out the occurrence of a performance issue, as several filtering techniques can be used in the visualization platform to avoid the creation of such massive graphs.

5 Conclusions and Future Work

Taking into account the work developed so far, and the insights gained during the development of this monitoring system and its demonstration via prototype in the context of Industry 4.0, the proposed architecture can be considered as suitable for solving the identified problem, i.e., the need to ensure adequate monitoring of CEP systems in Big Data contexts.

Given the complexity of the IEB in production contexts, it is considered essential to ensure adequate monitoring of the system. This monitoring was supported by storage, processing and analytical technologies and it is part of the proposal for the IEB Mapping and Drill-Down System depicted here. In this way, it is now possible to see what is happening in the IEB, or, when generalized, in any CEP system for Big Data contexts, making it easier to control the system and to visualize the data flowing throughout the components and at which scale.

The demonstration efforts presented in this work should continue in future works, so that the monitoring system can cover all the proposed components, thus continuing to validate the proposed architecture. Consequently, the development of the monitoring system should be extended to cover the Rules and Triggers components of the IEB, so that it becomes more comprehensive and advantageous.

It is therefore considered that this work may be relevant for future studies that focus on bridging the gap between CEP and Big Data, making monitoring of CEP systems in Big Data contexts more accessible to the community.

Acknowledgements. This work has been supported by FCT – Fundação para a Ciência e Tecnologia within the R&D Units Project Scope: UIDB/00319/2020, the Doctoral scholarship PD/BDE/135101/2017 and by European Structural and Investment Funds in the FEDER component, through the Operational Competitiveness and Internationalization Programme (COMPETE 2020) [Project nº 039479; Funding Reference: POCI-01-0247-FEDER-039479].

References

Andrade, C., Cardoso, M., Costa, C., Santos, M.Y.: An inspection and logging system for complex event processing in bosch's industry 4.0 movement. In: Themistocleous, M., Papadaki, M., Kamal, M.M. (eds.) EMCIS 2020. LNBIP, vol. 402, pp. 49–62. Springer, Cham (2020). https://doi.org/10.1007/978-3-030-63396-7_4

Andrade, C., Correia, J., Costa, C., Santos, M.Y.: Intelligent event broker: a complex event processing system in big data contexts. In: AMCIS 2019 Proceedings of Americas Conference on Information Systems, Cancun (2019)

Dickey, D.A., Dorter, B. S., German, J.M., Madore, B.D., Piper, M.W., Zenarosa, G.L.: Evaluating Java PathFinder on Log4J (2011)

Flouris, I., et al.: FERARI: a prototype for complex event processing over streaming multi-cloud platforms. In: Proceedings of the 2016 International Conference on Management of Data, pp. 2093–2096 (2016). https://doi.org/10.1145/2882903.2899395

Hadar, E.: BIDCEP: a vision of big data complex event processing for near real time data streaming. In: CAiSE Industry Track (2016)

Jayan, K., Rajan, A.K.: Sys-log classifier for complex event processing system in network security. In: 2014 International Conference on Advances in Computing, Communications and Informatics (ICACCI), pp. 2031–2035 (2014). https://doi.org/10.1109/ICACCI.2014.6968471

Lan, L., Shi, R., Wang, B., Zhang, L., Jiang, N.: A universal complex event processing mechanism based on edge computing for internet of things real-time monitoring. IEEE Access **7**, 101865–101878 (2019). https://doi.org/10.1109/ACCESS.2019.2930313

Miranskyy, A., Hamou-Lhadj, A., Cialini, E., Larsson, A.: Operational-log analysis for big data systems: challenges and solutions. IEEE Softw. **33**(02), 52–59 (2016). https://doi.org/10.1109/MS.2016.33

Oliner, A., Ganapathi, A., Xu, W.: Advances and challenges in log analysis. Commun. ACM **55**(2), 55–61 (2012). https://doi.org/10.1145/2076450.2076466

Rebelo, J., Andrade, C., Costa, C., Santos, M.Y.: An immersive web visualization platform for a big data context in Bosch's industry 4.0 movement. In: European, Mediterranean and Middle Eastern Conference on Information Systems (EMCIS), Dubai, December 2019

Trnka, A.: Big data analysis. Eur. J. Sci. Theol. (2014). http://www.ejst.tuiasi.ro/Files/48/15_Trnka.pdf

Evaluation of Machine Learning Methods for the Experimental Classification and Clustering of Higher Education Institutions

Jacek Maślankowski[1]([⊠]) [iD] and Łukasz Brzezicki[2] [iD]

[1] University of Gdańsk, ul. Armii Krajowej 101, 81-824 Sopot, Poland
jacek.maslankowski@ug.edu.pl
[2] Ustka City Hall, Wyszyńskiego 3, 76-270 Ustka, Poland
brzezicki.lukasz@wp.pl

Abstract. Higher education institutions have a big impact on the future of skills supplied on the labour market. It means that depending on the changes in labour market, higher education institutions are making changes to fields of study or adding new ones to fulfil the demand on labour market. The significant changes on labour market caused by digital transformation, resulted in new jobs and new skills. Because of the necessity of computer skills, general universities started to offer various courses on IT, including computer science that was originally offered by technical universities. It is also possible to have selected medical studies not only at medical universities but also in private colleges, e.g., nursing studies. As a result, the current classification of higher education institutions used in official statistics can be revised. The paper shows the experimental work on the use of machine learning methods to classify and cluster higher education institutions in Poland. Different attributes were used to classify the type of institution, including fields of studies, programme orientation and others. The aim of the paper was also to evaluate various machine learning methods in the process of classifying or clustering and validating the associated types of higher education institutions.

Keywords: Higher education · Machine learning · Clustering

1 Introduction

Higher education in Poland, starting with the act of 2005 consolidating and unifying, as well as adapting the system to European conditions, has been subject to changes and reforms many times (including in 2011, 2014 and 2018). The classification adopted at the beginning has not been verified so far, even though there has been a significant diversification of the activities of universities since 2005 through the adoption of different strategies and missions that have been implemented in individual academic centers. Among the many postulates for systemic changes, the academic community indicated, inter alia, institutional rationalization, leading to a change in the institutional status in the fragmented system of higher education through "the development of criteria and indicators relating to didactic and research achievements, enabling the determination of

© Springer Nature Switzerland AG 2022
M. Themistocleous and M. Papadaki (Eds.): EMCIS 2021, LNBIP 437, pp. 31–45, 2022.
https://doi.org/10.1007/978-3-030-95947-0_3

an objectified typology of universities and their relationships, as well as their basic units, necessary for the classification of universities" [1]. Therefore, it should be considered that the functional division of units according to the achievements of the university is the desired direction of their segmentation, which is expected by the academic community. The aim of the research is an attempt to present a new classification of universities, considering various criteria of their activity in response to contemporary challenges and expectations posed to academic centers. The proposed classification of universities should contribute to better creation of public policies and planning the development of individual universities and the entire higher education sector. In addition, the new experimental classification may also prove to be a useful tool for selecting units under other methods, such as Data Envelopment Analysis (DEA), which, by definition, examines the effectiveness of homogeneous economic units or creating more reliable and precise rankings of universities.

2 Motivation

According to the data contained in the integrated information system on higher education and science, POL-on, a total of 380 different universities operated in 2020 [2]. It should be noted, however, that the basic legal act regulating the entire higher education system in Poland is the Act of July 20, 2018, Law on Higher Education and Science [4], which divides universities according to various criteria.

The first criterion for the division is the founding unit, then the public university is established by a state body. On the other hand, a non-public one is established by a natural person or a legal person other than a local government unit or a state or local government legal person.

The second criterion is the nature of the didactic activity. A distinction is then made between a vocational university that provides education only for a practical profile, considering the needs of the socio-economic environment, and an academic university that offers first-cycle and second-cycle studies or uniform master's studies, and also conducts research activities. The basis for the above division is conducting research, but most of all being authorized to award the academic degree of doctor.

Within academic universities, the legislator distinguished 3 types, indicating that the word "academy" is reserved for the name of an academic university, but without specifying any characteristics that distinguish it from other units. Then, specifying that the word "polytechnic" is reserved for the name of an academic university with the scientific category A +, A or B + in at least 2 disciplines in the field of engineering and technical sciences. On the other hand, the word "university" is reserved for the name of an academic university with the academic category A +, A or B+ in at least 6 scientific or artistic disciplines. It is worth noting that this is one of the two main criteria used to classify universities.

In the academic community, he advocates the belief that the current classification does not correspond to the contemporary challenges of universities and does not reflect their achievements. Antonowicz [3] explicitly points out that "The formal classification of universities in Poland is essentially a bureaucratic fiction not only because of the criteria used, but also because of their politicization, because of which several universities (e.g., in Zielona Góra, Opole, Rzeszów) 2005 is not able to meet the conditions to be a full university, and Akademia im. Jakub from Paradyż in Gorzów Wielkopolski has the status of an academic university, although it does not have any authority to award the degree of Doctor of Sciences" [3, pp. 18].

The Act [4] indicates that supervision may be exercised by other ministries in addition to the ministry of higher education. In connection with the above, a university (Article 433), which is supervised by:

- the Minister of National Defense - is a military university;
- the Minister responsible for Internal Affairs or the Minister of Justice - is a university of state services;
- the Minister responsible for Culture and Protection of National Heritage - is an art university;
- the Minister in charge of Health - is a medical university;
- the Minister responsible for Maritime Economy - is a maritime university.

In addition, the Minister of Higher Education, as well as the authorities of churches and other religious associations, exercise supervision over a public university of theology and other public schools of theology.

The legislator also made it possible for universities to form a federation to jointly carry out the tasks of participating entities, except for conducting education during studies. Therefore, it can be assumed that this is another criterion for dividing universities into self-functioning units and federations. Of course, in addition to the criteria legally regulated in the Act on Higher Education and Science [4], universities can also be divided in other respects. One of them is to classify according to the classes promoted by Statistics Poland, including [5]: (1) Universities; (2) Higher schools of technology; (3) Higher schools of agriculture; (4) Higher schools of economics; (5) Higher schools of pedagogy; (6) Medical universities; (7) Maritime universities; (8) Higher schools of sport; (9) Higher schools of arts; (10) Higher schools of theology; (11) Higher schools of the Ministry of National Defense and Ministry of the Interior and Administration; (12) Other higher education institutions.

However, it should be noted that a significant part of the classification of universities (especially those subject to the Ministry of Science and Higher Education) according to Statistics Poland is based on the previous Act on Higher Education of 2011, which distinguished the nature of a given type of higher education institution based on the number and scope of scientific disciplines. It is interesting that in 2020 such a division of universities still functions in the POL-on system.

Universities can be divided according to the main area of activity or mission in the field of either education or science [6] - this division is currently supported by the Ministry of Science and Higher Education through organized projects, e.g. "Initiative of Excellence - Research University" or "Teaching Initiative excellence". The litera-ture [6–10] also suggests other criteria for the division of universities, e.g. due to the size of the center (small-large), location (city-village or the seat of territorial division authorities and smaller cities), focusing on a selected area of education (e.g. religious education) or scientific discipline (e.g. natural sciences and social sciences and (facul-ties, departments) and others. The above examples do not cover the entire spectrum of university classification. It should be noted, however, that in most cases, universities are classified only according to the nature of education and related disciplines, or their main mission, including education or science. It should be emphasized that the appropriate classification of universities allows to compare similar units in terms of a given evaluation criterion. In the higher education sector, various rankings are created for many [11], which measure various aspects of the university's activity. However, while making measurements and comparisons within a given group of universities is to some extent accepted by the academic community, the creation of general rankings that do not consider the specificity of various types of universities and fields of science is controversial. Therefore, an appropriate classification of universities is both important and necessary for a reliable comparison of the achievements of academic centers.

3 Methods

The wide use of Big Data tools and methods made more common natural classification of objects based on their attributes. There are several examples of classifying objects, that are well known, including machine learning algorithms and graph theory [12]. Machine learning algorithms can be divided into two major groups: supervised (classification) and unsupervised (clustering) [13]. Among the supervised learning algorithms for data science, the most common in the current literature are decision tress, Naïve Bayes and Support Vector Machines [14]. In more advanced examples, for example image segmentation, artificial neural networks are used [13]. Unsupervised machine learning, including cluster analysis, and semi-supervised algorithms with cluster labelling and classifications blocks are commonly used in the cases of dividing objects into classes. Still there is a necessity of the work by researchers to find optimal number of clusters [15]. Although, machine learning algorithms has very critical examination in selected research areas [16], still it is wide used in the scientific literature for classification and clustering.

The second method used in the case study is based on neural networks. The use of neural networks is common in Big Data text analytics, mostly based on data from social media. It involves other methods, such as sentiment analysis or NLP – Natural Language Processing to process and analyze the data into usable form [17]. However, neural networks can also be used to solve more complex problems, including the prediction on intraday stock return [18] or predicting consumer product demand [19].

It is necessary to understand that the methods of classifications with unsupervised machine learning are well known in the research papers for a long time. We can find several research papers on this topic in research papers published many decades ago. One of the common research tasks today is to classify web users based on their attributes. This problem in the literature is well known and many different methods has been used and tested. For example, conceptual clustering and cluster mining were used to classify user communities on the Internet [20]. When working with Big Data, one of the issues to be considered is also de-duplication of records as many data may occur several times in the dataset [21].

4 Methodology

Among the possible variables that can be used to classify institutions we have considered the following, listed in Table 1.

Table 1. Potential classifications of higher education institutions

Class	Description (examples)	Usability
Size	Number of students	+ (5)
Statistical classification	Universities, Technical universities, etc.	− (1)
Broad fields of study (ISCED-F)	00 Generic programmes and qualifications 01 Education 02 Arts and humanities 03 Social sciences, journalism and information ... 10 Services	+ (4)
Narrow fields of study (ISCED-F)	001 Basic programmes and qualifications 002 Literacy and numeracy 003 Personal skills and development 011 Education ... 103 Security services 104 Transport services	+ (3)
Detailed fields of study (ISCED-F)	0011 Basic programmes and qualifications 0021 Literacy and numeracy 0031 Personal skills and development 0111 Education science ... 1031 Military and defence 1032 Protection of persons and property 1041 Transport services	− (2)
Disciplines	Management and quality, Quantity methods	+ (4)
Research fields (domains)	Social sciences, etc.	+ (4)
Level of education (ISCED-2011)	5 – Short-cycle tertiary education 6 – Bachelor's or equivalent level 7 – Master's or equivalent level 8 – Doctoral or equivalent level	+ (2)
Programme orientation	General or Vocational	+ (3)
Non formal programmes	Courses taught	+ (2)
Sector	Public / Private	+ (3)
Finances	Total income amount	+ (4)
Research potential	Number of publications by research fields	+ (4)
Main source of financing	Government/students/other	+ (4)

Source: own study.

Some of the classes listed above cannot be used in selected traditional classification methods, for instance graphs, as they are too detailed. For example, higher education institutions in Poland can name detailed fields of study with their own names. It means that there are many unique fields of study that cannot be used to link different higher education institutions. On the other hand, it can be done with the list of ISCED (International Standard Classification of Education) detailed fields of study. However, mapping the fields of study created at higher education institution may not be possible without the acceptance of the authorities of this institution. It may lead to non-reliable results of higher education institutions classifications.

The methodology used in this paper includes the following steps:

1) Supervised machine learning to check the consistency among higher education institution types by different attributes,
2) Graph analysis to see the diversity between higher education institutions and concentration of different higher education institutions,
3) Unsupervised learning to classify higher education institutions into clusters,
4) Descriptive statistics to analyse each cluster.

To provide reliable results we decided to test all the attributes mentioned above to provide classes and check the consistency within each class. Several different methods have been used, as written above. We have started with supervised machine learning to check the consistency between different higher education institutions. The results show that the use of all fields of studies associated with different higher education institution types gave the best results (i.e., 70% of average weighted precision).

5 Results and Discussion

First step was to check how the current model of classification of higher education institutions (HEI) types fits to the fields of study assigned to each type. To accomplish this task, we decided to use supervised machine learning. The model was tested with 400 features (fields of study), according to the classification of higher education institutions by Statistics Poland. We have used 300 features that were tested in the 80 / 20 rate. It means that 80% of observations were used to train the model. Another 20% of observations were used to test if the model correctly recognized the types of higher education institutions by fields of study.

Testing the training dataset accuracy...

	precision	recall	f1-score	support
Universities	0.57	0.71	0.63	302
Higher schools of technology	0.46	0.51	0.48	127
Higher schools of agriculture	0.26	0.20	0.23	35
Higher schools of economics	0.46	0.05	0.09	114
Higher schools of pedagogy	0.00	0.00	0.00	41
Medical universities	0.75	0.10	0.17	31
Maritime universities	0.00	0.00	0.00	3
Higher schools of sport	1.00	0.11	0.20	18
Higher schools of arts	0.50	0.65	0.57	23
Higher schools of theology	0.38	0.75	0.50	4
Higher schools of the selected Ministries	0.45	0.64	0.53	248
Other HEI – class 12	0.00	0.00	0.00	9
Other HEI – class 13	0.00	0.00	0.00	2
accuracy			0.49	957
macro avg	0.37	0.29	0.26	957
weighted avg	0.48	0.49	0.45	957

The results above show that the accuracy is rather low – weighted 48%. It proves that the distribution of different fields of studies among higher education institutions is high. The best concentration of the fields of study is for class 8 (Higher schools of sport) – 100%, class 6 (Medical universities) – 75%, and class 1 (Universities) – 57%. It is the result of the fact that these types of higher education institutions (especially Higher schools of sport as well as Medical universities) have unique fields of studies.

Making analysis for all fields of study assigned to the higher education institution (i.e. University of Warsaw; Management, Administration, Law etc.) gave better results.

Testing the training dataset accuracy...

	precision	recall	f1-score	support
Universities	0.00	0.00	0.00	2
Higher schools of technology	0.33	0.60	0.43	5
Higher schools of agriculture	1.00	0.50	0.67	2
Higher schools of economics	0.33	0.45	0.38	11
Higher schools of pedagogy	1.00	0.33	0.50	3
Medical universities	0.00	0.00	0.00	0
Maritime universities	0.00	0.00	0.00	1
Higher schools of sport	1.00	1.00	1.00	1
Higher schools of arts	1.00	0.86	0.92	7
Higher schools of theology	1.00	0.86	0.92	7
Higher schools of the selected Ministries	0.74	0.78	0.76	40
Other HEI – class 12	1.00	0.60	0.75	5
Other HEI – class 13	0.00	0.00	0.00	1
accuracy			0.67	85
macro avg	0.57	0.46	0.49	85
weighted avg	0.70	0.67	0.67	85

Results above shows that the best fit is for class 3 (Higher schools of agriculture), class 4 (Higher schools of pedagogy), class 8 (Higher schools of sport), class 9 (Higher schools of arts), class 10 (Higher schools of theology) and class 13 (Higher schools of the Ministry of National Defence). In listed above higher education institutions, the fit is 100%.

As mentioned in the previous section, we decided to combine several different attributes to prepare a new classification of higher education institution. Typical classification of higher education institutions can be based on detailed fields of study. In Fig. 1 there is a graph showing clusters of higher education institutions.

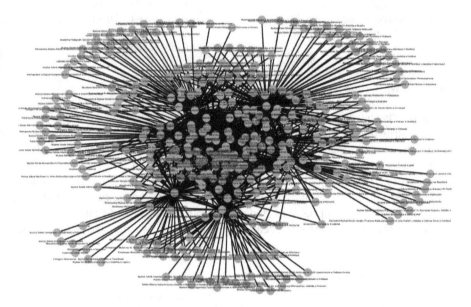

Fig. 1. Higher education institutions clusters by detailed fields of study

In this figure we can see the clusters of the most popular fields of study, such as administration, management, and economics. On the other side, more specific fields of study, clustering less higher education institutions, are medicine or physical sciences. The graph above is hard to study, but it shows the general clusters of different higher education institutions, concentrated among the most popular fields of studies.

The next step was to find the most consistent higher schools, i.e. to find the similarity rate between studied institution and referenced institution by fields of study present at both institutions. We decided to use only higher education institution with more than 30 fields of studies. The results were shown in Table 2.

Table 2. Consistency of higher education institution in terms of fields of studies

Studied institution	Referenced institution	Fields	Rate
Uniwersytet Pedagogiczny im. Komisji Edukacji Narodowej w Krakowie	Uniwersytet Mikołaja Kopernika w Toruniu	37	72,5%
Uniwersytet Rzeszowski	Uniwersytet Mikołaja Kopernika w Toruniu	37	68,5%
Uniwersytet Pedagogiczny im. Komisji Edukacji Narodowej w Krakowie	Uniwersytet Marii Curie-Skłodowskiej w Lublinie	34	66,7%
Uniwersytet Opolski	Uniwersytet Mikołaja Kopernika w Toruniu	31	60,8%
Uniwersytet Wrocławski	Uniwersytet Im. Adama Mickiewicza w Poznaniu	45	54,2%
Uniwersytet Mikołaja Kopernika w Toruniu	Uniwersytet Jagielloński w Krakowie	58	52,7%
Uniwersytet Śląski w Katowicach	Uniwersytet Im. Adama Mickiewicza w Poznaniu	40	51,3%
Uniwersytet Łódzki	Uniwersytet Jagielloński w Krakowie	42	51,2%
Uniwersytet Szczeciński	Uniwersytet Im. Adama Mickiewicza w Poznaniu	35	50,7%
Uniwersytet Wrocławski	Uniwersytet Jagielloński w Krakowie	42	50,6%
Uniwersytet Zielonogórski	Uniwersytet Warmińsko-Mazurski w Olsztynie	33	50,0%
Uniwersytet Śląski w Katowicach	Uniwersytet Mikołaja Kopernika w Toruniu	39	50,0%
Uniwersytet Śląski w Katowicach	Uniwersytet Jagielloński w Krakowie	39	50,0%
Uniwersytet Zielonogórski	Uniwersytet Mikołaja Kopernika w Toruniu	33	50,0%
Uniwersytet Jagielloński w Krakowie	Uniwersytet Im. Adama Mickiewicza w Poznaniu	56	49,6%
Uniwersytet Szczeciński	Uniwersytet Łódzki	34	49,3%
Uniwersytet Szczeciński	Uniwersytet Gdański	34	49,3%
Uniwersytet Szczeciński	Uniwersytet Mikołaja Kopernika w Toruniu	34	49,3%

(*continued*)

Table 2. (*continued*)

Studied institution	Referenced institution	Fields	Rate
Uniwersytet Warszawski	Uniwersytet Jagielloński w Krakowie	44	48,9%
Uniwersytet Zielonogórski	Uniwersytet Marii Curie-Skłodowskiej w Lublinie	32	48,5%
Uniwersytet Warszawski	Uniwersytet Mikołaja Kopernika w Toruniu	43	47,8%
Uniwersytet Wrocławski	Uniwersytet Mikołaja Kopernika w Toruniu	39	47,0%
Uniwersytet Warszawski	Uniwersytet Im. Adama Mickiewicza w Poznaniu	42	46,7%
Uniwersytet Warmińsko-Mazurski w Olsztynie	Uniwersytet Mikołaja Kopernika w Toruniu	35	45,5%
Uniwersytet Łódzki	Uniwersytet Im. Adama Mickiewicza w Poznaniu	37	45,1%
Uniwersytet Łódzki	Uniwersytet Gdański	37	45,1%
Uniwersytet Szczeciński	Uniwersytet Jagielloński w Krakowie	31	44,9%
Uniwersytet Śląski w Katowicach	Uniwersytet Łódzki	35	44,9%
Uniwersytet Wrocławski	Uniwersytet Łódzki	37	44,6%
Uniwersytet Warszawski	Uniwersytet Łódzki	40	44,4%
Uniwersytet Marii Curie-Skłodowskiej w Lublinie	Uniwersytet Jagielloński w Krakowie	31	44,3%
Uniwersytet Marii Curie-Skłodowskiej w Lublinie	Uniwersytet Łódzki	31	44,3%
Uniwersytet Wrocławski	Uniwersytet Warszawski	36	43,4%
Uniwersytet Wrocławski	Uniwersytet Śląski w Katowicach	36	43,4%
Uniwersytet Wrocławski	Uniwersytet Gdański	36	43,4%
Uniwersytet Warmińsko-Mazurski w Olsztynie	Uniwersytet Rzeszowski	33	42,9%
Uniwersytet Śląski w Katowicach	Uniwersytet Gdański	33	42,3%
Uniwersytet Warszawski	Uniwersytet Gdański	37	41,1%
Uniwersytet Mikołaja Kopernika w Toruniu	Uniwersytet Marii Curie-Skłodowskiej w Lublinie	44	40,0%
Uniwersytet Warszawski	Uniwersytet Szczeciński	36	40,0%
Uniwersytet Mikołaja Kopernika w Toruniu	Uniwersytet Im. Adama Mickiewicza w Poznaniu	42	38,2%

(*continued*)

Table 2. (*continued*)

Studied institution	Referenced institution	Fields	Rate
Uniwersytet Warszawski	Uniwersytet Śląski w Katowicach	34	37,8%
Uniwersytet Mikołaja Kopernika w Toruniu	Uniwersytet Łódzki	41	37,3%
Uniwersytet Mikołaja Kopernika w Toruniu	Uniwersytet Gdański	39	35,5%
Uniwersytet Jagielloński w Krakowie	Uniwersytet Gdański	38	33,6%
Uniwersytet im. Adama Mickiewicza w Poznaniu	Uniwersytet Gdański	42	32,8%
Uniwersytet Mikołaja Kopernika w Toruniu	Uniwersytet Jana Kochanowskiego w Kielcach	34	30,9%

Source: own study

Table 2 shows that the most consistent higher education institutions are universities. The highest number of fields of study with the rate calculated as number of fields of studies of studied to referenced institution shows that the second most consistent group are technical universities. The result was calculated with the following Eq. (1):

$$Cr = \frac{Ns}{Nt} * 100 \tag{1}$$

C_r – consistency rate by fields of study.
N_s – number of similar fields of studies in studied and referenced institutions.
N_t – number of total number of fields of studies in the studied institution.
The consistency between institutions having the most similar number of fields of studies is shown in Fig. 2.

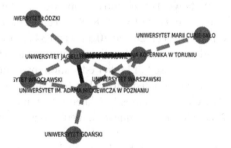

Fig. 2. Consistency of higher education institutions by fields of studies

The graph shows only institutions having 40 or more same fields of studies. The connection between institutions having more than 45 fields of studies are presented in solid line. The dashed line represents the connection having 40–45 same fields of studies.

The third figure shows the classification of higher education institutions according to their consent to posting doctorates in different research domains. Not all higher education institutions are listed in this graph, because only selected institutions have possibility to post doctorates.

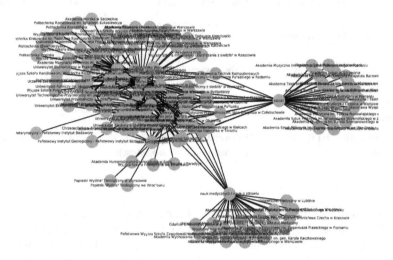

Fig. 3. Higher education institutions clusters by doctorates research domain

As it was shown in previous figure, most of the institutions are concentrated within the most popular domain, such as social sciences. Opposite to them are tertiary education schools of medicine and arts – shown in the left and in the bottom of Fig. 3.

Because of the huge concentration of higher education institutions in Fig. 1 we decided to control the number of clusters. The next step was to repeat the step of clustering higher education institution with the unsupervised machine learning method. Firstly, we examined the number of schools by different number of classes. The results are shown in Table 3 and Table 4. It shows that the most proportional with the lowest standard deviation (SD) is a dividing into 9 (SD 13) or 18 (SD 9) clusters. The number of higher education institutions differs between 26 and 70, or 9 and 34 respectively. We have used k-means algorithm to divide the higher education institutions into 9 clusters.

The cluster 0 is mostly composed of higher education institutions that have technical fields of studies (vocational oriented curricula). It includes especially the group of technical universities. The cluster 1 is mostly related to the universities having general curricula. The cluster 2 includes higher education institutions related to economic fields of studies.

The general description shown in Table 4 is just a brief overview. Some exceptions in each cluster occurs, as we did not make any changes to the results provided with unsupervised machine learning algorithm.

Table 3. The matrix of number of classes and number of schools within clusters

Sc/C	1	2	3	4	5	6	7	8	9	10	11	12	13	14	15	16	17	18	19	20
[0]	417	157	192	91	58	42	33	73	51	27	30	11	36	11	69	12	30	7	22	16
[1]		260	149	100	47	114	79	41	70	61	58	17	35	71	32	68	26	7	25	34
[2]			77	170	197	69	97	59	37	45	38	30	29	16	31	47	14	14	23	27
[3]				55	35	70	54	36	37	151	46	67	27	38	15	18	14	30	23	14
[4]					80	70	70	55	53	30	15	13	42	43	12	24	31	39	18	6
[5]						51	54	88	45	13	53	30	27	31	22	12	67	38	31	11
[6]							29	20	26	28	14	71	56	21	36	17	12	51	19	24
[7]								42	60	10	55	15	66	15	27	42	36	21	29	24
[8]									33	15	13	33	36	39	36	31	17	25	18	22
[9]										33	64	35	12	28	15	13	12	20	34	16
[10]											25	43	13	23	16	32	30	16	17	9
[11]												47	19	33	16	36	28	49	35	14
[12]													14	12	10	13	5	14	10	36
[13]														29	66	12	23	13	14	20
[14]															8	16	32	22	34	33
[15]																20	20	8	22	32
[16]																	16	4	10	8
[17]																		30	15	36
[18]																			9	9
[19]																				14
ANoS	417	209	139	104	83	69	59	52	46	41	37	34	32	29	27	26	24	23	21	20
St.dev.	0	52	47	42	59	23	23	20	13	39	18	19	16	15	18	15	14	14	8	10

Source: own study; Note: Sc/C. - Schools count / Cluster, ANoS - Average number of schools, St.dev. - Standard deviation

Table 4. Characteristics of each cluster

Cluster no.	General description
0	Vocational orientation of curricula
1	General
2	Economic
3	Technical
4	Management/Humanum
5	Medical
6	Physical sport
7	Music/Art/Humanum
8	Health/IT/General

Source: own study

6 Conclusions

In the paper we demonstrated that the most reliable and suitable method of classification of higher education institutions is to use fields of studies. It provides the most consistent groups of higher education institutions and makes the most diversification among clusters. The use of different attributes to classify, including number of students or disciplines makes the results less diverse.

The results shown in this paper confirms the opinion from various researchers that the classification of higher education institutions is very artificial. Therefore, this classification should be revised every few years to include the dynamic changes that occur every year. Current challenge in higher education sector is to provide fields of studies for the highest demand jobs in the labour market. As a result, we can observe the possibilities to study management at technical universities as well as vocational oriented IT at universities.

Our future studies will concentrate on the use of machine learning algorithms to predict student performance, dropout rate education and graduation rates. To propose more effective admission criteria and reduce the operating costs of higher education.

References

1. Woźnicki, J.: Deregulacja w systemie szkolnictwa wyższego. Program rozwoju szkolnictwa wyższego do 2020 r. Część V, FRP, KRASP, Warszawa (2015)
2. POL-on. Higher education institutions (2021). https://polon.nauka.gov.pl/opi/aa/rejestry/szk olnictwo?execution=e7s1. Accessed 20 Oct 2021
3. Antonowicz, D.: Stopniowe różnicowanie systemu szkolnictwa wyższego i jego konsekwencje. Seria Raportów Centrum Studiów nad Polityką Publiczną UAM. Poznań (2019)
4. Act of July 20, 2018, Law on Higher Education and Science (2018)
5. Higher education schools and their finances, Statistics Poland (2019)
6. Jalote, P., Jain, B.N., Sopory, S.: Classification for research universities in India. High. Educ. 79(2), 225–241 (2019). https://doi.org/10.1007/s10734-019-00406-3
7. Shin, J.C.: Classifying higher education institutions in Korea: a performance-based approach. High. Educ. 57, 247–266 (2009). https://doi.org/10.1007/s10734-008-9150-4
8. Hermanowicz, J.C.: Classifying universities and their departments: a social world perspective. J. High. Educ. 76(1), 26–55 (2005). https://doi.org/10.1353/jhe.2005.0005
9. Van Vught, F.A., Kaiser, F., File, J.M., Gaethgens, C., Westerheijden, D.F.: U-map: the European classification of higher education institutions. Center for Higher Education Policy Studies – CHEPS, Enschede (2010)
10. Ziegele, F.: Classification of higher education institutions: the European case. Pensamiento educativo. Rev. Invest. Educ. Latinoamericana 50(1), 76–95 (2013). http://dx.doi.org/10.7764/PEL.50.1.2013.7
11. Szadkowski, K.: Globalne rankingi uniwersytetów a długoterminowa strategia wzmacniania pozycji polskich uczelni. Seria Raportów Centrum Studiów nad Polityką Publiczną UAM, Poznań (2019)
12. Kumar, R., Pattnaik, P.K.: Graph Theory. Laxmi Publications Pvt Ltd. (2018)
13. Razmjooy, N., Estrela, V., Loschi, H.: A study of metaheuristic-based neural networks for image segmentation purposes. In: Memon, Q., Khoja, S. (eds.) Data Science. Theory, Analysis, and Applications. CRC Press, Taylor & Francis Group (2020)

14. Alloghani, M., Al-Jumeily, D., Mustafina, J., Hussain, A., Aljaaf, A.J.: A Systematic review of supervised and unsupervised machine learning algorithms for data science. In: Berry, M.W., Mohamed, A., Wah Yap B. (eds.) Supervised and Unsupervised Learning for Data Science. Unsupervised and Semi-supervised Learning, pp. 3–21. Springer, Cham (2020). https://doi.org/10.1007/978-3-030-22475-2_1

15. Albalate, A., Minker, W.: Semi-Supervised and Unsupervised Machine Learning: Novel Strategies, pp. 1–320. Wiley (2011)

16. Hu, W., Singh, R.R.P., Scalettar, R.T.: Discovering phases, phase transitions, and crossovers through unsupervised machine learning: a critical examination. Phys. Rev. E. **95**(6), 14 (2017). https://doi.org/10.1103/PhysRevE.95.062122

17. Nahili, W., Rezeg, K., Kazar, O.: A new corpus-based convolutional neural network for big data text analytics. Journal of Intelligence Studies in Business **9**(2), 59–71 (2019). https://doi.org/10.37380/jisib.v9i2.469

18. Ramesh, V.P., Baskaran, P., Krishnamoorthy, A., Damodaran, D., Sadasivam, P.: Back propagation neural network based big data analytics for a stock market challenge. Commun. Stat.: Theory Methods **48**(14), 3622–3642 (2019). https://doi.org/10.1080/03610926.2018.1478103

19. Chong, A.Y.L., Ch'ng, E., Liu, M.J., Li, B.: Predicting consumer product demands via big data: the roles of online promotional marketing and online reviews. Int. J. Prod. Res. **55**(17), 5142–5156 (2017). https://doi.org/10.1080/00207543.2015.1066519

20. Paliouras, G., Papatheodorou, C., Karkaletsis, V., Spyropoulos, C.D.: Discovering user communities on the Internet using unsupervised machine learning techniques. Interact. Comput. **14**(6), 761–791 (2002). https://doi.org/10.1016/S0953-5438(02)00015-2

21. Maślankowski, J.: Towards de-duplication framework in big data analysis: a case study. In: Wrycza, S. (ed.) SIGSAND/PLAIS 2016. LNBIP, vol. 264, pp. 104–113. Springer, Cham (2016). https://doi.org/10.1007/978-3-319-46642-2_7

Multi-language Sentiment Analysis – Lesson Learnt from NLP Case Study

Jacek Maślankowski[1]([✉]) [iD] and Dorota Majewicz[2] [iD]

[1] University of Gdańsk, ul. Armii Krajowej 101, 81-824 Sopot, Poland
jacek.maslankowski@ug.edu.pl
[2] The Academy of Tourism and Hotel Management in Gdansk, ul. Miszewskiego 12/13,
80-239 Gdańsk, Poland

Abstract. The aim of this paper is to present the use of sentiment analysis in both Polish and English languages. This goal is related to the fact that the authors of this article have observed many sentences in both Polish and English, used in social media and on websites in Poland. The paper presents the principles of various inflectional forms that should be used in the preparation of the training dataset being the subject of the analysis. Therefore, one of the goals of this article is to identify possible problems that an analyst of sentiment analysis machine learning methods may misinterpret. The motivation of the study was to see if the same methods could be used to analyse sentiment in different languages. We decided to evaluate the possibility of using one sentiment evaluation mechanism, assuming the use of similarly prepared training sets. In addition, the article shows the principles and differences between these languages, including in terms of the possibility of gender identification based on the text. We presented the results of a case study that showed how machine learning tools treat unstructured data to find the right sentiment and what problems can be identified when delivering text in these two languages. The conducted study also showed the possibility of using Big Data sources, such as comments in the form of comments on websites or social media, in order to correctly identify the sentiment, which is not always the case if the training set is not prepared properly.

Keywords: Big data · Text mining · Lexical analysis · Sentiment analysis

1 Introduction

The goal of the paper is to test sentiment analysis approach that can be used for both Polish and English, e.g., whether it is possible to identify correct sentiment or a gender based on the text provided. Such analyses are necessary to provide information on groups of people commenting on specific events, which is currently the subject of frequent analyses in the business community. This applies, among others, to opinions on specific products, public sentiment, consumer confidence or similar issues. We prepared a case study that shows how machine learning tools treat the unstructured data to find the right sentiment.

This paper was divided into six parts. After introduction and theoretical background, in the third part there is a theoretical background on IT issues and a comparison of

© Springer Nature Switzerland AG 2022
M. Themistocleous and M. Papadaki (Eds.): EMCIS 2021, LNBIP 437, pp. 46–54, 2022.
https://doi.org/10.1007/978-3-030-95947-0_4

the syntax and semantics of Polish and English. The fourth part concentrates on the case study, whose aim was to show deficiencies in machine learning methods when traditional tokenization rules are applied. It also shows the need for lemmatization and obstacles that such method can deal with. The fifth part shows the traps of natural language processing for different languages. Several examples have been included to show the possible problems in multi-language machine learning exercise. It shows that the problems can be reduced to a common denominator as long as the lemmatization and stemming process are properly processed and any redundant words are removed. The last part shows the conclusions.

The paper shows that we need dedicated solutions for machine learning purposes and differences between languages, namely Polish and English, do not allow for applying any unified method of text mining. The research question is: whether it is possible to use similar approach to provide the result of analysis having data in two languages – i.e. English and Polish. Additional analysis shows main differences between different flexible forms and structures, which have impact on the way the algorithm for sentiment analysis should be trained and tested.

2 Theoretical Background

Increasing complexity of big data methods and tools has given opportunities to process and extract valuable information from unstructured data, like text from the web. Currently, web data are one of the most widely used big data sources [1]. In research papers the feature of big data that allows to process web data is considered as a Business Intelligence & Analytics 2.0 [2]. Typical methods that can be used for text processing include lexical analysis, such as word counts or collocates [3]. One of the methods is a sentiment analysis that can be conducted based on explicit or implicit sentiment expressions. An explicit sentiment expression is when it is possible to express an emotion through a single emotion word. Implicit sentiment expression is when the message is not directly expressed but used as a suggestion or command [4]. Text mining and sentiment analysis can be used to process unstructured information to find, e.g., brand related topics and sentiments within the text [5]. Text analytics is especially important in enterprises. It is estimated that about 80% of data in enterprises is unstructured [6].

Natural Language Processing (NLP) may focus on three challenges: linguistic, statistical and computational [7]. Based on the semantic parsing method and statistical occurrences in the text, specific information can be provided. NLP can be used to extract data models and process them based on text [8]. There are several examples in which a useful data model can be formed based on the web data. This included detailed information on job vacancies or real-estates [9]. However, in many cases this information is extracted from websites that have a semi-structure form. Another aspect is to define correctly bag of words [10], which is important when there is a risk of typos in the sentence, typical to written short messages. This method is used nowadays to solve different problems, not only applied to text [11] like in this paper. However, we can observe the evaluation of the approaches to define bag of words for text classification, but mostly they start with text lemmatization as a key step at starting point [12].

Unstructured information is always more noisy than information that comes from databases. It leads to the misinterpretation of the key sentiment based on the sentence or text. Therefore, there is a need to apply a big data quality framework, which controls the data quality on every step of the data processing [13].

3 Syntax and Semantics of Natural Language

Theoretically, the comparison of structures in different languages seems to have no limitations imposed, with emphasis put on their value. We, therefore, face the problem of determining which structures in two or more languages are comparable, and one of the criteria seems to be semantic equivalence [14]. It is the principles of formal semantics which are used in the process of big data analysis. Described as the knowledge of meaning, cognitive in nature, it expresses a part of human knowledge that allows a person to match sounds and meanings [15]. Here, formal semantics, with its attempt to describe and provide explanation for semantic facts, appears as a part of Chomsky's linguistic competence of a natural language user [16]. In a natural language, linguistic competence—which constitutes knowledge of language—is implicit, i.e., language users do not have conscious access to the principles and rules that govern the combination of sounds, words, and sentences. They, however, recognize the violation of rules and principles. [17]. Thus, in the IT environment, one needs reliable solutions for a machine to "learn" processes for semantic identification, which are challenging in English and Polish analysis.

According to Bańczerowski, the larger the number of languages with which a given language is confronted, the more complete its description will be, and the fuller its typological status, and a similar statement can also be made about various models [14]. The issue arising is how the meaning relates to the world, as it is more than a mental phenomenon, and there is a need for the semantic theory to explain both the "internal" and "external" nature of meaning. In the comparative analysis of both languages by big data tools, we adopted the view that semantic rules must be sensitive to syntactic structure, as syntax affects interpretation, and the explanation lies in the fact that syntactic ambiguity leads to semantic ambiguity [18]. As we present in the next part of the paper, if two or more syntactic rules can be applied at some point, it follows that a sentence will be semantically ambiguous. Thus, regardless of the language analyzed, a major factor in programming language statements interpretation is pragmatics, which involves a broad scope of knowledge, and this includes "the programme's actions, the way he plans to implement the created programs using syntax and semantics and it addresses the programmer's background and attitude and what he is intended to create, their understanding of the context in which a programming language statement is created from, and their knowledge of the way in which language is used to communicate information" [19].

With regard to the main topic of the paper, we have considered several contrastive explorations between Polish and English language, which may serve as a challenge in the processes of big data analysis. First of all, Polish sentence structure is more flexible than the English one, and it allows for changes in the order of constituents without significant change in the meaning. Polish has a more complex morphological structure; nouns, adjectives and pronouns are inflected, which is related to their function in a sentence, with each gender having a different form for the Nominative, Genitive, Dative, Accusative, Instrumental, Locative, and Vocative case, make the analysis of Polish texts more challenging. However both Polish and English nouns have three genders, in Polish, grammatical gender has nothing to do with natural gender (sex); it is mainly of importance for purposes of grammatical agreement, where feminine nouns require that a modifying adjective have relevant endings (e.g., nowy komputer). In English, gender is sometimes shown by different forms or different words when referring to people or animals (e.g., boy, girl, child), while the form of modifying adjectives remains the same in all cases, with single exceptions, e.g. blond, blonde.. In English, many nouns that refer to people's roles and jobs can be used for either a masculine or a feminine subject, such as teenager, doctor, friend, or cousin, while Polish relevant nouns usually refer to either subject, e.g., nastolatek/nastolatka, lekarz/lekarka; przyjaciel/przyjaciółka; kuzyn/kuzynka. However, in a specific context, a masculine subject may occur in the general meaning, where gender has not been specified, for example: Dobrze jest mieć przyjaciół (It is good to have friends). In the sentence, masculine plural form has been presented, while the actual meaning is It is good to have friends, and speakers usually equally consider both male and female ones in this context, with no specification for male ones as suggested by the form. In English, the distinction for neutral words is possible by adding the words male or female (e.g., male friend to indicate that a man is not a boyfriend).

Nouns in Polish have seven different case forms for expressing grammatical case (but some case suffixes are the same), which is related to their function (theta roles) in a sentence, with each gender having a different form for the Nominative, Genitive, Dative, Accusative, Instrumental, Locative, and Vocative case. In short, the Nominative case is used to express the subject of a sentence, the Dative to express the indirect object (to or for whom something is done), the Accusative the direct object, i.e., the item perceived or acted on by the subject. The Instrumental expresses the means by which something is done (for example, ride by train, write with a pen). The Genitive expresses possession and, in general, and for example, end of the world, most of all, etc. The Locative is used with certain prepositions, especially prepositions expressing the simple locational senses with the use of prepositions such as on, in, at; while the Vocative is used to address someone directly. In English, however, there are only three grammatical cases used in personal pronouns (I, you, he, she, etc.) and who: subjective case, where pronouns used as subject (e.g., I); objective case, where pronouns used as objects of verbs or prepositions (me); and finally possessive case, with pronouns expressing ownership (mine). In nouns the first two cases (subjective and objective) are indistinguishable, and are called the common case, while the possessive in nouns occurs in the apostrophe form of the word (John's).

In the sentiment analysis, it is rather a semantic interpretation that plays a crucial role in the interpretation of various Polish sentences. Negation in English is applied through the verb phrase (by inserting the negative adverb not after the first auxiliary verb of the verb phrase or by inserting the operator do and the negative adverb not before the verb, e.g., I cannot go there/I will not read that book), through noun phrase negation (I have no time); through adjective phrase negation (They are not tall). Other English types of negation include negative indefinite pronouns: no one, nobody, nothing and none, the negative adverb never, together with nowhere, nothing, hardly, and scarcely. The grammatical rules of Standard English do not allow for the use for a double or triple negation (Don't do nothing never). In contrast, Polish negation rules are more complex.

While negative forms such as nic (nothing), nigdy (never) or nigdzie (nowhere) by rule require a negative verb form, the semantic interpretation becomes more tentative in the analysis in, for example, Ona nigdy nic nie zrozumie versus Ona nic nie neguje, with the former sentence being negative, while the latter positive. Moreover, expressions dość and nie zbyt (Ona jest dość ładna vs. Ona nie jest zbyt ładna) are semantically opposite, and they, as such, might be a challenge for machine learning tools. The sentence Ona jest dość brzydka would be univocally marked negative in the sentiment analysis, while Ona nie jest zbyt brzydka, normally suggesting a positive opinion, would be marked as negative in the sentiment analysis process (two negative markers). Similar interpretation problems will occur with expressions such as niekoniecznie (niekoniecznie brzydki = positive), mało (mało interesujące = negative), similarly to contrastive expressions such as chociaż, wprawdzie, or ale, which induce a semantic twist. Thus, a semantic web extended by a field based on sentiment markers appears extremely valuable in the natural language processing development.

With the focus on the semantics and pragmatics for additional linguistic markers, another challenge research arises, namely, the use of humor and irony in big data tool analysis, which skillfully manipulate the syntactic and structural ambiguity of the sentence (humor) and use words that say the opposite of what the addresser really means (irony).

4 Case Study

The case study has been used to make a comparison analysis of the possibilities to extract sentiment information from both Polish and English language. The survey was divided into two parts. In the first part an automatic sentiment detection library was used. We decided to do this part to know what the precision of the analysis regarding different expressions is. The software used in this case study was a big data ecosystems including Apache Spark/Hadoop with scripts written in Python. The primary library used to check the efficiency of correct identification of different expression was a MonkeyLearn library. The analysis were supported by Pandas and Numpy libraries for loading and processing the data. In the second part of the case study we decided to use Machine Learning with our own training dataset. To accomplish this task, we prepared a training dataset with different sentences regarding three types of sentiment: positive, negative, and neutral.

The first lookup in the training datasets allows the formulation of the conclusion that Polish language is much more complex to train. The reason lies in different forms of verbs, and, as a result, lemmatization is a key issue during the process of preparing the training dataset for Polish language. Both datasets required to prepare a stop words dictionary. Although numerous stop words dictionaries have been published on various websites, still there is a necessity to prepare a dedicated for a specific data source a set of a stop words. Looking into such dictionaries can be a bit confusing, especially that words such as "jeden" in Polish – which is translated into English as "one" is indicating a specific number. We could also find a word "nie" in Polish stop words dictionary. This word in English is "no" and is crucial in sentiment analysis. However, we could find this example of stop word in English dictionary either. Examples of stop words that can be ambiguous in terms of the accuracy of proper identification of sentiment are shown in Table 1.

Table 1. Selected stop words that can change the meaning of the sentence

Suggestion	Polish	English
Not include	nie	no
Include	i	and
Not include	więcej	more

In Table 1 we put three different examples of stop words that may result in ambiguous identification of the sentiment. For example – the word "nie" can change the meaning of a specific expression, e.g., "you have no chance" is negative. Omitting this word in the sentence will make the sentence written wrongly. Thus, we need to have a dedicated set of stop words that is a result of a deep analysis of natural language expressions used in a specific data source.

The issue is especially visible in various web portals, where the language used in the social media is quite different. Because Twitter social media uses short messages (up to 140 characters), the sentiment identification can be relatively difficult. However, our observation shows that it is highly recommended to make analysis of the hashtags first then look into the whole post to have additional information of the sentiment. The hashtags can be such as "depressed" or similar. Therefore, it is quite easy to identify whether the sentiment is negative, positive or neutral. In the case studies, we decided to have these three types of sentiment, because most of the machine learning libraries related to sentiment analysis allow for classification of the text according to these three classes.

In the second part of the study we repeated the same exercise for using Naive Bayes algorithm. We have prepared a training dataset with selected words and provide a sample testing examples. The results we discovered were similar to the ones described in the previous part of this paper.

5 Results of Analysis

The goal of the case study was to make a comparison of analysis of different typical expressions. In this chapter we concentrated on the expressions in English language that are tested with the MonkeyLearn (monkeylearn.com) machine learning library. Because this library is developed by experts and available in free as well as paid version, we decided to prepare some lexical expressions to show that lemmatization will not work on selected phrases. In Table 2 we present results of analysis of specific sentences. It includes sentences themselves, their length, probability of proper identification, and sentiments identified.

Table 2. Selected sentences and its sentiment

No.	Sentence	Length of the sentence	Probability of proper identification	Sentiment
1	Good, very good, I am so happy	30	0.997	Positive
2	Bad, that was so bad in my life	31	0.693	Negative
3	I feel not bad not good	23	0.820	Negative
4	Have you ever been to such a good place?	40	0.721	Positive
5	Today we have a long discussion whether it is good to be good or not good to be bad	84	0.935	Positive
6	Good!	5	0.999	Positive
7	Bad!	4	0.765	Negative
8	Not bad	7	0.885	Negative
9	No good	7	0.807	Positive
10	Frankly speaking, I am not happy	33	0.721	Positive

In Table 2 we have selected sentences that should be easy to identify by a machine learning tool. They include typical words that have positive or negative meaning, such as good, bad or different ones. Please note that we included in the table sentences that have different length to know how it affects the probability of proper identification. For example, sentence 1 contains three positive words – "good," "good" and "happy". It is easy to understand that such an expression will have a positive meaning. However, because the sentence has other words than those three mentioned, it was identified with the probability of 0.997. The second sentence is definitely negative – it has two words "bad". Still, it was not identified with the probability of 1 because it has other words included. The longer expression may a bit confusing for machine learning algorithm that extracts information by tokenization of specific words. For example such expressions were included in the table in 4th and 5th position. In sentence 4 there is one word "good" that makes this sentence positive. The probability is 0.721. The sentence 5 is longer and has a neutral meaning. We made also a test to receive a score of the words "good" and "bad" – position 6 and 7. Please note that the probability of good as a positive meaning resulted in a probability of 0.999 (exclamation mark included in the sentence), while the word "bad" had a negative meaning with the probability of 0.765 (also exclamation mark was included). The weaknesses of machine learning typical algorithms that divide the sentence into words was discovered in sentences 8 and 9. The sentence "not bad" was treated as a negative with the probability of 0.885. It means that the word "not" has a negative meaning and bad as well which scores to the amount of 0.885. In sentence 9, "no good" the probability was lower than the word good – 0.807 comparing to 0.999 for the sentence "Good!", which shows that the negation of the word does not have a huge impact on the overall meaning of the sentence.

As English is widely spoken around the world, there are many libraries that offer bag of words analysis, whether it is bi-gram or n-gram. The variation is also not troublesome, as it is mostly limited to removing endings, such as -ing or -s. The situation is different in the case of the second analyzed language. Here, due to numerous inflectional variations, the use of various forms of words, the use of bag of words requires very specialized algorithms allowing for stemming and lemmatization at a high level of abstraction. For example, the masculine and feminine forms already change the form of words that must first be checked to the basic form. In the case of our case study, the rule was to replace all words with their basic form, using dictionaries prepared based on publicly available data. Only in the second stage, the rules described in the context of the English language were applied.

In the case of Polish language, the results were similar to the ones received in English language. It means that different negative forms must be treated as a part of the sentence. Otherwise, the machine learning algorithm will detect the sentence in opposite way, just because of polarization of specific words, not recognizing the negative forms in correct way.

6   Conclusions

Our case study shows that selecting a proper training dataset is crucial when natural language processing and text mining methods are applied. We also need to manually detect whether the machine learning tool identifies sentences correctly or not, and simple identification based on keywords is insufficient. There are different expressions, such as "not bad" that should have a positive meaning, but, as it has been shown in Table 2, typical machine learning tool may treat each word separately, treating such expression as two words "bad" and "not" with different scores. Therefore, there is a need to instruct the machine learning tool how to deal with collocations and complex expressions. It shows that bi-grams and n-grams are necessary in NLP applications to the text provided from social media or Internet.

The second conclusion from the paper is that there is no unified method to deal with different languages syntax and lexical forms. We proved that Polish language needs stemming and lemmatization, while it is not so important for English. However, if we want to join the training dataset, it is a key issue to do the stemming and lemmatization for both languages. On the other side, we see a huge problem in applying lemmatization for the whole of the sentence, as it may change the overall meaning of the sentence.

Another very important aspect is that for national languages not so common as English, we are obliged to prepare our own training datasets. As it is widely known, preparation of the good training dataset, i.e. having the right proportion and transparent sentences may be not possible in many cases. Therefore, preparation of the same analysis for Polish and English (e.g. sentiment or emotional analysis) leads to a disproportionately large workload in relation to the results in the case of the Polish language. This rule may apply to other national languages as well, which are not so popular as English.

The final conclusion is that preparing a reliable and relevant tool for natural language processing leads to the necessity of preparing a dedicated training dataset that will include all lexical forms necessary in the referred testing data source.

References

1. Franks, B. (ed.): Web data: the original big data. In: Taming the Big Data Tidal Wave: Finding Opportunities in Huge Data Streams with Advanced Analytics. Wiley (2012)
2. Chen, H., Chiang, R., Storey, V.: Business intelligence and analytics: from big data to big impact. MIS Q. **36**(4), 1165–1188 (2012)
3. van Grinsven, V.T., Snijkers, G.: Sentiments and perceptions of business respondents on social media: an exploratory analysis. J. Off. Stat. **31**(2), 283–304 (2015)
4. Ordenes, V.F., Ludwig, S., De Ruyter, K., Grewal, D., Wetzels, M.: Unveiling what is written in the stars: analyzing explicit, implicit, and discourse patterns of sentiment in social media. J. Consum. Res. **43**(6), 875–894 (2017)
5. Liu, X., Burns, A.C., Hou, Y.: An investigation of brand-related user-generated content on Twitter. J. Advert. **46**(2), 236–247 (2017)
6. Müller, O., Debortoli, S., Junglas, I., vom Brocke, J.: Using text analytics to derive customer service management benefits from unstructured data. MIS Q. Exec. **15**(4), 243–258 (2016)
7. Liang, P.: Learning executable semantic parsers for natural language understanding. Commun. ACM **59**(9), 68–76 (2016)
8. Osman, C., Zălhan, P.: From natural language text to visual models: a survey of issues and approaches. Inform. Econ. **20**(4), 44–61 (2016)
9. Maślankowski, J.: Towards de-duplication framework in big data analysis. a case study. In: Wrycza, S. (ed.) SIGSAND/PLAIS 2016. LNBIP, vol. 264, pp. 104–113. Springer, Cham (2016). https://doi.org/10.1007/978-3-319-46642-2_7
10. Ishihara, S.: Score-based likelihood ratios for linguistic text evidence with a bag-of-words model. Forensic Sci. Int. **327**, 110980 (2021). https://doi.org/10.1016/j.forsciint.2021.110980
11. Ameer, R.S.A., Al-Taei, M.: Human action recognition based on bag-of-words. Iraqi J. Sci. **61**(5), 1202–1214 (2020). https://doi.org/10.24996/ijs.2020.61.5.27
12. Yan, D., Li, K., Gu, S., Yang, L.: Network-based bag-of-words model for text classification. IEEE Access **8**, 82641–82652 (2020). https://doi.org/10.1109/ACCESS.2020.2991074
13. Maślankowski, J.: Data quality issues concerning statistical data gathering supported by big data technology. In: Kozielski, S., Mrozek, D., Kasprowski, P., Małysiak-Mrozek, B., Kostrzewa, D. (eds.) BDAS 2014. CCIS, vol. 424, pp. 92–101. Springer, Cham (2014). https://doi.org/10.1007/978-3-319-06932-6_10
14. Bańczerowski, J.: Some contrastive considerations about semantics in the communication process. In: Fisiak, J. (ed.) Papers and Studies in Contrastive Linguistics. The Polish-English Contrastive Project, vol. 2, pp. 11–32. Adam Mickiewicz University Poznań; Center for Applied Linguistics, Washington D.C. (1974)
15. Piasecki, M.: Selektywne wprowadzenie do semantyki formalnej. In: Szymanik, J., Zajenkowski, M. (eds.) Kognitywistyka. O umyśle umyślnie i nieumyślnie, pp.114–117, Koło Filozoficzne przy MISH, Uniwersytet Warszawski (2004)
16. Larson, R., Segal, G.: Knowledge of Meaning. MIT Press, Cambridge (1995)
17. Fernández, E.M., Smith Cairns, H.: Fundamentals of Psycholinguistics, p.1–10. Wiley-Blackwell (2011)
18. Briscoe, T.: Introduction to formal semantics for natural language (2011). http://www.cl.cam.ac.uk/teaching/1011/L107/semantics.pdf
19. Kebande, R.V., Karani, N.Y.: Formal semantics, syntax, pragmatics: an essence of programming language design. Acad. Res. Int. **4**(2), 124–131 (2013)

Modeling User Engagement Profiles for Detection of Digital Subscription Propensity

Paweł Misiorek[1]([⊠]) [iD], Jakub Warmuz[2], Dominik Kaczmarek[2],
and Michał Ciesielczyk[2] [iD]

[1] Poznan University of Technology, Faculty of Computing and Telecommunications
Institute of Computing, ul. Piotrowo 2, 61-138 Poznan, Poland
pawel.misiorek@put.poznan.pl
[2] Deep.BI Poland, Warszawa, Poland
{jakub.warmuz,dominik.kaczmarek,michal.ciesielczyk}@deep.bi
https://deep.bi

Abstract. In this paper, we study how the application of a dynamic user engagement profiling can influence the efficiency of systems aimed at detecting the user's propensity to buy a subscription. Specifically, we address a task of identifying the digital media readers who are involved enough in the publisher's offer to pay for access to the content of a given webpage. We present the user engagement profile updating framework responsible for enriching raw events with time-agnostic temporal features. In particular, we experimentally evaluate the performance of machine learning algorithms for the task of predicting the user propensity to subscribe using the synthetic dataset based on publicly available data streams on users of KKBox's music service. Additionally, we provide the results of online tests in which the propensity-to-subscribe prediction model is used to control the paywall displays on a digital media website with live traffic. The results of experiments have proven that enrichment of data with engagement profiles leads to higher performance of prediction models than relying just on raw features and tuning the model's hyperparameters.

Keywords: Big data · User engagement modeling · User profiling · Subscription for digital content · Streaming data processing

1 Introduction

In the landscape of digital media publishers, only a small fraction of readers bother to register on the website. An even smaller portion of them converts into subscribers to the premium content, which constitutes one of the primary sources of income for the publishers. The identification and accurate targeting of the users who might be interested enough in the offer to pay for access are therefore crucial for the financial success of digital media publishers and other

© Springer Nature Switzerland AG 2022
M. Themistocleous and M. Papadaki (Eds.): EMCIS 2021, LNBIP 437, pp. 55–68, 2022.
https://doi.org/10.1007/978-3-030-95947-0_5

premium-content-generating businesses. As a result, those enterprises are adopting subscription propensity modeling more and more often.

As Gould Finch and Frankfurter Buchmesse point out in their white paper[1], the impact of Artificial Intelligence (AI) on the publishing industry will be immense. Major publishing houses have already implemented predictive solutions into their workflows with impressive results. Bloomberg Media has leveraged a Machine Learning (ML) model that calculates the subscription propensity scores to optimize the paywall height for each user, thus maximizing revenue [12]. In another study, a group at the New York Times has shown that with a dynamic paywall steered by propensity scores, they were able to increase the probability of subscribing to premium content by 10% in only 11 weeks, leading to a net profit of at least $230,000 during the seven-month study [3]. Additionally, researchers have already demonstrated the value of time-aware user engagement features in building subscription prediction models [7].

Given the industry sentiment in which such prominent characters as Andrew Ng advocate for more data-centric rather than model-centric approaches to AI [1], this paper investigates the impact of real-time profile enrichment with time-agnostic behavioral features on the efficiency of propensity-to-subscribe modeling. It has to be stressed that one of the pain points in building predictive models in the publishers' industry is the time-sensitivity of the solution. A prediction for a user needs to be generated before they lose interest and exit the website, upon which the marketing targeting becomes intractable. On the other hand, user preferences are highly dynamic. A user who was not interested in the offer yesterday may be inclined to buy today after reading an engaging article. In practice, this means that the ML pipelines need to score the users in seconds or even immediately. In order to meet these requirements, in this paper, we address the problem of building scalable and efficient dynamic user engagement profiling applicable to be used by machine learning models generating propensity-to-subscribe predictions in a streaming manner.

The paper contribution is as follows. Given the needs of digital media publishers, we demonstrate how user profiles can be enriched in real-time and used for propensity-to-subscribe modeling. We describe the user engagement profile dynamic updating framework being a part of the Deep Glue System responsible for managing the users of the digital content. We prove the importance of proper time-aware data preprocessing based on user engagement features through offline experiments conducted on the synthetic propensity-to-subscribe dataset derived from KKBox's dataset[2], and online testing conducted on the digital media website with live traffic. In particular, we find that with real-time user profile enrichment with behavioral data, we are able to significantly improve the efficiency of ML models on the KKBox's dataset and increase digital media publishers' monthly subscription rates by up to 100%. The profiling method delivers user engagement features, which are more context-independent

---

[1] https://www.buchmesse.de/files/media/pdf/White_Paper_AI_Publishing_Gould_Finch_2019_EN.pdf.

[2] https://wsdm-cup-2018.kkbox.events/.

and more time-agnostic. This makes them more generalizable and applicable to multiple niches within the industry, for which the ML models are usually served in an environment that differs from the one where the models were trained and tuned.

2   Related Work

Most of the literature about user profile enrichment focuses on social media applications. Usually, they are based on processing textual data [16] extracted from popular services such as Twitter [8]. Additionally, many research papers on real-time user scoring use the collaborative filtering approach derived from recommendation systems, in which content recommendations are based on similar users' content consuming patterns [17]. This is not applicable to our case, as we are not working with social media, where one can create a network graph of connections between users – our goal is to predict the propensity to subscribe or churn rather than recommending new content. Tang et al. [18] propose time-forgetting machines which use temporal behavior to discount the old preferences of the users in real-time recommendation systems. We use a similar concept in that our enrichment mechanism adds the time-agnostic temporal features, e.g., based on aggregation in a specific time window. The idea of data enrichment using features modeling user engagement is also used by competitors of KKBox's Churn Prediction Challenge [13] aimed at building Machine Learning models for churn prediction task based on a dataset containing events of user interactions in a music service given as daily user logs describing their listening behaviors [14]. The authors of [15] use a similar schema of building engagement features defined as aggregation over a time window to the one used in this paper. However, we propose a more general framework enabling the definition of counting features or custom features defined as functions of other features. Other studies on modeling and measuring user engagement in the context of digital media are presented in [4,11]. In particular, the author of [11] investigates the patterns of user engagement in a large dataset consisting of page views of news articles. In contrast to our research, his approach is focused on the relationship between engagement levels and information gain in articles' text.

The detection of user's propensity to subscribe for digital content is an under-explored research problem [6]. In [7], Davoudi et al. propose the time-aware subscription prediction model using user engagement measures. In more recent research presented in [5,6] the authors study the adaptive paywall control policies. In contrast to these results, our research is focused on investigating the influence of dynamic user engagement profiling on the efficiency of machine learning models aimed at prediction a user propensity to subscribe. Moreover, we present the results on tests conducted on website with live traffic.

3   User Engagement Profile Updating

The main goal of our user engagement profile updating framework is to enrich the events about users with new time-aware features modeling their current

Table 1. User engagement profile features.

Feature type	Description
Counters	Features counting the number of specific events in a given time window, e.g., the number of page opens (Volume), or the number of days with at least one visit (Frequency)
Total sums	Sums for a given original features in a given time window, e.g., total number of seconds spent using the service
Basic Statistics	Averages, minimum/maximum of a given raw feature, e.g., daily average of user visits in a given time window
Recency features	Time elapsed from a last occurrence of a given event, e.g. number of days from last visit (Recency)
Custom features	Features defined using formulas involving other features values, e.g., the change of some feature in a given time window, the RFV score being the function of the Recency, Frequency and Volume (RFV) values.
Segment features	Features obtained as a result of discretization of numeric features, e.g., segments based on RFV scores, etc.

engagement. For a given user u and a given timestamp t the user engagement profile $p(u, t)$ may be formally modeled as a sequence of features:

$$p(u, t) = (f_1, \ldots, f_m),$$

where m is a total number of features in the profile.

Profile features are generated based on events collected in various time windows, defined as some periods (e.g., 1 h, 7 days, entire history) before the time t, which usually corresponds to the timestamp of the enriched event. Most of them are the aggregation features, including counters of specific events (e.g., the number of paywalls shown) or total sums of a given original numeric feature (e.g., the number of seconds spent in the system) in the given time window. Additionally, profiles include features based on simple statistics such as a minimum, maximum or average in a given time window. Finally, they are complemented by custom features based on predefined formulas involving the current values of original or other enriched profile features. More details about engagement feature types are presented in Table 1.

The overview of the system architecture is depicted on Fig. 1. In the online environment, the stream of user events (denoting different interactions with the system) is collected in real-time and are stored on a distributed messaging system (Apache Kafka[3]).

All the raw events are enriched online with user profiles and ML model predictions using Apache Flink[4] framework. The user engagement profile is updated

---

[3] https://kafka.apache.org.
[4] https://flink.apache.org.

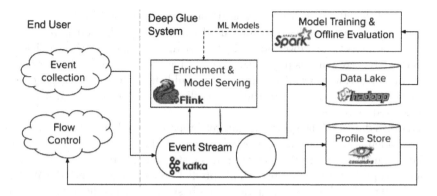

Fig. 1. System architecture diagram.

online on every interaction collected. As a result, the generated predictions for a specific user change depending on the actions she performs. The main reason for modeling the user profiles and embedding them into the raw events is to simplify the learning process. The current user profile represents the context in which the specific action has been performed. Since the predictions are generated online, all the user profile features also have to be calculated in a streaming manner.

The output predictions are indexed for fast access in a profile store (powered by Apache Cassandra[5]). For online decision-making, the last available prediction for a specific user is used. The same data stream is also stored on Hadoop Distributed File System[6] for subsequent batch processing. The ML models are trained, tuned, and evaluated offline (using Apache Spark[7]) using the latest data available. Since the data stored is as an event stream, the target label used during the training represents the information whether a specific sequence of user interactions resulted in a subscription event. After each model building cycle, the result serialized models are pushed to Apache Flink where they are used for online prediction generation.

4   Datasets

Two datasets are used for the purposes of research presented here.

1. Digital media publisher's dataset. The dataset based on events describing the behavior of users exploring the content of a digital news site of the large media publisher from Western Europe. The publisher's site is visited by about 1.5M unique users daily (both subscribers and non-subscribers), generating about 3.5M page views (both from desktop and mobile devices) on a daily average. The data used in this paper was collected in a period from November 21, 2020,

---

[5] https://cassandra.apache.org.

[6] https://hadoop.apache.org/.

[7] https://spark.apache.org/.

to March 2, 2021. Each event was dynamically enhanced by features from user engagement profiles and then used to learn the ML models predicting user's propensity to subscribe. This dataset directly matches the application scenario targeted in this paper. Moreover, it has to build ML models for online testing involving paywall control on the publisher site based on generated predictions. However, due to the non-public character of the data, it cannot be shared or published.

2. KKBox's dataset. The synthetic dataset prepared based on publicly available for academic research purposes KKBox's churn dataset [13,14]. The original data came from KKBOX, a leading music streaming company from Taiwan, and was prepared for KKBox's churn prediction challenge within the WSDM Cup 2018 [14]. We chose this dataset as a basis since it has the unique feature of providing many timestamped events for each user. Specifically, the dataset contains daily reports summarizing activities of a given user by means of the numbers of songs played or total time spent. This kind of data enables one to process it as data streams in order to enhance the events with features of the user engagement profile [14,15]. For the purposes of our synthetic dataset, we used only the part of available data containing the reports on user activities (provided in files user_logs.csv) enhanced by basic data on users (provided in file members.csv). Then we have labeled the samples with labels simulating users' subscriptions. Eventually, in order to make our results reproducible, we made our final dataset (after labeling and enhancing with user engagement profiles) publicly available[8].

The details of datasets' preprocessing including labeling and profile-based enhancement were presented in Sect. 5.

5   Experimentation Setup

In this section, the details of experimentation scenarios are described for both datasets used in our research.

5.1   KKBox's Dataset Experiments

The goal of the experiments introduced in this section is to demonstrate the significant improvement of machine learning algorithms' efficiency caused by enhancing the input data with additional features from our subsystem of user engagement profiles building. As we made our KKBox's dataset modification publicly available, these experiments should be replicable.

Dataset Prepartion. The data preparation includes feature engineering, filtering, and labeling. We used the user_logs.csv file from Kaggle's WSDM - KKBox's Churn Prediction Challenge [10,13,14] as a basis and complemented it with

---

[8] https://www.kaggle.com/pawelwmm/kkbox-user-engagement-modeling-dataset.

Table 2. KKBox dataset features.

Feature short name	Description	Feature type
num_unq	# of unique songs played	raw
num_25	# of songs played less than 25% of the song length	raw
num_50	# of songs played between 25% to 50% of the song length	raw
num_75	# of songs played between 50% to 75% of the song length	raw
num_985	# of songs played between 75% to 98.5% of the song length	raw
num_100	# of songs played over 98.5% of the song length	raw
total_secs	Total seconds played	raw
registered_via	Registration method	raw
registration_init_time	Registration timestamp	raw
avg_num_unq	Average # of unique songs listened to by the user	profile
smooth_avg_num_unq	Smoothed avg_num_unq	profile
days_since_first_visit	# of days since the user was first observed in the service	profile
max_num_unq	Maximum # of songs played in a day	profile
min_num_unq	Minimum # of songs played in a day	profile
visit_frequency.lastNdays	Frequency of visits in the last N days (for N=7,14,28,56,112,1000 days)	profile
volume.num_X.lastNdays	Total # of songs played to extend X over the last N days (for X=25,50,75,985,100 and N=7,14,28,56,112,1000 days)	profile
volume.total_secs.lastNdays	Total # of seconds spent using the service over the last N days (for N=7,14,28,56,112,1000 days)	profile

additional features concerning users from the members.csv file [13]. Then the raw data was enriched by user engagement features based on the framework described in Sect. 3. The short descriptions of dataset features are collected in Table 2, with the distinction to raw and user engagement profile features. Next, the target label simulating a subscription event was created. As a subscription event, we defined a moment in time in which a customer's average value on a target feature exceeds a certain threshold N days into the future from this user's event. We chose the number of unique songs played as the target feature and 14 days as a value of N. This means that in order for a user event to be labeled as a subscription, the moving average over the next 14 days on the target feature needs to exceed a given threshold. Such a method of data labeling prevents the look-ahead bias. The distribution of the target feature was strongly left-skewed, and thus, before the labeling, its values were cropped to below 125 unique songs. The threshold for labeling was set to 95 unique songs. This value was chosen in order to better correspond with the empirical user subscription rates that digital publishers experience. After the labeling, we obtained multiple events per user in the raw dataset. Therefore, a sampling method needed to be developed in such a way that only one event per user was left for the machine learning step. Here, we took a random event for a non-subscriber and an event in a day before the subscription for the subscribers (which corresponds to the last day before the 14-days-long period of the target feature average measurement).

Algorithms Under Evaluation. The choice of machine learning algorithms used in our study was motivated mainly by our experiences gained when preparing propensity-to-subscribe prediction models for business purposes. We chose the Logistic Regression (LR) algorithm as a basic solution and the Gradient Boosted Trees (GBT) algorithm as a solution used to build the final model applied for paywall control. What is crucial for the final application scenario is that prediction models based on the chosen algorithms can be easily serialized, distributed, and deployed on machines responsible for making online predictions. Moreover, both of these algorithms are known for working well on data with numerical features. In contrast to the LR algorithm, the GBT algorithm is able to exploit higher-order and more complex relations in data. Therefore, it provided models of better efficiency evaluated through standard ML measures. We built our models using the Hadoop computing cluster of 9 nodes with the total number of 54 CPU cores and 504GB RAM, and *LogisticRegression* and *GBTClassifier* implementations from Spark ML library [2].

The following approaches have been compared for the case of offline test performed using KKBox's dataset:

- LR algorithm on KKBox raw features (KKBox-only LR),
- LR algoritm on data enriched with features from user engagement profiles (Enriched LR),
- GBT algorithm on KKBox raw features (KKBox-only GBT),
- GBT algoritm on data enriched with features from user engagement profiles (Enriched GBT),
- LR algoritm using only the feature used in data labeling procedure (number of unique songs played) as a Baseline - our goal is to check how much the current value of these feature indicates that its average value in the next 14 days exceeds the threshold.

We conducted five experiments for different splits on training and test data for a training ratio equal to 0.7. The hyperparameters of the LR and GBT estimators were optimized by a 4-fold cross-validated grid search over predefined parameter ranges. The configurations of parameters chosen to build the final models included the following non-default settings:

- for LR: maximum number of iterations equal to 25, regularization parameter equal to 0.01;
- for GBT: maximum number of iterations equal to 85, maximum depth of the individual tree equal to 8.

Other parameters were set according their default values in the algorithms implementation [2]. The efficiency of algorithms was evaluated using the test set by the means of standard ML measures [9]. The evaluation results were presented in Sect. 6.

5.2   Publisher's Dataset Experiments

Dataset Prepreprocessing. The publisher's data used to build ML models was collected in a period from November 21, 2020, to March 2, 2021. The set of original raw page views was cleaned by removing events generated by web crawlers, users that cannot be reliably tracked, already active subscribers, unsupported devices, and sites that were not articles. Based on these events, we labeled the samples for the task of the propensity-to-subscribe prediction by setting all the page views of a given non-subscriber user opened no more than 2 h before the purchase as positive samples. Then, we randomly took one event for each user: the positive one for users with the subscription purchase and the negative one for each user without any subscription purchase. The final dataset contained about 1.5M samples with an imbalance ratio equal to about 0.00065.

Each event was dynamically enhanced with features from user engagement profiles used the system described in Sect. 3 (see Table 1). All temporal features were calculated for 7 and 30 days time windows. In total, out of 152 features in the data, 26 were chosen for the final model based on automated feature selection on the validation set.

Model Building. Before the training process, the data were divided into train, validation, and test sets. We chose time as a factor for partitioning the data. This way, we could mimic with history data the real-time nature of the target infrastructure. The distribution between sets was 70% for the training set, 10% for the validation set, and 20% for the test set. Since the raw data was highly imbalanced (with the imbalance ratio equal to 0.00065), we decided to downsample negative events in training data by removing them randomly with the downsampling ratio determined experimentally.

On-line Experiments. We deployed and tested our system in a real-world environment. We provided the tests, for which the ML model presented in the previous section – built using the Spark GBT algorithm trained on the historical data about publisher's users – was used to generate online predictions of users' propensity to subscribe. More precisely, the ML model predictions were calculated online for each opening of an article by a user, given the current context information (such as the time of the day or visit source) and the latest user engagement profile. Subsequently, the predictions indicating users' current propensity to subscribe were used to decide whether to display a paywall on the corresponding article.

The experiment was conducted online for four weeks, from May 17th, 2021, to June 13th, 2021. According to the experiment scenario, the dynamic paywall policy based on ML predictions was applied to article opens for a randomly selected subset of 454267 unique non-subscribers. The solution performance was evaluated by comparing with the parallel test on the randomly chosen control group of 100614 unique non-subscribers for which default paywall policy was applied. This default policy was to block access to specific content if and only if it belongs to the predefined set of premium articles, regardless of all other aspects. We collected the number of subscription purchases made during the experiment period in both groups separately. Finally, the user conversion rate was used as the performance measure for online testing, chosen since it reflects the business goals of a digital publisher. The results of the experiment are presented in Sect. 6.2.

6   Results

In this section, the results of experiments introduced in Sect. 5 are presented.

6.1   Results of KKBox's Dataset Experiments

The results of KKBox's off-line experiments are presented in Fig. 2 and 3 and Tables 3 and 4. The comparison of AUC curves shown in Fig. 2 confirms that the models based on enriched data (namely Enriched GBT and Enriched LR) have achieved better results than the models based on raw data. This observation is even more evident when looking at prediction qualities illustrated by means of precision recall curves (see Fig. 3). We can observe that KKBox-only LR model performs only a bit better than the baseline method based on the number of songs played at the last day before 'subscription'. Finally, we have observed that – when using the same set of features – models based on the GBT algorithm achieves better efficiency than the ones based on the LR algorithm.

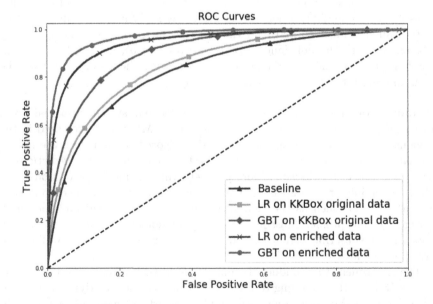

Fig. 2. ROC Curves for experiments on the KKBox's dataset.

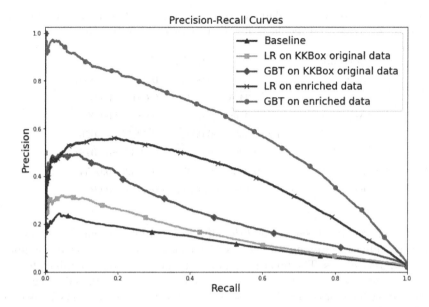

Fig. 3. Precision Recall Curves for experiments on the KKBox's dataset.

The values of most popular machine learning measures [9] collected in Tables 3 and 4 confirm the conclusions formulated when analysing the curves. In particular, the simple LR model based on data enriched with user profiles performs much better than more sophisticated GBT model limited to original data without profiles. These results demonstrate the key role of user engagement profiles in the performance of digital subscription propensity models.

Table 3. Results of KKBox's dataset experiments presented as means and standard deviations for series of 5 experiment iterations (Baseline and LR models).

Measure	Baseline	KKBox-only LR	Enriched LR
AUC	0.8289(±0.0018)	0.8535(±0.0018)	0.9458(±0.0006)
Average Precision	0.1267(±0.0023)	0.1620(±0.0025)	0.3824(±0.0022)
Accuracy	0.9758(±0.0002)	0.9756(±0.0002)	0.9772(±0.0002)
Balanced Accuracy	0.5058(±0.0002)	0.5185(±0.0010)	0.5749(±0.0135)
Precision	0.2105(±0.0059)	0.3219(±0.0080)	0.5421(±0.0115)
Recall	0.0129(±0.0005)	0.0389(±0.0020)	0.1529(±0.0276)
F1	0.0240(±0.0009)	0.0694(±0.0033)	0.2373(±0.0342)

6.2   Results of Publisher's Dataset Experiments

Evaluating Off-line Performance. The trained model has been evaluated using the test set in the dedicated module. The test set, as opposed to the

Table 4. Results of KKBox's dataset experiments presented as means and standard deviations for series of 5 experiment iterations (Gradient Boosted Trees models).

Measure	KKBox-only GBT	Enriched GBT
AUC	0.9034(±0.0012)	0.9679(±0.0006)
Average Precision	0.2421(±0.0022)	0.6013(±0.0039)
Accuracy	0.9766(±0.0002)	0.9823(±0.0002)
Balanced Accuracy	0.5393(±0.0002)	0.7216(±0.0026)
Precision	0.4963(±0.0114)	0.6837(±0.0072)
Recall	0.0695(±0.0037)	0.4482(±0.0054)
F1	0.1220(±0.0055)	0.5414(±0.0039)

training set, has not been not additionally downsampled to make the scenario closer to online environment. The test set contains 310,455 negative samples and 203 positive ones. The precision and recall scores have been obtained for the experimentally set threshold for positive prediction equal to 0.0335. The same threshold has been used for the online experiment described in the next section.

The offline evaluation results are collected in Table 5.

Table 5. Results of offline evaluation for the model used in the online test on the digital media website.

Measure	Score
AUC	0.8412
Average precision	0.0170
Precision	0.0038
Recall	0.5764
F1	0.0076

Evaluating On-line Performance. In this section we presents the results of online tests conducted according to the description provided in Sect. 5.2. In particular, we have compared the performance of dynamic paywall policy (called Deep Glue Dynamic Paywall) based on predictions generated be the ML model using features from the current user engagement profiles and the default paywall policy based on blocking the so called premium content. The results are presented in Table 6.

Table 6. Results of on-line experiments in the digital publisher environment.

Paywall policy	No of users	No of subscr.	User conversion rate
Deep Glue Dynamic Paywall	454,367	340	0.07483%
Premium Paywall	100,614	36	0.03578%

The results have confirmed that using Deep Glue Dynamic Paywall policy based on the ML model exploring user engagement features may increase the number of new subscriptions sold even more than twice.

7   Conclusions

In this paper, we demonstrate that real-time profile enrichment with time-agnostic user engagement features leads to significant improvement of machine learning models aimed at detecting the user's propensity to buy the subscription. Our studies follow the recent postulate of Andrew Ng for more data-centric rather than model-centric approaches to machine learning confirming validity of his observations [1]. The results of experiments have proven that enrichment of data with user engagement profiles has a significantly bigger impact on final predictive models' performance than the choice of algorithms and their hyper-parameters.

What is worth to mention, we have complemented our analysis by presenting the results of online tests conducted on live traffic for which the machine learning model based on the data enriched by user engagement profiles was used to control the paywall displays on a digital media website. The results have demonstrated the significant performance increase measured by means of user conversion rate. It has to be stated that the biggest limitations for our research are related to the fact that reliable model evaluation requires tests on live web traffic, which take more time than offline testing. Our plans for future work include studies the impact of particular profile features on online performance.

Acknowledgments. This work was supported by the Polish National Centre for Research and Development, grant POIR.01.01.01-00-1352/17-00, and by Poznan University of Technology, grant 0311/SBAD/0703.

References

1. Andrew Ng: MLOps: From Model-centric to Data-centric AI - DeepLearning.AI.   https://www.deeplearning.ai/wp-content/uploads/2021/06/MLOps-From-Model-centric-to-Data-centric-AI.pdf. Accessed Oct 2021
2. Apache Spark: PySpark ML Library. https://spark.apache.org/mllib/ (2021). Accessed Oct 2021
3. Aral, S., Dhillon, P.S.: Digital paywall design: implications for content demand and subscriptions. Manag. Sci. **67**(4), 2381–2402 (2020). https://doi.org/10.1287/mnsc.2020.3650
4. Carlton, J., Brown, A., Jay, C., Keane, J.: Using interaction data to predict engagement with interactive media. In: Proceedings of the 29th ACM International Conference on Multimedia, pp. 1258–1266. ACM, New York, NY, USA (2021). https://doi.org/10.1145/3474085.3475631
5. Davoudi, H., An, A., Zihayat, M., Edall, G.: Adaptive paywall mechanism for digital news media. In: Proceedings of the 24th ACM SIGKDD International Conference on Knowledge Discovery & Data Mining, pp. 205–214. ACM, New York, NY, USA (2018). https://doi.org/10.1145/3219819.3219892

6. Davoudi, H., Rashidi, Z., An, A., Zihayat, M., Edall, G.: Paywall policy learning in digital news media. IEEE Trans. Knowl. Data Eng. **33**(10), 3394–3409 (2021). https://doi.org/10.1109/TKDE.2020.2969419

7. Davoudi, H., Zihayat, M., An, A.: Time-aware subscription prediction model for user acquisition in digital news media. In: Proceedings of the 2017 SIAM International Conference on Data Mining (SDM), pp. 135–143. SIAM (2017). https://doi.org/10.1137/1.9781611974973.16

8. Fei, Y., Lv, C., Feng, Y., Zhao, D.: Real-time filtering on interest profiles in twitter stream. In: Proceedings of the 16th ACM/IEEE-CS on Joint Conference on Digital Libraries, pp. 263–264. JCDL 2016, ACM, New York, NY, USA (2016). https://doi.org/10.1145/2910896.2925462

9. Flach, P.: Machine Learning: The Art and Science of Algorithms That Make Sense of Data. Cambridge University Press, Cambridge, New York, NY, USA (2012)

10. Gregory, B.: Predicting customer churn: Extreme gradient boosting with temporal data. ArXiv (2018). https://www.arxiv.org/pdf/1802.03396.pdf

11. Grinberg, N.: Identifying modes of user engagement with online news and their relationship to information gain in text. In: Proceedings of the 2018 World Wide Web Conference, pp. 1745–1754. WWW 2018 (2018). https://doi.org/10.1145/3178876.3186180

12. Gupta, R., Parimi, R., Weed, Z., Kundra, P., Koneru, P., Koritala, P.: Driving subscriptions through user behavior modeling and prediction at bloomberg media. In: Nicosia, G., et al. (eds.) Machine Learning, Optimization, and Data Science. pp. 472–476. Springer International Publishing, Cham (2020). https://doi.org/10.1007/978-3-030-64583-0_42

13. Kaggle: WSDM - KKBox Churn Prediction Challenge. https://www.kaggle.com/c/kkbox-churn-prediction-challenge/. Accessed Oct 2021

14. KKBox: WSDM Cup 2018 Workshop within The 11th ACM International Conference on Web Search and Data Mining (WSDM). https://wsdm-cup-2018.kkbox.events/, Last accessed Oct. 2021

15. Li, H., Vu, Q.H., Pham, T.L., Nguyen, T.T., Chen, S., Lee, S.: An ensemble approach to streaming service churn prediction. In: WSDM Cup 2018 Workshop within The 11th ACM International Conference on Web Search and Data Mining, pp. 1–8. Los Angeles, California, USA (2018). https://wsdm-cup-2018.kkbox.events/

16. Liang, S.: Collaborative, dynamic and diversified user profiling. In: Proceedings of the AAAI Conference on Artificial Intelligence, vol. 33, no. 01, pp. 4269–4276 (2019). https://doi.org/10.1609/aaai.v33i01.33014269

17. Mezghani, M., Zayani, C.A., Amous, I., Péninou, A., Sèdes, F.: Dynamic enrichment of social users' interests. In: 2014 IEEE Eighth International Conference on Research Challenges in Information Science (RCIS), pp. 1–11 (2014). https://doi.org/10.1109/RCIS.2014.6861066

18. Tang, X., Xu, Y., Geva, S.: Integrating time forgetting mechanisms into topic-based user interest profiling. In: 2013 IEEE/WIC/ACM International Joint Conferences on Web Intelligence (WI) and Intelligent Agent Technologies (IAT), vol. 3, pp. 1–4 (2013). https://doi.org/10.1109/WI-IAT.2013.132

Using Result Profiles to Drive Meta-learning

Krzysztof Grąbczewski[(✉)]

Institute of Engineering and Technology, Faculty of Physics,
Astronomy and Informatics, Nicolaus Copernicus University,
ul. Grudziądzka 5, 87-100 Toruń, Poland
kg@is.umk.pl

Abstract. Knowledge gained by meta-learning processes is valuable when it can be successfully used in solving algorithm selection problems. There is still strong need for automated tools for learning from data, performing model construction and selection with little or no effort from human operator. This article provides evidence for efficacy of a general meta-learning algorithm performing validations of candidate learning methods and driving the search for most attractive models on the basis of an analysis of learning results profiles. The profiles help in finding similar processes performed for other datasets and pointing to promising learning machines configurations. Further research on profile management is expected to bring very attractive automated tools for learning from data. Here, several components of the framework have been examined and an extended test performed to confirm the possibilities of the method. The discussion also touches on the subject of testing and comparing the results of meta-learning algorithms.

Keywords: Meta-learning · Meta-search · Algorithm selection · Algorithm ranking · Result profiles

1 Introduction

Many learning algorithms have been proposed by scientific community to solve problems like classification, approximation, clustering, time series prediction and so on. Large amount of algorithms and their different performance in particular applications have risen questions about ways to select the most adequate and the most successful learning methods for particular tasks. Such algorithm selection problems, also solved with machine learning, are tasks of *meta-level learning* (or just *meta-learning*, ML) and by analogy to the vocabulary used in logic, the former group of learning approaches, can be referred to as *object-level learning* (though more often called *base-level learning*).

In fact, the term *meta-learning* has been used in many different contexts, so that it encompasses the whole spectrum of techniques aiming at gathering meta-knowledge and exploiting it in learning processes. Although many different particular goals of meta-learning have been defined, the ultimate goal is to

M. Themistocleous and M. Papadaki (Eds.): EMCIS 2021, LNBIP 437, pp. 69–83, 2022.
https://doi.org/10.1007/978-3-030-95947-0_6

use meta-knowledge for finding more accurate models at object-level and/or to find them with as little resources as possible. This article presents a general algorithm for meta-learning based on results profiles, and examines the gains of its particular implementation. The method facilitates arbitrary profile management for discovering datasets in available knowledge base characterized by similar results, to draw conclusions about which learning machines are likely to provide good results.

Some selected, interesting approaches to meta-learning, more related to the approach proposed here, are superficially reviewed in Sect. 2. Section 3 presents the motivation and general idea of the proposed algorithm, which is presented in detail in Sect. 4. Its several incarnations are tested on 77 datasets and 212 object-level learning machines. The test is described in Sect. 5 and its results analyzed in Sect. 6.

2   Meta-learning for Ranking Learning Machines

Many different approaches have been proposed as tools for meta-learning. Here, we focus on meta-learning techniques capable of reliable prediction which methods would provide best results for a given learning task. In other words, we need tools to generate accurate rankings of learning algorithms for particular problems. The task of ranking algorithms can be regarded as equivalent to the *algorithm selection problem* (ASP) discussed already in 1970s by Rice [16]. He presented an abstract model of the problem as in Fig. 1. The goal is to find a mapping $S : \mathcal{D} \to \mathcal{A}$, such that for given data $D \in \mathcal{D}$, $A = S(D)$ is an algorithm maximizing some norm of performance $||p(A, D)||$. The problem has been addressed by many researchers and undertaken from different points of view [9,17]. Often, the task gets reduced to the problem of assigning optimal algorithm to a vector of features describing data. Such approaches are certainly easier to handle, but the conclusions they may bring are also limited. Separating meta-learning (ranking) and object-level learning processes simplifies the task, but implies resignation from on-line exploitation of meta-knowledge resulting from object-learners validation.

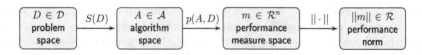

Fig. 1. Rice's model of algorithm selection problem

Building successful tools for automated selection of learning methods, most suitable for particular tasks, requires integration of meta-level and object-level learning in a single search process with built-in validation of object-level learning machines and meta-knowledge acquisition and exploitation. A general algorithm for such kind of meta-learning based on learning machine complexity estimation has been proposed [11], but it can not be successful in cases, where the complexity estimation can not successfully drive the meta-search.

The most popular approach to meta-learning was initiated by the meta-learning project *MetaL*. It was focused on learning rankings of algorithms from simple descriptions of data (collections of *meta-attributes*). In first approaches, meta-attributes were basic data characteristics like the number of instances in the dataset, the number of features, the types of features (continuous or discrete, how many of which), data statistics, some numbers obtained with some more advanced statistical analysis and information theory [5] and so on. Provided a description of a dataset, rankings were generated by *meta-learners* in such a way that for each pair of algorithms to be ranked, a classification algorithm was trained on two-class datasets describing wins and losses of the algorithms on some collection of datasets and after that, decisions of the meta-classifiers were combined to build final rankings.

An interesting step forward was *landmarking* [15]. The idea was to use meta-features measuring the performance of some simple and efficient learning algorithms (*landmarkers*) like linear discriminant learners, naive Bayesian learner or C5.0 decision tree inducer. The results provided by the landmarkers were used as features describing data for further meta-learning.

Interesting further improvements were: *relative landmarking* that introduced meta-attributes describing relations between results [7], *typed higher-order inductive learning* [2], deriving data characteristics from the structures of C5.0 decision trees [14], and many others [1].

Many other interesting algorithms of similar goal are also worth mentioning here. Some of them merge model selection and hyperparameter optimization, often relying on Bayesian optimization with different internal solutions. Random forests are successfully applied in Auto-WEKA [10,19] and AUTO-SKLEARN [6]. Gaussian processes find application in a meta-search for appropriate kernels in model space, treating model evidence as a function to be maximized [12]. An evolutionary algorithm was used within Tree-based Pipeline Optimization Tool (TPOT) to automatically design and optimize machine learning pipelines [13].

Algorithm Ranking Criteria. To generate rankings of learning algorithms, the results of meta-learners have usually been combined with such criteria as *average ranks* (AR), *success rate ratios* (SRR), *significant wins* (SW, counting statistically significant differences between pairs of algorithms) or *adjusted ratio of ratios* (ARR, combining ratios of accuracy and time) and *relative landmark* (RL, proposed for cases involving $n > 2$ algorithms) [18]:

$$ARR_{i,j}^d = \frac{\frac{A_i^d}{A_j^d}}{1 + \log\left(\frac{T_i^d}{T_j^d}\right) * X}, \quad (1) \qquad RL_i^d = \frac{\sum_{j \neq i} ARR_{i,j}^d}{n - 1}. \quad (2)$$

where A_i^d and T_i^d are accuracy and time of the i'th landmarker on data d and X is a parameter interpreted as "the amount of accuracy we are willing to trade for 10-times speed-up".

A serious disadvantage of methods like SRR, ARR and SW is their quadratic complexity, so when the number of candidate algorithms is large, they are not applicable. Moreover, they are strongly dependent on the collection of methods included in the comparison – when we need to test one more algorithm, all the indices must be recalculated.

The quality of rankings generated by meta-learning algorithms has usually been measured by means of its similarity to the ideal ranking calculated for the data. The similarity has been measured with some statistical methods like Spearman's rank correlation coefficient, Friedman's significance test and Dunn's multiple comparison technique. Such measures pay the same attention to rank differences at the beginning and at the end of the ranking, which is not what we really expect from meta-learning algorithms. We need the best methods at the top of the ranking while it is not so important whether the configuration is ranked 50000th or 100000th.

3   Motivation – From Passive to Active Ranking

A possibility of ranking algorithms ideally, without running them on the data at hand, would be found with great enthusiasm by many data analysts. But the task is very hard, even if significantly restricted to particular kind of data or/and small set of algorithms to be ranked. Very naive approaches basing on simple data characteristics are doomed to failure, because the information about the methods' eligibility is usually hidden deeply in complex properties of the data like the shapes of decision borders, not in simple characteristics of the current form of the data.

Landmarking is definitely an interesting direction, because it tries to take advantage of the knowledge extracted by landmarkers in their learning processes. But it is still passive in the sense that the selection of landmarkers and of meta-features is done once at the beginning of the process. The result is also static, because the ranking is not verified—no feedback is expected and no adaptation is performed.

To provide a trustworthy decision support system the rankings should be validated. No human expert would blindly believe in raw rankings. Instead they repeatedly construct and test complex models that encompass data preprocessing and final target learners. Meta-learning tools should proceed in a similar way. Therefore it seems reasonable to organize meta-learning approaches as search processes, exploring the space of complex learning machine configurations [4] augmented with heuristics created and adjusted according to proper meta-knowledge coming from human experts and artificial processes, protecting against spending time on learning processes of poor promise and against combinatorial explosion [11].

The Idea of Profiles. Profile analysis proposed here follows the idea that the relative differences between the results obtained by different machines may point the directions to more attractive machine configurations. Such informative results are gathered into collections called *profiles* and are used to predict the areas in the machine space worth further investigation. The idea is similar to relative landmarking, but in contrast to it, profiles are handled in an active way—there is no a priori definition of landmarkers, but a dynamic profile of results is created—its contents may change in time, when the feedback shows that the current profile predictions are not satisfactory. The profiles can contain the results of arbitrary selection of learning machines (any machine can be a landmarker), and on the basis of profile similarity between learning tasks, the machines most successful in solving similar problems are selected as candidates for best results providers. The details on the possibilities of profile definitions, ranking generation and the whole active search process are described in the following section.

4   Result Profile Driven Meta-learning

Result *profiles* are collections of results obtained in validation processes for selected machine configurations. The configurations are not fixed a priori as in classical landmarking methods, but are updated on-line during the search process. Thus, the profiles can be called *active*. Within the search, subsequent candidates are validated to verify which machines are really efficient in learning from the data at hand. Using profiles for ranking other methods may take advantage of relations between results to point promising directions of machine parameter changes. Because of the similarity to relative landmarking, the technique can also be called an *adaptive (or active) relative landmarking*.

The Algorithm. Result profile driven meta-learning (RPDML) searches for successful learning algorithms within a given set of candidate machine configurations $\mathcal{C}$. It runs a procedure called *validation scenario* (VS) for selected machine configurations to get some measure of the quality of the machine, in the form of an element of an ordered set $\mathcal{R}$. An important part of RPDML is a profile manager (PM) responsible for the profile contents and for using the profile for selection of subsequent candidate machine configurations for validation. The list of parameters includes also the time deadline for the whole process. The procedure of RPDML is written formally as Algorithm 1. It operates on four collections of machine configurations:

- C_R – a collection of pairs $\langle c, r \rangle \in \mathcal{C} \times \mathcal{R}$ of machine configurations c validated with results r,
- $C_P \subseteq C_R$ – the profile – a collection of selected results,
- C_Q – a sequence of candidate configurations (the queue) ordered with respect to estimated qualities and step numbers at which they were added,
- C_B – used temporarily in the algorithm to represent current ranking of candidate machine configurations.

To avoid long but fully formal statements, some shortcuts will be taken below, for example, the expression "a configuration in the profile" should be understood as an appropriate pair and so on. Although slightly informal, they will not introduce ambiguities and will significantly simplify descriptions.

Algorithm 1 (Result profile driven ML)

Input: *set C of machine configurations, validation scenario (VS), profile manager (PM), time deadline.*

Output: *Machine configuration ranking.*

The algorithm:

1. $C_R \leftarrow \emptyset$, $C_Q \leftarrow \emptyset$
2. $step \leftarrow 0$
3. *Initialize PM*
4. *While the time deadline is not exceeded:*
   (a) *If $step == 0$ or PM changed the profile C_P since last time:*
      i. $C_B \leftarrow$ *new ranking for current profile C_P*
      ii. *For each $c \in C_B$,*
         if c does not occur in C_R then add $\langle c, step + \frac{rank\ of\ c\ in\ C_B}{length(C_B)} \rangle$ to C_Q
   (b) *If C_Q is empty then break the loop*
   (c) *Pop an item c with maximum rank from C_Q*
   (d) $r \leftarrow VS(c)$ *(perform VS for c and get the result r)*
   (e) *Add $\langle c, r \rangle$ to C_R*
   (f) *Adjust the profile C_P within PM with $\langle c, r \rangle$*
   (g) $step \leftarrow step + 1$
5. *Return the configurations from C_R in the order of decreasing results*

New ranking is generated each time the profile is changed. Machine configurations are added to the queue with a rank in which the step number also plays an important role—first the most recent ranking is considered, and only if the ranking is fully served, the next configuration is taken from the newest of the older rankings.

Validation Scenario. The validation scenario defines what needs to be done to estimate the quality of a given machine configuration. It contains a test scenario, specifying the details of the test to perform for a candidate machine configuration (for example a cross-validation test) and a *result query* extracting the quality of machine configuration from the test (for example mean accuracy or a collection of accuracy results).

Time Limit. Usually, new algorithms are analyzed with respect to computational complexity – the question is how much time and/or memory it takes to reach the goal. In case of meta-learning, we deal with an inverse problem – how good model can be found in a given time, as it is natural that all possible models can not be tested and estimated, because that would take many orders of magnitude larger time than we can supply. Because of that, the main loop of the algorithm is limited by time deadline and the analysis of its efficiency has the form of empirical examination of the accuracy of models returned within that time. Different approaches are given the same amount of time for their work and their gains are compared.

Profile Management. Two important aspects of profile management are: care about the contents of the profile and the method of using it to determine advantageous directions of further search for machine configurations. It is not obvious what results should be kept in the profile and even what size of the profile can be most successful. There is much space for in-depth analysis of such dependencies. Given a profile, ranking configurations can also be done in a number of ways. The most natural one is to collect the results obtained for the profile configurations on other data files, determine the most similar profile, or more precisely, the data for which the profile is the most similar, and generate a ranking corresponding to the most successful configurations for that data. The similarity can also be used to combine results for several similar datasets into the final scores. So, the behaviour of PM may be determined by:

- profile similarity measure,
- configuration selection strategy (deciding how many and which configurations are included in the ranking),
- knowledge base used for calculations (the collection of datasets $D_1, \ldots, D_k$ and results obtained for these datasets with the methods of interest, that is a set of functions $f_{D_i} : \mathcal{C} \to \mathcal{R}$.

From practical, object-oriented point of view, it may be advantageous to design the methods of profile adjustment and ranking generation together, to let them interact better in their tasks. Therefore, they are enclosed in a single PM object. It can also be very profitable to use the feedback sent to PM not only for profile adjustment, but also for learning how to generate rankings on the basis of the profiles (to exploit the information about how successful the previous rankings were). Investigations on these subjects are very interesting direction of further research, but significant advantages will be possible only when we have gathered a huge database of results obtained with large number of learning methods on large number of datasets in experiments performed in systematic, unified manner. Therefore, the experiments presented here, though not small, are just the beginning. Nevertheless, they show that meta-learning driven by result profiles really works.

5   The Experiment Settings

To analyze the RPDML framework in action, its configuration described in Subsect. 5 was tested on 77 datasets from the UCI repository [3], also available from OpenML [20], representing classification problems and 212 configurations of object-level learning machines. A list of names identifying the datasets is given in Table 1. The sets represent various domains and pose different requirements to the learning methods. The feature spaces consist of from 2 to 10000 features. The instance counts range from 42 to almost 5 millions. The numbers of classes of objects to recognize are between 2 and 23. Such collection of datasets seems to provide a sufficient field for reliable meta-learning experiments.

Table 1. Summary of 77 UCI datasets, used in the experiment.

balone3c	census-income-all	heart	ml-prove-h2	shuttle-all	vehicle
acute1	contraceptive-method-choice	hepatitis	ml-prove-h3	sonar	vertebral-column-3c
acute2	credit-screening	image	ml-prove-h4	soybean-large	vote
anneal-all	ctg-1	ionosphere-all	ml-prove-h5	soybean-small	wall-following-2
appendicitis	ctg-2	iris	movement-libras	spect-all	wall-following-24
arcene-trn-val	cylinder-bands	kddcup99-10	mushroom	splice	wall-following-4
australian	dermatology	kddcup99	nursery	steel-plates-faults	waveform2
balance-scale	ecoli	kr-vs-kp	page-blocks	tae	wdbc
breast-cancer-wisconsin	flag	lbreast	parkinsons	telugu-vowel	wine
breast-tissue	german	lung-cancer	pima-indians-diabetes	thyroid-all	wpbc
bridges-mat	glass	mammographic-masses	qsar-biodeg	tic-tac-toe	yeast
bridges-rel	hayes-roth	ml-prove-h0	sat-all	transfusion	zoo
car	heart-270	ml-prove-h1	seeds	user-knowledge-all	

Some of the UCI datasets are originally split into parts (usually training and test sample). Here, all such datasets were joined into a single set to be analyzed with cross-validation. In Table 1, suffix "-all" informs about such joins.

RPDML Configuration. Each parameter of the Algorithm 1 (set $\mathcal{C}$ of candidate *machine configurations, validation scenario, profile manager* and *time deadline*) may significantly influence the gains of the method in particular application. Their values used for the experiment are specified below.

Object-Level Learning Machine Configurations. 212 learning methods of four types were applied: 102 decision tree (DT) induction algorithms, 40 k-nearest neighbor (kNN) methods, 5 naive Bayesian (NB) classifiers, 65 support vector machines (SVM). Decision tree algorithms were constructed with different split criteria, pruning methods and/or the way of validation. The 40 kNN methods were obtained with 10 different values of k (from 1 to 51) and 4 "metrics" used for distance calculations (Square Euclidean, Manhattan, Chebychev, Canberra). Bayesian classification used 5 settings of Naive Bayesian Classifier: one using no corrections, one applied with Laplace correction and 3 instances equipped with m-estimate corrections ($m \in \{1, 2, 5\}$). The 65 Support Vector Machines contained 5 configurations with linear kernel (with $C \in \{.5, 2, 8, 32, 128\}$) and 60 with Gaussian kernels: all combinations of $\sigma \in \{.001, .01, .1, .5, 1, 10\}$, square Euclidean or Canberra "metric" and $C \in \{.5, 2, 8, 32, 128\}$.

Application of all the classifiers but DTs was preceded by data standardization. For kNN and SVM methods, because of their computational complexity, each dataset containing more than 4000 vectors was filtered randomly to leave more or less 1000 vectors (each vector was kept with probability equal to 1000 divided by the original vectors count). The largest datasets (census-income-all and the two KDD cup datasets) were also filtered in a similar way for DTs, to keep around 10000 vectors.

More details on the methods configuration, experiment design and results can be found at http://www.is.umk.pl/~kg/papers/EMCIS21-RPDML.

Validation Scenario. Algorithm selection in the approach of RPDML is based on validation of learning machines, as shown in Sect. 4. In the experiment, this role was entrusted to 10-fold cross-validation. Since we are interested in not only high mean accuracy, but also in its small variance (i.e. stable results), the criterion used here was the mean accuracy reduced by its standard deviation.

Time Limit. In more sophisticated applications, it may be very important to comply with the time limit, to check some faster methods first and then, engage more complex ones [8]. Here, we have just 212 machine configurations, so instead of the time limit it was chosen to allow for validation of 12 configurations, before the final decision had to be taken.

Profile Management. Proper profile handling is a crucial idea of the RPDML. The rationale behind it is that similar relations between selected results for two datasets may be precious pointers of meta-search directions. We expect that the winners of the most similar tasks will perform well also on the new dataset being analyzed. A thorough analysis of profile solutions should take into consideration such aspects as profile construction and maintenance, profiles similarity measures, ranking candidates on the basis of profile similarity.

The experiment, presented here, is based on a knowledge base consisting of results of 212 learning machines obtained for 77 datasets, so possibilities of profile maintenance analysis are limited. To draw reliable conclusions, one needs to collect thousands or even millions of results. Such analysis has not been done yet. Since the task was to check just 12 of 212 configurations (the "time" limit) and point the most promising one, the profiles were composed of all the results obtained by the validation procedures.

Profile similarity was measured in one of two ways: with (the square of) the Euclidean metric and with the Pearson's correlation coefficient. Current rankings used to nominate the most promising configurations were calculated with respect to four indices:

- average accuracy reduced by its standard deviation,
- the same but expressed in the units of standard deviations in relation to the best of 212 results,
- average p-value of paired t-test comparing the method with the best one,
- average rank of the method.

All the averages were calculated over 5 or 10 most similar datasets from the knowledge base and were weighted with the similarity measures. These create 16 instances of RPDML configurations: all combinations of 2 similarity measures, 4 ranking indices and 2 sizes of the set of similar datasets.

State-of-the-Art Ranking Methods for Comparison. State-of-the-art methods for ranking algorithms usually prepare data descriptions to measure similarity between datasets and construct rankings on the basis of ranked methods accuracies obtained for the most similar data. They do not perform any validation of the methods on the data for which the ranking is being created, hence they can be called *passive.*

Since pairwise comparisons are possible only when the number of candidate machine configurations is extremely small, we can not base ranking on measures like ARR with RL, SRR or SW. Instead, the passive rankings, used for reference here, are based on less computationally complex formulae (3, 4, 5, 6).

$$AA(c) = \frac{1}{n} \sum_{i=1}^{n} A_c(i) \qquad (3) \qquad AR(c) = \frac{1}{n} \sum_{i=1}^{n} Rank(c, i) \qquad (5)$$

$$AD(c) = \frac{1}{n} \sum_{i=1}^{n} \frac{A_c(i) - A_{B(i)}(i)}{\sigma_{B(i)}(i)} \qquad (4) \qquad AP(c) = \frac{1}{n} \sum_{i=1}^{n} p(c, i), \qquad (6)$$

where c denotes the candidate configuration, n the number of datasets, $A_c(i)$ is the accuracy of the machine c tested on i'th dataset, $\sigma_c(i)$ – the standard deviation of this accuracy estimated in the test, $B(i)$ stands for a configuration that has reached the highest accuracy for i'th dataset, $Rank(c, i)$ is the rank of configuration c in the ordered results for i'th dataset and $p(c, i)$ is the p-value of the paired t-test comparing results obtained for c and $B(i)$. Each formula has its advantages and drawbacks. Some of them are pointed out further, in the discussion on the results.

To reliably compare active ranking methods and passive approaches, the latter are also validated. It means that the passive rankings are subject to step-by-step validation of top machine configurations to return the configurations in new order, corresponding to the validation results (the same validation scenario as in Algorithm 1).

Goals of the Experiment. The main goal of the test was to examine whether the profile approach of RPDML is capable of finding more attractive learning machines than other approaches devoid of profile analysis. Therefore, the first reference method for the comparison is a meta-search based on random ranking of methods. It is important to realize that it is not the same as random selection of a model. Here, a number of randomly selected machines go through the validation process which prevents from selecting a method that fails.

Another goal of the experiment was to examine the advantages of the profiles themselves. To achieve this, a comparison of the profile-based methods to static rankings based on the same criteria has been conducted.

Since the goal here is to check advantages of profiles, they are compared to similar algorithms with no profile based decisions. We do not compare to other complete solutions like Auto-WEKA or AUTO-SKLEARN, because that would not provide desired information on profiles and would require significant modifications of the systems to compensate the differences in goals and architectures.

Testing algorithm selection should not be performed with the use of a knowledge base containing information about the test data. That would be a sort of cheating. Thus, a leave-one-out style tests were executed (each RPDML instance was trained on the results obtained for 76 datasets and tested on the 77th).

Table 2. Summary of RPDML results for 77 UCI datasets.

Rank	Method	Mean - s.d.	Loss	p value	Wins	Mean
28.21	Corr-5NN-PV	0.82291	0.522	0.1474	28	0.8615
28.23	Corr-10NN-PV	0.82268	0.520	0.1582	28	0.8621
28.32	SqEuclid-10NN-PV	0.82590	0.410	0.1847	37	0.8638
28.65	Corr-5NN-Ranks	0.82080	0.569	0.1927	31	0.8603
28.88	SqEuclid-5NN-PV	0.82570	0.448	0.1957	33	0.8629
30.15	SqEuclid-5NN-Ranks	0.81911	0.657	0.1596	27	0.8581
30.24	Corr-5NN-AccStdDiff	0.82030	0.564	0.1904	28	0.8594
31.98	Corr-10NN-AccDiff	0.82017	0.641	0.1356	26	0.8588
32.12	Corr-5NN-AccDiff	0.81972	0.599	0.1577	28	0.8594
33.33	SqEuclid-5NN-AccDiff	0.81729	0.672	0.1394	30	0.8566
33.43	Static PV	0.82181	0.551	0.1873	36	0.8600
33.91	SqEuclid-5NN-AccStdDiff	0.81711	0.674	0.1621	28	0.8559
34.08	Corr-10NN-AccStdDiff	0.81858	0.641	0.1406	23	0.8578
34.19	Corr-10NN-Ranks	0.81884	0.637	0.1844	31	0.8583
34.42	SqEuclid-10NN-Ranks	0.81701	0.655	0.1571	34	0.8572
36.95	SqEuclid-10NN-AccStdDiff	0.81498	0.732	0.1618	30	0.8545
37.25	Static Ranks	0.81394	0.763	0.1159	22	0.8524
39.1	SqEuclid-10NN-AccDiff	0.81433	0.751	0.1544	25	0.8543
48.4	Random	0.80997	1.050	0.0526	15	0.8514
53.05	Static AccStdDiff	0.80243	1.098	0.0732	20	0.8420
55.16	Static AccDiff	0.80234	1.096	0.0813	19	0.8423

* s.d. stands for standard deviation

Table 3. Top ranked results of object-level classifiers for 77 UCI datasets.

Rank	Method	Mean - s.d.	Loss	p value	Wins	Mean	S.d.
46.77	M 1	0.80480	1.109	0.1198	19	0.8427	0.03793
52.64	M 2	0.80062	1.155	0.1458	22	0.8390	0.03837
53.4	M 3	0.80176	1.164	0.0988	15	0.8418	0.04005
53.48	M 4	0.80003	1.281	0.1078	13	0.8384	0.03835
53.52	M 5	0.79971	1.198	0.1517	19	0.8410	0.04131
54.23	M 6	0.80123	1.242	0.0883	14	0.8404	0.03913
55.84	M 7	0.80240	1.514	0.0668	14	0.8407	0.03828
56.36	M 8	0.79706	1.434	0.1021	12	0.8366	0.03953
56.66	M 9	0.79695	1.364	0.0962	12	0.8375	0.04051
58.68	M 10	0.79522	1.364	0.1242	14	0.8372	0.04198
59.13	M 11	0.79915	1.379	0.0904	9	0.8389	0.03971
59.28	M 12	0.80040	1.574	0.1019	15	0.8417	0.04132
59.34	M 13	0.79606	1.353	0.1209	19	0.8382	0.04212
59.48	M 14	0.79748	1.301	0.1228	15	0.8359	0.03839
59.53	M 15	0.79869	1.337	0.0985	12	0.8405	0.04180
59.58	M 16	0.79465	1.513	0.0963	14	0.8356	0.04100
...	...	...	...	...	...	...	...
72.13	M 44	0.79308	1.590	0.0423	11	0.8364	0.04330
72.47	M 45	0.79073	1.494	0.1615	22	0.8343	0.04357
72.6	M 46	0.78725	3.019	0.0662	8	0.8292	0.04191
73.71	M 47	0.78916	2.352	0.0886	15	0.8324	0.04323
74.27	M 48	0.78517	3.023	0.0504	9	0.8273	0.04216
74.88	M 49	0.78566	3.035	0.0518	8	0.8258	0.04016
75.08	M 50	0.78598	2.855	0.0601	8	0.8295	0.04356
...	...	...	...	...	...	...	...

6   Results and Analysis

Some of the most reasonable indicators of algorithm quality that can serve as comparison criteria, and have been calculated in the experiment, are:

- average test accuracy or the accuracy reduced by its standard deviation,
- average loss with respect to the best available result, represented in the unit of (the winner's) standard deviation,
- average rank obtained among other algorithms,
- average p-value of paired t-test comparisons with the winner methods,
- the count of wins defined as obtaining results not statistically significantly worse than those of the winners (examined with paired t-test with $\alpha = 0.05$).

There is no single best criterion and each of those listed above has some drawbacks. Average test accuracy (also reduced by standard deviation) may favor datasets with results of relatively larger variance. Calculating accuracy differences (loss) with respect to the winner and rephrasing them in the units of winner's standard deviations is not adequate in case of zero variance (happens e.g. when 100% accuracy is feasible). Ranks may be misleading when families of similar methods are contained in the knowledge base – a small difference in the accuracy may make big difference in rank. Average p-values are not perfect either – it is possible that a better model gets lower p-value when compared to the winner then a worse model (e.g. when large variance of the latter disturbs statistical significance). Naturally, the count of wins suffers from the same drawbacks as p-values.

To facilitate multicriteria comparison, all these scores are presented in Table 2. For reference, also the top-ranked results of the 212 object-level algorithms are shown in Table 3. Full tables of results (overall and particular for each dataset) are available online at http://www.is.umk.pl/~kg/papers/EMCIS21-RPDML.

First Glance Analysis. Even a short glance at the result tables makes clear impression that most of the values in Table 2 are more attractive the ones in Table 3. The mean accuracies of the best RPDML scores are higher by more than 2% and average ranks get reduced by almost half in relation to the best object-level algorithms.

It may seem surprising that the best average ranks are so large (46.77 for the object-level winner and 28.21 for RPDML). Their nominal values may be a bit misleading because of the strategy of assigning the ranks following the methods of rank-based statistical tests, where in case of a draw, all the methods with the same result obtain the average rank corresponding to their positions. As a result, in the most extreme case, for the "accute1" dataset, the best classifiers performing with 100% accuracy get the rank 59, because 117 of the 212 classifiers classify the data perfectly. Other examples are "accute2" with the top rank of 49.5, "steel-plates-faults" with 35 or two "wall-following" datasets, where 49 perfect classifiers share the rank of 25.

Average accuracies, average loss and mean rank show similar properties, so they are quite correlated. More different rankings are obtained with the criteria of p-values and numbers of wins (naturally, the two are also correlated). It can be observed in the tables by means of the bold-printed numbers which show the best scores according to the criteria.

Detailed analysis of the results confirms that none of the comparison criteria is perfect. Even the statistical methods like p-values and counts of wins (or more precisely the count of datasets for which the results can not be confirmed with a statistical test to be significantly less accurate then the best results) sometimes show peculiar effects. For example, the results for the "vertebral-columns-3c" data show that a method ranked 126th, according to the mean reduced by standard deviation, is not significantly worse than the winner while 70 methods ranked higher, including the one ranked at position 20, lose significantly to the winner. The winner's accuracy is 0.8323 ± 0.05832, while the algorithms ranked at positions 126 and 20 reach 0.8032 ± 0.08185 and 0.8086 ± 0.05148 respectively. The one ranked 20th seems better, because it is more stable (less variance), but paradoxically, the stability makes it lose to the winner, while larger variance of the 126th one grants it with a win. Another example is "wall-following-24", where the meta-learning based on random ranking gets accuracy of 0.9937 ± 0.01059 (hypothesis about losing to the winner is not rejected with paired t-test with $\alpha = 0.05$) while the others provide slightly higher accuracy and 4 times smaller deviation (e.g. 0.9964 ± 0.00248) and are confirmed with the t-test to lose.

Similar facts cause that the largest average p-value (among the object-level learning methods) was obtained by a method building full greedy DTs, which means maximum possible accuracy for the training data and large variance for the test data. As a result of the larger variance, the number of wins is the highest, but at the same time its mean accuracy is about 1% lower on average than that of other methods with lower win counts.

Meta-learning vs Single Object-Level Classifiers. Comparison of meta-learning approaches with single learners should be done with special care. The meta-learning algorithms are allowed to perform multiple validation tests and select one of many (here 12) models. Thus, it is natural that they can be more accurate. The difference can be clearly seen with the naked eye from the results. For example:

- average ranks for the RPDML methods range from 28.21 to 39.1 (most less than 34) while the top-ranked object-level method reaches the value of 46.77,
- average mean accuracy minus standard deviation ranges from 0.81433 to 0.82590 for RPDML while the best object-level result is 0.8048.

An interesting observation is that for some datasets, the accuracies of some RPDML machines are higher than the best object-level classifier's. Although RPDML just selects a machine from the 212 object-level algorithms, it sometimes happens, that in some folds of cross-validation, it recognizes that a machine, less accurate in general, can be more successful in application to this particular data sample. Obviously, it can not be treated as a regular feature, as it happened 8 times for 4 datasets (ctg-2, ml-prove-h1, nursery and sat-all), but it is interesting that such improvement is at all possible. In such cases, the lower p-value of the t-test, the better, so the index has been modified to $2 - p\text{-}value$, to be a greater reward instead of a penalty.

Profile-Based vs Static Ranking Methods. The most important analysis of this experiment concerns the advantages of the function of profiles. To facilitate the discussion, the methods based on static rankings have been introduced and tested. Table 2 presents the results of the static methods among those of RPDML and the random ranking. According to all the criteria, two of the static rankings (based on accuracy) perform slightly worse or slightly better than random ranking. The other two (based on ranks and p-values) do better, but they are outperformed by most of the RPDML configurations in most comparisons. Only the static ranking based on p-values is located higher than some of its RPDML counterparts in comparison with respect to p-values and wins, but keeping in mind the disadvantages of these criteria mentioned above, we can reliably claim that the profiles are precious tools in meta-learning.

7   Conclusions and Future Perspectives

RPDML is an open framework, that facilitates easy implementation of many meta-learning algorithms integrating meta-knowledge extraction and its exploitation with object-level learning. Different kinds of problems may be solved with appropriate implementation of the framework modules like validation scenario and profile manager. The implementations presented here have proven their value in the experiments. The framework facilitates active management of learning results profiles, leading to more adequately adapted meta-learning algorithms.

Since the framework is open, a lot of research can be done with it, hopefully leading to many successful incarnations of RPDML. First of all, there is a lot of space for development of intelligent methods for profile management. The way profile is maintained with the feedback coming from experiments, can be crucial for final efficiency of profile-based meta-learning machines. Some experiments with simple methods of profile size reduction have shown that it is very easy to spoil the results by inaccurate profile maintenance. For example, the idea of handling the profile by keeping the results with as high accuracy as possible can lead to profile degeneration. Experiments, not described here in detail, have shown that such technique may at some point generate poor ranking, which would be kept and followed to the end of learning time, because once machines of poor accuracy appear at the top, subsequent validations end up with weak results, not eligible for the profile, so the profile does not change and the poor ranking is followed on and on. The lack of changes in the profile implies no changes in ranking and inversely. A sort of dead lock appears. Hence, profile management must be equipped with techniques aimed at avoiding such situations. The profiles should be diverse, and continuously controlled, whether they result in rankings providing accurate models at the top. Otherwise, it can be more successful to return to some old but more suitable profile, instead of losing time for validation of many machines from a degenerate ranking.

Profile management includes adaptive methods of dataset similarity measurement for more suitable ranking generation. In parallel to profile analysis, knowledge base properties may also be examined in order to prepare knowledge bases most eligible for meta-learning. The knowledge bases may be equipped with additional information providing specialized ontologies useful not only in meta-learning but also in testing object-level learners.

References

1. Balte, A., Pise, N., Kulkarni, P.: Meta-learning with landmarking: a survey. Int. J. Comput. Appl. **105**(8), 47–51 (2014)
2. Bensusan, H., Giraud-Carrier, C., Kennedy, C.J.: A higher-order approach to meta-learning. In: Cussens, J., Frisch, A. (eds.) Proceedings of the Work-in-Progress Track at the 10th International Conference on Inductive Logic Programming, pp. 33–42 (2000)
3. Dua, D., Graff, C.: UCI machine learning repository (2017). http://archive.ics.uci.edu/ml
4. Duch, W., Grudziński, K.: Meta-learning via search combined with parameter optimization. In: Rutkowski, L., Kacprzyk, J. (eds.) Advances in Soft Computing, vol. 17, pp. 13–22. Springer, Heidelberg (2002). https://doi.org/10.1007/978-3-7908-1777-5_2
5. Engels, R., Theusinger, C.: Using a data metric for preprocessing advice for data mining applications. In: Proceedings of the European Conference on Artificial Intelligence (ECAI-98), pp. 430–434. Wiley (1998)
6. Feurer, M., Klein, A., Eggensperger, K., Springenberg, J., Blum, M., Hutter, F.: Efficient and robust automated machine learning. In: Cortes, C., Lawrence, N., Lee, D., Sugiyama, M., Garnett, R. (eds.) Advances in Neural Information Processing Systems, vol. 28, pp. 2962–2970. Curran Associates, Inc. (2015)

7. Fürnkranz, J., Petrak, J.: An evaluation of landmarking variants. In: Giraud-Carrier, C., Lavra, N., Moyle, S., Kavsek, B. (eds.) Proceedings of the ECML/PKDD Workshop on Integrating Aspects of Data Mining, Decision Support and Meta-Learning (2001)

8. Grąbczewski, K., Jankowski, N.: Saving time and memory in computational intelligence system with machine unification and task spooling. Knowl.-Based Syst. **24**, 570–588 (2011)

9. Guyon, I., Saffari, A., Dror, G., Cawley, G.: Model selection: beyond the Bayesian/frequentist divide. J. Mach. Learn. Res. **11**, 61–87 (2010)

10. Hutter, F., Hoos, H.H., Leyton-Brown, K.: Sequential model-based optimization for general algorithm configuration. In: Coello, C.A.C. (ed.) LION 2011. LNCS, vol. 6683, pp. 507–523. Springer, Heidelberg (2011). https://doi.org/10.1007/978-3-642-25566-3_40

11. Jankowski, N., Grąbczewski, K.: Universal meta-learning architecture and algorithms. In: Jankowski, N., Duch, W., Grąbczewski, K. (eds.) Meta-Learning in Computational Intelligence. Studies in Computational Intelligence, vol. 358, pp. 1–76. Springer, Heidelberg (2011). https://doi.org/10.1007/978-3-642-20980-2_1

12. Malkomes, G., Schaff, C., Garnett, R.: Bayesian optimization for automated model selection. In: Proceedings of the 30th International Conference on Neural Information Processing Systems, NIPS'16, pp. 2900–2908. Curran Associates Inc., Red Hook (2016)

13. Olson, R.S., Bartley, N., Urbanowicz, R.J., Moore, J.H.: Evaluation of a tree-based pipeline optimization tool for automating data science. In: Proceedings of the Genetic and Evolutionary Computation Conference 2016, GECCO '16, pp. 485–492. Association for Computing Machinery, New York (2016)

14. Peng, Y., Flach, P.A., Soares, C., Brazdil, P.: Improved dataset characterisation for meta-learning. In: Lange, S., Satoh, K., Smith, C.H. (eds.) DS 2002. LNCS, vol. 2534, pp. 141–152. Springer, Heidelberg (2002). https://doi.org/10.1007/3-540-36182-0_14

15. Pfahringer, B., Bensusan, H., Giraud-Carrier, C.: Meta-learning by landmarking various learning algorithms. In: Proceedings of the Seventeenth International Conference on Machine Learning, pp. 743–750. Morgan Kaufmann (2000)

16. Rice, J.R.: The algorithm selection problem - abstract models. Technical report, Computer Science Department, Purdue University, West Lafayette, Indiana (1974). cSD-TR 116

17. Smith-Miles, K.A.: Cross-disciplinary perspectives on meta-learning for algorithm selection. ACM Comput. Surv. **41**(1), 6:1–6:25 (2009)

18. Soares, C., Petrak, J., Brazdil, P.: Sampling-based relative landmarks: systematically test-driving algorithms before choosing. In: Brazdil, P., Jorge, A. (eds.) EPIA 2001. LNCS (LNAI), vol. 2258, pp. 88–95. Springer, Heidelberg (2001). https://doi.org/10.1007/3-540-45329-6_12

19. Thornton, C., Hutter, F., Hoos, H.H., Leyton-Brown, K.: Auto-WEKA: combined selection and hyperparameter optimization of classification algorithms. In: Proceedings of the 19th ACM SIGKDD International Conference on Knowledge Discovery and Data Mining, KDD '13, pp. 847–855. Association for Computing Machinery, New York (2013)

20. Vanschoren, J., van Rijn, J.N., Bischl, B., Torgo, L.: OpenML: networked science in machine learning. SIGKDD Explor. **15**(2), 49–60 (2013)

Blockchain Technology and Applications

Computation of Blockchain Readiness Under Partial Information

Elias Iosif[✉], Klitos Christodoulou, and Andreas Vlachos

Department of Digital Innovation, School of Business and Institute For the Future,
University of Nicosia, Nicosia, Cyprus
{iosif.e,christodoulou.kl,vlachos.a}@unic.ac.cy
https://www.unic.ac.cy/iff/

Abstract. As the blockchain ecosystem gets more mature many businesses, investors, and entrepreneurs are seeking opportunities on working with blockchain systems and cryptocurrencies. A critical challenge for these actors is to identify the most suitable environment to start or evolve their businesses. In general, the question is to identify which countries are offering the most suitable conditions to host their blockchain-based activities and implement their innovative projects. The Blockchain Readiness Index (BRI) provides a numerical metric (referred to as the blockchain *readiness score*) in measuring the maturity/readiness levels of a country in adopting blockchain and cryptocurrencies. In doing so, BRI leverages on techniques from information retrieval to algorithmically derive an index ranking for a set of countries. The index considers a range of indicators organized under five pillars: Government Regulation, Research, Technology, Industry, and User Engagement. In this paper, we further extent BRI with the capability of deriving the index – at the country level – even in the presence of missing information for the indicators. In doing so, we are proposing two weighting schemes namely, linear and sigmoid weighting for refining the initial estimates for the indicator values. A classification framework was employed to evaluate the effectiveness of the developed techniques which yielded to a significant classification accuracy.

Keywords: Blockchain readiness index · Blockchain business intelligence · Classification models

1 Introduction

Blockchain technology has contributed several interesting properties, not only in deriving peer-to-peer software architectures but also in enabling alternative business and transaction models. The blockchain ecosystem evolved from the idea of establishing decentralized "trust" [17]. A decentralized model where multiple distrusting actors, with different motives, are competing with each other in a decentralized, transparent environment. Since the inception of the decentralized trust idea as proposed in [14], blockchain technology and cryptocurrencies have

© Springer Nature Switzerland AG 2022
M. Themistocleous and M. Papadaki (Eds.): EMCIS 2021, LNBIP 437, pp. 87–101, 2022.
https://doi.org/10.1007/978-3-030-95947-0_7

seen a massive adoption in the cyberspace [4,13]. Despite the adoption and the evolving landscape rooted on social and business interactions among many actors, blockchain technology has been criticized by many nations, governments, law-makers, and financial institutions. However, the community and the dynamic ecosystem reinforced by many social relationships have driven the technology in a long-term evolving state. At the beginning of this disruptive technology this state was deeply rooted in the development of the technology and its advancements, such as, scalability, transaction speeds and interoperability [23]. However, as the adoption of the technology is fueling a variety of applications across many industries [5,7,12], along with many economic, social, and business activities being disrupted, several new and different kinds of challenges are coming into play.

These challenges underscore the focus to the operational and regulatory dimensions that follow from the widespread of the technology and market adoption. Under this state of affairs, many nations are showing interest in adopting the technology but still they respond differently, and face many challenges in harnessing the potential of this technological innovation [18]. On the negative side of the spectrum, many countries have issued a direct ban of the technology and cryptocurrencies, others have taken a more dichotomous approach of the Blockchain technology and cryptocurrencies with limited forms of regulation, and on the positive side of the spectrum countries have taken a more proactive strategy seeking opportunities in becoming "enabling environments" for embracing the technology. The following observations motivated this study:

- *Governmental authorities often fail to capture the set of variables[1] that measure a country's capacity to adopt blockchain and cryptocurrencies as a technological advancement.*
- *There is a lack of a benchmarking tool that enables businesses to identify which countries are becoming blockchain "friendly" to host their operations, and establish their investment decisions.*

As a response to the aforementioned observations, BRI [22] provides a numerical metric (referred to as the blockchain *readiness score*) in measuring the maturity/readiness levels of a country in adopting blockchain and cryptocurrencies.

This paper extends our previous contribution [22] of an algorithmically derived Blockchain Readiness Index (BRI) by accurately estimating the readiness score per country even in the presence of several missing indicators. Section 4 discusses the details of our enchanced model for deriving the BRI that makes no assumptions on no missing values for indicators. More specifically, this paper contributes the following: (a) a robust indexing model for the proposed BRI, that provides accurate estimates on missing values for indicators; and (b) an empirical evaluation for measuring the effectiveness of our numerical estimates (on linear/sigmoid weights and weighted similarities) adopting a classification framework.

---

[1] In this work we refer to such variables or factors as *indicators*.

Overall, our research work aims to provide business intelligence and insights on the opportunities and risks – identified by the fast-moving blockchain environment – to business executives, individuals, and start-ups.

2   Related Work

To date, there is limited research done in constructing an algorithmic readiness index to assess the level of preparedness for blockchain technology and cryptocurrencies among nations. This section briefly reports on well-known readiness indexes proposed in the literature for various industries and positions this work in the landscape of algorithmic readiness indexes for the disruptive blockchain technology.

2.1   Readiness Indexes

Readiness indexes are developed to provide a numerical representation of how engaged an examined item is – such as a nation – towards a specific subject matter. A number of technological indexes have been developed to date as an assessment of various technological metrics. The Networked Readiness Index (NRI) proposed by the Global Information Technology Report [1], attempts to measure the propensity of nations to exploit the opportunities offered by Information and communications technology (ICT) developments. The latest release of the NRI [9] reports 121 nations based on four pillars: Technology, People, Governance and Impact. The general aim of NRI is to mesure how ICT is penetrating into countries and what is the impact on their economies and on the ability to fulfill a set of defined Sustainable Development Goals (SDGs). Our research aims on developing a similar index for measuring the level of readiness of countries with regards to blockchain technology and cryptocurrencies. The proposed BRI is set to provide a general perspective on the current patterns and approaches nations taking with regards to blockchain and cryptocurrencies. In doing so, the BRI is focusing among others on various features, such as, regulation regimes, research competences and awareness of the local blockchain community. Furthermore, indexes aiming to provide rankings of nations/regions regarding their readiness to become front-runners on new technological advancements. The best known examples include the Autonomous Vehicles Readiness Index (AVRI) [19] which provides a tool for assessing the level of readiness for autonomous vehicles; the Automation Readiness Index (ARI) [20] which assesses the level of preparedness for intelligent automation; and the Smart Industry Readiness Index (SIRI) published by the Singapore Economic Development Board [3] which aims to support manufacturers to assess and compare their maturity levels against Industry 4.0 and global industry benchmarks. Other indexes that attempt to report the readiness and maturity levels for Industry 4.0 are discussed in [2].

A relevant study introduced the Blockchain and Cryptocurrencies Regulation Index (BCRI) [21]. In this work, authors describe a methodology for assessing the degree of enabling indicators and controls of cryptocurrencies for various countries. The ranking presented provides a single numerical score for each country, as well as, a general classification. The rationale of their approach is based on annotating each country with a positive or negative assessment on different enabling environments in the following dimensions: (i) legal environment, (ii) political environment, and (iii) infrastructure environment. However, the implementation details of the framework are abstracted without a clear indication on whether the index is algorithmically and/or dynamically derived or how the framework is treating missing values from indicators.

In contrast, our methodology is dynamic and not restricted to any number of indicators. As long as these indicators are expressed as numerals the index can be derived.

3 Indicators of Blockchain Readiness

This section provides a brief description of the indicators considered by BRI.

3.1 Technology Indicators

The significance of technological innovation within a governmental ecosystem is emphasized by [8]. For this enabler the following indicators are considered.

Node Distribution: The estimation of the size of Bitcoin (Global Bitcoin nodes distribution[2]) and Ethereum (The Ethereum Network and Node Explorer[3]) is derived by identifying all the reachable nodes within countries. For this version of the BRI we consider only Bitcoin and Ethereum as these public decentralized networks are widely transacted since their Genesis block. We note that our proposed methodology can be expanded to consider other data sources for all blockchain protocols available.

ICT Development Level: The ICT Development Index (IDI) is an index published by the United Nations International Telecommunication Union based on internationally agreed ICT indicators. In brief this composite index combines several indicators into one benchmark for monitoring the development of ICT over countries. The intuition is that this index can lead to signals indicating room for innovation towards Blockchain-specific activities, especially for high ranked countries.

Internet Penetration: Internet penetration rates indicate the prospect of Blockchain adoption within nations. Internet World Stats[4] is a useful source for country and regional statistics, international online market research, the latest Internet information, world Internet penetration data, world population statistics, telecommunications information reports, and Facebook statistics by country. This information may not be directly related to blockchain engagement but high internet penetration rates indicate a positive sign.

---

[2] https://bitnodes.io/.
[3] https://www.ethernodes.org/.
[4] https://www.internetworldstats.com/.

Bitcoin ATMs Launched: Bitcoin ATMs is a convenient first introduction for many people to the Bitcoin ecosystem. Installation rates indicate the rate at which a country is embracing Bitcoin and how easy it is for the population to deposit and withdraw Bitcoin in exchange for cash. Installation rates are obtained by Coin ATM Radar[5].

Global Innovation Index: The Global Innovation Index (2018) provides comprehensive metrics regarding the innovation performance of several countries worldwide. 80 indicators have been developed and evaluate the political environment, education, infrastructure and business sophistication.

eGovernment Development Index (EGDI): The EGDI [15] assesses eGovernment development at a national level and is composed by three components: online service index, telecommunication infrastructure index and the human capital index. This index provides signals on the transformation towards sustainable and resilient societies for each country.

3.2 Industry Indicators

The penetration of blockchain technology to the industry and emerging businesses is significant. Industry engagement and willingness to develop the blockchain sector of the economy, can play a dynamic role towards a society's social and economic status in the future [10].

Prevalence of Top 100 Cryptocurrency Exchanges by Volume: The number and volume of cryptocurrency transactions is able to indicate the degree in which an economy is financed from the blockchain industry. The top 100 cryptocurrency exchanges by volume can be derived by the metrics of Coinmarketcap[6].

Fintech Score: The Findexable Global Fintech Index City Rankings report (2020)[7] presents the results of an index algorithm which ranks the fintech ecosystems of more than 230 cities, 65 countries and 7000 fintech companies.

Cost to Mine 1 Bitcoin: This metric identifies how likely a country is to host mining operations. Energy consumption and mining facilities are developed on top countries. This provides a signal on how engaged the ecosystem is within a local community.

Doing Business Index: Doing Business Index (2020)[8] is taking into consideration the ease of starting a business, dealing with construction permits, getting electricity, registering property, getting credit, protecting minority investors, paying taxes, trading across borders, enforcing contracts, and resolving insolvency within a country.

---

[5] https://coinatmradar.com/.
[6] https://coinmarketcap.com/.
[7] https://findexable.com/.
[8] https://www.doingbusiness.org/en/rankings.

3.3 User Engagement Indicators

Individuals and local startups have initiated various community efforts. This enabler attempts to capture positive or negative signals on how community is reacting to blockchain technology and cryptocurrencies.

Community Interest in Blockchain: This indicators captures the increase over time of the number of Web search keywords that include the term "Blockchain". This indicates a trend within a country's interest to the technology.

Community Interest in Bitcoin: Similarly to the above, the increase over time of the number of Web searches that include the term "Bitcoin". This indicates a trend within a country's interest to Bitcoin as a concept and as a cryptocurrency. Other keywords such as "distributed ledgers" or "decentralization" are also considered.

Bitcoin Core Downloads: The total number of Bitcoin Core downloads indicates local engagement and interest and a rough approximation of where most Bitcoin users are located. The data period range can be adjusted; for the purposes for this study we use data for the previous 365 days.

3.4 Government Regulation Indicators

Cryptocurrency Regulation Analysis: Data reported by the Worldwide Cryptocurrency Regulation Analysis (2020)[9], are taken into consideration along with the following metrics: (i) legality of Bitcoin, (ii) ICOs restrictions, (iii) ICOs registration locations, (iv) exchanges locations, and (v) user voting (public opinion).

4 Robust Indexing: Proposed Model

This section discusses the proposed model leveraged by our algorithmic BRI in deriving the index even in cases of countries are missing values for some indicators. The indicators are used to construct a feature vector that is used to characterise each country. For our work this feature vector is an N-dimensional vector for each country (denoted by c) consisting of numerical values for each indicator, k.

Let us assume a dataset consisting of countries for which their respective BRI scores should be estimated. On the basis of those scores, the countries can be ranked (typically in descending order) resulting into a readiness index. At the abstract level, this process is composed by the following steps.

In the first step, any missing BRI indicators should be estimated for each country. During the second step, the BRI indicators (either initially available or estimated), are exploited for computing a single BRI score for each country. This

---

[9] https://cointobuy.io/.

score is meant to quantify the blockchain readiness of the corresponding country. The models proposed for executing the aforementioned steps are presented in Sect. 4.1, and Sect. 4.2 respectively.

4.1 Estimation of Missing Indicators

Consider a country c for which the values of one or more indicators are missing. Let us denote with $\hat{I}_{c,k}$ the value of the k–th indicator of c which is estimated as:

$$\hat{I}_{c,k} = \frac{1}{|T_c|} \sum_{t \in T_c} I_{t,k}, \tag{1}$$

where, T_c stands for the set of c's most similar countries computed according to (3), and $I_{t,k}$ is the value of the k–th indicator of country t being member of T_c.

In general, similarity computation is used as a tool for handling the cases of missing operators providing robustness to the proposed approach. The effect of $|T_c|$ in terms of performance is reported in Sect. 6.

4.2 Ranking

Consider the ideal country $\tilde{c}$ and some country c. For the purposes of BRI the feature vector of the ideal country exhibits the best possible value for each indicator [22].

For example, assume two countries characterized by three indicators. Let the vectorized representation (i.e., feature vector) of those countries be as follows: $[0.52, 0.63, 0.19]$ and $[0.71, 0.25, 0.80]$. The feature vector of the ideal country is computed by applying the maximum operator element-wise resulting into $[0.71, 0.63, 0.80]$.

The ranking of c is conducted with respect to a score S_c which is computed as:

$$S_c = f(\tilde{c}, c)g_c, \tag{2}$$

where, $f(\tilde{c}, c)$ denotes the cosine similarity between ideal country $\tilde{c}$ and some other country c. In general, the cosine similarity is widely-used measurement that has been utilized in various areas including semantic web (e.g., [6]) and natural language processing (e.g., [11]), especially for tasks related to unsupervised machine learning.

The similarity between $\tilde{c}$ and c, $f(\tilde{c}, c)$, is estimated as the cosine of their respective vectorized indicators' values[10] :

$$f(\tilde{c}, c) = \frac{\sum_{i=1}^{N} I_{\tilde{c},i} I_{c,i}}{\sqrt{\sum_{i=1}^{N} (I_{\tilde{c},i})^2} \sqrt{\sum_{i=1}^{N} (I_{c,i})^2}}, \tag{3}$$

---

[10] In general, any similarity (or distance) metric can be used. In this work, we have also experimented with Euclidean distance without observing any improvement for the experiments reported in Sect. 5.

where, $I_{\tilde{c},i}$ and $I_{c,i}$ are the values of the i–th indicator of $\tilde{c}$ and c, respectively, while N stands for the number of indicators.

The similarity scores computed by (3) lie in $[0,1]$, with 0 and 1 denoting zero and absolute similarity, respectively.

The g_c constituent of (2) is defined as:

$$g_c = \frac{N - n_c}{N}, \tag{4}$$

where, N is the number of indicators and n_c denotes the number of c's null indicators.

Both $f(\tilde{c}, c)$ and g_c range in the $[0,1]$ interval.

An alternative scheme of S_c, denoted as S_c', is defined as follows (g_c is substituted by a sigmoid function in which g_c also appears as a parameter):

$$S_c' = f(\tilde{c}, c) \left(1 + \left(\frac{g_c(1 - \gamma)}{\gamma(1 - g_c)} \right)^{-2} \right)^{-1}, \tag{5}$$

where, g_c is computed according to (4), as in the case of (2).

As in the initial scheme, S_c' computes scores that within $[0,1]$. γ is constant that typically takes values as $0 \leq \gamma \leq 1$ and it can be used for centering the sigmoid function in the the $[0,1]$ domain. The basic idea that underlies (5) is the weighting of $f(\tilde{c}, c)$ according to a non-linear scheme. In Sect. 6, the performance for various values of γ is presented and discussed.

Overall, either S_c score or S_c' score can be used for computing the final BRI i.e., the ranking of countries according to their blockchain readiness. A comparison between S_c and S_c' is also reported in Sect. 6.

5   Experimental Data and Setup

This section presents the experimental data used along with the setup of the experiments. In addition, the evaluation process and metric are described followed by two experimental baselines.

The dataset used in this work is summarized in Table 1.

Table 1. Overview of experimental dataset.

Number of countries annotated as "high BRI"	45
Number of countries annotated as "mid BRI"	55
Number of countries annotated as "low BRI"	90
Total number of countries	190

In total, there are 190 countries categorized with respect to the following BRI levels (labels): (i) "high BRI', (ii) "mid BRI", and (iii) "low BRI". Each country was assigned (in the form of annotations) a category grounded on the rational decisions made by human experts [11].

More specifically, 45 out of 190 were annotated as countries featuring "high BRI", while 55 and 90 countries were assigned the "mid BRI" and "low BRI" annotations, respectively.

The key parameters of the proposed models, defined in Sect. 4, are as follows:

1. Weighting scheme used for BRI: linear or sigmoid (use of (2) or (5))
2. γ used in sigmoid weighting (see (5))
3. Given a country c, the number of c's most similar countries (see $|T_c|$ in (1))

The performance for various values set to the above parameters are reported in Sect. 6. Next, we describe an experimental setup that is formulated in the context of supervised learning.

- **Features:** Two features were utilized, namely, the weighting scores (linear or sigmoid) and the respective BRI scores.
- **Classification task:** The experimental task of this work was defined as a classification problem. Given the aforementioned features for a country, the task is to assign a label to it i.e., "high BRI" or "mid BRI" or "low BRI".
- **Classification models:** We have experimented with various classifiers including Naive Bayes (NB), Support Vector Machines (SVM), and Random Forest (RF).
- **Evaluation process:** A 10-fold cross validation process was applied using the dataset presented in Table 1.
- **Evaluation metric:** Classification accuracy was used for evaluating the performance of classifiers. It is computed as the percentage of the correctly classified test instances. Specifically, in the framework of 10-fold cross validation, the performance is reported in terms of average classification accuracy by averaging the classification accuracy scores that correspond to each fold.

All experimental results are reported only for the case of SVM. This is because very similar performance was achieved for the case of NB, while the use of RF resulted in lower classification accuracy compared to SVM and RF. Regarding SVM, we used the SMO algorithm [16] with the following configuration: (i) use of polynomial kernel (degree of polynomial: 1.0), (ii) the complexity parameter: 1.0, (iii) epsilon for round-off error: 1×10^{-12}, (iv) tolerance parameter: 0.001. The aforementioned categorization from human experts was used as ground truth for training/testing purposes.

Within the present classification-based experimental framework, the following classification baselines were adopted:

---

[11] The annotations of three experts were used and an overall annotation was compiled considering the three individual annotations. The overall annotation (i.e., after consolidating the three individual annotations) was used for the experimental part of this work.

- **Baseline 1:** Assume no classification model. Given any (unknown) country, always assign to it the label of the most populous class (i.e., "low BRI", see Table 1).
- **Baseline 2:** Use no weighting i.e., $g_c = 1$ in (2).

Baseline 1 was meant for testing the usefulness of a classification model that goes beyond the naive most–populous–class strategy. Baseline 2 was adopted for checking whether $f(\widetilde{c}, c)$ needs weighting.

6   Evaluation Results

This section, reports the evaluation results derived in terms of average classification accuracy with respect to the granularity schemes presented in Table 2.

Table 2. Classification of granularity schemes.

Granularity scheme	Class labels
3-class	"high BRI", "mid BRI", "low BRI"
2-class	"high BRI", "low BRI"

The 2-class granularity scheme focuses on the "high–vs.–low" discrimination based on the hypothesis that there are cases where the discrimination of two ends of the BRI spectrum is adequate (as opposed to the case of trying to build a more fine-grained model). The results reported were obtained using the two features: (i) weighting scores (linear or sigmoid), and (ii) the respective BRI scores.

Table 3, summarizes the performance for both linear and sigmoid schemes. The performance is reported for the 3-class and 2-class granularity schemes. In addition, the performance of the two baselines is included for comparison purposes.

Table 3. Classification acc. (%) for 3-class and 2-class task ($|T_c|=10$, $\gamma = 0.7$).

Features	Linear scheme (use of S_c)	Sigmoid scheme (use of S_c')
3-class		
Baseline 1	47.4	47.4
Baseline 2	48.4	48.4
Proposed features	**66.8**	62.6
2-class		
Baseline 1	66.7	66.7
Baseline 2	68.9	68.9
Proposed features	**89.6**	**89.6**

Firstly, it is observed that the use of the proposed features outperforms the two baseline approaches. This holds for both weighting and granularity schemes. Regarding the 3-class granularity scheme, the highest classification accuracy (66.8%) is yielded by the linear scheme. The sigmoid scheme obtains slightly lower accuracy (62.6%). For the 2-class granularity scheme, the two weighting schemes achieve identical performance being equal to 89.6%

Table 4. Classification acc. (%) for γ values of sigmoid scheme ($|T_c|=10$).

γ	0.1	0.2	0.3	0.4	0.5	0.6	0.7	0.8	0.9
3-class	50.0	51.1	52.1	53.2	53.9	53.7	62.6	61.6	**64.2**
2-class	83.0	84.4	83.7	85.9	87.4	88.9	**89.6**	88.9	88.9

Table 4, presents the performance for various values of the γ factor that is used in sigmoid weighting scheme (see (2)). As before, this is shown for both classification granularity schemes. In terms of performance scores, the 3-class scheme exhibits greater variance when compared to the 2-class scheme. Regarding the 3-class scheme, the highest classification accuracy (64.2%) is achieved when $\gamma = 0.9$. For the 2-class case top performance (89.6%) is yielded for $\gamma = 0.7$.

Table 5. Classification acc. (%) for various $|T_c|$ values using the linear scheme.

$|T_c|$	1	2	3	5	10	15	20	30	40
3-class	65.8	65.8	64.2	64.7	**66.8**	66.3	66.8	65.8	64.7
2-class	91.1	91.1	**91.9**	91.1	89.6	91.1	91.1	90.4	90.4

The classification accuracy for various values of $|T_c|$, which appears in (1) and denotes the number of c's most similar countries, is shown in Table 5.

The accuracy scores are presented with respect to the two classification granularity schemes. For the case of 3-class, the highest performance (66.8%) is yielded by the use of $|T_c|= 10$. Regarding the 2-class granularity scheme, the top classification accuracy (91.9%) is achieved for $|T_c|= 10$.

A number of indicative classification outputs are as follows: Canada and France ("high BRI"), Belarus and Greece ("mid BRI"), and Andorra and Maldives ("low BRI"). Those outputs were computed by the model that yielded the top classification accuracy (66.8) for the 3-class case.

Furthermore, in Table 6 we present the confusion matrix that corresponds to the top-performing setting (91.9% in Table 5). This details the performance of the classifier in term of misclassification types ("low BRI instead of high BRI", and "high BRI instead of low BRI").

For the case of "high BRI", the classification outcome is correct for 36 countries, while only two countries were misclassified. Regarding the "low BRI" case,

Table 6. Confusion matrix of the top-performing classification setting.

Low BRI	High BRI
88 (correct)	2 (error)
9 (error)	36 (correct)

88 countries were correctly classified and nine countries were erroneously put under the opposite category.

Overall, excellent classification accuracy (up to 91.9%) was achieved for the case of 2-class granularity scheme; which focuses on the discrimination of "high BRI" vs. "low BRI" countries. The 3-class granularity scheme poses a more difficult classification problem and, as anticipated, a lower performance score (66.8% classification accuracy) was obtained. This difficulty can be attributed on the presence of countries that lie in the middle of the BRI spectrum. Regarding the hardest classification task, i.e., the one based on the 3-class granularity scheme, the linear weighting scheme appears to performs better than the sigmoid scheme.

In order to further investigate the performance achieved for the 2-class task, the respective evaluation setup was adopted as follows: (i) use of a stricter split of train/test data (50%/50%), and (ii) use of a deep architecture for investigating the potential effect of non-linearities not captured by the models used so far.

Table 7. Multilayer perceptron (MLP) with two hidden layers: average classification acc. (%) for the 2-class case.

Layer 1: # nodes	Layer 2 # nodes	Dropout	Avg. classification accuracy
2	2	0%	76.8
2	2	2%	80.1
2	2	5%	71.6
2	2	8%	71.6
2	5	0%	81.5
2	5	2%	**85.1**
2	5	5%	80.7
2	5	8%	74.9

A Multilayer Perceptron (MLP) with two hidden layers was utilized with the following setups regarding the number of nodes: (i) two nodes for each layer, and (ii) two and five nodes for the first and second layer, respectively. Furthermore, a number of dropout rates was utilized. The average classification accuracy (computed across ten runs of the 50%/50% train/test split) is shown in Table 7. In general, the second layer setup (two and five nodes) performs better than the first setup. Also, the dropout appears to enhance the performance when set to 2%. This is observed for both setups. Overall, the top average classification accuracy (85.1%) is obtained for the second setup when applying 2% dropout.

7 Conclusions and Future Work

In this work, we proposed an updated version of our previous approach on an algorithmic computation of a blockchain readiness score (referred to as Blockchain Readiness Index – BRI) at the country level. BRI utilizes a set of indicators being related to the blockchain maturity exhibited by the countries under investigation. The core contribution of this work is a technique for estimating the BRI in the presence of missing indicators (extending our previous approach which requires no missing indicators). We coined the term "robust BRI" to refer to the ability of estimating BRI scores even when information for the indicators is missing.

The estimation of missing indicators was based on the assumption that countries that share similar blockchain-related indicators are likely to exhibit similar blockchain readiness. Under this reasoning, we proposed two weighting schemes for refining the initial similarity estimates, that constitute the building block of BRI, namely, linear and sigmoid weighting. In order to evaluate the effectiveness of the core numerical estimates (linear/sigmoid weights and weighted similarities) a classification-based framework was adopted utilizing supervised learning where those estimates were used for training several classifiers.

It was experimentally shown that the proposed classification features significantly outperform the baseline approaches for both classifications tasks: (a) "high BRI" vs. "mid BRI" vs. "low BRI" (also referred to as 3-class task), and (b) "high BRI" vs. "low BRI" (also referred to as 2-class task). Especially for the latter task, up to 91.9% classification accuracy was achieved. This experimentally justifies the effectiveness of the proposed approach regarding the estimation of missing blockchain indicators. In addition, it was found that the weighting of the similarity scores plays a critical role. The use of no weighting (Baseline 2) resulted in poor performance. Regarding the investigated weighting schemes, the linear one appeared to perform better than the sigmoid scheme for the 3-class task. For future work, we plan to further enhance the proposed approach for robust BRI estimation by investigating the weighted fusion of the indicators within the similarity computation phase.

Acknowledgement. This research was funded by the Ripple's Impact Fund, an advised fund of Silicon Valley Community Foundation (Grant id: 2018-188546).

References

1. Baller, S., Dutta, S., Lanvin, B.: The global information technology report 2016: innovating in the digital economy (2016). http://www3.weforum.org/docs/GITR2016/WEF_GITR_Full_Report.pdf. Online by the World Economic Forum and INSEAD

2. Basl, J.: Analysis of Industry 4.0 readiness indexes and maturity models and proposal of the dimension for enterprise information systems. In: Tjoa, A.M., Raffai, M., Doucek, P., Novak, N.M. (eds.) CONFENIS 2018. LNBIP, vol. 327, pp. 57–68. Springer, Cham (2018). https://doi.org/10.1007/978-3-319-99040-8_5
3. Singapore Economic Development Board: The smart industry readiness index (2020). https://siri.gov.sg/. Online by the Singapore Economic Development Board
4. Carayannis, E.G., Christodoulou, K., Christodoulou, P., Chatzichristofis, S.A., Zinonos, Z.: Known unknowns in an era of technological and viral disruptions-implications for theory, policy, and practice. J. Knowl. Econ. (2021). https://doi.org/10.1007/s13132-020-00719-0
5. Casino, F., Dasaklis, T.K., Patsakis, C.: A systematic literature review of blockchain-based applications: current status, classification and open issues. Telem. Inform. **36**, 55–81 (2019)
6. Christodoulou, K., Paton, N.W., Fernandes, A.A.A.: Structure inference for linked data sources using clustering. In: Hameurlain, A., Küng, J., Wagner, R., Bianchini, D., De Antonellis, V., De Virgilio, R. (eds.) Transactions on Large-Scale Data- and Knowledge-Centered Systems XIX. LNCS, vol. 8990, pp. 1–25. Springer, Heidelberg (2015). https://doi.org/10.1007/978-3-662-46562-2_1
7. Christodoulou, P., Christodoulou, K., Andreou, A.: A decentralized application for logistics: using blockchain in real-world applications. Cyprus Rev. **30**(2), 181–193 (2018)
8. Dolfsma, W., Seo, D.: Government policy and technological innovation-a suggested typology. Technovation **33**(6–7), 173–179 (2013)
9. Dutta, S., Lanvin, B.: The network readiness 2019: towards a future-ready society (2019). https://networkreadinessindex.org/. Online by Portulans Institute
10. Friedlmaier, M., Tumasjan, A., Welpe, I.M.: Disrupting industries with blockchain: the industry, venture capital funding, and regional distribution of blockchain ventures. In: Venture Capital Funding, and Regional Distribution of Blockchain Ventures, 22 September 2017, Proceedings of the 51st Annual Hawaii International Conference on System Sciences (HICSS) (2018)
11. Iosif, E., Potamianos, A.: Similarity computation using semantic networks created from web-harvested data. Nat. Lang. Eng. **21**(1), 49 (2015)
12. Kapassa, E., Themistocleous, M., Quintanilla, J.R., Touloupos, M., Papadaki, M.: Blockchain in smart energy grids: a market analysis. In: Themistocleous, M., Papadaki, M., Kamal, M.M. (eds.) EMCIS 2020. LNBIP, vol. 402, pp. 113–124. Springer, Cham (2020). https://doi.org/10.1007/978-3-030-63396-7_8
13. Makridakis, S., Christodoulou, K.: Blockchain: current challenges and future prospects/applications. Future Internet **11**(12), 258 (2019)
14. Nakamoto, S.: Bitcoin: a peer-to-peer electronic cash system (2008). http://bitcoin.org/bitcoin.pdf
15. United Nations: Un e-government surveys (2018). https://publicadministration.un.org/
16. Platt, J.: Fast training of support vector machines using sequential minimal optimization. In: Scholkopf, B., Burges, C., Smola, A. (eds.) Advances in Kernel Methods-Support Vector Learning (1998)
17. Shin, D.D.: Blockchain: the emerging technology of digital trust. Telem. Inform. **45**, 101278 (2019)
18. Shin, D., Ibahrine, M.: The socio-technical assemblages of blockchain system: how blockchains are framed and how the framing reflects societal contexts. Digital Policy, Regulation and Governance (2020)

19. Threlfall, R.: Autonomous vehicles readiness index. Klynveld Peat Marwick Goerdeler (KPMG) International (2018)
20. Economist Intelligence Unit: Automation readiness index (2020). https://www.automationreadiness.eiu.com/. Online by the Economist Intelligence Unit
21. T.F. University: Blockchain & cryptocurrencies regulation index (2018). https://doingcrypto.org/
22. Vlachos, A., Christodoulou, K., Iosif, E.: An algorithmic blockchain readiness index. In: Multidisciplinary Digital Publishing Institute Proceedings, vol. 28, p. 4 (2019)
23. Zheng, Z., Xie, S., Dai, H., Chen, X., Wang, H.: An overview of blockchain technology: architecture, consensus, and future trends. In: 2017 IEEE International Congress on Big Data (BigData Congress), pp. 557–564. IEEE (2017)

Blockchain Application in Luxury Brand Strategy: What Does Blockchain Technology Mean to Luxury Brands?

Pei-Hsiu Shih, Markus Bick$^{(\boxtimes)}$, and Matthias Murawski

ESCP Business School, Berlin Campus, Heubnerweg 8-10, 14059 Berlin, Germany
pei_hsiu.shih@edu.escp.eu, {mbick,mmurawski}@escp.eu

Abstract. Many applications, across an array of different industries, access blockchain technology. This paper focuses on the luxury industry and explores how these blockchain-based applications add value. The study incorporates the findings of a Delphi study of luxury sector professionals. Eleven luxury brand core values were identified and validated, and six blockchain application areas along the customer journey were refined for the industry by panelists. The results show that the *product authenticity or certification* application meets the most important core values for luxury brands, especially in thriving online marketplaces and secondary markets. *Responsibility*, i.e. the value ranked lowest by the panelists, entails huge demands from the market, namely in the form of corporate social responsibility and sustainability. The study provides the luxury sector with valuations of technology applications according to added value, customer journey phases and concrete use cases as examples. The contribution of the study is that it provides indicators for luxury business strategies when considering taking part in the blockchain networks.

Keywords: Blockchain application · Luxury brands · Strategy

1 Introduction

Counterfeiting is a huge global issue. According to the OECD [1], the total value of counterfeited goods will reach an estimated $2.81 trillion in 2022. In terms of the luxury sector, these imitation goods are harmful to brand equity [2] and violate the core values of exclusivity and exceptional quality. Meanwhile, not only do counterfeited items lead to monetary losses for brands, but intellectual property and trademark infringement also have a negative influence on brand equity [3]. Therefore, proving the authenticity of items for sale on online marketplaces is crucial for both brands and consumers [4]. The main players on luxury e-commerce platforms include Farfetch, Yoox Net-a-Porter and MatchesFashion in Europe, as well as JD.com and Tmall in Asia [5].

Some measures have been taken to ensure a safe online shopping environment for clients. Chinese retailer JD.com, for example, on 25 August 2020, unveiled a partnership with blockchain company Everledger and the Gemological Institute of America (GIA) in relation to a diamond provenance transparency service. The initiative allows individual

© Springer Nature Switzerland AG 2022
M. Themistocleous and M. Papadaki (Eds.): EMCIS 2021, LNBIP 437, pp. 102–116, 2022.
https://doi.org/10.1007/978-3-030-95947-0_8

buyers to verify the authenticity of diamonds available for purchase on JD.com, and it prevents the use of fraudulent certificates, ultimately building more trust in professional online diamond sellers. The collaboration aims to provide direct access to individual diamonds' characteristics, in a bid to fight counterfeiting and to identify synthetic diamonds which may not be advertised as such [6].

Product authenticity must never be neglected; otherwise, it can cause serious loss and delegitimise a business [7]. Moreover, smooth customer journeys, typified by short delivery lead times, and supportive customer care, for instance, are the main criteria when customers evaluate different online platforms. Furthermore, distributed ledgers, immutability, transparency and traceability are directly relevant characteristics when it comes to disclosing product authenticity and information throughout the supply chain [7–9]. However, luxury brands are usually not willing to adopt new technologies [10]. In this paper, our main objective herein is to answer two questions:

What blockchain applications in the luxury industry are most likely to be adopted? And how does the application add value?

We take the perspective of luxury professionals to discuss whether the adoption of blockchain technology could be beneficial to their sector. In addition, we try to identify application areas that create value, and we address essential concerns and the information required to decide whether or not to embrace the technology. We also offer a deeper understanding of the relevancy of blockchain technology and the luxury goods industry by associating the added value for luxury brands with applicable blockchain application areas. To provide a list of the most suitable application areas and its potential values to the sector, values and possible application fields based on literature research were evaluated, revised and validated by a group of luxury professionals via the Delphi technique, in order to obtain luxury-insiders' viewpoints and insights.

2   Identification of Core Values and Opportunities in the Luxury Sector

2.1   Core Values of a Luxury Brand

In economics, in contrast to essential goods, when consumers' income increases, the demand for luxury goods increases. These items can fulfill not only functional needs, but also psychological satisfaction [11]. The main difference between a luxury brand and a cheaper good is the realisation of mental desire [12]. According to Danziger [13], ten core values are essential for a luxury brand, and they can be categorised according to different perspectives, including *product performance, refined design, human touch, brand history, uniqueness* and *exclusiveness*. These features are essential for a luxury brand to express its value creation. Tynan et al. [14] addressed five types of luxury brand values from customers' points of view, namely *utilitarian,* outer and self-expression, the hedonic effect, *relationship with a brands* and *cost-related characteristics*.

2.2 Exceptional Quality and Innovation

In terms of product quality, a luxury brand is likely to provide extraordinary performance, which makes it stand out from others. In many cases, what constitutes high quality is professional knowledge. Luxury brands have their own 'ateliers', or so-called "workrooms," where skillful artisans devote themselves to their products, for example high-end jewellery, watches and leather goods, thus making the spirit of craftsmanship highly desirable. Furthermore, the purchase of a luxury watch, for instance, can sometimes be seen as an investment. To prove value preservation over time, activity in the secondary luxury market is an important index. According to a survey conducted by Nwankwo et al. [15], among all of the motivations for buying luxury goods, quality was ranked in first place. In essence, the ability to provide high-quality products is one of the most important criteria when evaluating a luxury brand.

In order to be at the top of its class in terms of quality, a luxury brand is likely to invest in product research and development. At the same time, bringing out revolutionary concepts and ideas help these brands become the best of the best in consumers' minds. Thus, it is not only important to investigate functional performance, but designs and concepts can also offer the public a new way of thinking or living. Aside from fashion, Van Cleef & Arpels, a high-end jeweller and watchmaker, introduced the "Cadenas" watch model, designed for women to read the time in an era when women were usually not supposed to wear wristwatches like men; wristwatches were seen purely as a feminine accessory. After the introduction of the first waterproof Rolex 'Oyster' model, with its masculine design, this innovative product changed the way men wore timepieces. In short, the factor that earns luxury brands a place in history is their spirit of pursuing perfection and being "avant-garde" in their outlook.

2.3 Exclusivity and Heritage

The spirit of craftsmanship leads to another feature of a luxury brand, namely exclusivity, which can be recognised through the control of product distribution, product quantity, uniqueness and a premium price band. The more effort a customer has to expend in order to attain the brand, the more luxurious the brand [16]. Taking a Hermes handbag as an example in this regard, it is almost impossible for a new customer to purchase a Kelly bag as their first transaction with the company; instead, it is necessary for a customer to show their loyalty to the brand. Therefore, in order to qualify to buy a certain "quota bag" like a Kelly or a Birkin, purchasing other products initially is an important indicator of how much they are willing to spend for an exclusive item. This sense of superiority followed by owning a rare item creates value for a luxury brand, because the more inaccessible a particular product, the harder it becomes for a competitor or forfeiter to imitate [16].

Usually, a heritage brand is defined by its history. Not only does it act as an element of brand equity, but heritage is also recognised in terms of brand identity [17]. In other words, it is the heritage that differentiates the brand from other competitors. Heritage is very much a brand's roots, in that its origins and history provide a good way to revisit value propositions and then sort out core competencies. With a clear view of these elements, a brand is likely to differentiate itself from others, thus allowing its value to stand out. In the meantime, brand heritage could also serve as a connection between brands and customers in the sense of engaging customers and getting them involved in the history and prestige. Also, protecting symbolic heritage items is a very powerful way of marketing a brand. It also provides a key element in relation to authenticity.

2.4 Significant Symbols and Values Perceived by Customers

Significant identifiable elements of a luxury brand that link to its history cannot be neglected. Often, these elements' "vocabulary" is referred to as the "association" of a brand. They are usually original and connected to the brand's story and the history of a product. To illustrate this point, Chanel filmed the video 'The Vocabulary of Fashion', highlighting the key elements that shape the style of Chanel but which are also deeply linked to the life story of Gabrielle Chanel. This kind of brand vocabulary is not necessarily in the form of logos or signs; more so, it is commonly recognised by the public as the origin of a brand, thereby providing luxury brand status in public perception.

Following Tynan et al. [14], among all of the core values mentioned so far, high quality and exceptional performance are seen as essential when talking about a luxury brand, while heritage and other symbolic traits are the elements that differentiate a brand from its competitors. The value of a luxury brand is built mutually, from both the brand side and the customer side. Based on the research by Wuestefeld et al. [18], brand heritage has a great impact on customer perceived value: economically, socially and functionally. Moreover, a heritage brand is often seen as trustworthy and authentic, and if heritage is relevant and meaningful to a customer, they are likely to remain loyal, accept higher prices and reduce buying risk, thereby implying that perceived value is rather important [19].

3 Methodology

Our research objective is to explore the most valuable application areas for blockchain technology in the luxury sector, and so this paper applies a Delphi study [20, 21] to verify the core values and features of luxury shoppers' decision journey and to map values with potential application fields, in order to identify the optimum way to apply blockchain technology. The method is an appropriate approach for exploring insights and potential opportunities, as industry insiders identify the value of applying this technology and provide a luxury sector viewpoint. According to Durach et al. [22], the likelihood and time spam of implementing blockchain technology is specific to every industry, but the authors suggest narrowing down the methodology to a specific industry, in order to gain insightful opinions. Thus, panel members who have been immersed in the luxury industry for several years make them ideal candidates.

3.1 Verification of Luxury Market Features and Application Areas Through the Delphi Approach

In answer to the research questions, the aim of the Delphi method is to seek consensus on opportunities and to identify the market sweet spot for applying blockchain technology in the luxury sector. Thus, panelists who have experience in the luxury sector were the target group. Furthermore, as the topic is highly relevant to new technology, it requires the sensitivities of overall luxury market trends and strategic movement among major players in the market. Therefore, various positions and backgrounds within the luxury sector were the main criteria for recruiting the panelists.

Table 1 illustrates the panel members' demographics. Overall, their age range falls between 18 and 34 years of age, which also corresponds to the development of the Internet. All members are based in Europe, in three cities, namely London, Paris and Geneva. There are four nationalities in the member pool: French, Turkish, Swiss and Italian. Two of the members have experience in the innovation sector that combines technology and luxury domain knowledge. Others are keen on market trends, not only for internal brands, but also for the total luxury market. In terms of academic background, most of the panel members have completed a master's degree in either business or luxury management. One has a technical background.

Table 1. Delphi panel member demographics

Panel member	A	B	C	D	E	F
Age range	25–34	25–34	18–24	25–34	25–34	25–34
Gender	Female	Female	Female	Female	Female	Female
Firm location	London	Paris	Paris	Paris	Paris	Geneva
Education	Master	Master	Master	Master	Master	Master
Background	Business Design	Management	Luxurx and fashion management	Entrepreneurship management	Fashion and costume, marketing	Engineering
Focus	Luxury e-commerce	Luxury group marketing intelligence	Luxury group marketing intelligence	Luxury group marketing intelligence	Luxury group strategy	Luxury watch brand

In this study, two rounds of interviews were conducted to gather the six luxury insiders' opinions and insights. Twelve interviews took place, as each panel member was interviewed twice. Both interviews were semi-structured, thereby providing more flexibility and opportunities to delve deeper into details relating to the research questions. Each interview lasted around 20 to 30 min, and all of them were conducted in English. Given geographical differences and the COVID-19 situation, only one physical interview took place, with the rest facilitated via video conferencing. The interviewees' identities have been anonymised. Due to trade secret concerns, company names and brand names also remain confidential.

3.2 First-Round Interview Question Design

In the first-round interviews, starting with three open-ended questions, the panelists were asked to give their general impressions and understanding of the blockchain application in the luxury sector. The three questions were as follows: *How have you been exposed to blockchain technology? What blockchain use cases have you observed in the luxury market? Where do you see opportunity?*

The second part of the first-round interview ranked a number of core values collected and categorised from the literature (see Sect. 2). Short examples were given to illustrate the elements. The panelists were then asked to choose their top five core values that should be included when it comes to a luxury brand. The aim of the question was to seek consensus on the cognition on luxury brands, thereby providing common ideas when it comes to luxury. Furthermore, the question afforded the interviewees the chance to extend the list or remove some elements, if some values were not mentioned or they disagreed with. The following are the key core values that were provided [13]:

Exceptional performance	*Relatability/relevancy*
Craftsmanship	*Heritage*
Exclusivity	*Responsibility*
Innovation	*Sense of aesthetic*
Artistic interpretation & expression	*Other suggestions*
Timelessness	

In the third part of the interview, the panelists were asked to identify the most important stages for a luxury shopper, as well as the corresponding business application areas that represent value in the customer journey. The aim of the question was to shape blockchain application areas from the perspective of luxury clients' shopping behaviour, by identifying the most valuable elements in this regard. The last question in the first-round interview was another open question: *What obstacles and challenges do you foresee in implementing the technology in the luxury sector?* The purpose of the question was to probe reasons for hesitating to apply this new technology in this context.

3.3 Second-Round Interview Question Design

Based on the results from the first-round interviews, several potential blockchain application were mentioned, and these are summarised into six categories. Based on the six application areas, the panelists were asked to score their importance, link them to the core values of luxury brand and, finally, estimate the likelihood of – and time frame relating to – implementation. The objective in the second round of interviews was to prioritise those application fields linking to the brands' core values while evaluating application areas from practical and operational viewpoints. The following six potential application areas were mentioned during the first-round interviews and integrated into the results of existing studies [22, 23].

- Diamond tracking
- Product authenticity or certification
- Transfer ownership
- Supply chain information documentation
- Post-purchase communication
- Alternative currency

Three sets of questions were asked in the second-round interviews. In the first session, the panelists were asked to evaluate the six application areas business in accordance with the importance of their impact, namely what effect the application can have in the luxury sector; they were allowed to extend the list as well. The question was: *Please rank the importance of the business impact for the following possible blockchain applications in the luxury sector. Please explain why you have ranked them in this way. What other applications should be included?*

The second session associated applications and core values, and its aim was to understand what value these technological applications can offer. In addition, from the first-round interviews, the importance of the core values was evaluated; thus, industry relevance could also be interpreted through the value proposition point of view. The question was as follows: *What core values of a luxury brand can be linked to the applications?*

Lastly, in order to understand the likelihood of implementation, the panelists were asked to estimate if it would actually happen and, if so, how long it would take for the majority of market players to implement the technology. The questions were presented as follows: *What business application will most likely be implemented, and why? How long (years) do you think it take to apply, and why?*

4   Results and Discussion

4.1   Knowledge Level in Relation to Blockchain Technology

Four out of six panelists had encountered blockchain technology in the workplace, either by handling projects to do with the technology or being invited to events related to the topic. One panelist had taken lectures on the subject, while another had obtained information solely via fashion business news websites. Interestingly, different types of knowledge levels represent different stages of implementing the technology in the practical business world:

Opportunity Exploration Stage. Panelists B and E had worked on projects related to the secondary market. One had conducted research in order to provide a global view of trends in the secondary market for "hard luxury", finding that blockchain technology was a tool for authenticating products and therefore identifying counterfeit goods in the preowned marketplace.

Evaluation Stage. Panelist A was in charge of an innovation project for one of the biggest luxury online marketplaces. To meet the internal objective of reaching 100% sustainable operation, her team had sought solutions to meet the goal. Blockchain-based supply chain documentation and product digital identity had been identified, and so they had been sourcing startups that could meet this business need.

Execution Stage. Panelist F worked for a high-end watch brand that had already implemented blockchain-based product certification. Different from other panelists, for F, blockchain technology was not something unreachable; instead, the team was planning to extend information to include supply chain details in the near future.

The six panelists believed that *diamond tracking, digital identity* and *product authentication* for preowned items were the main application areas, based mainly on their intuition connected to their belief in luxury products as well as general observations of market trends. Interestingly, more than half of the panelists mentioned that the luxury goods they were referring to only focused on the hard luxury category. Fashion and footwear were not considered for applying blockchain technology in the luxury industry. As panelist E mentioned, jewelry and watches are seen as more durable and timeless, in that when it comes to the resale price versus the original price, the ratio is always higher. All panelists admitted that use cases in the industry are few and far between, thereby leading to the assumption that the industry is not familiar with the technology.

4.2 Customer Decision Journey in a Luxury Shopper Scenario

Following Durach et al. [22], the customer journey should be considered in a circular process to meet modern consumers' behaviour. In Table 2, we map the customer decision journey according to the relevancy level for luxury shoppers and list application fields stated by the panelists and taken from a case analysis.

Table 2. Mapping the customer decision journey to relevant blockchain application fields in the luxury sector

Customer decision journey (CDJ)	Relevancy to luxury shoppers	Relevant blockchain application identified
Consideration/Motivation		
Evaluation	High	• Product authenticity or certification • Diamond tacking
Payment		• Alternative currency • Transfer ownership: smart contract
Post-purchase experience	High	• Post-purchase communication
Loyalty loop	High	• Post-purchase communication • Loyalty program: virtual membership points
Others		• Supply chain information documentation • Diamond tracking

Evaluation, post-purchase experience and the *loyalty loop* were noted as crucial stages within the customer journey by all panelists. In the evaluation step, it was agreed by all that product quality certification would provide added value for luxury shoppers, and at the same time, a product authenticity application was addressed by several panelists as well, especially in preparation for the booming secondary market and online platforms according to panelist A. Post-purchase experience was agreed upon by all panelists. At this regard, product maintenance services and loyalty programmes were mentioned. It was also stated many times during the interviews that "service" is one of the most important values when it comes to a luxury experience, and so it should be included in "exceptional performance". Post-purchase experience is one of the most important experiences within the service scope.

When it comes to the payment stage, a privacy issue was raised by panelist E, who identified that many luxury purchases are often gifts, and some clients wish to remain anonymous while purchasing, especially so-called "ultra-high net worth" individual (UHNWI) clients.

Transparency across the whole supply chain is hard to categorise into only one stage of the customer decision journey, as the supply chain can be extended upstream from product and material origins and downstream to customer ownership. However, it was highlighted as a final and ideal goal of the industry to disclose information on raw materials and manufacturing, as luxury products have been highly criticised in terms of unethical product sourcing and employee welfare throughout the production process (panelist B).

4.3   Evaluation of the Core Values and Application Fields

All of the listed core values were mentioned at least one time during the interviews (Table 3). This means that the values can be considered relevant to a luxury brand.

According to the results, all of the panelists ranked *craftsmanship* in relation to the two most important values for a luxury brand. In addition to the highest quality of workmanship, the spirit of excellence, the concept of perfection and the amount of time spent on creating goods also ranked highly. Panelist B mentioned that craftsmanship is the core competence of a luxury brand, because it is how a brand differentiates itself from others and competes with other brands; also, it represents the spirit of a brand and its determination for the highest quality.

Exclusivity was mentioned four times. Due to scarcity and high price, according to panelist C, people acquire a luxury good due to the feeling of joining a prestigious community aligned with a sense of superiority. According to panelist E, individuals project their idealised values onto the group they want to be part of. When a luxury brand is accepted by broader groups, its aura is diluted, and so it no longer occupies a special place in the consumer's mind. As stated by Nielson [24], who report on Chinese consumer behaviour, what customers care about the most are high quality, uniqueness, exclusiveness and heritage, which corresponds to the results from the first-round interviews.

Again, four out of the six interviewees mentioned *heritage* when it comes to the top five core values. With more than three years of experience in a heritage and brand equity team, panelist E has addressed the importance of heritage as a core value of a luxury brand. Brand heritage is one of the most valuable assets when it comes to storytelling, especially for marketing and branding aspects. However, brands with a rich heritage are usually seen as traditional and old. Therefore, it is important for a brand to translate a possibly monotonous history into bitesize and relevant information to a new generation of customers.

Table 3. Ranking of the core values for each panelist

Core values/Panelists	A	B	C	D	E	F	Average ranking	Numbers of mentions
Craftsmanship	1	1	2	1	1	1	1.17	6
Exclusivity	3	3			3	4	3.25	4
Heritage		2		4	5	2	3.25	4
Innovation		5	1	3		5	3.50	4
Creativity			3	2	2		2.33	3
Timelessness	2	4					3.00	2
Relevancy	4				4		4.00	2
Sense of aesthetic			5			3	4.00	2
Exceptional performance			4	5			4.50	2
Responsibility	5						5.00	1
Dream factor								Newly identified

Innovation around heritage storytelling can be illustrated through the example of Gucci. Marketing activities that were built around Gucci's brand heritage were done through various channels, including flagship stores' interior design concepts, a targeted location strategy and renewed iconic collections. The "Forever Now" campaign, for instance, featured photos from the 1950s, showcasing craftsmen in their workshops. Similar exhibitions have been launched by many other brands, as they provide new forms of communication and presentation, and the brand can access a wider audience. In addition, by creating an "Instagrammable" environment, content can be easily shared between the offline and the online world. Therefore, brands can develop smart content strategies that not only showcase the heritage and history of the brand, but also educate the audience with product knowledge, attract young clients or expand local visibility in new markets.

The *dream factor* was cited by panelist D as an additional new core value, in that a luxury brand should be able to create a dream for its customers, by building up a Holy Grail-like iconic product and a desirable brand image. This new factor was noted by Okonkwo-Pezard [2], in that the dream factor arouses the curiosity and interest of customers, and it is one of the most important elements in a luxury item. In short, the dream factor represents the long-term desires of customers. It is clearly an important index that shows a brand's potential.

To answer the research question, i.e. to identify the added values of blockchain technology application, the panelists were asked to link the core values and applications. By highlighting the top five core values identified in previous questions in each application, the level of relevancy and importance of the application and the industry were distinguished. In Table 4, *product authenticity or certification, supply chain information documentation*, and *diamond tracking* are considered the most relevant to the top five core values identified in the previous results: *craftsmanship, exclusivity, heritage, innovation* and *creativity*. In terms of mentions of top core values in four highly relevant applications, *product authentication or certification* were mentioned 14 times, followed

Table 4. Associated core values for blockchain applications for luxury shoppers (*sign represents the top five core values from previous interview results)

Blockchain application	Associated core values (times of mention)	Numbers of top 5 core value mentions
Product authenticity or certification	Heritage (5)* Craftsmanship (3)* Exclusivity (3)* Innovation (3)* Exceptional performance (3) Responsibility (2) Sense of aesthetics (2)	14
Supply chain information documentation	Craftsmanship (5)* Responsibility (4) Innovation (3)* Timelessness (1) Relevancy (1)	8
Diamond tracking	Responsibility (4) Exclusivity (3)* Craftsmanship (1)* Innovation (1)* Exceptional performance (1) Timelessness (1)	5
Alternative currency	Innovation (5)* Relevancy (2) Exceptional performance (1)	5
Transfer ownership	Relevancy (3) Exclusivity (2)* Heritage (2)* Timelessness (2) Responsibility (2) Exceptional performance (1) Dream factor (1)	4
Post-purchase communication	Exclusivity (3)* Relevancy (2) Responsibility (2) Dream factor (2) Innovation (1)* Timelessness (1) Exceptional performance (2)	4

by *supply chain information documentation* with eight mentions, *diamond tracking* with five mentions and *alternative currency* with five.

The panelists were informed that the implementation rate refers to the possibility that major players in the market will start to take action. As shown in Table 5, in general, the mean possibility of implementation for the six applications was over 50%, *product authenticity or certification* were seen as the best possible applications with 92% and the lowest standard deviation of 8.8 pts, followed by *diamond tracking* with an 85% likelihood of implementation with a higher standard deviation of 15 pts. In terms of business impact, *diamond tracking* ranked number one, followed by *product authentication or certification*. All panelists agreed that *product authentication or certification* eliminate concerns around counterfeiting, especially in the secondary goods markets and online platforms. Panelist A stated that implementation would force second-hand online marketplaces to make direct changes to their business models.

The transparency of supply chain information was discussed widely when it comes to blockchain applications. However, panelists A and E held different points of view. Obviously, harmonising stakeholders throughout the supply chain is very difficult, but nevertheless, in the view of sustainability, it is essential to disclose as much information as possible, so that manufacturers share more responsibility for the production process, thereby providing consumers with more information at the same time. Despite the benefits that information disclosure can bring, for high-end jewel brands, detailed information such as the identity of jewellers and workplaces is confidential and is seen as a trade secret. In order to prevent jewellers from getting robbed or threatened, some information is better left unsaid, according to panelist E.

Table 5. Business impact and estimated likelihood and years of implementation

Blockchain application	Business impact level ranking	Mean of likelihood of implementation	Estimated years for implementation
Product authenticity or certification	2.33 (STD 1.03)	92.5% (STD 8.8)	3.33 (STD 1.47)
Diamond tracking	1.5 (STD 0.84)	85% (STD 22.8)	3.4 (STD 1.08)
Transfer ownership	4 (STD 1.1)	75% (STD 26.65)	3.6 (STD 0.96)
Post-purchase communication	3.5 (STD 1.22)	64.17% (STD 15.63)	2.88 (STD 0.95)
Supply chain information documentation	2.83 (STD 1.17)	60% (STD 22.36)	3.25 (STD 1.29)
Alternative currency	6 (STD 0)	58.75% (STD 36.37)	3.25 (STD 1.55)

5 Conclusion and Implications

In response to our research questions, eleven luxury brand core values were identified and validated by a set of panelists in a Delphi study. Assessing the core values' ranks gave us a sense of the industry's characteristics alongside possible strategic rationales. Moreover, core values and applications were connected. To investigate further the possibility of implementing blockchain technology, the panelists were asked to assess the business impact level and the likelihood of implementation on the defined application areas, in order to provide a practical point of view.

Overall, the application *product authenticity or certification* meets the most top five core values. Namely, the application helps provide a good deal of added value to the luxury industry, which directly answers the research question. The application was recognised by the panelists as highlighting the most important core values, such as protecting *heritage* and *craftsmanship*, providing *exclusivity* and *innovating*. With the boom of the luxury secondary market, the application also offers another channel for brands to connect with product owners, thus creating new touchpoints and extending the product lifecycle. Meanwhile, activating the secondary market also satisfies the expectations of consumers in terms of sustainability.

Essentially, all of the application areas can be linked to at least one of the top five luxury brand core values, among which "responsibility" was mentioned the most in various application fields. However, it is not the core value that brands value the most, as it only ranks tenth out of eleven core values. Interestingly, according to the literature findings, the demand to ensure corporate social responsibility and sustainability is usually in the form of external pressure. In response to market demand luxury brands are being forced to tackle the issue – and blockchain could be a possible solution.

Even though some use cases are illustrated to prove the potential of blockchain application in the luxury sector, there is still insufficient evidence to show that implementation is scalable. The panelists voiced their concerns about the application of the technology in terms of, for instance, the lack of talent within the industry, immaturity of the technology, privacy issues for UHNWI clients and the requirement for resources such as energy and money. Also, it was mentioned multiple times by the panelists that the lack of consensus, such as an alliance or a widely recognised protocol in the luxury industry, would slow down implementation of the technology.

However, our research suffers from some limitations. The panelists' backgrounds narrowed the focus on luxury product categories to mostly hard items such as jewellery and watches, or high-quality leather goods. Moreover, the panelists did not consider themselves experts on the technological level regarding blockchain, albeit this does represent actual industry talent restrictions in this regard. Lastly, the panelists tended to view blockchain application from a European market point of view, due to their professional experience and personal backgrounds.

Thus, observations on other continents such as Asia, the Americas and Africa could be considered during future research. Other luxury categories such as wines and spirits, automobiles and air transport, hospitality and concierge services should be considered as well. Eventually, panelists with a relevant technical background, as well as employees from technology providers, independent high jewellery studio owners or secondary market runners, should be included as well.

References

1. OECD: Mapping the Real Routes of Trade in Fake Goods. https://read.oecd-ilibrary.org/gov ernance/mapping-the-real-routes-of-trade-in-fake-goods_9789264278349-en#page3
2. Okonkwo-Pézard, U.: The luxury brand strategy challenge. In: Kapferer, J.-N., Kernstock, J., Brexendorf, T.O., Powell, S.M. (eds.) Advances in Luxury Brand Management, pp. 59–64. Palgrave Macmillan, Cham (2017)
3. Kapferer, J.-N., Michaut-Denizeau, A.: Is luxury compatible with sustainability? Luxury consumers' viewpoint. J. Brand Manag. 21, 1–22 (2014)
4. Schmidt, C.G., Klöckner, M., Wagner, S.M.: Blockchain for supply chain traceability: case examples for luxury goods. In: Voigt, K.-I., M. Müller, J. (eds.) Digital Business Models in Industrial Ecosystems. FBF, pp. 187–197. Springer, Cham (2021). https://doi.org/10.1007/ 978-3-030-82003-9_12
5. Paton, E., Friedman, V.: The luxury E-commerce wars heat up. On one side: Amazon. On the other: a new alliance of brands and platforms. Who will win? https://www.nytimes.com/ 2020/11/29/business/amazon-farfetch-richemont-ecommerce-wars.html
6. McKinsey: The State of Fashion 2020. https://www.mckinsey.com/~/media/mckinsey/indust ries/retail/our%20insights/the%20state%20of%20fashion%202020%20navigating%20unce rtainty/the-state-of-fashion-2020-final.pdf
7. Pun, H., Swaminathan, J.M., Hou, P.: Blockchain adoption for combating deceptive counterfeits. Prod. Oper. Manag. 30, 864–882 (2021)
8. de Boissieu, E., Kondrateva, G., Baudier, P., Ammi, C.: The use of blockchain in the luxury industry: supply chains and the traceability of goods. J. Enterp. Inf. Manag. 34, 1318–1338 (2021)
9. Azzi, R., Chamoun, R.K., Sokhn, M.: The power of a blockchain-based supply chain. Comput. Ind. Eng. 135, 582–592 (2019)
10. Holmqvist, J., Wirtz, J., Fritze, M.P.: Luxury in the digital age: a multi-actor service encounter perspective. J. Bus. Res. 121, 747–756 (2020)
11. Wiedmann, K.-P., Hennigs, N., Schmidt, S., Wüstefeld, T.: The perceived value of brand heritage and brand luxury. In: Diamantopoulos, A., Fritz, W., Hildebrandt, L., Bauer, A. (eds.) Quantitative Marketing and Marketing Management. Marketing Models and Methods in Theory and Practice; Dedicated to Udo Wagner, pp. 563–583. Springer, Wiesbaden (2012). https://doi.org/10.1007/978-3-8349-3722-3_27
12. Nia, A., Lynne Zaichkowsky, J.: Do counterfeits devalue the ownership of luxury brands? J. Prod. Brand Manag. 9, 485–497 (2000)
13. Danziger, P.N.: Putting the Luxe Back in Luxury. How New Consumer Values are Redefining the Way We Market Luxury. Paramount Market Pub, Ithaca (2011)
14. Tynan, C., McKechnie, S., Chhuon, C.: Co-creating value for luxury brands. J. Bus. Res. 63, 1156–1163 (2010)
15. Nwankwo, S., Hamelin, N., Khaled, M.: Consumer values, motivation and purchase intention for luxury goods. J. Retail. Consum. Serv. 21, 735–744 (2014)
16. Becker, K., Nobre, H.: Toward a luxury brand definition. In: 6th Annual EuroMed Conference on Confronting Contemporary Business Challenges through Management Innovation, pp. 143–157 (2013)
17. Dion, D., Borraz, S.: Managing heritage brands: a study of the sacralization of heritage stores in the luxury industry. J. Retail. Consum. Serv. 22, 77–84 (2015)
18. Wuestefeld, T., Hennigs, N., Schmidt, S., Wiedmann, K.-P.: The impact of brand heritage on customer perceived value. Markt 51, 51–61 (2012)
19. Muehling, D.D., Sprott, D.E.: The power of reflection: an empirical examination of nostalgia advertising effects. J. Advert. 33, 25–35 (2004)

20. Avella, J.R.: Delphi panels: research design, procedures, advantages, and challenges. Int. J. Dr. Stud. **11**, 305–321 (2016)
21. Skinner, R., Nelson, R.R., Chin, W.W., Land, L.: The Delphi method research strategy in studies of information systems. Commun. Assoc. Inf. Syst. **37**, 31–63 (2015)
22. Durach, C.F., Blesik, T., Düring, M., Bick, M.: Blockchain applications in supply chain transactions. J. Bus. Logist. **42**, 7–24 (2021)
23. McDowell, M.: 6 ways blockchain is changing luxury. https://www.voguebusiness.com/tec hnology/6-ways-blockchain-changing-luxury
24. Nielsen: In China's Premium Sector, One Size Doesn't Fit All. https://www.nielsen.com/hk/ en/insights/article/2017/in-chinas-luxury-sector-one-size-doesnt-fit-all/

Exploring the Need for Blockchain-Based National Population Census

Sana Rasheed$^{(\boxtimes)}$ and Soulla Louca

Digital Innovation Department, University of Nicosia, Nicosia, Cyprus
rasheed.s@live.unic.ac.cy, louca.s@unic.ac.cy

Abstract. National population census provides the basis for governments' financial, economic, health and education policies for its populace. It plays a vital role in mapping a country's growth and financial trajectories and it is the single most valuable and shared resource among government departments and apparatuses. The centralized, traditional methodologies currently in use are faced with several challenges including and not limited to high costs, privacy issues, enumerating unsafe areas and reduced cooperation. This research aims to analyze through a systematic literature review the drawbacks and challenges of the current traditional methodologies used in housing and population census to identify if a decentralized system would assist in mitigating them. The drawbacks identified are population coverage, ethnic and racial discrimination, privacy concerns, census data distribution, cost of census, and cooperation and participation. The research, even though at an embryonic stage, shows that blockchain-based solutions may be a candidate for solving several of the above mentioned challenges while laying at the same time the foundations of our research on blockchain-based systems for tackling with other challenges faced within census such as that of the missing people.

Keywords: Blockchain · National population census · Decentralized solution

1 Introduction

Population and housing census (hereby now referred to as census) is conducted to gather information on demographics, individuals, and their state of living for and in the respective jurisdiction. It gives a holistic picture of the economic and financial situation of the country and forms the basis for building policies and allocating financial resources. The United Nations has mandated the requirement for a decennial census which is a population census conducted every ten years to gather data on the residents of the jurisdiction [1]. It lays the foundation for policymaking in the dimensions of finances, economy, healthcare, and education, on a substantially granular level, beneficial for mapping the growth of the country.

Don Tapscott - a world's leading authority on innovation, mentions that the economic and social impact of technology is a voice on emerging technologies like blockchain-based systems and their impact on industries. He suggests, the technology industries can either be subject to disruption or conform to innovation and transform accordingly.

M. Themistocleous and M. Papadaki (Eds.): EMCIS 2021, LNBIP 437, pp. 117–129, 2022.
https://doi.org/10.1007/978-3-030-95947-0_9

Like any new and emerging technology, it is hard to extrapolate and forecast the future implications and drawbacks of switching to an entirely new system that has not been battletested [2]. Apart from testing and shifting to a blockchain based decentralized solution, Casey and Vigna have raised the concern that it is also crucial to define proper rules and steps to reveal only needed information in different circumstances. Otherwise, it would be hard to stop a malicious user to gain access of one's identity details that he/she can later use to impersonate [3].

Census plays an important role in mapping a country's growth and financial trajectories and it is the single most valuable and shared resource that is used among numerous departments and apparatuses of the government [4].

The solutions followed nowadays by government for census enumeration are either one of these [5]:

a) The traditional census is a full enumeration, based on a field operation at a given time on sample basis. This traditional approach also includes: i). long form or short form enumeration, cover within short time span, and ii). rolling census, cover whole country over long period of time. Among the countries that follow this methodology is the United States and France.
b) A full/sample field enumeration combined with data taken from registers.
c) Use registers and administrative sources (inclusive or exclusive to existing survey).

According to UNECE online survey report on national practices in 2010 census round, the traditional census approach was still the most common approach adopted in the UNECE region. Few countries have adopted a combined or register based census methodology [5].

To conduct the traditional census enumeration, there are only two methods:

● Interviewer/Enumerator-based: They conduct door-to-door interview and record information; or
● Self-completion: A household member completes the questionnaire on behalf of the family.

Enumerator-based surveys are widely common in developing countries and some parts of developed countries where a designated officer performs this task in a specified area during a restricted short period of time. This approach is widely used for illiterate populations or groups who may be unwilling to complete the census forms themselves, or find it difficult to do so [5]. Self-completion examples can be seen in United States where the questionnaires distributed and collected by post (mail-out/mail-back procedure) or by enumerators. This method can be adopted in the countries where literacy is relatively high [5].

A general concern with enumerator-based survey is, what did the officer hear and wrote down? Another critical concern is that the officers are paid by the number of houses they have visited. The more houses they cover, the more they earn. This can also become a barrier and cause miss-information. However, in both methods the data are recorded on paper which increases the chance of human errors.

Our aim is to explore the implementation of the population census over a blockchain to extend the inherent advantages of distributed ledgers for transparency, immutability, and security, thus solving the problem of forced/ethnical cleansing of marginalized communities from the national census data. The ultimate goal of the research is to mitigate the missing person problem that is one of the hardest to overcome all over the world. In order to identify if a decentralized solution is suitable for census, we have carried out a systematic literature review on traditional methods used for identifying the disadvantages of the centralized systems and explore the possibility of transitioning to decentralized systems.

Section 2 gives an overview of blockchain technology and Sect. 3 describes the methodology followed. Section 4 discuss the finding, and Sect. 5 debate the need for blockchain-based solutions, and concluded our discussion in Sect. 6. We would like to emphasize that this is the first stage of our work. Our ultimate goal is to design and implement a decentralized solution for the current census problems identified.

2   Blockchain Technology

Blockchain technology holds a very simple idea and has far-reaching implications. It is a distributed ledger (also known as decentralized databases) that allows users to add, verify or permanently record transactions [34]. These networks are consensus oriented and need community consent to perform any changes on the ledger. Once a transaction is recorded in a block of data and inserted on the chain, then the alteration in the processed transaction is not possible. This results in eliminating the need of central "gatekeeper" to provide trusted sources of transactional verification and support [6].

Blockchain was initially introduced as the technology behind bitcoin, the first digital currency to solve the double-spending problem without the need of a trusted authority [7]. The introduction of Ethereum's smart contracts in 2015, allowed developers to deploy their own logic-based concepts that were known as decentralized applications or dapps. These dapps could be deployed on the Ethereum network and would allow the users in the network to interact with them just like any other conventional application. This created a wide range of opportunities for developers and technology enthusiasts to engage in the space and use blockchain for non-financial purposes as well.

Soon afterwards, several industries recognized its potential for solving several other problems encountered such as logistics or tampered proof data. The decentralized nature of blockchain technology, along with its immutability and cryptographic characteristics makes data difficult to tamper with. Based on the above, blockchain can be characterized as a distributed ledger of any type of transactions, where a transaction is the exchange of data (medical data, consumer details, product data, etc.) Its main characteristics are:

- Decentralized: no single authority controls, influences or manipulates the data records that exists in a blockchain.
- Shared: blockchains are made up of multiple parties (or systems).
- Time-stamped: transactions are stored in chronological order.
- Append-only: you can only add new transactions to a blockchain.
- Immutable: Once written, a transaction cannot be deleted or modified.

- Cryptographically-secured: advanced cryptography enables tampered-proof records. security and secrecy.
- Enables smart contracts: blockchains are programmable enabling smart contracts to be implemented and executed.

The blockchain based model varies from industry to domain and its applications. We can find various implementations from the energy sector [8, 9] to finance [10], healthcare, supply chains, academia [35] and many more. Moreover, blockchain technology can be used for governmental services for improving trust, transparency and promoting accountability of government activities. Many governments around the world have proceeded into implementing a land registration system [11]. The UK government released a report on the potential of blockchain technology for government services, recommending its use [12]. Dubai on the other hand, is one of the first cities around the world to embrace the technology and has already several blockchain based government services [11]. Estonia, in collaboration with Bitnation works on a project for to offering public notary services to Estonian e-Residents [12, 13]. Estonian e-Residents have electronic IDs that can be used to notarize official documents such as birth certificates, marriage arrangements, business contracts, land titles, and other from anywhere in the world [14].

3   Research Method

A systematic approach has been followed for reviewing the existing literature. The specific methodology has been chosen as such review methods enables researchers to avoid arbitrary decision making [15]. The main objective of our research is to identify the drawbacks of centralized systems for conducting population census and whether those drawbacks could be mitigated through blockchain technology.

In order to ensure that all papers and official reports were taken into consideration, the following inclusion rules were used:

A.   Work that was published in the last twenty years. If published by a renowned organization, the 20-year constraint is relaxed. The rationale for using the twenty-year constraint is based on the fact that countries conduct decennial censuses which occur once every ten years; hence, changes within the census practicing methodologies are not significant. Therefore, older publications and literature about population census are substantially relevant.
B.   Papers had to be peer-reviewed.
C.   Only papers written in the English language were considered.

The United National Statistic Division (UNSD) official reports and selective national news media articles were considered in order to cover the reported issues and challenges. The reason of including news articles was to eliminate any biases picked up from post census findings. These findings are generally published under government authorities and may include manipulation issues for the sake of political or electoral gains. The United Nation website, American Census Survey, and a part of google search was used to find official news reports on the subject. The google search has been used for it.

For the literature review, the Ebscohost search engine has been used which includes 102 databases including access to Scopus, a bibliographic abstract and citation database that Elsevier provides [16]. The following keywords were used with the advance search option by filling them in multiple text boxes using the OR operator to get maximum listing.

- population census
- population census methods or mechanism
- population census challenges or barriers or difficulties or issues or problems or limitations
- privacy or security issues
- census undercount minorities
- census data differential undercount
- challenges of census in developing countries.

The search process followed was top-down, i.e., starting from broader searches such as "population census mechanism" and "population census types", to slowly refining focus to core objective using targeted keywords, such as "undercount in the census", "problems with centralized census enumeration".

Based on above criteria, the resultant set left with 6,245 searched items. Few The keywords "machine learning", "deep learning", "artificial intelligence", "neural network", "forecast", "prediction", "foreseeing", "data analysis", "outlier", "experimental studies", and "testing methods" were added in the exclusion filter to exclude irrelevant articles. This resulted in 2,121 records.

After screening the title list, more irrelevant keywords were identified and added in exclusion filter. These were "tourism", "pollutants", "pandemic", "agriculture", "spatial trends", "smart phones", "language", "educational planning", "mass media", "art, urbanization", "water supply" removing another 1,897 more items from the list.

Papers were shortlisted from the search results if the objective question was primarily addressed in the research paper or was discussed partially alongside the main research focus. We shortlisted a mix of papers and standards relating to our objective question totaling to 224. From the shortlisted literature, we conduct an in-depth study to select only those papers that resonate entirely with this paper's theme. It results in a total of 22 references that include papers, books, UN standards and official news articles (Fig. 1). It is worth noting that a quick debrief on the search results, shows that around 54% of relevant references are covering the UN standards, national census and official news reports, while 46% are the peer-reviewed papers and books discussing census. The rest of our references at the end relate to blockchain.

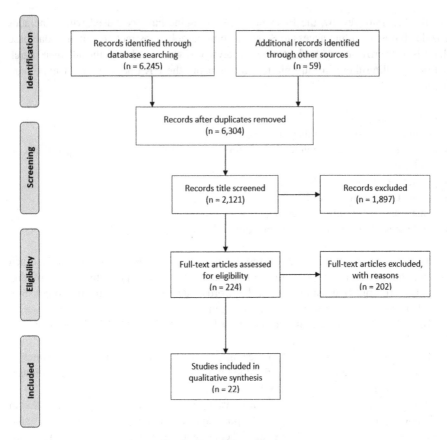

Fig. 1. Search flow diagram

4 Drawbacks and Gaps in Census Enumeration

This section highlights the drawbacks and gaps in census enumeration as identified from our review.

4.1 Population Coverage

One of the major concerns regarding census data is its inability to concisely cover all forms of living arrangements of individuals that are a part of a region or country resulting to discrepancies and loopholes that prevent holistic enumeration of individuals residing in a state. Individuals that do not have proper living arrangements, such as homeless communities, frequent travelers and in fact nomads who do not associate themselves to a single location are usually overlooked [1].

If we look at the recent period, Pakistan 6th national population census had been conducted in 2017 and Pakistan's official news media reported that as much as 1.5 million people from the city of Karachi have been reported missing [17, 18]. Since then,

4 years have passed and yet Pakistan's census data is not released and become a subject of politicized. Similar missing problems are reported from the United States news media. In the 2010 census 1.5 million children from minorities (2.1% of black Americans and 1.5% of Hispanics) were not accounted for [19, 20].

Another concern is the of over-coverage. Hogan [21] has discussed estimation issues of US census 2000. He analyzed the framework of the census system and concluded that the system failed to correctly identify 4.7 million erroneous enumerations in US census 2000. This was due to misidentification of residences of large numbers of people in the sample, leading to both false matches and false non-matches.

PC [22] has talked about the sensitivity of the census that has remained intractable in Nigeria. Since 1960 independence, Nigeria missed the opportunity to appraise the past, accurately. Census, being a crucial factor in determining, planning, and evaluating political and economic terms was deliberately exploited for political and monetary reasons.

Other problems are the erroneous inclusions of people who are included in the census inappropriately such as foreign tourists or people that have died [23].

4.2 Ethnic and Racial Discrimination

Throughout the history of data collection on behalf of the ruling authorities, discriminations have existed that tend to underestimate, or overestimate certain groups based on religion, race or ethnicity. Since figures obtained through census are utilized for policy-making, inclusive of monetary decisions concerning funding, such under-representations lead to disproportionate allocation of funds, depriving communities of the required financial assistance due to underrepresentation.

Barbara Crossette [24] discusses the various census concerns that exists of racial, ethnic and religious minorities who sense they are being undercounted or miscategorized. O'Hare [23] mainly focuses on "differential undercounts" problem which refers to people in some group have higher net undercount rates than people in other group. Rebecca Nagle [25] also highlights that, among other non-white communities, the native American population of Navaho origins along with Alaskan natives, were underrepresented by 4.9% in US census 2010. In the census of 2020, the likelihood of even more severe underrepresentation is higher given the data collection process has been made online, whereas these regions suffer from the lack of adequate broadband access. Moreover, just a 1% undercount in New Mexico census 2020 could result in the loss of $750m in federal aid to the state. In India, with the passage of the Citizenship Amendment Act (CAA) law that bans Muslim immigrants to settle in India the upcoming decennial census was likely to underrepresent Muslim population [24].

4.3 Privacy Concerns

With the advent of technology, data has become increasingly accessible and a topic of controversies and legal standings in the recent years A data leak in the database of the US Census Bureau exposed data on 4200 individuals. Data is not encrypted, and therefore readable after being hacked [26]. In addition, there are major concerns of poor measures of security in terms of data storage and organizations with access to the data.

Tim Singleton Norton [27] reported similar privacy issue from the Australian census. During the years 2013–2016, the Australian Census suffered from 14 data breaches which alone is a foremost concern to the citizens. Sabine Devins [28] highlights the concerns Germans have in regards to their data. In 1980s, a group of citizens managed to sue the German government over a 160-question long questionnaire in the census enumeration process. The concerns raised indicated that through the personal information collected in the census, it was possible to identify individuals.

4.4 Census Data Distribution

Another important prospect is to understand how census bureaus are sharing data to the relevant or requested authorities. Juran [29] have widely discussed the reports of 2010 World Program on population and housing censuses to understand the primary methods of census data dissemination. About 63 countries are reported to use paper publications as their primary method of data distribution. 34 countries use static web pages for distribution and only 17 countries used interactive online databases. Majority developing countries replying on paper based, CD-ROMs and DVDs based data distribution and almost all countries, including US don't have distributed and decentralized system to fulfill the need of all stakeholders, in a given time.

4.5 Cost of Census

The task of census is one that is country-wide and involves a commendable amount of resources from human capital to financial costs related directly and indirectly to material involved that is using for census and enumeration purposes. Skinner investigated the census challenges related cost pressures, concerns about intrusiveness, privacy and response burden, reduced cooperation, difficulties in accessing secure apartments and enumerating unsafe areas, more complex living arrangements, and timeliness concerns [4, 30].

Fienberg and Kenneth [31] tried to estimate the cost of US censuses. It has been estimated that in the decennial census of 2010, it cost United States approximately thirteen billion dollars, which was twice as much as the cost of census in the 2000. Furthermore, the cost of census for 2000 was twice of 1990. Hence, over time, the cost and complexity of census has grown considerably, with the population growing with a similar pace.

4.6 Cooperation and Participation

Historically, public reluctance has been noted among the population related to census data collection. The major concern in the earlier time for the reluctance was disclosing information that may result in increased taxation on the peers and extra efforts are required by the governments to improve coverage. The extra efforts are translated into cost of media coverage and advertisements for spreading public awareness. In the developing countries like Pakistan, Nepal, Bangladesh, given the scarcity of literate individuals in the population, schoolteachers were sent to households to spread awareness and later to perform duties related to enumeration such as in-person field research work resulting to a shortage of teachers which were later filled with literate and un-employed population of the country. In circumstances like this, additional costs must be borne by the government [32]. Nonetheless, all the above stated issues are the rips of centralized eco-system. A centralized system govern by the authorities can manipulate census data for political and economic gains and can marginalize minorities without leave a trace of evidence.

5 Blockchain-Based National Population Census

The decentralized nature of blockchain technology along with its characteristics of transparency, immutability, and cryptography minimizes concerns and enables unknown parties trust each other. without a third-party authority. Contrary to a centralized database, there is not one single point of entry for hackers. This feature and the fact that there is no central control, blockchain is a powerful technology for recording transactions in a secure manner. Leveraging on blockchain technology, the some of the challenges that traditional census methodologies are faced with could be mitigated.

As mentioned before, the main challenges identified through the systematic literature review are Population Coverage, Ethnic and Racial Discrimination, Privacy Concerns, Census Data Distribution, Cost of Census and Cooperation and Participation.

- *Population Coverage.* Based on the literature [1, 19–23], the problem exists due non-existing proper living arrangement in the homeless communities or due their frequent travels (nomads). In the last census of Pakistan (occurred in 2017), this case is quite evident. 1.5 million people are missing from the city of Karachi, and since then data is not yet published [17, 18], also raised concern of its correctness and trust. If, however, in a blockchain-based solution, the NGOs that deal with homeless communities or nomads, are doing the enumeration for the census bureau on the blockchain then the problem could be mitigated. The missing data could be capture and provide more accurate data to policy makers. In such a solution, the governance model could also include the NGOs so that all together can decide who is a trustworthy NGO and who is not. Moreover, if integrated with Artificial Intelligence, then candidates can be profiled to better understand the trajectory of growth or changes in the data, such as education, area of residence, etc. for improving data for missing entries. The UN technical report [33] on post enumeration surveys served as a reference document. They have documented that legalities pertaining to data access, the limitations, restriction of use, organizations involved, and the process of access and retrieval should be made clear beforehand. This ensures all legal formalities are dealt with prior to the commencement of the data collection process. When using a blockchain-based system the data quality and integrity in enhanced since an extra layer of verification can be added on the blockchain through the cross-check by the different nodes in the net. In addition, smart contracts can be used to check and normalize data [14].
- *Ethnic & Racial Discrimination.* This challenge exists due to alteration/deletion of records leading to underestimating, or overestimating certain groups based on religion, race or ethnicity [23, 24]. This results in deliberately exploitation of the census for

political and monetary reasons. The immutability of blockchain-based records and its timestamped attributes can help resolve such problems.

- *Privacy concerns* exist due to the non-encrypted data that are hacked and exposed to others [26–28]. If the data breaches are avoided, then the privacy concerns can be mitigated. A centralized system would alleviate the challenge of encryption but in order to minimize the risk of data breaches, then the decentralized nature of blockchain systems would make it more difficult for data breach.
- *The Census Data* Distribution relates to how census bureaus are sharing data to the relevant or requested authorities. Such methods range from paper based, to CD-ROMs, static webpages, online databases, and other [29]. Through blockchain smart contracts, 3rd parties can access to the needed data directly provided they meet the criteria set in the contract.
- *The Cost of Census* issue exists due to complex and heavy mature of planning the census requires and this process is iterative and need to be done every after 10 years [4, 30, 31]. It involves resources from human capital to financial costs to instruments and materials being used during the process. Re-engineering the whole census methodology and process via blockchain technology, it is expected that costs will be lowered. Some of the reasons for that is the decentralized nature of a blockchain-based system that enables the sharing of resources while that the same time it requires less maintenance. The pilot testing will help us further identify the cost savings.
- *Cooperation and Participation.* The population is reluctant to participate in census. This issue exists due to lack of trust in the census practice and centralize nature of the current census systems. Common concerns are under-representation, disclosing/leaking of personal information, no transparency in census process and system which leads governments to put more budget to reach to desirable coverage benchmark [32]. With blockchain technology, transparency and accountability are the things can be integrated in the census process and bring trust back to the society.

Table 1 presents the identified gaps and how blockchain technology can potentially resolve or improve the corresponding challenge.

Table 1. Challenges of national population census and potential solution

Sr.	Challenges of centralized system	Blockchain-based solution	Potential solution
1	Population coverage	Improve	Decentralized NGOs, part of the blockchain, doing the enumeration smart contracts
2	Ethnic & racial discrimination	Improve	Immutability of records, timestamped records
3	Privacy concerns	Resolve	Decentralization, cryptographically-secured, immutability

(*continued*)

Table 1. (*continued*)

Sr.	Challenges of centralized system	Blockchain-based solution	Potential solution
4	Census data distribution	Resolve	Smart contracts
5	Cost of census	Improve	Decentralization
6	Cooperation & participation	Improve	Transparency and Accountability

This work yields new potential solutions for census data using decentralized-based applications to present and monetize population's socio-economic characteristics like education, purchasing power, ethnicity, housing, employment, home ownership, house rent, median income, food consumption and travel behaviors. On the bases of this research, better solutions could be provided through decentralized systems mitigating the above mentioned challenges.

6 Conclusion

In this paper, we identified through a systematic literature review the drawback of traditional census methodologies, that is centralized ones, in order to explore the potential of redesigned them as decentralized systems. The challenges at hand vary from population coverage, ethnic and racial discrimination, security breaches and privacy concerns, data dissemination, cost of census and cooperation and participation. The identified issues and challenges are a global phenomenon and not only valid for developing countries. A blockchain-based solution, may alleviate a lot of the problems identified but perhaps not all. The human interaction involved in the data management of census from collection to storage to deriving insights is strong, and errors and leakages are likely to occur. This paper lays the foundations of our research on blockchain-based systems for tackling with the challenges faced within census such as that of the "missing people". Future work includes the design and the pilot testing of such a system along with its societal impact. Nonetheless, this research unveils future approaches for higher socio-economic and commercial gains and new socio-economic research routes using blockchain strategies.

References

1. United Nations: Principles and Recommendations for Population and Housing Censuses. Department of Economic and Social Affairs Statistics Division, New York (2017)
2. Tapscott, D., Tapscott, A.: Blockchain Revolution: How the Technology Behind Bitcoin Is Changing Money, Business, and the World. Penguin Random House, USA (2016)
3. Casey, M.J., Vigna, P.: The Truth Machine: The Blockchain and the Future of Everything. St. Martin's Press (2018)
4. Reynolds, F., Haaga, J. (eds): The American People: Census 2000. Russell Sage Foundation (2005)

5. United Nations Economic Commission for Europe: Conference of European Statisticians Recommendations for the 2020 Censuses of Population and Housing. UNECE (2015)
6. Weinstein, S.: Blockchain neutrality. Georgia Law Rev. **55**(2), 499–591 (2021)
7. Nakamoto, S.: Bitcoin: A peer-to-peer electronic cash system. Bitcoin. https://bitcoin.org/bitcoin.pdf. Accessed 20 July 2021
8. Scheller, F., Reichelt, D., Dienst S., et al.: Effects of implementing decentralized business models at a neighborhood energy system level: a model based cross-sectoral analysis. In: 14th International Conference on the European Energy Market (EEM), Dresden, pp. 1-6 (2017)
9. Scheller, F., Johanning, S., Seim, S., et al.: Legal framework of decentralized energy business models in Germany: challenges and opportunities for municipal utilities. J. Energy Ind. **42**, 207–223 (2018)
10. Chen, Y., Bellavitis, C.: Blockchain disruption and decentralized finance: the rise of decentralized business models. J. Bus. Ventur. Insights **13**, e00151 (2020)
11. Batubara, F.R., Ubacht, J., Janssen, M.: Unraveling transparency and accountability in blockchain. In: Proceedings of the 20th Annual International Conference on Digital Government Research. ACM (2019)
12. Alketbi, A., Nasir, Q., Talib, M.: Blockchain for government services - use cases, security benefits and challenges. In: 15th Learning and Technology Conference (L&T), pp. 112–119. IEEE (2018)
13. BITNATION: Governance 2.0 (2017). https://bitnation.co/.21. Accessed July 2021
14. Mattila, J.: The blockchain phenomenon – the disruptive potential of distributed consensus architectures. ETLA Working Papers 38, The Research Institute of the Finnish Economy (2016)
15. Shamseer, L., Moher, D., Clarke, M., et al.: Preferred reporting items for systematic review and meta-analysis protocols (PRISMA-P) 2015: elaboration and explanation. BMJ **349**, g7647 (2015). https://doi.org/10.1136/bmj.g7647
16. Elsevier's Scopus Now Accessible Within EBSCO Discovery Service. EBSCO Publishing. http://newsbreaks.infotoday.com/Digest/Elseviers-Scopus-Now-Accessible-Within-EBSCO-Discovery-Service-85415.asp. Accessed 12 Nov 2021
17. Karim, M.: Missing people in census. Daily DAWN (2017). https://www.dawn.com/news/1364371. Accessed 23 July 2018
18. Israr, F.: 15 million Karachiites missing in census. Daily Nation (2017). https://nation.com.pk/06-Nov-2017/15-million-karachiites-missing-in-census-claims-sattar. Accessed 23 July 2018
19. CBS News (2012). https://www.cbsnews.com/news/2010-census-missed-15-million-minorities. Accessed 23 July 2018
20. Elana, B.: Time for Another Head Count (2018). https://slate.com/technology/2018/05/2020-census-technology-could-help-with-address-verification.html. Accessed 25 July 2018
21. Hogan, H.: The accuracy and coverage evaluation: theory and design. Surv. Methodol. **29**, 129–138 (2003)
22. Etebong, P.C.: Demography in Nigeria: problems and prospects. Biostat. Biometr. Open Access J. **5**(1), 555654 (2018)
23. O'Hare, W.: Differential Undercounts in the U.S. Census-Who is Missed? Springer Briefs in Population Studies. Springer, Cham (2019). https://doi.org/10.1007/978-3-030-10973-8
24. Crossette, B.: For census-takers worldwide, 2020 could be a rough year (2019). https://www.passblue.com/2019/12/21/for-census-takers-worldwide-2020-could-be-a-rough-year. Accessed 02 Jan 2020
25. Nagle, R.: We are still here: native americans fight to be counted in US census (2020). https://www.theguardian.com/us-news/2020/jan/15/we-are-still-here-native-americans-fight-to-be-counted-in-us-census. Accessed 04 Jan 2020

26. Abel, J.: Yet another U.S. government cybersecurity breach; this time it's the Census Bureau (2015). https://www.consumeraffairs.com/news/yet-another-us-government-cybers ecurity-breach-this-time-its-the-census-bureau-072415.html. Accessed 20 Feb 2021

27. Norton, T.: The census is too important to boycott, despite serious privacy concerns (2016). http://www.smh.com.au/comment/the-census-is-too-important-to-boycott-des pite-privacy-concerns-20160804-gqllvs.html. Accessed 15 Dec 2019

28. Devins, S.: Why Germans are so private about their data (2017). https://www.handelsblatt. com/today/handelsblatt-explains-why-germans-are-so-private-about-their-data/23572446. html?ticket=ST-1119959-eZWdKzPuhLf4ofbXVloa-ap4. Accessed 02 Jan 2020

29. Juran, S., Pistiner, A.: The 2010 round of population and housing censuses (2005–2014). Stat. J. IOAS **33**, 399–406 (2017)

30. Skinner, C.: Issues and challenges in census taking. Ann. Rev. Stat. Appl. **5**, 49–63 (2018). https://doi.org/10.1146/annurev-statistics-041715-033713

31. Fienberg, S., Kenneth, P.: Save your census. Nature **466**, 1043 (2010)

32. Bair, R., Torrey, B.: The challenges of census taking in developing countries. Govern. Inf. Q. **2**(4), 433–452 (1985). https://doi.org/10.1016/0740-624X(85)90070-X. Elsevier (2000)

33. United Nations: Post Enumeration Surveys Operational Guidelines. United Nations Secretariat, New York (2010)

34. Makridakis, S., Polemitis, A., Giaglis, G., Louca, S.: Blockchain: the next breakthrough in the rapid progress of AI. Artif. Intell.-Emerg. Trends Appl. **10**, 197–219 (2018). https://doi. org/10.5772/intechopen.75668. IntechOpen

35. Themistocleous, M., Christodoulou, K., Iosif, E., Louca, S., Tseas, D.: Blockchain in academia: where do we stand and where do we go? In: The Proceedings of the Fifty-Third Annual Hawaii International Conference on System Sciences, (HICSS 53), 7–10 January 2020, Maui, Hawaii, USA. IEEE Computer Society, Los Alamitos (2020)

Blockchain Applications in Smart Grid
A Review and a Case Study

Qian Meng[1], Lasse Berntzen[1(✉)], Boban Vesin[1], Marius Rohde Johannessen[1],
Simona Oprea[2], and Adela Bara[2]

[1] School of Business, University of South-Eastern Norway, Horten, Norway
{qian.meng,lasse.berntzen,boban.vesin,marius.johannessen}@usn.no
[2] Bucharest University of Economic Studies, Bucharest, Romania
{simona.oprea,adela.bara}@csie.ase.ro

Abstract. An increasing number of prosumers participate in the energy market, either by offering flexibility or selling surplus energy. This is made possible through EU directives for electricity transactions in smart grids. The directives provide guidelines for individual and aggregated transactions, allowing customers to sell or share electric surplus at the local level or to the national grid. This is seen as an important part of the transition to renewable energy.

In this paper, we introduce blockchain as a mechanism for handling decentralized transactions in smart grids. Blockchain technology allows for a flexible peer-to-peer trading mechanism. It can handle transmission and distribution management with energy flow optimization and grid infrastructure security, prosumer and microgrid management with different trading and pricing mechanisms, and interactive load between electric vehicles and grid. We describe blockchain technology, provide a survey of blockchain applications in the energy sector, emphasize the achievements and limitations of this technology in EU research studies and industrial projects, and underline the findings of the Smart-MLA project in this field.

Keywords: Smart Multi-Layer aggregator · Smart MLA · Smart contract · Ethereum · Aggregator · Prosumer · Flexibility

1 Introduction

In recent years, the transition from fossil energy sources to renewable energy sources has become increasingly important. One reason is the commitment to reduce CO_2 emissions; another reason is the development of new technologies for renewable energy production. Digital transformation and other technologies have also made it possible for a community, building, family, or even individuals to generate electricity from wind power and solar energy [1]. The prosumers can share or sell their surplus power to the grid. Transactions between generators and consumers have changed from one direction to multi-direction. Thus, the centralized grids will become more decentralized, and smart grids enable a two-way flow of electricity and data whereby smart metering is taken as

© Springer Nature Switzerland AG 2022
M. Themistocleous and M. Papadaki (Eds.): EMCIS 2021, LNBIP 437, pp. 130–149, 2022.
https://doi.org/10.1007/978-3-030-95947-0_10

a first step. Traditional centralized grid infrastructure experiences significant pressure and challenges: more unpredictable input of renewable energy sources, grid digitalization enabling controllable power transmission and distribution, and more interactive and dynamic loads due to electric vehicle charging.

Smart grids have been frequently mentioned as an important area for blockchain technology use. Blockchain allows prosumers to trade energy without any centralized authority and may contribute to increased grid flexibility.

The authors are partners in Smart-MLA, a project funded through the ERA-NET Smart Grid Plus initiative. This project aims to enable all electricity consumers to have access to the energy markets to trade energy based on their flexibility [2]. In the Smart-MLA project, blockchain technology is used to demonstrate how to register settlements among customers, the aggregator, and the distribution system operator (DSO). A new framework for microgrid trading and management platform is studied and proposed to improve grid flexibility. Effective handling of transactions is essential for the success of the project. Thus, the purpose of this paper is to present a comprehensive literature review of blockchain technology in smart grids and a case study for microgrids.

The remaining parts of this paper are structured as follows: Sect. 2 presents our research approach. Section 3 contains the description of blockchain technology; Sect. 4 contains the review of blockchain use in the energy sector. Section 5 presents the achievements and limitations of blockchain technology in smart grids. Section 6 presents the Smart-MLA project as a case study, followed by our conclusion in Sect. 7.

2   Research Approach

This study is mainly conducted as a structured literature review. The purpose of a literature review is to examine relevant literature for a given topic, research area, or question and present the findings in a categorized and structured manner, reflecting the research topic [3]. This paper aims to provide an overview of blockchain technology and its usefulness for smart grids and transaction handling. According to Webster and Watson [3], literature review findings should be structured by themes, topics, ideas, or concepts. Given our research topic, we structured our review categorically into the following categories: Description of blockchain technology (Sect. 3), application areas in the energy sector with an emphasis on smart grids (Sect. 4), and finally, limitations and challenges of blockchain in smart grids (Sect. 5).

With the predetermined categories in mind, we conducted the literature review in June and July 2021. The search was conducted using Google Scholar. Google Scholar provides results from the academic databases available to our institution (including web of science, EBSCO, IEEE, Science Direct, Scopus) and additional sources available through self-archiving in academic repositories (ResearchGate, Academia, etc.). As blockchain in smart grids is a new phenomenon, we included conferences and journals, and industry white papers for the application category. We used the following search terms in various combinations: 'smart grid', 'blockchain', 'energy sector', 'microgrid', 'EU project', 'p2p trading', 'smart contract'.

The initial screening of papers included reading the title and abstract scanning for relevance to our categories and a second more detailed reading of papers which resulted in the selection presented below. The initial screening of papers included reading the title and abstract scanning for relevance to our categories and a second more detailed reading of papers which resulted in the selection presented below. The initial search resulted in about 200 articles, which was further narrowed down using the following screening process: First, we removed all articles older than 2011, as these did not address our research theme. We then scanned abstracts looking for the selected search phrases and excluded papers that we did not find relevant to the topic "blockchain technology in smart grids." The scanning left us with a total of 39 articles covering blockchain use in wholesale markets, smart grid management, microgrids, vehicle to grid handling, as well as studies from large EU H2020-funded projects on blockchain use in the energy sector.

3   Blockchain Technology

Blockchains have gained attention in academia and the energy sector with a core innovation: they help to guarantee the validity of a transaction by recording it not only in one main register but on a distributed system of registers, all of which are connected through a secure validation mechanism. Blockchain technology offers a way for untrusted parties to reach an agreement on a shared digital record that might otherwise be easily faked or duplicated.

A blockchain can be seen as a distributed ledger with transactions structured in blocks [4]. These blocks are linked using cryptographic hash functions, which guarantee the immutability of the past. The blockchain is decentralized. Instead of operating the ledger by a single trusted center, each node holds a copy of the records' chain and agrees on the valid state of the ledger with consensus. The methodology to reach consensus varies to fit different application domains. 'Proof of Work,' 'Proof of Stake,' 'Proof of Authority,' and 'Practical Byzantine Fault Tolerance' [4] are four main consensus algorithms with different properties.

Blockchains can be categorized as public, consortium, and private based on the degrees of decentralization, as shown in Table 1 [4]. A public blockchain is permissionless, implying that anyone can submit transactions to the blockchain and access the blockchain. In a permissioned blockchain, only predefined and authorized nodes can do this. Several characteristics of the blockchain categories are presented in Table 1.

After a decade of evolution, newer blockchain solutions offer better solutions than the first generation of blockchain technology. For example, Ethereum solved the inefficiencies by shifting to a better blockchain technology solution using smart contracts. It also adopts Proof-of-Stake (PoS), which requires less computing capacity and supports higher rates of transactions, which is more efficient than Proof-of-Work (PoW).

Blockchain acts as a distributed ledger that provides transparency, trust, and data security in all applications, specifically in safety-critical systems. The utilization of the blockchain in smart grids could offer various advantages to the power system with increased security, improved data accessibility, privacy, data transparency and immutability, removal of third-party control during the power generation, transmission,

Table 1. Characteristics of blockchain

Characteristics	Public blockchain	Consortium blockchain	Private blockchain
Permission	Permissionless	Permissioned to some nodes	Permissioned to a person/entity
Access to write	Anybody	Specific nodes	Internally controlled
Access to read	Anybody	Restricted access	Restricted access
Speed of transaction	Low	High	Very high
Decentralization	Fully decentralized	Less decentralized	Least decentralized

distribution, and consumption chains. A market analysis was conducted to investigate the parameters that affect the large-scale adoption of blockchain in smart energy grids [5]. Based on the characteristics of power systems, blockchain applications are mainly in four areas: wholesale trading, smart grid management, trading support for prosumers in microgrids, and interactive loads between grids and electric vehicles. Section 4 provides a systematic and up-to-date review with economic consideration of blockchain applications.

4 Application of Blockchain Technology in the Energy Sector

Power systems include the generation, transmission, distribution, and consumption chains. With the demand for digitalization and decentralized power systems, several proposals have been made for blockchain applications, as in Fig. 1. Several authors have discussed the feasibility of the different consensus mechanisms for energy transactions [6].

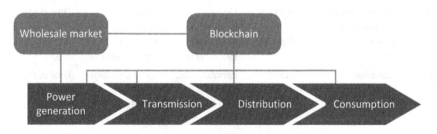

Fig. 1. Blockchain and the power industry

As to the application of blockchain for transactive energy systems, the impact of blockchain on the energy sector is presented from the perspectives of product, process, position, and paradigm [7]. The challenges are discussed from efficiency, integration, privacy, and cybersecurity [8]. In most blockchain application cases, data acquisition is through geographically distributed meters/sensors that form a distributed network, where each meter/sensor acts as a node. Each meter is identified by a unique address and capable of communicating for data collection and exchange.

4.1 Wholesale Market

Traditional wholesale markets consist of complex procedures that require third parties such as brokers, trading agents, exchanges, price reporters, logistic providers, banks, and regulators. The current procedures are time-consuming and unreliable since transactions need to be verified and reconciled multiple times from initialization to final settlement. Distributed blockchain and smart contracts can allow a generating unit to trade directly with consumers or retailers without the middleman. The application of blockchain in the wholesale market may transform the current energy market structure. A trading process for day-ahead and near real-time markets in smart grids was designed, built, and tested with the multichain architecture of blockchain [9]. The work in [10] envisages blockchain-based trading platforms eliminating the need for brokers and clearinghouses.

Moreover, by reducing transaction costs, blockchain could enable participants to trade in smaller volumes [11]. Some studies present the reduction of transaction costs for trading large volumes by making operational processes more efficient and connecting all parties' trading desks [12]. Table 2 provides a synthesis of the leading wholesale market approaches to the implementation of blockchain.

Table 2. Studies related to blockchain in the wholesale market

Work	Contribution	Platform	Technical approach	Focused application	Economic consideration
[9]	Day-head and near real-time market bidding	Smart contracts	Case study, IBM Hyperledger Fabric	Wholesale trading	Time cost
[10]	Energy trading and payment settlement	Enterprise private Ethereum	Unified permissioned blockchain, Experiments	Wholesale Western Australian energy market	Time cost
[11]	Traceable and transparent energy usage	Private Ethereum,	Permissioned blockchain edge model, Experiment	Communication privacy and security	Time cost and gas cost
[12]	Design a blockchain-based secure energy trading framework (SETS)	Private blockchain Smart contracts	Conceptual	Demand response management	Time cost

4.2 Smart Grid Management

The electricity grid consists of three levels in most countries: the transmission grid, the regional grid, and the distribution grid. Regional and distribution grids are considered as distribution systems, as defined by European Union legislation [21]. Figure 2 below shows the blockchain can contribute to high voltage grid management and lower voltage microgrid. Grid management refers to two main fields: the first is about energy flow optimization in the grid to reduce energy loss, and the second is the protection of the infrastructure from cyberattacks. Modern Transmission System Operators (TSOs) and Distribution System Operators (DSOs) are faced with the challenges of better understanding the present state of the system and storing and analyzing huge quantities of data. Simultaneously, increased digitization has increased power system vulnerability to cyberattacks [22]. Blockchains could enhance network management by automatically maintaining verifiable network asset condition data. Moreover, blockchain technology could naturally protect against grid-related cyber-threats due to its inherent redundancy and the fact that it is tamper-proof and does not have a single point of attack [23].

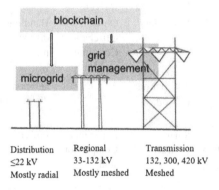

Fig. 2. Blockchain applicability in grid management

In the application of voltage regulation for power flow, a permissionless blockchain is more suitable than a permissioned blockchain for two main reasons. First, participation of the agents within the system should be qualified, invite-only, and agreed upon by all agents within the network to limit cybersecurity concerns with respect to malicious agents and Sybil attacks [15]. Second, the scalability of the overall system in terms of transaction speed and the computational burden should be kept as low as possible. To further improve the scalability of blockchain-based systems, a common strategy is to minimize the data stored on the ledger and reduce the complexity of the logic executed by the smart contracts [16]. To optimize the power flow in the grid, the algorithm of alternating direction method of multipliers (ADMM) has been proved more energy efficient than PoW and PoA through experimentation of utilizing the 39-bus New England transmission system and IEEE-57 and −118 benchmark systems [18]. Table 3 offers several studies that approach blockchain implementation in grid management.

Table 3. Studies related to blockchain in grid management

Work	Contribution	Platform	Technical approach	Focused application	Economic consideration
[13]	A general form for energy system management	Smart contracts Ethereum	Ethereum Virtual Machine	Medium-voltage direct-current (MVDC), 33 kV distribution networks	Network operation cost, Smart contract computation cost
[14]	Distributed voltage regulation	Smart contract	Experiment Case study Hyper ledger	Grid operation for transactive energy system	N/A
[15]	Data protection framework for grid against cyber attack	Blockchain with both public and private keys	Case study IEEE-118 benchmark system	Robustness and security of the grid	N/A
[16]	Privacy-preserving in smart grids	Ethereum	On-chain Off-chain Conceptual	Handling dishonest participants	Gas cost
[17]	Autonomous distribution network in smart grid	Autonomous distribution network	Case study	Power autonomous distribution	N/A
[18]	Solution of the optimal power flow problem	Smart contracts	Experiment Comparison study	Power flow optimization	Consumption with ADMM lower than PoW, PoA
[19]	Medium and low voltage grid management	Smart contracts	Experiment	Voltage management	N/A
[20]	Smart meter data for balance between production and demand for DSO	Ethereum Public blockchain Smart contract	Experiment	DSO demand response management	N/A

4.3 Trading Support for Prosumers in Microgrids

By enabling local markets in microgrids, blockchains could relieve stress on transmission networks, and thereby reduce network costs, improve the economics of small-scale renewables and demand energy response, and enrich customers with more choice and transparency. In microgrids, smart meters can be strategically dispersed throughout the spatial zones, and methods for optimal allocation and placement of smart meters in the distribution systems, as well as distributed state estimation techniques, can be found in [29]. Households with photovoltaic panels can make the energy self-sufficient in a low voltage community. Blockchain smart contracts and cybersecurity in Buildings-to-Grid (B2G) cybersecurity testbed are described in [33]. An open-source private Ethereum blockchain was implemented using four Raspberry Pi devices representing participating households to minimize external energy dependency [35].

Four trading mechanisms for local energy market transactions, including classic auctions with pricing mechanisms such as Uniform Price (UP), Pay-As-Bid (PAB), Generalized Second-Price (GSP), and Vickrey-Clark-Groves (VCG), are envisioned to evaluate the benefits and show their efficiency, which reveals VCG is the most beneficial [36].

The pricing mechanism was enhanced by gradually updating the bids and offers to create more room for local trade. Usually, if the matching process is over, the trade will stop. Still, by gradually increasing the prices of bids and decreasing the prices of offers, the trade will continue until the prices become very close to the retailer's prices for selling/buying electricity. Additionally, two novel and efficient settlement mechanisms: Global Balancing Settlement (GBS) and Splitting Settlement (SS) for Peer-to-Peer (P2P) electricity exchange, are proposed to enhance the performance of the classic Pairwise Settlement (PS) [37].

Table 4. Studies with blockchain implementation in electricity transactions

Work	Contribution	Platform	Technical approach	Focused application	Economic consideration
[27]	Inhouse microgeneration system with solar energy production and distribution architecture	Smart contract	Conceptual	Prosumers to produce, consume and trade energy	N/A
[28]	A privacy-preserving energy scheduling model for energy service companies	Smart contract	Lagrange relaxation algorithm, Case study	Aggregating multiple energy resources	Overall system energy cost
[29]	Microgrid operational architecture for the monopoly price manipulation and privacy leakage problem	Ethereum Private	Alternating direction method of multipliers (ADMM)	Microgrid operation optimization	N/A

(*continued*)

Table 4. (*continued*)

Work	Contribution	Platform	Technical approach	Focused application	Economic consideration
[30]	Framework for distributed energy resources in voltage regulation of microgrid	Smart contracts Private	PoW	Voltage control in microgrid	Mining cost and communication cost
[31]	A smart management system for prosumers in microgrid	Ethereum	Case study TestRPC	Peer-2-peer electricity trading	Satisfaction index
[32]	Transaction mode for distributed generation in microgrid	Smart contract	Continuous double auction Experiment	Aggressiveness Model for transaction	Transaction price and volume
[33]	Blockchain and smart contracts to improve smart grid cyber resiliency and secure transactions	Public blockchain Smart contracts	PNNL House to Grid cyber testbed	House to grids	Conceptual
[34]	Establish a unified energy blockchain with moderate cost, credit-based payment scheme	Unified blockchain	Stackelberg game, Case study	Payment in typical scenarios like microgrid	Maximum economic benefits
[35]	Efficient share of energy within a community	Open source blockchain, Ethereum	Experiment, PoA	Energy community controlling	Time cost, Prototype system
[36]	Pricing mechanism for the local market on blockchain to stimulate transaction	Smart contract	Experiment Comparison of UP, PAB, GSP, VCG	Blockchain trading mechanism	VCG provides more gains for prosumers
[37]	Settlement mechanism for local trading with blockchain	Smart contracts	Trading settlement methods	Local trade	Different settlement is envisioned

Table 5. Studies related to blockchain in interactive loads between electric vehicles and grids

Work	Contribution	Platform	Technical approach	Focused application	Economic consideration
[38]	Electric vehicle charging framework with optimal algorithm	Smart contracts Permissioned blockchain	Delegated Byzantine fault tolerance (DBFT) algorithm	Electric vehicles charging	N/A
[39]	Charging coordination mechanism for batteries and electric vehicles	Smart contracts	Knapsack algorithm, partially blinded signatures	Batteries and Electric vehicles charging	N/A
[40]	Modeling of security of trading between electric vehicles and charging piles	Smart contracts	Experiment	Electric vehicles and charging piles management	Consumption, charging, time cost
[41]	Charging stations selection on pricing and distance to electric vehicles	Smart contracts	Exploration, bidding, evaluation, charging	Charging station selection	N/A
[42]	The hierarchical authentication mechanism for electric vehicles	Public blockchain	Elliptic curve cryptography	Electric vehicles to grids	N/A
[43]	Localized energy trading among electric vehicles	Consortium blockchain	Double auction Experiment	Electric vehicles and energy trading	Selling price, buying price

The simulations are performed using a residential community with 30% of the electricity that can be locally traded to lower the bills and unstress the public grid. Table 4 provides several studies approaching blockchain implementation in electricity trading.

4.4 Interactive Loads Between Grids and Electric Vehicles

As electric vehicles become more popular, power system operators are faced with the challenges of supplying batteries or electric vehicle-related mobile load. Blockchain technology could improve batteries and electric vehicle charging coordination by facilitating energy payments at charging stations and enabling drivers to make charging decisions based on map and real-time pricing data [38–40]. A reliable, automated, and privacy-preserving selection of charging stations is presented based on pricing and the distance to the electric vehicle. The protocol builds on a blockchain where electric vehicles signal their demand and charging stations send bids similar to an auction [41]; therefore, the customers can find the cheapest charging station within a previously defined region and preserve the privacy of the electric vehicle. As the discharging mechanism, a designed hierarchical authentication mechanism has been employed to preserve the anonymity of electric vehicles and support mutual authentication between electric vehicles, charging stations, and the central aggregator [42]. A new model achieves demand response by providing incentives to discharging electric vehicles to balance local electricity demand out of their own self-interests. Moreover, consortium blockchain technology is explored to improve transaction security and privacy protection [43]. Table 5 emphasizes several studies related to electric vehicle operation and blockchain implementation.

5   Achievements and Limitations of Smart Grid Blockchain Projects

As to the academic research and practical implementation in industry, there are a lot of efforts made. The activities and achievements are described below.

5.1   Achievements from EU Academic Research Projects

Many opportunities are provided for funding projects regarding blockchain in the energy sector globally. In Europe, the European Union, through Horizon 2020, has supported academic research and innovation for blockchain technology into the energy sector, which brings up new trust paradigms and societal, technical, and infrastructural solutions (Table 6).

- For wholesale bidding, the project P2P-SmartTest [45] presents a model of a P2P energy trading system with four layers: power grid layer, ICT layer, control layer, and business layer. The project CROSSBOW [46] proposes the shared use of resources to foster cross-border management of variable renewable energies and storage units, enabling higher penetration of clean energies while reducing network operational costs and improving the economic benefits of renewable energy sources and storage units.
- As regards grid management, (i) in order to reduce the loss of power flow in the transmission process. The project Future Flow [47] gives a unique regional cooperation scheme that aims to design balancing and redispatching markets and open them to new sources of flexibility crossing Austria, Slovenia, Hungary, and Romania. In project TESTBED [48], the Alternating Direction Multiplier Method (ADMM) was put forward as a fully distributed optimal power flow (OPF) approach because a centralized control strategy cannot effectively optimize the power loss problem in real-time [24]. (ii) For infrastructure security, the project Defender [49] provides a modular version of the platform installed in each of four pilots in France, Italy, and

Slovenia. ENGIE (Generation), ASM (Distribution), BFP (Renewable Energy), and ELES (Transmission) assessed the system's ability to cope with several realistic attack scenarios against various cyberattacks. They are the first to propose the I2SP prototype, which is a novel Information Sharing Platform able to gather, pre-process, model, and distribute network traffic information [25]. The project SealedGRID [50] provides a security platform that combines Blockchain, Distributed Hash Tables, Trusted Execution Environments, and OpenID Connect for its realization of the fully integrated SealedGRID consortium.

- As to prosumers and microgrid management, the project eDream [51] has a vision for a novel near real-time Closed Loop optimal blockchain-based Demand Response ecosystem, where DSOs and aggregators cooperate within a novel yet appropriate market framework, with an aim to exploiting to the largest possible extent the flexibility potential, while keeping system reliability within prescribed limits and preserving continuity and security of supply. A model has been defined for capturing the prosumer level constraints in terms of available energy profiles and energy service requirements enabling their optimal aggregation in hierarchical structures [26]. The project Smart-MLA [52] developed multi-layer aggregator solutions to facilitate optimum demand response and grid flexibility and utilize blockchain-based smart contracts to enable interaction between internal energy assets and external flexibility markets.
- About the interactive loads between grids and IoT (electric vehicles, batteries), the project [53] presents a "spam attack" method to parties with sufficient cryptocurrency reserves like electric vehicles submitted to the Ethereum network. The project [54] provides the idea of setting up Public Key Infrastructure (PKI) to support the security and privacy aspects of vehicular communications, which can be used for electric vehicle charging in the smart grid.

5.2 Achievements from Industrial Practice

Industry participants have enhanced active projects on how blockchain technology is envisioned, contributing to different segments of the electricity sector. They illustrate how blockchain could add value to electricity stakeholders in Table 7 [22].

5.3 Limitations and Challenges

Blockchain is still an emerging technology, with at least five limitations. Blockchain has an environmental cost since public blockchains consume a lot of energy. Also, lack of regulation creates a risky environment. Blockchain is complex, and end-users may find it hard to appreciate the benefits. Blockchain may be slow and cumbersome to use due to scalability issues and computations needed to show "Proof-of-Work." Finally, established actors in the financial market may have an interest in not supporting blockchain technology [66]. The use of private blockchains solves the environmental cost problem and speeds up the transactions. However, a private blockchain has other issues related to security and possible lack of transparency.

Table 6. EU research projects of blockchain application in the energy sector

Field	Project	Application	Period
Wholesale bidding market	P2P-SmartTest [45]	Blockchain can simplify the metering and billing of the P2P energy trading market	2015–2017
	CROSSBOW [46]	Cross border management for the transnational wholesale market	2017–2021
Grid management	Future Flow [47]	To design models for consumers and distribute generators for balancing and redispatching services on a regional platform	2016–2019
	TESTBED [48]	To build and test sophisticated ICT, thereby facilitating the successful implementation of smart grid applications, including blockchain	2017–2019
	Defender [49]	Blockchain provides peer-to-peer trustworthiness in infrastructure security, resilience, and self-healing	2017–2020
	SealedGRID [50]	Provide a solution for security threats in the smart grids infrastructure	2018–2021
Prosumer and microgrid management	eDream [51]	To create community-driven energy systems exploring local capacities, constraints, and secure grid nodes stabilization.	2018–2020
	SMART-MLA [52]	Utilizing smart contracts to enable interaction between internal assets and external markets to facilitate demand response & grid flexibility	2018–2021
Interactive loads between grids and IoT (electric vehicles, batteries)	SOFIE [53]	To use interconnected distributed ledgers to build decentralized business platforms: food chain, gaming, and energy market	2018–2020

(continued)

Table 6. (*continued*)

Field	Project	Application	Period
	SerIoT [54]	Developing an adaptive smart software-defined network-based IoT framework in domains of transport, food chain, and energy	2018–2021

Table 7. The industrial practice of blockchain application in the energy sector

Field	Benefit	Project	Product
Wholesale bidding market	– Reduce transaction costs in wholesale energy trading	Enerchain(Ponton) [55]	Enerchain 1.0
		Interbit(BTL) [56]	Interbit
Grid management	– Improve DSO and TSO network management and security	Keyless Signature Infrastructure (Guardtime) [57]	KSI blockchain EU-SysFlex
	– Improve TSO ability to balance supply and demand	TenneT [58]	Equigy
		Electron [59]	ElectronConnet
Prosumers and microgrid management	– Reduce variable costs of retail payment processing and accounting – Greater transparency into billing – Fluid energy contract entry/exit – Greater customer choice of supply	Drift [60]	Blockchain drift
		Grid+ [61]	Grid+
	– Relieve stress on transmission networks – Improve DER economics – Greater customer choice of supply	Brooklyn Microgrid (LO3) Energy [62]	LO3
		Alliander and Spectral [63]	Jouliette
EVs charging and coordination	– Improve DSO ability to coordinate electric vehicle load and discharge	Share&Charge (MotionWerk) [64]	SaaS
		eMotorWerks (Enel X) [65]	eMotorWerks

6 Case Study: The Smart-MLA Microgrid Architecture

The research project Multi-layer aggregator solutions to facilitate optimum demand response and grid flexibility (Smart-MLA) aims to develop multi-layer aggregator solutions integrated into an informatics prototype to facilitate optimum demand response and grid flexibility and contribute to more renewable sources integration. This project will provide a new framework of blockchain-Agent/Aggregator Based Microgrid Architecture. A more detailed description of Smart-MLA can be found in [52].

We present this as our case because the authors are part of the Smart-MLA project, responsible for a work package where we examine business models and the development of blockchain applications for the handling of micro-transactions. The overall transaction model was defined in the project application, and the literature review presented here has been essential for the further development of the blockchain transaction model and the development of smart contracts. The blockchain model is more thoroughly explained in [44].

Through the adoption of blockchain, a decentralized platform is created where the community aggregators play an important role regarding demand response. Therefore, the ICT solutions developed in Smart-MLA will allow prosumers to benefit from aggregation. In this model, the prosumers are entitled to generate, store, consume and sell self-generated electricity through aggregators without disproportionately burdensome procedures. The smart contract-based blockchain shall provide the microgrid with a more flexible, reliable, and secure operation and control structure. Blockchain will be utilized between prosumers and the aggregator and between the aggregator and the DSO, as shown in Fig. 3.

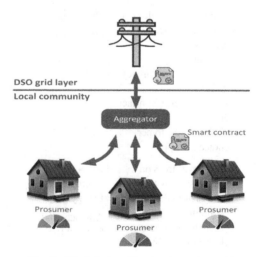

Fig. 3. Blockchain utilization in a microgrid

Inside the microgrid, there are three kinds of information to be taken into account: power flow, ICT data, and market trading. The smart contract between the aggregator and the prosumers contains the energy flow metering data, generation and consumption, and real-time monitoring. The smart contract between the aggregator and DSO keeps the data of demand response, transaction data of energy trading and bidding [36]. The blockchain does not have a mechanism for scheduling the execution of smart contracts, so for auctions, the smart contracts need to be initiated by an external party. The data flow between the local prosumers and DSO is provided in Fig. 4. Using the acronyms: LEM Local Electricity Market, RES Renewable Energy Sources.

The small-scale prosumers are registered as peer nodes of the network, and smart metering data are stored in the chain [36]. A prosumer has a smart contract with the data acquired from the smart meter. The contract will publish prosumer energy transactions on the chain by registering them and then broadcasting them across the entire network. Thus, each prosumer identification and their energy settlement, delivery, and financial settlement will be registered in the network.

A comparison through an experiment of a small-size community including 11 modern smart houses with more than 300 appliances, eight roof- or faced- photovoltaic systems, and smart-metered 15-min readings revealed that VCG (Vickrey-Clark-Groves) with price adjustment provides more gains for prosumers that could increase RES investment volume at the community level. After the market is initially cleared, an adjustment coefficient of the price is proposed for both sides (seller and buyer) to enlarge the trading potential at the community level using blockchain technology.

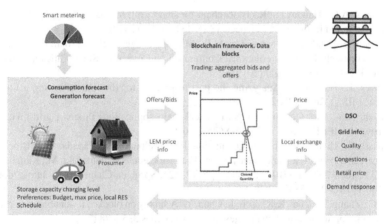

Fig. 4. Data flows in local electricity trading

The VCG pricing mechanism proves to bring excellent results to the local energy market participants and enhance trading with outstanding benefits [36].

7   Conclusion

Blockchain technology has various and unique features and attracts a lot of interest in academics and industry. The energy sector has started an impressive utilization of blockchain technology in electricity generation, transmission, distribution, and consumption. This paper surveyed the recent application of the blockchain in the smart grid from a research and industrial point of view. Furthermore, it illustrated the advantages of the blockchain in P2P trading, grid infrastructure security, prosumers management, and electric vehicles' interactive charging with the smart grid. A new framework for microgrid trading platform is put forward under the EU research project Smart-MLA. Currently, most of the applications are in the test, validation, or experimental phase. With the support of setting regulations and business standards, blockchain technology can play a significant role in the microgrid market.

Acknowledgments. This work was supported under the ERA-Net Smart Grids Plus scheme Grant number 89029 and funded through the Research Council of Norway Grant number 295750 with the project title "Multi-layer aggregator solutions to facilitate optimum demand response and grid flexibility."

This work was also supported by a grant from the Romanian National Authority for Scientific Research and Innovation, CCCDI – UEFISCDI, project title "Multi-layer aggregator solutions to facilitate optimum demand response and grid flexibility," contract number 71/2018, code: COFUND-ERANET-SMARTGRIDPLUS-SMART-MLA-1, within PNCDI III.

References

1. Agung, A.A.G., Handayani, R.: Blockchain for smart grid, Journal of King Saud University - Computer and Information Sciences. ISSN 1319-1578 (2020)
2. Berntzen, L., Brekke, T., Johannessen, M.R.: Multi-layer aggregation in smart grids a business model approach. In: 5th International Conference on Connected Smart Cities, pp.405–409. IADIS Press, Porto, Portugal (2019)
3. Webster, J., Watson, R.: Analyzing the past to prepare for the future: writing a literature review. MIS Q. **26**(2) (2002)
4. Musleh, A.S., Yao, G., Muyeen, S.M.: Blockchain applications in smart grid-review and frameworks. IEEE Access **7**, 86746–86757 (2019)
5. Kapassa, E., Themistocleous, M., Quintanilla, J.R., Touloupos, M., Papadaki, M.: Blockchain in smart energy grids: a market analysis. In: Themistocleous, M., Papadaki, M., Kamal, M.M. (eds.) EMCIS 2020. LNBIP, vol. 402, pp. 113–124. Springer, Cham (2020). https://doi.org/10.1007/978-3-030-63396-7_8
6. Liu, C., Zhang, X., Chai, K.K., Loo, J., Chen, Y.: A survey on blockchain-enabled smart grids: advances, applications and challenges. IET Smart Cities **3**, 56–78 (2021)
7. Themistocleous, M., Stefanou, K., Megapanos, C., Iosif, E.: To chain or not to chain? A case from energy sector. In: Themistocleous, M., Rupino da Cunha, P. (eds.) Information Systems. EMCIS 2018. LNBIP, vol. 341. Springer, Cham (2019). https://doi.org/10.1007/978-3-030-11395-7_3
8. Eiseie, S., et al.: Blockchains for transactive energy systems: opportunities, challenges, and approaches. IEEE Comput. **53**(9), 66–76 (2020)
9. Wang, S., Taha, A.F., Wang, J., Kvaternik, K., Hahn, A.: Energy crowdsourcing and peer-to-peer energy trading in blockchain-enabled smart grids. IEEE Trans. Syst. Man Cybern. Syst. **49**(8), 1612–1623 (2019)
10. Abdella, J., Tari, Z., Anwar, A., Mahmood, A., Han, F.: An architecture and performance evaluation of blockchain-based peer-to-peer energy trading. In: IEEE Trans. Smart Grid **12**(4), 3364–3378 (2021)

11. Gai, K., Wu, Y., Zhu, L., Xu, L., Zhang, Y.: Permissioned blockchain and edge computing empowered privacy-preserving smart grid networks. IEEE Internet Things J. **6**(5), 7992–8004 (2019)
12. Kumari, A., Gupta, R., Tanwar, S., Tyagi, S., Kumar, N.: When blockchain meets smart grid: secure energy trading in demand response management. IEEE Netw. **34**(5), 299–305 (2020)
13. Thomas, L., Zhou, Y., Long, C., et al.: A general form of smart contract for decentralized energy systems management. Nat Energy **4**, 140–149 (2019)
14. Saxena, S., Farag, H., Turesson, H., Kim, H.M.: Blockchain Based Grid Operation Services for Transactive Energy Systems. ArXiv, abs/1907.08725 (2019)
15. Liang, G., Weller, S.R., Luo, F., Zhao, J., Dong, Z.Y.: Distributed blockchain based data protection framework for modern power systems against cyber attacks. IEEE Trans. Smart Grid **10**(3), 3162–3173 (2019)
16. Li, C., Palanisamy, B., Xu, R.: Scalable and privacy-preserving design of on/off-chain smart contracts. CoRR, vol. abs/1902.06359 (2019)
17. Lo, C., Ansari, N.: Decentralized controls and communications for autonomous distribution networks in smart grid. IEEE Trans. Smart Grid **4**(1), 66–77 (2013)
18. Foti, M., Mavromatis, C., Vavalis, M.: Decentralized blockchain-based consensus for optimal power flow solutions. Appl. Energy **283**, 116100 (2020)
19. Pop, C., Cioara, T., Antal, M., Anghel, I., Salomie, I., Bertoncini, M.: Blockchain based decentralized management of demand response programs in smart energy grids. Sensors (Basel, Switzerland) **18**, 1–21 (2018)
20. El-Taweel, N.A., Farag, H.: Voltage regulation in islanded microgrids using distributed constraint satisfaction. IEEE Trans. Smart Grid **9**, 1613–1625 (2018)
21. The Norwegian Water Resources and Energy Directorate, The Norwegian power system. Grid connection and licensing, faktaark2018_03 (2018). http://www.nve.no. Accessed 28 July 2021
22. Nera, Blockchain in Electricity: a Critical Review of Progress to Date, Economic Consulting (May 2018). https://cdn.eurelectric.org/media/3115/paper1_blockchain_eurelectric-h-BA73FBD9.pdf. Accessed 28 July 2021
23. Morris, J.: How the blockchain could fight grid cyber-threats, GreenBiz leadership development, 31 May 2017. https://www.greenbiz.com/article/how-blockchain-could-fight-grid-cyber-threats. Accessed 28 July 2021
24. Xu, J., Sun, H., Dent, C.: ADMM-based distributed OPF problem meets stochastic communication delay. IEEE Trans. Smart Grid **10**(5), 5046–5056 (2019)
25. Fotiadou, K., Velivassaki, T., Voulkidis, A.C., Railis, K., Trakadas, P., Zahariadis, T.: Incidents information sharing platform for distributed attack detection. IEEE Open J. Commun. Soc. **1**, 593–605 (2020)
26. Cioara, T., Antal, M., Mihailescu, V.T., Antal, C.D., Anghel, I.M., Mitrea, D.: Blockchain-based decentralized virtual power plants of small prosumers. IEEE Access **9**, 29490–29504 (2021)
27. Kounelis, I., Steri, G., Giuliani, R., Geneiatakis, D., Neisse, R., Nai-Fovino, I.: Fostering consumers' energy market through smart contracts. In: 2017 International Conference in Energy and Sustainability in Small Developing Economies (ES2DE), pp. 1–6 (2017)
28. Tan, S., Wang, X., Jiang, C.: Privacy-preserving energy scheduling for ESCOs based on energy blockchain network. Energies **12**, 1530 (2019)
29. Münsing, E., Mather, J., Moura, S.: Blockchains for decentralized optimization of energy resources in microgrid networks. In: Proceedings of the IEEE Conference Control Technol. Appl. (CCTA), Mauna Lani, HI, USA, pp. 2164–2171 (2017)
30. Danzi, P., Angjelichinoski, M., Stefanović, Č., Popovski, P.: Distributed proportional-fairness control in microgrids via blockchain smart contracts. In: Proceedings of the IEEE International Conference Smart Grid Communications, Dresden, Germany, pp. 45–51 (2017)

31. Sabounchi, M., Wei, J.: Towards resilient networked microgrids: blockchain-enabled peer-to-peer electricity trading mechanism. In: Proceedings of the IEEE Conference on Energy Internet and Energy System Integration (EI2), Beijing, China, pp. 1–5 (2017)
32. Wang, J., Wang, Q., Zhou, N., Chi, Y.: A novel electricity transaction mode of microgrids based on blockchain and continuous double auction. Energies **10**(12), 1971 (2017)
33. Mylrea, M., Gourisetti, S.N.G.: Blockchain for smart grid resilience: Exchanging distributed energy at speed, scale and security. In: Proceedings of the Resilience Week (RWS), Wilmington, DE, USA, pp. 18–23 (2017)
34. Li, Z., Kang, J., Yu, R., Ye, D., Deng, Q., Zhang, Y.: Consortium blockchain for secure energy trading in industrial Internet of Things. IEEE Trans. Ind. Inform. **14**(8), 3690–3700 (2018)
35. Schlund, J., Ammon, L., German, R.: ETHome: open-source blockchain based energy community controller. In: Proceedings of the Ninth International Conference on Future Energy Systems (2018)
36. Oprea, S., Bâra, A.: Devising a trading mechanism with a joint price adjustment for local electricity markets using blockchain. Insights for policy makers. Energy Policy **152** (2021)
37. Oprea, S., Bâra, A., Andreescu, A.I.: Two novel blockchain-based market settlement mechanisms embedded into smart contracts for securely trading renewable energy. IEEE Access **8**, 212548–212556 (2020)
38. Su, Z., Wang, Y., Xu, Q., Fei, M., Tian, Y., Zhang, N.: A secure charging scheme for electric vehicles with smart communities in energy blockchain. IEEE Internet Things J. **6**, 4601–4613 (2019)
39. Baza, M., Nabil, M., Ismail, M., Mahmoud, M., Serpedin, E., Rahman, M.A.: Blockchain-based charging coordination mechanism for smart grid energy storage units. In: Proceedings of the IEEE International Conference Blockchain (Blockchain), Atlanta, GA, USA, pp. 504–509 (2019)
40. Huang, X., Xu, C., Wang, P., Liu, H.: LNSC: a security model for electric vehicle and charging pile management based on blockchain ecosystem. IEEE Access **6**, 13565–13574 (2018)
41. Knirsch, F., Unterweger, A., Engel, D.: Privacy-preserving blockchain-based electric vehicle charging with dynamic tariff decisions. Comput. Sci. Res. Dev. **33**(1–2), 71–79 (2017). https://doi.org/10.1007/s00450-017-0348-5
42. Garg, S., Kaur, K., Kaddoum, G., Gagnon, F., Rodrigues, J.J.: An efficient blockchain-based hierarchical authentication mechanism for energy trading in V2G environment. In: Proceedings of the IEEE International Conference Communications Workshops (ICC Workshops), Shanghai, China, pp. 1–6 (2019)
43. Kang, J., Yu, R., Huang, X., Maharjan, S., Zhang, Y., Hossain, E.: Enabling localized peer-to-peer electricity trading among plug-in hybrid electric vehicles using consortium blockchains. IEEE Trans. Ind. Inf. **13**(6), 3154–3164 (2017)
44. Berntzen, L., Meng, Q., Vesin, B., Johannessen, M.R., Brekke, T., Laur, I.: Blockchain for smart grid flexibility - handling settlements between the aggregator and prosumers. In: The Fifteenth International Conference on Digital Society (ICDS), Nice, France (2021)
45. P2P-SmarTest Project (2017). https://www.p2psmartest-h2020.eu/. Accessed 28 July 2021
46. CROSSBOW, CROSS BOrder Management of Variable Renewable Energies and Storage Units Enabling a Transnational Wholesale Market (2020). https://cordis.europa.eu/project/id/773430. Accessed 28 July 2021
47. FutureFlow, Designing eTrading Solutions for Electricity Balancing and Redispatching in Europe (2019). https://cordis.europa.eu/project/id/691777. Accessed 28 July 2021
48. Testing and Evaluating Sophisticated information and communication Technologies for enaBling a smartEr griD | TESTBED Project. https://cordis.europa.eu/project/id/734325. Accessed 28 July 2021
49. Defender, Defending the European Energy Infrastructures (2020). https://cordis.europa.eu/project/id/740898. Accessed 28 July 2021

50. Scalable, trustEd, and interoperAble pLatform for sEcureD smart GRID. https://cordis.eur opa.eu/project/id/777996. Accessed 28 July 2021
51. eDREAM—new Demand Response to technologies. https://edream-h2020.eu/. Accessed 28 July 2021
52. SMART-MLA, Multi-layer aggregator solutions to facilitate optimum demand response and grid flexibility. https://smart-mla.stimasoft.com. Accessed 28 July 2021
53. Secure Open Federation for Internet Everywhere. https://cordis.europa.eu/project/id/779984. Accessed 28 July 2021
54. SerIoT - Secure and Safe Internet of Things. https://cordis.europa.eu/project/id/780139. Accessed 28 July 2021
55. www.enerchain.ponton.de. Accessed 28 July 2021
56. www.interbit.io. Accessed 28 July 2021
57. www.guardtime.com. Accessed 28 July 2021
58. www.tennet.eu. Accessed 28 July 2021
59. www.electron.net. Accessed 28 July 2021
60. www.drifttrader.com. Accessed 28 July 2021
61. www.gridplus.io. Accessed 28 July 2021
62. www.brooklyn.energy. Accessed 28 July 2021
63. www.alliander.com. Accessed 28 July 2021
64. www.motionwerk.com. Accessed 28 July 2021
65. https://evcharging.enelx.com. Accessed 28 July 2021
66. Marr, B.: The 5 Big Problems With Blockchain Everyone Should Be Aware Of, Forbes Homepage. https://www.forbes.com/sites/bernardmarr/2018/02/19/the-5-big-pro blems-with-blockchain-everyone-should-be-aware-of/?sh=314b99941670. Accessed 28 July 2021

Exploring ICO's Phenomenon: Developing a Taxonomy of Academic and Non-academic Discourse

Guido Di Matteo[✉] and Stefano Za

University "G. d'Annunzio" of Chieti-Pescara, Pescara, Italy
{guido.dimatteo,stefano.za}@unich.it

Abstract. New ventures and private investors are showing increasing interest in innovative forms of fundraising. ICO is the abbreviation of Initial Coin Offering and it represents an innovation in entrepreneurial finance [1]. However, no study has ever developed a taxonomy of academic and not academic discourse related to this type of innovative financial tool. This paper aims to fill this gap by developing a taxonomy to investigate and categorize papers that discuss Initial Coin Offering phenomenon. This study is developed using a mixed methodology. The first stage of the research protocol regards the dataset definition and description. In the second stage we adopted the taxonomy process developed by Nickerson et al. [2]. The purpose of the present work is to develop a taxonomy with a set of dimensions each consisting of a set of characteristics that describes the objects in a specific study. We identified "Research Topics" as set of dimensions. It comprises eight dimensions: field of investigation, focus, actors, token type, extra topic, research issue, ICO phase, blockchain. In the taxonomy process we assigned a single value to every dimension. In the last section, we summarize some preliminary results, providing conclusions and discussions for future research.

Keywords: Initial coin offering · Blockchain · Cryptocurrency · Taxonomy · Token sale

1 Introduction

New ventures and private investors are showing increasing interest in innovative forms of fundraising. Traditional ways to fund a project can be represented through the 3 F's (family, friends and fools): banks or financial institutes, angel investors or venture capitalists, government grants, crowdfunding.

The process involving the development of ICO, as we know it today, was first described in January 2012 in the white paper entitled "The second Bitcoin White Paper" [3].

ICO stands for Initial Coin Offering and it represents an innovation in entrepreneurial finance [1].

The idea behind this was that the existing Bitcoin network could serve as a basic protocol to build new protocol levels with their respective rules.

© Springer Nature Switzerland AG 2022
M. Themistocleous and M. Papadaki (Eds.): EMCIS 2021, LNBIP 437, pp. 150–164, 2022.
https://doi.org/10.1007/978-3-030-95947-0_11

The first ICO was launched by Willett in 2013 under the name Mastercoin in which raised USD 500,000 [4]. Another important turning point in the field of ICO process is the creation of Ethereum company, which was founded by Vitalik Buterin in 2013. The company introduced Ether tokens raising more than USD 18 millions of start-up capital.

ICO is defined as a poorly regulated process (method) of obtaining start-up funding for companies engaged in blockchain technology [5].

ICOs, also called token sale, allow entrepreneurs to sell a predefined number of newly generated digital tokens to the public in exchange for cryptocurrencies [6].

The easiest way to define initial coin offerings (ICOs) is that they can be considered a financing activity that allows online projects and start-up companies to raise the required funds with the support of venture capitalists.

Since Bitcoin was first conceptualized in 2008 and implemented in 2009 [7], the price of Bitcoin has gone from almost zero (January 2009) to more than $56,000 (March 2021). The rise of Bitcoin has brought attention not only to digital currencies but also to the underlying technology empowering digital currencies: blockchain technology [8].

Companies adopt this revolutionary token sale process to try to avoid a more regulated process of raising capital by institutional investors in the classic public offering of shares.

An ICO is a new way to perform crowdfunding campaigns, based on blockchain technology. It allows financing startups using blockchain technology without intermediaries. The new venture will create and distribute its tokens with the aim to convince investors on the success of its innovative project. The token of the ICO can be developed through a smart contract, a computer program running on a public blockchain.

A blockchain is a distributed ledger that is usually managed by a peer-to-peer network [9]. In the distributed ledger, transactions are organized into blocks that are linked together in a chain. In a blockchain, trans-actions are validated and recorded by distributed consensus in the peer-to-peer network, eliminating the need for a trusted central entity [8].

Blockchain technology represents one of the greatest innovations that have occurred in recent years as this tool allows the creation and exchange of digital assets (cryptocurrencies), as well as the conclusion of contracts between customers. All this has led to the rapid introduction of a new fundraising method by startups, especially in the field of innovative technologies, known as initial Coin Offering. Before this revolutionary tool, companies raised funds for their innovative projects using traditional methods, where venture capital funds and business angels played a fundamental role.

Due to the innovations provided by the blockchain technology, the cost of the ICO process using the cryptocurrency exchange platforms is up to ten times cheaper than the costs of traditional IPO (Initial Public Offering) on the stock market [3].

ICOs are a disruptive financial tool through which new ventures can generate and sell blockchain-based tokens to investors. In ICOs, entrepreneurs raise money through the issuance of blockchain based tokens. Blockchain can be defined as a decentralized, distributed ledger technology that records the provenance of a digital asset. This innovative technology facilitates peer-to- peer transactions, without the need for financial intermediaries.

An ICO provides a new way for entrepreneurs to raise money for a startup by selling their own cryptocurrency to investors. This is similar to crowdfunding in two aspects:

both require a minimum funding threshold to be reached; and both are in a way engaged in testing the market demand for their product.

This is similar to crowdfunding in two aspects: both require a minimum funding threshold to be reached; and both are in a way engaged in testing the market demand for their product [10].

Only one study carried out a systematic literature review concerning this phenomenon [11] at Americas Conference on Information Systems. Current literature provides contributions on investor decisions to fund ICOs as well as on investee decision to obtain funds for their innovative projects, other studies provide an overview on ICO characteristics that influence the investors-investee relationship. Their research provides a systematic literature review revealing clusters of ICO characteristics that influence an investor's decision-making process.

G. Fridgen, F. Regner, A. Schweizer and N.Urbach developed a general taxonomy of empirically validated ICO design parameters, but the manuscript is dated [12] and their classification consider only technical aspects regarding three thematic categories: token, issuer and sales term.

However, no study has ever developed a taxonomy of academic and non-academic discourse related to this type of innovative financial tool. This paper aims to fill this gap by developing a taxonomy to investigate and categorize papers that discuss Initial Coin Offering phenomenon.

The present work is structured as follows: the next paragraph provides a description of the theoretical background concerning the ICO phenomenon. In the third paragraph we illustrate the methodology adopted to develop the taxonomy. Afterwards, we provide a description of the taxonomy development process classifying the dimensions and their values. In the last section, we summarize some preliminary results, providing conclusions and discussions for future research.

2   Theoretical Background

The literature related to ICOs is still quite limited. Most of the works refer to what the success factors of ICOs are and link success to the amount of money raised. Adhami, Giudici, and Martinazzi [13] examined the specific characteristics of an ICO that determine success. They found that the probability of an ICO's success is higher if the code source is available, when a token presale is organized, and when tokens allow contributors to access a specific service.

Fisch [14] analysed the factors that determine the amount raised. The results explored by Fisch showed that technical white papers and high-quality source codes increase the amount raised, while patents are not associated with increased amounts of funding. Fisch, Masiak, Vismara and Block [1] identified and categorized the motivations to invest in ICOs using factor analysis. They found that investors are driven by ideological, technological, and financial motives. Moreover, Fisch and Momtaz [15] examined the role of institutional investors in ICOs. They argued that institutional investors' superior screening and coaching abilities enable them to overcome the information asymmetry of the ICO context. They found that institutional investor backing is associated with higher post-ICO performance.

Roosenboom, Van der Kolk and De Jong [16] found evidence that ICOs are more successful in raising funding when they disclose more information to investors, have a higher quality rating by cryptocurrency experts, organise a presale, have shorter planned token sale durations and have a larger project team.

Some studies focused on aspects of the venture such as raising funds, others investigated the characteristics of the investor or investee or both. Hsieh and Oppermann [10]investigated how ICO characteristics, cryptocurrency markets, the jurisdictions, the ICO industry and conventional financial markets affect the initial returns of ICOs. Moreover, they discovered that having a short offering phase, not holding a presale, an accurately written whitepaper, and the creation of an independent blockchain all have a positive impact on ICOs' initial returns.

Momtaz [17] focused on asymmetric information between investor-investee. He found that loyal CEOs have to offer lower financial incentives to attract investors and are still able to raise more proceeds and are less likely to fail.

Another mainstream of study analyses ICOs in relation to IPO (Initial Public Offering) and crowdfunding phenomena.

An, Duan, Hou, and Xu [18] studied the effects of founders' characteristics on firm's success in ICOs, drawing parallels between ICOs, crowdfunding and venture capital, where a large literature examines the relationship between founder characteristics and firm performance. They discovered that the disclosure of founders' personal information is associated with larger amount of funds raised in ICOs.

Huang, Meoli and Vismara [19] demonstrated that the availability of investment-based crowdfunding platforms is positively associated with the growth of the number of ICOs, while debt and private equity markets do not provide similar effects.

Block, Groh, Hornuf, Vanacker, and Vismara [20] drew a comparison between crowdfunding and ICO. Their study demonstrated that although the two market segments initially appear to be similar, relevant differences exist between them. Their comparison focused on the stakeholders, microstructures, regulatory environments, and development of the markets.

Collomb, De Filippi, and Sok [21] compared Initial Public Offerings (IPOs) and equity crowdfunding with ICOs and explored the corresponding risks and limitations of these different fundraising practice. They discovered that many ICOs share lots of similarities with traditional IPOs and equity crowdfunding, so they should be regulated in a similar manner.

Hashemi Joo, Nishikawa and Dandapani [22] recognized the benefits of ICO as a way of raising funds and presented a comparison between the ICO and the initial public offering to realize the future possibilities of this innovative funding method. ICOs structure is much more elastic, and it represents a faster and less costly way of raising capital than IPOs.

Other academics also consider it essential to argue about Blockchain when analyzing the phenomenon of ICO.

Kher, Terjesen, and Liu [23] systematically reviewed 152 articles concerning blockchain and its applications and synthesized five topics: computer science, economics, entrepreneurship, and law and governance.

According Boreiko, Ferrarini and Giudici [24], ICOs are a new way for blockchain startups to finance project development by issuing coins or tokens in exchange for fiat money or Bitcoin or other cryptocurrencies. They compared the European and American regulation, highlighting the great differences between Europe and the US which make Europe less friendly to blockchain startups.

According to Yan Chen [25] blockchain tokens may democratize entrepreneurship by giving entrepreneurs new ways to raise funds and engage stakeholders, and can give to innovators a new way to develop decentralized applications.

Lo and Medda [26] examined venture related to blockchain tokens and developed the analysis through a stepwise testing of four hypotheses using panel ordinary least squares with cluster-robust standard errors. They found that token functions are statistically significant in relation to token prices.

Mangano [27] illustrated advantages and drawbacks concerning the use of blockchain technology in finance. The issuance of blockchain securities is creating a division between the world where securities are issued, offered and sold, and the world where law is enforceable. Albrecht, Lutz, & Neumann [28] investigated whether blockchain ventures can reduce information asymmetries between investor/investee by utilizing signaling mechanisms on Twitter and seeing how the resulting effects differ from those in conventional market environments.

3   Methodology

In conducting our review, we followed the approach used by Za et al. [29] which comprises four major steps: 1) material collection, 2) analysis collection, 3) taxonomy development (selecting structural dimensions and categories based on well-established theory, 4) preliminary evaluation and interpretation.

Although we adhered to this process, we gathered the first two steps so that our study comprises three major steps as described in Fig. 1.

This study is developed using a mixed methodology. In the first step we selected bibliographic sources using Scopus database since academics and practitioners consider this tool a comprehensive, expertly curated abstract and citation database.

The first stage of the research protocol regards the dataset definition and description. We chose the searching terms using Scopus, then we applied a practical and methodological screening giving a description of the dataset, eventually a refining selection.

In the second stage we used the taxonomy process developed by Nickerson et al. [2]. The purpose is to develop a taxonomy with a set of dimensions each consisting of a set of characteristics that describes the objects in a specific study. It consists of iterating empirical-to-conceptual and conceptual-to-empirical approaches in the analysis of the papers gathered in the dataset. The iterating process should be run until values and attributes of theoretical dimensions appear clear [30]. Our purpose is to identify a set of dimensions and their values to better categorize papers of the dataset.

We adopt a "useful taxonomy" in agreement with the definition by Nickerson et al. [2]: the dimensions and values should be concise, robust, comprehensive and extendible.

Finally, in our research each paper has one value for each dimension, so we did not assign two or more values to one dimension.

In the third section, we report the findings from a preliminary interpretation of studies regarding ICOs phenomenon. As part of this analysis, we consider ICOs' theoretical background to understand how research type and topics are related to this innovative finance tool. From the preliminary analysis we report for every value the number of papers involved distinguishing four dimensions concerning research type (research approach, research design, data collection, philosophy view) and eight dimensions concerning the different kind of topics (field of investigation, focus, actors, token type, extra topics, research issue, ICO phase, blockchain).

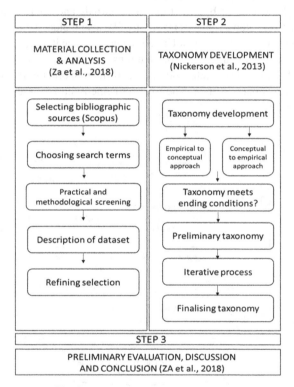

Fig. 1. Taxonomy development process.

4   Material Collection and Sample Description

In a literature review research, academics select different kinds of criteria to collect documents. To cover all studies regarding ICOs' phenomenon, we conduct our search using Scopus database, since this platform is widely used by academics and researchers in the field of social studies [30]. The first stage of our work involved data collection so that a congruous source of academic literature can be identified. We used Scopus database to gather relevant studies related to the ICOs phenomenon. To perform the search, we specified a query on Scopus to find documents which contain the string "Initial Coin Offering*" in the article title, abstract or keywords without any temporal restriction. We used wildcards to also include plural words, grammatical and spelling variations.

The first query returned 226 papers published between 2017 and 2021. A growing interest regarding this innovative finance tool can be noticed. Articles represented 63% of the works, followed by conference papers which constituted 20% of the total. Prevalent keywords used are Initial Coin Offering (130), Blockchain (108) and Cryptocurrency (67). The major publication outlets included Small Business Economics, Economist United Kingdom, Journal of Alternative Investments, European Business Organization Law Review, Journal of Corporate Finance.

We restricted our dataset by selecting only journals and conference proceedings document types, to develop a rigorous taxonomy. We also included only English studies and excluded the publisher Economist United Kingdom since it represents a newspaper. The first refined dataset included 133 contributions.

We analyzed all abstracts to refine our dataset further, in order to include only works consistent with ICOs phenomenon. The final refinement led to 99 relevant papers for our purpose (Fig. 2).

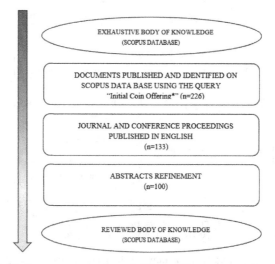

Fig. 2. Systematic selection of bibliographic sources on Scopus.

5   Taxonomy Description

In this study, we developed a taxonomy to better understand and describe the emerging phenomenon of ICOs. A taxonomy is the result of a design science research approach; it consists of dimensions containing characteristics that are "mutually exclusive and collectivly exhaustive" [31].

Our purpose is to synthesize the literature regarding ICOs phenomenon exploring which kind of research academics apply and which topics are investigated.

We identified "Research Topics" as set of dimensions. It comprises eight dimensions: field of investigation, focus, actors, token type, extra topic, research issue, ICO phase, blockchain. In the taxonomy process we assigned a single value to every dimension.

5.1   Research Topics

Field of Investigation. We used ICO bench categories to classify a specific field of investigation for every paper. ICO Bench is a rating platform which identify 26 categories (Investment, Cryptocurrency, Banking, Software, Legal, Communication, etc.)

Focus. We mean the main aspects discussed in our data set: Technological, Organizational, Individual, Social, Geopolitical and Legal aspects.

Actors. Every paper's content can be analysed from the point of view of two main actors: capital seekers (investee), capital providers (investor) or both.

Token Type. We considered the general classification of token type: utility, security and payment. Utility Tokens give holders access to a product or service but do not grant holders rights that are the same as those granted by specified investments. A Security Token provides rights and obligations similar to securities or investment like share or debt instruments. Payment Tokens are used as alternative means of payment and exchange.

Extra Topic. This dimension includes paper that discuss non only ICO's phenomenon but also other financial tools such as Crowdfunding, Initial Public Offering and Venture Capital.

Research Issue. This dimension refers to the kind of aspects every paper wants to explore, every work cover literature gap in a particular field and their purpose is to analyse: Technical aspects, Token market, Information asymmetry (investor-investee) and Ideological aspects (Entrepreneur behaviour, Investor's risk tolerance).

ICO Phase. Generally, every ICO can be divided in three phases: Pre ICO, ICO launch and post ICO. Every work can be associated to a particular ICO phase. Pre ICO refers to ICO planning and marketing services. ICO phase refers to the actual launch and development process. Once the ICO launch and development process is completed, it is then opened for ICO token sale and exchange (Post ICO).

Blockchain. This dummy dimension refers to the presence or not of blockchain as topic (Table 1).

Table 1. Research topics dimensions

Research topics		
Dimension	Values	Distinguishing attributes
Field of Investigation (Icobench categories)	Investment	According to finance, the practice of investment refers to the buying of a financial product or any valued item with anticipation that positive returns will be received in the future
	Cryptocurrency	Cryptocurrencies are digital financial assets, for which ownership and transfers of ownership are guaranteed by a cryptographic decentralized technology [24]
	Banking	"Banking means accepting, for the purpose of lending or investment, of deposits of money from the public, repayable on demand or otherwise, and withdrawable by cheque, draft, order or otherwise." (Banking regulation act, 1949)
	Software	Software comprises the entire set of programs, procedures, and routines associated with the operation of a computer system. (www.britannica.com)
	Media	The means of communication that reach large numbers of people, such as television, newspapers, and radio. (Collins's dictionary)
	Legal	It comprises papers that explores legal issues
	Platform	Platform stands for Blockchain platform. It represents a platform that exists to support a particular flavour of Blockchain such as Ethereum, R3, Ripple
	Internet	It comprises papers that explores only internet field as a media tool
	Smart contract	It comprises papers focused on Smart contracts. Smart contracts are computerized transaction protocols that execute terms of a contract. (Nick Szabo, 1998). Smart contracts permit trusted transactions and agreements to be carried out among parties without the need for a central authority or a legal system
	Artificial intelligence	The theory and development of computer systems able to perform tasks normally requiring human intelligence, such as visual perception, speech recognition, decision-making, and translation between languages. (Oxford dictionary, 2017)
	Communication	It comprises papers that explores almost one type of communication: verbal and non-verbal communication and written communication
	Energy	It comprises papers that explore energy sector. The energy sector is a category of stocks that relate to producing or supplying energy

(continued)

Table 1. (*continued*)

Research topics		
Dimension	Values	Distinguishing attributes
Focus	Technological	Papers that explore technical aspects related to the ICO: innovative tools, bonus, soft and hard cap, platform
	Organizational	Papers that point out organizational structure of companies: functional, divisional, matrix, flat
	Individual	Documents that consider more aspects related to the psychology of the individuals involved
	Social	Documents that explore social projects. Socially responsible ICOs aim to improve public wellbeing in education, environment, health and poverty
	Geopolitical	Documents that explore geopolitical issue related to ICOs: how governments can affect the development of new ICOs
	Legal	Documents that explores legal issues: how ICOs face different legal issues in different countries
Actors	Investor	The person who invests money in order to make a profit
	Investee	The business entity in which an investment is made
	Both	Both investor and investee
Token type	Utility	Utility Tokens grant holders access to a current or prospective product or service but do not grant holders rights that are the same as those granted by specified investments
	Security	A Security Token provides rights and obligations similar to securities or investment like share or debt instruments
	Payment	Payment Tokens are used as an alternative means of payment and exchange
Extra topic	Crowdfunding	Crowdfunding is most commonly defined as "the efforts by entrepreneurial individuals and groups—cultural, social, and for-profit—to fund their ventures by drawing on relatively small contributions from a relatively large number of individuals using the internet, without standard financial intermediaries" (Mollic, 2014)
	IPO	We refer to IPO as the first offer of shares of a private company to public
	Venture Capital	Venture capital investment consists in the purchase of shares of young, privately held companies by outsiders for the primary purpose of capital gain (The Oxford handbook of entrepreneurship, 2006 chapter 14)
	Not present	Absence of extra topics in documents
Research Issue	Information Asymmetry	Documents that explore investor-investee relationship
	Ideological aspects	Documents that explore ideological aspects (entrepreneur behaviour, investor's risk tolerance)
	Technical aspects	Documents that cover literature gap in technical aspects: platforms, smart contracts, token price
	Token market	Documents that give an overview of token market

(*continued*)

Table 1. (*continued*)

Research topics		
Dimension	Values	Distinguishing attributes
Ico phase	Pre ICO	It refers to a sale of a limited number of Tokens or Coins before the actual ICO (Initial Coin Offering) takes place
	ICO	It refers to the launch of ICO
	Post ICO	It refers to post ICO performance
Blockchain	YES	Documents that deepen Blockchain topic
	NO	Blockchain topic is not explored

6 Preliminary Evaluation and Discussion

From a preliminary analysis of our dataset, we identified several findings. First, the papers explore issues regarding mainly token market (42), technical aspects (32) and information asymmetry between capital seekers and capital providers (19). Dataset documents focus mostly on technological (30), social (19) and legal (18) aspects.

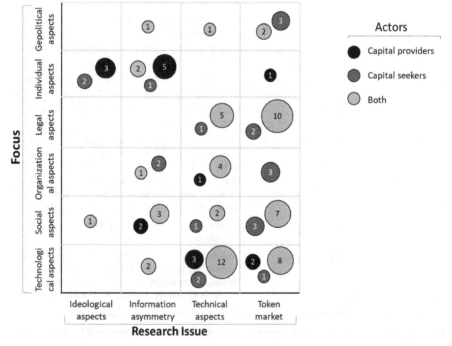

Fig. 3. Number and distribution of contributions discussing ICO phenomenon in relation to the actors considering focus and research issue dimensions.

Several features and aims discussed in our dataset documents can be explored by combining two or more dimensions. We proposed a preliminary analysis of ICOs literature using a subset of 3 dimensions in two different combinations:

- In the first analysis we considered the following dimensions: focus, research issue, actors (Fig. 3).
- In the second analysis we considered the following dimensions: focus, research issue, ICO phase (Fig. 4).

This analysis can provide some insight into the discussion on ICO phenomenon in the contributions focused on relationships between capital providers and capital seekers (actors) and on what stage of ICO process is explored.

Figure 3 shows the resulting diagram combining three specific dimensions: Focus (technological, social, organizational, legal, individual, and geopolitical aspects), Research issue (ideological aspects, information asymmetry, technical aspects, and token market) and Actors (capital seekers and capital providers). Looking at the diagram, it appears that most documents consider both investor/investee relationships (61), most of these focus on technological, social and legal aspects, exploring the token market and technical aspects.

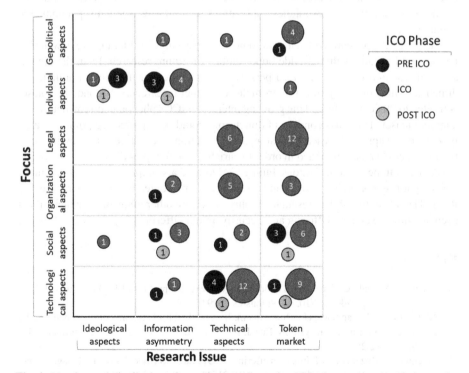

Fig. 4. Number and distribution of contributions discussing ICO phenomenon in relation to the ICO phase considering focus and research issue dimensions.

Figure 4 shows the resulting diagram combining three specific dimensions (the first two are the same of the first diagram): Focus (technological, social, organizational, legal, individual, and geopolitical aspects), Research issue (ideological aspects, information asymmetry, technical aspects and token market) and ICO phase (pre Ico, ICO, post ICO). Looking at the diagram, it appears that most documents explore ICOs without considering pre or post ICOs launch (74), most of these focus on technological and legal aspects, exploring technical aspects and the token market. Few documents (6) explore post ICO services.

7   Conclusion

The proposed taxonomy could be useful for practitioners as well as for academics.

These findings offer several theoretical contributions to ICOs phenomenon. First previous studies did not develop a taxonomy of academic and not academic discourse related to this innovative financial tool. Second, this study contributes to the innovation research by identifying eight dimensions in research topic, which combined in an appropriate way can disclose any gaps in literature or can identify the most explored topics. Third, the study contributes to pointing out the emerging research issue regarding information asymmetry and investor/investee relationships. The findings of this study also have implication for investor and investee to achieve more awareness about this finance tool, as well as some policies implications for countries where this phenomenon is unregulated.

Although the present work narrows some of the gaps in ICOs literature review, it also has several limitations that provide opportunities for future research. First, the dimensions of research topics relate to a personal interpretation of the present authors, so dimensions may differ significantly from those of other researchers. Second, the dataset is limited to 99 documents and the growing interest on ICOs phenomenon can determine a larger dataset. Third, a second set of dimensions could be explored regarding research type (research approach, research design, data collection). Therefore, a further literature review process is recommended in order to enrich research topics dimensions as well as the dataset number of contributions. Future works could also explore a new set of dimensions regarding research approach and research design adopted by researchers. Finally, it could be useful to use the present taxonomy to explore other innovative financial tools such as Initial Exchange Offering and Security Token Offering [29].

References

1. Fisch, C., Masiak, C., Vismara, S., Block, J.: Motives and profiles of ICO investors. J. Bus. Res. (2019). https://doi.org/10.1016/j.jbusres.2019.07.036
2. Nickerson, R.C., Varshney, U., Muntermann, J.: A method for taxonomy development and its application in information systems. Eur. J. Inf. Syst. **22**, 336–359 (2013). https://doi.org/10.1057/ejis.2012.26
3. Lahajnar, S., Rožanec, A.: Initial coin offering (ICO) evaluation model. Invest. Manag. Financ. Innov. **15**, 169–182 (2018). https://doi.org/10.21511/imfi.15(4).2018.14
4. Lee, I., Shin, Y.J.: Fintech: ecosystem, business models, investment decisions, and challenges. Bus. Horiz. **61**, 35–46 (2018). https://doi.org/10.1016/j.bushor.2017.09.003

5. Investopedia Homepage. https://www.investopedia.com/news/what-ico/. Accessed 9 Jan 2021
6. Kranz, J., Nagel, E., Yoo, Y.: Blockchain token sale. Bus. Inf. Syst. Eng. **61**(6), 745–753 (2019). https://doi.org/10.1007/s12599-019-00598-z
7. Low, R., Marsh, T.: Cryptocurrency and blockchains: retail to institutional. J. Invest. **29**, 18–30 (2019). https://doi.org/10.3905/joi.2019.1.102
8. Chen, Y.: Blockchain tokens and the potential democratization of entrepreneurship and innovation. Bus. Horiz. **61**, 567–575 (2018). https://doi.org/10.1016/j.bushor.2018.03.006
9. Zhao, W.: Blockchain technology: development and prospects. Natl. Sci. Rev. **6**, 369–373 (2019). https://doi.org/10.1093/nsr/nwy133
10. Hsieh, H.-C., Oppermann, J.: Initial coin offerings and their initial returns. Asia Pacific Manag. Rev. (2020).https://doi.org/10.1016/j.apmrv.2020.05.003
11. Bruckner, M., Straub, A., Veit, D.: Initial coin offerings, how do investors decide? - A systematic literature review. In: 26th Americas Conference on Information Systems. AMCIS 2020, p. 10 (2020)
12. Fridgen, G., Regner, F., Schweizer, A., Urbach, N.: Don't slip on the initial coin offering (ICO) -a taxonomy for a blockchain-enabled form of crowdfunding. In: 26th European Conference on Information Systems: Beyond Digitization - Facets of Socio-Technical Change, ECIS 2018 (2018)
13. Adhami, S., Giudici, G., Martinazzi, S.: Why do businesses go crypto? An empirical analysis of initial coin offerings. J. Econ. Bus. **100**, 64–75 (2018). https://doi.org/10.1016/j.jeconbus.2018.04.001
14. Fisch, C.: Initial coin offerings (ICOs) to finance new ventures. J. Bus. Ventur. **34**, 1–22 (2019). https://doi.org/10.1016/j.jbusvent.2018.09.007
15. Fisch, C., Momtaz, P.P.: Institutional investors and post-ICO performance: an empirical analysis of investor returns in initial coin offerings (ICOs). J. Corp. Financ. **64** (2020). https://doi.org/10.1016/j.jcorpfin.2020.101679
16. Roosenboom, P., van der Kolk, T., de Jong, A.: What determines success in initial coin offerings? Ventur. Cap. (2020). https://doi.org/10.1080/13691066.2020.1741127
17. Momtaz, P.P.: Initial coin offerings, asymmetric information, and loyal CEOs. Small Bus. Econ. **57**(2), 975–997 (2020). https://doi.org/10.1007/s11187-020-00335-x
18. An, J., Duan, T., Hou, W., Xu, X.: Initial coin offerings and entrepreneurial finance: the role of founders' characteristics. J. Altern. Invest. **21**, 26–40 (2019). https://doi.org/10.3905/jai.2019.1.068
19. Huang, W., Meoli, M., Vismara, S.: The geography of initial coin offerings. Small Bus. Econ. **55**(1), 77–102 (2019). https://doi.org/10.1007/s11187-019-00135-y
20. Block, J.H., Groh, A., Hornuf, L., Vanacker, T., Vismara, S.: The entrepreneurial finance markets of the future: a comparison of crowdfunding and initial coin offerings. Small Bus. Econ. **57**(2), 865–882 (2020). https://doi.org/10.1007/s11187-020-00330-2
21. Collomb, A., De Filippi, P., Sok, K.: Blockchain technology and financial regulation: a risk-based approach to the regulation of ICOs. Eur. J. Risk Regul. **10**, 263–314 (2019). https://doi.org/10.1017/err.2019.41
22. Hashemi Joo, M., Nishikawa, Y., Dandapani, K.: ICOs, the next generation of IPOs. Manag. Financ. **46**, 761–783 (2019). https://doi.org/10.1108/MF-10-2018-0472
23. Kher, R., Terjesen, S., Liu, C.: Blockchain, Bitcoin, and ICOs: a review and research agenda. Small Bus. Econ. **56**(4), 1699–1720 (2020). https://doi.org/10.1007/s11187-019-00286-y
24. Boreiko, D., Ferrarini, G., Giudici, P.: Blockchain startups and prospectus regulation. Eur. Bus. Organ. Law Rev. **20**(4), 665–694 (2019). https://doi.org/10.1007/s40804-019-00168-6
25. Chen, Y.: Blockchain tokens and the potential democratization of entrepreneurship and innovation. Bus. Horiz. **61** (2018). https://doi.org/10.1016/j.bushor.2018.03.006

26. Lo, Y.C., Medda, F.: Assets on the blockchain: an empirical study of tokenomics. Inf. Econ. Policy (2020). https://doi.org/10.1016/j.infoecopol.2020.100881

27. Mangano, R.: Blockchain securities, insolvency law and the sandbox approach. Eur. Bus. Organ. Law Rev. **19**(4), 715–735 (2018). https://doi.org/10.1007/s40804-018-0123-5

28. Albrecht, S., Lutz, B., Neumann, D.: The behavior of blockchain ventures on Twitter as a determinant for funding success. Electron. Mark. **30**(2), 241–257 (2019). https://doi.org/10.1007/s12525-019-00371-w

29. Za, S., Spagnoletti, P., Winter, R., Mettler, T.: Exploring foundations for using simulations in IS research. Commun. Assoc. Inf. Syst. **42**, 268–300 (2018). https://doi.org/10.17705/1CAIS.04210

30. Cipriano, M., Za, S., Ceci, F.: Exploring the discourse on digital transformation in the domain of non-profit organisations, pp. 1–32

31. Nickerson, R.C., Varshney, U., Muntermann, J., Isaac, H.: Taxonomy development in information systems: developing a taxonomy of mobile applications. In: 17th European Conference in Information Systems ECIS 2009 (2009)

How Decentralized is Decentralized Governance Really? - A Network Analysis of ERC20 Platforms

Johannes Werner$^{(\boxtimes)}$, Niclas Freudiger, and Rüdiger Zarnekow

Technische Universität Berlin, Berlin, Germany
{johannes.werner,ruediger.zarnekow}@tu-berlin.de

Abstract. Blockchain technology offers a vast amount of possible applications, which include the decentralization of platforms among many others. That decentralization can enable decentralized governance of platforms, which in turn may lead to a decentralized governance structure in which the rights to make decisions about the platform are decentralized. It remains unclear how decentralized the platform governance really is solely based on its possibility and intention to decentralize. We analyze how decentralized the governance structures of in reality occurring platforms are. For this we collected data of 16 platforms which are based on the Ethereum blockchain. These platforms were analyzed in terms of token and transaction distribution as well as transaction behavior. This allowed us to examine the distribution of platform resources associated with the governance structure. As a result, we could identify that not yet decentralized governance structures becomes more decentralized. Additionally, we enhance the knowledge on the development of the decentralization of platform resources.

Keywords: Blockchain · Distributed ledger · Governance · Network analysis

1 Introduction

Since Bitcoin was the first practical application of blockchain technology, this technology has received attention from practitioners and academics. Although there exists almost unlimited possibilities to apply this technology [1], most of the use cases are still attributed to finance [2]. However, more and more use cases in other branches of industries emerge (e.g., [3, 4]). Even now the technology is expected to have further enormous potential, leading to an increase of the global gross domestic product of up to 1.76 trillion USD [5].

Key features of blockchain technology include decentralization, data integrity, transparency, auditability, and automation [6]. These properties can enable decentralized platforms. In particular, it follows from decentralized platforms that areas of its governance can be decentralized, e.g., the decision rights of the platform based on the owned tokens [7]. Thereby, the question arises what level of decentralization these platforms do acquire. The technologically possible level of decentralized governance does not need to be attained [8]. For example, due to initial token issues on blockchain-based platforms,

© Springer Nature Switzerland AG 2022
M. Themistocleous and M. Papadaki (Eds.): EMCIS 2021, LNBIP 437, pp. 165–179, 2022.
https://doi.org/10.1007/978-3-030-95947-0_12

it may be possible that platforms start in a centralized form and only later become decentralized [7]. Consequently, the decentralization that occurs of a very instance does not dependent on the technological capabilities alone. In particular, a platform may stay centralized even though a decentralized form is desired. This leads to the following research questions:

How decentralized are platform resources of blockchain-based platforms?

and

Do the platform resources of blockchain-based platforms shift from a centralized to a decentralized form over time?

The remainder of this paper is structured as followed: First, foundations of blockchain technology and the governance of blockchain-based platforms are given. Moreover, the used methodology is outlined. Then, the results of the analysis are presented followed by a discussion and finally a conclusion is given.

2 Theoretical Background

2.1 Blockchain Technology

In this paper, we understand blockchain technology as a concept of distributed ledger technology [9]. It is a distributed network, which stores and synchronizes data among its participants, which are called nodes. Each node independently manages, extends, and stores updates to the ledger in the form of blocks of transactions. These transactions, which are commissioned by any network participant, wait in a buffer zone, the so-called mempool, before being bundled into blocks and applied collectively to the latest state of the blockchain. Depending on the amount of transaction costs appended by the initiator of the transaction, transactions will be included in one of the following blocks created by miners. These miners bundle transactions from the mempool into blocks and validate these blocks in a race against each other for an expected block reward. This process, the consensus, of finding a suitable next block may differ between blockchain platforms. The two most popular consensuses are Proof-of-Work (PoW) and Proof-of-Stake (PoS). While PoW uses computing power for validation and scales the power of a miner by adding additional computing power, in PoS nodes pledge a number of tokens for their honest creation of the block [10].

As an evolution of the Bitcoin blockchain the Ethereum platform was introduced in 2014. It provides various features, such as scripting or creating platforms. Additionally, the Ethereum Virtual Machine offers an autonomous computational engine that can be used to create and process smart contracts [11]. Thereby, a smart contract is an event driven program, which is stored on the blockchain [12]. It is represented by a 20-digit byte address, like wallets, and after it has been triggered by a transaction, it is executed without external interventions [13]. These smart contracts were often implemented according to standards, like ERC20 or ERC721. Additionally, they can be distinguished by their purposes, e.g., currency, voting, assets, etc. [14]. In case of voting, smart contracts can be used to grant rights on co-determination on decisions of the platform granting voting power in accordance to owned platform tokens [11]. Although there exists an extra standard for voting smart contracts with EIP-1022, they are currently implemented in different ways using the ERC20 standard [15].

Up to now, the level of decentralization of blockchains was mainly analyzed in terms of mining and focuses on Bitcoin [16]. Furthermore, the structure of ERC20 networks on the Ethereum blockchain were analyzed with graph analysis methods (e.g., [17, 18]).

2.2 Governance of Blockchain Platforms

Blockchain governance may be subdivided into governance of blockchain and governance by blockchain [19]. Here, we focus on the governance of blockchain. Preceding research has examined governance of blockchain from different perspectives. For example, Beck et al. [7] propose a framework using three dimensions decision rights, accountability and incentives. A different approach is used by Miscione et al. [20] and Ziolkowski et al. [21], who propose tribal governance as a new governance archetype for blockchain. Additionally, Pelt et al. [22] develop a framework for blockchain governance consisting of three layers and six associated dimensions. Furthermore, Werner et al. [23] and Werner and Zarnekow [24] analyze the governance of blockchain based platforms from the governance perspective of traditional platforms.

In case of platform governance, decision rights are the authority and responsibility to make decisions regarding the design of a platform [25]. This process also occurs on blockchain-based platforms (e.g., [26]). Due to the technological features of the blockchain, it can be implemented in various decentralized forms, e.g. voting, consensus or conflict resolving mechanisms [22]. In these cases, the distribution of rights to participate in such mechanisms may be related to the tokens owned by a participant [7, 27]. Thus, a decentralized structure of governance can be achieved, if the tokens are distributed in a decentralized manner [23, 28]. In contrast, a centralized structure of the decision rights is also possible, depending on the true distribution of tokens [24].

3 Methodology

3.1 Database

We used a three-step process to collect the data for our analysis. First, the platforms were selected and a time frame for the analysis was defined. Second, we collected the data and in a third step the data was prepared.

We selected platforms based on the Ethereum Blockchain with the largest market capitalization on Coinmarketcap.com. In addition, they have to be managed or intend to be managed by a decentralized governance. We point out that the database includes platforms, which exist for a long time and which have large transaction volumes. Furthermore, platforms, which were only recently published on the Ethereum blockchain were included in the analysis. While the development might not be very advanced on these platforms, early stages of token accumulation can be detected.

The chosen time frame for the analysis was 07/09/17 to 07/05/20, which corresponds to a block level of 4 million to 10.4 million on the Ethereum blockchain. In this period, the majority of the chosen platforms were published. If the number of transactions of a platform was too small in the analyzed time period, it was excluded from the analysis. An overview on the analyzed platforms is given in Table 1.

To collect the needed data, a local Ethereum node was created and the python library EthereumETL was used for export [29]. The initial dataset included ERC20 transactions that contain a transfer, which were grouped by smart contract addresses.

Table 1. Selected platforms.

Abbr.	Name	Abbr.	Name
AGI	*SingularityNet*	MKR	*Maker Protocol*
ANT	*Aragon Network*	PNK	*Kleros*
AST	*AirSwap*	POLY	*Polymesh*
BNT	*Bancor Protocol*	REQ	*Request Network*
DAT	*Datum Network*	RLC	*iExec*
DNT	*District0x Network*	RPL	*Rocketpool*
KNC	*KyberNetwork*	XYO	*XYO*
LEND	*Aave Protocol*	ZRX	*0x Project*

In the third step we added mint and burn events of tokens to the database. Burn events are transactions from the target to the genesis address and mint events are transactions from the genesis address to the intended target. These events were collected using google's BigQuery Ethereum dataset [30] and the python library EthereumETL Airflow [31] and were manually inserted into the database. In each case, the inserted transactions were matched to the existing data format. In total, the dataset consisted of approximately 89 GB, 422 million transactions and 167000 smart contracts. Furthermore, we collected the addresses of developers and exchanges via "Etherscan" [32] and "Bloxy" [33]. A complete overview of the database sources and structure is shown in Fig. 1.

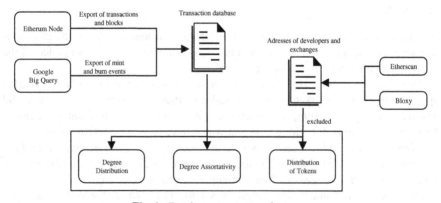

Fig. 1. Database structure and sources

3.2   Distribution and Network Analysis

In networks, a path is a sequence of nodes where each node is connected by an edge. The length of the path is the number of the used edges in a path and the closeness centrality is defined as the mean distance between vertices [34]. In an undirected network a degree of a vertex is the number of edges attached to that vertex. In directed networks, these edges are differentiated into incoming edges (in-degrees) and outgoing edges (out-degrees) [34]. The assortativity of a network describes how vertices behave with respect to a certain property. In the following analysis, the assortativity is considered with respect to the degree, and thus, the value ranges from −1 to +1. A higher value indicates degrees that are more similar and a value around 0 indicates that there is a neutral mixture between different vertices [35].

For the distribution of tokens and transaction participation, we use Gini and Nakamoto coefficients. For the Nakamoto coefficient an absolute value is used. It measures the inequality of the system based on the amount of the largest participants in the system that would have to be compromised to gain control of 51% of the existing tokens [36]. We use an adapted form of the Nakamoto coefficient based on 90% of the existing tokens in order to get a better insight into the distribution of tokens and to reduce the misleading by large participants like exchanges or development teams. Additionally, we calculated the relative share of the Nakamoto coefficient in the entire network.

Table 2. Gini coefficients for the distribution of tokens.

		Blocknumber (in Mio.)							
		4	5	6	7	8	9	10	10.4
Platforms	AGI		0.8946	0.9443	0.9574	0.9522	0.9448	0.9387	0.9375
	ANT	0.9454	0.9639	0.9662	0.9668	0.9669	0.9674	0.9695	0.9674
	AST		0.9818	0.9812	0.9838	0.9843	0.9846	0.9857	0.9859
	BNT	0.9450	0.9823	0.9837	0.9854	0.9840	0.9822	0.9807	0.9724
	DAT		0.9804	0.9864	0.9924	0.9933	0.9935	0.9935	0.9937
	DNT		0.9485	0.9501	0.9467	0.9481	0.9665	0.9671	0.9679
	KNC		0.9629	0.9781	0.9817	0.9847	0.9766	0.9808	0.9786
	LEND		0.9742	0.9755	0.9569	0.9564	0.9654	0.9694	0.9670
	MKR		0.9877	0.9877	0.9861	0.9774	0.9796	0.9792	0.9776
	PNK			0.9856	0.9856	0.9830	0.9812	0.9666	0.9753
	POLY			0.9857	0.9964	0.9952	0.9957	0.9957	0.9947
	REQ		0.9340	0.9398	0.9495	0.9535	0.9576	0.9617	0.9615
	RLC	0.8728	0.9662	0.9672	0.9716	0.9724	0.9660	0.9637	0.9619
	RPL		0.9557	0.9550	0.9588	0.9593	0.9612	0.9674	0.9751
	XYO			0.9937	0.9927	0.9929	0.9924	0.9896	0.9887
	ZRX		0.9291	0.9351	0.9576	0.9726	0.9735	0.9758	0.9714

Furthermore, we use the Gini coefficient as a relative concentration measure, which describes how equally distributed a certain feature is. We use it for the distribution of tokens and for the in- and out-degrees. After normalization, the value Gini coefficient ranges between 0 and 1, where a value up to 0.5 stands for a moderate and from 0.5 to 1 for a significant concentration of the characteristics [37, 38].

4 Results

4.1 Distribution of Tokens

The Gini coefficient was calculated for the number of native platform tokens on the wallets. Therefore, it provides information about the distribution of the tokens. Since the Gini coefficient is very susceptible to entities with expression 0, these were excluded for the calculation of the Gini coefficient. As can be seen in Table 2, all platforms considered show a high Gini coefficient in terms of token distribution with a value of at least 0.85 and were thus identified as being overly unequally concentrated. Even after excluding the largest exchanges and wallets which could be attributed to the developer teams, a strong concentration in the distribution of tokens was detected. The identification of the excluded wallets was performed using the public available list of wallets assigned to exchanges and developer teams on "Etherscan".

The calculation of the Nakamoto coefficients for 90% for the distribution of native platform tokens is presented in Table 3. It shows that the distribution of tokens of most of the platforms increases in absolute terms or that the relative share in relation to the network decreases over time. Exceptions are MKR and XYO, which have increasing Nakamoto coefficients, which is neutral or positive in comparison to the network growth. In contrast, DAT has a decreasing Nakamoto coefficient, but this also corresponds with a decreasing share of the network. Further, exceptions were found for AGI and ANT, which have a decreasing Nakamoto coefficient in the beginning, which increases later. For LEND, the opposite holds true.

Table 3. Nakamoto coefficients for 90% without exchanges.

		Blocknumber (in Mio.)							
		4	5	6	7	8	9	10	10.4
Platforms	AGI		1794; 18.61	1281; 8.11	623; 4.99	854; 6.37	1095; 8.08	1340; 9.53	1420; 9.78
	ANT	368; 7.4	815; 3.93	763; 3.55	748; 3.41	770; 3.36	768; 3.26	710; 2.94	843; 3.34
	AST		39; 0.49	67; 0.6	56; 0.53	57; 0.52	55; 0.57	39; 0.4	36; 0.36
	BNT	599; 6.63	203; 1.16	248; 1.13	229; 0.98	282; 1.12	328; 1.35	408; 1.59	802; 2.8
	DAT		61; 0.97	65; 0.79	40; 0.35	30; 0.26	27; 0.24	27; 0.24	26; 0.23
	DNT		2002; 6.4	2013; 6.07	2347; 6.9	2312; 6.63	1125; 3.74	1108; 3.62	1081; 3.48
	KNC		3338; 6.59	1706; 3.16	1166; 2.15	926; 1.66	1996; 3.45	1646; 2.43	2189; 2.76
	LEND		2136; 1.19	2956; 1.79	5522; 3.38	5798; 3.53	3696; 2.27	2589; 1.59	2107; 1.31
	MKR		20; 1.22	42; 1.16	68; 1.08	217; 1.85	229; 1.48	280; 1.4	348; 1.44
	PNK			18; 0.56	22; 0.76	37; 1.31	42; 1.43	188; 4.27	141; 2.87
	POLY			69; 0.15	39; 0.04	105; 0.11	98; 0.1	129; 0.14	214; 0.22
	REQ		3230; 10.19	3466; 8.81	2630; 7.17	2346; 6.37	2189; 5.56	1879; 4.77	1912; 4.8
	RLC	33; 18.33	311; 4.28	361; 4.01	305; 3.37	322; 3.29	493; 4.27	634; 4.59	727; 4.82
	RPL		30; 5.15	41; 5.71	40; 5.0	41; 4.92	50; 4.7	72; 3.72	83; 2.4
	XYO			2; 0.02	2; 0.01	2; 0.01	2; 0.01	2; 0.01	3; 0.01
	ZRX		4795; 10.2	6161; 8.81	5052; 6.18	3960; 3.71	4603; 3.64	4606; 3.26	6504; 4.13

4.2 Degree Assortativity

The results of the analysis of degree assortativity are shown in Table 4. Three types of platforms exist. Assortative platforms have a positive assortativity value. Disassortative platforms have a negative assortativity value and neutral mixing platforms have a neutral value.

Table 4. Degree assortativity.

		Blocknumber (in Mio.)							
		4	5	6	7	8	9	10	10.4
Platforms	AGI		−0.370	−0.306	−0.297	−0.281	−0.278	−0.275	−0.273
	ANT	−0.418	−0.396	−0.389	−0.384	−0.360	−0.348	−0.326	−0.326
	AST		−0.351	−0.315	−0.308	−0.299	−0.304	−0.299	−0.287
	BNT	0.447	0.272	0.168	0.085	0.084	0.057	0.102	0.125
	DAT		−0.270	−0.224	−0.270	−0.268	−0.270	−0.268	−0.268
	DNT		−0.407	−0.387	−0.384	−0.377	−0.387	−0.381	−0.377
	KNC		−0.358	−0.307	−0.286	−0.273	−0.223	−0.094	−0.042
	LEND		−0.318	−0.362	−0.345	−0.327	−0.311	−0.307	−0.308
	MKR		−0.344	0.428	0.450	0.223	−0.266	−0.313	−0.286
	PNK			−0.510	−0.447	−0.402	−0.398	−0.394	−0.360
	POLY			−0.335	−0.362	−0.326	−0.312	−0.294	−0.286
	REQ		−0.337	−0.287	−0.278	−0.269	−0.269	−0.262	−0.257
	RLC	−0.449	−0.350	−0.346	−0.342	−0.324	−0.313	−0.134	−0.078
	RPL		−0.391	−0.385	−0.372	−0.390	−0.480	−0.382	−0.359
	XYO		0.266	0.750	0.661	0.575	0.290	−0.144	−0.275
	ZRX		−0.245	−0.273	−0.268	−0.232	−0.218	−0.200	−0.186

Most platforms can be considered as disassortative, i.e. wallets tend to enter into transactions with wallets that have different characteristics in terms of the degree. Thus, high degree wallets interacted preferentially with low degree wallets and vice versa. The platforms of this group have a tendency of weakening their disassortative character towards the point of neutral mixing around a value of 0 with time. Around this value, wallets of different sizes interacted with each other evenly. The platforms were located in an interval of −0.38 to −0.04 with respect to their assortativity value. A stronger development starting from higher assortativity values could be observed in early phases of the platforms.

In the case of the assortative platforms, the wallets remained preferentially among their peers with regard to the examined property. That is, wallets with a high degree tend to transact with wallets that also have a high degree, and wallets with a low degree behave accordingly. The platform BNT could be identified as predominantly assortative.

The assortative character of this platform decreased during the development phases and fluctuated above the neutral mixing point. A clear trend in the development of assortativity could not be identified.

There were also platforms that cannot be described as neither assortative nor disassortative. These showed transitions from assortative and disassortative phases and thus fluctuate around the boundary of neutral mixing. Examples of such platforms are MKR and XYO.

Over the development phases a continuous development in the direction of a disassortative platform could be identified for XYO. For MKR, repeated transitions from assortative to disassortative phases could be observed. Altogether, a trend of the platforms towards a weakening disassortative behavior over the observed development phases could be identified for most of them.

4.3 Degree Distribution

The transaction participation of the network participants was examined using Gini coefficients of in- and out-degrees. In Table 5 the Gini coefficients for in-degrees and in Table 6 the Gini coefficients for out-degrees are shown.

The out-degrees have higher Gini coefficients compared to the in-degrees over all periods. Thus, they could be considered more concentrated. While a general increase

Table 5. Gini coefficients for in-degrees.

		Blocknumber (in Mio.)							
		4	5	6	7	8	9	10	10.4
Platforms	AGI		0.4365	0.4966	0.5554	0.5627	0.5718	0.5805	0.5823
	ANT	0.5047	0.4827	0.5062	0.5112	0.535	0.5596	0.5984	0.6262
	AST		0.497	0.5342	0.5608	0.5823	0.6027	0.61	0.6256
	BNT	0.617	0.7473	0.9212	0.9482	0.9612	0.9645	0.9661	0.9653
	DAT		0.5585	0.6618	0.6413	0.6457	0.649	0.6505	0.6508
	DNT		0.5091	0.5245	0.531	0.535	0.5485	0.5498	0.5502
	KNC		0.4835	0.5579	0.594	0.6574	0.6871	0.7398	0.7415
	LEND		0.1513	0.2743	0.2976	0.3097	0.3257	0.3826	0.4603
	MKR		0.571	0.8237	0.9002	0.902	0.889	0.8932	0.8898
	PNK			0.1009	0.2785	0.4456	0.5098	0.7474	0.783
	POLY			0.4041	0.4376	0.5123	0.5351	0.5525	0.5631
	REQ		0.4687	0.5213	0.5699	0.597	0.6123	0.625	0.6329
	RLC	0.5972	0.5704	0.6113	0.6318	0.6779	0.7271	0.7637	0.7655
	RPL		0.2629	0.4646	0.4899	0.4986	0.5779	0.6399	0.7796
	XYO			0.6489	0.6812	0.6876	0.6746	0.6693	0.6613
	ZRX		0.4365	0.4966	0.5554	0.5627	0.5718	0.5805	0.5823

Table 6. Gini coefficients for out-degrees.

		Blocknumber (in Mio.)							
		4	5	6	7	8	9	10	10.4
Platforms	AGI		0.8833	0.8569	0.7865	0.7807	0.777	0.7765	0.7776
	ANT	0.8265	0.7248	0.7092	0.7072	0.7204	0.7342	0.7517	0.7702
	AST		0.7422	0.7745	0.7662	0.7721	0.757	0.7586	0.7671
	BNT	0.9161	0.8656	0.956	0.97	0.9771	0.9777	0.9783	0.9781
	DAT		0.8986	0.8861	0.8876	0.8792	0.8775	0.8759	0.8751
	DNT		0.7813	0.763	0.7616	0.7592	0.7261	0.7248	0.7246
	KNC		0.8263	0.7974	0.8006	0.8215	0.835	0.8551	0.8513
	LEND		0.9856	0.9357	0.9272	0.9254	0.9217	0.9226	0.9195
	MKR		0.9053	0.9264	0.9415	0.9411	0.9218	0.9249	0.9234
	PNK			0.9946	0.9427	0.912	0.9036	0.9197	0.9161
	POLY			0.9144	0.9065	0.8946	0.8858	0.8831	0.8844
	REQ		0.8131	0.8166	0.8068	0.8105	0.818	0.8202	0.8231
	RLC	0.8161	0.7995	0.7893	0.7852	0.8029	0.8377	0.8563	0.8584
	RPL		0.938	0.8927	0.8816	0.8751	0.8884	0.8756	0.8991
	XYO			0.9654	0.9248	0.9101	0.9156	0.921	0.922
	ZRX		0.8833	0.8569	0.7865	0.7807	0.777	0.7765	0.7776

in concentrations could be identified for the in-degrees, a tendency towards weakening can be recognized in the concentration of out-degrees. Exceptions to this are the platforms AST, BNT, KNC, MKR and RLC, whose Gini coefficient of out-degrees increase continuously.

5 Discussion

This article analyzes the governance decentralization of platforms that are built on the Ethereum blockchain. The influence on governance decisions in this case is based on the number of native tokens owned. Therefore, the platforms were considered as networks and it was investigated whether participants control a large part of the networks in terms of number of tokens owned and participation in the transaction volume.

The Gini coefficient calculated for the distribution of tokens shows a value of more than 0.9 in almost all analyzed periods, indicating an excessively uneven concentration of tokens. Moreover, an increasing concentration over time can be recognized. This is similar to the behavior of Ethereum, which also shows an increase from 0.982 in 2015 to 0.998 in 2017 [39]. Since wallets are sometimes created for one-time use only and are not reused afterwards, entities with expression 0 were excluded from the calculations.

The Nakamoto coefficient is not susceptible to one-time use wallets that are empty or almost empty due to its construction. However, wallets with a particularly large number of tokens are strongly taken into account in this metric. The used relative index based on the Nakamoto coefficient does also not include empty wallets. Therefore, it can be used to compare the platforms with each other, as well as the development of the platforms over time. The Nakamoto coefficient shows an increase over time, which can be explained by wallets of the developers and early adopters who give up their initially held tokens over time. However, it cannot be excluded that individual wallets are divided into several smaller ones in order to disguise the volume of tokens. The platform AGI is particularly notable, where the Nakamoto coefficient initially decreases and then increases again. This may be caused by a consolidation to large wallets, where the tokens were distributed over several wallets during the initial distribution, which were later merged. Also a falling Nakamoto coefficient was observed, which indicates an accumulation of the platform tokens among a few network participants, e.g., on DAT.

In summary, all platforms show a strong concentration in the distribution of tokens and it can be assumed that this concentration comes from the initial token distribution, which only changes slowly.

The Gini coefficient of in- and out-degrees is above 0.5 in all periods and can thus the in- and out-degrees can be regarded as clearly concentrated. The out-degrees are clearly more concentrated than the in-degrees. Due to the strong concentration a "Preferential Attachment" can be seen, where new network participants first connect to the largest nodes [40]. The increasing concentration of in-degrees and the decreasing concentration of out-degrees over time can be equally accounted by the entry of new hubs, such as exchanges or smart contracts. While there is a further concentration of in-degrees in large hubs, the opposite occurs for out-degrees, where transactions are distributed from a few to more large hubs.

In case of assortativity most of the platforms can be regarded as disassortative or evolve from an assortative to a disassortative platform. For these platforms, a weakening of disassortativity over time could be observed. Early stages of development show many large hubs that are the center of the transaction volume. As the development of the platforms continues, new hubs appear, for example in the form of exchanges or smart contracts, through which the amount of disassortativity decreases. A quicker evolution of the assortativity value was observed for younger platforms. They started at a higher baseline value and declined more rapidly. This can be explained by the increased emergence of exchanges, which expand their offerings more quickly to new cryptocurrencies.

In addition to the disassortative platforms, BNT could be identified as an assortative platform. For example, the converters of BNT are a unique selling point of the platform. They are an interface in the form of smart contracts to exchange tokens from different platforms without the need for another party, with one converter for each pair of tokens to be exchanged [41]. This in turn results in a large number of small and medium-sized hubs rather than a few large ones as with other platforms.

The third group shows both assortative and disassortative phases. Similar to BNT, the assortative phases in MKR and XYO were caused by platform-native smart contracts. This effect was amplified by the absence of large centralized exchanges. Instead, there are smaller centralized exchanges and decentralized exchanges.

In summary, the transactional behavior of the platforms can largely be considered disassortative. In this way, it is similar to networks such as Ethereum [42] or the Internet [35], which can also be considered disassortative.

With regard to the question of how decentralized the governance of blockchain-based platforms is, it could be seen that the initial concentration of tokens is still predominant. The high concentration of incoming and outgoing transactions and the disassortative network behavior stand in the way of decentralization. However, decentralization can be seen over the development periods. Thus, the Gini coefficients of out-degrees are decreasing and the disassortative character of the platforms is weakening. Nevertheless, the Gini coefficients of the token distribution and the Nakamoto coefficient are increasing, which in turn does not indicate increasing decentralization. Consequently, it can be inferred that there is an uneven distribution among individual entities that can unduly influence decisions. This in turn implies that the decision rights of platforms cannot be considered as decentralized.

Despite the decentralized nature of the governance mechanisms of these platforms, the level of decentralization still depends on the real distribution of platform resources [24]. Over the development phases, developments toward decentralization have taken place in most platforms, but there have also been opposing developments toward centralization. This is in line with the approach of platform operators who initially start the governance of their platform centralized and switch later to decentralized forms of governance [7].

6   Conclusion and Outlook

In this study blockchain-based platforms, which use decentralized governance mechanisms, were analyzed whether or not their governance is truly decentralized. For this purpose, data of 16 blockchain-based platforms was collected and prepared. This data was analyzed in terms of the distribution of tokens as platform resources, transaction distribution and transaction behavior. By this, the resources of the analyzed platforms develops towards decentralization, but they cannot be considered decentralized yet.

While the data used is sufficient to answer the research questions of the beginning, one must be clear about its limitations. First, lost wallets could not be recognized and could therefore not be excluded from the analysis. Second, the splitting of single to several smaller wallets could also not be recognized, which also might have influenced the analysis of the token distribution. Third, the real ownership of tokens on centralized exchanges could not be seen in the data at hand, so it could not be taken into account. For further research, we suggest an in-depth analysis of the governance processes of the platforms, which can be analyzed once the governance modules on the platforms have been implemented and have a sufficient transaction volume for an analysis. More specifically, a detailed comparison of planned and actual applied governance of single platforms should be examined.

References

1. Swan, M.: Blockchain: Blueprint for a New Economy. O'Reilly Media, Inc., Sebastopol (2015)

2. Friedlmaier, M., Tumasjan, A., Welpe, I.M.: Disrupting industries with blockchain: the industry, venture capital funding, and regional distribution of blockchain ventures. In: Proceedings of the 52nd Annual Hawaii International Conference on System Sciences (2019)
3. Salviotti, G., De Rossi, L.M., Abbatemarco, N.: A structured framework to assess the business application landscape of blockchain technologies. In: Proceedings of the 51st Hawaii International Conference on System Sciences (2018)
4. Morabito, V.: Business Innovation Through Blockchain. The B3 Perspective. Springer International Publishing, Cham (2017)
5. PWC: Time For Trust: How blockchain will transform business and the economy. https://www.pwc.com/gx/en/industries/technology/publications/blockchain-report-transform-business-economy.html
6. Fridgen, G., Radszuwill, S., Urbach, N., Utz, L.: Cross-organizational workflow management using blockchain technology-towards applicability, auditability, and automation. In: Proceedings of the 51st Hawaii International Conference on System Sciences (2018)
7. Beck, R., Müller-Bloch, C., King, J.L.: Governance in the blockchain economy: a framework and research agenda. JAIS 1020–1034 (2018). https://doi.org/10.17705/1jais.00518
8. Bodó, B., Giannopoulou, A.: The logics of technology decentralization – the case of distributed ledger technologies. In: Blockchain and Web 3.0. Social, Economic, and Technological Challenges. Routledge Studies in Science, Technology and Society, pp. 114–129. Routledge, London (2020). https://doi.org/10.4324/9780429029530-8
9. Kannengießer, N., Lins, S., Dehling, T., Sunyaev, A.: What does not fit can be made to fit! Trade-Offs in distributed ledger technology designs. In: Proceedings of the 52nd Annual Hawaii International Conference on System Sciences (2019)
10. Zheng, Z., Xie, S., Dai, H.-N., Chen, X., Wang, H.: Blockchain challenges and opportunities: a survey. Int. J. Web Grid Serv. **14**, 352–375 (2018)
11. Buterin, V.: A next-generation smart contract and decentralized application platform (2014)
12. Luu, L., Chu, D.-H., Olickel, H., Saxena, P., Hobor, A.: Making smart contracts smarter. In: Katzenbeisser, S., Weippl, E. (eds.) Proceedings of the 2016 ACM SIGSAC Conference on Computer and Communications Security. CCS 2016, 24–28 October 2016, Vienna, Austria, pp. 254–269. Association for Computing Machinery, New York, NY (2016)
13. Antonopoulos, A.M., Wood, G.A.: Mastering Ethereum. Building Smart Contracts and DApps. O'Reilly Media, Inc., Sebastopol (2018)
14. Oliveira, L., Zavolokina, L., Bauer, I., Schwabe, G.: To token or not to token: tools for understanding blockchain tokens. In: Pries-Heje, J., Ram, S., Rosemann, M. (eds.) Proceedings of the International Conference on Information Systems - Bridging the Internet of People, Data, and Things. ICIS 2018. Association for Information Systems (2018). https://doi.org/10.5167/UZH-157908
15. Muth, R., Tschorsch, F.: Empirical analysis of on-chain voting with smart contracts. In: Bernhard, M., et al. (eds.) FC 2021. LNCS, vol. 12676, pp. 397–412. Springer, Heidelberg (2021). https://doi.org/10.1007/978-3-662-63958-0_32
16. Lin, Q., Li, C., Zhao, X., Chen, X.: Measuring decentralization in bitcoin and ethereum using multiple metrics and granularities. In: 2021 IEEE 37th International Conference on Data Engineering Workshops (ICDEW), pp. 80–87. IEEE (2021). https://doi.org/10.1109/ICDEW53142.2021.00022
17. Victor, F., Lüders, B.K.: Measuring ethereum-based erc20 token networks. In: Goldberg, I., Moore, T. (eds.) Financial Cryptography and Data Security. FC 2019. LNCS, vol. 11598, pp. 113–129. Springer, Cham (2019). https://doi.org/10.1007/978-3-030-32101-7_8
18. Chen, W., Zhang, T., Chen, Z., Zheng, Z., Lu, Y.: Traveling the token world: A graph analysis of Ethereum ERC20 token ecosystem. In: Proceedings of The Web Conference 2020, pp. 1411–1421 (2020). https://doi.org/10.1145/3366423.3380215

19. Ølnes, S., Ubacht, J., Janssen, M.: Blockchain in government: benefits and implications of distributed ledger technology for information sharing. Gov. Inf. Q. **34**, 355–364 (2017). https://doi.org/10.1016/j.giq.2017.09.007
20. Miscione, G., Ziolkowski, R., Zavolokina, L., Schwabe, G.: Tribal governance: the business of blockchain authentication. In: Proceedings of the 51st Hawaii International Conference on System Sciences (2018)
21. Ziolkowski, R., Miscione, G., Schwabe, G.: Consensus through blockchains: exploring governance across inter-organizational Settings. In: Pries-Heje, J., Ram, S., Rosemann, M. (eds.) Proceedings of the International Conference on Information Systems - Bridging the Internet of People, Data, and Things. ICIS 2018. Association for Information Systems (2018)
22. van Pelt, R., Jansen, S., Baars, D., Overbeek, S.: Defining blockchain governance: a framework for analysis and comparison. Inf. Syst. Manag. **38**, 21–41 (2021). https://doi.org/10.1080/105 80530.2020.1720046
23. Werner, J., Frost, S., Zarnekow, R.: Towards a taxonomy for governance mechanisms of blockchain-based platforms. In: Rowe, F., et al. (eds.) 28th European Conference on Information Systems - Liberty, Equality, and Fraternity in a Digitizing World. ECIS 2020 (2020)
24. Werner, J., Zarnekow, R.: Governance of blockchain-based platforms. In: Gronau, N., Heine, M., Poustcchi, K., Krasnova, H. (eds.) WI2020. Band 1: Proceedings der 15. Internationalen Tagung Wirtschaftsinformatik 2020, pp. 128–141. GITO Verlag (2020). https://doi.org/10.30844/wi_2020_b1-werner
25. Tiwana, A., Konsynski, B., Bush, A.A.: Research commentary–platform evolution. Coevolution of platform architecture, governance, and environmental dynamics. Inf. Syst. Res. **21**, 675–687 (2010). https://doi.org/10.1287/isre.1100.0323
26. MakerDAO: MakerDAO Documentation (2021). https://docs.makerdao.com/
27. Christodoulou, P., Christodoulou, K.: A decentralized voting mechanism: engaging ERC-20 token holders in decision-making. In: 2020 Seventh International Conference on Software Defined Systems (SDS), pp. 160–164. IEEE (2020). https://doi.org/10.1109/SDS49854.2020.9143877
28. Hsieh, Y.-Y., Vergne, J.-P.J.P., Wang, S.: The internal and external governance of blockchain-based organizations: evidence from cryptocurrencies. In: Campbell-Verduyn, M. (ed.) Bitcoin and beyond. Cryptocurrencies, blockchains, and global governance. RIPE series in global political economy, pp. 48–68. Routledge, London, New York (2018)
29. GitHub: ethereum-etl (2021). https://github.com/blockchain-etl/ethereum-etl
30. Medvedev, E., Day, A.: Ethereum in BigQuery: how we built this dataset (2018). https://cloud.google.com/blog/products/data-analytics/ethereum-bigquery-how-we-built-dataset
31. GitHub: ethereum-etl-airflow (2021). https://github.com/blockchain-etl/ethereum-etl-airflow
32. Etherscan: Ethereum (ETH) Blockchain Explorer (2021). https://etherscan.io/
33. Bloxy: Bloxy (2021). https://bloxy.info/
34. Newman, M.E.J.: Networks. An introduction. Oxford University Press, Oxford (2010)
35. Newman, M.E.J.: Assortative mixing in networks. Phys. Rev. Lett. **89**, 208701 (2002).https://doi.org/10.1103/PhysRevLett.89.208701
36. Srinivasan, B.S.: Quantifying Decentralization (2017). https://news.earn.com/quantifying-decentralization-e39db233c28e
37. Fahrmeir, L., Heumann, C., Künstler, R., Pigeot, I., Tutz, G.: Statistik. Der Weg zur Datenanalyse. Springer Spektrum, Berlin, Heidelberg (2016)
38. Mittag, H.-J., Schüller, K.: Statsunistik. Eine Einführung mit interaktiven Elementen. Springer, Berlin, Heidelberg (2020). ; Imprint: Springer Spektrum, Berlin, Heidelberg
39. Bai, Q., Zhang, C., Xu, Y., Chen, X., Wang, X.: Evolution of Ethereum: A Temporal Graph Perspective (2020)

40. Albert, R., Barabási, A.-L.: Statistical mechanics of complex networks. Rev. Mod. Phys. **74**, 47–97 (2002). https://doi.org/10.1103/RevModPhys.74.47

41. Hertzog, E., Benartzi, G., Benartzi, G.: Bancor protocol. Continuous liquidity for cryptographic tokens through their smart contracts (2018). https://website-bancor.storage.google apis.com/2018/04/01ba8253-bancor_protocol_whitepaper_en.pdf

42. Liang, J., Li, L., Zeng, D.: Evolutionary dynamics of cryptocurrency transaction networks: an empirical study. PLoS ONE **13**, e0202202 (2018). https://doi.org/10.1371/journal.pone. 0202202

Using a Hybrid Approach of Game Design, Blockchain Technology and Learning Analytics in Higher Education Institutions: A Case Study of the British University in Dubai

Khaled Al Shehhi[(✉)] and Khalid Almarri

The British University in Dubai, Dubai, UAE
khaled.almarri@buid.ac.ae

Abstract. The Learning Management System (LMS) tries to resolve the multiple challenges that occur due to limits of time, location, and frequency of teacher-student interactions. As a tool in the e- learning process, the LMS provides several benefits that can help overcome problems that often occur during the learning process.

However, the current deployment of LMS as a learning medium still has its limitations such as low engagement and motivation, secure documents, certification, and exam verification to replace a cumbersome manual process, and ultimately personalization of features that relevant to students' requirements. Recently, some new technologies developed as recent trends to tackle the various difficulties and challenges relevant to these issues and obstacles. In this sense, the Gamification design boosted users' interaction and engagement with the online system by adding a new game concept. Similarly, blockchain technology improves the security of online document exchange, verification, and storage. Ultimately, learning analytics demonstrated to allow the personalization of online platforms based on interactions and data logs. In this work, we studied how combining these strategies might boost the LMS performance and tackle existing issues and problems.

To do that, we employed a design science methodology as a rigor innovation strategy in digital innovation. The results reveal encouraging results of the new systems (LMSD) implementation in Dubai's British university.

Keywords: LMS · e-learning · Gamification · Blockchain · Learning analytics · Innovation

1 Introduction

There is no one disputing that technology plays a big influence in transforming the overall terrain in education. In this digital era, the use of online learning has expanded substantially and become more widespread over the Covid-19 epidemic, displacing the classroom (face to face environment) (face to face setting). Hence, educators should provide students excellent teaching techniques that inspire them to appropriately engage and learn important knowledge (Ulfa and Fatawi 2021; Mestan 2019). Numerous reports,

© Springer Nature Switzerland AG 2022
M. Themistocleous and M. Papadaki (Eds.): EMCIS 2021, LNBIP 437, pp. 180–193, 2022.
https://doi.org/10.1007/978-3-030-95947-0_13

expert opinions, and scholarly findings demonstrate, however, that online learning in its various forms and methods currently faces difficulties and obstacles related to trying to incorporate versatility, encouraging engagement, assisting students with their learning processes, and promoting an attitude-based learning environment (Bruggeman et al. 2019).

The United Arab Emirates' Ministry of Education has acknowledged the critical role of ICT in enhancing the teaching and learning process. Leading higher education institutions in the UAE, such as the University of Fujairah and the British University in Dubai, have begun integrating ICT into their educational systems through a blended approach that incorporates different ICT resources into the learning process. Blackboard and Moodle are two examples of successful learning management systems that optimize the learning process (Salloum et al. 2018).

2 Practical Problem

The Like academic findings, the application of e-learning systems in their current forms shows three major problems: low engagement of the students, security, integrity of documents and exams, and systems adaptation to students' needs and persona. Following the design science approach and it is deployment in innovating process, product, and service -as suggested by Hevner et al. (2019), the problem explicated in details as in Table 1.

Table 1. Problem explication

Problem	Explanation	Current solutions
Low engagement of the students	Students are now detached to different degrees, ranging from 25% to more than half. The classes and resources soon bore them. One of the established reasons is their "engrossment in technology."	Psychological Engagement techniques, variety of video and multimedia, and Forums
Security and integrity of documents and exams	Academic transcripts are one of the most time-consuming and labor-intensive processes in higher education. Each entrance must be personally verified consistently before a certified transcript of a student's grades can be published Online exams and students' identity is a cumbersome issue in online learning	Manual verification of documents and personal assurance of exam process integrity

(*continued*)

Table 1. (*continued*)

Problem	Explanation	Current solutions
Systems adaptation to students' needs and persona	The students differ in their requirements when interacting with the online system. Personalizing their profiles to adapt the current system to their actual needs is required	Collecting traditional data regarding students (such as gender, race, age) but does not give the institution a real understanding of who the people are behind the numbers

3 Literature Review

3.1 E-Learning Systems

The debate on the definition and application of e-learning concentrates on the intersection of education, teaching, and learning with ICT. It is unquestionably guided by two other disciplines: education technology and distance learning. Both have made a significant contribution to the intensified use of ICT for academic purposes, but none of it can be exclusively compared to e-learning (Sangrà et al. 2012). We adopt the three definitions found in Kumar Basak et al. (2018: 192) as follows:

1- E-learning is "the learning supported by digital electronic tools and media".
2- M-learning is the "e-learning using mobile devices and wireless transmission".
3- "Digital learning is any type of learning that is facilitated by technology or by instructional practice that makes effective use of technology," and it occurs in all learning areas and domains.

However, as full description of learning management systems was found in Ulfa and Fatawi (2021) as follows:

4- A learning management system (LMS) is a learning tool for conducting an instructional program in an online learning environment that mimics conventional classroom learning practices. Synchronous and asynchronous communication mechanisms, management features, and evaluation functions are all part of an LMS. These functions make it more comfortable for the instructor to arrange the course. As a result, an LMS can be described as a learning setting that empowers both students and teachers to participate in personalized learning.

3.2 Gamification (Game Design)

Gamification is characterized as "the use of game-based mechanics, aesthetics, and game thinking to engage people, inspire action, encourage learning, and solve problems" (Kapp 2012). In essence, gamification applies game thinking, methods, and components in a non-game sense and formal and informal contexts, using gameplay mechanics, which increases motivation and engagement (Kiryakova et al. 2014).

Empirical studies show that Gamification tools are being used to promote learning in a wide range of educational environments and academic subjects and resolve cross-cutting attitudes and behaviors like teamwork, imagination, and self-guided learning (Caponetto et al. 2014). Figure 1 shows the elements used in gamification to support the e-learning processes.

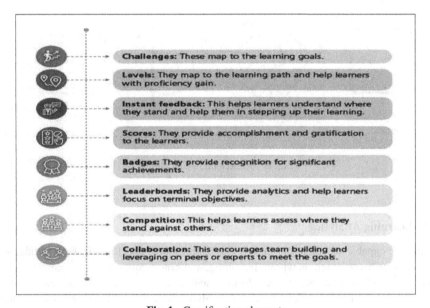

Fig. 1. Gamification elements

3.3 Blockchain Technology

Blockchain, according to Tapscott and Tapscott (2017), is the Internet's second generation. The first-generation stressed interaction and teamwork, but it was created for transferring and storing information rather than meaning. It provides a stable database where one can store important information (such as money accounts, transcripts, and certificates), and having confidence embedded into the technology can help reshape higher education and provide different learning models.

Furthermore, the technology could ensure that the student who enrolled in the course finished it and understood the material. It may include a payment option and enable students to build smart contracts to establish long-term learning strategies. For instance, the university's course materials may contain an enormous number of pages at the university level. Each page should be manually checked and approved for each student who requires this document (to ensure accuracy). However, if this information is stored on a blockchain, an individual might receive a complete, validated record of content courses and academic qualifications only with a few clicks. Figure 2 shows how the process is accomplished.

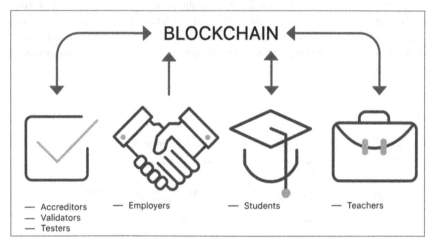

Fig. 2. Blockchain in education

3.4 Learning Analytics

LMSs are capable of collecting and storing activity data and logs. It tracks students' engagement habits, such as where, how long, and how frequently they access various resources, such as content, quizzes, forums, and other tools. Each online learner will produce their own, unique data. Learning Analytics (LA) is a software application that pulls data from a huge volume of log data generated by a learning management system (LMS) (Aldowah et al. 2019).

Learning analytics is used to enhance learning by addressing matters that occur during the education process. A data-driven approach is characterized as the use of data to decide the best plan and objectives (Ulfa and Fatawi 2021). According to Jagadish et al. (2014), a data-driven approach can address a multitude of challenges. The use of LA can help build a more personalized, adaptive, and engaging learning environment, enhancing teaching and learning effectiveness and teachers' and students' output. Figure 3 illustrates the learning analytics types in aggregate form.

4   Innovation Approach

This We use a design science method to create our new artifact in order to address the explicated challenge in this work. According to Peffers et al. (2007), the solution's

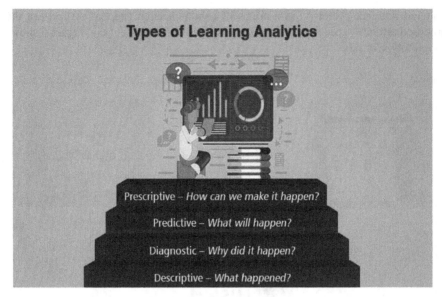

Fig. 3. Learning analytics types

objectives are formed from the established issue and knowledge of what is achievable and practical. The aim might be quantified in terms of how the current solution is superior to the prior one or qualitatively in terms of how the new artifact is intended to aid in the exploration of a solution to an unresolved challenge. Figure 4 depicts the stages of the invention process.

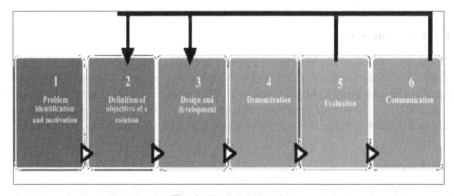

Fig. 4. Design approach

4.1 Design and Development

This stage involves the creation of the artifact, based on problem identification and objective of the design. The ultimate aim of this iteration is to construct a human-centered interface prototype as a means of communication and explore and test the proposed artifacts' specifications and suggestions from real-life users. Figure 5 shows the prototype design.

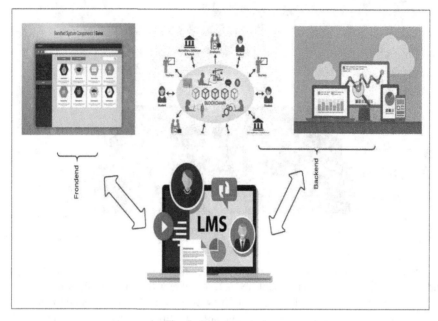

Fig. 5. Prototype design

4.2 Demonstration

We created a proof-of-concept software prototype (called LMSD) mobile advertisement platform to obtain feedback and further develop the prototype to demonstrate the proposed artifact in solving highlighted problems. The prototype is a working model (Walker et al. 2002) and the system's first version before it is released. The demonstration phase included three stakeholders of the software, namely students, employees, and teachers.

4.3 Evaluation

Further to the development and refinement phase, verify that the application meets the study objectives and that the prototype is valuable in contributing to measurements and producing satisfactory results.

5 Findings and Analysis

The system's overall evaluation shows positive responses from the three parties involved in the evaluation process. The involved participants were asked to evaluate their perceived usefulness from the system from 1 to 5. Table 2 shows the results of this analysis.

Table 2. LMSD overall evaluation

Stakeholder	N	Mean	Std. Deviation
Students	20	4.2000	.83666
Employees	8	4.4000	.89443
Teachers	8	4.0000	.70711

Furthermore, a set of criteria found in related systems development have been used to confirm the usefulness of LMSD. Table 3 illustrates these criteria and the corresponding descriptive statistics.

Table 3. Overall evaluation criteria of LMSD

Criteria	N	Mean	Std. Deviation
Usefulness to your personal needs	36	4.2222	.66667
Relevancy and convenience	36	4.5556	.72648
Ease of use	36	4.6667	.50000
Utility in term of feedback provided and incentives	36	4.3333	.70711
Privacy concern	36	4.6667	.70711
Not annoying	36	4.7778	.44096
Comprehensiveness	36	3.8889	.60093
Applicability	36	4.5556	.52705

These measurements have reverberated in participants' comments; one of them stated;

"It is not annoying; it saves my time and effort to search a material and make a purchase decision."

Another participant commented;

"It has a great incentive, and who will not be pleased to receive these incentives on a daily basis? Besides, it is secure and protects my privacy and documents."

The descriptive statistics revealed that the students are happy with the gamification elements. However, these elements are ranked according to their priorities and desires of the students. Some features have been discarded in the final version of the system based on students' feedback. Capture from the analysis is shown in Fig. 6.

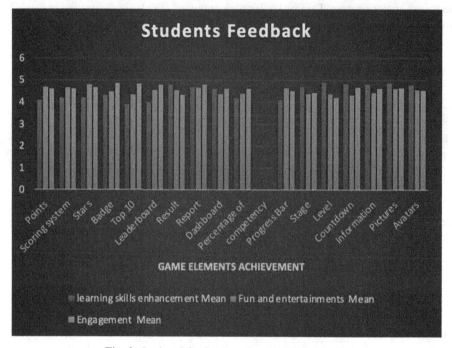

Fig. 6. Students' feedback on Gamification elements

With regard to blockchain, the evaluation was reflected encouraging results. All our participants were very interested in the new options added to the system. Their assessment of the three new options is shown in Table 4.

Table 4. Blockchain features evaluations

Blockchain Features	Students	Employees	Teachers
Payment	4.5	4.8	4.5
Certificate issuance	4.8	4.9	4.6
Exam's security	4.2	4.1	4.9

Despite their good comments, an in-depth chat with them revealed a need for further functionality to be introduced to the system. In this regard, several members of the university's IT department recommended adopting blockchain-based cloud storage to free up storage space on the university's servers. Additionally, professors and some postgraduate students demonstrated that blockchain security might be utilized to guard against piracy of unpublished material. All of these features were incorporated into the system's final version.

Finally, the evaluation of learning analytics choices revealed a high level of acceptability among participants. Following numerous focus group meetings that included a quick presentation and lengthy conversation, feedback shows widespread interest, particularly among students and instructors.

Students and instructors were intrigued by the possibility of enhancing learning outcomes through LA review. How can students' performance be improved, or how can instructors be motivated to tailor a learning plan and appropriate instructional materials to students' needs and personas? In this example, stakeholders employ LA as an analytical technique to aid in policy development by identifying student inadequacies or learning requirements in online learning. The evaluation of the three stakeholders is depicted in Fig. 7.

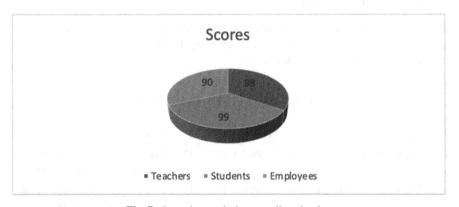

Fig. 7. Learning analytics overall evaluation

6 Case Study: LMSD Deployment in the British University in Dubai

The implementation process starts after the innovation proposal has been successfully delivered to the potential stakeholders and went through several iterations. This is the transition from a conventional e-learning system to a new LMSD system. Continuous improvement extends the life of creativity until the next product substitutes it.

6.1 Final LMSD System

The new system incorporated all inputs from the participants. The final LMSD is an e-learning system containing all the traditional features of LMS such as Module and Blackboard and Gamification elements that support engagement and motivation, blockchain technology to provide more security to resources, and learning analytics to adapt to students' requirements.

Features of the new system.

1- It makes learning more enjoyable and engaging.
2- It allows students to see how real-world technologies are used.
3- It provides Real-time feedback.
4- It Improves the learning environment.
5- It Speeds up information retrieval.
6- It provides a more secure system.
7- It Replaces manual verification and issuance.
8- It has an effective storage.
9- It has a Personalization.
10- Cost-effectiveness.

6.2 Cost of Implementation

In this section, we present the cost-benefit analysis. The analysis shows myriad benefits that justify the cost of implementation and adopting the new system. Table 5 illustrates this analysis in numbers and added values.

Table 5. LMSD cost and benefits analysis

7	Resources	8	Cost	9	Benefits
10	Gamification system	11	50000 AED	12	Students' retention, effective teaching, more engagements
13	Blockchain technology	14	100000 AED	15	Effective and secure file storage, remove cumbersome manual tasks
16	Learning analytics	17	750000 AED	18	Personalization of the systems. Increased student retention, effective resource allocation

6.3 Other Required Resources

In order to implement the LMSD system, other supportive resources were utilized; Table 6 shows these resources and their related costs.

The numbers showed a significant return on investment (ROI). The current project's actual cost is within the estimated cost limit, and the deployment of the system offers an enhanced overall learning process and higher students retention rate. These results justify all related costs and efforts.

Table 6. LMSD supportive resources associated costs

19	Resources	20	Cost
21	System Training	22	100000 AED
23	New infrastructure	24	200000 AED
25	Programmers	26	20000 AED/month

6.4 Challenges of Implementation

As with any new digital innovation project, this project faces relatively minor challenges compared to others as this system used a combination of pull and push strategy for development. Using a customer-oriented approach and open innovation strategies has increased the new technology resistance from final users. However, a few challenges are listed as follows:

1- The low self-efficacy of some users is a normal issue in deploying new technology.
2- Employee's resistant to accept new technology as they think it will replace their roles.
3- Some system errors prevent participants from completing some tasks.
4- Low trust in technology from some teachers to store their sensitive material in the system.

6.5 Post-implementation Phase

At this stage, all challenges and hurdles are treated in professional ways using the best practice available. To avoid the obstacles in the implementation stages a regular meetings and training sessions were held. The main aim is to permeate how the new system will provide value for all university members and not threaten employees' traditional roles. Additionally, low self-efficacy and trust were handled by professional trainers.

In order to assess the post-implementation Ex post evaluation was used. Ex post assessment is a method of determining a system's value after it has been applied using both financial and non-financial criteria. Ex post assessment methods in information systems can be drawn from a crucial application of the "context, information, and method" model built for assessing organizational change (Venable et al. 2016).

Post-implementation is a crucial phase in innovation that is taken to not rely on first success and become complacent and futile. According to this phase, the system was reinvigorated, and new features were added. For instance, the gamification elements were not standard to all students, and the need to personalize them is in urgent demand. As such, a new feature was added, which is called gamification behavioral analytics. This feature is vital to increase the efficiency of the system.

7 Conclusion

Modern technologies such as gamification, blockchain, and learning analytics have demonstrated their viability in a variety of sectors, one of which is education. We integrated these new technologies into LMS systems in this study to address fundamental issues and obstacles that impede the learning process directly and indirectly. In terms of gamification design, the application increased students' interest and motivation significantly. Additionally, blockchain technology has demonstrated its efficacy in protecting the transmission and storage of digital information. Additionally, several new services, such as payment and cloud-based blockchain storage, have been introduced depending on potential customers' pull approach. Finally, learning analytics plays a significant role in evaluating students' data logs in order to tailor and adjust the features of LMS systems. Additionally, after multiple revisions, the gamification design was evaluated and its features customized depending on student engagement using learning analytics concepts. Overall, the final LMSD system was introduced, and as a fundamental concept of controlling the innovation process, constant assessment is used to make any necessary adjustments. Although some employees and students expressed modest opposition to the method, this resistance was overcome via the provision of essential training and encouragement. The system's early adoption demonstrates a high return on investment and a plethora of benefits that surpass the system's development and deployment expenses.

References

Aldowah, H., Al-Samarraie, H., Fauzy, W.M.: Educational data mining and learning analytics for 21st century higher education: a review and synthesis. Telematics Inform. **37**, 13–49 (2019)

Bruggeman, B., Tondeur, J., Struyven, K., Pynoo, B., Garone, A., Vanslambrouck, S.: Experts speaking: Crucial teacher attributes for implementing blended learning in higher education. Internet High. Educ. **48**, 100772 (2021)

Caponetto, I., Earp, J., Ott, M.: Gamification and education: a literature review. In: European Conference on Games Based Learning, vol. 1, p. 50. Academic Conferences International Limited (October 2014)

Hevner, A., vom Brocke, J., Maedche, A.: Roles of digital innovation in design science research. Bus. Inf. Syst. Eng. **61**(1), 3–8 (2019)

Jagadish, H.V., et al.: Big data and its technical challenges. Commun. ACM **57**, 86–94 (2014)

Kapp, K.M.: The Gamification of Learning And Instruction: Game-Based Methods And Strategies for Training and Education. John Wiley & Sons, Hoboken (2012)

Kiryakova, G., Angelova, N., Yordanova, L.: Gamification in education. In: Proceedings of 9th International Balkan Education and Science Conference (2014)

Kumar Basak, S., Wotto, M., Belanger, P.: E-learning, M-learning and D-learning: conceptual definition and comparative analysis. E-Learn. Digit. Media **15**, 191–216 (2018)

Mestan, K.: Create a fine blend: an examination of institutional transition to blended learning. Australas. J. Educ. Technol. **35** (2019)

Peffers, K., Tuunanen, T., Rothenberger, M.A., Chatterjee, S.: A design science research methodology for information systems research. J. Manag. Inf. Syst. **24**, 45–77 (2007)

Salloum, S.A., Al-Emran, M., Shaalan, K., Tarhini, A.: Factors affecting the E-learning acceptance: a case study from UAE. Educ. Inf. Technol. **24**(1), 509–530 (2018). https://doi.org/10.1007/s10639-018-9786-3

Sangrà, A., Vlachopoulos, D., Cabrera, N.: Building an inclusive definition of E-learning: an approach to the conceptual framework. Int. Rev. Res. Open Distrib. Learn. **13**, 145–159 (2012)

Tapscott, D., Tapscott, A.: How blockchain will change organizations. MIT Sloan Manag. Rev. **58**, 10 (2017)

Ulfa, S., Fatawi, I.: Predicting factors that influence students' learning outcomes using learning analytics in online learning environment. Int. J. Emerg. Technol. Learn. (ijet) **16**, 4–17 (2021)

Venable, J., Pries-Heje, J., Baskerville, R.: FEDS: a framework for evaluation in design science research. Eur. J. Inf. Syst. **25**, 77–89 (2016)

Walker, M., Takayama, L., Landay, J.A.: High-fidelity or low-fidelity, paper or computer? Choosing attributes when testing web prototypes. In: Proceedings of the Human Factors and Ergonomics Society Annual Meeting, 2002, pp. 661–665. SAGE Publications Sage CA, Los Angeles, CA (2002)

Blockchain Technology and Waste Management: A Systematic Literature Review

Irénée Dondjio$^{(\boxtimes)}$ and Marinos Themistocleous

University of Nicosia, Nicosia, Cyprus
{dondjio.i,themistocleous.m}@unic.ac.cy

Abstract. Population growth and increased trash generation are expected to worsen living conditions in LCDs. However, waste management organizations have been hindered by a lack of stakeholder participation and coordination as well as obsolete disposal methods. By automating the collection and transportation of rubbish, current technology only aids to reducing human participation. People could be more engaged in waste management activities if they were remunerated for it. The enabling system should automatically record significant activities and respond appropriately. The blockchain technology could be the solution as it may help waste management by increasing public knowledge, transparency, and stakeholder confidence. This study looks at how the blockchain technology could improve waste management by increasing public awareness, transparency, and trust among stakeholders. By ensuring immutability using a cryptographically secure distributed ledger system, blockchain links people, processes, and technical developments. Through a systematic literature review on blockchain technology deployment in waste management, this research seeks to add to the content of previous studies and to enlighten the path for future studies. Furthermore, the study's findings will help addressing research gaps on using new technology to conserve the environment. They would also help authorities and politicians to raise awareness and involve stakeholders in social issues.

Keywords: Blockchain · Waste management · Incentive models · LDC's

1   Introduction and Research Problem

Despite the growing worry over pollution's effects on the globe, waste production and use, continue to expand due to their many applications today. For example, the increased usage of plastics nowadays is attributed to their durability, lightweight, strength, affordability, and corrosion resistance (Babayemi et al. 2019). But, due to their inability to degrade, the increasing use of plastics has a severe impact on worldwide waste management practices, as well as endangering the entire ecosystem.

From early separation to ultimate disposal, waste management requires multiple processes. Authorities need to understand these phases to identify problem areas and implement solutions. Waste management organizations in LDCs cannot track these processes due to the huge data volumes and diversity of procedures involved in disposal (Taylor

© Springer Nature Switzerland AG 2022
M. Themistocleous and M. Papadaki (Eds.): EMCIS 2021, LNBIP 437, pp. 194–212, 2022.
https://doi.org/10.1007/978-3-030-95947-0_14

et al. 2020a, b). Growing populations in LDCs will increase waste generation and data management requirements, making this a challenge that will only worsen in the future. Waste management is a complicated matter, where the involvement of all relevant stakeholders can play a crucial role in supporting policymakers in defining an effective and long-running waste management plan at the local level. Ongena et al. (2018) argued that the current waste management systems in most developing countries are, characterized by poor reward systems encompassing a lack of transparency, trust, and sustainability, the corrupt collaboration between governments and companies involved in waste handling, and ignorance among citizens about waste handling. Blockchain may alleviate this problem by providing a single platform for waste management professionals to log all activities. By doing so, governments may use the technology to stimulate stakeholder engagement in garbage collection and environmental protection. A fundamental feature of the blockchain is its ability to engage and inspire users via "reward-token" characteristics such as social engagement and competition (Christodoulou et al. 2022; Cunha et al. 2021). There are different waste disposal procedures, but companies must choose the more appropriate method to use depending on the kind of waste. To lessen their environmental effect, waste management organizations should, for example, dispose of hazardous trash in landfills and recycle plastics. To identify an ideal waste eradication approach, these bodies need accurate information concerning waste management issues, practices, facilities, legislation, and monitoring. In some instances, this information might be inaccurate due to human error. There is a need for individuals to employ evidence-based research in making decisions to reduce the costs of ineffective policies. In this regard, a blockchain-based technology will ensure the waste management body's access accurate data by eliminating the possibility of human errors, thereby facilitating appropriate decision-making (Soja et al. 2020).

The study will fill these gaps by delivering accurate and timely data to stakeholders. Due to the huge data quantity associated with solid waste creation, stakeholders are now having difficulty following the system's phases (Taylor et al. 2020a, b). Besides, the complex waste management supply chain magnifies the problem further because it hinders the development of comprehensive garbage management initiatives. Therefore, there is a need for platforms that facilitates the tracking of all activities associated with waste disposal to facilitate the management of garbage issues. Because traditional technologies such as Artificial Intelligence (AI) and the Internet of things (IoT) do not provide an adequate level of transparency and cooperation among many groups, municipalities may improve the efficiency of their waste management operations by implementing blockchain as a tamper-proof solution. According to Gopalakrishnan et al. (2020), the blockchain not only has the potential to connect the appropriate parties in order to foster cooperation and information exchange, but it will also provide stakeholders with a decentralized channel that promotes traceability and trust along the entire waste management supply chain.

The study results will positively impact the political landscape because they will offer policymakers with information to guide their approach toward waste management. For instance, some policymakers could be unaware of the direct impacts of improper waste management initiatives on the local economy. Hence, they might be reluctant to prioritize proper garbage disposal incentives when developing regulations. The study will inform this audience because the researcher will gather information regarding the impacts of waste management practices on job creation, changes in property taxes, and the relationship between change in property value and unemployment. The blockchain management technology can provide policymakers with the capacity to manage waste disposal efficiently and transparently to achieve sustainability.

Based on the aforementioned study gaps, this article aims "*To investigate the adoption of the blockchain technology in the waste management sector.*" *The paper is organized as follows: Sect. 2 highlights related studies on the use of blockchain in waste management. Section 3 presents the methodology of the systematic approach. Section 4 displays the key findings while Sect. 5 presents the conclusion, discussion and further work.*

2   Literature Review

The researcher applies a systematic literature review as it aims to proliferate the acceptance of the trend toward innovative systems and identify the main research trends and gaps (Casino et al. 2019, p. 77). Furthermore, the research is based on the understanding of different variables, such as people and technology. Also, the issues related to a blockchain solution and the prerequisite for integration in the solid waste sector will be elucidated and the drawback of the existing solutions will be identified and suggestions will be advised.

2.1   Waste Management and Its Impacts on Nature and human's Health

Waste management refers to the many waste management and disposal systems. They may be controlled, reused, recycled, processed, destroyed or discarded. The primary goal of waste management is to minimise the quantity of material that cannot be used and to prevent environmental and health risks (Kassou et al. 2021).

The "collecting, monitoring, regulation and disposal" operations encompass several activities. Waste collection services are often offered free of charge by the municipal authorities (Gopalakrishnan and Ramaguru 2019). The trash gathered is disposed of by several ways, e.g. via settlement and incineration. In particular, solid waste is burned in order to decrease its volume by 80 to 95 percent and transform it into gas, steam, ash and heat. Air pollution is, however, a problem when trash is disposed of via incineration (Ongena et al. 2018).

Other methods, such as reuse, reprocessing and recycling, are thus promoted. Organic waste, in particular those that are biodegradable, may be degraded so that they may be utilised in agriculture as mulch or compost and the biodegradable methane gas collected and used as a source of power and heat. Liquid waste such as wastewater is subjected to treatment that may be disposed of via trash disposal, composting and incineration (Gopalakrishnan and Ramaguru 2019).

Governments worldwide recognize the negative impacts of the accumulation of plastic wastes on the planet, but their efforts to mitigate these challenges have been futile. Among the challenges that management organizations face in their efforts to control plastic wastes are the exercise's unprofitability and technological challenges associated with eliminating the pollutants (Idumah and Nwuzor 2019). Plastic waste management has gradually become a sensitive issue because the materials are not just hazardous to society. They also have an essential role in people's lives. Hence, the demand for plastics encourages the quest for the products, which appears to overwhelm existing waste management efforts, resulting in the accumulation of pollutants on the planet.

2.2 Obstacles of Current Waste Management Practices

Numerous cities in LDC's are unable to implement sound waste management owing to a variety of factors, including institutional, financial, technological, regulatory, and knowledge gaps, as well as lack of public engagement (Ngoc and Schnitzer 2009). Below are some other significant difficulties in implementing a solid waste management system:

2.2.1 Lack of Enforcement and Awareness

One of the major causes for the poor management of trash begins with a lack of knowledge. People that generate trash are unaware of why and how to separate waste and waste collectors and handlers do not know how to process the useful waste and how to dispose the useless waste. In general, there is a lack of understanding of the health and environmental consequences of poor waste management. According to Indian waste management regulations of 2016, waste separation from sources was required to channel waste into wealth via recovery, reuse and recycling (Gopalakrishnan et al. 2021a, b).

2.2.2 Lack of Waste Segregation at Various Holding Sources

The major sources of garbage are homes and industry where trash is segregated at source. Most municipal trash now is not adequately separated into biodegradable and non-biodegradable waste. In a few instances the government does not provide the common people with enough infrastructure for the disposal of separated trash. The government has set regulations as trash generators must pay 'User Fee' to collecting rubbish and 'Spot Fine' to litter and not be separated (Gopalakrishnan and Ramaguru 2019).

2.2.3 Lack of Scientific Landfills

The accessible sites today are not properly built since it contaminates groundwater and pollutes the air via the release of methane gas. Bad smell, fire explosion, animal scavenging, among others, are problems faced in waste dumps. The quantity of dump sites available is not equal to the country's need. More than 70% of the municipal trash collected is deposited directly into the sites (Ahmad et al. 2021a, b, c).

2.2.4 Lack of Technological Development in Determining Flow of Waste

Garbage producers and waste handlers do not understand how and where the waste is treated when it is released. There is no adequate waste management tracking system. While Radio-frequency identification (RFID) technology is utilised to control trash, its application is restricted. Data are manually input in the present waste management system leading to data mistakes that create discrepancies and incorrect entry and manipulation of data for financial advantage. Official letters are also handed on as tangible documents that may be lost during transit (Sahoo and Halder 2020).

2.3 Current Technologies Used in SWM (Solid Waste Management)

Technology is gradually gaining popularity in waste management because it offers a comprehensive solution to material processing, distribution, and recollection. Chidepatil et al. (2020) describe the ongoing developments in the use of technology to manage wastes. The authors focus on how agencies use blockchain and Artificial Intelligence systems to solve problems arising from increased plastic use today. The convergence of blockchain with AI and other technologies like IoT has received a lot of attention during the last years (Pressmair et al. 2021; Themistocleous et al. 2019; Themistocleous et al. 2018). Municipalities frequently seek to enhance waste management process efficiency via innovative methods. In certain countries, routing, dynamic scheduling, a smartphone navigation system, GPS, recyclable devices, smart buckets, and waste vehicles have been integrated in the Cloud. Wastes originate from many sources, for example nondurable products, durable goods, food scraps and packing, where they have to be properly handled (Lamichhane 2017). They must be processed and assigned to various processing facilities that are not a simple job since different handling procedures, deletion alternatives and treatment options may be involved. With new software technology and internet dispersion throughout the years, small, dependable and cost effective hardware solutions have been created, thus generating efficient integrated systems for SWM (Ongena et al. 2018). Such integrated technologies are extensively used in the SWM optimisation process. Web-GIS systems with RFID tags are for instance used for the collection, storage, integration, analysis and collection of the location or user-related data. Different trash (chemical, hospital, industrial, and residential) are handled at greater collection and transport prices (Kassou et al. 2021). Optimisation methods were extensively utilised in literature to decrease the cost of collecting. The shortest route technique, for example, has been used to decrease collecting and transport costs or even more complicated issues that include elements such as routing, dispatch, maintenance and management. Models of optimisation were also linked with other technologies to increase efficiency in waste management (Lamichhane 2017). For example, several researchers have coupled genetic algorithms with life cycle evaluation. They created a computer-based interface for an integrated model for optimising waste management, which makes it easy to use.

2.4 Background of the Blockchain Technology

Blockchain technology traces its origin to 2008 when Satoshi Nakamoto, an author, published an article "Bitcoin: A Peer-to-Peer Electronic Cash System" to address challenges arising from the digital currency system (Oyelere et al. 2019). In the publication, Nakamoto provided readers with recommendations concerning how to develop a transparent and secure digital currency system that does not require the management of a central body or bank. The author coined the phrase "block chain" to describe his idea of the transparent and secure digital currency. In the preceding years, other fields adopted the phrase, including the Bitcoin industry, which acted as a blockchain due to its ability to offer users security and transparency (Christodoulou et al. 2020, Papadaki et al. 2021). Since then, other industries have adopted the term, such as education and healthcare, to facilitate transparency and security in their information sharing processes.

2.4.1 Key Blockchain Characteristics

Traceability – blockchain technology allows users to trace transactions within its network. Users can retrieve important information concerning a transaction when they inspect the block containing a particular unit of data (Oyelere et al. 2019). Furthermore, each block in the technology has a close connection to adjacent blocks, vital for tracking information.

Transparency – the technology fosters transparency because it allows members within the system to monitor and control transactions. Notably, blockchain allows members to broadcast transactions when they feed them into the system (Oyelere et al. 2019). Additionally, it permits them to identify and reject transactions that they distrust. In this regard, the technology promotes openness and security because it allows stakeholders to participate in determining the type of data within a network. External parties cannot alter information within a network without the permission of other members, thereby guaranteeing security.

Immutability – This is a significant characteristic of the blockchain that guarantees transactions within a blockchain unit. The technology ensures that users cannot delete or modify validated transactions in the system (Themistocleous 2018).

Trust – The decentralized feature of blockchain technology does not just prevent failure in the entire system but also builds trust among stakeholders. Unlike in a centralized system where a few parties control data, blockchain ensures that all parties actively participate in permitting or rejecting transactions (Oyelere et al. 2019). Hence, all nodes in the network in a decentralized ledger act as trust bearers.

Security – the technology allows users to employ a hash function, which transforms a variable sequence into a fixed-length sequence (Kapassa et al. 2020). In doing so, the blockchain prevents any relationship between output and input. It is impossible for individuals to not only use the binary output to trace the variable-length input but also reverse the process.

2.5 Blockchain and Waste Management

The blockchain technology has many important features among current technologies that may assist to improve the waste management system (Sahoo and Halder 2020). Blockchain is a time-scale sequence of unchanging data recordings kept using cryptographic principles in a distributed ledger. Initially employed by financial organisations to record transactions, blockchain permanently saves information in blocks in which everyone who is a part of the network has a copy of the leader. The idea of the distributed ledger is currently utilised for any kind of data and in many commercial applications other than financial transactions with progress in a blockchain (Akram et al. 2021). The blockchain technology offers possibilities for various industries such as finance, food, healthcare, logistics and other supply chains. Blockchain streamlines the supply chain and provides a more efficient, transparent system that enables the stakeholders of the system to monitor waste with more responsibility (Akram et al. 2021). blockchain technologies provide a unique collaborative method that enables governments, regulators and companies to cooperate on more structured waste management without less incoherence. Waste monitoring prevents recyclable material from turning up in the sites (Ahmad et al. 2021a, b, c). The platform is usually categorised as public or private, depending on the intricacy of projects and security requirements. Researchers reviewed the criteria for selecting between two platforms and performed performance analyses with varied workloads to determine the usability in various supply chain applications for each platform (Akram et al. 2021). In reverse logistics and solid waste management literature, blockchain was already presented. The technology, for example, is used to record each recyclable element on a current blockchain platform. This common directory provides access to all stored waste disposal, recyclable and other relevant transactions available to all network members (Dua et al. 2020). This method helps to monitor devices and recyclables and reduces the danger of data mixing or processing as part of waste management projects, blockchain technology plays an important role and can help developing nations reduce an environmental load of plastics on their environment and communities. The current blockchain applications in SWM are typically focused on (1) payment or reward facilitation such as the Plastic Bank case, or (2) waste monitoring and tracking such as the initiatives by the SNCF and the Dutch Ministry of Infrastructure (Taylor et al. 2020a, b).

In the first case, Plastic Bank offers a monetary incentive to citizens engaged in plastic waste collection. This initiative facilitates the recycling of plastics and selling them in the form of social plastics. Blockchain technology distributes, authenticates, and stores these rewards to achieve a greater social impact in waste management worldwide (PlasticBank, Fight Ocean Plastic and Poverty 2020). The transparency and the immutability aspect of the blockchain prohibit fraudulent and corrupt activities from taking place on the platform.

In the second scenario, the blockchain records trash collection and waste transport data. Using blockchain technology, Arep, an SNCF subsidiary, tracked the amount, type, and frequency of waste collected in train station waste bins. SNCF captured the trash data and transfers in blockchain transactions using the digital IDs of bins on railway stations (Taylor et al. 2020a, b).

Numerous benefits will accrue from using blockchain in trash management in low-income countries (Sandhiya and Ramakrishna 2020). As a first step, it will increase communication between all parties involved, including producers and customers. Additionally, because blockchain is a digital solution, it will help stakeholders feel more secure when exchanging information about waste. Moreover, it will encourage the sharing of waste management stakeholders' knowledge on the subject of waste. As a fourth benefit, it will operate as a motivator for people to practise proper garbage disposal. Furthermore, the technology enables members to communicate information without intermediaries, thereby creating a trustworthy atmosphere for pollution control. Also, the decentralised nature of blockchain technology, which allows users to participate in processing waste management data while prohibiting the unauthorised alteration of confirmed information, contributes to the security of blockchain technology. It will also help governments create confidence with residents because it will give everyone access to information about the circulation of waste.

3   Methodology - Systematic Review

A systematic Literature Review (SLR) is regarded as a viable and comprehensive methodology for a research thesis according to (Puljak and Sapunar 2017). A systematic literature review, as described by (Okoli and Schabram 2010), seeks to 'identify, appraise, and synthesize all scientific data that satisfies pre-specified eligibility requirements to address a given research query'. Parallel to the above mentioned, the researcher applies a SLR as a research methodology for researching the literature related to the use of a blockchain solution in waste management. Consequently, this study aims to map the state of art in published papers about the use Blockchain technology in SWM with variables such as: novelty, drivers, models and procedures. Besides, the research is based on the understanding of different variables, such as people and technology. Moreover, the issues related to a blockchain solution and the prerequisite for integration in the waste sector will be elucidated and the drawback of the existing model will be identified and suggestions will be advised.

In order to fulfil the goals of this dissertation the researcher commits to follow the steps shown in Fig. 1 (Group 2007). As the figures displays, The SLR (Systematic Literature Review) method, will consist of three (3) phases. The researcher recognizes the necessity for an SLR at the first phase (planning phase), therefore a review procedure is designed and tested. The researcher performs a search and gathering of primary studies in the second phase (conducting phase), and data is collected and assessed. The third stage (report phase), which is the last step, focuses on combining the material gathered in previous phases with the primary aim of communicating the findings. The technique for conducting the SLR for this study has been specified (Kitchenham et al. 2010).

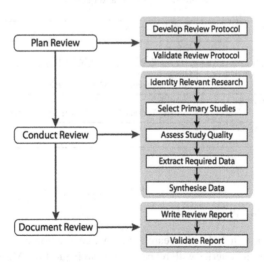

Fig. 1. The systematic literature review

3.1 Planning Phase

- *Identifying the Research Question and goals for the review*
  As stated Global waste and resource problems require and encourage improved and more sustainable waste management. Resources and waste streams that were previously disposed of are now being reused, repurposed, or reclaimed. While numerous laws and regulations have been enacted to help enable the required broad transitions to sustainable waste management, a number of persistent problems remain. The tracking and monitoring of wastes is essential to many of these initiatives. Keeping track of data is essential for adhering to current regulations and policies, and it also has the potential to influence new regulations and policies aimed at reducing the amount of trash that is disposed of in landfills or burned. However, tracking wastes and keeping tabs on their owners is a difficult task. A blockchain technology may help overcoming these challenges. This stage is meant to identify the research questions that the researcher aims to answer. In Parallel to the research aim, the following research question is identified: *"How Can the blockchain technology be implemented in waste management?"*.
- *Identifying Keywords and Search Queries*
  The query that guided the search process was how the blockchain can serve as a solution for waste management. Hence, the keywords to informed the search process included "blockchain," and "waste management." The Boolean operator **(OR)** was used to widen the search browsing by utilising such key terms, while the Boolean operator **(AND)** was used to refine and restrict the search (Table 1).

Table 1. Keywords and queries

Keywords	Search Queries
Blockchain	Query-1 "Blockchain" AND "Waste Management"
Waste Management	Query-2 "Cryptocurrencies" AND "Waste Management"
Cryptocurrencies	Query-3 "Smart Contracts" AND "Waste Management"
Smart Contracts	

3.2 The Conducting Phase

The conducting phase includes the search strategy, conduction process and results of identified keywords and queries with respect to research question. Moreover, this phase also determines the inclusion and exclusion criteria, database search log, application of Boolean operators, literature selection, PRISMA framework, and other quality processes.

After the initial screening (removing articles published before 2018), there were total **449** papers remaining for investigation.

- *Literature Selection*

    A detailed search of the databases originally revealed a total of **190** publications, instructed by the "Preferred Reporting Items for Systematic Reviews and Meta-Analyses (PRISMA)" to recognise, filter, and choose the most relevant literature. The articles were imported into "Endnote", where they were merged, checked, reassessed, rectified, and duplicates were eliminated at the same time. The inclusion and exclusion criteria were used to further filter and pick the most relevant articles, as well as to exclude those that were not (Fig. 2).

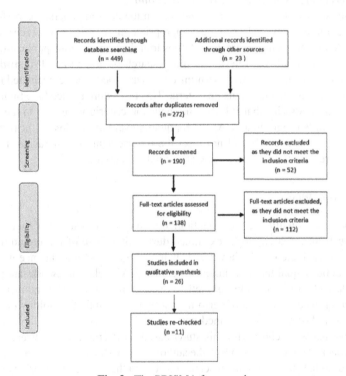

Fig. 2. The PRISMA framework

- **Inclusion and Exclusion Criteria**
  The scope of the systematic review be defined by providing parameters that determine what information should be located in the literature search and which research to include or omit from the findings.

  Inclusion Criteria - Peer- Reviewed studies only, English language only, Date of publication: 2018 onwards, Study scope: "the use of blockchain in Waste Management", Grey literature, White papers and material from non academic sources.
  Exclusion Criteria - Full- Text not available, Non English, Date of publication: before 2018, Diverged from the study scope.

- **Study Screening, Selection and Data Extraction**
  A manual search of the lists of references from the chosen papers was performed to check a comprehensive selection, and appropriate more articles were rechecked and added. There were many abstracts and titles found among various publications to see whether the material was relevant to this research or not. In all, **190 studies** were chosen, and their full-texts were scrutinised, downloaded, and re-evaluated further in light of the inclusion and exclusion criteria. This procedure reduced the findings even further, and **26 studies** that fulfilled the inclusion criteria were sent to the "Critical Appraisal Skills Programme (CASP)" for quality evaluation. Most of the papers were not accepted because they did not meet the requirements for inclusion. In last, **11 studies** were selected for this review after final rechecking.

3.3 Reporting Phase

Using appropriate qualitative and quantitative methods, the researcher tried to extract information from research works examined during this stage of the literature review. To investigate each element of how blockchain technology might enhance waste management practices, qualitative techniques were used. Models/frameworks are protocols that include a theory that supports methods and/or proposals. The number of study works relating to each element of performance of a blockchain technology in the waste management industry was determined using quantitative techniques. Table 2 lists the publications that were chosen for this study based on Brereton et al. (Brereton's et al. 2007) approach. The first column lists the authors who performed the research paper, the second column lists the title of the research piece, and the third column briefly describes the study work's emphasis.

Table 2. Selected papers for the SRL

Authors	Title	Subject/Goal
Ahmad et al. 2021	"Blockchain-Based Forward Supply Chain and Waste Management for COVID-19 Medical Equipment and Supplies"	For the COVID-19 medical equipment, research offers a decentralised blockchain-based system that automates forward supply chain operations and enables safe, traceable, transparent, and reliable information sharing among all parties engaged in waste management. The researcher uses blockchain technology.
Akram et al. 2021	"Blockchain Enabled Automatic Reward System in Solid Waste Management"	Using real-time series data, for waste level and waste volume, a blockchain g system is suggested in this research.
Dua et al. 2020	"Blockchain-based E-waste Management in 5G Smart Communities"	In the 5G future, the research study proposes an effective e-waste management method based on blockchain to address the aforementioned issue. This technology maintains track of the e-waste produced and offers an game-based mechanism to encourage recycling.
França et al. 2020	"Proposing the use of blockchain to improve the solid waste management in small municipalities"	This study examines how the Blockchain may be used to improve the management of solid waste in a Brazilian municipality.
Gopalakrishnan and Ramaguru, 2019	"Blockchain based waste management"	In this study, research study looked at current blockchain-based waste management systems to see how well they work in solving the issues the waste disposal.
Gopalakrishnan et al. 2021	"Cost analysis and optimisation of Blockchain-based solid waste management traceability system"	In this study, assisting municipalities become more efficient at waste management, this research report provides a Blockchain-based Solid Waste Management model.
Gupta and Bedi, 2018	"E-waste management using blockchain based smart contracts"	This research report provides a new method to e-waste management based on blockchain technology. Smart contracts can be written using blockchain technology, which is what it takes to implement them.
Kassou et al. 2021	"Blockchain-based medical and water waste management conception"	The research presents a Blockchain Technology and Internet of Things (IoT) idea for a waste management system that guarantees waste control in order to better manage waste coordination. This paper also includes a preliminary design for the system and an analysis of the system's performance.
Lamichhane, 2018	"A smart waste management system using IoT and blockchain technology"	The ultimate goal is to create a Solid Waste Management System by combining the latest Blockchain Technology ..
Ongena et al. 2018	"Blockchain-based smart contracts in waste management"	Researchers construct challenges and assess the applicability of a blockchain technology to alleviate the issues highlighted in waste management practices.
Sahoo and Halder, 2020	"Blockchain-based forward and reverse supply chains for E-waste management"	In this article, researchers suggest a new e-waste management system that takes into account both the reverse and forward supply chains and makes use of blockchain technology.

4 Key Findinds

4.1 Finding-1: Environmental Obstacles

There are a number of environmental and social obstacles to the fast global development of cities. The higher urbanisation rates, economic development, global population expansion and the improvement in living standards in emerging countries are significant reasons for the quantity, rates and range of garbage produced (Akram et al. 2021). The study emphasises important possibilities for building trust amongst participating companies engaged in trash management in intelligent cities provided by blockchain technology. In the next paragraphs, more explanation is given (Akram et al. 2021).

4.2   Finding-2: Benefit of Traceability on the System

The traceability function ensures that trash produced by intelligent cities is managed in accordance with the waste management standards to safeguard the environment from contamination. It also allows users to monitor the end of life of the intelligent city trash effectively (Ongena et al. 2018). For example, blockchain may be used to identify the kind of health waste handled in a recycling plant and utilised in the production of medical equipment and gadgets. The blockchain technology tracking or game-simulation function allows users to record the current position of vehicles transporting intelligent cities trash along with other information like the quickest way and weight of rubbish (Gupta and Bedi 2018).

4.3   Finding-3: Technical and Physical Barriers

In a well-functioning waste management system, manufacturers, consumers, and recyclers' access facilities and equipment needed to manage pollutants (Sahoo and Halder 2020). Unfortunately, there is a lack of a well-functioning waste management system characterised by irregular waste collection, lack of collection points, inadequate collection vehicles, insufficient waste bins, and non-functional separation facilities. Furthermore, there is a lack of sufficient waste bins, which prompts most people to use plastic bags or adopt inappropriate disposal strategies.

Social-Cultural Barriers - Lack of participation and awareness among residents is another barrier to effective waste management in developing countries. Existing literature shows that motivating individuals to waste management can increase their awareness and improve their reception (Ongena et al. 2018). Unfortunately, most residents in developing countries ignore the severity of inappropriate waste disposal practices. For example, they often ignore signs that show littering and non-littering spots and fail to participate in waste separation (França et al. 2020). Moreover, residents seldom attend community meetings aimed at educating them concerning proper waste management approaches.

Financial Barriers - For a government to effectively manage waste and achieve its environmental conservation objectives, it must invest heavily in practices aimed at collecting data concerning materials in circulation and recycling or incinerating pollutants (Sahoo and Halder 2020). Nevertheless, waste management organisations suffer from insufficient funding arising from mismanagement of money, inadequate budget allocation, and ineffective revenue collection structures.

Legal/Political Barriers - Even though governments in developing countries demonstrate the willingness to reduce waste disposal and address environmental pollution, most of them have weak legislation and experience conflicting interests that hinder effective waste management. Some regions lack rules regarding the production, disposal, or recycling of waste materials, allowing inappropriate dumping of pollutants (Gopalakrishnan and Ramaguru 2019). Those that have established regulations regarding waste management lack proper mechanisms to implement the policies. Hence, there is no punishment for individuals who dump waste materials or dispose of them illegally.

4.4   Finding-4: Limitation of the Use of Blockchain in Waste Management

Blockchain technology may be suitable for certain use cases, while traditional technologies will be more fit for others. A significant challenge for practitioners in deciding whether or not to utilize blockchain is the lack of product data or accurate technological assessment accessible to evaluate the suitability of blockchains. (Lo et al. 2017). This finding is corroborated by a substantial number of papers collected from electronic databases during the SLR's conduct phase. In contrast to rewards facilitation presented (Sect. 2.6.7), which only requires the waste to be checked once (for example, the Plastic Bank checks the plastic waste received once at the collection location before making a payment), recording the waste chain necessitates the identification of individual or groups of waste items multiple times at defined life-cycle stages. Physical items may be kept on the blockchain through their digital identities, but creating trustworthy digital IDs is difficult, especially when required throughout a resource's life-cycle. QR codes and RFID tags, for example, are only reliable if they can be read, which is not assured if trash is broken up. (Taylor et al. 2020b). Other major limitations of the use of the blockchain technology in waste management include:

- **Slow Adoption** - Blockchain technology has played a critical role in enhancing the trust, security, fairness, operational transparency, and auditability of waste management mechanisms presently in place in smart cities. It may assist authorities in properly disinfecting hazardous waste prior to disposal at a recycling facility, hence minimizing the danger of disease transmission (Gupta and Bedi 2018).
- **Smart Contracts Security** - In blockchain-based waste management systems designed for Smart cities, smart contracts are utilized to automate processes and duties. Some examples of these smart contracts include IoT-based trash bin monitoring, real-time tracking of waste shipments, waste fraud detection, and the eradication of illegal waste dumps. The immutability of smart contracts on the blockchain offers both benefits and drawbacks. Even while smart contracts are impermeable to hackers, once they are launched, developers will be unable to alter them to meet changing business requirements (Ahmad et al. 2021a, b, c).
- **Storage issues** - Trash collection, sorting, transportation, and disposal generate a large amount of data. Images, videos, or documents that show adherence to environmental and human safety regulations at the local or national level may be included in these records. The information gathered includes information on the kind of rubbish dumped, where it was sent, and where recycling and landfilling facilities are located. (Schmelz et al. 2019). In fact, a large number of sensors throughout smart cities gather this data to monitor rubbish generation and disposal. Blockchain storage capacity is limited since each node in the network keeps a copy of the data. Blockchain technology is excellent for storing and processing data for small businesses. However, large-scale commercial applications have a major influence on blockchain performance.
- **Scalability** - Stakeholders in smart city waste management want high quality service when implementing blockchain-based technologies. Transaction throughput, transaction execution time, and transaction cost all have an impact on a blockchain platform's service quality. Because blockchain technology is decentralized and

self-governing, increasing these requirements while maintaining high transaction transparency, security, and privacy is difficult (Ahmad et al. 2021a, b, c).

5 Conclusion and Discussion

The project seeks *to investigate the application of Blockchain in Waste Management.* Eleven selected papers were examined to address the research question, and the use of blockchain technology in waste management was identified. According to the overall findings of this SLR, every stakeholder must be engaged in the process of providing critical information regarding waste management methods. Waste stakeholders include importers, electronic assemblers, recyclers, dismantlers, scavengers, consumers, policymakers, authorities, non-governmental organizations, and ultimate disposal facilities. The researcher examined the perspectives of various stakeholders on waste management challenges in respective zones/territories. While the authors think solid waste recycling may help decrease pollution, the method faces a number of challenges in most LDC's. As a result, barriers that may impede the adoption of technology-based waste management systems were identified.

One of the barriers to effective waste management technology adoption in developing and less developed countries is the regulatory environment. According to the majority of stakeholders, implementing appropriate regulatory controls may help govern how technology is used to address the pollution issue. Regulations regarding solid waste management have played an important role in developed countries such as the United Kingdom. As a result, developing and less developed nations must establish strong legislative frameworks in order to construct long-term waste management systems. However, many less developed countries are unable to avoid plastic dumping owing to ineffective industrial management. The use of blockchain technology in waste management techniques such as plastic garbage may be hampered by public awareness.

Despite the fact that the research addressed the primary issue, there are certain constraints to consider. To begin, the papers examined were restricted to those found in JSTOR, EBSCOhost, IEEE Xplore Digital Library, ScienceDirect, and SpringerLink. Second, despite the fact that this study utilized a wide list of keywords in major research databases, there is a risk losing some essential work due to the dispersion in function of the keywords used in this area. Furthermore, the scalability and continuously evolving aspect of the blockchain technology remain significant issues, and there is a lack of work (for example, Framework) that combines the improvements offered by all research efforts. Besides, the use of blockchain in the waste management industry, including testing, is still in its early stages.

All of these findings point to a research gap and open research questions that need further investigation. Consequently, a conceptual model is needed that combines all relevant research findings, synthesizes and orchestrates them in an efficient way, that will assist all stakeholders engaged in waste management on their path towards broad use of a blockchain technology.

References

Agora Tech Lab. Waste Management Fueled by Blockchain. Barcelona Research Group on Informal Recyclers (2020). Waste Pickers Under Threat (2018)

Ahmad, R.W., Salah, K., Jayaraman, R., Yaqoob, I., Omar, M.: Blockchain for waste management in smart cities: a survey. TechRxiv (2021a). Preprint https://doi.org/10.36227/techrxiv.143455 34.v1

Ahmad, R.W., Salah, K., Jayaraman, R., Yaqoob, I., Omar, M., Ellahham, S.: Blockchain-based forward supply chain and waste management for COVID-19 medical equipment and supplies. IEEE Access **9**, 44905–44927 (2021b)

Ahmad, R.W., Salah, K., Jayaraman, R., Yaqoob, I., Omar, M.: Blockchain for waste management in smart cities: a survey. IEEE Access **9**, 131520–131541 (2021c). https://doi.org/10.1109/acc ess.2021.3113380

Akram, S.V., et al.: Blockchain Enabled Automatic Reward System in Solid Waste Management. Security and Communication Networks (2021)

Babayemi, J.O., Nnorom, I.C., Osibanjo, O., Weber, R.: Ensuring sustainability in plastics use in Africa: consumption, waste generation, and projections. Environ. Sci. Eur. **31**(1), 1–20 (2019). https://doi.org/10.1186/s12302-019-0254-5

Biswas, B., Gupta, R.: Analysis of barriers to implement blockchain in industry and service sectors. Comput. Ind. Eng. **136**, 225–241 (2019). https://doi.org/10.1016/j.cie.2019.07.005

Briones, A.G., et al.: Use of gamification techniques to encourage garbage recycling. A smart city approach. In: Uden, L., Hadzima, B., Ting, I.-H. (eds.) KMO 2018. CCIS, vol. 877, pp. 674–685. Springer, Cham (2018). https://doi.org/10.1007/978-3-319-95204-8_56

Chidepatil, A., Bindra, P., Kulkarni, D., Qazi, M., Kshirsagar, M., Sankaran, K.: From trash to cash: how blockchain and multi-sensor-driven artificial intelligence can transform circular economy of plastic waste? Adm. Sci. **10**(2), 23 (2020). https://doi.org/10.3390/admsci10020023

Christodoulou, C., Katelaris, L., Themistocleous, M., Christodoulou, P., Iosif, E.: NFTs and the metaverse revolution: research perspectives and open challenges. In: Lacity, M., Treiblmaier, H. (eds.) Blockchains and the Token Economy: Theory and Practice (2022)

Christodoulou, K., Iosif, E., Inglezakis, A., Themistocleous, M.: Consensus crash testing: exploring ripple's decentralization degree in adversarial environments. Future Internet **12**(3), [53] (2020)

Cristofini, O., Roulet, T.J.: Playing with trash: how gamification contributed to the bottom-up institutionalization of zero waste. Acad. Manag. Proc. **2020**(1), 12616 (2020). https://doi.org/ 10.5465/ambpp.2020.39

Cunha, P.R., Soja, P., Themistocleous, M.: Blockchain for development: a guiding framework. Inf. Technol. Dev. **27**(3), 417–438 (2021)

Dilotsotlhe, N.: Factors influencing the green purchase behavior of millennials: an emerging country perspective. Cogent Bus. Manag. **8**(1), 1908745 (2021). https://doi.org/10.1080/233 11975.2021.1908745

Douti, N.B., Abanyie, S.K., Ampofo, S., Nyarko, S.K.: Solid waste management challenges in urban areas of Ghana: a case study of Bawku municipality. Int. J. Geosci. **08**(04), 494–513 (2017). https://doi.org/10.4236/ijg.2017.84026

Dua, A., Dutta, A., Zaman, N., Kumar, N.: Blockchain-based E-waste management in 5G smart communities. In: IEEE INFOCOM 2020-IEEE Conference on Computer Communications Workshops (INFOCOM WKSHPS), pp. 195–200. IEEE (2020)

Schmelz, D., Pinter, K., Strobl, S., Zhu, L., Niemeier, P., Grechenig, T.: Technical mechanics of a trans-border waste flow tracking solution based on blockchain technology. In: 2019 IEEE 35th International Conference on Data Engineering Workshops (ICDEW), pp. 31–36 (2019). https://doi.org/10.1109/ICDEW.2019.00-38

Ferronato, N., Torretta, V.: Waste mismanagement in developing countries: a review of global issues. Int. J. Environ. Res. Public Health **16**(6), 1060 (2019). https://doi.org/10.3390/ijerph 16061060

França, A.S.L., Neto, J.A., Gonçalves, R.F., Almeida, C.M.V.B.: Proposing the use of blockchain to improve the solid waste management in small municipalities. J. Cleaner Prod. **244**, 118529 (2020)

Godfrey, L.: Waste plastic, the challenge facing developing countries—ban it, change it, collect it? Recycling **4**(1), 3 (2019). https://doi.org/10.3390/recycling4010003

Gopalakrishnan, P., Ramaguru, R.: Blockchain based waste management. Int. J. Eng. Adv. Technol. **8**(5), 2632–2635 (2019)

Gopalakrishnan, P.K., Hall, J., Behdad, S.: A blockchain-based traceability system for waste management in smart cities. In: 25th Design for Manufacturing and the Life Cycle Conference (DFMLC), vol. 6 (2020). https://doi.org/10.1115/detc2020-22553

Gopalakrishnan, P.K., Hall, J., Behdad, S.: Cost analysis and optimization of Blockchain-based solid waste management traceability system. Waste Manag. **120**, 594–607 (2021a). https://doi.org/10.1016/j.wasman.2020.10.027

Gopalakrishnan, P.K., Hall, J., Behdad, S.: Cost analysis and optimization of Blockchain-based solid waste management traceability system. Waste Manag. **120**, 594–607 (2021b)

Gupta, N., Bedi, P.: E-waste management using blockchain based smart contracts. In: 2018 International Conference on Advances in Computing, Communications and Informatics (ICACCI), pp. 915–921. IEEE (2018)

Helmefalk, M., Rosenlund, J.: Make waste fun again! a gamification approach to recycling. In: Brooks, A., Brooks, E.I. (eds.) ArtsIT/DLI -2019. LNICSSITE, vol. 328, pp. 415–426. Springer, Cham (2020). https://doi.org/10.1007/978-3-030-53294-9_30

Hinchcliffe, T.: Dutch Govt to use Blockchain for Waste Transportation Automation with Belgium. The Sociable (2018). https://sociable.co/technology/blockchain-waste-transportation/. Accessed 11 May 2020

Idumah, C.I., Nwuzor, I.C.: Novel trends in plastic waste management. SN Appl. Sci. **1**(11), 1–14 (2019). https://doi.org/10.1007/s42452-019-1468-2

Innovation Insight for Blockchain Security (2017). Gartner. https://www.gartner.com/en/docume nts/3792664

Kassou, M., Bourekkadi, S., Khoulji, S., Slimani, K., Chikri, H., Kerkeb, M.L.: Blockchain-based medical and water waste management conception. In: E3S Web of Conferences, vol. 234, p. 00070. EDP Sciences (2021)

Kapassa, E., Themistocleous, M., Quintanilla, J.R., Touloupos, M., Papadaki, M.: Blockchain in smart energy grids: a market analysis. In: Themistocleous, M., Papadaki, M., Kamal, M.M. (eds.) EMCIS 2020. LNBIP, vol. 402, pp. 113–124. Springer, Cham (2020). https://doi.org/10.1007/978-3-030-63396-7_8

Kwabena, B., Clifford, A., Kwasi, K.A.: Stakeholders perceptions on key drivers for and barriers to household E-wast E management in Accra, Ghana. Afr. J. Environ. Sci. Technol. **12**(11), 429–438 (2018). https://doi.org/10.5897/ajest2018.2409

Lamichhane, M.: A smart waste management system using IoT and blockchain technology (2017)

Lo, S.K., Xu, X., Chiam, Y.K., Lu, Q.: Evaluating suitability of applying blockchain. In: 2017 22nd International Conference on Engineering of Complex Computer Systems (ICECCS) (2017). https://doi.org/10.1109/iceccs.2017.26

Lynch, S.: OpenLitterMap.com – open data on plastic pollution with blockchain rewards (littercoin). Open Geospatial Data Softw. Stand. **3**(1), 1 (2018). https://doi.org/10.1186/s40965-018-0050-y

Malloy, C.: Even garbage is using blockchain now. Bloomberg CityLab. Even Garbage Is Using Blockchain Now – Bloomberg, 18 March 2021

Namasudra, S., Deka, G.C., Johri, P., Hosseinpour, M., Gandomi, A.H.: The revolution of blockchain: state-of-the-art and research challenges. Arch. Comput. Methods Eng. **28**(3), 1497–1515 (2020). https://doi.org/10.1007/s11831-020-09426-0

Ngoc, U.N., Schnitzer, H.: Sustainable solutions for solid waste management in Southeast Asian countries. Waste Manag. **29**(6), 1982–1995 (2009). https://doi.org/10.1016/j.wasman.2008.08.031

Niranjanamurthy, M., Nithya, B.N., Jagannatha, S.: Analysis of Blockchain technology: pros, cons and SWOT. Clust. Comput. **22**(6), 14743–14757 (2018). https://doi.org/10.1007/s10586-018-2387-5

Okoli, C., Schabram, K.: Working Papers on Information Systems a Guide to Conducting a Systematic Literature Review of Information Systems Research a Guide to Conducting a Systematic Literature Review of Information Systems Research (2010)

Oyelere, S.S., Tomczyk, L., Bouali, N., Joseph, A.F.: Blockchain technology and gamification – conditions and opportunities for education. University of Eastern Finland's eRepository (2019)

Ongena, G., Smit, K., Boksebeld, J., Adams, G., Roelofs, Y., Ravesteyn, P.: Blockchain-based smart contracts in waste management: a silver bullet? In: Bled eConference, p. 19 (2018)

Papadaki, M., Karamitsos, I., Themistocleous, M.: Covid-19 digital test certificates and blockchain. J. Enterp. Inf. Manag. **34**, 1–10 (2021)

Parizi, R.M., Dehghantanha, A.: On the understanding of Gamification in blockchain systems. In: 2018 6th International Conference on Future Internet of Things and Cloud Workshops (FiCloudW) (2018). https://doi.org/10.1109/w-ficloud.2018.00041

Puljak, L., Sapunar, D.: Acceptance of a systematic review as a thesis: survey of biomedical doctoral programs in Europe. Syst. Rev. 253 (2017). https://doi.org/10.1186/s13643-017-0653-x

Pressmair, G., Kapassa, E., Casado-Mansilla, D., Borges, C., Themistocleous, M.: Overcoming barriers for the adoption of local energy and flexibility markets: a user-centric and hybrid model. J. Cleaner Prod. **317**, 128323 (2021)

Saberi, S., Kouhizadeh, M., Sarkis, J., Shen, L.: Blockchain technology and its relationships to sustainable supply chain management. Int. J. Prod. Res. **57**(7), 2117–2135 (2018). https://doi.org/10.1080/00207543.2018.1533261

Sandhiya, R., Ramakrishna, S.: Investigating the applicability of blockchain technology and ontology in plastics recycling by the adoption of ZERO plastic model. Mater. Circular Econ. **2**(1), 1–12 (2020). https://doi.org/10.1007/s42824-020-00013-z

Sadhya, V., Sadhya, H.: Barriers to adoption of blockchain technology. In: AMCIS 2018 Proceedings, New Orleans, LA (2018)

Santti, U., Happonen, A., Auvinen, H.: Digitalization boosted recycling: gamification as an inspiration for young adults to do enhanced waste sorting. In: 13th International Engineering Research Conference (13th EURECA 2019) (2020). https://doi.org/10.1063/5.0001547

Seaborn, K., Fels, D.I.: Gamification in theory and action: a survey. Int. J. Hum. Comput. Stud. **74**, 14–31 (2015). https://doi.org/10.1016/j.ijhcs.2014.09.006

Sahoo, S., Halder, R.: Blockchain-based forward and reverse supply chains for E-waste management. In: Dang, T.K., Küng, J., Takizawa, M., Chung, T.M. (eds.) Future Data and Security Engineering, FDSE 2020, pp. 201–220. Springer, Cham (2020). https://doi.org/10.1007/978-3-030-63924-2_12

Soja, P., Rupino da Cunha, P., Themistocleous, M.: Blockchain for development: preliminary insights from a literature review. In: The Proceedings of the Twenty Sixth Americas Conference on Information Systems (AMCIS 2020), Virtual Conference, 10–14 August 2020 (2020)

Tang, J., Zhang, P.: Exploring the relationships between gamification and motivational needs in technology design. Int. J. Crowd Sci. **3**(1), 87–103 (2019). https://doi.org/10.1108/ijcs-09-2018-0025

Taylor, P.J., Dargahi, T., Dehghantanha, A., Parizi, R.M., Choo, K.-K.R.: A systematic literature review of blockchain cybersecurity. Digit. Commun. Netw. **6**(2), 147–156 (2020a). https://doi.org/10.1016/j.dcan.2019.01.005

Taylor, P., Steenmans, K., Steenmans, I.: Blockchain technology for sustainable waste management. Front. Polit. Sci. **2**, 15 (2020b). https://doi.org/10.3389/fpos.2020.590923

UNEP. Africa is currently recycling only 4% of its waste. United Nations Environment Programme (2018). Retrieved from Africa_WMO_Poster.pdf (unep.org)

Themistocleous, M., Stefanou, K., Megapanos, C., Iosif, E.: To chain or not to chain? A blockchain case from energy sector. In: Themistocleous, M., Rupino da Cunha, P. (eds.) 15th European, Mediterranean, and Middle Eastern Conference, EMCIS 2018, Limassol, Cyprus, 4–5 October 2018. LNBIP, vol. 341, pp. 29–35, Springer, Heidelberg (2019). ISBN 978-3-030-11394-0

Themistocleous, M., Stefanou, K., Iosif, E.: Blockchain in solar energy. Cyprus Rev. **30**(2), 207–214 (2018)

Themistocleous, M.: Blockchain technology and land registry. Cyprus Rev. **30**(2), 199–206 (2018)

Vanapalli, K.R., et al.: Challenges and strategies for effective plastic waste management during and post COVID-19 pandemic. Sci. Total Environ. **750**, 141514 (2021). https://doi.org/10.1016/j.scitotenv.2020.141514

Yukalang, N., Clarke, B., Ross, K.: Barriers to effective municipal solid waste management in a rapidly urbanizing area in Thailand. Int. J. Environ. Res. Public Health **14**(9), 1013 (2017). https://doi.org/10.3390/ijerph14091013

Cloud Computing

The Adoption of Cloud Computing in South Africa's Oil and Gas Industry

Shaheen Jamalodeen🆔 and Jean-Paul Van Belle(✉)🆔

University of Cape Town, Cape Town, South Africa
Jean-paul.vanbelle@uct.ac.za

Abstract. Cloud computing has become an increasingly attractive option for oil and gas organizations looking to reduce costs while increasing operational excellence. The cloud is not only a tool for faster computing power and higher performance, but also as an instrument to faster application deployment, lower service costs and a step towards digital transformation. This study aimed to determine the level of cloud computing adoption within selected organizations within the oil and gas industry in South Africa. The study also attempted to understand the factors that influence this adoption and how SA oil and gas companies are utilizing cloud technologies, as well as the factors that influence the presumed lack of adoption. This research was guided by the Technology, Organization, and Environment (TOE) framework and used a qualitatively approach, based on semi-structured interviews from seven participants, from four oil and gas companies in SA. The findings of this research show a high level of awareness but low level of adoption of cloud computing. The factors that were found to have a positive and significant influence on the intention to adopt cloud computing included security, relative advantage, compatibility, top management support, vendor support and competition. The factors that were found to be a risk or challenge towards the adoption of cloud computing included complexity, government regulations, organizational readiness, bandwidth, trust and vendor lock-in.

Keywords: Cloud computing · Oil & Gas industry · South Africa · TOE framework · Cloud computing benefits · Cloud computer risks

1 Introduction

Despite the hi-tech nature of the oil and gas industry, it is still at an early stage in its adoption of cloud computing when compared to other industries. The main reason for this is largely related to a deeply ingrained aversion to risk. However, demand for cloud computing is growing given that it is a processing driven, data-rich industry [1].

Despite its many benefits, there are still several concerns that have slowed the adoption of cloud computing in the upstream oil & gas industry [2]. There are concerns regarding data security (reluctance to have data stored outside the firewall), disaster recovery, reliance on an extremely large dataset, high availability and poor bandwidth, especially in developing countries, as well as the huge investment that have already been

© Springer Nature Switzerland AG 2022
M. Themistocleous and M. Papadaki (Eds.): EMCIS 2021, LNBIP 437, pp. 215–228, 2022.
https://doi.org/10.1007/978-3-030-95947-0_15

made in on-premise solutions. However, the more significant hurdles are not technical but rather regulatory and geopolitical [2].

The purpose of this study was to determine the level of cloud computing adoption within the oil and gas industry in South Africa. The study also attempted to understand the factors that influence this adoption and how SA oil and gas companies are utilizing cloud technologies, as well as the factors that influence the presumed lack of adoption.

2 Literature Review

Cloud computing offers an attractive proposition to the oil and gas industry. Benefits include reduced IT costs, adaptability, improving job training, scalability and fast business reactions based on real-time data [3]. Collaboration is also becoming critical tool in oil and gas companies as sensitive information needs to be shared with remote teams, stakeholders and joint venture partners to maximise productivity and transfer knowledge [4].

Howevere, there are several concerns as the oil and gas industry moves towards the cloud, *"There is reluctance in the industry to have data stored outside of the firewall. There is a concern not only with intrusions that could compromise IT, but also with protection of trade secrets, especially when it comes to sensitive areas such as well logs. There is also an issue of scale for some applications. For example, much of exploration and production depends on 3D rendering and graphics accelerators, which have yet to make it off the workstation because of the size of the files and speed required for viewing. Another consideration is the sunk investment in legacy IT applications and infrastructure that the industry has already made."* [5:32]. However, the security concerns can be addressed with a hybrid model with end-to-end data encryption [6].

By embracing cloud computing in a cautious and slow way, the oil and gas industry is preventing itself from gaining the benefits that cloud computing technologies and services can offer [Perrons]. *"Other sectors like healthcare and retail faced many of the same technical and regulatory issues that the energy industry is wrestling with on its journey to the cloud—like, for example, data security, technical bottlenecks resulting from massive volumes of data, and legal problems arising from moving data across international borders—but still found ways to overcome these challenges and realize the full potential that this technology can deliver"* [3:225].

Wariness of the cloud is now diminishing, as there is more evidence that the oil and gas industry is moving towards the cloud [7]. A 2011 survey showed that 32% are currently using private or public cloud services and another 36% have plans to use cloud services in the future [8]. Other studies concur. *"It is inevitable that many major industries – energy included – will migrate to cloud computing"* [9:3]. *"Cloud computing technologies are particularly well suited for oil and gas companies"* [10:2]. *"At present, most of the world's top ten oil companies have applied cloud computing on oil and gas exploration and management operations"* [11:101].

However, as the pressure mounts for oil and gas companies to find new ways to streamline their businesses, many oil and gas organizations are now turning to public cloud services in order to boost collaboration between multinational offices and maximize productivity [12]. Reportedly, in 2016 more than 80% of oil and gas business were using some form of public cloud services to improve cost-savings and agility and to gain a competitive edge, although mainly in non-critical areas [13].

3 The Technology-Organization-Environment (TOE) Framework

There are several models and frameworks that have been proposed by researchers to study the adoption of new technologies in organisations, including the resource-based view and the diffusion of innovation (DOI) theory [14]. The technology, organisation and environment (TOE) framework [15] was deemed to be most appropriate for this study, as it analyze the acceptance of new IT technologies at an organizational level. The TOE model identifies three types of context (the technological context, the organisational context and the environmental context) that may influence an organisation to adopt and implement new technological innovations [15]. These three contexts present both limitations and opportunities for adoption of technological innovation. In particular, the TOE framework *"provides a holistic picture for user adoption of technology, its implementation, foreseeing challenges, its impact on value chain activities, the post-adoption diffusion among firms, factors influencing business innovation-adoption decisions and to develop better organisational capabilities using the technology"* [16:6].

4 Research Methodology

This research aims to determine the level of cloud computing adoption within selected organizations within the oil and gas industry in South Africa. The study will also attempt to understand the factors that influence this adoption and how SA oil and gas companies are utilizing cloud technologies, as well as the factors that slow or prevent adoption.

The primary question for this research is to determine the level of adoption of cloud computing technology within selected organizations within the oil and gas industry in South Africa. The secondary questions for this research are: (a) How South African oil and gas companies are adopting cloud computing and what are the factors influencing this adoption? (b) What are the challenges or factors that influence the lack of adoption?

This research has a positivist philosophy as it aims to investigate the level of adoption of cloud computing technology within the oil and gas industry. This research is guided by the existing theories defined by the Technology, Organization, and Environment (TOE) framework and therefore will use a deductive approach. This research uses a qualitative research method to provide answers to the research questions. Qualitative research can be defined as *"any kind of research that produces findings not arrived at by means of statistical procedures or other means of quantification"* [17:17]. Semi-structured interviews were used in this study. The interview questions were designed using related research in the field and literature review and were based on the TOE framework. A pilot test was conducted, with the help of colleagues within the oil and gas industry, in order to ensure that the questionnaire was clear, accurate and complete.

Ethics approval for this research was obtained from UCT Ethics Committee. Participants were informed what the research entails and that their participation is entirely voluntary.

Six oil and gas companies were chosen for this study. Out of the six companies, two chose not to participate in the research study. However, the information gathered from the remaining four companies were enough for the research. Two are local South African companies and the other two are international oil companies. Seven participants from four oil and gas companies were interviewed for this study. The participants selected for this study are all oil and gas professionals, with good knowledge and experience with working within the cloud (Table 1). Saturation was achieved and no new themes emerged in the last few interviews. The data was analyzed using thematic analysis using [18]'s six steps.

Table 1. List of participants selected for the research study

Participant Code	Organisation	Role in organisation	Experience in current role	Cloud computing experience
P1	O&G - A	IT Consultant	5	Yes; < 2 years
P2	O&G - B	Geoscience Systems Lead	10	Yes; < 2 years
P3	O&G - C	Database Systems Manager	12	Yes; < 2 years
P4	O&G - D	Infrastructure Specialist	12	Yes; < 2 years
P5	O&G - D	Systems Engineer	8	Yes; < 2 years
P6	O&G - D	Exploration Data Manager	5	Yes; < 2 years
P7	O&G - D	IT architect	14	Yes; > 10 years

5 Findings and Discussions

This section contains five subheadings that focus on discussion of findings and analyses of interviews that were conducted in order to identify the level of adoption of cloud computing within the selected oil and gas companies in South Africa. The first section focuses on the current level of adoption (Table 5) and the second, third and fourth section focuses on findings based on the on the technological, organizational and environmental framework, while the fifth section focuses on the risks and challenges identified in this study.

5.1 Current Level of Adoption

All participants reported that their organization have adopted some **cloud computing services** but that SaaS is the only cloud service model being used. No PaaS or IaaS service models were used. The SaaS applications adopted by all four oil and gas companies are Microsoft Office 365 and Skype for Business. The main reason for adopting SaaS is because it allows for collaboration and communication in a secure environment. This is consistent with the literature, as the first step for many organizations toward the adoption and usage of cloud computing is SaaS [8]. However, P1 and P6 added that they feel that there are currently not a lot of cloud services available that would fit the oil and gas industry and the applications that they would be interested in, are not mature for cloud computing yet.

In terms of deploying cloud solutions, the results show that only one of the four oil and gas companies are using a **cloud deployment model**. Oil and gas company 3 (O&G-3) recently implemented a private cloud Electronic Content Management (ECM) solution. Participant P3 indicated that a big part of their business is selling geological data and since their old ECM solution was outdated and no longer supported, they urgently required a content management solution. P3 – *"We explored various options and decided that going with a private cloud solution was our best and cost effective option. The advantage of using a cloud solution was that our clients no longer have to come to us to access our data. Now, they are able to access our data from anywhere in the world by using a secure web portal."*

Participants from the remaining oil and gas companies were then asked: *"What kind of cloud deployment model do you intend to use?"* The participants from the remaining three oil and gas companies (O&G-1, O&G-2 and O&G-4) all replied that they will only consider an internal on-premise (OP) private cloud model, with participant P2 (O&G-2) adding, that they might consider the possibility of evolving into a hybrid model. All seven participants agreed that they would not use a public cloud model. This is consistent with what we find in the literature [5] and until concerns such as security, loss of control of their data, privacy and regulatory compliance associated with migrating to public cloud model are undertaken, oil and gas companies will always tend to look towards a private cloud model [19] (Table 2).

Participants where then asked: *"What to your knowledge are the future plans for use and implementation of cloud computing in the organization?"* Participant P1 (O&G-1) indicated that they will not be implementing any cloud solutions anytime soon because he feels that some of the cloud services they would be interested in, are not mature enough to be used within the oil and gas industry. Participant P2 (O&G-2) indicated that they want to explore virtualization and look into cloud storage but feel there aren't any cloud vendors that, *"tick all the boxes for them."* So, they will continue to investigate their cloud options and make a decision in the near future. Participants P3 (O&G-3) indicated that they recently implemented a private cloud ECM solution. They are now considering cloud storage and desktop virtualizations as their next step into their cloud journey but are still investigating and have made no decisions yet. Participant P6 (O&G-4) indicated that they have recently implemented a VxRail hyper-converged Infrastructure Appliance and are currently in the testing phase. Participant P6 added that their end goal is to move away from an on-premise environment to an internal on-premise private cloud environment.

Overall, all oil and gas companies were investigated showed a positive attitude towards cloud-computing adoption. P6 – *"We didn't implement cloud because of cloud.*

Table 2. Current level of cloud computing adoption within the four O&G companies.

Adoption question	O&G - 1	O&G - 2	O&G - 3	O&G - 4
Have you implemented cloud computing?	Yes	Yes	Yes	Yes
What cloud computing services do you use?	SaaS only	SaaS only	SaaS only	SaaS only
What cloud deployment model do you currently use?	None	None	On Premise Private cloud	None
What cloud deployment model do you intend to use?	OP Private cloud	OP Private/Hybrid cloud	OP Private cloud	OP Private cloud

We became aware of the technology and we could identify specific benefits of a technology that sounded like it would work for us. We investigated further, and we actually saw a good fit."

5.2   Technology Factors Influencing the Cloud Computing Adoption

Security. Security concerns have been constantly reported as one of the key challenges impeding organizations from adopting cloud computing. Participant P1 and P2 believe that cloud security is a major risk to their business, as they fear that their crucial data and other information, which gives them a competitive edge, could be compromised in the cloud. These findings are in agreement with [3] who also reported that the need to protect trade secrets and intellectual assets is a barrier to cloud adoption. Participants P3, P6 and P7 on the other hand, who are a lot further in their cloud strategy, had another point of view. They agree that security is a risk but one you can manage and believe that it's not a key concern when it comes to cloud computing adoption. Participants P3 and P6 added that one way to manage security concerns is by ensuring that the cloud vendors provide evidence that they comply with the relevant ISO security compliance policies and certifications. Participant P7 further added that, in his opinion, things are more secure in the cloud than they are on premise. P6 – "*Security is a risk but one you can manage. With cloud computing, you more aware of the security, therefore when you approach a cloud vendor, you ask for specific security certifications. You are identifying the risk and managing it.*"

Relative Advantage. All seven participants agree that adopting cloud solutions will provide greater benefits to their organizations. The benefits mentioned by the participants are savings on software and hardware costs, agility, flexibility, time saving and manageability. Other benefits that were also mentioned is manageability and time saving. P5 – *"You only need to upgrade one profile and then deploy to the rest of your VDIs. It's easy to set up new VMs which can be preconfigured and customized. It will save you lots of time. If you need more computer resources, it's just a click of a button."*

Another benefit is the maintenance costs. P5- *"The benefits are that we don't have to provide all the hardware, the air con's etc. to make things work. By moving from a physical hardware to a virtualized environment will help us to save on costs...".*

Another benefit that was mentioned by participants P3 and P6 was flexibility. The cloud solution allowed staff and clients the opportunity to access the applications and data anytime and from anywhere in the world. P3 - *The advantage of using a cloud solution was that our clients no longer have to come to us to access our data. Now, they are able to access our data from anywhere in the world by using a secure web portal."*

Compatibility. All seven participants pointed out that they already using some cloud applications and believe that cloud computing is easily compatibility with their organisation existing IT infrastructure. All the participants also pointed out that if cloud technology was not compatible with their current systems, then their organizations would not have implemented it. In addition, no participants reported that they needed to change any of their existing systems in order to deploy any cloud systems. Participant P7 added, *"Cloud vendors have put a lot more effort into packaging their software. They make it more compatible, in a way that makes it easier to deploy, easier to use and easier to manage."*

Participant P3 revealed that before choosing their ECM solution, they first did research and due diligence to make sure that the ECM cloud solution was compatible with their current systems and IT infrastructure, otherwise they would not have implemented it. Participant P3 also added that the cloud ECM solution met their current business needs by allowing their clients easy secured access to their database from anywhere in the world.

Complexity. The results show that all the participants are already familiar with cloud computing and are running some cloud services and therefore do not believe that complexity will be a major factor when adopting cloud computing. P4 – *"It was fairly simple. You should not feel the impact of going cloud. If you feel it then it was not done competently and properly by the provider of the cloud solution."*

However, participant P3 revealed that while implementing their cloud CMS system was relatively straight forward, migrating their legacy CMS database to the private cloud CMS database was much more complex and required careful planning. P3 - *"It required careful planning and testing prior to implementation. We also did not have the necessary skills required to, after implementation, to run and maintain the application. We had to send staff for training and not until after they received their certification, could they work on the system."* In addition, participant P3 stated that the key to their successful implementation was choosing the right vendor, one that had the necessary experience and skill to guide them through the migrating process. Participant P3 also added that training of staff was important. The findings in this study reveal that complexity will be seen as a challenge in the adoption process of cloud computing within the selected organizations in the oil and gas industry in SA, that still have legacy systems.

Summary of Technology Factors
Four factors were identified under the technology theme. The technology theme refers to the internal and external technologies that an organization has to assess when investigating adoption and includes relative advantage, compatibility, complexity and security. Our findings indicate that compatibility, relative advantage and security are all positive factors that would influence the adoption of cloud computing in the four oil and gas companies we investigated. Despite security and compatibility being identified as a challenge in previous studies (Al-Mascati & Al-Badi, 2016; Nedev, 2014), the results from this study do not perceive these factors as a challenge but rather as an enabler of the technology, therefore having a positive effect on cloud computing adoption. It was also established that adopting cloud services would provide greater benefits for the organization. Complexity is the only factor that was seen to be a challenge in the adoption process but only for those oil and gas companies that still have legacy systems. Oil and gas companies have a long history of legacy systems and processes with complex applications [20]. Most legacy systems are outdated and no longer supported and according to participant P3, *"Migrating these legacy databases to the cloud can be a real challenge"*. There is a risk that the software and data programs will not be able to work properly and match with what the cloud model requires, which could potentially lead to the failure of the cloud computing adoption.

5.3   Organizational Factors Influencing the Cloud Computing Adoption

Top Management Support. The results of this study identified top management support as a crucial factor in the adoption of cloud computing within the selected organizations in the oil and gas industry in South Africa. All seven participants are in agreement and believe that without top management support, adopting any cloud services would be impossible. Top management will not only ensure a supportive climate but will also provide adequate resources to successfully adopt cloud computing solutions [21]. P3 – *"Top Management Support was very important, we urgently required a new system and without their support we would have never implemented the software."*

However, from the interviews we can observe different levels of support when it comes to top management. Participant P2 indicated that when they implemented their cloud solutions the requirement analysis came from the board and that they were very much involved from the start. P2 – *"We had their buy in from the word go. The requirement analysis came from the board. So, we had these sessions where we got their inputs, their buy in and they were kept up to date throughout the whole project. They were very much involved from the start because a lot of these tools they use as well."*

Organisational Readiness. All study participants agree, that in order to be ready to adopt cloud computing, their organizations needed to be prepared. Organization readiness refers to the availability of technological infrastructure (hardware, software, network resources and services) and the IT skills of human resources that are required to support the adoption of cloud computing [22]. P7 – *"When you're building infrastructure, particularly on premise infrastructure like the VxRail, we made sure we had the IT Infrastructure and local expertise available."*

Before O&G-3 could launched their private cloud CMS system, participant P3 stated that they did not have the necessary skills required to run and maintain the application after installation. Staff had to be sent for training and only after they received certification on the software weere they allowed to work on the system. Providing adequate training and education is a key factor that influences cloud computing adoption in organizations [23].

Thus organizational readiness is important and vital to the process of adopting cloud computing within the selected oil and gas organizations in SA. This is in line with previous studies [21, 23] that confirm that technological infrastructure and the staff's IT skills are key to the adoption of cloud computing.

Summary of Organizational Factors

Two factors were identified under the organizational theme. The organizational theme looks at several resources and characteristics of an organization that could affect the technology adoption, such as top management support and organizational readiness. Top management support was identified as a very important factor. Our findings suggested that without top management support, adopting any cloud services would be impossible because they are responsible for providing the necessary resources needed. Organizational readiness was also identified as a vital factor that must be considered. Our findings suggested that before any decision is made, an organization needs to evaluate if their current technology infrastructure and the IT skills of human resources are ready to implement cloud computing.

5.4 Environmental Factors Influencing the Cloud Computing Adoption

Government Regulations. Participants P1 (O&G-1) and P2 (O&G-2) indicated that they were uncertain around government regulations on cloud computing and how it would affect their cloud adoption solutions, as they have not done any investigations or their due diligence when it comes to this. Participants (P3, P6, P7) from organizations O&G-3 and O&G-4 indicated that, although they are not up to date about regulations and policies for cloud computing in South Africa, they are aware around certain regulations surrounding data sensitivity and that industry data must remain within the borders of South Africa. This was one of the reasons why their organizations are deciding to move towards an internal on-premise private cloud model rather than a public cloud model, to ensure that their critical data will remain in-house and therefore believe that it will not be affected by any government regulations. P7 – *"We need to have our data within our sovereign control. Our data must be within the borders of South Africa and then remain within the borders of South Africa. And the reason for that is, that when it's inside of our borders, it is governed by the country's laws, in terms of access to the data, use of the data or misuse of the data."*

This study reveals that there is a clear lack of understanding relating to government regulations and policies around cloud computing in South Africa. The South Africa government introduced the POPI Act in 2013 to provide cloud clients with assurances regarding sensitive data, hoping to improve the public's confidence and trust and help promote cloud computing adoption in South Africa. However, the POPI Act has raised more questions than answers regarding how organizations should prepare or what steps are required in order to comply with the POPI Act and what impact it will have on organizations, after it's enforced. Despite this, as long as their critical data remains in-house, participants are under the assumption that government regulation will not be a challenge towards the adoption of cloud computing within the selected organizations in the oil and gas industry in South Africa.

Vendor Support. All seven participants agree that vendor support is critical and essential, not only when adopting cloud computing but with any new technology. Participant P3 explained, that because they had a lot of legacy systems, choosing the correct vendor was essential, one that has the necessary experience to guide you through the implementation process and also provide adequate training, to learn the skills needed to migrate a legacy database and to maintain the cloud platform afterwards. P3 – *"We are running a lot of legacy systems, so transferring our data from a legacy database system to the cloud was rather a complex operation.... Choosing the right vendor was essential. One that has the necessary experience that could guide us through this process."*

Participant P7 also added, that when dealing with vendors, it is important to have a service level agreement (SLA) in place, eliminating any disputes that could arise. SLAs goes hand in hand with clearer decision making and accountability [24]. This study confirms that vendor support, in the form of technical support, training and knowledge transfer is essential when adopting cloud computing within the oil and gas industry in SA.

Competitive Pressure. The results from our findings reveal that four out of the seven participants believe that that they cannot stand aside and watch while their competitors take advantage of the benefits of cloud computing, they have to act as well in order to remain competitive. However, two out the seven participants would prefer to take a wait and see approach. Participant P7 explains that oil and gas companies are typically risk adverse organizations, they will first observe what others have done before following themselves. Participant P2 also adds that, *"no one wants to be the frontrunner because that leaves you becoming the guinea pig."* Organizations are maybe more willing to adopt cloud computing when they see their competitors having success with the technology. However, participant P7 cautioned that there are other variables that are often not taken into consideration. P7 – *"Remember that if we see benefits that another oil company is achieving, it does not guarantee that we will see the same benefits even if we did exactly the same thing. Because our culture is different. Our people are different. Our skillset is different and our skill level is different. So those variables are very often not taken into consideration."*

Thus we found that competitive pressure plays a role in the adoption decision of cloud computing within the selected organizations within the oil and gas industry in SA.

Summary of Environmental Factors

Three factors were identified under the environmental theme. The environmental theme refers to factors outside the organization that might affect the organizations decision to adopt cloud computing, such as the external environment that the organizations operates in and includes its competitors, vendor support and government rules and regulations. Vendor Support was identified as a critical and essential factor. An organization needs to access if the vendor they have chosen are able to provide technical support, training and knowledge transfer before any decision is made to implement cloud computing. Our findings also indicate that government regulations and competitive pressure are all important factors that is not seen as a challenge to the adoption of cloud computing within the selected organizations within the oil and gas industry in SA. However, when it comes to government regulations it might be worthwhile to determine how the POPI Act will affect cloud solutions, once it is implemented.

5.5 Risks and Challenges

This research identified various issues and concerns raised by the participants that could impact on cloud-computing adoption within the selected organizations in the oil and gas industry in SA. The risks and challenges identified in the study was bandwidth, trust and vendor lock in.

All seven participants believe that bandwidth poses a risk for cloud computing adoption in the oil and gas industry in SA. These participants agree that the lack of adequate bandwidth and the high broadband costs is major concern for the oil and gas industry in South Africa when adopting cloud computing. Participant 7 explained that oil and gas companies handle large amounts of data and therefore will require large bandwidth to process and store data in the cloud and with the high cost of broadband in SA, this can be very expensive.

Another concern that was identified in this study is that none of the four oil and gas companies selected in this study, have a proper and clear corporate strategy that guides their cloud adoption process. O&G-1 and O&G-3 have currently no cloud strategy in place but are thinking of having one in place in the future, while O&G-2 (P2) confirmed that they have "*a bit of strategy in place*" but it's not well defined and still being discussed. Participant P3 indicated, that he believes O&G-4 does have a cloud technological architecture in place but "*it still early days and I think there might be a few changes on the way.*" In addition, participant P2 mentioned that there also need to change the mind-sets from people within the organization, "*getting users away from the mindset of a workstation server mentality*", otherwise organizations could struggle to adopt the new technology, which could lead to negative impact.

This study confirms that vendor support is essential, however there were some concerns that were raised, such as trust and vendor lock, that could impact on cloud computing adoption. Participant P2 and P6 addressed vendor lock in and stated it's a real concern if you rely too much on a particular vendor. They both agreed that this will prevent you from diversifying and migrating to a new vendor. P2 – *"Once you relied too much on a particular vendor you lock yourself in. It's difficult to get out. And so whatever competitors are out there offering you a better service, it's not easy for you just to sort of diversify into another."* However, participant P3 indicated, that he believes that vendor lock in is not an issue. Before implementing their cloud CMS system, they made sure to discuss with the vendor that if required, they would be able to migrate their database to another cloud vendor without any hidden costs involved.

6   Conclusion

The primary question for this research is, *"To determine the level of adoption of cloud computing technology within selected organizations in the oil and gas industry in South Africa."* The findings from this study confirm that cloud computing adoption within the selected organizations within the oil and gas industry in SA is low because they are still in the early stages of their cloud computing implementation. Although cloud computing adoption is low, the oil and gas organizations selected in this study showed a positive attitude towards adopting cloud computing because they believe that cloud computing services have the capabilities to give their business a cost and a competitive advantage.

The secondary questions for this research are, *"How South African oil and gas companies are adopting cloud computing and what are the factors influencing this adoption?"* The most common type of cloud computing service model used by the SA oil and gas industry is SaaS, while no organization in this study is using any PaaS or IaaS service models. As identified in the findings, there are currently not a lot of cloud services available that would fit the oil and gas industry and the applications that the industry would be interested in, are not mature for cloud computing yet. In terms of deploying cloud solutions, the results reveal that until security concerns, loss of control of their data, privacy and regulatory compliance associated with migrating to public cloud model are undertaken, oil and gas companies in SA will always tend to look towards an internal private cloud model, which can also explain the low adoption of cloud solutions. Based on the results of this study, the following factors were observed to have a positive influence on the adoption of cloud computing in the oil and gas industry in SA (Table 3). They are security, relative advantage, compatibility, top management support, vendor support and competition.

"What are the challenges or factors that influence the lack of adoption?" The analysis identified the following factors that can be seen as a challenge to the adoption of cloud computing such as complexity, government regulations and organisational readiness. In addition, we also identified factors that could impact or be seen as a risk or barrier to the adoption of cloud computing such as bandwidth, trust and vendor lock-in.

Although none of the oil and gas organizations in this study have a clear corporate strategy, there is still a need for such a strategy in order to properly guide these organizations in their cloud adoption process. Furthermore, since many oil and gas companies still have legacy systems, there is also a need for a cloud migration and deployment strategy, to ensure a smooth and successful migration. Migrating data from an in-house legacy system to a cloud-based solution is a complex process that needs to be implemented with a clear strategy. It also recommended that by communicating the results of the cloud

Table 3. Enablers, challenges and risks to cloud computing adoption in O&G industry

Influence on Cloud Computing Adoption	Factors
Positive influences/drivers	Security, relative advantage, compatibility, top management support, vendor support, competition
Challenges	Complexity, government regulations, organisational readiness
Risks/Barriers	Bandwidth, trust, vendor lock-in

computing initiative will allow employees to understand the benefits and how it impacts on their business. We also identified that the key to a successful cloud implementation is choosing the right service provider, one that has the necessary experience to guide you through the implementation process. In addition, the service provider should provide you with adequate training, skills and resources to meet the organization's needs, as well as provide evidence that they comply with the relevant ISO security compliance policies and certifications.

As this is a preliminary study and considering the small sample size, we would like to suggest more research be done on a larger sample, in order to validate this finding across the entire industry in South Africa. Another factor that could be considered a limitation is that all the participants interviewed for this research were men. This is not unusual, as [21] and [23] also observed from there research that the oil and gas industry, especially in technical functions are often male dominated.

References

1. Subhalakshmipriya, C., Tamilarasi, R.: Next generation tools for oil and gas companies? – Cloud computing. Int. J. Comput. Sci. Inf. Technol. **5**(6), 8214–8220 (2014)
2. Sing, S.: Cloud services are on a slow, but steady march (2014). Accessed http://www.pdgm.com/resource-library/articles-and-papers/2014/cloud-services-are-on-a-slow-but-steady-march/
3. Perrons, R., Hems, A.: Cloud computing in the upstream oil & gas industry: a proposed way forward. Energy Policy **56**, 732–737 (2013)
4. Poorebrahimi, A., Roozbahani, F.S.: Effects of security and privacy concerns on using of cloud services in energy industry, an oil and gas company: a case study. Int. J. Adv. Netw. Appl. **7**(03), 2779–2783 (2015)
5. Feblowitz, J.: Oil and gas: into the cloud? J. Petrol. Technol. **63**(5), 32–33 (2011)
6. Black, P.: Digital oilfield ten years on: a literature review. Accessed https://www.energysys.com/project/the-digital-oilfield-ten-years-on-a-literature-review/
7. Gordii, M.: Use of cloud computing in oil and gas industry. Geomat. Environ. Eng. **7**(2), 35–41 (2013)
8. Microsoft: The Microsoft Upstream Reference Architecture. Microsoft, Redmond WA (2013)
9. Accenture: A new era for energy companies: Cloud computing changes the game. Accenture, Boston MA (2012)
10. IBM: Shaping the future of the oil and gas industry with smarter cloud computing. IBM, Armonk NY (2013)

11. Ma, Y.-W., Chen, J.-L., Chang, Y.-Y.: Cloud computing technology for the petroleum application. In: 18th International Conference on Advanced Communication Technology (ICACT), pp. 101–104. Pyeongchang, South Korea (2016)

12. Wagner, P.: Cloud Myth # 4: The Energy Industry is Not in The Cloud (2016). Accessed https://www.accttwo.com/blog/cloud-myth-4-energy-industry-cloud

13. EMC: Hybrid cloud adoption: why the oil and gas industry is turning to cloud to cope with the sea of change (2016). Accessed https://uk.emc.com/collateral/industry-overview/emc-oil-gas-report.pdf

14. Rogers, E.M.: Diffusion of Innovations. Free Press, New York (2003)

15. DePietro, R., Wiarda , E., Fleischer , M.: The context for change: organization, technology and environment. In: Tornatzky, L.G., Fleischer, M. (eds.) The Processes of Technological Innovation, pp. 151–175. Lexington Books, Lexington MA (1990)

16. Gangwar, H., Date, H., Ramaswamy, R.: Understanding determinants of cloud computing adoption using an integrated TAM-TOE model. J. Enterp. Inf. Manag. 28(1), 107–130 (2015)

17. Strauss, A., Corbin, J.: Basics of Qualitative Research: Grounded Theory Procedures and Techniques. Sage Publications, Newbury Park, CA (1990)

18. Braun, V., Clarke, V.: Using thematic analysis in psychology. Qual. Res. Psychol. 3, 77–101 (2006)

19. Perrons, R.K.: How the energy sector could get it wrong with cloud computing. Energy Explor. Exploit. 33(2), 217–226 (2015)

20. Jalal, M.K.: Factors Affecting Adoption of Cloud Computing Technology by Organizations of Saudi Petro-Chemical Supply Chains. University of Portsmouth (2017)

21. Al-Mascati, H., Al-Badi, H.: Critical success factors affecting the adoption of cloud computing in oil and gas industry in Oman. In: 3rd MEC International Conference on Big Data and Smart City (ICBDSC), pp. 1–7. Muscat (2016)

22. Senyo, P.K., Effah, J., Addae, E.: Preliminary insight into cloud computing adoption in a developing country. J. Enterp. Inf. Manag. 29(4), 505–524 (2016)

23. Toluwase, T.O.: Exploring strategies for outsourcing oil and gas functions in the cloud and analysing the implications for the Oil & Gas industry. University of Liverpool (2017)

24. Atta, A.: An exploratory study on cloud computing adoption by a large South African Retailer. Honours Thesis, University of Cape Town (2016)

A Semantic Driven Approach for Efficient Cloud Service Composition

Wafa Hidri[✉], Riadh Hadj M'tir, and Narjès Bellamine Ben Saoud

National School of Computer Science, RIADI Laboratory, Manouba University,
Manouba, Tunisia
wafa.hidri@ensi-uma.tn, riadh.hadjmtir@riadi.rnu.tn,
narjes.bellamine@ensi.rnu.tn

Abstract. Today, the business requirements of consumer are often very complex, requiring a composition of multiple component cloud services to create new composite value-added applications. In the process of cloud service composition, service composability forms the basis of the efficient development of emerging composite services. Developing such services is a challenging task due to the lack of tools and techniques for understanding the composability relationships among component cloud services, which influence the whole composite service's efficiency.

In this paper, we propose a composability model for cloud services that characterize the composition relationships among services. We propose a set of composability rules which compare the semantic features of cloud services to verify the interconnection of them. Our proposed model deals essentially with functional and technical cloud services aspects. These rules compare the capabilities and requirements of cloud services to determine whether two services are composable.

Keywords: Semantic cloud environment · Cloud service composition · Component cloud service · Composability

1 Introduction

Given the complexity of consumer's business requirements and the limitation of the capability of a single cloud service, the fulfillment of the consumer's requests has become more difficult. To overcome these problems, a composition of cloud services is required [1]. Recently, both research community and industry pay attention to service-oriented architecture (SOA) [2] because it can provide a set of solutions for service compositions in cloud environments. Thus, the opportunities offered by both SOA and cloud computing can be combined to create flexible service combinations. Therefore, cloud services offered from diverse providers in the web, have been effectively applied as reusable components to solve the problems of composite applications development. The steps of discovering and selecting individual component cloud services in a service composition process are more challenging and time-consuming tasks. However, the more hard task

© Springer Nature Switzerland AG 2022
M. Themistocleous and M. Papadaki (Eds.): EMCIS 2021, LNBIP 437, pp. 229–243, 2022.
https://doi.org/10.1007/978-3-030-95947-0_16

is how to automatically integrate cloud services to create a coherent composite application that meets complex business requirements which are not achieved by the existing applications.

Generally, cloud services are provided as a monolithic cloud stack [3] that contains essentially three service offerings: Software as a Service (SaaS), Platform as a Service (PaaS), and Infrastructure as a Service (IaaS). In order to create new value-added applications that meet companies business demands, developers need to compose a set of SaaS cloud services that perform a set of specific business activities defined by the consumer. Furthermore, these software services need to be combined with other cloud resources (platform and infrastructure services) to guarantee their good functioning. For this reason, it is necessary to compose software services with their corresponding PaaS/IaaS services. As a result of this, these cloud services integrated together create a novel end-to-end service-based composite application for companies without taking into account the underlying technical problems.

In this paper we show how it is possible to guide a developer in building composite services according to the proposed composability model by analysing cloud services relationships and dependencies. The paper is structured as follows: Sect. 2 reports a motivating example that illustrates the different dependencies between component cloud services that can exist when developing composite application in Cloud. Section 3 introduces the main concepts' definitions of our composability model and presents the defined composability rules used to generate a composite service. Section 4 discusses related works. Finally, Sect. 5 concludes our work.

2   Motivating Scenario

Let us consider a company that decides to develop an integrated virtual classroom application, due to the global pandemic situation, for online education using cloud services. First, the business designers analyse the goals and design the abstract business process that corresponds to the required application. Then, after identifying the activities (business goals) which are in our context a set of abstract cloud services, the developers look for a set of concrete cloud services that perform these activities. To find concrete cloud services for each activity, developers not expert in cloud service domain can not find the corresponding cloud services to their needs because of the large number of providers offers. However, discovering the most relevant cloud services and integrating them manually is a hard and time consuming task and the retrieved solutions can not always satisfy the developers's needs.

Figure 1 illustrates the required composite service (the virtual classroom composite service) described by Business Process Model and Notation (BPMN), it is constituted of the following abstract activities where the provided functionalities are performed by a set of component software cloud services:

1. Access to virtual classroom: allows students to access their virtual space.
2. Attend virtual courses: allows students to attend an active virtual learning session.

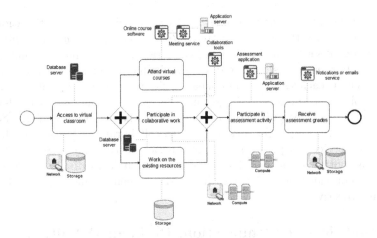

Fig. 1. The virtual classroom composite application

3. Participate in collaborative work: allows students to collaborate with their colleagues and to work as active work groups by swapping work, feedback and remarks.
4. Work on the existing learning resources: allows students to work with the existing courses and activities delivered by the teacher.
5. Participate in an assessment activity: allows students to participate in an assessment activity delivered by the teacher.
6. Receive assessment grades: allows students to receive their provided assessment grades and the teacher's feedbacks.

To run the aforementioned component software services, cloud resources (PaaS and IaaS) are required. Each abstract activity denotes a requested concrete cloud service or many cloud service components such as virtual servers, applications, middleware, databases, compute resource and so on. The new required composite application involves software services for meeting, learning, communication, collaboration, assessment (SaaS-level), and should run on specialized platform services such as application server, database server (PaaS-level) and infrastructure services, e.g., compute resources, network and storage capacity (IaaS-level). First, we need to define the platform services needed to be integrated to the application ones to be executed. For instance, two software services `Online course software` and `Meeting service` are integrated to perform the abstract activity *Attend virtual courses*. The execution of these two software component services need respectively the platform services application server and database. These cloud servers need storage and compute resources to be deployed on cloud. The *access to virtual classroom* activity needs virtual networking cloud resource to check access of students. The abstract activity *participate in an assessment* can be performed by an `assessment application` which requires respectively a virtual application server to be executed and a compute resource (virtual machine) to evaluate the students's exams. Moreover, the software service `Notifications or emails service`, which sends notifications or emails, can perform the abstract activity *Receive assessment grades*. This software component service stores its data in a storage resource and to communicate with students their assessment grades via a virtual networking cloud resource.

To conclude, each software component service has a set of application requirements (deployment services) to be executed. Each deployment entity needs a set virtual cloud resources (infrastructure services) to be deployed on cloud. Sometimes, a software component service needs to collaborate with a set of software component services to perform a set of functionalities required by a complex abstract activity. Non skilled developers need a guide to discover, select and compose component cloud services that perform their business goals, which is our main objective.

3   Cloud Service Composition: Problem Definition and Formulation

Composing SaaS services is a process that allows the invocation of a set of software component cloud services to implement the business process tasks or activities. However, discovering the suitable concrete services is a challenging task because of the rigidity in matching an activity to a software cloud service.

3.1   Cloud Service Discovery and Selection

The service discovery module is the basis for a successful composition process. It is the step of finding software cloud services that satisfy specific cloud consumer requirements expressed by a set of activities. The service selection step is a the next phase that consists in ordering the discovered services to obtain the most relevant service that meets cloud consumer preferences. Really, service providers offer their services via Internet, and the user access to web portals to discover and find the software required. Based on this principle, we formulate the cloud discovery and selection module in a cloud service-oriented approach where the services are crawled from the web portals and stored in a cloud services registry. Cloud services are described by their profile description including Capabilities, Requirements, the Non-Functional properties, and Cloud Features (CRNFCF). When the user want to find services in the cloud services registry, he/she initiates a service request which will be sent to the matchmaking engine, and matched services are returned. After that, the selection is done to the user's preferences based on non-functional attributes and user context specifications. Finally, the selected service is invoked and the results returned to the user.

3.2   Semantic Description of Cloud Service

In our previous work [4], a semantic cloud service description is proposed where cloud service is presented by its capabilities, requirements, and its different relationships. The main concepts and object properties presented in the proposed ontology are shown in Fig. 2.

Fig. 2. Main concepts of cloud service ontology

3.3 Composability Model for Cloud Services

A component cloud service is a cloud service that can be accessed over the Internet, it can be Software, Platform or Infrastructure as a Service (SaaS, PaaS or IaaS). A component cloud service can be defined as follows:

Definition 1 *(Component Cloud Service): is a service belonging to a given cloud service composition.*

A Component Cloud Service s is represented as follows:

$$Cm_s = (Cap_s, Req_s, Ct_s)$$

Where Cap_s indicates a set of capabilities and Req_s indicates a set of requirements of component cloud service s, and Ct_s is an optional set of constraints.

A composite cloud service is created by matching a component cloud service requirement to a component cloud service capability. Two types of relationships (horizontal, vertical) are considered when composing component cloud services as shown in Fig. 3. For example, a user requires the following requested cloud service defined as $Cm_r = (Cap_r, Req_r, Ct_r)$, if there are two component cloud services $Cm_{s_1} = (Cap_{s_1}, Req_{s_1}, Ct_{s_1})$, and $Cm_{s_2} = (Cap_{s_2}, Req_{s_2}, Ct_{s_2})$ that meet the requirements of the requested cloud service Req_r which means that Cm_r requires the capabilities of two component cloud services to be executed: $Req_r \equiv (Cap_{s_1} \wedge Cap_{s_2})$. As a result, the requested cloud service can be composed with these two component services Cm_{s_1} and Cm_{s_2}: $Cm_r \bowtie Cm_{s_1}$ and $Cm_r \bowtie Cm_{s_2}$. The generated composite cloud service is composed with $(Cm_r, Cm_{s_1}, Cm_{s_1})$.

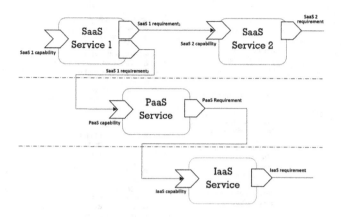

Fig. 3. Component cloud service composition relationships

In Fig. 3, the component cloud service $SaaS_1$ has two requirements. The first requirement $SaaS_1 requirement_1$ is a functional requirement, and the second $SaaS_1 requirement_2$ is a deployment requirement. The capability of the component cloud service $SaaS_2$ can meet the first requirement, so $SaaS_1$ is composed horizontally with $SaaS_2$. The capability of the component cloud service $PaaS$ can meet the second requirement, so $SaaS_1$ is composed vertically with $PaaS$. This later needs an IaaS component service to be hosted. Therefore, the $PaaS$ component service is composed vertically with $IaaS$.

Definition 2 *(Composite Cloud Service): is a combination of various component cloud services.*

The composite cloud service structure can be seen as a graph, which can be defined as G = (S, R), where S represents a set of component cloud services and R a set of composition relationships, where $s_i \in S$, s_i represents each component cloud service, $r_{ij} \in R$, represents the ith component cloud service is combined with the jth component cloud service where Req_{s_i} is satisfied by Cap_{s_j}, as shown in Fig. 4.

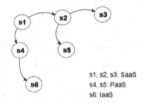

Fig. 4. Composite cloud service structure

Definition 3 *(Horizontal Composability): is a functional composability between component cloud services belonging to the same level.*

Three types of horizontal composability are defined as follows:

- Composability at SaaS level $(Cm_{saas_i} \bowtie Cm_{saas_j})$:
  Two component cloud SaaS services Cm_{saas_i} and Cm_{saas_j} are composable if $\exists\, c_{saas_j} \in Cap_{saas_j}$ and $r_{saas_i} \in Req_{saas_i}$: $c_{saas_j} = r_{saas_i}$
  The result composite cloud service c is represented as follows: $Cp_c = (Cap_c, Req_c)$ where $Cap_c = Cap_{saas_i} \cup Cap_{saas_j}$ and $Req_c = (Req_{saas_i} \cup Req_{saas_j}) - r_{saas_i}$ means the union of all the requirements not matched as shown in Fig. 5.

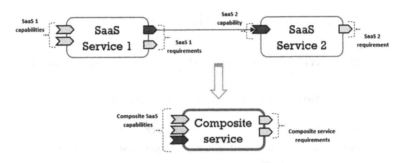

Fig. 5. Horizontal composability at SaaS level

- Composability at PaaS level $(Cm_{paas_i} \bowtie Cm_{paas_j})$:
  Two component cloud PaaS services Cm_{paas_i} and Cm_{paas_j} are composable if $\exists\, c_{paas_j} \in Cap_{paas_j}$ and $r_{paas_i} \in Req_{paas_i}$: $c_{paas_j} = r_{paas_i}$
- Composability at IaaS level $(Cm_{iaas_i} \bowtie Cm_{iaas_j})$:
  Two component cloud IaaS services Cm_{iaas_i} and Cm_{iaas_j} are composable if $\exists\, c_{iaas_j} \in Cap_{iaas_j}$ and $r_{iaas_i} \in Req_{iaas_i}$: $c_{iaas_j} = r_{iaas_i}$.

Definition 4 *(Vertical Composability): is a deployment and execution composability between component cloud services across different levels.*

Two types of vertical composability are defined as follows:

- Composability across SaaS-PaaS levels $Cm_{saas_i} \bowtie Cm_{paas_j}$:
  Two component cloud services Cm_{saas_i} and Cm_{paas_j} are composable if $\exists\, c_{paas_j} \in Cap_{paas_j}$ and $r_{saas_i} \in Req_{saas_i}$: $c_{paas_j} = r_{saas_i}$
  The result composite cloud service c is represented as follows: $Cp_c = (Cap_c, Req_c)$ where $Cap_c = Cap_{saas_i}$ and $Req_c = Req_{paas_j}$ as shown in Fig. 6.
- Composability across PaaS-IaaS levels $Cm_{paas_i} \bowtie Cm_{iaas_j}$:
  Two component cloud services Cm_{paas_i} and Cm_{iaas_j} are composable if $\exists\, c_{iaas_j} \in Cap_{iaas_j}$ and $r_{paas_i} \in Req_{paas_i}$: $c_{iaas_j} = r_{paas_i}$.

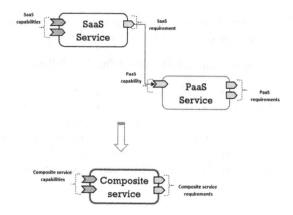

Fig. 6. Vertical composability across SaaS-PaaS levels

The composability types detailed previously are summarized in Table 1.

Table 1. Cloud services composability types

Composability	Type	Description
$SaaS \bowtie SaaS$	Horizontal, cross SaaS	Functional dependency
$SaaS \bowtie PaaS$	Vertical, across SaaS and PaaS	Execution and deployment dependency
$PaaS \bowtie PaaS$	Horizontal, cross PaaS	Platform dependency
$PaaS \bowtie IaaS$	Vertical, across PaaS and IaaS	Execution and deployment dependency
$IaaS \bowtie IaaS$	Horizontal, cross IaaS	Resource dependency

When there is a vertical and horizontal composition, the result composite cloud service c is represented as follows: $Cp_c = (Cap_c, Req_c)$ where $Cap_c = \bigcup Cap_{saas}$ and $Req_c = \phi$ if the composite cloud service hasn't any requirement, or $Req_c = r_c$ if it requires a capability of another component cloud service as shown in Fig. 7.

Definition 5 *(Component Cloud Service Matching): is a matching between capability and requirement parameters of two component cloud services Cm_s and $Cm_{s'}$.*

Four matching types are defined as follows:

- Exact match: Cm_s exactly combines with $Cm_{s'}$ if all list of Cap_s matches all list of $Req_{s'}$, thus $Cap_s \equiv Req_{s'}$.

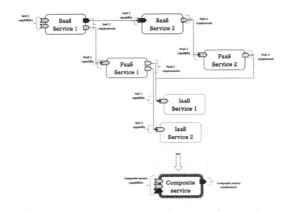

Fig. 7. Vertical and horizontal composition

- Subsume match: Cm_s combines with $Cm_{s'}$ such that $Cap_s \subset Req_{s'}$.
- Invert-subsume match: Cm_s combines with $Cm_{s'}$ such that $Req_{s'} \subset Cap_s$.
- Fail match: if the match cannot be categorized under the above four matches.

These four types of matching are considered to verify the semantic similarity between the concept capability and the concept requirement which are two ontology concepts. The semantic similarity is evaluated by the degree of connectivity between the parameters (capability, requirement) of the connected component cloud service which is calculated by the similarity function SIM according to the following scores:

- Exact match: SIM(capability, requirement) = 1
- Subsume match: SIM(capability, requirement) = 2/3
- Invert-subsume match: SIM(capability, requirement) = 1/3
- Fail match: SIM(capability, requirement) = 0

For example, let us consider that $saas_a$ and $saas_b$ are two connected services. A Subsume matching relation between them means that a capability $cap \in saas_a.Cap$ subsumes a requirement $req \in saas_b.Req$. In other words, $cap \in saas_a.Cap$ is a super-class of $req \in saas_b.Req$, than Cap_a is a set that includes Req_b, and there is at least one capability of $saas_a$ which cannot be connected to any requirement of $saas_b$. While the Invert-subsume matching relation means that a capability $cap \in saas_a.Cap$ is subsumed by a requirement $req \in saas_b.Req$, or, in other words $cap \in saas_a.Cap$ is a sub-class of $req \in saas_b.Req$, than Req_b is a set that includes Cap_a, and there is at least one requirement of $saas_b$ which cannot be connected to any capability of $saas_a$.

The calculation of semantic similarity is used to deduce which services whose capabilities feed the requirements of another service; in other words, which services are composable with other services. Thus, two services are composable if it is at least one pair matched from the set the requirements of one service and the set of the capabilities of another service. Therefore, the semantic similarity is (Exact, Subsume or Invert-subsume). We conclude that:

$$\exists cap_j \in Cm_s.Cap, \exists req_i \in Cm_{s'}.Req, , SIM(cap_j, req_i) > 0$$

3.4   Composite Service Generation

Our matching algorithm is based on the similarity function SIM to verify the composability of two services according to the different semantic matching relations: Exact, Subsume and Invert-subsume. To illustrate the functioning of the above algorithm, we treat for example the case of the abstract activity *Attend virtual courses* of the scenario mentioned previously (see Fig. 1). To implement this activity, we need two services `Online course software` and `Meeting service` that meet the user's needs in order to achieve his goals. A composite service will be generated by combining the suitable composable component services according to the following requirements: i) the service `Online course software` has respectively two requirements *Activity Dashboard* and *Learning Management*, and ii) the service `Meeting service` has respectively two requirements *Video Conferencing* and *Live Chat*. Let us consider the following service instances and their corresponding capabilities as shown in Table 2. The algorithm searches the corresponding service capability that matches each of these service requirements respectively by measuring the semantic similarity SIM between them. Each matched pair (capability, requirement) means that their corresponding services are composable. A composite service is generated containing the appropriate composable component services that meet all these service requirements such as (*Meeting service* ⋈ *GoToWebinar*) and (*Online course software* ⋈ *TalentCards*) as presented in Fig. 8.

Algorithm 1. Matchmaking algorithm

Require: S_x, S_y
Ensure: generated_plan
   generated_plan ← ϕ
   matched ← *false*
  for each requirement $req_i \in S_y.$Req **do**
    for each capability $cap_j \in S_x.$Cap **do**
     if SIM(cap_j, req_i) > 0 **then**
      matched ← *true*
      generated_plan ← *generated_plan* ∪ (S_x, S_y)
     else
      output('no matching')
     end if
    end for
  end for

Table 2. Component cloud service instances

Component cloud service	Capabilities	Is composable with
TalentCards	Activity Dashboard, Activity Tracking, Assessment Management	OnlineCourseSoftware
Canvas	Reporting and Statistics, Activity Dashboard, Learning Management, Assessment Management	OnlineCourseSoftware
GoToWebinar	Contact Management, Mobile Access, Live Chat, Video Conferencing	MeetingService
360Learning	Activity Dashboard, Learning Management, Reporting/Analytics	OnlineCourseSoftware
Lessonly	Self Service Portal, Reporting and Statistics, Activity Dashboard, API, Alerts/Notifications	OnlineCourseSoftware
WebHR	Alerts/Notifications, Third Party Integrations	
SAP Litmos	Self Service Portal, Reporting and Statistics	

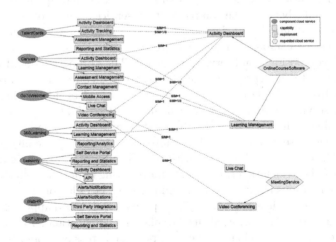

Fig. 8. Matching composable component cloud services

4   Related Work

Given the cloud computing layered architecture, cloud service composition is different from traditional composition approaches. There are many research works in cloud service composition that can be categorized into two classes. The first class focuses on service composition at the same layer where most of works consider the problem of web service composition at SaaS level [5,6]. These works are based on web services to provide composite SaaS services, due to the dominance of web service as the most used technology in service composition domain. The second class focuses on service composition at multiple layers [7,8] (e.g., across SaaS and IaaS layers) to provide an end-to-end vertical service composition[8,9], which includes the composition of SaaS and IaaS services. Some works consider the service composition problem under cloud as a process: discover, select one component cloud service from a number of many candidate cloud services respectively and compose these component services on the basis of a certain business logic specified by the consumer. However, the most of research works don't take into consideration the core of this process which are the discovery and selection phases. In [1], the authors proposed a framework which allows the selection of a combination of virtual appliances and infrastructure services that are compatible and satisfy unskilled users with vague preferences. They develop an ontology based approach to analyze cloud service compatibility by applying reasoning on the expert knowledge. In addition, they apply combination of evolutionary algorithms and fuzzy logic for composition optimization. The authors in [10] exploited cloud patterns which leverage best practices in services composition to ease the design and deployment of cloud-oriented applications. Their proposed methodology is supported by semantic Web technologies to solve incongruence between interfaces' and parameters' descriptions, and to automatize the whole composition process. Also, Serrano et al. [11] exploit the potential of semantic models and knowledge engineering to support service and application linkage by studying links between the complementary services. The proposed approach is based on studying linked data mechanisms and looking for alternatives to solve the service composition problem. Karim et al. [8] proposed a complete solution by composing cloud services vertically. They proposed a model for predicting an end-to-end QoS values of cloud-based software solutions composed of services from multiple cloud layers. They are based on identifying internal features of services and end users to calculate service similarity and then predict QoS values. The authors in [12,13], used an heuristic method to resolve the QoS-aware cloud service composition. Moreover, in [14], genetic algorithm was used to achieve global optimization with regard to service level agreement. The authors used the association rules mining for selecting appropriate clusters based on semantic relations between them in composite services history to enhance service composition efficiency. Ye et al. [7] proposed a QoS-based approach to cloud service composition that involved the trip planning application for a company to demonstrate the vertical cloud service composition across SaaS and IaaS layers. That work enables long-term quality-driven composition of cloud services based on economic models, however [15] proposed an agent-based technique, for dealing with one-time, persistent, vertical, and horizontal cloud service compositions in multi-Cloud environments. In addition, [16] presented a middleware platform (Cloud Integrator) for composing services provided by different cloud platforms. Cloud Integrator lies in the PaaS layer, allowing HaaS, SaaS and DaaS resources to be available for the users so that they can build applications consisting of the composition of services provided by these platforms. Based on ontology, the authors in [17] proposed a System for cloud service discovery and composition. However, [18] proposed a service matchmaking algorithms for SaaS selection, composition and ranking based on a new concept called 'existence degree'.

A summary of the comparative study of the related works is shown in Table 3 that presents a comparison of the studied approaches with reference to the following criteria:

- Semantic: supports semantics in service composition process.
- Functional level: takes into consideration the functional level when composing services.
- Computing level: takes into consideration the computing level when composing services.
- Service relationships: supports the relationships between the different component cloud services such as connectivity, compatibility and composability.

Table 3. Comparative analysis of the related works

Related works	Criteria			
	Semantic	Functional level	Computing level	Service relationships
[1]	~	+	+	+
[10]	+	+	+	−
[18]	−	+	−	+
[14]	~	+	−	−
[17]	+	+	−	−
[12]	−	+	−	−
[11]	+	+	~	−
[16]	−	+	~	+
[8]	−	+	+	−
[13]	−	+	−	−
[7]	−	+	+	+
[15]	−	+	−	−
Our approach	+	+	+	+

+ Supported, − Not Supported, ~ Limited Support.

5   Conclusion

In this paper, we propose a semantic approach for composing cloud services in order to create new composite application. We define a model for verifying cloud service composability. It provides a set of composability rules that compare semantic main features of cloud services which are respectively requirements and capabilities. After that, we present an algorithm to automatically generate composite services according to these proposed semantic matching rules. Future work includes an implementation of the proposed approach and an extension of our composability model to include additional semantic features such as policy and resource properties.

References

1. Dastjerdi, A.V., Buyya, R.: Compatibility-aware cloud service composition under fuzzy preferences of users. IEEE Trans. Cloud Comput. **2**, 1–13 (2014). https://doi.org/10.1109/TCC.2014.2300855
2. Papazoglou, M.P., Traverso, P., Dustdar, S., Leymann, F.: Service-oriented computing: state of the art and research challenges. Computer **40**, 38–45 (2007)
3. Papazoglou, M.P., van den Heuvel, W.-J.: Blueprinting the cloud. IEEE Internet Comput. **15**, 74–79 (2011)
4. Hidri, W., Hadj M'tir, R., Bellamine Ben Saoud, N.: An ontology for composite cloud services description. In: Barolli, L., Woungang, I., Enokido, T. (eds.) AINA 2021. LNNS, vol. 226, pp. 482–494. Springer, Cham (2021). https://doi.org/10.1007/978-3-030-75075-6_39
5. Wakrime, A.A., Jabbour, S.: Minimum unsatisfability based QoS web service composition over the cloud computing, pp. 540–545 (2015)
6. Wu, C.-S., Khoury, I.: Tree-based search algorithm for web service composition in SaaS, pp. 132–138 (2012)
7. Ye, Z., Bouguettaya, A., Zhou, X.: Economic model-driven cloud service composition. ACM Trans. Internet Technol. (TOIT) **14**, 1–19 (2014). https://doi.org/10.1109/ISCC.2014.6912608
8. Karim, R., Ding, C., Miri, A.: End-to-end QoS prediction of vertical service composition in the cloud, pp. 229–236 (2015)
9. Kamienski, C., et al.: E2ECloud: composition and execution of end-to-end services in the cloud, pp. 1–6 (2014)
10. Di Martino, B., Cretella, G., Esposito, A.: Cloud services composition through cloud patterns: a semantic-based approach. Soft. Comput. **21**(16), 4557–4570 (2016). https://doi.org/10.1007/s00500-016-2264-1
11. Serrano, M., Shi, L., Foghlú, M.Ó., Donnelly, W.: Cloud services composition support by using semantic annotation and linked data. In: Fred, A., Dietz, J.L.G., Liu, K., Filipe, J. (eds.) IC3K 2011. CCIS, vol. 348, pp. 278–293. Springer, Heidelberg (2013). https://doi.org/10.1007/978-3-642-37186-8_18
12. Faruk, M.N., Vara Prasad, G.L., Divya, G.: A genetic PSO algorithm with QoS-aware cluster cloud service composition. In: Advances in Signal Processing and Intelligent Recognition Systems. AISC, vol. 425, pp. 395–405. Springer, Cham (2016). https://doi.org/10.1007/978-3-319-28658-7_34

13. Toh, S.Y., Tang, M.: Software-as-a-service composition in cloud computing using genetic algorithm. In: Cheng, L., Leung, A.C.S., Ozawa, S. (eds.) ICONIP 2018. LNCS, vol. 11302, pp. 542–551. Springer, Cham (2018). https://doi.org/10.1007/978-3-030-04179-3_48

14. Karimi, M.B., Isazadeh, A., Rahmani, A.M.: QoS-aware service composition in cloud computing using data mining techniques and genetic algorithm. J. Supercomput. **73**(4), 1387–1415 (2016). https://doi.org/10.1007/s11227-016-1814-8

15. Gutierrez-Garcia, J.O., Sim, K.M.: Agent-based cloud service composition. Appl. Intell. **38**, 436–464 (2013)

16. Cavalcante, E., et al.: Cloud integrator: building value-added services on the cloud, pp. 135–142 (2011)

17. Guerfel, R., Sbaï, Z., Ayed, R.B.: Towards a system for cloud service discovery and composition based on ontology. In: Núñez, M., Nguyen, N.T., Camacho, D., Trawiński, B. (eds.) ICCCI 2015. LNCS (LNAI), vol. 9330, pp. 34–43. Springer, Cham (2015). https://doi.org/10.1007/978-3-319-24306-1_4

18. Saouli, H., Kazar, O., Benharkat, A.C.N.: SaaS-DCS: software-as-aservice discovery and composition system-based existence degree. Int. J. Commun. Netw. Distrib. Syst. **14**, 339–378 (2015)

Digital Governance

Digital Transformation Strategy and Organizational Change in the Public Sector: Evaluating E-Government IS and User Satisfaction

Konstantinos Ioannou[1,2(✉)], Fotis Kitsios[1,3], and Maria Kamariotou[1]

[1] Department of Applied Informatics, University of Macedonia, Thessaloniki, Greece
{k.ioannou,mkamariotou}@uom.edu.gr, kitsios@uom.gr
[2] Department of Cybersecurity, Ministry of Interior, 10183 Athens, Greece
[3] School of Social Science, Hellenic Open University, Parodos Aristotelous 18, 26335 Patras, Greece

Abstract. The effectiveness of e-government projects is hampered by a lack of know-how, reduced funding, and a lack of sound policy initiatives and decisions. Many e-government projects have been devalued because they were designed incorrectly, and effectively transfer existing bureaucracy to the digital world. The purpose of this paper is to explore the factors affecting the acceptance and satisfaction of IS users in e-government. Data was collected by 498 users in the Greek public sector. This study is useful for professionals who design these systems to improve their effectiveness and to carefully consider these variables in the design and usage of IS in the public sector.

Keywords: E-government · Satisfaction · Electronic document management system · Information systems acceptance · Public sector

1 Introduction

Recent advances in Information Technology (IT) and Information Systems (IS) have influenced several industries and the public sector. IT and IS transform individuals, businesses and all public agencies providing with quick and secure access to all resources from a single point on. Implementing IS in government is part of a larger transformation cycle aimed at supporting government to provide safer, more reliable and more productive services to people, organizations and businesses [2, 3, 6, 20, 26, 27].

Previous researchers have used current IT/IS related models to help organizations to adopt effective IS. Some of these models include the Technology Acceptance Model (TAM) [7], the Theory of Planned Behavior (TPB) [5], and the unified theory of acceptance and use of technology [3]. The factors affecting IS and user behavior are significant for IT/IS implementation to be effective. Essentially, evaluation models were introduced to consider user needs and to analyze the dimensions and aspects in system growth to increase their acceptance and satisfaction [15–17, 22]. The DeLone and McLean model

© Springer Nature Switzerland AG 2022
M. Themistocleous and M. Papadaki (Eds.): EMCIS 2021, LNBIP 437, pp. 247–257, 2022.
https://doi.org/10.1007/978-3-030-95947-0_17

of IS success (1992) [9] is among the highest used to explain the effects of IS, and has been utilized as the reason for many researches in different countries [28]. Although IS researchers have paid a lot of attention at the IS success model, limited papers have been applied in order to assess the effectiveness of IS in the public sector. Therefore, recognizing the efficacy of e-government systems, as well as the dimensions influencing the performance of employees in the public sector, clarifies a significant field of inquiry to bridge the gaps in literature and tackle future study.

Current research in the field of e-government has looked at public satisfaction as the end users. There are minimal research about the acceptance and satisfaction of internal users. Furthermore, current IS success models pay attention at system-centric assessment or organizational structure. Scholars have not yet addressed user-centric evaluations of IS in the public sector. To develop a successful e-government system, it is necessary to accomplish a level of performance that mainly satisfies most internal users [29, 32]. Results have attracted the attention of several researchers and practitioners in e-government, who have started to study the correlation between technology and individual and organizational success in the public sector (e.g., [29, 30]). While these topics have a significant contribution to the literature of public management, there are still no empirical papers examining the relation between technology and performance in the public sector and, especially, the impact of IS on staff's actions in terms of the use of e-government.

This paper explores the factors affecting the acceptance and satisfaction of IS users in e-government. Specifically, this article examines the satisfaction of IRIDA's users. IRIDA is a new, more efficient, faster, safer and more transparent electronic document management system which is used in the Ministry of Interior for the central management and handling of documents. Data was collected by 498 users in the Greek public sector.

The following is the structure of the paper. Section 2 includes the theoretical background on satisfaction in e-government. The methodology is explained in Sect. 3 and Sect. 4 discusses the findings. The final section presents limitations and avenues for future researchers.

2 Theoretical Background

The introduction of IT and computer technology into public administration brought new administrative practices and led to what is now called e-government. E-government strengthens transparency, efficiency and public accessibility and is increasingly acknowledged as a central pillar to facilitating the transformation of public governance [32]. IT, moreover, has transformed government; it provides new opportunities for delivering better, more reliable and competitive services to people and businesses and its acceptance by employees and citizens is a top priority for governors. Therefore, the creation of a theoretical model for the acceptance of digital technology in the public sector, such as that proposed by Sang et al (2009) [21], is particularly useful for developing future political and strategic decisions to enhance the usage of such services.

Much of the literature focuses on users' satisfaction with the development of services in e-government, as the success of such initiatives depends largely on the percentage of their use [32]. User acceptance is expressed mainly through the TAM. It is applied to understand individuals' attitudes towards the use of technology, which can lead to further acceptance and adoption. That is to say, the attitude formed by TAM represents the attitude formed towards the use of technology. It is considered as one of the earliest and most widely accepted research approaches; it is a dominant model in the field of technology and in the use of IS, along with the theory of IS success suggested by DeLone and McLean. According to the TAM model, the important aspects that impact on the adoption and usage of digital technologies are perceived ease of use and perceived usefulness, with Davis (1989) [7] being its main exponent. According to Davis, the model can be used to investigate the frequency at which users use a specific technology, the characteristics of the system, and the reasons users ultimately accept or reject it. In conducting a research on users of two information systems in a Canadian company and evaluating the variables used in the initial research, Davis said that both perceived usefulness and ease of use are strongly associated with self-reported system indicators; and, therefore, the final degree of acceptance and frequency of use of a system by its end users depends directly on what motivates each user.

Weerakkody et al. (2016) [25] attempt to fill a research gap by exploring the significance of users' trust in the efficiency of a system and its information in the UK, and to what extent cost affects satisfaction. The five dimensions highlighted in their paper have significantly affect users' satisfaction with services in the public sector. According to Anwer et al. (2016) [24], a thorough evaluation of these services will help to highlight their strengths and weaknesses, identify their new guidelines and compare their organization locally, nationally and internationally. For this reason, they are proceeding with an analysis and assessment of the current state of Afghanistan's e-government services, through a combination of evaluation approaches. Sachan et al. (2018) [32] investigate users' satisfaction of e-government services and therefore suggest a model, incorporating the TAM into the process. This research can help app developers to gain an idea of the needs of users in order to enhance the design and implementation of these systems. According to Wirtz et al. (2016) [23], the key difficulty for local e-government portals is to define the most important dimensions affecting user satisfaction. For this reason, they develop a model to satisfy the users of such gates, using mixed methods. Also, the research of Danila et al. (2014) [19] explores user intentions and the usage of e-government services; it presents a framework that combines the TAM, the designed behavior theory and the DeLone and McLean success model, in order to explore the dimensions affecting the purpose and the use of such services. Skordoulis et al. (2017) [18] study the TAXIS information system and examine the satisfaction of users with its use, using a multi-criteria methodology. Wang et al. (2008) [28] develop and validate a success model of e-government systems, based on the revised DeLone and McLean success model, that records the multidimensional and interdependent nature of these systems. The main aim of Horan et al (2006)'s [14] work is to create a means for the success of e-government, as shown by the users of such e-services. Regardless of whether their model will be used in the future, they point out that as these services are more widespread, it is necessary to understand the manner in which they are perceived by the taxpayer. The research of AL Athmay et al. (2016) [13] was conducted to investigate the dimensions affecting the adoption of e-government services in the United Arab Emirates, considering the end-user. They are interested in knowing the significance of satisfied users and the effect they have on user intention for these services.

However, system developers are also considered employees, since they are primarily called upon to use the new applications either voluntarily or out of compulsion. Dukic et al. (2017) [12] examine the level of computer skills of staff in the public sector and the degree to which they uphold e-government. Using a questionnaire from Croatian central government officials, they concluded that the official felt they were very specialized and did not resist the change. It is considered that some improvements in e-services need to be made. Stefanovic et al. (2016) [29] also explore the success of such systems from the angle of employees. The findings verify the validity of the DeLone and McLean model in e-government. Floropoulos et al. (2010) [11] investigate the TAXIS system using employees in Public Financial Services. This is interesting since this system is applied in a country with a strong taxation system that is mandatory. Terpsiadou et al. (2009) [10], in their study, concluded that most users are generally satisfied with the features of the system. Al-Busaidy et al. (2009) [8] carried out a survey of civil servants from three e-government-related ministries. It is revealed in the survey that there is a strong link between the following factors: efficiency, accessibility, availability and trust.

[28] using the DeLone and McLean (2003) IS success model [9] investigated the effect of information quality, quality of service, quality of system and use on user satisfaction for e-government technologies. The results conclude that authorities in the public sector should develop IS which will execute accurate and useful information and a user-friendly system for users to accept. Additionally, the findings of their study highlighted that quality of information has a greater impact on user satisfaction and perceived net benefit than quality of service and system. Therefore, managers in the public sector will concentrate on executing up-to-date and accurate information. Many scholars explored the effect of information quality, service quality, system quality and use on the satisfaction of employees who used municipal e-government systems. The findings of these studies concluded that the quality of service and the technical quality are increasing the satisfaction of staff. Employees have therefore the intention to use systems with a high degree of usability, user-friendliness, and ease of use. User satisfaction is a significant factor for the benefits of local government workers, such as increased efficiency, work performance and effectiveness [29, 32].

In e-government in particular, scholars have measured user satisfaction which adapt three factors: quality of the information, quality of the service and quality of the system. The first factor tests the content of IS containing variables such as precision, currency, timeliness of performance, reliability, completeness, mindfulness, ease of use and adequate amount of information. Level of service quality allows workers in the public sector to carry out their day-to-day work activities. Therefore, factors such as information production, the user-friendly interface, system compatibility and technical staff skills are essential to help users. The third aspect pertains to IS production efficiency. Quality of service involves variables such as information completeness, precision, format, currency, importance, timeliness, accuracy, validity, usability, and conciseness to calculate the user satisfaction impact on this aspect. IS users in the public sector indicated that the quality of system and service has a direct but not high and positive impact on user satisfaction. Their expectations are focused on the quality of information, perceived ease of use and the interface of the system because the main goal is the improvement of their work. Users require timely information by accessing data in real-time; correct information, fewer incorrect data entries and more consistent data entry across users over time.

Analyzing the current literature [29, 30, 32], the following hypotheses are defined:

H1: System quality significantly and positively influences user's satisfaction.
H2: Information quality significantly and positively influences user's satisfaction.
H3: Service quality significantly and positively influences user's satisfaction.
H4: Perceived ease of use significantly and positively influences user's satisfaction.
H5: Perceived usefulness significantly and positively influences user's satisfaction.

3 Methodology

To evaluate the satisfaction of with the use of IRIDA, a questionnaire was developed. The questionnaire was distributed to 3500 users of the system and 498 completed it. The proposed research model comes from previous research and incorporates the two main research trends derived from the literature about user satisfaction and technology acceptance [7, 9, 29, 30, 32]. In other words, it is based on both the DeLone and McLean success model for IS and Davis' TAM. Such a combination model helps to identify the degree to which a specific system fulfills its demands and proves its value, through the visual gaze of its immediate recipients, its users. Moreover, the use of variables in both models allows for a more comprehensive view of the application of such information systems, as it incorporates both objective and subjective elements of their definition. Applying the DeLone and McLean model, the key variables for evaluating an information system are the quality of the system, the quality of the information, and the quality of the service. Respectively, the variables of perceived ease of use and perceived utility by the TAM are used. All of the above variables are key to evaluating technical success, semantic success, and application effectiveness and have a direct causal relationship with satisfaction [29, 30, 32]. The instrument used 5-point Likert-scales to operationalize these variables. Analysis of the data was carried out using Regression Analysis.

4 Results

The reliability was measured using Cronbach's alpha and the values ranged from 0.959 to 0.970, exceeding the minimally required 0.70 level [4]. These values are displayed in Table 1. Independent variables are perceived usefulness, perceived ease of use, system quality, service quality and information quality and the dependent variable is satisfaction.

Table 1. Cronbach a.

Variables	No. of items	Cronbach a
Satisfaction	5	0.959
System quality	5	0.963
Information quality	7	0.960
Service quality	7	0.970
Perceived ease of use	5	0.960
Perceived usefulness	3	0.963

Table 2 presents the correlations between variables.

Table 2. Correlations.

	Satisfaction	System quality	Information quality	Service quality	Perceived ease of use	Perceived usefulness
Satisfaction	1.000	0.876	0.894	0.765	0.897	0.900
System quality	0.876	1.000	0.912	0.788	0.858	0.819
Information quality	0.894	0.912	1.000	0.794	0.867	0.857
Service quality	0.765	0.788	0.794	1.000	0.794	0.765
Perceived ease of use	0.897	0.858	0.867	0.794	1.000	0.895
Perceived usefulness	0.900	0.819	0.857	0.765	0.895	1.000

From the normal P-P and scatter plots (Fig. 1) and (Fig. 2), the data are usually distributed (all residuals cluster around the 'line') and conform with the assumptions of homogeneity of variance (homo-scedasticity) and linearity. The residual errors are evenly spread and not linked to the predicted value, thereby suggesting that the correlation is linear, and the variance of y is the same among all values of x, which supports the homoscedasticity assumption [1]. Z-score was used to evaluate the univariate outliers and all values were within the acceptable range. Mahalanobis and Cook's distances were used to evaluate the multivariate outliers. No influential outliers were identified. Variance inflation factors (VIFs) was used to evaluate Multicollinearity.

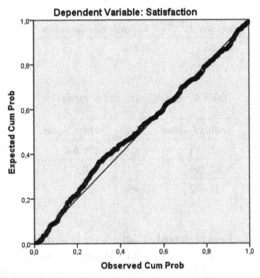

Fig. 1. Standard P-P plot of the regression standardized residual

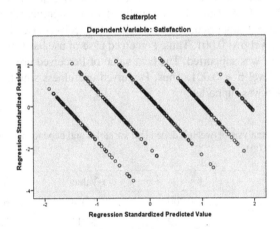

Fig. 2. Residual scatter plot

Table 3 presents that R^2 is 0.885 and adjusted R^2 is 0.884. The F statistic is 757.029 with 498 degrees of freedom (5 from the regression and 493 from residuals) and the significance value is less than $p < 0.05$ (0.000). Therefore, the model is significant. The findings of regression analysis in Table 4 also confirm the satisfactory prediction performance of the regression model.

Table 3. Regression analysis.

R	R^2	Adjusted R^2	Estimate standard error	Durbin-Watson
0.941	0.885	0.884	0.414	2.040

Table 4. ANOVA statistics of regression.

Model		Sum of square	Df	Mean Square	F	Sig.
1	Regression	648.233	5	129.647	757.029	0.000
	Residual	84.259	493	0.171		
	Total	732.492	498			

According to the findings presented at Table 5, the beta value of System quality was 0.200 with significance level $p < 0.001$. Thus, System quality has significant effect on Satisfaction and H1 was supported. The beta value of Information quality was 0.229 with significance level $p < 0.05$. Thus, Information quality has significant effect on Satisfaction and H2 was supported. The beta value of Service quality was -0.031 with significance level $p > 0.05$. Thus, Service quality does not significantly influence Satisfaction and H3 was not supported. The beta value of Perceived ease of use was -0.239 with significance level $p < 0.001$. Thus, Perceived ease of use has significant effect on Satisfaction and H4 was supported. The beta value of Perceived usefulness was 0.350 with significance level $p < 0.001$. Thus, Perceived usefulness significantly influence Satisfaction and H5 was supported.

Table 5. Regression analysis between independent variables and dependent variable. $*p < 0.05$, $**p < 0.01$, $***p < 0.001$.

Model 1	β	t-Value	VIF
System quality	0.200	5.014	6.816
Information quality	0.229	5.311	7.933
Service quality	-0.031	-1.131	3.184
Perceived ease of use	0.239	5.913	6.984
Perceived usefulness	0.350	9.464	5.835

5 Conclusion

The results of the analysis show that the correlation between the variables is positive in most of the hypotheses presented and analyzed in the previous sections. It is found that four of the five cases examined are confirmed and their variables positively affect the overall satisfaction of users. These are, in particular, the quality of the system, the quality of information, the perceived ease of use and the perceived usefulness of the system. On the contrary, although the correlation between service quality with overall satisfaction is assessed as positive, for statistical reasons it should have been rejected. In fact, the perceived ease of use and the perceived usefulness seem to be the variables with the greatest impact on overall satisfaction. Confirmation of the positive effect of the above variables can be easily explained when it comes to the users of the system. This is because they are the ones who mainly enter the data in this electronic document management system and therefore are particularly interested in having a system with that will ultimately make it functional and useful for the exercise of their duties.

Comparing the results of the present work with those of the authors of the articles in the literature review, it is worth noting that their findings are mainly coincidental. Indeed, according to previous research, all three dimensions of quality have immediate and positive effects on the satisfaction of internal users of respective systems, with each of these dimensions playing a more important role in overall satisfaction, depending on the research under consideration [29–31]. Nevertheless, the ease of use and perceived usefulness, the two key dimensions in accepting IS have a positive sign in most surveys, that refer to the extent to which users think the system can help them perform their work better [30, 32].

The use of the system essentially completely eliminates the printing of documents, their printed circulation, their handwritten assignment and signature, and their time-consuming archival and retrieval. In this way, the employee is freed from a series of unnecessary and tedious procedures, enhancing his efficiency, transparency in procedures, hierarchical control and central coordination of public services, and therefore his overall administrative capacity to respond with speed, accuracy, and flexibility to the operational requirements of a modern organizational environment while achieving significant savings.

During the survey, there was a restriction on the size of the sample. This paper investigated the satisfaction of users with this system. However, the choice to conduct the survey only in the Ministry of Interior made the sample relatively small compared to most empirical surveys that have used the questionnaire method. In addition, without the creation of a broader analysis, it has not been possible to evaluate system performance at a broader organizational level. Although evaluating the satisfaction of users in the electronic document management system under study is a first step in understanding the performance of all users, future research is needed to assess the proposed model in a representative national sample of users, so any generalization of results should be done with special care.

Behavioral IS usage models could be used by future researchers in order to clarify IS usage in various settings (such as operational, tactical and strategic level) where IS usage can be measured through time spent on the system. The results of the study reflect the attention provided to enhancing the efficiency and performance of public IS by users and suppliers of applications to consider these factors in the design and use of IS. Besides, this study is helpful to professionals in order to develop those systems more effectively and to carefully consider these factors in the development and use of IS. Due to the growing use of IT for the supply of public services, a greater understanding of such constructs necessary for increased acceptance.

References

1. Kachigan, S.K.: Multivariate Statistical Analysis: A Conceptual Introduction, 2nd edn. Radius Press, Santa Fe (1991)
2. Angelopoulos, S., Kitsios, F., Kofakis, P., Papadopoulos, T.: Emerging barriers in E-government implementation. In: Wimmer, M.A., Chappelet, J.-L., Janssen, M., Scholl, H.J. (eds.) EGOV 2010. LNCS, vol. 6228, pp. 216–225. Springer, Heidelberg (2010). https://doi.org/10.1007/978-3-642-14799-9_19
3. Angelopoulos, S., Kitsios, F., Babulac, E.: From E to U: towards an innovative digital era, chapter 103. In: Symonds, J. (ed.) Ubiquitous and Pervasive Computing: Concepts, Methodologies, Tools, and Applications, pp. 1669–1687. IGI Global Publishing (2010)
4. Newkirk, H.E., Lederer, A.L., Srinivasan, C.: Strategic information systems planning: too little or too much? J. Strat. Inf. Syst. 12, 201–228 (2003)
5. Ajzen, I.: The theory of planned behavior. Organ. Behav. Hum. Decis. Process. 50, 179–211 (1991)
6. Charalabidis, Y., Loukis, E., Lachana, Z., Alexopoulos, C.: Future research directions on the science base and the evolution of the digital governance domain. In: International Conference on Information Systems (ICIS 2019), Munich, Germany, pp. 1–6 (2019)
7. Davis, F.D.: Perceived usefulness, perceived ease of use, and user acceptance of information technology. MIS Q. 13, 319–340 (1989)
8. Al-Busaidy, M., Weerakkody, V., Dwivedi, Y.K.: Factors influencing eGovernment progress in Oman: an employee's perspective. In: 15th Americas Conference on Information Systems (AMCIS 2009), San Francisco, California, USA (2009)
9. Delone, W.H., McLean, E.R.: The DeLone and McLean model of information systems success: a ten-year update. J. Manag. Inf. Syst. 19, 9–30 (2003)
10. Terpsiadou, M.H., Economides, A.A.: The use of information systems in the Greek public financial services: the case of TAXIS. Gov. Inf. Q. 26, 468–476 (2009)
11. Floropoulos, J., Spathis, C., Halvatzis, D., Tsipouridou, M.: Measuring the success of the Greek taxation information system. Int. J. Inf. Manag. 30, 47–56 (2010)
12. Dukić, D., Dukić, G., Bertović, N.: Public administration employees' readiness and acceptance of e-government: findings from a Croatian survey. Inf. Dev. 33, 525–539 (2017)
13. AL Athmay, A.L.A.A., Fantazy, K., Kumar, V.: E-government adoption and user's satisfaction: an empirical investigation. EuroMed J. Bus. 11, 57–83 (2016)
14. Horan, T.A., Abhichandani, T., Rayalu, R.: Assessing user satisfaction of E-government services: development and testing of quality-in-use satisfaction with advanced traveler information systems (ATIS). In: 39th Hawaii International Conference on System Sciences (HICSS 2006), Kauia, HI, USA, pp. 1–10 (2006)
15. Kamariotou, M., Kitsios, F.: Information systems planning and success in SMEs: strategizing for IS. In: Abramowicz, W., Corchuelo, R. (eds.) BIS 2019. LNBIP, vol. 353, pp. 397–406. Springer, Cham (2019). https://doi.org/10.1007/978-3-030-20485-3_31
16. Kamariotou, M., Kitsios, F.: An empirical evaluation of strategic information systems planning phases in SMEs: determinants of effectiveness. In: 6th International Symposium and 28th National Conference on Operational Research, Thessaloniki, Greece, pp. 67–72 (2017)
17. Kamariotou, M., Kitsios, F.: Strategic information systems planning: SMEs performance outcomes. In: 5th International Symposium and 27th National Conference on Operation Research, Athens, Greece, pp. 153–157 (2016)

18. Skordoulis, M., Alasonas, P., Pekka-Economou, V.: E-government services quality and citizens' satisfaction: a multi-criteria satisfaction analysis of TAXISnet information system in Greece. Int. J. Prod. Qual. Manag. **22**, 82–100 (2017)
19. Danila, R., Abdullah, A.: User's satisfaction on E-government services: an integrated model. Procedia Soc. Behav. Sci. **164**, 575–582 (2014)
20. Kitsios, F., Angelopoulos, S., Papadogonas, T.: Innovation and strategic management in e-government services. Int. J. Trade Serv. **1**, 35–42 (2009)
21. Sang, S., Lee, J.-D.: A conceptual model of e-government acceptance in public sector. In: 3rd International Conference on Digital Society (ICDS 2009), Cancun, Mexico, pp. 71–76 (2009)
22. Kitsios, F., Kamariotou, M.: Strategic IT alignment: business performance during financial crisis. In: Tsounis, N., Vlachvei, A. (eds.) Advances in Applied Economic Research. Springer Proceedings in Business and Economics, pp. 503–525. Springer, Cham (2017). https://doi.org/10.1007/978-3-319-48454-9_33
23. Wirtz, B.W., Kurtz, O.T.: Local e-government and user satisfaction with city portals – the citizens' service preference perspective. Int. Rev. Public Nonprofit Mark. **13**(3), 265–287 (2016). https://doi.org/10.1007/s12208-015-0149-0
24. Anwer, A.M., Esichaikul, V., Rehman, M., Anjum, M.: E-government services evaluation from citizen satisfaction perspective: a case of Afghanistan. Transforming Gov. People Process Policy **10**, 139–167 (2016)
25. Weerakkody, V., Irani, Z., Lee, H., Hindi, N., Osman, I.: Are U.K. citizens satisfied with E-government services? Identifying and testing antecedents of satisfaction. Inf. Syst. Manag. **33**, 331–343 (2016)
26. Loukis, E., Charalabidis, Y.: Why do eGovernment projects fail? Risk factors of large information systems projects in the Greek public sector: an international comparison. Int. J. Electron. Gov. Res. (IJEGR) **7**, 59–77 (2011)
27. Loukis, E.N., Tsouma, N.: Critical issues of information systems management in the Greek Public Sector. Inf. Polity **7**, 65–83 (2002)
28. Wang, Y.S., Liao, Y.W.: Assessing eGovernment systems success: a validation of the DeLone and McLean model of information systems success. Gov. Inf. Q. **25**, 717–733 (2008)
29. Stefanovic, D., Marjanovic, U., Delić, M., Culibrk, D., Lalic, B.: Assessing the success of e-government systems: an employee perspective. Inf. Manag. **53**, 717–726 (2016)
30. Rai, A., Lang, S.S., Welker, R.B.: Assessing the validity of IS success models: an empirical test and theoretical analysis. Inf. Syst. Res. **13**, 50–69 (2002)
31. Stefanovic, D., Mirkovic, M., Anderla, A., Drapsin, M., Drid, P., Radjo, I.: Investigating ERP systems success from the end user perspective. Tech. Technol. Educ. Manag. **6**, 1089–1099 (2011)
32. Sachan, A., Kumar, R., Kumar, R.: Examining the impact of e-government service process on user satisfaction. J. Glob. Oper. Strateg. Sourcing **11**, 321–336 (2018)

Towards Smart Cities 4.0: Digital Participation in Smart Cities Solutions and the Use of Disruptive Technologies

Charalampos Alexopoulos[1]([envelope]) [ORCID], Panagiotis Keramidis[1] [ORCID],
Gabriela Viale Pereira[2] [ORCID], and Yannis Charalabidis[1]

[1] University of the Aegean, 83200 Samos, North Aegean, Greece
alexop@aegean.gr
[2] Danube University Krems, 3500 Krems, Lower Austria, Austria

Abstract. The realization of the complexity of the modern societies' needs and problems leads to an understanding that the current civil societies' ecosystem could be compared to a network, where every stakeholder is connected to the others and they collaborate by exchanging information, services and engagement. Recent research studies suggest the adoption of a new model, the Quadruple Helix model, in the action plans of smart cities. This model puts the community and the citizens in the command position alongside with the business, research and government stakeholders. It also entails the participation of the citizens not only in the service provision, through monitor and engagement, but also in the policy making, leading to a more bottom-up decision-making system towards Smart Cities 4.0 level. Information and Communication Technologies, and more specifically the Disruptive Technologies, emerge as a major means of achieving digital transformation in order to co-create user-driven decisions for the communities and the smart cities of the future. The aim of this study is to compare existing solutions of digital participation systems, identify the points of convergence and differentiation and extract useful insights for future research and applications.

Keywords: Smart Cities · Disruptive technologies · Digital participation

1 Introduction

From a technological perspective, a Smart City is a civil ecosystem that combines technology solutions for improving the efficiency and the connectivity inside the city [1]. The first level of this field of expertise (Smart City 1.0), which was led mostly by the private sector, was succeeded by a municipality-led ecosystem (Smart City 2.0), where the public administration and the local representatives were dominating the initiatives in order to achieve improvement of the lives of the citizens and the efficiency of public services. In the next phase (Smart City 3.0), this phenomenon changed into a more automated-driven system that "thinks and acts" for the better result. In this phase, citizen engagement started to emerge.

© Springer Nature Switzerland AG 2022
M. Themistocleous and M. Papadaki (Eds.): EMCIS 2021, LNBIP 437, pp. 258–273, 2022.
https://doi.org/10.1007/978-3-030-95947-0_18

Although those were the dominant levels of Smart Cities, gradually, some cities, which tend to be innovators in this field, built an ecosystem where the decision-making process involves the citizens' participation with a more agile way [2]. Referring to Smart Cities 4.0, where the decision-making process is led bottom-up, from the citizens to the administration, in a collaborative way.

Consequently, the stakeholders in the previous levels of Smart Cities, have to adjust to a more citizens-centric way of designing, executing, maintaining and monitoring the services in such an ecosystem [3]. Furthermore, the policy-making is also in charge of the citizens' votes [4]. As a result, finding a consensus in public affairs concerns not only for research institutes, government or municipal administrators and the private sector, but also the citizens' engagement and collaborative opinion expression [5].

Finding an equilibrium between these four stakeholders might uplift some challenges towards the future civil ecosystems and public administrations [6], but there are paradigms that nominate that this level is suitable, concerning the accuracy of the orientation of public policies [7], which may increase, as a result of a more wide and collaborative participation of the citizens in deciding the needs and the initiatives of their own city [8].

Literature indicates that there is a plethora of solutions that could be applied in order to achieve a more collaborative, connected and transparent system of governance in a local but also in a wider level [9]. The use of the disruptive technologies is a key factor in terms of efficiency, security and accuracy [10]. Technologies like Blockchain, Internet of Things, Artificial Intelligence, Social Networks etc. are just a few examples of ways that could influence the cities towards a more citizens-oriented governance.

There are some similar interesting studies that address the subjects that are hereby presented. Namely, "A Taxonomy of Smart Cities Initiatives" [11] is a complete study about the initiatives and their categorization in several axes based on the Quadruple Helix model, but it focuses on the general solutions and the initiatives of Smart Cities. Another interesting related example is "Smart Sustainable Cities - Reconnaissance Study" [12], which is a reconnaissance study based on the relationship between Smart Cities initiatives and Sustainable Development objectives, with a wide variety of case studies and interviews, and with an extension of policy recommendations. Of course, there are some interesting studies, for instance, "Using Disruptive Technologies in Government: Identification of Research and Training Needs" [10], that focus on the use of disruptive technologies in Government, but they are not directly linked in Smart Cities 4.0. To our knowledge, there is no study that combines the Smart Cities 4.0 initiatives' classification with the disruptive technologies' contribution.

The aim of this paper is to collect, classify and study the solutions that have been applied in cities and have designated the new level of governance and policy and decision making. It also aims to examine the characteristics of these solutions and extract some insights that could be beneficial for future research and applications. Moreover, it aims to present the results of the digital participation in some cities and show how they have affected the society and the economy, providing a simple taxonomy of those results. Lastly, it aims to point out the connection between disruptive technologies and digital participation applications, concluding that with the right use of these technologies, the results could be promising for future citizens' participation applications.

This paper is structured as follows: Sect. 2 presents the landscape of Smart Cities in terms of Stakeholders, Digital Participation and Disruptive Technologies; Sect. 3 describes the basic methodological approach towards the classification of Digital Participation Initiatives; Sect. 4 provides the classified results of Digital Participation Initiatives; Sect. 5 discusses the taxonomy of the results emerged by the Digital Participation in Smart Cities 4.0, while Sect. 6 concludes the paper.

2   Background on Smart Cities

In order to achieve better understanding of the Smart Cities 4.0 initiatives concerning digital participation of the citizens, the involvement of the academia, the industry, the policy makers and the actual use of disruptive technologies, there are hereby analyzed briefly some of the key-relations of the main classification. All those relations are related to the initiatives, but most of them are extended in every Smart Cities ecosystem.

2.1   Smart Cities Stakeholders

One of the most accurate definitions of a Smart City ecosystem is "an inclusive and participatory arena for local governments and all interested stakeholders (including citizens) to co-create communities" [13].

A significant percentage of literature studies tend to focus on three fundamental stakeholders: Universities, private sector, and local municipalities [14]. Most of the existing studies, suggest that Universities have major a role in the identification of a solution, industry is mostly responsible for designing and implementing the solution, while the municipality inspect the development [15]. This is best known as the "The Triple Helix" model. Yet, it does not include the end-user of every initiative and every project, citizens. Which creates a complication, having in mind that the Smart Cities 4.0 model itself is consisted based on the notion that cities are increasingly bottom-up governed, meaning that citizens have the power not only to monitor and regulate the policy and administration of the City, but also to collaborate and create regulations and initiatives themselves [16].

"The Quadruple helix model" is the model that includes the Communities' participation in the ecosystem's development [17]. Of course, the rest of the actors continue to play a vital role in the development, with the same formation or with partial differentiations, for instance separating the Municipality role into Policy makers and Public Authorities [18]. This model could be considered more suitable for the next step of Smart Cities.

In the initiatives that will be mentioned in the next sections, the citizen-centricity is apparent, while the innovative characteristic is that the citizens are not the only stakeholders that are gaining from this collaboration. Small businesses, policy makers, public administration are also gaining from being part in such an ecosystem, in either economic growth or more accurate metrics about the citizens' views in the city's needs. Furthermore, except the individuals' profit of being part of such an ecosystem [8], there is a macroscopic development of the ecosystem itself, in terms of Economic, Social and Environmental Sustainability [18].

2.2 Smart Cities and Digital Participation

What differentiates the Smart Cities 4.0 model from the previous models is the role of Digital Participation in the ecosystem. It is the citizen-centricity in the decision-making process that evolves the model of Smart City. The Government provides openness and transparency, while the citizens provide citizen-centric services, through collaboration mechanisms, and finally the public value is ready to adopt the services [3].

When it comes to Digital Participation, it is essential to underline the difference between Smart Cities 3.0 and Smart Cities 4.0. In the former, the term includes citizens' engagement with the policy making process and feedback for the administration's work. A simple example of this would be a digital platform where the users can rate the proposals regarding the Smart City governance. The latter, namely Smart Cities 4.0, involves a citizen-centric-based approach in policy making. There is collaboration between the Communities and the citizens in order to achieve the most citizen-empowered initiatives inside the ecosystem. The overall governance is majorly influenced by the citizens' participation, either in the voting and decision-making process or in the initiatives' coordination [16]. The policy making process becomes bottom-up, while the public value creation and adoption is also influenced by the citizens-centric vision [19]. Eventually, the Smart Cities' needs are monitored, and the action plans are designed majorly from the citizens themselves, through collaboration with the stakeholders. A prominent example of this can be considered a digital platform where the users can provide not just feedback but collaborate independently in order to propose policies for the functions of a city. This collaboration might be enhanced by the usage of Disruptive Technologies, for instance Artificial Intelligence in order to extract patterns from the users' collaboration outcomes.

2.3 Smart Cities and Disruptive Technologies

The conceptualization of the Smart Cities comes with twenty years of multidisciplinary collaboration. One of the disciplines that is deeply embedded in the notion of Smart Cities is ICT. Most of the initiatives are related to a digital solution, and the Smart Cities 4.0 initiatives more than any others, as it will be demonstrated in the next sections. In the last years, the disruptive technologies have evolved the means of creating public value and have played a primary role in governance of the Smart Cities [5].

The disruptive technologies may support a unique or combine different aspects regarding their contribution to the digital participation solutions. The aspects of these technologies are covering the whole spectrum of digital transformation from data generation to data analytics and service provision. It would be constructive to analyze some of the basic disruptive technologies, underlining the essence of their contribution in Smart Cities' ecosystem:

- Social Networks: As a result of Policy making 2.0 evolution and the direct link to the technological field, the research community can observe a significant potential in using social media on this regard [20]. Social networks do not only provide opportunity of creating a communication channel. They could play a major role in government information flows and the availability of government information [21]. However, even though social media are a representative example of a bottom-up-driven community, there are still some barriers and risks that research community and policy makers should examine [22]. Nonetheless, one could consider many examples of social networks incorporated in the Smart Cities 4.0 context, for instance a digital platform that will enable citizens to identify their own needs for the city governance based on the engagement of the networks' users.

- Blockchain: By applying blockchain and distributed ledger technologies (DLT) in the Smart Cities environment, systems gain a set of benefits for decentralized applications, and the security of distributed ledger technologies which includes consensus algorithms and smart contracts, performance increase, and reduce cost of systems [23]. All these contributions are necessary, especially in Smart Cities 4.0 ecosystem, since the digital participation system needs robust security and integrity for the voting function. Indeed, the inclusion of blockchain technologies when the solutions for Smart Cities 4.0 is possible. For example, the usage of blockchain to store the votes and propositions for the cities' needs.
- Internet of Things (IoT): The use of IoT in the Smart Cities' context provides two major benefits. Firstly, it increases the effectiveness and precision of the operation and the management of the smart city ecosystem, while providing the necessary support of the new and innovative services and applications [24]. IoT is closely related with the installation of sensors which in turn are closely connected with the production of big data. A sensor is a component able to detect a change in its environment and convert it into an electrical signal [25]. They play a major role in a lot of electronic projects which produce and analyze environmental big data, which are useful source for policy making. There is a wide range of costs for sensors, so it is possible that citizens can create their own electronic projects using sensors and collect and share data of their local environment for the community. A potential usage of IoT in Smart Cities 4.0 can be identified by considering the advantageous role of IoT in monitoring the city's environmental parameters. They can be of great value for the citizens, since they can consult these parameters to come up with effective policy proposals.
- Artificial Intelligence (AI): According to Kaplan and Haenlein, Artificial Intelligence is a system's ability to interpret and learn from external data and use that for completing tasks in a flexible and adaptable way [26]. AI is a large technological category that includes other widely used technologies, like Natural Language Processing, Machine Learning, Data Mining, Deep Learning and others. All those technologies can be incorporated in a Smart Cities 4.0 solution. For instance, a Natural Language Processing mechanism can detect the citizens' opinion for some issues related to Smart Cities and thus the citizens using the solution can provide policy proposals based on these insights.
- Augmented Reality/Virtual Reality (AR/VR): Virtual Reality (creates a digital environment and replaces the user's real environment), Augmented Reality (overlays digital created content into user's real environment) or any of the other subcategories of Digital Reality have several applications in Digital Government and some of them focus in Smart Cities [27]. Tourism, Education, Environmental awareness, Digital participation are just a few examples of fields that AR/VR Technologies could be applied in the context of Smart Cities 4.0. Even though this is a major technology, it has not been used in the identified solutions. However, there are examples that could

be considered feasible, especially for modelling virtual environments so the citizens can be educated for aspects related to policy making.

It should also be noted that there is a plethora of instances where combinations of all the aforementioned technologies, or even additional technologies, can provide beneficial results for the digital solutions. Experts have recorded prominent cases of solutions incorporating several Disruptive Technologies like AI, IoT and Blockchain simultaneously [28].

3 Methodological Approach

This section contains the methodology of the classification of Digital Participation Initiatives that were available online and the actual classification. The method is consisted with influence of other well-structed classification models from some relevant exploratory studies, for instance "A Taxonomy of Smart Cities Initiatives" [11]. The main goal of the classification is to present the initiatives with some of their common attributes and characteristics, in a simple, well-structed and centralized system.

The methodological approach of this study is based on documentary analysis for the identification of the current actions of Digital Participation towards Smart Cities 4.0 context. The purpose of this is to extract evidences for validating the research claims.

The main source of online clustered Digital Participation initiatives is "Bee Smart City" (Available at: https://www.beesmart.city/). Although there were other hubs and clusters for innovation in the context of Smart City solutions considered too, varying from providing intelligence for innovators (e.g., Smart City Hub – available at: https://smartcityhub.com/) to actually supporting projects, initiatives and start-ups (e.g., Smart City Taiwan – available at: https://www.twsmartcity.org.tw/en), the Bee Smart City was chosen due to its wide range of solutions implemented around the globe. Following the trends and searching for "citizen engagement", which is almost similar term with the Digital Participation, the online platform provided some results ranked based on popularity. These projects are representative of the world's initiatives worldwide. It would not be possible to rank all projects, due to their number, but also because there are a lot of projects that are not registered in similar online libraries.

In order for the classification to be accomplished there are many research directions to follow. One method could be seeking experts' opinions on those basic characteristics. A second method could be questionnaires, asking a wide variety of people, from different educational and professional backgrounds, about which attributes they would deem worthy of comparison. Another could be searching on the bibliography and forming a set of common attributes. Finally, the latter method was chosen, in order to achieve the flexibility and precision for such an innovative analysis.

The next step was searching the bibliography for the right structure of the classification. For this scope, several research libraries were examined. Due to the wide variety of the aspects included in this research study, there were numerous keywords used for search in those libraries. Some of them were "digital participation", "smart cities", "citizen engagement" and plenty of others.

Finally, the basic structure of the classification was formed based on two pivotal subcategories: their primary aspects and the aspects concerning the Smart Cities 4.0

context. In the former, the initiatives present some primary aspects of their launching, their aim and their benefits. The structure of this matrix would include for each initiative its name, the location/locations of launching, the year of launching, the presented cost of the final product or the final service, a short description of the aim of the project or the problem that intends to solve and some categories of key-benefits of each project. In the latter, they are classified based on their major aspects that concern the Smart Cities 4.0 ecosystem's architecture. Namely, the stakeholders that are involved in the initiative, noting that the stakeholders are considered those who were mentioned in Sect. 2.1 of this study, the exact Disruptive Technologies that are being used, if any, the Citizens' role in the initiative, based on the specifications that are provided by the initiatives, and the main Axes of the Smart Cities' Quadruple Helix [11] that each initiative concerns. All the information needed was found in the relevant "Bee Smart City" page.

There was a certain evaluation of the aspects that would be chosen for this classification, which are presented in each column separately in both tables, while the initiatives themselves are presented in each row. In the first table, the aspects are based on the related fields that the web platform "Bee Smart City" presented. Categories like Location, Year of launching, Key Benefits and others exist in the platform per se. For reasons of simplicity the most relevant were chosen for this table, while others are available online. In the second table, the aspects that were chosen to be examined were explicitly based on the fundamental Smart Cities 4.0 architecture. The stakeholders' involvement, observing that as the landscape changes the roles are evolving, namely the Universities, the Municipalities/Public Administrators, the Industry and the Citizens. The Disruptive Technologies that were used in each initiative, although some initiatives did not use any of the emerging technologies that were noted in this study, namely social media, Blockchain, IoT, Sensors, Digital Reality. The Citizens' role in the initiative, since the contribution of Citizens and their Communities are deeply embedded in Smart Cities 4.0 notion. This contribution could be monitoring public administration, or engagement with the policy making process, which already was accomplished in the previous generation of Smart Cities, but in some initiatives the users collaborated with each other and cooperated in the policy making process from a more relevant position. Lastly, the Axes of the Smart Cities' Quadruple Helix [11] that the initiatives concerned, an aspect significantly useful for understanding not only the ecosystems' areas that where initiatives find applications, but also the exact stakeholders' contribution to this area based on the initiatives' ecosystem.

4   Classification of Digital Participation Initiatives

In this section, we classify the selected initiatives based on the attributes articulated in the literature. Table 1 presents the classification based on the primary aspects, while Table 2 presents the aspects regarding the analysis of the Smart Cities 4.0 context.

In order to accomplish an overall understanding of the classification presented, there are some additional notes that should be mentioned. Initially, the initiatives were representative and so were the aspects that were examined related to them. Especially in the second table, the classification does not imply ranking of the projects presented. Every one of them is unique and so is the environment in which it is applied. Consequently, it

Table 1. Classification of Digital Participation Initiatives and their primary aspects.

Initiative Name	Location	Launch	Key Benefits	Problem - Aim
PaloAlto311	Palo Alto	2013	Efficiency Gains, Citizen Engagement, Life Quality, Connectivity, Knowledge Sharing, Easy Replication	Reporting issues of the city to the municipality
ZenCity	Tel Aviv	2014	Citizen Engagement, Knowledge Sharing, Life Quality, Inclusion / Equality	Collect real-time and frequent citizen feedback. Empower data-driven decision making.
CityMaking.Wien	Vienna	2018	Easy Replication, Efficiency Gains, Connectivity, Environmental Impact, Cost Savings, Inclusion / Equality, Knowledge Sharing	The city of Vienna lacks public green areas. Facilitation of the conception, design and request of permissions to build parklets.
Websays	Barcelona, Tarragona	2011	Knowledge Sharing, Citizen Engagement, Inclusion / Equality, Life Quality	Citizens' feedback and empowerment
Citibeats	Barcelona	2017	Citizen Engagement, Knowledge Sharing, Life Quality, Inclusion / Equality	Citizens' feedback for public and private entities
Inspirehub	Tecumseh	2016	Easy Replication	Residents' engagement both in terms of frequency and personal relevance.
CHAOS	Helsinki, Hämeenlinna	2016	Easy Replication, Cost Savings, Connectivity, Environmental Impact, Citizen Engagement, Inclusion / Equality	Building resilient cities of the future and increasing livability by breaking the data silos.
Civocracy	Potsdam, Brussels, Lyon, Geertruidenberg, Nice, La Rochelle, Monheim Am Rhein, North Holland, Losser, South Holland, Strasbourg	2015	Citizen Engagement	Government's empowerment to effectively and efficiently connect with their citizens, and make better decisions collaboratively.
CitizenLab	Winchester, Brussels	2016	Citizen Engagement	Citizen-centricity for governments, through user-friendly cloud software, insightful data analytics and focus on mobile.
PlaceSpeak	Vancouver	2011	Citizen Engagement	Facilitate legitimate and defensible online citizen engagement processes by connecting the digital identity of participants to their physical location.
Digitax	Alba Iulia	2017	Easy Replication, Life Quality, Cost Savings, Efficiency Gains, Connectivity, Citizen Engagement	Digitizing the three essential components of the public institutions in Romania: the relationship with the citizens, the internal activity of the institution and the communication between the institutions.
H.A.R.D.	Undisclosed	2017	Easy Replication, Life Quality, Cost Savings, Efficiency Gains, Connectivity, Citizen Engagement, Environmental Impact, Knowledge Sharing, Inclusion / Equality	Cities and other institutions (e.g., mining companies) around the world face several challenges whilst dealing with disasters, as they lack technical and financial resources.
Agenda Teresina 2030	Teresina	2018	Easy Replication, Citizen Engagement, Knowledge Sharing	Encourage the citizens to adopt a more sustainable lifestyle and hence contribute to the sustainable development of the city.
Mobile CrowdSensing (MCS)	Undisclosed	2018	Life Quality, Environmental Impact, Citizen Engagement, Knowledge Sharing, Inclusion / Equality	Citizens' participation with different types of reports with one tool.
EngageCitizen	Braga	2013	Citizen Engagement, Knowledge Sharing	Developing a Citizen-Centric approach at the municipality in order to increase its efficiency, improve its relation with Citizens and empower its population.

Table 2. Classification of Digital Participation Initiatives and their aspects towards Smart Cities 4.0 context.

Initiative Name	Stakeholders Involved	Disruptive Technologies Used	Citizens' Role	Axes
PaloAlto311	Citizens, Business, Municipality	Web – Mobile Technologies	Participate, Monitor	E-Government, Tourism, Transportation – Mobility, Environment
ZenCity	Citizens, Municipality	AI, social media	Engage, Policy making contribution	E-Government
CityMaking. Wien	Citizens, Municipality	Web Technologies	Participate	E-Government, Tourism, Health, Environment
Websays	Citizens, Municipality	Social media	Engage, Policy making contribution	E-Government
Citibeats	Citizens, Business, Municipality, Academia	AI, social media	Engage, Policy making contribution	E-Government, Tourism, Economy Development, Energy Sustainable Development
Inspirehub	Citizens, Business, Municipality	Web – Mobile Technologies	Engage, Communicate	E-Government, Economy Development
CHAOS	Citizens, Business, Municipality	Big Data Analysis	Engage, Policy making contribution	E-Government, Economy Development, Energy Sustainable Development
Civocracy	Citizens, Municipality, Academia	AI	Engage, Policy making contribution, Workshops participation	E-Government, Environment, Security, Transportation – Mobility, Energy Sustainable Development, ICT Infrastructure
CitizenLab	Citizens, Municipality, Academia	Natural Language Processing Technology	Engage, Monitor, Policy making contribution	E-Government
PlaceSpeak	Citizens, Municipality	Web – Mobile Technologies	Engage, Policy making contribution	E-Government
Digitax	Citizens, Municipality	Cloud Technology	Engage	E-Government
H.A.R.D.	Citizens, Business, Municipality	Web – Mobile Technologies	Engage, Monitor, Participate	E-Government, Environment, Security, Energy Sustainable Development
Agenda Teresina 2030	Citizens, Municipality	Social Media	Engage, Participate	E-Government, Environment, Energy Sustainable Development
Mobile CrowdSensing (MCS)	Citizens, Business, Municipality	Sensors, IoT Data	Engage, Participate, Data provision	E-Government, Environment, Security, Energy Sustainable Development, Transportation – Mobility, ICT Infrastructure
EngageCitizen	Citizens, Business, Municipality	AI, Social Network	Engage, Policy making contribution, Monitor	E-Government, Environment, Security, Energy Sustainable Development, Transportation – Mobility, ICT Infrastructure

is safe to assume that the success of every initiative is not visible having these aspects in mind, not even having the results of each initiative, which are presented in the next Section.

There are some primary correlations between the projects and some points in which they tend to be similar or differ. For instance, the different combinations of Stakeholders involved in the initiatives is visible. Obviously, the Citizens' and Municipalities' involvement is more common, but some of them involve the private sector or in some instances, the Academia, but in a lesser extent, since the Universities are usually involved in the early stages of an initiative, providing the research background [29].

One that could also be noticed, referring the Disruptive Technologies, is the extend involvement of social media and AI, which tend to be the most commonly used in this set of examples. Another useful notice is that a significant number of recent initiatives, for instance "CityMaking.Wien", "Agenda Teresina 2030", "Mobile CrowdSensing (MCS)", tend to focus on the Environment Axis as well, possibly signaling the need of creating a more environmentally sustainable ecosystem in the context of Smart Cities 4.0. Eventually, there are some examples of correlations between some aspects in the same table or between the two that could be discussed in a separate section, for instance which axes are evolved by a certain Disruptive Technology, like AI or social media, or in which cities certain axes are evolved, like ICT Infrastructure or Economy Development. Thus, some heterogeneous factors about the differentiations of ecosystems or technologies and their roles to play in the context of Smart Cities 4.0 can be explained.

5 Taxonomy

Having the classification of the initiatives being conducted, it would be significantly constructive to study the results of those initiatives and try to create a taxonomy of those results in terms of the current status of the initiatives, the citizens' actual participation, measured through different ways, for instance questionnaires, some representative case studies of the initiatives as well as some diversity characteristics about the cities applied and how the ecosystem's feasibility has been improved. The taxonomy used the same methodological approach as the classification analyzed in Sect. 3. The set of initiatives is the same.

5.1 Taxonomy of the Results Emerged from Digital Participation

The systematic taxonomy of the results of citizens' engagement and collaboration through the Digital Participation applications was merely a partial observation of the projects' involvement to the Smart Cities' ecosystem's evolution. There are many factors that can describe the success of a Smart Cities initiative, and since the particular subject is Digital Participation, it consequently involves Communities and Citizens, making it a multidimensional subject to study and examine. Thus, the results of the initiatives and their success conceptualize a notion that tends to behave like a spectrum, breaks down into several sub-parameters, which need to be examined separately. For instance, examining the economic feasibility of an initiative is not the same with examining its adaptability to diverse ecosystems. Or examining the efficiency of the collaborative channel between the citizens is not the same with examining the overall solutions that are led to the administration of a municipality. Yet, all those factors are necessary for the overall success of the initiative. As a result, in this section, the results are not directly linked to the overall success of the initiative, they are just classified with some primary aspects of their development.

With this taxonomy some correlations between the different aspects of an initiative's results can be examined. Obviously, there were not all of the initiatives completed, so some of them lack of results and case studies. However, the rest of the set of the initiatives are able to demonstrate some correlations. At first, the major role of the private sector in the continuity of the initiatives is apparent. Several initiatives do include adaption in the business sector, with some of them being mostly used by private companies.

Furthermore, the cities' diversity itself is worth examining. There are initiatives that are adopted by only one city and others that are adopted by over 100 cities. Consequently, it could be constructive to study the differences between those two cases. On the one hand the replicable, adaptable solution that can collect an enormous amount of data, from diverse ecosystems, on the other hand the specific and explicitly designed solution that serves one city with a distinctive architecture for this city, that will allow the study and optimization of the efficiency of the public organizations inside the city in terms of Digital Participation, but also in terms of operation efficiency. The cities' diversity is not the only one that is interesting. The wide diversity of the improved sectors within the city is also significant.

From Empowered Citizens to Mobility and from AI application in Citizens' participation to parklets inside the city, the initiatives prove that there is always room for evolution for the public sphere in the context of Smart Cities. Plus, this also proves something more. There are a lot of initiatives with similar orientation, for instance in empowering citizens' participation and knowledge sharing. Yet, a wide variety of improvements on several sectors is noticeable. That could be due to different orientation of the policy making process in each city. That process could be result of citizens' contribution. So, it is safe to consider that even if the products or the tools have similar structure or functionalities, the final improvement of the city's indicators is a result of the stakeholders', and especially the citizens' decisions, since they are the linchpin of policy making towards Smart Cities 4.0. Of course, that is up to further research to be examined.

The taxonomy could be related to demographics, city size, city climate, city industry, political-government orientation, but in this study those factors are only superficially considered in the conjunction between the results of the initiatives and the contribution of Digital Participation applications in Smart Cities 4.0.

5.2 Prioritization of Needs Based on Digital Participation

Since this study has collected a representative set of initiatives in the Digital Participation sector, and since citizen-centric policy making and citizen collaboration and involvement in the decision-making process are fundamental in the Smart Cities 4.0 context, it would be constructive to conduct a plain prioritization of the needs that emerge from these initiatives and their results, so far.

Table 3. Taxonomy of Digital Participation Initiatives' Results.

Initiative Name	Current Status	Results Noted	Improved Sectors	Case Studies	Applied Cities Diversity
PaloAlto311	Implemented	Successfully deployed and widely used.	City facilities	City of City of Palo Alto	Only one
ZenCity	Implemented	Successful results of using the product. Different actions have been participatory organized.	Homelessness, Mass Shooting, Proactive Government	City of Beaverton, Town of Cary, City of Aurora, Modi'in	Wide variety of cities, towns in different states and countries
CityMaking. Wien	Imple-mented	Widely used by both enterprises and governments	Administration information about citizens' views	UBER, LEGO, Government of Peru, Government of the Republic of Ecuador	Mostly used for enterprises
Websays	Imple-mented	500+ application visitors. Roughly the half of them did not know about the possibility of using parking places as parklets. 50+ questionnaires collected.	Parklets	City of Vienna	Only one
Citibeats	Implemented	Widely used for helping cities and organizations to extract insights from people's opinions.	SDGs observatory, Informing educational policies	Barcelona and another 3 big cities in Spain	Same country, similar size
Inspirehub	Implemented	Widely used from enterprise and some cities to communicate with citizens.	Citizens' communication	Town of Tecumseh	Only one
CHAOS	Implemented	Successful combination of human intelligence and big data to produce forerunning urban analytics and forecasts.	Data-driven cities, Empowered citizens, Livability	Helsinki City, KONE, Maria01	Mostly used for enterprises
Civocracy	Implemented	Citizen engagement with local governments to create more inclusive societies.	Collective governance, Empowered citizens	North Holland,Potsdam , Lyon	Different European Cities, with different objectives
CitizenLab	Implemented	Helped 100+ cities and governments achieve their citizen participation goals	AI to citizen participation, Housing Crisis, Mobility	Winchester, Brussels, Over 100+ Cities	Wide variety of cities and governments
PlaceSpeak	Implemented	Organizations can easily tap into the knowledge and experience of thousands of civically engaged participants.	Community planning, Public Health, Transportation, Parks & Recreation	City of Chilliwack, City of Calgary, City of Fort St. John	Variety in subjects of work
Digitax	In Development	-	-	pilot	-
H.A.R.D.	In Development	-	-	-	-
Agenda Teresina 2030	Implemented	In the end of these 30 days, Teresina's citizens are a little more conscious about the ways to contribute to the sustainable development of Teresina.	Tree planting, Sustainable Development, Citizen Awareness	Teresina	Only one
Mobile CrowdSensing (MCS)	Implemented	Successful application of IoT and Sensors data to research, smart cities and education	Wild dump reporting and controlling, Environmental monitoring, Ganga river monitoring	Undisclosed	Variety of applications and different fields of environmental uses.
EngageCitizen	Implemented	Around 40 city councils using it	Petitions, Events, Local News, Municipal Information	Braga, Guimarães, Ponte de Lima, London	Variety of councils

Based on the results in the Table 3, one of the most common indicators that is seemed to be improved by the most of the initiatives is Empowering Citizens including Citizens' communication and Collective Governance. Thus, it is safe to consider that the Public Administration has already done some progress on this regard, since the actions of the Public Administration is monitored and engaged by the citizens and their collaborative communities. One specific sub-category of this aspect that is not so obvious is the use of AI in citizens' participation. And this could be extended to the involvement of any Disruptive Technologies in the citizens' participation.

Something less common in the Table 3 is the Mobility and Transportation, even though that some of the initiatives have been involved in the evolution of this sector. On the same level, the facilitation of the city towards a more environmentally friendly structure, with more parklets and places that citizens and tourists can enjoy their days is notable. Still there are some projects that through collaboration have achieved improvement in this regard.

The needs that are not common in the previous Section are the most urgent to be involved with the Digital Participation of the Citizens towards a Smart Cities 4.0 ecosystem. For instance, SDGs observation is something that should be more institutionalized in the future initiative of Digital Participation. It comprises a wide variety of problems that the modern urban societies are called to face. Facing those needs collectively as citizens of the same participatory ecosystem would solve a lot of social and practical problems, while it would evolve the indicators of the Smart City.

Of course, there are some fundamental aspects of Smart Cities that are not directly discussed in the Digital Participation in these initiatives. For instance, the Development of ICT towards Public Sector's evolution is something that stands as an invisible need, having extensions in the most indicators of Smart Cities. However, this development should happen with an institutionalization of the ICT Governance [30]. This way the Public Authorities, alongside with the Citizens will accomplish a great milestone towards the appropriate usage of ICT in the public sphere, thus a significant evolution will be conducted in Smart Cities 4.0.

In the future, the role of the Disruptive Technologies is going to be more vital than ever, in terms of transformation of the public administration initiatives and the Digital Participation initiatives. And since the context of Smart Cities 4.0 includes citizen-centric policies and collaborative decision making from citizens, then the Disruptive Technologies are going to find steer applications in these areas. With examples as AI, Blockchain and IoT to ensure transparency, accuracy and efficiency, the future of the Digital Participation is connected with those Technologies.

6   Conclusions

In the context of Smart Cities 4.0, where the Citizens take a major role in policy making process through collaborative contribution to more citizens-centric policies, with the decisions made increasingly bottom up and the stakeholders' roles being continuously reconsidered, it is essential to study the evolution of the ecosystems through its examples. The examples of the evolution are the initiatives that are coordinated by members of the ecosystem. And since the Citizens' engagement is embedded in the new generation of

Smart Cities, it is constructive to study the initiatives of Digital Participation to have an overview of their contribution to the ecosystem's evolution.

The proposed classification of the initiatives helps to underline the key elements in every similar project, based on the representative initiatives that are examined. Examining these initiatives and their possible contribution to the evolution towards the Smart Cities 4.0 achievement, it comes to analyzing common aspects, like the Disruptive Technologies used, or the key-roles in the products. Collectively, however, those aspects construct the fundamental areas of Smart Cities 4.0, underlining the importance of empowering the Citizens to adopt Digital Participation Solutions.

Referring to the results of these initiatives, it is safe to consider that they demonstrate some correlations between the results of the use of the projects and the improvement of the Smart Cities' indicators. The study suggests some obvious correlations and their contribution to the ecosystem's needs, based on the results, thus the Citizens' Engagement itself.

The implications of this study to the scientific field of Digital Governance as well as the Smart Cities field of study and practice pertain on two fundamental aspects. Firstly, by evaluating the role of the citizens in the policy making process of a Smart City and proposing some insights based on the existing solutions the future research can orient itself towards providing the citizens with a wider range of capabilities in a proactive manner. Additionally, the technological insights emerged from this study can assist the future development of new solutions oriented towards the goal of actively incorporating the citizens' input in the policy making process. There is certain room for expansion of this study direction, especially for more exploratory literature research in order to identify the fundamental principles already mentioned in literature that assist the evolution of Smart Cities towards Smart Cities 4.0 in a more formalized manner.

Studying this new generation of Smart Cities, it is feasible to evolve nowadays' initiatives to possible new ones or modifications to existing ones. Having in mind the major role of the Disruptive Technologies and their contribution to the evolution of the ecosystems' development, the future of the ICT and Public Administration towards a more citizen-centric Governance can be discovered.

References

1. Cohen, B.: The 3 Generations of Smart Cities. https://www.fastcompany.com/3047795/the-3-generations-of-smart-cities. Accessed 27 July 2021
2. Pereira, G.V., Eibl, G., Stylianou, C., Martínez, G., Neophytou, H., Parycek, P.: The role of smart technologies to support citizen engagement and decision making. Int. J. Electron. Gov. Res. **14**, 1–17 (2018). https://doi.org/10.4018/ijegr.2018100101
3. Lopes, K.M.G., Macadar, M.A., Luciano, E.M.: Public value: citizens at the center of public management. Pesquisa Sobre o Uso das Tecnologias de Informação e Comunicação no Setor Público Brasileiro. CGI. Br, São Paulo (2018)
4. Simonofski, A., Asensio, E.S., De Smedt, J., Snoeck, M.: Citizen participation in smart cities: evaluation framework proposal. In: 2017 IEEE 19th Conference on Business Informatics (CBI). IEEE (2017). https://doi.org/10.1109/cbi.2017.21
5. Pereira, G.V., Parycek, P., Falco, E., Kleinhans, R.: Smart governance in the context of smart cities: a literature review. IP **23**, 143–162 (2018). https://doi.org/10.3233/ip-170067

6. Pereira, G.V., Rinnerbauer, B., Ginner, M., Parycek, P.: Categorizing obstacles in e-Government. In: Proceedings of the 10th International Conference on Theory and Practice of Electronic Governance. ACM (2017). https://doi.org/10.1145/3047273.3047367

7. Alawadhi, S., Scholl, H.J.: Smart governance: a cross-case analysis of smart city initiatives. In: 2016 49th Hawaii International Conference on System Sciences (HICSS). IEEE (2016). https://doi.org/10.1109/hicss.2016.370

8. Macadar, M.A., Pereira, G.V., Pinto, F.B.: The role of eParticipation in the expansion of individual capabilities. In: Panagiotopoulos, P., et al. (eds.) ePart 2019. LNCS, vol. 11686, pp. 155–166. Springer, Cham (2019). https://doi.org/10.1007/978-3-030-27397-2_13

9. Radu, L.-D.: Disruptive technologies in smart cities: a survey on current trends and challenges. Smart Cities 3, 1022–1038 (2020). https://doi.org/10.3390/smartcities3030051

10. Ronzhyn, A., Wimmer, M.A., Spitzer, V., Viale Pereira, G., Alexopoulos, C.: Using disruptive technologies in government: identification of research and training needs. In: Lindgren, I., et al. (eds.) EGOV 2019. LNCS, vol. 11685, pp. 276–287. Springer, Cham (2019). https://doi.org/10.1007/978-3-030-27325-5_21

11. Alexopoulos, C., Pereira, G.V., Charalabidis, Y., Madrid, L.: A taxonomy of smart cities initiatives. In: Proceedings of the 12th International Conference on Theory and Practice of Electronic Governance. ACM (2019). https://doi.org/10.1145/3326365.3326402

12. Estevez, E., Lopes, N., Janowski, T.: Smart Sustainable Cities: Reconnaissance Study. http://collections.unu.edu/view/UNU:5825. Accessed 27 July 2021

13. Marsal-Llacuna, M.-L.: Conceptualizing, modeling and simulating sustainability as tools to implement urban smartness. In: Gervasi, O., et al. (eds.) ICCSA 2015. LNCS, vol. 9157, pp. 477–494. Springer, Cham (2015). https://doi.org/10.1007/978-3-319-21470-2_35

14. Lawton Smith, H., Leydesdorff, L.: The Triple Helix in the context of global change: dynamics and challenges. Prometheus 32, 321–336 (2014). https://doi.org/10.1080/08109028.2014.972135

15. Dameri, R.P.: The conceptual idea of smart city: university, industry, and government vision. In: Dameri, R.P. (ed.) Smart City Implementation, pp. 23–43. Springer, Cham (2017). https://doi.org/10.1007/978-3-319-45766-6_2

16. Janowski, T., Estevez, E., Baguma, R.: Platform governance for sustainable development: reshaping citizen-administration relationships in the digital age. Gov. Inf. Q. 35, S1–S16 (2018). https://doi.org/10.1016/j.giq.2018.09.002

17. Alizadeh, T., Sipe, N.: Brisbane's digital strategy: an economic strategy for the digital age? Aust. Planner 52, 35–41 (2015). https://doi.org/10.1080/07293682.2015.1019753

18. Núñez Ferrer, J., Alessi, M., Egenhofer, C., Rizos, V.: Orchestrating Infrastructure for Sustainable Smart Cities. https://www.ceps.eu/ceps-publications/orchestrating-infrastructure-sustainable-smart-cities/. Accessed 27 July 2021

19. Lopes, K.M.G., Macadar, M.A., Luciano, E.M.: Key drivers for public value creation enhancing the adoption of electronic public services by citizens. IJPSM 32, 546–561 (2019). https://doi.org/10.1108/ijpsm-03-2018-0081

20. Ferro, E., Loukis, E.N., Charalabidis, Y., Osella, M.: Policy making 2.0: from theory to practice. Gov. Inf. Q. 30, 359–368 (2013). https://doi.org/10.1016/j.giq.2013.05.018

21. Criado, J.I., Sandoval-Almazan, R., Gil-Garcia, J.R.: Government innovation through social media. Gov. Inf. Q. 30, 319–326 (2013). https://doi.org/10.1016/j.giq.2013.10.003

22. Falco, E., Kleinhans, R., Pereira, G.V.: Challenges to government use of social media. In: Proceedings of the 19th Annual International Conference on Digital Government Research: Governance in the Data Age. ACM (2018). https://doi.org/10.1145/3209281.3209298

23. Ghandour, A.G., Elhoseny, M., Hassanien, A.E.: Blockchains for smart cities: a survey. In: Hassanien, A.E., Elhoseny, M., Ahmed, S.H., Singh, A.K. (eds.) Security in Smart Cities: Models, Applications, and Challenges. LNITI, pp. 193–210. Springer, Cham (2019). https://doi.org/10.1007/978-3-030-01560-2_9

24. Hernández-Muñoz, J.M., et al.: Smart cities at the forefront of the future internet. In: Domingue, J., et al. (eds.) FIA 2011. LNCS, vol. 6656, pp. 447–462. Springer, Heidelberg (2011). https://doi.org/10.1007/978-3-642-20898-0_32

25. Berntzen, L., Johannessen, M.R., Florea, A.: Sensors and the smart city: creating a research design for sensor-based smart city projects. In: ThinkMind//SMART 2016, The Fifth International Conference on Smart Cities, Systems, Devices and Technologies (2016)

26. Kaplan, A., Haenlein, M.: Siri, Siri, in my hand: who's the fairest in the land? On the interpretations, illustrations, and implications of artificial intelligence. Bus. Horiz. **62**, 15–25 (2019). https://doi.org/10.1016/j.bushor.2018.08.004

27. Briggs, R., Dul, J., Mariani, J., Kamleshkumar Kishnani, P.: Digital reality in government. https://www2.deloitte.com/us/en/insights/industry/public-sector/augmented-virtual-reality-government-services.html. Accessed 27 July 2021

28. Themistocleous, M., Stefanou, K., Megapanos, C., Iosif, E.: To chain or not to chain? A case from energy sector. In: Themistocleous, M., Rupino da Cunha, P. (eds.) EMCIS 2018. LNBIP, vol. 341, pp. 31–37. Springer, Cham (2019). https://doi.org/10.1007/978-3-030-11395-7_3

29. Dameri, R.P.: Smart City Implementation. Springer, Heidelberg (2017). https://doi.org/10.1007/978-3-319-45766-6

30. Wiedenhöft, G., Luciano, E., Pereira, G.V.: Institutionalization of information technology governance and the behavior of individuals in the public organizations context. In: Proceedings of the 25th European Conference on Information Systems (ECIS), Guimarães, Portugal, 5–10 June 2017, pp. 1453–1467 (2017)

E-GovSTP: An E-Government Model for a Small Island State, the Case of São Tomé and Principe

Daniel Neto Vaz[1]([✉]) [iD], Bruno Sousa[2] [iD], and Henrique Mamede[1] [iD]

[1] INESC TEC, Universidade Aberta, Lisbon, Portugal
1701120@estudante.uab.pt, jose.mamede@uab.pt
[2] University of Coimbra, CISUC, DEI, Coimbra, Portugal
bmsousa@dei.uc.pt

Abstract. Literature posits that most data and research on E-Government dominantly focuses on large economies where social, political, organizational and economic aspects of these local contexts significantly differ from other parts of the world. One such part is the group of island states specifically referred to as Small Islands Developing States (SIDS), sharing common challenges of reduced size, diseconomies of scale, impact of climate changes and other challenges. E-Government models should be adapted to local context, and for SIDS this entails understanding the local context so as to formulate a sustainable model. Even though we find studies and models for SIDS, significant differences exists among SIDS that warrant individual approaches. An example of a SIDS is São Tome and Principe, where the government is involved in E-Government initiatives. This is visible at the Ministry of Finance where different interacting Departments have developed systems and software tools to manage business processes. These systems and tools are used for interactions internally and with public and private sectors. However, for implementation, there is a lack of a centralized, interoperable vision or directive. Consequences are high total cost of ownership, subsequent costs with interoperability and maintenance, and, in the end, deficient long-term sustainability. Considering the impact of costs of information technology initiatives to the public budget, financed in its majority by development and bilateral assistance, there is a need for an E-Government model that prescribes directives for a sound, interoperable and sustainable E-Government implementation. We propose the development of E-GovSTP, a framework/model that intends to combine technical considerations and aspects of the local context to formulate guidelines for E-Government implementations in the Ministry of Finance. This artifact shall be developed through sound theoretical foundation, application of established standards and guidelines to areas of privacy and security, interoperability and system and communications. Additionally, the fundamental aspects of the local context (political, social and organizational) shall be factored into the model in order to guarantee the sustainability having in mind existing technical, material and financial constrains the country faces.

Keywords: E-Government · e-Governance · Small island economies · SIDS · Government ICT · E-Government framework

© Springer Nature Switzerland AG 2022
M. Themistocleous and M. Papadaki (Eds.): EMCIS 2021, LNBIP 437, pp. 274–288, 2022.
https://doi.org/10.1007/978-3-030-95947-0_19

1   Introduction and Problem Formulation

São Tome and Principe (STP) is a Small Island Developing State (SIDS) located in the central west coast of Africa. Since 2015, with the assistance of the World Bank, through a Project budgeted at 27 million USD, the country was connected to the "African Coast to Europe" (ACE) fiber backbone (World Bank [36]; Sub-marine Networks [35]). This has improved the quality of communications in the islands and increased the potential for further innovation, in particular in the E-Government processes. The government has focused on service modernisation through the implementation of E-Government initiatives. A few of these institutions include Customs, Internal Revenue, Port Authority, National Parliament, Social Security, Immigration, among others.

There is not, however, a centralized or integrated framework for such implementations, which lead to duplication of efforts and resources and high total cost of ownership. There are instances of excessive CAPEX and mainly OPEX costs to maintain required equipment, to acquire additional (and somehow duplicated) licenses. The reduced number of experts with specialised knowledge required to maintain and upgrade the system also aggravates the situation and OPEX costs.

The scarce financial resources available for the country are not able to support costly technological endeavours. Most Information Technology projects are financed with external assistance, with the potential of further increasing the foreign debt and dependency from external investors. In the long term, the sustainable implementation of information systems, of transparent E-Government initiatives, cannot rely on the dependency of São Tomé and Principe from external suppliers.

At the Ministry of Finance in particular, there is a need of a framework with clear directives for E-government implementation. Literature review shows the existence of frameworks and recommendation (Nielsen [27], Bwalya and Mutula [10], Glyptis et al. [16]) for developing states and SIDS. However, authors such as Bwalya and Mutula [10] underline that E-Government should be based on the specific contextual characteristic of its area of applicability, and these con textual requirements differ among SIDS. Therefore, any applicable model should consider factors of the local context, so that the guidelines should address and solve local issues at the Ministry of Finance. In this regard, the model herein proposed, E-GovSTP, takes into consideration the functions of different entities, the intra- and inter-relationships with other entities in public and private sectors, and contextual aspects of political, social and organizational nature. E-GovSTP is a contextualized E-Government model, adapted to the local reality, and takes into consideration financial, human resources, and technological constraints of São Tomé and Principe (STP) context.

This paper proposes a strategy to devise such model, which will be implemented in collaboration with experts in E-Government and assistance from financial and economic specialists, inside and outside the Ministry of Finance. The specification is in a early design phase, where the problem was clearly identified, but without objective recommendations, as well as the assessment of their impact.

The remainder of the paper is organised as follows: Sect. 2 documents the E-Government projects, Sect. 3 details the research methodology, while Sect. 4 details the current design of the E-GovSTP model, and Sect. 5 concludes the paper.

2   E-Government Models and Small Island States

According to Priyambodo and Suprihanto [31] the definition of E-Government refers to the use of Information and Communication Technologies to change and improve government services, from production to delivery. Datar et al. [11] define E-Government as a tool to address digital divide, and that it is affected by different aspects, such as broadband connectivity, the underlying technological infrastructures. The quality of education is also a key relevant aspect to consider, as identified by Salas-Pilco and Law [32], since one of its component, computer literacy, is crucial for E-Government adoption. In addition, educational solutions should be designed considering local conditions and strategic priorities.

InfoDev [12] describes three stages in the E-Government implementation: 1 - Publish (information online), 2 - Interact (civic participation), 3 - and Transact (online services), further informs that the diverse interactions with citizens follows five transformation elements: Process reform (vs simple automation), Leadership (to push reforms), Strategic investment (prioritise funding), Collaboration (inter-agency, with private sector), and Civic engagement (citizen engagement opportunities). Some constrains in the development of E-Government initiatives in developing nations can arise due to lack of a holistic planning and myths as to the meaning of E-Government. For instance, Becker and Ponschock [9] explain the myth that simply connecting people does not end the digital divide, because it is not a mere technological problem but a mix of factors from technology and social aspects such as age, income, skills and politics. Authors like Okunola et al. [29] described several issues that constrain E-Government adoption in a developing nation, such as the challenge of poor technology infrastructure, poor internet connectivity, unreliable electricity supplies and low ICT literacy levels. Other contributing factors are socio-demographic variables of education, employment and income, which reflects the relevance of local context. Another E-Government challenge is security, regarding information confidentiality, integrity and availability in the diverse platforms, which requires considerable resources, as discussed by Efe [2].

2.1   E-Government Models and Frameworks

This section discusses the existing work and frameworks towards E-Government models, as summarised in Table 1. Research works on E-Government are mainly based on data from countries in North America, in Europe and in Asia, as pointed by Dias [13], thus not considering the particularities of Small Islands Developing States (SIDS). As also underlined by Glyptis et al. [16] in studying the challenges of E-Government in small countries, the characteristics of a country's public sector and the characteristics of the country itself are determinant factors for the digital transformation of governments. Nielsen [27] presented a study on E-Government in a country apparently similar to São Tomé and Principe in terms of size, the Faroe Island. However, the islands are only similar in size, since the economic, political and financial structures are different from STP. Bayaga and Ophoff [8] specifically address E-Government in developing countries and underline the lack of research on privacy and security aspects, as well as the implications of infrastructures in rural and urban environments.

Several frameworks focus mainly on the identification of factors affecting E-Government implementation. For instance, Glyptis et al. [16] list the categories of factors including financial, legal, political, organizational, socio-cultural, and environmental for E-Government implementation. Abu-Shanab and Bataineh [1] present a framework for E-Government that address some key success factors, covering infrastructure, human and governmental challenges, which is inline with the views of Priyambodo and Suprihanto [31].

Table 1. Sample of reviewed literature and their points.

Proposal	Useful points	Missing points
Efe [2]	E-Government security with Blockchain principles	Not a model per se
Abu-Shanab and Bataineh [1]	Security as part of the infrastructure component of E-Government	Details on implementation of security
Nawaf et al. [3]	Hardware and software and implications in security	Does not address SIDS-specific constrains and adoption factors
Almrabeh and AbuAli [5]	What, Why and How of E-Government	Methodology to apply recommended measures
Alzahrani et al. [6]	Includes data from developed and developing countries	Developed countries do not include small island states
Angelopoulos et al. [7]	VISION platform, privacy level agreement	SIDS context-specific aspects
Bayaga and Ophoff [8]	Country-specific social construct	Applicability in country-specific context
Bwalya and Mutula [10]	E-Government implementation in resource-constrained country	Not totally adequate for STP due to specificities of island states
Glyptis et al. [16]	E-Government issues for small countries	Example country differ significantly from a SIDS
AlKalbaniet al. [4]	Can be adapted to small island states	Local context-specific aspects
Nielsen [27]	Proposal for a small island	Not applicable to local context
Priyambodo and Suprihanto [31]	Information centric network, ISO 27001: 2009 and 14443, education for privacy and security	Applicability in hardware and software acquisition in resource - constrained countries

Authors such as InfoDev [12], Almarabeh and AbuAli [5] describe the challenges to the implementation of E-Government and the need to set up the necessary governance structure for the continual operation in maintaining E-Government platforms. Bwalya and Mutula [10] concluded that E-Government implementation should be based on the specific contextual requirements of the area where it is being implemented.

Considerations of privacy and security are important for the adoption of E-Government and this should be subject to careful analysis. Nawaf et al. [3] explain that the use of acceptance models to study the adoption of E-Government is not totally correct because these models lack strong security consideration. Alzahrani et al. [6] discusses trust in E-Government and underline the complexities in the trust definition, as it varies based on the different approaches (psychological, sociological, economic and computer science, organisational science, business and marketing). In order to satisfy the information security requirements in public organisation for E-Government, AlKabani et al. [4] suggests the adoption of a compliance approach. The proposed information security compliance framework includes aspects of organisational security culture (commitment and accountability), technology (compatibility and capability), operational processes (integration, audit, monitoring), and environment (legal and social pressures).

2.2   The Local Context of São Tomé and Principe

São Tome and Principe (STP) is a small island developing state facing challenges related to being a SIDS, and also due to its particular local context. Such challenges include heavy dependence on donors for public budget, unemployment of its young population and human and technical constrains. Based on the UN 2020 Electronic Government Development Index (EGDI) [14], Sao Tome and Principe ranks 24 out of 54 African countries. The individual indexes of the EGDI show a growing tendency for Online Service Presence, IT Infrastructure and Human Development for Sao Tome and Principe. The structure of the index itself is an indication of differences between countries as to their social, economic and technical characteristics, as drivers that influence E-Government implementation. The EGDI 2020 indicates that STP is among the 9 lowest ranked countries among SIDS (0,4074, Medium EGDI), having scored higher values before 2014. However, for EGDI 2020, the country ranks in middle position among African countries, ranked 24th among 52 countries, and above some larger regional economies. This is a steady growth from 2014 (36th) onwards, scoring 34th in 2016 and 26th since 2018.

Some E-Government models were reviewed for this article (Almarah Beth and Abuali [5], Bwalya and Mutula [10]), and these, however, lack aspects that are specific to a particular island state. Models are not universal, that is, E-Government models cannot be blindly applied without the precise notion of the local reality of a country. One might argue that a model developed for another SIDS (e.g., Nielsen [27]) can be applied to STP, but, again, this lacks the elements unique to STP given the differences among SIDS countries. These differences are in areas of technical challenges, human and resource constrains, and specific economic, political and cultural characteristics. The E-GovSTP model, herein proposed, aims to fill this gap. The research work in progress intends to design and validate a model that can be followed by the public finance Departments of STP's Ministry of Finance. These are Departments responsible for revenue collection and expenditure management activities, which are considered by Jian [22] ascore activities in the management of public finance. In particular, the E-GovSTP model aims to assist new implementations or improvements in the on-going E-Government initiatives. The E-GovSTP model brings the advantage of better E-Government and has the potential to contribute to anti-corruption environment, by increasing transparency and accountability, pointed by Lupu and Lazar [25] as being the pillars in E-Government policies.

The design of the E-GovSTP model considers characteristics particular to SIDS, and specific to São Tome and Principe, having in mind an analysis by GCPSE [15] that, even among SIDS, significant differences exist when addressing issues of wealth and income, capacity of public service, history and degree of smallness. If we group islands by the communities they belong to, we also find differences regarding stages of E-Government development. São Tome and Principe is a member of the Portuguese-speaking community, and OECD [28] explains that these countries do not present the same stages of development, political stability and institutional coherence, which lead to distinct progress in terms of E-Government implementation. The E-GovSTP model builds upon the premise that the adaptation to the local context greatly contributes to the success of long-term digital transformation initiatives discussed by OECD [28].

Data from the National Institute of Statistics of STP, STPemNumeros [34], shows a country with a very young population averaging 20 years old, with 63% residing in urban areas, 90% literacy rate, and a population almost evenly divided between man and women. There are over 200 educational establishments distributed among educational levels from kindergarten to university. Based on 2017 data, we see a considerable trade deficit, with imports over ten times the value of exports, and, relatedly at the national budget, expenses are slightly higher than revenue, which in its composition has external financial assistance at around 60%. Also, as per WFP-STP [37] unemployment in STP is one of the highest in its region at 15%. The same publication shows that, by 2017, STP already had 2 licensed telecoms, 2% penetration rate for landlines and close to 90% penetration rate for mobile communication. As to electricity, a very relevant aspect to consider for systems and technology, there has been a considerable increase in demand and supply. However, the heavy dependency of fuel generated electricity and other technical issues has resulted in periodic outages with its effect across all sectors and adverse effect on systems and business continuity.

Financially STP is betting on the service sector, based on projected data for the 2022 national budget (MoF-OGE2022 [26]), which makes up 69,9% of GDP, and the majority of current revenue planned to come from a combination of import, value added and consumption taxes. These three categories of taxes are collected by Customs and Internal Revenue and managed by Treasury, Budget and Accounting Departments, all in the Ministry of Finance.

The presence of a young population, oriented towards new technology, coupled with higher penetration rates of mobile communication represents potential advantages to factor into an E-Government model. The dire situation of public accounts is clear and requires rigorous control of expenses, with a keen eye on investments in the areas of information systems and technology and their hidden and total costs of ownership. The effect of governmental discontinuity consequent to falls of government through parliamentary no-confidence votes or new governments resulting from elections has its effect on policy and governance related to the implementation of E-Government; this has to do with new governments frequently revamping and replacing considerable structures of central public administration and bringing new personnel, which negatively impacts ongoing initiatives in the public administration.

The consideration of the above social, economic, technological and political aspects, makes this paper one of the first contributions towards the design of an E-Government model applicable to a specific sector in STP, by detailing the research methodology that will be followed to design and validate the model for São Tomé and Principe.

Proposed research falls under the fiscal and tax thematic axis of digital service, as defined by the proposed National Strategy for Digital Governance for Sao Tome and Principe (INIC-STP [21]), drafted together by the Government of Sao Tome and Principe and the E-Government Center of UN University in Guimaraes, Portugal. This national strategy identified ten thematic axes supported by three enabling pillars, being them technological, legislative and administrative, with the requirements of political commitment and strong leadership as key success factors.

3   Towards the Design of the E-GovSTP Model

This section details the methodology to design the E-GovSTP model, towards a transparent and accountable E-Government model for São Tomé and Principe. The E-GovSTP model aims to provide guidelines enabling a sustainable and interoperable E-Government initiative in the Departments (Directorates) of Ministry of Finance performing revenue collection and expenditure management. In a nutshell, the proposed research seeks to create an integrated vision and guideline on how to implement E-Government in STP, adapted to the local socioeconomic context, and based on sound theoretical foundations. In addition, the E-GovSTP model also aims to provide objective information with a clear sequence and priority of instruments to be implemented, and directives on interoperability between systems in different Departments.

The E-GovSTP model addresses an important need in the public finance sector of STP, seeing that, as to the best of authors' knowledge, there is no such model suited to the specific reality of STP Ministry of Finance.

The design of the E-GovSTP model will leverage from theoretical foundations and standards, seeking to produce knowledge through a set of research questions, relevant to the E-Government in STP. Three initial research questions are formulated:

RQ1 Which socioeconomic and technological factors, and constrains influence E-Government implementation at the central public administration of the Ministry of Finance?

RQ2 Which are the priorities in terms of needs for the delivery of digital services, and in which sequence should these be implemented, considering the scarcity of resources?

RQ3 Which guidelines and specifications should be included in an E-Government model that can be adapted to the local context, promoting its successful implementation?

3.1   A Suitable Research Methodology

The E-GovSTP model is motivated by the need of an E-Government model adapted to the specificity of São Tomé and Principe. This subsection details the research methodology that will be followed to design and validate the E-GovSTP model.

Different research methodologies can be applied to answer the formulated questions (RQ1–RQ3). The Grounded Theory Research (GTR) and the Design Science Research (DSR) are the dominant research methodologies in the area of information systems, as presented by Gregory [18]. The author further explains that GTR requires iterative subsequent data collections until theoretical saturation based on the theoretical sampling and constant comparative method. The efforts using GTR to produce theory based on considerable data require longer research periods, in comparison to DSR. We should note that GTR timeframe is longer than the timeframe allotted for this research activity. The proposed model aims at seeking a solution fit for the local context and based on its features in face of a clear and existing problem. In this regard, DSR is fit as a methodology of choice, since, as explained by (Gregory [20], it is tailored to solve practical real-world problems by proposing relevant solutions). Stol et al. [33] indicate that GTR shares common features among its variants, and that one of these features is to limit exposure to literature in order to limit exposure to existing concepts. The objective of the research at hand is to formulate a model based on established concepts and standards and adapted to the local context, and therefore requires rigorous literature review and insight of applicable standards in order to design the model. We also seek to further understand the issues of the local context that affect the design of E-GovSTP, in line with Hevner et al. [19], which indicates that in DSR.

"... knowledge and understanding of a problem domain and its solution are achieved in the building and application of the designed artifact. (Hevner et al., 2004, pp. 75)".

and underlines that DSR aims at creating and evaluating artifacts, based on the understanding that design involves processes and products, by following a creative application of suggested seven guidelines. Besides this, the design of E-GovSTP model will consider relevant methods and instantiation of information technology models/artifacts, as suggested by Lacerda et al. [23], which can then be evaluated considering their quality attributes.

In addition, we will adapt the extended version of DSR, proposed by Peffers et al. [30], used to design and demonstrate a process model. This extended version encompasses six activities or phases, not necessarily sequential, namely, motivation and problem definition, objectives of the proposed solution, design and development, demonstration, evaluation and communication.

In order to develop the E-GovSTP model that fits the local context, the first step includes knowledge acquisition regarding E-government models through the theoretical foundations approach, as well as an in-depth analysis of the local context. Researching theoretical foundations and contextual information will allow the identification and analysis of common elements included in E-Government models for SIDS and work out their contextualized inclusion in the model for this local context. From the viewpoint of local context it is necessary to understand the state of local public administration and citizen's need for the electronic delivery of services in order to identify and set a priority for these needs and solutions. One should also understand, public budget aspects in order to better understand financial constrains facing the island. In a second step, The E-GovSTP model must include information regarding the coverage and state of telecommunication infrastructures, online services and aspects of human resource development, as included in EGDI [14]. Such research shall combine observations, interviews and literature and document analysis, thus configuring a mixed methods research, which Creswell [17] explains as being able to achieve "a more complete understanding of a research problem than either approach alone".

The specification of E-GovSTP model will follow the activities suggested by Peffers et al. [30], as illustrated in Fig. 1. Some of the activities can have entry points for research, as outlined in the bottom part and coloured in gray.

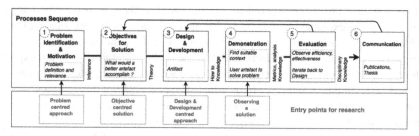

Fig. 1. Design science research model (adapted from (Peffers et al. [30]))

The activities to design and evaluate the E-GovSTP model, according to the DSR methodology are as follows:

1. **Problem identification** – the problem has been identified as the lack of model to guide E-government implementation with a centralized vision and strategy. During additional research work, refinements can be applied to the identified problem (e.g., research questions can be reformulated), the proposed solution can be reviewed and the model artifact can be enhanced. This entails collaboration with the IT Department of the Ministry of Finance, INIC (Government institution in charge of information and communication technology), and other public and private actors.

2. **Objectives of proposed solution** – development of an artifact, a model, that includes applicable standards for the identified technical areas and factoring aspects of local context in terms of political reality, social conditions, and organization of our public administration. The application of theoretical foundation and standards (e.g. ISO 27001, ITIL 4) is illustrated in Table 2.

3. **Design and development of the artifact** – Having determined the artifact's components or architecture, an *exante* evaluation is going to be carried out with main stakeholders. Once agreed on architecture, the next phase is the additional acquisition of knowledge on the subject through of systematic literature and document review and data collection, in order to determine the specific features of the local context and the basis to engineer the artifact. The subsequent step is the second phase of the literature review to determine approaches to implement existing standards applicable to identified technical issues of privacy and security, interoperability, and systems and communications, as listed in Table 2, in a way that is adapted to the needs and constrains of the local context. This process is iterative with the demonstration and evaluation phases, until the last step of fully developing and documenting the model.

As an example of local context factors, Lee [24], using a dataset of 22 SIDS countries including STP, determined that the E-Government development has direct and indirect effect on environment sustainability. The author also describes environment sustainability as related to several issues, such as isolation from major markets and small resource base. These challenges have to be met with strong policies, making clear the importance of identifying local political and social issues applicable across other technical aspects of E-Government.

4. **Demonstration** – Discuss the finalized model with experts and technical staff inside and outside the Ministry, including technical and managerial focus groups in the Ministry, and iterating such discussion between development and demonstration phases. The demonstration of the E-GovSTP will be promoted in workshops, with knowledgeable staff in the Ministry of Finance and other government entities.

5. **Evaluation** – will be promoted as an iterative activity to allow the revision of the model. Evaluation criteria intends to determine the efficiency, validity and utility of the model against the problem identified and the specific technical issues identified. The evaluation may take the form of small focus groups or small workshops, submission to expert analysis and questionnaires to users where Likert scales can measure identified criteria. To promote participation and to evaluate the acceptance of the E-GovSTP model, the Unified Theory of acceptance and use of technology (UTAUT) mechanism is proposed to be employed [20].

6. **Communication** – to be done throughout the research period and by progressive and final publications of results.

4   Preliminary Steps of the E-GovSTP Model

As outlined previously, the design of the E-GovSTP model includes, as a first step, the identification of the problem, the interactions between Departments of the Ministry of Finance and other entities.

Figure 2 illustrates the complex structure of the Ministry of Finance. The Departments/Directorates in the Ministry of Finance interact with other entities in the public and private sectors.

In the Ministry of Finance, Customs and Internal Revenue Departments carry out revenue collection activities. Other Departments, such as Treasury, Budget, Accounting, and Financial and Administrative Department (FAD) perform Budget and expenses management. As stated, the external interaction with public sector involves exchanges with public FADs, local authorities in municipalities, public institutes and agencies, and public companies with financial autonomy. This interaction involves the exchange of information regarding collected taxes, public accounting and budget information.

On the other side, the external interaction with the private sector involves private companies and taxpayers paying taxes and duties, importers/exporters paying overseas trade duties and the exchange of financial information such as incoming taxes.

Internally, there is a need for a model to shape E-Government systems/infrastructures for use by internal departments/directorates and to prescribe directives for their seamless interoperability. The exchange of information among such systems/infrastructures (intra-ministerial) is associated with technical issues, in particular with privacy and security, interoperability, due to the heterogeneity of systems and communications protocols

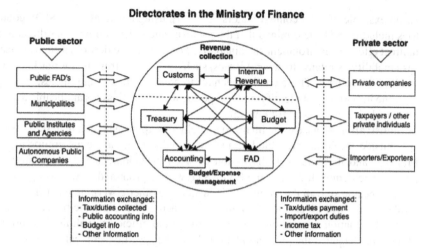

Fig. 2. Relationships of the Directorates at the Ministry of Finance

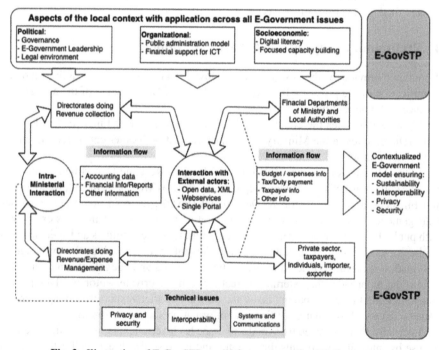

Fig. 3. Illustration of E-GovSTP model for contextualised E-Government

employed. Such issues are also associated with the interaction with external actors, either in the public or private sector.

The E-GovSTP, illustrated in Fig. 3, focus on the rigor of applying theoretical foundations and established standards, and to promote the consideration of aspects of the context of São Tomé and Principe, to enable a contextualized E-Government model. E-GovSTP aims to ensure sustainable policies, interoperable directives (recall interactions between the diverse entities in Fig. 2), adhering to privacy and security standards that are relevant in the IT domain. A non-exhaustive list of applicable standards for each technical area follows in Table 2.

E-GovSTP will consider diverse aspects of the local context with impact on E-Government. The implementation of E-GovSTP model will take into consideration the following contextual aspects: **Political Context** (Governance, E-Government leadership, Legal environment), **Organisational Context** (Model and evolution of local public administration, Financial support for information and communication technology initiatives), and **Social Context** (Digital literacy, Focused capacity building, Democracy).

Table 2. Non-exhaustive list of applicable standards and practices.

Systems and Communications

- ITIL 4 (2019) – information technology service and asset management
- COBIT 5 – information technology management and governance
- Dev Ops – for system development and related operations
- ISO/IEC/IEEE 18882:2017 – section on scalability
- ISO 22301:2019 – requirements for business continuity

Interoperability

- Open standards, XML, Web service
- Dematerialized information exchange (UNECE, UNCTAD, WCO)
- ISO/IEC/IEEE 18882:2017 - exchanges between systems

Privacy and security

- ISO 27001 – information security, used in combination with 27002, and 27005 for risk management
- IEC 27032 – standards for cybersecurity
- IEC 27033 – network security
- Digital signature (example: NIST digital signature standard)

The identification of features of the local context, will also inform additional guidelines:

1. Layout country-specific requirements for the implementation of E-Government based on aspects that constitute metrics for the UN E-Government Development index
2. Determine key success factors for E-Government initiatives taking into consideration specific local environment (cultural, social, political, technical) with emphasis on security and privacy
3. Establish methodology to vet, monitor and manage software and hardware used in Government systems for security and other vulnerabilities.

5   Conclusions

E-GovSTP model is mainly motivated by the lack of an E-Government model suitable to the reality of São Tome and Principe. The design and validation of the E-GovSTP will follow the Design Science Research approach, in order to provide a contextualised model that is sustainable, enhances STP sustainable growth and reduces dependence on external assistance.

We are committed to E-GovSTP and we believe that such a model should be of importance to policy-makers, technical personnel and concerned citizens so that all stakeholders are aware of and enabled to solve challenges in the implementation of E-Government. It should also be noted that E-GovSTP is equally relevant to donor and development institutions as an instrument for a better assessment of E-Government initiatives they are proposed to finance.

The next steps of this research work entails the specific activity of design and development, with two specific tasks developed in an interactive manner. The first task is a systematic literature review, along with the revision of available information both on the local and technical contexts so that the basis for the artifact are designed. This knowledge acquisition process will support the second tasks, which is devoted to the development of the artifact in an iterative way.

Additionally, we will seek to obtain information from intervening actors in the Ministry of Finance, INIC, as well as survey current E-Government projects. The proposed model is based on proven theory, and represents a solution that is relevant for E-Government policy-makers.

References

1. Abu-Shanab, E., Bataineh, L.Q.: Challenges facing e-government projects: how to avoid failure? Int. J. Emerg. Sci. 4(4), 207–217 (2014)
2. Ahmet, E., Kazdal, H.: It security trends for e-government threats. Int. J. Multi. Stud. Innov. Technol. 3(2), 105–110 (2019)
3. Alharbi, N., Papadaki, M., Dowland, P.: Security factors influenc ing end users' adoption of e-government. J. Internet Technol. Secured Trans. (JITST) 3(4), 320–328 (2014). https://doi.org/10.20533/jitst.2046.3723.2014.0040
4. AlKalbani, A., Deng, H., Kam, B.: A conceptual framework for information security in public organizations for e-government development. In: ACIS (2014)
5. Almarabeh, T., AbuAli, A.: A general framework for e-government: definition maturity challenges, opportunities, and success. Eur. J. Sci. Res. 39(1), 29–42 (2010)

6. Alzahrani, L., Al-Karaghouli, W., Weerakkody, V.: Analyzing the critical factors influencing trust in e-government adoption from citizens' perspective: a systematic review and a conceptual framework. Int. Bus. Rev. **26**(1), 164–175 (2017). https://doi.org/10.1016/j.ibusrev.2016. 06.004

7. Angelopoulos, K., et al.: A holistic approach for privacy protection in e-government. In: Proceedings of the 12th International Conference on Availability, Reliability and Security, pp. 1–10 (2017)

8. Bayaga, A., Ophoff, J.: Determinants of e-government use in developing countries: the influence of privacy and security concerns. In: 2019 Conference on Next Generation Computing Applications (NextComp), pp. 1–7. IEEE (2019)

9. Becker, P.: Digital divide: more than just a technology chasm. J. Strategic Int. Stud. **XI**(5), 19–29 (2016)

10. Bwalya, K.J., Mutula, S.: A conceptual framework for e-government development in resource-constrained countries: the case of zambia. Inf. Dev. **32**(4), 1183–1198 (2016). https://doi.org/ 10.1177/0266666915593786

11. Datar, M., Panikar, A., Farooqui, J.: Emerging trends in e-government. Foundations of e-government, pp. 37–46. Computer society of India, India (2008). http://www.csisigegov.org/ critical_pdf/4_37-46.pdf

12. De Kleine, A., Streifel, S., Ju Kim, E., Riordan, M., Savescu, C.: The e-government handbook for developing countries: a project of infodev and the center for democracy and technology (2010)

13. Dias, G.P.: A decade of Portuguese research in e-government: evolution, current standing, and ways forward. Electron. Gov. Int. J. **12**(3), 201–222 (2016). https://doi.org/10.1504/EG. 2016.078415

14. EGDI2020: United nations department of economic and social affairs, division for public institutions and digital government. https://publicadministration.un.org/egovkb/en-us/data-center/

15. Fosu, A.K., Gafa, D.W.: Development strategies for the vulnerable small island developing states. In: Roberts, J.L., Nath, S., Paul, S., Madhoo, Y.N. (eds.) Shaping the Future of Small Islands, pp. 37–70. Springer, Singapore (2021). https://doi.org/10.1007/978-981-15-4883-3_3

16. Glyptis, L., Christofi, M., Vrontis, D., Del Giudice, M., Dimitriou, S., Michael, P.: E-government implementation challenges in small countries: the project manager's perspective. Technol. Forecast. Soc. Chang. **152**, 119880 (2020). https://doi.org/10.1016/j.techfore.2019. 119880

17. Gregar, J.: Research Design: Qualitative, Quantitative and Mixed Methods Approaches, vol. 228, 4th edn. SAGE Publications (2014)

18. Gregory, R.W.: Design Science Research and the Grounded Theory Method: Characteristics, Differences, and Complementary Uses, pp. 111–127. Physica-Verlag HD, Heidelberg (2011). https://doi.org/10.1007/978-3-7908-2781-1_6

19. Bichler, M.: Design science in information systems research. Wirtschaftsinformatik **48**(2), 133–135 (2006). https://doi.org/10.1007/s11576-006-0028-8

20. Hlomela, T., Mawela, T.: Citizens' perceptions of mobile tax filing services. In: Themistocleous, M., Papadaki, M., Kamal, M.M. (eds.) Information Systems, pp. 256–269. Springer, Cham (2020)

21. INIC-STP: Estratégica digital para a governação digital em sao tome e principe, inic-instituto da inovcacao e conhecimento (2020). http://inic.gov.st/docs/EstrGovDigital-STP-Jan2020. pdf. Accessed 16 Nov 2021

22. Jian, W.: E-government and public finance management. Public Administration: Challenges of Inequality and Exclusion (2003)

23. Lacerda, D., Dresch, A., Proença, A., Antunes Júnior, J.A.V.: Design science research: a research method to production engineering. Gestão & Produção **20**, 741–761 (2012). https://doi.org/10.1590/S0104-530X2013005000014

24. Lee, Y.B.: Exploring the relationship between e-government development and environmental sustainability: a study of small island developing states. Sustainability **9**(5) (2017). https://doi.org/10.3390/su9050732. https://www.mdpi.com/2071-1050/9/5/732

25. Lupu, D., Lazar, C.G.: Influence of e-government on the level of corruption in some eu and non-eu states. Procedia Econ. Finan. **20**, 365–371 (2015). https://doi.org/10.1016/S2212-5671(15)00085-4. https://www.sciencedirect.com/science/article/pii/S221256711500 00854. Globalization and Higher Education in Economics and Business Administration - GEBA 2013

26. MoF-OGE2022: Ministry of finance of STP 2022 national budget. https://www.financas.gov.st/index.php/publicacoes/documentos/file/1384-stp-apresentacao-orcamento-2022. Accessed 16 Nov 2021

27. Nielsen, M.M.: Digitising a small island state: a lesson in Faroese. In: Proceedings of the 9th International Conference on Theory and Practice of Electronic Governance, pp. 54–59 (2016). https://doi.org/10.1145/2910019.2910042

28. OECD: Promoting the digital transformation of African Portuguese-speaking countries and timor-leste. https://doi.org/10.1787/9789264307131-en

29. Okunola, O.M., Rowley, J., Johnson, F.: The multi-dimensional digital divide: perspectives from an e-government portal in nigeria. Gov. Inf. Q. **34**(2), 329–339 (2017). https://doi.org/10.1016/j.giq.2017.02.002

30. Peffers, K., et al.: Design science research process: a model for producing and presenting information systems research. CoRR abs/2006.02763 (2020). https://arxiv.org/abs/2006.02763

31. Priyambodo, T.K., Suprihanto, D.: Information security on e-government as information-centric networks. Int. J. Comput. Eng. Res. Trends **3**(06), 360–365 (2016)

32. Salas-Pilco, S.Z., Law, N.: ICT curriculum planning and development: policy and implementation lessons from small developing states (2018). https://doi.org/10.1007/978-3-319-676 57-9 4

33. Stol, K.J., Ralph, P., Fitzgerald, B.: Grounded theory in software engineering research: a critical review and guidelines. In: 2016 IEEE/ACM 38th International Conference on Software Engineering (ICSE), pp. 120–131 (2016). https://doi.org/10.1145/2884781.2884833

34. STPemNumeros: Instituto nacional das estatísticas de sao tomé e príncipe, são tome e principe em numeros 2017. https://ine.st/index.php/publicacao/documentos/category/99-stp emnumeros

35. SubmarineNetworks: Submarine cable networks: Cables connecting west coast of Africa. https://www.submarinenetworks.com/euro-africa. Accessed 27 July 2021

36. TheWorldBank: Central African backbone apl2: Sao tome and principe (2010). https://documents1.worldbank.org/curated/en/238571468201832640/pdf/STP010PID0post010apprais al0Stage.pdf. Accessed 27 July 2021

37. WFP-STP: Wfp-stp, world food program in sao tome and principe (2019). https://www.fao.org/sao-tome-e-principe/noticias/detail-events/en/c/1181260/. Accessed 16 Nov 2021

Mobile Government Service Delivery Challenges in Municipalities

Siphelele Mtshengu and Tendani Mawela(✉) ⓘ

University of Pretoria, Hatfield, South Africa
u15096387@tuks.co.za, tendani.mawela@up.ac.za

Abstract. Scholars have reiterated the potential of mobile government solutions to extend the adoption of electronic government services in the context of the proliferation of mobile phones across various countries. This study aimed to understand the challenges faced by municipalities in the implementation, deployment and maintenance of m-government applications. The research followed an interpretive case study strategy and collected data from a municipal entity and its citizens, focusing on the m-government services of the entity. The findings indicate that various stakeholders are key to the successful delivery and uptake of m-government services. The municipal entity faced various challenges including ICT skills shortages, budget overruns, system interoperability and constrained resource capacity. From the citizens' perspective, the study noted concerns with the training of users, service resolution delays as well as privacy and security concerns. Several recommendations for consideration on m-government projects are put forth based on the lessons from the case study.

Keywords: E-Government · M-Government · Local government · Developing country · Government to Citizen (G2C)

1 Introduction

1.1 Background

The use of Information and Communication Technologies (ICTs) to enhance government processes may improve the government's interaction with the citizens and quality of service delivery [1]. Government entities in developing countries face challenges of providing sustainable development and improving the accessibility, quality and speed at which they deliver services to their citizens [2]. Through ICTs, the government can expand services to its citizens, improve the economic development of the country and thus, the ability to perform competitively within a global context [3]. Governments have undertaken the implementation of ICT systems to deliver services and information to citizens [4], which manifests as electronic government (e-government). At the same time, it is also noted that various countries have more than 100% mobile phone penetration rates [5], and this continues to increase. With the proliferation of mobile phones and an upward trend in mobile internet access, the world has seen increasing implementation

© Springer Nature Switzerland AG 2022
M. Themistocleous and M. Papadaki (Eds.): EMCIS 2021, LNBIP 437, pp. 289–301, 2022.
https://doi.org/10.1007/978-3-030-95947-0_20

of mobile government solutions (m-government). M-government can be viewed as a subsection of e-government. E-government may incorporate mobile applications and devices; however, it is not limited to those and can accommodate various solutions [6]. M-government brings the services of e-Government even closer to citizens using the already widely adopted and accessible mobile devices such as tablets, smartphones and other handheld devices [7, 8]. Various governments have implemented strategies that utilize smart devices in their communication and public service delivery channels [9].

Municipal or local government entities are at the forefront of service delivery and citizen interaction. As such, it is important to understand how this level of government may deploy ICT based solutions such as m-Government to support developmental and service delivery efforts. The objective of the study was to assess the deployment and use of m-government in a local government setting with an emphasis on a municipal entity and its mobile electronic government application for service delivery. The study was guided by the following research question: *"How may mobile government applications support municipal service delivery?"* The study sought to understand the resources and capabilities necessary to deploy m-government services successfully in developing countries. Of interest were the challenges faced by governments in the implementation and maintenance of m-government applications. The study also reviewed the impact of m-government application on the municipal entity, its service delivery mandate as well as the citizens. The paper contributes to the extant literature on m-government opportunities and challenges.

2 Informing Literature

2.1 E-Government Overview

According to the literature [10], e-government involves governments using "the internet and other ICTs as enablers to deliver their public services more smartly, improve citizen-state relations, and transform the scope of administrative actions and political processes". E-Government offers a variety of benefits for both governments and citizens. Some of the cited benefits include improved accessibility to public services, more cost-effective services, better quality government services, enhanced transparency and improved citizen trust in government [4, 11]. Many successful e-government projects have been implemented in various countries through the application of ICTs [12]. These have been based on national strategies, the development of frameworks that support the digital government, building the required skills, promoting an improved ICT culture, and developing infrastructure that supports ICT migration. However, the implementation of e-government systems faces various challenges, particularly in developing nations. For example, a lack of supporting infrastructure, high operational costs, inadequate ICT skills, citizen mistrust, a persistent digital divide which results in limited access for some citizen groups as well as low implementation success and adoption rates [11, 13].

2.2 M-Government Adoption, Opportunities and Challenges

Some scholars have indicated that m-government offers opportunities to extend e-government [23–25]. M-government involves using wireless and mobile technologies, applications, and devices to improve service delivery for the various government stake-holders [14]. M-government can offer many of the services provided by traditional e-government and it holds the promise of improving government services [15]. M-government may also assist in bridging the digital divide gap [16]. M-government services can enable the timely delivery of information to citizens. It has various advantages, such as personalized and affordable services as well as convenient government services that are available anywhere and at any time [6, 17, 18]. Citizens in developing countries have increased access to mobile phones, and it is argued that m-government can help extend the benefits of e-government for developing nations [8]. However, m-government does face several limitations. For instance, the volume of information mobile phones can transfer [19], capacity constraints and screen size as well as manifold standards and technologies [20–22]. The use of wireless networks may further expose users to security threats [14]. Additionally, it has been noted that the significant factors that influence citizens to adopt m-government include the perceived usefulness, perceived ease of use, cost of the service, social influence, perceived trust as well as users attitude towards the systems [52, 53]. This paper reflects on the experiences of a local government municipal entity in implementing an m-government solution towards enhancing service delivery. In the next section, the research methods that were adopted for the study are discussed.

3 Research Methods

3.1 Research Approach

This research study was underpinned by an interpretative philosophical stance and followed an exploratory, qualitative approach. It was structured as a single case study of a municipal entity focusing on the m-government services of the entity that are offered through a mobile application. Data was collected via interviews from the municipal entity's m-government project stakeholders including Information and Communications Technology (ICT) personnel; the Customer Relationship Management (CRM) team, which is responsible for logging and distribution of the service requests logged on the mobile application; as well as the technical teams which resolve the service requests. Nine semi-structured interviews were held with representatives from the municipal entity. Furthermore, citizens who were registered users of the m-government application were invited to complete a qualitative questionnaire and share their experiences. Forty citizens responded to the questionnaire. The interview data was analyzed using the deductive thematic analysis approach [26]. Additionally, project-related documents were reviewed and analyzed to understand the context of the m-government deployment.

4 Findings and Discussion

4.1 Mobile Government Application Background

The municipal entity launched the mobile application project to improve service delivery by enabling citizens to log service requests directly with the entity. The project was derived from the public's need to have additional accessible channels to log service requests. It was also influenced by the organization's desire to improve public perception of the entity and develop an online presence through m-government. The organization's management anticipated multiple benefits from the project, and these included improved governance of the municipal entity, increased and improved interaction with citizens, improved and efficient services to citizens as well as improved internal processes. An external service provider developed the application for the municipal entity. The purpose of the application was to enable citizens to log service requests to the entity efficiently and conveniently. Users had to download and register on the application to log service requests. Various key project stakeholders were identified as outlined in the Table 1 below.

Table 1. Project stakeholders (Source: Authors)

Actor	Role in the project	Interests in the mobile application
Previous Managing Director	Business Case Approval and Funding	• Service delivery improvement • Enhance organizational public perception management
Current Managing Director	Project finance	• Successful management of current organizational service delivery systems
Head of Department: Information Technology	Application owner	• Improved IT perception (internally)
Manager: Information Technology	Technical project manager	• Performance requirements (key performance indicator)
Operations Manager: Marketing and Communication	Project manager	• Improved customer perception • Business Performance Requirement of the Operations Manager
External Service Provider	Project implementers and technical support	• Business development • Financial development
Manager: Customer Relationship Management	User/customer liaison	• Performance requirements (key performance indicator)
Citizens	Users	• Improved service delivery

4.2 Local Government Challenges and Perceptions

The research findings noted various challenges from the municipal entity's perspective, and these included the following:

Financial Implications and Budget Overruns. The project budget grew to be substantially more than the initial estimated costs for application development and maintenance. Since the project had reached a state of irreversibility [27] when the contract was finalized, the project could not be cancelled. Cost overruns are not uncommon in ICT projects, and these are common in both developed and developing countries. Cost overruns also contribute a significant percentage to government ICT project failures [28].

Contract Management. When the project was initiated, the service provider was supposed to develop the mobile application and transfer the application management skills to the municipal entity. However, the skills transfer clause was never incorporated in the contract, and thus the skills transfer was never required contractually. Therefore, it was not implemented. According to the Head of Department IT: *"In the initial discussions with the service provider, they were supposed to transfer the skills to our guys over time, but there were challenges that also included limited capacity on our side"* (Respondent A, Interview 1). The lack of skills transfer being incorporated into the contract and ultimately resulting in higher consulting costs could be attributed to poor project planning. Cost overruns and poor project planning are interrelated and can both contribute to project failure [28]. Therefore, contract management is a critical element when public entities outsource functions to private sector service providers [29].

Interoperability of Systems. When the mobile application was launched, it could not interface with the organization's ERP system, which was used for logging and allocating all service requests to the relevant municipal technical teams. This created a challenge as service requests had to be manually captured and this resulted in time lost between the service request being logged and its resolution. A second version of the mobile application was released, enabling an automatic upload of all valid service requests to the ERP system. However, the system was still unable to update the user once the service request was closed. One of the critical success factors that need to be considered in developing m-government solutions is interoperability, which implies assessing the compatibility of information on the legacy systems and the new application [13]. Failure to ensure compatibility leads to redundancy. Thus, a mapping of the current systems to the desired applications should have been conducted prior to implementation at the business and system impact analysis stage.

Stakeholder Management. The organization did not anticipate the increased volumes of service requests that would be received through the mobile application. Thus, the capacity of the various regional operations and municipal technical teams was insufficient, resulting in these teams being unable to meet the turnaround times of service delivery. The service delivery units and technical teams were not engaged at the initial stages of the project. Therefore, the units were not able to assess how the mobile application would impact them. As a result, adequate resource planning and management could not cater for the increase in the volumes of service requests received. The regional operations manager indicated that: *"none of the service delivery units was consulted, the system was imposed on us, and we were required to prioritize the mobile application service logs ahead of others, and that is not how we work- all service requests are important"* (Respondent I, Interview 9). One of the strategic success factors in implementing an m-government solution is adequate stakeholder management. Stakeholder resistance challenges could have been minimized by conducting a stakeholder analysis. When conducting a stakeholder analysis at the project inception or planning stages, all potential stakeholders need to be analyzed as well as their role and impact on the success of the project. In addition, these stakeholders need to be involved throughout the various project phases [31].

Service Expectation Failure. Critical success factors for projects should be identified for the organization to assess if it has met its goals or not. One of the key success factors of the mobile application project was reduced service request resolution time, and the data reflected that this was not achieved. It was noted, for instance, that 52.68% of the queries related to potholes were resolved later than the agreed 3-day service level agreement (SLA) period. One of the common contributors to e-government project failures is "Expectation Failure", where the functionality and design are adequate, however, user expectations are not met by the system [32, 33]. The mobile application could not meet the citizens' expectations with regard to the turnaround times. This meant that the technical features were well implemented. However, the soft features regarding the acceptability of the project were neglected.

Resource Capacity. From the interviews held with the respondents from various regional operations, IT, and technical teams, it was noted that there were human resource capacity challenges that were also affecting the success of the project. There was only one dedicated personnel to the mobile application, who was an Assistant Manager. Due to the lack of skills transfer as well as the contract terms and conditions, the IT department was unable to assist even with first-line support of the mobile application and all technical queries, and system change requests were submitted to the external service provider. Resource shortages in the IT department meant that when the Assistant Manager was away from work, there was no other liaison to assist until his/her return. This was a risk with regards to succession planning as the organization's IT department had also experienced high staff turnover. The challenge of shortages in skilled ICT personnel and high ICT staff turnover is not unique to the organization. The challenge is prevalent and increasing in developing countries [34]. The lack of ICT skills is common in local government entities, and this lack of skills may result in higher costs. It could also compromise the service delivery as turnaround times of external contractors may not be as quick [35] due to processes that need to be adhered to.

SLA with Service Providers. There was no Service Level Agreement (SLA) entered into with the external service provider, which made it a challenge for the organization to measure the service provider's performance accurately. The main basis of measurement was on the availability of the mobile application to enable service request logging and the functionality of the mobile application. A performance service level agreement is one of the critical internal tools that the organization can utilize to set the standard of performance required from the contractor and enforce it [36].

Unintended Consequences. When a project is implemented, there may be unintended consequences that emanate, and these at times pose negative effects that may be to the detriment of the project [37]. An example that was picked up from the project was the issue of trivial service requests. One of the available categories in the mobile application was the "General" service request category. Some citizens used this category to log service requests that were not within the mandate and scope of the municipal entity as well as other requests that were considered "trivial". These included requests to clean resident's property driveways, and clear leaves that had fallen on resident's pavements. These were classified as non-issues and were closed without responses and resolutions. These consequences could have been minimized by user training and eliminating excess categories such as "general" in the mobile application.

4.3 Citizens' Challenges and Perceptions

The research findings noted the following challenges from the citizens' perspective:

User Training. 45% of the citizen respondents indicated that they initially struggled with using the mobile application. For instance, some users noted that they were unsure of the level of detail needed to be captured for their requests. The mobile application allowed the users to take a photo of the incident they want to log and upload it on the application. It also allowed them to capture the geographical location of the incident using the Geographic Information System (GIS) function and provide an explanation of the incident they would like to report through the "Description" input field on the screen. Users did not obtain training and sufficient information on the level of detail to capture when logging a request. Where users did not capture sufficient information, there was a risk of the issues being classified as "Non-Issues" and closed without being resolved. The lack of user training and information negatively impacted user adoption, which was compounded by applications that were not user-friendly. Research has shown that where users were given an opportunity to be trained, they would opt to use e-government more [38]. Successful e-government solutions that have been implemented by organizations were designed to be user-centric, thereby increasing adoption and user satisfaction [39].

Logging of Geographical Location. 40% of the respondents reflected that they could not log faulty traffic lights or potholes as these mainly were identified while driving. Thus subsequently, they had to be logged when stationary or when they arrived at their residence. This required remembering the exact coordinates of the fault, which often resulted in an incorrect location being captured. When the users followed up with the municipal entity on these service requests, they found that they had been logged as "non-issues" since the correct location could not be established. Where users managed to log a request while they were stationary, 25% of them indicated that the GIS functionality was often incorrect by approximately 100 to 200 m. Thus, on streets with multiple traffic lights, this caused errors regarding which traffic light was faulty. Comprehensive testing, including citizen involvement and user acceptance testing of solutions, is essential to the successful implementation of applications [40].

Service Resolution Delays. 75% of the users indicated that while their service requests were resolved, they were not resolved in less than a day, except for traffic lights which mainly were resolved in two days. Users also indicated that there was no communication regarding the service request turnaround time indicated to them by the municipal entity via the mobile application. Thus, they relied on either seeing the service requests resolved physically or calling the entity to follow up on the request. 25% of the users still had their service requests active on the mobile application several weeks after logging the service request. Users also indicated that they could also not track their service requests on the application. They had to do so via e-mail which is duplication of effort and thus defied the notion of managing service requests efficiently through the mobile application. Prior research has shown that in instances where the government does not deliver on their commitments, trust by citizens is diminished. It is noted that citizens already have challenges with trust in government [41, 42]. The inability for the entity to meet the service levels defined by the entity may have a long-term detrimental impact on the use of the mobile application by citizens [43].

User Registration Issues. One of the benefits of e-government and m-government solutions is efficiency and thus translating to improved service delivery [44]. Without the efficiency in e-government, users are discouraged from using the implemented technologies, which further worsens trust issues [45]. 20% of the users relayed that the registration process took time as they also had to wait for the e-mail confirmation sent by the mobile application upon registering. Users noted that the e-mail took several minutes to reach them, thus delaying the registration process as they could not log a service request without verifying the e-mail address. 30% of the users noted that they could not log a service request when they logged on using their Facebook account on the mobile application and that they had to register afresh on the mobile application. System efficiency is one of the components that citizens use to decide whether to adopt an m-government solution or not [46]. Where the users perceive that the system is inefficient and therefore time-consuming, they will not adopt the m-government solution [45, 46].

Privacy and Security. Challenges of privacy, confidentiality and security constitute a major concern in the adoption of e-government and m-government solutions. Where citizens cannot be assured of privacy, they are more likely not to use the e-government solution [47]. Citizens were not able to use the mobile application unless they register on the mobile application. The minimum required fields on the application included the name, surname and e-mail address. Users could also link the application to their Facebook account. When downloading the application, it required the user to grant the application access to their phone contacts and their gallery. 50% of the users surveyed were not comfortable with this privacy permission as the mobile application could identify the user's geographical location. It was not communicated clearly to the users how the mobile application would handle privacy issues. Surveyed users lamented that: *"I understand accessing my location, but why does the app need to access my contacts? That is a violation of my privacy"*. As the author in [20] indicated, privacy and security concerns can hinder the adoption of government mobile application projects.

5   Conclusion, Recommendations and Future Research

5.1   Concluding Remarks

The study focused on understanding the challenges associated with implementing an m-government application from the perspectives of both the government and the citizens. The discussion noted several challenges that were detrimental to the project outcomes as well as unintended consequences. These challenges also threatened the future benefits that could have been derived from the mobile application should they not be adequately managed. Several factors influence the development and implementation of IS solutions. These influences may either hinder or enable a successful deployment. Leadership support is one of the key enablers of e-government solutions since leaders set the tone for and avail the required resources to implement the project [44, 48]. The project barriers and constraints that were identified threatened the success of the project. One of the factors that hindered the project was system compatibility. The mobile application could not interface with the organization's ERP system, thus leading to manual inputs that were time-consuming. One of the components that needed to be assessed when measuring m-government readiness was the technology infrastructure. There was need for an assessment of the hardware and software requirements to enable successful deployment [49].

The failure to correctly identify and manage stakeholders can be detrimental to the successful deployment of government ICT solutions [30]. Internally the project had a negative impact, including resource constraints that were not envisaged at the inception of the project. The mobile application resulted in increased service delivery requests that could not be resolved on time by the current human resources in the organization. The mobile application costs were also much higher than anticipated, which negatively impacted the sustainability of the project. Efforts towards enhancing user communication and training were essential to support user satisfaction in the longer term. The findings have also shown that the inability of entities to align the goals of the m-government solution to those of the organization can be detrimental to the project's success. The users expected a turnaround time of one day, while the municipal entity could only manage three days at best. M-government solutions can be used to manage user expectations, and where these are not met, m-government can lower citizens' trust in government services.

Based on the assessment of the mobile application implemented by the municipal entity, it can be deduced that m-government applications face various challenges but do hold the potential to improve service delivery in several aspects if implemented successfully. This can be through the improved confidence in local government, in opening more channels for users to interact with the government thereby improving transparency, and increased accountability as users can monitor services requested and rendered to them.

5.2 Recommendations

It is recommended that government entities planning to implement e-government and m-government solutions should ensure adequate budgeting for the solutions envisioned [50]. Where the projects will be outsourced to external service providers, there is a need for comprehensive contracts to be put in place that govern performance levels, rights to the software, skills transfer and cost structuring [36]. Organizations also need to ensure sufficient capacity to handle the service requests and queries from citizens to promote citizen interaction and trust in government services. Internal training also needs to be conducted by entities whose staff will handle customer queries in alignment with citizens service expectations. A lack of customer relationship management could negatively impact the success of the project. There needs to be a common goal communicated and adopted by all stakeholders involved in the project to minimize resistance from within. The goal needs to be aligned to the strategic objectives of the organization to promote accountability. A readiness assessment is an important factor to be considered prior to deploying m-government solutions. Government entities need to assess the need for the solution, assess the resources required to achieve their objectives, and the resource required to sustain the project [49, 51]. Stakeholder management should be considered carefully when implementing mobile government projects. In addition, stakeholder management needs to include both internal and external stakeholders.

5.3 Contribution, Limitations and Future Research

The study reviewed m-government implementation challenges and adoption dynamics by concentrating on a municipal entity's case study in a developing country. The research added to the literature on mobile government and highlighted the complexities involved in deploying m-government solutions. The study focused on one municipal entity, and this is noted as a limitation. Thus, future studies may seek to solicit the views of other municipal entities and stakeholders on their experiences of m-government. The study focused on the local government level. There is an opportunity to investigate the implementation of m-government at the provincial and national government levels.

Acknowledgements. This work is based on the research supported in part by the National Research Foundation of South Africa (Grant Numbers 127495).

References

1. Chun, S.A., Luna-Reyes, L.F., Sandoval-Almazán, R.: Transforming government: people, process and policy. Collaborative E-government **6**(1), 5–12 (2012)
2. Waema, T.M., Mitullah, W., Adera, E.: Research in African e-local governance: outcome assessment research framework. Afr. J. Sci. Technol. Innov. Dev. **1**(1), 220–248 (2009)
3. Naidoo, G.: Implementation of E-government in South Africa-successes and challenges: the way forward. Int. J. Adv. Comput. Manag. **1**(1), 62–66 (2012)
4. Dwivedi, Y.K., Rana, N.P., Janssen, M., Lal, B., Williams, M.D., Clement, M.: An empirical validation of a unified model of electronic government adoption (UMEGA). Gov. Inf. Q. **34**(2), 211–230 (2017)
5. Chen, Z.J., Vogel, D., Wang, Z.H.: How to satisfy citizens? Using mobile government to reengineer fair government processes. Decis. Support Syst. **82**, 47–57 (2016)
6. Sheng, H., Trimi, S.: M-government: technologies, applications and challenges. Electron. Gov. **5**(1), 1 (2008)
7. Mukonza, R.M.: M-government in South Africa's local government. In: Proceedings of the 7th International Conference on Theory and Practice of Electronic Governance - ICEGOV 2013, pp. 374–375 (2013)
8. Shareef, M.A., Archer, N., Dwivedi, Y.K.: Examining adoption behavior of mobile government. J. Comput. Inf. Syst. **53**(2), 39–49 (2012)
9. Kim, S.K., Park, M.J., Rho, J.J.: Does public service delivery through new channels promote citizen trust in government? The case of smart devices. Inf. Technol. Dev. **25**(3), 604–624 (2019)
10. Chou, T.C., Chen, J.R., Pu, C.K.: Exploring the collective actions of public servants in e-government development. Decis. Support Syst. **45**, 251–265 (2008)

11. Rana, N., Dwivedi, Y., Lal, B., Williams, M., Clement, M.: Citizens' adoption of an electronic government system: towards a unified view. Inf. Syst. Front. **19**(3), 549–568 (2015). https://doi.org/10.1007/s10796-015-9613-y
12. Komba, M.M., Ngulube, P.: Factors for e-government adoption: lessons from selected African countries. Mousaion **30**(2), 24–32 (2012)
13. Almarabeh, T., AbuAli, A.: A general framework for e-government: definition maturity challenges, opportunities, and success. Eur. J. Sci. Res. **39**(1), 29–42 (2010)
14. Kumar, M., Hanumanthappa, M., Reddy, B.L.: Security issues in m-government. Int. J. Electron. Secur. Digit. Forensics **1**(4), 401–412 (2008)
15. Alotaibi, S.R.D., Roussinov, D.: Using focus group method to identifying citizen requirements to Saudi mobile government services. In: 19th International Conference on e-Business and e-Government (2017)
16. Mossey, S., Bromberg, D., Manoharan, A.P.P.: Harnessing the power of mobile technology to bridge the digital divide: a look at US cities' mobile government capability. J. Inf. Technol. Politics **16**(1), 52–65 (2019)
17. Babullah, A., Dwivedi, Y.K., Williams, M.D.: Saudi Citizens' perceptions on mobile government (mGov) adoption factors. In: UKAIS, p. 8 (2015)
18. Ntaliani, M., Costopoulou, C., Karetsos, S.: Mobile government: a challenge for agriculture. Gov. Inf. Q. **25**(4), 699–716 (2008)
19. Ghyasi, A.F., Kushchu, I.: Uses of mobile government in developing countries (2004). http://www.movlab.org
20. Kumar, M., Sinha, O.P.: M-government–mobile technology for e-Government. In: International Conference on e-Government, India, pp. 294–301 (2007)
21. Isagah, T., Wimmer, M.A.: Mobile government applications: challenges and needs for a comprehensive design approach. In: Proceedings of the 10th International Conference on Theory and Practice of Electronic Governance, pp. 423–432 (2017)
22. Charland, A., LeRoux, B.: Mobile application development: web vs. native: web apps are cheaper to develop and deploy than native apps, but can they match the native user experience? Queue **9**(4), 20–28 (2011)
23. Hlomela, T., Mawela, T.: Citizens' perceptions of mobile tax filing services. In: Themistocleous, M., Papadaki, M., Kamal, M.M. (eds.) EMCIS 2020. LNBIP, vol. 402, pp. 256–269. Springer, Cham (2020). https://doi.org/10.1007/978-3-030-63396-7_17
24. Hobololo, T.S., Mawela, T.: Exploring the use of mobile phones for public participation in the buffalo city metropolitan municipality. AGRIS Online Papers Econ. Inform. **9**(1), 57–68 (2017)
25. Ochara, N.M., Mawela, T.: Enabling social sustainability of e-participation through mobile technology. Inf. Technol. Dev. **21**(2), 205–228 (2015)
26. Braun, V., Clarke, V.: Using thematic analysis in psychology. Qual. Res. Psychol. **3**(2), 77–101 (2006)
27. Walsham, G.: Actor-network theory and IS research: current status and future prospects. In: Lee, A.S., Liebenau, J., DeGross, J.I. (eds.) Information systems and qualitative research. ITIFIP, pp. 466–480. Springer, Boston (1997). https://doi.org/10.1007/978-0-387-35309-8_23
28. Mimicopoulos, M.G.: E-government funding activities and strategies. Department of Economic and Social Affairs, Division for Public Administration and Development Management, United Nations, New York (2004)
29. Cordella, A., Willcocks, L.: Outsourcing, bureaucracy and public value: reappraising the notion of the "contract state." Gov. Inf. Q. **27**(1), 82–88 (2010)
30. Gil-García, J.R., Pardo, T.A.: E-government success factors: mapping practical tools to theoretical foundations. Gov. Inf. Q. **22**(2), 187–216 (2005)

31. Scholl, H.J.: E-government: a special case of ICT-enabled business process change. In: Proceedings of the 36th Annual Hawaii International Conference on System Sciences, pp. 12-pp. IEEE (2003)

32. Yeo, K.T.: Critical failure factors in information system projects. Int. J. Project Manag. **20**(3), 241–246 (2002)

33. Bannerman, P.L.: Defining project success: a multilevel framework. In: Proceedings of the Project Management Institute Research Conference, pp. 1–14 (2008)

34. Kirlidog, M., van der Vyver, C., Zeeman, M., Coetzee, W.: Unfulfilled need: reasons for insufficient ICT skills in South Africa. Inf. Dev. **34**(1), 5–19 (2018)

35. Ferro, E., Sorrentino, M.: Can intermunicipal collaboration help the diffusion of E-Government in peripheral areas? Evidence from Italy. Gov. Inf. Q. **27**(1), 17–25 (2010)

36. Chen, Y.C., Perry, J.: Outsourcing for e-government: managing for success. Public Perform. Manag. Rev. **26**(4), 404–421 (2003)

37. Rose, W.R., Grant, G.G.: Critical issues pertaining to the planning and implementation of E-Government initiatives. Gov. Inf. Q. **27**(1), 26–33 (2010)

38. Carter, L., Weerakkody, V.: E-government adoption: a cultural comparison. Inf. Syst. Front. **10**(4), 473–482 (2008)

39. Verdegem, P., Verleye, G.: User-centered E-Government in practice: a comprehensive model for measuring user satisfaction. Gov. Inf. Q. **26**(3), 487–497 (2009)

40. Olphert, W., Damodaran, L.: Citizen participation and engagement in the design of e-government services: the missing link in effective ICT design and delivery. J. Assoc. Inf. Syst. **8**(9), 27 (2007)

41. Nzimakwe, T.: Transforming the public service through e-government: challenges for the future. Africanus **42**(1), 56–68 (2012)

42. Mpinganjira, M.: Use of e-government services: the role of trust. Int. J. Emerg. Mark. **10**(4), 622–633 (2015)

43. Rajapakse, J., Van Der Vyver, A., Hommes, E.: e-Government implementations in developing countries: success and failure, two case studies. In: 2012 IEEE 6th International Conference on Information and Automation for Sustainability, pp. 95–100. IEEE (2012)

44. Belachew, M.: E-government initiatives in Ethiopia. In: Proceedings of the 4th International Conference on Theory and Practice of Electronic Governance, pp. 49–54 (2010)

45. Bertot, J.C., Jaeger, P.T., Grimes, J.M.: Using ICTs to create a culture of transparency: E-government and social media as openness and anti-corruption tools for societies. Gov. Inf. Q. **27**(3), 264–271 (2010)

46. Kamau, G., Njihia, J., Wausi, A.: E-government websites user experience from public value perspective: case study of iTax website in Kenya. In: 2016 IST-Africa Week Conference, pp. 1–8. IEEE (2016)

47. Mengistu, D., Zo, H., Rho, J.J.: M-government: opportunities and challenges to deliver mobile government services in developing countries. In: 2009 Fourth International Conference on Computer Sciences and Convergence Information Technology, pp. 1445–1450. IEEE (2009)

48. Cloete, F.: E-government lessons from South Africa 2001–2011: institutions, state of progress and measurement: Section II: Country perspectives on e-government emergence. Afr. J. Inf. Commun. **2012**(12), 128–142 (2012)

49. Koh, C.E., Prybutok, V.R., Zhang, X.: Measuring e-government readiness. Inf. Manag. **45**(8), 540–546 (2008)

50. Nkwe, N.: E-government: challenges and opportunities in Botswana. Int. J. Humanit. Soc. Sci. **2**(17), 39–48 (2012)

51. Dwivedi, Y.K., Weerakkody, V., Janssen, M.: Moving towards maturity: challenges to successful e-government implementation and diffusion. ACM SIGMIS Database: Database Adv. Inf. Syst. **42**(4), 11–22 (2012)

52. Almarashdeh, I., Alsmadi, M.K.: How to make them use it? Citizens acceptance of M-government. Appl. Comput. Inform. **13**(2), 194–199 (2017)
53. Saxena, S.: Enhancing ICT infrastructure in public services: factors influencing mobile government (m-government) adoption in India. The Bottom Line (2017)

Digital Services and Social Media

Why Do People Not Install Corona-Warn-App? Evidence from Social Media

Chuanwen Dong$^{(\boxtimes)}$, Sanjana Bharambe, and Markus Bick

ESCP Business School, Berlin Campus, Heubnerweg 8-10, 14059 Berlin, Germany
{cdong,mbick}@escp.eu, sanjana.bharambe95@gmail.com

Abstract. This study investigates why the Corona-Warn-App, which was meticulously designed in Germany to interrupt the COVID-19's chain of infection, was not installed by the majority of the population and therefore failed to achieve what it was created to do. We collect natural language data by scraping 70,529 related comments from Twitter, and apply sentiment analysis to understand the content. We distinguish negative comments into two categories: technical issues, e.g. crashes and errors, and trust-related issues, e.g. concerns about privacy protection. After a more detailed manual check, we find that some criticisms of the app are not accurate. Surprisingly, more than 40% of trust-related denunciations are based purely on misinformation spread by users. For example, a user complains about a violation of data privacy, when, in fact, the app is fully GDPR-compliant. Our study provides evidence for the intentional promulgation of misinformation to lower trust in life-saving technologies during a pandemic, and calls for a more careful evaluation of the technology's performance.

Keywords: COVID-19 · Social media · Sentiment analysis · Trust · Pandemic

1 Introduction

The COVID-19 pandemic has detrimentally affected global healthcare systems. As of June 2021, more than 181 million cases have been confirmed worldwide, resulting in over 3.93 million deaths [1]. It is regarded as one of the deadliest pandemics in human history [2].

To fight this pandemic effectively, it is essential to break the chains of infection by means of quarantine, patient isolation, social distancing, etc. [3]. One possible solution is using mobile phone data to track and find people who have been infected by the virus [4]. To do so, countries all over the world have expended a great deal of effort to develop and promote digital contact tracing apps [5], which help people to determine whether they have come in contact with an infected person and whether this could result in a risk of infection [6]. If the app notifies a user about the risk, the user must refrain from meeting other people, to stop the potential spread of the disease.

Nevertheless, to play an effective role in ceasing the pandemic, corona apps must be used by at least 60% of the population [7]. However, the real installation rates across countries are only moderate [8]. For example, until May 2021, only 27.7 million, or

M. Themistocleous and M. Papadaki (Eds.): EMCIS 2021, LNBIP 437, pp. 305–318, 2022.
https://doi.org/10.1007/978-3-030-95947-0_21

about one-third of the total population in Germany, had installed their country's app [9]. Obviously, with such a low installation rate, the app cannot fulfill its designed requirement.

Several studies have already started to investigate the reasons for not installing the corona apps. The research methods are exclusively surveys or interviews, and the reported reasons are mainly users' risk attitude [10], technical issues [11], and privacy concerns [12]. In this study, we aim to provider a more comprehensive understanding of the factors preventing people from doing so by analyzing a large amount of comments from Twitter. The use of social media, to the best of our knowledge, has never been applied to investigate user preferences in relation to a corona app. The focus of this study is on the German Corona-Warn-App (CWA) for the following reasons: 1) Whereas most apps are constantly criticized for undermining users' privacy, the German app has one of the highest security scores in terms of GDRP compliance [13] and 2) Germany has a large population and a high number of social media users [14], which allows us to collect more data for analysis.

We scrape 70,529 related tweets in 2020 commenting on the CWA. After cleaning the data, we apply sentiment analysis using an artificial intelligence tool, and carry out content analysis manually to understand the barriers prohibiting users from installing the app. We find that technical issues, such as crashes and errors, are the most frequently mentioned reasons, especially shortly after the launch of the app. In addition, trust-related issues, such as doubts about its effectiveness and privacy protection, are also prominent. Much to our surprise, following a more detailed manual examination, we find that more than 40% of the trust-related issues in the tweets are incorrect. Such a high ratio demonstrates an intentional reduction in trust levels in order to avoid installing the app. Our study provides evidence for deliberately misleading information to lower trust in life-saving technologies during a pandemic, and calls for a more careful evaluation of the technology's performance.

2 Literature

The outbreak of COVID-19 has triggered much interest in related scientific studies. Researchers are calling for the appropriate use of mobile phone data to support the fight against the pandemic [4, 15]. Recent studies have analyzed and compared various contact tracing apps from the perspectives of data privacy and security [11]. In a comparison of 28 current popular contact tracing apps, the German CWA obtains one of the highest security scores [13]. However, it was noted that all apps are generally not well accepted by the public [8].

Researchers have started to investigate the reason for this low installation rate. An initial barrier is a need for a smartphone with iOS or an Android operating system [16]. In a survey of 1,972 Germans, older, female and healthier people were found to be more reluctant to install the app [10]. This result is consistent with a survey of 1,963 US Americans [17]. Technical issues are also confirmed to discourage people from installing the app [18]. The CWA was found with the most technical problems among government apps developed in eight countries [11]. Much concern has been placed on the privacy protection ability of the app [12, 19]. In addition, better data governance [20], additional monetary incentives [6], and enhanced consumer awareness on the functionality [21] are cited as ways of increasing the installation rate.

To date, the literature has heavily focused on surveys and/or interviews. In contrast, we extract data from social media, a much richer dataset. The analysis of 70, 529 tweets uncovers users' intentional promulgation of misinformation to lower their trust in the app. Such user behavior on a life-saving technology has, to the best of our knowledge, never been reported in the literature before.

3 The Corona-Warn-App

The CWA, Germany's official contact tracing app, was published by Robert Koch Institute and the Federal Ministry of Health in collaboration with Deutsch Telekom subsidiary T-systems and the software company SAP (Ferretti et al. 2020). It is an open-source project started in April 2020 and released on 16th June 2020. Despite its short development time, the app was constantly reviewed for possible developments and incoming development proposals [22]. The CWA is designed to curb the spread of the COVID-19 virus by interrupting infection chains [23].

As shown in Fig. 1, the app broadcasts a rolling proximity identifier (RPI) and simultaneously scans for the identifiers of other mobile devices using Bluetooth low energy (BLE) technology. In this way, all smartphones with an app know their close contacts and store this information locally. If a mobile phone user is positively tested, he/she is asked to voluntarily upload their temporary keys of up to the last 14 days to the server. Thereafter, the other mobile phones are then aware of the positive case, and they check locally if they have had close contact before. If yes, the mobile phone users are notified with detailed medical instructions.

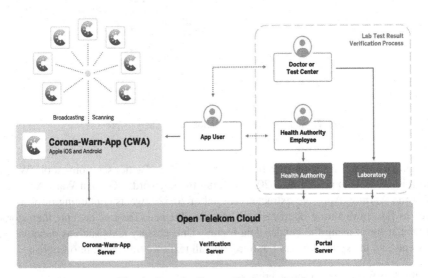

Fig. 1. How the Corona-Warn-App works

A notable advantage of the app is its high level of security. In its privacy statement, the app designers explicitly highlight that the CWA is GDPR-compliant[1]. The Chaos Computer Club (CCC) proposed minimum privacy requirements that should be considered when designing contact tracing apps, and the CWA is believed to fulfill all of these conditions[2].

4 Research Method

The aim of this study is to comprehensively identify the factors preventing people from installing the CWA, rather than testing existing theories. As a result, we apply an inductive approach to identify new themes via text mining [24, 25]. Figure 2 illustrates the chosen research method in detail.

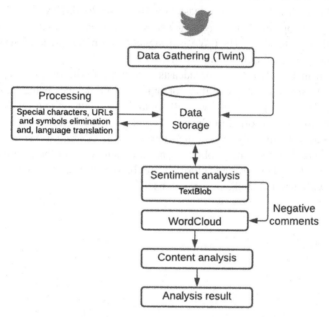

Fig. 2. Schematic representation of the analysis process

The first step is to scrape data from Twitter using the Twitter scrapping tool TWINT. All relevant tweets posted in 2020 containing the keywords "Corona Warn App" and "Corona Warning App" are extracted. A total of 70,529 tweets containing information such as ID, conversation ID, date, time, etc. are obtained. The raw data are then stored in tabular form, using the Pandas data frame[3]. Unnecessary texts such as punctuation, retweets and the symbol @ are removed, and all texts are translated into English.

---

[1] https://www.coronawarn.app/en/privacy/.

[2] https://github.com/corona-warn-app/cwa-documentation/blob/master/pruefsteine.md.

[3] https://pandas.pydata.org/docs/reference/api/pandas.DataFrame.html.

The 70,529 tweets were posted by 20,371 users. On average, a user posts 3.5 comments on CWA, a tweet is liked 9.4 times and retweeted 1.8 times. In total, 13 languages are detected in the tweets. German (89%) is naturally the most used language, followed by English (7%), Italian (0.4%), French (0.4%) and Spanish (0.4%). The number of tweets is rather equally distributed between 7 a.m. and 7 p.m., with slightly more during the morning peak hour from 9 a.m. to 11 a.m. Interestingly, about one third of the tweets are posted on Tuesdays, probably because Robert Koch Institute always update the corona infection numbers on Mondays (no updates on Saturdays and Sundays) and therefore revokes new waves of discussions on the next day.

The next step is sentiment analysis to understand the subjective opinions of the CWA users. A text message is represented by a bag of words. Each word is assigned a sentiment score, and the sentiment of a text message is then the weighted average of the scores from all constituting words. Naturally, a negative score presents a negative sentiment. Since we aim to investigate the reasons for not installing the CWA, the comments with negative scores are filtered for further analysis. The sentiment analysis is carried out by TextBlob, the natural language processing toolkit of Python. It works on a predefined dictionary of sentiment lexicons.

Next, a word cloud is plotted to visualize the most frequently discussed entities. The words with the highest frequency are those stressed the most by the users. The word cloud presents a descriptive analysis of the main concerns of users.

The keywords obtained from the word cloud are used to guide the content analysis, which extracts thematic information from the data. The negative comments are then distinguished into two major and five minor categories. We allocate all negative comments into the categories and check how their numbers develop over time. In a further step in the content analysis, we manually examine all of the comments and distinguish between correct and misinformed comments.

5 Results

In this section, we present the results from the abovementioned analysis.

5.1 Sentiment Analysis

After the initial cleaning of the 70,529 scrapped tweets, we obtain 67,854 valid comments. In the sentiment analysis, the Python TextBlob library is then used to distinguish the tweets into positive, negative, and neutral comments (Fig. 3).

The CWA was launched in June 2020, and most of the comments are naturally posted in that month. Thereafter, the numbers of comments drop, but they rise again in October. As the second COVID-19 wave started in Germany in October, it is likely that people started to use the app again at that time. Even though most of the comments are positive, there are still a significant number of negative comments, indicating that many users are indeed not satisfied with the CWA. After the sentiment analysis, 11,989 negative comments are selected.

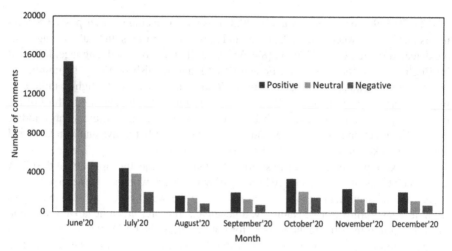

Fig. 3. Month-wise sentiment analysis of the positive, negative, and neutral tweets.

5.2 Word Cloud

Texts such as Corona-Warn-App, Corona, Corona warning app, and COVID-19 are removed before plotting the word cloud. Figure 4 shows the word cloud for every negative comment during the six months. The size of the words in the word cloud is based on their frequency and importance in the comments.

Fig. 4. Word cloud for all negative comments on Twitter on the Corona-Warn-App

On a monthly level, Table 1 summarizes the most frequently mentioned keywords. From the figure and table, we make the following two observations:

Observation 1: The negative comments can be roughly distinguished between two categories: technical concerns and trust-related concerns.

Table 1. High-frequency and important words in the word cloud

Month	Most frequently mentioned words in the comments
June, 2020	Smartphone, cellphone, people, installed
July, 2020	Problem, work, user
August, 2020	Work, test, risk
September, 2020	People, work, user
October, 2020	Contact, people, work
November, 2020	Data protection, risk
December, 2020	Data protection, risk

The keywords "smart phone," "cell phone," "work," etc. are related to the interactions between a phone and the CWA. The tweets with these keywords are obviously concerned about the technical issues of the app. On the other hand, the keywords "people" and "data protection" reflect users' concerns about trust in the CWA.

Observation 2: Shortly after the launch of the CWA, the negative comments are mainly on technical issues; thereafter, the comments focus on trust-related issues.

Interestingly, there is a clear change in the keywords along the time horizon. Shortly after the launch of the CWA, technical concerns are mainly mentioned, possibly because of potential technical problems associated with a newly developed product. When more and more people interact with the app, the trust-related concerns emerge.

The word cloud and the highlighted keywords provide us with preliminary guidance on users' concerns surrounding the CWA. Content analysis is now applied to understand the detailed reasons.

5.3 Content Analysis

It is challenging to examine the contents of the 11,989 negative tweets from the sentiment analysis, since none of the current artificial intelligence tools is able to provide a highly accurate content analysis. As a result, we take a manual approach, albeit we only focus on tweets with a high frequency of repetition. We use the keywords that appeared the most in the word cloud (Table 1) and filter all the negative comments that have these keywords. After this step, we obtain 3,621 tweets for further manual review.

We find that the selected comments can be distinguished into two main categories: technical issues and trust-related issues. Furthermore, technical issues can be further distinguished into three sub-categories: technical flows, compatibility issues, and user experience. Trust-related issues mainly revolve around doubts about the effectiveness of the CWA, as well as concerns about privacy (Fig. 5).

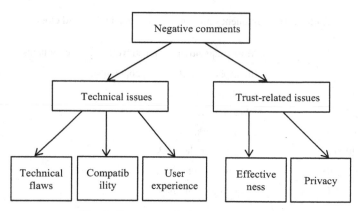

Fig. 5. Taxonomy of all negative comments

An illustration of the categorization of the various negative comments is provided below. Each reason category is described along with examples.

1) Technical flaws

Bugs and crashes can be found in any app, but the impact of these technical problems might be more severe in an app such as CWA, since it directly prohibits users from gaining/sharing essential information. Many people complain that the app crashes unexpectedly and displays lots of error messages. Such complaints are especially prominent shortly after the launch of the app; for example, a typical tweet is:

> *"In my experience, the CoronaWarnApp is a disaster. Endless cryptic error messages. No more transmission of the data. After the 1st update it was over. Allegedly bug in the Google interface and they don't care. Have now uninstalled. Unfortunately."*

Some other users complain that the CWA causes additional technical problems on their phones; for example, it drains the battery:

> *"Lauterbach Unfortunately, the Corona Warn app is still a bad joke. Downloaded the app to a new Samsung Galaxy S10 this morning. With 54% battery charge, 3 hours later still 25%. Deleting the app again doesn't work at all. A joke!"*

2) Compatibility

The compatibility issue is quite a severe problem in the CWA. The app is only supported by the latest versions of operating systems (iOS and Android) but not by old Apple products.

> *"This morning I tried to download the #CoronaWarnApp. I am retired and belong to the #risk group. Unfortunately, I had to find out that an installation on my # iPhone6 is not possible. Software out of date, thank you Mr. #Spahn. # New purchase subsidy."*

In addition, some users find that the CWA is not compatible with other corona apps:

"Unfortunately, the CoronaMelder does not work next to the German Corona-aWarnApp. Not useful for the thousands of people who live close to the border and regularly cross it."

3) User experience

Many users are confused, since the CWA's functions are not user-friendly; for example, it must always have an internet connection:

"I got the CoronaWarnApp yesterday evening and have to honestly say that I am disappointed and angry. What idiot thought that this would only work with the internet[...] great for the people who can afford it[...]."

Some users complain that the FAQ and Hotline features do not provide sufficient information:

"Can't find an answer in any FAQ." "It was a really rude person on the phone[...] I guess you have to work on that too."

4) Doubts about effectiveness

The abovementioned examples mainly focus on technical issues with the CWA. However, a large number of the comments reflect a lack of trust in the app. Many consumers have reservations about the effectiveness of the app in fighting the pandemic. A typical criticism in this regard is that the warning message is sent too late to protect app users:

"Unfortunately, the CoronaWarnApp only warns after days, so don't protect myself. Just like the scraps of cloth on your face. Useless."

Despite the detailed explanation, many users still believe that the app is ineffective in protecting them from the virus:

"Bluetooth measurement simply does not work with crowds of people in subways etc. It could well be that the measurement wrongly identified me as a contact and the app reports. It just makes you unnecessarily stressful. Nobody needs this CornaWahnApp!"

5) Privacy concerns

Besides the misgivings about the effectiveness of the CWA, many users do not fully trust it in terms of privacy protection. Almost all criticisms exclusively focus on the violation of privacy by collecting illegal personal data:

"Paid by the federal government to advertise the CoronaWarnApp? Solidarity has nothing to do with an expensive toy, which Telekom, SAP and the federal government deliver the data of the citizens free of charge. Big business in denouncing the citizens."

Figure 6 shows how the numbers of the technical and trust-related issues develop over time. Shortly after the launch of CWA, a large number of users complain about various technical problems (Fig. 6). About two months after the initial launch of the CWA, most of the bugs have been fixed, and the number of complaints on the technical issues drops significantly. The curve goes slightly up in October, consistent with the second wave of COVID-19 in Germany.

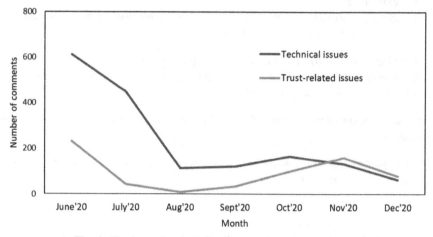

Fig. 6. Numbers of technical and trust-related issues over time

Similar to the number of criticisms of technical issues, trust-related issues also surge in June 2020, drop in August 2020 and then slightly increase in October 2020. It is understandable that both numbers share similar driving forces, such as the launch of the CWA, the development of the pandemic, etc. Generally speaking, there are more detractors on technical issues than on trust-related issues. However, the difference between the two curves decreases over time. In June 2020, there were in total 613 disapproving posts about technical issues, and 232 about trust-related matters. In October 2020, the difference was only about 50. In November and December 2020, there were actually more criticisms on trust-related issues. It can be inferred that as time progresses, many of the technical problems are solved; however, consumer trust in the product remains poorly established.

5.4   Misinformation

The natural next question is, why can these trust-related issues not be solved? In order to answer the question, we dive deeper into the detractors' comments and try to understand the reasons behind them. Much to our surprise, we find that many of them are misinformation, according to definitions provided by the World Health Organization [26]. We list a few examples as follows.

Misinformation About Technical Flaws
Many users complain that the CWA needs the internet all the time. However, this is not the

case, as the internet is only required for a short time, to match the diagnosis keys to provide results. When no internet access is available, exposure logging goes to a "restricted state" but still receives/sends Bluetooth beacons to exchange ID codes/diagnosis keys anonymously, and the diagnosis keys are matched later, once the internet is restored[4].

Misinformation About Compatibility
Many users complain that their phones cannot run two corona apps from different countries at the same time. However, the German CWA does not interfere with the working of other apps; hence, it can run simultaneously with Corona-tracing apps from other countries. The CWA is currently compatible in 29 countries, but developers are currently working on releasing it in more territories[5].

Misinformation About the User Experience
The main complaint is that the app consumes too much battery. However, thanks to the joint efforts of Google and Apple, they have developed an exposure notification API that employs the energy-saving Bluetooth Low Energy (BLE) technology. The CWA consumes battery power in two ways: running the app and recording encounters via the ENS. The battery power consumed by the latter is optimized using BLE technology. Many Apple users have reported a significant amount of battery drain after updating their iOS, but, in fact, the issue does not relate to the CWA but to Apple's ENS[6]. Moreover, in an experiment to observe battery consumption, no device lost more than 5% of its battery over a period of 24 h [27].

Misinformation About Privacy Violation
Despite the developer's efforts to make the Corona-Warn-App data protection-friendly, a significant number of people still believe that it violates data privacy. For example, people complain that the CWA is a violation of the European General Data Protection Regulation (GDPR), when, in fact, it was the first app developed under government supervision to consider specifically "Art. 25: Data protection by design and by default" of the GDPR in the early stages of its development [28]. Minimum amounts of data are retained by the Robert Koch Institute, and no data are shared without the user's permission. The pseudonymization mechanism and decentralized architecture ensure that the data are managed in an efficient manner [29]. Additionally, the Google/Apple exposure notification (GAEN) feature strives to provide complete data privacy. Moreover, both companies have assured that they do not share user information with third parties.

We calculate the number of misinformed tweets and plot them in Fig. 7. About $115/(115 + 1550) = 7\%$ of the technical issues are not valid. This ratio is significantly higher regarding trust-related issues. In total, $274/(274 + 387) = 41\%$ of all the trust-related issues are actually misinformed.

---

[4] https://github.com/corona-warn-app/cwa-documentation/issues/465.

[5] https://www.coronawarn.app/en/faq/#ios135.

[6] https://www.coronawarn.app/en/faq/#background_updates.

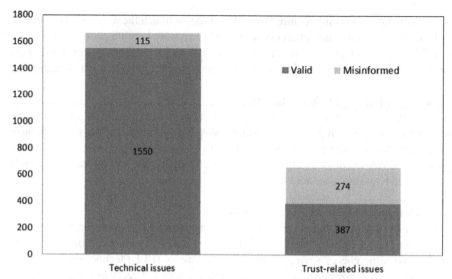

Fig. 7. Whereas most of the technical issues are valid, more than $274/(274 + 387) = 40\%$ of all trust-related issues are due to misinformation.

5.5 Discussion

Our results are consistent with the literature, in that technical problems were a major barrier shortly after the launch of the app [11, 18]. However, different from previous studies, our analysis demonstrates that these technical issues were solved in later updates, but the installation rate still remained low. Our result is also consistent with the literature finding [6, 12, 19, 20], that privacy is a major concern. However, we further examine the accuracy of the comments in detail.

The unique finding of our study is a surprisingly high number of misinformed tweets. Specifically, more than 40% of negative comments on trust-related issues are confirmed as inaccurate. Such a high ratio cannot simply be explained by carelessness. We argue that, besides the real technical and trust-related issues explored to date, a key reason for not installing the app is deliberate misinformation, promulgated intentionally to lower trust in the app. Our study therefore offers new evidence for misinformation in a life-threating pandemic [30].

6 Conclusion

The main contribution of this paper is its investigation of the reasons why the Corona-Warn-App has not been installed by the majority of the German population. Considering the disruptive COVID-19 pandemic – which is one of the most devastating in human history – and the novelty of the app, this study explores a field that has not been touched by the literature to date.

We scrap 70,529 related tweets and apply sentiment and content analysis to understand the reasons for not installing the app. We find that technical problems represent one issue, but, much to our surprise, we find evidence of misinformation being spread to lower user trust in the app. In fact, more than 40% of trust-related issues can be attributed to fabrication. Our study suggests that decision-makers should carefully align and evaluate information on such a novel technology applied in an emergency outbreak.

Our study is only restricted to one app in one country, and so future studies could be extended to other apps worldwide. Follow-up studies could investigate the reasons for the misinformation. New theories could also be developed to explain misinformation and the lack of trust in such a disruptive pandemic. It would also be interesting to investigate the adoption rate of the CWA after its incorporation of the digital vaccination certificate.

References

1. Johns Hopkins University. COVID-19 dashboard by the center for systems science and engineering (2021)
2. United Nations. UN launches COVID-19 plan that could 'defeat the virus and build a better world' (2020)
3. Ferretti, L., et al.: Quantifying SARS-CoV-2 transmission suggests epidemic control with digital contact tracing. Science **368**, eabb6936 (2020). https://doi.org/10.1126/science.abb 6936
4. Oliver, N., et al.: Mobile phone data for informing public health actions across the COVID-19 pandemic life cycle. Sci. Adv. **6**, eabc0764 (2020). https://doi.org/10.1126/sciadv.abc0764
5. Wen, H., Zhao, Q., Lin, Z., Xuan, D., Shroff, N.: A study of the privacy of COVID-19 contact tracing apps. In: Park, N., Sun, K., Foresti, S., Butler, K., Saxena, N. (eds.) SecureComm 2020. LNICSSITE, vol. 335, pp. 297–317. Springer, Cham (2020). https://doi.org/10.1007/978-3-030-63086-7_17
6. Munzert, S., Selb, P., Gohdes, A., Stoetzer, L.F., Lowe, W.: Tracking and promoting the usage of a COVID-19 contact tracing app. Nat. Hum. Behav. **5**, 247–255 (2021). https://doi.org/10.1038/s41562-020-01044-x
7. Hinch, R., et al.: Effective Configurations of a Digital Contact Tracing App: A report to NHSX (2020)
8. Blom, A.G., et al.: Barriers to the large-scale adoption of a COVID-19 contact tracing app in Germany: survey study. J. Med. Internet Res. **23**, e23362 (2021). https://doi.org/10.2196/23362
9. Statista. Anzahl der Downloads der Corona-Warn-App über den Apple App Store und den Google Play Store in Deutschland von Juni 2020 bis Mai 2021 (2021). https://de.statista.com/statistik/daten/studie/1125951/umfrage/downloads-der-corona-warn-app/
10. Horstmann, K.T., Buecker, S., Krasko, J., Kritzler, S., Terwiel, S.: Who does or does not use the 'Corona-Warn-App' and why? Eur. J. Pub. Health **31**, 49–51 (2021). https://doi.org/10.1093/eurpub/ckaa239
11. Wang, H., Wang, L., Wang, H.: Market-level analysis of government-backed COVID-19 contact tracing apps. In: Proceedings of the 35th IEEE/ACM International Conference on Automated Software Engineering Workshops, Virtual Event Australia, pp. 79–84. ACM (2020). https://doi.org/10.1145/3417113.3422186
12. Altmann, S., et al.: Acceptability of app-based contact tracing for COVID-19: cross-country survey study. JMIR Mhealth Uhealth **8**, e19857 (2020). https://doi.org/10.2196/19857
13. Hatamian, M., Wairimu, S., Momen, N., Fritsch, L.: A privacy and security analysis of early-deployed COVID-19 contact tracing Android apps. Empir. Softw. Eng. **26**(3), 1–51 (2021). https://doi.org/10.1007/s10664-020-09934-4

14. Datareportal. Digital 2020: Germany (2021). https://datareportal.com/reports/digital-2020-germany

15. Dong, C.: Mobile phone data as an opportunity to fight the pandemic. In: Bunkanwanicha, P., Coeurderoy, R., Ben Slimane, S. (eds.) Managing a Post-Covid19 Era, ESCP Business School, pp. 14–18 (2020)

16. Keusch, F., Bähr, S., Haas, G.-C., Kreuter, F., Trappmann, M.: Coverage error in data collection combining mobile surveys with passive measurement using apps: data from a German national survey. Soc. Methods Res. 004912412091492 (2020). https://doi.org/10.1177/0049124120914924

17. Li, T., et al.: What makes people install a COVID-19 contact-tracing app? Understanding the influence of app design and individual difference on contact-tracing app adoption intention. Pervasive Mob. Comput. 75, 101439 (2021). https://doi.org/10.1016/j.pmcj.2021.101439

18. Rosenbach, M., Schmergal, C.: Germans Disappointed by Coronavirus Tracking App (2020). https://www.spiegel.de/international/germany/lots-of-work-but-little-utility-germans-disappointed-by-coronavirus-tracking-app-a-7c30191e-b225-4c37-917d-41dc2a6078a1

19. Simon, J., Rieder, G.: Trusting the Corona-Warn-App? Contemplations on trust and trustworthiness at the intersection of technology, politics and public debate. Eur. J. Commun. 36, 334–348 (2021). https://doi.org/10.1177/02673231211028377

20. Amann, J., Sleigh, J., Vayena, E.: Digital contact-tracing during the Covid-19 pandemic: an analysis of newspaper coverage in Germany, Austria, and Switzerland. PLoS ONE 16, e0246524 (2021). https://doi.org/10.1371/journal.pone.0246524

21. Häring, M., et al.: Never ever or no matter what: investigating adoption intentions and misconceptions about the corona-warn-app in Germany. In: Proceedings of the Seventeenth Symposium on Usable Privacy and Security (2021)

22. The Federal Government of Germany. The Corona-Warn-App helps us in the fight against corona (2021). https://www.bundesregierung.de/breg-de/themen/corona-warn-app/corona-warn-app-englisch

23. Robert Koch Institute. Interrupt chains of infection digitally with the Corona-Warn-App (2021). https://www.rki.de/EN/Content/infections/epidemiology/outbreaks/COVID-19/CWA/CWA.html

24. Debortoli, S., Müller, O., Junglas, I., vom Brocke, J.: Text mining for information systems researchers: an annotated topic modeling tutorial. CAIS 39, 110–35 (2016). https://doi.org/10.17705/1CAIS.03907

25. Berente, N., Seidel, S., Safadi, H.: Research commentary—data-driven computationally intensive theory development. Inf. Syst. Res. 30, 50–64 (2019). https://doi.org/10.1287/isre.2018.0774

26. World Health Organization. How to report misinformation online (2021). https://www.who.int/campaigns/connecting-the-world-to-combat-coronavirus/how-to-report-misinformation-online?gclid=CjwKCAjwlrqHBhByEiwAnLmYUPNoegGcIEnXIacxds3XrjnY3c-hii0JdfYKL3-mJaQQz32idpeIeBoCqfQQAvD_BwE

27. Bletzinger, M.: Corona-Warn-App: Akku- und Internetfresser? Massive Sicherheitslücken? Das ist dran an der Kritik (2020). https://www.merkur.de/politik/corona-warn-app-deutschland-test-kritik-daten-sicherheit-akku-internet-appl-android-ios-zr-13801796.html

28. Intersoft Consulting. General Data Protection Regulation (GDPR) – Official Legal Text (2021). https://gdpr-info.eu/

29. Dix, A.: Die deutsche Corona Warn-App – ein gelungenes Beispiel für Privacy by Design? Datenschutz und Datensicherheit - DuD 44(12), 779–785 (2020). https://doi.org/10.1007/s11623-020-1366-1

30. WHO. Fighting misinformation in the time of COVID-19, one click at a time (2021). https://www.who.int/news-room/feature-stories/detail/fighting-misinformation-in-the-time-of-covid-19-one-click-at-a-time

User Perception of Algorithmic Digital Marketing in Conditions of Scarcity

Veronika Pavlidou[1]([✉]) [iD], Jahna Otterbacher[1,2] [iD], and Styliani Kleanthous[1,2] [iD]

[1] Open University of Cyprus, Latsia, Cyprus
veronika.pavlidou1@st.ouc.ac.cy
[2] CYENS Centre of Excellence, Nicosia, Cyprus

Abstract. Digital Marketing, and specifically, *targeted* marketing online is flourishing in recent years, and is becoming evermore precise and easy to implement, given the rise of big data and algorithmic processes. This study assesses users' perceptions regarding the *fairness* in algorithmic targeted marketing, in conditions of scarcity. This is increasingly important because as more decisions are made by data-driven algorithms, the potential for consumers to be treated unfairly by marketers grows. Awareness of users' perceptions helps to create a more open, understandable and fair digital world without negative influences. Also, it may help both marketers and consumers to communicate effectively.

Keywords: Digital marketing · Users' perceptions · Fairness in algorithmic processes · Microtargeting · Scarcity messages

1 Introduction

Businesses, and especially brands, have long embraced technology to remain competitive and deliver the best customer services. "Cognitive technologies" is a more recent industry term for narrow AI[1], implying that the technologies take the automation to a new level of "human-like" behaviours. Algorithmic-mediated, targeted marketing online, based on models created via machine learning (ML), has greatly influenced marketing practices. Today, most people conduct online research before making a purchase, and this fundamental change in buying behaviour forces marketers to adapt their business marketing strategies for the digital age. Marketers (i.e., advertisers) always try to reach their target audience based on demographics (gender, age, race, ethnicity), preferences, etc. and by using cognitive biases (e.g., scarcity bias), that influence potential consumer behaviour and decisions in order to increase sales. It is generally accepted that AI systems have many potential benefits for business, the economy, and for tackling society's most pressing social challenges, including the mitigation of

---

[1] Artificial intelligence systems focused on a singular or limited task. https://deepai.org/machine-learning-glossary-and-terms/narrow-ai.

© Springer Nature Switzerland AG 2022
M. Themistocleous and M. Papadaki (Eds.): EMCIS 2021, LNBIP 437, pp. 319–332, 2022.
https://doi.org/10.1007/978-3-030-95947-0_22

inequality. But that will only be possible if people trust these systems to produce 'fair results' - or at least, results that are explained to the user.

As (O'Neil 2016) states *"no model can include all the real world's complexity or the nuance of human communication"*. Thus, new issues have come up regarding the fairness of algorithmic decisions. According to IEEE Global Initiative on Ethics of Autonomous and Intelligent Systems document (2019), intelligent systems must respect human rights, freedoms, human dignity, and cultural diversity. They must be verifiably safe and secure throughout their operational lifetime and stakeholders should prioritize human well-being (e.g. mental health, emotions, sense of themselves, their autonomy, etc.) as an outcome in all system designs, using the best available and widely accepted well-being metrics as their reference point. And since machine learning algorithms used to automate decisions already affect individuals, businesses and other organizations globally, concerns regarding the fairness of the algorithmic decisions raised by the expert community are numerous. They include the lack of algorithmic fairness (leading to discriminatory practices such as racial and gender biases), content personalisation resulting in partial information asymmetry (e.g. 'filter bubble'), lack of transparency, the infringement of user privacy, and potential user manipulation (Lepri et al. 2017).

It is important for marketers to understand consumers' perceptions, and specifically *fairness perceptions*, to determine the factors that influence consumers to make purchase decisions. Moreover, the concept of fairness is essential to the relationship between consumers and marketers. Currently, we present an online study that aims to identify the existence of concerns about the targeted marketing online in conditions of scarcity. The study works towards understanding the perceptions of users, considering their level of awareness of issues related to bias and unfairness in algorithmic targeted marketing. Moreover, it examines the level of tailored-made ads with scarcity with which users are comfortable. The more people made aware of how these algorithms operate, the better chance there is to foster trust in these systems, as informed users will be in position to make an assessment as to whether they are being treated fairly or not.

2   Related Work

2.1   Targeted Marketing Online

Microtargeting techniques are really powerful, but can be potentially dangerous (Howard 2006). As (Kleinberg et al. 2018) state "algorithms are fundamentally opaque, not just cognitively but even mathematically." In other words, these processes are typically "black boxes," with the model of the consumer typically being constructed algorithmically (e.g., by exploiting her or his online behaviours to infer demographic characteristics and preferences) (Bayer 2020). For example, Wing's model of "Data and ML relation" (Wing 2018) shows that training data are input to a machine learning algorithm to produce a model that can classify the data subject (i.e., consumer) or make predictions. If the data is somehow biased, the algorithm will be affected, implying a biased model that produces biased results.

One of the upcoming trends in the E-Commerce industry is "contextual and programmatic advertising", which aims to provide the right audience with the right ad at the right moment. These techniques are expected to use huge amounts of data to identify target customers (Big Data in E-commerce: Global Markets, 2019). Marketers create ads based on their users' collected datasets, comprising observations on their demographic, historical, current, geographic location, etc. After publishing an ad, the contextual advertising system (e.g., Google's AdSense) then directs the ads, through keywords, to the right websites.

2.2 Users' Perceptions of Fairness in Algorithmic Processes

While targeted marketing has generally been viewed as beneficial to both consumers and marketers, there are concerns raised of how consumers perceive and reason about fairness in algorithmic processes. According to (Lee 2018), how users perceive, and process issues of FATE (Fairness, Accountability, Transparency and Ethics) is considered more important than the technical properties/qualities of the algorithmic processes driving targeted ads, such as accuracy and predictability. As (Shin and Park 2019) argued, users expect algorithms to offer accurate, convenient, and credible results; in other words, users are inclined to trust the system because they know how the data are analyzed and thus how recommendations are generated. Moreover, users with higher levels of trust were observed to be more likely to see algorithms as fair, accurate, and transparent, while trust moderating the relationship between FATE and satisfaction. However, public understanding is limited by a technical barrier as well as economic factors, with many algorithmic processes protected as trade secrets.

2.3 Persuasive Marketing Techniques

Consumer cognitive biases help marketers to develop successful campaigns. This strategy is known as cognitive marketing. *"Cognitive marketing is one of the best ways to connect with a customer on a personal level. It essentially uses what people are already thinking about in a positive way to give a brand a position that reflects the customer's position. This helps the customer to see a similarity between themselves and the brand, helping to form a strong connection"* (What is Cognitive Marketing and Why Should You Be Using It?, 2017). For example, companies such as Dove and its 2004 "campaign for real beauty", tried to connect with a customer by reducing the consumer's gap between the actual and ideal self or the Always company and its 2014 campaign "#likeagirl", with a very powerful meaning. Cognitive marketing campaigns focus on full targeting (i.e., demographic, geographic) and use different cognitive biases to be effective as possible. However, the most well-known is a *scarcity bias*.

Scarcity Bias or Effect Technique in Digital Marketing. The definition of Scarcity can be found in early marketing literature, and refers to a commodity's unavailability. Scarcity may be operationalized as: (1) limits on the supply of a commodity; (2) costs of acquiring, or of providing, a commodity; (3) restrictions limiting possession of a commodity, and/or (4) delays in providing a commodity (Brock 1968). Commodities refer to any marketable goods or services such as promotions, offers, events, etc. There are several types of scarcity: supply-caused scarcity (Cialdini 2008), demand-caused scarcity and time scarcity (Gierl and Huettl 2010), exclusivity or uniqueness (Fromkin 1970). Demand-caused scarcity and time scarcity can be defined as the presence of limited resources and competition on the demand side (e.g., not enough for two people) (Mittone and Savadori 2009). This type of scarcity is often used in promotion by big brands' "limited edition products" (Aggarwal et al. 2011). In contrast, Exclusivity is a specific type of scarcity, in which only a selected group of people receives a promotion (Broeder and Derksen 2018) or Uniqueness can be defined as a humans' need to feel that they are not too similar to others (Schumpe and Erb 2015).

As (Mittone and Savadori 2009) state, scarcity does work as an attractor as humans place a higher value on an object that is scarce. As (Aggarwal et al. 2011) explain, scarcity creates a sense of urgency among buyers that results in increased quantities purchased, shorter searches, and greater satisfaction with the purchased products. Today's world can be described as a time of unprecedented abundance, yet scarcity persists, and it is used in digital marketing as a tool for boosting consumption, creating wants and needs for the product or service that marketers would like to promote. As (O'Neil 2016) characteristically described "lead aggregators push people toward needless transactions... the data-driven algorithms, while producing revenue for search engines, lead aggregators, and marketers, is a leech on the economy as a whole". Announcements such as "In high demand", "Two seats left at this price!" or "Sale, by Invitation only" represent scarcity use in digital marketing. Such tactics are commonly found on platforms such as booking.com, amazon.com, ebay.com etc.

Perceptions of Persuasive Marketing Techniques. On the one hand, a scarcity bias (effect) in digital marketing is likely to elicit positive thoughts about the product (Gierl and Huettl 2010). And on the other, it can also provoke a negative thought, such as suspicion about marketers' manipulative intent (i.e., persuasive attempt). For example, it is possible for marketers to artificially restrict the quantity of a product being offered in a given retail outlet or sales territory, and thus send a false signal of popularity among consumers. In this way, according to (Gupta 2013), scarcity communicated by the retailer threatens consumers' freedom. Another example of an ethical issue is that when consumers compete against one another, the seller stands to benefit from such competition (Aggarwal et al. 2011). Clearly, persons should not be forced, tempted, or seduced into performing actions solely for the benefit of a third party (Becker 2019). Generally, in the digital marketing literature, it is clear that controversial ethical issues arise when tactics such as scarcity are employed by marketers.

Effectiveness of Scarcity in Digital Marketing. The framework of (Shi et al. 2020) indicates that the effective use of product scarcity in marketing depends on a combination of consumer characteristics, types of scarcity, and types of product, which results in different impacts on consumers. Also, as (Broeder and Derksen 2018) state, the effectiveness of scarcity may differ depending on the type of product and advertising context and they found that even though advertisements are not likable, they can be effective, indicating that the likability of advertisements is not necessarily related to effectiveness. Similarly, (Trinh Anh 2014) notes that the ease of searching for alternative online deals may change the effectiveness of scarcity messages.

According to (Lynn 1991) scarcity tactics are more effective when targeted at consumers who possess greater than average needs for uniqueness. Such targeting would be facilitated by an understanding of the demographic, lifestyle, and other characteristics of high need-for-uniqueness individuals. Also, as (Lynn 1991) states, scarcity has an effect only when subjects had been primed to think about the price implications of the scarcity. In other words, scarcity enhances the value (or desirability) of anything that can be possessed (Brock 1968). Thus, marketers can increase the perceived value of products, services, and promotions by manipulating the perceived scarcity of the offerings.

Lastly, microtargeting doesn't act as a magic bullet in consumer persuasion but is not pointless for advertisers or harmless for consumers (Winter et al. 2021). The previous studies propose to investigate the effectiveness of scarcity appeals in the context of consumer-choice setting and behavioral retargeting. Also, the fairness variable is suggested to be investigated since it is essential to the relationship between consumers and marketers.

3   Methodology and Research Questions

To explore users' perceptions regarding fairness in algorithmic processes that are commonly used in e-commerce contexts and in conditions of scarcity, a two-phase, mixed-methods study was conducted, in order to answer the following research questions (RQ): RQ1. How do users perceive algorithmically mediated digital marketing? RQ2. How do consumers perceive and respond to Scarcity in algorithmically mediated digital marketing? RQ3. What are users' perceptions about the fairness in use of scarcity in algorithmic micro-targeting.

In the first phase of the study, we conducted an online experiment, involving a simulated e-commerce context, which participants were asked to visit. We then assessed their perceptions and feelings surrounding the use of algorithmic micro-targeting, via a questionnaire. In the second phase, follow-up interviews were conducted with five participants, to explore more in-depth their views towards these practices. The participants of the study were recruited at the first author's college. Our research protocol and informed consent materials received ethical approval from [redacted for blind review.

Phase 1: Online Experiment. Our online experiment was implemented in three stages: a pre-experiment questionnaire (PQ1), participation in a simulated, online browsing experience, and finally, a post-experiment questionnaire (PQ2) (see Table 1). PQ1 (consisting of 16 questions) consisted of two parts 1) demographics of the respondent 2) shopping preferences. After participants completed PQ1, two types of ads were designed according to the majority's reported preferences. These ads were placed in between the text as advertising banners on the specific webpage designed for research purposes (i.e., simulated browsing experience), where participants had to sign in. Participants were then directed to the research website. First, they were told that they would be asked to read a text concerning higher education issues. Following that, they would be prompted to complete the post-questionnaire (PQ2) that would take them approximately 10 minutes. PQ2 (consisting of a series of 32 seven-point Likert item questions, with possible responses ranging from "strongly disagree" (1), "neutral" (4), to "strongly agree" (7)) was implemented in three sections: 1) confirmation that the article was read by participants 2) assessing microtargeting concerns 3) assessing their fairness and scarcity perceptions.

Although our experiment aimed to assess participants' views towards the practice of microtargeting, it is also important to understand the behaviour of the participants on the specific webpage, during the experiment. Thus, a website tracking tool has been used. The analysis was focused on the two main points: i) whether participants observed the ads on the page or not and ii) whether participants clicked on the ads or not. Per the responses to PQ2 [Q1-5] we found that most participants (N = 44; 88%) noticed the ads on the page and 47% believed that ads were tailored to their preferences. Moreover, 65% found the ads interesting because of the offer and 50% because of the product.

Participants (Analysis of PQ1). 57 questionnaires in total were returned to the researchers; 50 of these were complete and valid, and the participants agreed to continue to the online experiment. Table 2 presents the demographic attributes of the 50 English-speaking study participants. As can be observed, the participants are mostly Undergraduate-level (BSc) students from [redacted for blind review] (N = 30; 60%) and [redacted] (N = 12; 24%), female (N = 32; 64%) and male (N = 18; 36%) of age 18–29 (N = 34; 68%). In terms of their interests, they like to listen to music (N = 33; 66%), watch movies (N = 27; 54%), and use social media (N = 25; 50%). Many of them (N = 27; 54%) report spending up to 6 h per day online for entertainment and only (N = 4; 8%) more than 6 h online.

Phase 2: Interviews. Semi-structured interviews (IQ3) consisted of opinion, values and feeling questions aimed at understanding the cognitive and interpretive processes of people's opinions, judgments, values, and feeling responses of people to their experiences and thoughts. Specifically, the goals was to assess i) perceptions on use of algorithmic micro-targeting in online advertising ii) per-

Table 1. Post-Questionnaire (PQ2).

a/a	Section 1 confirmation that the article was read by participants
1	The article you just read was about
2	On the page was an ad/s for (choose all that apply)
3	I find the ad interesting because of the product
4	I find the ad interesting because of the offer
5	The ad is tailored to my preferencest
a/a	Section 2 microtargeting concerns
6	When I use social media, I prefer Facebook
7	I like that Facebook connects me with my friends and with friends of my friends
8	I like that Facebook connects people and events
9	I like that Facebook connects photos and People
10	I like that Facebook ranks the post each user sees
11	I like that Facebook picks and chooses the ads it thinks users will be interested in seeing
12	I like that Facebook has access to my activity when I use the social network
13	I like that Facebook has access to my activity when I visit other websites
14	I am aware of the consequences of being tracked online
15	I have no concerns regarding privacy or ethical issues
a/a	Section 3 fairness and scarcity perceptions
16	While browsing online, I find that there are many advertisements with messages like Buy Now!, Only one left!, Today' offer etc.
17	When I see the scarcity phrases, I feel that I have to buy this product
18	When I find ads with scarcity phrases, I tend to ignore them
19	While shopping online, I find that the products of my interest are often scarce
20	I like online ads tailored to my preferences
21	I don't trust the online ads with offers
22	When I see online ads, I have a feeling that my personal information is taken without permission
23	When I see online ads, I feel manipulated by the advertiser
24	I got nervous by seeing the online ads
25	When I see online ads, I feel that marketers intentionally created scarcity
26	I think it is not fair to use scarcity to convince me to purchase the product
27	While browsing online, I develop a desire to buy them immediately
28	While browsing online, I buy things offered for sale, even I can't afford them
29	While browsing online, offers and recommendations induce me to do just the opposite
30	While browsing online, I don't want to run the risk missing out on offers
31	While browsing online, I become frustrated when I am unable to get my preferred choice
32	While browsing online, I would be upset if I missed buying some products of interest
33	I often feel a regret after shopping online
34	I feel guilty that I can't control my spending

ceptions of its effects iii) perceptions of fairness in use of scarcity in algorithmic micro-targeting. The interview participants were recruited through a request for interview participation sent by email. Before starting (IQ3) the Informed Consent Forms with audio recording use permission were completed. Table 3 presents the demographic attributes of the 5 interview participants.

Table 2. Demographic profiles of Phase 1 participants (N = 50).

Survey participants			
Variables	Category	N	%
Gender	Male	18	36%
	Female	32	64%
Marital status	Single	30	53%
	Married	10	20%
	Divorced	4	7%
	Engaged/in a relationship	6	10%
Country	Cyprus	30	60%
	Nepal	12	24%
	India	4	8%
	Other	4	8%

Table 3. Demographic profiles of Phase 2 participants (N = 5).

Interview participants		
Variables	Category	N
Gender	Male	3
	Female	2
Country	Cyprus	5
Age	18–25	3
	40–50	2

3.1 Data analysis

Both quantitative (PQ2) and qualitative (IQ) data resulted from the study. For the responses to the questionnaire items, we consider the distribution of responses on the Likert item questions. To examine the degree of association between responses across items we use Correlation Analysis (Spearman's r). For now, we do not present a complete analysis of the interview data but use it to enrich the findings stemming from the quantitative data/PQ2.

4 Analysis

RQ1. How do users perceive algorithmically mediated digital marketing?
Most participants prefer to use Facebook (62%) and generally like the way the Facebook algorithm works [Q6-10]. Also, all interviewees reported using Facebook and generally also like the way the algorithm of Facebook works. Although 40% of participants like the Facebook post ranking algorithm, 16% do not know about it [Q10] and only 34% like how Facebook picks and chooses the ads for

each user [Q11]. The following quotes from interviews illustrate these findings: *"I would prefer to have control on what I want to see or not online, but I believe that it is too complicated. Sometimes, I intentionally hide the ads just to 'disorientate' the algorithm." (interviewee 48, male)*. In other hand, *"I don't know how Facebook works and it is not so important to me" (interviewee 21, male)*.

46% answered negatively to the fact that Facebook has access to their activities when they use this social network [Q12] and 54% answered negatively to the off-Facebook activity [Q13]. *"I have many concerns regarding the Facebook algorithm, generally, it makes me fill violated, I don't like the fact that it asks me so many personal questions, shows me ads and sends notifications that all related to my online activities. It seems that it collects everything about me, and I don't know why." (interviewee 19, female)*. In other hand, *"I have nothing to hide so I don't care who accesses my information". (interviewee 21, male)*. Although 68% are aware of the consequences of being tracked online [Q15], 62% have concerns regarding privacy or ethical issues [Q16].

There seems to be a relation between feeling nervous by seeing the online ads and feeling manipulated by the advertiser [Q23-24]. *"Definitely, I don't like to be tracked by Facebook…it is a little bit scary". "I feel awkward sometimes when I see ads related to my previous browsing." (interviewee 22, female)* Similarly, *"Marketers manipulate people by brain-washing techniques (i.e. offers, scarcity messages)". (interviewee 19, female) "Although I have been setting off everything on Facebook etc. I still feel tracked and I don't like it because it seems to control my needs in a way". (interviewee 48, male)* (Interviewee 40, male) believes that the internet censorship and online ads are related, and they limit our freedom in a way that is scary (Table 4).

Also, study participants who have no concerns regarding privacy or ethical issues [Q16] seem to like that Facebook picks and chooses the ads it thinks users will be interested in seeing [Q11]. *"I will interact with online ads only if they are interested to me" (interviewee 21, male)*. *"I have some concerns regarding privacy or ethical issues on Facebook. I would prefer if I could have full control of what I see there without giving my personal information"*. (Interviewee 22, female) (Table 4). Moreover, people who feel manipulated by the advertiser [Q23] feel that their personal information is taken without permission [Q22]. *"I would prefer if I could have account with not sharing my information". (interviewee 19, female) "I believe that people who trust Facebook and other platforms do not give an appropriate attention to the small text that says to you to consist to any sharing of your personal data." (interviewee 48, male) "Sometimes, I am just afraid that one day Facebook will know my needs better than I know." (interviewee 19, female)* (Table 4).

RQ2. How do consumers perceive and respond to Scarcity in algorithmically mediated digital marketing?

72% of study participants believe that there are many advertisements online with scarcity phrases [Q16]. All interviewees believe that people are bombarded with ads with scarcity phrases. There seem to be a relation between people who tend to ignore scarcity phrases [Q18] and people who don't trust the online ads with

Table 4. Result details RQ1.

Items	rs	p (2-tailed)
Q24-23	0.36856	0.00845
Q16-11	0.33204	0.01849
Q23-22	0.63174	0

offers [Q21]. *"Lately, I don't trust the offers because I believe marketers try to manipulate people by this way so if I want to buy something I check it twice before any purchasing". (interviewee 22, female). "Most of online ads I see have scarcity messages. Several times I have been trusted these messages, when I realized that there are many tricks (prices vs quantity). It's really annoying." (interviewee 19, female).* In other hand, *"I like and trust online ads with offers mostly from trustworthy companies like Amazon or Zara". (interviewee 48, male)* (Table 5).

Q20-30, 31, 32, 34 The experiment showed that the study participants who like tailored ads don't want to run the risk missing out on offers [30], they are upset if they miss buying some products of interest [31], they become frustrated when they are unable to get their preferred choice [32] and feel guilty that they can't control their spending [34]. *"I like offers only when I am looking for a specific product and I would be upset if miss them out". (interviewee 22, female). "I like online shopping, but unfortunately it hides many traps." (interviewee 21, male).* Similarly, *"I like ads and ads with offers, I enjoy mostly 'online window shopping' with no purchasing". (interviewee 48, male)* In other hand, *"I feel insecure when I see tailored ads since I like shopping and sometimes, I buy things that I regret after. So, I cannot control my spending especially if I see things that I like." (interviewee 19, female).* (Interviewee 40, male) believes that tailored ads are helpful, and one can benefit but only when having control over them; otherwise, it is "annoying" (Table 5).

Table 5. Result details RQ2.

Items	rs	p (2-tailed)
Q18-21	0.40163	0.003845
Q30-31	0.29963	0.03452
Q20-31	0.42467	0.00211
Q20-32	0.39759	0.00425
Q20-34	0.33233	0.01838

RQ3. What are users' perceptions about the fairness in use of scarcity in algorithmic micro-targeting?
Q19-23 There seem to be a relation between people who find that the products of their interest are often scarce [19] and people who feel manipulated by the adver-

tiser [23]. *"I know that marketers use sales tools such as scarcity messages ....
although I feel triggered to see more details it doesn't mean that I will purchase the
product. In other words, the scarcity message will not affect my decision to buy".
(interviewee 48, male). "I believe that marketers sometimes create fake scarcity
messages/offers to make more sales. It makes me feel insecure etc." (interviewee
22, female)* Similarly, *"There are people who have different weaknesses (shopa-
holic or in depression), and marketers use these people to gain money in some
way." (interviewee 19, female).* (interviewee 40, male) believes that there is a
current need to protect people with shopping weaknesses and to provide them
(for example technology education, training etc.) (Table 6).

Q26-24 58% of study participants think that it is not fair to use scarcity to
convince them to purchase the product [26] and it seems to be related to people
who got nervous by seeing the online ads [24]. *"It is not fair to use scarcity,
especially in the case of people with weaknesses." (interviewee 19, female).* In
other hand, *"It is fair to use scarcity phrases only if they are not fake or misleading." (interviewee 48, male).* Similarly, (interviewee 40, male) believes that
it is totally unethical to create intentionally the misleading scarcity messages
and there is a need to control these issues. *"I can understand that marketers
try to use different sale techniques and to stimulate their customers' needs, but
ethical limitations definitely should be applied." (interviewee 40, male)* (Table 6)

Q25-21 Moreover, people who feel that marketers intentionally created
scarcity [25] seem to don't trust the online ads with offers [21]. *"I don't trust
ads with offers I believe most of them are fake or spam" (interviewee 21, male).
"Usually, if I click to ad with offers or scarcity message and I am going to buy
the product I try to read customers' reviews before purchasing" (interviewee 22,
female). "Since I see ads based on my previous browsing and they have scarcity
messages or offers on them, I believe that they are fake or intentionally created.
Most of times I just ignore them." (interviewee 40, male)* (Table 6).

Table 6. Result details RQ3.

Items	rs	p (2-tailed)
Q19-23	0.44122	0.00134
Q26-24	0.39622	0.00439
Q25-21	0.40083	0.00392

5   Discussion

The paper contributes to digital marketing theory by developing an awareness
of the crucial link between cognitive marketing and understanding of fairness in
algorithmic processes since that may affect consumers' and marketers' behaviour.
It was revealed that whereas most people like the way how the algorithm of

Facebook or any other similar platform works they have concerns regarding privacy or ethical issues and they feel violated and no control over the algorithmic processes and personal data. Also, people who don't trust the online ads with offers tend to ignore scarcity phrases. On the other hand, people who like tailored ads don't want to run the risk missing out on offers and they become frustrated and feel guilty that they can't control their spending. Also, people who find that the products of their interest are often scarce feel manipulated by the advertiser. Moreover, people who feel that marketers intentionally create scarcity (64%) seem to don't trust the online ads with offers. The majority thinks that it is not fair to use scarcity to convince people to purchase the product and it makes them feel nervous by seeing the online ads. Moreover, people believe that marketers create misleading scarcity messages, and in their opinion, it is unethical. Another conclusion of our study is that people even who like online ads tailored to their preferences don't give attention to ad banners or to scarcity messages and don't have immediate desire to buy.

There doesn't appear to be a strong relation between participants liking online ads tailored to their preferences and an immediate desire to buy something ($rs = 0.20622$, p (2-tailed) $= 0.15076$). The below heatmap, which is a data visualization technique, uses a warm-to-cool colour spectrum to show which parts of a page receive the most attention. Specifically, it shows that the study participants looked mostly on the map image of the top page and mostly ignored the ad banners. Also, ads got no clicks. *"I interact with ads only when I am going to buy something". (interviewee 40, male). "Usually, I give attention to ads when I have time and mood." (Interviewee 22, female) "Ad banners are so common, people don't give attention to them, especially if they just interested to read an article they will not interact with ads". (Interviewee 48, male)* This phenomenon known as 'Banner blindness' and it could an instance of selective

Fig. 1. The heatmap.

attention. According to (Kara Pernice 2018) people direct their attention only to a subset of the stimuli in the environment - usually those related to their goals (i.e. read the article). Also, according to (Interviewee 48, male) *"Ad banners with offers that are not eye-catching and not branding are not effective"* (Fig. 1).

6   Limitations and Conclusions

There are a number of limitations associated with this study. First, the sample is small in size and it mostly consists of undergraduate students. Second, there is a chance of recall bias in the process of gathering data since the participants were directed to the specific website instead of browsing on their own. Since marketers expect consumers to enjoy their marketing efforts and at the same time consumers expect marketers not only to anticipate their needs, but to be accountable for the ads content and techniques they use, there is a need to continue exploring and monitoring the fairness perceptions and beliefs of not only the users but also other stakeholders involved, such as marketers, algorithmic mediators, and government regulators. Finally, future studies will need target a larger sample of participants allowing the collection of more reliable data.

Acknowledgements. This project is partially funded by the European Union's Horizon 2020 research and innovation programme under grant agreement No. 810105 (CyCAT).

References

Aggarwal, P., Jun, S.Y., Huh, J.H.: Scarcity messages. J. Advert. **40**(3), 19–30 (2011)

Bayer, J.: Double harm to voters: data-driven micro-targeting and democratic public discourse. Internet Policy Rev. **9**(1), 1–7 (2020)

Becker, M.: Privacy in the digital age: comparing and contrasting individual versus social approaches towards privacy. Ethics Inf. Technol. **21**(4), 307–317 (2019). https://doi.org/10.1007/s10676-019-09508-z

Broeder, P., Derksen, R.: Exclusivity in online targeted promotions: cross-cultural preferences of consumers. Int. J. Bus. Emerg. Mark. **10**(4), 396–408 (2018)

Brock. T.C.: Implications of commodity theory for value change. In: Psychological Foundations of Attitudes, pp. 243–275 (1968)

Cialdini, R.B.: Influence: Science and Practice, 4th edn. Allyn & Bacon (2008)

Fromkin, H.L.: Effects of experimentally aroused feelings of undistinctiveness upon valuation of scarce and novel experiences. J. Pers. Soc. Psych. **16**(3), 521 (1970)

Gierl, H., Huettl, V.: Are scarce products always more attractive? The interaction of different types of scarcity signals with products' suitability for conspicuous consumption. Int. J. Res. Mark. **27**(3), 225–235 (2010)

Gupta, S., Melewar, T.C., Bourlakis, M.: A relational insight of brand personification in business-to-business markets. J. Gener. Manag. **35**(4), 65–76 (2010)

Howard, P.: New Media Campaigns and the Managed Citizen (Communication, Society and Politics). Cambridge University Press, Cambridge (2006)

Kleinberg, J., Ludwig, J., Mullainathan, S., Sunstein, C.R.: Discrimination in the age of algorithms. J. Legal Anal. **10**, 113–174 (2018)

Trinh Anh, K.: Scarcity effects on consumer purchase intention in the context of E-commerce. Aalto University (2014)

Lee, M.K.: Understanding perception of algorithmic decisions: fairness, trust, and emotion in response to algorithmic management. Big Data Soc. 5(1) (2018)

Lepri, B., Oliver, N., Letouzé, E., Pentland, A., Vinck, P.: Fair, transparent, and accountable algorithmic decision-making processes. Philos. Technol. 31(4), 611–627 (2017). https://doi.org/10.1007/s13347-017-0279-x

Lynn, M.: Scarcity effects on value: a quantitative review of the commodity theory literature. Psychol. Mark. 8, 43–57 (1991)

Mittone, L., Savadori, L.: The scarcity bias. Appl. Psychol.: Int. Rev. 58(3), 453–468 (2009). Open J. Bus. Manag. 3, 96–108 (2015)

Mussomeli, A., Neier, M., Takayama, B., Sniderman, B., Holdowsky, J.: Building a cognitive digital supply network. Augmenting automation in an AI world. Deloitte Insights (2019)

O'Neil, C.: Weapons of Math Destruction: How Big Data Increases Inequality and Threatens Democracy, 1st edn. Crown, New York (2016)

Schumpe, B.M., Erb, H.P.: Humans and uniqueness. Sci. Prog. 98(1), 1–11 (2015)

Shi, X., Li, F., Chumnumpan, P.: The use of product scarcity in marketing. Eur. J. Mark. ahead-of-print (2020)

Shin, D., Park, Y.J.: Role of fairness, accountability, and transparency in algorithmic affordance. Comput. Hum. Behav. 98, 277–284 (2019)

The IEEE Global Initiative on Ethics of Autonomous and Intelligent Systems. Ethically Aligned Design: A Vision for Prioritizing Human Well-being with Autonomous and Intelligent Systems, First Edition. IEEE (2019)

Wing, J.M.: Data for good: FATES, elaborated. Columbia University Data Science Institute, 23 January 2018

Winter, S., Maslowska, E., Vos, A.: The effects of trait-based personalization in social media advertising (2021)

The Influence of Locus of Control in the Actualisation of Mobile Dating Applications Affordances to Mitigate Privacy and Security Concerns

Maureen Tanner[(✉)] [iD] and Sujala Singh

University of Cape Town, Rondebosch, Cape Town, South Africa
mc.tanner@uct.ac.za

Abstract. Mobile dating applications have changed how romantic relationships are pursued. However, despite the popularity of these applications, users have expressed numerous privacy and security concerns that warrant further investigation. This study explored how users' locus of control influences the actualisation of affordances to mitigate privacy and security concerns. Through a qualitative study based on 12 semi-structured interviews, seven propositions are formulated. The study contributes to MDA literature and affordance theory. The propositions articulate that users can actualise affordances from a network of tools to mitigate privacy and security concerns given their locus of control.

Keywords: Mobile dating applications · Affordances · Privacy concerns · Security concerns · Locus of control

1 Introduction

Social Network Services (SNSs) allow users to connect and form bonds. SNSs is far-reaching, and there are approximately 4.2 billion active social media users as of July 2021 [1]. Therefore, it is no surprise that some of this user base has also ventured into the world of mobile dating.

Mobile Dating Applications (MDAs) are location-based social networks. There are numerous MDAs available on the market (e.g., Tinder and Bumble), most of which are free of charge or offer a freemium option [2]. With the widespread use of SNSs and MDAs, there is a need to study users' privacy and security concerns [3].

Indeed, after the Ashley Madison scandal, people engaging in online dating have become warier about their privacy and security [4]. These concerns might be valid as Tinder has numerous security and privacy vulnerabilities. According to [5], Tinder stores the location information of users in plaintext. Tinder also utilises deep-linking transactions and collects PII data (e.g., birthday, data, country, data provider, gender language, location radius, device model, operating system version, and age) without disclosing this in the company's privacy policy [5].

© Springer Nature Switzerland AG 2022
M. Themistocleous and M. Papadaki (Eds.): EMCIS 2021, LNBIP 437, pp. 333–345, 2022.
https://doi.org/10.1007/978-3-030-95947-0_23

The study investigates this phenomenon by focusing on the actualisation of MDAs affordances to mitigate users' privacy and security concerns. Affordances are "the potential for behaviours associated with achieving an immediate concrete outcome and arising from the relation between an object (e.g., an IT artefact) and a goal-oriented actor or actors" [6] (p. 823). A reliance on 'affordances' is relevant as it allows us to investigate the "multifaceted relational structure between the object/technology and the users that enables or constrains potential behavioural outcomes in a particular context" [7] (p. 46). The actualisation of affordances is dependent on certain facilitating conditions [8]. This study considers the users' locus of control as a possible facilitating condition for the actualisation of MDA affordances to mitigate security and privacy concerns. Locus of control relates to the extent to which a person ascribes the cause or control of events occurring in their lives to themselves or external sources [9]. Hence, users with an internal or external locus of control might actualise MDA affordances differently in their attempt to mitigate privacy and security concerns.

Given the research problems and purpose, the research questions were formulated as follows: "How does users' locus of control influence the actualisation of affordances to mitigate privacy and security concerns?".

Several MDAs are available on the market, but this study focuses on Tinder and Bumble. Tinder is the most downloaded dating application worldwide, while Bumble is the third most downloaded application [10]. Both applications were chosen because of their broad reach and popularity amongst users globally. In addition, both Tinder and Bumble use "swipe logic" and their users' geo-locations to recommend potential matches [11].

The paper is organised as follows. First, an overview of the literature on MDAs and their affordances, specific security and privacy concerns of MDA users and theories on locus of control are provided. The methodology employed is then discussed, followed by an overview of the findings. The final section discusses the theoretical contributions emanating from this paper.

2 Literature Review

2.1 Affordances of Mobile Dating Applications

Affordances are "situated, interactional properties between objects and actors that facilitate certain kinds of social interactions in a complex environment" [12] (p. 3). The concept was first coined by [13], who defined affordances of the environment as "what it offers the animal, what it provides or furnishes, either for good or ill" [13]. When used in the context of Information Systems, affordances relate to the possibilities for goal-oriented actions offered by the features of the Information Technology (IT) artefact [14].

This study focuses on the actualisation of affordances. Actualisation is the process of turning a perceived affordance into action [15] to achieve a specific outcome [16]. Affordances are actualised through the interaction between an IT artefact and a goal-oriented user [17]. The actualisation of affordances can be facilitated or inhibited (i.e., facilitating conditions) by the features of the tool, the abilities and goals of the user, as well as the characteristics of the environment [18, 19].

In the context of MDAs, affordances are defined as the perceived range of possible actions offered by the features of the tool [20]. For example, the affordances offered by Tinder and Bumble include synchronicity, chatting, multimediality, locatability, immediacy, and visual dominance [3, 11, 21, 22].

- **Synchronicity** relates to the rapidity with which messages are sent on the applications. Therefore, the synchronicity affordance is dependent on the availability and the spontaneity of the users [23].
- The **Chatting** affordance relates to users' ability to communicate with each other through text messages. Through the chatting affordance, users are also able to share pictures and videos [20].
- **Multimediality** is a communicative affordance and relates to users' ability to link their profile to other SNS profiles such as Instagram, Spotify and Facebook [23]. In doing so, users can communicate over a broader range of media in addition to texting [21].
- **Locatability** relates to MDAs reliance on the users' geographic location to identify potential matches [24].
- **Immediacy** relates to the fact that users are immediately notified when new messages and matches are received, even when they are not active on the application [11].
- **Visual dominance** relates to the users' ability to use text and images to design their profiles [11].

2.2 Privacy Concerns of MDA Users

Privacy concerns relate to the fear that one's right to control one's personal information and how it is used may be violated [25]. MDA users can have social as well as institutional privacy concerns [26].

Social privacy concerns relate to fears around identity theft, cyberstalking, blackmail, information leakage, bullying and hacking [26]. For example, Tinder users worry about being cyberstalked, that others might use their private information without their consent, and that their accounts might be hacked [3]. Concerns about catfishing are also prevalent among MDA users. Catfishing occurs when users intentionally misrepresent themselves online while pursuing virtual relationships [27].

Institutional privacy concerns relate to fears of how institutions like Bumble and Tinder store and share the data they gather from user profiles. MDA users might be concerned about data security and whether these institutions share their data with third parties and government agencies [3, 21].

2.3 Security Concerns of MDA Users

Security concerns stem from a fear that data protection protocols could be breached through malicious activities [28]. Past studies have found that MDA users share numerous security concerns.

MDAs use location-based services to display profiles in proximity. In that regard, past studies have shown that users are concerned that their location might be leaked to malicious external parties [29]. Malicious parties can use the general location information displayed on profiles to triangulate the exact location of their target [29, 30]. [31] also found that malware may be used to gather data from MDA users. Examples of malware include spyware, phishing, botnets, and surveillance [28].

2.4 Social Media Users' Locus of Control

A person's locus of control relates to their perceived responsibility in various experiences [32]. Individuals with internal locus of control perceive that they are responsible for their decisions and circumstances [33]. They may also feel responsible for causing events [34]. In the context of MDA, a user with internal locus of control might feel responsible for taking measures to actively mitigate their privacy and security concerns to remain in control of the situation.

Individuals with external locus of control ascribe the control of circumstances to external sources (i.e., people and environment) [33]. They perceive external factors as the cause of what happens to them and feel controlled by their environment [32]. In the context of MDA, users with external locus of control might perceive that they cannot do much to mitigate any privacy and security concerns while using the app.

3   Methodology

This study was interpretive, deductive and exploratory. The chosen research strategy was that of qualitative interviews. Twelve in-depth, semi-structured interviews were conducted between May and August 2020 and respondents were encouraged respondents to elaborate on their experiences [35].

The interviews lasted approximately 1 h and were conducted over Skype until saturation was reached. The interviews were recorded, transcribed and shared with the respondents to validate the data.

The interview questionnaire comprised open-ended questions that explored the experiences of the Bumble and Tinder users concerning privacy and security concerns as well as their locus of control. The questions were formulated based on the affordances and the privacy and security concerns derived from literature. Moreover, questions around the functional features of Bumble and Tinder and how they actualised the affordances were formulated to understand the influence of the affordances on these concerns.

A purposive sampling strategy was followed. The sampling criteria related to the need for participants to have an active Bumble or Tinder account. Users between the ages of 18 and 34 were considered as they make up 60% of MDA users [1].

Participants were identified through word of mouth (e.g., casual conversations) and the Tinder and Bumble platforms. The snowballing technique was also applied thereafter to identify participants [35]. An overview of the participants' demographics is provided in Table 1.

Table 1. Respondents' demographics

Participant	Age	MDA Platform	Time on MDA	Gender
P1	27	Tinder	1 year	Male
P2	23	Tinder	5 months	Female
P3	21	Tinder	3 months	Female
P4	23	Tinder	7 months	Female
P5	22	Tinder	1 year	Female
P6	22	Tinder	2 months	Female
P7	34	Bumble	1 month	Male
P8	21	Tinder	3 years	Male
P9	31	Bumble	5 months	Male
P10	26	Bumble	1 month	Male
P11	22	Bumble	3 months	Female
P12	26	Bumble	3 months	Male

Data collection and data analysis were conducted concurrently to allow for corroboration. The recorded interviews were transcribed, cleaned and imported into NVIVO. The data was then analysed using a 6-step thematic analysis process [36]. First, the researchers familiarised themselves with the data during the cleaning, transcription and validation phase. Second, the initial codes were generated by identifying keywords from the transcripts. Third, the keywords were organised into themes. Fourth, relevant themes were reviewed, regrouped and validated. Fifth, the final themes were defined and chosen, and lastly, the final themes were finalised and compared with literature to allow for theorisation.

Ethical considerations were an important part of the study. For that purpose, all participants could withdraw from the study at any time, anonymity was preserved, and ethics clearance was secured from the researchers' academic institution.

4   Findings

The study explored how users with internal and external locus of control actualise affordances to mitigate privacy and security concerns. The findings derived from the data analysis are described in the following sub-sections.

4.1   Internal Locus of Control and MDA Affordance Actualisation

MDA users with internal locus of control were aware of security and privacy risks they incurred while accepting the Terms and Conditions to engage on these platforms. In some instances, they demonstrated limited to no privacy and security concerns as they felt that they had put measures in place to protect themselves. However, when they were concerned about privacy and security risks, they thought it was their responsibility to do what is required to mitigate these risks. Users with internal locus of control devised mitigating strategies by actualising a range of affordances described in the following sub-sections.

Privacy Concerns

Institutional Privacy Concerns. Institutional privacy concerns relate to how MDAs store and share users' data. Some respondents with internal locus of control did not seem to trust the measures put in place by the MDAs to secure their data: *"I would imagine that they don't seem to put too much emphasis on their security if that makes sense?"* [P10]. However, some perceived that it was not the responsibility of MDAs to ensure users' privacy online. They believed that users are in charge of the information being uploaded and have the responsibility to safeguard their privacy: *"If you're going to be negligent with your information, you can't go back to them and say that they have been negligent when it's you who should be in charge"* [P7]. While no specific measures were reported to mitigate institutional privacy concerns, users with internal locus of control instead actualised affordances to handle their social privacy concerns, as discussed in the following sub-section.

Social Privacy Concerns: Blackmail. Users with internal locus of control were aware of the risk of being blackmailed and had actualised a range of affordances to mitigate this social privacy concern. These users actualised the visual dominance affordance by carefully selecting the pictures they uploaded on their profile, which they described as *"decent"*. Visual dominance could also be actualised by screening and limiting the personal information displayed on their profiles (i.e., self- presentation). In doing so, they felt that no potentially compromising content was accessible to others: *"The pictures that I have on Tinder will not cause me any issues, nothing scandalous"* [P4].

Content being shared was also regulated by actualising the chatting affordance. Similarly to not sharing compromising information on their profiles, users with internal locus of control also ensured that they carefully screened the content being exchanged with their matches while texting: *"I don't send any photos on Tinder besides what's on my profile, and I do not ask for pictures...Some people might be sending nudes, and then all of a sudden they're in trouble"* [P4].

The actualisation of the multimediality affordance also compromised users' social privacy and increased the risk of them being blackmailed. Through multimediality, users could link their MDA profiles to their other SNS profiles. In doing so, a need to secure the content on these other SNS sites emerged. Hence, the actualisation of the MDA multimediality affordance led to the need to actualise other SNS affordances to fulfil the goal of not being blackmailed. For that purpose, some users also actualised the visual dominance affordance of the linked SNS sites to ensure that consistent pictures and content were uploaded online. In doing so, they ensured that there were no loopholes in this network of applications that pose a risk to their privacy: *"I make sure not to post something that's putting me at risk. So, my pictures are decent; they're all the same on every social media, including Instagram, Facebook and everything"* [P10].

Social Privacy Concerns: Cyberstalking. Users with internal locus of control actualised various affordances to mitigate the risk of being cyberstalked. Similarly to blackmail, the actualisation of the multimediality affordance also increased the risk of cyberstalking. Hence, to mitigate this concern, users actualised various affordances across various SNS linked to their MDA. The actualisation of the visual dominance affordance (i.e., the use of text and pictures on profiles) across the SNS profiles played a key role in that regard. Some users had different username handles across various SNS to avoid being tracked: *"A lot of people have the same name across all their social media. If someone finds your Instagram, they've found your Facebook, found your LinkedIn, they found your Twitter [...] So, because of that, I crafted my handle name so that people wouldn't find me"* [P3].

Social Privacy Concerns: Identity Theft. Identity theft was also exacerbated through the actualisation of the multimedia affordance. Respondents with internal locus of control put measures to mitigate the risks of their identity being stolen, and these measures also span across various SNS. For example, they actualized the visual dominance affordance by limiting personal information on their different SNS profiles. This gave them a sense of security, resulting in a lower concern about their identity being stolen: *"I think it's just also in terms of information that you give out there. So, I don't have a lot of profile photos"* [P7].

Social Privacy Concerns: Catfishing. Users with internal locus of control perceive that it is their responsibility to ensure the trustworthiness of their matches. To fulfil this goal, they actualise the MDA multimediality affordance to access the SNS profiles of their matches. They actualise the SNS visual dominance affordance to screen the SNS profiles of their matches: *"Being linked to social media can help prove somebody's true identity so if they have an Instagram, where they post a lot of their pictures or something like Facebook, with mutual friends, it shows that they are legit and real"* [P1]. The actualisation of the MDA visual dominance affordance is also helpful to ascertain the credibility and trustworthiness of potential matches before swiping. It is interesting to note that the actualisation of the multimedia affordance allows users to actualise the affordances of other SNS to ascertain the trustworthiness further and fulfil their goal. The findings reveal that the trajectory of affordances extends beyond the MDA, and users may actualise a range of affordances across a network of tools to achieve one goal.

Security Concerns

Location Tracking. Location tracking is a concern, especially when users match with people who are near them. They worry about accidentally meeting a match with whom the conversation did not go well and about being pressured to meet if the match can deduce their location through the application. Such a concern is exacerbated through the actualisation of the locatability affordance, which is central to the functioning of MDAs. However, users with internal locus of control understand and accept the risks associated with using MDAs: *"I mean, again, if you look at the whole point of Tinder, it is to get connected to the people within your proximity. So, does this exacerbate my security concerns? Definitely! But it's a risk that you sign up for the moment you join Tinder. Once you sign up, you're prepared for that risk; it's like you're accepting it in a way"* [P6].

In some cases, concerns are exacerbated by the risk of their location information being illegally obtained. In line with the notion of internal locus of control, they willingly accept that other MDA users will have some insight into their actual physical location. Still, when they are denied control over who is aware of their location, their security concern is exacerbated: *"I did hear that people were able to find your exact specific GPS location. Not just the proximity, but they were somehow able to find the actual location. So that was a bit concerning. But in terms of other users being able to see your approximate distance in kilometres, it's okay"* [P1].

Hence, depending on their primary goal, the locatabilty affordance can be seen as an advantage (e.g., matching with users within their search radius), although users are aware of the risks. If the location tracking security concern remains a secondary issue, users with internal locus of control actualise other affordances to meet this secondary goal. For example, users might actualise the chatting functionality by not disclosing their physical address to strangers: *"I think in general if somebody wants to know, I'll probably give them a very broad answer. So, I'll say from the northern suburbs, instead of like my actual area"* [P11].

Malware. Users with internal locus of control were concerned about the security risks associated with malware. As such, they took measures to mitigate these risks by actualising the affordances of the MDA. As users actualised the chatting affordance, they were careful not to download suspicious files from matches: *"I know not to open any sort of files or, I don't even open pictures on Tinder"* [P8].

Users with internal locus of control also actualised affordances of other applications (e.g., antivirus software) to fulfil their goal of not being victims of malware: *"Obviously I have my device security. So, I have Kaspersky, which I've loaded on so, if there's any sort of malware attack on my phone, hopefully, it will be detected via that"* [P7].

4.2   External Locus of Control and MDA Affordance Actualisation

The findings revealed that users with external locus of control did not necessarily actualise affordances to mitigate privacy and security concerns. This is further discussed in the following sub-sections.

Security Concerns

The findings revealed that some users with external locus of control tend to trust the MDA to mitigate their security concerns: *"I think there's a point where you must trust the likes of Facebook and Bumble and Tinder and all those big companies [...] there is a chance that they can get hacked, obviously, but yeah. What else could you do?"* [P12]. Some admitted having security concerns but did not necessarily actualise affordances to mitigate them: *"I had concerns, but I didn't take precaution. It's like I'm worried, but I'm also not doing anything about it"* [P5].

Some users with external locus of control rely on others to inform them about the existence of malware: *"I didn't see malware from the Tinder application with it being so popular and stuff like that. I'm sure news would have spread, and people would have figured out and avoided it"* [P9]. Some also share the opinion that since MDAs do not force them to download add-ons, they are not at risk of any malware-related security breach. However, these users did not seem to consider the risks associated with downloading content from other MDA users: *"Tinder, I found, never puts you under any pressure to install any third-party apps or any applications for that matter"* [P9]. Location tracking can also be a concern for some users with external locus of control, but some of these users do not do much to mitigate that concern: *"Everyone could see where I was, so no, I didn't take any extra steps"* [P5]. Some users with external locus of control also believe that MDAs monitor profiles and delete suspicious profiles that could be used for catfishing: *"I think the pictures are monitored, and they'll remove some accounts that do not respect the standards"* [P5].

Cyberstalking did not seem to be a significant concern for users with external locus of control. As social media users, some expect to be cyberstalked as their information is available to all. Therefore, they do not seem to mind if other users actualise the multimediality affordance to cyberstalk them: *"Because I'm on social network and you must expect people to look up everything about you"* [P5]. Others accepted that, as MDA users, they are expected to actualise the visual dominance affordance to share personal information to get a match. They trusted that other users would follow the norm and not use the app for malicious purposes: I think you just rely on the fact that people are using the application for the same reason as you, so this is more like writing about your bio and things that interest you [P12].

Privacy Concerns

Some users demonstrated external locus of control concerning privacy concerns. These users typically found MDAs like Tinder and Bumble to be reputable and secure. Therefore, they had low institutional privacy concerns: *"I thought Tinder and Bumble like to me were secure applications"* [P2].

While some users with external locus of control were somewhat concerned about their identity being stolen, they did not specifically actualise affordances to mitigate this risk. Instead, they would trust that other users would notify them if their identity had been stolen: *"I feel scared of such a thing to happen. But, I feel like if it happened, I'm going to be aware because people can tell me that they've seen me"* [P5]. Some also believed that MDAs would take the necessary steps to block fake accounts: *"Apparently, or so I've heard, that if you steal someone's identity, they automatically block you. So, if one picture gets repeated on Tinder, that person who repeated the photo gets blocked"* [P8].

5   Discussion and Conclusion

The study uncovered how MDA users with internal and external locus of control mitigate privacy and security concerns through the actualisation of affordances. The initial intent of the study was to explore the actualisation of MDA affordances. However, one major finding is that users can actualise a broader range of affordances that span across a network of SNS to fulfil their privacy and security goals through the actualisation of the multimedia affordance. This is particularly the case for users with internal locus of control. The study contributes to MDA literature through the following propositions derived from our empirical observations.

- P1: MDA users with internal locus of control did not actualise affordances to mitigate institutional privacy concerns. They instead perceived that it is the users' responsibility to ensure their privacy online.
- P2: Users with internal locus of control actualise the visual dominance affordance of a network of applications (MDA and SNS) by regulating their self-presentation online. This limits the risk of having compromising information on their profile and mitigates social privacy concerns
- P3: Users with internal locus of control actualise the chatting affordance by regulating the content of their messages. This limits the risk of sharing and downloading compromising content and mitigates social privacy and security concerns
- P4: Users with internal locus of control actualise the visual dominance affordance of a network of applications (MDA and SNS) to ascertain the credibility/trustworthiness of their matches and mitigate social privacy concerns
- P5: Users with external locus of control expressed limited security and privacy concerns and trusted the MDA and other users to maintain their security and privacy online. Hence, they did not specifically actualise affordances to mitigate their concerns.
- P6: The actualisation of the MDA multimediality affordances allows for the use of a network of SNS applications whose affordances can also be actualised by users with internal locus of control to mitigate privacy and security concerns

Past studies have shown that users are often more worried about the unintended use of their data by MDAs (institutional privacy concerns) instead of privacy invasions from other users [3]. This study found that users with internal locus of control are indeed concerned about the use of their data without their consent. On the other hand, they feel that it is the responsibility of the users to mitigate this risk. In contrast, users with external locus of control tended to trust the MDA application to ensure their data privacy (P1 & P5). Indeed, trust in the provider and other users can contribute to users' decision to share information online [37].

Social Privacy is a significant concern for SNS users [38]. For example, users might be concerned about blackmail, risky physical meetings, sexual violence, catfishing and harassment [37]. The same applies to personal security risks (e.g., scams, bots) [38]. However, some studies have found that while users are concerned about their privacy and security, they do not necessarily take measures to maintain their privacy [39]. Our findings indicate that this behaviour is manifested in users with external locus of control. Instead, users with internal locus of control actualise a network of MDA and SNS affordances to mitigate their social privacy concerns (see P2, P3 and P4). For users with internal locus of control, the actualisation of the visual dominance and the chatting affordances is primarily based on regulated content sharing and self-presentation. Past studies have also found that sharing content online is influenced by personal preferences, intentional behaviours, expectations of others' preferences, and the application's demands [37]. Moreover, while self-presentation has typically been described as a mechanism to highlight positive traits [40], this study found that this is counter-balanced by the need to regulate content to maintain privacy and security.

Past studies have found that users may decide to share their approximate location to reduce uncertainty around their online persona and establish a social presence [37]. This study found that such an approach (P3) can also serve as a strategy to mitigate the location tracking security concerns that emerge from the actualisation of the locatability affordance.

In addition to contributing to MDA literature, the findings also contribute to affordance theory. Past studies have found that affordances are both enabling and limiting. This implies that affordances have the potential to either mitigate or exacerbate privacy and security concerns [41]. This study found that while the actualisation of the multimedia and locatability affordances can be enabling, they are also limiting as they exacerbate security and privacy concerns. This gives rise to new goals related to the mitigation of these concerns. Therefore, it can be posited that upon encountering limiting outcomes during the actualisation of affordances, new goals might emerge to mitigate these outcomes.

Moreover, trajectories of affordances might be helpful to fulfil these goals (P6) [8]. The study found that trajectories of affordances may span beyond the current application and may involve a network of tools whose affordances can be actualised to fulfil a goal. The following propositions are formulated:

- P7: User goals are dynamic and can emerge through the actualisation of affordances. The need to fulfil one goal may give rise to other goals which can be fulfilled through the actualisation of affordances from a network of tools

This study addressed an important need to understand the privacy and security concerns of MDA users. Through the lens of affordances and the influence of users' locus of control, insights have been provided into measures taken by users to maintain their privacy and security online. The findings contributed to both MDA literature and affordance theory through the formulation of seven propositions. It is recommended that further studies be conducted to operationalise these propositions using a larger sample size.

References

1. Clement, J.: Global Digital Population, 19 July 2021
2. Mobile Device Management: Security and privacy issues associated with mobile applications. Digital Business. https://www.Statista.Com/Statistics/617136/Digital-Population-Worldwide/
3. Liu, C.Z., Au, Y.A., Choi, H.S.: Effects of freemium strategy in the mobile app market: an empirical study of Google Play. J. Manag. Inf. Syst. **31**(3), 326–354 (2014). https://doi.org/10.1080/07421222.2014.995564
4. Lutz, C., Ranzini, G.: Where dating meets data: investigating social and institutional privacy concerns on tinder. Soc. Media Soc. **3**(1), 1–12 (2017). https://doi.org/10.1177/2056305117697735
5. Mansfield-Devine, S.: The Ashley Madison affair. Netw. Secur. 8–16 (2015). http://tools.ietf.org/html/
6. Hayes, D., Cappa, F., Le-Khac, N.A.: An effective approach to m. **1**(1), 1–8 (2020). https://doi.org/10.1016/j.digbus.2020.100001
7. Volkoff, O., Strong, D.: Critical realism and affordances: theorizing it - associated organizational change processes. MIS Q. **37**(3), 819–834 (2013)

8. Evans, S.K., Pearce, K.E., Vitak, J., Treem, J.W.: Explicating affordances: a conceptual framework for understanding affordances in communication research. J. Comput.-Mediat. Commun. **22**(1), 35–52 (2017). https://doi.org/10.1111/jcc4.12180

9. Thapa, D., Sein, M.K.: Trajectory of affordances: insights from a case of telemedicine in Nepal. Inf. Syst. J. **28**(5), 796–817 (2018). https://doi.org/10.1111/isj.12160

10. Rotter, J.B.: Generalized expectancies for internal versus external control of reinforcement. Psychol. Monographs: General Appl. **80**(1), 1-undefined (1966)

11. Tankovska, H.: Most popular dating apps worldwide as of May 2021, by number of monthly downloads, 23July 2021. https://www.Statista.Com/Statistics/1200234/Most-Pop ular-Dating-Apps-Worldwide-by-Number-of-Downloads/

12. Timmermans, E., Courtois, C.: From swiping to casual sex and/or committed relationships: exploring the experiences of Tinder users. Inf. Soc. **34**(2), 59–70 (2018). https://doi.org/10. 1080/01972243.2017.1414093

13. Scacchi, W.: Collaboration practices and affordances in free/open source software development. In: Mistrik, I., Grundy, J., van der Hoek, A., Whitehead, J. (eds.) Collaborative Software Engineering, pp. 307–327. Springer, Heidelberg (2010)

14. Gibson, J.J.: The theory of affordances. In: Shaw, R., Bransford, J. (eds.) Perceiving, Acting, and Knowing: Toward an Ecological Psychology, pp. 67–82. Lawrence Erlbaum Associates, Inc. (1979)

15. Hatakka, M., Thapa, D., Saebo, O.: A framework for understanding the link between ICT and development: how affordances influence capabilities. In: SIG GlobDev Ninth Annual Workshop, pp. 1–20 (2016)

16. Henningsson, S., Kettinger, W.J., Zhang, C., Vaidyanathan, N.: Transformative rare events: leveraging digital affordance actualisation. Eur. J. Inf. Syst. (2021). https://doi.org/10.1080/ 0960085X.2020.1860656

17. Thapa, D., Zheng, Y.: Capabilities and affordances in the ICT4D context: similarities, differences, and complementarities. In: IFIP Advances in Information and Communication Technology, vol. 552, pp. 49–59 (2019). https://doi.org/10.1007/978-3-030-19115-35

18. Karlsen, C., Haraldstad, K., Moe, C.E., Thygesen, E.: Challenges of mainstreaming telecare. Exploring actualization of telecare affordances in home care services. Scand. J. Inf. Syst. **31**(1), 31–66 (2019)

19. Alraddadi, A.S.: Mechanisms of Technology Affordance Actualization Critical Realist Case Studies of Information Systems in Saudi Arabian SMEs (Issue March). Loughborough University (2020)

20. Strong, D.M., et al.: A theory of organization-EHR affordance actualization. J. Assoc. Inf. Syst. **15**(2), 53–85 (2014)

21. Pruchniewska, U.: "I like that it's my choice a couple different times": gender, affordances, and user experience on bumble dating. Int. J. Commun. **14**(1), 2422–2439 (2020)

22. Chamourian, E.: Identity Performance and Self Presentation Through Dating App Profiles: How Individuals Curate Profiles and Participate on Bumble. The American University of Paris (2017)

23. LeFebvre, L.E., Fan, X.: Mirror on the wall, which dating app affords them all? Exploring dating applications affordances and user motivations. In: Hetsroni, A., Tuncez, M. (eds.) It Happened on Tinder: Reflections and Studies on Internet-Infused Dating, pp. 63–77. Institute of Network Cultures (2019)

24. Ranzini, G., Lutz, C.: Love at first swipe? Explaining Tinder self-presentation and motives. Mob. Media Commun. **5**(1), 80–101 (2017). https://doi.org/10.1177/2050157916664559

25. Duguay, S., Burgess, J., Suzor, N.: Queer women's experiences of patchwork platform governance on Tinder, Instagram, and Vine. Convergence Int. J. Res. New Media Technol. **26**(2), 237–252 (2020). https://doi.org/10.1177/1354856518781530

26. Syamnovich, S.: Privacy vs. security: what's the difference? Norton (2020). https://us.norton.com/internetsecurity-privacy-privacy-vs-security-whats-the-difference.html
27. Krasnova, H., Günther, O., Spiekermann, S., Koroleva, K.: Privacy concerns and identity in online social networks. Identity Inf. Soc. **2**(1), 39–63 (2009). https://doi.org/10.1007/s12394-009-0019-1
28. Mosley, M.A., Lancaster, M., Parker, M.L., Campbell, K.: Adult attachment and online dating deception: a theory modernized. Sex. Relatsh. Ther. **35**(2), 227–243 (2020). https://doi.org/10.1080/14681994.2020.1714577
29. He, D., Chan, S., Guizani, M.: Mobile application security: malware threats and defenses. IEEE Wirel. Commun. **22**(1), 138–144 (2015)
30. Kim, K., Kim, T., Lee, S., Kim, S., Kim, H.: When harry met tinder: security analysis of dating apps on Android. In: Gruschka, N. (ed.) NordSec 2018. LNCS, vol. 11252, pp. 454–467. Springer, Cham (2018). https://doi.org/10.1007/978-3-030-03638-6_28
31. Qin, G., Patsakis, C., Bouroche, M.: Playing hide and seek with mobile dating applications. In: Cuppens-Boulahia, N., Cuppens, F., Jajodia, S., Abou El Kalam, A., Sans, T. (eds.) SEC 2014. IAICT, vol. 428, pp. 185–196. Springer, Heidelberg (2014). https://doi.org/10.1007/978-3-642-55415-5_15
32. Hayes, D.R., Snow, C.: Privacy and security issues associated with mobile dating applications. In: Conference on Information Systems Applied Research, pp. 1–13 (2018)
33. Yeşilyaprak, B.: Locus of control. In: Individual Differences in Education, pp. 239–258 (2004)
34. Rouhizadeh, M., Jaidka, K., Smith, L., Schwartz, H.A., Buffone, A., Ungar, L.H.: Identifying locus of control in social media language. In: Proceedings of the 2018 Conference on Empirical Methods in Natural Language Processing, pp. 1146–1152 (2018). https://github.com/tensorflow/models/
35. Yıldız Durak, H.: What would you do without your smartphone? Adolescents' social media usage, locus of control, and loneliness as a predictor of nomophobia. Addicta Turk. J. Addict. **5**(3) (2018). https://doi.org/10.15805/addicta.2018.5.2.0025
36. Saunders, M., Lewis, P., Thornhill, A.: Research Methods for Business Students, 5th edn. Pearson Education Limited (2009)
37. Braun, V., Clarke, V.: Using thematic analysis in psychology. Qual. Res. Psychol. **3**(2), 77–101 (2006)
38. Stoicescu, M.V., Matei, S., Rughiniş, R.: Sharing and privacy in dating apps. In: Proceedings - 2019 22nd International Conference on Control Systems and Computer Science, CSCS 2019, pp. 432–437 (2019). https://doi.org/10.1109/CSCS.2019.00079
39. Young, A.L., Quan-Haase, A.: Privacy protection strategies on Facebook: the Internet privacy paradox revisited. Inf. Commun. Soc. **16**(4), 479–500 (2013). https://doi.org/10.1080/1369118X.2013.777757
40. Cobb, C., Kohno, T.: How public is my private life? Privacy in online dating. In: 26th International World Wide Web Conference, WWW 2017, pp. 1231–1240 (2017). https://doi.org/10.1145/3038912.3052592
41. Stenson, C., Balcells, A., Chen, M.: Burning up privacy on tinder. In: 11th Symposium on Usable Privacy and Security, Ottawa, Canada (2015). http://www.ethicapublishing.com/inconvenientorinvasive/2C
42. Ellison, N., Heino, R., Gibbs, J.: Managing impressions online: self-presentation processes in the online dating environment. J. Comput.-Mediat. Commun. **11**(2), 415–441 (2006). https://doi.org/10.1111/j.1083-6101.2006.00020.x
43. Volkoff, O., Strong, D.M.: Affordance theory and how to use it in IS research. In: The Routledge Companion to Management Information Systems, pp. 232–246 (2018). https://doi.org/10.4324/9781315619361

Technology Acceptance of MS Teams Among University Teachers During COVID-19

Pawel Robert Smolinski[1], Marcin Szóstakowski[2], and Jacek Winiarski[3(✉)]

[1] University of Gdansk, Gdansk, Poland
p.smolinski.674@studms.ug.edu.pl
[2] Doctoral School of Humanities and Social Sciences, University of Gdansk, Gdansk, Poland
marcin.szostakowski@phdstud.ug.edu.pl
[3] Department of Business Informatics, University of Gdansk, Sopot, Poland
jacek.winiarski@ug.edu.pl

Abstract. The choice of software for implementing online learning has always been one of the fundamental problems in education sciences. Efficiency and quality of education largely depend on the properties of the tool (software) that the teacher uses. The COVID-19 pandemic has led to the rise in numbers of users of e-learning tools. Decision makers had to choose which available product their corporation, university or school would use. After several months of widespread implementation of different e-learning software, users are ready to give an evaluation. The aim of this paper is to provide such evaluation on MS Teams, which can be obtained by applying Technology Acceptance Models. Among the set of Technology Acceptance Models developed in science and verified in practice, the Unified Theory of Acceptance and Use of Technology (UTAUT) deserves special attention due to its flexibility and large predictive power. We propose an enriched UTAUT model for MS Teams, which adds two new variables to the original: Product Superiority (PS) and System Comprehensiveness (SC). This paper presents the development of Technology Acceptance Models as a software evaluation method, followed by the presentation of hypotheses and description of the research method used. The research was carried out using the questionnaire distributed among university teachers from northern Poland. We present the analysis of the results along with the conclusions formulated on their basis. At the end, we highlight the interpretative limitations and indicate further research directions.

Keywords: Technology acceptance · UTAUT model · MS teams · Education · e-learning

1 Introduction

The COVID-19 pandemic has drastically changed the form of teaching. As of spring 2020, e-learning has completely dominated education. One element that determines the effectiveness of e-learning is the use of the right software. There are many programs available on the market such as MS Teams, Google Classroom, Zoom or ClickMeeting. The question is, which program to use? This is an important issue especially for decision

© Springer Nature Switzerland AG 2022
M. Themistocleous and M. Papadaki (Eds.): EMCIS 2021, LNBIP 437, pp. 346–361, 2022.
https://doi.org/10.1007/978-3-030-95947-0_24

makers in corporations, service centers or universities educating tens of thousands of students. We believe that the objective choice criteria can be provided by the Technology Acceptance Models (TAM). Among the collection of many Technology Acceptance Models developed in science, the Unified Theory of Acceptance and Use of Technology (UTAUT) has stood out as the most flexible and predictive model, hence we decide to use it in this study.

In this paper, the original UTAUT model was modified (enriched) by adding two new variables - Product Superiority (PS) and System Comprehensiveness (SC) - hoping that they will reflect more accurately behavioral intention to use MS Teams software. The primary motivation for conducting this described research was to assess the acceptance level of MS Teams software among university teachers and highlight its strengths and weaknesses in e-learning.

2   Related Research

Technology acceptance models have been extensively used in science for over 20 years and their applications have found their way into various scientific disciplines. One of the more salient models is the Technology Acceptance Model (TAM) [1], originating from the Theory of Reasoned Action (TRA) [2]. In addition to its two subsequent versions: TAM2 [3] and TAM3 [4], UTAUT [5] stands out as one of the most relevant models of technology acceptance, which was derived from the aforementioned theories (TAM & TRA) and drew from the others such as: Social Cognitive Theory (SCT) [6], Theory of Planned Behavior (TPB) [7], Model of PC Utilization (MPCU) [8], Motivational Model (MM) [9], Innovation Diffusion Theory (IDT) [10] and Combined TAM and TPB [11].

The UTAUT is intended to allow a better understanding of user behavior by clarifying his intentions towards a given technology/information system. The theory assumes that Behavioral Intention (BI) is influenced by four main variables: (1) Performance Expectancy (PE), (2) Effort Expectancy (EE), (3) Social Influence (SI) and (4) Facilitating Conditions (FC). The variables define, respectively, the users' belief about the possibility of obtaining the desired outcomes, the degree of difficulty about using the technology, and the belief about the willingness of those in the consumer's immediate environment to use the technology and other facilitating factors. The popularity that UTAUT has gained has resulted in widespread use of the theory by other researchers, who have been adding new constructs to the model, designed for the better explanation of the behavioral intention of users of the studied technology. Eventually, UTUAT was developed into a further version–UTAUT 2 - that supplemented the original model with three new variables to explain the intention and use of a given technology: hedonic motives, price value and habit [12].

UTAUT is one of the most widely used technology acceptance models in science, which is used to analyze the intention and behavior of users of a wide range of different technologies, including, among others: websites, mobile technology, or Health Information Systems. At the time of writing this paper, the original article regarding UTAUT by Vankatesh et al. [5] was cited nearly 36000 times according to Google Scholar. A study conducted by Williams et al. [13] demonstrates the relevance and prevalence of this theory. The researchers reviewed the literature on the UTAUT and its empirical applications. They utilized a keyword search to find the occurrences of articles on the application of UTAUT in over 130 scientific journals and conferences. As a result, they selected 174 scientific articles. In the analyzed period, there was a tendency towards an annual increase in the number of scientific publications using UTAUT empirically. The analysis revealed the ubiquity of the use of UTAUT in technology acceptance studies in areas such as e-commerce, e-banking, e-government and e-learning. A significant number of empirical applications of the theory, besides the major variables, included additional external variables proposed by the authors of the studies. Williams et al. [13] emphasize that despite its multiple applications, UTAUT is still in a developmental phase. Researchers have conducted numerous attempts to test the original assumptions of the model, as well as utilizing extended models by adding new variables to original UTAUT in order to analyze the relationship among variables in different contexts. According to Williams et al. [13], there is still an opportunity to develop the area of technology acceptance.

This article focuses on the application of UTAUT in e-learning with the aid of complex ICT (Information and Communication Technology) tools - in this article, Microsoft Teams has been chosen as an analyzed e-learning tool. As of now, the use of UTAUT in e-learning has focused on the analysis of the acceptance of educational ICT systems such as virtual learning environment (VLE) or learning management system (LMS). The study conducted by Yee and Abdullah [14] aimed to determine the development of the use of UTAUT in examining the acceptance of educational ICT platforms (including Google Classroom) among teachers and students. In a review of articles, the authors selected studies that used UTAUT, UTAUT 2 or extended UTAUT models to analyze technology acceptance in education. The 39 research papers obtained were divided into three sections: (1) teachers' acceptance of ICTs, (2) teachers' acceptance of Google Classroom and (3) students' acceptance of using ICTs. The largest number - 23 articles - concerned students' acceptance of ICTs. 16 articles examined the level of acceptance of ICTs by teachers, of which 2 articles focused on the analysis of Google Classroom acceptance. The selected literature is predominated by applications of the original UTAUT or UTAUT 2 models. Notable among the studies on the level of acceptance of technology in education is that of Raman et al. [15] who analyzed the use of Smart Board by teachers using the original UTAUT, which showed a positive effect of PE and FC on behavioral intention. Saleem et al. [16], on the other hand, used the original UTAUT to measure the acceptance level of the Moodle platform among academic teachers, where all the main variables (PE, EE, SI, FC) had a significant effect on behavioral intention. Some of the analyzed articles incorporated the use of UTAUT 2 from which worth mentioning is the study of Mobile Technology acceptance level among secondary school teachers by Omar et al. [17] and the study of online courses acceptance level among Taiwanese academic teachers by Tseng et al. [18]. Extended UTAUT models with additional external variables also have been deployed as a research tool in measuring the level of acceptance of educational ICTs among teachers. Oye et al. [19] included the variables Anxiety, Self-efficacy and Attitude in the analysis of the original UTAUT model. Other studies in this area have similarly modified the UTAUT2, including the study of Oudhuis [20], in which the variable Proximity Of Support was added to the original model, and the study of Gunasinghe et al. [21], in which the model was extended to include the variable Personal Innovativeness, albeit in those cases the added external variables had no significant effect on the behavioral intention.

The research on the level of acceptance of technologies for e-learning has not been fully explored. The COVID-19 pandemic, which triggered the global daily need for e-learning, is likely to be a factor stimulating the intensity of research in this area, which is already resulting in the emergence of new studies examining the level of acceptance of ICTs learning platforms in multiple contexts. Some studies have analyzed through UTAUT the determinants of e-learning adoption during the COVID-19 pandemic [22], while others have focused on measuring the level of acceptance of specific platforms helping to address the e-learning needs, such as Google Classroom [23, 24] or Zoom [25]. The global nature of the widespread adoption of e-learning and the multiplicity of tools for its implementation, the comparison of the level of acceptance among available tools (i.e. Microsoft Teams, Zoom, Google Classroom), and analysis of the level of acceptance of e-learning technologies in different contexts are all areas that need further research in order to reduce the existing research gap.

3 Hypotheses

Based on the assumptions of the original UTAUT model, four main hypotheses were stated:

H1: Performance Expectancy (PE) has a positive effect on the behavioral intentions to use MS Teams in e-learning.
H2: Effort Expectancy (PE) has a positive effect on the behavioral intentions to use MS Teams in e-learning.
H3: Social Influence (SI) has a positive effect on the behavioral intentions to use MS Teams in e-learning.
H4: Facilitating Conditions (FC) have a positive effect on the behavioral intentions to use MS Teams in e-learning.

Performance Expectancy (PE), as defined by Vankatesh et al. [5], is the degree to which an individual perceives that using a technology will help him or her to attain a gain in job performance. It is users' beliefs about the usefulness and effectiveness of particular software in the particular context. In our case, it is the belief that MS Teams makes e-learning better and more efficient.

Effort Expectancy (EE) is the degree of ease associated with the use of an information system [5]. It is the belief that software does not require sophisticated knowledge, can be easily learned by inexperienced users and is intuitive.

Social Influence (SI) is the degree to which an individual perceives that important others believe he or she should use an information system [5]. In the context of e-learning and MS Tams, Social Influence might manifest through the recommendations from the university authorities and colleagues or just through the prevalence of the software in e-learning.

Facilitating Conditions (FC) are defined as the degree to which an individual believes that an organizational and technical infrastructure exists to support use of an information system [5]. Facilitating Conditions for MS Teams might be a training provided by the university, an ability to use the software on many devices or an ease with which a person can acquire help.

In addition, considering the specificity of MS Teams in e-learning, we proposed the enrichment of the original UTAUT model by two new variables: Product Superiority and System Comprehensiveness (Complexity).

Product Superiority (PS) represents the degree to which an individual believes that an information system (product) possesses a superior functionality (utility) in relation to other products available on the market intended for the same or similar tasks. Introduction of the PS variable enriches the UTAUT model with a market competition element, important from the economic-marketing perspective. We assume that a product with a high PS level will be desired more by customers and will have a greater Behavioral Intention (BI) if market priced. Similarly, a product with a low PS will be characterized by a low intention of using it. In our case, because studied universities provide each teacher with access to MS Teams software, we assume that the dimension of price availability does not matter, and that the influence of the PS variable will be reflected regardless of the price. Formally, the influence of the PS variable in the UTAUT model can be expressed in the following hypothesis:

H5: Product Superiority (PS) has a positive effect on the behavioral intentions to use MS Teams in e-learning.

System Comprehensiveness (Complexity) (SC) represents the degree to which an individual can carry a task through the information system. It defines the holistic usability of the tested software. In the absence of an appropriate SC level, an individual cannot complete tasks entirely using only one software and is forced to use alternatives. We assume that the higher the SC level, the lower the user's effort required for completing a task, because it is done through one software, and in effect greater behavioral intention to use the software. The effect of the SC variable in the UTAUT model is expressed in the following hypothesis:

H6: System Complexity (SC) has a positive effect on the behavioral intentions to use MS Teams in e-learning.

We also assume that the UTAUT model, enriched by two new variables, will have a better fit and explain a significantly higher percentage of the variation in the Behavioral Intention (BI) variable.

H7: The UTAUT with a PS variable has a better fit than the original UTAUT model.
H8: The UTAUT with a SC variable has a better fit than the original UTAUT model.

We consider the effect of Product Superiority (PS) on Behavioral Intention (BI) as particularly important. Because there are many available programs for e-learning on the market, Product Superiority (PS) will play a significant role in deciding which of them to use and thus significantly influence Behavioral Intention (BI). A slightly weaker influence is expected from the variable System Comprehensiveness (SC). Because SC reflects the global software capacity to meet the user's expectations, its effect on Behavioral Intention (BI) can already be expressed with other variables (e.g., Performance

Expectancy). Perhaps there is a potential for creating internal pathways in the UTAUT model with SC as a mediator. However, because of the exploratory character of this paper, we do not test such hypotheses. And for the same exploratory reason, we do not include model moderators like gender and age, present in the original UTAUT model.

4 Participants

245 academic teachers from northern Poland took part in this study (134 women and 106 men, 5 people did not report gender). Data was collected by administering an online questionnaire to the employees of all selected university departments.

8 responses were removed due to an unusual response pattern. The criterion for rejection was established based on the Guttman error, which identifies the discrepancies between respondent's answers to items and the expected response pattern for the entire scale [26, 27]. The threshold for rejection was arbitrarily established at $G > 0.4$.

The final models were estimated on a sample of 237 responses (131 women, 104 men, 2 people did not report gender). The average job tenure was 16.51 years, with a standard deviation of 11.65 years (maximum $= 51$ years, minimum $= 1$ year).

5 Instrument

Based on the literature review, a well-known method for creating UTAUT models and a pilot study ($n = 25$), a questionnaire was developed. It comprises 27 items on a 7-step Likert scale measuring 7 latent constructs. The questionnaire items, together with the results of a factor analysis, are presented in Table 1.

Table 1. Factor and reliability analysis

Latent construct	Item	Item Mean (Standard Deviation)	Factor Loading	Cronbach's Alpha
Performance Expectancy (PE)	PE1	6.26 (0.86)	0.802	0.87
	PE2	5.89 (1.23)	0.911	
	PE3	5.53 (1.30)	0.847	
	PE4	4.76 (1.69)	0.748	
Social Influence (SI)	SI1*	6.22 (0.94)	0.360	0.747 (0.79)
	SI2	4.65 (1.43)	0.794	
	SI3	4.84 (1.23)	0.765	
	SI4	5.00 (1.25)	0.692	
Effort Expectancy (EE)	EE1	5.64 (1.33)	0.798	0.887
	EE2	5.59 (1.30)	0.910	

(continued)

Table 1. (*continued*)

Latent construct	Item	Item Mean (Standard Deviation)	Factor Loading	Cronbach's Alpha
	EE3	5.51 (1.32)	0.723	
	EE4	5.07 (1.58)	0.827	
Facilitating Conditions (FC)	FC1	5.99 (1.20)	0.692	0.772
	FC2	5.65 (1.52)	0.589	
	FC3	5.72 (1.23)	0.715	
	FC4	5.65 (1.36)	0.737	
Behavioral Intention (BI)	BI1	4.97 (1.54)	0.788	0.874
	BI2	5.47 (1.42)	0.768	
	BI3	5.16 (1.56)	0.955	

Note: '* ' next to an item represents a removed variable

The results of the factor analysis have led to removing two items that have not reached a sufficient factor loading (PS2 and SI1, $\lambda < 0.5$). PS2 is an inverted item (see Appendix), which might have caused an inconsistency in respondent's answers, hence low loading. It also might be true that the respondents believe that although MS Teams is the best e-learning software, it can be replaced by other programs without loss of efficiency. Such an explanation, although plausible, undermines the assumption of a factor analysis that all items must be consistent.

Item SI1 has achieved a significantly higher mean than the other items included in the construct (Kruskal-Wallis Test: $\chi^2 = 197.95$, df $= 3$, p-value < 0.001; Pairwise Wilcoxon test: p-value < 0.001 for all comparisons with SI1), which probably led to a low factor loading. After removing two controversial items, the reliability of latent constructs containing them has improved: Product Superiority (PS) from 0.79 to 0.91 and Social Influence (SI) from 0.747 to 0.79.

6   Results

All hypotheses were verified by validating 3 structural equation models (SEM): the original UTAUT model, and two enriched UTAUT models with variables Product Superiority (PS) and System Comprehensiveness (SC). Models were estimated using Robust Maximum Likelihood Estimator in R package lavaan. Figure 1 presents a relation pathway for tested models, while Table 2 presents fit measures for individual models. Table 3 contains regression coefficients for postulated relations.

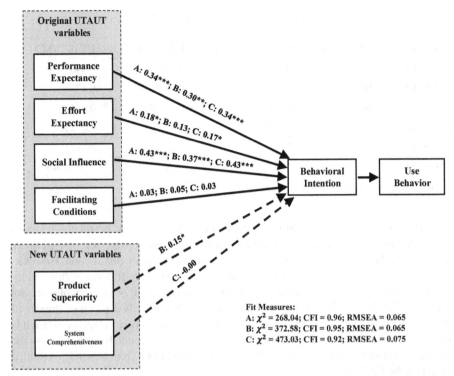

Fig. 1. SEM Regression Structure (A: original UTAUT, B: UTAUT with PS, C: UTAUT with SC)

Table 2. SEM fit measures

Statistics	Critical Value	Original UTAUT	UTAUT (PS)	UTAUT (SC)
CMIN/DF	<2	2.144	2.141	2.438
GFI	>0.8	0.892	0.878	0.849
AGFI	>0.8	0.853	0.838	0.803
NFI	>0.9	0.909	0.940	0.910
PNFI	>0.7	0.743	0.746	0.731
CFI	>0.9	0.955	0.950	0.924
RFI	>0.8	0.889	0.879	0.846
RMSEA	<0.08	0.065	0.065	0.075
ECVI	N/A	1.519	2.053	2.494
AIC	N/A	11848	13776	14584
BIC	N/A	12008	13974	14789

Note: Presented critical values come from different sources. For comprehensive review of all fit measures see: Konarski [28]. For individual measures see: Bollen [29], Browne & Cudeck [30], Byrne [31], Smith and McMillan [32]

Table 3. SEM regression pathways

Pathway	Hypothesis	Original UTAUT	UTAUT (PS)	UTAUT (SC)
BI ← PE	H1	0.343***	0.301**	0.340***
BI ← EE	H2	0.175*	0.133 n.s	0.173*
BI ← SI	H3	0.428***	0.367***	0.434***
BI ← FC	H4	0.032 n.s	0.052 n.s	0.032 n.s
BI ← PS	H5	N/A	0.149*	N/A
BI ← SC	H6	N/A	N/A	−0.003 n.s

Note: significance code: <0.001 '***', <0.01 '**', <0.05 '*'

All 3 models obtained a satisfying fit and conclusions about postulated relations can be drawn. The only statistic that systematically deviates from the acceptable critical value is CMIN/DF. CMIN statistic has an asymptotic chi-square distribution. However, this type of statistics may not be reliable in all circumstances. It deviates from a chi-square distribution when, for example, the sample is too small, or the variables are not normally distributed. The value of the CMIN statistic also heavily depends on the size of the sample. When it is large, the null hypothesis can be wrongly rejected, and when it is too small, wrongly accepted. CMIN also does not take into account the complexity of the model. Considering all the mentioned weaknesses, model fit cannot be solely examined based on the CMIN statistic.

In the original UTAUT model, 3 out of 4 main hypotheses (H1, H2, H3) were confirmed. The H4 hypothesis about the positive effect of Facilitating Conditions (FC) on Behavioral Intention (BI) was not confirmed in the model. This means that Facilitating Conditions are not a decisive factor in the acceptance of MS Teams as an e-learning software. The hypothesis about the effect of FC on BI was also not confirmed in the remaining two enriched UTUAT models.

In the UTAUT model with a PS variable, hypotheses about the positive effect of Performance Expectancy (PE), Social Influence (SI) and Product Superiority (PS) on Behavioral Intentions (BI) are confirmed (H1, H3, H5). Interesting is a sudden loss of predictive power of EE on BI (H2) after adding the PS variable to the model. It can be assumed that the proportion of the variation of BI, in the original UTAUT model explained by the EE variable, is explained by the PS variable in the enriched model. This suggests the existence of an additional mediatory relation between EE and PS. However, it must be emphasized that the effect of the Effort Expectancy (EE) on Behavioral Intention (BI) is already weak in the original model ($\beta = 0.175$, p-value = 0.03) and introducing an additional variable PS, partially correlated with EE (R = 0.637, p-value < 0.000, in the UTAUT model with PS), will result in a loss of predictive power of the EE variable on BI.

In the last UTAUT model, enriched with a SC variable, the hypotheses about the effect of Performance Expectancy (PE), Effort Expectancy (EE) and Social Influence were confirmed (H1, H2, H3). Hypothesis about the influence of System Comprehensiveness (SC) on Behavioral Intention (BI) (H6) was not confirmed. System Comprehensiveness, like Facilitating Conditions, is not a decisive variable in the acceptance of MS Teams in e-learning.

Hypotheses H7 and H8 about a better fit of the enriched models were verified using fit measures presented in Table 2. Basic fit statistics, such as GFI, AGFI, NFI, CFI, RFI and RMSEA, do not show significant differences in fit of the three postulated models. Only more specific measures like ECVI, AIC and BIC show some differences. The original UTAUT model has a significantly better probability of validation in an independent sample assessed by ECVI statistics (ECVI $= 1.519$). Also, the original UTAUT has the smallest value of the Akaike information criterion (AIC $= 11847.995$), suggesting the best model quality. Similar conclusion is provided by the results of ANOVA conducted on χ^2 (CMIN) values of three estimated models. It suggests significant differences in χ^2 (CMIN) values in favor of the original UTAUT model (see Table 4).

Table 4. Fit assessment ANOVA

	df	AIC	BIC	CMIN	ΔCMIN	df	p-value
UTAUT	125	11848	12008	268.04			
UTAUT PS	174	13776	13974	372.58	91.279	49	0.000***
UTAUT SC	194	14584	14789	473.03	123.372	20	0.000***

The hypotheses about a better fit of the enriched models are rejected. We assume all models explain the acceptance of MS Teams to a similar extent, subject that the original UTAUT model is the most parsimonious. A similar conclusion is provided by the analysis of determination coefficients R^2. The values of determination coefficients for 3 models are included in Table 5.

Table 5. Determination coefficients

	Original UTAUT	UTAUT (PS)	UTAUT (SC)
R^2	0.785	0.794	0.786
Adjusted R^2	0.733	0.728	0.715

The determination coefficients oscillate slightly below $R^2 = 0.8$. This is a good result for a technology acceptance model. It is assumed that a good UTAUT model will explain around 70% of the variation in the dependable variable, which corresponds to the results obtained by each of the three postulated models [5].

7 Discussion

MS Teams can be characterized by a level of technology acceptance and strong behavioral intention to use it in e-learning settings. Created UTAUT models suggest that Performance Expectancy (PE) and Social Influence (SI) are the two most significant variables in the models and are the best in explaining users' intentions. Performance Expectancy, in e-learning, might concern issues like the capacity of a program to host large online meetings, privacy and security, homework assignments, ability to share course materials or methods of evaluating students' progress. These users' expectations are important factors determining users' intentions and, in the end, users' decision to use MS Teams. A significant effect of Social Influence (SI) on Behavioral Intention implies that users value opinions and recommendations in decision-making process and positive direction of this effect implies that these opinions and recommendations are positive.

Facilitating Conditions (FC) do not bear on users' intentions to use MS Teams. It may mean that there is not enough support from the software developer or software provider (in our case universities) to facilitate user behavior, the technology lacks infrastructure and organization to solve users' issues or, simply, that Facilitating Conditions are not an important factor in the decision-making process. Software developers and providers should consider increasing user support, for instance, making better and more accessible instructor videos on the software developer side or providing better guidelines on the software provider side, if they wish to improve the technology acceptance.

The effect of Effort Expectancy (EE) on Behavioral Intention (BI) is harder to explain. In the original UTAUT model, Effort Expectancy is a significant variable, with a positive effect, which implies that ease with which users learn and use software has an influence on the user's behavioral intention. However, this effect is weak and introduction of new variable Product Superiority (PS) in the enriched model weakens it even further (into no significance). Product Superiority, which represents a competitive advantage of MS Teams over other e-learning software, is itself a significant variable. Most respondents believe MS Teams is a superior product, but this belief has a rather weak effect on users' intentions, nonetheless significant.

The second added variable System Comprehensiveness (SC) has no effect on users' intention. It also seems to deteriorate the model fit; however, this can be explained by violation of model parsimony, which always happens when adding insignificant variable. At this stage of the research, it is hard to tell if this new variable was poorly conceptualized or it is just a particular property of MS Teams or e-learning software in general.

We also confirmed that the UTAUT theory and models built upon it are very good at explaining the users' intention to use MS Teams. Although we did not compare UTUAT with other technology acceptance models (e.g. TAM or TAM II), we still can conclude that the above 70% of behavioral intention that UTAUT explains is sufficient in most academic or business settings. It provides enough information about what the user expects from the technology and which expectations (defined by the model variables) are the most important. Software developers or software providers can go through each variable at the time and see which aspects of their product are satisfying and which can be improved. We suggest the UTAUT models can be used as a part of SWOT analysis for IT products, where they serve as an objective criterion for inferring product strengths and weaknesses. The model variables that have a positive and significant effect on users' behavioral intention can be considered as product strengths, and insignificant or negative effect variables can be seen as product weaknesses. Taking MS Teams as an example, we can judge its performance (PE), ease (EE), good users' opinions (SI) and dominant market position (PS) as definitive strengths and the facilitating conditions (FC) as a weakness.

8   Conclusions and Further Research

This research is just a small step towards eliminating the exiting gap in our knowledge about technology acceptance in e-learning. As we have pointed out at the beginning of this paper, technology acceptance models play an important role in deciding which software is the best and are a powerful method for pointing out strengths and weaknesses of a particular software. Our research has shown that technology acceptance of MS Teams can be explained by the UTAUT model and its enriched versions. We have pointed out what drives the user's intention to use MS Teams and how the technology acceptance can be improved. Further research should extend our analysis by exploring other technology acceptance models (e.g. TAM and TAM II) and other programs (e.g. Zoom, Google Classroom) in e-learning. A multi-group analysis can answer questions about how the technology acceptance differs between e-learning software, how different groups (e.g., students, high schools and elementary teachers) accept e-learning technology and how the technology acceptance is related to students' outcomes. We believe that especially the comparison of different, available software is important. In this paper, we have only shown that MS Teams is well accepted software.

9   Limitations

The presented analysis is mainly exploratory. To keep it simple we purposefully limited the scope of our research by not including mediators and not performing multigroup analyses. As we state above, we want to expand on it in further studies (that includes collecting more representative samples).

Acknowledgments. We would like to express our deepest gratitude to Professor Bartosz Marcinkowski and Dr. Damian Gajda for sharing their extensive knowledge and experience, as well as for their scientific support and valuable advice, which greatly helped us in writing this article.

Appendix

Latent construct	Abbrev.	Items included in the questionnaire
Product Superiority (PS)	PS1	MS Teams is the best of all available e-learning software
	PS2	MS Teams can be replaced by other e-learning software without losing effectiveness. (reversed item)

(continued)

(continued)

Latent construct	Abbrev.	Items included in the questionnaire
	PS3	MS Teams offers the highest utility of all available e-learning software
	PS4	MS Teams has the largest number of functions necessary for e-learning of all available e-learning software
System Comprehensiveness (SC)	SC1	MS Teams provides access to all necessary functions and tools in e-learning
	SC2	MS Teams integrates all functions and tools necessary for e-learning
	SC3	MS Teams provides integration with other Office 365 software (PowerPoint, OneDrive, etc.)
	SC4	MS Teams provides integration with software from other manufacturers (not included in the Office 365 package)
Performance Expectancy (PE)	PE1	MS Teams is useful in e-learning
	PE2	MS Teams makes e-learning easier to implement
	PE3	MS Teams enables effective implementation of e-learning
	PE4	MS Teams increases academic teachers' productivity
Social Influence (SI)	SI1	MS Teams is recommended by university authorities as a tool for e-learning
	SI2	MS Teams is recommended by colleagues as the best e-learning software
	SI3	User reviews posted online indicate the popularity of MS Teams in e-learning
	SI4	Students confirm the prevalence of using MS Teams for e-learning
Effort Expectancy (EE)	EE1	I have learned to use MS Teams with ease
	EE2	It is easy to implement e-learning using MS Teams
	EE3	Any university employee involved in teaching can become proficient in MS Teams
	EE4	MS Teams is intuitive to use
Facilitating Conditions (FC)	FC1	MS Teams can be used on different types of devices (computer, tablet, smartphone)

(continued)

(*continued*)

Latent construct	Abbrev.	Items included in the questionnaire
	FC2	The university provides training in MS Teams
	FC3	You can easily find help with MS Teams on the internet (e.g., forums, YouTube, Microsoft help)
	FC4	I can count on the help of colleagues/students if I have problems using MS Teams
Behavioral Intention (BI)	BI1	I would use MS Teams for e-learning, even if it was not recommended by the university authorities
	BI2	I anticipate using MS Teams after the end of the COVID-19 pandemic
	BI3	I will be recommending MS Teams for conducting e-learning to my friends

References

1. Davis, F.D., Bagozzi, R.P., Warshaw, P.R.: User acceptance of computer technology: a comparison of two theoretical models. Manag. Sci. **35**, 982–1003 (1989). https://doi.org/10.1287/mnsc.35.8.982
2. Fishbein, M., Ajzen, I.: Belief, Attitude, Intention and Behaviour: An Introduction to Theory and Research. Addison-Wesley, Reading (1975)
3. Venkatesh, V., Davis, F.D.: A theoretical extension of the technology acceptance model: four longitudinal field studies. Manage. Sci. **46**(2), 186–204 (2000). https://doi.org/10.1287/mnsc.46.2.186.11926
4. Venkatesh, V., Bala, H.: Technology acceptance model 3 and a research agenda on interventions. Decis. Sci. **39**(2), 273–315 (2008). https://doi.org/10.1111/j.1540-5915.2008.00192.x
5. Venkatesh, V., Morris, M.G., Davis, F.D., Davis, G.B.: User acceptance of information technology: toward a unified view. MIS Q. **27**, 425–478 (2003). https://doi.org/10.2307/30036540
6. Bandura, A.: Social Foundations of Thought and Action: A Social Cognitive Theory. Prentice-Hall, Englewood Cliffs (1986)
7. Ajzen, I.: The theory of planned behavior. Behav. Human Decis. Process. **50**(2), 179–211 (1991). https://doi.org/10.1016/0749-5978(91)90020-T
8. Thompson, R.L., Higgins, C.A., Howell, J.M.: Personal computing: toward a conceptual model of utilization. MIS Q. **15**(1), 125–143 (1991). https://doi.org/10.2307/249443
9. Davis, F.D., Bagozzi, R.P., Warshaw, P.R.: Extrinsic and intrinsic motivation to use computers in the workplace. J. Appl. Soc. Psychol. **22**(14), 1111–1132 (1992). https://doi.org/10.1111/j.1559-1816.1992.tb00945.x
10. Rogers, E.M: Diffusion of Innovations, 4th ed. The Free Press, New York (1995)
11. Taylor, S., Todd, P.A.: Understanding information technology usage: a test of competing models. Inf. Syst. Res. **6**(2), 144–176 (1995). https://doi.org/10.1287/isre.6.2.144

12. Venkatesh, V., Thong, J.Y., Xu, X.: Consumer acceptance and use of information technology: extending the unified theory of acceptance and use of technology. MIS Q. **36**(1), 157–178 (2012). https://doi.org/10.2307/41410412

13. Williams, M., Rana, N., Dwivedi, Y.: The unified theory of acceptance and use of technology (UTAUT): a literature review. J. Enterp. Inf. Manag. **28**, 443–488 (2015). https://doi.org/10.1108/JEIM-09-2014-0088

14. Yee, M.L.S., Abdullah, M.S.: A review of UTAUT and extended model as a conceptual framework in education research. Jurnal Pendidikan Sains Dan Matematik Malaysia **11**, 1–20 (2021). https://doi.org/10.37134/jpsmm.vol11.sp.1.2021

15. Raman, A., Don, Y., Khalid, R., Hussin, F., Omar, M.F., Ghani, M.: Technology acceptance on smart board among teachers in terengganu using UTAUT model. Asian Soc. Sci. **10**(11), 84–91 (2014). https://doi.org/10.5539/ass.v10n11p84

16. Saleem, N.E., Al-Saqri, M.N., Ahmad, S.E.A.: Acceptance of moodle as a teaching/learning tool by the faculty of information studies at sultan qaboos university, oman based on UTAUT. Int. J. Knowl. Content Dev. Technol. **6**(2), 5–27 (2016). https://doi.org/10.5865/IJKCT.2016.6.2.005

17. Omar, M.N., Ismail, S.N., Kasim, A.L.: The influence of mobile technology adoption among secondary school teachers using the UTAUT 2 model. Int. J. Recent Technol. Eng. (IJRTE) **8**(4), 3827–3831 (2019). https://doi.org/10.35940/ijtte.D8204.118419

18. Tseng, T.H., Lin, S.J., Wong, Y.S., Liu, H.X.: Investigating teachers' adoption of MOOCs: the perspective of UTAUT2. Interact. Learn. Environ. (2019). https://doi.org/10.1080/10494820.2019.1674888

19. Oye, N.D., Iahad, A.N., Rahim, A.N.: ICT literacy among university academicians: a case of Nigerian public university. ARPN J. Sci. Technol. **2**(2) (2012)

20. Oudhuis, I.: Educational technology in Dutch higher education: the influence of PE, EE, SI, FC, Proximity of Support, HM, Habit and BI on the use of educational technology in Dutch Higher Educationa. Master's thesis, Tilburg University, Netherland (2017)

21. Gunasinghe, A., Ab Hamid, J., Khatibi, A., Ferdono Azam, S.M.: The adequacy of UTAUT-3 in interpreting academicians' adoption in e-learning in higher education environments. J. Interact. Technol. Smart Educ. **17**(1), 86–106 (2019). https://doi.org/10.1108/ITSE-05-2019-0020

22. Sangeeta, Tandon, U.: Factors influencing adoption of online teaching by school teachers: a study during COVID-19 pandemic. J. Public Affairs **1**(11) (2020). https://doi.org/10.1002/pa.2503

23. Mokhtar, R., Karim, M.H.A.: Exploring students behaviour in using google classroom during Covid-19 pandemic: unified theory of acceptance and use of technology (UTAUT). J. Mod. Educ. **3**(8), 182–195 (2021). https://doi.org/10.35631/IJMOE.380015

24. Fauzi, A., Wandira, R., Sepri, D., Hafid, A.: Exploring students' acceptance of google classroom during the covid-19 pandemic by using the technology acceptance model in West Sumatera Universities. Electron. J. e-Learn. (EJEL) **19**(4), 233–240 (2021). https://doi.org/10.34190/ejel.19.4.2348

25. Wijaya, F., Solikhatin, S.A., Tahyudin, C.: Analysis of End-user satisfaction of zoom application for online lectures. In: 2021 3rd East Indonesia Conference on Computer and Information Technology (EIConCIT), pp. 348–353. IEEE, Indonesia (2021). https://doi.org/10.1109/EIConCIT50028.2021.9431903

26. van der Flier, H.: Environmental factors and deviant response patterns. In: Poortinga, Y.H. (ed.) Basic Problems in Cross-Cultural Psychology. Swets & Zeitlinger, Amsterdam (1977)

27. Molenaar, I.W.: A weighted Loevinger H-coefficient extending Mokken scaling to multicategory items. Kwantitatieve Methoden **12**(37), 97–117 (1991)

28. Konarski, R.: Modele równań strukturalnych: teoria i praktyka. Wydawnictwo Naukowe PWN, Warszawa (2010)

29. Bollen, K.A.: Structural equation models. In: Encyclopedia of Biostatistics; 2nd Ed. Wiley, Hoboken (2005)

30. Browne, M.W., Cudeck, R.: Alternative ways of assessing model fit. Sociol. Methods Res. **21**(2), 230–258 (1992). https://doi.org/10.1177/0049124192021002005

31. Byrne, B.M.: Structural Equation modeling with AMOS: Basic Concepts, Applications and Programming, 2nd edn. Routledge, New York (2010)

32. Smith, T.D., McMillan, B.F.: A primer of model fit indices in structural equation modeling (2001). http://files.eric.ed.gov/fulltext/ED449231.pdf

Sense of Presence in VR Mobile Application

Urszula Krzeszewska[ID], Aneta Poniszewska-Marańda[(✉)][ID],
and Joanna Ochelska-Mierzejewska[ID]

Institute of Information Technology, Lodz University of Technology, Lodz, Poland
urszula.krzeszewska@dokt.p.lodz.pl,
{aneta.poniszewska-maranda,joanna.ochelska-mierzejewska}@p.lodz.pl

Abstract. Presence is one of the most important psychological constructs for understanding human-computer interaction. It is especially important for applications that use advanced techniques of iteration between humans and computers, such as Virtual Reality (VR) applications. The paper addresses the problem of difficulty for users to experience a sense of presence in VR applications, especially when the worlds they are transported to are unknown to them. It presents the experiments made for three selected mobile application together with their results and analysis.

Keywords: Human-computer interaction · VR mobile applications · Presence · Sense of presence · Multimodal Presence Scale for Virtual Reality questionnaire

1 Introduction

Presence is one of the most important psychological constructs for understanding human-computer interaction. It has great practical relevance for the design and evaluation of media products, especially in education, entertainment, telecommunications, psychology, and health care [1,2]. It is especially important for applications that use advanced techniques of iteration between humans and computers, such as Virtual Reality (VR) applications.

Virtual reality (VR) is a three-dimensional virtual environment that uses VR "goggles" or glasses to mimic reality as closely as possible. Augmented reality (AR), a related technology, enhances (or augments) reality by providing digital information on top of what the user is seeing, allowing learners to practice skills and understand the outcomes of their actions in a simulated environment.

Virtual Reality immerses users in a virtual environment that is completely generated by a computer. The most advanced VR experiences even provide freedom of movement – users can move in a digital environment and hear sounds. Moreover, special hand controllers can be used to enhance VR experiences, and haptic peripherals can add enhancement and feedback to movements.

To experience virtual reality, special headsets are required. Most VR headsets are connected to a computer (e.g. Oculus Rift) or a gaming console

© Springer Nature Switzerland AG 2022
M. Themistocleous and M. Papadaki (Eds.): EMCIS 2021, LNBIP 437, pp. 362–375, 2022.
https://doi.org/10.1007/978-3-030-95947-0_25

(e.g. PlayStation VR) to harness computational power to enable high-fidelity experiences.

However, standalone devices such as *Google Cardboard* have become the most popular. Most standalone VR headsets work in combination with smartphones – we insert a smartphone into the headset and immediate enter the virtual world. This is slowly evolving to standalone, tetherless headsets that allow the user greater freedom of movement like for example the *Oculus Quest*.

The paper addresses the problem that it is difficult for users to experience a sense of presence in VR applications, especially when the worlds they are transported to are unknown to them which is measured by Multimodal Presence Scale for Virtual Reality questionnaire. Additionally, mobile phone applications have a much bigger problem with creating an environment that allows for a true sense of presence.

The paper is structured as follows: Sect. 2 describes the methodology of experiments made to evaluate the sense of presence of three selected mobile applications. Section 3 presents the results of pilot study, Sect. 4 the results of final study while Sect. 5 deals with the discussion of the obtained results.

2   Virtual Reality Applications

The definition of virtual reality comes, naturally, from the definitions for both "virtual" and "reality". The definition of "virtual" is near and reality is what we experience as human beings. So the term "virtual reality" basically means "near-reality". This could, of course, mean anything but it usually refers to a specific type of reality emulation.

Virtual Reality (VR) applications or systems combine the image of the real environment (seen by man) with computer generated information. This information can take the form of text, sounds or images, and can even be three-dimensional objects. They are generated on the basis of a location in the space determined by the VR system (using a built-in compass, gyroscope, GPS, etc.) and recognized objects visible in the lens of the digital camera [13,14].

The latest scientific research clearly confirms that when a person is better involved in a given message – he is able to absorb knowledge much faster and more effectively. In the case of using virtual reality in education, an average increase in content retention at the level of about 50% compared to the methods known so far is observed. This is influenced not only by the possibility of being in the VR world, but also by interacting with objects and elements of the virtual world.

Virtual reality is the so-called native medium. No other medium (neither radio nor television, cinema or internet) allows such a degree of involvement as when using VR. In the world of virtual reality, we move in exactly the same way as in the real world. Depending on the type of application and equipment we have – we can move freely, pick up objects, drop them, etc. With experience in the VR world we enter exactly the same interactions as in the real world. We are 100% committed to this world.

The steps of creation process of Virtual Reality applications are as follows:

Step 1. Clarification of the final concept of VR application: When creating an VR application, at the initial stage we need to know how the application will work. Therefore, it is extremely important to clarify the concept properly. Together with the client we determine step by step what the user will do, what he will be able to interact with and what will happen on the screen of the device as a result of these interactions. It is equally important to determine where the data, 3d models, photos, videos and other materials displayed in the application will be downloaded from. As part of the concept, we also determine the appearance of the application, the appropriate template, colours, appearance of icons, sounds, etc.

Step 2. Choosing the right engine for virtual reality: The VR engine allows not only to create the entire application that will work properly on various devices, but also guarantees the possibility of its use, expansion, data exchange with the user. When creating VR applications, we use the Unity environment. At Unity, depending on which platform we create, we use various additional engines.

Step 3. Preparation of graphics and 3D models the VR application: The success of VR application depends largely on this step. By using ready-made 3d models purchased from banks or publicly available databases, we run into problems with optimization. It is much more reasonable to model from scratch, for another project. When creating 2D graphics, things are simpler. They do not burden the performance of the device as much.

Step 4. Programming works – writing, creating and programming VR applications: Sometimes enter this stage simultaneously when graphic designers are already working on 3D models and 2D graphics. Usually, we start programming work by developing the application logic and testing the assumed functionalities. At this stage, we already have the VR engine selected, so we also have programming available at our disposal. Programming works are accompanied by parallel internal tests. Each new functionality must be tested very thoroughly in many different ways, on many devices, under different circumstances.

Step 5. External tests performed by the client and project finalization: After the programming work is over, it is time for the client to test the application. At this stage, we try to cause various possible errors, which we then solve.

We know the world through our senses and perception systems. In school we all learned that we have five senses: taste, touch, smell, sight and hearing. These are however only our most obvious sense organs. The truth is that humans have many more senses than this, such as a sense of balance for example. These other sensory inputs, plus some special processing of sensory information by our brains ensures that we have a rich flow of information from the environment to our minds.

Everything that we know about our reality comes by way of our senses – our entire experience of reality is simply a combination of sensory information and our brains sense-making mechanisms for that information. It stands to reason then, that if we can present our senses with made-up information, our perception of reality would also change in response to it. We would be presented with a version of reality that isn't there, but from our perspective it would be perceived as real [13].

Therefore, the virtual reality entails presenting our senses with a computer-generated virtual environment that we can explore in some fashion. Answering "what is virtual reality" in technical terms it is the term used to describe a three-dimensional, computer generated environment which can be explored and interacted with by a person. That person becomes part of this virtual world or is immersed within this environment and whilst there, is able to manipulate objects or perform a series of actions [14].

3   Methodology of Sense of Presence Studies

We decided to use the questionnaire created and evaluated in [6]. This questionnaire has been used in different studies, among others in [7–9]. It allows to examine three dimensions of presence:

- physical presence,
- social presence,
- self-presence

considering the aspects such as: physical realism, not paying attention to real environment, sense of being in the virtual environment, not aware of the physical mediation, sense of coexistence, human realism, not aware of artificiality of social interaction, not aware of the social mediation, sense of bodily connectivity, sense of bodily extension.

According to the provided questionnaire (Table 1) [6], each of the sentences should be rated on a five-point Likert scale, where 1 – "I completely disagree", 2 – "I disagree", 3 – "I neither disagree nor agree", 4 – "I agree", 5 – "I strongly agree".

The following applications were selected to verify the research question:

- VR Space [3],
- VR Galaxy Wars [4],
- Titans of Space® Cardboard VR [5].

All of the selected applications take place in the space – people do not have the opportunity to experience being in space on a daily basis, they may have some ideas of what it looks like, therefore by using these types of applications they confront their expectations with how the application works.

VR Galaxy Wars [4] is a game in which additional interactions beyond just immersion in the virtual environment could potentially increase the sense of presence.

Titans of Space® Cardboard VR [5] and *VR Space* [3] are the applications that allow to explore the solar system. They promise full immersion. Titans from

Space is more educational where VR space focuses more on the sense of presence in a given space – it differentiates these applications and can affect the sense of presence in the realities they create.

Additionally, all applications only require to have a Google Cardboard – they do not require any additional devices to allow the more advanced controls. We wanted to rule out the possibility that the selected applications due to the use of a pad or keyboard would be perceived more as toys, which would diminish the sense of presence in the virtual world.

One of the presence dimensions listed within the selected questionnaire, due to the choice of application, may be difficult to study. It is a *social presence*. Applications have places within the space. It means that human interactions are very limited there. In two of the selected applications (VR Space [3] and VR Galaxy Wars [4]) there is only interaction with aliens, and in the third application (Titans of Space® Cardboard VR [5]) there is interaction with humans, but not directly, because through the ship's on-board computer. Therefore, it was necessary to check whether this dimension of presence is sufficiently marked to obtain reliable results for the selected applications within social presence.

4   Pilot Study

The pilot study was conducted on two subjects. Each person had all 3 applications installed on their phone. In addition to the phone, Google Cardboard glasses were used (inspired by them) – Legato Cardboard 2 [10]. Due to the nature of the application, a computer chair was added, with the ability to make a full rotation, to help the application in a way to reflect the conditions in space.

4.1   Test Setup

Before performing the tests (using all the applications), the test subjects were explained what the experiment is about, what would be tested (to sensitize the user to certain aspects of the application) – without giving specific questions or statements that would be tested later. Then the order in which the applications will be used was randomly selected, to prevent in the future that the first application is always rated the best or the worst, as it gives a new experience of being in a given space. The applications were numbered ("1" – VR Space [3], "2" – VR Galaxy Wars [4] and "3" – Titans of Space® Cardboard VR [5]), the corresponding numbers were written on cards, and the subject selected consecutive cards deciding the order in which to use the applications.

The next step is to get familiar with the applications and perform the tests. Subjects have about 5–10 min to get familiar with the application and use it as intended (usually it takes about 2 min to learn how to navigate in the application, select the appropriate modes, etc.). After going through all the applications, they were given a questionnaire with questions with a game specified. Their task was to rate how much they agree with the given statement on a 5-point Likert scale, where 1 indicates "I completely disagree" and 5 – "I strongly agree".

Table 1. Selected questionnaire to measure presence within VR applications [6]; Physical realism (PR), not paying attention to real environment (NARE), sense of being in the virtual environment (SBVE), not aware of the physical mediation (NAPM), sense of coexistence (SC), human realism (HR) not aware of artificiality of social interaction (NAASI), not aware of the social mediation (NASM), sense of bodily connectivity (SBC), sense of bodily extension (SBE).

Label	Item	Area attribute
Physical Presence		
PHYS_2	The virtual environment seemed real to me	PR
PHYS_3	I had a sense of acting in the virtual environment, rather than operating something from outside	NAPM
PHYS_4	My experience in the virtual environment seemed consistent with my experiences in the real world	PR
PHYS_5	While I was in the virtual environment, I had a sense of "being there"	SBVE
PHYS_10	I was completely captivated by the virtual world	NPARE
Social Presence		
SOC_1	I felt like I was in the presence of another person in the virtual environment	SC
SOC_2	I felt that the people in the virtual environment were aware of my presence	HR
SOC_3	The people in the virtual environment appeared to be sentient (conscious and alive) to me	HR
SOC_5	During the simulation there were times where the computer interface seemed to disappear, and I felt like I was working directly with another person	NASM
SOC_7	I had a sense that I was interacting with other people in the virtual environment, rather than a computer simulation	NAASI
Self-presence		
SELF_2	I felt like my virtual embodiment was an extension of my real body within the virtual environment	SBE
SELF_3	When something happened to my virtual embodiment, it felt like it was happening to my real body	SBC
SELF_4	I felt like my real arm was projected into the virtual environment through my virtual embodiment	SBE
SELF_6	I felt like my real hand was inside of the virtual environment	SBC
SELF_7	During the simulation, I felt like my virtual embodiment and my real body became one and the same	SBC

4.2   Results of Pilot Tests

The results of the experiments during the pilot tests are presented in Table 1. The questionnaire to be completed by the pilot study participants is presented in Table 1. It shows that the conducted experiments were successful. The people testing the applications had no questions about the course as well as the sentences specified in the questionnaire. It is worth noting, however, that in the questions about social presence, one of the subjects did not answer at all, stating that they had seen interactions with other people or creatures. In contrast, the second respondent rated all of these aspects as "1", adding that the interactions were poor because there were virtually none. This confirmed the previously noted difficulty in seeing social interactions in the selected applications.

As a consequence of right concerns about the validity of this part of questionnaire, we decided not to use it in the rest of the research. We found the other two parts of the questionnaire examining other aspects of presence (*Physical Presence* and *Self-presence*) sufficient to verify the thesis.

The other properties can be considered consistent across applications. Trends are already apparent as to which of the selected applications best or worst captures the sense of presence (Table 2).

Table 2. Results of experiments conducted for 2 subjects – question numbers correspond to sentence numbers assigned in the questionnaire; numbers 1, 2, 3 correspond to individual applications (VR Space, VR Galaxy Wars and Titans of Space® Cardboard VR).

Label	First subject			Second subject		
	1	2	3	1	2	3
PHYS_2	3	2	3	3	1	2
PHYS_3	3	3	2	2	3	2
PHYS_4	3	2	2	3	1	1
PHYS_5	4	3	3	3	3	1
PHYS_10	5	4	3	3	3	2
SOC_1	1	1	1	N.A	N.A.	N.A.
SOC_2	1	1	1	N.A	N.A.	N.A.
SOC_3	1	1	1	N.A	N.A.	N.A.
SOC_5	1	1	1	N.A	N.A.	N.A.
SOC_7	1	1	1	N.A	N.A.	N.A.
SELF_2	3	2	2	3	2	2
SELF_3	3	1	2	2	1	1
SELF_4	2	2	2	1	1	1
SELF_6	3	3	2	3	2	2
SELF_7	3	2	3	2	2	3

5   Final Study

The final study was conducted on 14 subjects. Similar to the pilot testing, the final study had each person install the 3 studied applications on their own device, as well as each phone was equipped with Google Cardboard – *Legito*. All of the participants took the opportunity to use the office wivel chair to get a better feel for the application and its nature – space.

5.1   Participants

As written earlier, 14 participants took part in the study. All participants in the study were from the same age range of 20–30 years - two of them aged 20–24 and twelve of them aged 25–30.

The study attempted to ensure equal numbers of male and female participants as much as possible. Ultimately, 6 women and 8 men participated in the study. 4 of the female participants had previous contact with a VR game and 2 had not. Whereas in the men, 5 had previously played using VR glasses and 3 had not. Which consequently gives the statistic that 9 people had previous exposure to this type of application and for 5 it was their first experience with VR.

The study was announced to few studentsgroups of computer science at the Lodz University of Technology. Participants volunteered to take part in the study.

5.2   Test Setup

As with the pilot tests, it was explained to each participant in the study what their task was – what the experiment was about, and what would be tested, at the same time not giving specific wording to sensitize participants to the relevant parts of the application, while not revealing the questionnaire.

Then the order in which the applications will be used was randomly selected, to prevent in the future that the first application is always rated the best or the worst, as it gives a new experience of being in a given space. The applications were numbered ("1" – VR Space [3], "2" – VR Galaxy Wars [4] and "3" – Titans of Space® Cardboard VR [5]), the corresponding numbers were written on cards, and the subject selected consecutive cards deciding the order in which to use the applications – the same as in the pilot study.

Each subject was given approximately 10 min to become familiar with the application and use it as intended. After using all the applications (after about 30 min), each participant was asked to fill out a questionnaire, choosing one of the values on a five-point Likert scale ("1" indicates "I completely disagree" and "5" – "I strongly agree"). The questionnaire, after pilot testing, was adapted and restricted only to test two of the three aspects of presence – *physical presence* and *self-presence*.

5.3 Results of Final Study

Basic statistics for each application by individual questionnaire sentence and histograms of results by physical presence and self-presence are presented in the tables and figures below. Table 3 and Fig. 1 show the results for the VR Space application. Next, Table 4 and Fig. 2 show the results for the Galaxy Wars VR application, while Table 5 and Fig. 3 show the results for theTitans of Space® Cardboard VR application.

Table 3. Results of experiments for VR Space application during final study.

Label	1 – VR Space			
	Mean	Median	Min	Max
PHYS_2	2.86 ± 0.35	3	2	3
PHYS_3	2.57 ± 0.49	3	2	3
PHYS_4	2.93 ± 0.88	3	2	4
PHYS_5	3.21 ± 0.41	3	3	4
PHYS_10	3.50 ± 0.63	3	3	5
SELF_2	2.71 ± 0.70	3	2	4
SELF_3	1.93 ± 0.80	2	1	3
SELF_4	1.57 ± 0.49	2	1	2
SELF_6	2.71 ± 0.45	3	2	3
SELF_7	2.21 ± 0.41	2	2	3

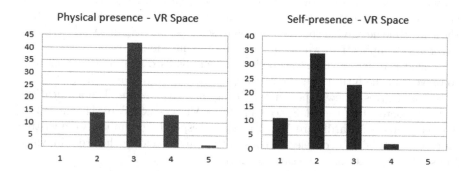

Fig. 1. Results histogram for VR Space application for physical presence and self-presence.

As can be seen from the data presented in the tables and histograms, all three applications did not score high on any of the examined dimensions. Most of the studied aspects were evaluated by the participants of the survey with an average score not exceeding 3 (this is the middle value within the five-point

Table 4. Results of experiments for VR Galaxy Wars application during final study.

Label	2 – VR Galaxy Wars			
	Mean	Median	Min	Max
PHYS_2	2.00 ± 0.65	2	1	3
PHYS_3	2.79 ± 0.41	3	2	3
PHYS_4	2.14 ± 0.91	2.5	1	3
PHYS_5	3.07 ± 0.59	3	2	4
PHYS_10	3.50 ± 0.73	3	3	5
SELF_2	2.21 ± 0.41	2	2	3
SELF_3	1.64 ± 0.81	1	1	3
SELF_4	1.71 ± 0.59	2	1	3
SELF_6	2.14 ± 0.74	2	1	3
SELF_7	2.14 ± 0.35	2	2	3

Table 5. Results of experiments for Titans of Space Cardboard VR application during final study.

Label	3 – Titans of Space Cardboard VR			
	Mean	Median	Min	Max
PHYS_2	2,36 ± 0,48	2	2	3
PHYS_3	1,79 ± 0,41	2	1	2
PHYS_4	1,36 ± 0,48	1	1	2
PHYS_5	1,93 ± 0,88	2	1	3
PHYS_10	2,14 ± 0,74	2	1	3
SELF_2	2,00 ± 0,00	2	2	2
SELF_3	1,43 ± 0,49	1	1	2
SELF_4	1,36 ± 0,48	1	1	2
SELF_6	1,79 ± 0,41	2	1	2
SELF_7	2,71 ± 0,45	3	2	3

questionnaire). The exceptions here are the sentences marked **PHYS_5** (*While I was in the virtual environment, I had a sense of "being there".*) and **PHYS_10** (*I was completely captivated by the virtual world.*), which for two of the examined applications (VR Space and VR Galaxy Wars) received average scores exceeding 3. Additionally, these are the only aspects for which former study participants gave a value of 5 (it is the highest possible value on the used scale).

One of the lowest rated aspects for all 3 applications are those labeled **SELF_3** (*When something happened to my virtual embodiment, it felt like it was happening to my real body.*) and **SELF_4** (*I felt like my real arm was projected into the virtual environment through my virtual embodiment.*). Furthermore, **SELF_3** is an aspect for which 2 out of 3 applications (VR Galaxy Wars

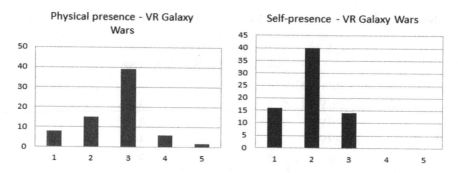

Fig. 2. Results histogram for VR Galaxy Wars application for physical presence and self-presence.

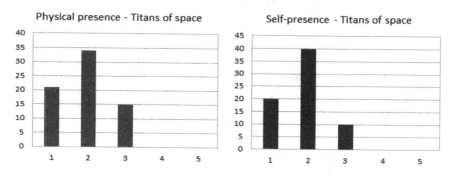

Fig. 3. Results histogram for Titans of Space Cardboard VR application for physical presence and self-presence.

and Titans of Space) received a median score of 1 (this is the lowest possible value on the used scale).

It is also worth mentioning that for most of the surveyed aspects the maximum value chosen by the participants was 3. It means that the studied applications for the vast majority of aspects are rated no higher than the middle of the scale.

Analysing the distribution of data for selected dimensions of presence – physical presence and self-presence one can see a general trend. For all tested applications, the results for self-presence are shifted to the left relative to the median value, meaning that the values are lower than the selectable value that is the middle. However, in the case of physical presence, the histograms show that most responses were in the middle, and among the arms, we have a predominance of lower values (1 and 2, compared to 4 and 5). The exception here is the last application, where again there was a shift of the graph to the left.

Additionally, it's worth noting that looking overall, the VR Space application was rated best and Titans of Space was rated the worst. It is a trend that was already visible in the pilot study. There, too, the first mentioned application received the highest scores, while Titans of space received the lowest.

6   Discussion and Conclusions

The results of the study show that the evaluation of sense of presence in selected mobile applications is not high. It may suggest that it is not easy to create a mobile application that allows a full sense of presence. The results for all tested applications not exceeding the average value possible to select within the given scale, show that we are still far from creating a mobile application that realistically allows us to feel present in it.

Let's look at the aspects that determine a sense of presence and contrast them with the possibilities offered by mobile applications like VR. As defined in [11] and [12] the aspects listed below are considered:

1. The extent and fidelity of sensory information – the amount of useful and salient sensory information presented in a consistent manner to the appropriate senses of the user, e.g. monocular and binocular cues to spatial layout, resolution, field of view or spatialized audio.
2. The match between sensors and the display – the sensory-motor contingencies, e.g. the mapping between the user's actions and the perceptible spatio-temporal effects of those actions.
3. Content factors – the objects, actors and events represented by the medium.
4. User characteristics – for example the user's perceptual, cognitive and motor abilities, prior experience with and expectations towards mediated experiences, and a willingness to suspend disbelief.

When considering the range and fidelity of sensory information, it is worth noting that mobile VR applications are very limited in this regard. If the application is to run on a cell phone the only sensory information it provides is an image shown binaurally, using Google Cardboard, and audio, maximally delivered binaurally (mostly unanimously). It means that all mobile applications are inherently worse off in terms of sense of presence within the determinant under study. A general solution would be to add other sensory information carriers. For VR applications happening in space, it was a good idea to use a swivel chair so that walking is not necessary. However, it was not sufficient. More sound emitting points could be added. In the general case, a chair that reacts to falling asteroids with shaking, etc. would be very helpful to get a better feel for the application.

As for the second determinant – the match between sensors and the display – it is difficult with such a small number of sensors to talk about their alignment. In the selected applications, most of the sounds are just quiet music, which most people associate with large space, and thus with outer space. However, there is nothing else here that needs to be well synchronized. It means that the sounds can feel completely disconnected from what is happening within the application. A solution to increase the contribution of this parameter to the positive evaluation of the sense of presence could be to add more sensors that are well synchronized with the image (which is hardly possible in mobile applications), but also to add other sounds related to specific actions, the sound of engines, etc.

When looking at the content factors, all social interactions affect the sense of presence, especially social presence. However, since special presence is not considered within this study, we will focus on other aspects of this determinant. Given the user's ability to change the space, within selected applications is severely limited. Two of the applications are only exploratory applications, meaning that there is no ability to interact with the space. When it comes to the user representation, only Tittans of Space had a realistic representation of the user as a human. Nevertheless, this application was rated the lowest. It may be due, among other things, to the fact that there was no possibility to realistically operate the viewing position (including giving the user the possibility to rotate the "head" by 360°, which is not possible in the real world). Other applications represented the user as an entire spaceship, which also does not give a realistic representation of a human. Here, it would be useful to create a realistic human representation for all applications, along with limiting head movements, along with a view of body parts as in a human. It would be nice to be able to move these body parts, but it is not feasible within a mobile application that does not have additional sensors.

Given individual user characteristics, it is something beyond our control. Keeping in mind that this type of application is available for everyone to use, regardless of what characteristics they have. It means that applications should be adaptable even to those users who are extremely resistant when it comes to feeling present while using the application.

Taking all these aspects into consideration, one can say without hesitation that mobile VR applications are very difficult to create in terms of sense of presence. Additionally, applications that simulate space place additional constraints that make this task even more difficult. It means that if we would like to create a VR application in space, it is worth considering a different form than a smartphone application, and in case of a mobile application, to use all possible carriers of information and interaction, including social relations.

References

1. Lee, K.M.: Presence, explicated. Commun. Theory **14**(1), 27–50 (2004)
2. Klimmt, C., Vorderer, P.: Media psychology "is not yet there": introducing theories on media entertainment to the presence debate. Presence Teleoperators Virtual Environ. **12**(4), 346–359 (2003). https://doi.org/10.1162/105474603322391596
3. VR Space. http://play.google.com/store/apps/details?id=com.bce.VR. Accessed 20 Apr 2021
4. VR Galaxy Wars. http://play.google.com/store/apps/details?id=com.blackantgames.vrgalacticwars. Accessed 20 Apr 2021
5. Titans of Space® Cardboard VR. http://play.google.com/store/apps/details?id=com.drashvr.titansofspacecb&hl=en. Accessed 20 Apr 2021
6. Makransky, G., Lilleholt, L., Aaby, A.: Development and validation of the multimodal presence scale for virtual reality environments: a confirmatory factor analysis and item response theory approach. Comput. Hum. Behav. **72**, 276–285 (2017). https://doi.org/10.1016/j.chb.2017.02.066

7. Volkmann, T., Wessel, D., Franke, T., Jochems, N.: Testing the social presence aspect of the multimodal presence scale in a virtual reality game. In: Proceedings of MuC 2019: Mensch und Computer, pp. 433–437 (2019). https://doi.org/10.1145/3340764.3344435

8. Volkmann, T., Wessel, D., Franke, T., Jochems, N.: Social presence in a virtual reality game with different levels of abstraction: testing the social presence aspect of the multimodal presence scale. In: Alt, F., Bulling, A., Döring, T. (Hrsg.) Mensch und Computer 2019 - Tagungsband. ACM, New York (2019). https://doi.org/10.1145/3340764.3344435

9. Adame, A.: Fully immersed, fully present: examining the user experience through the multimodal presence scale and virtual reality gaming variables. Electron. Theses Projects Dissertations **918** (2019). https://scholarworks.lib.csusb.edu/etd/918

10. Legato Cardboard 3D. http://legato.pl/pl/produkt/rejestratory/legato-cardboard-3d. Accessed 22 Apr 2021

11. Ijsselsteijn, W., Ridder, H., Freeman, J., Avons, S.: Presence: concept, determinants and measurement. In: Proceedings of SPIE - The International Society for Optical Engineering, vol. 3959 (2000). https://doi.org/10.1117/12.387188

12. Misztal, S., Carbonell, G., Schild, J.: Visual delegates - enhancing player perception by visually delegating player character sensation. In: Proceedings of the Annual Symposium on Computer-Human Interaction in Play (CHI PLAY 2020), pp. 386–399. Association for Computing Machinery, New York (2020). https://doi.org/10.1145/3410404.3414238

13. Orus, C., Ibanez-Sanchez, S., Flavian, C.: Enhancing the customer experience with virtual and augmented reality: the impact of content and device type. Int. J. Hosp. Manag. **98**, 103019 (2021). https://doi.org/10.1016/j.ijhm.2021.103019. ISSN 0278-4319

14. Radianti, J., Majchrzak, T.A., Fromm, J., Wohlgenannt, I.: A systematic review of immersive virtual reality applications for higher education: design elements, lessons learned, and research agenda. Comput. Educ. **147**, 103778 (2020). https://doi.org/10.1016/j.compedu.2019.103778. ISSN 0360-1315

Positive Online Customer Experience as an Antecedent of the Willingness to Share Information with an E-Commerce Retailer

Jussi Nyrhinen[1]([✉]) [iD], Tiina Kemppainen[2] [iD], Miia Grénman[2] [iD], Lauri Frank[3] [iD], Markus Makkonen[3] [iD], and Terhi-Anna Wilska[1] [iD]

[1] Department of Social Sciences and Philosophy, University of Jyväskylä,
PO Box 35, 40014 Jyväskylä, Finland
jussi.nyrhinen@jyu.fi
[2] School of Business and Economics, Jyväskylä University,
PO Box 35, 40014 Jyväskylä, Finland
[3] Faculty of Information Technology, University of Jyväskylä,
PO Box 35, 40014 Jyväskylä, Finland

Abstract. This paper examines how a positive online customer experience (OCE) can lead customers to consent retailers to collect their personal data and to receive personalized services in exchange. The paper addresses a gap in literature by acknowledging the customer's perspective while most of the prior literature has overemphasized the benefits of customer data for the firm. The aim of this paper is to provide a literature review to inform understanding of the antecedents and consequences of the willingness to share information (WSI). The paper offers four important contributions for both academics and practitioners. First, it adds to understanding of the importance of OCE and WSI for customer loyalty in e-commerce. Second, the paper examines the e-store antecedents of WSI by drawing on existing literature. Third, it proposes the potential consequences of WSI and constructs a conceptual framework for future testing. Finally, the paper proposes managerial implications.

Keywords: Online commerce · Online customer experience · Servicescape · Share of wallet · Willingness to share information

1 Introduction

Customer data plays a crucial role in e-store management and success. In today's highly competitive e-commerce field where customer behavior is unpredictable and ever-changing, customer data has become an increasingly important strategic decision-making tool for companies aiming to stay in business. The more a company knows about its customers, the better it can provide them with services and products that meet their interests, needs, and expectations and stand out from competitors' offerings. This requires in-depth customer understanding beyond their buying habits and demographic

M. Themistocleous and M. Papadaki (Eds.): EMCIS 2021, LNBIP 437, pp. 376–383, 2022.
https://doi.org/10.1007/978-3-030-95947-0_26

factors, for instance; what customers value, in what kind of life situation they are in, and how a company's offerings can become a part of customers' lives [15, 25].

Customer data allows companies to identify their customers, to reach them more effectively, and to improve company's offerings and personal services to them. However, even though both companies and customers can benefit from customer data collection and analysis, the problem from a company's perspective is how to convince customers to share their personal information with the company - to show that customer's inputs will be used for his/her own benefit. As companies in all fields of business are increasingly collecting customer data, customers may experience privacy concerns and other risks that negatively contribute to the idea of sharing one's information [21]. While today's technology offers countless opportunities for companies to collect customer data and to utilize it in service design and improvement, these opportunities are useless if customers do not want to pass on their information. Hence, it is essential to understand the customers' willingness to share their information and the factors that contribute to it in a positive or negative way. Here, customer willingness to share information (WSI) refers to personal information that customers voluntarily reveal and distribute to companies [28].

This paper discusses how a positive online customer experience (OCE) can lead customers to allow retailers to gather their personal data and receive personalized services in exchange. Most of the literature has overemphasized the benefits of customer data and the sharing of customer information for the firm, while mostly ignoring the customers' perspective [19]. To increase a customer's WSI, customer data can be obtained and utilized in a more customer-centric manner so that customers also receive benefits from the data that is collected, thus further supporting the currently prevailing customer-dominant logic of marketing (CDL; e.g., [16]). Customer data allows companies to further develop their servicescapes to provide more personalized OCEs. In online retailing, consent is not a one-off agreement; it must first be earned by providing a satisfactory experience and then maintained by providing perpetually outstanding experiences through better customer insight.

The structure of the paper is as follows. The first section presents the research method used for the literature review. Thereafter, a discussion of the main concepts of WSI, OCE, online servicescape, trust, and customer loyalty is provided. The following section provides the literature review, structured according to the framework. Finally, the paper ends with a proposed conceptual framework and a discussion on it as well as makes proposals for further research.

2 Literature Review

A literature review was conducted by using the following method. The research team comprised of five academics. A review question was identified ('What are the antecedents and consequences of WSI in online retailing?') and according search terms were chosen by the team. These included 'willingness to share information', 'online customer experience', 'online servicescape', 'trust', and 'customer loyalty'. The peer-reviewed journal articles were in the focus of the search. The articles were analyzed according to a selection criterion that was to examine the theme of the article as written in both the title and the abstract of the article. The content analysis was then conducted manually to draw the key concepts and to develop a conceptual framework.

3   Constructing the Conceptual Framework

3.1   Willingness to Share Information and Customer Loyalty

Customer data collection is a process between a company and a customer that requires the involvement of both parties; data cannot be collected from non-active customers, and, on the other hand, customer consent to share information is required.

Willingness to Share Information (WSI). WSI is based on a process during which customers weigh their risks and opportunities [22, 34] and decide whether personal information is exchanged with the benefits provided by a company [22]. Evaluations of risks and benefits are typically based on one's beliefs and dispositions rather than fact-based costs of benefits [23]. Personal information can include, for instance, demographic details, payment information, contact information, such as address and location, and purchase history. From a customer's perspective, e-stores and traditional brick-and-mortar stores are different in terms of required information sharing. While one can walk to a local supermarket and make a purchase with cash without sharing any information about oneself to the retailer, an e-store purchase always requires some information-sharing (such as payment and delivery details) to be completed.

Previous studies in marketing and information systems research [21] have identified factors that influence customers' WSI. Studies show that lack of trust and customers' concerns about the privacy of their information are key factors preventing consumers from sharing their information with companies [3]. Customers with high levels of privacy concerns avoid disclosing their personal information with online stores [9]. The consumption context, the type of information and its sensitivity, and the characteristics of the consumer can also influence customers' stances towards information sharing [22, 27]. Studies have shown, for instance, that the more sensitive information is, the less willing consumers are willing to share it [27] and that young people are willing to share more personal information than older consumers [13].

Customer Loyalty. Although there is limited evidence on how customers' WSI affects loyalty, those who manifest high levels of loyalty intentions and behaviors toward a company are familiar with the relational benefits that the company offers [7]. Conversely, participating in a loyalty program does not necessarily enhance loyalty because these programs usually reward customers who are already loyal. Thus, consumers often enroll in multiple loyalty programs to take advantage of all available offers and reward schemes [7]. However, prior studies suggest a connection between WSI and loyalty in the context of specialty retail [21], even though these effects are considered rather weak.

3.2   Antecedents of the Willingness to Share Information

Online Customer Experience (OCE). The concept of the customer experience, which originates from a set of personal and multidimensional interactions between a customer and a service provider or a product, is commonly used in marketing and management studies. Customer experience is evaluated by the customer, who compares their expectations against their interaction with the service provider and/or its offering at different touchpoints or moments of contact within various servicescapes [11, 20, 31].

The importance of customer experiences has widely been acknowledged in the marketing and management literature. The changing nature of customer involvement in value creation has led to a more recent paradigm shift in marketing: from service-dominant logic (SDL; [32]) to customer-dominant logic (CDL; [16]).

This trend is also visible in online commerce and in relation to customer data. OCE has been identified as an essential contributor to a company's success in e-commerce [24, 27]. Unsatisfying experiences encourage customers to switch retailers, while customer satisfaction has positive consequences like increased revenue, customer loyalty, and positive word-of-mouth [5, 18, 24, 29].

In this study, OCE is defined as the cumulative outcome of a customer's exposure to the e-store servicescape [26]. Online customers engage in cognitive and affective processing of e-store servicescapes, resulting in an internal and subjective takeaway impression [26, 29]. The cognitive experiential stage (CES) of the experience includes conscious mental processes, such as thinking, while the affective experiential stage (AES) includes the customer's generation of moods, emotions, and feelings [11, 29]. The emotional characteristics of customer experiences have recently received increasing attention [8, 18], although it has also been concluded that both cognitive and emotional evaluations contribute to customer satisfaction [29].

Online Servicescape Determinants. In her seminal work, Bitner [6] defined the servicescape as the physical setting for a marketplace exchange to be performed, delivered, and consumed within a service organization. In addition, Bitner conceptualized the servicescape to constitute three types of objective, physical, and measurable stimuli that are organizationally controllable and able to enhance employee and customer approach/avoidance decisions and that can facilitate or hinder employee/customer social interaction [10]. According to the current understanding, a servicescape comprises not only objective, measurable and managerially controllable stimuli but also subjective, immeasurable and often managerially uncontrollable social, symbolic, and natural stimuli, all of which influence customer approach/avoidance decisions and social interaction behaviors [10].

From a customer's perspective, an ideal servicescape can be characterized as being physically appealing, socially supportive, symbolically welcoming, and naturally pleasing. The customer's evaluation in the service context is shown to be influenced by the substantive staging of the servicescape (i.e., the functional and mechanical clues) and its communicative aspects (i.e., human clues) [10]. Substantive staging refers to the physical creations of the service environment [1], which include physical, objective, and managerially controllable factors, such as layout, products, and prices that affect the perceived service [10]. Contemporary servicescapes also augment these elements in the virtual space of an e-store, where they manifest in website design and virtual interaction [3].

According to Dong & Siu [9], communicative staging of the servicescape refers to how the service environment is presented and interpreted, and it involves a transmission of meaning that is directly related to service delivery and that transcends the instrumental context [1]. Store personnel are central to communicative staging, and their behavior, competency, and habits affect the service evaluation [10]. A servicescape also provides a platform to support activities and interactions with customers. Therefore, it acts as a link between people through its symbolic meanings [17]. A customer's evaluation of both the substantive and communicative staging of a servicescape should, thus, positively predict their assessment of the AES and the CES because servicescape elements have been shown to strongly affect both cognitive and affective responses toward a service encounter [10].

Trust. In e-stores and brick-and-mortar (B&M) stores, customers can form their trust perceptions based on interactions with the retailer [29]. The literature differentiates the antecedents of trust into cognitive and emotional (affective) factors [4]. Trust may be based upon the rational assessment of a partner's reliability and competence (i.e., cognitive factors increase the confidence that a retail transaction will be successful, and emotional factors help reduce awkwardness, complexity, and uncertainty and increase confidence in the retailer's goodwill and abilities). Prior studies [14] have shown that particularly meaningful experiences engendered by social interaction with other customers and store personnel can enhance trust in a brand, which emphasizes the role of the AES in trust formation. A prior empirical study by Rose et al. [29] found that both the AES and the CES have direct positive effects on trust toward the retailer while testing the effects of online shopping antecedents.

4   Conceptual Framework and Discussion

From the results of the above literature review, we have formed a conceptual model on WSI and its antecedents and consequences, which is presented below in Fig. 1. This conceptual model provides insight and promotes the understanding of the antecedents and consequences of WSI in e-store which helps to develop a conceptual framework for future testing.

Specifically, the following conclusions can be drawn. First, the proposed framework suggests that trust is playing a significant role in the connection of WSI and loyalty in online shopping environments. Satisfying OCE enhances a customer's trust towards the retailer, and this is affecting also WSI and loyalty in a positive manner. Evidently, consumers consent to share information, such as their data, with retailers that they regard reliable, but also in-return for a received positive OCE. Further, this is a reciprocal connection: With customer data a retailer is able to tailor and provide better customer experiences. In advanced online commerce, OCE may be automatically tailored based on customer data.

Second, the literature review implies that there is a linkage between WSI and loyalty, and WSI can be considered as an antecedent for loyalty in online commerce. Loyalty, in turn, is something which retailers want to pursue, as it yields positive outcomes such as an increase in share of wallet (SOW) and positive word-of-mouth (WOM). Thus, as a retailer, by taking care of the antecedents to WSI, namely trust and OCE, one is likely

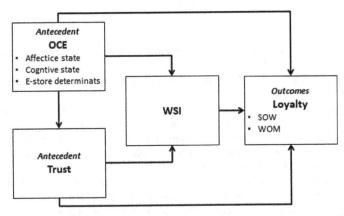

Fig. 1. A conceptual framework of the willingness to share information online.

not only to increase the likelihood of customers sharing valuable data with you but also to eventually have a positive effect on your SOW and WOM.

Third, we discussed how servicescape elements constitute OCE. The antecedents to WSI were found to consist of OCE and trust. OCE is composed of the online servicescape (online store determinants) and the consumer's affective and cognitive processing of this servicescape. Thus, by taking into account the negative and positive emotions of a consumer during the online service path, a retailer can affect OCE, and subsequently WSI and loyalty. For example, by providing a technically smooth online experience and necessary product information as well as desired logistics and payment options to the consumer, the retailer can affect OCE.

Based on the literature review and the conceptual model, we draw the following managerial implications. First, this conceptual model highlights the importance of emotional social factors in online commerce when building OCE. These factors may help a retailer to diversify from its competitors. However, especially in e-tailing, the research has focused on market-relevant factors and website interface, leaving the social interaction with little focus. Our framework provides guidance to consider social factors and the AES when aiming to enhance customer loyalty in e-commerce. Second, the conceptual model presents a relationship between WSI and loyalty. When customers are willing to share personal information about themselves on their shopping behavior, loyalty to the retailer is simultaneously increased. Further, the online retailer may utilize the collected customer data to improve OCE, for example, through personalization of the advertisements shown to the customer.

As it is based on a literature review, the conceptual model provided in this paper is not tested empirically and, thus, the general limitations related to conceptual research apply. Further research should empirically test the relationship of the constructs of the conceptual model presented in this paper. Further empirical research could also compare different environments (online vs. offline vs. omnichannel), domains (services vs. products), and markets.

References

1. Arnould, E.J., Price, L.L., Tierney, P.: Communicative staging of the wilderness servicescape. Serv. Ind. J. **18**(3), 90–115 (1998)
2. Ballantyne, D., Nilsson, E.: All that is solid melts into air: the servicescape in digital service space. J. Serv. Mark. **31**(3), 226–235 (2017)
3. Bansal, G., Zahedi, F.M., Gefen, D.: Do context and personality matter? Trust and privacy concerns in disclosing private information online. Inf. Manag. **53**(1), 1–21 (2016)
4. Basso, A., Goldberg, D., Greenspan, S., Weimer, D.: First impressions: emotional and cognitive factors underlying judgments of trust e-commerce. In: Proceedings of the 3rd ACM conference on Electronic Commerce, October 2001, pp. 137–143 (2001)
5. Bilgihan, A.: Gen Y customer loyalty in online shopping: an integrated model of trust, user experience and branding. Comput. Hum. Behav. **61**, 103–113 (2016)
6. Bitner, M.J.: Servicescapes: the impact of physical surroundings on customers and employees. J. Mark. **56**(2), 57–71 (1992)
7. Bellini, S., Cardinali, M.G., Ziliani, C.: Building customer loyalty in retailing: not all levers are created equal. Int. Rev. Retail Distrib. Consum. Res. **21**(5), 461–481 (2011)
8. Chaney, D., Lunardo, R., Mencarelli, R.: Consumption experience: past, present and future. Qual. Mark. Res. **21**(4), 402–420 (2018)
9. Dinev, T., Hart, P.: An extended privacy calculus model for e-commerce transactions. Inf. Syst. Res. **17**(1), 61–80 (2006)
10. Dong, P.N., Siu, Y.-M.: Servicescape elements, customer predispositions and service experience: the case of theme park visitors. Tour. Manag. **36**, 541–551 (2013)
11. Fisk, R.P., Patrício, L., Rosenbaum, M.S., Massiah, C.: An expanded servicescape perspective. J. Serv. Manag. **22**(4), 471–490 (2011)
12. Gentile, C., Spiller, N., Noci, G.: How to sustain the customer experience: an overview of experience components that co-create value with the customer. Eur. Manag. J. **25**(5), 395–410 (2007)
13. Goldfarb, A., Tucker, C.: Shifts in privacy concerns. Ame. Econ. Rev.: Papers Proc. **102**(3), 349–353 (2012)
14. Ha, H.-Y., Perks, H.: Effects of consumer perceptions of brand experience on the web: brand familiarity, satisfaction and brand trust. J. Consum. Behav. **4**, 438–452 (2005)
15. Heinonen, K., Strandvik, T.: Reflections on customers' primary role in markets. Eur. Manag. J. **36**(1), 1–11 (2018)
16. Heinonen, K., Strandvik, T., Mickelsson, K.J., Edvardsson, B., Sundström, E., Andersson, P.: A customer-dominant logic of service. J. Serv. Manag. **21**(4), 531–548 (2010)
17. Johnstone, M.-L.: The servicescape: the social dimensions of place. J. Mark. Manag. **28**(11–12), 1399–1418 (2012)
18. Kemppainen, T., Frank, L.: How are negative customer experiences formed? A qualitative study of customers' online shopping journeys. In: Abramowicz, W., Corchuelo, R. (eds.) BIS 2019. LNBIP, vol. 373, pp. 325–338. Springer, Cham (2019). https://doi.org/10.1007/978-3-030-36691-9_28
19. Kunz, W., et al.: Customer engagement in a Big Data world. J. Serv. Mark. **31**(2), 161–171 (2017)
20. LaSalle, D., Britton, T.A.: Priceless: Turning Ordinary Products into Extraordinary Experiences. Harvard Business School Press, Boston (2003)
21. Leppäniemi, M., Karjaluoto, H., Saarijärvi, H.: Customer perceived value, satisfaction, and loyalty: the role of willingness to share information. International Review of Retail, Distribution and Consumer Research **27**(2), 164–188 (2017)

22. Li, H., Sarathy, R., Xu, H.: Understanding situational online information disclosure as a privacy calculus. J. Comput. Inf. Syst. **51**(1), 62–71 (2010)
23. Li, H., Sarathy, R., Xu, H.: The role of affect and cognition on online consumers' decision to disclose personal information to unfamiliar online vendors. Decis. Support Syst. **51**(3), 434–445 (2011)
24. Makkonen, M., Riekkinen, J., Frank, L., Jussila, J.: The effects of positive and negative emotions during online shopping episodes on consumer satisfaction, repurchase intention, and recommendation intention. In: Pucihar, A., Kljajic Borstnar, M., Bons, R., Seitz, J., Cripps, H., Vidmar, D. (eds.) 32nd Bled eConference: Humanizing Technology for a Sustainable Society. Maribor: University of Maribor, pp. 931–954 (2019)
25. Martin, K.D., Murphy, P.E.: The role of data privacy in marketing. J. Acad. Mark. Sci. **45**(2), 135–155 (2016). https://doi.org/10.1007/s11747-016-0495-4
26. Meyer, C., Schwager, A.: Understanding customer experience. Harv. Bus. Rev. **85**(2), 116–126 (2007)
27. Mothersbaugh, D.L., Foxx, W.K., Beatty, S.E., Wang, S.: Disclosure antecedents in an online service context: the role of sensitivity of information. J. Serv. Res. **15**(1), 76–98 (2012)
28. Phelps, J., Nowak, G., Ferrell, E.: Privacy concerns and consumer willingness to provide personal information. J. Public Policy Mark. **19**(1), 27–41 (2000)
29. Rose, S., Clark, M., Samouel, P., Hair, N.: Online customer experience in e-retailing: an empirical model of antecedents and outcomes. J. Retail. **88**(2), 308–322 (2012)
30. Rose, S., Hair, N., Clark, M.: Online customer experience: a review of the business-to-consumer online purchase context. Int. J. Manag. Rev. **13**(1), 24–39 (2011)
31. Shaw, C., Ivens, J.: Building Great Customer Experiences. MacMillan, New York (2005)
32. Trevinal, A.M., Stenger, T.: Toward a conceptualization of the online shopping experience. J. Retail. Consum. Serv. **21**(3), 314–326 (2014)
33. Vargo, S.L., Lusch, R.F.: Evolving to a new dominant logic for marketing. J. Mark. **68**(1), 1–17 (2004)
34. Zimmer, J.C., Arsal, R.E., Al-Marzouq, M., Grover, V.: Investigating online information disclosure: effects of information relevance, trust and risk. Inf. Manag. **47**(2), 115–123 (2010)

Introducing Sentient Requirements for Information Systems and Digital Technologies

Elena Kornyshova(✉) and Eric Gressier-Soudan

CEDRIC, Conservatoire National des Arts et Métiers, Paris, France
{elena.kornyshova,eric.gressier_soudan}@cnam.fr

Abstract. Traditionally requirements for Information Systems are considered as functional and non-functional. However, with current omnipresent Digital Technologies, we believe that new requirements dealing with individuals' well-being are emerging. We call them sentient requirements using the term from the animal rights protection field. In this paper, we analyze the existing literature to understand better the deep nature of humans' interactions with digital technologies and we introduce sentient requirements. It is based on a literature review including scientific and science-fiction literature. We apply these requirements to improve user experience in museums through a visiting game as a use case. Our proposal could be used by researchers and practitioners to enforce the design of Information Systems in various application fields to provide a better interaction between humans and digital technologies.

Keywords: Sentient requirement · Well-being · Information system · Digital technology · Museum · Visiting game

1 Introduction

We are dealing with visitors' experience improvements in museums through serious visiting games. Our goal is to find an accurate way to enrich user experience (UX). Personalization is usually the way this goal is processed. Information and Communication Technologies (ICT) devices are generally supporting this approach. An important step during design and engineering of IS is requirement engineering at the early phases of the development life cycle [1]. Thus, the first step was to identify requirements to provide a personalized experience when using UX featured applications and their associated devices.

From our point of view, the personal use of ICT implies a new kind of need dealing with the well-being of people using them. For example, when a visitor tries to use a portable device in a museum and if the screen is not enough responsive because it is too dirty, the device becomes a source of stress, and its initial goal to provide a better experience to visitors cannot be reached. This kind of concern about ICT devices should deal with self-awareness to provide welfare or well-being to users. The same

© Springer Nature Switzerland AG 2022
M. Themistocleous and M. Papadaki (Eds.): EMCIS 2021, LNBIP 437, pp. 384–395, 2022.
https://doi.org/10.1007/978-3-030-95947-0_27

kind of idea can be found in [2]. It evokes digital and social media technologies can take control upon human consciousness and, by this way, they imply dissatisfaction about these technologies. For example, social networks stimulate depression when "we feel we have to check, but checking does us no good" [2]. The current and future Information Systems (IS) and supporting devices should be designed, developed, and updated in a way to enhance and especially not to damage humans and their well-being.

The requirements are traditionally seen as functional and non-functional. A functional requirement is a "description of a behavior that a software system will exhibit under specific conditions [3], a non-functional requirement (NFR) is a "description of a property or characteristic that a system must exhibit or a constraint that it must respect" [3]. The former type represents the set of functionalities to be provided by ICT devices, and the latter covers additional aspects like security, availability, scalability.

The main research gap addressed in this paper is based on the following statement: the traditional requirements do not cover the need to provide ICT and ICT devices (called globally ICT in the following) dealing with the well-being of their users. This kind of requirement is not functional by nature. Their purpose does not cover the suitable functionalities addressing the application needs. They don't either address non-functional requirements which deal with the operationality of the system architecture. This new kind of feature adds an additional dimension to the usual requirements and also impacts a sub-set of traditional functional and non-functional requirements.

In the case of museum visit experience, the literature review did not identify sources expressing this sort of requirements explicitly. To be able to feed our proposal, we took our main inspiration from science-fiction literature and completed it by related literature reviews. As an example, I. Asimov defined the four laws of robotics (the three first ones [4] and later the zeroth law). The Asimov's laws influenced ethic rules for Artificial Intelligence (AI). We have been inspired by the Powers Trilogy of Anne McCaffrey and Elisabeth Ann Scarborough [5–7]. This trilogy describes a living planet, Petaybee, which is also depicted by the authors as a sentient planet. Sentience is defined as an ability "of experiencing an affective state" [8]. This term was especially developed in the field of animals' rights protection [9, 10]. The sentience concept matches our approach of the relationship between humans and technologies; thus, we qualified the new family of requirements as "sentient". This term was first developed in the field of animals' rights protection [9, 10] and is already used in the field of Artificial Intelligence [11]. The Sentient Machine is introduced to define the evolution of machines from Artificial Narrow Intelligence to Artificial Generalized Intelligence by A. Husain [11]. The goal of our work is to specify sentient requirements for applications interacting with human through ICT devices. Sentient requirements would add an additional view to the design and development of ICT. In a broader acceptance, our goal is to explore what sentience abilities, or sentientness, imply for ICT.

In Section 2, we present our research approach. Section 3 is dedicated to the presentation of identified sentient requirements that are applied to a use case of ICT in the context of a museum to improve user experience. We discuss results in Section 4. Section 5 concludes the paper and gives future directions of our research work.

2 Research Approach

In this section, we detail our research process depicted in Fig. 1.

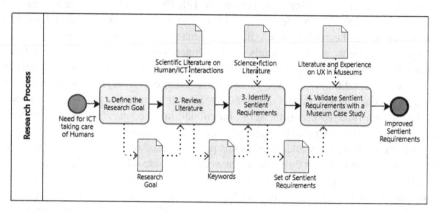

Fig. 1. Research process.

1. **Define the Research Goal.** Our initial research goal was to identify requirements for ICT in Museums in order to provide a better, personalized experience to visitors. After a first literature review, we aimed to provide humans with digital technologies and devices that could contribute to their well-being and could help to avoid negative consequences. To reach this goal, theories and practices of design and engineering should be updated to take into account this new dimension which should be integrated very early in the requirements definition step. For the current research, we refined the research goal as: "Is it possible to identify sentient requirements for the well-being of ICT users?".

2. **Review Literature.** As sentient requirements represent an emerging field, it is difficult to carry out precise research of the literature. Thus, this first step of the literature review was wide. We proceeded by using the following search string: "ICT" AND "Human" on google scholar in January 2021 and we used the backward/forward strategies to complete the study. We have checked the 20 retrieved pages and stopped after 5 pages without relevant results. We included works directly dealing with requirements and those with the associated terms, like "need", for instance. We excluded several works related to our topic but not specifying any requirements-related information. We classified the gathered literature into the following perspectives: philosophical perspective [2, 12–18]; IT and business perspective [19–25]; ethical perspective [26–29]; and societal perspective [30, 31]. Then, we carried out the textual analysis of the selected sources and extracted sentences that could be useful to capture the nature of human interactions with ICT with regards to their well-being. In addition, this step allowed us to identify the list of keywords to be used during a more detailed literature review: sentient requirement, well-being requirement, welfare requirement, smart requirement, affective requirement, and synergy requirement.

3. **Identify Sentient Requirements.** For this step, we used the science-fiction literature to feed the list of sentient requirements. As I. Asimov [4] inspired thoughts on Artificial Intelligence, we have been inspired by the Powers Trilogy of Anne McCaffrey and Elisabeth Ann Scarborough [5–7]. This trilogy describes a living planet, Petaybee, which is also depicted by the authors as a sentient planet. We extracted from the first book sentences characterizing the sentient planet abilities and its interactions with humans and other beings. Together with the literature collected from the previous steps, we grouped different ideas depending on their nature.

   For instance, to formulate the requirement "Interaction and Involvement", we generalized the following retrieved sentences and ideas: (i) The synergy requirement studied with application to interactions between human beings: ICT should be designed to support synergy between human beings. The synergy could be understood as interaction and involvement as it also covers the relationship between human beings and ICT [25]; (ii) Human beings and ICT should co-evolve together through time [2, 17, 32]; (iii) Human-Technology symbiosis "defining how humans will live and work harmoniously together with technology" and Human-Environment Interactions referring to "the interaction of people not only with a single artifact, but with entire technological ecosystems featuring increased interactivity and intelligence" [19]; (iv) "It[planet]'s only courteous to communicate", "There's a relationship [between the planet and humans] involved", "Living here, most of us know that and accept the gifts, the protection, and in return, we offer it companionship", "I just know that Petaybee works for us, and for itself, in a unique symbiosis…" [5]. We proceeded in the same way for the other requirements. The details cannot be present here due to the lack of space. Based on the analysis we did not include several requirements detailed in different perspectives as we consider them belonging to the two other types of requirements (exclusion criterion). For instance, a requirement "ICT should help to learn on technologies" [33] is a functional requirement as learning objectives are covered by the ICT functionalities. Another example is "ICT should ensure end-to-end encryption" [29] is typically a non-functional requirement as is it related to the security of data usage.

4. **Validate Sentient Requirements with a Museum Case Study.** To check the applicability of the sentient requirements, we apply them to a role-playing visiting game in a museum.

3   Emergence of Sentient Requirements

To qualify the new kind of requirements we used the term of sentience. Broom [9] defines: "a sentient being is one that has some ability: to evaluate the actions of others in relation to itself and third parties, to remember some of its own actions and their consequences, to assess risk, to have some feelings and to have some degree of awareness". This author underlines different aspects of sentience [10]: the sentience is related to ethics and moral issues; sentient abilities could be acquired and also be lost; the sentience requires "to act in an acceptable way towards each other person and toward each animal that is used"; and effects should be adapted to a given animal, "some components of sentience being dependent upon cognitive ability". [8] mentions that sentience covers all aspects of sensory consciousness; to be sentient means to be "capable of experiencing an affective state".

By [34], the capacity to have pleasant or unpleasant experiences "entails having a quality of life or experiential welfare, from which it follows that sentient beings have interests".

Based on the identified from the literature needs for a better consideration of humans in ICT, we define the sentient requirements as follows:

- **Interaction and Involvement:** ICT should interact and communicate with human.
- **Awareness:** ICT should be aware of human beings, know and learn about them, and sense/perceive humans.
- **Safety:** ICT should protect from danger and harm and take care of human; the laws of I. Asimov fall in this requirement.
- **Belongingness and Felicity:** ICT should provide a feeling of being comfortable or happy with ICT.
- **Adaptability:** ICT should be adaptable, thus be able to detect distinctive characteristics of each human and to adapt itself to this given individual.
- **Sustainability:** ICT should be able to stand for a long time and to protect the environment and earth ecosystem.
- **Respectfulness:** ICT should be respectful. Respectfulness is very important as it works in both directions: not only ICT should be respectful with humans, but also humans have the responsibility to make ICT ethic, non-dangerous for other beings.
- **Inclusiveness:** ICT should be inclusive and ensure equality between humans, it should be done with regards to different origins, languages, health situation, and more.
- **Self-Reflectiveness:** ICT should learn about itself and contribute to human development by providing additional capabilities and skills.

The sources of sentient requirements are summarized in Table 1.

Table 1. Sources of sentient requirements.

Sentient requirement	Philosophical perspective	IT and business perspective	Ethical perspective	Societal perspective	Science-fiction
Interaction and Involvement	X	X			X
Awareness	X	X	X		X
Safety					X
Belongingness and Felicity					X
Adaptability					X
Sustainability				X	
Respectfulness					X
Inclusiveness	X	X	X	X	
Self-Reflectiveness	X	X		X	

We applied the sentient requirements to the case of a role-playing visiting game in a museum based on our experience with museums and the related literature [35–43], etc.

The purpose of the game is to learn the process of manufacturing an artifact. The visitors can choose between three different roles. The game is provided through touchable tablets to each player. The visitor has a role and follows different steps of the game to build his knowledge. Across the museum, the visitor solves puzzles related to the content encountered corresponding to different resources and manufacturing tasks. In Table 2, we illustrate the sentient requirements expressed for our use case and deduce related functional requirements to show how the sentient requirements could be implemented in practice.

Table 2. Illustration of sentient requirements with a visiting game in a museum.

Sentient requirement	Sentient requirement expression	Corresponding functional requirement(s)
Interaction and Involvement	The tablet should be able to guess visitor's unforeseen needs and provide answers/guidelines	Include a chatbot service
Awareness	The tablet should be able to identify satisfying conditions to be used by a visitor (clean, enough power, functional)	Alarm if it is dirty, compute the amount of available power, detect any misbehavior
Safety	The tablet should alarm in case of any kind of danger	Display/broadcast an alarm and personalized instructions to avoid danger in time
Belongingness and Felicity	Users should feel proud of their accomplishment through the game	Monitor game achievements, stimulate users, and provide incentives during the game
Adaptability	The tablet should sense emotions and adapt the game to the mood of the user	Have sensors, compute emotional states, adapt puzzles
Sustainability	The tablet should optimize network communications to lower radio waves emission	Compute and adapt radio communication intensity to the appropriate level
Respectfulness	The tablet should react to inappropriate usage	Have sensors to detect unexpected movements, bumps, and drops, display/broadcast warnings
Inclusiveness	The tablet should detect disabilities and adapt the interaction with the visitor (for instance, switch to speech)	Have sensors, detect how the interaction is going on, and provide accurate help
Self-Reflectiveness	The tablet should help to improve the user experience	Gather game data, analyze player behavior, enhance gameplay

Based on this example, we have obtained the following results: (i) We have succeeded to express the identified sentient requirements applied to the visiting game in a museum, and (ii) We have shown that sentient requirements could be translated as a set of functional requirements.

Therefore, our proposal about sentient requirements could be applied to a real case and it provides useful insights to improve user experience design.

4 Discussion

To illustrate the role of sentient requirements in the ICT field, we suggest to model requirements hierarchy as a pyramid (Fig. 2). This pyramid is built by analogy with the Maslow pyramid of needs [44]. It shows the importance of sentient requirements and allows to position them in accordance with the existing requirements typology. As in the Maslow's five levels allow to satisfy human needs, we believe that all three levels of sentient requirements should be achieved in order to provide mindful ICT.

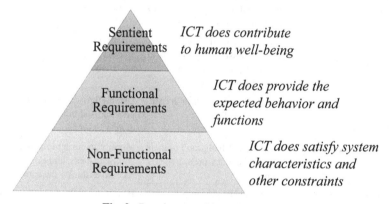

Fig. 2. Requirements hierarchy pyramid.

With regards to the Human-Computer Interaction challenges [19], four sentient requirements (interaction and involvement, awareness, inclusiveness, and self-reflectiveness) could contribute to develop the five challenges, namely: Human-Technology symbiosis, Human-Environment Interactions, Well-being, Health and Eudaimonia, Accessibility and Universal Access, and Learning and Creativity.

Considering current trends in ICT, a set of concepts arose recently: digital humanities, Life 3.0, Health 3.0, Welfare Society 2.0 etc. Digital humanities refer to "the intersection of digital technology and humanities: arts, literature, music, dance, theater, architecture, philosophy, and other expressions of human culture" [45]. Tegmark [46] presents the role of Artificial Intelligence can play for human. He defines three stages of Life: Life 1.0 (biological evolution), Life 2.0 (cultural evolution), and Life 3.0 (technological evolution). The last stage (not yet reached) refers to design not only "software" (meaning knowledge used to process the information issued from senses to decide about action, a kind of living "biological software"), but also "hardware", that is to say, the ability of organisms to change their physical components. To attain this future Life 3.0, Artificial Intelligence (AI) will play a particular role and should be friendly. One of the main requirements to the friendly AI is to align goals, thus, to better accomplish human goals using superintelligence. The goals alignment could be done by resolving three problems: "making AI learn our goals, making AI adopt our goals, making AI retain our goals". Within a visionary editorial, Nash [47] defines Health 3.0 as using social networking technologies to exchange about symptoms, medication, and providing medical care. Misuraca [26] foresees different socio-technical trends as, for instance, "Care 3.0 – Robotics for personalized care solutions" and calls it Welfare Society 2.0. These trends underline the necessity to go forward with the definition and application of sentient requirements and make us consider the necessity to take into account the goal-oriented dimension into process-relational philosophy underlying our research.

The ICT device is a kind of blurred border between the real world, and the virtual universe. Sensors from the real-world feed actuators in the virtual world and vice versa [48]. The device also supplied by the computing resources behind, is the place to get control from the application and where to instantiate the sentient properties. In some way, this concern dives into the research field of Machine Consciousness [49]. But machine consciousness is different. It is more a concern of bringing some intelligence to machines including artificial sentience. Instead, we focus on interaction and sentient properties provided by technology to enhance user experience in the digitalized emerging world of everyday life.

Michel Serres, the French philosopher, states that along his history, Humankind lost abilities, but each time it occurred, it was for a greater benefit [50]. For example, Human "lost" the head with the invention of the computer. But at the same time, the computer raised new opportunities that we now experience through the digital era and the new tools emerging from it. It extended our minds. Michel Serres also states that Humans have completely changed since the mid 20th century. Humankind lost its connection to earth and nature. We do not feel life the same way anymore. Over the world, most people live in cities and this phenomenon seems far from being stopped [51]. Our creed is that this statement shows a missing link in mankind approach to the digital era. As we are losing the connection with nature, we need to reinforce the way we sense our environment.

We believe that the introduction of sentient requirements could contribute to the maintenance of the human sovereignty by aligning properties of technologies to the human needs, by creating this kind of harmony between human beings and technologies. For instance, the application of sentient requirements to social medias inducing the FOMO (Fear Of Missing Out) syndrome (discussed in [2]) could decrease the risk of becoming depressive. Based on infomateriality of [16, 32] and close to the relational synergy of [17], our point of view is that human beings and ICT should co-evolve together through time. In line with these works, we claim that symbiosis between human beings and ICT is often foreseen as two opposite sides. This leads us to sentience that we define as a new kind of harmonious co-existence of human beings and ICT through time.

In our view, the specification of sentient requirements would allow to overcome this gap. According to [52] detailing a five-point assessment of contributions (with regards to theory, method, framing, phenomenon, and composition), we position our contribution mainly on the phenomenon axis as we deal with a new emerging concept (sentient requirements) applied to ICT. Sentience becomes a topic in scientific Information Technology-related publications. We believe that this term reflects well the concept of requirements contributing to building an emotional link between human beings and ICT. Our proposal will contribute also to the method axis, as the sentient requirements will impact the existing methods of requirements engineering and the whole cycle of IS engineering.

However, the introduction of sentient requirements will produce many additional, often new, questions to be solved, as, for example, can ICT and devices be designed to be sentient, especially when we think about robots and smart Internet of Things? Can we expect a smarter and more sustainable life with the digital surroundings we are providing? The way we embrace the future and the relationship with artificial intelligence-based technology is different from transhumanism [53] where human beings are extended or augmented with ICT parts.

5 Conclusion and Future Works

We believe that, using the sentient requirements, we can design a peaceful and sustainable digital technology that will help human beings to reach some kind of bliss in the future. IS and digital technologies are not only a tool that serves the consumer economy; there are tools that should gracefully help humans, and their environment including animals and nature to sustain and to enhance. The applications are numerous, we can cite smart healthcare, smart personal devices, smart home applications, drones, entertainment, cultural heritage, industry 4.0, and all fields covered by augmented, mixed, or, in general, extended reality (XR), and so on. We believe that researchers and practitioners who are interested in the design and engineering of IS should take into account the sentient requirements to design more suitable devices. Sentience is a powerful metaphor that deconstructs the way IS are designed and used nowadays.

In our short-term research, we will study how sentient requirements could be implemented to provide personalized usage of digital technologies based on machine learning techniques. In our further research, we intend to experiment sentient requirements with academics and practitioners working on topics around smart life and robotics.

References

1. Davis, A.M.: Software Requirements: Objects Functions and States. PTR Prentice Hall, Upper Saddle River (1993)
2. Kreps, D., Rowe, F., Muirhead, J.: Understanding digital events: process philosophy and causal autonomy. In: HICSS 2020, Maui, Hawaii, USA, pp. 1–10 (2020)
3. Wiegers, K.E., Beatty, J.: Software Requirements. Microsoft Press, USA (2013)
4. Asimov, I.: Runaround. Street & Smith Publisher, New-York (1942)
5. McCaffrey, A., Scarborough, E.A.: Powers that Be, p. 384. Del Rey Books, New York (1993)
6. McCaffrey, A., Scarborough, E.A.: Power Lines, p. 384. Del Rey Books, New York (1994).
7. McCaffrey, A., Scarborough, E.A.: Power Play, p. 292. Del Rey Books, New York (1995)
8. Feinberg, T.E., Mallatt, J.M.: The Ancient Origins of Consciousness: How the Brain Created Experience, p. 392. MIT Press, New York (2016)

9. Broom, D.M.: The evolution of morality. Appl. Anim. Behav. Sci. **100**(1–2), 20–28 (2006)
10. Broom, D.M.: Considering animals' feelings: Précis of Sentience and Animal Welfare. Anim. Sentence J. **5**(1), 1 (2016)
11. Husain, A.: The Sentient Machine: The Coming Age of Artificial Intelligence. Scribner, New York (2017)
12. Hultin, L.: On becoming a sociomaterial researcher: exploring epistemological practices grounded in a relational, performative ontology. Inf. Organ. **29**(2), 91–104 (2019)
13. Baxter, G., Sommerville, I.: Socio-technical systems: from design methods to systems engineering. Interact. Comput. **23**(1), 4–17 (2011)
14. Kaptelinin, V., Nardi, B.: Activity theory as a framework for human-technology interaction research. Mind Cult. Activity **25**(1), 3–5 (2018)
15. Cresswell, K., Worth, A., Sheikh, A.: Actor-network theory and its role in understanding the implementation of information technology developments in healthcare. BMC Med. Inform. Decis. Mak. **10**, 1–11 (2010)
16. Kreps, D.: Infomateriality. In: International Conference on Information Systems, San Francisco, CA, USA (2018)
17. Markus, M.L., Rowe, F.: Is IT changing the world? Conceptions of causality for information systems theorizing. MISQ **42**(4), 1255–1280 (2018)
18. Lee, E.: Observation and interaction. In: Martín-Vide, C., Okhotin, A., Shapira, D. (eds.) LATA 2019. LNCS, vol. 11417, pp. 31–42. Springer, Cham (2019). https://doi.org/10.1007/978-3-030-13435-8_2
19. Stephanidis, C.C., et al.: Seven HCI grand challenges. Int. J. Human-Comput. Interact. **35**(14), 1229–1269 (2019)
20. Cecchinato, M.E., et al.: Designing for digital wellbeing: a research & practice agenda. In: Extended Abstracts of the 2019 CHI Conference (2019)
21. Kagermann, H., Wahlster, W., Helbig, J.: Recommendations for implementing the strategic initiative Industrie 4.0: Securing the Future of German Manufacturing Industry. Final report of the Industrie 4.0 Working Group. Forschungsunion, Germany (2013).
22. Lu, Y.: Industry 4.0: a survey on technologies, applications and open research issues. J. Ind. Inf. Integr. 1–10 (2017)
23. Ozdemir, V., Hekim, N.: Birth of Industry 5.0: making sense of big data with artificial intelligence, "the internet of things" and next-generation technology policy. Omics: J. Integr. Biol. **22**(1) (2018)
24. Geoghegan, L., Lever, J., McGimpsey, I.: ICT for Social Welfare: A Toolkit for Managers, p. 208. Bristol University Press (2004)
25. Whitworth, B.: The Social Requirements of Technical Systems, Virtual Communities: Concepts, Methodologies, Tools and Applications. IGI Global (2011)
26. Misuraca, G.: The future of welfare systems: exploring the role of ICT-enabled social innovation. https://ec.europa.eu/social/BlobServlet?docId=15983&langId=en/. Accessed 25 Nov 2019
27. Misuraca, G., Gagliardi, D.: ICT-enabled social innovation (IESI): a Conceptual and Analytical Framework, TU Dortmund Publisher. https://www.socialinnovationatlas.net/fileadmin/PDF/einzeln/01_SI-Landscape_Global_Trends/01_13_ICT-Enabled-SI_Miscuraca-Gagliardi.pdf/. Accessed 26 Nov 2019
28. Jørgensen, R.F., Pedersen, A.M., Benedek, W., Nindler, R.: ICT and Human Rights, Frame Fostering Human Rights among European (External And Internal) Policies, Large-Scale Fp7 Collaborative Project. https://www.humanrights.dk/sites/humanrights.dk/files/media/dokumenter/udgivelser/research/frame/frame_-_ict_and_human_rights.pdf/. Accessed 26 Nov 2019

29. ICT and human rights: an ecosystem approach. Ericsson AB. https://www.ericsson.com/ass ets/local/about-ericsson/sustainability-and-corporate-responsibility/documents/download/ conducting-business-responsibly/human_rights0521_final_web.pdf/. Accessed 26 Nov 2019
30. Patel, S.: ICT and human development: a global perspective. Indian J. Appl. Res. **IV(X)** (2014)
31. Ratan, A.L., Bailur, S.: Welfare, agency and "ICT for Development". In: International Conference on Information and Communication Technologies and Development, Bangalore, pp. 1–12 (2007)
32. Kreps, D.: Against Nature: The Metaphysics of Information Systems. Routledge, London (2018)
33. Buchanan, R.A.: History of technology, Encyclopaedia Britannica Publisher. https://www.bri tannica.com/technology/history-of-technology/. Accessed 25 Nov 2019
34. DeGrazia, D.: Sentience and consciousness as bases for attributing interests and moral status: considering the evidence and speculating slightly beyond. In: Johnson, L.S.M., Fenton, A., Shriver, A. (eds.) Neuroethics and Nonhuman Animals. AN, pp. 17–31. Springer, Cham (2020). https://doi.org/10.1007/978-3-030-31011-0_2
35. Vassilakis, C., et al.: Stimulation of reflection and discussion in museum visits through the use of social media. Soc. Netw. Anal. Min. **7**(1), 1–12 (2017). https://doi.org/10.1007/s13 278-017-0460-3
36. Kuflik, T., Wecker, A., Lanir, J., Stock, O.: An integrative framework for extending the boundaries of the museum visit experience: linking the pre, during and post visit phases. Inf. Technol. Tour. **15**(1), 17–47 (2014). https://doi.org/10.1007/s40558-014-0018-4
37. Karaman, S., et al.: Personalized multimedia content delivery on an interactive table by passive observation of museum visitors. Multimed. Tools Appl. **75**(7), 3787–3811 (2014). https://doi. org/10.1007/s11042-014-2192-y
38. Antoniou, A., et al.: Capturing the visitor profile for a personalized mobile museum experience: an indirect approach. In: Workshop on Human Aspects in Adaptive and Personalized Interactive Environments (HAAPIE), Halifax, Canada (2016)
39. Falk, J.H., Dierking, L.D.: The Museum Experience Revisited. Routledge, London (2016)
40. Falk, J.H., Dierking, L.D.: Learning from Museums. Rowman & Littlefield, Lanham (2018)
41. Paliokas, I., Sylaiou, S.: The use of serious games in museum visits and exhibitions: a systematic mapping study. In: International Conference on Games and Virtual Worlds for Serious Applications (2016)
42. Damala, A., Stojanovic, N.: Tailoring the adaptive augmented reality (A 2 R) museum visit: identifying cultural heritage professionals' motivations and needs. In: International Symposium on Mixed and Augmented Reality-Arts, Media, and Humanities (ISMAR-AMH) (2012)
43. Doran, K., et al.: Creation of a game-based digital layer for increased museum engagement among digital natives. In: Second International Workshop on Games and Software Engineering: Realizing User Engagement with Game Engineering Techniques (GAS) (2012)
44. Maslow, A.H.: A theory of human motivation. Psychol. Rev. **50**(4), 370–96 (1943)
45. Drucker, J., Kim, D.: Intro to digital humanities: concepts, methods, and tutorials for students and instructors, UCLA center for digital humanities. http://dh101.humanities.ucla.edu/. Accessed 25 Nov 2019
46. Tegmark, M.: Life 3.0: Being Human in the Age of Artificial Intelligence, p. 384. Knopf Publishing Group, New York (2017)
47. Nash, D.: Health 3.0. Pharm. Therap. J. **33**(2), 69, 75 (2008)
48. Natkin, S., Yan, C.: Adaptive narration in multiplayer ubiquitous games. Int. J. Cogn. Inform. Nat. Intell. (2009)
49. Rushby, J. Sanchez, D.: Technology and Consciousness. SRI-CSL Technical Report (2018)

50. Serres, M.: L'Innovation et le Numérique. Programme Paris Nouveaux Mondes. Initiative d'excellence (Idex) du Pôle de recherche et d'enseignement supérieur «hautes études», Sorbonne (2013).
51. Serres, M.: Humain et révolution numérique. Poscast at Conference USI (2011)
52. Leidner, D. E.: What's in a contribution? J. Assoc. Inf. Syst. **21**(1), Article 2 (2020)
53. Bostrom, N.: A history of transhumanist thought. J. Evol. Technol. https://www.nickbostrom.com/papers/history.pdf. Accessed 25 Nov 2019

Emerging Computing Technologies and Trends for Business Process Management

Counterfactual Explanations for Predictive Business Process Monitoring

Tsung-Hao Huang$^{(\boxtimes)}$, Andreas Metzger, and Klaus Pohl$^{(\boxtimes)}$

paluno - The Ruhr Institute for Software Technology,
Gerlingstraße 16, 45127 Essen, Germany
{tsunghao.huang,andreas.metzger,klaus.pohl}@paluno.uni-due.de

Abstract. Predictive business process monitoring increasingly leverages sophisticated prediction models. Although sophisticated models achieve consistently higher prediction accuracy than simple models, one major drawback is their lack of interpretability, which limits their adoption in practice. We thus see growing interest in explainable predictive business process monitoring, which aims to increase the interpretability of prediction models. Existing solutions focus on giving factual explanations. While factual explanations can be helpful, humans typically do not ask why a particular prediction was made, but rather why it was made instead of another prediction, i.e., humans are interested in counterfactual explanations. While research in explainable AI produced several promising techniques to generate counterfactual explanations, directly applying them to predictive process monitoring may deliver unrealistic explanations, because they ignore the underlying process constraints. We propose LORELEY, a counterfactual explanation technique for predictive process monitoring, which extends LORE, a recent explainable AI technique. We impose control flow constraints to the explanation generation process to ensure realistic counterfactual explanations. Moreover, we extend LORE to enable explaining multi-class classification models. Experimental results using a real, public dataset indicate that LORELEY can approximate the prediction models with an average fidelity of 97.69% and generate realistic counterfactual explanations.

Keywords: Predictive process monitoring · Counterfactual explanation · explainable AI

1 Introduction

Predictive business process monitoring forecasts how an ongoing business process instance (aka. case) will unfold by utilizing prediction models trained from historical process data (typically in the form of event logs) [8,15]. One may, e.g., predict the remaining time [32], outcome of an ongoing case [29] or the next activity executed [27].

© Springer Nature Switzerland AG 2022
M. Themistocleous and M. Papadaki (Eds.): EMCIS 2021, LNBIP 437, pp. 399–413, 2022.
https://doi.org/10.1007/978-3-030-95947-0_28

Increasingly, sophisticated prediction models are employed for predictive process monitoring. These sophisticated models include tree ensembles [29,30] and deep artificial neural networks [6,19,28]. Compared to simple prediction models, such as decision trees or linear regression, these sophisticated prediction models achieve consistently better accuracy in various types of predictive process monitoring problems [27,28,32].

However, one drawback of these sophisticated prediction models is their lack of interpretability. Using black-box prediction models without being able to interpret their decisions has potential risks [11,17,22].

To facilitate the interpretability of black-box prediction models, research under the name of explainable AI is gaining interest [11,17]. Consequently, explainable AI techniques have started to be applied also in the context of predictive process monitoring, helping to deliver accurate predictions which can be interpreted. Existing explainable predictive process monitoring techniques give explanations for why a particular prediction was made. While factual explanations can be helpful, people typically do not ask why a particular prediction was made, but rather why it was made instead of another prediction [17,18]. Counterfactual explanations help people to reason on cause-effect or reason-action relationships between events [4,17].

We introduce LORELEY, a technique to generate counterfactual explanations for process predictions. LORELEY is based on the model-agnostic technique LORE introduced by Guidotti et al. [10]. LORE generates explanations using genetic algorithms. We demonstrate the feasibility of LORELEY using a real and public dataset, the BPIC2017 event log. Results indicate that we can reach a fidelity of the explanations of 97.69%, i.e., LORELEY can very accurately and faithfully approximate the local decision boundary of the black-box prediction model. In addition, LORELEY generates high-quality explanations, matching the domain knowledge about the process.

Section 2 gives a discussion of related work. Section 3 provides a detailed problem statement. Section 4 introduces the LORELEY technique. Section 5 describes the setup and Sect. 6 the results of our evaluation. Section 7 discusses current limitations.

2   Related Work

We structure related work on explainable predictive process monitoring along with two types of techniques: *model-specific* and *model-agnostic* [11,21].

Model-Specific Explanation Techniques. Model-specific techniques are tied to a specific type of prediction model. One direction of work uses attribute importance derived from neural networks as an explanation. Weinzierl et al. use layerwise relevance propagation to derive attribute importance from LSTMs [34]. Sindhgatta et al. use the attention mechanism of LSTMs to extract attribute importance [25]. Harl et al. apply gated graph neural networks and extract attribute importance from the softmax layer for each event in a process instance [12].

Another direction of work suggests designing transparent models, which are interpretable by users and at the same time provide accurate predictions. Breuker et al. propose combining process mining and grammatical inference [3]. Their solution consists of a predictor and an analyzer. While the predictor provides the predictions using a probabilistic finite automaton, the analyzer provides visualizations of the predictor. Verenich et al. propose an interpretable way to predict the remaining cycle time of a process instance by building on a mined process model [31]. For each activity in the process model, a regression model is trained to predict its execution time, and for each decision point, a classification model is trained to predict branching probabilities. Böhmer and Rinderle-Ma propose sequential prediction rules to predict the temporal behavior and the next activity of an ongoing case [2].

The above work demonstrates the feasibility and relevance of explainable predictive process monitoring but focuses on factual explanations only. Our technique complements this work by generating counterfactual explanations. In addition, our technique is model-agnostic and thus – compared to the above work – can generate explanations for any type of prediction model. One benefit is that the form of explanations remains the same even if the underlying prediction model changes, and thus model-agnostic techniques facilitate evaluating alternatives among different prediction models before their deployment [21].

Model-Agnostic Explanation Techniques. Model-agnostic techniques can generate explanations for any type of prediction model. One direction of work aims to compute attribute importance by querying the prediction model with randomly generated samples. Many of the techniques leverage the popular technique LIME introduced by Ribeiro et al. [22]. LIME generates a perturbation of samples around the instance to be explained. Then, using the generated samples and their corresponding black-box predictions, LIME trains a locally faithful model that can approximate the local decision boundary of a prediction model. Rehse et al. apply LIME to a smart production process, where an LSTM is trained to solve a binary classification problem [20]. Sindhgatta et al. apply LIME to interpret the results of eXtreme Gradient Boosting trees applied for outcome-oriented and time-oriented prediction problems [26]. Rizzi et al. use LIME to understand the weakness of random forest classifiers for outcome-oriented predictions [23]. They find the most frequent attributes that are identified as important by LIME when the classifier makes wrong predictions (false positives and false negatives). Then, they randomize these attributes to train the model again to neutralize the effects. Despite its popularity, one concern is that LIME's sampling process ignores possible correlations among the input attributes [18] e.g., process constraints in the case of predictive process monitoring [13]. Thus, unrealistic synthetic instances might be used to train a local interpretable model, thereby leading to unrealistic explanations. Another sampling-based approach is followed by Galanti et al., who use Shapley Values (from game theory) to provide explanations to the users [9]. They visualize explanations as an aggregated heatmap of attribute importance summarizing all the cases in the test set. Another direction of work involves Partial Dependence Plots, which are used by Mehdiyev and Fettke to derive the marginal effects between attributes and predictions from a neural network [16].

Again, the above work focuses on factual explanations only. By generating counterfactual explanations, our technique complements this work.

3 Motivation and Problem Statement

Our technique is based on the LORE technique introduced by Guidotti et al. [10]. LORE is a local model-agnostic technique that uses genetic algorithms to generate synthetic data for training decision trees that locally approximate the behavior of a black-box prediction model. LORE uses genetic algorithms to iteratively generate a set of neighboring input data instances, which are in close proximity to the instance to be explained.

Using decision trees as the interpretable models offer two main advantages: First, decision trees are intrinsically interpretable models. Second, explanations in the form of rules (factual and counterfactual) can be generated from a decision tree by following the split conditions from the root to the leaf node [10].

These rule-based explanations provide a step forward from simply generating a single counterfactual data instance as an explanation [33], as rules provide a higher level of abstraction of the explanation[1].

However, directly applying LORE to prediction models for predictive process monitoring faces two problems:

Problem 1. Perturbation-based techniques, like LIME and LORE, generate random samples without considering existing process constraints [13]. Typically, there are constraints in which order the activities in a business process may be executed imposed by the control flow. As an example, activity B may only follow after activity A was executed. As a result, such process-constraint-agnostic perturbation-based techniques face the risk of generating unrealistic instances that represent process traces that could never happen. In turn, the generated interpretable models deliver misleading or useless explanations; e.g., the counterfactual explanation may indicate that executing a specific activity B before A may lead to the desired outcome, while such execution order is not possible.

Problem 2. LORE is limited to binary classification. In BPM applications, however, one very often faces multi-class prediction problems. Examples include next activity predictions [28], where the classes are the number of activity types that may occur, and outcome-oriented predictions, where more than two process outcomes may be predicted [29].

4 Approach

To address the above problems, we introduce the LORELEY technique, which offers several enhancements from LORE, thereby delivering a specific technique for generating counterfactual explanations for predictive process monitoring. In the following, we first briefly explain LORE and then introduce LORELEY.

---

[1] If concrete counterfactual data instances are needed, these can be generated, e.g., by randomly sampling concrete values for the attributes that comply with the rules.

4.1   The LORE Technique as Starting Point

Given a black-box prediction model b, and an input instance to be explained x, LORE provides an explanation for the black-box prediction $b(x) = \hat{y}$. LORE consists of two main stages: (1) neighborhood generation, and (2) interpretable model induction and explanation generation [10].

Stage 1. In this stage, a group of data instances Z is generated using a genetic algorithm. The goal of the genetic algorithm is to a generate a balanced neighborhood $Z = Z_= \cup Z_{\neq}$, where instances $z \in Z_=$ satisfy $b(x) = b(z)$ and instances $z \in Z_{\neq}$ satisfy $b(x) \neq b(z)$. To initiate the first generation P_0 for the genetic algorithm, Guidotti et al. propose making N copies of x as the initial generation. Following the initialization step, generation P_0 goes through the evolutionary loop. The loop starts with selecting a group A from P_i with the highest fitness score according to the fitness function. Then, the crossover operation is applied to A with a probability of p_c. For the crossover operation, two-point crossovers are used to select two attributes from the parents randomly and swap the selected attributes to generate the children. The resulting instances and the ones without crossover are placed in a set B. Then, a proportion of B is mutated with probability p_m. The attributes are randomly replaced by the values generated by the empirical distribution derived from the data [10]. Finally, The unmutated and mutated instances become the next generation P_{i+1} and go through the next evolutionary loop. These evolutionary loops are repeated until the user-defined generation G is reached. The genetic generation process is run for both $Z_=$ and $Z_{\neq}$ to form the neighborhood Z of x.

Stage 2. After the neighborhood generation stage, an interpretable model c in the form of a decision tree classifier is induced to derive explanations for x, the instance to be explained. Once the decision tree classifier is trained, the factual rule for the instance to be explained x can be derived by following the split conditions of the tree from root to the leaf where x belongs. As for the counterfactual rule, it is defined as the rule derived from the path leading to a different outcome with the minimum number of violated split conditions (not satisfied by x) on the path. One advantage of using a decision tree as the interpretable model c is that both factual and counterfactual explanations in the form of decision rules are consistent with c by construct [10]. Also, one can tune how detailed and precise the explanation should be by setting the complexity of the tree (e.g. max depth, minimum impurity decrease, etc.).

4.2   Preliminaries

Based on [29, 32], we define key concepts related to predictive process monitoring:

- **Event:** An event e is a tuple $(a, c, t, (d_1, v_1), ..., (d_n, v_n))$, where a is the event class, c is the case id, t is the timestamp, $(d_1, v_1)....(d_n, v_n), n \geq 0$ are the name and value of the event attributes.
- **Trace:** A trace is a sequence $\sigma = \langle e_1, e_2, ..., e_m, \{(b_1, w_1), ..., (b_s, w_s)\}\rangle, \forall i, j \in \{1, ..., m\}, e_i.c = e_j.c$, which means all events in a trace carry the same case id. $\{(b_1, w_1), ..., (b_s, w_s)\}, s \geq 0$ are the name and value of the case attributes.

- **Event log:** An event log is a set of completed traces. $L = \{\sigma_1, \sigma_2, ..., \sigma_g\}$, where g is the number of traces in the event log.
- **Trace prefix:** $\sigma|_k = \langle e_1, e_2, ..., e_k \rangle$ is the prefix of length k (with $0 < k < m$) of trace σ; e.g., $\langle e_1, e_2, e_3, e_4 \rangle|_2 = \langle e_1, e_2 \rangle$.

4.3   The LORELEY Technique

LORELEY includes three extensions of LORE that jointly address the two problems as motivated in Sect. 3. A graphical overview of the artifacts and activities of LORELEY is shown in Fig. 1. The upper part of the figure depicts how individual predictions are generated. As this is not the focus of LORELEY, it is depicted by dashed lines. The lower part of the figure depicts how explanations are generated and highlights the extensions from LORE in gray. This consists of three main stages: Stage 0 is an additional stage compared with LORE and is responsible for finding similar prefixes for initialization. Stage 1 generates neighborhood instances using a modified form of the genetic algorithm from LORE. Stage 2 follows LORE to train a decision tree for deriving counterfactual explanations.

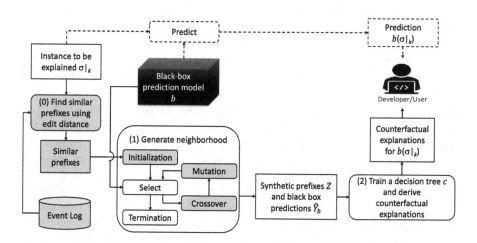

Fig. 1. Overview of LORELEY (extensions from LORE highlighted in grey)

Initialization with Similar Prefixes. To ensure that mutation possibilities for the control flow come from real traces, we modify the initialization step of LORE as follows. While LORE duplicates the instance to be explained to reach the target population size for the first generation, LORELEY selects similar prefixes in the event log by comparing the edit distance (see below) on the control flow sequences, thereby incorporating more variation in the first generation. This is key because the control flow variations in the first generation are used during the mutation step of the genetic algorithm.

The concept of edit distance was used by [7, 14] to group similar traces during trace bucketing as part of encoding the input data for the prediction model. The assumption behind such bucketing is that prefixes with similar control flow are more likely to have similar behaviors in the future. We follow this reasoning and adopt the Levenshtein edit distance to find prefixes that are similar to the instance to be explained (in terms of control flow).

Considering Control Flow Constraints During Crossover and Mutation. During the crossover and mutation steps, LORELEY considers additional constraints related to attributes that represent control flow. In many predictive process monitoring models, the control flow is represented as a combination of several one-hot encoded categorical attributes or as aggregations (e.g., frequency) of the control flow attributes [28,29]. Without further constraints, crossover and mutation would treat each of these encoded attributes independently without considering the potential constraints implied by the underlying process. As a result, crossover and mutation would lead to instances that represent unrealistic control flows.

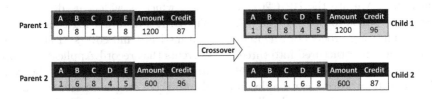

Fig. 2. Example for control-flow-aware crossover in LORELEY

To address this problem, we propose to treat the attributes representing the control flow as a single attribute in the crossover and mutation steps. Figure 2 shows an example. In the crossover step, the attributes representing the control flow (encoded as frequency vectors in the example) are combined and swapped with other bundles of control flow attributes from the other parent to produce children. In the mutation step, the possible control flow attributes are replaced by the values randomly drawn from the control flow attributes of the first generation. By doing so, we ensure that the control flows of the synthetic prefixes are similar to the instance to be explained $x = \sigma|_k$ (within the user-defined similarity threshold) and are realistic by construction.

Explaining Multi-class Predictions. We extend LORE from binary prediction to multi-class prediction: The neighborhood becomes $Z = \bigcup_{i \in I} Z_{b(z)=i}$, where I is the set of possible predicted outcomes and z are the instances with black-box prediction $b(z) = i, i \in I$. To generate each $Z_{b(z)=i}$, the fitness function of LORE is extended to

$$fitness_i^x(z) = \mathbb{1}_{b(z)=i} + (1 - d(x,z)) - \mathbb{1}_{x=z} \tag{1}$$

where d is a distance function, $\mathbb{1}$ is an indicator function $\mathbb{1}_{true} = 1, \mathbb{1}_{false} = 0$. The intuition behind is to find the instance z that is as close as possible to the instance to be explained x, yet not equivalent, while the corresponding black-box prediction $b(z)$ should be equal to a predefined outcome, i.e. $b(z) = i$ [10].

5   Experiment Setup

To facilitate transparency, reproducibility, and replicability, the code of our pro-
totypical implementation, the used dataset as well as our experimental results
are publicly available[2].

Research Questions. We aim to answer the following research questions:

> *RQ1. How faithful are the explanations generated by* LORELEY *to the underly-
> ing black-box prediction model?* We analyze how accurately the interpretable
> model c can approximate the local decision boundary of the black-box
> model b.
>
> *RQ2. How is the quality of* LORELEY*'s explanations?* We analyze how far the
> generated explanations match what would be expected considering domain
> knowledge and insights about the process.

Data Set. We use the BPIC2017 event log[3], which is widely used in predictive process monitoring research [29,32]. The BPIC2017 event log concerns the
loan application process of a Dutch financial institute and covers 31,509 cases.
The events are structured into three types: events that record **A**pplication state
changes, events that record **O**ffer state changes, and **W**orkflow events. The overall application process can be decomposed into three stages, receiving applications, negotiating offers, and validating documents respectively [24]. Each stage
has its corresponding working items (workflow events) and the application state
is updated according to the stages that the application has gone through. At
the end of the process, an application could be successful ($A\_Pending$)[4] or not
(A_Denied). Additionally, an application state $A\_Canceled$ is set if the customer
neither replied to the call nor sent the missing documents as requested.

Training the Black-Box Prediction Model. We train a black-box prediction
model b, for which we generate explanations. The model b predicts the process
outcome at different prediction points (i.e., prefix lengths). Following [24,29],
we consider the occurrence of the three events, A_Pending, A_Canceled, and
A_Denied as the respective process outcomes.

We train a two-layer LSTM model, a
widely used black-box prediction model
for predictive process monitoring (e.g.,
see [5,6,28]). We split the event log into
a training set (80% of the traces) and a
testing set (20% of the traces). As we are
not aiming at improving the prediction
accuracy of the black box with LORELEY,
we did not perform exhaustive hyper-
parameters/structures tuning.

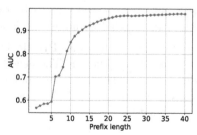

Fig. 3. AUC by different prefix lengths

---

[2] https://git.uni-due.de/adi645f/cf4bpm-artifacts.
[3] https://doi.org/10.4121/uuid:5f3067df-f10b-45da-b98b-86ae4c7a310b.
[4] The assessment is positive, the loan is final and the customer is paid.

Following Teinemaa et al. [29], we measure the prediction accuracy of the LSTM using the area under the ROC curve (AUC) metric. Figure 3 shows AUC across different prefix lengths. The overall AUC is 0.857, which is calculated as the weighted average of the obtained AUC for each prefix length up to 40.

Generating Explanations. As the prediction accuracy of the trained black-box model from above differs for the different prefix lengths, this allows us to evaluate LORELEY in different scenarios. In particular, we can evaluate our technique when the black-box model delivers low accurate predictions and also when predictions are getting more and more accurate. As such, we evaluate LORELEY for prefix lengths 5, 10, 20, 30, and 40. As shown in Fig. 3, there is a jump in AUC between prefix lengths 5 and 6. After that, accuracy gets constantly higher. For each prefix (in the test set) belonging to the aforementioned prefix lengths, we generate an interpretable model c using LORELEY. This means we generate a total of 23,426 interpretable models (see Table 1 below).

As parameters for the genetic algorithm, we use the suggested default values from [10] with some small adjustments. We use default values for crossover and mutation probabilities, $p_m = 0.7$ and $p_c = 0.2$, but increase the number of generations G from 10 to 15 due to the highly imbalanced dataset (Pending: 55%, Canceled: 33%, Denied: 12%). The fitness calculation (see Eq. 1) has to query the black-box model to retrieve the corresponding prediction for every generated prefix. To keep the experiment computationally tractable, we set a target population size of 600 for each of the three possible outcomes, resulting in 1800 prefixes Z to train and evaluate the explanation. The generated prefixes are split into 80% training set and 20% test set. The interpretable model c (i.e., a decision tree) is trained using the training set and evaluated on the test set.

6 Experiment Results

Results for RQ1 (Faithfulness of Explanations). We use the widely used fidelity metric from explainable AI [10,11,22] to evaluate the faithfulness of LORELEY. We evaluate how faithful the interpretable model c and thus the explanations generated from it are to the black-box model b.

Table 1 reports the evaluation results. The average results reported are calculated as weighted average considering the number of prefixes per prefix length in the test data. Overall, the interpretable model generated by LORELEY reaches 97.69% *Fidelity* for all the evaluated prefix lengths on average. *Fidelity* remains stable across all prefix lengths with a variance of less than 0.5%, suggesting that LORELEY can generate good explanations independent of the accuracy of the black-box model.

The results show that LORELEY can approximate the black-box model's local decision boundary accurately. This implies that the explanations generated by LORELEY can faithfully represent the knowledge learned by the black-box model within the local decision boundary for the instance to be explained.

Results for RQ2 (Quality of Explanations). To assess the quality of explanations generated by LORELEY, we look deeper into its explanations. First, we

Table 1. Metrics for different prefix lengths

Prefix length	Nbr. of prefixes	Fidelity
5	6,283	0.9754
10	6,277	0.9735
20	5,338	0.9849
30	3,454	0.9755
40	2,074	0.9730
Total: 23,426		**Avg.: 0.9769**

examine whether the most important attributes indicated by the explanations correspond to the domain knowledge. It is expected that the logic learned by the black box b would reflect a certain degree of domain knowledge as accuracy increases along the prefix length. Since involving the process owner of the BPIC2017 event log was not possible, we compare our results with the findings of the winners of the BPIC2017 challenge, for which this dataset was published.

Figure 4 shows the top five most frequent attributes for each input length examined. The most important attributes can be computed from the decision tree according to the decrease of impurity used to select split points. For every interpretable model c, the most important attributes are tracked. Then, the attributes are counted, grouped by the prefix length, and divided by the number of instances of each prefix length. The result shown in Fig. 4 gives a broader view regarding what the black box b has learned for different input lengths. As the figure shows, the most important attribute for prefix lengths 20, 30, and 40 is $CreditScore$. This corresponds to the findings of the professional group winners [1], where they found $CreditScore$ is among the most important attributes as a result of the predictive analysis. The other frequent attribute is $ApplicationType\_Limit\ raise$ and it is the second most frequent important attribute for prefix length 30 and 40. This corresponds to the findings of the academic group winners [24], who found that the institute approved a significantly higher fraction of applications of the type "limit raise" (73.37%) than "new credit" (52.61%). It is therefore another reasonable predictor used by the black box b. Figure 4 also shows that the $LoanGoal$ attributes are used by the black-box model quite often to predict the outcome (especially for prefix lengths 5 and 10) although $Loan$-$Goal$ has little influence on the outcome of the case according to the analysis [24]. However, they could be the most frequent decisive attributes available for the black box considering prefixes 5 and 10 are still quite early in the process.

Complementing this high-level assessment of explanation quality, we analyze the explanations generated by LORELEY for a particular input data of prefix length 30. The instance to be explained has the following event attributes for $O\_Create\ Offer$ { $First\ Withdrawal\ Amount = 0$, $NumberOfTerms = 126$, $Monthly$-$Cost = 250$, $CreditScore = 0$, $OfferedAmount = 25000$, $Selected = $ true, $accepted = $ false}, and it has the following case attributes { $case\_RequestedAmount = 25000$, $case\_LoanGoal = Existing\ loan\ take\ over$, $case\_ApplicationType = new$

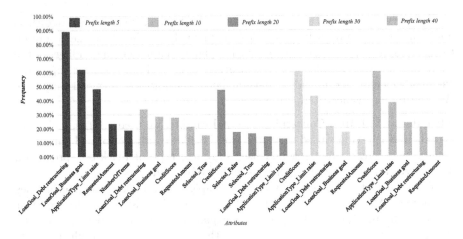

Fig. 4. Top five frequent important attribute for different input length

credit}. The corresponding black-box prediction is *A_Denied*. By observing the control flow of the prefix, one can find that the prefix is at the later stage of the application process. The application process has gone through application creation and assessment. An offer is created and the customer has been contacted a few times to send incomplete files.

For this instance to be explained, LORELEY generates the interpretable model *c* shown in Fig. 5. The *Fidelity* of *c* is 0.9343.

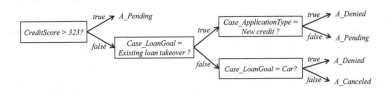

Fig. 5. An example of a generated interpretable model *c*

The factual rule for the instance to be explained is:

$$\{ CreditScore \leq 323,\ Case\_LoanGoal = Existing\ loan\ takeover,$$
$$Case\_ApplicationType = New\ credit\} \rightarrow A\_Denied$$

The following are examples of two counterfactual rules (with changes from the factual rule highlighted in grey):

$$\{ CreditScore > 323\} \rightarrow A\_Pending$$

$$\{ CreditScore \leq 323,\ Case\_LoanGoal = Existing\ loan\ takeover,$$
$$Case\_ApplicationType\ != New\ credit\} \rightarrow A\_Pending$$

These two counterfactual rules provide the least changes (split conditions not fulfilled by the data instance to be explained) one has to make to obtain the desired outcome. Again, the derived explanations match the findings of the BPIC2017 academic winner [24]: Applications of type "limit raise" or applicants with higher credit scores indeed have higher acceptance rates (recall that state *A_Pending* means accepted; see above).

Threats to Validity. Concerning external validity, we used a large, real event log (BPIC2017) widely used in related work. Still, we only performed our experiments for a single event log and used only one type of black-box prediction model, which thus limits the generalizability of our findings.

With respect to internal validity, sample-based explanation techniques (including LIME, LORE, and LORELEY) face potential instability due to their stochastic nature. That is, the generated explanations can be expected not to be the same when applying the techniques to the same input. As a result, the metrics reported above might be different. Examining the stability of the technique requires significant additional compute resources and time.

7   Limitations

Similarity Threshold Depends on the Encoding of Prefixes. Since the fitness calculation in Eq. 1, specifically the distance calculation $d(x, z)$, needs the attribute vectors to be the same length, the similarity threshold depends on how the prefix is encoded. For example, when using index-based encoding [29], setting the similarity threshold to 0 may be necessary because the fitness function cannot compute the distance between two prefixes with different lengths. This dependency is due to the distance calculation in the fitness function. A way to avoid this is to map the prefix vectors of different lengths to the same dimensions for fitness calculation by using dimensionality reduction techniques.

Finding Influential Predictors Based on Control Flow. Another limitation of LORELEY is that it may not be able to find influential predictors that are based on control flow. We use edit distance to identify prefixes that have similar control flow. However, two prefixes with very large edit distance could be very "similar" based on a process model. Take BPIC2017 as an example, we might want to explain an instance with only one offer event in the prefix. While [24] shows that the number of offers is one of the decisive factors to the outcome of the process, LORELEY is unlikely to include prefixes with more than one offer due to the way it calculates similar prefixes. A possible extension of LORELEY could be to use the process model to identify similar prefixes instead of using the edit distance.

8   Conclusion and Outlook

This paper introduced LORELEY, a counterfactual explanation technique for process predictions. LORELEY extends LORE [10] to ensure the explanations conform to the underlying process constraints. Experimental results indicate that LORE-LEY is able to approximate the prediction models with high fidelity and generate realistic counterfactual explanations.

As future work, we plan to address the current limitations of the technique. In addition, we will evaluate LORELEY with further benchmark datasets and different black-box prediction models, as well as analyze the stability of the technique by comparing the difference of explanations generated by different runs for the same input.

Acknowledgments. We thank Felix Feit, Tristan Kley, and Xhulja Shahini for comments on earlier drafts. Research leading to these results received funding from the European Union's Horizon 2020 R&I programme under grant no. 871493 (DataPorts).

References

1. Blevi, L., Delporte, L., Robbrecht, J.: Process mining on the loan application process of a Dutch financial institute. BPI Challenge (2017)
2. Böhmer, K., Rinderle-Ma, S.: LoGo: combining local and global techniques for predictive business process monitoring. In: Dustdar, S., Yu, E., Salinesi, C., Rieu, D., Pant, V. (eds.) CAiSE 2020. LNCS, vol. 12127, pp. 283–298. Springer, Cham (2020). https://doi.org/10.1007/978-3-030-49435-3_18
3. Breuker, D., Matzner, M., Delfmann, P., Becker, J.: Comprehensible predictive models for business processes. MIS Q. **40**(4), 1009–1034 (2016)
4. Byrne, R.M.J.: Counterfactuals in explainable artificial intelligence (XAI): evidence from human reasoning. In: The Twenty-Eighth International Joint Conference on Artificial Intelligence, IJCAI 2019. ijcai.org (2019)
5. Camargo, M., Dumas, M., González-Rojas, O.: Learning accurate LSTM models of business processes. In: Hildebrandt, T., van Dongen, B.F., Röglinger, M., Mendling, J. (eds.) BPM 2019. LNCS, vol. 11675, pp. 286–302. Springer, Cham (2019). https://doi.org/10.1007/978-3-030-26619-6_19
6. Evermann, J., Rehse, J., Fettke, P.: Predicting process behaviour using deep learning. Decis. Support Syst. **100**, 129–140 (2017)
7. Francescomarino, C.D., Dumas, M., Maggi, F.M., Teinemaa, I.: Clustering-based predictive process monitoring. IEEE Trans. Serv. Comput. **12**(6), 896–909 (2019)
8. Di Francescomarino, C., Ghidini, C., Maggi, F.M., Milani, F.: Predictive process monitoring methods: which one suits me best? In: Weske, M., Montali, M., Weber, I., vom Brocke, J. (eds.) BPM 2018. LNCS, vol. 11080, pp. 462–479. Springer, Cham (2018). https://doi.org/10.1007/978-3-319-98648-7_27
9. Galanti, R., Coma-Puig, B., de Leoni, M., Carmona, J., Navarin, N.: Explainable predictive process monitoring. In: ICPM 2020. IEEE (2020)
10. Guidotti, R., Monreale, A., Giannotti, F., Pedreschi, D., Ruggieri, S., Turini, F.: Factual and counterfactual explanations for black box decision making. IEEE Intell. Syst. **34**(6), 14–23 (2019)
11. Guidotti, R., Monreale, A., Ruggieri, S., Turini, F., Giannotti, F., Pedreschi, D.: A survey of methods for explaining black box models. ACM Comput. Surv. **51**(5), 93:1–93:42 (2019)
12. Harl, M., Weinzierl, S., Stierle, M., Matzner, M.: Explainable predictive business process monitoring using gated graph neural networks. J. Decis. Syst., 1–16 (2020)

13. Jan, S.T.K., Ishakian, V., Muthusamy, V.: AI trust in business processes: the need for process-aware explanations. In: Conference on Artificial Intelligence, AAAI 2020, pp. 13403–13404. AAAI Press (2020)
14. Maggi, F.M., Di Francescomarino, C., Dumas, M., Ghidini, C.: Predictive monitoring of business processes. In: Jarke, M., et al. (eds.) CAiSE 2014. LNCS, vol. 8484, pp. 457–472. Springer, Cham (2014). https://doi.org/10.1007/978-3-319-07881-6_31
15. Márquez-Chamorro, A.E., Resinas, M., Ruiz-Cortés, A.: Predictive monitoring of business processes: a survey. IEEE Trans. Serv. Comput. **11**(6), 962–977 (2018)
16. Mehdiyev, N., Fettke, P.: Prescriptive process analytics with deep learning and explainable artificial intelligence. In: 28th European Conference on Information Systems, ECIS 2020 (2020)
17. Miller, T.: Explanation in artificial intelligence: insights from the social sciences. Artif. Intell. **267**, 1–38 (2019)
18. Molnar, C.: Interpretable Machine Learning. Online (2019)
19. Park, G., Song, M.: Predicting performances in business processes using deep neural networks. Decis. Support Syst. **129** (2020)
20. Rehse, J., Mehdiyev, N., Fettke, P.: Towards explainable process predictions for industry 4.0 in the dfki-smart-lego-factory. Künstliche Intell. **33**(2), 181–187 (2019)
21. Ribeiro, M.T., Singh, S., Guestrin, C.: Model-agnostic interpretability of machine learning. In: ICML Workshop on Human Interpretability in Machine Learning (WHI) (2016)
22. Ribeiro, M.T., Singh, S., Guestrin, C.: Why should i trust you?: explaining the predictions of any classifier. In: The 22nd ACM SIGKDD International Conference on Knowledge Discovery and Data Mining. ACM (2016)
23. Rizzi, W., Di Francescomarino, C., Maggi, F.M.: Explainability in predictive process monitoring: when understanding helps improving. In: Fahland, D., Ghidini, C., Becker, J., Dumas, M. (eds.) BPM 2020. LNBIP, vol. 392, pp. 141–158. Springer, Cham (2020). https://doi.org/10.1007/978-3-030-58638-6_9
24. Rodrigues, A., et al.: Stairway to value: mining a loan application process. BPI Challenge (2017)
25. Sindhgatta, R., Moreira, C., Ouyang, C., Barros, A.: Exploring interpretable predictive models for business processes. In: Fahland, D., Ghidini, C., Becker, J., Dumas, M. (eds.) BPM 2020. LNCS, vol. 12168, pp. 257–272. Springer, Cham (2020). https://doi.org/10.1007/978-3-030-58666-9_15
26. Sindhgatta, R., Ouyang, C., Moreira, C.: Exploring interpretability for predictive process analytics. In: Kafeza, E., Benatallah, B., Martinelli, F., Hacid, H., Bouguettaya, A., Motahari, H. (eds.) ICSOC 2020. LNCS, vol. 12571, pp. 439–447. Springer, Cham (2020). https://doi.org/10.1007/978-3-030-65310-1_31
27. Tax, N., Teinemaa, I., van Zelst, S.J.: An interdisciplinary comparison of sequence modeling methods for next-element prediction. Softw. Syst. Model. **19**(6), 1345–1365 (2020). https://doi.org/10.1007/s10270-020-00789-3
28. Tax, N., Verenich, I., La Rosa, M., Dumas, M.: Predictive business process monitoring with LSTM neural networks. In: Dubois, E., Pohl, K. (eds.) CAiSE 2017. LNCS, vol. 10253, pp. 477–492. Springer, Cham (2017). https://doi.org/10.1007/978-3-319-59536-8_30
29. Teinemaa, I., Dumas, M., Rosa, M.L., Maggi, F.M.: Outcome-oriented predictive process monitoring: review and benchmark. ACM Trans. Knowl. Discov. Data **13**(2), 17:1–17:57 (2019)

30. Verenich, I., Dumas, M., La Rosa, M., Maggi, F.M., Di Francescomarino, C.: Complex symbolic sequence clustering and multiple classifiers for predictive process monitoring. In: Reichert, M., Reijers, H.A. (eds.) BPM 2015. LNBIP, vol. 256, pp. 218–229. Springer, Cham (2016). https://doi.org/10.1007/978-3-319-42887-1_18

31. Verenich, I., Dumas, M., La Rosa, M., Nguyen, H.: Predicting process performance: a white-box approach based on process models. J. Softw. Evol. Process **31**(6) (2019)

32. Verenich, I., Dumas, M., Rosa, M.L., Maggi, F.M., Teinemaa, I.: Survey and cross-benchmark comparison of remaining time prediction methods in business process monitoring. ACM Trans. Intell. Syst. Technol. **10**(4), 34:1–34:34 (2019)

33. Wachter, S., Mittelstadt, B., Russell, C.: Counterfactual explanations without opening the black box: automated decisions and the GDPR. Harv. JL & Tech. **31**, 841 (2017)

34. Weinzierl, S., Zilker, S., Brunk, J., Revoredo, K., Matzner, M., Becker, J.: XNAP: making LSTM-based next activity predictions explainable by using LRP. In: Del Río Ortega, A., Leopold, H., Santoro, F.M. (eds.) BPM 2020. LNBIP, vol. 397, pp. 129–141. Springer, Cham (2020). https://doi.org/10.1007/978-3-030-66498-5_10

Factors that Affects the Use of AI Agents in Adaptive Learning: A Sociomaterial and Mcdonaldization Approach in the Higher Education Sector

Nahil Kazoun[1]([✉]), Angelika Kokkinaki[2], and Charbel Chedrawi[2,3]

[1] PhD Programme, School of Business, University of Nicosia, Nicosia, Cyprus
kazoun.n@live.unic.ac.cy
[2] School of Business, University of Nicosia, Nicosia, Cyprus
{kokkinaki.a,chedrawi.c}@unic.ac.cy
[3] Faculty of Business and Management, Saint Joseph University, Beirut, Lebanon
charbel.chedrawi@usj.edu.lb

Abstract. In the Higher Education Sector (HES), we see increasingly Artificial Intelligent (AI) agents in the form of chatbots or interactive virtual agents indistinguishable from people and a unique example of human-machine interaction using natural language processing. They are becoming one of the main technological tools to ensure accreditation and e-learning, while providing better adaptive learning. This conceptual paper aims to examine the factors that affect the intention to use AI agents/chatbots for adaptive learning in HEI from a sociomateriality perspective taking into consideration the mcdonaldization effect. An extended UTAUT (Unified Theory of Acceptance and Use of Technology) model is proposed to be evaluated in the HES context.

Keywords: Higher education sector · Higher education institution · AI agents · Chatbots · Sociomateriality · Macdonaldization · UTAUT

1 Introduction

The higher education sector (HES) has undergone numerous changes and modifications, as a result of internationalization, students' mobility [1], quality assurance processes, accreditation frameworks, and lately the COVID19 pandemic. The mode of delivery in HES has gradually shifted from conventional face-to-face settings, to distance learning, e-learning, and hybrid [2].

Henceforth, an urgent need to innovate and to adopt new teaching and evaluation approaches has emerged, rendering Higher Educational Institutions (HEI) more adaptive to the new external environment and to students and teachers needs for learning and teaching [3]. Indeed, ensuring adaptive learning while seeking accreditation, provided HEI many opportunities for innovations and for acceleration in novelty and invention [4]. From this perspective, we are witnessing the increased pace of technological transformation within HEI, particularly the emerging coupling of e-learning technologies with

© Springer Nature Switzerland AG 2022
M. Themistocleous and M. Papadaki (Eds.): EMCIS 2021, LNBIP 437, pp. 414–426, 2022.
https://doi.org/10.1007/978-3-030-95947-0_29

Artificial Intelligence (AI) and more specifically AI agents or Chatbots. Quite often, chatbots are not distinguished from human discussants thanks to advances in AI that can simulate a conversation or imitate a natural language discussion through messaging applications, websites, mobile apps, and the telephone [5].

In fact, Chatbots, or interactive virtual agents (also known as interactive agents, digital assistants, artificial conversation entities, and smart bots) that participate in conversational dialogues with humans, are a unique example of human-machine interaction using natural language processing. They are becoming one of the main technological tools to ensure accreditation and e-learning, while supporting HEI in providing better adaptive learning [6].

However, two major concerns are emerging with regards to the above: the first one is the social impact of such technologies on various HEI stakeholders (students, professors, and others). The social impact will be discussed using the Sociomateriality theory that tries to comprehend the interactions between social and material actors [7], and to explain the entanglement of human and non-human agents [8]. In our study AI agents/chatbots represent the material part, and their use and impact on HEI stakeholders represent the social part. The second concern addresses the institutional mcdonaldization and rationalization trap caused by the innovation and accreditation trends in HEI. In fact, for [9], mcdonaldization is the processes of becoming hyper-rationalized where each activity is being broken down into its component parts, taking into consideration the four McDonaldization's concepts: efficiency, calculability, predictability, and improved control [10]. Mcdonaldization in HEI is associated with rationalization of teaching and research to serve straightforward ends; as a result, universities are doing the same processes, using common technological tools for accreditation and innovation to achieve mutual objectives for adaptive learning [9]. For [11], academic degrees lost their relationship to knowledge and education due to the McDonaldization of education, which solely pushed the credentials needed to attain a certain aim (accreditation).

In such new normal context, and with the adoption of AI agents/chatbots in HES, we propose to study the factors that affect the intention to use AI agents/chatbots for adaptive learning in HEI from a sociomateriality perspective taking into consideration the mcdonaldization effect.

For this purpose, we will start with a brief contextual and theoretical backgrounds. We will first address an overview about AI, AI agents/chatbots, and the use of these chatbots in HEI. Then, we shall briefly present a summary review about our core theories: the adaptive e-learning, the Mcdonalidzation, and the sociomateriality. Then we shall present our proposed model. Finally, we shall conclude our work with our contributions and further research.

2   Contextual Background: HEI and AI Agents/Chatbots

Despite, or perhaps because of the tremendous rise of academic research in relation to intelligent automation (AI and AI agents, etc.), we still don't have a complete understanding of the implications of its use and impact on our lives [12]. Researchers, consumers, and architects of information systems have long been captivated by the idea of interacting with a computer as effortlessly as one would with another human [13]. In fact, there is a lack of literature on the use of AI agents/chatbots and their impact especially in the HES. Besides, there is yet a dearth of study on adaptive learning in the HES; as for the mcdonaldization and sociomateriality theories, they are covered by previous articles [14, 15], but their link to AI agents/chatbots specifically in HES is rare to find. Finally, researches covering the use AI agents/chatbots for adaptive learning in HES, from a mcdonaldization, and sociomteriality perspectives, do not exist at all, implying that theory-driven research on the factors that affect the usage of these technologies is still having a lack [12].

We propose to fill these gaps through our article that examines theoretically the factors that affect the use of AI agents/chatbots in HEI for adaptive learning, based on the adaptive e-learning, the mcdonaldization, and the sociomateriality theories.

2.1 Artificial Intelligence and AI Agents/Chatbots

The nature of technologies that are recognized as Artificial Intelligence (AI) has changed over time [16]. For [17], AI is the ability to independently comprehend and learn from external data in order to attain particular results through flexible adaptation. It is also the ability of computers to execute human-like cognitive tasks, such as manipulating and moving objects, sensing, perceiving, problem solving, decision-making, and invention [18]. The emergence of AI is profoundly affecting our lives, through inventing intelligent machines, developing innovative services, and improving efficiency across nearly every aspect of life [19].

The rise of AI-powered digital transformation has become an important driver of change in various industries [20]. For instance, several AI tools such as evolutionary algorithms, fuzzy sets, artificial neural networks, and chatbots are being employed in a variety of organizational functions [21]. With this regards, AI agents/Chatbots or Virtual Assistants are the new tools that have hit the market, designed to simplify the interaction between humans and computers. A chatbot is an AI software that can simulate a conversation (or a chat) with a user or imitate a natural language discussion (or chat) through messaging applications, websites, and mobile apps or through the telephone [5].

Conceptually, the core technical capacity of AI chatbots focuses on virtual conversational agents or avatars that emphasize on synthesizing multimodal signals such as images, videos, and sounds to mimic human-to-human conversation. The widespread use of "digital assistants", the growth of bots on chat platforms, and the integration of voice control into a wide range of consumer products all demonstrate this (Amazon's Alexa, Apple's Siri, Microsoft's Cortana, …) [22].

Natural language processing (NLP) techniques have advanced rapidly in recent years, resulting in AI agents/chatbots that facilitate natural human-computer conversation and frameworks that allow these techniques to be easily applied. In addition, Intelligent Tutoring Systems (ITS) have enormous potential, especially in large-scale distance teaching institutions, which run modules with thousands of students, where human one-to-one tutoring is impossible [23].

With this regard, it is interesting to examine if the advancements in AI have a positive impact on HEI; Indeed, AI agents/chatbots that rely on Deep Learning (DL) to assist provision of information are being implemented in the HES. These chatbots are accessible through different digital hubs: websites, mobile and messaging applications,

SMS, etc. In fact, the COVID-19 pandemic triggered many online applications based on cloud computing AI, blockchain, big data, and deep learning (DL) [24]. But what kind of impact these particular features have on the users' intentions? And what are the factors that affect the use of these technologies? These are some of the questions that we study in the sequel.

2.2 Higher Education and the Use of AI Agents/Chatbots

AI applications in education have been increasing in number and have received a lot of attention recently [23]. In fact, in order to adapt to the new norm of teaching and learning, the COVID19 pandemic serves as an example for the digital transformations that were initiated due to the need for social distancing and they are still employed nearing post pandemic. Moreover, the rise in the use of AI agents/chatbots, and other technological tools for online education (language apps, interactive tutoring, video conferencing platforms, online learning tools…) is impressive [25] in view of the overall demand for online education that is expected to reach US $350 billion by 2025 [26].

In the context of HEI, the educational use of chatbots is an emerging area of experimentation [22]. AI agents/chatbots can quiz existing knowledge, trigger higher student engagement with a learning task or support higher-order cognitive activities [27]. When used within a large group of students, AI agents/chatbots can solve the problem of individual student support and contribute to personalized learning [28]. AI agents/chatbots also facilitate administrative duties for student advising and support while offering the framework of the learning process, picking and arranging content to match the students' needs and speed, and aiding in learning motivation and functioning as a learning companion through dialogue and collaboration [29].

Initiation, response, and feedback (IRF) are the aspects that make up the interaction between the AI agents/chatbots and the student according to [30]. These AI agents/chatbots also allow students to connect with one another; such interaction includes a discussion component (D), resulting in IDRF [31]. In sum, chatbots in education can help with queries, administrative and management duties, student mentoring, incentive, student learning assessments, simulations, training specific skills and abilities, and giving reflection and metacognitive tactics, among other things [28].

Moreover, several studies show that chatbots can support the teaching–learning process across a range of subjects with various degrees of success [22]. Indeed, AI in HEI can promote collaborative learning by supporting adaptive group formation based on learner models, by facilitating online group interaction or by summarizing discussions that can be used by a human tutor to guide students towards the aims and objectives of a course [23], and where Virtual agents can act as teachers, facilitators or students' peers. In reality, educational leaders were actively engaged in AI adoption discussions and began to develop organizational structures to assure the successful adoption and application of AI [32].

The following table shows a comparison between the "Traditional Learning System" predominantly teacher-centered and the new AI Bot System where the focus is on both student and tutor [33] (Table 1):

Table 1. Traditional learning system (teacher centered) vs. AI bot system [33].

Teacher Centred Learning/ Traditional System	AI-Bot System
Focus is on the instructor	The centre focus is on both the student and tutor
System is built on what the instructor knows about language forms and structures	The system focuses on how the student will use the language
Depends on passive learning	Incorporates both active and passive learning styles
Students rely on the teacher	There is interdependence between the teacher and the student
The tutor is responsible for the student's excellence	The student is solely responsible for his/her excellence
Online platforms are just repository areas	Online platforms accommodate interaction and experimentation
The learning environment is centred on the curriculum	The learning environment is centred on the student's profile, learning experiences and needs
The student's behaviour is not a factor in the formulation of the pedagogical model	The student's behaviour is modulated to tailor the pedagogical model to the learner's model
The learning environment is not adaptive	There is implementation of adaptive learning environments

3 Theoretical Background

3.1 Adaptive E-Learning

E-learning or online education is changing the way we approach teaching and learning, where modifications in the way of delivering educations have been fast and transformational [34]. According to [35], the market of e-learning all over the world will be over US $ 243 billion in 2022.

In fact, the adaptive e-learning theory is based on individualized education in order to manage education in an individualized fashion. Adaptive learning is based on features and information about the student's learning style to cover primarily sensory preferences of perceptions (verbal, visual, etc.) and social aspects of the motivation to study [36]. Other factors include affective aspects of the motivation to study, learning tactics, including orderliness, the way of processing information, the approach to study, the degree of self-regulation, the ability to self-manage the study process, the success rate, and other factors [36]. Teachers and students have had to rapidly adapt to an environment where traditional face-to-face classroom environments are significantly more challenging [37].

Adaptive e-learning in higher education is based on personalized learning paths derived from algorithms, course analytics, assessment data, and student feedback, and can be used to give remediation as well as assist learners in achieving topic mastery [38]. It allows pupils to use existing knowledge and learn new material faster. It is an innovative technique of improving student engagement, motivation, and performance by personalizing the student experience in response to specific student reactions [39]. In an online environment, what was once very easy to accomplish face to face (F2F) like practical demonstrations, becomes quite challenging requiring subject matter experts to become adept at the use of rapidly evolving learning technologies that are not commonly used to teach hands-on activities in their field [40].

Because of the constant changes in teaching and learning of the same curriculum that are conducted in a different manner to suit the needs of each student, HEI, professors, doctors, educators, and students have all had to adapt to it, forming an adaptive e-learning phase [36]. Hence, the future of e-learning must be built on principles of openness and equality with an education in digital competence [22].

Indeed, since the outbreak of the COVID19 pandemic and the astonishing transition to online education, the usage of innovative tools like AI agents/chatbots has become critical for e-learning adaptation and survival in the new normal. As a result, there has been a growing awareness of the potential benefits of adaptability in e-Learning. This is mostly due to the awareness that traditional methodologies cannot reach the objective of personalized learning, especially on a "massive" scale [41].

The context of HES is witnessing continuous changes and innovations. For instance, the COVID19 pandemic led to the shift to e-learning method, where technology was the major solution to adapt to these changes. New tools, and pool of resources such as Microsoft teams, Zoom, Google Hangout, AI agents/chatbots were taken into consideration in universities to ensure innovative methods for an adaptive learning to the changes that are happening in this sector, initiating then innovation never seen before within HEI.

Indeed, the fact of seeking accreditation open doors for innovation through technological instrumentals or tools such as the use of AI agents/chatbots at universities, and make us wonder about its impact on the members of the social system in HEI (mainly educators and students).

3.2 Mcdonaldization Theory

McDonaldization is the tendency for the processes to become hyper-rationalized, with each activity being broken down into its component parts; it's entirely based on Max Weber's idea of academic legitimacy [9].

[10] analyzes the social processes he characterizes in four important features as 'McDonaldization': efficiency, calculability, predictability, and improved control through the replacement of human labor with technology, using a neo-weberian perspective. He emphasized that McDonaldization is an irreversible process that pervades most of the modern world, including HEI, to varied degrees. For [9], if we relate these four concepts to the HES, we can note that 'Efficiency' states to reorganizing the university to achieve market-defined 'value' goals, both financially and in terms of government funding, and to the student 'stakeholder', and the competent 'production line' of graduates to meet the continuous changes of needs, or the 'challenges' of globalization and guarantee 'knowledge transfer'. The 'predictability' of the 'McDonaldization' route in higher education, where the rationalization of teaching and research to suit straightforwardly economic purposes may be seen. We may see this process of instrumental planning and rationalization in the rising loss of academic autonomy and bureaucratic "performance assessment" when we apply the fourth part of Ritzer's thesis to higher education critically.

[42, p. 233], emphasized how the McDonaldization of universities emerges through adoption of replicated technology to manage processes and to reduce ambiguity. Indeed, as universities continue to face changes, all HEI attempt to re-skill educators and students in order to prepare them to adapt to new learning and teaching methods. In terms of virtual engagement and creativity, the latest technological tools and practices have the potential to benefit both staff and students, as well as the whole university, which lead all HEIs' to be part of the mcdonaldization and rationalization [43].

Thus, the loss of human control in some places and the replacement of human labor with technology (AI agents in our case), demonstrate that a macdonaldization effect is on the rise within the HES. Max Weber link the manifestation of such mcdonaldization to bureaucratic reasoning and thinking within organizations and the structure they impose on human interaction that leads to an increasingly rational thinking [9].

3.3 Sociomateriality Theory

In organizational contexts, sociomateriality tries to comprehend and explain the inter-actions between social and material actors [7]. The social is the result of interactions between people and nonhumans that shape and are shaped by each other [44]. The Material refers to everything in our life, according to [45], whether natural or technological, organic or inorganic. The role of non-humans as an active part of the social debate has been on the agenda of many scholars [15, 45, 46] who seek to understand social phenomena as the product of interaction between humans and non-humans.

Beyond understanding the entanglement of human and non-human agents, ways they might form organizations, their practices, and changes, sociomateriality is also a valuable alternative for (re)thinking organizational phenomena [8]. This theory is the outcome of investigating the social and material components of technology and organization while assessing how human bodies, spatial arrangements, physical items, and technologies intertwine with language, interaction, and practices [46]. It provides a fresh approach to studying technology in the workplace, as it allows researchers to look at both the social and the material aspects at the same time [47].

Alignment and misalignment of technology's material properties and social inter-actions are discussed by [46]. He emphasized the importance of comprehending how technology is deployed in enterprises while not overlooking the human component. This theory tries to illuminate the social, which is represented by the various stakeholders within HEI, and its infrastructure as a sociomaterial assemblage with academic learn-ing, teaching, institutional goals, architectural intent, technology, personnel, students, and pedagogic outcomes, constructed by all actors in an active symbiosis of becoming [48]. Indeed, the Sociomateriality theory emphasizes the use of material change to foster collaborative and inclusive academic environments, where staff and students can learn, belong, and grow as members of a scholarly community, with a focus on how individuals learn in organizations [49].

[15] emphasizes the significance of comprehending how people and technology interact in daily life. [47] raise concerns about the separation of the technical from the social by debating the concept of constitutive entanglement between the social and the material, which refers to the interaction of human and technological elements in organizations.

Within the context of e-Learning, a sociomaterial perspective gives the relation between HEI's stakeholders, especially educators and students (the social), and the use of technology, particularly AI agents (the material). It also outlines the interaction between teachers and learners and these technological tools, a new dimension through balancing any modification to preexisting methods and models to ensure a successful adaptive learning within the continuous changes happening in the HES. It is interesting to examine what are the factors that affect such use.

4   Factors that Affects the Use of AI Agents/Chatbots for Adaptive Learning in HES: The Proposed Research Model

Understanding the reasons for rejecting or adopting emerging technologies has become critical. As a result, technology acceptance concepts, theories, and models expect to bring the idea of how individuals may accept, understand, and use the latest technology. [50] proposed the **Unified Theory of Acceptance and Use of Technology** (UTAUT) framework to explore and analyze the acceptance of technology and its reasons in information systems (IS) research. The UTAUT model has been used in a variety of fields and cross industry; from interactive whiteboards [51], and mobile health [52], to ERP software acceptance [53].

[50] developed a unified model that brings together different perspectives on user acceptance and innovation adoption. Four essential concepts are included, that is,

- "performance expectancy" (one of the main influencing factors towards information system adoption and use);
- "effort expectancy" (or the degree of easiness and the amount of work involved with using the technology; individuals are less likely to want to use technology if it is seen to require more effort);
- "social influence" (or the individual's perception of how crucial superiors, peers, and subordinates believe he or her should use the technology), and
- "facilitating conditions" (in terms of computer hardware and software required for the technology use) are direct predictors of behavioral intention and, ultimately, conduct, and that gender, age, experience, and voluntariness of usage modify these dimensions

According to many authors [50–52], theses constructs are directly associated with Behavioral Intentions (BI) which is defined as users' intention to use the system, and Use Behavior (UB) (Fig. 1).

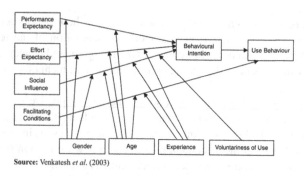

Source: Venkatesh *et al.* (2003)

Fig. 1. Basic UTAUT model [50]

Our proposal for the research model is an extension of the Unified Theory of Acceptance and Use of Technology (UTAUT) to address the specificities of the use of AI agents for adaptive learning in higher education institutions. UTAUT has been widely used as a theoretical lens by academics undertaking empirical investigations of user intention and behavior in technology adoption research. However, many other factors can be explored to determine use behavior in HEI from the above-mentioned theoretical perspective. We propose to add new variables and/or factors that could influence users' behaviors and acceptance of technology, and test them within the HES through teachers and students' behaviors and acceptance of AI agents/chatbots usage.

These factors/variables are security and privacy (of the data collected and the concerns raised), Trust in Technology (or confidence in the AI agents and whether users are prepared to share and offer their data and information [54], individualized or personalized education (or tailored learning techniques to meet the students' specific needs [55], Perception of equality and fairness, and engagement. Furthermore, we propose to add two moderators to the existing four; these moderators are: Collaborative Learning (to enhance learning processes) and Learning Motivation (that accelerate the adoption process).

Thus, in our context, we propose the following theoretical extended UTAUT Model, where HEI's stakeholders (users) acceptance for AI agents/chatbots technology (adoption of a new technology) within the HES (Fig. 2).

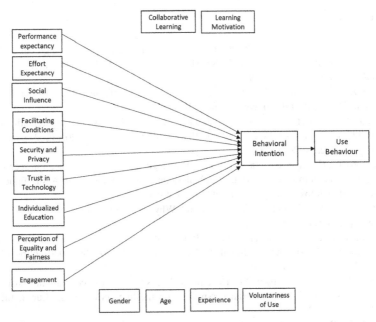

Fig. 2. Proposed extended UTAUT model

5 Conclusions and Future Developments

In this article, we outlined and examine the factors that affect using AI agents/chatbots applications in HEI. The main objective of this research was to highlight the factors that affects the use of AI agents/chatbots for adaptive learning in the higher education sector. This approach will be ultimately considered as a step closer to the process of using AI agents in HEI.

In fact, the contributions of this study are threefold; first we contributed to theory by adding one more context to test the UTAUT model in HEI for the usage of AI agents/chatbots. We contributed to the theory by suggesting additional variables to the UTAUT through the theoretical perspective we used (sociomateriality and macdonaldization). Furthermore, this study advances the literature by offering key insights for practitioners and scholars interested in studying HEI when it comes to the use of chatbots for adaptive learning. In fact, we filled a gap in the current literature on the use of chatbot technology in HEI. Finally, on a practical level, this study gives HES' professionals important information on the factors that influence the use of chatbots in HEI.

Upon addressing the theoretical perspectives based on the proposed framework and proposing hypotheses, we shall carry on with a quantitative methodology and a hypothetico-deductive approach [56, 57] in order to collect data through a survey and test the validity of the hypotheses. In fact, the next step will be addressing around 1000 questionnaires to different stakeholders of HEI including academic faculty educators (professors, doctors, etc.), students, accrediting agencies, vendors and suppliers, employers, government, alumni, parents, donors, technical administrative body, etc.

References

1. De Wit, H., Philip, G.: Altbach: internationalization in higher education: global trends and recommendations for its future. Pol. Rev. High. Educ. **5**(1), 28–46 (2021). https://doi.org/10.1080/23322969.2020.1820898
2. Mendoza, N.F.: Zoom Losing to Teams in the Video Conference Race to the Top, Tech Republic Publishing (2020). www.techrepublic.com
3. Kabudi, T., Pappas, I., Olsen, D.: AI-enabled adaptive learning systems: a systematic mapping of the literature. Comput. Educ. Artif. Intell. **2**, 100017, ISSN 2666-920X (2021). https://doi.org/10.1016/j.caeai.2021.100017
4. Chedrawi, C., Howayeck, P., Tarhini, A.: CSR and legitimacy in higher education accreditation programs, an isomorphic approach of Lebanese business schools. Qual. Assur. Educ. **27**(1), 70–81 (2019). https://doi.org/10.1108/QAE-04-2018-0053
5. Expert AI Team.: Chatbot: What is a Chatbot? Why are Chatbots Important? (2020). https://www.expert.ai/blog/chatbot/
6. Subedi, S., Hetényi, G., Shackleton, R.: Impact of an educational program on earthquake awareness and preparedness in Nepal. Geosci. Commun. **3**, 279–290 (2020). https://doi.org/10.5194/gc-3-279-2020
7. Oberländer, A.M., Röglinger, M., Rosemann, M., Kees, A.: Conceptualizing business-to-thing interactions–A sociomaterial perspective on the internet of things. Eur. J. Inf. Syst. **27**(4), 486–502 (2018)
8. Moura, E., Bispo, M.: Sociomateriality: theories, methodology, and practice. Canadian J. Adm. Sci. (2020). https://doi.org/10.1002/cjas.1548
9. Garland, C.: The mcdonaldization of higher education? Notes on the UK Experience, Fast Capitalism, **4**(1) (2008). https://doi.org/10.32855/fcapital.200801.011
10. Ritzer, G.: The McDonaldization Thesis: Explorations and Extensions. Pine Forge Press, Thousand Oaks (1998)
11. Azim, M., Hussain, Z., Bhatti, A., Iqbal, M.: McDonaldization of education in Pakistan: a step towards dehumanization. Int. J. Innov. Creat. Change. **15**(2) (2021). www.ijicc.net
12. Vrontis, D., Christofi, M., Pereira, V., Tarba, S., Makrides, A., Trichina, E.: Artificial intelligence, robotics, advanced technologies and human resource management: a systematic review. Int. J. Human Resour. Manag. (2021). https://doi.org/10.1080/09585192.2020.1871398
13. Schuetzler, R., Grimes, M.G., Giboney, J.S.: The impact of chatbot conversational skill on engagement and perceived humanness. J. Manag. Inf. Syst. **37**(3), 875–900 (2020). https://doi.org/10.1080/07421222.2020.1790204
14. Ritzer, G.: The McDonaldization of Society. Pine Forge Press, Thousand Oaks (1993)
15. Orlikowski, W.J.: Sociomaterial practices: exploring technology at work. Organ. Stud. **28**(9), 1435–1448 (2007). https://doi.org/10.1177/0170840607081138
16. Sharma, M., Biros, D.: AI and Its Implications for Organisations. In: Lee, Z.W.Y., Chan, T.K.H., Cheung, C.M.K. (eds.) Information Technology in Organisations and Societies: Multidisciplinary Perspectives from AI to Technostress, pp. 1–24. Emerald Publishing Limited, Bingley (2021). https://doi.org/10.1108/978-1-83909-812-320211001
17. Kaplan, A., Haenlein, M.: Siri, Siri, in my hand: Who's the fairest in the land? On the interpretations, illustrations, and implications of artificial intelligence. Bus. Horiz. **62**(1), 15–25 (2019)
18. Benbya, H., Leidner, D.: How Allianz UK used an idea management platform to harness employee innovation. MIS Q. Executive **17**(2), 141–157 (2018)
19. Haddad, G., Chedrawi, C.: Artificial Intelligence and the inclusion-exclusion paradox: a sociomaterial perspective. In: ICTO Conference 2019: The Impact of Artificial Intelligence on Business (2019)

20. Rai, A., Constantinides, P., Sarker, S.: Next-generation digital platforms: toward human–AI hybrids. MIS Q. **43**(1), iii–x (2019)
21. Rajpurohit, N., Saxena, M., Yadav, R., Chande, P.K.: Investigating impact of artificial intelligence in deployment of effective project teams. Int. J. Adv. Sci. Technol. Scopus **29**(8), 382–391 (2020)
22. Vázquez-Cano, E., Mengual-Andrés, S., López-Meneses, E.: Chatbot to improve learning punctuation in Spanish and to enhance open and flexible learning environments. Int. J. Educ. Technol. High. Educ. **18**(1), 1–20 (2021). https://doi.org/10.1186/s41239-021-00269-8
23. Zawacki-Richter, O., Marín, V.I., Bond, M., Gouverneur, F.: Systematic review of research on artificial intelligence applications in higher education – where are the educators? Int. J. Educ. Technol. High. Educ. **16**(1), 1–27 (2019). https://doi.org/10.1186/s41239-019-0171-0
24. Gan, W., Lin, J.C.-W., Chao, H.-C., Vasilakos, A., Yu, P.: Utility-driven data analytics on uncertain data. IEEE Syst. J. (2020). https://doi.org/10.1109/JSYST.2020.2979279
25. Callo, E., Yazon, A.D.: Exploring the factors influencing the readiness of faculty and students on online teaching and learning as an alternative delivery mode for the new normal. Univ. J. Educ. Res. **8**(8), 3509–3518 (2020)
26. World Economic Forum: The COVID-19 pandemic has changed education forever. This is how (2020). https://www.weforum.org/agenda/2020/04/coronavirus-education-global-cov id19-online-digital-learning/
27. Pereira J.: Leveraging chatbots to improve self-guided learning through conversational quizzes. In: ACM International Conference Proceeding Series (2016). https://doi.org/10.1145/3012430.3012625
28. Reiswich, A., Haag, M.: Evaluation of chatbot prototypes for taking the virtual patient's history. Stud. Health Technol. Inform. **260**, 73–80 (2019)
29. Molnár, G., Szüts, Z.: The role of chatbots in formal education. In: 2018 IEEE 16th International Symposium on Intelligent Systems and Informatics (SISY). IEEE (2018)
30. Fleming, M., et al.: Streamlining student course requests using chatbots. In: 29th Australasian Association for Engineering Education Conference (AAEE 2018), Engineers Australia (2018)
31. Mullamaa, K.: Student centred teaching and motivation. Adv. Soc. Sci. Res. J. **4**(1), 16 (2017)
32. Tyson, M.M., Sauers, N.J.: School leaders' adoption and implementation of artificial intelligence. J. Educ. Adm. **59**(3), 271–285 (2021). https://doi.org/10.1108/JEA-10-2020-0221
33. Sandu, N., Gide, E.: Adoption of AI-chatbots to enhance student learning experience in higher education in India. In: 2019 18th International Conference on Information Technology Based Higher Education and Training (ITHET), pp. 1–5 (2019). https://doi.org/10.1109/ITHET4 6829.2019.8937382
34. Palvia, S., et al.: Online education: worldwide status, challenges, trends, and implications. J. Glob. Inf. Technol. Manag. **21**(4), 233–241 (2020). https://doi.org/10.1080/1097198X.2018.1542262
35. Statista E-learning and digital education (2020). https://www.statista.com/topics/3115/e-lea rningand-digital-education/
36. Šarmanová, J., Kostolányová, K.: Adaptive e-learning: from theory to practice. ICTE J. **4**(4), 34–47 (2015). https://doi.org/10.1515/ijicte-2015-0018
37. Bryson, J.R., Andres, L.: Covid-19 and rapid adoption and improvisation of online teaching: curating resources for extensive versus intensive online learning experiences. J. Geogr. High. Educ. **44**(4), 608–623 (2020). https://doi.org/10.1080/03098265.2020.1807478
38. Educause: 7 things you should know about adaptive learning (2017). https://library.educause.edu/~/media/files/library/2017/1/eli7140.pdf
39. Yakin, M., Linden, K.: Adaptive e-learning platforms can improve student performance and engagement in dental education. J. Dent. Educ. **85**, 1309–1315 (2021)

40. Mitchell, J.E.: How do we think about labs and practical skills in an online context? In: Gibbs, B., Wood, G.C. (eds.) Emerging Stronger: Lasting Impact from Crisis Innovation, p. 35. Engineering Professors' Council, Godalming (2020)

41. Paramythis, A., Loidl-Reisinger, S.: Adaptive learning environments and e-learning standards. Electron. J. e-Learn. **2**(1), (2004)

42. Ralph, N.: The McDonaldization of nursing education in Australia, Unpublished doctoral thesis, Monash University, Australia (2013)

43. Holmes, C., Lindsay, D.: Do you Want Fries with that?: The McDonaldization of University Education—Some Critical Reflections on Nursing Higher Education. SAGE Publications (2018). https://doi.org/10.1177/2158244018787229journals.sagepub.com/home/sgo

44. Fenwick, T., Edwards, R., Sawchuk, P.: Emerging Approaches to Educational Research: Tracing the Socio-Material. Routledge, London (2011)

45. Fenwick, T.: Sociomateriality in medical practice learning: attuning to what matters. Med. Educ. **48**(1), 44–52 (2014)

46. Leonardi, P.M.: Why do people reject new technologies and stymie organizational changes of which they are in favor? Exploring misalignments between social interactions and materiality. Human Commun. Res. **35**(3), 407–441 (2009)

47. Orlikowski, W.J., Scott, S.V.: Sociomateriality: challenging the separation of technology, work and organization. Acad. Manag. Ann. **2**(1), 433–474 (2008)

48. Acton, R.: Place-people-practice-process: using sociomateriality in university physical spaces research. Educ. Philos. Theory **49**(14), 1441–1451 (2017). https://doi.org/10.1080/00131857.2017.1309637

49. Scott, D., Hargreaves, E.: The sociomateriality theory. In: The SAGE Handbook of Learning (2020)

50. Venkatesh, V., Morris, M.G., Gordon, B.D., Davis, F.D.: User acceptance of information technology: toward a unified view. MIS Q. **27**(3), 425–478 (2003)

51. Šumak, B., Šorgo, A.: The acceptance and use of interactive whiteboards among teachers: differences in UTAUT determinants between pre- and post-adopters. Comput. Hum. Behav. **64**, 602–620 (2016). https://doi.org/10.1016/j.chb.2016.07.037

52. Hoque, R., Sorwar, G.: Understanding factors influencing the adoption of mHealth by the elderly: an extension of the UTAUT model. Int. J. Med. Inform. **101**, 75–84 (2017). https://doi.org/10.1016/j.ijmedinf.2017.02.002

53. Chauhan, S., Jaiswal, M.: Determinants of acceptance of ERP software training in business schools: empirical investigation using UTAUT model. Int. J. Manage. Educ. **14**, 248–262 (2016). https://doi.org/10.1016/j.ijme.2016.05.005

54. Wang, W., Siau, K.: Trust in health chatbots. In: International Conference on Information Systems (ICIS 2018), San Francisco, CA (2018)

55. Smutny, P., Schreiberova, P.: Chatbots for learning: a review of educational Chatbots for the Facebook Messenger. Comput. Educ. **151**, 103862, ISSN 0360-1315 (2020). https://doi.org/10.1016/j.compedu.2020.103862

56. Klein, H.K., Myers, M.D.: A set of principles for conducting and evaluating interpretive field studies in information systems. MIS Q. **23**(1), 67–93 (1999)

57. Straub, D., Boudreau, M., Gefen, D.: Validation guidelines for IS positivist research. Commun. Assoc. Inf. Syst. **13**, 24 (2004). https://doi.org/10.17705/1CAIS.01324

Artificial Intelligence in the Innovation Process - Do We Pay Attention to This Participant in Innovative Projects?

Zornitsa Yordanova$^{(\boxtimes)}$ (iD)

University of National and World Economy, 8mi dekemvri 23, Sofia, Bulgaria
zornitsayordanova@unwe.bg

Abstract. Innovation requires a specific management approach and it seems that emerging technologies are able to provide additional value to innovators for better handling the unknown and unpredictable environment in which innovation is developed. The innovation process is the best known methodological and systematic way for innovations to be developed and whether artificial intelligence is already used and how exactly in this process, is the focal point in this study. The research was motivated by the frequency of innovation's failure during development and the diverse case studies in the literature in which artificial intelligence has been used to support the successful development outcome. We used a bibliometric analysis for sheding the light and bringing more understanding for the new managerial techniques through artificial intelligence as part of the innovation management in the last 20 years research. The results of this study are particularly important for innovation managers who are not first adopters and need more analysis of the application of artificial intelligence, the outcomes, benefits and disadvantages of this use as part of the innovation development and innovation process. The paper contributes by summarizing the current research on the topic and outlines the research agenda for its further evolution.

Keywords: Artificial intelligence · Innovation process · Innovation management · Project management · Stakeholder management · Technology management · Innovative projects

1 Introduction

Artificial intelligence (AI) is increasingly involved in various management processes to make them more effective, both to replace manual or mental human labour and to intensify the results. Innovation and technology development are widely recognized as an activity leading to competitiveness and leadership in business, as well as to sustainability and pioneering in public policy, education and the environmental context [1]. AI technology has already been applied in all these areas since the science literature is full of case studies and analysis from technical [2] managerial [3], and societal perspective [4]. However, project management and innovation process as managerial horizontal activities, influencing all sectors and functions of an enterprise, have both being highly impacted by AI in several contexts and still their nexus is under-researched [5]. This

© Springer Nature Switzerland AG 2022
M. Themistocleous and M. Papadaki (Eds.): EMCIS 2021, LNBIP 437, pp. 427–438, 2022.
https://doi.org/10.1007/978-3-030-95947-0_30

study aims to reveal how AI is involved in the management of innovation projects and the innovation process itself. We will go the extra mile after the comprehensive and broad article of AI and innovation management, which offers a review, framework and research agenda by Haefner et al. [6] in 2021 by diving deeper to the main tool of developing innovation – the innovation process.

We conducted a bibliometric analysis to shed light on the achievements on the topic and to answer these three main research questions (RQ) in order to open the further development of AI as a participant and supporter of the innovation process.

RQ 1: What are the areas/phases of innovation development process where AI has mostly been used so far?
RQ 2: How is AI used in innovation projects or project management?
RQ 3: What are the trends for further development of applying AI for innovation development as part of the innovation process?

The research design is based on some common bibliometric methods as these are recommended for business research by Donthu et al. [7]. For addressing the research questions and also to gain a one-stop overview and identify some knowledge gaps, we investigated 83 articles and conference reports which met the inclusion criteria for consideration in this study. The results are one of the first attempts of raising the bar on AI as a participant in projects as well as its importance for replacing some of the sup-phases and activities, which are part of the innovation development and innovation processes from managerial perspective.

2   Theoretical Background

2.1   Artificial Intelligence in Process Management

Artificial intelligence has already been applied in several contexts to boost and optimize process management.

2.2   Project Management for Innovation

Over the last decades, the project structure has established itself as an effective tool for managing complex new activities such as the development of innovations [8]. Innovation development and innovation processes are usually conducted through project organization [9], because the usual uncertainty in which they are processed is easily manageable through project management [10]. These projects are often called innovation projects and their identification is not always so evident [11]. For many companies, improving and increasing innovativeness and the ability to develop innovations is the most substantial factor for growth [12]. Unfortunately, while the value of these projects for companies is significant and even growing, these kind of projects failure rate is also extremely high [13].

Project management is the part of the project knowledge that explores the more optimal and successful management of these initiatives. However, conventional project management methods are often insufficient for managing innovation projects [14]. As a result, project management and innovation development/process are two separate areas of knowledge and the two streams of research have been relatively isolated from each other, but still the boundary between these two domains often overlaps and blurs [15]. Notwithstanding, innovation and project management have been identified as cross-bordered research areas and are often analysed from a single managerial perspective [16] living in ambivalent environment [17].

2.3 Innovation Process

The innovation process is usually considered as a sequence of activities that lead to an innovation result, often categorized as a product, process, organizational or marketing innovation. Rodgers [18] defines innovation development as a process containing solutions, activities, relationships and environmental considerations, as well as their impact on an object that materializes after identifying a need or problem, has been in the process of research and development, and then this is being commercialized. The phases and structure of the innovation process generally depend on the field of the project, the science and environmental obstacles, the level of uncertainty [19]. It may also dependent on the actors and contributors involved, the objective or the environment where the innovation development takes part [20].

3   Research Design

The research design is organized following the main principles of bibliometric analysis as this method can extract relevant information from a large number of publications and to elicit the information for answers to the research questions in this study.

3.1   Data Selection

The scope of this research was defined by conducting a Boolean search in the Scopus database for extracting high-quality publications [21] on the matters of innovation process and artificial intelligence that are mutually discussed and analysed in a single publication. The formula used was the following:

TITLE-ABS-KEY ("innovation process" AND "artificial intelligence" OR "AI").

After conducting the search, 83 publications met the search criteria. The details about the scope are described in Table 1.

The topic of AI in the innovation process has been increasingly researched over the last 5 years and especially after 2018. The data about 2021 was gathered in the middle of 2021 which is the reason of the smaller number in this last period. We still decided to keep the results to cover the topic in its entirety (Fig. 1).

In Fig. 2 are presented countries of origin, keywords and keywords plus of these 83 publications. The larger amount of publications come from Austria and Germany. Beside the words that used in the search criteria, keywords are also: machine learning, sustainability, deep learning, big data, problem solving, knowledge management, patents which reveal the general path of the research in the area of AI I the context of the innovation process. Deeper insights are analysed in the results' section of the study.

Table 1. Data selection and scope for bibliometric analysis

Timespan	2000:2021
Sources (Journals, Books, etc.)	69
Documents	83
Average citations per documents	7.181
References	3245
Article	40
Book chapter	4
Conference paper	39
Authors	246

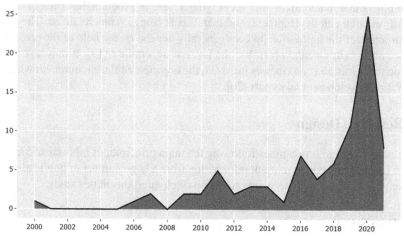

Fig. 1. Annual scientific production on AI in innovation process

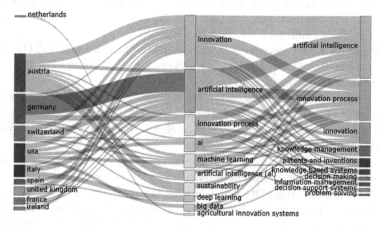

Fig. 2. Countries of origin, keywords and keywords plus of the publications in scope

3.2 Bibliometric Analysis

Bibliometric analysis was applied as a systematically proven type of research from many scholars [22] and is currently considered one of the most effective scientific methods for understanding the research field from a historical, holistic and interdisciplinary perspective [23]. Bibliometric analysis facilitates the mapping of the current research as well as identifies knowledge gaps, streams of research already done, authors information, and recognizes further research agenda [24]. Bibliometric analysis is effectively used method to explore the emergence of the domain of digitalization and innovation [25] and has the ability to monitor the research and forecast future research trends [26].

In this study, we applied the following bibliometric analysis to address the core topic of digitalization of the firm's innovation process in the particular field of using AI and to find insights to answer the research questions:

- Wave analysis – three-plot (countries, sources, keywords, journal labelling)
- Citation analysis
- Keywords analysis
- Top-tier Journals
- Country of research analysis

For the purpose of bibliometric analysis, R software has been used and its package Biblioshiny in particular.

4 Results and Discussion: Artificial Intelligence in Innovation Process

The results are based on the selected 83 that met the criteria of the simple Boolean search in the Scopus database. Looking at the words in titles, only the bigrams show that

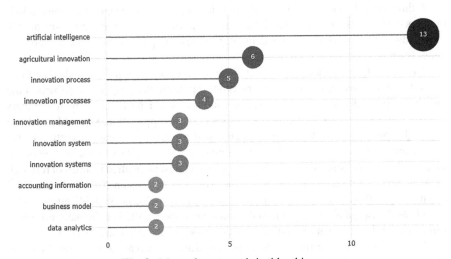

Fig. 3. Most relevant words in titles, bigrams

innovation system, business models and data analytics are other innovation management concepts already researched in the context of AI and innovation process. Agricultural innovation was definitely the field where most of the research took place to render the innovation process with the means of AI (Fig. 3).

The very same analysis, but in the abstracts of the 83 publications reveal same trending topics such as business model, innovation systems and agricultural innovation, but also some new directions of research: model innovation, sustainable development and multi business. Deeper analysis within the abstracts reveals that in the context of agricultural innovation, wide topics are the foci of the research such as: smart innovation, agricultural innovation systems, policy making, innovation framework, etc (Fig. 4).

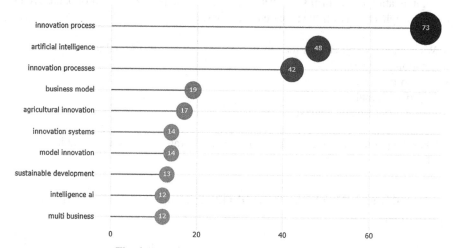

Fig. 4. Most relevant words – abstracts, bigrams

A three map shows the most spread words in titles in the scoped publications. Beside the expected words participating in the search criteria, widely used were also: model, knowledge, systems, design, management, analysis, support, sustainable, technology, agile, learning (Fig. 5).

The word dynamics method indicates the diversity in the topics over the last three years. Main reasons for this new comers as hot topics are the adoption of AI within the innovation process in more industries, firms and teams which supported the researchers to make more analysis on the further development of this application. Since AI is rather a new and expensive technology, the research is still based on study cases mostly (Fig. 6).

We analysed the thematic evolution following the statistical recommendation of the used software R and since the last two years were the most intensified in terms of research on AI in the innovation process, we based the evolution analysis on 2016, 2020 and 2021 (even though 2021 data covered only publications until 06.2021). 33 publications out of the whole dataset of 83 were published in only year and a half. The thematic evolution went from radical innovation to data analytics, from AI to deep learning (Fig. 7).

The thematic map, sorting out four groups using the technique proposed by Cobo et al. [27], is a strategic thematic map, plotting the themes into four quadrants (clusters

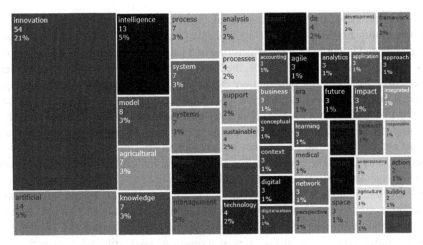

Fig. 5. Three map on titles, unigrams

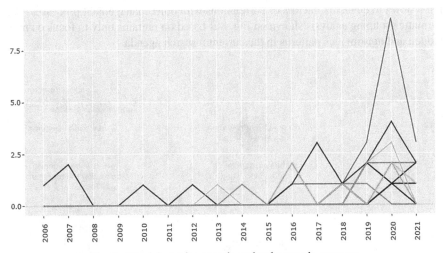

Fig. 6. Word dynamics growth, author keywords, per year

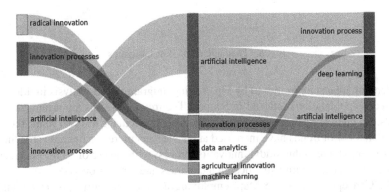

Fig. 7. Thematic evolution 2016, 2020 and 2021

of keywords) including Motor, Transversal, Niche, and Peripheral themes according to their centrality and density rank values along two axes. The Motor Themes are both well developed and important for the structuring of the analysed research field [28]: innovation systems, agricultural innovation, intellectual property, AI, innovation management. Themes in the upper-left quadrant are Niche Themes and they have well developed internal ties but unimportant external ties which put them into position of being only marginally important for the field [28]. They have peripheral character in the context of AI use in the innovation process: accounting information, information system, business model and model innovation. Themes in the lower-left quadrant are both weakly developed and marginal. The Emerging Themes (low and left on Fig. 8) have low density and low centrality, mainly representing either emerging or disappearing themes [28] and these are: data analytics, design thinking and space technologies. Themes in the lower-right quadrant are important for the research field but are not developed [28] enough, they are called as transversal and general, basic themes: innovation process. The thematic grouping reveals that innovation process in terms of AI use is still under-researched and the basic topics are still centred only around the innovation process itself, without breaking it down to elements, factors or correlations with other management processes. This thematic grouping analysis shown on Fig. 8 is based on bigrams only to focus on more hidden and not-obvious patterns in the current research agenda.

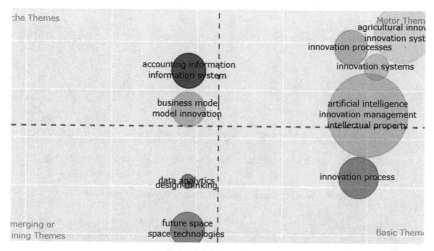

Fig. 8. Thematic map – titles, bigrams

Trending topics are proposed by Fig. 9 using unigrams word analysis in titles of the analysed 83 publications indexed in Scopus. The trending words are arranged in time periods. An interesting observation brings the insight that in the last two years, the diversity and number of trends have increased and have been more oriented towards the core of the research topic in this study: innovation process with the use of AI for management purposes (potentially with using design techniques and innovation systems).

The Conceptual Structure Map, employing the multiple correspondence analysis (MCA) method visualizes the conceptual structure in a two-dimensional plot. Conceptual

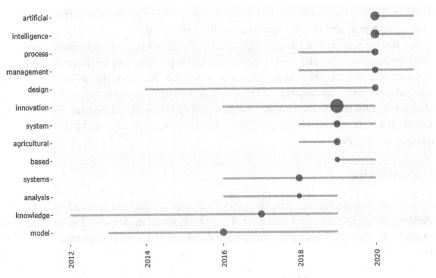

Fig. 9. Trending topics, unigrams in titles

structure is used to understand the topics covered by researchers (so-called research front) and to identify what are the most important and the most recent issues [29]. There is an identified nexus between research on innovation management topics such as: smart tools, innovation systems, factors for dynamics, conditions of the environment. However, the

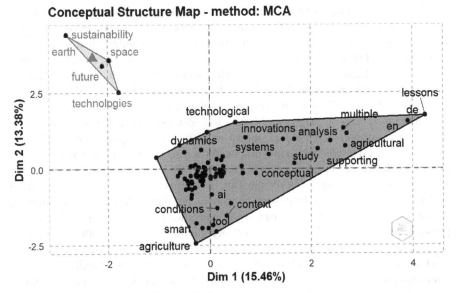

Fig. 10. Conceptual structure map

AI use in the innovation process has been analysed also in completely different context of the managerial, and it is the space technology (Fig. 10).

For further research in the next years when the growing trends of publications and experimentation of the use of AI in the innovation process will continue to exponentially increase, we recommend a systematic analysis to be conducted in order for some clear patterns and concrete use to be revealed. In such a systematic analysis, border publications and out of scope science fields should be extracted and several inclusion and exclusion criteria should be applied for the purpose of organizing best practices for managerial purposes.

5   Conclusion

This study provides a bibliometric analysis on the science literature indexed in the Scopus database for the use and application of AI in the innovation process. The results show that such a use has predominantly a managerial context and is still under-researched. The analysis on 83 publications show some nexus to close concepts that are jointly analysed by scholars such as: innovation systems, model innovation, data analytics, information technologies. We started this study with the motivation to address our research questions and we partially achieved the necessary outcomes and insights to answer them.

RQ 1: The current research has not revealed any proper phases, part of the innovation process where AI has already been applied and could render the process and make it optimal. Thus, we call for further research on the question on how AI is incorporated and designed for the purpose of improving the innovation process with all challenges which this process is facing.

RQ 2: AI is used in agricultural innovation project and in health innovation according to the literature. Still, this research focused only on the innovation process and does not cover AI use in pure project management. However, we can suggest that a knowledge gap is identified in the AI application for managing innovations since the topic is of a growing interest and still not sufficient results show clear application path. Following some research evidence from the literature that more than 50% of the SMEs are non-innovative [30], we call for further research on the field of the application of AI in the innovation processes of enterprises in order to boost, provoke and support innovation when this is not part of the organizational motivation and purpose of the enterprise. This would be even more relevant in crisis and for measuring the impact assessment in different industries and performance on a firm level [31].

RQ 3: We identified several knowledge gaps from practical application perspective on the managerial use of AI in the innovation process. For further development of applying AI for innovation development as part of the innovation process is essential the process phases to be clearly identified from the prism of applying of AI. From another perspective, AI application is also dependent on data gathered within the innovation process, such as ideas, selection criteria of ideas, market analysis on innovation potential in different industries and on diverse markets, customer expectations and innovation diffusion, etc. As a first step in the AI development for managerial use in the innovation process, we call for urgent research on the types and content of data needed in order such first versions of algorithms to be created and applied.

Acknowledgement. This work was supported by the UNWE Research Programme (Research Grant No 9/2021).

References

1. Clark, J., Guy, K.: Innovation and competitiveness: a review. Technol. Anal. Strateg. Manag. **10**(3), 363–395 (1998). https://doi.org/10.1080/09537329808524322
2. Yogesh, K., et al.: Artificial intelligence (AI): multidisciplinary perspectives on emerging challenges, opportunities, and agenda for research, practice and policy. Int. J. Inf. Manag. **57**, 101994 (2021). ISSN 0268-4012. https://doi.org/10.1016/j.ijinfomgt.2019.08.002
3. Popkova, E.G., Alekseev, A.N., Lobova, S.V., Sergi, B.S.: The theory of innovation and innovative development. AI Scenar. in Russia Technol. Soc. **63**, 101390 (2020). ISSN 0160-791X. https://doi.org/10.1016/j.techsoc.2020.101390
4. Fukuda, K.: Science, technology and innovation ecosystem transformation toward society 5.0. Int. J. Prod. Econ. **220**, 107460 (2020). ISSN 0925-5273. https://doi.org/10.1016/j.ijpe.2019.07.033
5. Prem, E.: Artificial intelligence for innovation in Austria. Technol. Innov. Manag. Rev. **9**(12), 5–15 (2019). https://doi.org/10.22215/timreview/1287
6. Haefner, N., Wincent, J., Parida, V., Gassmann, O.: Artificial intelligence and innovation management: a review, framework, and research agenda. Technol. Forecast. Soc. Change, **162**, 120392 (2021). ISSN 0040-1625. https://doi.org/10.1016/j.techfore.2020.120392
7. Donthu, N., Kumar, S., Mukherjee, D., Pandey, N., Lim, W.M.: How to conduct a bibliometric analysis: an overview and guidelines. J. Bus. Res. **133**, 285–296 (2021). ISSN 0148-2963. https://doi.org/10.1016/j.jbusres.2021.04.070
8. Gemünden, H.G., Lehner, P., Kock, A.: The project-oriented organization and its contribution to innovation. Int. J. Project Manag. **36**(1), 147–160 (2018). https://doi.org/10.1016/j.ijproman.2017.07.009
9. Allahar, H.: A management innovation approach to project planning. Techno. Innov. Manag. Rev. **9**(6), 4–13 (2019). https://doi.org/10.22215/timreview/1245
10. Van Lancker, J., et al.: The organizational innovation system: a systemic framework for radical innovation at the organizational level. Technovation (2015). https://doi.org/10.1016/j.technovation.2015.11.008i
11. Deák, C.: Managing innovation projects versus ordinary project management. In: Conference: 2nd ISPIM Innovation Symposium: Stimulating Recovery - The Role of Innovation Management –At, New York City, USA (2009)
12. Lopesa, A.: Innovation management: a systematic literature analysis of the in-novation management evolution. Braz. J. Oper. Prod. Manag. **13**(1), 16–30 (2016). https://doi.org/10.14488/BJOPM.2016.v13.n1.a2
13. Rhaiem, K., Amara, N.: Learning from innovation failures: a systematic review of the literature and research agenda. RMS **15**(2), 189–234 (2019). https://doi.org/10.1007/s11846-019-00339-2
14. Kerzner, H.: Innovation Project Management: Methods, Case Studies, and Tools for Managing Innovation Projects. 1st edn. Wiley (2019). ISBN-13 978-1119587293
15. Filippov, S., Mooi, H.: Innovation project management: a research agenda. In: 6th International Conference for Innovation and Management (ICIM2009), Sao Paolo, 2009/12/08–10 (2009)
16. Yordanova, Z.: Project management for innovation projects – state of art. In: Huang, T.-C., Wu, T.-T., Barroso, J., Sandnes, F.E., Martins, P., Huang, Y.-M. (eds.) ICITL 2020. LNCS, vol. 12555, pp. 277–285. Springer, Cham (2020). https://doi.org/10.1007/978-3-030-63885-6_32

17. Davies, A., Manning, S., Söderlund, J.: When neighboring disciplines fail to learn from each other: the case of innovation and project management research. Res. Pol. **47**(5), 965–979 (2018). https://doi.org/10.1016/j.respol.2018.03.002. ISSN 0048-7333

18. Rogers, E.: Diffusion of Innovations, 5th edn. Free Press, London (2003)

19. Kaplan, L.R., Farooque, M., Sarewitz, D., Tomblin, D.: Designing participatory technology assessments: a reflexive method for advancing the public role in science policy decision-making. Technol. Forecast. Soc. Change, **171**, 120974 (2021). ISSN 0040-1625. https://doi.org/10.1016/j.techfore.2021.120974

20. Broekaert, W., Andries, P., Debackere, K.: Innovation processes in family firms: the relevance of organizational flexibility. Small Bus. Econ. **47**(3), 771–785 (2016). https://doi.org/10.1007/s11187-016-9760-7

21. Meho, L.I., Rogers, Y.: Citation counting, citation ranking, andh-index of human-computer interaction researchers: a comparison of scopus and web of science. J. Am. Soc. Inform. Sci. Technol. **59**(11), 1711–1726 (2008). https://doi.org/10.1002/asi.20874

22. Pritchard, A.: Statistical bibliography or bibliometrics. J. Doc. **25**, 348–349 (1969)

23. Caviggioli, F., Ughetto, E.: A bibliometric analysis of the research dealing with the impact of additive manufacturing on industry, business and society. Int. J. Prod. Econ. **208**, 254–268 (2019). https://doi.org/10.1016/j.ijpe.2018.11.022

24. Donthu, N., Kumar, S., Pattnaik, D.: Forty-five years of journal of business research: a bibliometric analysis. J. Bus. Res. **109**, 1–14 (2020). https://doi.org/10.1016/j.jbusres.2019.10.039

25. Zhang, X., et al.: A bibliometric analysis of digital innovation from 1998 to 2016. J. Manag. Sci. Eng. **2**(2), 95–115 (2017). ISSN 2096-2320. https://doi.org/10.3724/SP.J.1383.202005

26. Tseng, Y.H., Lin, Y.I., Lee, Y.Y., Hung, W.C., Lee, C.H.: A comparison of methods for detecting hot topics. Scientometrics **81**(1), 73–90 (2009). https://doi.org/10.1007/s11192-009-1885-x

27. Cobo, M., López-Herrera, A., Herrera-Viedma, E., Herrera, F.: Science mapping software tools: review, analysis, and cooperative study among tools. J. Am. Soc. Inf. Sci. **62**, 1382–1402 (2011). https://doi.org/10.1002/asi.21525

28. Cobo, M.J., López-Herrera, A.G., Herrera-Viedma, E., Herrera, F.: An approach for detecting, quantifying, and visualizing the evolution of a research field: a practical application to the fuzzy sets theory field. J. Inform. **5**(1), 146–166 (2011). https://doi.org/10.1016/j.joi.2010.10.002

29. Aria, M., Cuccurullo, C.: Science mapping analysis with bibliometrix R-package: an example (2018). https://bibliometrix.org/documents/bibliometrix_Report.html#section-5-thematic-map. Accessed 1 Oct 2021

30. Carvalho, N.M.; Yordanova, Z.: Why say no to innovation? Evidence from industrial SMEs in European Union. J. Technol. Manag. Innov. **13**(2), 43–56 (2018). https://doi.org/10.4067/S0718-27242018000200043. https://www.jotmi.org/index.php/GT/article/view/2440

31. Boneva, S.: Impact assessment of directive 2010/12/EC of the council on the structure and rates of excise duty applied on manufactured tobacco. The Global Economic Crisis and the Future of European Integration, Sofia (2013)

Healthcare Information Systems

Assessment of Machine Learning Classifiers for Heart Diseases Discovery

Roseline Oluwaseun Ogundokun[1]([✉]) [ID], Sanjay Misra[2] [ID], Peter Ogirima Sadiku[3], and Jide Kehinde Adeniyi[1]

[1] Department of Computer Science, Landmark University Omu Aran, Omu-Aran, Nigeria
ogundokun.roseline@lmu.edu.ng
[2] Department of Computer Science and Communication, Ostfild University College, Halden, Norway
[3] Department of Computer Science, University of Ilorin, Ilorin, Nigeria

Abstract. Heart disease (HD) is one of the utmost serious illnesses that afflict humanity. The ability to anticipate cardiac illness permits physicians to deliver better knowledgeable choices about their patient's wellbeing. Utilizing machine learning (ML) to minimize and realize the symptoms of cardiac illness is a worthwhile decision. Therefore, this study aims to analyze the effectiveness of some supervised ML procedures for detecting heart disease in respect to their accuracy, precision, f1-score, sensitivity, specificity, and false-positive rate (FPR). The outcomes, which were obtained using python programming language were compared. The data employed in this investigation came from an open database of the National Health Service (NHS) heart disease which originated in 2013. Through the machine learning (ML) technique, a dimensionality reduction technique and five classifiers were employed and a performance evaluation between the three classifiers- principal component analysis (PCA), decision tree (DT), random forest (RF), and support vector machine (SVM). The NHS database contains 299 observations. The system was evaluated using confusion matrix measures like accuracy, precision, f1-score, sensitivity (TPR), specificity, and FPR. It is concluded that ML techniques reinforce the true positive rate (TPR) of traditional regression approaches with a TPR of 98.71% and f-measure value of 68.12%. The true positives rate which is the same as the sensitivity was used to evaluate the accuracy of the classifiers and it was deduced that the PCA + DT outperformed that of the other two with a sensitivity of 98.71% and since the value is on the high side, this implies that the classifier will be able to accurately detect a patient with HD in his or her body.

Keywords: Machine learning · Heart disease · Confusion matrix · Classification · Dimensionality reduction

Abbreviations

PCA Principal Component Analysis
ML   Machine learning
DT   Decision Tree

© Springer Nature Switzerland AG 2022
M. Themistocleous and M. Papadaki (Eds.): EMCIS 2021, LNBIP 437, pp. 441–452, 2022.
https://doi.org/10.1007/978-3-030-95947-0_31

RF   Random Forest
SVM   Support Vector Machine
FE   Feature extraction
FS   Feature Selection
HD   Heart Disease
DM   Data Mining

1 Introduction

Cardiovascular illnesses are the biggest cause of mortality globally, as reported World Health Organization (WHO) [1], with 17.9 m persons dying per annum. Obesity, high blood pressure, hyperglycemia, and excessive saturated fat are all linked to an increased risk of heart disease [1]. Additionally, the American Heart Association [2] associates an increase in weight for instance 1–2 kg daily, sleeping difficulties, limb edema, persistent cough, and a fast heart rate with HD symptoms. Due to the symptoms' nature being similar to other diseases or mistaken with indications of age, diagnosis is a challenge for practitioners. Physicians now have a new chance to enhance patient diagnosis because of the rise in medical data gathering [3]. Physicians have expanded their use of computer technology to aid administrative activities in recent years.

Machine learning (ML) is becoming an essential tool in the healthcare sector to assist with patient diagnosis. ML is a diagnostic technique that is employed once a job is big and complex to analyze, for instance, converting a healthcare account of events into knowledge, making epidemic forecasts, or analyzing genetic data [4–6]. Machine learning methods have been utilized in recent research to detect and forecast various heart issues. Melillo et al. [7] were instrumental to the development of an automated classifier for affected roles with congestive heart failure (CHF) that distinguishes between those at low and high risk. The sensitivity and specificity of the classification and regression tree (CART) were calculated to be 93.3% and 63.5%, respectively. To discover the optimum set of characteristics and enhance performance, Al Rahhal et al. [8] developed a deep neural network (DNN) categorization of electrocardiogram (ECG) data. Guidi et al. [9] were instrumental to the development of a clinical decision support system (CDSS) for heart failure (HF) examination. They examined the performance of several ML classification techniques, including neural networks (NN), SVM, CART-based fuzzy rules, and RF. With an accuracy of 87.6%, the CART method and RF achieved the greatest results. Zhang et al. [10] used natural language processing (NLP) and the rule-based approach to find an NYHA class for HF from amorphous medical records, with an accuracy of 93.37%. Parthiban et al. [11] investigated an SVM method for diagnosing HD in diabetic individuals, achieving a 94.60% accuracy and accurately predicting characteristics like age, gore pressure, and gore sugar.

The large dimensionality of the dataset is a significant issue in machine learning [12]. Because analyzing numerous features takes a lot of retention and results in overfitting, weighting attributes, reducing repetitive data, and converting period, increasing the algorithm's accomplishment [13–17]. Different illnesses of health management, gene expression, medical imaging, and the Internet of Things may all be characterized by a limited number of characteristics. Feature extraction (FE) is used to modify and simplify data, while feature selection is used to decrease the dataset by eliminating irrelevant characteristics [18]. By capturing a large variance, principal component analysis (PCA) generates new components that contain the most important information of the characteristics [19].

Therefore, the purpose of this investigation is to liken the effectiveness of five supervised ML techniques which include DT, RF, NB, SVM, and KNN for detecting heart disease. The outcomes, which were obtained using python programming language were compared. The system was evaluated using confusion matrix measures like accuracy, precision, f1-score, DR, and FPR.

The remaining part of this article is structured as thus: Sect. 2 presents the literature review with related works discussed extensively. Section 3 discussed the material and methods utilized for the implementation of the study. Section 4 presented the results gotten from the system implementation and the interpretation of the results deduced. The article was concluded in Sect. 5 with future works suggested.

2 Literature Review

Artificial Intelligence (AI), Data Mining (DM), and ML algorithms and methods have started to be used in clinical settings in the past three years, including diagnostic radiography [20–22], cardiac electrophysiology [23], diabetes [24, 25], dermatology [26, 27], and psychoanalysis [28, 29]. In 2019, a surge in ML techniques was anticipated in the medical industry because of their practicality and accessibility as well as the remarkable outcomes achieved so far.

Prakash et al. published research on heart disease prediction in 2017 that used Optimality Criterion feature selection (OCFS) for prognostication and accurately detecting HD. On the assumption of selective information, an investigator advances their technique for choosing a rough feature set (RFS-IE). They evaluate the OCFS with the RFS-IE in terms of computing time, prognostication quality, and error rate utilizing a variety of datasets in their research. When compared to other methods, the OCFS technique takes the least amount of time to execute its process [30].

Seyedamin et al. published research in 2017. They experiment with various machine learning techniques and evaluated the accuracy of their findings. In this research, several machine learning methods were applied to a small data set and the results were compared. A classifier was created using SVM and a medical heart disease dataset. The aforementioned methods of Bagging, Boosting, and Stacking was used to enhance accuracy. MLP outperformed other methods with 84.15% accuracy when the stacking technique SVM was employed [31].

Nguyen Cong Long et al. published a study in 2015 on illness prediction using the firefly algorithm. Rough set theory is used to train the classifier. Other classification methods, such as Naive Bayes and SVM, are compared to the findings. The proposed approach increases accuracy to 87.2% while reducing convergence speed and processing time. The study's limitation is that when there are a significant number of characteristics, the rough set attribute becomes unmanageable [32].

Jesmin Nahar, Tasadduq Imama, and Kevin S. Tickle researched in 2012 that compared various classifiers for identifying heart disease. SVM offered promising accuracy when it comes to improving absolute accuracy as a performance metric. Their article also discussed automated and motivating feature selection techniques such as MFS and CFS. In terms of accuracy, both methods have shown to be extremely promising [33].

Jesmin Nahar et al. utilized an association rule mining (RM) classifier to infer major heart disease factors in 2013. The heart disease dataset was used to conduct a rule extraction experiment utilizing RM techniques such as predictive, Tertius, and apriori. The rule is chosen by Predictive Apriori built on its excessive accuracy [34].

H. Hannah Inbarani et al. proposed an innovative feature selection technique for illness prognostication. Their study was built on hybridization of Particle Swarm Optimization (PSO) and PSO-built Quick-reduct (PSO-QR). The findings of this study indicate that the suggested method outperforms current feature selection (FS) strategies on a variety of typical medical datasets [35].

Researchers [36] proposed five novel FS approaches on the origin of the performance impact of G-BLUP and Bayes C techniques. The authors predicted the body mass index (BMI) and high-density lipoprotein cholesterol (HDL) and it was discovered that guided FS of SNPs in the G-BLUP provided a versatile and computation efficiency alternative to Bayes C. The drawback in their research was that once the supervised selection was employed, predicted performance necessitates a great deal of rigorous assessment, otherwise results may not be obtained [36].

Sina Tabakhi postulated three FS models which are unsubstantiated, filter, and multivariate. The author examined an unproven FS method built on ant colony optimization (ACO). The researcher made a trade-off between the computing period and the rate of the findings. The UFSACO technique shows an increase in efficiency and efficacy, as well as an improvement over earlier similar methods [37].

M. Akhil Jabbar et al. presented a study on the classification of HD by utilizing artificial neural network (ANN) and feature subset selection (FSS). The authors presented FSS as a technique for reducing dimensionality and input data. This article presented a classification technique for HD classification that employed ANN and FS. The number of diagnostic tests required by physicians from patients was decreased when the number of components was reduced. The data set utilized in this study was from Andhra Pradesh, and the findings indicated that accuracy is improved over older categorization methods. Furthermore, the findings indicated that this method is more accurate and quicker [38].

Divia Tomar and Sonali Agarwal released a comprehensive article that downplays the relevance of different data mining methods such as classification, clustering, association, and regression in the field of medicine. They similarly provided an overview of various methods, as well as their benefits and drawbacks. They also drew attention to roadblocks and other issues with data mining methods used on medical data. This article was suggested as a good starting point for learning about the various data mining methods [39].

The main contribution in this study are as follows:

- Improving old manual system.
- Detection of heart disease.
- Introduction of PCA feature extraction.
- Improving efficiency and effectiveness.

3 Material and Method

3.1 Dataset

The NHS England dataset Catalogue is a publicly available online resource that is linked to HD. They're based on real-world hospital administrative data in England. A sample population of emergency admissions for HD is included in the simulated extract. The dataset is available and can be accessed: https://data.england.nhs.uk/dataset?_organizat ion_limit=0&res_format=CSV.

3.2 Methodology

Feature Extraction
For machine learning concerns, feature extraction is a required step. Feature extraction discovers new m dimensions from a set of n original dimensions. This may be divided into two types of methods. They are the projection technique for unsupervised learning, which comprises principal component analysis (PCA), linear discriminate analysis, and others, and the compression approach for supervised learning, which uses mutual information and information theory [40].

PCA
PCA was chosen because it produces excellent results when dealing with linked charac- teristics. We selected PCA since we are dealing with test characteristics for heart disease diagnosis. It discovers similarities and contrasts between each characteristic by identify- ing patterns in the data set. It is a strong tool for data analysis. The NHS repository was used to choose the heart disease data collection. The original data is selected, as well as the average of the original data. It's time to calculate the covariance matrix. After that, the covariance matrix is used to choose the Eigenvectors and Eigenvalues. The main component of the heart disease data set is selected as the eigenvector having the greatest Eigenvalue. It demonstrates the strongest link between the data characteristics. The Eigenvalues are ordered from highest to lowest. The data with the highest level of relevance is selected, whereas the data with the lowest level of importance is rejected or deleted. This is done to reduce higher-dimensional data to lower-dimensional data [41–45].

3.3 Proposed System

To identify the appropriate characteristics, a framework is created that is coupled with feature extraction using PCA. This is accomplished via a step-by-step procedure. The outliers must first be eliminated. The observed data that varied significantly from the observed data are referred to as outliers. It's also known as "noise". Data noise or attribute noise are both possible sources of noise. To eliminate outliers, the data is cleaned as the first stage in the machine learning process. The feature extraction phase is the second step, in which the PCA is utilized to extract the key feature or the most significant features. The final stage is to categorize the HD using the five ML classifiers, and then determine whether or not a person has HD. The system flow diagram for the proposed system is shown in Fig. 1.

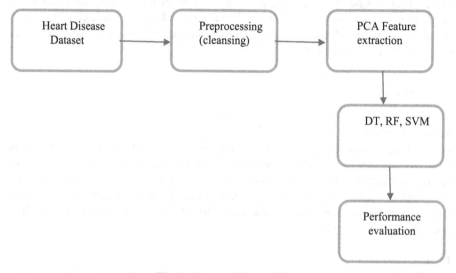

Fig. 1. Proposed System Flow

3.4 Performance Evaluation

The accuracy, sensitivity (detection rate), precision, and f-measure were employed to assess the performance of the study. The true positives (TP) signify an individual has been diagnosed of having HD and is having HD present in his body, the true negatives (TN) signify an individual that was diagnosed as not having HD and was not having HD, the false positives (FP) signify an individual that was diagnosed as having HD but was not having HD in his body and false negatives (FN) signifies an individual that was diagnosed of not having HD and is having HD [46].

4   Results and Discussion

An NHS HD dataset was obtained from the Kaggle repository, an open-source database. Irrelevant rows are removed based on a particular need of HD, which is to reduce the number of characteristics to the fewest that are most relevant for detecting HD, such as age, sex, and so on. The models were implemented using the Python programming language. The PCA is then performed, and the output is verified on the weighted dataset using the five ML classifiers as a subprocess, after which the results are produced. The results produced are evaluated using confusion matrix (CM) values which were used to calculate the performance matrices like accuracy, sensitivity, specificity, f-measure, precision, and false-positive rate. These CM values are shown in Figs. 2, 3, and 4. Table 1 shows the confusion matrix with the actual and predicted values. As it is seen in Table 1 HD binary classification comprises 2 classes: one is a positive class and the other one is the negative class.

Table 1. Confusion matrix

	Predicted HD patient	Predicted healthy patient
Actual HD patient	TP	FN
Actual healthy patient	FP	TN

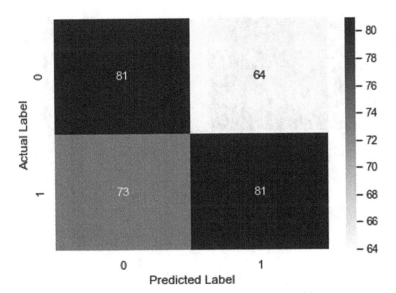

Fig. 2. Confusion matrix for classifier PCA+RF

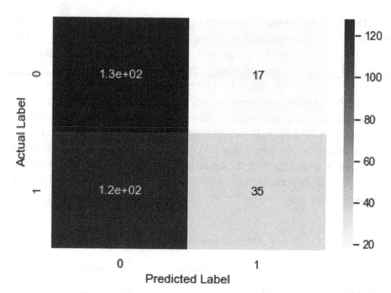

Fig. 3. Confusion matrix for classifier PCA+SVM

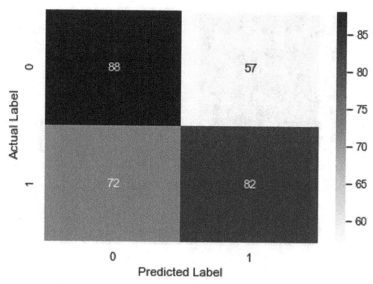

Fig. 4. Confusion matrix for classifier PCA+DF

Table 2. Performance evaluation for the classifiers

Measures	PCA+RF	PCA+DT	PCA+SVM
Sensitivity	55.86	**98.71**	60.69
Precision	52.6	52	**55**
Accuracy	54.18	52.31	**56.86**
F-measure	54.18	**68.12**	57.7

Table 3. Performance evaluation with the existing system

Authors	Methods	Sensitivity
Ayon, Slam, & Hossain [47]	DT	96.23
Shamrat, F. J. M., Raihan, M. A., Rahman, A. S., Mahmud, I., & Akter [48]	DT	98%
Budholiya, K., Shrivastava, S. K., & Sharma, [49]	XGBoost	85.71
Proposed method	**PCA+DT**	**98.71**

4.1 Discussion

The system employed the use of PCA feature extraction and three classification ML techniques. Table 2 shows the performance evaluation for the three classifiers with PCA FE and it was discovered that out of the three classifiers, PCA+SVM outperformed the remaining two in terms of precision and accuracy with 55% and 56.86% respectively, PCA+DT outperformance the remaining two in terms of sensitivity which is the detection rate of 98.71% and f-measure of 68.12% and this shows that the PCA+DT classifiers are the best ML technique for the detection of HD in the medical field as it was demonstrated in this study. Table 3 likewise demonstrate the performance evaluation of the proposed system with existing ones and it was discovered that the proposed system outperformed those of the existing systems with a sensitivity of 98.71% over that of Ayon, Slam & Hossain [47] having 96.23%, Shamrat, Raihan, Rahman, Mahmud & Akter [48] with 98% and Budholiya, K., Shrivastava, S. K., & Sharma, [49] with 85.71%. This shows that it is recommended that the feature extraction technique be encouraged to be used with ML techniques to have high sensitivity, accuracy, and precision values to perform effectively and efficiently.

5 Conclusion and Future Work

The use of PCA to enhance machine learning model detection is suggested in this article. The classifier aimed to determine whether a patient had heart disease. When system resources are taken into account, it is impossible to use all of the features. In this research, we were able to enhance the raw data findings by using the feature extraction method. Different machine learning methods, such as DT, RF, and SVM, are performed separately on an NHS HD dataset using Python, and the results are compared to determine which ML classifier works best and it was deduced that the best ML in this study is PCA+DT with a sensitivity or detection rate of 98.71% and an f-measure of 68.12% which are relatively a good system performance. The true positives rate which is the same as the sensitivity was used to evaluate the accuracy of the classifiers and it was deduced that the PCA+DT outperformed that of the other two with a sensitivity of 98.71% and since the value is on the high side, this implies that the classifier will be able to accurately detect a patient with HD in his or her body.

The use of a limited HD dataset that includes the FE method is a drawback of this research. Because FE performs better with a bigger dataset, the authors suggest using a larger dataset in the future to get greater accuracy, precision, f1-score, DR, and FPR results. Deep learning methods for classification may potentially be used in the study.

References

1. Cardiovascular Diseases (CVDs). http://www.who.int/cardiovascular_diseases/en/. Accessed 16 July 2019
2. American Heart Association. Classes of heart failure. https://www.heart.org/en/health-topics/heart-failure/what-is-heart-failure/classes-of-heart-failure. Accessed 11 Aug 2018
3. Heart failure. http://www.heart.org/HEARTORG/Conditions/HeartFailure/Heart-Failure_UCM_002019_SubHomePage.jsp. Accessed 19 June 2018
4. Shalev-Shwartz, S., Ben-David, S.: Understanding Machine Learning: From Theory to Algorithms. Cambridge University Press, Cambridge (2014)
5. Friedman, J., Hastie, T., Tibshirani, R.: The elements of Statistical Learning. Springer Series in Statistics, vol. 1, no. 10. Springer, New York (2001). https://doi.org/10.1007/978-0-387-84858-7
6. Marsland, S.: Machine Learning: An Algorithmic Perspective. Chapman and Hall/CRC, Boco Raton (2011)
7. Melillo, P., De Luca, N., Bracale, M., Pecchia, L.: Classification tree for risk assessment in patients suffering from congestive heart failure via long-term heart rate variability. IEEE J. Biomed. Health Inform. **17**(3), 727–733 (2013)
8. Al Rahhal, M.M., Bazi, Y., AlHichri, H., Alajlan, N., Melgani, F., Yager, R.R.: Deep learning approach for active classification of electrocardiogram signals. Inf. Sci. **345**, 340–354 (2016)
9. Guidi, G., Pettenati, M.C., Melillo, P., Iadanza, E.: A machine learning system to improve heart failure patient assistance. IEEE J. Biomed. Health Inform. **18**(6), 1750–1756 (2014)
10. Zhang, R., Ma, S., Shanahan, L., Munroe, J., Horn, S., Speedie, S.: Automatic methods to extract New York heart association classification from clinical notes. In: 2017 IEEE international conference on bioinformatics and biomedicine (bibm), pp. 1296–1299. IEEE (2017)
11. Parthiban, G., Srivatsa, S.K.: Applying machine learning methods in diagnosing heart disease for diabetic patients. Int. J. Appl. Inf. Syst. (IJAIS) **3**(7), 25–30 (2012)
12. Domingos, P.: A few useful things to know about machine learning. Commun. ACM **55**(10), 78–87 (2012)
13. Wettschereck, D., Dietterich, T.G.: An experimental comparison of the nearest-neighbor and nearest-hyperrectangle algorithms. Mach. Learn. **19**(1), 5–27 (1995). https://doi.org/10.1007/BF00994658
14. Wettschereck, D., Aha, D.W., Mohri, T.: A review and empirical evaluation of feature weighting methods for a class of lazy learning algorithms. Artif. Intell. Rev. **11**(1), 273–314 (1997). https://doi.org/10.1023/A:1006593614256

15. Yang, M.S., Nataliani, Y.: A feature-reduction fuzzy clustering algorithm based on feature-weighted entropy. IEEE Trans. Fuzzy Syst. **26**(2), 817–835 (2017)

16. Chen, R., Sun, N., Chen, X., Yang, M., Wu, Q.: Supervised feature selection with a stratified feature weighting method. IEEE Access **6**, 15087–15098 (2018)

17. Imani, M., Ghassemian, H.: Feature extraction using weighted training samples. IEEE Geosci. Remote Sens. Lett. **12**(7), 1387–1391 (2015)

18. Liu, H., Motoda, H. (eds.): Feature Extraction, Construction, and Selection: A Data Mining Perspective, vol. 453. Springer, Heidelberg (1998). https://doi.org/10.1007/978-1-4615-5725-8

19. Guyon, I., Gunn, S., Nikravesh, M., Zadeh, L.A. (eds.): Feature Extraction: Foundations and Applications, vol. 207. Springer, Heidelberg (2008)

20. Rajpurkar, P., et al.: ChexNet: radiologist-level pneumonia detection on chest x-rays with deep learning. arXiv preprint arXiv:1711.05225 (2017)

21. Grewal, M., Srivastava, M.M., Kumar, P., Varadarajan, S.: RadNet: radiologist level accuracy using deep learning for hemorrhage detection in CT scans. In: 2018 IEEE 15th International Symposium on Biomedical Imaging (ISBI 2018), pp. 281–284. IEEE (2018)

22. Li, Z., et al.: Thoracic disease identification and localization with limited supervision. In: Proceedings of the IEEE Conference on Computer Vision and Pattern Recognition, pp. 8290–8299 (2018)

23. Rajpurkar, P., Hannun, A.Y., Haghpanahi, M., Bourn, C., Ng, A.Y.: Cardiologist-level arrhythmia detection with convolutional neural networks. arXiv preprint arXiv:1707.01836 (2017)

24. Ting, D.S.W., et al.: Development and validation of a deep learning system for diabetic retinopathy and related eye diseases using retinal images from multiethnic populations with diabetes. JAMA **318**(22), 2211–2223 (2017)

25. Alade, O., Sowunmi, O., Misra, S., Maskeliūnas, R., Damaševičius, R.: A neural network based expert system for the diagnosis of diabetes mellitus. In: Antipova, T., Rocha, Á. (eds.) Information Technology Science, pp. 14–22. Springer, Cham (2018). https://doi.org/10.1007/978-3-319-74980-8_2

26. Esteva, A., et al.: Dermatologist-level classification of skin cancer with deep neural networks. Nature **542**(7639), 115–118 (2017)

27. Adegun, A.A., Viriri, S., Ogundokun, R.O.: Deep learning approach for medical image analysis. Comput. Intell. Neurosci. **2021**(2021), 6215281 (2021)

28. Al Hanai, T., Ghassemi, M.M., Glass, J.R.: Detecting depression with audio/text sequence modeling of interviews. In: Interspeech, pp. 1716–1720 (2018)

29. Huang, Y.H., Wei, L.H., Chen, Y.S.: Detection of the prodromal phase of bipolar disorder from psychological and phonological aspects in social media. arXiv preprint arXiv:1712.09183 (2017)

30. Long, N.C., Meesad, P., Unger, H.: A highly accurate firefly-based algorithm for heart disease prediction. Expert Syst. Appl. **42**(21), 8221–8231 (2015)

31. Nahar, J., Imam, T., Tickle, K.S., Chen, Y.P.P.: Computational intelligence for heart disease diagnosis: a medical knowledge-driven approach. Expert Syst. Appl. **40**(1), 96–104 (2013)

32. Nahar, J., Imam, T., Tickle, K.S., Chen, Y.P.P.: Association rule mining to detect factors that contribute to heart disease in males and females. Expert Syst. Appl. **40**(4), 1086–1093 (2013)

33. Inbarani, H.H., Azar, A.T., Jothi, G.: Supervised hybrid feature selection based on PSO and rough sets for medical diagnosis. Comput. Methods Programs Biomed. **113**(1), 175–185 (2014)

34. Bermingham, M.L., et al.: Application of high-dimensional feature selection: evaluation for genomic prediction in man. Sci. Rep. **5**(1), 1–12 (2015)

35. Tabakhi, S., Moradi, P., Akhlaghian, F.: An unsupervised feature selection algorithm based on ant colony optimization. Eng. Appl. Artif. Intell. **32**, 112–123 (2014)

36. Jabbar, M.A., Deekshatulu, B.L., Chandra, P.: Classification of heart disease using artificial neural network and feature subset selection. Glob. J. Comput. Sci. Technol. Neural Artif. Intell. **13**(3), 4–8 (2013)

37. Tomar, D., Agarwal, S.: A survey on data mining approaches for healthcare. Int. J. Bio-Sci. Bio-Technol. **5**(5), 241–266 (2013)

38. Hand, D.J.: Principles of data mining. Drug Saf. **30**(7), 621–622 (2007)

39. Roiger, R.J.: Data Mining: A Tutorial-Based Primer. Chapman and Hall/CRC, Boco Raton (2017)

40. Kavitha, R., Kannan, E.: An efficient framework for heart disease classification using feature extraction and feature selection techniques in data mining. In: 2016 International Conference on Emerging Trends in Engineering, Technology, and Science (ICETETS), pp. 1–5. IEEE (2016)

41. www.cs.cmu.edu/afs/cs/academic/class/15385-s12/...slides/lec-18.ppt

42. Tilki, Ö.: PCA-based face recognition: an application, Master's thesis (2014). www.doc.ic. ac.uk/~dfg/ProbabilisticInference/IDAPILecture15.pdf

43. Karegowda, A.G., Manjunath, A.S., Jayaram, M.A.: Comparative study of attribute selection using gain ratio and correlation-based feature selection. Int. J. Inf. Technol. Knowl. Manag. **2**(2), 271–277 (2010)

44. www.isical.ac.in/~k.ramachandra/slides/Feature%20Extraction.pptx

45. http://dai.fmph.uniba.sk/courses/ml/sl/pca.pdf

46. Abdulsalam, S., et al.: Performance evaluation of ANOVA and RFE algorithms for classifying microarray dataset using SVM. In: Themistocleous, M., Papadaki, M., Kamal, M.M. (eds.) EMCIS 2020. LNBIP, vol. 402, pp. 480–492. Springer, Cham (2020). https://doi.org/10.1007/978-3-030-63396-7_32

47. Ayon, S.I., Islam, M.M., Hossain, M.R.: Coronary artery heart disease prediction: a comparative study of computational intelligence techniques. IETE J. Res. 1–20 (2020)

48. Shamrat, F.J.M., Raihan, M.A., Rahman, A.S., Mahmud, I., Akter, R.: An analysis on breast disease prediction using machine learning approaches. Int. J. Sci. Technol. Res. **9**(02), 2450–2455 (2020)

49. Budholiya, K., Shrivastava, S.K., Sharma, V.: An optimized XGBoost based diagnostic system for effective prediction of heart disease. J. King Saud Univ.-Comput. Inf. Sci. (2020)

Digital Transformation Approach to Public Hospitals Environment: Technology Acceptance Model for Business Intelligence Applications

Nikolaos Kapetaneas[1,2](✉) and Fotis Kitsios[1,3]

[1] Department of Applied Informatics, University of Macedonia, Thessaloniki, Greece
nkapetaneas@uom.edu.gr, kitsios@uom.gr
[2] Department of Finance, Ministry of Health, 10187 Athens, Greece
[3] School of Social Science, Hellenic Open University, Parodos Aristotelous 18, 26335 Patras, Greece

Abstract. Organizations have implemented business intelligence (BI) applications to realize a variety of organizational benefits. However, a majority of BI application implementation projects are unsuccessful. One of the main reasons for the failure is end user resistance to adopt BI applications that their organization chose. Therefore, it is important to understand how to facilitate individual adoption of BI application. This study proposes a technology acceptance model for the systematic evaluation of administrative activities in public hospitals, using the example of a (BI) software package. The proposed model is based on an expanded Technology Acceptance Model (TAM) and previous surveys of IT implementation success factors and reviews of relevant change management variables.

Keywords: Information system success model · Technology acceptance model · Business intelligence adoption · Change management- healthcare information systems

1 Introduction

Information systems (IS) are a central part of today's organizational life. Organizations are making increasing use of the benefits associated with Information Technology (IT) to improve business processes and organizational efficiency [2, 38, 42, 43]. In particular, the application of standardized software throughout the organizations, usually involves significant organizational changes, which have to be managed successfully [3]. However, their use has not grown to a high point and their potential has been underused [4]. The introduction of e-health in hospitals means new and innovative work processes, where both employees and managers need to know that their work will change radically compared to today, which means learning, skills development and continuous changes in working practice.

The BI literature has already highlighted improvements in decision-making based on the information provided by BI. Furthermore, Bronzo et al. (2013) [5] show that

© Springer Nature Switzerland AG 2022
M. Themistocleous and M. Papadaki (Eds.): EMCIS 2021, LNBIP 437, pp. 453–462, 2022.
https://doi.org/10.1007/978-3-030-95947-0_32

business analytics as part of BI have a positive impact on organizational performance when aligned with process orientation initiatives. The key question then is whether after the implementation of the BI users really accept, use and reach their full potential. The business value of BI should therefore be reflected in an improved business process and, therefore, in an improved business performance [6].

A number of research has been carried out in the past to understand users' acceptance of IT [1, 10, 13, 14, 17, 25]. As a result, many different models and theories have been developed that incorporate a variety of behavioral, social and other control factors to explain the use of IT [7, 8]. However, the benefits can only be fully exploited where these promising innovations are fully accepted and adopted [4].

One of the main reasons for failure is the resistance of end-users to use the BI applications chosen by their organization [9]. As with most technology adoption projects, resistance to the use of the BI application must be overcome in order to realize the promised benefits of BI applications. Therefore, it is important to understand how to facilitate the individual adoption of BI applications.

Systematic evaluation of IT acceptance information on factors related to employees' decisions to adopt new IT technologies. However, few efforts have been made to provide information to managers to improve their decisions factors and their relationship to specific management variables could contribute significantly to successful implementation of standardized software throughout the enterprise. In this respect, organizational surveys, together with their subsequent analysis and data-driven monitoring activities, have proven to be an effective and useful tool in managing organizational change processes [15, 16, 18, 41].

While several studies have examined factors influencing organizational adoption of BI application, factors associated with individual adoption of BI application have not received much attention. This study attempts to close this literature gap. This study is mainly based on the external variables covered by the Information Systems success model proposed by DeLone and McLean (TAM 1), [12], including system quality, information quality and service quality, together with perceived usefulness, perceived ease of use and intention to use as research dimensions demonstrated by Grublješič & Jaklič (2015) [1] and Venkatesh & Bala (2008) [7].

In this context, we propose a framework for integrating variables into updated TAM that are relevant to managing user acceptance when implementing BI software packages. In addition, this approach will provide a useful tool for guiding management activities during the implementation of such complex software systems. In addition, a number of suggested propositions (P) will conducted in line with previous research, that focus on specific effects of management variables on end-user acceptance factors of standard software at the public hospitals. Therefore, this research will demonstrate the usefulness of such an assessment framework in guiding management decisions to increase user acceptance when implementing a BI system at the workplace.

The acceptance of healthcare employees in future changes is questioned [4, 20, 21] despite the fact that traditional management and control style is ineffective and does not meet the need to transform future workplaces [4]. Previous studies have identified a gap between complex administrative responsibilities and employees who do not accept all changes for future transformation of the health sector, however healthcare employees face complex challenges in both adopting new technology and developing new products and services [11, 17, 21]. The study will focus on the suggested factors that influence the acceptance or not of BI and the relationship between people, acceptance of information systems and work in public hospitals and will explores possible factors that could have a positive impact on the acceptance of the BI, since public health organizations require employees to learn and respond more quickly to new challenges. Despite the consensus on the importance of digital transformation in the workplace in public hospitals, there is a need for a greater understanding of how employees can accept through work how to deal with issues related to digital reform and addressing future challenges.

The following is the structure of the paper. Section 2 includes relevant literature in the area of information system adoption and provide the theoretical foundation of our research model. The methodology is explained in Sect. 3 and Sect. 4 discusses practical implications and limitations of our research.

2 Theoretical Background

TAM is the most commonly used and researched model for accepting technology. In this context, we rely on an extensive model (TAM), to examine the factors that are significant for individuals to adopt BI applications. Much of the previous research related to the acceptance of technology focuses on the TAM proposed by Venkatesh & Bala (2008) [7] and later expanded by Engin, & Gürses (2019) [19], Hsieh & Lai (2020) [20] and Grublješič & Jaklič (2015) [1].

TAM assumes that the intent to use an IT system depends on two major factors: the first factor is the perceived utility of a system, which refers to "the degree of in which a person believes that using a particular system would improve his or her work performance" (p. 320) [21]. The second factor is perceived ease of use, which refers to "the extent to which a person believes that using a particular system would be effortless" (p. 320) [21]. TAM also suggests that perceived utility is influenced by perceived ease of use. Thus, these factors influence the intent to use an IT system, which ultimately determines actual system usage [21].

Kwak et al. (2012) [34] used TAM in a project-based sector and found that the support of consultants in the Perceived Usefulness (PU) was negative. They extended the TAM in terms of implementation projects and internal and external variables of management support and Pasaoglu (2011) [14] conducted a Turkey-based study using demographics, knowledge about Enterprise Resource Planning (ERP), organizational culture, perceived ease of use and actual use of the ERP system. The main findings showed a positive relation between the research variable and the actual use of ERP. Moreover, Bach et al. (2016) [10] discuss a framework for investigating the adoption of business intelligence systems in organizations, from the technology acceptance model perspective. They propose a research framework based on the technology acceptance model that is expanded using the concepts of technology driven strategy, information quality and project management. Furthermore, do Nascimento et al. (2020) [2] were conducted an ongoing research study focus on supporting a digital transformation gap found in a public primary healthcare system. They found that the adoption of some business intelligence technologies require mainly changes on the present behavior, both from organizations and people, to be implemented successfully.

The expanded TAM is a key building block of the framework proposed for the assessment of management interventions based on the model. Although TAM provides an established and well-supported picture of psychological variables affecting user acceptance, the model only targets the main determinants of IT use and user intent, but does not explicitly identify external variables related to the application of IT in the workplace [22]. Therefore, TAM can be seen as a model that identifies psychological acceptance variables that mediate the effect between external variables and the actual acceptance of users. Although many external variables related to user acceptance have been identified [22, 23, 35], few efforts have been made to integrate specific variable management at TAM, although these variables are particularly important in guiding the successful implementation of standardized software throughout the organization [7]. Therefore, less is known about the applicability of TAM in such complex software packages, especially in the case of BI systems, and, in addition, which management variables have an incremental impact on the psychological intermediaries identified by the expanded TAM.

Many external variables were previously considered as previous factors of TAM's key belief factors [7] are less important or are only indirectly related to specific management decisions when implementing company-level standardized software in organizations. Individual differences, for example, are not directly subject to management decisions and can only be indirectly influenced through specific interventions, such as training, information or user support. From a managerial point of view, in order to evaluate and improve the IT implementation process and its relationship with user acceptance, it seems reasonable to focus on external variables that are most likely to be subject to management decisions and interventions. Based on the general research on technology acceptance in standard software implementations, as well as the broader area of literature on organizational change, the following section provides a framework for structuring and integrating important administrative variables in the context of IT implementation processes in the enlarged TAM.

3   Proposed Theoretical Model

Many factors have been suggested as relevant to the successful management of standard software implementation processes and user acceptance [16, 24, 25, 37]. Venkatesh and Bala (2008) [7] listed four categories of determinants of user acceptance: individual differences (e.g. computer stress), system characteristics (e.g. output quality), social influences (e.g. image) and accommodative conditions (e.g. organisational support). This categorization summed up several variables that have been shown to be generally related to perceived ease of use, perceived usefulness and subjective norms. The proposed categories provide a useful framework for the general earlier elements of the TAM variables. However, this categorization of external variables does not specifically focus on management aspects when applying corporate standard software to organizations and includes categories of variables that are not directly subject to management interventions (e.g. individual differences). In a different approach, Kwahk and Lee (2008) [37] proposed computer self-efficacy, organizational commitment and perceived personal competence as prior factors of perceived ease of use and perceived usefulness.

Overall, the factors listed by the various authors appear to differ significantly between the studies, and little effort has been made to provide a systematic categorization of the management factors associated with the acceptance of IT users in organizations during the implementation process [35, 36]. A model-based evaluation of managerial variables will benefit from providing a framework that structures external management variables in IT implementations related to user acceptance and behavior.

An integrated approach should include central and relevant variables in order to analyze the strengths and weaknesses of the implementation process against user acceptance. Based on assessing the factors of content, process, and context, management can identify areas for improvement and extract specific measures to optimize them. Figure 1 illustrates the full research model proposed for evaluating management's activities to improve user acceptance of BIs software implementations.

Hsieh & Lai (2020) [20] and Grublješič & Jaklič (2015) [1] pointed to relevant research into the Technology Acceptance Model (TAM) that the quality of information positively affects the perceived usefulness. That is, when the quality of the information management system information is accurate, the results and the outputs will be reliable and could be reused, therefore users believe that the system is capable of providing correct information and results. The study therefore makes suggested proposition (P) 1 on the basis of the above relevant research.

P1. Information quality has a positive effect on the perceived usefulness of the BI system. Standard software systems typically incorporate different business functions and procedures based on a common database [2, 39, 40]. Therefore, the quality of the system results for a particular user largely depends on the degree of data quality. Exploring the factors for a successful standard software, Chou et al. (2011) [26] said that when the quality of service includes timely and reliable information, as well as user convenience, it positively affects the perceived usefulness. The same was found in the Gefen and Keil studies (1998) [27], they updated the TAM to be a function of the standard software framework. The results of their studies show that the quality of services affects not only user engagement, but also the perceived ease of use of the BIs systems. The following suggested proposition (P) 2 is therefore formulated:

P2. Services quality is positively related to BI user's perceived usefulness. One more important aspect is the system performance quality, which includes system stability, downtime, and reporting availability, and is defined as system performance. Wixom and Todd (2005) [28] identified five general quality characteristics for IT systems: Reliability explains how reliably a system works for the user—flexibility refers to possible system customizations of user requirements. Integration focuses on the capabilities of the system to collect and process data from different sources. Accessibility refers to the simplicity of accessing information from the system and extracting it from the system. Finally, speed indicates how the system responds to user requirements, and in particular how tasks are performed. End users prefer systems that perform well and therefore use them more regularly [1].

P3 Service quality has a positive effect on the perceived ease of use of the BI system. Chiu and Fang (2005) [29] explored internet users' behavior and found that system quality includes design quality, response time, and accessibility. Design quality refers to the inquiry function of the system and file transfer speed. Online response time means how soon the response is and how long the response takes. Accessibility refers to whether the software and hardware of the website are accessible. These have significant impacts on an IS user's perceived ease of use. Thus, the following suggested proposition (P) 4 follows:

P4. System quality is positively related to BI user's perceived ease of use.
Schepers and Wetzels (2007) [30] and Lee and Kim (2009) [31] studied previous research articles on TAM, and found evidence that user's perceived ease of use affects perceived usefulness positively. Based on above results, suggested proposition (P) 5 is presented as follows:

P5. Perceived ease of use is positively related to BI user's perceived usefulness.
A number of studies analyzed the association between individual motivation and user acceptance of a knowledge management system. The results demonstrate that whether the use of a knowledge management IS can improve users' work performance, productivity and efficiency will affect users' frequency in using the system. The results show a positive relationship between perceived usefulness and users' intention to use. Chiu and Fang (2005) [29] explored users' behavior in using internet, and concluded that frequently updating useful information on a website can affect users' willingness to use the website. The study proved the positive relation between perceived usefulness and users' intention to use. Hence, this relationship comes as suggested proposition (P) 6 as follows:

P6. Perceived usefulness is positively related to BI user's intention to use.
Anur and Alwi (2017) [32] explored researches on hospital employees' use of electronic case histories, and found the users' intention to use electronic case histories were affected by their feelings about whether they are easier to use than the conventional method. The study therefore concludes that perceived ease of use has a positive impact on user's intention to use. Chen et al. (2008) [33] studied electronic public service, and the results show that a simplified electronic public service system attracts user to reuse the system. Thus, this leads us to establish the following suggested proposition (P):

P7. Perceived ease of use is positively related to BI user's intention to use.

In conclusion the model proposed is following:

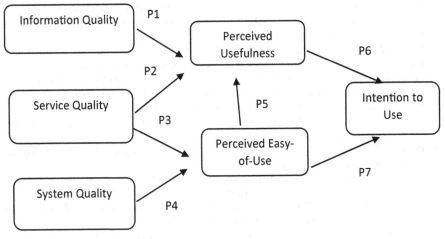

Fig. 1. Proposed research model

4   Conclusions

The purpose of this research is to provide with information about the factors that are currently most relevant to users' acceptance of BI across public hospitals. In addition, the TAM helps to specifically identify the possibilities for improving the planning and arrangement of administrative activities.

Therefore, it is necessary to discuss the BIs use environment considering not only technical aspects but also end users' viewpoints as well as sensitive factors. Despite of some limitations, it is expected that this study will give meaningful evidence based on the users' viewpoints regards the intention to use BI standard software.

Moreover, this research could have major contribution to top management in public hospitals, to know the current level of usage of BIs, since the study will focus basically in public hospitals, thus providing new information about the current level of implementation. In addition, the study could also have practical implications on future planning and design of BI applications, with regards to major determinants of employee's adoption of BIs in public hospitals.

Some of the limitations of this study could be that all data will be collected from the management administrators work in finance departments in public hospitals. Therefore, the ability to generalize the findings of this study may be limited. Also, this study will omit some factors that might be significant to individual's intention to adopt BI applications. Future studies could examine other potential factors such as prior BI experience, individual innovativeness, technical knowledge and social influence.

References

1. Grublješič, T., Jaklič, J.: Business intelligence acceptance: the prominence of organizational factors. Inf. Syst. Manage. **32**, 299–331 (2015)

2. do Nascimento, M.G., et al.: Covid-19: a digital transformation approach to a public primary healthcare environment. In: 2020 IEEE Symposium on Computers and Communications (ISCC), pp. 1–6. Rennes, France (2020)
3. Venkatesh, V., Davis, F.D., Morris, M.G.: Dead or alive? the development, trajectory and future of technology adoption research. J. Assoc. Inf. Syst. **8**, 268–286 (2007)
4. Gjellebæk, C., Svensson, A., Bjørkquist, C., Fladeby, N., Grundén, K.: Management challenges for future digitalization of healthcare services. Futures, **124** (2020)
5. Bronzo, M., de Resende, P.T.V.V., Deoliveira, M.P.V., McCormack, K.P., de Sousa, P.R., Ferreira, R.L.: Improving performance aligning business analytics with process orientation. Int. J. Inf. Manage. **33**, 300–307 (2013)
6. Popovic, A., Turk, T., Jaklic, J.: Conceptual model of business value of business intelligence systems. Management **15**, 5–30 (2010)
7. Venkatesh, V., Bala, H.: Technology acceptance model 3 and a research agenda on interventions. Decis. Sci. **39**, 273–315 (2008)
8. Venkatesh, V., Morris, M.G., Davis, G.B., Davis, F.D.: User acceptance of information technology: towards a unified view. MIS Q. **27**, 425–478 (2003)
9. Yoon, T.E., Jeong, B.K., Ghosh, B.: User acceptance of business intelligence application: motivation to learn, technology, social influence, and situational constraints. Int. J. Bus. Inf. Syst. **26**, 432–450 (2017)
10. Bach, MB., Čeljo, A, Zoroja, J.: Technology acceptance model for business intelligence systems: preliminary research. Procedia Comput. Sci. **100**, 995–1001 (2016)
11. Pai, F.Y., Huang, K.I.: Applying the technology acceptance model to the introduction of healthcare information systems. Technol. Forecast. Soc. Chang. **78**, 650–660 (2011)
12. DeLone, W.H., McLean, E.R.: The DeLone and McLean model of information systems success: a ten-years update. J. Manage. Inf. Syst. **19**, 9–30 (2003)
13. Kitsios, F., Kamariotou, M., Manthou, V., Batsara, A.: Hospital information systems: measuring end-user satisfaction. In: Themistocleous, M., Papadaki, M., Kamal, M.M. (eds.) EMCIS 2020. LNBIP, vol. 402, pp. 463–479. Springer, Cham (2020). https://doi.org/10.1007/978-3-030-63396-7_31
14. Pasaoglu, D.: Analysis of ERP usage with technology acceptance model. Glob. Bus. Man. Res. **3**, 157–169 (2011)
15. Holt, D.T., Armenakis, A., Feild, H.S., Harris, S.G.: Readiness for organizational change: the systematic development of a scale. J. Appl. Behav. Sci. **43**, 232–255 (2007)
16. Bueno, S., Salmeron, L.S.: TAM-based success modeling. Interact. Comput. **20**, 515–523 (2008)
17. Kitsios, F., Stefanakakis, S., Kamariotou, M., Dermentzoglou, L.: E-service evaluation: user satisfaction measurement and implications in health sector. Comput. Stand. Interfaces J. **63**, 16–26 (2019)
18. Papadopoulos, T., Angelopoulos, S., Kitsios, F.: A strategic approach to e-health interoperability using e-government frameworks, In: Information Resources Management Association, User-Driven Healthcare: Concepts, Methodologies, Tools, and Applications, IGI Global Publishing, chapter 19, pp. 791–807 (2013)
19. Engin, M., Gürses, F.: Adoption of hospital information systems in public hospitals in Turkey: an analysis with the unified theory of acceptance and use of technology model. Int. J. Innov. Technol. Manage. **16**, 1–19 (2019)
20. Hsieh, P.J., Lai, H.M.: Exploring people's intentions to use the health passbook in self-management: An extension of the technology acceptance and health behavior theoretical perspectives in health literacy. Technol. Forecast. Soc. Change **161**, 120328 (2020)
21. Kohnke, O., Wolf, T.R., Mueller, K.: Managing user acceptance: an empirical investigation in the context of business intelligence standard software. Int. J. Inf. Syst. Change Manage. **5**, 269–290 (2011)

22. Yousafzai, S.Y., Foxall, G.R., Pallister, J.G.: Technology acceptance: a meta-analysis of the TAM: Part 1. J. Model. Manage. **2**, 251–280 (2007)

23. Lee, Y., Kozar, K.A., Larsen, K.R.T.: The technology acceptance model: Past, present and future. Commun. Assoc. Inf. Syst. **12**, 752–780 (2003)

24. Kerimoglu, O., Basoglu, N.: A framework for understanding adoption of organizational enterprise resource planning systems. In: Picmet Conference, Portland, Oregon, USA (2005)

25. Kitsios, F., Papadopoulos, T., Angelopoulos, S.: A roadmap to the introduction of pervasive Information Systems in healthcare. Int. J. Adv. Pervasive Ubiquit. Comput. **2**, 21–32 (2010)

26. Chou, H.-P., Wu, M.-Y., Weng, Y.-C., Huang, Y.-H.: TAM2-based study of website user behavior-using web 2.0 websites as an example. WSEAS Trans. Bus. Econ. **8**, 133–155 (2011)

27. Gefen, D., Keil, M.: The impact of developer responsiveness on perceptions of usefulness and ease of use: An extension of the technology acceptance model. Data Base Adv. Inf. Syst. **29**, 35–49 (1998)

28. Wixom, B.H., Todd, P.A.: A theoretical integration of user satisfaction and technology acceptance. Inf. Syst. Res. **16**, 85–102 (2005)

29. Chiu, Y.W., Fang, K.D.: A study of portal user behavior patterns. Web J. Chin. Manage. Rev. **8**, 43–60 (2005)

30. Schepers, J., Wetzels, M.: A meta-analysis of the technology acceptance model: investigating subjective norm and moderation effects. J. Inf. Manage. **44**, 90–103 (2007)

31. Lee, S., Kim, B.G.: Factors affecting the usage of intranet: a confirmatory study. Comput. Hum. Behav. **25**, 191–201 (2009)

32. Anur, M., Alwi, M.Y.: Technology acceptance in healthcare service: a case of Electronic Medical Records (ERM), **7**, 863–877 (2004)

33. Chen, Y.C., Shang, R.N., Ho, T.Y., Hesieh, S.C.: The behavioral intention to use e systems for employees in public utility company: Analysis based on TAM and TTF. J. E Bus. **10**, 305–327 (2008)

34. Kwak, Y.H., Park, J., Chung, B.Y., Ghosh, S.: Understanding end-users' acceptance of enterprise resource planning (erp) system in project based sectors. IEEE Trans. Eng. Manage. **59**, 266–277 (2012)

35. Sindakis, S., Kitsios, F.: Entrepreneurial dynamics and patient involvement in service innovation: developing a model to promote growth and sustainability in mental health care. J. Knowl. Econ. **7**(2), 545–564 (2014). https://doi.org/10.1007/s13132-014-0228-1

36. Stefanakakis, S., Trevlakis, S. Kitsios, F.: Analyzing quality characteristics: the case of an e – health application. In: Vlachopoulou, M., Kitsios, F., Kamariotou, M. (Eds.) Proceedings of the 6th International Symposium and 28th National Conference on Operational Research, Thessaloniki, Greece, pp. 246–251 (2017)

37. Kwahk, K., Lee, J.: The role of readiness for change in ERP implementation: theoretical bases and empirical validation. Inf. Manage. **45**, 474–481 (2008)

38. Escobar-Rodríguez, T., Monge-Lozano, P., Romero-Alonso, M.M.: Acceptance of e-prescriptions and automated medication-management systems in hospitals: an extension of the technology acceptance model. J. Inf. Syst. **26**, 77–96 (2012)

39. Jackson, J.D., Mun, Y.Y., Park, J.S.: An empirical test of three mediation models for the relationship between personal innovativeness and user acceptance of technology. Inf. Manage. **50**, 154–161 (2013)

40. Kraus, S., Schiavone, F., Pluzhnikova, A., Invernizzi, A.C.: Digital transformation in healthcare: analyzing the current state-of-research. J. Bus. Res. **123**, 557–567 (2021)

41. Li, X., Hsieh, J.P.A., Rai, A.: Motivational differences across post-acceptance information system usage behaviors: an investigation in the business intelligence systems context. Inf. Syst. Res. **24**, 659–682 (2013)

42. Kitsios, F., Grigoroudis, E., Giannikopoulos, K., Doumpos, M., Zopounidis, C.: Strategic decision making using multicriteria analysis: new service development in Greek hotels. Int. J. Data Anal. Tech. Strat. **7**, 187–202 (2015)
43. Mitroulis, D., Kitsios, F.: Evaluating digital transformation strategies: a MCDA analysis of Greek tourism SMEs. In: Proceedings of the 14th European Conference on Innovation and Entrepreneurship (ECIE19), Kalamata, Greece, vol. 2, pp. 667–676 (2019)

Health is Wealth: A Conceptual Overview of Virtual Healthcare & Future Research Directions [1995–2021]

Josue Kuika Watat[1] (✉) ⓘ, Ebenezer Agbozo[2] ⓘ, Sunday Olaleye Adewale[3] ⓘ, and Gideon Mekonnen Jonathan[4] ⓘ

[1] HISP Centre and Department of Informatics, University of Oslo, Ole-Johan Dahls Hus Gaustadalleèn 23B, 0373 Oslo, Norway
josuekw@ifi.uio.no
[2] Ural Federal University, Yekaterinburg, Russian Federation
eagbozo@urfu.ru
[3] School of Business, JAMK University of Applied Sciences, Rajakatu 35, 40100 Jyväskylä, Finland
sunday.olaleye@jamk.fi
[4] Stockholm University, Stockholm, Sweden
gideon@dsv.su.se

Abstract. The appearance of pandemics of various kinds that have shaken the world and transformed health paradigms has led many organizations and states to review their health strategies to ensure sustainable assistance to the population. Organizations are turning more towards a sustainable digital transformation, which considers multiple dimensions, including health. This study presents a topic-oriented mapping of a range of conceptual and practice-based efforts and strategies implemented in the virtual health paradigm. The systematic literature review conducted since the first insights in 1995 reveals the eagerness related to the digital transformation of health care and the popularization of digital health strategies. The resolutions of our study will enrich the emerging literature on virtual health in a wide range of settings.

Keywords: Virtual HealthCare · Covid19 · Artificial intelligence · Information systems · Bibliometric

1 Introduction and Related Work

Socio-economic and cultural transitions, and climate change have placed the use of digital technologies at the center of developmental concerns and paradigm shifts in health care [1, 2]. The crowding of hospital beds, physical distance and the inability of doctors to provide meticulous follow-up to the growing number of patients have put the need and importance of telehealth to address global health crises back on the agenda [3]. At the height of the covid19 crisis, telehealth proved its decisive role in the whole chain of patient follow-up. Diverse researches highlight the importance of telehealth in a

M. Themistocleous and M. Papadaki (Eds.): EMCIS 2021, LNBIP 437, pp. 463–473, 2022.
https://doi.org/10.1007/978-3-030-95947-0_33

multi-contextual way, as it describes new frameworks that amply respond to emergency situations with better prospects of structural transformation [4]. This exponential transformation therefore poses an urgent need to study new digital approaches associated with health in order to theorize lessons learned and experiences in various theoretical anchors [5, 6].

This research aims to present a systematic review of the emerging literature from an analytical perspective of virtual health care in a global health emergency. We perform a global review since the first investigations that were conducted in 1995, until 2021. The presentation of the state of the art of the studied problem aims to draw up a non-exhaustive typology of the different theoretical and practical approaches of virtual health care carried out showing the evolution over time. In comparison with the literature available since the beginning of the year 2020, there is a need to highlight the different approaches carried out in a global health crisis situation following a consolidated and unique research.

After an outline of previous research conducted on the problem studied, we conduct a systematic analysis of the impact of virtual health care in a multi-contextual setting. Subsequently, we present some trends from the emerging literature with associated analyses. The concluding section of this research focuses on the theoretical and practical implications of our research. We also present the conclusions stemming from our work.

The spread of various diseases and pandemics like covid19 have revealed the use of tools and techniques associated with virtual health care. They incorporate ubiquitous patient collaboration. This is the case of the "CIGNA" project [7]. In addition, there is a project called "SAPHIRE" which allows patients to be monitored from their homes thanks to a connection of the various medical sensors associated with the decision support devices in hospitals [8]. Also, research such as that by [9] and [10] have focused on patient peer support and health care delivery, respectively.

Another study examined the practicality of using mobile devices as a rescue mission during an emergency on the road. This novel idea called "My Contact Person" is a naming convention saved on a mobile device that paved the way for the paramedical professionals or good Samaritans to link a victim of an accident or people in danger to their loved ones or connect the victims with an ambulance for first [11]. A good Samaritans can also make a video call to show the present situation of the victims. Virtual healthcare is growing and seems to be the future of Medicare care especially for the rural dwellers where there is abject poverty and lack of infrastructural facilities. Further, Virtual healthcare is a panacea for Africa and other countries with large crowds and where hospital beds are not sufficient for the patients that need care.

The ongoing COVID-19 corroborates the expansion of virtual healthcare. Meg, Vimal, Stacy and Jared [12] confirmed the increase and importance of virtual health care in the United States as an intervention for COVID-19 social distancing. Also, the authors mentioned that the inevitability of virtual health care has set the policy makers thinking on the virtual care services charges in the future. Seeking solution for this daunting task has stirred the American Medical Association (AMA), Manatt Health, a legal and consulting firm to come up with a framework that enables accessibility of the value of digital care [12]. In America, before COVID-19 the virtual health care adoption was extremely low, but the COVID-19 panic has increased the adoption rate. The literature synthesized and the existing studies attest to the under-development of virtual health care.

2 Methodology

To achieve the aims of this research, we leverage on the systematic literature review methodology known as PRISMA (Preferred Reporting Items for Systematic Reviews and Meta-Analyses) to gather literature on virtual healthcare research over time in order to understand the core concepts. The systematic review approach was adopted due to its ability to essentially summarize evidence relating to efficacy of any domain of discourse accurately and reliably [13]. The PRISMA statement guidelines were adopted for this study to select the core themes that pertain to virtual healthcare globally [14].

We used the keyword "virtual healthcare" OR "virtual health" focused on Scopus as our main source of scientific articles for our research goal. The metadata query results produced 1043 results and was limited to scientific papers in English language, papers published until 2021 (as of this article's submission date) and full author information available (i.e. excluding book summary prefaces) – making 866 papers. To obtain research papers relevant to the goal of our study, our exclusion criteria:

- Duplicated articles.
- Articles (abstract, introduction, discussion, and conclusion) irrelevant to the theme of virtual healthcare or virtual health.

Our inclusion criteria:

- All articles published until 2021 (at the time of submission).
- Cited and uncited articles.
- Abstracts (abstract, introduction, discussion, and conclusion) and titles relevant to the theme of virtual healthcare or virtual health.

The total number of papers were 865 – 357 reviews, 343 articles, 117 conference papers, 12 notes, 11 conference reviews, 9 book chapters, 6 editorials, 6 short surveys, 3 letters, and 1 erratum. Figure 1 illustrates the process discussed.

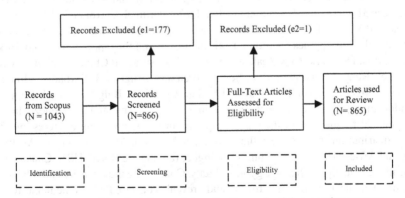

Fig. 1. Research methodology – data collection and article screening process

The research follows a thematic analysis approach which involves the comprehension of themes that represent ways of understanding the combined meaning of the text [15]. Thematic analysis aids in identifying patterns within data [16]. The study followed six-step approach: (a) data familiarization, (b) generating initial codes, (c) theme search, (d) reviewing themes, (e) defining and naming themes, and (f) reporting [17].

This study made use of the biblioshiny, a web based interface built on the bibliometrix (the open-source scientometrics and bibliometrics research tool) package for R [18]. Results from our data analysis are presented in the next section.

3   Results

The bibliometric analysis conducted generated insightful results that indicates the country's scientific production, author's word growth, thematic map keywords, conceptual structural map, trends topics and thematic map evolution. This section discusses the six (6) stages of virtual healthcare transformation based on the academic literature synthesized with Biblioshiny algorithms. The descriptive statistics in Table 1 below shows that total documents of 842 accounts for 4.65 average years from publication, 8.43 average citations per documents and 1.53 average citations per year per document. The documents type consists of article (340), book chapter (9), conference paper (117), editorial (6), letter (3), note (11), review (350) and short survey (6). Collaboration wise, the single-authored documents accounts for 82, documents per author 0.25, authors per document 3.96, co-authors per documents 4.63 and the collaboration index 4.29. For document type, review was predominant and followed by article. Further, co-authorship excelled the single authorship.

Figure 2 shows how Biblioshiny visualize country scientific production as a world map. The darkest blue shows the saturation of virtual healthcare paper production and followed in turn with blue and lighter blue colors. The grey color shows country gaps of virtual healthcare literature. Southern America tops the list of virtual healthcare literature and specifically Brazil with 776. Next to South America is Northern America and United States of America frequency accounts for 470 while Canada records 156. United Kingdom in Europe has 122, Australia has 77 and China in Asia has 56. Other countries like Spain records 48, Japan 43, Egypt 40, Italy and Netherlands 35, Sweden 33, Greece 31, Germany 30, Colombia 28, India 25, Portugal 22, Romania 18, France 16, Finland and Mexico 15, Cuba, Ireland, and Malaysia 10, Saudi Arabia, South Africa and Switzerland 9, Philippines 8, Jordan, Pakistan, Qatar, and Singapore 7, Iran and Turkey 6, Argentina, Denmark, New Zealand and Peru 5, Austria and Chile 4, Belgium, Croatia, Israel, Kenya, Norway, Serbia, South Korea and Uruguay 3, Barbados, Hungary, Lebanon, Nigeria, Panama, Poland and Sudan 2, Bolivia, Bulgaria, Czech Republic, Ecuador, Ethiopia, Georgia, Guatemala, Jamaica, Malta, Thailand and Venezuela. The geographical frequencies of the papers captured in this study is quite interesting. The papers distribution cut across Southern America, Northern America, Europe, Australia, Asia, and Africa. The first ten countries in higher ranking are Brazil, USA, Canada, UK, Australia, China, Spain, Japan, Egypt, and Italy. Confirming the intensity and robustness of virtual healthcare in Brazil, a recent study reveals concerted 79 telemedicine-related

Table 1. Virtual healthcare literature descriptive statistics

Description	Results
DATA OVERVIEW	
Timespan	1995:2021
Sources (Journals, Books, etc.)	537
Documents	842
Average years from publication	4,65
Average citations per documents	8,425
Average citations per year per doc	1,534
References	1
Document types	
article	340
book chapter	9
conference paper	117
editorial	6
letter	3
note	11
review	350
short survey	6
Document contents	
Keywords plus (ID)	5065
Author's keywords (DE)	2216
AUTHORS	
Authors	3333
Author appearances	3897
Authors of single-authored documents	73
Authors of multi-authored documents	3260
Authors collaboration	
Single-authored documents	82
Documents per author	0.253
Authors per document	3.96
Co-Authors per documents	4.63
Collaboration index	4.29

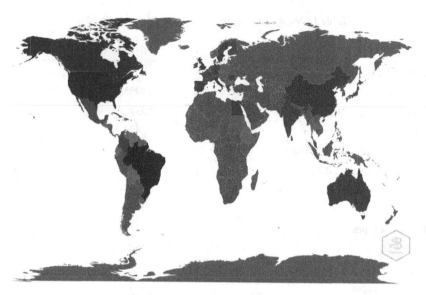

Fig. 2. Country scientific production

legislations emanates from the Brazil federal government as a combination of laws, decrees, and ordinances. These legislations are in combination with another 31 regulations from the Federal Councils of Health Professionals [19]. Telemedicine commenced in Brazil in 2011 and it has survived for one decade. Our bibliometric results show virtual healthcare research gap in Greenland, Iceland, Russia, Panama, Oman, Yemen, Papua New Guinea. Apart from Egypt, Sudan, Ethiopia, Nigeria and South Africa, most of the other African countries have not played a significant role in academic productivity related to virtual healthcare.

Figure 3 elaborates the Author's word growth from 2000–2021 and shows different patterns of growth for ten keywords of systematic review, telemedicine, COVID-19, Telehealth, Virtual Health, Review, Nursing, Meta-Analysis, Digital Health and Public Health. Systematic review, Review and Meta-Analysis which indicates secondary study started evolving in different years. For example, systematic review first appeared in 2014 with 1 frequency and since 2014 it has been growing till date. Within eight years, it has grown from 1 to 50. Review appearance was earlier in 2010 and within 12 years it has grown from 1 to 32. For meta-analysis, its growth was a bit slow, and it emerged it emerged in 2016 and by 2021 it has grown from 1 to 25. Telemedicine, Telehealth, Virtual Health, and Digital Health belongs to the same group and telemedicine and telehealth pattern of growth was similar. The duo emerged in the same year (2003) and by 2021, telehealth has grown from 1 to 36 while telemedicine outgrown telehealth with 13 (36 vs 49). For virtual health which is the focus of this study appeared for the first time in 2014 with 1 and by 2021, it has increased to 32. Digital health featured in 2018 and increased to 18 in 2021. Also, nursing as a keyword growth commenced with 1 in 2011 and reached 26 in 2021 but COVID-19 reflects in virtual healthcare literature in 2020

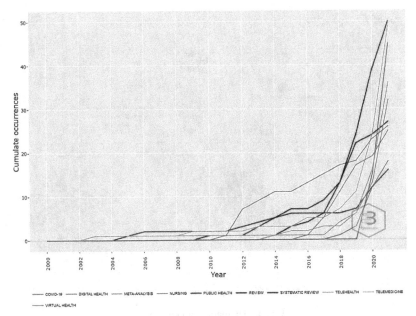

Fig. 3. Author word growth

and till date records 45. Finally, Public Health commenced in 2005 and by 2021, it has grown to 16. Because of COVID-19 disruption, it only reflects in less than two years but its frequency almost catching up with the keywords that covers 19 years. The word growth shows the infancy of virtual healthcare research domain. The virtual health is growing linearly.

Biblioshiny classified the Thematic Map of Keywords in Fig. 4 into four quadrant of Motor themes in the upper right, Niche themes in the upper left, Peripheral themes in the lower left and Transversal and basic themes in the lower right. Density divides the vertical part of the quadrant while Centrality divides the quadrant horizontally. The motor themes in the first quadrant plays a central role to the structure of the virtual healthcare research field and reflect both high centrality and density. Healthcare, artificial intelligence and Internet were clustered together in motor theme. Brief intervention is the only niche theme, and it indicates a marginal theme in the field of virtual healthcare. The peripheral themes clustered virtual health communities and systematic review together. These are the emerging and declining themes. The systematic literature review and meta-analysis are more pronounced than the virtual health communities, social media, and virtual health record. The last quadrant clustered telemedicine and nursing together. These concepts of telemedicine are not well developed. Overall, telemedicine has the highest centrality with 6.08, density of 65.84, centrally ranked 9 and density ranked 2. Healthcare has the highest density with 127.48, 2.49 centrality, centrally ranked 5 and density ranked 8. Virtual health communities centrally ranked 2 and density ranked 4. Also, nursing density ranked 1. The metrics of centrality, density, rank centrality and rank density differs.

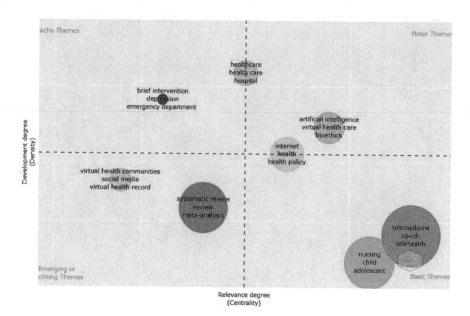

Fig. 4. Thematic map keywords

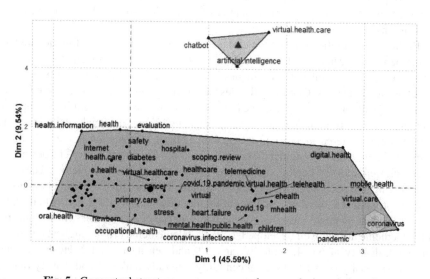

Fig. 5. Conceptual structure map – correspondence analysis and clustering

From Fig. 5, the red cluster highlights majority of the keywords which are popular within the healthcare scope. An evident set of keywords within the red cluster is concepts related to the covid-19 pandemic; revealing the sporadic rise in virtual healthcare initiatives to support healthcare delivery. The blue cluster (chatbot, artificial intelligence, and virtual healthcare) culminate in a confirmatory manner to support the assertions of researchers with respect to the diffusion of artificial intelligence within healthcare to support decision making. In areas such as pharmaceutical prescriptions, elderly care, and in communicating with the general populace regarding the covid-19 pandemic, conversational AI has been beneficial and will continue to play a vital role in supporting healthcare delivery [20, 21].

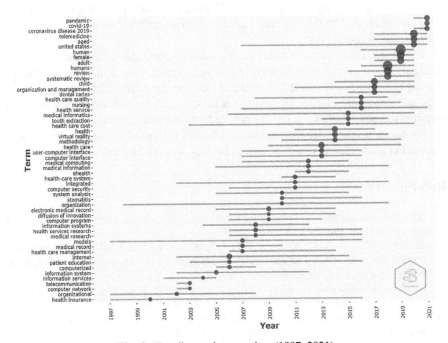

Fig. 6. Trending topics over time (1997–2021)

From Fig. 6, one very key concept to take note of is the topic "human". This can be attributed to the shift from technology as a means of solving tasks (i.e. techno-centric) to technology that contributes to the wellness (physically, socially, and mentally) of individuals – i.e. human-centric [22–24].

4 Conclusion

The diffusion of modern technology, has played a key role in improving the living and working conditions of humanity; and is greatly influencing areas such as healthcare. The future of healthcare delivery is dependent on technology as a support medium for decision making. The SARS-COV-2 (Covid-19) pandemic that hit the entire globe in 2020 has revealed the need for healthcare delivery to be heavily invested into as well as novel techno-centric and human-centric solutions to be developed. Virtual healthcare is one of such promising technologies. Virtual healthcare is the vehicle through which healthcare delivery could be accessible to all communities and societies; so long as there exists affordable platforms for end users.

Our study delved into the world of virtual healthcare by presenting a bibliometric and thematic study on the state of the art. It was evident that with respect to virtual healthcare, artificial intelligence and internet health policy will be of great interest in the coming years in order to protect improve livelihood using data-driven techniques while not compromising on the privacy of individuals. Another revelation has to do with Brazil as a leader in the virtual healthcare space and this can be linked with the legal enabling environment created by the Brazilian Federal Government. This should be a lesson for emerging economies to adopt.

With respect to theoretical contributions, our study provides a thematic and biblio-metric overview of virtual healthcare and provides researchers with emerging themes they could ride on to steer the field forward. With respect to practical contributions, these facts and figures presented, will be relevant to policymakers, software developers and investors to know where to target efforts in order to improve human livelihood.

For future research, we recommend researchers to expand the search databases to sources our study did not cover, as well as languages aside the English language.

References

1. Izzo, F., Camminatiello, I.: Gaming for healthcare: a Bibliometric analysis in business and management. Int. Bus. Res. **13**, 27–41 (2020)
2. Chatterjee, P., Tesis, A., Cymberknop, L.J., Armentano, R.L.: Internet of Things and artificial intelligence in healthcare During COVID-19 pandemic-a south american perspective. Front Public Health **8**, 600213 (2020)
3. Babalola, D., Anayo, M., Itoya, D.A.: Telehealth during COVID-19: why Sub-Saharan Africa is yet to log-in to virtual healthcare? AIMS Med. Sci. **8**, 46–55 (2021)
4. Arshad Ali, S., et al.: Global interest in telehealth during COVID-19 pandemic: an analysis of Google trends™. Cureus **12**, e10487–e10487 (2020)
5. Mele, S., Izzo, F.: Virtual healthcare: a literature review in business and management field. Int. J. Bus. Manage. **16**, 25 (2021)
6. Abdel-Rahman, O.: Patient-related barriers to some virtual healthcare services among cancer patients in the USA: a population-based study. J. Comp. Effectiveness Res. **10**, 119–126 (2021)
7. McClure, S., Scambray, J., Kurtz, G.: Hacking Exposed: Network Security Secrets and Solutions, Fourth Edition (2009)
8. Laleci, G.B., Dogac, A., Olduz, M., Tasyurt, I., Yuksel, M., Okcan, A.: SAPHIRE: A multi-agent system for remote healthcare monitoring through computerized clinical guidelines. In: Annicchiarico, R., Cortés, U., Urdiales, C. (eds.) Agent Technology and e-Health, pp. 25–44. Birkhäuser Basel, Basel (2008)
9. Schopp, L.H., Hales, J.W., Quetsch, J.L., Hauan, M.J., Brown, G.D.: Design of a peer-to-peer telerehabilitation model. Telemed. J. E Health **10**, 243–251 (2004)
10. Demiris, G., Oliver, D.R.P., Fleming, D.A., Edison, K.: Hospice staff attitudes towards telehospice, **21**, 343–347 (2004)

11. Olaleye, S.A., Sanusi, I.T., Agjei, R.O., Adusei-Mensah, F.: Please call my contact person: mobile devices for a rescue mission during an emergency. Inf. Discov. Deliv. **49**, 114–122 (2021)

12. Meg, B., Vimal, M., Stacy, L., Jared, A.: How to Measure the Value of Virtual Health Care. Havard Business Review, USA (2021)

13. Liberati, A., et al.: The PRISMA statement for reporting systematic reviews and meta-analyses of studies that evaluate health care interventions: explanation and elaboration. J. Clin. Epidemiol. **62**, e1–e34 (2009)

14. Hutton, B., et al.: The quality of reporting methods and results in network meta-analyses: an overview of reviews and suggestions for improvement. PLoS ONE 9, e92508 (2014)

15. Bearman, M., Dawson, P.: Qualitative synthesis and systematic review in health professions education. Med. Educ. **47**, 252–260 (2013)

16. D'Agata, A.L., Coughlin, M., Sanders, M.R.: Clinician perceptions of the NICU infant experience: Is the NICU hospitalization traumatic? Am. J. Perinatol. **35**, 1159–1167 (2018)

17. Braun, V., Clarke, V.: Using thematic analysis in psychology. Qual. Res. Psychol. **3**, 77–101 (2006)

18. Aria, M., Cuccurullo, C.: bibliometrix: An R-tool for comprehensive science mapping analysis. J. Informet. **11**, 959–975 (2017)

19. Silva, A.B., et al.: Three decades of telemedicine in Brazil: mapping the regulatory framework from 1990 to 2018. PLoS ONE **15**, e0242869–e0242869 (2020)

20. Nadarzynski, T., Miles, O., Cowie, A., Ridge, D.: Acceptability of Artificial Intelligence (AI)-led chatbot services in healthcare: a mixed-methods study. Digit. Health **5**, 2055207619871808 (2019)

21. Battineni, G., Chintalapudi, N., Amenta, F.: AI Chatbot Design during an Epidemic Like the Novel Coronavirus. Healthcare, Basel, Switzerland, 8 (2020)

22. Castro, L.A., Tapia, A., Perez, C.B., Beltrán-Márquez, J.: Towards human-centric interfaces for decision making support in geriatric centers. In: Ochoa, S.F., Singh, P., Bravo, J. (eds.) UCAmI 2017. LNCS, vol. 10586, pp. 643–654. Springer, Cham (2017). https://doi.org/10.1007/978-3-319-67585-5_63

23. Fahl, S., Harbach, M., Smith, M.: Towards human-centric visual access control for clinical data management. Stud. Health Technol. Inf. **180**, 756–760 (2012)

24. Ukil, A., Marin, L., Jara, A., Farserotu, J.: On the knowledge-driven analytics and systems impacting human quality of life. In: Proceedings of the 29th ACM International Conference on Information and Knowledge Management, pp. 3539–3540. Association for Computing Machinery (2020)

Using 3D-Technology to Support Facial Treatment

Paul Alpar[1] ⓘ, Thomas Driebe[1](✉) ⓘ, and Peter Schleussner[2]

[1] Philipps-University, Hans-Meerwein-Straße 6, 35032 Marburg, Germany
alpar@staff.uni-marburg.de, tdriebe@gmx.de
[2] Praxis Linzbach and Schleussner, Frankfurterstr. 47, 61118 Bad Vilbel, Germany

Abstract. Facial treatments, even for aesthetic purposes, often involve unnecessary patient risk due to treatment by unexperienced practitioners and/or a lack of standardized procedures. We develop a software to support and standardize facial treatments based on knowledge of experts. The prototype utilizes WebGL and 3D-equipment, but it also focuses affordability to make its wide-spread use more likely. It aims to help in treatment planning along with professional self-development. In this paper, we describe the underlying problem, a possible medical model as a solution, the prototype architecture, and how the prototype is utilized in the treatment process. Finally, we conduct a test of the prototype.

Keywords: 3D-documentation · Treatment support · Non-surgical aesthetical procedures

1 Introduction

In this paper, we present a prototype for making facial treatment knowledge available to novice practitioners consisting of a web-based software and low-cost hardware. It showcases the prototype itself as well as additional validation. We use soft filler tissue treatment to demonstrate the prototype, since this is often performed by novice clinicians. Soft-filler tissue treatments are non-surgical aesthetic interventions in the face, but nonetheless can involve critical patient risk if done wrong. The prototype focuses on providing cost-effective 3D-intervention planning and documentation, since other available, but more expensive hardware likely will not be used by novice practitioners. The aim is to provide a prototype that enables both knowledge transfer and professional development. Additionally, in order to address the problems stated in the next section, the prototype needs to be as accessible as possible in terms of hardware requirements. The prototype should also be able to validate different treatment models.

The training of practitioners is similar across surgical disciplines; therefore, we will first address the problems in current training to demonstrate the necessity of our prototype. In recent years, the number of digital support systems in the medicine sector increased, but the development is clearly biased towards diagnostic medicine compared to surgical medicine [1]. Diagnostics provide a better fit for most digital technologies: A main example is the development of medical AI, where diagnostic AI systems like

M. Themistocleous and M. Papadaki (Eds.): EMCIS 2021, LNBIP 437, pp. 474–487, 2022.
https://doi.org/10.1007/978-3-030-95947-0_34

IBM Watson are well-known for condensing information. The AI support allows the physician to utilize a body of scientific literature beyond a single person's capacity [2]. Also, all systems lined up for FDA approval are from the diagnostic sector [3]. This is broadening the gap between surgical and diagnostic medicine. While diagnostics are continuously improved, the basic access to skilled surgical care is lacking globally [4]. Our prototype should, therefore, contribute to the digital innovations geared towards surgical treatment with a focus on affordability.

2 Practitioner Training

The gap between diagnostic and surgical practice is not only reflected in the availability of digital support systems, but also in the professional training of diagnostic and surgical clinicians. Professional training for surgeons and adjacent disciplines like plastic treatments relies on Halsted's apprenticeship model [5]. This approach means that apprentice surgeons learn to replicate good clinical practice by observing and imitating experts. There are two shortcomings to this method: The process does not establish a good framework for further self-improvement without the help of additional experts. This missing framework opens risks for patient safety [6]. Continuous professional development requires a framework within which to improve. Another requirement for healthcare software is to seamlessly integrate into daily routine. If software use adds to the time needed for a procedure, it will only be used if necessary or mandated [7]. Surgical medicine in general also sees a trend of more complex techniques, while apprenticeship periods get shorter [6]. This change has an increased impact on fields like aesthetic and reconstructive plastic procedures, where procedures are often performed by novices and/or non-surgeon clinicians. This is sometimes permitted in lifting treatments, where only needle injections are needed. In Germany, for example, only physicians may conduct soft-filler therapies with substances like Hyaluron. In other countries, being a trained physician is not a requirement to perform such procedures. Practitioners are often trained in workshops by companies who sell beauty-treatment products.

The training is related to Halsted's model [5], since the treatment is usually demonstrated by an expert and then replicated by the participants. This short training period has implications for patient health. While an incorrect surgical treatment may have more dire consequences, faulty needle injections can result in deformation or release of the filler compound into a vein, which may lead to paralysis or worse [8]. While knowledge management in health care has been long discussed [9], the health care sector is one of the later adopters of digital knowledge management systems [10]. The healthcare sector in general suffers from missing transfer of the rich scientific knowledge to clinical practice [11]. Knowledge management increased the differences between diagnostical and surgical healthcare: While the diagnostic decision processes were easy to digitalize, the apprenticeship model [5] proved more difficult to transfer. Still, 3D-data makes it possible to capture the inputs during surgeries mentioned in the introduction. It allows to capture the position and shape of every object involved and, if measured over time, may also collect data on haptic and density due to the speed of deformations. An important part of knowledge management is also to provide the ability to improve the knowledge of the clinicians. When teaching by observing, a model for the intervention is not strictly needed. Nonetheless, novice clinicians need to respect knowledge from various sources, e. g., anatomy of bloodstream pathways and bone structures, to perform a low-risk injection.

3   Medical Model: The MD Codes

As elaborated above, the results of face-lifting interventions depend heavily on the practitioner's experience and mentor, rather than being similar due to standardized procedures. This also leads to the development of own treatment techniques by many practitioners, depending on what seems to produce the most volume in their patients' faces in the shortest amount of time. Besides different techniques, the preferred filler substances may vary, creating another variable. Substances differ in different categories like thickness or evaporation time, which affect treatment results. Furthermore, to be economic, practitioners try to curtail the injection volume in a way that leaves no residue in a substance bottle, i. e., they try not to waste any product.

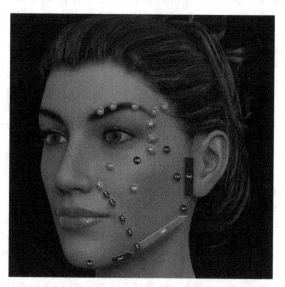

Fig. 1. MD-codes for facial aesthetic treatment in the cheek area [12].

To approach these challenges, de Maio developed a treatment framework called the MD(MeDical)-codes [12]. The codes condense his own professional experience into a template for novice clinicians and are an example of transferring tacit to explicit knowledge. The MD-codes were first introduced for approaching and planning treatments in 2015 [13], but they were not sufficiently detailed to be a reliable knowledge base for new clinicians. They were focussing on providing safe locations for injections when treating different parts of the face. The codes provide several groups of injection points, with the intention that one group alters a specific facial feature (see Fig. 1 for examples). These points are currently the most advanced standard in soft tissue filler therapy and specify some of the variables needed for a Hyaluron treatment. As shown in Fig. 1, the points have different geometries and colours. The geometry indicates the necessary injection technique while the colour suggests an injection depth, which depends on the bone structure in the area. An improved system was released in 2021 [14]. The new version of the codes offers additional specifications and is now comprehensive enough to guide the complete treatment process. The MD-model [14] consists of two parts, that cover the complete treatment process. The codes themselves are a set of injection points with each point being assigned information regarding the treatment, such as needle type, injection volume, warnings, needle movement during injection and more. Figure 2 shows an example of the specifications for the tear trough area, which is a vulnerable area between an eye and a cheek.

Anatomical unit MD code	Injection area	Target depth of injection	Injection device	Injection delivery	Alerts	Active number per side (mL)[a]
Tear trough (Tt)[i]						
Tt1	Central infraorbital	Supraperiosteal[b]	Cannula	∴	⚠	0.2
					Be wary of the infraorbital artery branches[i]	
Tt2	Lateral infraorbital	Supraperiosteal[b]	Cannula	∴		0.2
Tt3	Medial infraorbital	Supraperiosteal[b]	Cannula	∴	⚠	0.1
					Be wary of the angular artery and vein[i]	

Fig. 2. Treatment variables per point [14].

The other part of the model [14] is a number of decision rules. They suggest a set of injection points based on the current state of the patient's facial features. Figure 3 shows the decision process for the tear through area outlined in Fig. 2. Since it is a vulnerable area (see Fig. 4), most decision paths try to avoid direct needle injections. Therefore, it provides novice clinicians with instructions about both, what exactly to treat and how to perform a treatment. The rules are presented as decision trees and, when combined, always aim at a holistic treatment that conceals the effects of aging [14]. Our prototype uses the MD-model [14] as a basis to enable standardized treatment procedures. Since the MD-codes are a new model based on a single person's experience, our prototype will also be used to test and validate them. Additionally, since many practitioners have developed own techniques due to different teachers, the prototype should be able to represent individual point sets as well, or a combination of MD-codes [14] and own techniques. These documentation possibilities should enable practitioners to have a structured and traceable professional development and provide an alternative to the apprenticeship model [5]. Here, knowledge management is not applied within an organization, but across a medical discipline. Inter-organizational knowledge sharing is beneficial to the patient, especially in the case of individual practitioners who often cannot develop their own codified knowledge management systems [15].

The MD-codes are applied in non-surgical soft tissue filler based volumization. Volumization is used to remove aging effects, for example, the shrinking of the skin in the face. It is intended to restore a more juvenile look. Soft tissue fillers include Hyaluron, collagen, or autologous fat. They are applied via sharp or dull needles. The treatments vary in their injection points and point-specific injection depth, filling volume, firmness

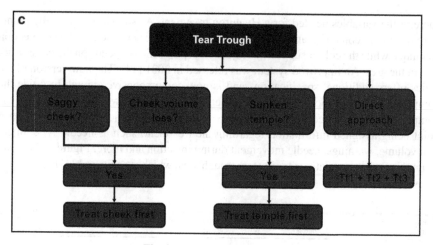

Fig. 3. Decision algorithm [14]

of the used filler, and the injection technique. Techniques vary in the way the needle is moved during the injection. The treatment variables mentioned above together with a pre- and post-intervention 3D-scan constitute the data used in our project.

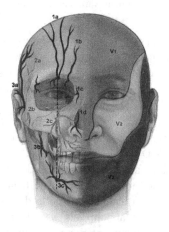

Fig. 4. Example of facial bloodstream and bone features [16].

4 Prototype Architecture

The treatment by non-surgeons mentioned in the introduction leads to the additional problem that specialized equipment to support a treatment is usually missing. Better equipment would allow the practitioner for more accurate planning and ultimately reduced patient risk. While equipment is commercially available, it is usually too costly for non-specialized practitioners to purchase. Therefore, it is also necessary to provide a technology that is affordable, easy to use, and based on the medical procedure. Using the example of treatments with soft tissue fillers, we will showcase our current prototype using WebGL and affordable 3D-scanning equipment. In the following, we will cover the needed software and hardware and how the prototype is used during a treatment.

4.1 Hardware

The application of 3D-data depends on the equipment: Consumer-level 3D-scanners may only be suited to capture pre- and post-surgery models, while higher-end scanners are able to compile 3D-models at a high frame rate and possibly support live operations. Applicable 3D-scanners range from mobile phones to handheld devices and the price range is between 200€ (for consumer devices) and around 4000€ (for professional models). As stated in the section above, a single pre-treatment scan is enough to enable treatment support guided by MD-codes. A post-treatment scan is desirable for documentation purposes. 3D-scanners usually fall within three categories [17]: very precise industry models, small-model scanners for supplementing 3D-printing and small webcam-based scanners like Kinect or Intel Realsense. The Intel Realsense camera series is prized at around 200€. It utilizes IR-based stereo-photogrammetry. Such a scanner can process 1920×1080 pixels at 40 fps and has a depth resolution between 0.2 and 1.5 mm. The 3D-model only takes a few minutes to be captured providing a quick and cost-effective solution. Such a system based on a stereo-camera, supported by IR-sensors, offers the best price-performance ratio [18]. The handheld scanner we use to demonstrate our prototype is a XYZ-3D-scanner 2.0 (see Fig. 5) that cost 235€. It represents an Intel Realsense SR300 camera with a handle. The specified scanning range of 0.3–0.2 m allows an easy scan in a practitioner's office.

Fig. 5. Handheld 3D-scanning device [19].

4.2 Software

First, the 3D-scan needs to be compiled into a 3D-model. Intel did only provide a rudimentary SDK for their Realsense scanners; therefore, a third-party software needs to be used. To keep the flexibility, we utilize the ItSeez3D-scanner suite, which is based on the Intel SDK. It is compatible to all Realsense camera models and allows to compile the model either locally or on a web server, which allows for our prototype to be also run from mobile devices with low processing power. The advancement of WebGL further supplements a platform-independent mobile device 3D-software system, since most modern browsers offer WebGL. For our prototype, we use the WebGL-based Three.js JavaScript package. With the additional use of HTML5, the prototype provides a responsive design and can be used on whatever device the clinician has available, though big screens are recommended. Three.js also provides the necessary interfaces to use most available 3D-imports. The file format is standardized. Three.js is able to import this standardized file range, be it the classic .obj-Format or the more recent .gltf. Since many soft tissue filler treatments are executed in small offices, the equipment and software need to be easy to use and affordable.

5   Usage

In the following, we will describe how the prototype is used during an aesthetic treatment. As outlined in the introduction, the prototype needs to be seamlessly incorporated in the existing workflow. Therefore, it is advantageous that during treatment some time is usually reserved to document the interventions for legal reasons.

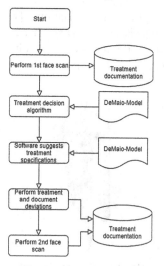

Fig. 6. Treatment process

A short overview of the treatment process is shown in Fig. 6. The clinician first needs to perform a face scan and load it into the prototype. Then, the practitioner can choose the relevant MD-codes [14] based on the given aesthetic goal via the decision tree. Figure 3 shows the decision tree for the tear through area, where the rules can either guide to a set of points (Tt1–3) or further decision trees (Treat cheek/temple first). Based on the result, the practitioner receives a suggestion of points including treatment variables like technique or needle type. For precise documentation, each point represented in the model [14] can be dragged to its injection point on the scanned face. If the clinician deviates from suggested values for treatment variables, those changes can also be documented. Additionally, to be able to represent individual techniques, practitioners can add their own injection points along with other data. An example of this is shown in Fig. 7: On the top left are the data values applicable for injection points (one field per point, the size is increased for better screenshot readability). The point itself is placed as a red 3D-line on the left cheek area of the patient scan in the middle. Finally, on the top right, a menu is available to let the practitioner add individual points or point groups as well as change the camera perspective and scan orientation. The position change of a single vertex depends on several factors: The volume and injection vectors of each injection point, the interaction between each injection point and below-surface resistance like fat tissue and bones, individual attributes like skin tightness, and time since injection (because the water part evaporates in a soft tissue filler). While the prototype currently is not able to simulate the changes, a structured documentation will enable practitioners to trace their work and better predict future results. To accomplish this, a second scan is performed after the treatment. A comparison of the documentation enables the practitioner to evaluate his work after the treatment.

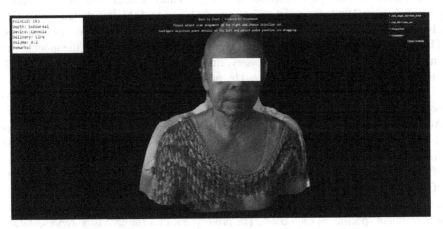

Fig. 7. Example screenshot with individual injection point.

6   Prototype Features

The design represents the priorities set in the sections above. The prototype is browser-based and, therefore, a setup-free application. To run, it needs a web server, which may be online or local and it is available as open-source software, like XAMPP. The Three.js API is used to import and export 3D-face models, while standard HTML5 interfaces are utilized to input additional data like patient name and age. A WebGL-enabled browser is common standard on most modern devices (e. g., Chrome, Firefox).

HTML5 LocalStorage API offers the persistent short-term database. The LocalStorage key-value-pairs are used to store the necessary data as JSON-strings. Since LocalStorage is browser-based and domain-specific, it is immediately available online and local.

The browser-based architecture does not require deeper IT-knowledge from practitioners and contributes to making the software more accessible. Even low-cost desktops can offer the required browser. The suggested third-party compilation tool, ItSeez3D-Scanner, is available as an app for mobile devices or desktops. WebGL in Three.js allows multiple data types for 3D-model import, then uses them in the buffer geometry format. Buffer geometry stores vertices as a single list of coordinate values, which allows for better performance. 3D-models may also be exported in the Standard Tesselation Language (STL) format which is the IEEE-recommended format to use for medical 3D-surface imaging due to its usability [20]. MD-code injection point sets are represented as 3D-lines in the model. They are aligned towards the centre of the face and can be adjusted in all but the y layer, enabling the practitioner to precisely set the injection point. Each line is linked to a set of injection point attributes shown in Figs. 2 and 7. The initial suggestions are based on MD-codes, but may be adjusted. The suggestions also produce alerts if they are too close to sensitive underlying parts of the face, like blood streams. An attribute influencing the documentation process is the degree of hardness of the used product. It determines how much the facial structure changes during the week after the injection due to the vaporizing water part. Therefore, another scan may be taken after the vaporization process finishes. While the initial suggestions are based on de Maio's clinical experience [14], individual adjustment allows practitioners to refine the model with own techniques. The results may then be compared at conferences and further develop the model. The changes by individual users are necessary, since some treatments are highly individual. Still, this option should only be utilized by more experienced practitioners.

The precise position and the injected volume on the other hand are expected to be changed by the practitioner, since those depend on each individual patient's face. Additionally, the points in MD-codes each cover a small area in which to inject, as shown in Fig. 1. This renders these two attributes to be the best opportunities for the clinician's self-improvement and professional development. Therefore, the prototype offers additional data to support these decisions. It allows for comparisons with results of previous cases and between pre- and post-treatment scans. To reduce the impact of language barriers and preparation time, MD-codes contain several visual cues to indicate the treatment specifics at each point. The prototype uses a similar visual representation of main point attributes on the 3D-model: line diameter correlates to the injected volume of hyaluronic acid, its colour represents injection depth, and a hazard triangle indicates an injection point close to an artery. This is useful during the treatment itself, since the practitioner can quickly access necessary information when preparing the next syringe. It also facilitates the comparison of different treatments.

To obtain the decision support data mentioned above, the prototype needs to respect several system restrictions. The supporting data includes measurements of depth and volume change in the face. The prototype cannot be effectively calibrated from the start, since it is designed to work with any scanner the practitioner has available. This may also result in a low mesh resolution of the 3D-model. Still, to enable professional self-improvement, a transparent relationship between face measurements and injection volume is needed. The implemented solution is as follows: Each injection point is a line anchored in a plane parallel towards the scanned face. Each line is defined by two points in the coordinate system, one point on the surface of the face model to anchor the alignment and one outside point on the plane to define the injection point. To standardize imported models from different scanners, imports are first scaled and rotated to fit an uncalibrated baseline face, upon which the overlays are projected. Then, the distance from each outer line point towards the scanned face model is measured. To account for low-mesh scans, the measurement is done as a raycast towards the closest point on the face model. The closest point is identified by using the ICP [21] algorithm to match each point on the line to each point of the face model. As a result, the clinician receives an information about the fold depth at the injection point. He further receives information about facial symmetry, since the distances are calculated on both sides. The injection volume can then be adjusted accordingly. If the clinician did the same point set treatment in the past, the distance and volume values of past treatments may be looked up as well. The same distance calculation is then performed for both post-treatment scans. Therefore, the clinician gets the initial fold depth, applied volume of hyaluronic acid and the post-treatment and post-evaporation change per injection point. In total, each treatment is documented as a series of up to three 3D-face models, each with the point set overlay according to the applied treatment and connected relational data regarding the different attributes of the injection points as well as general data like the patient's age.

7 Prototype Test

To validate our prototype, we performed a test procedure with a patient in need of a full facial lift. As outlined above, the test has two objectives:

1. The prototype should provide the guidance necessary to perform a treatment.
2. The prototype should perform the task sufficiently well with low-cost equipment.

7.1 Test Conditions

The software was tested with a treatment procedure performed by an experienced dermatologist, who often performs soft-tissue filler treatments. The patient received a full facial lift. 3D-scanning was performed before and after the treatment, with a series of three different postures at each point. The three postures included a frontal image with level head, head tilted up 45° and head tilted up 45° while smiling. The last one is used to accentuate the treatment improvements. Below, we will show the criteria and results of the two testing procedures.

7.2 Medical Model

To test the medical model [14], the MD-codes, we assess its suggestions against the assessments of an experienced practitioner in the testing procedure. Table 1 shows the properties suggested by de Maio as well as the properties used by the practitioner. A before-and-after 3D-scan is shown in Fig. 8.

Table 1. Testing of the MD-codes

Injection	Depth		Volume		Needle	
	De Maio	Used	De Maio	Used	De Maio	Used
Ck1	D	D	0.3	0.2	N	N
CK2	D	D	0.2	0.2	N	N
Ck3	D	S	0.3	0.1	N	N
T1	D	D	0.5	0.1	N	C
T2	D	D	0.5	0.15	N	C
Tt1	D	S	0.2	0.05	C	C
Tt2	D	S	0.2	0.05	C	C
Tt3	D	S	0.2	0.05	C	C
NL	D	S	0.3	0.4	N	C
Jw1	D	D	0.5	0.2	N	N
Jw2	S	S	0.5	0.3	C	C
Jw3	S	S	1	0.2	C	C
Jw4	S	D	0.5	0.1	C	N
ML		S		0.2		C
W		S		0.5		C
MI		S		0.2		C

D = Deep (Supraperiosteal), S = Subcutaneous, C = Cannula, N = Needle, Volume is measured in mL

The suggested and performed treatment show several differences. The practitioner added three own injection points not covered by the medical model. Concerning the injection point properties, the De Maio-model uses a bigger share of deep injections and much more material in several points [14]. Even considering the additional injection points, the practitioner only used 3 mL Hyaluron, while MD-codes suggested 4,9 mL for the same treatment [14]. The material is sold in bottles of 1 mL priced at around 300 € each, therefore the MD-code treatment is about 600€ more expensive in materials.

7.3 3D-Technology

The second objective tests the hardware performance. To successfully support the treatments, the scanned 3D-models need to be precise enough to represent the correct facial details.

Table 2. Data of the treatment scans shown in Fig. 8

	Vertices	Triangles	Time to compute
Pre-treatment	24876	49181	18 s
Post-treatment	25109	49820	19 s

An important aspect, as mentioned above, is the seamless and fast integration of the software into the standardized procedures. Computing time was measured on an Intel i7-8550U CPU at 1.8 GHz. As shown in Table 2, the scanner provides a consistent performance. A big advantage of commercial-grade scanners is their scanning speed. The utilized Realsense Setup requires to walk around the patient and the patient needs to remain motionless during this process. Motion will lead to distortion as visible in the shoulders area in Fig. 8. The scanning time was reduced by only scanning the frontal face instead of the full bust, but still around 20 s were needed for each scan.

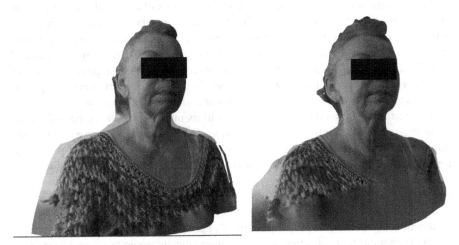

Fig. 8. Treatment scans. Pre-treatment (left) and post-treatment (right), level-head posture

7.4   Discussion

The experiment was done to test two objectives. In the medical part, we tested if the software and MD-codes could provide the necessary guidance for a treatment. When utilized by an experienced practitioner, several differences were found. As mentioned above, practitioners often use their own point sets, and in our test treatment, the practitioner also diverged from the De Maio model [14]. The option of free setting of points in the prototype allows to track these individual sets. Therefore, a novice could stay within the De Maio model [14] using the prototype, while experienced practitioners could also use our system to document their more individual treatments. The MD-codes also suggested the use of more material. As visible in Fig. 8, a change in cheek volume was achieved by the practitioner with three fifths of the suggested material. Since this lowers the material cost per treatment, less material use is desirable for most practitioners and patients. Novices can at first use the guiding frame of the MD-codes and then compare their results in the 3D-documentation of the prototype and gradually lower the amount of material used.

In the technical part, we tested if the low-cost equipment was able to perform the task sufficiently well. As the Figs. 8 and 7 show, the model textures are partially distorted in the right part of the face. This may either be due to the dim light or to patient movement during the scanning phase. Apart from that, the vertex resolution can display the change in volume, and a processing time of 18 s on an average modern processor seems acceptable.

8 Conclusion

We introduced a web-based software prototype to plan and document soft-tissue filler treatments with 3D-models. The prototype implements a medical model to standardize the treatment and reduce patient risk. The implication for practise is that unexperienced practitioners using guidance by MD-codes, our software, and relatively cheap 3D-cameras can perform good and safe face treatments. Another implication is that there is less need for an experienced practitioner to execute the apprenticeship learning model. It is possible to transfer the necessary knowledge via recommendations by an expert and with digital systems. This is also of theoretical interest because it changes the transfer of knowledge. Besides codification, which is typically used in diagnostic medicine, photos (scans) and 3D-treatment documentation present another transfer option.

Our test showed that the prototype can fulfil its intended functions, but still needs some improvement, mainly on the medical side. The MD-codes can serve as a guiding framework for novices, but the differences in the test between suggested and performed treatment show the need for a more refined model, which we will discuss below.

9 Future work

As mentioned in Sect. 5, the prototype currently can neither simulate the precise changes that will occur due to an injection, nor can it automatically generate a complete suggestion for treatment. The position change of a single vertex depends on several factors: The volume and injection vectors of each injection point, the interaction between each injection point, and below-surface resistance like fat tissue and bones, individual attributes like skin tightness and time since injection. Therefore, a future version of the software may collect this data and use it in a machine-learning process to predict the changes. A complete suggestion for injections is also dependent on beauty standards, which are subjective at the individual patient level. While several attempts have been made to develop an objective measure (e. g., the golden ratio), the measures were not reproducible in experimental studies [22]. However, since MD-codes provide standardized injection volumes [14], they may be viewed as another attempt to standardize beauty procedures. Hyaluron enables this by being a flexible soft-tissue filler that can adapt to different faces. Therefore, the documented results of the treatments should be tested against beauty standards in future studies. This may enable the software to produce automatic suggestions in accordance with most conceptions of beauty.

References

1. Wall, J., Krummel, T.: The digital surgeon: how big data, automation, and artificial intelligence will change surgical practice. J. Pediatr. Surg. **55S**, 47–50 (2020)
2. Druss, B.G., Marcus, S.C.: Growth and decentralization of the medical literature: implications for evidence-based medicine. J. Med. Libr. Assoc. **93**(4), 499–501 (2005)
3. Topol, E.J.: High-performance medicine: the convergence of human and artificial intelligence. Nat. Med. **25**(1), 44–56 (2019)
4. Bath, M., Bashford, T., Fitzgerald, J.E.: What is 'global surgery'? Defining the multidisciplinary interface between surgery, anaesthesia and public health. BMJ Glob. Health **4**(5), e001808 (2019)
5. Pellegrini, V.D., Ferguson, P.C., Cruess, R., Cruess, S., Briggs, T.W.R.: Sufficient competence to enter the unsupervised practice of orthopaedics: what is it, when does it occur, and do we know it when we see it? AOA critical issues. J. Bone Joint Surg. Am. **97**(17), 1459–1464 (2015)
6. Velazquez-Pimentel, D., Hurkxkens, T., Nehme, J.: A virtual reality for the digital surgeon. In: Atallah, S. (ed.) Digital Surgery, pp. 183–201. Springer, Cham (2021). https://doi.org/10.1007/978-3-030-49100-0_14
7. Hult, H.V., Hansson, A., Gellerstedt, M.: Digitalization and Physician Learning: Individual Practice, Organizational Context, and Social Norm (2020)
8. Price, R.D., Berry, M.G., Navsaria, H.A.: Hyaluronic acid: the scientific and clinical evidence. J. Plast. Reconstr. Aesthet. Surg. **60**(10), 1110–1119 (2007)
9. Kitchiner, D., Davidson, C., Bundred, P.: Integrated care pathways: effective tools for continuous evaluation of clinical practice. J. Eval. Clin. Pract. **2**(1), 65–69 (1996)
10. Mohajan, H.: An Analysis of Knowledge Management for the Development of Global Health (2016)
11. Abidi, S.S.R.: Healthcare knowledge management: the art of the possible. In: Riaño, D. (ed.) K4CARE 2007. LNCS (LNAI), vol. 4924, pp. 1–20. Springer, Heidelberg (2008). https://doi.org/10.1007/978-3-540-78624-5_1
12. Bertossi, D., Nocini, P.F., Rahman, E., Heydenrych, I., Kapoor, K.M., de Maio, M.: Non-surgical facial reshaping using MD Codes. J. Cosmet. Dermatol. **19**(9), 2219–2228 (2020)
13. de Maio, M.: Unlocking the code of facial revitalisation: a step-by-step approach to using injectables. Allergan Medical Institute (2015)
14. de Maio, M.: MD Codes™: A Methodological Approach to Facial Aesthetic Treatment with Injectable Hyaluronic Acid Fillers. Aesth. Plast. Surg. **45**(2), 690–709 (2021). https://doi.org/10.1007/s00266-020-01762-7
15. Al-Busaidi, K.A.: Knowledge workers' perceptions of potential benefits and challenges of inter-organizational knowledge sharing systems: a Delphi study in the health sector. Knowl. Manage. Res. Pract. **12**, 398–408 (2014). https://doi.org/10.1057/kmrp.2013.4
16. Marur, T., Tuna, Y., Demirci, S.: Facial anatomy. Clin. Dermatol. **32**(1), 14–23 (2014)
17. Straub, J., Kading, B., Mohammad, A., Kerlin, S.: Characterization of a large, low-cost 3D scanner. Technologies **3**(1), 19–36 (2015)
18. Wong, J.Y., et al.: Validity and reliability of craniofacial anthropometric measurement of 3D digital photogrammetric images. Cleft Palate-Craniofacial J. **45**, 232–239 (2008)
19. XYZ Printing. 3D Scanner 2.0 (2020). https://www.xyzprinting.com/en/product/3d-scanner-2-0. Accessed 17 Dec 2020
20. IEEE Recommended Practice for Three-Dimensional (3D) Medical Modeling. IEEE (2015)
21. Rusinkiewicz, S., Levoy, M.: Efficient variants of the ICP algorithm. In: Third International Conference on 3-D Digital Imaging and Modeling: 28 May - 1 June 2001, Quebec City, Canada Proceedings. IEEE (2000)
22. Laurentini, A., Bottino, A.: Computer analysis of face beauty: a survey. Comput. Vis. Image Underst. **125**(14), 184–199 (2014)

Online Health Communities: The Impact of AI Conversational Agents on Users

Alain Osta[1]([⊠]), Angelika Kokkinaki[2], and Charbel Chedrawi[2,3]

[1] Graduate School, University of Nicosia, Nicosia, Cyprus
osta.a@live.unic.ac.cy
[2] School of Business, University of Nicosia, Nicosia, Cyprus
{kokkinaki.a,chedrawi.c}@unic.ac.cy, charbel.chedrawi@usj.edu.lb
[3] Business and Management Faculty, Saint Joseph University, Beirut, Lebanon

Abstract. The literature lacks evidence on the acceptability of AI conversational agents (chatbots) and the motivations for their adoption in healthcare industry. This paper aims to examine the acceptance of these chatbots based on the UTAUT model in Online Health Communities (OHCs) and to explore what kind of impact these particular features have on the users' intentions, and the actual use of these communities. Based on a quantitative methodology approach, we rely on the UTAUT model to study OHCs users' behavior and intentions towards such AI conversational agents/chatbots. The study shows that the UTAUT has proved to be a strong and reliable model for evaluating the adoption and application of AI conversational agents (chatbots) in OHCs. A questionnaire was employed to collect data, and respondents are chosen using the cluster sampling approach. On a 7 Likert scale, respondents were asked to select which choice best suited their reaction to any of the topics presented. A total of 632 answers from 62 countries were received, with 443 of them being complete. Many tests were used to examine the data such as the bivariate and multivariate analysis. Since the returned p-value for most of the hypotheses tested was 0.05, the majority of the hypotheses tested were accepted. Findings showed the interrelations between AI conversational agents/chatbots and OHCs on users' Behavioral Intention (BI). The main constructs of the UTAUT model (Performance Expectancy, Effort Expectancy, Social Influence, and Facilitating Conditions) had a significant impact on the participants' BI and Usage Behavior (UB) for AI conversational agents/chatbots in OHCs. As for moderators, gender and age had no effect on BI and UB. Understanding the main factors that have a significant impact on users' intentions to use chatbots in OHCs determines the significance of those results.

Keywords: Online Health Communities · AI conversational agents · Chatbots · UTAUT

© Springer Nature Switzerland AG 2022
M. Themistocleous and M. Papadaki (Eds.): EMCIS 2021, LNBIP 437, pp. 488–501, 2022.
https://doi.org/10.1007/978-3-030-95947-0_35

1   Introduction

Healthcare undergoes a continuous transformation and faces many challenges; incidents of miscommunication between health professionals and friends or family of patients, misinformed patient about health-related issues on social media platforms, without forgetting the upheaval caused by the recent COVID-19 pandemic. In fact, healthcare providers usually need lots of time to address such challenges on their own and surely better coordination and communication between all healthcare stakeholders (patients, practitioners, patients' family or friends…) would positively contribute to the all involved stakeholders' experience.

With this regard, the advancements in Artificial Intelligence (AI) are expected to have a positive impact on the healthcare industry, whereas the informational requirements and the need for online health communication is intensified [1]. Indeed, AI conversational agents or Chatbots are considered a promising development to that respect. Chatbots are a class of AI applications that rely on Deep Learning (DL) to assist provision of information [2], gather information or perform routine tasks and are being implemented in the Online Health Communities (OHCs) as an alternative means to provide information instead of human healthcare personnel [3]. Chatbots are accessible through different digital hubs: websites, mobile and messaging applications, SMS, etc. It is estimated that there will be an increase in the deployment of chatbots in the health sector in the future. However, a number of questions in relation to the intentions to use health-related AI conversational agents is not fully exploited in the literature.

In view of the above, the aim of this research is to examine the intention of using health chatbots applications in OHCs and to explore what kind of impact these particular features have on the users' intentions, and the actual/potential use of these communities. The focus of the article is therefore to study such intention of use and its impact on users' behavior in OHCs through one of the most used models (UTAUT) that analyzes the behavioral intention to adopt any system related to technology [4].

For this purpose, we will first sum up the related literature covering OHCs and AI agents/chatbots. Then we shall present the UTAUT model with the related technology acceptance studies applied in health organizations and the proposed model and hypotheses to be tested. Afterwards, we will briefly explain the methodology used and present our results through a proper discussion of the findings. Finally, we shall conclude our work with our contributions, managerial implications, and limitations.

2   Contextual Background: OHCs AI Agents/Chatbots

Online health communities (OHCs) - a special case of virtual communities - offer opportunities to patients, friends or family to post and explain their concerns, ask questions, receive feedback, or share their experiences. Users/patients can choose a physician and interact only with him/her to protect their privacy [5].

OHCs' positioning is reinforced through the adoption of AI and DL techniques. As digital health innovation continues to improve, it has initiated changes in providing care by changing the doctor-patient relationship with shared decision-making, communication, health management, and cost-effectiveness [6]. OHCs have three diversions based on the users' perspective: i) an OHC could aim healthcare subjects through discussion forums and sharing ideas and experiences; ii) address patients and physicians for exchange of support and information; or iii) designed only for physicians in order to share their professional knowledge and experiences.

The integration of heterogeneous systems is crucial for enterprise preparedness during a crisis [7]. The COVID-19 pandemic promoted healthcare delivery solutions and healthcare apps based on blockchain and AI [8]. The outcome of digitalization produces benefits for the healthcare systems and electronic medical test records improve the access to the health records both for patients and health practitioners [9]. DL algorithms is capable of feature extraction with no human interaction. It exploits a structure imitating a human's neuronal structure of the brain [10].

Within the same context of OHCs, chatbots are AI applications based on DL able to interact and converse with a human through text, voice, and animation [11]; they are software applications created to reproduce and imitate human interaction and communication through or into speech or text [12]. In the context of healthcare, personalized health and therapy information are being provided by chatbots or healthbots to provide support to patients by suggesting diagnoses and treatments based on patient indications [13].

Interactive conversational agents, digital assistants, artificial conversation entities, and smart bots are also defined as chatbots. These chatbots are considered more attractive and user-friendly. They provide users with an efficient and comfortable communication by offering accurate information and assistance to their questions and problems [14].

Limitation in healthcare resources such as medical professionals and facilities usually impedes people living in remote areas from receiving professional medical advice and having access to real-time and efficient health care services [15]. Thus, patients generally opt for other options [16]. In fact, some of the motivations for using chatbots include the novelty of such interaction, social factors and entertainment, but most importantly efficiency. In a business context, these applications became commonly used because they minimize service costs and can deal with several consumers at the same time [14].

Forty-one different chatbots have been used for different purposes in mental health. Mental disorders, stress, depression, and acrophobia could be managed by using chatbots, and this idea was proven by twelve studies that demonstrated the efficiency of automation and use of chatbots [17].

Finally, the COVID-19 has had the largest impact on technological advancements and acceptance. In the next section we shall introduce the UTAUT model and our research methodology.

3   The Impact of AI Agents/Chatbots on OHCs' Users

3.1   The Proposed UTAUT Model and Our Main Hypotheses

Understanding the reasons for rejecting or adopting each new technology has become critical. As a result, technology acceptance concepts, theories, and models expect to bring the idea of how individuals may accept, understand, and use the latest technology. Venkatesh [4] proposed the **Unified Theory of Acceptance and Use of Technology** (UTAUT) framework to explore and analyze the acceptance of technology and its reasons in information systems (IS) research; it is one of the most widely used technology acceptance frameworks that investigates and explains the intention to use technology in organizational contexts [4].

In fact, the UTAUT model has been used in a variety of fields including near-field communication technologies [18], interactive whiteboards [19], e-health [20], and ERP software acceptance [21], and home telehealth services [22]. Many factors influence people's decision-making process in relation to the adoption of new technologies. Research has been presented in various contexts [4, 23]. To the best of authors' knowledge there is limited research on this research area.

The UTAUT model presents four independent constructs: Performance Expectancy (PE), Effort Expectancy (EE), Social Influence (SI), and Facilitating Conditions (FC) that predict technology acceptance. According to many authors [4, 18–20], these constructs are directly associated with Behavioral Intentions (BI) which is defined as users' intention to use the system, and Use Behavior (UB). User demographics such as gender and age have been conceptualized as moderators in the UTAUT framework [24].

In our article we shall study the impact of these constructs on the level of the acceptance of health AI agents/chatbots in OHCs through the UTAUT model [4]. The choice of this model is explained by the fact that it provides a comprehensive synthesis of users' intentions to adopt new technologies. The following table will present the basic UTAUT model including the interrelations between the six main constructs and two moderators (Gender and Age) (Fig. 1).

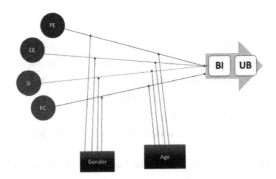

Fig. 1. Basic UTAUT model. Source [4]

The following table will present the variables and moderators of the UTAUT model (Table 1).

Table 1. Presentation of UTAUT main constructs

Variables/Moderators	Description [4]
PE	The degree to which a person believes that using the system would improve job performance. The acceptance framework has been utilized in various studies to explain end-users' BIs for adopting new technologies in the healthcare business [25]
EE	The level of ease in relation with the use of the system. It comprises three variables: complexity, ease of use, and perceived ease of use. EE is seen in the context of the health industry as the perceived level of ease in adopting a healthcare system
SI	The degree to which a person believes that other people believe he or she should adopt the new system. Along with increased support from friends, volunteers, and family, E-Health applications are viewed as a valuable instrument for achieving the technology use [26]
FC	The degree to which a person believes that an organizational and technological infrastructure has been developed to support the system's use. FC is also presented as the perception that resources will be available to complete the task [27]
BI	BI relates to how people intend to use technology in the future
Gender	One of the main moderating variables in the UTAUT. Guo [28] investigated the moderating role of gender in the adoption of mobile social networking sites and to recognize gender differences
Age	Age is identified as a moderator on BI and technology use. In the adoption of IS, the impact of PE on BI has been shown to be larger for males than females

The following table will also present the main hypotheses adopted for the use of chatbots in OHCs (Table 2).

Table 2. Table of hypotheses

Hypothesis
H1. PE posits a positive relationship towards BI to use platforms/chatbots in OHCs
H2. EE posits a positive relationship towards BI to use platforms/chatbots in OHCs
H3. SI posits a positive relationship towards BI to use platforms/chatbots in OHCs
H4. FC will have a significant effect on BI to use platforms/chatbots in OHCs
H5. BI posits a positive relationship towards UB
H1a, H1b, H1c and H1d: Gender will moderate the relationship between PE, EE, SI, and FC respectively, to use chatbots in OHCs
H2a, H2b, H2c and H2d: Age will moderate the relationship between PE, EE, SI, and FC respectively, to use chatbots in OHCs

3.2 Research Methodology

As a philosophy, positivism complies to the view that only "factual" knowledge collected through observation, including measurements, is trustworthy [29–31]; the researchers are working with precise frameworks or models (the UTAUT) while presuming that these frameworks or models are solid and sustainable [32], with a philosophical realism adhering to the hypothetico-deductive approach. Indeed, after addressing the theoretical perspectives based on the UTAUT framework and after proposing the hypotheses, the survey is generated to collect data and test the validity of the hypotheses. In fact, it is noted by IS publications that most of IS researches are positivistic [32], and most of the quantitative researches in IS used hypothetico-deductive approach [33].

Statistical analysis was performed using IBM SPSS version 25. In fact, a descriptive analysis was enrolled, and the variables were presented as per their type. All the scores followed a Likert scale from 1 to 7 (from 1 "strongly disagree" to 7 "strongly agree"). Reliability test was done for each score in order to validate the score (Cronbach alpha value was higher than 0.7 for all the scores).

Bivariate analysis was enrolled in order to test the correlation between UTAUT scores (PE, EE, SI, FC, BI, and UB) and the variables considered as moderators (gender, age). In the bivariate settings we used Student t-test and ANOVA test. Linear regression test was used to test the correlation between UTAUT scores and BI and between BI and UB. Furthermore, a multivariate analysis was enrolled in order to test the factors affecting BI. A statistically significant correlation was set at 5% (p-value less than 0.05).

Our statistical analysis was performed on a convenience sample of 443 participants (OHCs members). A total of 632 responses have been received of which 443 were complete. The completion rate is about 70% and the responses came from 62 countries. The data collection started on March 15th, 2021 and lasted until April 25th, 2021 for a total duration of 40 days.

4   Results, Findings and Discussion

This part presents the statistical analysis performed on the complete sample; based on the results, we shall analyse the hypotheses and the correlations between the main constructs of UTAUT model with BI and UB with a proper discussion; then, we will address the analysis of the main moderators defined by Venkatesh [4].

Participants were almost evenly distributed: 49% females and 46% males (Appendix A). The mean age was 34.3 (minimum 18 - maximum 68 years). However, one interesting finding was recorded that out of the 443 participants, 57.8% had limited experience in the use of Chatbots and/or online communities, and only 3.6% considered themselves experts in the use of chatbots in OHCs (Appendix B); These low experience levels that there is too much to do regarding this matter; this finding will be further emphasized in the managerial implication part.

The impact of the UTAUT variables was tested; all four variables were supported in the multivariate analysis. The study findings matched most of the hypothesized interrelations with UTAUT variables (H1, H2, H3, H4, and H5). Through linear regression, the findings showed that the variables of the conceptual model have a positive correlation on the BI to use chatbots in OHCs (PE: p = 0.000, EE: p = 0.001, SI: p = 0.000, and

FC: p = 0.001). These variables were considered as very important in determining the acceptance of using technology in the healthcare context through various researchers [34, 35].

The following Tables 3 and 4 are showing the multivariate analysis of the main UTAUT constructs and their correlations with BI, and the representation of the main UTAUT score categories (Table 5).

Table 3. Multivariate analysis of UTAUT main constructs

Study population	Unstandardized Coefficients		Standardized Coefficients	t	P.value
	B	Std. Error	Beta		
(Constant)	1.872	0.930		2.014	0.045
PE	0.292	0.036	0.341	8.019	0.000
SI	0.126	0.026	0.235	4.867	0.000
FC	0.118	0.036	0.165	3.249	0.001
EE	0.130	0.040	0.139	3.210	0.001
Dependent variable : BI					

Table 4. Representation of UTAUT score categories

UTAUT constructs	Representation and score categories (%)		
	Poor	Good	Very good
PE	**60.9**	26.9	12.2
EE	38.8	**31.4**	**29.8**
SI	**83.1**	8.8	8.1
FC	58	**28**	**14**
BI	**56.9**	21.9	21.2
UB	**93.2**	3.8	2.9

Regarding PE (a 5-item scale with a mean of 21.6 ± 7.23 over 35, and a median of 23 with a minimum of 5 and a maximum of 35) (Appendix C), participants almost agree that using chatbots enhances productivity and facilitates the accomplishment of tasks more quickly. Having 60.9% in the poor area means that a great potential exists to enhance the awareness and promote the use of these technologies. So, PE is very important to the use of online platforms. In fact, users are always interested to enhance their performance through the use of these technologies. Accordingly, this variable is considered as one of the strongest one on BI [4, 34, 36].

According to regression analysis, PE is positively correlated to BI (p < 0.001) to use chatbots in OHCs. From a user perception, this finding confirms that using the system will enhance performance, attitude, and intention to use the system in the healthcare context [4, 37]. It also confirms previous literature that showed PE as a strong predictor of BI to adopt healthcare technology [22, 38]. In summary, when PE increase, BI increase and the null hypothesis is rejected. In other words, when users or patients find that the use of chatbots/OHCs increases their productivity and enhances their health, they increase their intentions to use them.

Regarding EE (a 5-item scale with a mean of 25.46 $\pm$ 6.61 over 35, and a median of 26, with a minimum of 5 and a maximum of 35), participants highly agree that the process of learning and becoming familiar in using Chatbots is easy for them. Having 61.2% in the Good and Very Good area means that the users are already considering that EE is highly important to use these technologies. EE is considered as a crucial step to the use of these online platforms. According to regression analysis, EE (H2) is significantly correlated to BI (p = 0.001) as in many other researchers [35, 39, 40]. It implies that the ease of using chatbots in the healthcare field is more likely to have an impact on the perception of BI [19]. This finding confirms [41], that EE has a positive impact on the BIs of patients interacting with physicians in OHCs.

In summary, when users' or patients find that the use of chatbots in OHCs is easy, they will increase their intentions to use them.

As for SI (a 7-item scale with a mean of 22.88 $\pm$ 11.52 over 49, and median of 22 with a minimum of 7 and a maximum of 49), participants highly disagree that the majority of friends or colleagues surrounding them use or believe that they should use chatbots. Having 83.1% in the poor area means that the users are already considering that SI is not affecting them to use these technologies. In fact, a statistically significant and positive correlation was found between SI (H3) and BI in the regression analysis (p < 0.001). Although health is always a personal thing but patients are not experts. So, their BI and UB in OHCs are influenced by their social relationships mainly other patients in the family, friends or even family members nurse, doctors, technician etc. [34, 35, 40].

In other words, when users' friends, family, and colleagues (who matter), propose to users that they should use chatbots in OHCs, the users increase their intentions to use OHCs.

Finally for FC (a 4-item scale with a mean of 18.67 $\pm$ 4.61 over 28, and a median of 19 with a minimum of 4 and a maximum of 28), participants highly agree that they have the necessary resources (laptops, smartphones, etc.) to use chatbots for getting support on all levels. Also, they highly agree that they have the necessary knowledge to use chatbots for getting support on all levels. Having 42% in the Good and Very Good areas means that the users are already considering that FC is highly important to use these technologies. Also, having 58% in the poor area means that this factor is highly important to increase the BI.

Regarding FC (H4), a statistically significant and positive correlation was found between FC and BI in the regression analysis (p = 0.001). The literature confirmed as per the findings of this study that FC has a significant influence on BI [40]. According to [39], the BI to adopt this tool is related to the specific devices that sometimes need technical support more than other ones. In other words, having laptops, smartphones and the necessary knowledge and experts available for assistance, increase the users' BI to use chatbots in OHCs. When users receive more FCs to use chatbots, they will increase their intentions to use them.

The following table is showing the significant correlation between BI and UB. It highlights that UB is positively correlated with BI (p < 0.001), and UB will increase with the increasing of BI (B = 0.514).

As for BI (a 4-item scale, with a mean of 17.88 ± 6.19 over 28, and a median of 18 with a minimum of 4 and a maximum of 28), participants agree that they are planning to use chatbots in OHCs in the future, provided that they have access to these online platforms. However, 56.9%, of participants are located in the poor area, highlighting the need to understand the motivations and discover the opportunities to increase the acceptance of using chatbots in OHCs. Regarding H5, a statistically significant correlation was found between BI and UB in the linear regression (p < 0.001). This finding is associated with the findings of the literature review that found all variables having a significant correlation [41].

Additionally, the categorization of answers in this study showed that almost 45% of responders currently do not consider that becoming familiar with the use of chatbots is easy for them. Hence, having this significant correlation between BI and UB is a great potential to get people more involved into employing this technology.

Finally, for UB (a 3-item scale with a mean of 10.84 ± 3.48 over 21, and a median of 11 with a minimum of 3 and a maximum of 21), participants do not agree that they are currently or frequently using chatbots in OHCs. It is indicative that 93.2% are located in the poor area. Further researches are required to understand the factors and examine opportunities that lead to UB.

To conclude, once we have a significant correlation between BI and UB, the variables that had a direct significant correlation on BI should have an indirect correlation with UB (Table 5). So, once participants are having the intention to use chatbots in OHCs, it will not be hard to convince them using these applications. Multiple strategies must be defined and aligned with the independent variables that had a direct impact on BI. In other words, when users' have more intention in using chatbots in OHCs, they use them more frequently.

Henceforth the 5 main hypotheses (H1, H2, H3, H4 and H5) were validated.

Finally, a detailed analysis was conducted about the role of UTAUT moderators in the use of chatbots in OHCs. In fact, Venkatesh [4] included many moderators in the UTAUT framework such as gender and age. So, we analyzed all the related hypotheses.

In general, the factor gender did not show any significant correlation with independent variables in this study (ANOVA Test). The chosen sample is in fact more familiar with

Table 5. Correlation between BI and UB

	Unstandardized Coefficients		Standardized Coefficients	t	P.value
	B	Std. Error	Beta		
(Constant)	5.675	0.435		13.046	0.000
Behavioral Intention	0.289	0.023	0.514	12.570	0.000
Dependent Variable: Use Behavior					

technology. The same analysis was applied for the age moderator. The findings do not correlate with the literature. In other terms, age does not have any impact on the use of chatbots in OHCs. In the bivariate analysis, a statistically non-significant correlation was found between Age and PE, EE, SI, FC and UB. Other researchers identified that the age is the most significant moderator in the healthcare context due to the fact that older patients may have some challenges when using technology [20, 22].

As mentioned before, the participants are already technology users'; their age does not increase or decrease their intentions to use chatbots in OHCs.

5   Contributions, Conclusion, Limitations and Future Research

In this article, we tried to highlight and examine the intention of using health AI agents/chatbots applications through the UTAUT model in OHCs. Based on the UTAUT framework, the technology use experience of OHCs members was showed through the intention of using AI conversational agents/chatbots in OHCs. BI and UB are highly correlated with the main constructs of UTAUT and play a major role in affecting the relationship between the variables and BIs of the participants.

The study showed that when PE, EE, SI, and FC increase, BI will increase. In other terms, when productivity is enhanced, the users will increase their intentions to use chatbots in OHCs. Also, these applications must be user friendly as it will increase participants BIs to use them. Apparently, family members, friends and colleagues have a major impact on the intentions of our participants. When the participants are well equipped with technology, they certainly increase their BIs to use these applications.

The contribution of this study is twofold; first we contributed to theory by adding one more context to test the UTAUT model in OHCs for the usage of AI agents/chatbots. By testing the UTAUT model, this study has answered the demand for further research and empirical studies on intelligent automation in the healthcare industry. It also fills a gap in the current literature on the use of chatbot technology in healthcare. The UTAUT has once again proven to be a strong and reliable model for evaluating the adoption and application of new technology, since the findings revealed a better understanding of users' acceptability and readiness to use chatbots in OHCs. Therefore, this study advances the literature by offering key insights for practitioners and scholars interested in studying patients' behavior when it comes to the use of chatbots in OHCs.

Another contribution of this study is important information on the factors influencing the use of chatbots in OHCs. Technology developers should ensure that chatbots in OHCs interact in a variety of languages, providing customers with a user-friendly interface. The practitioners must ensure that chatbots do not cause any technology-related anxiety. Designers must create user-friendly chatbots in order to reduce patients' concerns about technology.

Patients can also use health chatbots to connect directly with physicians for diagnosis or treatment support by talking or texting smart algorithms as the first point of contact for primary care in the future. Physicians, nurses, or any other medical experts may be revealed from answering every single health question, including FAQ; instead, they will look to chatbots first. If the little medical assistant is unable to reply to the issues mentioned, the case will be transferred to a real-life doctor. Chatbot providers must ensure distinct and distinctive service features to meet the patients' needs and encourage patient usage. As for healthcare practitioners, chatbots must be developed with customization and personalization provisions based on the needs of patients in order for patients to feel at ease when using chatbots for health purposes.

Finally, although the literature review indicates that the UTAUT model is robust and has been validated in the literature, there are some intrinsic limitations need to be acknowledged; For instance, the intention-behavior gap and the external factors influence as identified by [42], should be taken into consideration in future studies. Furthermore, it is believed that other variables such as trust and FOTA, and other moderators such as technology experience, educational level, occupation, culture, and geographical zone, should be added to the UTAUT model in order to be tested in future studies and other contexts.

Finally, our research shows a methodological limit in terms of the generalization of the results; in fact, this research was carried out over a set length of time, therefore there is a need for a longitudinal evaluation in future research to guarantee UB. To conclude future research should explore the ethical principles and practical implications of chatbots, as well as the cultural and the regional impact on BI and UB.

Appendixes

Appendix A: Demographic Characteristics of the Study Population

		Frequency	Percent
	Female	217	49.0
Gender	Male	204	46.0
	Prefer not to answer	22	5.0

Appendix B: Experience Related to the Use of Chatbots in OHCs

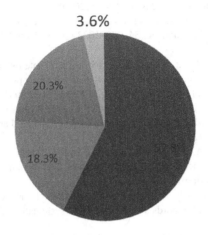

Appendix C: Descriptive Analysis of UTAUT Main Constructs

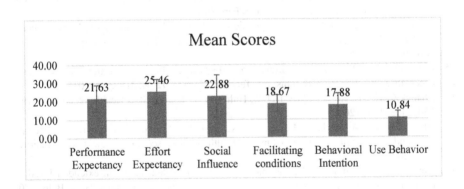

References

1. Wright, R.: The coronavirus pandemic is now a threat to national security, The New Yorker, 7 October (2020). https://www.newyorker.com/news
2. Long, M.: Deep learning in healthcare- How it's changing the game (2020). https://www.aidoc.com/blog/deep-learning-in-healthcare/
3. Sennaar, K.: Chatbots for healthcare – comparing 5 current applications. business intelligence and analytics. Healthcare. Customer Service. Emerj, the AI Research and Advisory Company (2019)
4. Venkatesh, V., Morris, M.G., Gordon, B.D., Davis, F.D.: User acceptance of information technology: toward a unified view. MIS Quart. **27**(3), 425–478 (2003)

5. Wu, B.: Patient continued use of online health care communities: Web mining of patient-doctor communication. J. Med. Internet Res. **20**, e126 (2018)

6. Mesko, B., Gyorffy, Z.: The rise of the empowered physician in the digital health era: viewpoint. J. Med. Internet Res. **21**(2), e12490 (2019)

7. Papadaki, M., Karamitsos, I., Themistocleous, M.: Covid-19 digital test certificates and blockchain. J. Enterp. Inf. Manage. **34**, 993–1003 (2021). https://doi.org/10.1108/JEIM-07-2021-554

8. Jabarulla, M.Y., Lee, H.-N.: A blockchain and artificial intelligence-based, patient-centric healthcare system for combating the COVID-19 pandemic: opportunities and applications. Healthcare **9**, 1019 (2021). https://doi.org/10.3390/healthcare9081019

9. Karamitsos, I., Papadaki, M.: Blockchain digital test certificates for COVID-19. In: Tallón-Ballesteros, A.J. (Ed.) Modern Management based on Big Data II and Machine Learning and Intelligent Systems III (2021)

10. Koteluk, O., Wartecki, A., Mazurek, S., Kołodziejczak, I., Mackiewicz, A.: How do machines learn? artificial intelligence as a New Era in medicine. J. Personalized Med. **11**(1), 32 (2021). https://doi.org/10.3390/jpm11010032

11. Abd-Alrazaq, A.A., Bewick, B., Farragher, T., Gardner, P.: Factors that affect the use of electronic personal health records among patients: a systematic review. Int. J. Med. Inform. **126**, 164–175 (2019)

12. Palanica, A., Flaschner, P., Thommandram, A., Li, M., Fossat, Y.: Physicians' perceptions of chatbots in health care: cross-sectional web-based survey. J. Med. Internet Res. **21**(4), e12887 (2019). https://doi.org/10.2196/12887

13. Amato, F., Marrone, S., Moscato, V., Piantadosi, G., Picariello, A., Sansone, C.: CEUR workshop proceedings. Chatbots Meet eHealth: Automatizing Healthcare (2017). http://ceur-ws.org/Vol-1982/paper6.pdf. Accessed 26 Feb 2019

14. Brandtzaeg, P.B., Følstad, A.: Why people use chatbots. In: Kompatsiaris, I., et al. (eds.) INSCI 2017. LNCS, vol. 10673, pp. 377–392. Springer, Cham (2017). https://doi.org/10.1007/978-3-319-70284-1_30

15. Park, S.H., Lee, L., Yi, M.Y.: Group-level effects of facilitating conditions on individual acceptance of information systems. Inf. Technol. Manage. **12**(4), 315–334 (2011)

16. Zhang, Z., Lu, Y., Kou, Y., Wu, D.T.Y., Huh-Yoo, J., He, Z.: Stud Health Technol Inform. **264**, 1403–1407 (2019)

17. Abd-Alrazaq, A.A. Alajlani, M., Denecke, K., Nashva, A., Denecke, K. Bewick, B.: Perceptions and opinions of patients about mental health chatbots: scoping review. J. Med. Internet Res. (2021)

18. Khalilzadeh, J., Ozturk, A.B., Bilgihan, A.: Security-related factors in extended UTAUT model for NFC based mobile payment in the restaurant industry. Comput. Hum. Behav. **70**, 460–474 (2017). https://doi.org/10.1016/j.chb.2017.01.001

19. Šumak, B., Šorgo, A.: The acceptance and use of interactive whiteboards among teachers: differences in UTAUT determinants between pre- and post-adopters. Comput. Hum. Behav. **64**, 602–620 (2016). https://doi.org/10.1016/j.chb.2016.07.037

20. Hoque, R., Sorwar, G.: Understanding factors influencing the adoption of mHealth by the elderly: an extension of the UTAUT model. Int. J. Med. Inform. **101**, 75–84 (2017). https://doi.org/10.1016/j.ijmedinf.2017.02.002

21. Chauhan, S., Jaiswal, M.: Determinants of acceptance of ERP software training in business schools: empirical investigation using UTAUT model. Int. J. Manage. Educ. **14**, 248–262 (2016). https://doi.org/10.1016/j.ijme.2016.05.005

22. Cimperman, M., Brenčič, M.M., Trkman, P.: Analyzing older users' home telehealth services acceptance behavior—applying an extended UTAUT model. Int. J. Med. Inform. **90**, 22–31 (2016). https://doi.org/10.1016/j.ijmedinf.2016.03.002

23. Taylor, S., Todd, P.: Assessing IT usage: the role of prior experience. MIS Q. **19**(4), 561–570 (1995)

24. Lee, Y., Kozar, K.A., Larsen, K.R.T.: The technology acceptance model: past, present, and future. Commun. Assoc. Inf. Syst. **12**, 752–780 (2003)

25. Esmaeilzadeh, P., Sambasivan, M., Kumar, N., Nezakati, H.: Adoption of clinical decision support systems in a developing country: antecedents and outcomes of physician's threat to perceived professional autonomy. Int. J. Med. Inf. **84**(8), 548–560 (2015)

26. De Veer, A.J.E., Peeters, J.M., Brabers, A.E., Schellevis, F.G., Rademakers, J.J., Francke, A.L.: Determinants of the intention to use e-Health by community dwelling older people. BMC Health Serv. Res. **15**, 103 (2015)

27. Chan, F.K.Y., Thong, J.Y.L., Venkatesh, W., Brown, S.A., Hu, P.J., Tam, K.Y.: Modeling citizen satisfaction with mandatory adoption of an E-government technology. J. Assoc. Inf. Syst. **11**(10), 519–549 (2010)

28. Guo, Y.: Moderating effects of gender in the acceptance of mobile based on UTAUT model. Int. J. Smart Home **9**(1), 203–216 (2015)

29. Klein, H.K., Myers, M.D.: A set of principles for conducting and evaluating interpretive field studies in information systems. MIS Q. **23**(1), 67–93 (1999)

30. Straub, D.W., Boudreau, M.-C., Gefen, D.: Validation guidelines for IS positivist research. Comm. AIS **13**, 380–427 (2004)

31. Creswell, J.W.: Research Design: Qualitative Quantitative and Mixed Methods Approaches, Second edition Sage Publication, Thousand Oaks (2003)

32. Orlikowski, W.J., Baroudi, J.J.: Studying information technology in organizations: research approaches and assumptions. Inf. Syst. Res. **2**(1), 1–28 (1991)

33. Walsh, I.: Using quantitative data in mixed-design grounded theory studies: an enhanced path to formal grounded theory in information systems. Eur. J. Inf. Syst. **2014**, 1–27 (2014)

34. Tavares, J., Oliveira, T.: Electronic health record portal adoption: a cross country analysis. BMC Med. Inform. Decis. Mak. **17**, 97 (2017). https://doi.org/10.1186/s12911-017-0482-9

35. Okumus, F., Ali, F., Bilgihan, A., Ozturk, A.B.: Psychological factors influencing customers' acceptance of smartphone diet apps when ordering food at restaurants. Int. J. Hospital. Manage. **72**, 67–77 (2018). https://doi.org/10.1016/j.ijhm.2018.01.001

36. Reyes-Mercado, P.: Adoption of fitness wearables. J. Syst. Inf. Technol. **20**(1), 103–127 (2018)

37. Pai, F.-Y., Huang, K.-I.: applying the technology acceptance model to the introduction of healthcare information systems. Technol. Forecast Soc. Change. **78**, 650–660 (2011)

38. Quaosar, G.A.A., Hoque, M.R., Bao, Y.: Investigating factors affecting Elderly's intention to use m-health services: an empirical study. Telemed. E Health **24**(4), 309–314 (2018). https://doi.org/10.1089/tmj.2017.0111

39. Gao, Y., Li, H., Luo, Y.: An empirical study of wearable technology acceptance in healthcare. Ind. Manage. Data Syst. **115**(9), 1704–1723 (2015). https://doi.org/10.1108/IMDS-03-2015-0087

40. Hsieh, P.J.: An empirical investigation of patients' acceptance and resistance toward the health cloud: the dual factor perspective. Comput. Hum. Behav. **63**, 959–969 (2016). https://doi.org/10.1016/j.chb.2016.06.029

41. Lu, X., Zhang, R., Zhu, X.: An empirical study on patients' acceptance of physician-patient interaction in online health communities. Int. J. Environ. Res. Public Health **16**, 5084 (2019). https://doi.org/10.3390/ijerph16245084

42. Venkatesh, V., Bala, H.: Technology acceptance model 3 and a research agenda on interventions. Decis. Sci. **39**(2), 273–315 (2008)

Information Systems Security and Information Privacy Protection

GDPR-Compliant Data Processing: Practical Considerations

João Almeida[1], Paulo Rupino da Cunha[1]([✉]) [ID], and Alexandre Dias Pereira[2] [ID]

[1] Department of Informatics Engineering, University of Coimbra, Coimbra, Portugal
rupino@dei.uc.pt
[2] Faculty of Law, University of Coimbra, Coimbra, Portugal

Abstract. We provide actionable guidance to organizations needing to comply with the European General Data Protection Regulation (GDPR). We use a data processing pipeline – Data collection, Data protection, and Data operations – to structure the discussion around regulation requirements (with references to specific articles and recitals), socio-technical challenges, and applicable security best practices and techniques. Ensuring compliance is critical since fines for infringements can mount up to 4% of the total worldwide annual turnover of the organization in the preceding financial year.

Keywords: GDPR · Practical guidelines · Privacy

1 Introduction

The European General Data Protection Regulation (GDPR) [29] superseded the Data Protection Directive (95/46/EC) [10], reinforcing data protection as a fundamental right of citizens. Introduced in 2016 and enforced since 25 May 2018, it had a significant impact on organizations around the world, since it applies in any geography as long as personal data of European citizens is processed. Additionally, fines for infringement are steep, at up to 4% of the organization's worldwide annual turnover.

In a nutshell, to be compliant, organizations need to [30]: obtain informed consent for personal data collection, timely inform of data breaches, provide users with access to their personal data and its uses, erase personal data of users at their request, provide users with a copy of their personal data to port to another organization, ensure that privacy is built-in by design and that proper security protocols are in place from the onset, eventually appoint independent data protection officers.

GDPR gives organizations leeway on how to comply, partly because it aims to be technologically neutral [15], but this stance has the side-effect of making it harder for organizations trying to define implementation roadmaps [32].

For our guidance, we start by extrapolating, from the set of operations defined in its Art. 4 [15], a data processing pipeline that needs to be established for compliance: Data collection, Data protection, and Data operations. See Fig. 1.

© Springer Nature Switzerland AG 2022
M. Themistocleous and M. Papadaki (Eds.): EMCIS 2021, LNBIP 437, pp. 505–514, 2022.
https://doi.org/10.1007/978-3-030-95947-0_36

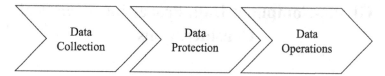

Fig. 1. A data processing pipeline extrapolated from Art. 4 of GDPR

As we move along the pipeline, we reference the relevant regulation articles and recitals (reasons for the adoption of the articles), all of which can be conveniently consulted on-line [15].

Remaining concerns, including the management of processing by external entities (Art. 8), are out of scope.

The remainder of the paper is structured as follows: In Sect. 2, we provide some common ground. Sections 3, 4, and 5, explore the data processing pipeline, namely Data Collection, Data Protection, and Data Operations, respectively. We present conclusions in Sect. 6.

2   Common Ground

Before discussing the practical aspects of GDPR compliance, we provide some background on the regulation and the challenges in addressing it.

2.1   Causes and Goals

To ensure alignment with GDPR, and given the lack of guidance mentioned earlier, it is important to understand the motivations behind the introduction of the regulation, particularly what needed to be changed and why. The Recitals of the regulation are especially useful, setting out *"the reasons for the contents"* of the articles [28].

First and foremost, data protection is established as a fundamental right (Recital 1), which this regulation aims to strengthen (Recital 2), in the face of the challenges brought from the current scale of data processing (Recital 6). Moreover, we can definitely see how much the digital landscape has changed in recent years – how ubiquitous it is in our daily lives, and how intrusive it can be. Strong enforcement of this fundamental right is deemed necessary to return the control of personal data to the citizens (Recital 7).

Though many of GDPR's underlying ideas were already present in the previous Data Protection Directive, this latter had to be transposed into national law and interpreted and enforced by each Member State. This situation led to fragmentation (Recital 9), which GDPR aims to fix by assuming the form of regulation, ensuring *"Consistent and homogenous application of the rules"* (Recital 10).

In essence, GDPR emerges due to the changing digital landscape, which was inadequately controlled by existing legislation and led to subjects losing control over their own data.

2.2 Relevance and Difficulties

A pragmatic reason for the relevance of GDPR for organizations lies in its active enforcement, which is accompanied by fines that are now calculated as a percentage of the yearly turnover (Art. 48) and issued by the Member States' independent Supervisory Authority (Art. 51), taking into account mitigating and aggravating factors (Art. 48; Recital 148) [4]. Consequently, larger organizations should no longer feel comfortable accepting the fines. Criminal penalties can also ensue, brought by the Member States (Recital 149), as can the compensation for damages (Art. 82; Recital 146).

Despite these incentives to compliance, reinforced by the good public image which it conveys [32], cases of non-compliance are still common, more than one year after the end transitional period. The complexity of the process may result from the lack of guidelines, and the amount of restructuring an organization may need to undergo [32]. It is well-known that security should be designed early on into a system, to avoid the risk of considerable refactoring later on to accommodate it. In a similar vein, once data on a user is collected, it may end up spread over many of the organization's services and supporting systems, for uses which may not be entirely controlled. This situation raises considerable challenges when trying to add data protection measures after the fact, and when trying to provide users with accounts of how their data is used (Art. 15).

3 Data Collection

Sound data collection practices are fundamental to achieve GDPR compliance, as its correct implementation is what determines the legality (Art. 6) of all subsequent processing operations as defined in (Art. 4).

To collect personal data, i.e., data related to an identifiable natural person (Article 4), the organization needs their explicit consent (Art. 6; Recital 40), whereby they are made aware of "*risks, rules, safeguards and rights*" (Recital 39). Furthermore, the controller is held accountable for the processing requirements enumerated in Article 5, namely the key 'purpose limitation' and 'data minimization,' meaning that processing should be limited to the specific purposes, and be done solely on the necessary personal data, to which the data subject gave explicit consent for (Article 6).

Consent is a problematic topic. GDPR requires (Art. 4) that it must be "*freely given, specific, informed and unambiguous,*" and Art. 7 enumerates conditions, including how to present it. However, in practice, we often see it implemented using annoying pop-ups with pre-ticked boxes, or in forms that force individual disabling of hundreds of advertisers, which runs counter the spirit of Recital 32.

The malicious intent of such default settings, predicated on users not caring to change them, is discussed in [2], as are the 'capture errors' caused by intending to close pop-ups but inadvertently accepting their policy. Specifically, for GDPR, in [33], the authors describe the effect that nudging can have, whereby small changes to a consent notice led to different user behavior.

These cases highlight the need for precise requirements on how to obtain free and informed consent, which the regulation does not provide, leading to abuses. Fines issued for inadequate consent requests are few and far between [14], diminishing what was supposed to be a significant incentive for compliance.

This situation raises the question of what informed consent is. Should organizations guarantee that the user reads the whole privacy agreement? For most, this would be unfeasible. Given the high abandonment rate during initial web page screening [18], organizations need to capture the user's attention quickly. Cookie banners used by cookie consent libraries are less obtrusive, but the majority do not meet GDPR requirements [9].

The situation gets worse because many users are not concerned with privacy issues [19, 24], as their level of exposure on social media attests [7]. Causes may include the reduced attention given to privacy until recently, leading to mistakes for cognitive reasons [2], either for lack of knowledge or disregard.

Automatic data collection upon visiting a site (such as the IP address and location) is another source of concern. On the one hand *"merely proceeding with a service cannot be regarded as an active indication of choice"* (Art. 29 of [5]); on the other hand, location data is explicitly stated as an example of personal data (Art. 4), and IP addresses can similarly identify a person (Recital 30).

4   Data Protection

Having decided what data to collect and to what purposes, the next step is to ensure adequate protection. The regulation addresses the so-called 'CIA triad' (confidentiality, integrity, and availability). The former two properties, concerned with preventing unauthorized disclosure and modification [34], are the subject of Art. 5, while availability takes second place in the eyes of the regulation (Art. 32). This prioritization is essential since the goals of availability are often orthogonal with those of confidentiality and integrity [37].

4.1   Security by Design

Security needs to be designed into a system from early on, since retrofitting it becomes significantly more expensive [25]. A critical step is to rigorously define the security requirements, using one of several existing methods [12]. Next, the implementation should follow best practices, such as the thorough, yet technologically agnostic, 'OWASP Secure Coding Practices' [25].

Sadly, companies frequently favour more features and performance over security, which is usually only considered after a significant incident, as shown by the Zoom videoconference debacle during the COVID pandemic [36].

The system should also be thoroughly tested for vulnerabilities, preferably using both approaches: white-box (e.g., inspections and code reviews) and black-box (e.g., automated tools and red teams). Alas, no system will be completely secure, as the regular identification of 0-day vulnerabilities demonstrates. To mitigate this, organizations can offer bug bounty programs as a way to crowdsource the discovery of vulnerabilities, to discourage hackers' participation in existing black markets [13].

Defense in depth is also essential, meaning that multiple layers of protection should be deployed to prevent the failure of one compromising the entire system [3]. However, we often see cases where a single mechanism is employed, leading to a false sense of security. A prime example if the use of HTTPS in web services, which, without additional input processing, is useless to counter SQL injection attacks that are capable of compromising the entire database.

4.2 Pseudonymization

Pseudonymization is one of the few technical measures specifically mentioned in GDPR (Art. 25; Art 32; Recital 28). It aims to de-identify personal data, making it no longer attributable to a data subject (Art. 4). However, this is more complex than merely removing unique identifiers [22] (e.g., national ID) since the combination of other less sensitive attributes (quasi-identifiers) can often still be used to identify a subject. For instance, [31] found that 87% of the US population was uniquely identified through the combination of their gender, date of birth, and zip code prefix.

Different privacy models exist to achieve pseudonymization. They are based on several sanitizing operations [20]: generalization, suppression (removal of values), anatomization (de-association of attributes by separation), and perturbation (alteration of values). These methods include:

- K-anonymity [31], one of the most well-known methods. It ensures that each such quasi-identifier combination occurs in at least k records [22]. As such, each record is indistinguishable from at least k-1 others [20] (making the dataset, in theory, publishable with a high value of k). However, this does not take into account sensitive values (non-identifying, but whose confidentiality is critical) and their distribution, so extensions with additional constraints were created [20].
- Differential privacy is particularly interesting, given the prevalence of data mining for knowledge extraction from datasets. The idea is that a single record does not considerably affect (based on a parameter $\in$) the output of some processing operation [20]. That is, we are concerned with sharing results of processing, instead of the dataset itself, without inadvertently disclosing data about a specific record.

Several tools exist to apply such models, and as is often the case when considering security, we should always look for existing, validated, implementations (i.e., avoid coding from scratch). An example is the 'ARX Data Anonymization Tool' [27], which allows configuring and applying several privacy models and then analyzing the re-identification risk.

4.3 Encryption

GDPR mentions encryption alongside pseudonymization (Art. 32). Encrypting collected personal data significantly reduces the risk of unauthorized disclosure, while also enabling the use of integrity checking mechanisms (e.g., by appending the hash when encrypting). Of course, there are other aspects to consider:

First, data must be encrypted both in transit (commonly done with HTTPS) and while stored in the system. The latter is not as usual [8], once again, because of a false sense of security about the system perimeter. Nevertheless, it is critical to prevent insiders or those who manage to penetrate the system from disclosing the data [8].

Second, the encryption algorithm's choice is paramount, since discovered weaknesses can render them obsolete, as can the mere increase in computational power that may enable brute force attacks (i.e., trying all possible key combinations to decrypt the original text). Furthermore, public and standardized algorithms should be preferred since these are subject to extreme scrutiny. On the contrary, practical attacks are usually found for algorithms with closed designs, like the COMP128 used for mobile communications [8]. There are techniques to work with encrypted data:

- Homomorphic encryption that enables the manipulation of encrypted data as if it were not. This technique is particularly useful to leverage the computational power of the cloud while preserving confidentiality [21]. There is, however, a severe efficiency penalty [17].
- Trusted execution environments, "*hardware-assisted devices robust against attacks*" [17] and tamper-proof, that protect loaded data. An example is Intel Software Guard Extensions, available with all recent Intel processors. Performance is higher than that of the homomorphic encryption, but memory is limited to 90MB [17].

These two approaches provide very high levels of security, but their drawbacks mean that they must be applied selectively, especially when using highly sensitive data, such as medical (Art. 9).

4.4 Measuring Security

Having a metric for system security would be useful. It would enable comparisons of *as-is* and *to-be* scenarios, namely in the degree of improvement of changes. Ideally, it would also indicate the level of compliance with GDPR. However, given the constant identification of vulnerabilities and ways to explore them in increasingly complex IT systems, any such metric would likely be inadequate. As Bellovin argues [6], "*We need layers of assured strength, but we don't have them.*"

An alternative is using the effort put on securing the system as a proxy for that metric. The latter is the fundamental idea underlying trust-based benchmarking [23], and since GDPR is non-prescriptive, it seems an appropriate approach, especially given the need to "*demonstrate that processing is performed in accordance with this Regulation*" (Art. 24).

4.5 Data Breaches

The eventuality of a data breach needs to be considered, since perfect security is unattainable. Human and technical attack vectors change constantly, and systems are designed with pragmatic trade-offs (e.g., in terms of cost or usability). Consequently, we need to be able to detect security incidents and mitigate their effects.

System logging is extremely useful for the detection of abnormal behavior, i.e., unauthorized data accesses that compromise confidentiality. Meanwhile, integrity checkers, like AIDE [1], use cryptographic hashes to detect modifications to data that should not be altered. Once again, choosing secure algorithms is essential; many cryptographic hash functions have been made obsolete.

Adequate encryption can be effective for mitigating breaches, since data should be useless to anyone who does not hold the key.

When a data breach is detected, GDPR requires that supervisory authority be notified within 72 h (Art. 33), unless it is unlikely to result in a risk to the rights and freedoms of natural persons (e.g., the data was encrypted). In case of risk, the affected subjects (e.g., users whose data was exposed) should also be notified (Art. 34).

5 Data Operations

GDPR mandates keeping records of all data processing activities when "*is likely to result in a risk to the rights and* freedoms *of data subjects*" or when the organization has more than 250 employees (Art. 30). Additionally, processes must be in place to handle requests from users exercising the rights of access and portability and the rights to rectification and erasure (Art.12), which we examine next.

5.1 Rights of Access and Portability

The right of access is essential in the context of GDPR. It enables users to find out which personal data an entity holds on them (Art. 15) and to what purpose. Building on that, the right to data portability (Art. 20), enables the users to obtain a copy of their personal data from an entity in such a way that is transferable to another, namely in a "*commonly used and machine-readable format*" (Art. 20). The goal is to prevent lock-in effects, mainly when market concentration is high [16], since "*Switching costs are negatively correlated with data portability*" [11].

Strong authentication is essential to support data portability and should not be unduly compromised in favor of availability. Confidentiality (e.g., by not risking unauthorized disclosure) takes precedence over availability. As discussed in Sect. 4, the 'CIA triad' of security properties may conflict, and priorities must be set [37].

5.2 Rights to Rectification and Erasure

GDPR calls for personal data to be accurate and up to date (Art. 5), leading to the right to rectification (Art. 16). Similarly, the right to be forgotten addresses the cases when the data is no longer needed for its original purposes or consent has been withdrawn (Art. 17).

On the one hand, the ease of storing and accessing digital data compromises our "*ability to forget*" [26]; but on the other hand, merely erasing a piece of data may not be the adequate procedure, since it can compromise of the integrity of a database or the ability to comply with other legal and fiscal regulations. Thus, it is essential to understand the lifetime of the collected data and how exactly it is stored.

Equally relevant are issues that arise from the use of artificial intelligence that learns from collected data and later applies those learning to new data [35]. This raises significant research questions, such as, for example, [35]:

- "*How can we ensure a balance between the Right to Be Forgotten and a machine learning model's need to remember information used to train it?*", or

- *"Can artificial intelligence models be created that 'learn' from new data without storing personal information that could be used in a Right to Be Forgotten request?"*.

Finally, it is essential to ensure that 'erased' data was not backed-up or that existing backups are also deleted, which raises additional technical challenges.

6 Conclusion

We provided guidance for organizations needing to comply with GDPR. Using a data processing pipeline extrapolated from the set of operations defined in the regulation, we referenced the relevant recitals and articles (using a convenient online source), discussed sociotechnical challenges for compliance, and presented adequate security best practices and techniques, supported on relevant literature.

The rather ambitious scope required some tradeoffs between breadth and depth. Nevertheless, this contextualization, with the inclusion of diverse security techniques and practices, should prove useful reading to those seeking to achieve compliance and may serve as a starting point for more specialized work regarding some aspects.

Future work can also address explicitly out-of-scope concerns, including the management of data processing by external entities (Art. 8). Finally, additional insights may emerge from the reports that the European Commission must submit to the European Parliament and the Council on the evaluation and review of GDPR. The most recent was due by the end of May 2020 (Art. 97).

References

1. AIDE - Advanced Intrusion Detection Environment, available on-line at https://github.com/aide/aide. Accessed 7 July 2020
2. Anderson, R.: Security engineering: A Guide to Building Dependable Distributed Systems, 3rd edn. Wiley, Indianapolis, Indiana (2020)
3. Antunes, N., Vieira, M.: Defending against web application vulnerabilities. Computer **45**(2), 66–72 (2012)
4. Article 29 Data Protection Working Party. Guidelines on the application and setting of administrative fines for the purposes of the Regulation 2016/679. http://ec.europa.eu/newsroom/just/document.cfm?doc_id=47889. Accessed 7 July 2020
5. Article 29 working party. guidelines on consent under regulation 2016/679 (wp259rev.01). https://ec.europa.eu/newsroom/article29/document.cfm?action=display&doc_id=51030. Accessed 7 July 2020
6. Bellovin, S.M.: On the brittleness of software and the infeasibility of security metrics. IEEE Secur. Priv. **4**(4), 96 (2006)
7. Beye, M., Jeckmans, A., Erkin, Z., Hartel, P.H., Lagendijk, R., Tang, Q.: Privacy in Online Social Networks, pp. 87–113. Computational Social Networks. Springer, London (2012)
8. Boavida, F., Bernardes, M.: Introdução à Criptografia, FCA–Editora de Informática (2019)
9. Degeling, M., Utz, C., Lentzsch, C., Hosseini, H., Schaub, F., Holz, T.: We value your privacy. Now take some cookies: measuring the GDPR's impact on web privacy (2018). arXiv preprint arXiv:1808.05096

10. Directive 95/46/EC of the European Parliament and of the Council of 24 October 1995 on the protection of individuals with regard to the processing of personal data and on the free movement of such data). https://eur-lex.europa.eu/legal-content/en/TXT/?uri=CELEX%3A3 1995L0046. Accessed 7 July 2020

11. Engels, B.: Data portability among online platforms. Internet Policy Rev. **5**(2) (2016)

12. Fabian, B., Gürses, S., Heisel, M., Santen, T., Schmidt, H.: A comparison of security requirements engineering methods. Requirements Eng. **15**(1), 7–40 (2010)

13. Fryer, H., Simperl, E.: Web science challenges in researching bug bounties. In: Proceedings of the 2017 ACM on Web Science Conference, pp. 273–277 (2017)

14. GDPR Enforcement Tracker. https://www.enforcementtracker.com. Accessed 7 July 2020

15. Intersoft Consulting. General Data Protection Regulation – Official Legal Text. https://gdpr-info.eu. Accessed 1 June 2020

16. Janal, R.: Data portability-a tale of two concepts. J. Intell. Property, Inf. Technol. E-Commer. Law, **8**(1), 59–69 (2017)

17. Flora, J.: Trusted execution environments. CSAM 6 Jan 2020

18. Liu, C., White, R.W., Dumais, S.: Understanding web browsing behaviors through Weibull analysis of dwell time. In: Proceedings of the 33rd International ACM SIGIR Conference on Research and Development in Information Retrieval, pp. 379–386 (2010)

19. Malandrino, D., Petta, A., Scarano, V., Serra, L., Spinelli, R., Krishnamurthy, B.: Privacy awareness about information leakage: who knows what about me? In: Proceedings of the 12th ACM workshop on Workshop on privacy in the electronic society, pp. 279–284 (2013)

20. Mendes, R., Vilela, J.P.: Privacy-preserving data mining: methods, metrics, and applications. IEEE Access **5**, 10562–10582 (2017)

21. Naehrig, M., Lauter, K., Vaikuntanathan, V.: Can homomorphic encryption be practical? In: Proceedings of the 3rd ACM Workshop on Cloud Computing Security Workshop, pp. 113–124 (2011)

22. Narayanan, A., Shmatikov, V.: How to break anonymity of the Netflix Prize dataset, arXiv e-print. http://arxiv.org/abs/cs/0610105. Accessed 8 July 2020

23. Neto, A.A., Vieira, M.: Untrustworthiness: a trustbased security metric. Fourth Int. Conf. Risks Secur. Internet Syst. **2009**, 123–126 (2009)

24. Omoronyia, I.: The case for privacy awareness requirements. In: Censorship, Surveillance, and Privacy: Concepts, Methodologies, Tools, and Applications, pp. 697–716. IGI Global (2019)

25. Open Web Application Security Project (OWASP) Secure Coding Practices - Quick Reference Guide. https://owasp.org/www-pdf-archive/OWASP_SCP_Quick_Reference_Guide_v2.pdf. Accessed 8 July 2020

26. Politou, E., Alepis, E., Patsakis, C.: Forgetting personal data and revoking consent under the GDPR: Challenges and proposed solutions. J. Cybersecurity, **4**(1), tyy001 (2018)

27. Prasser, F., Kohlmayer, F., Lautenschlaeger, R., Kuhn, K.A.: Arx-a comprehensive tool for anonymizing biomedical data. In: Proceedings of the AMIA Annual Symposium, pp. 984–993 (2014)

28. Publications Office of the European Union, 2.2. Preamble (citations and recitals). https://publications.europa.eu/code/en/en-120200.htm. Accessed 8 July 2020

29. Regulation (EU) (2016/679) (2016). https://eur-lex.europa.eu/eli/reg/2016/679/oj. Accessed 8 July 2020

30. Saltis, S.: GDPR explained in 5 minutes: everything you need to know. https://www.coredna.com/blogs/general-data-protection-regulation. Accessed 1 June 2020

31. Sweeney, L.: K-anonymity: a model for protecting privacy. Internat. J. Uncertain. Fuzziness Knowl.-Based Syst. **10**(05), 557–570 (2002)

32. Teixeira, G.A., Silva, M.M., Pereira, R.: The critical success factors of GDPR implementation: a systematic literature review. Digit. Policy, Regul. Governance. **21**(4), 402–418 (2019)

33. Utz, C., Degeling, M., Fahl, S., Schaub, F., Holz, T.: (Un) informed consent: studying GDPR consent notices in the field. In: Proceedings of the 2019 ACM SIGSAC Conference on Computer and Communications Security, pp. 973–990 (2019)

34. Vieira, M., Antunes, N.: Introduction to software security concepts. In: Cotroneo, D. (eds.) Innovative Technologies for Dependable OTS-Based Critical Systems. Springer, Milano (2013)

35. Villaronga, E.F., Kieseberg, P., Li, T.: Humans forget, machines remember: artificial intelligence and the right to be forgotten. Comput. Law Secur. Rev. **34**(2), 304–313 (2018)

36. Warren, T.: Zoom announces 90-day feature freeze to fix privacy and security issues. https://www.theverge.com/2020/4/2/21204018/zoom-security-privacy-feature-freeze-200-million-daily-users. Accessed 1 June 2020

37. Wilson, K.S.: Conflicts among the pillars of information assurance. IT Professional **15**(4), 44–49 (2012)

Naïve Bayes Based Classifier for Credit Card Fraud Discovery

Roseline Oluwaseun Ogundokun[1]([⊠]) [iD], Sanjay Misra[2] [iD],
Olufunmilayo Joyce Fatigun[3], and Jide Kehinde Adeniyi[1]

[1] Department of Computer Science, Landmark University, Omu Aran, Nigeria
Ogundokun.roseline@lmu.edu.ng
[2] Department of Computer Science and Communication, Ostfold University College, Halden, Norway
sanjay.misra@covenantuniversity.edu.ng
[3] Directorate of Financial Services, Agricultural and Rural Management Training Institute, Ilorin, Nigeria

Abstract. As financial services and operations expand, financial fraud is on the rise. Despite the use of preventative and security measures to reduce monetary fraud, criminals are constantly acquiring and developing new ways to circumvent fraud detection systems, posing a challenge to quantitative methods and predictive approaches. As a result, new methodologies must be researched and tested to leverage the insights gained from the study to assist further incorrect fraud forecasting and the establishment of fraud discovery schemes with extra measures to alleviate distrustful events. Naïve Bayes (NB) is a significant Machine Learning (ML) classifier that is not yet explored in the literature, unlike the use of common ML techniques like Decision Tree (DT), Random Forest (RF), Artificial Neural Network (ANN), and the likes. This paper, therefore, explores the use of a technique yet to be employed for credit card fraud detection (CCFD) namely Naïve Bayes. The classifier was compared using a confusion matrix for performance matrices like accuracy, precision, recall, f-measure, and ROC-AUC. It was discovered that NB outperformed most of the ML classifiers employed in state-of-the-art compared with an accuracy of 97.99%, recall of 98.02%, the precision of 99.97%, f-measure 98.98%, and FPR of 0.1971.

Keywords: Naïve Bayes · Classification · Machine learning · Credit card fraud detection · Credit card

Abbreviation

Abbreviation	Meaning
ML	Machine Learning
DT	Decision Tree
KNN	K-Nearest Neighbor
CC	Credit Card
CCF	Credit Card Fraud
FPR	False Positive Rate

© Springer Nature Switzerland AG 2022
M. Themistocleous and M. Papadaki (Eds.): EMCIS 2021, LNBIP 437, pp. 515–526, 2022.
https://doi.org/10.1007/978-3-030-95947-0_37

TP	True Positive
TN	True Negative
FP	False Positive
FN	False Negative
FL	Fuzzy Logic
LR	Logistic Regression
DM	Data Mining

1 Background and Related Works

Every year, fraudulent transactions cost the financial sector billions of dollars, and preventing these deficits introduces continuous disputes for data analysis [1–9]. In 2017, fraud losses resulting from car loans are expected to reach about $4–6 billion [10]. According to Bloomberg [11], approximately 1% of US auto mortgage usage consists of some kind of deception, and this number is on its way to surpassing mortgage scams. Given the significant rise in the numbers, which skyrocketed to about $2–4 billion in 2015, PointPredictive [10] contends in support of the problem's importance and effect. In general, fraud occurs in a variety of private and governmental organizations, as well as in many areas of the economy. Credit cards, healthcare insurance, telecommunications, internet transactions, and vehicle insurance are among the five major sectors that are vulnerable to fraud, according to Abdallah, Maarof, and Zainal [12]. Banking and fiscal facilities, government and public management, and manufacturing businesses are the sectors most vulnerable to fraud occurrences, as stated in the ACFE's Statement to the Countries [13]. The authors also point out that document creation and modification were the most common methods of concealing. It was similarly discovered that the extended a fraud goes undiscovered, the more money the organization loses. Because of the nature of their business, financial institutions are especially vulnerable to fraud. As a result, it is critical for these institutions to not only identify but also mitigate such occurrences. Every time a scam occurs, it results in a loss. As a result, banks and other organizations at risk of fraud are always on the lookout for efficient fraud prediction techniques. Financial fraud has been combated through a variety of ways, among them are decision trees (DT) [14–16], neural networks (NN) [17–19], self-organizing maps [20], signal processing on graphs [21]. As a result, numerous researchers have looked at various techniques and compared their predictive abilities. Adewumi and Akinyelu [22] provided a review on machine learning (ML) and nature-inspired methods for CCFD that summarized the accuracy of various techniques. Support Vector Machine (SVM) is one of the utmost widely employed methods for detecting monetary scams, although it has been surpassed by DT, according to Adewumi and Akinyelu [22]. Sahin and Duman [18] obtained accuracy in the range of 83.02% and 94.76% using hybrid methods built on SVM and DT. Lu and Ju [23] obtained an accuracy of 91.28% while utilizing Imbalanced Class Weight SVM (ICW-SVM) on certain datasets, demonstrating that ICW-SVM beat the decision tree technique for these datasets. Thabtah, Hammoud, Kamalov, and Gonsalves [24] conducted tests using a variety of datasets to investigate the relationship among class unevenness and accuracy, finding that the relationship is convex. Kirkos et al. [14] compared the effectiveness of three data mining (DM) techniques in identifying fake financial statements. The classification accuracy of a Bayesian belief network beat 2 alternative methods built on DT and NN. When both performance measures and profitability were taken into consideration, Mahmoudi and Duman [25] used linear Fisher discriminant analysis in a CCFD method, which accomplished exceptionally than alternative methods evaluated. Carneiro et al. [26], on the other hand, examined 3 supervised approaches: logistic regression (LR), Random Forest (RF), and SVM. The RF method outperformed the other two models in terms of performance. Van Vlasselaer et al. [27] reported the use of a network-based method to identify deceitful credit card (CC) dealings in electronic shops, while Baesens et al. [28] investigated these transactions further using analytical tools. The outcomes of three models were also benchmarked: LR, NN, and RF. The RF technique accomplished better than the other 2 in terms of prediction accuracy. To identify social security fraud, Van Vlasselaer et al. [27] used a network-built method. Bahnsen et al. [1] looked at customer behavior characteristics and found that adding these variables would increase prediction performance substantially. They also presented a novel technique for estimating if the period of an innovative business is within the sureness interlude of prior business dealings timings based on the von Mises distribution. Furthermore, it was discovered that using the suggested strategy results in greater savings. These authors evaluated several procedures, for instance, LR, DT, RF with and without Bayes minimal risk threshold and cost-conscious procedures, cost-conscious LR, and ultimately the conscious DT, using various sets of characteristics.

Dal Pozzolo et al. [29] compared several procedures and modeling methods (RF, NN, and SVM) to determine the unsurpassed method and the most suitable model performance metric. They stated that detecting fraud is a very unbalanced issue. As a result, standard categorization methods ought not to be used. As an alternative, they recommended concentrating on instances with an extreme likelihood of being deceitful. They argue that prioritizing such dealings is extra important than concentrating on their categorization accuracy. Artificial neural networks (ANN) beat LR in an investigation by Sahin and Duman [18]. Random Forests beat other classification techniques including SVM, LR, and K-nearest neighbor (KNN) in research by Whitrow et al. [19]. Both of these are focused on detecting CCF. To develop CCFD models, Sahin et al. [15] used a cost-conscious DT method. Traditional methods for instance DT, ANN, and SVM were surpassed by their suggested methodology. In research by Bhattacharyya et al. [2], the performance of LR, SVM, and RF in identifying deceitfulness in CC businesses was examined. The RF technique was demonstrated to be the utmost success. Transaction aggregation has been used by several researchers to identify CCF [8, 19, 30, 31]. Transaction aggregation was shown to be a stronger fraud forecaster than the discrete operation or communicative methods in these experiments. This method is considered to be especially effective when using the RF Method as a classifier. Lim et al. [31] utilized the conditional weighted transaction aggregation approach to improve the method employed by Whitrow et al. [19]. In contrast to previous approaches, the suggested one was determined to be successful. They also found that aggregation-based approaches outperform business-level or other business-built aggregation approaches. Jha et al. [8] corroborated similar results, demonstrating that using a transaction aggregation approach may help detect fraudulent credit card transactions. Correspondingly, Hartmann-Wendels et al. [19] looked at the use of transaction aggregation in the detection of CCF. The authors discovered that demographic and socio-economic factors are important drivers in predicting fraudulent occurrences using data supplied by a German bank that solely operates online. Carcillo et al. [32] demonstrated how to deal with big data (BD) in monetary deceitful discovery for CC dealings, culminating in the Scalable Real-Time Fraud Finder (SCARFF), which integrates BD technologies with ML techniques. It had better be mentioned that due to data availability issues, deceitful data analysis is not as prevalent in monetary data examination. In addition, the quantity of deceitful instances in the dataset is much smaller than the number of non-deceitful instances [17, 26, 29] investigated deep learning (DL) NN for detecting fraudulent credit card usage, whereas Wang and Xu [33] combined DL with text analysis for auto insurance fraud discovery. To solve class imbalance, Wong et al. [34] presented 2 cost-conscious DL techniques, which were evaluated on business province datasets. Dal Pozzolo et al. [5] used a real-world data stream of more than 75 million dealings allowed for more than 3 years to show the effect of three characteristics on CCF data examination. Kim et al. [35] investigated an amalgam ensemble and DL method for CCFD, allowing them to evaluate the two methods and find that the deep learning approach performed the best.

As the preceding discussion demonstrates, detecting and preventing financial fraud is a difficult issue for a variety of reasons, and no one solution will work for all types of financial fraud. The motivation of these studies is that after many previous works have been surveyed Naïve Bayes ML classifiers have not been employed for the detection of credit card fraud. Therefore, this study intends to use the Naïve Baye ML classification technique for the detection of fraud in credit card transactions.

The main aim of this study is to recognize fraudulent transactions by employing CCF. To achieve this, the system is obligatory to classify fraudulent and non-fraudulent transactions. The main intention of the study is to make a fraud discovery process efficient and effective within a minimal time delivering high accuracy and true positive rate (TPR) based on classification algorithms.

The paper is subdivided into three remaining sections: Sect. 1 presents the literature review currently available in the discussed field. Section 2 details the material and methods used for the execution of the projected model. Section 3 explains the results gathered from the execution of the model and the discussion of the result. Section 4 provides the conclusion and future work that can be deployed in the impending period.

2 Materials and Method

2.1 Dataset

The dataset employed for the implementation of this system comprises 284, 807 credit card dealings made by the owners in Europe in September 2013. 492 out of the datasets were fraudulent which is referred to as the positive class and 284, 315 of the datasets were legitimate. Table 1 displays the summary of the datasets employed for the system implementation.

2.2 Machine Learning (ML)

We can determine whether an impending transaction is fraudulent or legitimate using a fraud detection module that uses ML and deep learning. Because of its numerous

Table 1. Summary of datasets

Total transactions	Legitimate transaction	Fraudulent transaction	Number of features	Link
284, 807	284, 315	492	31	https://www.kaggle.com/rahulmakwana/creditcard-fruad-detection

utilizations and low-time usage, ML is the most popular and widely utilized technology. ML is a field of computer science that deals with algorithms that allow computers to learn and improve without having to be explicitly programmed. Machine learning can be used in a variety of fields. For instance, medical, diagnosis, and regression. ML is a combination of process and statistical models that allows a computer to accomplish a task without having to hard code it. A model is developed using training data and then tested on the trained model.

2.3 Naïve Bayes

Naive Bayes is a statistical approach based on Bayesian theory that makes decisions based on the greatest likelihood. Bayesian probability estimates probabilities that are unknown using known values. Uncertain statements are subjected to logic and past knowledge in this method. The conditional independence assumption is used in this strategy to ensure that the data features are independent of one another [36, 43]. The naive Bayes classifier makes use of the conditional probabilities (1) and (2) of the fraud and non-fraud classes.

$$P(f_k/c_i) = \frac{P(f_k/c_i) * P(c_i)}{P(f_k)} \tag{1}$$

$$P(f_k/c_i) = \prod_{i=1}^{n} P(f_k/c_i), k = 1, 2, \ldots, n \tag{2}$$

Where n is the extreme sum of features, $P(f_k/c_i)$ is the possibility of creating feature value f_k assumed class c_i, $P(c_i/f_k)$ is the possibility of feature value f_k being in class c_i, $P(c_i)$ and $P(f_k)$ are the possibility of incidence of class c_i, and the possibility of feature value f_k happening correspondingly. The succeeding classification rules are employed by the classifiers to accomplish binary classification.

$$\text{The classification is } C_2 \text{ if } P(c_1/f_k) > P(c_2/f_k) \tag{3}$$

$$\text{The classification is } C_2 \text{ if } P(c_1/f_k) > P(c_2/f_k) \tag{4}$$

2.4 Proposed Method

Naïve Bayes (NB) is the ML classification algorithm employed in this study. The credit card fraud (CCF) dataset was inputted into the system after which preprocessing such as cleansing, training phase was performed on the data. The 30% of the cleansed and trained dataset was passed into the NB classifier for classification. The results gotten from the classified dataset were then evaluated using the confusion matrix values for system performance and the percentage for accuracy, precision, sensitivity, f-measure, and ROC were gotten and compared with existing systems. Figure 1 shows the proposed CCFD system flow diagram.

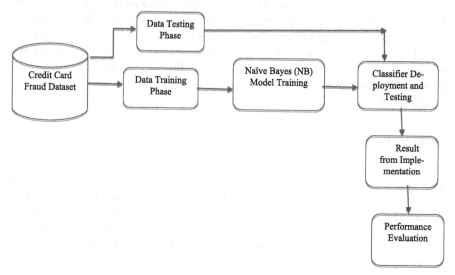

Fig. 1. CCFD flow diagram

2.5 Performance Evaluation

To appraise the performance of the system, dissimilar measures were employed. Using the accuracy metric alone will not be accurate to measure the performance of the system once the dataset employed was extremely imbalanced. The confusion matrix consists of four outputs as shown in Table 2. AUC measures how well predictions are ranked rather than their absolute values. It also measures the quality of the model's predictions. The output of the confusion matrix are as follows [41]:

1. True Positive (TP): This refers to the sum of CCF dealings that are classified as fraudulent and are fraudulent.
2. True Negative (TN): This refers to the sum of fraudulent dealing that is classified as not fraudulent and was not a fraudulent transaction.
3. False Positive (FP): These are genuine transactions that are wrongly classified as fraud

4. False Negative (FN): These are fraud transactions but are wrongly classified as genuine transactions.

Table 2. Confusion matrix

	Fraudulent	Legitimate
Fraudulent set	TP	FN
Legitimate set	FP	TN

3 Result and Discussions

Different criteria for algorithm comparison have been used to evaluate which algorithm is best suited for the challenge of identifying fraud transactions. Accuracy, recall, f-measure, precision, and false-positive rate are the most commonly used metrics for determining the results of machine learning algorithms (FPR) [37, 40]. A Confusion matrix can be used to calculate all of the above-described metrics. According to these metrics, the performance of a suggested model was evaluated [39, 42]. The CCF dataset was used to test the models. The dataset's training ratio was 70%, with the testing set accounting for 30% of the total dataset.

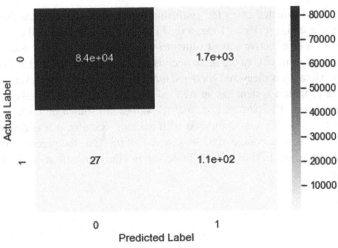

Fig. 2. NB confusion matrix

Figure 2 shows the confusion matrix computed during implementation for the NB classifier and it is demonstrated that the classifier has a TP value of 84000, TN value of 110, FP value of 27, and FN value of 1700. Figure 3 shows the ROC of the classifier and it is deduced that the classifier has an AUC value of 0.95.

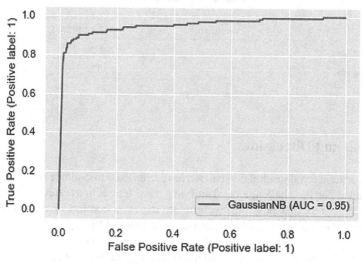

Fig. 3. NB ROC graph

3.1 Discussion

The system was evaluated using the confusion matrix value to compute the measures like accuracy, recall, precision, f-measure, FPR, and AUC used for the performance analysis. AUC is an effective way of summarizing the overall detection accuracy of the system. Generally, an AUC of 0.5 recommends no discernment, 0.7 to 0.8 is considered satisfactory, 0.8 to 0.9 is measured good and more than 0.9 is measured exceptional [38], therefore our proposed system has an AUC of 0.95 as seen in Fig. 3 makes the system an outstanding one. The performance metrics values are shown in Table 4 and when the proposed system NB was compared with existing systems, it was deduced that it outperformed with an accuracy of 97.99%, recall of 98.02%, the precision of 99.97%, f-measure 98.98%, and FPR of 0.1971. Table 5 shows the comparison of the system with existing ones.

Table 4. Performance evaluation of the proposed system

Measures	DT (%)
Accuracy	97.99
Precision	99.97
Recall	98.02
F1-measure	98.98
FPR	0.1971
AUC	0.95

Table 5. Comparative analysis with state-of-the-art

Authors	Algorithm	AUC (%)	Accuracy (%)	Precision (%)	f-measure (%)
Taha, & Malebary [41]	(OLightGBM	92.88	98.40	97.34	56.95
Rtayli, N., & Enneya [42]	RFE+HPO	81	99	95	N/A
Rai, A. K., & Dwivedi [43]	AE	N/A	97	5.3	10
Proposed System	NB	95	97.99	99.97	98.98

4   Conclusion and Future Research Direction

Companies are now focusing their efforts on marketing their products on websites and mobile applications, thanks to the ever-growing industry of online advertising. As a result, fraudulent transactions have become increasingly prevalent in recent years. By classifying CCF into legitimate and fraudulent transactions, machine learning techniques have been effective and efficient. We propose the Naïve Bayes machine learning classification model for the detection of credit card fraud. The result gotten demonstrated the proposed system outperformed existing ones that have used traditional ML-like SVM, RF, DT, ANN, and the likes with an accuracy of 97.99%, recall of 98.02%, the precision of 99.97%, f-measure 98.98%, and FPR of 0.1971.

References

1. Bahnsen, A.C., Aouada, D., Stojanovic, A., Ottersten, B.E.: Feature engineering strategies for credit card fraud detection. Expert Syst. Appl. **51**, 134–142 (2016). https://doi.org/10.1016/j.eswa.2015.12.030

2. Bhattacharyya, S., Jha, S., Tharakunnel, K., Westland, J.C.: Data mining for credit card fraud: a comparative study. Decis. Support Syst. **50**, 602–613 (2011). https://doi.org/10.1016/j.dss.2010.08.008. arXiv:1009.6119
3. Chan, P.K., Fan, W., Prodromidis, A.L., Stolfo, S.J.: Distributed data mining in credit card fraud detection. IEEE Intell. Syst. **14**, 67–74 (1999)
4. Chen, R.C., Shu-Ting, L., Shiue-Shiun, L.: Detecting credit card fraud by using support vector machines and neural networks. http://www.medwelljournals.com/abstract/?doi=ijscomp.2006.30.35
5. Dal Pozzolo, A., Boracchi, G., Caelen, O., Alippi, C., Bontempi, G.: Credit card fraud detection: realistic modeling and a novel learning strategy. IEEE Trans. Neural Netw. Learn. Syst. **29**, 3784–3797 (2018). https://doi.org/10.1109/TNNLS.2017.2736643
6. Elshaar, S., Sadaoui, S.: Semi-supervised classification of fraud data in commercial auctions. Appl. Artif. Intell. **34**, 47–63 (2020). https://doi.org/10.1080/08839514.2019.1691341
7. Eshghi, A., Kargari, M.: Introducing a new method for the fusion of fraud evidence in banking transactions with regard to uncertainty. Expert Syst. Appl. **121**, 382–392 (2019). https://www.sciencedirect.com/science/article/abs/pii/S0957417418307590. https://doi.org/10.1016/J.ESWA.2018.11.039
8. Jha, S., Guillen, M., Christopher Westland, J.: Employing transaction aggregation strategy to detect credit card fraud. Expert Syst. Appl. **39**, 12650–12657 (2012). https://doi.org/10.1016/j.eswa.2012.05.018
9. Wu, Y., Xu, Y., Li, J.: Feature construction for fraudulent credit card cashout detection. Decis. Support Syst. **127**, 113155 (2019). https://doi.org/10.1016/j.dss.2019.113155
10. PointPredictive: Estimating auto lending fraud losses for 2017. Technical Report. PointPredictive (2017a)
11. Bloomberg: Auto loan fraud soars in a parallel to the housing bubble (2017). https://www.bloomberg.com/news/articles/2017-05-10/auto-loan-fraud-issoaring-in-a-parallel-to-the-housing-bubble
12. Abdallah, A., Maarof, M.A., Zainal, A.: Fraud detection system: a survey. J. Netw. Comput. Appl. **68**, 90–113 (2016). https://doi.org/10.1016/j.jnca.2016.04.007
13. ACFE: Report to the Nations on occupational fraud and abuse. Technical Report. Association of Certified Fraud Examiners (2016)
14. Kirkos, E., Spathis, C., Manolopoulos, Y.: Data mining techniques for the detection of fraudulent financial statements. Expert Syst. Appl. **32**, 995–1003 (2007). https://doi.org/10.1016/j.eswa.2006.02.016
15. Sahin, Y., Bulkan, S., Duman, E.: A cost-sensitive decision tree approach for fraud detection. Expert Syst. Appl. **40**, 5916–5923 (2013). https://doi.org/10.1016/j.eswa.2013.05.021
16. Wheeler, R., Aitken, S.: Multiple algorithms for fraud detection. Knowl.-Based Syst. **13**, 93–99 (2000). https://doi.org/10.1016/S0950-7051(00)00050-2
17. Gómez, J.A., Arévalo, J., Paredes, R., Nin, J.: End-to-end neural network architecture for fraud scoring in card payments. Pattern Recogn. Lett. **105**, 175–181 (2017). https://doi.org/10.1016/j.patrec.2017.08.024
18. Sahin, Y., Duman, E.: Detecting credit card fraud by decision trees and support vector machines. In International multiconference of engineers and computer scientists, pp. 442–447 (2011). http://www.iaeng.org/publication/IMECS2011/, https://doi.org/10.1016/j.dss.2015.04.013, arXiv:1009.6119
19. Whitrow, C., Hand, D.J., Juszczak, P., Weston, D., Adams, N.M.: Transaction aggregation as a strategy for credit card fraud detection. Data Min. Knowl. Disc. **18**, 30–55 (2009). https://doi.org/10.1007/s10618-008-0116-z
20. Quah, J.T.S., Sriganesh, M.: Real-time credit card fraud detection using computational intelligence. Expert Syst. Appl. **35**, 1721–1732 (2008). https://doi.org/10.1016/j.eswa.2007.08.093

21. Vergara, L., Salazar, A., Belda, J., Safont, G., Moral, S., Iglesias, S.: Signal processing on graphs for improving automatic credit card fraud detection. In: Proceedings - International Carnahan Conference on Security Technology, pp. 1–6 (2017). https://doi.org/10.1109/CCST.2017.8167820

22. Adewumi, A.O., Akinyelu, A.A.: A survey of machine-learning and nature-inspired based credit card fraud detection techniques. Int. J. Syst. Assu.r Eng. Manage. **8**, 937–953 (2017). https://doi.org/10.1007/s13198-016-0551-y

23. Lu, Q., Ju, C.: Research on credit card fraud detection model based on class weighted support vector machine. J. Convergence Inf. Technol. **6**, 62–68 (2011). http://www.aicit.org/jcit/ppl/05-JCIT2-870048.pdf, https://doi.org/10.4156/jcit.vol6

24. Thabtah, F., Hammoud, S., Kamalov, F., Gonsalves, A.: Data imbalance in classification: experimental evaluation. Inf. Sci. **513**, 429–441 (2020). https://doi.org/10.1016/j.ins.2019.11.004

25. Mahmoudi, N., Duman, E.: Detecting credit card fraud by modified fisher discriminant analysis. Expert Syst. Appl. **42**, 2510–2516 (2014). http://www.scopus.com/inward/record.url?eid=2-s2.0-84912535379&partnerID=tZOtx3y1, https://doi.org/10.1016/j.eswa.2014.10.037

26. Carneiro, N., Figueira, G., Costa, M.: A data mining-based system for creditcard fraud detection in e-tail. Decis. Support Syst. **95**, 91–101 (2017). https://doi.org/10.1016/j.dss.2017.01.002

27. Van Vlasselaer, V., et al.: APATE: A novel approach for automated credit card transaction fraud detection using network-based extensions. Decis. Support Syst. **75**, 38–48 (2015). https://doi.org/10.1016/j.dss.2015.04.013

28. Baesens, B., Van Vlasselaer, V., Verbeke, W.: Fraud analytics using descriptive, predictive, and social network techniques. Wiley (2015). https://doi.org/10.1017/CBO9781107415324.004, arXiv: arXiv:1011.1669v3

29. Dal Pozzolo, A., Caelen, O., Le Borgne, Y.A., Waterschoot, S., Bontempi, G.: Learned lessons in credit card fraud detection from a practitioner perspective. Expert Syst. Appl., **41**, 4915–4928 (2014). https://doi.org/10.1016/j.eswa.2014.02.026, arXiv: z0024

30. Hartmann-Wendels, T., Mählmann, T., Versen, T.: Determinants of banks' risk exposure to new account fraud - evidence from Germany. J. Bank. Finance **33**, 347–357 (2009). https://doi.org/10.1016/j.jbankfin.2008.08.005

31. Lim, W.Y., Sachan, A., Thing, V.: Conditional weighted transaction aggregation for credit card fraud detection. IFIP Adv. Inf. Commun. Technol. **433**, 3–16 (2014). http://www.scopus.com/inward/record.url?eid=2-s2.0-84911085381&partnerID=tZOtx3y1

32. Carcillo, F., Dal Pozzolo, A., Le Borgne, Y.A., Caelen, O., Mazzer, Y., Bontempi, G.: SCARFF: a scalable framework for streaming credit card fraud detection with spark. Inf. Fusion **41**, 182–194 (2018). https://doi.org/10.1016/j.inffus.2017.09.005

33. Wang, Y., Xu, W.: Leveraging deep learning with LDA-based text analytics to detect automobile insurance fraud. Decis. Support Syst. **105**, 87–95 (2018). https://doi.org/10.1016/j.dss.2017.11.001

34. Wong, M.L., Seng, K., Wong, P.K.: Cost-sensitive ensemble of stacked denoising autoencoders for class imbalance problems in business domain. Expert Syst. Appl. **141**, 112918 (2020). https://doi.org/10.1016/j.eswa.2019.112918

35. Kim, E., et al.: Champion-challenger analysis for credit card fraud detection: Hybrid ensemble and deep learning. Expert Syst. Appl. **128**, 214–224 (2019). https://linkinghub.elsevier.com/retrieve/pii/S0957417419302167, https://doi.org/10.1016/j.eswa.2019.03.042

36. Bagga, S., Goyal, A., Gupta, N., Goyal, A.: Credit card fraud detection using pipeling and ensemble learning. Procedia Comput. Sci. **173**, 104–112 (2020)

37. Arowolo, M.O., Ogundokun, R.O., Misra, S., Kadri, A.F., Aduragba, T.O.: Machine learning approach using KPCA-SVMs for predicting COVID-19. In: Garg, L., Chakraborty, C., Mahmoudi, S., Sohmen, V.S. (eds.) Healthcare Informatics for Fighting COVID-19 and Future Epidemics. EICC, pp. 193–209. Springer, Cham (2022). https://doi.org/10.1007/978-3-030-72752-9_10

38. Mandrekar, J.N.: Receiver operating characteristic curve in diagnostic test assessment. J. Thorac. Oncol. 5(9), 1315–1316 (2010)

39. Taha, A.A., Malebary, S.J.: An intelligent approach to credit card fraud detection using an optimized light gradient boosting machine. IEEE Access 8, 25579–25587 (2020)

40. Rtayli, N., Enneya, N.: Enhanced credit card fraud detection based on SVM-recursive feature elimination and hyper-parameters optimization. J. Inf. Secur. Appl. 55, 102596 (2020)

41. Rai, A.K., Dwivedi, R.K.: Fraud detection in credit card data using unsupervised machine learning-based scheme. In: 2020 International Conference on Electronics and Sustainable Communication Systems (ICESC), pp. 421–426. IEEE (2020)

42. Ogundokun, R.O., Misra, S., Ogundokun, O.E., Oluranti, J., Maskeliunas, R.: Machine learning classification based techniques for fraud discovery in credit card datasets. In: Florez, H., Pollo-Cattaneo, M.F. (eds.) ICAI 2021. CCIS, vol. 1455, pp. 26–38. Springer, Cham (2021). https://doi.org/10.1007/978-3-030-89654-6_3

43. Onah, J.O., Abdulhamid, S.M., Misra, S., Sharma, M.M., Rana, N., Oluranti, J.: Genetic search wrapper-based naïve bayes anomaly detection model for fog computing environment. In: Abraham, A., Piuri, V., Gandhi, N., Siarry, P., Kaklauskas, A., Madureira, A. (eds.) ISDA 2020. AISC, vol. 1351, pp. 1371–1382. Springer, Cham (2021). https://doi.org/10.1007/978-3-030-71187-0_127

Investigating Cyber Security Awareness Among Preservice Teachers During the COVID-19 Pandemic

Moses Moyo(✉) ⓘ, Osman Sadeck ⓘ, Nyarai Tunjera ⓘ, and Agnes Chigona ⓘ

Cape Peninsula University of Technology, Cape Town, South Africa
{moyom,tunjeran,chigonaa}@cput.ac.za

Abstract. South African institutions of higher education suffered serious disruptions during the COVID-19 pandemic which, resulted in migrating most teaching and learning activities to various online platforms, of which many depended on the open web. This has the potential to expose lecturers and students to cyber security threats and risks. As such cyber security awareness (CSA) becomes important. This study investigated the CSA among preservice teachers pursuing a Bachelor of Education studies in Further Education and Training (FET) at a university in Cape Town, South Africa. The purpose of the study was to gain an insight into CSA among preservice teachers who had been using digital technologies to support learning during the COVID-19 pandemic. An electronic questionnaire was administered to a random sample of 300 preservice teachers. The findings show that preservice teachers were limited in their awareness of cyber security threats and risks likely to affect their use of various digital technologies for remote learning. Furthermore, preservice teachers implemented basic strategies to mitigate basic cyber security threats and attacks. These basic strategies were found not to be sufficient for advanced attacks. The study concluded that lack of proper CSA and knowledge among preservice teachers presented them with challenges in solving threat attacks associated with denial-of-service (DoS), data theft and phishing when using personal digital devices.

1 Introduction

The effects of COVID-19 on South African education cannot be overemphasised. Without immediate solutions to curb the spread of the disease, the South African institutions of higher education resorted to online remote teaching and learning using various digital technologies readily available to students [1, 2]. Online remote teaching remains an ad hoc solution to the COVID-19 lockdown restrictions, alongside other measures such as a restricted number of people per gathering and social distancing that prevent face-to-face (f2f) classes. Migrating educational activities to different digital platforms on the open web and accessing them using unmanned digital devices can expose lecturers and students to cyber security threats and risks that can have negative effects on the use of these platforms. Unmanned devices refer to unsecured personal devices not registered on the university network which has protocols for protection against cyber-attacks. The

© Springer Nature Switzerland AG 2022
M. Themistocleous and M. Papadaki (Eds.): EMCIS 2021, LNBIP 437, pp. 527–550, 2022.
https://doi.org/10.1007/978-3-030-95947-0_38

student population in South African universities is diverse, that is, from different social-economic backgrounds and digital divide, with varying levels of CSA. Mistakes due to cyber security ignorance by students can lead to serious security breaches to university online services as well as to the information stored on students' devices. Unlike some students pursuing different degree programmes, preservice teachers continue using digital technologies with learners in schools who need even more protection from cyber security threats and risks. In this context, CSA among preservice teachers becomes important for safe use of digital technologies in teaching and learning as well as personal use at home, outside the university firewall protection.

Universities usually protect their information systems by deploying advanced security technologies and training information technology (IT) security professionals but pay little attention to the CSA of the actual users of the information systems and online platforms [3, 4]. Universities tend to have cyber security policies and strategies that may be difficult for students who have little information security knowledge [5, 6]. A study conducted by [5] reports that lack of information security knowledge among most ICTs end-users was due to inadequate CSA. Similarly, a study conducted with students in higher education by [7] reveals that the cyber security behaviour of the participants was not satisfactory because most of the threats faced could have been eliminated if they were aware of such threats. According to [8], most university lecturers lack Information and Communication Technology (ICT) knowledge to assist students in cyber safety. Online teaching and learning require safe cyberspace to safeguard the quality of the education offered on uncoordinated digital platforms. The vulnerabilities and security of the preservice teacher's digital devices are not known to the university IT security departments. This further renders preservice teachers vulnerable to cyber-attacks when accessing online learning material through their unsecure devices. Given the increased cyber security breaches reported locally and globally, it is essential to have insights into how pre-service teachers understand and protect themselves from cyber security threats and risks when using digital technologies for learning and personal purposes [9]. University management should be aware of the cyber security threats and risks to the university and and those likely to be experienced by students in order to put in place appropriate intervention strategies to protect these users. According to [10], the lack of CSA among digital technology users represents a serious problem to many organisations and this should be properly assessed as part of the organisation's overall security management and assessment strategy. This study intends to contribute to CSA awareness and knowledge among preservice teachers through these research questions:

1. *What is preservice teachers' level of CSA?*
2. *What cyber security threats and risks are preservice teachers familiar with?*
3. *How do preservice teachers deal with cyber security threats and risks when using digital technologies?*
4. *How do cyber security threats and risks affect the use of digital technologies among preservice teachers?*

This article is organised into the following major sections: Related literature; Methods; Results and findings; Discussions and Conclusions.

2 Related Literature

Cyber security awareness is a well-documented subject but its practicality remains elusive in educational circles where there is a rapid increase in the use of digital technologies for teaching and learning [9, 11]. Much of the literature on the use of digital technologies in teaching and learning has underplayed the importance of CSA for the safe use of technology in virtual learning environments (VLEs). In this section, basic concepts are explained and detailed analysis and evaluation of existing literature on CSA is made.

2.1 Cyber Security

The ISO [12] defines cyber security as the preservation of the confidentiality, integrity and availability of information in cyberspace. Von Solms and Van Niekerk [13], view cyber security as the protection of cyberspace itself, of the tangible or intangible technologies that support the cyberspace, of electronic information, and the users in their personal, societal and national capacities. The European Union Agency for Network and Information Security [14] refers to cyber security as the collection of tools, policies, security concepts, security safeguards, guidelines, risk management approaches, actions, training, best practices, assurance and technologies that can be used to protect the cyber environment and organisation and user's assets. In addition to the protection of the infrastructure and information assets, the definitions show that cyber security extends to the protection of the people who use the information assets as well. Another important aspect of CSA is privacy, the degree to which students believe that online digital technologies are safe and protects their sensitive information [15]. As such the use of various digital devices to access the internet can lead to security and privacy breaches of personal data stored on devices that are viewed by unauthorised persons, tempered with or even deleted [16]. Therefore, the major purpose of cyber security has to do with the protection of an organisation or person connected to the internet against cyber threats and risks. Universities, which provide services via the web have to put in effort and commitment to mitigate cyber security given the risk of students being exposed to cyber threats. During the COVID-19 pandemic, device owners were expected to put security measures in place to ensure that their personal information is secure. This implies that preservice teachers need to be actively involved in the protection and appropriate use of their digital devices. To attain this feat, cyber security knowledge is essential among preservice teachers.

2.2 What is Cyber Security Awareness?

Awareness comprises knowledge, self-perception of skills, actual skills and behaviour, and attitudes, and their interrelationship [9]. Kim [17] refers to CSA as to how much end-users know about the cyber security threats their networks face and the risks they introduce. In this regard, CSA is a measure of the degree of understanding of users about the importance of information security and their responsibilities and actions to exercise sufficient levels of information security control to protect the data and networks of their organisation [18]. Cyber security awareness among university students is important in that it can cater for both knowledge and skills needed to protect the university and personal information assets. Literature shows that essential knowledge and skills of using different digital technologies in accessing online information and applications lag among users in different education institutions despite different CSA training provided [19]. This is compounded by limited knowledge of existing tools that can be used to protect against cyber threats among end-users in universities [20, 22]. Large organisations such as universities are reliant on online systems which are easily targeted by cyber threats and criminals who utilise any inherent vulnerabilities [23]. Users ignorant of cyber security risks and with potential irresponsible behaviour in using digital technologies for educational and personal purposes increases the surface attack for cybercriminals [24].

Although CSA has long been regarded as an essential defence aspect in the protection of information systems, devices and their users [9], large organisations may lack the capacity to provide adequate CSA training to their workforce and other end-users [25]. Universities are not an exception to this, because they tend to have large populations of online platform users with students being the most vulnerable group. This becomes even more difficult with a large population of students accessing online learning material during the COVID-19 pandemic using their own devices which may not be secure, thereby leading to data security and privacy breaches in the devices they use [16]. Abawajy [20] posits that a considerable proportion of cyber security breaches are due to inside users of the system due to ignorance or careless behaviours such as sharing passwords and opening unknown e-mails and attachments. For universities, this includes students being among users who are most vulnerable to cyber-attacks due to lack of CSA evident in their careless and reckless use of digital technologies which they spend most of their time on [26]. When students utilise different online services, their activities can potentially act as a weakness to threats such as hackers and malware and can endanger information assets they access. To curb the risks to information assets and protect students from cyber-attacks, CSA becomes important.

2.3   The Need for Cyber Awareness Among Preservice Teachers

Online remote learning during the COVID-19 pandemic has a host of conundrums that require immediate and long-lasting solutions [27]. While most of the online remote learning meant to deal with education delivery issues at South African institutions of higher education seem to be ad hoc, the cyber security threats and risks associated with the use of web-based technologies can have devastating effects. Such consequential effects can reverse the novel idea of migrating learning activities to online platforms. Literature has highlighted that developing countries experience a wide digital divide and university students in these countries may be compelled to use available digital device capable of connecting to the Internet [2]. The shortage of secured digital technologies provided by universities and limited knowledge to safely use digital technologies exacerbate the possibility of cyber security attacks and this highlights the urgent need for CSA among students [28, 29]. A 2017 Data Breach Investigations Report by [30] shows that approximately 90% of cyber-attacks were due to human error and this implies that mistakes made on digital technologies by users can initiate and intensify the risk of cyber-crime and the damage it poses to various organisations. Technology-based information security solutions alone can hardly provide the complete security needed to defend an organisation or personal electronic information assets from cyber threats [9, 21]. Relying on system users and the decisions they make can assist organisations to avoid a false sense of strong protection by technology-based security systems against cyber-attacks. For universities, it makes sense that lecturers and students who use online digital technologies be cyber security aware so that they understand cyber threats, the potential impact cyber-attacks can have on business activities; the steps needed to reduce risks as well as preventing cyber-crime infiltrating their online workspace [9, 30].

The rise in cyber security breaches and cyber-crimes and the means being used to commit the crimes necessitates that organisations involve collaboration between all end-users and the IT security departments to curb the risks involved [24, 31]. This implies that cyber security should not be the sole responsibility of IT security departments. The disadvantage of having online systems users who are not CSA is that they fail to report cyber threats, but continue with activities that make their cyberspace vulnerable [31, 32]. Some authors emphasise the importance of communication and collaboration of all cyber security functions and practices with users across the organisation [32]. A strong CSA campaign among users in various departments is essential and this should be speared by IT security specialists and heads of departments of different units that depend on online systems.

A poor university culture on student mobility has the potential of creating security vulnerabilities that can be exploited by malicious internal and external users [21, 33]. According to [34], end-users of digital technologies are an essential part of any organisation because they can contribute to cyber security or cyber insecurity in several ways, and this makes it imperative for the development of cyber security-aware users. By allowing students to use unmanned mobile devices on university networks and the open web, might make traditional security measures ineffective [9, 35]. Providing CSA to a large population of employees and end-users is a very big challenge for universities.

The over-reliance on mobile devices has become an issue prevalent among young people who aspire to be connected yet seem not to be worried about using the security settings on these devices to counter cyber security threats and risks [36, 37]. Studies show that most students are not aware of the fact that poorly secured mobile devices can easily be breached resulting in data and information theft [36, 38, 39]. University students using unmanned mobile devices for online remote learning need to be vigilant of the potential cyber-attacks targeting educational institutions [40]. These unmanned devices accessing the networks on and off-campus can be used by hackers committing cybercrimes such as stealing important personal and financial data from university databases [9, 40]. Literature shows that students who are CSA are likely to be cautious in their use digital technologies [6, 41]. However, to achieve, this feat, universities need to put in place proper CSA for all end-users such as students. Aldawood and Skinner [5] affirm that CSA is an effective method of dealing with cyber threats because people are potential victims of cybercriminals. This suggest that CSA programmes are needed to develop a positive information security culture among end-users such as students [42].

2.4   Common Cyber Security Threats that May Target University Students

Several cyber security threats and attacks prevalent in public organisations such as universities and colleges resulting from lack of, or, poor CSA have been documented [24].

Most of the cyber-attacks apply social engineering techniques in which the criminals persistently use tricks in luring the unsuspecting victims to divulge important personal information needed to commit cybercrimes. Dlamini and Modise [43] posit that a host of social engineering techniques are prevalent cyber security attacks and threats among South African communities. These include phishing, identity theft, and money fraudulent activities, adware, botnet, hacking, hoax email, keylogging, malware, spam spyware and Trojan Virus. Besides social engineering techniques, cyber-attacks can occur in the form of cyberbullying, cyberstalking, data theft and ransomware [10, 17, 44]. According to [11] phishing attacks are the most widespread form of attack vectors that cybercriminals successfully use on university networks, financial systems and databases. Cybercriminals target users to steal information they can sell, use to commit frauds or monetise in an alternative manner [10, 11, 45]. While these cyber-attacks can be widespread to digital technologies, this study is confined to university students particularly preservice teachers, who on completion of their studies continue using digital technologies with learners and other members of the society.

A study by [46] reports cyberbullying as a prevalent cyber-attack among preservice teachers in American and Australian institutions of higher education. Cyberbullying is reported to have a direct and indirect social and emotional impact on individuals and these may affect how preservice teachers operate within and outside classrooms [47]. Online sexual harassment is another form of cyber-attack associated with the misuse of digital technologies intended for educational use [48].

2.5 Current Practices of Cyber Security Awareness and Challenges

Currently, there is limited literature on CSA targeting students in South African universities particularly preservice teachers who assume more responsibilities with learners who use digital technologies for educational purposes. There is overwhelming evidence that the behaviour of digital technology users is essential in reducing or increasing information security breaches [49, 50]. Some studies allude to the lack of CSA among digital technology users as the main contributing factor that can increases cyber security risks [9, 35, 51]. This has seen a rise in the studies and effort in remedying user behaviour to reduce cyber breaches by increasing CSA among different groups of users in an organisation [50, 52]. Much of the efforts implemented target university employees including lecturers and support staff. According to [53] most of the CSA initiatives in South Africa are delivered through independent and uncoordinated means in which institutions are responsible for security awareness training depending on their specific objectives and focus areas.

CSA campaigns are the most commonly used method in many organisations [54]. These usually take the form of workshop presentations, newsflash through organisational emails and training. These methods are meant to change the behaviour of online application users for the better when they become aware of cyber security risks posed by hackers and malware [32, 55]. Some of the existing CSA methods have been criticised for boredom on intended audiences because they are either police statements or workshops that require participants to watch videos and then were asked to answer a few multiple-choice questions to pass the security training [56]. This has raised concerns in that the intended audience does not pay enough attention to the content of the video because they want to complete the training or workshops in the shortest possible time [56].

Bada, Sasse and Nurse [54] posit that changing security behaviour requires more than disseminating knowledge about risks and precaution measures and should involve a general understanding of how preventive technologies are used and whether individuals are capable of using them. Ismail [32] suggests that organisations must engage with staff and other users of online systems and induct them into cyber security culture instead of using superficial presentations. This can empower and encourage users on the need to report any suspicious online activities on their or enterprise device, emails and applications. According to [10] and [57], online system users need to be familiar with the measures put in place by their organisations to protect them when under cyber-attacks or even if they make mistakes.

3   Methods

The study employed a descriptive survey strategy in which an online Google form questionnaire was used to collect data from a simple random sample of preservice teachers. The context was their use of digital technologies for online remote learning. The online survey questionnaire was designed following techniques used in previous studies [9, 58]. The items used in the questionnaire design were sourced from different studies on CSA such as [3, 9] and [35]. This was intended to reduce potential common method variance, a major source of biases and errors in surveys [59, 60]. The design of the questionnaire, therefore involved, determining the types of data needed to answer research questions, categorising the items under important research questions, deciding the form of response and layout of the questionnaire [58, 61].

The major form of response for the questionnaire was a 5-point Likert scale in which respondents indicated their honest opinion about cyber security knowledge, attitude, strategies used and effects on remote online learning. Content validation of the questionnaire was done by three cyber security specialists from local universities. All items sourcing technical knowledge and skills were deleted from the questionnaire. The online questionnaire was then piloted with 21 first-year preservice teachers in the Infant Teacher Programme. The reliability test for the questionnaire based on the Cronbach's Alpha was 0.919, indicating a very high closeness of items used in the instrument. The questionnaire was edited for grammar and validated to avoid skipping questions. Permission to conduct the study was obtained from the Faculty Ethics Committee Reference Number: EFEC1–6/2020. Respondents, complete the informed consent form to acknolwdge their particpation in the study as being voluntary. Respondents made aware that they were free to withdraw from the study whenever they wanted. Informed consent to publish the study was also sort from respondents prior to data collection.

3.1   Research Participants

The population comprised 1204 students in the FET department. The sample size **n**, was computed using the formula $n = \frac{N}{1+N(e)^2}$ as 300 and was increased by 10% to 330 respondents (*see Table* 1). A simple random sample was obtained using student registration numbers drawn randomly from the four cohorts of registered students, namely first to fourth year. The link to the online questionnaire questionnaire was sent to each of the respondent.

Table 1. Population and sample size

Year level	Number of students	Percentage	No of respondents
1st	347	28.8	95
2nd	289	24.0	79
3rd	303	25.2	83
4th	265	22.0	73
Total	**1204**	**100**	**330**

3.2 Data Collection and Analysis Procedures

The online questionnaire was further discussed among the researchers for final refinement before it was distributed to the respondents through WhatsApp and e-mail groups. Data were available from the responses populated in the Google Sheet linked to the form. The data was downloaded as an Excel spreadsheet, and further cleansed and coded. Data was imported into Statistical Package for Social Sciences (SPSS) Version 27 and then analysed quantitatively, to produce frequency charts, tables and descriptive statistics.

3.3 Ethical Consideration

An ethical clearance certificate was obtained from the Faculty Research Committee. Each respondent was asked to complete an informed consent form to indicate voluntary participation in the study.

4 Results

Quantitative data analysis was done using SPSS Version 27. Results are presented as simple distribution tables and charts as well as descriptive statistics. Interpretations are provided for each set of results presented.

4.1 Demographic Information

The response rate was 91% (300) of the 330 respondents sampled. Of the three hundred preservice teachers who completed the questionnaire, 65.7% were female and 34.3% male. The distribution of the respondents according to level of study is shown in Fig. 1.

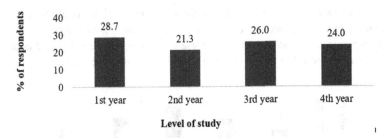

Fig. 1. Distribution of respondents by the level of studies

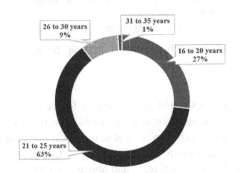

Fig. 2. Distribution of respondents by age range

The respondents were fairly distributed among their level of study providing a sample with good representativeness of the student population in the department. The distribution of the sample by age range is depicted in Fig. 2.

The results in Fig. 2 show that most of the respondents, 90% were aged between 16 and 25 years with 21 o 25 years accounting for the majority.

The results in Fig. 3 show that smartphones (53.7%) and laptops (41.7%) were preferred devices for accessing online learning material to desktop computers and tablets.

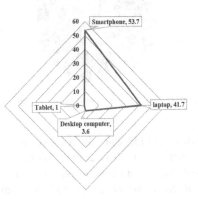

Fig. 3. Devices used by preservice teachers to access online learning material

The use of mobile devices by the majority of the respondents could have a security implication and this required more security awareness among the users.

The experience of respondents in the use of devices for personal and educational purposes was important in this study. The results are shown in Fig. 4.

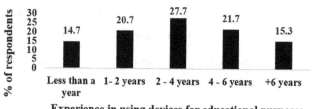

Experience in using devices for educational purposes

Fig. 4. Distribution of respondents by experience in using electronic devices for educational purposes

Respondents' experiences in the use of devices to access online learning material range from less than a year to more than six years. The results show that more than 60% of the respondents had experience of at least 2 years of using digital devices for educational purposes. Respondents with experience up to 4 years started using devices at the university while those with 4 years and above could have started before coming to university.

It was important for this study to solicit information on the Internet access from the sample as this has cyber security risks bearing among the student population during remote learning, see Fig. 5.

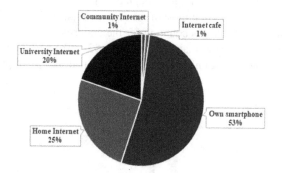

Fig. 5. Internet access for accessing remote learning material

The results indicate that most (53%) of the respondents accessed the Internet from their smartphones, 25% from router Wi-Fi at home and only 20% used the university internet facility. It can be deduced from these results that most of the preservice teachers could have been using unsecured internet access and could have been exposed to cyber threats.

The study went on to solicit information on the most frequently used platforms by rating each platform on a 5-Likert scale (Every day = 5, twice a week = 4, once a week 3, once a month = 2 and never used 1).

Table 2. Means scores for online platforms used by preservice teachers

Platforms used	N	Minimum	Maximum	Mean	Std. Dev
WhatsApp	300	3	5	4.98	0.18
University emails	300	1	5	4.23	0.97
Facebook	300	1	5	4.22	1.30
University web site	300	1	5	4.03	1.13
YouTube	300	1	5	3.93	1.06
Ordinary emails	300	1	5	3.86	1.15
Open Websites	300	1	5	3.81	1.30
Instagram	300	1	5	3.47	1.49
FB Messenger	300	1	5	3.37	1.51
Blogs	300	1	5	2.64	1.22
Twitter	300	1	5	2.50	1.39
LinkedIn	300	1	5	2.18	1.17

The results in Table 2 show the mean scores and standard deviations on the frequency of use of different platforms for educational and personal purposes. The mean ± SD score of 4.98 ± 0.18 shows that most of the respondents used WhatsApp daily. This was followed by university emails, Facebook and University websites which were used at least twice a week (mean scores between 4.03 ± 1.13 and 4.23 ± 0.97)). The rest of the platforms were used at most once a week except LinkedIn which was used once a month. These results confirm that preservice teachers were likely to be exposed to cyber threats associated with most of the platforms they used particularly when accessed in unprotected networks outside the university firewalls. Using own devices to access learning material during remote learning required a certain level of CSA for preservice teachers to work safely on the web.

Respondents were asked to rate their cyber security knowledge and CSA using a 5-point Likert scale with 5 being excellent and 1 being very poor. The results for the ratings are shown in Figs. 6.

The results show that most of the respondents (74% to 78%) perceived their CSA and knowledge as fairly good and good. This was confirmed by close mean scores of 3.54 and 3.53 with close standard deviants of 0.88 and 0.92 respectively. The Spearman correlation coefficient of 0.836 at a p-value of 0.00 showed a significant association of perceived security awareness and perceived cyber security knowledge among the respondents. There was a weak correlation between educational level and perceived cyber security knowledge $r = 0.126$, $p = 0.030$; and also between educational level and CSA $r = 0.130$, 0.024. These results show that preservice teachers regarded themselves

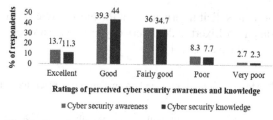

Fig. 6. Perceived cyber security knowledge and awareness

as being vigilant to cyber security threats based on the basic cyber security knowledge they have.

4.2 Actual Cyber Security Awareness Among Preservice Teachers

To determine the actual CSA, we asked respondents to indicate the extent to which they agreed or disagreed on what CSA meant for a preservice teacher who uses digital technologies to access online learning material. Thirteen statements to measure actual CSA were provided for rating on a 5-point Likert scale, strongly agree (5) to strongly disagree (1). The results for the mean rating presented in Table 3 are ranked in descending order.

The results show that actual cyber security awarness in the sample was generally lower than the perceived CSA. The mean scores for fewer variables were above 3.0 indicate that respondents lack basic security awareness in terms of what should be trusted concerning the use of devices and the responsibilities of security issues when using online digital technologies. For example, most of the respondents trusted friends with their unprotected devices because they believed that they will not be attacked, thought that the security and and privacy of their data was the responsibility of IT security specialists. Because of that, respondents tended to use weak passwords they can easily remember mean SD (2.80 + 1.7). However, some of the respondents were aware of that their devices could be attacked when accessing online educational material. Overall, the results show that actual CSA was lower than that of the perceived CSA as indicated by close to 51% of the respondents who professed ignorance in most of the basic security items asked. The respondents' actual CSA was unambiguously in contrast to their perceived CSA. A mean score of 3.02 ± 0.78 indicated an agreement among respondents that the actual CSA was lower than the perceived one, which was fairly good to good (mean = 3.54 ± 0.88).

4.3 Knowledge of Cyber Security Threats and Risks Among Preservice Teachers Using Online Digital Technologies

Cyber security knowledge about threats and risks plays an important role for preservice teachers for the safe use of various digital devices to access online educational materials during remote learning. To measure actual cyber security knowledge, respondents were asked to indicate their knowledge about common threats, attacks and risks based on a

Table 3. Ratings on actual cyber security awareness among respondents

Descriptive Statistics on actua + B2:G17l cyber security awareness (n = 300)

Statement	N	Minimum	Maximum	Mean	Std. Dev
My friends will not send me anything malicious or scams through email	300	1	5	3.88	1.08
I will not be attacked by cyber threats because my device is well protected	300	1	5	3.25	1.14
I trust all my friends I lend my devices that they will use them safely	300	1	5	2.84	1.24
Cyber security is the sole responsibility of IT specialist	300	1	5	2.83	1.25
It is too difficult to remember difficult passwords; therefore, I use my name or something easy to remember	300	1	5	2.80	1.47
It is a good practice to download movies and TV series because the companies that make them are rich and I really cannot afford it (I am a student)	300	1	5	2.73	1.28
Updating my security software on my device is time consuming annoying and uses up my data bundle	300	1	5	2.72	1.27
Cyber criminals will not attack my device because it is used for educational purposes only	300	1	5	2.63	1.22
Cyber security issues are for IT specialists and NOT for simple digital technologies users such as preservice teachers	300	1	5	2.48	1.20
The security settings and tools slow me down and are pesky I turn them off or disable them	300	1	5	2.47	1.21
It is a waste of time to change passwords because you can still get hacked	300	1	5	2.47	1.28
If I pirate software I will not get updates and security patches but I don't need (updates and patches)	300	1	5	2.40	1.15
Posting pictures and bad messages online about my college students makes it anonymous and is much better than saying it to their face	300	1	5	1.96	1.15

5-point Likert scale. The results for ratings, means and standard deviations are shown in Table 4.

The respondents rated their knowledge differently in most of the items provided. The knowledge for spam emails, smishing, identity theft and cyberbullying varied between moderate and good as indicated by 51% to 61.4% of the respondents. This was also confirmed by mean scores between 3.3 and 3.6. However, 21% to 32%, indicated that poor knowledge or complete lack of knowledge of cyber security posed by spam emails, smishing, identity theft and cyberbullying among preservice teachers. The knowledge about certain cyber security threats and attacks such as identity theft, vishing, phishing, hacking, unauthorised installation of software and malware attacks become moderate as the percentage of respondents with poor knowledge increase. The mean decreased appreciably from 3.1 to 2.9. A considerable percentage (23 to 37%) of respondents was had poor or no knowledge of most of the common cyber security threats and risks they were likely to fall victim to.

Table 4. Knowledge of cyber security threats and risks among preservice teacher

Knowledge cyber threats, risks or attack	% Rating on knowledge of cyber threats, attacks or risks (n = 300)					Mean	Std. Devi
	Very good knowledge	Good knowledge	Moderate knowledge	Poor knowledge	No knowledge at all		
Spams e-mails - messages in your inbox you did not ask for from senders you do not know	36.7	24.7	15.1	10.2	13.3	3.6	1.41
Smishing – cyber attack using misleading text messages (SMS) or email to deceive you eg SMS purporting that you won a competition and ask you to claim your prize	35.0	24.3	13.0	18.7	9.0	3.5	1.50
Identify theft – requests made to confirm banking details or SIM number used to steal money from your bank account	28.3	24.7	15.3	21.4	10.3	3.3	1.50
Cyberbullying - chain letters, negative, harmful, false, or mean content about someone else shared on your email or shared on WhatsApp or SMS	30.0	21.0	17.0	11.3	20.7	3.3	1.51

(*continued*)

Table 4. (*continued*)

Knowledge cyber threats, risks or attack	% Rating on knowledge of cyber threats, attacks or risks (n = 300)					Mean	Std. Devi
	Very good knowledge	Good knowledge	Moderate knowledge	Poor knowledge	No knowledge at all		
Password theft - being tricked into revealing your passwords on false pretence	23.3	23.0	18.7	23.3	11.7	3.1	1.49
Vishing - fraud where a fraudster convinced you to provide critical information such as banking details over the phone	21.7	26.7	17.0	25.3	9.3	3.1	1.50
Unauthorised installation of software on your device	18.0	22.3	24.0	23.7	12.0	3.0	1.42
Phishing - being tricked to volunteer information by the victim into opening an email, instant message, or text message to a fraudster who pretends to be a trusted entity	18.3	25.7	18.7	10.3	27.0	3.0	1.48
Hacking – Someone stealing information from your devices or preventing you from accessing the information on devices or emails	17.3	26.0	19.3	10.4	27.0	3.0	1.46
Deletion of content from your device without your knowledge	18.7	21.7	20.7	24.2	14.7	3.0	1.45
Malware attack - stealing of data and damaging or destroying applications on a device by cybercriminals using intrusive malicious software	18.3	19.7	21.4	28.3	12.3	2.9	1.48

4.4 Strategies Used to Deal with Cyber Security Threats and Risks When Using Digital Technologies

Strategies used by preservice teachers to deal with cyber security threats and risks were investigated by asking respondents to indicate their tendency of performing certain security activities when working online with their digital devices. Table 5 shows the results.

Table 5. Ratings on possible strategies used to counter cyber security threats and risks

Possible strategy used to deal with cyber threats and risks	Ratings on the frequency of use of each strategy					Mean	Std. Dev
	Always	Often	Sometimes	Rarely	Never		
I always lock my devices with a strong password to protect them when not in use	69.0	19.0	9.0	2.7	0.3	4.54	0.79
I ensure that sensitive data is protected on my mobile devices	59.3	26.3	11.3	2.3	0.8	4.41	0.83
I update software on my devices	57.0	25.0	13.0	2.7	2.3	4.32	0.96
I physically secure my mobile devices	54.7	23.3	15.7	3.3	3.0	4.23	1.03
I avoid malicious web sites	52.3	27.3	13.7	4.4	2.3	4.23	1.00
I only access trusted, reputable sites when browsing or downloading from the Internet	50.0	29.3	15.0	5.0	0.7	4.23	0.93
I disconnect my devices from the network/ internet when suspicious activities occur	54.0	22.3	16.0	4.7	3.0	4.20	1.06

(continued)

Table 5. (*continued*)

Possible strategy used to deal with cyber threats and risks	Ratings on the frequency of use of each strategy					Mean	Std. Dev
	Always	Often	Sometimes	Rarely	Never		
I delete all suspicious emails without opening	50.0	21.7	19.3	5.7	3.3	4.09	1.10
I use antivirus software on my devices	48.0	28.0	13.3	4.7	6.0	4.07	1.16
I back up all my data on my devices regularly	40.0	23.3	19.3	10.3	7.1	4.05	1.11
I log-off from all online applications	45.0	25.3	22.1	4.3	3.3	4.04	1.07
I abide by all license/copyright laws when downloading software	39.7	28.0	23.0	6.7	2.6	3.95	1.07
I update any protection software on my device every 3 or 6 months	45.7	29.0	13.3	8.7	3.3	3.79	1.26
I read software security policy agreements before downloading them on my device	36.3	23.7	24.7	9.6	5.7	3.75	1.20
I use filters on my devices to block websites that may present security threats	27.0	30.0	21.0	10.7	11.3	3.51	1.30
I use pop-up blockers on my devices	28.3	23.7	21.7	11.7	14.6	3.39	1.39

The results show that all possible strategies with a mean greater than 4 were always or often used to curb potential cyber security threats, risks and attacks as indicated by 70% of the respondents. Notably, most respondents 54% to 69% confirmed that they always used the stated strategies to prevent unauthorised access to their devices and data by using passwords. Furthermore, results show that respondents always updated software on their devices, and also avoided malicious websites. These results confirm that most of the preservice teachers took precautionary measures to protect their devices from potential cyber security threats. However, strategies involving logging off from devices or platforms, abiding with licence and copyright requirements, use of pop-up blockers were not as popular as the other strategies considering that these were used by less than 50% of the respondents. Overall, the mean score for the strategies was 4.08 and a standard deviation of 0.803, indicating that respondents often used some strategies to protect themselves and devices against cyber security threats, attacks and risks. A Chi-square test reveals a significant dependency of strategies used on the knowledge about cyber security threats ($X^2 = 32.657$; df = 12; N = 300; p = 00). Individual students with good cyber security knowledge were more likely to use recommended strategies than those who have limited knowledge. The Chi-test also revealed a significant association of strategies used to deal with cyber security threats and CSA of preservice teachers ($X^2 = 23.863$; df = 12; N = 300; p = 0.021).

4.5 Impact of Cyber Security Awareness on the Use of Digital Technologies for Remote Learning

Cyber security threats and risks can bring about educational challenges for students accessing learning material over different learning platforms using their devices at home. Respondents were asked to indicate how cyber security threats and risks had impacted their use of digital technologies for remote learning based on a 5-point Likert scale from Severe impact = 5 to no impact = 1. The results in Table 6 show the frequency distribution and mean scores of the ratings of the selected statements.

The results depicted in Table 6 show that cyber security and risks were negatively impacting preservice teachers in using digital technologies for remote learning. This is evidenced by mean scores above 3.0 and more than 62% of the respondents who indicate having experienced moderate to severe impact of the cyber security threats when attempting to use digital technologies for remote online learning during the COVID-19 pandemic era. The most impacts were due to fear of being exposed to cyber security threats when accessing online platforms and loss of important educational information from devices being used. This resulted in pre-service teachers being reluctant to use their own devices for remote learning outside the university firewalls. Furthermore, most of the preservice teachers, 62%, seem to be unable to stop unauthorised installation of harmful third-party software which courses denial-of-service, particularly during synchronous virtual classes. These results highlight the dilemmas faced by students with limited CSA in using digital technologies for remote learning provisioned over the web.

Table 6. Possible impact of cyber security threats and risks on the use of digital technologies

Statement	Ratings on the impact of cyber threats and risks on remote learning (n = 300)					Mean	Std. Dev
	Severe	Major	Moderate	Minor	None		
Fear of being exposed to cyber threats when accessing online educational platforms	32.0	28.3	16.0	13.7	10.0	3.91	1.12
Loss of important educational information from my device due to unknown reasons	23.3	20.3	35.7	12.0	8.7	3.78	1.14
Reluctance to use my devices to access online educational material due to fear of cyber-attacks I hear about	23.3	36.0	26.1	10.3	4.3	3.71	1.21
An application that was installed unknowingly slow my device in opening online learning material	18.0	23.2	29.5	18.0	11.3	3.64	1.25
Many applications opening on my device prevented me from attending virtual classes	13.3	23.7	31.0	18.3	13.7	3.53	1.28
A malware I cannot remove from my device prevents me from accessing the web for research purposes	10.3	20.3	32.7	22.7	14.0	3.34	1.33

5 Discussion of Findings

The findings are briefly discussed to answer the four research questions posed in the introduction of the article.

5.1 What is the Level of Cyber Security Awareness Among Preservice Teachers?

The level of actual CSA was fairly good as indicated by less than 50% of the respondents but generally lower than expected CSA. This was consistent with previous studies [3, 9, 35] that report low CSA among students in institutions of higher learning.

5.2 What are Cyber Security Threats and Risks that Preservice Teachers are Familiar With?

This study found that preservice teachers were considerably aware of a common number of cyber security threats and risks that could affect the use of digital technologies for remote learning purposes during the COVID-19 pandemic era. A study by [10] emphasises the importance of university students being aware of different cyber security threats that cant target them when using digital technologies. Preservice teachers understood cyber security threats in the same context as the daily risks and attacks likely faced particularly cyberbullying, hacking, spamming, phishing and vishing and data theft. The effects of such risks are emphasised primarily outside educational contexts [20, 35] and taken for granted that even university students are familiar with these risks. This study found that preservice teachers were not aware that their devices could be used to target university networks by attackers.

5.3 How do Preservice Teachers Deal with Cyber Security Threats and Risks When using Digital Technologies?

Although there is a plethora of literature on how individuals can protect themselves against cyberattacks, there is scarce literature referring to preservice teachers [9, 62]. Surveyed preservice teachers were convinced that passwords protection was the best way to protect their devices from cyberattacks a recommended practice in several literature sources [10, 20]. Although most preservice teachers (60%) used plausible strategies to deal with potential cyber threats, attacks and risks, a considerable percentage (up to 40%) remained in dire danger of being attacked as they sometimes, rarely or did not take any step to protect their devices. According to [63], the COVID-19 pandemic which has shifted most f2f activities to remote online work has changed the opportunities of cybercriminals focusing on the digital tools and platforms used, and this needed users to use other strategies to counter the malicious activities. The author further suggests that users be critical of requests for information by verifying the sources and updating security controls on devices and software. Some of the strategies confirmed by preservice teachers in this study were consistent with those practised elsewhere.

5.4 How do Cyber Security Threats and Risks Affect The Use of Digital Technologies among Preservice Teachers?

The impact of cyber security attacks and risks experienced by preservice teachers in the use of digital technologies to access educational material during remote learning was mostly moderate to severe. A study by [64] reports that COVID-19 has impacted online distance learning due to the spread of cyber-attacks including DoS, spoofing and phishing which resulted in the frustration of students. DoS can prevent students access to information or performing important educational tasks made available on various learning platforms. With little assistance from the IT security departments to solve various cyber security challenges, students' educational progress with remote learning became a nightmare. Similar effects of cyber threats are reported in other literature sources, for example, [65] posits that institutions of higher education cannot defend all users of their systems off-campus. This has a bearing particularly on a group of users who barely have cyber security knowledge. During the COVID pandemic, preservice teachers spend most of the time learning on their own and any cyber security challenges they face severely retard their educational progress.

6 Conclusions, Limitations and Recommendations

From the findings in this study, we conclude that preservice teachers have a fairly good basic CSA which can be useful in mitigating basic cyber security attacks. The use of passwords on smartphones when not in use is highly practice highly, but the changing of such passwords is rarely done. However, this basic security awareness is not enough for threats and attacks experienced during remote learning. DoS and poor data confidentiality were prevalent cyber security issues that preservice teachers were unable to tackle. Without support from the IT security department, preservice teachers remain marginalised and vulnerable to advanced cyber security attacks and risks. This study recommends that, to raise cyber awareness, basic cyber security be taught formally and as a compulsory component of computers in education.

References

1. Mnguni, L.: Online learning in lockdown is far from Ideal (2020). https://mg.co.za/article/2020-04-08-online-learning-in-lockdown-is-far-from-ideal/. Accessed 05 May 2021
2. Lorente, L.M.L., Arrabal, A.A., Pulido-Montes, C.: The right to education and ICT during COVID-19: an international perspective. Sustain. **12**(21), 1–17 (2020)
3. Potgieter, P.: The Awareness behaviour of students on cyber security awareness by using social media platforms: a case study at the central University of Technology. In: Proceedings of 4th International Conference on the Internet, Cyber Security and Information Systems 2019, vol. 12, K. Njenga, Ed. Kalpa Publications in Computing, pp. 272–262 (2019)
4. Aloul, F.: The need for effective information security awareness. J. Adv. Inf. Technol. **3**(3), 176–183 (2012)
5. Aldawood, H., Skinner, G.: Educating and raising awareness on cyber security social engineering: a literature review. In: 2018 IEEE International Conference on Teaching, Assessment, and Learning for Engineering (TALE), pp. 62–68 (2018)
6. Sridevi, K.V.: Cyber security awareness among in-service secondary school teachers of Karnataka. Indian J. Educ. Technol. **2**(2), 82–94 (2020)
7. Muniandy, L., Muniandy, B., Samsudin, Z.: Cyber security behaviour among higher education students in Malaysia. J. Inf. Assur. Cyber Secur. **2017**(3), 1–13 (2017)
8. Sawahel, W.: COVID-19 Brings New Cyber-Security Threats to Universities. University World News Africa Edition, Durban, 08 Jun 2020
9. Chandarman, R., Van Niekerk, B.: Students' cybersecurity awareness at a private tertiary educational institution. African J. Inf. Commun. (AJIC) **2017**(20), 133–155 (2017)
10. Al-Janabi, S., Al-Shourbaji, I.: A study of cyber security awareness in educational environment in the Middle East. J. Inf. Knowl. Manag. **15**(1), 1–30 (2016)
11. Singh, H.: Cyber security in universities: threats, threat actors and defence 2020. https://thecyphere.com/blog/cyber-security-universities/. Accessed 24 May 2021
12. ISO: ISO/IEC 27032:2012 Information technology - Security techniques - Guidelines for cybersecurity (2012)
13. Von Solms, R., Van Niekerk, J.: From information security to cyber security. Comput. Secur. **2013**(33), 97–102 (2013)
14. European Union Agency for Network and Information Security, Definition of cybersecurity. Gaps and overlaps in standardisation (2015). www.enisa.europa.eu/publications/definition-of-cybersecurity. Accessed 21 May 2021

15. Arpaci, I., Kilicer, K., Bardakci, S.: Effects of security and privacy concerns on educational use of cloud services. Comput. Hum. Behav. **45**(2015), 93–98 (2015)

16. Dawson, M., Bacius, R., Gouveia, L.B., Vassilakos, A.: Understanding the challenge of cybersecurity in critical infrastructure sectors. L. Forces Acad. Rev. **26**(1), 69–75 (2021)

17. Kim, L.: Cybersecurity awareness: protecting data and patients. Nurs. Inf. **47**(6), 65–67 (2017)

18. Shaw, R., Chen, C., Harris, A., Huang, H.: The impact of information richness on information security awareness training effectiveness. Comput. Educ. **52**(2), 92–100 (2009)

19. Zwilling, M., Klien, G., Lesjak, D., Wiechetek, Ł, Cetin, F., Basim, H.: Cyber security awareness, knowledge and behavior: a comparative study. J. Comput. Inf. Syst. **00**(00), 1–16 (2020)

20. Abawajy, J.: User preference of cyber security awareness delivery methods. Behav. Inf. Technol. **33**(3), 237–248 (2014)

21. Abawajy, J., Kim, T.-H.: Performance analysis of cyber security awareness delivery methods. In: Kim, T.-H., Fang, W.-C., Khan, M.K., Arnett, K.P., Kang, H.-j, Ślęzak, D. (eds.) SecTech 2010. CCIS, vol. 122, pp. 142–148. Springer, Heidelberg (2010). https://doi.org/10.1007/978-3-642-17610-4_16

22. Furnell, S., Bryant, P., Phippen, A.: Assessing the security perceptions of personal Internet users. Comput. Secur. **26**(5), 410–417 (2007)

23. von Solms, B., von Solms, R.: Cybersecurity and information security – what goes where? Inf. Comput. Secur. **26**(1), 2–9 (2018)

24. Ulven, B., Wangen, G.: A systematic review of cybersecurity risks in higher education. Futur. Internet **13**(2), 39–51 (2021)

25. Bada, M., Nurse, J.: Developing cybersecurity education and awareness programmes for small and medium-sized enterprises (SMEs). Inf. Comput. Secur. **27**(3), 393–410 (2019)

26. Aliyu, M., Abdallah, N., Lasisi, N., Diyar, D., Zeki, A.: Computer security and ethics awareness among IIUM students: an empirical study. In: The Information and Communication Technology for the Muslim World (ICT4M) 2010 International Conference (2010)

27. Smalley, A.: Higher education responses to Coronavirus (COVID-19) (2021). https://www.ncsl.org/research/education/higher-education-responses-to-coronavirus-covid-19.aspx

28. Bangani, Z.: Covid-19 school closures pose a big threat to learning gains (2021). https://www.timeslive.co.za/news/south-africa/2021-04-21-covid-19-school-closures-pose-a-big-threat-to-learning-gains/. Accessed 26 Apr 2021

29. TeachThought Staff: The Difference between Technology Use and Technology Integration (2014). https://www.teachthought.com/technology/difference-technology-use-technology-integration/. Accessed 20 Apr 2021

30. CyberGuard: The importance of cyber security awareness (2021). https://www.ogl.co.uk/the-importance-of-cyber-security-awareness. Accessed 21 May 2021

31. Metivier, B.: Cybersecurity roles and responsibilities for the board of directors (2018). https://www.tylercybersecurity.com/blog/cybersecurity-roles-and-responsibilities-for-the-board-of-directors%0A. Accessed 21 May 2021

32. Ismail, N.: Who is responsible for cyber security in the enterprise? (2018). https://www.information-age.com/responsible-cyber-security-enterprise-123474640/. Accessed 21 May 2021

33. Shahabuddin, A., et al.: Exploring maternal health care-seeking behavior of married adolescent girls in Bangladesh: a social-ecological approach. PLoS ONE **12**(1), e0169109 (2017)

34. He, W., Zhang, Z.: Enterprise cybersecurity training and awareness programs: recommendations for success. J. Organ. Comput. Electron. Commer. **29**(4), 249–257 (2019)

35. Taha, N., Dahabiyeh, L.: College students information security awareness: a comparison between smartphones and computers. Educ. Inf. Technol. **26**(2), 1721–1736 (2020). https://doi.org/10.1007/s10639-020-10330-0

36. Koyuncu, M., Pusatli, T.: Security awareness level of smartphone users: an exploratory case study. Mob. Inf. Syst. **2019**, 16–28 (2019)

37. Breitinger, F., Tully-Doyle, R., Hassenfeldt, C.: A survey on smartphone user's security choices, awareness and education. Comput. Secur. **101647**, 88 (2019)

38. Mi, T., Gou, M., Zhou, G., Gan, Y., Schwarzer, R.: Effects of planning and action control on smartphone security behaviour. Comput. Secur. **97**, 101954 (2020)

39. Moletsane, T., Tsibolane, P.: Mobile information security awareness among students in higher education: an exploratory study. In: 2020 conference on information communications technology and society (ICTAS), pp. 1–6 (2020)

40. Crompton, H., Burke, D.: The use of mobile learning in higher education: a systematic review. Comput. Educ. **123**(2018), 53–64 (2018)

41. Kamarulzaman, M.H.: Cyber security awareness among Malaysian pre-university students. In: E-Proceeding of the 6Th Global Summit on Education, p. 199, September 2017

42. Da Veiga, A.: Comparing the information security culture of employees who had read the information security policy and those who had not: Illustrated through an empirical study. Inf. Comput. Secur. **24**(2), 139–151 (2016)

43. Dlamini, Z., Modise, M.: Cyber security awareness initiatives in South Africa: A synergy approach. In: Case Studies in Information Ware fare and Security: For researchers, teachers and students, M. Warren, Ed. Reading UK: Academic Conferences and Publishing International Limited (2013)

44. Talib, A.M., Atan, R., Abdullah, R., Murad, M.A.A.: Towards a comprehensive security framework of cloud data storage based on multi-agent system architecture. J. Inf. Secur. **3**(4), 295–306 (2012)

45. Samme-Nlar, T.: Cyberspace security in Africa – where do we stand? african academic network on internet policy (2020). https://aanoip.org/cyberspace-security-in-africa-where-do-we-stand/. Accessed 23 May 2021

46. Redmond, P., Lock, J., Smart, V.: Pre-service teachers' perspectives of cyberbullying. Comput. Educ. **119**, 1–13 (2018)

47. Deschamps, Y., McNutt, K.: Cyberbullying: what's the problem? Can. Public Adm. **59**(1), 45–71 (2016)

48. Bele, J., Dimc, M., Rozman, D., Jemec, A.: Raising awareness of cybercrime - the use of education as a means of prevention and protection. In: Proceedings of the 10th International Conference on Mobile Learning 2014, ML 2014, pp. 281–284 (2014)

49. Crossler, R., Johnston, A., Lowry, P., Hu, Q., Warkentin, M., Baskerville, R.: Future directions for behavioral information security research. Comput. Secur. **32**(2013), 90–101 (2013)

50. Öğütçü, G., Testik, Ö., Chouseinoglou, O.: Analysis of personal information security behavior and awareness. Comput. Secur. **56**(2016), 83–93 (2016)

51. Hanus, B., Wu, Y.: Impact of users' security awareness on desktop security behavior: a protection motivation theory perspective. Inf. Syst. Manag. **33**(1), 2–16 (2016)

52. Kim, E.: Recommendations for information security awareness training for college students. Inf. Manag. Comput. Secur. **22**(2014), 115–126 (2014)

53. Dlamini, M.T., Venter, H.S., Eloff, J.H.P., Eloff, M.M.: Security of cloud computing: seeing through the fog (2011)

54. Bada, M., Sasse, A., Nurse, J.: Cyber security awareness campaigns: why do they fail to change behaviour? Int. Conf. Cyber Secur. Sustain. Soc. (2019)

55. Piccoli, G., Pigni, F.: Information Systems for Managers. Prospect Press, Burlington (2019)

56. Adams, R.: Our approach to employee security training (2018). https://www.pagerduty.com/blog/security-training-at-pagerduty/

57. Ismail, N.: The importance of cyber security culture (2017)

58. Zefeiti, A.M.B., Mohamad, N.A.: Methodological considerations in studying transformational leadership and its outcomes. Int. J. Eng. Bus. Manage. **7**, 10 (2015)

59. Youssef, A., Alageel, M.: A framework for secure cloud computing. Int. J. Comput. Sci. 9(4), 487–500 (2012)
60. Podsakoff, P.M., MacKenzie, S.B., Lee, J.Y., Podsakoff, N.P.: Common method biases in behavioural research: a critical review of the literature and recommended remedies. J. Appl. Psychol. 88(5), 879–903 (2003)
61. Chang, S., Van Witteloostuijn, A., Eden, L.: From the editors: Common method variance in international business research. J. Int. Bus. Stud. 41(2), 178–184 (2010)
62. Peker, Y., Ray, L., Da Silva, S., Gibson, N., Lamberson, C.: Raising cybersecurity awareness among college students. J. Colloq. Inf. Syst. Secur. Educ. 4(1), 17 (2016)
63. Brown, S.: How to think about cybersecurity in the era of COVID-19? (2020). https://mitsloan. mit.edu/ideas-made-to-matter/how-to-think-about-cybersecurity-era-covid-19. Accessed 10 Aug 2021
64. Alexei, A., Alexei, A.: Cyber security threat analysis in higher education institutions as a result of distance learning. Int. J. Sci. Technol. Res. 10(3), 128–133 (2021)
65. Povejsil, E.: Cybersecurity in higher education understanding vulnerabilities and preventing attacks (2021). https://collegiseducation.com/news/technology/cybersecurity-higher-ed-und erstanding-vulnerabilities-preventing-attacks/. Accessed 16 Aug 2021

Diversity of Students' Unethical Behaviors in Online Learning Amid COVID-19 Pandemic: An Exploratory Analysis

Pawel Robert Smolinski[1]([✉]), Jakub Kowalik[2], and Jacek Winiarski[2]

[1] University of Gdansk, Gdansk, Poland
p.smolinski.674@studms.ug.edu.pl
[2] Department of Business Informatics, University of Gdansk, Sopot, Poland
{jakub.kowalik,jacek.winiarski}@ug.edu.pl

Abstract. The COVID-19 pandemic and the proliferation of online learning have made preventing unethical behaviors an additional task for many teachers. This article investigates the specificity of unethical behavior in online learning and formulates proposals for actions to eliminate this phenomenon. The authors assume that the Internet, as a tool for finding information and communication, enables students to engage in unethical behavior, especially at the stage of assessing the acquired knowledge. The article presents a spectrum of unethical behaviors in online learning carried out via electronic media. The historical perspective of the development of online education in connection with the development of the Internet is presented. The research was carried out using the method of a designed survey among full-time and part-time undergraduate and graduate students of selected universities in northern Poland. A set of ten most common unethical behaviors is determined, then the frequency of their occurrence is examined, and the relationships between them are defined. The article ends with the classification of students' unethical behaviors in online learning, proposed on the basis of the conducted research.

Keywords: Online learning · Unethical behavior · COVID-19 pandemic

1 Introduction

There are numerous definitions of e-learning in the literature. The term "online learning" appeared in the late 1980s. It is defined by Nichols as part of the e-learning process with education fully provided through the Web, without any physical learning materials and face-to-face contact [23].

E-learning is a broader term that generally means the use of various online technological tools for educational purposes. The terms "online learning" and "e-learning" are sometimes used interchangeably. For the purpose of this article, it has been decided to use only the term "online learning".

The aim of the article is to formulate a classification of students' unethical behaviors during online education. The authors intend to answer three main research questions:

© Springer Nature Switzerland AG 2022
M. Themistocleous and M. Papadaki (Eds.): EMCIS 2021, LNBIP 437, pp. 551–566, 2022.
https://doi.org/10.1007/978-3-030-95947-0_39

RQ1: How many distinct factors of unethical students' behavior could be formed?
RQ2: What logical connections could be found between items in each of the selected factors?
RQ3: What practical implications for education could such a classification have?

The hypothesis was formulated as follows: classification of students' unethical behaviors during online education can be formulated based on the factors selected in the statistical analysis of the survey results. There are many classifications of unethical behavior in online learning proposed, based on theoretical considerations. The research gap is the lack of systematization of unethical behavior of students, based on empirical research.

The article starts with a description of online learning evolution. Then a literature review on the subject of students' unethical behavior is presented. The research part includes presenting the results of a survey on the frequency of selected unethical activities, analysis of the obtained data with the use of statistical tools and identification of categories of unethical student behaviors. The article closes with a discussion of results, justification of the qualitative relationships between the categorized behaviors, and suggestions of prevention methods for further online education.

1.1 Research Background

The education systems in Europe have been changed due to the COVID-19 pandemic in a very short time. According to a report published by the International Association of Universities [25], nearly 90% of Higher Education Institutions were teaching in online or blended (mixed) models. Even though online learning is known and practiced for more than 20 years, it has never been used on a large scale before. Commonly, students could choose some online courses at university, but most courses were in a traditional, on-site model.

There were high hopes for online learning at the end of the 20th century. The 1998 Delphi-II study published by the Federal Ministry of Education and Research in Germany [29] presented a vision in which the education online system until 2020 will be prevalent globally. All levels of education were supposed to incorporate online learning as a standard mode of study (2005), and digital (virtual) universities (2010) were expected to be a norm.

Contrary to fears that online learning will result in less involvement of students and, consequently, difficulties in teaching and acquiring knowledge, many studies show that online education can be effective. One research shows that students were responsible for 85–90% of the exchanged messages during the online courses, which is even higher indicative than on-site learning [10]. Other studies have found that students communicate and exchange new ideas more often in online classes [28]. It is worth noting that online learning allows overcoming some individuals' dominance, allowing others to join the discussion, which may explain the increase in overall student activity (the number of messages exchanged).

One of the world's first universities to offer online courses was the New Jersey Institute of Technology in the USA. For this purpose, the University applied the "Virtual Classroom" software, the prototype released between 1985 and 1987 [12]. Even though it was a practical and exclusive solution, it did not draw much attention. The Internet did not become popular until 1995. However, just eight years later, over 1.6 million students in the USA participated in at least one online course, and 500,000 graduated from online universities [2]. This growth in online education is closely related to the change in Internet access in society.

In 2015, the number of Internet users exceeded 3.22 billion. According to Statista.com, in 2020, there were 4.66 billion users connected to the Internet (which corresponds to 59% of the entire world population) [31]. According to the OECD report, the percentage of digitalization and Internet use in developed countries is the highest in the 16–24 age group (97%) and the lowest in the 55–74 age group (67%) [13].

In its report [7], the Federal Communications Commission draws attention to the fact that faster Internet connection is closely correlated with extended online activity. Since 1997 the speed of available Internet connections has doubled every four years. Research from 2016 shows that people from OECD countries aged between 14–24 spent more than 4 h a day using the Internet, whereas, in the Netherlands, the declared amount of time exceeded 6 h [24].

From the education's point of view, it is crucial to change the Internet's perception in its entire system. There is a strong correlation between education level, measured as the average number of years of school completed by people over 15 in a given society, and the rate of access to the Internet [5].

Despite the drastic development and the removal of many technical barriers, the wide adaptation of online learning has slowed down. Research suggests that teachers did not have any major concerns about the quality of online education (only 8% expected it to be lower), the majority was ready to conduct online classes (although over 37% declared no experience in online teaching at all), and as many as 20% of respondents expected that more than 80% of students would learn completely online in 2013 [18]. However, many teachers were still forced to maintain their classes in on-site conditions, which resulted in a reluctance to prepare additional materials or rework current ones for online courses. Teachers also reported the lack of support from universities (e.g. providing training) as a reason for their resistance [3, 17]. Nelson and Thompson [22] add the unclear accounting of teaching time, rewards, additional burden, or the cost and availability of computer hardware as the main barriers to this teaching model. The above doubts and obstacles resulted in the withdrawal of most universities from the extensive implementation of online learning until schools' forced closure due to the COVID-19 pandemic.

This situation entailed the necessity to use different tools than before and the modification of teaching materials. The new condition also required a change in behaviors and habits. While the teacher and the students are in different locations, the control becomes hard. The lack of control and proctoring may trigger inappropriate or unethical behaviors that students would otherwise not commit.

2 Literature Review

Public media was the first to report students' unethical behavior in online learning during the COVID-19 pandemic. One of the first articles published on this topic was a text by Appiah [26] in The New York Times Magazine. The author analyzed the research conducted by The International Center for Academic Integrity and signaled a possibility of a quick escalation of students' unethical behavior in online learning during the pandemic. Another research carried out by Academic Integrity In the Age of Online Learning [1] surveyed 789 teachers on academic integrity. 93% of respondents said that students cheat more often online than in the traditional educational environment. It is also worth mentioning the work of Lederman [14], who previously analyzed reports on unethical student behavior, but did not try to comprehensively systematize them.

A search for academic articles with the keywords "unethical student behavior" at ResearchGate (RG) and Google Scholar (GS) resulted in 63,200 articles on GS alone. To narrow down results to the topic of this study, a further search was made with a subset of keywords: online, student, unethical, behavior. This resulted in 41,000 hits at GS but overall convergence with the topic was still not satisfactory. Finally, upon adding two more keywords: COVID-19 and pandemic, ten publications broadly related to search results have been found (RG) and one was fully matched [6].

Fask, Englander and Wang [9] research of exams taken 'on-site' (in a fully controlled environment) and online (unable to be controlled) was focused on the difference in unethical behavior frequency. They proved that students from the online group had had 14% better results on average, which they consider an indicator of unethical behavior.

Bilen and Matros [6] analyzed the degree of volatility in dishonesty during an online exam conducted under control (webcam) or non-controlled conditions. The research method was a comparative analysis of the time needed to complete each question in both groups. Researchers found more cheating attempts in the uncontrolled group, signified by the shorter time to complete questions. An article concludes that students have a substantial benefit from a camera-controlled exam, which allows them to prove their innocence, when accused of cheating. In the article, the researchers find that dishonesty is more common when exam results are more significant – negative result means serious consequences (e.g.: to retake a year), positive has much more substantial impact on an ongoing evaluation. The research was done on exams only; other forms of students' activity (lectures, classes, projects) were not studied.

Another research was done by Hebebci, Beritz and Alan [11] on Turkish students in different study levels. Researchers tested 530 students in terms of unethical behavior during online learning. The initial hypothesis was the correlation between the tendency to cheat and gender, education level, or knowledge of ethics. Authors proved that male students are involved in unethical behavior in online learning more often than female students. The authors explain that both genders have different roles in society, and different expectations are made for both. Additionally, men spend more time online (they are more digitally proficient). The authors do not find any difference between groups based on the study level or an ethical course passed earlier.

In another article about students' dishonesty in online learning, Jones [15] used a survey with ten questions as a method of research. However, she was interested only in plagiarism. Details about plagiarism in high schools can be found in Josephson Institute's 2012 report card on The Ethics of American Youth [16]. In Jones's study, 92% of students know somebody who plagiarized at least once. Although 59% of students confessed that their plagiarism was entirely intentional, 41% declared they never plagiarized. Jones defined different reasons for plagiarism in the tested group, e.g. lack of information or unclear instructions, a subject beyond an area of student's interest or a general learning overload. She described how students make a self-excuse; they say "everybody does it and nobody is punished" or "nobody cares about plagiarism". Surprisingly, many students classified plagiarism as ethically neutral. In conclusions, she describes ten strategies aimed to strengthen pro-ethical behavior.

Arefeen, Mohyuddin and Khan [4] studied the students' unethical behavior at the University of Bangladesh. They searched for the relationship between participation in an ethics course and students' and graduates' unethical behavior. Based on the conducted research, they concluded that it is essential to shape students' ethical behavior through ethics courses at all stages of education, particularly in situations like the COVID-19 pandemic. They warn that the acquisition and consolidation of unethical behaviors during the study years may result in such behaviors being exhibited later in professional life. They describe the implications of unethical behavior for university and professional life but do not propose a comprehensive division based on obtained results.

The main goal of the research conducted by Bylieva, Lobatyuk, Tolpygin, and Rubtsova [8] was to formulate methods of preventing academic dishonesty, divided on the basis of theoretical analyzes into three sets: cheating, plagiarism and collusion. The researchers examined fifty examples of unethical behavior from different countries and education systems. They concluded that teachers could not entirely avoid students' unethical behavior in online learning by implementing only technical solutions. They recognized tasks that require creative thinking as the most effective method of preventing academic dishonesty in online education.

Watson and Sottile [27] investigated whether students cheat more often in online classes than in traditional classrooms, then whether gender and year of study impact the frequency of cheating. The researchers conducted surveys on 635 students, and the results were analyzed using t-tests and ANOVA. They identified undesirable behaviors that occur more frequently in online education, e.g., giving answers to other students and using instant messaging to consult. Watson and Sottile [27] showed that women admit cheating more often in an online course and are more likely to receive help during the exam. Researchers have shown that year of study is essential in the frequency of unethical behavior, as younger age groups perpetuate more cheaters.

King and Guyette [19] studied the opinions of management students about online exam behavior. They determined and compared the scope of cheating committed in online and traditional classes. A sample of 121 undergraduate students showed that students feel more liberal in their behavior when the online examiner does not establish precise rules for taking the exam. In the students' opinion, behaviors that were considered ethically acceptable during the online examination were: using the textbook, own notes and printed sources (e.g. articles, abstracts). The behaviors that most of the respondents considered inappropriate (unethical) were: sending exam answers to other students, obtaining exam questions, asking another person to take an exam for them. No significant gender differences were found in the attitudes examined.

Lau and Yuen [20] investigated the unethical behavior of high school students. They defined three groups of such activities. These are unauthorized acts (copying, hacking, piracy), internet stickiness (internet addiction), and plagiarism (unauthorized use of materials). Each of the three groups has been defined through several dimensions (variables). However, the classification was not based on empirical research results, and the only basis was theoretical considerations. Besides, the proposed classification goes beyond unethical behavior, extending the scope of analysis to include other online behaviors, e.g. excessive use of the Internet. The authors prove that male students tend to be more unethical than female students. Also, students from low socioeconomic status families are more likely to be dishonest than students from high-status families.

According to Malgwi and Rakovski [21], cheating is the result of three factors, known as the triangle of academic dishonesty: pressure (e.g. creating an atmosphere of competition), opportunities (e.g. availability of cheat sheets) and rationalization (e.g. other students are also cheating). The opportunity factor is particularly problematic in online settings due to the limited control of lecturers over students. King, Guyette, and Piotrowski [19] showed that 73.6% of students consider online conditions as creating more opportunities for cheating. In a study by Witherspoon, Maldonado and Lacey [30] 80% of respondents admitted to cheating during the exam when the opportunity arose.

The presented literature review shows the lack of a classification of unethical students' behavior in online learning based on empirical results, which would consider the scale of this phenomenon during the COVID-19 pandemic. Researchers mainly focused on identifying unethical behaviors, identifying their causes, building the characteristics of people perpetrating them and formulating proposals for preventive actions. Therefore, the authors of this article believe that it is necessary to classify unethical behavior on the basis of empirical data and propose practical methods to prevent unethical behavior in online learning.

3   Methodology

3.1   Research Design

To identify the most common unethical behaviors while learning online, a survey was conducted as it was the most convenient method under COVID-19 conditions. Surveys do not generate high costs and enable researchers to access a large sample needed for statistical analyzes. In order to reduce the obtained data, an exploratory factor analysis was used. The reason for using that method was the lack of a statistically confirmed classification of unethical behavior in previous studies. This is the first study to statistically analyze the relationship between unethical behaviors in online learning.

3.2   Sample

The study was conducted on a group of students from selected universities in northern Poland. Out of 369 responses, 365 comprised the main sample, and 4 were eliminated from the analysis due to missing data. 56.9% of the respondents were women, 41.9% were men. The mean age in the sample was 22.44 years, with a standard deviation of 4.55 years (see Table 1).

Table 1. Sample statistics

		Number (percent)
Course of study	Economics	44 (13.1%)
	International Economic Relations	41 (12.2%)
	Tourism Management Studies	2 (0.6%)
	Management	248 (74.0%)
Cycle of study	I cycle – bachelor	248 (74.0%)
	II cycle – master	86 (25.7%)
	III cycle - doctoral	1 (0.3%)
Year of study	First	226 (67.5%)
	Second	37 (11.0%)
	Third	71 (21.2%)
	Fourth	1 (0.35)
Residence	City	167 (49.9%)
	Town	90 (26.9%)
	Village	78 (23.3%)

3.3 Instrument

Before conducting the in-depth interview, the authors of this paper used brainstorming to make a list of questions. Sixteen neutral open-ended questions were formulated to identify unethical student behaviors during remote teaching. An in-depth interview scenario was developed, and the research location (a social room) was planned.

Experts in the field of online learning were selected as respondents. These individuals were identified based on the maxima of two variables: the number of publications in the field of online learning registered in the library database of the University of Gdansk and the amount of experience in teaching measured by the activity in the Moodle LMS (https://mdl.ug.edu.pl/). A ranking was performed, and seven persons were selected. Five respondents agreed to participate in the research. Interviews were conducted in January 2021. Based on answers a 10-item questionnaire was designed.

It contained descriptions of behaviors most often indicated by experts as unethical in online learning (see Table 2). Responses were scored on a 5-point Likert scale, with the higher values indicating the higher frequency of student's behavior (see Table 2). The questionnaire was verified in a pilot study ($N = 71$) and demonstrated satisfactory reliability (Cronbach's $\alpha = 0.75$). No items have been deleted.

3.4 Procedure

The primary study was conducted online using Microsoft Forms. The questionnaire was administered to students during online classes. Participation in the survey was voluntary and anonymous.

4 Results

4.1 Descriptive Statistics

The results of the study are presented in Table 2. The most common unethical behaviors are: lack of students' engagement in an online class (1) ($M = 3.05$, $SD = 0.96$) and the use of prohibited materials during an exam (10) ($M = 2.54$, $SD = 1.29$). The least common behaviors are: simulating activity during a class (5), hacking an exam (6), enabling an unauthorized person to participate in a class (7), activities disrupting the course of a class (8) and giving login details to another person in order to participate in an exam for a student (9). The means for the remaining behaviors are: simulating technical problems (2) ($M = 1.58$, $SD = 0.839$), recording classes without the consent of the teacher (3) ($M = 1.85$, $SD = 1.06$) and providing exam's content to other people/groups (4) ($M = 1.64$, $SD = 1.05$). The mean for the entire questionnaire is 1.62, with a standard deviation of 0.44.

Table 2. Questionnaire items with percentage of answers

No	How often during online classes did you act as follows:	Never	Occasionally	Moderately	Frequently	Always
1	Lack of engagement. Logging into a class and then lack of the required activity (e.g. being away from a hardware device, using social media, carrying out other activities)	11 (3.3%)	94 (28.1%)	116 (34.6%)	94 (28.1%)	20 (6%)
2	Simulating technical problems in order to not perform the required activity (e.g. missing/damaged microphone, turned off cameras, inefficient internet connection)	203 (60.6%)	81 (24.2%)	41 (12.2%)	8 (2.4%)	2 (0.6%)

(continued)

Table 2. (*continued*)

No	How often during online classes did you act as follows:	Never	Occasionally	Moderately	Frequently	Always
3	Recording a class without the teacher's consent (e.g. recording, taking screenshots)	168 (50.1%)	91 (27.2%)	41 (12.2%)	28 (8.4%)	7 (2.1%)
4	Providing exam content to other people/groups without teacher's consent	223 (66.6%)	45 (13.4%)	39 (11.6%)	20 (6.0%)	8 (2.4%)
5	Simulating activity during a class (e.g. using OBS - virtual camera software)	315 (94.0%)	13 (3.9%)	3 (0.9%)	1 (0.3%)	3 (0.9%)
6	Hacking an exam (e.g. gaining access to correct answers, extending test duration)	315 (94.0%)	11 (3.3%)	5 (1.5%)	2 (0.6%)	2 (0.6%)
7	Enabling an unauthorized person to participate in a class (e.g. disseminating a link to the class)	316 (94.3%)	12 (3.6%)	1 (0.3%)	1 (0.3%)	5 (1.5%)
8	Activities disrupting the course of a class (e.g. not muting the microphone on purpose, taking control over the presentation, performing the so-called *raids*, conducting off topic conversations with other participants)	315 (94.0%)	11 (3.3%)	6 (1.8%)	2 (0.6%)	1 (0.3%)

(*continued*)

Table 2. (*continued*)

No	How often during online classes did you act as follows:	Never	Occasionally	Moderately	Frequently	Always
9	Giving login details to another person in order to enable them to participate in an exam	316 (94.3%)	9 (2.7%)	4 (1.2%)	4 (1.2%)	2 (0.6%)
10	Using prohibited materials during an exam and cheating (e.g. using open book, using cheat sheets, using Internet search results, consultations with other people, group work)	95 (28.4%)	75 (22.4%)	81 (24.2%)	54 (16.1%)	30 (9.0%)

4.2   Factor Analysis

To reduce data obtained from the responses, exploratory factor analysis was used (EFA with Oblimin Rotation and Kaiser Normalization, using SPSS). Factor loadings equal to or greater than 0.5 were considered sufficient for extraction. Three hidden factors of unethical behavior during online learning were extracted (see Table 3). The KMO sample adequacy measure showed an acceptable correlation at the level of 0.8, and the Bartlett sphericity test is statistically significant (χ^2 (df = 45) = 1121.657, p<0.001). The extracted factors explain 64.77% of the variance.

Reliability analysis for the entire test showed adequate internal reliability with Cronbach's α equal to 0.715. Internal reliability for each factor, measured by Cronbach's α, showed good reliability for factor 1 ($\alpha = 0.867$) and acceptable reliability for factor 2 ($\alpha = 0.672$). Factor 3 ($\alpha = 0.472$) obtained the lowest reliability.

Table 3. Factor loadings

No	How often during online classes did you act as follows:	Factor 1	Factor 2	Factor 3
1	Lack of engagement. Logging into a class and then lack of the required activity (e.g. being away from a hardware device, using social media, carrying out other activities)	−0.070	0.037	0.838
2	Simulating technical problems in order to not perform the required activity (e.g. missing/damaged microphone, turned off cameras, inefficient internet connection)	0.111	−0.017	0.754
3	Recording a class without the teacher's consent (e.g. recording, taking screenshots)	−0.010	0.762	−0.060
4	Providing exam content to other people/groups without teacher's consent	0.117	0.842	−0.059
5	Simulating activity during a class (e.g. using OBS - virtual camera software)	0.799	−0.006	0.026
6	Hacking an exam (e.g. gaining access to correct answers, extending test duration)	0.792	0.750	−0.025
7	Enabling an unauthorized person to participate in a class (e.g. disseminating a link to the class)	0.882	−0.031	0.097
8	Activities disrupting the course of a class (e.g. not muting the microphone on purpose, taking control over the presentation, performing the so-called *raids*, conducting off topic conversations with other participants)	0.817	−0.008	−0.053
9	Giving login details to another person in order to enable them to participate in an exam	0.732	−0.008	0.004
10	Using prohibited materials during an exam and cheating (e.g. using open book, using cheat sheets, using Internet search results, consultations with other people, group work)	−0.085	0.714	0.180

5 Discussion

5.1 Discussion of Result

The obtained results suggest that the most common behaviors are lack of engagement (1), the use of prohibited materials during exams (10) and recording a class without the teacher's consent (3). These behaviors are relatively easy to conduct, and the probability of their detection is low. Some of these behaviors may also be considered appropriate or somewhat acceptable, which further contributes to their frequency. For example, in the study by King, Guyette and Piotrowski [19], using an open book during an online exam was endorsed by the vast majority of respondents as appropriate behavior.

The least common behaviors, used only by a small number of students, are: simulating activity (5), hacking (6), enabling an unauthorized person to participate in a class (7), activities disrupting a class (8) and giving login details to another person in order to participate in an exam. (9). The first two behaviors require preparation and knowledge of computer science, so they are naturally difficult to carry out. Behaviors 7 and 8 are harmful to other students participating in the classes and are easy to detect. Besides, behaviors 6 and 9 may incur certain expenses, for example: purchasing a hacking program or paying the person who will write the exam for the student. The above factors may contribute to the low frequency of these behaviors.

Various classifications of unethical behavior in online learning have been proposed in the literature, e.g. Lau, Yuen [20] or Bylieva, Lobatyuk, Tolpygin, Rubtsova [8]. However, researchers have only suggested classifications based on logical implications without applying statistical methods. As is shown in our research, such classification is possible using exploratory factor analysis (See Table 3). Based on extracted factors, three categories of unethical behaviors are proposed and named. The first category is called: **Hacking and spoofing** (5) (6) (7) (8) (9), the second category: **Dishonest use of materials** (3) (4) (10) and the third category: **False presence** (1) (2).

Category 1 (Hacking and spoofing), based on factor 1, includes only unethical behavior characterized by a very low incidence in online learning (M = 1.11, SD = 0.40). Category 2 (Dishonest use of materials), based on factor 2, comprises behaviors designed to unfairly increase the quiz/exam grade and are relatively easy to undertake. These behaviors are rare (M = 2.01, SD = 0.89) but present in online learning and may result in obtaining non-representative grades by students who undertake them. Factor items also strongly correlate with each other, which may suggest that these behaviors co-occur. Category 3 (False presence), based on factor 3, consists of the most common behaviors (M = 2.317, SD = 0.731). It explains the smallest percentage of the variance (10.31%) and Cronbach's α equal to 0.472. Despite mentioned weaknesses, category 3 has a strong logical explanation and remains a subject for further analysis.

5.2   Discussion of Classification

Hacking and spoofing contain behaviors that require above-average computer skills (5) (6) (7) as well as enabling the participation of unauthorized persons in classes or exams (8) (9). The relationships within this category indicate that students proficient at hacking combine unethical behavior with activities enabling unauthorized people to participate in classes/exams. It proves that hackers do not care about authorizing their Internet activities (spoofing/anonymity is a significant feature of their online behavior) and enables other Internet users to perform spoofing processes. Prevention methods for this group of unethical behaviors should primarily concern technical security. Good protection against hacking (e.g. use of programs dedicated to online learning) and ensuring that only fully authorized people can access classes or exams (e.g. only students with university domain email) can effectively limit the behaviors classified to this group.

Dishonest use of materials is a group of behaviors consisting of cheating (10), stealing the content of classes/presentations/exams (3) and making them available to interested people (4). This relationship indicates that students, who use prohibited materials (e.g. cheat sheets, Internet search results) during the evaluation stage, are also more likely to register the content of a class without the teacher's consent and spread it among other students. It proves that cheating is connected with the desire to popularize unethical behavior. A student who engages in academic dishonesty, cheats and records lectures will most likely popularize unethical behavior among other students, probably because of a need to self-justify their actions. If this happens frequently enough, it may create social proof for this kind of behavior, and students may rationalize their actions. Prevention methods should rely significantly on technical support in the form of safeguard/proctoring programs preventing the acquisition of the content of classes/credits/exams and social engineering techniques that demotivate students from undertaking unethical behavior (e.g. moral codes).

False presence includes behavior such as lack of engagement in online classes (1) and possible simulation of technical problems to avoid the required activity (2). A student, whom a teacher calls out, may simulate various problems (e.g. microphone malfunction or internet disconnection) to avoid engagement. Prevention methods should revolve around social engineering techniques (e.g. providing a restricted time frame for the answer) and class organization (e.g. relying on group work, interactive presentation, active vs passive learning model).

5.3 Additional Findings

The last part of the statistical analysis concerns whether gender and age impact the frequency of unethical behavior. Mann-Whitney U test was used to determine the significance of a difference in the frequency of unethical behavior between women and men. No significant difference was found ($Z = 1.102$, $p = 0.270$). Similarly, the analysis of the two most differentiating items: lack of engagement (1) and the use of prohibited materials during exams (10), did not show any significant differences in the answers of women and men (χ^2 (df = 4) = 3.873, $p = 0.423$ for item 1 and χ^2 (df = 4) = 8.425, $p = 0.077$ for item 10). Age correlates with the frequency of unethical behavior only for the first item ($r = -0.184$, $p = 0.001$). It means that the older the respondent, the less frequently he/she disengages in classes. However, it should be noted that the obtained correlation is very weak, and the age variance in the studied group is not too high ($M = 22.44$, SD = 4,55).

6 Limitations

The presented study possesses a few limitations and generalization of the results should be made with caution. A survey design relies solely on students' evaluation of their behavior during online learning. No methods have been used to directly and objectively measure the prevalence of unethical behavior. Additionally, the presented research is limited by geographical and cultural constraints. Only Polish students participating in online courses at universities from northern Poland have been surveyed. The geographical location of the universities does not determine the location of study in online education, however, most of the surveyed students began their education before the COVID-19 pandemic and expected a stationary education. During the data analysis, the authors identified a problem with the reliability of factor 3, which is below the critical value of $\alpha = 0.6$. However, according to the authors, factor 3 has significant practical implications, and therefore its analysis is justified.

7 Conclusions and Further Research

One of the consequences of the COVID-19 pandemic has been the rapid increase of online learning. And as many studies have shown, online education is positively correlated with various unethical behaviors. It is proposed in this research that unethical behaviors can be classified using exploratory factor analysis into three distinct categories. These categories can help educators better understand academic dishonesty, identify unethical behaviors and plan efficient preventive actions against them.

As far as the behavior classified as hacking and spoofing is concerned, preventive measures can be taken by individual teachers, but first and foremost this is an area for the university authorities. University managers should order the implementation of software and hardware security solutions and instruct the IT department to watch over their functioning. Tested and updated system solutions covering the entire organization certainly have a chance to be one of the key elements eliminating the occurrence of unethical behavior. Activities grouped under Dishonest use of materials require preventive action in two areas. The first is the technical area, the scope of which is similar to preventive actions from the Hacking and spoofing group. The second area, on the other hand, requires actions demotivating the occurrence of unethical behavior by, for example, formulating and publishing legal regulations specifying the rules of using educational content. These rules should respect copyright, considering open access and public domain regulations. The proposed preventive measures should be designed and implemented by the university authorities which will oblige all students to respect them by, for example, obligatory signing of the regulations. Preventive actions against the unethical activities grouped under False presence should be implemented primarily by the teachers teaching online. These actions should include actions to demotivate the occurrence of unethical behavior and to stimulate individual student activity.

The authors intend to expand further research by conducting comparative analysis of students' unethical behaviors from different geographic locations and cultural backgrounds (Europe and North America). Further research should aim to design a catalog of preventive measures reducing the possibility of undesirable behavior in online learning. To conclude, the analyzed research area has significant exploratory potential. Therefore, it is advisable to continue and deepen the understanding of the outlined problem.

References

1. Academic integrity in the age of online learning. http://read.uberflip.com/i/1272071-aca demic-integrity-in-the-age-of-online-learning/0. Accessed 10 Apr 2021
2. Allen, I., Seaman, J.: Seizing the opportunity: the quality and extent of online education in the United States, 2002 and 2003. Sloan Consortium, Wellesley (2003)
3. Allen, I., Seaman, J.: Staying the course: online education in the United States, 2008. Sloan Consortium, Needham (2008)
4. Arefeen, S., Mohyuddin, M., Khan, M.: An Exploration of unethical behavior attitude of tertiary level students of Bangladesh. Glob. J. Manage. Bus. Res. Adm. Manage. **20**(17), 39–47 (2020)
5. Barro, R., Lee, J.: A new data set of educational attainment in the world, 1950–2010. J. Develop. Econ. **104**(C), 184–198 (2013)

6. Bilen, E., Matros, A.: Online cheating amid COVID-19. J. Econ. Behav. Organ. **182**, 196–211 (2021)
7. Broadband Performance OBI Technical Paper no. 4. https://transition.fcc.gov/national-bro adband-plan/broadband-performance-paper.pdf. Accessed 12 Apr 2021
8. Bylieva, D., Lobatyuk, V., Tolpygin, S., Rubtsova, A.: Academic dishonesty prevention in e-learning university system. In: Rocha, Á., Adeli, H., Reis, L.P., Costanzo, S., Orovic, I., Moreira, F. (eds.) WorldCIST 2020. AISC, vol. 1161, pp. 225–234. Springer, Cham (2020). https://doi.org/10.1007/978-3-030-45697-9_22
9. Fask, A., Englander, F., Wang, Z.: Do online exams facilitate cheating? an experiment designed to separate possible cheating from the effect of the online test taking environment. J. Acad. Ethics **12**(2), 101–112 (2014). https://doi.org/10.1007/s10805-014-9207-1
10. Harasim, L.: A history of e-learning: shift happened. In: Weiss, J., Nolan, J., Hunsinger, J., Trifonas, P. (eds.) The International Handbook of Virtual Learning Environments, pp. 59–94. Springer, Dordrecht (2006)
11. Hebebci, M., Bertiz, Y., Alan, S.: Investigation of university students' online unethical behaviors. In: International Conference on Social and Education Sciences (IConSES), Chicago (2020)
12. Hiltz, S.: Evaluating the virtual class room. In: Harasim, L. (Ed.) Online education, pp. 133–183. Praeger, New York (1990)
13. ICT Access and Usage by Households and Individuals. https://stats.oecd.org/Index.aspx?Dat aSetCode=ICT_HH2. Accessed 27 Mar 2021
14. Inside Higher Ed. https://www.insidehighered.com/digital-learning/article/2020/07/22/tec hnology-best-way-stop-online-cheating-no-experts-say-better. Accessed 12 April 2021
15. Jones, D.: Academic dishonesty: are more students cheating? Bus. Commun. Q. **74**(2), 141–150 (2011)
16. Josephson Institute's 2012 report card on the ethics of American youth. https://charactercou nts.org/wp-content/uploads/2014/02/ReportCard-2012-DataTables.pdf. Accessed 11 April 2021
17. Keengwe, J., Kidd, T., Kyei-Blankson, L.: Faculty and technology: implications for faculty training and technology leadership. J. Sci. Educ. Technol. **18**(1), 23–28 (2009)
18. Kim, K., Bonk, C.: The future of online teaching and learning in higher education: the survey says. Educause Q. **29**, 22–30 (2006)
19. King, C., Guyette, R., Piotrowski, C.: Online exams and cheating: an empirical analysis of business students' views. J. Educators Online **6**, 1–11 (2009)
20. Lau, W., Yuen, A.: Internet ethics of adolescents: understanding demographic differences. Comput. Educ. **72**, 378–385 (2014)
21. Malgwi, C., Rakovski, C.: Combating academic fraud: are students reticent about uncovering the covert? J. Acad. Ethics **7**(3), 207–221 (2009)
22. Nelson, S., Thompson, G.: Barriers perceived by administrators and faculty regarding the use of distance education technologies in pre-service programs for secondary agricultural education teachers. J. Agric. Educ. **46**(4), 36–48 (2005)
23. Nichols, M.: A theory for eLearning. Educ. Technol. Soc. **6**(2), 1–10 (2003)
24. OECD: Measuring the Digital Transformation. OECD Publishing, Paris (2019)
25. Regional/National Perspectives on the Impact of COVID-19 on Higher Education. https://www.iau-aiu.net/IMG/pdf/iau_covid-19_regional_perspectives_on_the_imp act_of_covid-19_on_he_july_2020_.pdf. Accessed 22 March 2021
26. The New York Times Magazine Ed.. https://www.nytimes.com/2020/04/07/magazine/if-my-classmates-are-going-to-cheat-on-an-online-exam-why-cant-i.html. Accessed 10 April 2021
27. Watson, G., Sottile, M.: Cheating in the digital age: do students cheat more in online courses? Online J. Distance Learn. Adm. **13**(1) (2010)

28. Winkelmans, T.: Educational computer conferencing: an application of analysis methodologies to a structured small group activity. Unpublished MA Thesis, University of Toronto (1988)

29. Winnes, M., Schimank, U.: National report: federal republic of Germany, pp. 209–220. Max-Planck-Institute for the Study of Societies, Köln (1999)

30. Witherspoon, M., Maldonado, N., Lacey, C.: Academic dishonesty of undergraduates: methods of cheating. Paper presented at the Annual Meeting of the American Educational Research Association May 2010, Denver, Colorado (2010)

31. Worldwide digital population as of January 2021. https://www.statista.com/statistics/617136/digital-population-worldwide/. Accessed April 12, 2021

An Empirical Investigation of Agile Information Systems Development for Cybersecurity

Abdulhamid A. Ardo$^{(\boxtimes)}$, Julian M. Bass , and Tarek Gaber

Department of Computer Science and Software Engineering,
University of Salford, Manchester, UK
a.a.ardo@edu.salford.ac.uk

Abstract. Cybersecurity has been identified as a major challenge confronting the digital world, neglecting cybersecurity techniques during software design and development increases the risk of malicious attacks. Thus, there is a need to make security an integral part of the agile information system development process. In this exploratory study, we empirically explore the agile security practices adopted by software developers and security professionals. Data was collected by conducting ten semi-structured interviews with agile practitioners from seven companies in the United Kingdom (UK). The study was conducted between August–November 2020. An approach informed by grounded theory was used for data analysis including Open coding, Memoing, Constant comparison and Theoretical saturation. The security practices identified in this study were categorized into roles, ceremonies and artefacts and mapped onto the different phases of the Software Development Lifecycle (SDLC). We discovered practitioners use five artefacts: security backlog documentation, software security baseline standards, security test plan templates, information security and security audit checklists; and that there are more artefacts than roles and ceremonies. Also, while most practitioners rely on automated tools for software security testing, only one practitioner mentioned conducting security tests manually. These practices that we have identified comprise a novel taxonomy which form the main research contribution of this paper.

Keywords: Agile security practices · Agile information systems development · Cybersecurity · Software security testing · Security specialist · Grounded Theory · Automated test tools

1 Introduction

Agile information systems development is increasingly becoming influential, and its main goal is the improvement of software product's quality and productivity [1]. Conventionally, the agile development process consists of roles, ceremonies or practices and artefacts. The three typical agile team roles are the scrum master, product owner and development team members. These roles describe the key responsibilities of agile team members. Agile ceremonies are periodic meetings conducted to check project quality

© Springer Nature Switzerland AG 2022
M. Themistocleous and M. Papadaki (Eds.): EMCIS 2021, LNBIP 437, pp. 567–581, 2022.
https://doi.org/10.1007/978-3-030-95947-0_40

and schedule, while artefacts define the elements adopted for sharing project information [2]. The three popular agile methodologies are extreme programming (XP), scrum and lean. These methodologies, however, do not put much emphasis on cybersecurity issues as there are limitations to their use of security activities [3, 4]. Many of the cybersecurity challenges are attributed to lack of integrating security activities during the development process. Also, the risk of unintentionally using insecure practices in most situations leads to the production of insecure software systems. To develop a secure software, practitioners need to adopt many of the quality-improving features of agile software development. Some of these features include iterative development, continuous integration, retrospectives, and constant refraction, among others. It is therefore imperative to integrate security best practices into the agile software development lifecycle to prevent cyberattacks [5]. Backman in [6], have tried to answer the question why software security breaches remain a challenge. By conducting interviews and surveys at a software company he found insufficient knowledge, and inadequate testing policies as some of the issues responsible for software vulnerabilities. Therefore, to address the above enumerated problems of using agile for building secure software, some of the existing studies have highlighted the need to involve the entire agile team and integrate security activities throughout the development process [7–9].

The existing literature have explored agile security as highlighted in this section. Villamizar et al. [10] have discussed the lack of security requirements integration into agile practices. Bartsch in [11] have explored agile security issues through practitioner interviews. His findings highlighted the need for more focus on improving practitioner's cybersecurity awareness and expertise. Also, the study suggested adequate focus on stakeholders' involvement which is inadequate in security-critical agile projects. Queslati et al. [12] conducted a systematic literature review to identify software security development challenges reported in literature. The study found 20 challenges, 14 of which are valid problems to the agile research community and the remaining 6 were neither caused due to agile principles or security assurance practices. Rindell et al. [7] have identified the security activities from OWASP, Microsoft SDL and Common Criteria models and mapped them into agile development processes, practices, and artefacts. While the three studies discussed in this section are related to agile methods security [10–12], none of these studies have developed a taxonomy of agile security practices categorized by roles, ceremonies, and artefacts. Detailed literature review on the intersection of agile and security issues are discussed in the related work section.

Thus, this study aims to fill this gap by improving the security of agile information systems development. In this paper, the main research question we seek to answer is: "What security practices are adopted by practitioners during agile information systems development?". This paper will also answer the following sub-questions:

RQ1: How is software security testing performed in agile teams?
RQ2: How the software security specialist role can be integrated into agile process?

To achieve the research aim, we conducted ten practitioner interviews and adopted a data analysis method informed by the grounded theory. This study contributes to the existing literature in three ways: (i) presenting a taxonomy of empirically identified security practices categorized into roles, ceremonies, and artefacts; (ii) Describing the different ways of software security testing in agile teams; (iii) Describing how the security specialist role can be integrated into the agile process.

The rest of this paper is organized as follows: In Sect. 2, a review of related work is discussed, along with a brief on secure software development models. The paper then introduces the research method adopted for the study in Sect. 3, providing information on the selected research sites, data collection and analysis process used. The paper findings organized into sections on software security testing and integrating the security specialist role in agile process are presented in Sect. 4. Section 5 discusses the study findings in relation to the literature and the research questions. Section 6 concludes the study by explaining the three main research findings.

2 Related Work

This section introduces software security and discusses the prior studies on the intersection between security and agile information systems development.

2.1 Overview of Software Security

The ubiquitous nature of software is bringing enormous benefits to the way human transact their daily activities. However, this also comes with the consequence of increasing system flaws and misuse by malicious users. With the daily reported cases of cybersecurity breaches in the news and social media, software security has attracted the attention of industry players and the academia [13]. The increasing software vulnerability can also be attributed to the astronomic increase in computer connectivity as well as complexity of information systems. The concept of "building security in" is one strategy advocated by researchers towards confronting the challenges of cyberattacks [14].

The term "Cybersecurity" is defined as the set of practices, guidelines technologies and tools used for protecting organizational assets [15]. Cybersecurity needs to guarantee three security attributes which includes confidentiality, integrity, and availability. Most computer security vulnerabilities are attributed to the use of poor programming practices by software practitioners [16]. The CWE/SANS lists the top 25 software errors causing majority of cyber-attacks [17]. Similarly, the Open Web Application Security Project (OWASP) also lists the top 10 web application security risks for managing websites [17]. The purpose of annually publishing the lists is to serve as a guide for practitioners writing codes to be acquainted of current software bugs to avoid. All reported vulnerabilities are usually assigned an identification number and stored in a database known as the National Vulnerability Database (NVD) [18]. Looking at the cybersecurity issues discussed in this section, there is a need to study what efforts have been made in literature to develop security models.

2.2 Secure Software Development Models

Prior study had described the existing software security models and techniques [8]. Three of the popular models are the Microsoft Security Development Lifecycle (SDL) model [19], Software Assurance Maturity Model (SAMM) [20] and the Building Security in

Maturity Model (BSIMM) [21]. Out of these models, only the BSIMM was created through empirical observation and real-world data from software security practices. Also, the above listed models were criticized in literature for being theoretical in their approach and adoption strategies [22]. Each of the models have their own peculiar limitations. The Microsoft Security Development Lifecycle (SDL) framework requires huge documentation and is heavy on processes and organization [23]. Also, some practitioners consider Microsoft SDL threat modelling (risk analysis processes) as too expensive to implement in smaller projects. For SAMM, just like other maturity models adopted for agile software development, the checklist contained in the model are not appropriate for all security-context [8]. While for BSIMM, there seems to be lack of empirical research evaluating the model from a scholarly viewpoint [22]. While the aim of this paper is not solely to build a comprehensive security model, our study has added to the scholarly body of empirical research on secure agile information systems development.

2.3 Security and Agile for Information Systems Development

Existing studies have highlighted the lack of security activities in agile information systems development [3, 24, 25]. Baca & Carlsson in [3] looked at the compatibility of security practices with the characteristics of the agile manifesto. Bansal & Jolly in [26] evaluated security practices with the aim of proposing ways of developing secure information systems processes. The limitation of the study in [3] is that the security enhanced agile development process produced has not been empirically evaluated and compared with other existing development processes. For the study done by Bansal & Jolly in [26], factors such as cost, time and recurrence which may affect the compatibility between two security activities that can help project managers in decision making has not been considered.

Terpstra et al. [4] conducted a systematic review on security in agile methods which revealed several methods for integrating security in agile methods. The paper went further to corroborate the aim of this study that little is known about security from practitioner perspectives. The study identified three contextual factors important for shaping security in agile projects. These factors are solutions addressing the artefacts, solutions addressing the human factors in agile and solutions addressing the agile process itself [4]. However, the identified solution factors were only focused on people, but nothing was mentioned with regards to tools or other sophisticated methods used. Also, collected data was only based on practitioners' posts on LinkedIn which will not allow for in-depth understanding of the phenomena.

Rindell et al. [8] conducted a survey of security engineering activities as practiced by some Finnish agile practitioners. The study surveyed their use of 40 security engineering practices and 16 agile development activities. The study observed the discrepancy between the level of use and perceived impact of security activities. However, the study findings were not compared with other existing baseline surveys conducted in other countries.

Baca et al. [9] proposed an enhanced secure agile development process for a money transfer system at Ericsson Corporation. The study identified security roles which were categorized into four competences including security manager, security architect, security master and penetration tester. However, an obvious drawback of the proposed system is the extra resources required with through the introduction of four different security competences.

Cruzes et al. [27] studied how software security testing was performed in agile teams across different organizations. The existing literature on software security testing broadly focuses on two areas. The first testing focus area are those done for security services such as confidentiality, integrity, availability, authentication, authorization, and non-repudiation [28]. The second focus area is in the aspect of testing for software resilience to withstand attacks [24]. In the context of secure agile software development, security testing issues include validating if security requirements have been implemented properly to avoid attacks. Also, there are issues of identifying unintended software system's vulnerabilities.

Bezerra et al. in [29] have grouped the agile security practices based on practitioners' assessment in a particular cyber security organization. Thus, a common finding of agile information systems development studies in the existing literature is that agile methods do sometimes comply with security requirements, but it is faced with the issues of higher cost and slower development due to inadequate agile security processes [8].

Based on the discussions above, no study has created an empirical taxonomy of agile security practices categorized into roles, ceremonies, and artefacts in a single study. Therefore, this gap in knowledge is what our study aims to fill. While there exists a practitioner study that developed taxonomy of agile methods artefacts based on empirical interviews [2]. Also, there is an article that used practitioner descriptions of agile methods tailoring by focusing on the product owner role [30]. Since there is still paucity of empirical evidence on agile methods security in practice and so we think our study can add value to the existing body of knowledge.

3   Method

To answer the earlier enumerated research questions, we conducted ten empirical interviews with selected UK practitioners working in seven companies as shown in Table 1. The research adopted a data analysis method informed by grounded theory methodology. Grounded Theory is a systematic methodology which is aimed at theory construction using qualitative data. Due to the paucity of literature on agile security from practitioner perspective, the Grounded Theory methodology allows for the emergence of concepts grounded in data [31, 32]. Also, the Grounded Theory is an appropriate methodology in software engineering for constructing theories relevant to practitioners [24].

3.1   Research Sites

We identified and selected appropriate research sites as shown in Table 1. Due to the Covid-19 pandemic, the first author conducted online interviews with the participants. The snowballing sampling technique was used to select additional research participants. The selected research sites consisted of agile practitioners working in companies operating in different sectors including IT consulting, CRM Company, Healthcare services and the FinTech industry. Most of them are large companies but there are a couple of medium-sized and one small and medium-sized enterprise (SME). The diversity of the research sites provided richness to the data collected and lends credence to the results.

3.2 Data Collection

In this study, the source of data collection was through practitioner interviews. Each of the research participants was sent an information sheet which detailed what the study was about. It further asked for their informed consent to record their responses and indicate their choice of anonymity on a consent form. An interview guide containing topics to be covered was followed. Each participant was asked the same questions even though the wording and sequencing of the questions were not uniform for all participants. The initial interview guide questions were generated from light literature review and the researcher's experience with investigating agile information systems development. The initial questions were subjected to several reviews by the authors. The questions were again modified as data collection progressed following the constant comparison technique of grounded theory. The interview transcribes were manually analyzed at the initial stage before moving to the qualitative data analysis software, Nvivo. The Nvivo software package was chosen because of its ability to facilitate many iterative aspects of the grounded theory process [33]. Nvivo can analyze various types of data i.e., text, audio, video, and photos, whereas tools like Leximancer can only be used for text analysis. Also, the qualitative data analysis tool like ATLAS.ti 4.0 seem to work with data files of limited ranges. This means files must be converted to ASCII format before been inputted.

Table 1. Description of participants' and organizations in the study

Code	Job title	Software development experience (Years)	Business type	Organization size
ITCONCco1_SSE1	Senior software engineer	10	IT consulting	Medium-sized
Finco1_SSE2	Senior software engineer	16	Financial services	Large
ITCONCco1_SDA	Senior developer analyst	25	IT consulting	Medium-sized
CRMco1_FSSD1	Full Stake software developer	3	Customer relationship management	Large
HEALTHco1_SD1	Software developer	3	Health	Small

(continued)

Table 1. (*continued*)

Code	Job title	Software development experience (Years)	Business type	Organization size
ITSERVco1_VP-COS1	Vice president cyber operations security	25	IT services	Large
LAWENFco1_CSS1	Cyber security specialist	4	Law enforcement	Large
CYBERFOUDco1_ADL1	Cyber foundry, analyst developer lead	10	Cyber foundry	Large

3.3 Data analysis

After conducting each interview, the first author listened to the recordings many times to ensure accurate transcription to avoid distortion in meanings [34]. By adopting the grounded theory methodology for this study, the authors performed the four major activities described by the Glaserian Grounded theory to analyze the collected data. They are (i) reviewing the data to identify repeated themes, (ii) use keywords to categorize the themes, (iii) code the themes and (iv) categorize the themes through the relationships identified. These activities are summarized as open coding, memoing, constant comparison and theoretical saturation.

3.3.1 Open Coding

This stage involved line-by-line reviewing of the interview transcripts [32] with the aim of identifying key themes from the interviewee's responses. Going through the first interview, we came up with 42 codes. A second interview was analyzed where 29 codes emerged. Subsequently analyzed transcripts had lesser number of codes as many themes were already identified in the initial interviews.

3.3.2 Memoing

In this paper, memos were written to capture interviewee's responses and show the relationship between the different concepts and categories. Brief notes were written on different related topics containing verbatim quotes from interviewees pulled together to make-up a memo. Using the interview transcripts as primary evidence, 6 memos were written out of which 2 are related to the theme of this paper. Memo writing helped elucidate the authors ideas and re-focused further data collection.

3.3.3 Constant Comparison

This research used the constant comparison technique to iterate between data collection and analysis. The data collected was constantly compared within itself as well as other instances of same and similar events. The technique was essentially helpful for refining generated codes and categories.

3.3.4 Theoretical Saturation

It defines the point in the data analysis process when no new categories emerge, and the data categorization is not impacted by adding more interviews [32].

4 Findings

This section explains the research findings which includes a novel taxonomy of agile security practices developed from the analysis of interview transcribes which have been categorized into roles, ceremonies, and artefacts. Two agile security related memos will be discussed in this section. They memos describe the different software testing methods and tools used in practice. The second memo explains the functions performed by security specialists in the different companies and how they interact with other roles in an agile process.

As earlier mentioned, the key finding of this study is the identification of security practices categorized into roles, ceremonies, and artefacts. We particularly discovered more artefacts than roles and ceremonies. The five artefacts are security backlog documentation, software security baseline standards, security test plan templates, information security and security audit checklists. All the artefacts were mapped in detail onto the stages of the agile SDLC.

The backlog documentation describes all security-related activities contained in the product backlog. According to practitioner (ITSERVco1_VP-COS1) *"All our security activities are prioritized in a sort of security backlog document ... it is normally updated based on a project's peculiar requirements."* Another important artefact discovered from analyzing empirical interviews is the security baseline standard. *"We adhere strictly to the government-regulated standard requirements like the GDPR ... Additionally, we have our company baseline standards like basic stuff such as encryption and using strong passwords..."* (ITCONCco1_SSE1). These baseline security standards help organizations protect their critical resources such as servers and workstation from cyberattacks.

While baseline standards are sometimes classified as either High-level or Technical, the security test plan template is categorized under the technical group. *"We adopt test plans that will ensure our software operates securely..."* (ITCONCco1_SSE1). The objective of adopting a template for the testing phase is to ensure a process of identifying security threats and the elimination of issues specifically on the safety and integrity of the software. Lastly, the chief technology officers are commonly responsible for issuing the checklist used in their company for information security and audit checks. *"It is part of my duties to issue security audit checklist to the security and development teams..."* (ITSERVco1_VP-COS1).

There are other activities identified which were accordingly mapped to specific ceremonies and roles on the SDLC. The four ceremonies include security sprint planning meeting at the pre-requirements phase, conducting API security meetings at the design stage, conducting secure code review sessions at the implementation phase, and performing security retrospective meeting at the release phase. For the role's activities, we identified security specialist or a times dedicated security team who are involved in all security related discussions from the requirements to the release phases. While we have done a detailed empirical study on practitioner security practices, however, it will be difficult to include the diagrammatic representation of the taxonomy in this paper because of space limitation.

4.1 Software Security Testing

At the testing phase of software development, the use of automated test tools is common among interviewed practitioners. The reliance on these tools indicates a somewhat straightforward absence of other testing methods as reported by this study's general findings. The identified testing tools in this study were categorized into two groups which are the specialized vulnerability testing and standard software testing tools. There are also practitioners that combine manual and automated testing at different stages of software development.

The specialized testing tools mentioned by practitioners in this study were mainly used for vulnerability assessment, scanning and management. According to practitioner (ITCONCco1_SSE1) *"We use a tool known as OpenVAS and what it does is to give you a free vulnerability assessment test..."* Basically what the user needs to do is to supply the port numbers and other details and the tool does the testing. Practitioner (ITCON-Cco1_SSE1) have highlighted the advantage of using the OpenVAS tool where he said, *"OpenVAS is pretty easy and freely available to use as well..."* Apart from the OpenVAS tool, other software companies use software tools such as Qualys, Rapid7 and Nessus to conduct vulnerability assessment. Among the reason's software practitioners mentioned for using these tools are providing specialized functions such as automating network auditing, identifying threat actors through cloud-based solutions, and providing other penetration testing services such as website scanning to identify potential vulnerable spots, confidential data searches and compliance checks as well. According to practitioner (ITSERVco1_VP-COS1) *"vulnerability testing using Qualys or Rapid7 or Nessus takes place at all points, so we know that we are not introducing any vulnerabilities ..."* The adoption of automated testing tools in other companies is informed by the diverse capabilities of open-source frameworks such as Kali Linux. According to practitioner (CYBERFOUDco1_ADL1).

"We use an array of different tools for security vulnerability checks, most of which can be found in Unix ... Kali Linux is one which has a whole platter of tools in that to analyze and exploit software security issues..."

In standard software testing, GitHub is a common collaborative code hosting platform that allows co-located practitioners to work together on projects. Some practitioners prefer using specialized plug-in on the GitHub platform to perform vulnerability checks. According to practitioner (CRMcol_FSSD1) *"We use a GitHub plug-in called Snyk for vulnerability checks. Previously, we used Greekeeper but recently moved to Snyk because we felt it is a bit better..."* The GitHub platform has various features for things like code verification and modelling of threat actors. This is explained by practitioner (Finco1_SSE2) who said, *"Basically some tools are used for code verification from the security perspective and others for internal tasks to check and identify imposters ..."*.

There are certain practitioners that favour combining the use of certain testing tools for security checks on parts of their application like APIs with manual software testing. Postman is an API testing tool which enables the automating of various forms of tests such as functional tests, regression tests and end-to-end tests, among others. *"We use Postman to do certain checks on APIs ... we use that to set up automated tests to prevent human errors..."* (ITCONCcol_SDA). Moving to the implementation phase, (ITCONCcol_SDA) prefers to perform software test manually. *"I don't use any tools for security tests on codes because coding analysis needs to be done manually by going through the code and working that in..."*.

Practitioners involved in security testing who participated in this study discussed very little about the techniques they use for mitigating or managing risks during software testing. According to practitioner (CRMcol_FSSD1), *"We use slow increments and the maker checker approach to develop our projects... You are not allowed to develop, push, approve and merge your code all by yourself..."* Apart from (CRMcol_FSSD1), there are other practitioners that manage risk also by relaying on the iterative feature of agile software methods. *"The short lifecycle and iterative way of development minimizes the risk of project delay by been able to provide exactly what the customers requested"* (Finco1_SSE2). The second agile risk management technique described by practitioners in this study is a method where a company uses the developed software internally before pushing it out known as "Dogfooding".

"We dogfood a lot of our products internally... We have like a lot of Sales and Support Staff who use our products internally first before it is pushed out and that helps us mitigate risk..." (CRMcol_FSSD1).

4.2 Security Specialist Role

Typically, agile teams are composed of three roles which are product owner, scrum master and self-organizing team members. In this study, we have discovered another role known as the security specialist. *"In my organization we have an expert that handles issues related to security design and architecture and also responsible for implementing it..."* (CRMcol_FSSD1). The security specialist is responsible for handling all security related tasks, but their function sometimes overlaps with that of the product owner to ensure that the information systems development process does not impose any security risks. Practitioner (CYBERFcol_ADL1) mentioned that their security officer does more than just handling security but performs other tasks for the company. *"So, the security guy is also involved in software development ... the person does PR and some other assigned tasks for us..."*.

There are situations where a company has a dedicated team that handles all cyber-security related issues of the information systems development process. According to practitioner (Finco1_SSE2), *"we have a group of experts when it comes to security to act like internal hackers to try to expose any holes in the system..."*. Thus, security roles vary across different projects and organizations. During the data collection phase of this study, we found that a lot of decisions about security are mostly handled by those having security tasks assigned to them. According to practitioner (CYBERFco1_ADL1) *"Security is handled by ...... practitioners having job titles like security specialist..."*. While having a security specialist within the software development team is one way of doing it, in some other organizations all stakeholders are involved in security decision as explained by (ITSERVco1-COS1), *"All stakeholders are required, you got the Business, the Development Lead, Legal team to handle legal requirements that might need to be met..."* (ITSERVco1-COS1). Since security is not something done in isolation, it will be better done with all the key stakeholders. Security decisions are mostly considered as business decisions because there are some financial impacts to them.

At the security requirements gathering phase, a better way of developing secure application will be to involve all stakeholders. Therefore, all the stakeholders need to know the threats and vulnerabilities in their domain. Practitioner (ITSEVco1-VP-COS1) indicated that when he said:

> *"So, it's engaging the right stakeholders at the right time and it's not just a security talking to a techy and saying these are the requirements. It needs to be understood across the board..."*

At the design phase, the data collected did not point to an exclusive security role. However, the software security specialist and software developer roles traverse from the requirements to the release phases of the development lifecycle.

5 Discussion

The novel taxonomy developed in this study has categorized the security practices into roles, ceremonies, and artefacts. The taxonomy has helped to structure the identified secure agile practices. While our study identified eight security practices at the implementation phase, there is a published work that showed only three practices at the same phase [29]. Our taxonomy will help to improve organization's security activities as it encompasses different practices (roles, ceremonies & artefacts) rather than previous research endeavor which focused only on the security roles in a team [9].

5.1 Software Testing Methods Used in Practice (RQ1)

To answer the research question "How is software testing done in agile teams?", we found that almost all the practitioners use testing tools which were categorized as either security specialized or standard software tests. Only one practitioner stated his preference for manual software testing rather than using security test tools. Our study findings show that there is a consensus among the participants involved in our study on their use of automated testing tools. Thus, the findings reveal how practitioners have adopted different specialized testing tools to identify and prevent attacks to their software systems.

Comparing our findings with the literature, a positive security trend exists due to the extensive use of security tools and reliance on automation [8].

In practice, the agile testing quadrants developed by Crispin and Gregory is popularly used [27]. Our study findings have shown that software companies rely on two of the quadrants which focuses on manual testing and the use of testing tools. For the testing tools quadrant, some of the tests underneath it includes security, performance, or load and illity testing. While the manual testing quadrant has test such as user acceptance testing (UAT), usability and exploratory testing. However, none of the practitioners mentioned anything about adopting illity software testing or the tools used. Existing empirical studies have shown that practitioners heavily rely on specialized testing tools to verify developed software systems [8]. Other testing phase activities mentioned in literature include test cases, but penetration testing is adopted to a lesser degree [8]. However, practitioners involved in our study mentioned adopting specialized tools for security testing. This might be because penetration testing is becoming more common nowadays with the increased number of cyberattacks.

Apart from adopting automated tools, an existing study have emphasized the need to adopt risk management approaches to drive the security testing process [27]. While there is a need for further studies to understand how risk management techniques can be applied to security projects that have adopted agile methods, practitioners in this study only mentioned techniques such "dogfooding" and iterative development approach. The adopted techniques need to be properly understood and their structure well-conceptualized to protect against threats arising from risky activities.

5.2 Integration of Security Specialist Role into Agile Process (RQ2)

The second question posed in this study was to discover "How the software security specialist role can be integrated into agile process?", we discovered from the practitioner interviews conducted that security specialist are involved in different activities depending on their organization and operational environment. We have seen that organizations constrained by budget assign security duties to a single security personnel. Riisom et al. in [5] have however highlighted the drawback of the security specialist role as sometimes not involved in daily project activities and that other team members might not have the necessary skills to fix software security flaws. There are other software development companies in this study that instead have security teams composed of various roles responsible for managing project's security resources. While a security team ensures better management of security resources on one hand, additional roles increase project costs [26]. Backman in [6] showed the relationship between developer security awareness and their involvement in penetration testing activities. Since developers are assumed to have some security knowledge, adopting secure testing guidelines such as OWASP in addition to training can improve security knowledge levels of practitioners.

6   Conclusion

One of the objectives of agile methods is to improve quality and responsiveness during the development process. However, we have found there tends to be a gap between agile and security practitioners thinking. Our study has provided a taxonomy of agile security practices categorized into roles, ceremonies and artefacts and mapped onto the SDLC, which was derived from empirical practitioner interviews Our exploratory study comprised ten semi-structured, recorded, and transcribed interviews to better understand practitioner perceptions of agile security issues. Our study made three main findings as follows.

Firstly, we were surprised to discover that our taxonomy shows that there are more artefacts than roles and ceremonies. We identified three ceremonies which included security sprint meeting, secure APIs, and security retrospectives. We further identified two security roles which are the security specialist and penetration tester. The five artefacts we identified are: security backlog documentation, software security baseline standards, security test plan templates, information security and security audit checklists.

Secondly, our study discovered that more security practices identified fit onto the implementation and verification phases of the SDLC. Again, we were surprised that the practitioners in our study did not discuss more practices in the requirements and design stages. This finding is different to what was discovered in previous literature where more security practices fitted onto the requirements and implementation phases.

Thirdly, it is important to point out the importance attached to using testing tools by practitioners. Given that software companies in the UK used specialized automated tools to test for security and software performance, there was only one practitioner that expressed his preference for manual software testing. Our study also highlighted iterative development and dogfooding as the techniques used by practitioners for risk management. Finally, this study confirms earlier studies that mention the use of iterative development by practitioners for risk management and mitigation. We also identified an interesting practice where a group of practitioners are sometimes assigned the task of using the software in-house before pushing it out to clients commonly referred to as "dogfooding".

In the future, we propose to expand the study beyond UK practitioners to examine a developing country context specifically Nigeria. We aim to empirically explore agile security practices and the software security testing techniques adopted by practitioners in Nigeria. We plan to evaluate the security testing techniques identified to support the adoption of secure agile practices for the Nigerian software industry.

References

1. Dingsøyr, T., Nerur, S., Balijepally, V., Moe, N.B.: A decade of agile methodologies: towards explaining agile software development. J. Syst. Softw. **85**, 1213–1221 (2012)
2. Bass, J.M.: Artefacts and agile method tailoring in large-scale offshore software development programmes. Inf. Softw. Technol. **75**, 1–16 (2016)
3. Baca, D., Carlsson, B.: Agile development with security engineering activities. In: International Conference on Software and Systems Process, pp. 149–158. Association for Computing Machinery (ACM), New York (2011)
4. Terpstra, E., Daneva, M., Wang, C.: Agile practitioners' understanding of security requirements: insights from a grounded theory analysis. In: 25th International Requirements Engineering Conference Workshops (REW), pp. 439–442. IEEE, Lisbon, Portugal (2017)

5. Riisom, K.R., Hubel, M.S., Alradhi, H.M., Nielsen, N.B., Kuusinen, K., Jabangwe, R.: Software security in agile software development: a literature review of challenges and solutions. In Proceedings of the 19th International Conference on Agile Software Development, pp. 1–5. ACM, Porto, Portugal (2018)

6. Backman, L.: Why is security still an issue? a study comparing developers' software security awareness to existing vulnerabilities in software applications. In: Research Thesis, Linkoping University, Linkoping, Sweden (2018)

7. Rindell, K., Hyrynsalmi, S., Leppänen, V.: Fitting security into agile software development. In: Research Anthology on Recent Trends, Tools, and Implications of Computer Programming, pp. 1026–1045. IGI Global (2021). https://doi.org/10.4018/978-1-7998-3016-0.ch047

8. Rindell, K., Ruohonen, J., Holvitie, J., Hyrynsalmi, S., Leppänen, V.: Security in agile software development: a practitioner survey. Inf. Soft. Technol **131**, 106488 (2020)

9. Baca, D., Boldt, M., Carlsson, B., Jacobsson, A.: A novel security-enhanced agile software development process applied in an industrial setting. In: 10th International Conference on Availability, Reliability and Security, pp. 11–19. IEEE, Toulouse, France (2015)

10. Villamizar, H., Kalinowski, M., Viana, M., Fern´andez, D.: A systematic mapping study on security in agile requirements engineering. In: 44th Euromicro Conference on Software Engineering and Advanced Applications (SEAA), pp. 454–461. IEEE, Prague, Czech Republic (2018). https://doi.org/10.1109/SEAA.2018.00080

11. Bartsch, S.: Practitioners' perspectives on security in agile development. In: Sixth International Conference on Availability, Reliability and Security, pp. 479–484. IEEE, Vienna, Austria (2011)

12. Oueslati, H., Rahman, M.M., ben Othmane, L., Ghani, I., Arbain, A.F.B.: Evaluation of the challenges of developing secure software using the agile approach. Int. J. Secure Softw. Eng. (IJSSE), **7**(1), 17–37 (2016)

13. Amoroso, E.: Recent progress in software security. IEEE Softw. 35(2), 11–13 (2018). https://doi.org/10.1109/MS.2018.1661316

14. McGraw, G.: Software Security: Building Security, 1st edn. Addison-Wesley Professional, Upper Saddle River, NJ (2006)

15. Von Solms, R., Van Niekerk, J.: From information security to cyber security. Comput. Secur. **38**, 97–102 (2013)

16. Stallings, W., Brown, L., Bauer, M.D., Bhattacharjee, A.K.: Computer security: principles and practice: pearson education upper saddle river. NJ, USA (2012)

17. Siavvas, M., Tsoukalas, D., Jankovic, M., Kehagias, D., Tzovaras, D.: Technical debt as an indicator of software security risk: a machine learning approach for software development enterprises. Enterp. Inf. Syst. J. **15**(9), 1–43 (2020)

18. Zhang, S., Caragea, D., Ou, X.: An empirical study on using the national vulnerability database to predict software vulnerabilities. In: Hameurlain, A., Liddle, S.W., Schewe, K.-D., Zhou, X. (eds.) DEXA 2011. LNCS, vol. 6860, pp. 217–231. Springer, Heidelberg (2011). https://doi.org/10.1007/978-3-642-23088-2_15

19. Howard, M., Lipner, S.: The Security Development Lifecycle, vol. 8. Microsoft Press, Redmond (2006)

20. Owasp Samm Project.: Software Assurance Maturity Model (SAMM): A guide to building security into software development - v1.5. Technical Report Version 1.5., p. 72 (2017). https://owaspsamm.org/

21. McGraw, G.: Software security and the building security in maturity model (BSIMM). J. Comput. Sci. Coll. **30**(3), 7–8 (2015)

22. Rindell, K., Ruohonen, J., Hyrynsalmi, S.: Surveying secure software development practices in finland. In: 13th International Conference on Availability, Reliability and Security, pp. 1-7. ACM, Hamburg, Germany (2018)

23. Rindell, K., Hyrynsalmi, S., Leppänen, V.: A comparison of security assurance support of agile software development methods. In: Proceedings of the 16th International Conference on Computer Systems and Technologies, pp. 61–68. ACM, Dublin, Ireland (2015)

24. Adolph, S., Hall, W., Kruchten, P.: Using grounded theory to study the experience of software development. Empirical Softw. Eng. **16**(4), 487–513 (2011)

25. Oueslati, H., Rahman, M.M., ben Othmane, L.: Literature review of the challenges of developing secure software using the agile approach. In: 10th International Conference on Availability, Reliability and Security, pp. 540–547. IEEE, Toulouse, France (2015)

26. Bansal, S.K., Jolly, A.: An encyclopedic approach for realization of security activities with agile methodologies. In: 5th International Conference - Confluence The Next Generation Information Technology Summit (Confluence), pp. 767–772. IEEE, Noida, India (2014)

27. Cruzes, D.S., Felderer, M., Oyetoyan, T.D., Gander, M., Pekaric, I.: How is security testing done in agile teams? a cross-case analysis of four software Teams. In: Baumeister, H., Lichter, H., Riebisch, M. (eds.) XP 2017. LNBIP, vol. 283, pp. 201–216. Springer, Cham (2017). https://doi.org/10.1007/978-3-319-57633-6_13

28. Felderer, M., Büchler, M., Johns, M., Brucker, A.D., Breu, R., Pretschner, A.: Chapter one - security testing: a survey. Adv. Comput. **101**, 1–51 (2016)

29. Bezerra, C.M.M., Sampaio, S.C.B., Marinho, M.L.M.: Secure agile software development: policies and practices for agile teams. In: Shepperd, M., Brito e Abreu, F., Rodrigues da Silva, A., Pérez-Castillo, R. (eds.) QUATIC 2020. CCIS, vol. 1266, pp. 343–357. Springer, Cham (2020). https://doi.org/10.1007/978-3-030-58793-2_28

30. Bass, J.M.: How product owner teams scale agile methods to large distributed enterprises. Empir. Softw. Eng. **20**(6), 1525–1557 (2015)

31. Glaser, B.G.: Theoretical Sensitivity: Advances in the Methodology of Grounded Theory 1978. Sociology Pr., New York (1967)

32. Corbin, J.M., Strauss, A.: Grounded theory research: procedures, canons, and evaluative criteria. Qual. Sociol. **13**(1), 3–21 (1990). https://doi.org/10.1007/BF00988593

33. Hutchison, A.J., Johnston, L.H., Breckon, J.D.: Using QSR-NVivo to facilitate the development of a grounded theory project: an account of a worked example. Int. J. Soc. Res. Methodol. **13**(4), 283–302 (2010)

34. Oates, B.J.: Researching information systems and computing. Sage (2005)

Innovative Research Projects

Increasing the Security of Smart Cities of the Future Thanks to UWB Technology

Krzysztof Hanzel$^{(\boxtimes)}$ ⓘ and Damian Grzechca ⓘ

Department of Electronics, Electrical Engineering and Microelectronics, Faculty of Automatic Control, Electronics and Computer Science, Silesian University of Technology, Akademicka 16, 44-100 Gliwice, Poland

{Krzysztof.Hanzel,Damian.Grzechca}@polsl.pl

Abstract. We expect many autonomous vehicles in the modern cities of the future. These, in order to ensure the safety of other road users, will have to be equipped with perception systems enabling the detection and identification of obstacles, and the determination of the resulting threat. Currently, these two key aspects are carried out by systems that properly deal with only one of them at a time. Therefore, the article presents the concept of using UWB (Ultra-wideband) technology as a component of the ADAS (Advanced Driver Assistance Systems) to detect and identify road users. The paper also presents a test of driving a car equipped with a UWB tag at city speeds. As a result, the accuracy of the acquired position that can be obtained in such conditions is presented. Then, the obtained data was filtered with the use of simple filters, and the obtained results indicate the possibility of a significant improvement in positioning accuracy.

Keywords: Smart city · Positioning · Ultra-wideband · Driving safety · Automotive

1 Introduction

One of the key tasks of automotive technology is constantly increasing the level of safety. Regardless of whether we are talking about seat belts invented already in the 70s or about the latest technological achievements based on artificial intelligence, we constantly increase its level. Work is currently underway on many systems aimed at improving the safety of not only the driver (who is often in a privileged position in relation to other road users), but also pedestrians, cyclists and, more and more often, people using electric personal transport devices. All these systems are based on the exchange of information using ADAS (Advanced Driver Assistance Systems), which plays a superior role over modern, electronic vehicles and ensures not only safety, but also increases the comfort of driving [1, 2]. As part of ADAS, these systems can use many methods of perception of the environment realized with the use of sensors such as radars and lidars [3, 4], wide-application vision cameras, MEMS or ultrasonic sensors [5]. But these are not all systems, because modern cars also have well-known consumer technologies such as Wi-Fi [6], Bluetooth, GPS, they have access to cellular networks [7], etc. All these systems

© Springer Nature Switzerland AG 2022
M. Themistocleous and M. Papadaki (Eds.): EMCIS 2021, LNBIP 437, pp. 585–596, 2022.
https://doi.org/10.1007/978-3-030-95947-0_41

are used to improve the safety and comfort of driving. Comfort is expressed in all systems that replace or relieve the driver (e.g. lane assistant or autonomous parking), while safety is often also understood as the implementation of activities that the driver would perform, but electronic systems will do it much faster and more reliably in situations where the person will either not notice the threat or their reaction time is too high.

2 Detection and Identification of the Environment

Ensuring safety in the context of a modern vehicle is therefore largely based on the perception of the vehicle's surroundings. The systems are designed to first detect what is around the car, and then identify this object. As in most cases, the systems deal with the first task almost flawlessly, so identification is still quite a challenge [4, 8]. This is due to their redundancy and concentration within the ADAS - in weather conditions where, for example, lidar is not able to make full perception [9] (e.g. in the case of fog that causes the laser beam to scatter), detection of objects can be provided by a radar, for which this obstacle is not a problem as opposed to, for example, physical obstructions through which the radar is unable to function. Similarly, in night conditions, the vision camera may not be able to see objects located several dozen or several hundred meters from the vehicle, but laser sensors can handle it flawlessly.

After the detection stage, it is necessary to identify, because otherwise the vehicle should behave when it is detected at the side of a hydrant, tree or substation, otherwise if it is a pedestrian who, in addition, moves towards the road (or worse, is on a collision trajectory with ours vehicle). This identification is carried out in various ways, but most of the latest systems, regardless of whether the input data are properly crafted video frames or, for example, a cloud of lidar points, use mechanisms based on artificial intelligence methods. These have the characteristic that they are characterized by a specified degree of accuracy. For example, we can get an object on the internal map of the vehicle that is 10% a tree, 20% a substation and 70% a human [10]. It is then that problems start to appear not only of a programming nature (to what extent this object threatens our trajectory of movement, should the car start emergency braking, should a manoeuvre be performed to avoid this object) but also of an ethical nature - from how many percent of a person cannot be hit whether an object tagged as a human should be prioritized by the system, or finally, in a crisis situation, save an object that is a human in 74% or focus only on an object that is represented in the system as a human 85%? Of course, you can consider a philosophical nature, but the priority action should be to make it possible to abandon such considerations.

Therefore, reliable identification, especially of safety-critical objects, is essential. As already noted, many modern cars are equipped with commercial systems such as Wi-Fi or Bluetooth, which each of us has in our smartphones. Their use in the case of identification could give a 100% result - Jack's iPhone moving along the road represents Jack - human identification in this case would be flawless. However, these systems - repeatedly considered in the context of positioning, have more disadvantages than advantages, and the context of their use - mainly for data transmission with the highest possible bandwidth, and constraints resulting from energy performance (e.g. signal power limitation) actually prevents certain localization in time real. Of course, these systems are used as, for example, GPS assistants in metropolises where the satellite signal is limited due to high buildings, or in places where this signal is completely unavailable (underground car parks, tunnels), but it is only used for a rough location - determining the street where the vehicle is located, an interpretation in the form of a heatmap, suggesting in which direction to go, etc. Although the latest proposed solutions [11, 12] in the field of positioning using Wi-Fi already achieve an accuracy of around 1 meter, they are subject to a number of factors - e.g. a large number of reference points, IPS conditions or offline handling process, which is necessary to create the basis on which the system is later based.

3   Proposal to Use UWB System

The situation would seem to be a stalemate, but the UWB system, which has been developed for about 10 years, may become a solution to this problem. This system, based on broadband data transmission, enables both precise location [13] (with an accuracy of several centimeters) and identification [14], and its low energy consumption additionally ensures the possibility of implementing and tagging all important elements of infrastructure or vehicles [15]. The parameters of the system used by our team based on the DWM1000 module by DecaWave are presented in Table 1.

Table 1. DWM1000 main configuration parameters.

Property	Value
Frame length	27 octets
Preamble length	256 symbols
Transmission channel	3
Baud rate	6.8 Mbps
Transmitter antenna delay	16418*15.65 ps
Receiver antenna delay	16418*15.65 ps

The growing popularity of this solution can be noticed thanks to the more and more common implementation of this technology in consumer electronics devices - the latest phones from companies such as Apple [16] (that are also compatible with the latest DecaWave systems) or smartphones based on the Android [17] operating system already allow you to use this technology. At the same time, implementations using UWB are appearing in places such as the New York subway or cars of BMW or Volkswagen groups. This system is also already used in medical applications, e.g. to monitor the rehabilitation process [18]. Also, more and more companies are presenting locating devices based on this technology [19]. Unfortunately, the use of UWB in automotive applications is so far slight. The first autonomously moving platforms are being created [20], but so far there are few uses in OPS conditions [21].

The basic unit of the UWB system is based on the reference points and tag (example photo of used in research device shown on Fig. 1).

Fig. 1. Elements of the UWB localization system. Hardware of the node (DecaWave DWM1000 with STM32 Microcontroller).

In the case of standard positioning in urban traffic, the minimum number of anchors is 3. Using packet exchange between devices (e.g. using the TWR method which allows to receive data without the need to synchronize the device clocks – principles of communication shown on Fig. 2), the distance between them is determined.

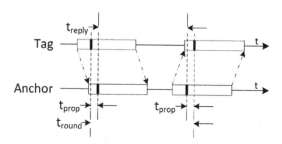

Fig. 2. Communication between UWB Anchor and Tag

The obtained wave propagation time – t_{prop}, was converted to the distance between nodes – tag, and particular anchor. The time of flight can be calculated with the use of the (1). When the time of flight was calculated, the distance between tag and particular anchor could be calculated with the use of the (2).

$$t_{prop} = \frac{t_{round} - t_{reply}}{2} \tag{1}$$

$$d = c \cdot t_{prop} \tag{2}$$

where: d – the distance between nodes; c – the speed of electromagnetic wave propagation; and t_{prop} – the wave propagation time between nodes.

On the basis of the distance between nodes, the position in relation to the reference point is determined using the trilateration algorithm.

The principle of operation flows from the fundamental geometry and the main idea is depicted in the Fig. 3 [22]. There were three reference points (anchors) which were selected from all available, for example $A1$, $A2$ and $A3$. The position of the anchors were well known in three dimensions $A1 \rightarrow (x_1, y_1, z_1)$, $A2 \rightarrow (x_2, y_2, z_2)$, $A3 \rightarrow (x_3, y_3, z_3)$ as well as distance from tag to particular anchor d_{A1}, d_{A2} and d_{A3}.

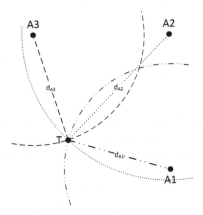

Fig. 3. Trilateration – an example of the operation given for the point - the tag T, and for the three distances d_{A1}, d_{A2} and d_{A3} from the three reference points (anchors) $A1$, $A2$ and $A3$

Assuming a scenario in which the reference points are on the vehicle and the marker is, for example, our smartphone equipped with UWB technology, we are able to precisely and in real time determine the position and identify the object representing it. One of the innovative solutions is also the ability to monitor the speed and trajectory of the vehicle and support for autonomous driving, especially in cities where autopilot systems must register and process many more signals than, for example, on highways. As mentioned earlier, a very important aspect is also the possibility of identification, which takes place in the UWB system at the stage of exchanging position messages. The information contained therein may be limited to a simple device identifier (where the rest of the data is downloaded from the network), but they can also provide important information both about the object passed by (dimensions, potential danger), but also about the immediate vicinity, road infrastructure or road conditions [14].

4   Conducted Research and Obtained Results

An example may be a study in which we set up the UWB system based on the DWM1000 chips from decaWave on a square plan with a side of 5 meters. This arrangement reflects an example of the intersection of two streets with one lane (2.5 m) in each direction and traffic light poles in which UWB modules can be installed. Then we made test drives by car at different speeds encountered in city traffic (speeds from 10 to 60 km/h presented in the Table 2). The result of the study was a trajectory showing the vehicle's passage and the speed with which it was moving on a given road section.

Table 2. Speed of the object in different measuring series

Series	Speed	
	[km/h]	[m/s]
R1	10	2.78
R2	20	5.56
R3	30	8.33
R4	40	11.11
R5	50	13.89
R6	60	16.67

On the basis of the collected data, the mentioned before trilateration were carried out, and then the resulting paths were marked on the map An example of a straight line trip by a car at a speed of 10 km/h, subjected to trilateration is presented in Fig. 4.

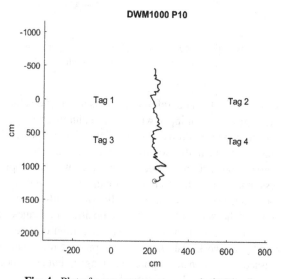

Fig. 4. Plot of a car passage at a speed of 10 km/h

For the obtained data, we performed an analysis in the form of determining the RMSE (Root Mean Square Error) given by formula (3) for the position in the both X and Y axis and the maximum deviation from the point on the travel axis (4). Both the path and the error of the journey were determined based on the ISO/IEC 18305 standard.

$$RMSE_P = \sqrt{\frac{1}{N} \sum_{i=1}^{N} (x_i - \hat{x}_i)^2 + (y_i - \hat{y}_i)^2} \qquad (3)$$

$$MAX_P = \max_{i \in N} \left(\sqrt{(x_i - \hat{x}_i)^2 + (y_i - \hat{y}_i)^2} \right) \qquad (4)$$

The obtained results for all series are presented in Table 3.

Table 3. Results of statistical measures for raw data

Statistical measures	Series					
	R1	R2	R3	R4	R5	R6
MAX [cm]	75.76	42.06	47.91	39.28	40.95	45.33
RMSE [cm]	30.58	24.05	21.90	18.62	18.17	15.92

On the basis of the obtained results, it can be concluded that the UWB system for the proposed model of traffic at city speed while traveling along a straight line represents an average accuracy of 21.54 cm, which in the authors' opinion is a sufficient value in city traffic to increase the safety of pedestrians and other road users. In addition, it is also worth noting that the average value of the RMSE parameter for data from the UWB system decreases with increasing speed. It may be caused by the concentration of points around the axis of the passage due to certain characteristics of the traffic.

The next step that was checked was the filtration using two methods - a median filter and filtration using a moving average. The data was filtered with a filter window from 1 (meaning no filtration) through odd values (3, 5, 7, 9, 11, 13) to 15 (which in this case was taken as the largest filtration). In the case of a median filtration with window size k of x_i sample, where $i = 1, \ldots, k$ and $x_i \leq x_{i+1}$ is presented in (5).

$$med(x_i) = \begin{cases} x_{j+1} & \text{for } k = 2j + 1 \\ \frac{1}{2}(x_j + x_{j+1}) & \text{for } k = 2j \end{cases} \tag{5}$$

In this case – as mentioned before – the k value was always an odd number, so the form for $k = 2j + 1$ was used.

The second type of filtration that was used to process data from the UWB system was the average filter. The task of this type of filtration is to reduces the amplitude of any random outliers, which we noted in the raw data (6).

$$avg(x_i) = \frac{1}{k} \sum_{\substack{j = -\lfloor \frac{k}{2} \rfloor \wedge \\ j \in \mathbb{Z}}}^{\lfloor \frac{k}{2} \rfloor} x_{i+j} \tag{6}$$

After the filtration with the median filter, the RMSE parameter values presented in Table 4 were obtained.

Table 4. RMSE values for all series after median filtration [cm]

Filter window	Series					
	R1	R2	R3	R4	R5	R6
1	27,11	19,61	17,90	16,12	15,85	15,62
3	27,04	19,46	17,61	15,50	15,40	14,86
5	26,99	19,24	17,24	15,31	15,24	14,26
7	26,90	19,04	16,92	14,92	15,10	13,99
9	26,88	18,92	16,66	14,48	15,01	13,83
11	26,83	18,79	16,41	14,07	14,77	13,56
13	26,66	18,71	16,13	13,91	14,72	13,51
15	26,66	18,62	**15,89**	**13,69**	14,68	**13,24**

For filtration with the use of the median filter, the best results were obtained for series 3, 4 and 6. The obtained improvement was on average 1.57 cm, which is 8%. The next step was to perform the moving average filtration, the results of which are presented in Table 5.

Table 5. RMSE values for all series after moving average filtration [cm]

Filter window	Series					
	R1	R2	R3	R4	R5	R6
1	27,11	19,61	17,90	16,12	15,85	15,62
3	26,92	19,07	17,08	14,70	14,79	13,74
5	26,77	18,68	16,43	13,69	14,29	12,37
7	26,62	18,31	15,74	12,70	13,90	11,19
9	26,48	17,93	15,07	11,72	13,63	10,20
11	26,36	17,53	14,45	10,81	13,40	9,53
13	26,24	17,12	13,92	9,98	13,17	9,13
15	26,12	16,71	13,44	**9,22**	12,92	**8,87**

The results for the moving average filtration turned out to be better than for the median filtration. The best results were obtained this time for series 4 and 6. The obtained improvement was on average 4.16 cm, which is more than 2.5 times better than the median filtration result. This is a 22% improvement over the raw data. The results of the filtration were also presented graphically on Fig. 5.

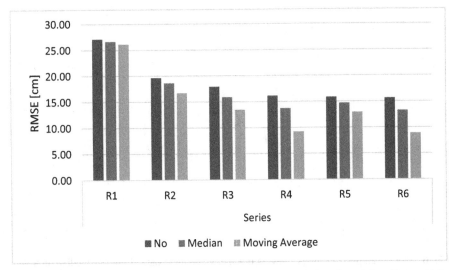

Fig. 5. Comparison of RMSE values for raw and filtered data using the median filter and the moving average.

The graph shows that on average, with the increase in speed, data filtration allowed to obtain better results (lower value of the RMSE parameter). Regardless of the data series, it can be noticed that the most effective filtration is using a moving average (in some cases, for example, the R6 series after filtration, the data was improved by almost 50% – a decrease in RMSE from 15.62 cm to 8.87 cm). It is also worth noting that the data obtained from the UWB system are obtained with a frequency of over 66 Hz, which allows for free filtration and further processing, which is planned as part of further research on the use of UWB technology in the automotive industry by the author. The next figure (Fig. 6) shows a plot of an exemplary data series showing the data before and after filtration using the two mentioned methods.

The presented figure shows how the filtration affects the data, especially the outliers, visible around the value of -200 cm in relation to the reference point spacing and around the value of 800–1000 cm. The currently used filtering with a window 15 allows for a significant improvement, but it should be borne in mind that the use of this type of filtration (filters with a sliding window) carries the risk of data deformation, especially if the data acquisition frequency is low and the dynamics of movement is very high.

Based on the currently conducted research, it can also be concluded that the frequencies of data acquisition from the newer system – based on DWM3000 systems are much higher, which will allow for even more frequent updating of position information in the ADAS system. This entails the ability to precisely track the paths of objects' movement and predict their possible impact on the trajectory on which the vehicle is moving. This is important from the point of view of autonomous driving algorithms (route planning and generating responses to emerging threats), but also increasing safety in classic cars, especially in conditions where classic systems are not able to predict a threat (e.g. a situation in which an impending the human is obscured by another obstacle).

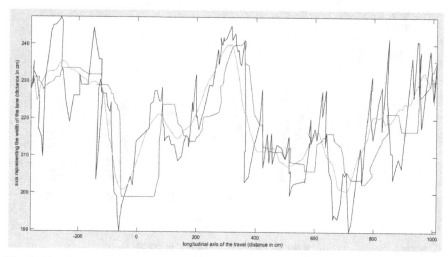

Fig. 6. Plot of sample data series showing raw data (blue line), data filtered by median filter with window 15 (orange line) and filtered data with moving average, also with window 15 (yellow line).

It is also worth noting that the ability to identify objects with such accuracy as the position will allow for more reliable driving with the use of autonomous systems – having the guarantee that the object passed by is – for example – a tagged hydrant, we are much more sure that it will not enter the road soon, creating a threat that would have to be skipped.

5   Conclusion

Based on the study and the articles cited, it can be concluded that UWB technology can become a driving force for improving safety based on positioning with the identification of road users. The obtained accuracy of about 20 cm allows you to avoid collisions involving, for example, pedestrians through their earlier detection and reactions of safety systems. Also, appropriate filtration of the data obtained from the UWB system is possible due to the frequency of operation, however, one should take into account the characteristics of the traffic. The filtration proposed in the article allowed to improve the RMSE parameter by over 20%. Based on the conducted research, it was shown that the best results were obtained for filtration using a moving average, where an improvement in position accuracy was observed with the increase of the window. Certain identification also makes it possible to increase safety, thanks to the possibility of adapting the algorithms to the potential mobility of other road users.

It is also worth emphasizing that even taking into account the maximum distances of the UWB system, it is a serious competition in terms of accuracy for other commercial systems that enable reliable identification (such as Wi-Fi or Bluetooth). Further plans for the development of the system are largely related to the implementation of the above solutions on DWM3000 devices - these, thanks to compatibility with devices such as iPhones, will enable the preparation of many real scenarios (e.g. based on the model of pedestrian crossings, intersections, etc.

Acknowledgement. This research was partially funded by European Social Funds, project no POWR.03.02.00–00-I007/17–00 "CyPhiS – the program of modern PhD studies in the field of Cyber-Physical Systems"; Polish Ministry of Science and Higher Education by Young Researchers funds of Department of Electronics, Electrical Engineering and Microelectronics, Faculty of Automatic Control, Electronics and Computer Science, Silesian University of Technology.

References

1. Ziebinski, A., Cupek, R., Erdogan, H., Waechter, S.: A survey of ADAS technologies for the future perspective of sensor fusion. In: Nguyen, N.-T., Manolopoulos, Y., Iliadis, L., Trawiński, B. (eds.) ICCCI 2016. LNCS (LNAI), vol. 9876, pp. 135–146. Springer, Cham (2016). https://doi.org/10.1007/978-3-319-45246-3_13
2. Ziebinski, A., Cupek, R., Grzechca, D., Chruszczyk, L.: Review of advanced driver assistance systems (ADAS). Presented at the (2017). https://doi.org/10.1063/1.5012394
3. Rasshofer, R.H., Gresser, K.: Automotive radar and lidar systems for next generation driver assistance functions. ResearchGate. **3**, 205–209 (2005). https://doi.org/10.5194/ars-3-205-2005
4. Fan, H., Yao, W., Tang, L.: Identifying man-made objects along urban road corridors from mobile LiDAR data. IEEE Geosci. Remote Sens. Lett. **11**, 950–954 (2014). https://doi.org/10.1109/LGRS.2013.2283090
5. Grzechca, D., Paszek, K.: Short-term positioning accuracy based on mems sensors for smart city solutions. Pol. Acad. Sci. Comm. Metrol. Sci. Instrum. (2019). https://doi.org/10.24425/mms.2019.126325
6. Mok, E., Retscher, G.: Location determination using WiFi fingerprinting versus WiFi tri-lateration. J. Locat. Based Serv. **1**, 145–159 (2007). https://doi.org/10.1080/17489720701781905
7. Combain Mobile AB: CPS - Combain Positioning Service. https://combain.com. Accessed 08 July 2017
8. Deilamsalehy, H., Havens, T.C.: Sensor fused three-dimensional localization using IMU, camera and LiDAR. In: 2016 IEEE SENSORS, pp. 1–3 (2016) https://doi.org/10.1109/ICSENS.2016.7808523
9. Halimeh, J.C., Roser, M.: Raindrop detection on car windshields using geometric-photometric environment construction and intensity-based correlation. In: 2009 IEEE Intelligent Vehicles Symposium. pp. 610–615 (2009). https://doi.org/10.1109/IVS.2009.5164347
10. Constandache, I., Bao, X., Azizyan, M., Choudhury, R.R.: Did you see bob?: human localization using mobile phones. In: Proceedings of the Sixteenth Annual International Conference on Mobile Computing and Networking, pp. 149–160. ACM, New York (2010). https://doi.org/10.1145/1859995.1860013
11. Ninh, D.B., He, J., Trung, V.T., Huy, D.P.: An effective random statistical method for Indoor Positioning System using WiFi fingerprinting. Future Gener. Comput. Syst. **109**, 238–248 (2020). https://doi.org/10.1016/j.future.2020.03.043
12. Qin, F., Zuo, T., Wang, X.: CCpos: WiFi fingerprint indoor positioning system based on CDAE-CNN. Sensors. **21**, 1114 (2021). https://doi.org/10.3390/s21041114
13. Grzechca, D., et al.: How accurate can UWB and dead reckoning positioning systems be? comparison to SLAM using the RPLidar system. Sensors. **20**, 3761 (2020). https://doi.org/10.3390/s20133761

14. Hanzel, K., Paszek, K., Grzechca, D.: The influence of the data packet size on positioning parameters of UWB system for the purpose of tagging smart city infrastructure (2020). https://doi.org/10.24425/BPASTS.2020.134173

15. Darif, A., Saadane, R., Aboutajdine, D.: Energy consumption of IR-UWB based WSN in a start topology. In: 2014 International Conference on Multimedia Computing and Systems (ICMCS), pp. 663–667 (2014). https://doi.org/10.1109/ICMCS.2014.6911296

16. Zafar, R.: iPhone 11 Has UWB With U1 Chip - Preparing Big Features For Ecosystem. https://wccftech.com/iphone-11-u1-chip-uwb/. Accessed 13 Apr 2021

17. Google has added an Ultra-wideband (UWB) API in Android. https://www.xda-developers.com/google-adding-ultra-wideband-uwb-api-android/. Accessed 13 Apr 2021

18. Grzechca, D., et al.: Monitoring the Gait process during the rehabilitation of patients using computer vision techniques and UWB technology. In: Themistocleous, M., Papadaki, M. (eds.) EMCIS 2019. LNBIP, vol. 381, pp. 419–437. Springer, Cham (2020). https://doi.org/10.1007/978-3-030-44322-1_31

19. UWB Indoor-Localization and Tracking shown at CES 2020 – YouTube. https://www.youtube.com/watch?v=KWf9fcx26wg. Accessed 14 June 2020

20. She, L., Zhang, Y., Wu, S., Zhang, M.: Design of auto cruise system for robots based on UWB with Kalman filtering. In: 2020 7th International Conference on Information Science and Control Engineering (ICISCE), pp. 1822–1826 (2020). https://doi.org/10.1109/ICISCE50968.2020.00358

21. Paszek, K., Grzechca, D., Tomczyk, M., Marciniak, A.: UWB positioning system with the support of MEMS sensors for indoor and outdoor environment. J. Commun. 15, 511–518 (2020). https://doi.org/10.12720/jcm.15.6.511-518

22. Norrdine, A.: An algebraic solution to the multilateration problem (2015). https://www.researchgate.net/publication/275027725_An_Algebraic_Solution_to_the_Multilateration_Problem, https://doi.org/10.13140/RG.2.1.1681.3602

Exploring the Impacts of Artificial Intelligence (AI) Implementation at Individual and Team Levels: A Case Study in the UAE Government Sector

Aisha Al Ali and Sulafa Badi[✉]

Faculty of Business and Law, The British University in Dubai, Dubai, UAE
2016156044@student.buid.ac.ae, Sulafa.badi@buid.ac.ae

Abstract. Despite the growth of Artificial Intelligence (AI) implementation in operational workplace processes, there is limited understanding of its effects at the micro-individual and meso-team levels in government sector organisations. This study examines the impacts of implementing AI within a single case study of a governmental entity in the United Arab Emirates (UAE). Qualitative data was collected through semi-structured interviews with 15 participants and analysed using thematic analysis. The findings identify AI implementation as an incremental process requiring organisational leaders' adequate understanding of change management. AI has a considerable influence on the individual as it improves the ability of employees to carry out their work and increases their autonomy, competence, relatedness and ultimately productivity. It also enhanced team performance through efficient team communication and cooperative decision-making. The findings add to our understanding of the effects of AI implementation at the individual and team levels and signal the need for organisations to embrace change management approaches to support the transition to AI-enabled operations.

Keywords: AI · Implementation · Individual · Team · Workplace · Operational · Processes

1 Introduction

With the increasing digital transformation in 21st century organisations, Artificial Intelligence (AI) has continued to gain significance within the workplace. AI has allowed performing tasks using machines rather than entirely depending on humans, increasing efficiency and reducing the variability of products and services (Coombs et al. 2017; Bruun and Duka 2018). AI is a modern technology that has prompted an increase in scholarly research on its development and deployment inside organisations (Shabbir and Anwer 2015; Skilton 2017). However, limited studies have explored the impact of AI implementation in operational workplace processes at the micro- individual and meso-team levels. Success within the workplace largely depends on understanding the impact of AI and related aspects applied at individual and team levels, thus ensuring

© Springer Nature Switzerland AG 2022
M. Themistocleous and M. Papadaki (Eds.): EMCIS 2021, LNBIP 437, pp. 597–613, 2022.
https://doi.org/10.1007/978-3-030-95947-0_42

that needs at both levels are well met (Chowdhury 2014). Therefore, in-depth analysis into AI at the individual and team level will provide organisations with the opportunity to develop necessary motivational strategies to aid in successful organisational performance (Shabbir and Anwer 2015). Hence, the main research questions that underpin this study are:

- What are the impacts of AI implementation at the micro-individual level?
- What are the impacts of AI implementation at the meso-team level?

An exploratory approach is adopted within a single case study of a governmental entity in the United Arab Emirates (UAE). The governmental organization pioneered the implementation of AI in its operational processes utilising AI cognitive computing system technology, namely the IBM Watson. A total of 15 individual employees working independently or in teams were involved in the study through semi-structured interviews. The study findings make several contributions to the knowledge of AI implementation and its influence in the workplace at individual and team levels. First, the study contributes to the understanding of how AI implementation contributes to the motivation of employees in the organisation, particularly how the AI re-shapes employee's autonomy, competence, and relatedness and ultimately productivity. Second, the study also underlines how AI enhances team effectiveness through increased communication and cooperative decision making. Finally, the study develops strategic guidelines on how AI implementation could be supported and challenges reduced through increased understanding of change management, particularly change implementation stages and tactics to reduce employee resistance to change.

2   AI Implementation in Organisations

AI is a field of study that describes the capacity within machines to learn in a manner similar to human capacity (Alsedrah 2017). AI can imitate human intelligence, solve problems, and to an extent, make decisions. AI software is inserted into computers and robots, enabling them to develop a thinking ability. Accordingly, it is expected that AI can undertake necessary tasks without any errors (Shabbir and Anwer 2015). AI can conduct various forms of cognitive tasks that can spread over several fields running based on human attributes. It considers such fields as those requiring complex communication and image recognition (Coombs et al. 2017). In this case, AI can reproduce the human reasoning capacity in a fast and flawless manner.

There are several approaches to AI implementation in the workplace, thus resulting in the transformation of performance in organisations (Shabbir and Anwer 2015; Claudé and Combe 2018). The application of AI in the workplace has mainly been influenced by how this technology can quickly and rapidly handle repetitive and mundane tasks (Habeeb 2017). An example of such tasks is handling frequently asked questions by customers using chatbots (Habeeb 2017). The significance of AI is that it can free up employees' time to deal with more complex tasks and thus produce more efficiency in operations (Claudé and Combe 2018). In such a manner, AI makes it possible for modern human resources to focus on those parts of their work that are the most engaging

(Claudé and Combe 2018). This transformation takes place at a pace that makes organisations more productive and effective (Claudé and Combe 2018). Further applications of AI in the workplace also relate to receiving real-time insight (Ernst et al. 2018). It is a significant application because the current times are characterised by changing trends and customer expectations that require organisations to have data-driven insight to keep up with these changes (Shabbir and Anwer 2015). Accordingly, AI has been beneficial in improving the responsiveness to customer queries and enhancing the customer experience.

However, it is noted in the literature by Shabbir and Anwer (2015) that AI implementation is not an easy process. Organisations must be prepared for the disruption that will come about because of its implementation. Some of the challenges experienced in AI implementation include; lack of algorithmic transparency, lack of trust for AI among employees, and misunderstandings of AI because of its complex nature (Reim et al. 2020). Other challenges are privacy and data protection issues, cybersecurity vulnerabilities, adverse effects on workers such as loss of jobs, and intellectual property issues (Rodrigues 2020). Indeed, while AI as a disruptive technology has gained considerable significance in the operations of organisations today, there remains little understanding of this technology and its impacts on operational workplace processes at the individual and team levels (Shabbir and Anwer 2015; Claudé and Combe 2018; Smids et al. 2020). At the individual level, there remains a paucity in addressing AI's challenges, including job loss and replacement and the loss of human interaction. For instance, there have been limited explanations of how AI impacts an employee's motivation and skill development and how AI reshapes social relationships within teams (Smids et al. 2020). Therefore, AI impacts at micro-individual and meso-team levels require sufficient attention of the scholarly community to aid successful implementation.

3   Research Method

The study adopts an interpretive research philosophy in which the researcher sees reality exclusively via social construction. The study is qualitative and inductive, beginning with observations and searching for patterns from observations and coming up with relevant explanations (Creswell 2014). This research adopted a single case study design approach based on the uniqueness of the case study and its ability to offer an in-depth understanding of the phenomenon studied (Yin 2003). The case study explored the implementation of AI in a governmental organisation in the UAE. The case study organisation forms a rich context of a workplace whereby AI is implemented successfully and provides an opportunity to analyse early adopters of AI. Several AI technologies were adopted, including IBM's Watson, which combines Natural Language Processing (NLP), Machine Learning (ML) and various forms of machine vision techniques to recognise a large amount of data and undertake communication in the natural language (Claudé and Combe 2018). In the context of the case study organisation, AI is used to deliver integrated government services as digital bundles without having citizens physically visit government offices. Through the DubaiNow App, citizens can easily utilise various services such as utilities, health, residency, business, education, security and justice. The study participants were mainly drawn from the case study organisation and included 15 employees directly involved with AI work-related processes. The study participants were drawn from different departments, including the Services Center, the App Development Center, and Data Management Department. See Table 1 for details of the case study participants.

Table 1. Case study participants

Participant (no.)	Age range	Gender	Job title and department
Participant 1	25–30	Male	Employee – Services Center
Participant 2	30–35	Female	Employee – App Development Center
Participant 3	20–25	Male	Employee – Data Management Department
Participant 4	25–30	Male	Employee – Services Center
Participant 5	25–30	Female	Employee – App Development Center
Participant 6	30–35	Male	Employee - Services Center
Participant 7	35–40	Female	Senior Manager – Data Management Department
Participant 8	40–45	Male	Employee – Services Center
Participant 9	25–30	Female	Employee – Services Center
Participant 10	30–35	Female	Senior Manager – Data Management Department
Participant 11	45–50	Male	Employee - App Development Center
Participant 12	35–40	Male	Employee - App Development Center
Participant 13	40–45	Male	Middle-level Manager - Services Center
Participant 14	25–30	Female	Employee - App Development Center
Participant 15	25–30	Male	Employee - App Development Center

Data was collected through semi-structured interviews. An interview protocol was developed to guide data collection and allowed the researcher to ask more detailed questions (Halcomb and Hickman 2015). The interview questions explored how AI was implemented in the organisation and how AI impacted the participant's work at the individual and team levels. In instances where the questions were not clear, the researcher was able to clarify and provide further explanations. Through interviews, the researcher was able to weigh the authenticity of the responses based on the participants' facial expressions and their moods (Creswell 2014), thus supporting the validity of the study's contextual data. The textual data were subsequently analysed through thematic content analysis by following four steps: creating a data repository, developing initial codes, analysing the coded data, and ultimately making conclusions based on the coded data. The emergent codes from the key themes of the study will be presented in the next section to offer insights into the major aspects of how AI was implemented in the case study organisation and how AI impacted the participants work at the individual and team levels.

4 Case Study Findings

4.1 AI Implementation in the Case Study Organisation

There were several drivers for AI implementation in the case study organisation, as listed in Table 2. Participants viewed AI implementation as necessary in the current business environment, enabling success by improving business capabilities and meeting strategic business objectives. AI also created an innovative work environment through automation of business processes, accuracy in data analysis, and more engagement with employees and customers. AI is also perceived as a technology that acts as a road map to support data sharing in the organisation. AI implementation was also driven by the vision of Sheikh Rashid Al Maktoum, the ruler of Dubai, to make Dubai the happiest city in the world. AI is, hence, a technological initiative to translate this vision by incorporating AI into the customers' services. AI implementation was also seen as a means through which Dubai can gain regional influence through AI leadership. AI is also espoused to increase employee productivity and efficiency, increasing customer satisfaction ultimately. As participant No. 4 noted:

"There are various benefits such as it will surely enhance the productivity of the workers, and it also provides a solution to the intense problems of the organisation. Due to an increase in efficiency, customer satisfaction is also increased" (Participant No. 4)

Table 2. Drivers of AI implementation in the case study organisation

Drivers of AI implementation	Example statement quotes
AI as a 'necessity in the current business environment	*"Artificial Intelligence is the need of the current environment. I am well aware that my organisation is highly focused on the establishment and development of AI-based programs. Not only because it is the current need but also because it has reshaped the business. It has brought success in the organisation."(participant No. 2)* *"The organisation is looking for innovation and development. In addition, the advancement of technology and the invention of systems drive organisations to implement AI and remain competent." (Participant No. 10)*
AI improving business capabilities	*I think my company has introduced AI implementation to improve business capabilities with the help of technology advancement. I think it is to support the business by automation of business processes, accuracy in data analysis and more engagement with employees and customers." (Participant No. 13)*

(continued)

Table 2. (*continued*)

Drivers of AI implementation	Example statement quotes
AI enabling regional leadership	*"The minister of UAE wants to implement the AI technologies at a practical level. This is a major topic of discussion at the world summit in Dubai. The minister of artificial intelligence considers that an agile approach for adopting AI can help a government to acquire the position of leadership in the region. According to the minister, the Al Olama government wants to become a capital of AI in services and Government sector organisation in the coming ten years." (Participant No. 3)*
AI as an enabler of data sharing	*"Since we are working in a data-sharing team, we work for providing the guidelines for data sharing toolkit in the application of smart Dubai. Data sharing is the backbone of AI, and without a particular road map on data sharing, AI will not be successful." (Participant No. 1)* *"Currently, our department work with feedback from the operations department about the problems that they are facing daily while sharing the data on the application. We have designed a data-sharing toolkit which we keep on updating according to the requirement of the addition of new information". (Participant No. 1)*
AI enabling efficiency and leading to customer satisfaction	*"The managerial body of my organisation is intended to adopt and upgrade the artificial intelligence in the organisation. There are various benefits, such as it will surely enhance the productivity of the workers, and it also provides a solution to the intense problems of the organisation. Due to an increase in efficiency, customer satisfaction is also increased." (Participant No. 4)* *"There are different advantages of AI, such as it will certainly increase the employees' efficiency, and it also try to find solutions to the organisation's strenuous complications. Customer satisfaction is also enhanced due to an increase in workers' efficiency." (Participant No. 4)* *"My organisation has used step by step method to implement AI in the organisation. The purpose of adopting AI in an organisation is to increase efficiency. It will enable the organisation to increase the overall efficiency." (participant No. 11)* *" Therefore, the execution of AI will positively contribute to increased performance and productivity. The AI will enable the organisation to have the creation of new roles enhance compliance and manage risk."(participant No. 8)*

AI implementation in the case study organisation was executed through multiple stages involving key departments and other stakeholders, as explained in Table 3. The early stages involved gaining insight into the technology and its implementation. AI implementation was seen as an incremental improvement process with small steps rather than a radical transformation of the overall operational processes. Several measures have been put in place to assist employees working with AI. One of these tactics is collaborating with technology companies to facilitate the training of employees. Training employees on how to work with AI in the organisation was seen as an effective tactic that allowed employees to work with the technology adequately. As participant No. 6 commented:

> *"My organisation has taken great measures with respect to the introduction and implementation of various practices of AI in place. The most beneficial and useful practice that I feel is that my organisation provides training beforehand before any new technology is implemented in the organisation." (Participant No. 6)*

In terms of employee resistance to change, study participants did not perceive AI as a threat to their jobs because measures have been put in place to ensure they work in tandem with AI. Employees from several internal units were involved in the AI implementation process, such as the IT Department, Engineering Department and Operations. There was also support from external experts in the market. As participant No. 2 explains:

> *"The internal units that are involved in the implementation of AI in my organisation are employees from the IT department, engineering department and operational units. The combined efforts of all three units have successfully attained the objective of the organisation.*
> *Other than this, the external help is also attained from the AI experts in the market."*
> *(Participant No. 2)*

The availability of user manuals and experts was also seen to make it easier for employees to work with the given technology as participant No. 4 explicated:

> *"There are multiple measures that have been placed in the organisation to help me while working with the AI. Such as the availability of the user manuals also helps me a lot to deal with AI. Moreover, the organisation also provides the experts of the AI that help each person and me in the organisation regarding the issues and challenges to deal with the AI."(Participant No. 4)*

AI was implemented through collaboration among members of the different departments with cross-departmental collaboration facilitated by using an application that acts as a data-sharing toolkit. According to Participant 1, the collaboration stage occurs as follows:

> *"In the implementation process, the data sharing is based on three major steps checklist for senior buy-in, incentives for data sharing, and equitable contributions. The next step is project foundations and requirements of the data sharing. These requirements are legal, financial, and technical requirements about the data sharing between two collaborating parties." (participant No. 1).*

Table 3. AI implementation tactics in the case study organisation

AI implementation tactics	Example statement quotes
AI implementation as an incremental improvement process, not a radical transformation of the operation	*"I feel like the implementation of AI in my organisation is still in the beginning stage. A lot needs to be done in this respect." (Participant No. 15)* *"It is impossible that the organisation adopts the AI technologies at the blink of an eye. However, since new inventions in the field of artificial intelligence are based on a daily basis, the organisation has made it possible to implement them to some extent in order to improve the customer satisfaction and make the working environment of the organisation more efficient." (Participant No. 7)*
AI implementation in stages	*"In any organisation first, it is important to understand the need for AI implementation and secondly by analysing the environment for the adoption of AI tools and techniques. In particular to my organisation, different initiatives and steps have been taken to ensure the success of AI in operations, customer services and other supporting systems. The first step was to provide training and education on AI to all the employees, and the next step was to perform regular trials with the help of AI and machine learning." (Participant No. 2)* *"There are several steps that have been considered before implementation of the AI in the organisation such as, recognising the need of AI in the business model, the organisation analysed the internal capabilities, consultation with the experts of the AI and at last the preparation of the data. However, the successful implementation of AI in the organisation can be understood by some features such as building real intelligence such as human resources. Further, the organisation creates a work plan for the adoption of AI, and third is that the organisation avail services of the expert of AI." (Participant No. 4)* *"In the implementation process, the data sharing is based on three major steps checklist for senior buy- in, incentives for data sharing, and equitable contributions. The next step is project foundations and requirements of the data sharing. These requirements are legal, financial, and technical requirements about the data sharing between two collaborating parties." (participant No. 1)*

(continued)

Table 3. (*continued*)

AI implementation tactics	Example statement quotes	
Tactics for reducing resistance observed in the case	*Education and communication*	*"In order to understand how AI work, I believe that an individual must have a sound understanding of how the technology works. Learning data analytics and machine learning is advisable to work with AI. In my workplace, I attended several training sessions with respect to the education and knowledge of AI." (Participant No. 2)* *We are offered training programs and training sessions from collaborated teams of the government and IBM for getting updates on the customer services and customer satisfaction protocols and government initiatives on the implementation of AI." (participant No. 3)* *"In collaboration with IBM, the government has designed the training session for the employees of the government to create awareness in the employees about the initiates of the AI." (participant No.1)* *"My organisation has taken great measures with respect to the introduction and implementation of various practices of AI in place. The most beneficial and useful practice that I feel is that my organisation provides training beforehand before any new technology is implemented in the organisation." (Participant No. 6)* *"I have attended training sessions that helped me enhance my experience of using the system. Moreover, on-the-job training was also required to use AI in an organisation easily." (participant No. 8)* *"There are different steps in the company that have been put in place to assist me when dealing with the AI. Which includes the help of the experts, professionals of the AI, training sessions, along with that the user manual of the AI is also provided by the organisation." (participant No. 10)*
	Participation and involvement	*"The internal units that are involved in the implementation of AI in my organisation are employees from the IT department, engineering department and operational units. The combined efforts of all three units have successfully attained the objective of the organisation. Other than this, the external help is also attained from the AI experts in the market." (Participant No. 2)*

4.2 Impacts of AI at the Individual Level

The study participants agreed that working with AI has significantly impacted them individually, as Table 4 summarises. First, AI impacted daily work activities by reducing the work required to complete a given task and improving employees' efficiency. For example, participant No. 2 and participant No. 9 commented on how AI helped in reducing the time needed to deal with their customers:

"Under my job designation, I have to deal with customers on a daily basis and address their requests or complaints on an urgent basis. At an individual level, I believe that my work efficiency is improved because the time to deal with a single customer is reduced." (Participant No. 2)

"My job in an organisation is managing customers on a daily basis and effectively addresses their issues. I believe that work efficiency has developed and enhanced with AI and customers are satisfied." (Participant No. 9)

In addition, AI was seen to improve the speed of communication with customers through automation using predictive mail technology and voice-to-text technology. Thus, AI has been essential in increasing the speed at which daily activities are conducted as participants No. 2 and No. 5 elaborated:

"In my opinion, various practices of AI have affected the overall business and the daily activities of the business in a very positive manner. Take the example of mail; we do not have to type individual mail anymore. We can use predictive mail technology any time or can use voice-to-text technology so that the mail can be typed and sent to the desired recipient. It has hugely transformed the overall procedures." (Participant No. 5)

"Yes. In my opinion, almost all of my daily activities have been affected by the implementation of AI, but in a positive manner. Almost all of the activities like planning, implementation and decision-making have become much more simple and speedy than before." (Participant No. 2)

AI was also seen to improve the competency of employees through automation of manual tasks and help employees perform better in their work. According to participants, AI boosted their problem-solving skills and increased their speed in completing their tasks. As Participant No. 4 commented:

"AI significantly affects my problem-solving approach as I can now solve the difficult issues more efficiently. Besides, AI also helps me a lot to enhance my efficiency in the repetitive works and make it my behaviour to get the work done in a short period." (Participant No. 4)

AI also boosted our study participants' interest and confidence in learning new skills and using these new skills in the workplace. An example is participant 6, who works as part of the sales team and uses AI in planning and increasing sales using innovative sales strategies. Participant No. 10 also opined:

Table 4. Observed impacts of AI at the micro-individual employee level

Observed impacts of AI at the micro-individual employee level	Example statement quote	
Reducing the amount of work required to complete in a given task	*"Under my job designation, I have to deal with customers on a daily basis and address their requests or complaints on an urgent basis. At an individual level, I believe that my work efficiency is improved because the time to deal with a single customer is reduced." (participant No. 2)* *"My job in an organisation is managing customers on a daily basis and effectively addresses their issues. I believe that work efficiency has developed and enhanced with AI and customers are satisfied." (Participant No. 9)*	
Increasing speed of communication with customers	*"In my opinion, various practices of AI have affected the overall business and the daily activities of the business in a very positive manner. Take the example of mail; we do not have to type individual mail anymore. We can use predictive mail technology any time or can use voice-to- text technology so that the mail can be typed and sent to the desired recipient. It has hugely transformed the overall procedures. (Participant No. 5)* *"Yes. In my opinion, almost all of my daily activities have been affected by the implementation of AI, but in a positive manner. Almost all of the activities like planning, implementation and decision-making have become much more simple and speedy than before." (participant No. 2)"*	
Increasing employee motivation	*Autonomy: increased*	*"The adoption of the AI in my organisation significantly affects my sense of autonomy, such as the AI enhances my level of confidence to take decisions which are beneficial in the context of the organisation. Similarly, AI helps me a lot to take timely decisions, such as now I can take decisions regarding customer satisfaction such as to provide the best facility. Furthermore, working with the AI also encourages me to put forth my novel ideas and opinions, such as I shared my opinions regarding the issues and challenges and the need for the up-gradation of the AI-based technologies that can further enhance the organisation performance" (participant No. 4)* *"As far as I think the implementation of AI in my organisation has given a considerable amount of autonomy not only to me but almost all the employees, especially the managerial level employees. I can now make my decisions independently with much confidence and can freely express my ideas and opinions. (participant No. 6)*

(continued)

Table 4. (*continued*)

Observed impacts of AI at the micro-individual employee level		Example statement quote
	Competency: increased	*"My daily work activity has improved with AI. It has enhanced my workability and competency. For example, the technical task that I used to complete the manual was completed automatically in a short time." (participant No. 10)*
		"Yes, undoubtedly. Definitely. AI and its implementation have been very beneficial for me, especially in terms of the performance of my job. It has helped me at lots of points in my career. In short, you can say that definitely, it has increased my competence regarding my job. To be specific, it has undoubtedly increased my ability to perform my job well. Moreover, it has boosted my interest and confidence in learning new skills and also expressing them. As I am in the sales team, so AI has helped me in planning and increasing sales using innovative sales strategies." (Participant No. 6)
		"The employment of the AI in the organisational significantly increases my level of competencies such as working with the advanced technologies enhanced my ability to learning and skills. Besides, the use of the AI significantly enhanced my working behaviour and also it enlightens the critical issues of the organisation to be solved with less time and efficiencies." (Participant No. 7
		"AI significantly affects my problem-solving approach as I can now solve the difficult issues more efficiently. Besides, AI also helps me a lot to enhance my efficiency in the repetitive works and make it my behaviour to get the work done in a short period." (Participant No. 4)
	Relatedness: Increased	*"Due to rigorous training and the learning process, the employees of the team consider themselves much connected and related to the initiatives that are taken for implementation of the AI." (Participant No. 3)*
		"As far as the relatedness or the question with other employees in the organisation is concerned, I think that AI has improved it a lot. " (Participant No. 6)

"My daily work activity has improved with AI. It has enhanced my workability and competency. For example, the technical task that I used to complete the manual was completed automatically in a short time." (Participant No. 10)

The implementation of AI was also seen to increase employees' sense of autonomy, especially those employees at the managerial level who can make decisions more independently because of AI. As participant No. 4 and participant No. 6 commented:

"The adoption of the AI in my organisation significantly affects my sense of autonomy, such as the AI enhances my level of confidence to take decisions which are beneficial in the context of the organisation. Similarly, AI helps me a lot to take timely decisions, such as now I can take decisions regarding customer satisfaction such as to provide the best facility. Furthermore, working with the AI also encourages me to put forth my novel ideas and opinions, such as I shared my opinions regarding the issues and challenges and the need for the up-gradation of the AI-based technologies that can further enhance the organisation performance" (Participant No. 4)

"As far as I think the implementation of AI in my organisation has given a considerable amount of autonomy not only to me but almost all the employees, especially the managerial level employees. I can now make my decisions independently with much confidence and can freely express my ideas and opinions. (Participant No. 6)

There was also an increased sense of relatedness as a consequence of AI implementation. Employees felt more connected with each other due to the utilisation of this technology. This point is demonstrated by the response that was given by participant No. 3:

"Due to rigorous training and the learning process, the employees of the team consider themselves much connected and related to the initiatives that are taken for implementation of the AI." (Participant No. 3)

"As far as the relatedness or the question with other employees in the organisation is concerned, I think that AI has improved it a lot." (Participant No. 6)

4.3 Impact of AI at the Team-Level

The study participants agreed that working with AI has significantly impacted them at the team level, as Table 5 summarises. AI was seen to support team communication through data sharing, and this was seen to improve team cooperation by using instant chatbots and virtual assistance devices. Team communication was also seen to be improved through the employment of inter- departmental communication mediums and virtual collaboration technology. Teams were seen to become more engaged, more motivated and more involved in their work. Participant No. 2 commented:

"The cooperation, coordination and teamwork have been enhanced by using instant chatbots and virtual assistance devices. Moreover, the team has become

more engaged, more motivated and more involved in the work." (Participant No. 2)

The implementation of AI was also seen to enhance team decision-making through the employment of real-time interactive dashboards and systems-based data to make efficient decisions. The interaction between the team and AI also occurs through bots and AI-powered Microsoft meetings. Participant No. 2 explained:

"There are conversational bots and AI-powered Microsoft team meetings that have helped the team in interacting with members in video conferences. Bots and Virtual Assistants are examples of AI used at Team Level at my workplace" (Participant No. 2)

Table 5. Observed impacts of AI at the meso-team level

Observed impacts of AI at the meso-team level	Example statement quote
Improved team interaction	*"There are conversational bots and AI-powered Microsoft team meetings that have helped the team in interacting with members in video conferences. Bots and Virtual Assistants are examples of AI used at Team Level at my workplace"(Participant No. 2)*
Improved team cooperation	*"The cooperation, coordination and teamwork have been enhanced by using instant chatbots and virtual assistance devices. Moreover, the team has become more engaged, more motivated and more involved in the work." (participant No. 2)* *"The implementation of the AI significantly enhances my cooperation within my team, such as the AI linked me with my team through the employment of the inter- departmental communication medium. Furthermore, the use of virtual technology also enhanced my collaboration with my team members." (participant No. 3)*
Improved team decision-making	*"The implementation of the AI and its role in decision making significantly affects the growth of the organisation. Similarly, AI-enhanced the decision making power of my team through the employment of the real-time interactive dashboards and the use of systems-based data to make efficient decisions." (Participant No. 3)*

5 Discussion and Conclusion

The findings of this exploratory research study describe the implementation of AI in a governmental entity in the UAE. According to the findings, the competitive business world, the need to gain regional influence, and the promotion of productivity made it necessary for the case study organisation to implement AI. The process of AI implementation was progressive and incremental rather than a radical change in business operations. Additionally, the implementation of AI was done following several phases and entailed an adequate plan to reduce employee resistance and involve key stakeholders.

According to the study findings, AI implementation had substantial impacts at the individual level encompassing its role in helping employees to conduct their daily activities, improve their skillset, improve their decision-making, autonomy, competence, and relatedness. These findings are in tandem with those by Coombs et al. (2017), who assert that AI is meant to provide a means through which people can realise their potential. It is this which makes people experience improvement in the daily tasks they undertake in the workplace. The positive impact of AI implementation on employees' autonomy also serves to demonstrate the influence of this technology at the individual level. The introduction of AI positively affects employees as it boosts their confidence in many areas such as decision making. That is, they can make use of the recommendations provided by AI to reach decisions on their own without the need to go to their immediate supervisors for guidance. Employees develop the confidence to make decisions independently. Additionally, employees can come up with and share their novel ideas and opinions regarding different aspects of work that also points to the fact that they become more autonomous. This autonomy is illustrated in literature as the employees are willing to engage in their work (Deci et al. 2017).

In addition, the implementation of AI was seen to impact team interaction, cooperation and enhancement in decision-making. These findings are in line with those of Tyukin et al. 2018, who indicated that the ability of a team to cooperate would determine their ability to realise any considerable objectives. AI facilitates improved communication among team members through feedback loops. The increased collaboration, relatedness, and overall cooperation bring team members together and encourage them to reach common organisational objectives. With such a sense of togetherness, the benefits of teamwork can be well-realised, as mentioned by Smids et al. (2020), who note that teams work more effectively with automation.

Another significant finding that was made by this study is that AI implementation has an impact on the enhancement of individual and team performance. This AI technology enables productivity improvement at individual and team levels, therefore, contributing positively to organisational performance. There are various reasons for this positive change in productivity. One of them is that the application of AI has a beneficial effect on employee efficiency and productivity. In its turn, increased productivity leads to enhanced customer satisfaction. Highly productive employees are those who are in a better position to meet the customers' needs adequately. Employees can work well at the individual and team levels due to AI allowing for enhancement in areas such as the involvement of employees in organisational processes. Staff can collaborate more with each other and share their ideas because AI positively impacts data-sharing. That is, AI is useful in facilitating the development of appropriate infrastructure for adequate data sharing, and as a result, daily activities are carried out better. In such a manner, workers' productivity and subsequently their performance improves. These findings are similar to those in the study by Jia et al. (2018), which demonstrated that introducing AI in the workplace could change how employees do their tasks, whether as individuals or as teams. AI supports the use of machine-based operations, which are more efficient when compared to human capabilities in doing strenuous work or work that requires considerable analysis of information. Additionally, employees report improvement in their daily activities due to AI implementation, highlighting that it has enhanced their workability and level of competence. Therefore, the impact of AI on the employees' daily activities has been largely positive.

There are several managerial implications of the findings of this study. Organisations implementing AI should sufficiently understand change management, including change implementation in planned stages and managing employee resistance to change. Employee resistance to change could be reduced through education, communication, participation and involvement of employees in AI implementation processes. There should be continuous training and preparation of employees on AI adoption to avoid any form of resistance. As resistance is managed, cross-departmental cooperative mechanisms should also be put in place to align with different departments' operations to attain the maximum possible benefits from the implementation of AI.

Finally, this study has several limitations that should be acknowledged and may form the basis for future research directions. The study generalizability is limited to the context of the case study organisation explored and restricted by the small number of interviews conducted. Furthermore, the findings of our study remain propositions to be tested through future quantitative research. Future research that explores different organisational contexts will be valuable in enriching our understanding of the AI implementation phenomenon.

References

Alsedrah, M.K.: Artificial intelligence (2017). https://www.researchgate.net/publication/323498 156_Artificial_Intelligence. Accessed 2 Sept 2021

Bruun, E.P., Duka, A.: Artificial intelligence, jobs and the future of work: racing with the machines. Basic Income Stud. 13(2), 1–15 (2018)

Claudé, M., Combe, D.: The roles of artificial intelligence and humans in decision-making; towards augmented human? A focus on knowledge-intensive firms. UMEA School of Business (2018)

Chowdhury, M.F.: Interpretivism in aiding our understanding of the contemporary social world. Open J. Philos. 4, 432–438 (2014)

Coombs, C.R., Hislop, D., Barnard, S., Taneva, S.: Impact of artificial intelligence, robotics, and automation technologies on work - rapid evidence review. CIPD (2017)

Creswell, J.W.: A Concise Introduction to Mixed Methods Research. Sage, London (2014)

Deci, E.L., Olafsen, A.H., Ryan, R.M.: Self-determination theory in work organisations: the state of a science. Ann. Rev. Organ. Psychol. Organ. Behav. 4, 19–43 (2017)

Ernst, E., Merola, R., Samaan, D.: The economics of artificial intelligence: implications for the future of work. International Labour Organization, Geneva (2018)

Habeeb, A.: Introduction to Artificial Intelligence. Research Gate (2017). https://www.resear chgate.net/publication/325581483_Introduction_to_Artificial_Intelligence. Accessed 18 Sept 2021

Halcomb, E., Hickman, L.: Mixed methods research. Nurs. Stand.: Promot. Excell. Nurs. Care **29**(32), 41–47 (2015)

Jia, Q., Guo, Y., Li, R., Li, Y., Chen, Y.: A conceptual artificial intelligence application framework in human resource management. In: Proceedings of the International Conference on Electronic Business, ICEB, Guilin, China, pp. 106–114 (2018)

Reim, W., Åström, J., Eriksson, O.: Implementation of artificial intelligence (AI): a roadmap for business model innovation. AI Rev. **1**, 180–191 (2020)

Rodrigues, R.: Legal and human rights issues of AI: Gaps, challenges and vulnerabilities. J. Responsible Technol. **4**, 100005 (2020)

Shabbir, J., Anwer, T.: Artificial intelligence and its role in near future. J. Latex Class Files **14**(8), 1–11 (2015)

Skilton, M.: The impact of artificial intelligence on business. Warwick, Coventry (2017)

Smids, J., Nyholm, S., Berkers, H.: Robots in the workplace: a threat to—or opportunity for—meaningful work? Philos. Technol. **33**, 503–522 (2020)

Tyukin, I.Y., Gorban, A.N., Sofeykov, K.I., Romanenko, I.: Knowledge transfer between artificial intelligence systems. Front. Neurorobotics **12**, 49 (2018)

Yin, R.: Case Study Research: Design and Methods, 3rd edn. Sage Publishing, Beverly Hills (2003)

IT Governance and Alignment

Smart Government and Smart Citizens as a Smart Cities Building Blocks. A Survey

Patrycja Krauze-Maślankowska[(✉)] [ID]

University of Gdańsk, Armii Krajowej 101, 81-824 Sopot, Poland
patrycja.krauze-maslankowska@ug.edu.pl

Abstract. IT systems are an integral part of modern cities, managed by public administration units, equipped with tools allowing for taking efficient and accurate actions. The idea of creating smart cities, equipped with innovative technological solutions, is increasingly becoming the subject of strategic assumptions of many cities around the world. This means that a smart city is not only a vision of a well-managed city responding to the changing needs of its inhabitants, but also real activities that are becoming better and better suited to the specific economic, environmental and social conditions of a given place. The goal of this paper is to identify and find actions for better management of smart governance and smart citizens. To accomplish this goal, the survey was conducted among 280 Polish cities. The questionnaire was filled by public administration staff responsible for smart cities strategy and concept. The results allow to formulate conclusions that most of the actions oriented to smart governance are related to e-services, social participation, social media and civic budget. In the case of smart citizens, workshops and training were the most frequently indicated. The so-called city labs in the context of smart citizens were indicated mainly by representatives of large cities. Moreover, it has been proved that smart governance and smart citizens are the domain of big cities rather than medium and small units.

Keywords: Smart cities · Smart government · Smart citizens

1 Introduction

A smart city does not exist without the cooperation of the local government and residents. Cities of the future, plan their activities in such a way that the decisions made by local governments are conducive to the development, improvement of the satisfaction and quality of life of the inhabitants. The population of the city is constantly growing. This tendency contributes to the government's search for innovative solutions that will prove to be friendly to the local community. The directions of activities undertaken as part of the pursuit of the implementation of the smart city concept, affect many areas of the city's functioning. They include the development of enterprises, care for the natural environment and creation of new knowledge. Therefore, the purpose of this article is to answer the following research question:

Which activities under the implementation of the smart city concept in terms of smart governance and smart citizens are most often undertaken by cities in Poland?

M. Themistocleous and M. Papadaki (Eds.): EMCIS 2021, LNBIP 437, pp. 617–625, 2022.
https://doi.org/10.1007/978-3-030-95947-0_43

The research method used to answer the question is the own research, which consisted in collecting information by conducting a survey on the activities undertaken by public administration units in the context of the smart city concept.

The work consists of four parts. The first covers the characteristics of the concept of a smart city and its two key dimensions, which are government and people. The second part presents activities that can be taken as part of the implementation of the smart city concept in the government and people dimension. Selected research methods are characterized in the third part. The last part contains the conclusions obtained and the directions of future research.

2 Idea of the Smart Cities

The concept of a smart city is gaining more and more popularity. Both the scientific community as well as the private and public sector conduct various types of considerations on the positive and negative impact of smart city initiatives on the areas of society functioning. The very definition of the concept of smart city differs depending on the context of the technological services offered, normative conditions or resources characteristic for a given city. However, there is a division that systematizes the dispersed meaning of the city's intelligence through the use of certain thematic frameworks. The aforementioned division was proposed already in 2007 by Giffinger and covers six dimensions of a smart city in which actions taken to implement the discussed concept are concentrated. These dimensions include smart economy, smart mobility, smart environment, smart people, smart life and smart governance [1]. The initiatives taken in all these domains ultimately boil down to improving the quality and satisfaction with life in each city [2]. Undoubtedly, the cooperation of the government and citizens is of great importance for the development of modern cities. The implementation of this assumption may take place through the implementation of activities aimed at increasing trust in local administration and involving residents in the decision-making process. In turn, residents should demonstrate responsibility for the environment in which they live, as well as intelligence, knowledge and commitment as part of functioning in a given society.

The governmental and social layer of the city requires constant care for maintaining mutual relations. The mere implementation of innovative technological solutions to urban space, the aim of which is to improve the quality of life of residents, is not enough for citizens to feel part of a specific community. Initiatives undertaken as part of the pursuit of the assumptions of the smart city concept, by definition, build their foundations on the appropriate construction of the technical infrastructure. Many cities in the world limit their activities only to the installation of various types of sensors, meters and cameras without taking into account the real needs of their inhabitants. An example of such an approach is the city of Masdar, built since 2006 in the Emirate of Abu Dhabi in the United Arab Emirates. The assumption behind the construction of this city is to reduce energy consumption, implement an innovative approach to water treatment, turn waste into energy, reduce the carbon footprint by supplying construction machines with solar energy and installing a CO_2 capture, use and storage system. The main areas in which the use of modern technology is reflected include [3]:

– intelligent buildings and smart networks,

- green supply chain,
- clean transport infrastructure,
- energy storage technologies,
- integration of transport systems,
- sustainable management systems,
- intelligent municipal solutions,
- energy-saving lighting,
- thermal energy and geothermal cooling.

The city of Masdar seems to be a unique space that responds to the most important needs of the modern world. However, although the technologies used in the city in question are a source of valuable knowledge, they provide inspiration to cities struggling with a high level of pollution or energy consumption, the city itself is not a friendly place to live, because, like the cities of Sangdo or the planned Skolkovo, a kind of laboratory and science and experience park. The presented example of a fully ecological city is a revolutionary project and necessary from the point of view of the development of urban technology. However, modern cities, especially medium-sized and small ones, which do not have adequate resources to implement innovations should focus on cooperation with the inhabitants in the first place. City citizens are a unique source of knowledge and skills that, if used correctly, can contribute to the dynamic development of the city, which is one of the main assumptions of the construction of a smart city.

3   Smart Governance and Smart Citizens

Public administration units have limited possibilities in relation to generating innovative solutions. Such a situation arises as a result of the need to finance various types of projects from external sources, which generates additional problems with the settlement of the funds obtained, the involvement of the private sector and convincing residents about the legitimacy of the implemented projects. According to research by the Roosevelt Institute, Generation Y, which is now a working-age society, overwhelmingly (70%) support actions taken by public administration [4]. Therefore, the task of local administration is not only to undertake activities that seem important from an economic point of view, but also to pay more and more attention to the specific needs of citizens, which change with technological progress and globalization. Aspects related to urbanization have also changed. More and more often, young people give up living in a crowded, polluted and noisy city, choosing places located near the agglomeration. This tendency is an opportunity for development for medium and small towns, which are often well connected with the metropolis that the inhabitants choose as their place of work. Thanks to this, small and medium-sized cities can establish a closer relationship with their citizens. By offering places for recreation and sports, green parks, playgrounds for children and developing cultural and entertainment institutions, they allow you to spend time in peace away from the hustle and bustle.

The values described above relate to two important aspects of a smart city - citizens and local government. In the light of the considerations on the concept of a smart city, a number of factors can be distinguished that represent the domain of intelligent citizens and intelligent government, the summary is presented in Table 1.

Table 1. Components of a smart city by domains smart citizens and smart governance.

Smart city domain	Factors
Smart citizens	*Education* *Creativity* *Diversity*
Smart governance	*E-services* *E-democracy* *Participation*

Source: [2].

The factors identified for intelligent citizens allow the conclusion that cities should provide their citizens with unlimited access to knowledge, learning new skills and learning about new cultures and languages. The elements important from the point of view of public administration are the ability to create services that actually respond to the needs of residents, openness to changes and freedom to express their opinions by citizens and to include them in the decision-making process [5].

Including residents in the dialogue on improving their everyday lives gives the opportunity to share opinions, gain new experiences and create new products. The actions most often taken in the framework of the smart citizen dimension [6–8]:

- availability of universities,
- the development laboratories operating in the city,
- trainings and workshops for residents,
- campaigns promoting lifelong learning.

However, the activities undertaken around intelligent government include, among others, initiatives such as [9–11]:

- e-services offered by the municipal office,
- activity in social media,
- citizen-oriented participatory approach,
- applications made available to residents,
- possibility of 24/7 contact,
- open data,
- Universities of the Third Age and Youth City Councils.

Considering the above-mentioned activities that should be undertaken in order to develop a smart city, research has been carried out to answer the research questions posed:

Question 1. Which activities under the implementation of the smart city concept in terms of smart governance and smart citizens are most often undertaken by cities in Poland?

4   Research Method and Results

In order to answer the research question, a study was conducted using the CAWI (Computer-Assisted Web Interview) technique, which took place from July 1 to August 31, 2020. A request for public information pursuant to Art. 14 of the Act of September 6, 2001 on access to public information. A randomly selected sample for the study, using the simple drawing method without returning, covered 280 cities out of all 940 Polish cities as of June 30, 2020. There were 210 responses, resulting in a return rate of 22% of the total population. In addition, small cities (up to 20,000 inhabitants) account for 70%, medium-sized cities (from 20,000 to 100,000 inhabitants) 21%, and large cities (over 100,000 inhabitants) 9% of all responses, which is proportionally consistent with the actual the number of cities in the population for each stratum. The structure of the response against the layers is shown in Table 2.

Table 2. Structure of the study population.

Layers	Sample size	Number of returns	Population size	Proportion
Small towns	200	**145**	722	**20%**
Medium-sized cities	60	**47**	179	**26%**
Big cities	20	**18**	39	**46%**
Total	280	**210**	940	**22%**

Source: Own study.

The survey questionnaire consisted of 30 questions. The main goal was to assess the level of implementation of the smart city concept by cities in Poland, which is why the greater part (16 questions) was devoted to this subject. The remaining questions were used to assess the factors important from the point of view of the ability to undertake innovative activities, as well as to indicate barriers and opportunities that cities perceive in relation to development opportunities. Large cities, due to their specific conditions, which refer to a larger population, access to education, higher budget, etc., can afford to implement a greater number of development projects in terms of the implementation of the smart city concept.

5   Results of the Study

As part of the study, local public administration units were asked questions about general activities around smart governance and smart citizens and detailed tasks carried out in relation to the indicated smart city domains. Figure 1 shows the tendency to implement initiatives in the area related to improving the activity and effectiveness of local government and activities undertaken to meet the needs of residents.

As shown in Fig. 1, actions taken by local governments focused on improving their own processes and services are undertaken by almost every city, regardless of its size. In the case of large and medium-sized cities, all surveyed entities indicated that initiatives

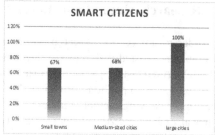

Fig. 1. Activities of local governments in the context of smart governance and smart citizens. *Source: Own study.*

were implemented within the domain of intelligent government, small cities declared 89% of such activities, which still constitutes the majority of the surveyed cities. In the context of activities undertaken within the smart citizens dimension, the entire surveyed sample of large cities indicated that they perform activities related to improving the satisfaction and skills of their inhabitants. Medium and small towns undertake such initiatives in 68 and 67%, respectively. It follows from the above that activities aimed at improving the quality of services offered to citizens and caring for satisfying their needs in relation to education, creativity and participation are carried out by the majority of the surveyed entities.

The next stage of the study was to identify detailed projects implemented within the indicated domains. Selected units were asked to indicate which of the listed activities are performed by them. The list of initiatives included the elements indicated in the second part of this document and was created as a result of the analysis of the literature relating to the development of the smart city concept. Figure 2 shows the results obtained for the smart order domain.

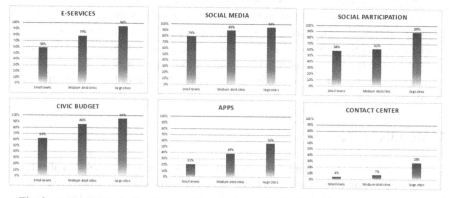

Fig. 2. Actions taken by local governments around smart governance. *Source: Own study.*

As shown in Fig. 2, most activities around smart governance are carried out as part of activities in social media. The second standout area is the services offered to residents. Big cities implement the most initiatives. The smallest number of units indicated having a 24-h contact center with residents in the organizational structure and dedicated city applications. The respondents were also able to independently indicate the tasks they perform in a given area. In addition to those listed in the prepared questionnaire, public administration units indicated the appointment of youth and senior councils influencing decisions made, having an integrated management system, and sharing information and alerts in the form of text messages.

Activities related to the improvement of the smart citizens domain in relation to the studied units are presented in Fig. 3. As in the case of the smart governance domain, the list of possible tasks was prepared based on a literature analysis.

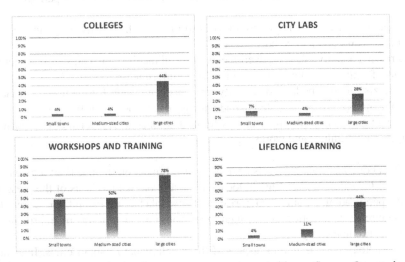

Fig. 3. Actions taken by local governments around smart citizens. *Source: Own study.*

The activities most often undertaken in the area related to the improvement of creativity, knowledge and experience of inhabitants include, in particular, the organization of workshops and training courses supporting the development of citizens. Higher education institutions in Poland are found only in large cities, which is caused by greater spatial, financial and organizational resources of these agglomerations. Many large cities also declare promoting lifelong learning, which allows us to constantly cooperate with citizens in order to co-create solutions that make cities a better place to live, work and spend free time. In addition to the tasks listed in the questionnaire, the cities indicated the organization of hackathons, dedicated training for children, issuing training vouchers as part of public-private cooperation and intensified information campaigns on the existing social, digital and social problems.

6 Conclusions and Future Work

The cooperation of the government with the inhabitants is one of the key values that should be created by modern smart cities. Dynamically changing technological conditions, related to a specific change in the attitude of residents to work and the common phenomenon of globalization, force public administration to change the way of reaching its citizens. The concept of a smart city and the domain of intelligent government and intelligent citizens within its scope allows to systematize the actions taken. Thanks to the analysis of the literature in terms of indicating specific assumptions which should characterize the indicated smart city domains, it was possible to conduct a survey consisting in collecting information from local government institutions regarding their activities undertaken within the smart city concept. The collected results allowed to obtain an answer to the research question posed in the introduction to this document. Namely, the activities that are most often taken by public administration in the context of the dimension of intelligent government and intelligent citizens include, in particular:

- providing electronic services for citizens to improve the quality of communication with residents and reduce bureaucracy,
- increasing activity of local governments in social media, which allows for faster and more effective reaching citizens with relevant information,
- organizing a civic budget, where city residents can decide for themselves what the public money will be allocated to and what needs are their priority
- providing citizens with opportunities for professional and personal development by organizing trainings and workshops.

The above-mentioned aspects have a positive impact on the image of a given city, they also increase citizens' trust in local administration. On the basis of the presented results, public administration, enterprises and city stakeholders can influence areas that still require more attention due to their significant impact in terms of improving the quality of life in the city.

Technology is an important aspect of the development of smart cities. Innovative solutions implemented in urban space are now expected to not only support the functioning of various types of activities, but also enable their transformation in relation to changing expectations and new challenges. Intelligent citizens are not only well-educated and willing to cooperate in the management process. The smart city domain related to smart people is also the ability of urban stakeholders (residents, enterprises, non-governmental organizations) to transform generally available resources such as open data provided by public administration in order to create various types of applications and solutions responding to the specific needs of general mobility. Such initiatives are still lacking in Poland, due to the still limited access to data allowing for easy processing and analysis.

Therefore, future research on the topic discussed in this article includes research on the impact of the obtained results and actions taken by local administration on the behavior of citizens. Work on this issue will allow for better adjustment of services to the real needs of the city's inhabitants.

References

1. Giffinger, R., Fertner, C., Kramar, H., Kalasek, R., Pichler-Milanović, N., Meijers, E.: Smart cities. Ranking of European medium-sized cities. Centre for Regional Science, Vienna (2007)

2. Vito, A., Umberto, B., Dangelico, R.M.: Smart cities: definitions, dimensions, performance, and initiatives. J. Urban Technol. **22**, 3–21 (2015)
3. Dziedzic, S.: Ekologiczne miasta przyszłości. Masdar City – Studium Przypadku. Research Papers of the Wroclaw University of Economics. Prace Naukowe Uniwersytetu Ekonomicznego We Wroclawiu, pp. 264–76 (2015)
4. Noveck, B.S.: Smart Citizens, Smarter State: The Technologies of Expertise and the Future of Governing. Harvard University Press (2015)
5. Danielewicz, J., Sikora-Fernandez, D., Churski, P., Zaucha, J.: Zarządzanie rozwojem współczesnych miast. Łódź (2019)
6. Ferraris, A., Belyaeva, Z., Bresciani, S.: The role of universities in the smart city innovation: multistakeholder integration and engagement perspectives. J. Bus. Res. **119**, 163–171 (2020)
7. Sarkar, A.N.: Innovations in designing smart cities as living labs. Smart City J. (2021)
8. Zhuang, R., Fang, H., Zhang, Y., et al.: Smart learning environments for a smart city: from the perspective of lifelong and lifewide learning. Smart Learn. Environ. **4**(1), 1–21 (2017). https://doi.org/10.1186/s40561-017-0044-8
9. Erastus, L.R., Jere, N., Shava, F.B.: A secure smart city infrastructure framework for E-service delivery within a developing country: a case of windhoek in Namibia. In: Yang, X.S., Sherratt, S., Dey, N., Joshi, A. (eds) Proceedings of Fifth International Congress on Information and Communication Technology. Advances in Intelligent Systems and Computing, vol. 1184, pp. 454–469. Springer, Singapore (2020). https://doi.org/10.1007/978-981-15-5859-7_45
10. Molinillo, S., Anaya-Sánchez, R., Morrison, A.M., Coca-Stefaniak, J.A.: Smart city communication via social media: analysing residents' and visitors' engagement. Cities **94**, 247–255 (2019)
11. Lebrument, N., Zumbo-Lebrument, C., Rochette, C., Roulet, T.J.: Triggering participation in smart cities: political efficacy, public administration satisfaction and sense of belonging as drivers of citizens' intention. Technol. Forecast. Soc. Change **171**, 120938 (2021)

Management and Organisational Issues
in Information Systems

ICT and Creativity: How ICT Impacts Creativity in a Saudi University

Ibrahim Almatrodi[✉]

King Saud University, Riyadh, Saudi Arabia
ialmatrodi@ksu.edu.sa

Abstract. This paper discusses how Information, Communication and Technology (ICT) systems interact with and impact creativity in one higher education institution at Saudi Arabia. It adopts a qualitative case study methodology and utilizes the organizational creativity theory, which guides the data collection and analysis. The study finds that personality, cognition, and motivation play a role in the impact of ICT on creativity in a major Saudi university. It is useful and beneficial for organizations to understand how ICT impacts creativity in order to be competitive and ensure growth in their industries. Through ICT, universities have become more innovative in their administrative and academic functions; this is important for stakeholders in order to gain benefits from ICT systems in key areas, such as creativity. This study is useful in enabling university managers and employees, as well as ICT specialists, to gain an overall view of the consequences of implementing ICT in universities in a country like Saudi Arabia.

Keywords: ICT · Organizational creativity · Case study · Universities

1 Introduction

Organizations such as universities, particularly those in developing countries, face the need to innovate in their practices and managerial processes. This creates the further need for a creativity culture in universities to improve productivity and be more effective and efficient. Organizational creativity means employees creating valuable and useful new products and services, or new ideas and procedures in an environment that tends to be complex [1]. However, the question of how ICT systems can interact with and impact the process of creativity and innovation in universities' managerial and administrative functions is important. It is widely known that organizational creativity benefits from ICT systems, which help organizations achieve their potential and improve the process of creativity in general; however, there is a need to define and realize the processes to achieve this. Briefly, this paper studies the existing problem via a case study of a university in a Saudi Arabia.

Most previous work on this subject has explored related research topics such as the definition of organizational creativity [1], individual and organizational creativity mechanisms [2], issues influencing organizational creativity [3], the influence of technological systems such as knowledge management (for example by authors such as Shahzad et al.

© Springer Nature Switzerland AG 2022
M. Themistocleous and M. Papadaki (Eds.): EMCIS 2021, LNBIP 437, pp. 629–639, 2022.
https://doi.org/10.1007/978-3-030-95947-0_44

[4]), issues influencing creative thinking [5], and the influence of organizational issues such as climate and resources [6]. In relation to the influence of ICT on creativity in organizations, studies by Chulvi et al. [7] and Dewett [15] have investigated this issue, and the topic of virtuality and its influence on creativity has been studied by researchers such as Martins and Shalley [14].

The purpose of this paper is to study how ICT impacts creativity in a Saudi university. Being aware of how ICT systems interact with and impact creativity means knowing the factors that lead organizations to be more sustainable and powerful in terms of achieving their vision and objectives. It has been proved that creativity helps organizations be more competitive and increase their revenue. Whether it is a private organization that aims to generate profit or a public organization that aims to improve the services it provides citizens and reduce its expenses, creativity must be part of a long-term strategy for the organization.

The contribution of the paper is knowledge of how ICT systems can impact creativity. It shows how certain factors can impact creativity, which can in turn influence the growth of the organization and increase the competitiveness of the organization in the higher education industry.

2   ICT Systems and Organizational Creativity

Organizational creativity is recognized as the formation of a valuable, worthwhile novel product, service, idea, procedure, or process by people working together in a complex environment [31]. ICT is defined as a wide-ranging combination of hardware, software, network infrastructure, and media that allows the processing, storage, and sharing of information and communication between humans and computers, locally and internationally [13].

Organizational creativity focuses on a number of issues, for example on the idea of novelty in organizations and on the creativity produced; however, this creativity has to be useful. It is important to mention that innovation is produced as the result of organizational creativity practices performed in organizations [9]. However, ICT systems can impact innovation and competitiveness; ICT tends to encourage innovation in enterprises, as it helps produce new products and/or services, as well as new processes, which help organizations become more competitive [16].

Organizational creativity has a number of features, such as that organizations must provide the tools, capabilities, and formal methods that encourage creativity [2]. ICT provides the systems and tools needed to achieve and encourage organizational creativity, and some authors have published guidance on how to design these ICT systems (such as Olszak et al. [17]), as they must solve a particular problem by providing the right information resources and information analysis to help produce new ideas, evaluate and select from new ideas, communicate the new knowledge in a way conducive to innovation and, finally, creating knowledge evolution in the organization.

It is believed that the originality of the team comes mainly from the incorporation of individually held expertise of team members at the team level [19]. However, organizational creativity also has some mechanisms for individuals or organizations, as explained by Bharadwaj and Menon [2]. As stated, these mechanisms must be meaningful, novel, and related to the working environment, and organizations must have mechanisms, such as tools and approaches, which facilitate creativity in the organization. It is argued that substantial ICT use negatively moderates the relationship between knowledge collection and organizational creativity [18]. Knowledge Management Systems (KM) have a positive impact on creativity, which leads to better organizational performance [4]. However, high-performance work practices lead to more organizational creativity when the enterprises experience organizational change; workers' collective learning also has a role to play and can influence organizational creativity [8].

Having an innovation lab in an organization has a positive impact on creativity and on members' attitudes to it. This kind of facility has important conceptual elements, specifically providing a *time* and *place* to engage in creative thinking and the *technology* to facilitate such a process. Also, ICT with organizational changes lead to productivity progress, as well as high degrees of innovation [20].

Organizational climate and work resources are closely linked to creativity and innovation in organizations, and also lead to improved organizational employee well-being [6, 21]. This climate, if accompanied by conflict in the project life cycle, can be one of many predictors of group creativity [10]. There are five further factors that are related to innovation if accompanied by work motivation, which can play a role in organizational creativity, namely: organizational encouragement, supervisory encouragement, work group support, sufficient resources, and challenging work [11]. However, some studies have shown that ICT permits strategic innovators to rapidly evolve their business models rand so protect themselves from competition [22].

Handzic and Chaimungkalanont [12] demonstrated that there exists a convincing and significant positive relationship between informal as well as organized forms of socialization and creativity. ICT may facilitate socialization and knowledge-gathering, as well as improving routines to enable innovation [23]. Thus, ICT can have an important role in creative development actions. Specifically, ICT has the capability to connect employees, codify knowledge, and increase boundary spanning, ICT may also present an important motivation for promoting creative action [15]. This is through the information and knowledge that ICT systems provide to organizations which can connect employees, improve communication and increase geographical reach and participation.

From this review of the literature on organizational creativity and ICT, it is clear that there is a lack of studies explaining the processes of how ICT interacts with and impacts creativity in organizations such as higher education institutions, especially in developing countries such as Saudi Arabia.

3   Theoretical Framework

To theoretically understand organizational creativity and its impact and interactions with ICT, a theory with this focus is needed. The interactionist model of creative behaviour developed by Woodman et al. [31] includes descriptions of creativity from personality, cognitive, and social psychology perspectives. In this model, creative behaviour is seen as a complicated person–situation interaction. Antecedent conditions occur depending on the current form of the person and their interaction. Antecedent conditions that influence creativity contain past underpinning history (learning), early socialization experiences, and background characteristics such as gender and socioeconomic status (SES) [31].

The interactionist model of creativity explains individual creativity as being the result of certain antecedent conditions that impact the personality and cognitive features of the individual and can determine the present situation of the organizational actors [32]. These include mental styles and abilities, which relate to creativity. Research has highlighted eight main factors involved in idea production, which are: associative fluency, fluency of expression, figural fluency, ideational fluency, speech fluency, word fluency, practical ideational fluency, and originality or personality. In addition, there are certain traits, including experience, broad interests, attraction to complexity, high energy, independence of judgement, autonomy, intuition, self-confidence, and capability to fix conflict that all help an individual to be creative.

There are also a number of motivational factors, for example evaluations and reward systems, that may impact intrinsic motivation to achieve a creative task, as they draw attention away from the heuristic elements of the creative task and toward the technical elements of task performance and knowledge, where it is important to look closely at the part that knowledge and expertise show the capability of employees to be creative [33]. Some authors, such as Amabile [34] identified both "domain-relevant skills" and "creativity-relevant skills", as being important for creativity. These two types of skill include the knowledge, technical skills, and talent needed to yield creative products (domain-relevant skills) as well as the cognitive skills and personality traits related to creative performance (creativity relevant skills) [31].

4 Methodology

This research adopts a qualitative methodology, which is used to understand meaning, with an emphasis on knowing how organizational employees understand the way ICT interacts with and impacts organizational creativity in a Saudi university, as the main study of the research. Additionally, it is important in this qualitative study that the researcher interprets and understands the experiences of different events related to ICT and creativity, with a focus on the relevant actors and participants individually [24].

An interpretive case study research strategy is adopted [34, 35], focusing on the phenomena of ICT and creativity in one Saudi university. Theory is used as the main tool for enabling and guiding data collection and analysis. The data collection tools used were semi-structured interviews and the main sample that was targeted for this research was organizational employees as users and managers in the university and IT professionals such as systems analysts, programmers, implementers, and testers. The snowballing sampling method was applied, beginning with the manager of electronic services, who recommended the next interviewee. This process was followed in each interview, giving a total number of participants of 30. Data was analyzed first by transcribing the interviews, then arranging the data into themes, then explaining and interpreting those themes by using the theory and using literature to support the findings.

The formulation of the questions, and thus the data collection and analysis, were influenced by the interactionist model of creativity. The questions were as follows:

1. How do you see the status of creativity in the university?
2. How do you see the influence of ICT on creativity generally in the university?

3. How does ICT influence personality and how does this influence on personality impact on creativity at the university?
4. How does ICT influence cognitive styles and their impact on creativity, how can ICT influence thinking at the university, and how does the way employees think impact on creativity?
5. How does ICT influence the motivation of university employees, and how does this impact on creativity?

5 The University, ICT, and Creativity

The data was collected at a university in Saudi Arabia; the university was founded in the mid-1950s and is one of the largest in Saudi Arabia. The university is funded by many sources, including government funding, its own endowments, and student fees. It is managed by a president who leads its highest council, the main decision-making body in the university with high authority. Under the president of the university, there are four vice presidents with duties related to academic issues, postgraduate study and research, and development and quality, and one vice president who is responsible for managerial and financial issues. The university also has many supportive deanships, such as one for electronic services. The deanship for electronic services played a key role in this study, as most respondents worked within this deanship, which plays a leading role in the use and implementation of ICT systems in the university. The university has more than 50,000 students (male and female) and employs more than 10,000 people, making it one of the largest universities in Saudi Arabia and the region. The university has ICT systems for many functionalities across management, research, and teaching. For example, it has a large Enterprise Resources Planning (ERP) system that supports managerial and financial functionalities, and various systems for different purposes in specific operational activities. One IT employee (YT) explained further that:

> ICT systems play a role in the running of everyday activities, as they provide information and knowledge and support decision-making. They also help managers and employees to operationalize everyday activities via automation. It has moved the operations of the university from manual work to automation of most activities in the university.

It was first necessary to establish how ICT systems influence creativity in general. According to one interviewee, an IT manager at the university (AC):

> In general, ICT systems are built based on algorithms in one form or another. The main aim of those algorithms is to increase the effectiveness of work and reduce human intervention. It is important to mention that if the organization understands the potential of ICT systems and agrees upon their correct use, and if the ICT systems are introduced in the university (or any organization) in the right way, they can lead the organization to focus on its routines. This is reflected in the ICT systems and in this way, you give employees time to think, reflect, and be more creative. However, if different people at the organization see the ICT systems as a threat to their interests, this could negatively influence their creativity.

ICT systems also play an important role in the creative activity in organizations, where managers encourage and are enthusiastic about risk-taking and push for idea generation at all levels of the organization. The information and knowledge produced by ICT systems will promote greater creativity as a result. Another influence on creativity at work is the degree to which managers are able to closely monitor their subordinates through ICT systems, which will encourage creativity [15]. One interviewee, a systems analyst (QW) provided some insight on this point:

The main aim of ICT systems is to help operations and carry out processes in the system instead of manually, but this requires organizations to show employees how to use such systems in the right way and realize their potential at all levels, even in risky situations. We have produced many new ideas for how ICT systems can help and serve the university; we have introduced and innovated various applications and systems for different functions. Idea generation, which leads to creativity, requires a high level understanding of the organization and benefits from the ICT systems used in the university processes. ICT provides the information and knowledge needed to improve decision-making, and this must be clear in the requirements analysis before systems development and implementation. This will enable the organization to focus on new products or innovating in current processes and develop new solutions to challenges faced by the university.

Employees with a high level of extraversion and openness to new experiences tend to be creative [25]. People with a high level of ICT experience understand how ICT can benefit the organization and enjoy using ICT applications in the organization; as a result, they tend to advance creativity in their organization. Employees with an intrapreneurial personality in relation to ICT are more likely to produce new ideas for how ICT can benefit the organization and, as a result, this intrapreneurial personality plays a role in innovative behaviour in the organization [36]. There is also a need for organizational employees and managers to be more committed to innovation; appetite for risk and reward, competition, and self-confidence all are important if organizations wish to advance creativity. Thus, creative intention among ICT specialists requires openness to experience, extraversion, conscientiousness, and knowledge collection behavior [26]. One interviewee, a systems tester (AQ), explained:

ICT systems increased the level of experience and knowledge of all aspects of work in the university. This has led to employees feeling happier and enjoying work, which in turn has led to creativity. Knowing how to use technology increases awareness of how ICT systems can benefit work and this has encouraged employees to think of new solutions to challenges faced by the university. ICT systems have many processes related to many operational activities and operate in a fast and quick way, which has increased both productivity and employees' business knowledge of the university. As a result, creativity has increased in terms of how to employ ICT systems to move the organization in an innovative direction.

The technical potential of ICT systems is not only a trigger of creativity, but also of other outcomes, such as the financial gains that result from cost savings in the running of managerial activities in the university. ICT systems have led to fewer people being needed to carry out work in the university and a reduction in the time needed to finish such work. These savings encourage and provide the grounds for creativity to be a reality in the university, with the aid of ICT systems. Another interviewee, a systems implementer (AW), reported that ICT systems have many advantages that can help enormously with creativity:

ICT decreases costs and increases competencies and effectiveness. The idea that I am trying to express is that ICT systems lead to automation of work that used to be performed by humans, for a lower cost. Also, previously employees had to process transactions manually to produce knowledge, such as calculations; now, systems can perform this function, giving the employees more time to think and make decisions based on the knowledge produced by the systems. This has given employees the time to be creative and innovative as a result.

However, one important factor is losing trust in the organization due to not believing the mission put forwards or the information and knowledge provided by the system; this can reduce the acceptance of ICT systems and thus the creativity needed by the employees in the organization. One interviewee (QE), a systems developer, said:

Stakeholders have an interest in ensuring that the ICT systems in the university work and perform their mission properly. ICT systems may increase or reduce the strength of alliances in the organization. There is a need to reach an agreement on the mission of ICT systems, otherwise they can be a negative factor affecting the creativity of employees. If the systems do not perform the required functions and work as expected to, the employees will lose trust in the ICT systems used in in the organization; this loss of trust will discourage innovative behaviour in the organization.

Cognitive theories tend to focus on thinking and information processing. In regard to creative thinking, thinking becomes creative if it tends to be original and generates adaptive ideas, new solutions, or insights. Creative behaviours and products are usually described as original and adaptive [27, 37], and the processes which generate original and adaptive ideas, solutions, and insights are considered creative processes. One IT systems analyst (ER) described and explained this point further:

ICT systems influence thinking in the organization and this influences creativity within the organization. ICT systems process data, which plays a role in creativity in the university. A famous psychologist, Daniel Kahenma, says that humans have two systems for thinking, one for fast thinking and decision making and the second for slow thinking and analysis. ICT systems work according to fast thinking and decision making, meaning they give people more time to think and focus on the decision-making that ICT systems support. You can notice that the majority of workers have become decision makers as a result of introducing such systems.

It is also important to say that different cognitive styles can improve user performance in information systems use [30]. However, sometimes, cognitive style insights are proposed as likely explanations for the communication difficulty that commonly exists between system specialists and the users of information systems [29]. When there is a clear communication of the thinking and information processing among organizational employees and the university, a path for innovation and creativity is opened, as one ERP manager (AA) explained:

> Effective communication between management and other university employees and members clearly influences innovation. I remember when the university leadership was clear about its objectives; as it intended to improve operations and be open to future development, this allowed many employees to suggest ways to improve the performance of such systems and improve the organizational generally. It is clear that once one ICT system becomes successful, employees start to think about the next system and how it can benefit the organization. Therefore, clear communication from the university leadership regarding the vision and mission for new ICT systems played a role in later innovative behaviour related to the implementation and use of these systems.

Motivation plays a critical role in the creative process; it is not sufficient for an individual to have uncommonly great skill or a profound theoretical understanding. To achieve a high level of creativity, as shown in a study of creativity and students, it is necessary to participate in tasks for pleasure and enjoyment of the task [28]. Thus, motivation plays a role in enabling creativity in the different tasks performed by employees. According to one participant (AR):

> In the university environment, when we felt that there were practices supporting our work and provided incentives for us, this motivated us to engage and focus all our thoughts on ICT systems and the university's implementation of such systems. We were creative in terms of how to use the systems and in understanding our requirements and how these were reflected in the ICT system. We understood routines and how ICT systems could play a role in improving those routines and the university performance. You could see that this was our main creative achievement. We used to participate in agile meetings at the time of ICT systems implementation, which were enjoyable; we listened to everyone's views, which led to a successful implementation.

All the aforementioned impacts can result in improving the competitiveness of the organization in comparison to its rivals. For example, motivation improves the performance of the employees of the organization; this leads to creativity, which can improve the competitive situation in the industry the organization operates in. In the university, according to one participant, a systems developer (RT):

> Once, the university provided incentives to employees who supported the system implementation. Incentives, which included pay rises, played a critical role in making the implementation and later use successful, as they motivated employees to perform better. This better performance encouraged employees to think in creative ways about how the system, and future systems, could serve the university's needs. The university became a leader in higher education in terms of ICT and

university operations, and we were asked to help other universities to implement such systems and achieve similar savings.

This improvement in performance and competitiveness as a result of creativity facilitated during the implementation of ICT systems led to university growth by improving decision-making processes and staffs' skills in dealing with the problems associated with the ICT systems' implementation and later use, and also improved the quality of work produced with the aid of such systems. One participant, a systems implementer (AQ), said:

I remember how unorganized the work used to be before the implementation of the ICT systems in the university. The quality of work produced, in regard to the information and knowledge gained and its accuracy, has improved on the previous situation before such systems were used. This has influenced the growth of the whole university in terms of improved employee skills and cost savings, which can be used in different areas.

6 Conclusion

This research has shown that ICT systems interact with and have an impact on creativity. It has highlighted that certain personality traits, such as risk taking and idea generation, can emerge as a result of the information and knowledge provided by ICT systems. People who are open to new experiences tend to be creative; ICT systems also impact creativity also when people enjoy using such applications, as when employees experience problems related to the implementation or use of such systems, this will negatively impact creativity – the opposite is also true. Competition and having an intrapreneurial personality are also shown to have an impact on creativity during the process of implementation or use of such systems, and as well as trust in the process of implementing and using ICT and its results.

ICT systems also impact creativity when the system leads the organization to generate new and original ideas that can be adapted within the organization. When the systems help to communicate new insight for the organization, this plays a role in producing innovative behaviour.

The limitations of this study include its focus on one organization only. There is a need to include more case studies across different types of organization and employ a variety of methods, such as surveys or mixed methods.

Nevertheless, the findings of this study are useful for universities and similar organizations to help them understand how ICT systems can impact creativity. They can use the ideas and results to ensure that new ICT systems will lead to multiple benefits, such as encouraging creativity. It has been proven that creativity can impact the competitiveness of the overall organization and it influence its growth and effectiveness.

References

1. Woodman, R.W., Sawyer, J.E., Griffin, R.W.: Toward a theory of organizational creativity. Acad. Manag. Rev. **18**(2), 293–321 (2016)

2. Bharadwaj, S., Menon, A.: Making innovation happen in organizations: individual creativity mechanisms, organizational creativity mechanisms or both? J. Prod. Innov. Manag.: Int. Publ. Prod. Dev. Manag. Assoc. **17**(6), 424–434 (2000)
3. Lang, J.C., Lee, C.H.: Workplace humor and organizational creativity. Int. J. Hum. Resour. Manag. **21**(1), 46–60 (2010)
4. Shahzad, K., Bajwa, S., Siddiqi, A., Ahmid, F., Sultani, A.: Integrating knowledge management (KM) strategies and processes to enhance organizational creativity and performance: an empirical investigation. J. Model. Manag. **11**(1), 154–179 (2016)
5. Magadley, W., Birdi, K.: Innovation labs: an examination into the use of physical spaces to enhance organizational creativity. Creat. Innov. Manag. **18**(4), 315–325 (2009)
6. Rasulzada, F., Dackert, I.: Organizational creativity and innovation in relation to psychological well-being and organizational factors. Creat. Res. J. **21**(2–3), 191–198 (2009)
7. Chulvi, V., Mulet, E., Felip, F., García-García, C.: The effect of information and communication technologies on creativity in collaborative design. Res. Eng. Design **28**(1), 7–23 (2016). https://doi.org/10.1007/s00163-016-0227-2
8. Jeong, I., Shin, S.J.: High-performance work practices and organizational creativity during organizational change: a collective learning perspective. J. Manag. **45**(3), 909–925 (2019)
9. Borghini, S.: Organizational creativity: breaking equilibrium and order to innovate. J. Knowl. Manag. **9**(4), 19–33 (2005)
10. Chen, M.H.: Understanding the benefits and detriments of conflict on team creativity process. Creat. Innov. Manag. **15**(1), 105–116 (2006)
11. Lin, C.Y.-Y., Liu, F.-C.: A cross-level analysis of organizational creativity climate and perceived innovation: the mediating effect of work motivation. Eur. J. Innov. Manag. **15**, 55–76 (2012)
12. Handzic, M., Chaimungkalanont, M.: Enhancing organizational creativity through socialization. Electron. J. Knowl. Manag. **2**(1), 57–64 (2004)
13. Zahedi, S.R., Zahedi, S.M.: Role of information and communication technologies in modern agriculture. Int. J. Agric. Crop Sci. (IJACS) **4**(23), 1725–1728 (2012)
14. Martins, L.L., Shalley, C.E.: Creativity in virtual work: effects of demographic differences. Small Group Res. **42**(5), 536–561 (2011)
15. Dewett, T.: Understanding the relationship between information technology and creativity in organizations. Creat. Res. J. **15**(2–3), 167–182 (2003)
16. Ollo-López, A., Aramendía-Muneta, M.E.: ICT impact on competitiveness, innovation and environment. Telemat. Inform. **29**(2), 204–210 (2012)
17. Olszak, C.M., Bartuś, T., Lorek, P.: A comprehensive framework of information system design to provide organizational creativity support. Inf. Manag. **55**(1), 94–108 (2012)
18. Giustiniano, L., Lombardi, S., Cavaliere, V.: How knowledge collecting fosters organizational creativity. Manag. Decis. **54**(6), 1464–1496 (2016)
19. Tiwana, A., McLean, E.R.: Expertise integration and creativity in information systems development. J. Manag. Inf. Syst. **22**(1), 13–43 (2005)
20. Gera, S., Gu, W.: The effect of organizational innovation and information technology on firm performance. Int. Prod. Monit. **9**, 37–51 (2004)
21. Önhon, Ö.: The relationship between organizational climate for innovation and employees' innovative work behavior: ICT sector in Turkey. Vezetéstudomány-Budapest Manag. Rev. **50**(11), 53–64 (2019)
22. Markides, C.C., Anderson, J.: Creativity is not enough: ICT-enabled strategic innovation. Eur. J. Innov. Manag. **9**(2), 129–148 (2006)
23. Dingler, A., Enkel, E.: Socialization and innovation: insights from collaboration across industry boundaries. Technol. Forecast. Soc. Chang. **109**, 50–60 (2016)
24. Hignett, S., McDermott, H.: Qualitative Methodology. Evaluation of Human Work, 4th edn., pp. 119–138. CRC Press, Boca Raton (2015)

25. Abdullah, I., Omar, R., Panatik, S.A.L.: A literature review on personality, creativity and innovative behavior. Int. Rev. Manag. Mark. **6**(1S), 177–182 (2016)

26. Amin, A., et al.: The impact of personality traits and knowledge collection behavior on programmer creativity. Inf. Softw. Technol. **128**, 106405 (2019)

27. Runco, M.A., Chand, I.: Cognition and creativity. Educ. Psychol. Rev. **7**(3), 243–267 (1995)

28. Hennessey, B.A.: The social psychology of creativity. Scand. J. Educ. Res. **47**(3), 253–271 (2003)

29. Zmud, R.W.: Perceptions of cognitive styles: acquisition, exhibition and implications for information system design. J. Manag. **5**(1), 7–20 (1979)

30. Yuan, X., Liu, J.: Relationship between cognitive styles and users' task performance in two information systems. In: Paper the Annual Meeting of Association for Information Science & Technology (ASIS&T), Montreal, Canada (2013)

31. Woodman, R.W., Sawyer, J.E., Griffin, R.W.: Toward a theory of organizational creativity. Acad. Manag. Rev. **18**(2), 293–321 (1993)

32. Woodman, R.W., Schoenfeldt, L.F.: Individual differences in creativity. In: Glover, J.A., Ronning, R.R., Reynolds, C.R. (eds.) Handbook of Creativity, pp. 77–91. Springer, Boston (1989). https://doi.org/10.1007/978-1-4757-5356-1_4

33. Carrol, J.B.L.: Domains of cognitive ability. In: Paper Presented at the Meeting of the American Association for the Advancement of Science, Los Angeles (1985)

34. Amabile, T.M.: A model of creativity and innovation in organizations. In: Staw, B.M., Cummings, L.L. (eds.) Research in Organizational Behavior, vol. 10, pp. 123–167. JAI Press, Greenwich (1988)

35. Walsham, G.: Interpretive case studies in IS research: nature and method. Eur. J. Inf. Syst. **4**(2), 74–81 (1995)

36. Åmo, B.W., Kolvereid, L.: Organizational strategy, individual personality and innovation behavior. J. Enterp. Cult. **13**(01), 7–19 (2005)

37. Rothenberg, A., Hausman, C.R.: The Creativity Question. Duke University Press, Durham (1976)

Democratizing Enterprise AI Success Factors and Challenges: A Systematic Literature Review and a Proposed Framework

Tarek Kaddoumi[1] and Torben Tambo[2(✉)] ⓘ

[1] Dubai, UAE
tarek.kaddoumi@gmail.com
[2] Aarhus University, Birk Centerpark 15, 7400 Herning, Denmark
torbento@btech.au.dk

Abstract. To democratize or not to democratize, this is not the problem anymore for the enterprises that consider democratizing their enterprise AI practice; the problem that these enterprises face nowadays, is how to successfully democratize their enterprise AI. In this paper we conduct a systematic literature review to provide an in-depth analysis of the success factors and the challenges of democratizing the artificial intelligence practices in the enterprises, we also build on this review and propose a framework for the enterprise AI democratization that suggests a set of the success factors and challenges. The research design of this paper is to conduct a systematic literature review by including 41 papers as an initial set of studies for review; we screen the papers and implement inclusion and quality checks on these studies, and we qualify 15 papers for the final review. The key findings of this paper, from the systematic literature review, list a set of success factors and challenges that enterprises should consider to strengthen or to avoid. We propose these factors in a form of proposed framework suggesting four categories: strategy, enterprise architecture, data, and trust. Because of the publication specification and limitation, we limited the scope of our primary studies to a limited set to match the constraints and limitations. The paper includes implications for the academic literature review and the extraction of factors that can impact the process of the enterprise artificial intelligence democratization, and the need to increase the awareness of the enterprise AI practices in order to overcome the challenges that might prevent enterprises from having a successful enterprise AI. While there are some efforts to assess and review the success factors and challenges of the AI practices in general, one of the major findings of the literature review conducted is that there is evident research gap in the literature on the perception and associated factors of artificial intelligence. This paper seeks to fill this gap.

Keywords: Enterprise · Emerging technologies · Artificial intelligence · Enterprise architecture · Intelligent enterprise

T. Kaddoumi—Independent IT Expert.

1   Introduction

Companies and organizations act with strong motivation and encouragement to start grasping the benefits of promising emerging technologies like artificial intelligence, blockchain, IoT, and AR/VR [1, 2]. It is noted nowadays that businesses are involved in exploring, evaluating, and implementing one, many, or all of these technologies. Research [3–8] indicates that these technologies can enable businesses in achieving better results and agility for businesses. Among these emerging technologies, Artificial Intelligence (AI) is considered to be the most commonly adopted and explored by businesses [5], through the applications of cognitive technologies, machine learning, and deep learning. One of the approaches to adopt AI in enterprises is AI democratization in the enterprise and making the AI technologies and services accessible and in hand of the employees; this was technically supported with the wide adoption of online platform technologies such as IaaS, PaaS, and SaaS. However, with the wide spectrum of opportunities of democratizing AI in the enterprise, the adoption of enterprise AI doesn't come free of challenges [9], and implications on the enterprise architecture [10–12].

Adopting a new approach is not a straightforward task. Some enterprises achieve success with implementing new approaches, others fail. Extracting the lessons learnt from the successful and the failed experiences gave us the motivator to conduct this study. This entails lack of systematic literature review to highlight the success factors and the challenges of democratizing the AI in enterprises. This paper is based on a systematic literature review and is to propose the enterprise AI democratization framework that can systematically enhance the quality, replicability, reliability, and validity of these reviews [13].

2   Theoretical Background

Emerging technologies, artificial intelligence, the internet of things (IoT), big data, blockchain, and augmented reality are driving businesses and enterprises to change how they operate. Among these disruptive and emerging technologies, artificial intelligence (AI) is considered the most disrupting technology and promises a remarkable business transformation potential [5] and researches indicate that there are several opportunities that AI presents [1]. Artificial intelligence - "the capacity of computers or other machines to exhibit or simulate intelligent behavior" [3] – is "one of the most consequential technologies of our time" [4].

While Artificial intelligence applications and deployment are highly regarded in consumer space, however, firms, businesses, and enterprises have actively considered embedding it into their operations and business models, with very striking results and promises [14]. AI is considered to be a game changer for many businesses industries. In marketing industry and business function for example, artificial Intelligence has achieved high gained adaptability because of the great value that added to the present and future business models and opportunities [5]. Another industry with potential impact of AI is the community well being, where AI holds the potential to either exacerbate or mitigate many threats to community well-being [6]. Banking is another example as well, as AI technologies have been playing an important role in the new banking era by enabling banks to become a customer-centric industry based on data. Banking sector considers personalizing services as an important strategy for leveraging the existing customer engagement, and attracting potential customer become new customers [7]. Another area of AI impact on businesses is predictive maintenance, for example analyzing large amounts of high-dimensional audio and image data where predictive analytics and deep learning can strongly detect anomalies in assembly processes and factories. Additionally, considering the customer service field of business, AI proved the ability to play the role of a critical add on in call centers employing speech recognition technologies and services. Sales industry also witnessed great value of AI implementations, by mashing customer demographic data and the historical transactions in addition to monitoring social media to help generate personal recommendations to identify the consumers next buy [14].

Introducing the AI technologies and services into the core operations and processes of enterprises is expected to impact and to be impacted by the enterprise architecture and should be well managed in integration with the existing enterprise architecture [10] and [12]. These technology advancements can't be introduced without finding the right framework of governance and democratization of tools and technologies. According to [2] "recent advances in Artificial Intelligence (AI) have led to intense debates about benefits and concerns associated with this powerful technology". [14] suggest that with the very motivating promises of AI technologies, applications, and services, by positively impacting the businesses economic, however the embracement of AI in enterprises should come with measures and controls to manage the adoption of the new technology, and to ensure soft transitioning and disruption – if any – that might be resulted. One of the very disruptive ways of adopting and embedding AI technologies and services within the enterprise is democratizing the AI among the enterprise citizens and empowering and enabling these business citizens to be enterprise AI citizens. Democratizing AI is considered by some researchers more than a way of adopting AI, as it is considered to be the need of the day [15].

3   Method

Methodologically we are going to follow the systematic literature review method, which is a method that attempts to make sense of a body of existing literature through the aggregation, interpretation, explanation, or integration of existing research [13]. According to [13], we are going to follow the following process steps in conducting our systematic literature review see Fig. 1.

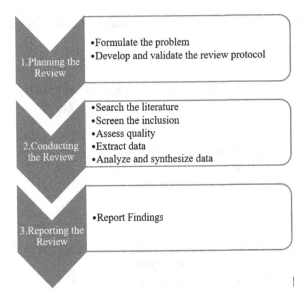

Fig. 1. Systematic literature review method

3.1 Planning the Review

According to [13], the research questions drive the entire literature review process. To be able to control the scope of the research and have better literature inclusion criteria, the research questions are narrowed down to have a manageable research topic. Accordingly, focus in this paper is reviewing the AI democratization in enterprises in academia. Also striving to identify the implication factors that can support or impact the practice of enterprise AI democratization. This can highlight the role of the enterprise architecture in impacting and being impacted by the enterprise AI democratization [12]. The systematic literature review will have three pillars. We will focus on understanding the potential role and the current perception of the Enterprise AI democratization. Answering this first part will help us in moving toward answering the other two questions, as we are going to target identifying the potential success factors that enterprises can consider to be part of their practice of democratizing AI among their firms' employees and teams. Secondly, identifying the challenges and potential obstacles that firms and businesses should be aware of to avoid or mitigate and account for during the process of democratizing their Enterprise AI programs.

3.2 Research Questions

In this review we study the research questions of:

RQ1. What is the concept of democratic thinking of AI in enterprise?
RQ2. What success factors have been reported for artificial intelligence democratization in enterprises?
RQ3. What challenges have been reported for artificial intelligence democratization in enterprises?

Validation Protocol. The criteria we applied contains the following elements:

1. Identification:

   a. Creating a pool of the studies that are included as results of the inclusion

2. Screening:

   a. Removing duplicates from the included studies.
   b. Remove results from books.
   c. Remove the results where abstracts show irrelativity.

3. Eligibility:

   a. Removing studies that do not offer guidance on literature review.
   b. Removing studies that are not in English.
   c. Removing studies that review on a very specific topic.

3.3 Conducting the Review

Channels for Literature Search. Among many channels available for literature search, we choose the electronic databases. Seeking rich results and as complete a search set as we can, we did the literature search by conducting the search among multiple electronic databases, those are: IEEExplore, ACM, Scopus, Web of Knowledge, and Google Scholars.

Keywords Used for the Search. We conducted our studies database searches using keywords identified in alignment with the research, the keywords are identified in the following table grouped in pillars that lead the research.

In this search, we emphasized on the inclusion of the enterprise AI and excluding the studies of cities, countries, human democratization, and nationwide discussions, and including the private sector only (Table 1).

Table 1. Keywords used for search.

Pillar	Keyword
Enterprise	Business, organization, company
Artificial Intelligence	AI, ML, MLOps, AutoML, Artificial Intelligence, Machine Learning
Governance	Ethics, rules, control
Democratization	Democratize**, citizenship, leverage, transform

3.4 Screen for Inclusion

Screen Procedure. As we completed the compilation of the primary studies, we moved to the process of screening these studies for inclusion and to identify which studies to be included in this review, extraction, and. analysis.

To achieve this goal, we applied reviewing the abstracts of the studies, to give a first set of inclusion results, this will be followed in the next step by conducting a quality assessment process by having a full-text review (Table 2).

Table 2. Search facets and topics.

Facet	Relevant topic	Examples of non-relevant topic
Enterprise	Business, firm, companies, marketing, retail	City, country, nation, public
Artificial Intelligence	AI, ML, emerging technologies	Blockchain, Human Intelligence, neural network
Governance	Ethics, rules, governing, transparency, control	Government, policing, regulations
Democratization	Value realization, transformation	Government, policing, regulations

Criteria for Quality Assessment. In this step, we obtained the full texts of the included research and studies. Therefore, we are able to understand the studies in order to list the studies for the next steps of extracting and analysis. We applied a quality review based on checking the following factors: the studies duplication and the studies eligibility.

Quality assessment procedure (Fig. 2).

Fig. 2. Quality Assessment Procedure

Quality assessment results
After implementing we came with the following results (Table 3).

Extract, Analyze, and Synthesize Data. To synthesize our research data, we developed a primary organization of coding for the screened studies, each code is 1:1 mapped to a category, those categories are: strategy and strategy alignment, enterprise architecture, data, and perception of AI trust. We extracted the factors that we highlighted from the papers and assigned them to the right category and we were able to build a proposed framework showing the assignment relationship of each factor (success/challenge) to the categories.

Table 3. Results quality assessment.

Stage	Task	Results	Comments
Identification	Records identified through database searching	(n = 41)	
Screening	Records after duplicates removed	(n = 2)	
	Records screened	(n = 39)	Record excluded with reasons (n = 9) Books (n = 5) Abstract not related (n = 4)
Eligibility	Full text articles assessed for eligibility	(n = 30)	Full text articles excluded, with reasons (15) Did not offer guidance on literature review (n = 8) Not in English (n = 1) Review on a very specific topic (n = 6)
Inclusion	Studies included	(n = 15)	

4   Results

Our systematic literature review extracted a set of success factors and challenges out of a total of 15 papers. For better reporting on these results and findings, we categorized the success factors to fall under four categories, those are:

- Strategy: the role of AI strategy and the alignment between AI strategy and business strategy.
- Enterprise Architecture: the role of the alignment between the AI practice and the enterprise architecture.
- Data: data is well considered as a core for the AI practice; this category highlights the role of the data for better AI democratization.

We worked on formalizing these factors in a proposed framework to illustrate them in an enterprise innovative driven context; to identify the business capabilities involved in the business innovation capability (as complementary capabilities), we refer to [16] identification of the four business capabilities that complement the innovation capability, those business capabilities are: technology development capability, operation capability, management capability, and transaction capability (Fig. 3).

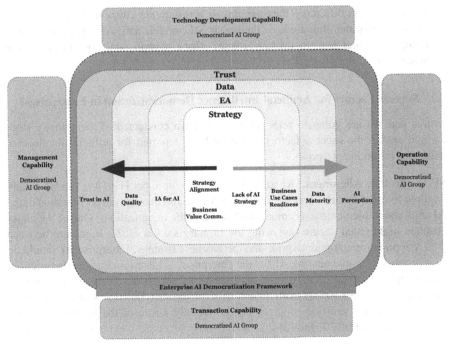

Fig. 3. Proposed framework for the enterprise AI democratization.

5 Discussion

5.1 What is the Concept of Democratic Thinking of AI in Enterprise?

According to reviewing the primary studies and the literature review process, it is solidly remarked that there has been a focus in highlighting the consumer AI for a very long time, however, according to [17], since 2018 the spotlight shifted to the enterprises. The driver is that AI can be deployed at enterprises for enhancing and improving business outcomes and performances. Businesses and enterprises are in serious need to grasp more value from the data they own and to predict business operations, and to enable data-driven decision making. Accordingly, AI and ML adoption grew in businesses with that hope [18]. With more AI and ML applications needed to provide more and better value, it is noted that AI application development takes time, and requires a broad set of skills, and calls for multiple iterations, and it is suggested that the democratization of AI and ML skills and applications resolves this challenge as AI practitioners and data scientists usually work in silos that are dedicated for a specific problem to solve. Borrowing from political science, something can be considered that has become democratized when it becomes available to the average person, therefore it is suggested that AI democratization promotes reusability and sharing best practices among enterprise AI citizens: engineers, analysts, scientists, and stakeholders.

Many companies and organizations that realized how to improve and advance to Enterprise AI have recognized that they are going to employ more than one ML model to get the business difference they are aiming for; they are aware that they are going to consider more than hundreds or thousands ML models and. AI apps, this majorly scales up the AI and data practices and requires that everybody at the organization to be included [17].

5.2 Success Factors for Artificial Intelligence Democratization in Enterprises?

In this part we are going to refer to the review we conducted of the primary studies and extract the success factors that have been reported for artificial intelligence democratization in enterprises.

SF 1 - Strategy Alignment. AI strategy is not an option, per [19], it is fundamentally required for modern firms that are looking to govern and manage the proliferation of the AI apps and implementations among the firms and the organizations. One of the major enablers highlighted during reviewing the primary studies is the alignment between the IA application in the enterprise and the business strategy. Enterprise AI should do as it promises: "implementing AI for the enterprise". This critical nexus (between AI and enterprise) can be done by ensuring that the AI adoption and embedding into the enterprise practices happens in alignment with the business objectives of the enterprise and that AI has a strategic program that is strongly aware of the business strategy, objectives, and KPIs [20] and [21].

SF 2 - Business Value Communication. Enterprise AI is about implementing the value drivers of AI applications and technologies for the business; however, it was reported by the review that the lack of understanding of the AI promise and programs among the business workspace citizens and executives is one of the major issues that should be addressed to facilitate better and successful Enterprise AI [22] and [23]. Democratizing the AI for the enterprises should be business citizens friendly, where value engineering behind the Enterprise AI should be communicated with the AI citizens of the enterprise in a language and a way of storytelling that is understood by the business employees and executives for better AI enabled and supported business decision making. Per [22] AI consideration and augmentation for better business decision making exposes a factor that should be critically accounted for -crucially-, which is how business executives and decision makers are able to deal and interact with the AI applications and services in a friendly and fluid manner.

SF 3 - Enterprise Information Architecture. In order to enable the enterprise AI citizens to deliver value out of their AI applications, and to participate in supporting the enterprise decisions and providing the ROI leverage and impact, they should have a foundation of information architecture to preset a shared democratized layer of business understanding to give the AI use access impact a democratized dimension by being enterprise wide [24].

SF 4 - Trust in AI Automation. One of the highly considered success factors is to empower the enterprise AI citizens by having a more productive enterprise AI platform, where they can enjoy automating the repeatable data science and AI tasks and focusing more on using the ML and AI results to generate value and insights for the enterprise. This automation means shifting some tasks to the automation platform; however, this doesn't come without issues related to enterprise trusting the AI automation black boxes [4].

A modern pattern has been introduced recently that empowers enterprises to have this automation issue/challenge solved and addressed, this kind of platform is referred to as AutoML or MLOps. This new AI design pattern is used when teams apply DevOps kind of practices to their AI/ML implementations.

SF 5 - Data Quality. Related to the previous point, the AI (and MLOps and AutoML) trust issue can be directly linked to the quality of an ML model (model accuracy, model fairness, and model robustness) which is – per [25] - often a reflection of the quality of the underlying data, e.g., noises, imbalances, and additional adversarial perturbations. Suggested by different researchers that improving the enterprise data sets (cleaning, integration, and features engineering) can be a main driver behind improving the ML model trust factors (accuracy, integration and fairness) [25].

According to [25], "it is not surprising to see data quality playing a prominent and central role in MLOps", and he clarified that "many researchers have conducted fascinating and seminal work around MLOps by looking into different aspects of data quality".

5.3   Challenges Reported for Artificial Intelligence Democratization in Enterprises?

In this part we are going to refer to the review we conducted of the primary studies and extract the challenges that have been reported for artificial intelligence democratization in enterprises.

CH 1 - Lack of AI Strategy. According to the systematic literature reviewed primary studies, the lack of strategizing the AI for enterprise was remarkably considered as one of the main challenges. According to [14] businesses should develop a clear AI strategy to clearly identify the gains and to be able to find the right talents to engage in this strategic AI practice. This will allow overcoming the business functions silos that might occur in business silos that limit an end-to-end AI program, and will support the process of democratizing the AI within the enterprise [18].

CH 2 - Lack of ROI Proven Use Cases. As per [26], some businesses tend to implement AI in the enterprise by developing pilots and proof of concepts for the AI technologies without having a business value driven use case.

Picking the right use cases for implementing and exploring the AI democratization in the enterprise is a vital factor in the process of realizing value from the enterprise AI practice. There is a relationship between the AI impact on the business use cases and the AI revenue impact [21]. The appreciation of this relationship between the applicability of the revenue impact per the AI impact on the business cases is recognized as one of the challenges that democratizing the AI in enterprises would face.

CH 3 - Data Volume for ML Models. ML is a core model of the enterprise AI enterprise practices that companies are looking for adoption, democratizing, and having enterprise citizens empowered and enabled to use. Among the challenges that enterprises are facing, the reviews reported that the ML models are developed and designed for a huge dataset by design, and that the learning nature of these models requires huge volume of data; according [14], enterprise ML models might need huge volumes of data in order to generate the results that are anticipated from it, this will certainly can't be always feasible for all enterprises and firms.

CH 4 – Employees Perception of AI. Progress and advancement in AI are going to create core effects on enterprise employees and individuals and their culture [1]. According to the review results, the researchers should hold ethical responsibility to analyze and assess the AI impact on the work workspaces. AI is – correctly or wrongly - tagged as a main driver for taking over and replacing human jobs; this argument varies from being a true fact as AI can enhance work efficiency by helping to automate repetitive work, and support business executives taking more insightful decisions to an exaggerated view where employees fear AI regardless the value benefits that can be delivered. Per [1] we have these perspectives presented as technology pessimists believe that emerging technologies will take away jobs. However, technology optimists suggest that "non-routine" jobs may not only exist but also surge.

5.4   The Mutual Impact Between AI and EA

This paper is presenting a solid belief in the interchangeable implications between enterprise architecture - as the enterprise platform of change in terms of management, control, and governance – and the artificial intelligence technologies and service democratization as a practice of democratizing set of emerging and disruptive technologies with rich capabilities for change and business value enhancement [12]. The paper still sees that the mutual impact between these two enterprise management practices requires more and in-depth research, we had a goal in this review to extract more factors in relationship with this mutual impact, however we were able to address and analyze some of the factors, and we are aware that these are not all the factors, and that this area requires more focus and research dedication. We consider this work as a platform for more work we are planning to conduct to enrich the research around the mutual impact. Between EA and AI.

A critical view is that both EA and AI are vaguely defined constructs. EA is mostly empirically driven and sets the enterprise scene for business – technology alignment. AI is an assemblage of technologies with different base platforms, algorithmic approaches and reach. AI is it's existing form and relatively new implementation experiences are modest. So, AI being more theoretically driven is a clash to EA's empiricism. AI is the unknown determinant in this interrelation. So, requirements and demands on the AI world must be technological and application-wise specificity and explicitness. Thereby the stipulated framework can help challenge the technological precision and operational maturity of AI.

6 Conclusions

This paper conducted a systematic literature review of the field of the enterprise AI democratization, it proposed a framework of success factors and challenges to help enterprises in their journey toward the AI democratization. Although the research was carefully and thoughtfully prepared, we are still aware of its limitations. First, the size of the primary studies to be studied could have been larger and more than 41. Secondly, the time limitation was vital in scoping the work of the study, accordingly some potential further research in this area is recommended as follows. Firstly, we, i.e. the authors of this paper, are aware - per our academic and professional experiences - of some of the factors (success and challenges) that have not been referred to or mentioned in any of the literature that we were able to screen, review, and extract from. Examples of these factors are algorithmic transparency, AI and business processes integrability, accountability, and maintainability. Therefore, we recommend allocating the time and focus on exploring potential existing academic literature related to these factors or proposing them in the right mythological format. Secondly, we propose scaling the proposed framework to be tested and validated with multiple empirical experiences and applications; this can validate the proposed factors in this study, add to the, and support the framework with weights for each factor.

References

1. Jain, A., Ranjan, S.: Implications of emerging technologies on the future of work. IIMB Manag. Rev. **32**(4), 448–454 (2020). https://doi.org/10.1016/j.iimb.2020.11.004
2. Ulnicane, I., Eke, D., Knight, E., Ogoh, G., Stahl, B.: Good governance as a response to discontents? Déjà vu, or lessons for AI from other emerging technologies. Interdiscip. Sci. Rev. **46**(1–2), 71–93 (2021). https://doi.org/10.1080/03080188.2020.1840220
3. Finley, T.: The democratization of artificial intelligence: one library's approach. Inf. Technol. Libr. **38**(1), 8–13 (2019). https://doi.org/10.6017/ital.v38i1.10974
4. Ahmed, N., Wahed, M.: The De-democratization of AI: Deep Learning and the Compute Divide in Artificial Intelligence Research (2020). http://arxiv.org/abs/2010.15581
5. Verma, S., Sharma, R., Deb, S., Maitra, D.: Artificial intelligence in marketing: Systematic review and future research direction. Int. J. Inf. Manag. Data Insights **1**(1), 100002 (2021). https://doi.org/10.1016/j.jjimei.2020.100002
6. Musikanski, L., Rakova, B., Bradbury, J., Phillips, R., Manson, M.: Artificial intelligence and community well-being: a proposal for an emerging area of research. Int. J. Commun. Well-Being **3**(1), 39–55 (2020). https://doi.org/10.1007/s42413-019-00054-6
7. Indriasari, E., Gaol, F.L., Matsuo, T.: Digital banking transformation: application of artificial intelligence and big data analytics for leveraging customer experience in the Indonesia banking sector. In: Proceedings of the 2019 8th International Congress on Advanced Applied Informatics, IIAI-AAI 2019, pp. 863–868 (2019). https://doi.org/10.1109/IIAI-AAI.2019.00175
8. Luce, L.: How AI is Revolutionizing the Fashion Industry (2019)
9. Unesco: Artificial intelligence in education: challenges and opportunities for sustainable development. Working Paper Education Policy, vol. 7, p. 46 (2019) https://en.unesco.org/themes/education-policy
10. Snoeck, M., Stirna, J., Weigand, H., Proper, H.A.: Panel discussion: artificial intelligence meets enterprise modelling. In: CEUR Workshop Proceedings, vol. 2586, pp. 88–97 (2020)

11. Auth, G., Czarnecki, C., Bensberg, F.: Impact of robotic process automation on enterprise architectures. Lecture Notes Informatics (LNI), Proceedings - Series Gesellschaft fur Inform., vol. 295, pp. 59–65 (2019). https://doi.org/10.18420/inf2019_ws05

12. Winter, R., Fischer, R.: Essential layers, artifacts, and dependencies of enterprise architecture. In: Proceedings of the 2006 10th IEEE International Enterprise Distributed Object Computing Conference Workshops, EDOCW2006, no. May, pp. 30–38 (2006). https://doi.org/10.1109/EDOCW.2006.33

13. Xiao, Y., Watson, M.: Guidance on conducting a systematic literature review. J. Plan. Educ. Res. **39**(1), 93–112 (2019). https://doi.org/10.1177/0739456X17723971

14. Manyika, J., Bughin, J.: The Promise and Challenge of the Age of Artificial Intelligence, no. October, p. 8. McKinsey Co. (2018)

15. Vuppalapati, C., Ilapakurti, A., Kedari, S., Vuppalapati, J., Kedari, S., Vuppalapati, R.: Democratization of AI, albeit constrained IoT devices & Tiny ML, for creating a sustainable food future. In: Proceedings of the 3rd International Conference on Inventive Computation Technologies, ICICT 2020, pp. 525–530 (2020). https://doi.org/10.1109/ICICT50521.2020.00089

16. Zawislak, P.A., Alves, A.C., Tello-gamarra, J., Barbieux, D., Reichert, F.M.: Innovation capability: from technology development to transaction capability. **7**(2), 14–27 (2012)

17. Pimpale, D.: Reshape enterprise using AI, data analytics, enterprises science and learning platforms. **3**(1) (2019)

18. Patel, J.: The democratization of machine learning features. In: Proceedings of the 2020 IEEE 21st International Conference on Information Reuse and Integration for Data Science, IRI 2020, pp. 136–141 (2020). https://doi.org/10.1109/IRI49571.2020.00027

19. Bellomarini, L., Fakhoury, D., Gottlob, G., Sallinger, E.: Knowledge graphs and enterprise AI: the promise of an enabling technology. In: 2019 IEEE 35th International Conference on Data Engineering (ICDE), pp. 26–37 (2019). https://doi.org/10.1109/ICDE.2019.00011

20. Guenole, N., Feinzig, S.: The business case for AI in HR—with insights and tips on getting started. IBM WATSON Talent, p. 36 (2018). https://public.dhe.ibm.com/common/ssi/ecm/81/en/81019981usen/81019981-usen-00_81019981USEN.pdf

21. Pandey, S.: ROI of AI: Effectiveness and Measurement, vol. 10, no. 05, pp. 749–761 (2021)

22. Chander, A., Srinivasan, R., Chelian, S., Wang, J., Uchino, K.: Working with beliefs: AI transparency in the enterprise. In: CEUR Workshop Proceedings, vol. 2068 (2018)

23. Larsson, S., Heintz, F.: Transparency in artificial intelligence. Internet Policy Rev. **9**(2), 1–16 (2020). https://doi.org/10.14763/2020.2.1469

24. Ding, R., Palomares, I., Wang, X., Yang, G., Liu, B.: Large-scale decision-making: characterization, taxonomy, challenges and future directions from an artificial intelligence and applications perspective, vol. 59, no. January, pp. 84–102 (2020). https://doi.org/10.1016/j.inffus.2020.01.006

25. Renggli, C., Rimanic, L., Gürel, N.M., Karlaš, B., Wu, W., Zhang, C.: A Data Quality-Driven View of MLOps, no. 1, pp. 1–12 (2021). http://arxiv.org/abs/2102.07750

26. Kerzel, U.: Enterprise AI canvas integrating artificial intelligence into business. Appl. Artif. Intell. **35**(1), 1–12 (2021). https://doi.org/10.1080/08839514.2020.1826146

Organizational Aspects in Achieving a Successful Digital Transformation: Case of an ERP System Change

Parisa Aasi(✉), Erik Gråhns, Robin Geijer, and Lazar Rusu

Department of Computer and Systems Sciences, Stockholm University, Stockholm, Sweden
{parisa,lrusu}@dsv.su.se

Abstract. Digital transformation has been an interesting concept from the organizational perspective for a long time. The benefits of a successful digital transformation can take your organization into the next step by providing an increased organizational growth, aid market reachability by penetrating new and exciting markets, or enable your business operations to function to a greater extent than before with higher efficiency and lower lead times. Digital transformation is however a complex and diverse concept that means to integrate new innovations by using digital technology into the organization with the need of making greater organizational changes to succeed. This research, has explored how different organizational aspects like structural, technological and cultural ones can impact the success of a digital transformation during an ERP system change. A case study has been conducted in a company to identify how the current structural, technological, and cultural aspects influence the current digital transformation in that the company. The data was collected through interviews with employees having managerial roles and from internal documents of company and was analyzed using thematic analysis. The results show an agile approach, a more decentralized structure and high readiness for change, along with a transparent communication between management and co-workers to be beneficial for a successfully digital transformation.

Keywords: Digital transformation · Organizational aspects · ERP · System integration · Organizational change

1 Introduction

Digital transformation refers to the strategic business transformation that requires cross-cutting organizational change as well as the implementation of digital technologies. Verhoef et al. [1, p. 889] defines digital transformation as "a change in how a firm employs digital technologies, to develop a new digital business model that helps to create and appropriate more value for the firm". Stating that we notice that digital transformation is multidisciplinary as it involves changes in strategy, organization, information technology,

M. Themistocleous and M. Papadaki (Eds.): EMCIS 2021, LNBIP 437, pp. 653–666, 2022.
https://doi.org/10.1007/978-3-030-95947-0_46

supply chains and marketing. According to a study of the Massachusetts Institute of Technology (MIT), digital-transformed businesses are 26% more profitable than norms [2]. However, to reduce the risks, a clear strategy is needed to for a successful digital transformation initiative and these strategies vary depending on the organization and its business [2]. In fact, 70% of all digital transformation initiatives do not reach their goals [3]. Therefore, the biggest concern amongst senior executives are the risks that digital transformation implies. Yet, because today almost every organizations embark on the journey of digital transformation. The topic concerning a successful integration is of a great importance as it has been proven that corporations that have failed their digital transformation are less profitable than those that have succeeded in this [2]. This because there are cases when even high-profile companies have failed in their digital transformation initiatives [4]. However, the knowledge about the role of organizational design in supporting the pursuit of digital transformations is scarce [5]. Therefore, in this research we have investigated in a case study how a specific company deals with their organizational change and strategy in preparing and adapting the organization in the best way during a digital transformation like is a new Enterprise Resource Planning (ERP) system change. The research that this study is intended to answer is *"What impact does structural, technological, and cultural aspects have in achieving a successful digital transformation in the case of an ERP system change?"*.

The next sections of the paper include the research background, research methodology, results and conclusions.

2   Research Background

2.1   Digital Transformation

The synoptic concept of digital transformation is that it is the use of technology to radically improve performance or reach of enterprises [6]. As this sounds very familiar to digitalization, it differentiates itself by affecting every aspect of an organization [1, 7], rather than only making business operations more digitalized [8]. A digital transformation is the reinvention of certain aspects of the company, according to Gurbaxani & Dunkle [9] these are organizational structure, processes, capabilities, and culture. In conclusion, this means that the transformation will not only change companies, but also markets and industries. To achieve this level of success, the digital transformation is dependent on digital matureness, as illustrated by [10]. Digitally mature businesses focus on integrating digital technologies in transforming their businesses. At the same time, less mature organizations focus on solving discrete problems with individual technologies.

2.2   Enterprise Resource Planning System

Enterprise Resource Planning (ERP) is a broad term used for the software package that creates the organizational capability to automate and integrate most of their business processes, share common data, and access information in real time [11]. An organization would want to go through with their ERP implementation or change because the rewards in this case would outweigh the risks. A successful implementation of an ERP system can help with managing company resources and increase the operational and financial capabilities, and thereby increase the business' profits and performance [12].

2.3 Digital Transformation

Digital transformation should no longer be only adjusted with the business strategy. Instead, these two strategies should merge into a new overarching strategy called digital business strategy which reflects organizational strategy. Digital business strategy needs to be formulated and executed based on the organizational strategy and leverage digital resources to create differential value [13]. According to Schwertner [2] a digital transformation strategy always has certain elements in common, no matter the industry. One of these elements is titled structural changes and it is listed among these elements because they are most often needed to fit the previous but still in use operations with the newly integrated ones. Naturally the need and scale of the restructure is dependent on the scope of the planned digital transformation. Verhoef et al. [1] concludes that the organization will benefit if their structure is considered flexible for digital change, in which flexibility is described as an organizational structure that is composed of separate business units, agile organizational forms, and digital functional areas, rather than a more centralized structure with a top-down hierarchy.

2.4 Conceptual Framework for Digital Transformation Success

There are three main organizational aspects that are affected during a digital transformation according to our findings from previous research literature. These are the technological aspects [1, 9, 10, 14, 15]; the structural aspects [2, 9, 14, 16]; and the cultural aspects [9, 10, 17, 18]. As we also could notice that are a number of drivers that influence digital transformation that is also influencing these organizational aspects of the organization. To visualize some of the drivers found in the research literature review a conceptual research framework is presented in Fig. 1, with the drivers of Verina & Titko [19] and the three categories of affected organizational aspects (technological, structural and cultural) as a result of the digital transformation.

A brief definition of each digital transformation drivers mentioned in the conceptual framework is presented in Table 1.

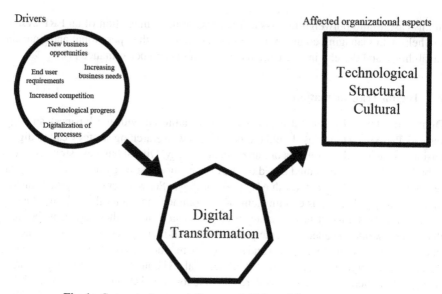

Fig. 1. Conceptual research framework (Adapted from [19, p. 724]).

Table 1. Digital transformation drivers (Adapted from [19, p. 724])

Digital Transformation Drivers	Definition
Increasing business needs	The organizational goals and objectives have increased and a digital transformation of the business would be a good response to cope.
Increased competition	The industry of the company has become harder, and to maintain its market share, a digital transformation would be a good idea.
New business opportunities	The possibility to enter a new market or evolve your current business model through new innovative ideas, which will often lead to a digital transformation.
Technological progress	When the organization develops or implement new software into their business.
Digitalization of processes	When the organization develops or implement new software into their business.
End user requirements	To make changes in the organization through their end user feedback and knowledge.

3 Research Methodology

3.1 Case Study Description

To answer the research question, a case study is conducted giving the possibility to gain a holistic view of the subject, compare different opinions and explore certain aspects of a specific situation [20]. By doing this, the generalization from a single case study can be interpreted with greater meaning and lead to a desired cumulative knowledge [21]. Moreover, according to Flyvbjerg [22] a single case study can be important for scientific development and also could be a complement to existing research.

The company in this case study operates in the insurance industry and has about 200 employees as well as close to 100 consultants at the moment. The company is in the middle of a transformation journey with several ongoing projects running in parallel. The project that contributes most to the digital transformation is the company's change of ERP system. The current ERP system is outdated and is difficult to further develop and they want to be able to meet new requirements with an increased number of modern digital services and have a high delivery capacity and gain new businesses. They started the project a couple of years ago with a comprehensive analysis and are about to go live with the first parts of the new system during 2023. This change of system will lead to major changes in their organization and how they will work. Before a restructure of the project, there were 77 employees and consultants involved, but after the restructure that number has dropped to about 42. The process of changing the ERP system has begun in 2018 with an extensive feasibility study and planned to be delivered a first part of the new ERP system in the autumn of 2020. However, this was canceled due to the impact of a government decision in the EU. This partial delivery is now planned to go live in 2023 instead. Due to this, the project was recently restructured in the spring of 2021 to better match the new conditions. The entire project is planned to be completed in 2027.

3.2 Data Collection

The data collection method in this research was done by conducting six semi-structured interviews with several decision makers on different levels in the company. An interview protocol was used containing questions based on the conceptual framework of this research. The interviewees were selected based on their experiences and roles in the project regarding the change of the company's ERP-system and the corresponding digital transformation in the company. The study was conducted by interviewing six employees having managerial roles from different departments of the company. All the interviews were held online using Microsoft Teams due to the circumstances of Covid-19. However, to achieve data triangulation [23] internal documents were also collected from the company to have other sources of information and multiple perspectives about the research under investigation. Before the interviews was held mutual consent was attained from all the respondents. The interviews were also recorded using Microsoft Teams and then transcribed for analysis. In Table 2, is shown the interviewees with their position and responsibilities in the company, and the length of interviews.

Table 2. List interviewees, their position and responsibilities in the company, and the length of interviews

Interviewee Nr.	Position	Responsibilities	Interview length
Interviewee 1	Chief of Business Development and Analysis	Manages resources related to the ERP resources related to ERP system change project	49 min
Interviewee 2	Chief of IT development	Responsible for seven development teams where most of them are involved in the ERP system change project	1 h and 26 min
Interviewee 3	Chief of Digital Services	Responsible for a team that develops new digital services in the organization. Former solution architect in the ERP system change project	1h and 15 min
Interviewee 4	Chief Customer Officer	Responsible for all the customer related divisions as well in the project management group for the ERP system project change	54 min
Interviewee 5	Business Investigator	Responsible for a team that receives deliveries from the system supplier as well to inform the business functions	51 min
Interviewee 6	Chief Information Officer	Responsible for the IT-department as well as being part of the project management group for the ERP system change project	1 h

3.3 Data Analysis

The data collected was analyzed using thematic analysis by following the guidelines of Braun & Clarke [24] for the data analysis. According to Bryman [25] the goal of thematic analysis is to find patterns, themes from the collected data by carefully reading through the material and cross referencing the answers from the different interviews. The discoveries should be of importance and relevance for the study and the research question. Therefore, the data analysis process has looked to find patterns and identify themes from the data collected in the studied company. The identified themes in the data analysis are the followings: organizational structure, technological advancement, cultural mindset, increased business needs, new business opportunities, change management and data management. A description of these themes is included below.

3.3.1 Theme 1: Organizational Structure

Most of the respondents mentioned that the company has a traditional organizational structure following a hierarchical model. This organizational structure impedes the digital transformation progress. They have planned and now are undergoing a change in their organizational structure by breaking down the more centralized organization of the company and implement smaller independent working teams at the ground level of the organization (as is shown in Fig. 2).

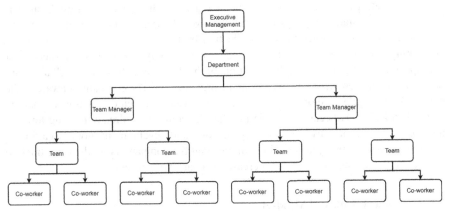

Fig. 2. The team-based model following the organization restructure

This organizational restructure should in turn reduce the directives from the top-level management since these teams are supposed to take responsibility for a specific component within the organization on its own. Interviewee 3 have noticed that "It should not be the greater organization above that decides upon what is to be and how it should be achieved." In the early stages of the project, the company was more focused on the business perspective. But with time and a restructure of the project, the main perspective changed to the IT side. The aspects of cross functional collaboration between the business and IT by saying that to decide on a solution with an already established way of achieving this would be bad practice. But to involve too many users in the developing stages would not be sufficient for the time frame of the project. They are however in the middle of an organizational restructure that will decentralize the organization and making their business more agile. This will effectively ensure a higher digital flexibility as according to Verhoef et al. [1]. By transforming their organizational structure into a more cross functional one, they can also assure that their structure is better prepared for new digital technologies as to have an established digital organization is a success factor of digital transformation according to Morakanyane et al. [10]. The ERP system change will also strengthen the company's journey towards becoming a more digital developed organization, as [26] states that ERP systems have been proved to be the solution to increase cross-connectivity and to have up-to-date-information within the organization.

3.3.2 Theme 2: Technological Advancement

A driver in the conceptual framework that can lead to a digital transformation is technological advancement. An important aspect that was highlighted during most of the interviews is to have an agile development within the organization. The consensus was that the iterative processes were beneficial for their current ERP project. Interviewee 6 mentioned: "Everyone is happy when there is a fairly fast rise in efficiency when entering an agile delivery model." This is further verified by Interviewee 2, who stated that the agile principles ensured continuous coordination and value creation for the customer in portions. The difference in their agile efficiency is depended on the digital matureness curve and where their current position. It was apparent during this study that there is a difference between digital matureness depending on the where in the organizational you look. The findings from the literature review regarding the success of digital transformation, as it was stated by [10] shows that the level of success is dependent on the level of digital matureness. Since the data collection from the case study implies that there was a range of different levels of matureness, one can only assume that the success, or perhaps more so the ease of implementation, of the digital transformation will also vary between the different departments within the organization. The company is aware of the benefits that an agile development can have on the success of their digital transformation, as implied by [1]. Especially considering that the company's already moving towards the goal of a more iterative oriented organization and development model to aid their ongoing transformation journey. This implies that the company is on the right track to reduce the risk of failure, or rather increase the chance of success.

3.3.3 Theme 3: Cultural Mindset

The coherent though within the organization is that a digital transformation is both time consuming and costly. As part of this, a new concept has recently been presented on the intranet and that they will follow, called minimum viable product. This means to develop a good enough solution to launch, but one that is not necessarily for long-term and as final solution. Interviewee 2 had an interesting perspective of the time frame of digital transformation and explained: "I do not know if these so-called digital transformations will ever lead to an end, but one is perhaps only at different stages within it." If a digital transformation were to be continuous, it would also demand continuous investments from the company and further imply that it is a huge cost for the organization. Even though not every interviewee shared the view that a digital transformation is continuous, they agreed upon the fact that it is a time-consuming process and that there are some economical concerns of digital transformation apparent during some of the interviews. Even though there were some economical concerns to be found, it was mentioned that the company was open to change. Just because customer service and IT department are ready for change doesn't mean that the organization as a whole is ready. There are in fact difference between the readiness amongst the departments. One reasoning that is that there are a range of different personal opinions towards the digital transformation project, where some have concerns about their future role within the company. Another reason that is mentioned by Interviewee 1 is that there may be some prerequisites missing. Where the competence, ability, and will may be missing from some ways of the organization.

However, the company is aware of some weaknesses and no matter the doubts or concerns that are connected to the digital transformation, they still do want change. The cultural aspect is one out of four aspects in which the company needs to reinvent during their digital transformation journey. This aspect is very broad since it involves roles, work ethics, competencies, opinions, concerns, and more. One finding from the case study is that there is a wide range of opinions towards the digital transformation project, where some areas of the company is more reluctant to change while others are not at all. This gap in differences is directly affecting the organizations readiness to change and making the reasoning behind the digital transformation harder to defend. The difference in opinions may hinder their success of digital transformation since they are obstructing a solid level of readiness to change. By considering the employees and the effect that the digital transformation may have on their daily assignments, the company would better understand what needs to change. If these changes are relevant and wanted by the affected employees, they will instead help the company to successfully perform a digital transformation because it would increase the readiness for change. Since it was found during the case study that the company still have a consensus that they do want this transformation and they do want this change, it can be assumed that there are some sort of transparency of the reasoning and process of the digital transformation which improve the mindset towards it.

3.3.4 Theme 4: Increased Business Needs

To increase automation and thereby improve operations efficiency was also an occurring subject, where the goal of an ERP system change was to reduce the amount of manual labor during repetitive tasks and reduce customer lead times. This would also ensure that the organization would be ready for bigger changes in their operational ways by enabling the work force to instead focus on more manual heavy workloads. One improvement that is to be made by digitalization is the possibility for pension deposits to be placed with the individual's pension company with much shorter lead times using new digital services. One subject which also affects the company in multiple ways are external requirements. These involves the rules and laws of handling pension contracts. To be held back from digitalizing and improving their efficiency by external requirements is an actual problem in which the organization must deal with. The steady increase of business needs can be a main driver of digital transformation, and the case study proves that this may also be one of the stronger reasonings of this specific transformation. The company analyze its business operations to find which parts that are no longer viable or sufficient in their goal of greater efficiency. There is also the constant need of answering regulations to continue with their digital advancement. This is considered a hindering factor and is impossible for the company to avoid. However, it could be considered as an addition to their already established internal requirements. By treating the external requirements as such, it would create a better end solution.

3.3.5 Theme 5: New Business Opportunities

Some business opportunities that are enabled by the digital transformation can also be extracted from the case study. During their digital transformation, there have been other technological heavy projects that have been implemented to further improve the service for their customers. During several interviews, it is clearly stated that the end goal of performing a digital transformation and to achieve more efficient workflow, is to reduce the brokerage-fee in which they offer to their customers. Interviewee 5 has mentioned that: "And then it is supposed to be cheaper, we just simply want to lower our brokerage-fee". The future goal mentioned above would highlight yet another business opportunity. By investing in, and developing a new digital platform in which the customer interacts with, they should be able to increase the customer satisfaction. The Interviewee 6 has stated that this platform could change on a day-to-day basis if it would be needed, since the operations are handled by the company, and the development is also made in-house. This platform is also developed as to fit the new ERP system in order to drive innovation and increase the digital services that the company can provide to their customers. Furthermore, it was mentioned that to change their current ERP system to a customized standard system, or better called Software as a Service (SaaS), is a great business opportunity because of future possibilities to share development costs. Currently the solution is guiding the development of some specific releases from their SaaS-provider, and if these releases are of value for other companies and of good standard, it would be possible to share the costs for upcoming highly sector specific developing costs. By acting on some new business opportunities that has occurred and some that has been a driving factor for the digital transformation, the business can fulfill some transformation goals that are set. Their main goal of reducing brokerage-fee for their customers would benefit from the increased efficiency provided by some of these investment opportunities. For example, the digital platform that the customer interacts with reduces manual labor. This in turn means reduced lead times and cost for the organization and therefore also more cost-efficient for the customer. This new digital platform is also developed to fit in with the new ERP system, which according to Schwertner [2] is an element of digital transformation that is common within all industries. This shows that the company is on the right path with their current opportunity investments. The possibility of a lowered development cost for future releases is also an example of investments that are made within the company today for a chance of future benefits. If this happens, the reduced cost for the company would in turn also present a reduced cost for the customer, thus again achieving their main goal of reducing their brokerage-fee.

3.3.6   Theme 6: Change Management

The company did not have a clearly expressed digital strategy. Instead they put a lot of effort in conducting studies about capabilities, objectives, existing ERP system, and future requirements. From the findings they continue by making a prioritization evaluation and set up a plan of a desired future state of the company in order to determine which projects that are going to be worked on at the moment. As part of the project they made sure to involve end users to get them on board for the upcoming changes. After all, it is the end user that will use the system, making it important that the system match the needs of the business. Anther communication change included their habit of sending out weekly letters with updates on what's happening in the organization and the project. It is mentioned that this can portray things in a larger perspective within the company to increase the understanding and give new insights to the employees. Another important aspect of change management is the need for education for the employees since the duties of many employees will change fundamentally. It is apparent that the company had no clear digital strategy prior to the digital transformation, and according to Schwertner [2] this is needed to be successful. However, since the company conducted several analytical studies before they started the transformation journey, they had somewhat of an idea of what to do and expect moving on with the project. As to why this is not considered a strategy is mainly due to the absence of clear directions showing the involved parties how to progress in the company's digital transformation. During this project, they are constantly prioritizing the areas of development as well as investigating which users are to be involved in what project.

3.3.7 Theme 7: Data Management

It was apparent this theme in conjunction with a digital transformation and by performing an ERP system change, that data management it is an important aspect for the company to have sufficient amount of- and good quality data. The current state of their ERP system has been customized to such an extent that it makes it difficult to further develop. By not documenting these prior customizations correctly, it directly impacts the data quality and indirectly hindering the ongoing ERP change because of poor data. Furthermore, there is a lot of data missing within the current system solution in order for the company to go fully digital. In some places, there is such a lack of information, that these cavities have been merged together and the current existing data has been summed up into a more generalized collection of data. This forces the company to constantly work with manual corrections, which is highly time consuming. This is one aspect that will hopefully change for the better with the new ERP system fully implemented. One of the main restrictions of digitalizing the company's business operations is that the old ERP system is not viable. There are too many customizations of the system, and because of this it is hard to create and store their data. Berić et al. [11] have noticed that an ERP system is a software package that makes the company capable to share common data and access this information in real time. The case study shows how the old system is incapable of achieving these results and therefore the digital transformation is needed from a data management perspective of the company. The data management will yet again also help the company in achieving their goals of increased efficiency and reduced cost for the customer. Specifically, the manual corrections mentioned in the case study is a time-consuming process and it is a cause of bad quality of data and it being hard to access for the users. The digital transformation connected with the ERP change should enable the organization to have less redundant- and more accessible data after the implementation.

4   Results

In order to achieve a successful digital transformation, it is necessary that organizational change, data integration, and technology should be focused equally [2]. From the case study results, and the codes mentioned within their respective theme was created a summary of the most significant factors affecting the company's digital transformation success (see Fig. 3). By doing so, a deeper understanding of the impact that a digital transformation can have on an organization is achieved.

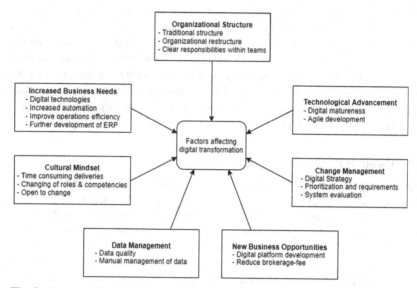

Fig. 3. Most significant factors affecting digital transformation in the studied company

As we can see in Fig. 3 (with the most significant factors affecting digital transformation) the company is working with several aspects simultaneously during their digital transformation and it is hard to determine what areas the company has focused more of its resources on. The company has some kind of balanced focus in use within their digital transformation projects, thus improving their chances of a successful digital transformation as is mentioned by [2].

The studied company has done a lot of work for increasing the likelihood for a successful digital transformation. In fact, the company's management were aware of its historically slow development processes, but with a newly implemented organizational structure and an agile approach they wish to reinforce their capabilities using digital technologies. However, the company's management has found a risk with the ongoing digital transformation that was due to a sudden need for delaying the first delivery of the new ERP system. This means that the timeline of the project has suddenly undergone through major changes, and instead of delivery the new ERP system in 2020 this was rescheduled to 2023. Therefore, the management group of the project had to reevaluate the time schedule and the involvement of every project participant needed to be overlooked. With this in mind, there is a higher risk that the budget will not hold and the pressure will increase when they will need to deliver a bigger part of the ERP system at a later state.

5 Conclusions

The study has looked to identify how structural, technological, and cultural organization aspects influence a successful digital transformation in a company. In this specific case, an ERP system change was planned to be done within the company, and thus inducing the need for a digital transformation. A case study was performed to identify the structural, technological and cultural aspects of the company being studied.

In order to achieve a successful digital transformation, the company will need to move from the more traditional, hierarchical organizational structure and to follow a more decentralized and team-based model. Another key factor for a successful digital transformation is the company's ability to implement new technology. Through an agile approach, a new digital platform is considered to be implemented in order to promote the digital transformation. By working towards these agile operations and developing new technologies, the digital matureness of the company will increase, further strengthening their position to successfully implement the new ERP system. Additionally, the impacts of the cultural aspect of an organization in their digital transformation is important to be connected to the information that is provided to the affected parties prior to the initiation of the project. The time restraint of the study limited to exclusively examine how the company took on the change of their ERP system and subsequently their digital transformation journey. Almost of the employees have worked from home because of the circumstances from Covid-19 and therefore, it was harder to observe and get a clear picture of the culture aspects within the organization. In a future research, it would be of interest to explore more the cultural aspects and also it would also be of interest to follow up the company throughout their process of the ERP system change project until they finalized the new ERP system implementation.

References

1. Verhoef, P.C., et al.: Digital transformation: a multidisciplinary reflection and research agenda. J. Bus. Res. **122**, 889–901 (2021)
2. Schwertner, K.: Digital transformation of business. Trakia J. Sci. **15**(1), 388–393 (2017)
3. Tabrizi, B., Lam, E., Girard, K., Irvin, V.: Digital transformation is not about technology. Harvard Business Review (2019). https://hbr.org/2019/03/digital-transformation-is-not-about-technology
4. Li, F.: Leading digital transformation: three emerging approaches for managing the transition. Int. J. Oper. Prod. Manag. **40**(6), 809–817 (2020)
5. Singh, A., Klarner, P., Hess, T.: How do chief digital officers pursue digital transformation activities? The role of organization design parameters. Long Range Plan. **53**(3), 101890 (2020)
6. Westerman, G., Bonnet, D., McAfee, A.: The nine elements of digital transformation. MIT Sloan Manag. Rev. **55**(3), 1–6 (2014)
7. Henriette, E., Feki, M., Boughzala, I.: The shape of digital transformation: a systematic literature review. In: MCIS 2015 Proceedings, Paper 10, pp. 431–443 (2015)
8. Bloomberg, J.: Digitization, digitalization, and digital transformation: confuse them at your peril (2018). https://www.forbes.com/sites/jasonbloomberg/2018/04/29/digitization-digitalization-and-digital-transformation-confuse-them-at-your-peril/?sh=162fdcc12f2c
9. Gurbaxani, V., Dunkle, D.: Gearing up for successful digital transformation. MIS Q. Exec. **18**(3), 209–220 (2019)

10. Morakanyane, R., O'Reilly, P., McAvoy, J., Grace, A.: Determining digital transformation success factors. In: Proceedings of the 53rd Hawaii International Conference on System Sciences (HICSS) (2020)

11. Berić, D., Stefanović, D., Lalić, B., Ćosić, I.: The implementation of ERP and MES Systems as a support to industrial management systems. Int. J. Ind. Eng. Manag. **9**(2), 77–86 (2018)

12. Putra, D.G., Rahayu, R., Putri, A.: The influence of enterprise resource planning (ERP) implementation system on company performance mediated by organizational capabilities. J. Account. Investment **22**(2), 221–241 (2021)

13. Bharadwaj, A., El Sawy, O.A., Pavlou, P.A., Venkatraman, N.: Digital business strategy: toward a next generation of insights. MIS Q. **37**(2), 471–482 (2013)

14. Kretschmer, T., Khashabi, P.: Digital transformation and organization design: an integrated approach. Calif. Manag. Rev. **62**(4), 86–104 (2020)

15. Baculard, L.P., Colombani, L., Flam, V., Lancry, O., Spaulding, E.: Orchestrating a successful digital transformation (2017). https://www.bain.com/insights/orchestrating-a-successful-dig ital-transformation/

16. Moşteanu, N.R.: Challenges for organizational structure and design as a result of digitalization and cybersecurity. Bus. Manag. Rev. **11**(1), 278–286 (2020)

17. Sainger, G.: Leadership in digital age: a study on the role of leader in this era of digital transformation. Int. J. Leadersh. **6**(1), 1–6 (2018)

18. Shea, C.M., Jacobs, S.R., Esserman, D.A., Bruce, K., Weiner, B.J.: Organizational readiness for implementing change: a psychometric assessment of a new measure. Implement. Sci. **9**(1), 1–15 (2014)

19. Verina, N., Titko, J.: Digital transformation: conceptual framework. In: Proceedings of the Int. Scientific Conference "Contemporary Issues in Business, Management and Economics Engineering' 2019", Vilnius, Lithuania, pp. 719–727 (2019)

20. Denscombe, M.: The Good Research Guide: for Small-Scale Research Projects, 5th edn. McGraw-Hill Education, Maidenhead, Berkshire (2014)

21. Yin, R.K.: Validity and generalization in future case study evaluations. Evaluation **19**(3), 321–333 (2013)

22. Flyvbjerg, B.: Five misunderstandings about case-study research. Qual. Inq. **12**(2), 219–245 (2006)

23. Yin, R.K.: Case Study Research: Design and Methods, 4th edn. SAGE Publications, Thousand Oaks (2009)

24. Braun, V., Clarke, V.: Using thematic analysis in psychology. Qual. Res. Psychol. **3**(2), 77–101 (2006)

25. Bryman, A.: Social Research Methods. Oxford University Press, Oxford (2016)

26. Ali, M., Miller, L.: ERP system implementation in large enterprises–a systematic literature review. J. Enterp. Inf. Manag. **30**(4), 666–692 (2017)

Understanding Well-Being in Virtual Teams: A Comparative Case Study

Almudena Cañibano[1] , Petros Chamakiotis[1(✉)] , Lukas Rojahn[1],
and Emma Russell[2]

[1] ESCP Business School, c/ Arroyofresno, 1, 28035 Madrid, Spain
pchamakiotis@escp.eu
[2] University of Sussex, Brighton BN1 9SL, UK

Abstract. Although virtual teams (VTs) have been around for over two decades, there are no studies explicitly examining their members' well-being. Motivated, therefore, by a knowledge gap in the VT literature, and a practical need to understand well-being in this context due to the Covid-19 pandemic which has led to an unprecedented transition into virtual working, in this paper, we draw on 14 interviews and present initial findings of a comparative case between two European organizations involving different types (global vs. local) of VTs (Phase 1). Using the job demands-resources (JDR) model as our theoretical lens, we make the following contributions: We identify the situated character of job demands and resources among our participants, explaining how VT members experience simultaneously increased job demands and reduced job resources, which, in combination, may substantially impair their well-being. We also find that understandings of demands and resources are idiosyncratic and vary depending on prior individual experiences of VT members. We discuss initial theoretical and practical contributions of Phase 1 of our study and outline our next steps (Phases 2 and 3).

Keywords: Virtual teams · Well-being · Job demands-resources

1 Introduction

Virtual teams (VTs) have been around for over two decades and have recently regained popularity because of an unprecedented transition into virtual working due to the Covid-19 pandemic. VTs are generally known for their benefits for both the employer and the employee [1], but also for their challenges, including trust [2], leadership [3], conflict [4], creativity [5], and, more recently, engagement [6, 7]. During the last two decades, scholars from information systems (IS), general management and kindred fields have sought to understand how these challenges can be managed and what they mean for organizations, leaders, and individuals, generally concluding that the management of VTs is different due to the unique characteristics (e.g., dispersion, technology-mediation), suggesting that older management practices based on traditional, face-to-face (F2F) environments may not always be suitable.

© Springer Nature Switzerland AG 2022
M. Themistocleous and M. Papadaki (Eds.): EMCIS 2021, LNBIP 437, pp. 667–680, 2022.
https://doi.org/10.1007/978-3-030-95947-0_47

The existing literature on VTs mainly refers to global VTs (aka GVTs) which were typically formed to bring together global talent despite geographical boundaries in organizations' effort to develop a competitive advantage and/or to become more global [8]. In the current context, it has been argued that VTs were not developed for competition or globalization purposes, but for survival [9]. According to these authors, VTs that were formed in early 2020 as a response to the Covid-19 pandemic are more local in character compared to the GVTs that dominated the literature in the pre-Covid-19 era, and they are known for different types of challenges, including new phenomena such as Zoom fatigue [9]. What we see therefore is that different types of VTs engender different types of challenges based on their (different) characteristics. Irrespective of VT type, employee well-being constitutes a significant topic and is seen as a prerequisite for effective working in the traditional management literature [10, 11]. Individual well-being at work results from the interplay of personal, job and organizational characteristics [12]. Perceptions of well-being are constructed by actors while they make and attribute meaning to the world, drawing upon their previous experiences [13]. In this sense, well-being is a subjective experience [14] that needs to be explored through the eyes of employees [15, 16].

In this paper, we present a comparative case study on VT members' perceptions of well-being [14] (Phase 1). Recognizing that different types of VTs experience different challenges, we focus on two European organizations – one involving GVTs and a local one involving locally (nationally) dispersed VTs – in our quest to understand how well-being is experienced in VTs with dissimilar levels of geographical dispersion. We conducted a total of 14 interviews with (G)VT members of the two organizations and used the job demands-resources (JDR) model [17] in order to classify thematically [18] the factors that influence workers' sense of well-being within the (G)VT context.

This comparative study is Phase 1 of a larger study involving an additional 28 interviews following a cross-sectorial multi-case study approach (Phase 2) and an envisaged follow-up quantitative diary study (Phase 3). Our study is the first one to explicitly study the topic of well-being in VTs building on a recognition of its importance within both the GVT [19] and the local (largely Covid-19-driven) VT context [9]. Drawing on the JDR model, we find that our Phase 1 participants' experiences and perceptions of job demands, and job resources are oftentimes situated. Phase 1 findings explain how VT members experience simultaneously increased job demands and reduced job resources, which, in combination, may substantially impair their well-being. We also find that understandings of demands and resources are idiosyncratic and vary depending on prior individual experiences of VT members. These findings are important and of value to a multidisciplinary audience of academics (e.g., IS, management, human resources (HR)), (G)VT members and leaders, HR professionals and professional bodies that may need to revisit their policies given the recent interest in VTs worldwide, as well as to educators teaching students on new ways of working, involving work in VTs.

In what follows, we present relevant theory (Sect. 2), our methodological approach (Sect. 3), our findings from Phase 1 (Sect. 4) and preliminary contributions (Sect. 5), and close the paper with our conclusions, the limitations of Phase 1 and our next steps (Sect. 6).

2 Relevant Literature

2.1 The Literature on (G)VTs

Commonly defined as groups of coworkers who are geographically, temporally and/or organizationally dispersed and work together via information and communication technologies (ICTs) [e.g., 20], VTs are known for their unique characteristics: the aforementioned types of dispersion, as well as their reliance on ICTs [1]. Scholars agree that there exist different types of VTs based on the above dimensions – e.g., global vs. local; inter- vs. intra-organizational; pure virtual vs. hybrid; and temporary vs. temporary; VTs consisting of subgroups vs. geographically isolated members – each with a distinct set of characteristics, and therefore, different types of challenges.

VT scholars have primarily sought to understand how management practices should be adapted to accommodate those challenges, and indeed, a wealth of empirical studies has emerged that advances theoretical knowledge in this literature and has been used to inform practitioners on the ground too. What these studies have in common is their focus on the issue of performance, i.e., scholars have focused on how, for example, leadership should be practiced in order to ensure that VTs are high-performing and able to deliver their tasks on time and successfully. Although recently we have seen a shift in focus on topics such as engagement within the VT context [7], this too has been studied in an effort to understand what VT leaders can do to ensure that their VTs continue to perform well. The Covid-19 pandemic has brought hidden aspects of work in VTs to the surface due to the sudden proliferation of this type of work across industries and the globe in an enforced way. Contrary, therefore, to previous VTs that were more global in character and were developed for different purposes, as explained in Sect. 1, new VTs are the result of an enforced work from home approach that introduces new challenges [21].

Focusing on these new challenges, emerging literature in response to the Covid-19 VTs highlights that VT members who work from home find it hard to coexist and deliver their work successfully when sharing their home-based workspace with others (e.g., family, housemates) or in parallel with other commitments (e.g., home-schooling, caring responsibilities), and that, although work may be delivered, their personal sense of well-being might be at stake [9]. Well-being has been recognized previously by HR scholars as an important and yet overlooked aspect of virtual teamwork [19], however, it remains an underexplored area in the VT literature [22].

Our position in this paper is that well-being constitutes an important area in all types of VTs for different reasons and it is important because without it we may have high-performing, but not necessarily sustainable, VTs [10, 23]. An important contributor to VT success is the selection of pertinent ICTs as without ICTs work in VTs would not be feasible [8]. While ICTs feature as the primary enabler of work in VTs, they have also been identified as causing burnout due to prolonged and inadequate use [9]. Media synchronicity theory suggests that ICTs vary in terms of their degree of synchronicity from lean (asynchronous, e.g., email) to rich (synchronous, e.g., videoconferencing) ones and that different ICTs work better for different tasks [24].

Questions therefore arise as to how the unique characteristics of (different types of) VTs, such as reliance on ICTs, influence their members' sense of well-being. Explored next is a model we borrow from the HR field that will help us frame those characteristics in a way that enables understanding of how VT members' well-being is influenced within this context.

2.2 Job Demands-Resources (JDR) Framework

The JDR is a heuristic model [25] that provides grounds to investigate the impact of work factors on employee well-being in any type of occupation [26], ranging from dentists [27] to cabin crew members [28]. This model encompasses two traditionally separate literatures on job stress and work motivation to dynamically explain how changing working conditions may be related to individual and organizational outcomes.

The JDR model was originally developed to explore how job characteristics are connected to burnout [29]. This connection relies on two fundamental propositions. First, the JDR model claims that all types of job aspects (physical, psychological, social or organizational) can be categorized in one of two groups: job demands and job resources [17]. Job demands refer to elements of the job that require continued effort, let it be cognitive, emotional or physical. Role overload [30], role conflict [31], urgency or uncertainty [12], exemplify job demands. Job resources refer to aspects of the job that are useful in terms of: (a) meeting work objectives; (b) diminishing job demands and their associated cost; or (c) encouraging employee learning and growth. Job resources can be offered to employees at three different levels: organizational, interpersonal and individual [32]. Job security, role clarity, autonomy or performance feedback are commonly cited job resources.

Second, the JDR model proposes that these job characteristics are connected to employee well-being through two differential psychological mechanisms [17]. On the one hand, the health-impairment process posits that excessive sustained job demands (e.g., ongoing uncertainty) deplete employees of energy, leading to exhaustion and strain. On the other hand, the motivation process assumes that job resources contribute to employees fulfilling needs of autonomy, competence and relatedness [33]. For instance, receiving constructive feedback can help individuals see the purpose of their effort, motivating them to engage further. In addition, the model postulates two interactive mechanisms: (a) job resources may mitigate the positive relationship between job demands and job strain (e.g., having a supportive boss may reduce the negative influence of uncertainty) [34]; and (b) job resources have a stronger influence on motivation when job demands are high (receiving constructive feedback is more beneficial for those who deal with ongoing tight deadlines) [17].

Following our literature review in the area of VTs and with the JDR serving as our theoretical lens, we develop following research question which we seek to address in this paper: How is well-being perceived in different types of VTs (global vs. local)?

3   Methodological Approach

3.1   Phase 1 Case Organizations and Participants

We followed a qualitative case study approach with two European organizations: a national transportation company (Company A) involving national VTs spread across the country, and a strategic management holding (Company B) involving GVTs. Case studies are suitable when wanting to gain in-depth understanding of a phenomenon within an organizational context, which may also contain truth that also can be applicable elsewhere [35]. This approach was a suitable one given the exploratory character of our study.

The only criterion for participant recruitment was current VT membership (global or local) and we also aimed for some balance between VT leaders and VT members. The former had more than four years of leadership experience in roles like recruitment, assistance, purchasing or controlling. Eleven German and three Italian participants were interviewed (in German and English respectively), and 57% of the participants were female. GVT participants were based in Asia, the USA, Italy, or Germany and all had more than one year VT experience at the time of interviewing. We selected participants of different VTs in order to paint a rich picture of the VTs in the selected organizations. We recruited 14 participants across the two organizations until we felt that saturation had been reached.

3.2   Phase 1 Data Collection and Analysis Process

Semi-structured interviews constituted our main data collection method and we also sent out questionnaires to gather bio-demographical information of our participants. An interview guide was developed after carefully reviewing the relevant literature. The interview guide was designed to cover all relevant areas (e.g., VT experience, whether their work was demanding). All 14 interviews lasted a little over one hour each, took place between June and August 2016.

Interviews were transcribed and analyzed on NVivo. We followed an interpretivist approach [36] and were guided by the principles of grounded theory to analyze our data [37] in order to get an understanding of what would come out of the dataset without being biased from relevant literature. While open-coding, we created two large thematic categories – "positive experiences" and "negative experiences" – and included all open codes in them. Once open coding was completed, and following numerous meetings among the authors, we used the JDR model to thematically categorize all open codes into axial codes. These constituted our final codes and included: task overload, role ambiguity, personal factors, and interpersonal factors, among others, all being factors associated with either job demands or job resources as per the JDR model.

4   Phase 1 Research Findings

Participants' accounts suggest that virtual teamworking has an influence on employee well-being because it substantially impacts individual experiences at work. Our interviewees described how working in VTs involved the emergence of additional job demands, which created an extra source of strain and potential distress. At the same time, they reported how this type of work involved the appearance of supplementary job resources, which may act as a source of motivation.

4.1 Emerging Job Demands in VTs

The participants described various experiences and factors related to virtual teamworking that required substantial effort, in addition to their standard task related effort. In this sense, our participants' experiences suggest that working in a VT may generate *task overload* (in VTs, workers perform extra activities that add to their load) and *role ambiguity* (in VTs, workers have less opportunities to learn what is expected of them from contextual interactions).

Task overload happens when a person experiences difficulties in fulfilling the requirements of their various tasks because of the collective demands such tasks impose on them. Our participants described five main factors that create new tasks for VT members and may lead to overload: technological problems, dealing with time differences, adapting to varying local working styles, overcoming the lack of body language and managing arising conflicts.

The use of ICTs is an inherent characteristic of VTs. Our participants' accounts suggest that, when present, technical problems with ICTs create additional tasks for VTs, which can generate task overload. One interviewee explained: *"if you have a meeting with a lot of people here and a lot of people at the other plant, and you have a bad connection - this can really be a problem sometimes to go ahead with the meetings if you have these connection problems."* (PB10). Another participant shared: *"...it is always a bit annoying when you spend the first 15 min trying to get someone to fix the technical problem and there are four or five other people on the line."* (PB02).

'*To go ahead with the meetings*' these workers are expected to either solve the technical problems or to be creative about information exchange. They often have to perform an IT-support function to their co-workers, which would not exist for a collocated team. However, they do not receive specific training for this. One of them said: *"I have not participated in any training measures in this direction, but I have also not heard from anyone that has."* (PA02).

Often, the additional demands creating task overload described by our participants were specifically connected to the global nature of their VT. For instance, technical problems were more frequently mentioned by the GVT participants. This is probably linked to their interaction with countries having varying strengths of Internet connection and their use of more heterogeneous devices. Other demands were linked to the increased locational and cultural diversity experienced in GVTs. For instance, time or local working style differences were described by several GVT members as difficult to deal with, challenging, problematic and creating new tasks to fulfil.

Regarding time differences, finding common time slots clashed with respecting each participant's normal working hours because they required very early-morning or late-evening meetings. One of the participants said: *"Of course, when it came to China, I knew that I had to be there tomorrow at 8:30am because they wanted to go home, they had already finished work, so you always had to take that into account. That's why these monthly meetings with China always took place in the morning, and the others with*

Brazil and America in the late afternoon." (PB09). This participant's account indicates how both she and her Chinese colleagues had to work overtime in order to manage their team responsibilities and to interact.

For PB10, the mere fact of finding time slots that were within everyone's core working time was an additional role to be fulfilled which required extra time or making concessions and working outside their usual working hours. When this participant was probed about his feelings regarding this problem he said: *"it is a little bit difficult, but we don't have many options, we need to do it like this"* (PB10).

Cultural differences were also described as a source of additional tasks: *"To be honest, I find it much more difficult to work in a VT than in a team that is really on site. Um, the reasons for that [...] We simply had different ways of working and bringing that together was sometimes a bit difficult."* (PB01). This account underlines how virtual teamworking has opened the door to teams being increasingly diverse. Although enriching, this diversity can require additional effort from employees who need to navigate different working styles and practices.

Our interviewees also described how missing body language in communicating with their teams created additional tasks: *"Yes, I think you do miss [body language] a bit. Because you really have to work on yourself to get it across when you don't have the opportunity to do it with gestures and facial expressions....so, it's better to talk too much than too little, because otherwise it doesn't come across!"* (PB09). Her account highlights how VT members need to work on their communication skills because they can seldom rely on non-verbal cues.

Other participants pointed out additional demands that emerge when cameras are not turned on: *"[Virtual working is] a bit more exhausting when [...] for example, there's a discussion and you only hear 5 different voices on the phone, for example, then I don't know... Oh God, who said what now? I think that's different when you have a live discussion [...] when someone hasn't even dialed in with the video (camera off) and you don't know where something is coming from that doesn't really add value basically."* (PA01). This interviewee experienced the lack of body language as *'exhausting'* because she could not identify the person who transmitted information, suggesting the need for more concentration and cognitive dedication.

Finally, for GVTs, the management of conflicts also appeared to create additional tasks. One participant shared: *"What is demanding is conflict management, or the demanding, tough discussion - we sometimes have conflicts or opinions in the team [...] and it is demanding online to deal with them properly, or to structure them properly."* (PB04). Solving conflicts requires VT workers to perform tasks outside of what would be expected from them in a physical context. They experience this as less natural than having a F2F conversation and need to work on how to *'deal with them properly'* or how *'to structure them properly'*. While local VTs can circumvent this demand by dealing with conflict when they meet F2F (which in the case of company A happened approximately once a month), GVTs cannot because they only see each other sporadically (once a year for Company B).

In addition to role overload, our findings suggest VT workers experience role ambiguity. Role ambiguity exists when the expectations that need to be fulfilled in order to perform are doubtful or uncertain. VT workers, particularly in global contexts, can experience increased role ambiguity because they miss informal communication opportunities and may encounter language barriers.

Informal communication opportunities, such as unplanned chats in the hallway, seem to play an important role in clarifying expectations. Our participants pointed out that missing such interactions may create role ambiguity. For instance, an interviewee said: *"Mini-information that is exchanged informally, such as in the coffee kitchen 'Oh, just seeing you...I've just spoken to customer XY, have you heard?'...I think that gets lost."* (PA04).

This interviewee felt that information that would be passed on naturally by co-workers in a physical context by for example walking down a hallway or randomly meeting a co-worker in the coffee kitchen is not exchanged in a VT context. She explained this as information that *'gets lost'*, leaving her with lingering doubts about evolving tasks and responsibilities.

Language barriers can also create role ambiguity. Our GVT interviewees suggested that speaking different native languages or having varying levels of English may create confusing messages and miscommunication. For instance, one participant said: *"you speak a different language than the people or the headquarters and so (...) you don't have information"* (PB10). This respondent indicates how speaking a different language may entail missing information, which can lead to unclear tasks. Another explained how she tries to deal with this problem: *"...I sometimes speak much more slowly than I normally would, and when I notice that it's really extremely difficult linguistically, I also try to adapt by not only speaking slowly but also simple"* (PB02).

Overall, VT workers, particularly those belonging to GVTs, experience added tasks in comparison to physically collocated teams and have less chances to clarify what is expected of them and what different steps they should take in conducting their work. These additional job demands are found to be connected to the experience of job intensification, exhaustion and loneliness.

4.2 Reduced Job Resources in VTs

Participant accounts indicate that a variety of personal and interpersonal job resources diminish in a VT context. However, existing resources mitigate job demands' negative impact on well-being. In addition, the extent to which different factors are understood as resources by the participants depend on their prior VT working experiences.

First, regarding personal job resources, the key recurrent factor in participants' accounts is giving and receiving feedback. Many perceived lack of feedback because they were physically separated from co-workers or leaders: *"Well, it's actually more difficult because of that, which is why I also say that it should be systematized, because - so feedback among colleagues, you don't even notice all the work they do, everyone is more to themselves - and if someone doesn't notice that anymore [because of the physical distance], then they can't be given feedback anymore."* (PA04). This respondent expressed a feeling of being 'more to [her]self' because of being in a VT. The decreased visibility of each worker's work and achievements make it harder to give and receive feedback and thus motivating appreciation and improvement tips.

Second, insofar as interpersonal resources are concerned, the informal interactions that enable colleagues to get to know one another often disappear in VTs. A member of a GVT highlighted: *"If I'm in a non-VT and the conversation is five minutes late because the meeting room is still occupied, the colleagues stand outside the door and talk about football or their children or the weather and get to know each other over time. Exactly at such a moment, every colleague hangs in the virtual queue and is annoyed that it is not happening now and that he is sitting there and is left alone."* (PB06).

The lack of an informal interaction is reinforced by the experience of feeling *'alone'*, waiting in the virtual void. The bonds that are developed at the interstices of work, seem to decline, both in quality and quantity due to physical separation and the lack of opportunities to develop more personal connections. One interviewee described this in the following terms: *"Because you have this physical distance, you certainly don't have such a close bond. You do a lot over the phone, yes, but it doesn't replace human contact..."* (PA04).

'Human contact' is valued as superior to virtual contact. For this reason, VT workers are keen on creating opportunities to meet in person and consider these meetings as a key resource, particularly when they start working together: *"at the beginning people have to get to know each other personally and therefore we usually do a kick-off at one of the locations where we say, 'Now let's all sit down together for a day and define how we are actually working'"* (PB06).

A F2F kick-off meeting allows VT members to establish the basis for building a personal relationship. The regular physical meetings that are possible for the local VT help maintain this interpersonal relationship. An interviewee said: *"F2F meetings in between [virtual meetings] are particularly important in order to strengthen the bond and also to get to know each other."* (PA02).

This participant experienced regular physical contact with her teammates as a valuable resource for *'strengthen[ing] the bond'* between them. This appears to be a motivating factor having a positive impact on well-being. On the contrary, the members of the GVT who did not have this opportunity expressed feelings of loneliness and demotivation. One of them said *"The risk is that you feel a bit alone sometimes [...] you are alone in another country, you are not motivated anymore"* (PB10).

Although interpersonal resources seemed to decline for all participants, that does not mean that they do not experience such resources at all. On the contrary, they are sometimes indispensable to mitigate the negative effects of growing job demands. For example, one participant described in detail how the support of others enabled a person that was new to virtual interactions to cope with the demands of technology: *"We had, um, someone from another area invited to a WebEx, (...) although I did brief her beforehand, the lady couldn't cope with the technology (...) but all the other staff members were (...) already dialed in, and it was very nice how everyone then wrote her a message, a note or somehow said things like "Do this and that" and also absolutely supported her, which was really nice. I think the first quarter of an hour of the meeting was actually a funny cooperation, because we had to explain to the lady how everything works, and, um, I think that was still really nice for the whole team, because everyone had the feeling of being there and maybe being able to help the lady, and then, exactly [on time], the meeting started."* (PA01).

The general positive disposition of the team members motivated everyone to be patient and left the participant a feeling of '*being there*' for one another, despite the distance. This example illustrates the capacity of resources to limit the downsides of demands.

In sum, VT members seem to generally have less access to individual and inter-personal resources than if they were working in the same space as the rest of their team. Experiencing work with such diminished resources reduces motivation and creates feelings of loneliness and detachment from the team. However, when VT members experience resources, these have the potential to mitigate the negative influence of job demands individual well-being.

It must be noted that the extent to which each VT worker interprets certain factors as resources seems to be related to their prior experience in working virtually. For example, this is the case with F2F meetings. One participant was discouraged with the lack of F2F interaction with her supervisor, explaining that *"especially now, since [name hidden] is my boss, I think out of 30 days, maybe I see her for two days [in person]"* (PA01). This individual, who had limited experience working virtually did not interpret those two days of F2F contact a month as a resource that could counterbalance the demands of virtual work. On the contrary, a participant who had substantial experience working virtually understood punctual F2F meeting as relevant resources. He highlighted: *"we are at least trying to send the staff to Germany once, to get to know as many people as possible [in person] and to use this to build the first foundations [of interpersonal connections]."* (PB03). For him, a rare interaction ('at least once') was understood as an important step in building interpersonal job resources. These accounts underline that the understanding of resources is idiosyncratic and situated. Virtual workers will build on their prior experiences to develop contextual interpretations which may affect their well-being differently.

5   Discussion

5.1   Theoretical Contributions

Driven by a recognized need to study well-being in the context of (G)VTs [e.g., 22], in this study we have used the JDR model from the HR literature to study (G)VT members' experiences and perceptions of job demands and job resources in particular. We have chosen two organizations, one involving GVT members and another involving locally (nationally) dispersed VT members, to identify similarities and differences in these two different types of VTs.

Our findings indicate that VT members experience additional job demands (e.g., role overload and role ambiguity) and reduced job resources. Our interviewees spoke about hidden aspects of their experiences in VTs, in relation to issues caused by ICTs for example. Although the VT literature has explained that different ICTs might be better for different tasks [24], the existing VT literature does not explain how hidden, formally unacknowledged issues related to ICT use may affect VT members' experience of demands. A similar study has introduced the term 'digi-housekeeping' to refer to formally unrecognized, and yet time-consuming and often troublesome, tasks associated with flexible working [38]. Our study highlights that similar issues add to the demands experienced by the VT worker. Consequently, VT workers may experience more strain leading to decreased well-being. In our study, these additional demands were particularly salient for GVT. Time differences and expecting GVT colleagues from other locations to be available after hours is an example that can potentially lead to violations of one's work-life boundaries. It has been argued that work-life boundaries might be violated in alternative working environments, such as Covid-19 VTs [9], however our study shows that this is the case with traditional GVTs as well. Our findings therefore both corroborate and extend suspicions in the recent literature that demands in the VT context may indeed be higher than in F2F teams [9].

We also found that VT members also experience reduced resources such as support from colleagues or feedback, which may reduce their motivation and in turn their well-being. These findings relate to the lack of social context in the VT environment. Researchers have posited that establishing and maintaining a social context in VTs is essential [39]. Our study extends these findings by showing that establishing and maintaining a social context has a paramount effect on how resources are experienced by (G)VT members. At the same time, our study has shown that the same resources whose lack may be detrimental can be used to mitigate the negative impact of job demands. Our argument is therefore that these resources are critical to render VT working sustainable. Finally, our analysis of the two cases has highlighted that individual understandings of demands and resources are idiosyncratic and situated; they depend to a certain extent on prior experience with VTs. Understanding individual experiences is important to depict the connection between VT working and well-being.

5.2 Practical Contributions

Our study has important practical value for both VT leaders and VT members. The former should make sure that their VTs are sufficiently equipped with the necessary resources and that demands – even invisible and formally unrecognized demands – do not exceed the resources available to VT members. Although leaders have little room to reduce certain demands, offering VT members sufficient resources can mitigate the strain created by demands. They should also appreciate that the issue of well-being is largely a personal issue and may be experienced differently by different individuals in the same VTs. Therefore, an understanding of the situated character of well-being in relation to the VT configuration (e.g., local, global, inter-/intra-organizational) is necessary in this regard. VT members, on the other hand, should be comfortable sharing honestly and transparently with their leaders how they feel and what could improve the equilibrium between demands and resources while taking into consideration their own personal circumstances that may affect their ability to deliver on their tasks.

6   Conclusion, Limitations, and Next Steps (Phases 2 and 3)

Using data on employee-lived experiences of working in VTs and drawing on JDR theory, we have shown that specific demands, such as task overload and role ambiguity, emerge from this type of work. Such demands, which differ between global and local teams, impair workers' well-being. At the same time, we found that VT members experience more difficulties accessing important resources such as feedback and inter-personal connections. As a result, they are more likely to struggle to fulfil basic needs of competence and relatedness, which mitigate the well-being downsides of job demands. Although understandings of demands and resources are idiosyncratic and vary depending on prior individual experiences of VT members, in combination, the experience of increased demands and reduced resources challenges the sustainability of VTs.

Our study has some limitations, such as our relatively small sample, which we will be overcoming with Phases 2 and 3 of our larger study. For Phase 2, we have already conducted 28 interviews with members of (G)VTs following a qualitative, cross-sectorial (e.g., consulting, aviation, IT) multi-case study approach. These interviews were conducted during the Covid-19 pandemic, capturing issues affecting well-being, which are more relevant today. We are currently in the process of analyzing those data and by the time of the conference we expect to be able to present findings from Phase 2 too. For Phase 3, we have envisaged a quantitative study whereby we will ask a larger number of participants to keep a diary of issues affecting their well-being for a week, with the aim of (a) overcoming some of the limitations characterizing interviews and (b) testing the statistical generalizability of our findings from Phases 1 and 2.

Acknowledgements. The authors would like to thank the research participants at the two organizations and Franziska Forchhammer for helping with data collection in Phase 1.

References

1. Ebrahim, N.A., Ahmed, S., Taha, Z.: virtual teams: a literature review. Aust. J. Basic Appl. Sci. **3**, 2653–2669 (2009)
2. Hacker, J.V., Johnson, M., Saunders, C., Thayer, A.L.: Trust in virtual teams: a multidisciplinary review and integration. Aust. J. Inf. Syst. **23** (2019). https://doi.org/10.3127/ajis.v23i0.1757
3. Kayworth, T.R., Leidner, D.E.: Leadership effectiveness in global virtual teams. J. Manag. Inf. Syst. **18**, 7–40 (2002)
4. Kankanhalli, A., Tan, B.C.Y., Wei, K.K.: Conflict and performance in global virtual teams. J. Manag. Inf. Syst. **23**, 237–274 (2007)
5. Chamakiotis, P.: Virtual teams as creative and agile work environments. In: Grant, C., Russell, E. (eds.) Agile Working and Well-Being in the Digital Age, pp. 133–142. Springer, Cham (2020). https://doi.org/10.1007/978-3-030-60283-3_10
6. Gibbs, J.L., Gibson, C.B., Grushina, S.V., Dunlop, P.D.: Understanding orientations to participation: overcoming status differences to foster engagement in global teams. Eur. J. Work Organ. Psychol. 1–19 (2021). https://doi.org/10.1080/1359432X.2020.1844796
7. Panteli, N., Yalabik, Z.Y., Rapti, A.: Fostering work engagement in geographically-dispersed and asynchronous virtual teams. Inf. Technol. People **32**, 2–17 (2019). https://doi.org/10.1108/ITP-04-2017-0133
8. Lipnack, J., Stamps, J.: Virtual Teams: People Working Across Boundaries with Technology. Wiley, New York (2000)
9. Chamakiotis, P., Panteli, N., Davison, R.M.: Reimagining e-leadership for reconfigured virtual teams due to Covid-19. Int. J. Inf. Manag. (2021). https://doi.org/10.1016/j.ijinfomgt.2021.102381

10. Pfeffer, J.: Building sustainable organizations: the human factor. AMP **24**, 34–45 (2010). https://doi.org/10.5465/amp.24.1.34
11. Van De Voorde, K., Paauwe, J., Van Veldhoven, M.: Employee well-being and the HRM-organizational performance relationship: a review of quantitative studies: HRM, employee well-being and organizational performance. Int. J. Manag. Rev. **14**, 391–407 (2012). https://doi.org/10.1111/j.1468-2370.2011.00322.x
12. Cartwright, S., Cooper, C.L.: Introduction: perspectives on organizational health. In: Cartwright, S., Cooper, C.L. (eds.) Oxford Handbook of Organizational Well-being. Oxford University Press, Oxford (2009)
13. Gillett-Swan, J.K., Sargeant, J.: Wellbeing as a process of accrual: beyond subjectivity and beyond the moment. Soc. Indic. Res. **121**(1), 135–148 (2014). https://doi.org/10.1007/s11205-014-0634-6
14. Diener, E., Suh, E.M., Lucas, R.E., Smith, H.L.: Subjective well-being: three decades of progress. Psychol. Bull. **125**, 276–302 (1999). https://doi.org/10.1037/0033-2909.125.2.276
15. Atkinson, C., Hall, L.: Flexible working and happiness in the NHS. Empl. Relat. **33**, 88–105 (2011). https://doi.org/10.1108/01425451111096659
16. Avgoustaki, A., Cañibano, A.: Motivational drivers of extensive work effort: are long hours always detrimental to well-being? Ind Relat. **59**, 355–398 (2020). https://doi.org/10.1111/irel.12263
17. Bakker, A.B., Demerouti, E.: The job demands-resources model: state of the art. J. Manag. Psych. **22**, 309–328 (2007). https://doi.org/10.1108/02683940710733115
18. Braun, V., Clarke, V.: Using thematic analysis in psychology. Qual. Res. Psychol. **3**, 77–101 (2006)
19. Adamovic, M.: An employee-focused human resource management perspective for the management of global virtual teams. Int. J. Hum. Resource Manag. **29**, 2159–2187 (2018). https://doi.org/10.1080/09585192.2017.1323227
20. Powell, A., Piccoli, G., Ives, B.: Virtual teams: a review of current literature and directions for future research. ACM SIGMIS Database **35**, 6–36 (2004)
21. Waizenegger, L., McKenna, B., Cai, W., Bendz, T.: An affordance perspective of team collaboration and enforced working from home during COVID-19. Eur. J. Inf. Syst. **29**, 429–442 (2020). https://doi.org/10.1080/0960085X.2020.1800417
22. Gilson, L.L., Maynard, M.T., Jones Young, N.C., Vartiainen, M., Hakonen, M.: Virtual teams research: 10 years, 10 themes, and 10 opportunities. J. Manag. **41**, 1313–1337 (2015). https://doi.org/10.1177/0149206314559946
23. MacIntosh, R., MacLean, D., Burns, H.: Health in organization: towards a process-based view. J. Manag. Stud. **44**, 206–221 (2007). https://doi.org/10.1111/j.1467-6486.2007.00685.x
24. Dennis, A.R., Fuller, R.M., Valacich, J.S.: Media, tasks, and communication processes: a theory of media synchronicity. MIS Q. **32**, 575–600 (2008)
25. Bakker, A.B., Demerouti, E.: Job demands–resources theory: taking stock and looking forward. J. Occup. Health Psychol. **22**, 273–285 (2017). https://doi.org/10.1037/ocp0000056
26. Bakker, A.B., Demerouti, E.: Job demands-resources theory. In: Cooper, C.L. (ed.) Wellbeing, pp. 1–28. Wiley, Chichester (2014). https://doi.org/10.1002/9781118539415.wbwell019
27. Hakanen, J.J., Bakker, A.B., Demerouti, E.: How dentists cope with their job demands and stay engaged: the moderating role of job resources. Eur. J. Oral Sci. **113**, 479–487 (2005). https://doi.org/10.1111/j.1600-0722.2005.00250.x
28. Yelgin, Ç., Ergün, N.: The effects of job demands and job resources on the safety behavior of cabin crew members: a qualitative study. Int. J. Occup. Saf. Ergon. 1–11 (2021). https://doi.org/10.1080/10803548.2021.1902674
29. Demerouti, E., Bakker, A.B., Nachreiner, F., Schaufeli, W.B.: The job demands-resources model of burnout. J. Appl. Psychol. **86**, 499–512 (2001). https://doi.org/10.1037/0021-9010.86.3.499

30. Duxbury, L., Halinski, M.: When more is less: An examination of the relationship between hours in telework and role overload. Work **48**, 91–103 (2014). https://doi.org/10.3233/WOR-141858

31. Ilgen, D.R., Hollenbeck, J.R.: The structure of work: job design and roles. In: Dunnette, M.D., Hough, L.M. (eds.) Handbook of Industrial and Organizational Psychology, pp. 165–207. Consulting Psychologists Press (1991)

32. Schaufeli, W.B., Bakker, A.B.: Job demands, job resources, and their relationship with burnout and engagement: a multi-sample study. J. Organiz. Behav. **25**, 293–315 (2004). https://doi.org/10.1002/job.248

33. Ryan, R.M., Deci, E.L.: Self-determination theory and the facilitation of intrinsic motivation, social development, and well-being. Am. Psychol. **55**, 68–78 (2000). https://doi.org/10.1037/0003-066X.55.1.68

34. Bakker, A.B., Demerouti, E., Euwema, M.C.: Job resources buffer the impact of job demands on burnout. J. Occup. Health Psychol. **10**, 170–180 (2005). https://doi.org/10.1037/1076-8998.10.2.170

35. Cavaye, A.L.M.: Case study research: a multi-faceted research approach for IS. Inf. Syst. J. **6**, 227–242 (1996). https://doi.org/10.1111/j.1365-2575.1996.tb00015.x

36. Symon, G., Cassell, C., Johnson, P.: Evaluative practices in qualitative management research: a critical review: qualitative management research. Int. J. Manag. Rev. **20**, 134–154 (2018). https://doi.org/10.1111/ijmr.12120

37. Glaser, B.G.: Basics of Grounded Theory Analysis. Sociology Press, Mill Valley (1992)

38. Whiting, R., Symon, G.: Digi-Housekeeping: The Invisible Work of Flexibility. Work, Employment and Society, 095001702091619 (2020). https://doi.org/10.1177/0950017020916192

39. Zander, L., Zettinig, P., Mäkelä, K.: Leading global virtual teams to success. Organ. Dyn. **42**, 228–237 (2013). https://doi.org/10.1016/j.orgdyn.2013.06.008

Technology as Driver, Enabler and Barrier of Digital Transformation: A Review

Vasilis Tsiavos[1](✉) and Fotis Kitsios[1,2]

[1] Department of Applied Informatics, University of Macedonia, Thessaloniki, Greece
vtsiavos@uom.edu.gr, kitsios@uom.gr
[2] School of Social Science, Hellenic Open University, Parodos Aristotelous 18, 26335 Patras, Greece

Abstract. In recent years, organizations and researchers have become increasingly interested in digital transformation. Technology has found its way into the lives of customers, but at the same time is disrupting industries by enabling organizations, that have embraced it, to gain more and more competitive advantages. However, technology is only one factor of a successful digital transformation strategy, where culture, management, human resources etc. also play an important role. While digital transformation has been researched over the years from multiple points of view, limited studies have focused in detail on the impact of technology on digital transformation. Questions such as how fast an organization should adapt to the evolution of technology, which technologies should be preferred and finally, in which cases technology might delay the digital transformation process, remain unanswered. The present paper aims to fill this gap by conducting a systematic literature review of 74 related articles, based on the Webster & Watson methodology, followed by a concept analysis of technology related themes in digital transformation. The results of the analysis reveal that technology does not only act as an enabler or driver of digital transformation, but can also be a barrier of it. While we contribute with our paper to the research body in digital transformation, at the same time, we identify potential research gaps that leave space for further investigation.

Keywords: Digital transformation · Technology · Industry 4.0

1 Introduction

We live in a rapidly moving world where entire industry sectors are being disrupted by digital technologies. Organizations in a multitude of industries are experiencing the impact of digital technologies that are continuously transforming their external environment regarding customer expectations and competition. This trend, called digital disruption, is altering the rulebook of business [1, 2]. Digital transformation is about how companies manage to respond to this new reality created by digital disruption [32]. It is likely that companies that will fail to adapt to the new digital reality will become

M. Themistocleous and M. Papadaki (Eds.): EMCIS 2021, LNBIP 437, pp. 681–693, 2022.
https://doi.org/10.1007/978-3-030-95947-0_48

victims of "digital Darwinism", where established firms may disappear and only those firms that are more adaptable and responsive to technological trends will survive and remain in this new competitive landscape. [3, 4].

The digital transformation of an organization is a complex process that starts with the awareness that a digital transformation is needed followed by a detailed digital strategy along with the identification of potential barriers. The formulation of a digital transformation strategy must consider, besides the technological factor, also shaping a digital culture and other factors [1, 2, 5, 9]. Although, technology is undoubtedly at the heart of digital transformation, little research attention has been paid on how in detail technology impacts digital transformation.

The goal of this paper is to reveal important aspects of the contribution of technology to digital transformation, through a systematic literature review. Seventy-four articles were reviewed based on the Webster and Watson (2002) [10] methodology. Digital transformation is a challenge for companies all over the world and technology, which is a key pillar of it, requires careful attention as it is constantly evolving. Hence, it is necessary to capture the current level of research on the technology's impact on digital transformation.

This paper is structured as follows: Sect. 2 outlines the methodology we used to conduct the literature review. The results of the analysis of the articles are discussed in Sect. 3. Finally, in the last section we state our conclusion and provide suggestions for future research.

2   Methodology and Data

We followed the systematic literature review process, as introduced by Webster and Watson [10]. It is a three-stage process: 1) The current literature reviews were examined to identify databases and keywords. 2) This was followed by an extensive backward search to examine citations and forward search to identify citations of the selected articles. 3) Finally, all articles were classified by concept based on their content and potential research opportunities were identified.

2.1   Previous Literature Reviews

To the best of our knowledge, no current literature review has exclusively addressed the technological aspects of digital transformation but has researched the phenomenon by studying a wide range of factors affecting it. There are, however, existing literature reviews that place greater emphasis on digital technology as an important factor of digital transformation (Table 1).

Pihir et al. (2019) [12] point out that the concepts of business innovation and agility in change management, are equally important as technologies. They list the technologies that are important for the digital transformation process of a business and emphasize on the fact that technologies evolve over time following a technological life cycle. Vial (2019) [11] argues that digital technologies allow for new forms of collaborative working between distributed networks of different actors and offer an enormous potential for

Table 1. Previous literature reviews

Authors	Year	Title	Methodology	Findings
Pihir et al. [9]	2020	Digital transformation playground - literature review and framework of concepts	2 Databases 528 Articles Quantitative Analysis 10 most cited Articles Qualitative Analysis	Business innovation and agility are as important as new technologies. A list of current technology trends is presented
Vial [11]	2019	Understanding digital transformation: A review and a research agenda	3 Databases 282 Articles	Technologies can be classified according to categories. Technologies are often source of disruption

innovation and organizational performance. He supports that technology can be classified under the acronym "SMACIT" (Social, Mobile, Analytics, Cloud, IoT). However, what existing literature reviews did not manage to address, is when an organization should respond to the evolution of technology, which technologies should it utilize on priority and how failing to adapt to technological advances in time, affects its digital transformation efforts.

2.2 Article Selection

The articles were retrieved from the Scopus and Web of Science databases using combinations of the keywords digital, transform, industry 4.0, business strategy etc. in the title, keyword and abstract fields. All articles were published in peer reviewed journals and conference proceedings. No constraints were imposed on the year of publication.

In total 2276 articles were gathered by searching for the above keywords. After applying the language, source and category restrictions in 510 articles were left. The remaining articles were examined for their contents, which resulted in the exclusion of 236 articles based on their title, 139 articles based on their abstract and 71 articles based on content. Thereafter, 3 duplicate articles were removed, leaving a total of 61. To these 11 articles were added from the backward search and 2 articles from the forward search. This yielded 74 articles for analysis (Fig. 1).

The search was completed when repeating articles for the various keyword combinations were found. Consequently, the critical number of articles had been obtained [10].

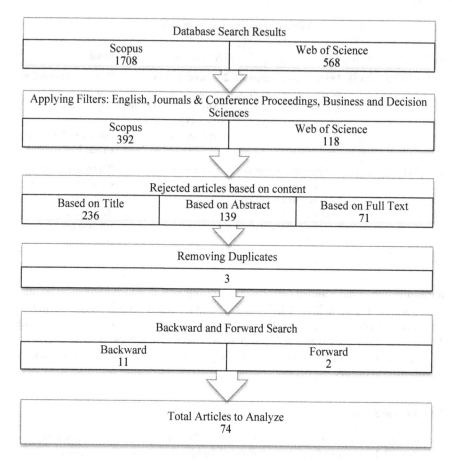

Fig. 1. Article selection process

2.3 Classification Framework

Seventy-four articles were analyzed using a classification framework. All articles were classified into 3 broad concepts (Technology as driver of digital transformation, Technology as enabler of digital transformation, Technology as barrier of digital transformation), that will provide a better understanding about the role of technology in digital transformation and aid future researchers to expand the related research body.

3   Results

3.1   Technology as Driver of Digital Transformation

Beyond competition, an organization is subject to pressures from external touch points, such as with customers or suppliers that require it to adapt to their level of technology, but also to improve its internal processes to support this adaptation. Customers nowadays intensively use digital technology, live and move digitally, while demanding from every company a customer value proposition and a service via new digital communication channels and at increased speed [13–19]. Therefore, firms are forced to adopt technologies that allow immediate and fast communication with the customer [6–8]. In the same sense, the concept of disintermediation has emerged in recent years, where companies that used to sell services and products through middlemen, e.g. airlines through travel agencies, have built entire technological infrastructures to process and support direct customer sales [20]. Similarly, supplier technology infrastructures are pushing businesses towards a technological revamp and digital transformation. The need for production forecasting is driving many suppliers to install supply chain software and end to end monitoring systems. Therefore, the development of a corresponding technological infrastructure and processes by their customers for proper communication with the supplier is imperative [14]. This requires alignment between the supplier and the firm in terms of the supplier's IT strategy, which needs to be factored into the firm's digital transformation efforts.

The new technologies needed for a firm to interact with its externals touch points and to face competition, also lead to the adaptation of new digitally supported internal processes that shape the firm's digital value chain [16, 21].

The above processes and interactions produce a fair amount of data, which requires new technological infrastructure, usually cloud based, for data analysis and storage [14, 22]. Beyond data storage and analysis, complex technological infrastructure and data protection legislation, also require investments in security [23–25]. However, while organizations are generally positive about the changes brought by technological developments and the competitive environment, changes imposed by regulatory frameworks are viewed negatively [26].

3.2 Technology as Enabler of Digital Transformation

In our literature review, we identified the wide variety of technologies referred to by scholars. The most frequent references are to Data, Cloud, IoT, artificial intelligence, as well as fast communications and 5G. The technologies of 3D Printing, the use of APIs, Augmented Reality, Blockchain, Analytics, Product Platforms, Robotics Automation and SOA Architecture are also referred to (Table 2). While Pihir et al. (2020) also lists a subset of our findings, he stresses the fact that technologies preferences change over time and follow a "technological life cycle" [12] In our research, however, we have not been able to identify what the speed of the adaptation to the life cycle of the evolution of technology should be and whether it varies according to the industry in which the organization operates.

Table 2. Technologies enabling digital transformation

Technologies	References	Technologies	References
3D Printing	[27–30]	Digital Analytics	[31, 33]
AI Artificial Intelligence	[16, 28, 29, 34–40]	Fast Communication & 5G	[21, 37, 40–44]
APIs	[45, 46]	IoT-Smart Connected Products	[14, 28–30, 34, 36, 38–40, 42, 43, 47, 50]
Augmented Reality	[27–29]	Product Platforms	[29, 51–53]
Data, Big Data, Effective Data Management	[14, 16, 22, 24, 28–30, 34–42, 44, 46, 48, 54–59]	Robotics Automation	[29, 37, 42]
Blockchain	[28, 51]	Services Oriented Architecture SOA	[24]
Cloud Computing	[14, 24, 28–30, 34, 38, 44, 47, 48, 50, 55]		

It is noteworthy that many scholars mention that the use of technologies also requires an IT strategy in full compliance with business objectives and the use of appropriate software that exploits these technologies [24, 60–69]. Firms which choose to develop their own software, should adopt the agile process [29, 35, 40, 70] to quickly adapt to requirement changes and, if they offer digital products and services, reduce time to market.

3.3 Technology as Barrier of Digital Transformation

While technology is best known as an enabler of digital transformation, we found that many researchers emphasize another facet of technology as barrier of digital transformation. A number of researchers stressed the issues of the incompatibility of preexisting technological infrastructure and monolithic legacy or inflexible "tailor-made" software with modern one and its lack of integration. Conventional monolithic architecture does not meet the demand for scalability and rapid development. A scalable IT architecture needs to be implemented using APIs, based on a microservices architecture and integration, both within the company and for the interaction with external partners [45, 71–73].

Moreover, a frequent issue that hinders mainly industrial sectors in the context of Industry 4.0 and the use of IoT, is the lack of high-speed communication networks and broadband infrastructure as well as missing unified communication protocols which are needed for Industry 4.0 technologies integration of systems, both inside and outside the organization [22, 49, 74].

Another significant challenge is the risk involved with IT security and data protection, where many organizations find it difficult to accept the risk of implementing new technologies and the costs involved [34, 75].

Our literature review with the concept analysis of 74 articles, has given us solid ground for a theoretical model, which is visualized below (Fig. 2).

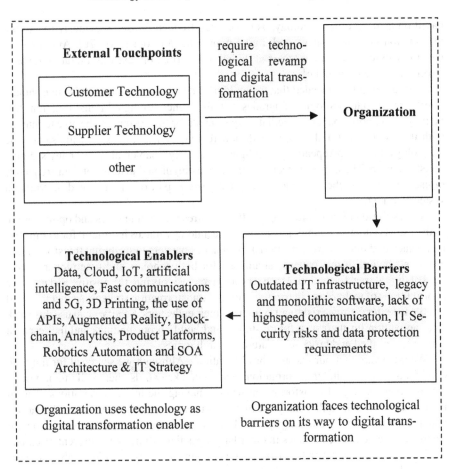

Fig. 2. Theoretical model

As illustrated in the figure above, an organization is influenced by actors at its external touch points, such as customers and suppliers and the technology they use. The organization must decide how to adapt, by upgrading its technology and adjusting its digital transformation strategy. In this endeavor it may face obstacles, such as outdated technological infrastructure, lack of broadband communication, but also issues related to IT system security and the data protection regulatory framework. The organization, after overcoming these obstacles, is leveraging modern technologies as enabler on its way to digital transformation. As evidenced in our research, it is important that this process flow is considered when designing a digital transformation strategy.

4 Conclusion

The purpose of this paper was to examine the role of technology as a driver, enabler and barrier of the digital transformation of an organization. We conducted a literature review, based on a specific methodology, as it has been frequently used previously to explore information systems strategy and digital transformation topics [10, 76]. Although our paper discusses an essential factor of digital transformation, existing literature reviews haven't analyzed it in detail.

Our research has revealed that technological developments in a firm's environment often force it to technological upgrades and, in essence, to digital transformation. It is no longer an option, but an immediate requirement for the business to be able to interact with its environment and comply with new regulatory frameworks. At the same time technology has been repeatedly highlighted as a key enabler of a company's digital transformation. Thus, specific technologies are distinguished in terms of their frequency of use. In any case, the technologies applied must be part of an integrated information systems strategy.

The evolution of technology itself often requires frequent updates and optimization, as the use of outdated technology or missing technology makes it difficult for a company to advance and introduces security risks that act as barriers to its digital transformation. The contribution of this paper is significant for both scholars and practitioners in the field of digital transformation. Managers are given insights into the positive and negative contributions of technology in forming a digital transformation strategy, so that they will be able to better estimate risks and benefits in their endeavors. Scholars can use this work as a motivation for their own future studies and build on our findings and the research gaps we identified and propose as future research topics.

We are aware that our research has limitations. Although we searched for multiple combinations of "digital transformation" and related keywords, there still might be articles referring to digital transformation without having the term, or variations of it, in their title or abstract. Additionally, we limited our search to business related publications which excluded more technical papers. Moreover, we only examined papers written in English, which excluded articles in other languages that contribute to current research.

Our analysis focused on how external touchpoints of an organization with customers and suppliers impact its technological progress, future studies are recommended to investigate how external touchpoints with other actors, such as the government and its technology (tax collection, social security etc.) impact a firm's technological requirements. While we conducted a cross-industry analysis of the most frequent technologies used, future research might find it useful to classify existing technologies and their use, based on industry.

References

1. Hess, T., Matt, C., Benlian, A., Wiesböck, F.: Options for formulating a digital transformation strategy. In: Galliers, Robert D., Leidner, Dorothy E., Simeonova, Boyka (eds.) Strategic Information Management: Theory and Practice, 5th edn., pp. 151–173. Routledge, London (2020). https://doi.org/10.4324/9780429286797-7
2. Kane, G.: The technology fallacy: people are the real key to digital transformation. Res.-Technol. Manag. **62**(6), 44–49 (2019). https://doi.org/10.1080/08956308.2019.1661079
3. Ismail, M.H., Khater, M., Zaki, M.: Digital business transformation and strategy: what do we know so far? (2018). https://doi.org/10.13140/RG.2.2.36492.62086

4. Schwartz, E.I.: Digital Darwinism: 7 Breakthrough Business Strategies for Surviving in the Cutthroat Web Economy, Updated edition. Broadway, New York (2001)
5. Chanias, S., Myers, M.D., Hess, T.: Digital transformation strategy making in pre-digital organizations: the case of a financial services provider. J. Strateg. Inf. Syst. **28**(1), 17–33 (2019). https://doi.org/10.1016/j.jsis.2018.11.003
6. Dengler, K., Matthes, B.: The impacts of digital transformation on the labour market: substitution potentials of occupations in Germany. Technol. Forecast. Soc. Change **137**, 304–316 (2018). https://doi.org/10.1016/j.techfore.2018.09.024
7. Gurbaxani, V., Dunkle, D.: Gearing up for successful digital transformation. MIS Q. Exec. **18**(3), 209–220 (2019). https://doi.org/10.17705/2msqe.00017
8. Nadkarni, S., Prügl, R.: Digital transformation: a review, synthesis and opportunities for future research. Manag. Rev. Q. **71**(2), 233–341 (2020). https://doi.org/10.1007/s11301-020-00185-7
9. Rautenbach, W.J., de Kock, I., Jooste, J.L.: The development of a conceptual model for enabling a value-adding digital transformation: a conceptual model that aids organisations in the digital transformation process. In: 2019 IEEE International Conference on Engineering, Technology and Innovation (ICE/ITMC), Valbonne Sophia-Antipolis, France, pp. 1–10 (2019). https://doi.org/10.1109/ICE.2019.8792675
10. Webster, J., Watson, R.T.: Analyzing the past to prepare for the future: writing a literature review. MIS Q. **26**(2), xiii–xxiii (2002)
11. Vial, G.: Understanding digital transformation: a review and a research agenda. J. Strateg. Inf. Syst. **28**(2), 118–144 (2019). https://doi.org/10.1016/j.jsis.2019.01.003
12. Pihir, I., Tomičić-Pupek, K., Furjan, M.: Digital transformation playground: literature review and framework of concepts. J. Inf. Organ. Sci. **43**(1), 33–48 (2019). https://doi.org/10.31341/jios.43.1.3
13. Berman, S.J.: Digital transformation: opportunities to create new business models. Strategy Leadersh. **40**(2), 16–24 (2012). https://doi.org/10.1108/10878571211209314
14. Bharadwaj, A., El Sawy, O., Pavlou, P., Venkatraman, N.: Digital business strategy: toward a next generation of insights. MIS Q. **37**(2), 471–482 (2013). https://doi.org/10.25300/MISQ/2013/37:2.3
15. Loonam, J., Eaves, S., Kumar, V., Parry, G.: Towards digital transformation: lessons learned from traditional organizations. Strateg. Change **27**(2), 101–109 (2018). https://doi.org/10.1002/jsc.2185
16. Parviainen, P., Tihinen, M.: Tackling the digitalization challenge: how to benefit from digitalization in practice. IJISPM - Int. J. Inf. Syst. Proj. Manag. **5**(1), 63–77 (2017). https://doi.org/10.12821/ijispm050104
17. Furjan, M.T., Tomičić-Pupek, K., Pihir, I.: Understanding digital transformation initiatives: case studies analysis. Bus. Syst. Res. J. **11**(1), 125–141 (2020). https://doi.org/10.2478/bsrj-2020-0009
18. Kotarba, M.: Digital transformation of business models. Found. Manag. **10**(1), 123–142 (2018). https://doi.org/10.2478/fman-2018-0011
19. Piccinini, E., Hanelt, A., Gregory, R.W., Kolbe, L.M.: Transforming industrial business: the impact of digital transformation on automotive organizations. Presented at the 2015 International Conference on Information Systems: Exploring the Information Frontier, ICIS 2015 (2015). https://www.scopus.com/inward/record.uri?eid=2-s2.0-85071974071&partnerID=40&md5=a1cba70e111f7ad65f414266cd231182
20. Andal-Ancion, A., Cartwright, P.A., Yip, G.S.: The digital transformation of traditional businesses. MIT Sloan, 10 (2003)
21. Lanzolla, G., Anderson, J.: Digital transformation. Bus. Strategy Rev. **19**(2), 72–76 (2008). https://doi.org/10.1111/j.1467-8616.2008.00539.x

22. Horváth, Dóra., Szabó, R.Z.: Driving forces and barriers of Industry 4.0: do multinational and small and medium-sized companies have equal opportunities? Technol. Forecast. Soc. Change **146**, 119–132 (2019). https://doi.org/10.1016/j.techfore.2019.05.021

23. Imgrund, F., Fischer, M., Janiesch, C., Winkelmann, A.: Approaching digitalization with business process management (2018). https://www.semanticscholar.org/paper/Approaching-Digitalization-with-Business-Process-Imgrund-Fischer/1031f03b2f5a5f1686dd4d2a00f2d5 8d7510fc4d. Accessed 06 Dec 2020

24. Leyh, C., Schäffer, T., Bley, K., Forstenhäusler, S.: Assessing the IT and software landscapes of Industry 4.0-enterprises: the maturity model SIMMI 4.0. In: Ziemba, E. (ed.) AITM/ISM -2016. LNBIP, vol. 277, pp. 103–119. Springer, Cham (2017). https://doi.org/10.1007/978-3-319-53076-5_6

25. Veile, J.W., Kiel, D., Müller, J.M., Voigt, K.-I.: Lessons learned from Industry 4.0 implementation in the German manufacturing industry. J. Manuf. Technol. Manag. **31**(5), 977–997 (2019). https://doi.org/10.1108/JMTM-08-2018-0270

26. Bollweg, L., Lackes, R., Siepermann, M., Weber, P.: Drivers and barriers of the digitalization of local owner operated retail outlets. J. Small Bus. Entrep. **32**(2), 173–201 (2020). https://doi.org/10.1080/08276331.2019.1616256

27. Gigova, T., Valeva, K., Nikolova-Alexieva, V.: Digital transformation – opportunity for industrial growth. In: 2019 International Conference on Creative Business for Smart and Sustainable Growth (CREBUS), Sandanski, Bulgaria, pp. 1–4 (2019). https://doi.org/10.1109/CREBUS. 2019.8840065

28. Hervé, A., Schmitt, C., Baldegger, R.: Digitalization, Entrepreneurial Orientation and Internationalization of Micro-, Small- and Medium-Sized Enterprises, p. 13 (2020)

29. Ivančić, L., Vukšić, V., Spremić, M.: Mastering the digital transformation process: business practices and lessons learned. Technol. Innov. Manag. Rev. **9**(2), 36–50 (2019). https://doi. org/10.22215/timreview/1217

30. İnel, M.N.: An empirical study on measurement of efficiency of digital transformation by using data envelopment analysis. Manag. Sci. Lett. 549–556 (2019). https://doi.org/10.5267/ j.msl.2019.1.008

31. Dethine, B., Enjolras, M., Monticolo, D.: Digitalization and SMEs' export management: impacts on resources and capabilities. Technol. Innov. Manag. Rev. **10**(4), 18–34 (2020). https://doi.org/10.22215/timreview/1344

32. Eling, M., Lehmann, M.: The impact of digitalization on the insurance value chain and the insurability of risks. Geneva Pap Risk Insur. - Issues Pract. **43**(3), 359–396 (2018). https:// doi.org/10.1057/s41288-017-0073-0

33. Whyte, J.: How digital information transforms project delivery models. Proj. Manag. J. **50**(2), 177–194 (2019). https://doi.org/10.1177/8756972818823304

34. Andriushchenko, K., et al.: Peculiarities of sustainable development of enterprises in the context of digital transformation. Entrep. Sustain. Issues **7**(3), 2255–2270 (2020). https://doi. org/10.9770/jesi.2020.7.3(53)

35. Björkdahl, J.: Strategies for digitalization in manufacturing firms. Calif. Manage. Rev. **62**(4), 17–36 (2020). https://doi.org/10.1177/0008125620920349

36. Correani, A., De Massis, A., Frattini, F., Petruzzelli, A.M., Natalicchio, A.: Implementing a digital strategy: learning from the experience of three digital transformation projects. Calif. Manage. Rev. **62**(4), 37–56 (2020). https://doi.org/10.1177/0008125620934864

37. Pousttchi, K., Gleiss, A., Buzzi, B., Kohlhagen, M.: Technology impact types for digital transformation. In: 2019 IEEE 21st Conference on Business Informatics (CBI), Moscow, Russia, pp. 487–494 (2019). https://doi.org/10.1109/CBI.2019.00063

38. Stentoft, J., Adsbøll Wickstrøm, K., Philipsen, K., Haug, A.: Drivers and barriers for Industry 4.0 readiness and practice: empirical evidence from small and medium-sized manufacturers. Prod. Plan. Control **32**, 1–18 (2020). https://doi.org/10.1080/09537287.2020.1768318

39. Tortorella, G.: Organizational learning paths based upon Industry 4.0 adoption: an empirical study with Brazilian manufacturers. Int. J. Prod. Econ. **219**, 284–294 (2020). https://doi.org/10.1016/j.ijpe.2019.06.023

40. Verhoef, P.C., et al.: Digital transformation: a multidisciplinary reflection and research agenda. J. Bus. Res. **122**, 889–901 (2021). https://doi.org/10.1016/j.jbusres.2019.09.022

41. Akberdina, V.V.: Digitalization of industrial markets: regional characteristics. **9**(6), 10 (2018)

42. Biahmou, A., Emmer, C., Pfouga, A., Stjepandić, J.: Digital master as an enabler for Industry 4.0, p. 11 (2016)

43. Lichtenthaler, U.: Building blocks of successful digital transformation: complementing technology and market issues. Int. J. Innov. Technol. Manag. **17**(01), 2050004 (2020). https://doi.org/10.1142/S0219877020500042

44. Peter, M.K., Kraft, C., Lindeque, J.: Strategic action fields of digital transformation: an exploration of the strategic action fields of Swiss SMEs and large enterprises. J. Strategy Manag. **13**(1), 160–180 (2020). https://doi.org/10.1108/JSMA-05-2019-0070

45. Dolganova, O., Deeva, E.: Company readiness for digital transformations: problems and diagnosis. Bus. Inform. **13**(2), 59–72 (2019). https://doi.org/10.17323/1998-0663.2019.2.59.72

46. Koilada, D.K.: Value-based digital transformation: innovating customer experiences. In: 2019 IEEE Technology & Engineering Management Conference (TEMSCON), Atlanta, GA, USA, pp. 1–5 (2019). https://doi.org/10.1109/TEMSCON.2019.8813559

47. Culot, G., Nassimbeni, G., Orzes, G., Sartor, M.: Behind the definition of Industry 4.0: analysis and open questions. Int. J. Prod. Econ. **226**, 107617 (2020). https://doi.org/10.1016/j.ijpe.2020.107617

48. Frank, A.G., Mendes, G.H.S., Ayala, N.F., Ghezzi, A.: Servitization and Industry 4.0 convergence in the digital transformation of product firms: a business model innovation perspective. Technol. Forecast. Soc. Change **141**, 341–351 (2019). https://doi.org/10.1016/j.techfore.2019.01.014

49. Kiel, D.: What do we know about 'Industry 4.0' so far? In: Conference Proceedings, p. 23 (2017)

50. Nataliia, Y., Oleksii, Y.: Conceptual groundwork of digital transformation of project management. In: 2019 IEEE 14th International Conference on Computer Sciences and Information Technologies (CSIT), Lviv, Ukraine, pp. 85–88 (2019). https://doi.org/10.1109/STC-CSIT.2019.8929818

51. Hinings, B., Gegenhuber, T., Greenwood, R.: Digital innovation and transformation: an institutional perspective. Inf. Organ. **28**(1), 52–61 (2018). https://doi.org/10.1016/j.infoandorg.2018.02.004

52. Li, L., Su, F., Zhang, W., Mao, J.-Y.: Digital transformation by SME entrepreneurs: a capability perspective. Inf. Syst. J. **28**(6), 1129–1157 (2018). https://doi.org/10.1111/isj.12153

53. Karimi, J., Walter, Z.: The role of dynamic capabilities in responding to digital disruption: a factor-based study of the newspaper industry. J. Manag. Inf. Syst. **32**(1), 39–81 (2015). https://doi.org/10.1080/07421222.2015.1029380

54. Heavin, C., Power, D.J.: Challenges for digital transformation – towards a conceptual decision support guide for managers. J. Decis. Syst. **27**(sup1), 38–45 (2018). https://doi.org/10.1080/12460125.2018.1468697

55. Jin, J., Ma, L., Ye, X.: Digital transformation strategies for existed firms: from the perspectives of data ownership and key value propositions. Asian J. Technol. Innov. **28**(1), 77–93 (2020). https://doi.org/10.1080/19761597.2019.1700384

56. Kontić, L., Vidicki, Đ: Strategy for digital organization: testing a measurement tool for digital transformation. Strateg. Manag. **23**(2), 29–35 (2018). https://doi.org/10.5937/StraMan1801029K

57. Sebastian, I., Ross, J., Beath, C., Mocker, M., Moloney, K., Fonstad, N.: How big old companies navigate digital transformation. In: Galliers, R.D., Leidner, D.E., Simeonova, B. (eds.) Strategic Information Management: Theory and Practice, 5th edn., pp. 133–150. Routledge, London (2020). https://doi.org/10.4324/9780429286797-6

58. Nwankpa, J.K., Roumani, Y.: IT capability and digital transformation: a firm performance perspective, p. 16 (2016)

59. Romero, D., Flores, M., Herrera, M., Resendez, H.: Five management pillars for digital transformation integrating the lean thinking philosophy. In: 2019 IEEE International Conference on Engineering, Technology and Innovation (ICE/ITMC), Valbonne Sophia-Antipolis, France, pp. 1–8 (2019). https://doi.org/10.1109/ICE.2019.8792650

60. Eller, R., Alford, P., Kallmünzer, A., Peters, M.: Antecedents, consequences, and challenges of small and medium-sized enterprise digitalization. J. Bus. Res. **112**, 119–127 (2020). https://doi.org/10.1016/j.jbusres.2020.03.004

61. Hansen, A.M.: Rapid adaptation in digital transformation: a participatory process for engaging IS and business leaders, p. 12 (2011)

62. Singh, A., Klarner, P., Hess, T.: How do chief digital officers pursue digital transformation activities? The role of organization design parameters. Long Range Plann. **53**(3), 101890 (2020). https://doi.org/10.1016/j.lrp.2019.07.001

63. Chanias, S., Hess, T.: Understanding digital transformation strategy formation: insights from Europe's automotive industry, p. 17

64. Haffke, I., Kalgovas, B., Benlian, A.: The role of the CIO and the CDO in an organization's digital transformation, p. 21 (2016)

65. Li, F.: The digital transformation of business models in the creative industries: a holistic framework and emerging trends. Technovation **92–93**, 102012 (2020). https://doi.org/10.1016/j.technovation.2017.12.004

66. Li, Z., et al.: An enhanced reconfiguration for deterministic transmission in time-triggered networks. IEEEACM Trans. Netw. **27**(3), 1124–1137 (2019). https://doi.org/10.1109/TNET.2019.2911272

67. Ndemo, B., Weiss, T.: Making sense of Africa's emerging digital transformation and its many futures. Afr. J. Manag. **3**(3–4), 328–347 (2017). https://doi.org/10.1080/23322373.2017.1400260

68. Sanchez, M.A., Zuntini, J.I.: Organizational readiness for the digital transformation: a case study research. Rev. Gest. Tecnol. **18**(2), 70–99 (2018). https://doi.org/10.20397/2177-6652/2018.v18i2.1316

69. Angelopoulos, S., Kitsios, F., Babulac, E.: From e to u: towards an innovative digital era. In: Symonds, J. (ed.) Ubiquitous and Pervasive Computing: Concepts, Methodologies, Tools, and Applications, Chapter 103, pp. 1669–1687. IGI Global Publishing (2010)

70. Shaughnessy, H.: Creating digital transformation: strategies and steps. Strategy Leadersh. **46**(2), 19–25 (2018). https://doi.org/10.1108/SL-12-2017-0126

71. Tapia, F., Mora, M., Fuertes, W., Aules, H., Flores, E., Toulkeridis, T.: From monolithic systems to microservices: a comparative study of performance. Appl. Sci. **10**(17), 5797 (2020). https://doi.org/10.3390/app10175797

72. Agostino, D., Arnaboldi, M., Lema, M.D.: New development: COVID-19 as an accelerator of digital transformation in public service delivery. Public Money Manag. **41**(1), 69–72 (2021). https://doi.org/10.1080/09540962.2020.1764206

73. Horlach, B., Drews, P., Schirmer, I.: Bimodal IT: business-IT alignment in the age of digital transformation, p. 13 (2016)

74. Raj, A., Dwivedi, G., Sharma, A., Lopes de Sousa Jabbour, A.B., Rajak, S.: Barriers to the adoption of Industry 4.0 technologies in the manufacturing sector: an inter-country comparative perspective. Int. J. Prod. Econ. **224**, 107546 (2020). https://doi.org/10.1016/j.ijpe.2019.107546

75. von Leipzig, T., et al.: Initialising customer-orientated digital transformation in enterprises. Procedia Manuf. **8**, 517–524 (2017). https://doi.org/10.1016/j.promfg.2017.02.066

76. Kitsios, F., Kamariotou, M.: Business strategy modelling based on enterprise architecture: a state of the art review. Bus. Process Manag. J. **25**(4), 606–624 (2019). https://doi.org/10.1108/BPMJ-05-2017-0122

Towards a New Value Chain for the Audio Industry

Mahdieh Darvish(✉), Matthias Murawski, and Markus Bick

ESCP Business School Berlin, Heubnerweg 8-10, 14059 Berlin, Germany
{mdarvish,mmurawski,mbick}@escpeurope.eu

Abstract. Since the late 1990s, audio industry has been subject to severe changes, due to the advent of new technologies such as the mp3 compression codec and the related arrival of peer2peer sharing platforms. The latter ones were replaced by streaming platforms which now drive the digital transformation in this industry. However, there is still turmoil on how digital transformation in this field again facilitates new forms of business. Thus, there is an ongoing change regarding the way value is created and captured within a new market structure. The main objective of our work is to map this new market structure and the new ways of value creation considering the recent developments in the audio industry. Based on a literature review we derive our first drafts of both models which were modified across two focus group workshops afterwards. Moreover, expert interviews are employed to evaluate and continuously modify our models for the current as well as future audio industry. The two models presented in this paper, capture the current value creation mechanisms in the audio industry and provide insights to better understand the future developments facilitated by digital technologies for academia and in practice.

Keywords: Value chain · Market structure · Audio · Entertainment & media industry · Digital transformation · Technology

1 Introduction

Technology shifts have caused dramatic changes in many different industries in recent years, not only innovating production processes [1], but also introducing new forms of business models and value creation from a more extensive perspective [2]. In particular, industries with mostly digital products, such as audio industry are providing value to customers from a new perspective [3] which is creating a disruption in the pre-established rules of doing business [4]. For example, while the popularity of digital music is growing steadily, the retail sales of recorded music in physical format has dropped from €14.6 billion in 1999 to €1.2 billion in 2019, accounting for only 10% of the total revenue of €11.1 billion for all formats including download music, on-demand streaming as well as paid subscriptions (U.S. Sales Database).

Distributing music as digital information goods has impacted the value chain and, therefore the market structure of audio industry significantly [5]. In the past years,

© Springer Nature Switzerland AG 2022
M. Themistocleous and M. Papadaki (Eds.): EMCIS 2021, LNBIP 437, pp. 694–704, 2022.
https://doi.org/10.1007/978-3-030-95947-0_49

platforms like Spotify.com challenged the business models in the audio industry continuously by making the music streaming a source of revenue, transforming the established music value chain from ownership to music as a service [6]. The growing importance of subscriber revenue in this sector drives the creation of new forms of business models from a different aspect across the industry [3]. Other audio products such as audio narratives and podcasts have been also growing continuously in terms of producer and listener as well as platforms facilitating digital publication [7, 8] and driving vastly the digital transformation in this industry [7].

Furthermore, digitization – defined as "the material process of converting analog streams of information into digital bits" [8] – blurs different product and industry boundaries [9] by creating opportunities for reconfiguration of the design and production, decoupling form from function and media from content as well as coupling traditionally unrelated products [9, 10]. Audio products as a type of goods with a high possibility of being digitized have been experiencing this transformation with radical aftereffects for the business in this field in the past decade [11].

Consequently, digitalization or digital transformation – defined as "the changes associated with the application of digital technology"– has led to a new value chain for the audio industry which captures the dynamic between different market players in a co-creating context enabled by new digital technologies [11, 12].

Examples, such as the extended role of distribution platforms in the production process (e.g., Amazon Music Original) and new forms of customer products (e.g., new audio experience: music and talk content from spottify.com) demonstrate the current dynamic and fluid views on audio products [10]. However, this new form of value chain has not been carved out academically so far. Thus, the impact of digitalization on value creation in business models, particularly in the audio industry is still a topic of high relevance in management and information systems research [12].

The main objective of our research is to capture the market structure and the current form of value creation in the audio industry comprehensively. Our study contributes to the understanding of how digital technologies facilitate new forms of value creation in today's audio industry. Therefore, we study the market players as well as their activities to create value in forms of a product or service in the audio industry. Based on our preliminary results, we start to answer the following research question: How is the current market structure and the value chain of the audio industry defined?

Building from this, we will use both developed artefacts (market structure and value chain) as a basis for our further research and proceed by investigating the current and future effects of recent technology trends on the value creation and caption in the audio industry.

Furthermore, we argue that the audio industry serves as an ideal setting for a study of the new ways of value creation through digital technologies. Considering its broad roots in the long-established sectors (e.g., record labels), audio industry enjoys expansive developments in digital native sectors (e.g., streaming) like any other industry. The remainder of this paper is structured as follows. We first provide a brief outline of related work. Section 3, then moves on to define our literature-derived market structure and value chain for audio industry. In Sect. 4, we present and modify the aforementioned artefacts in a workshop with two focus groups of experts from the audio industry. This serves as the basis for the following section in which the revised market structure and value chain are evaluated in interviews with academic as well as professional experts. Evaluation and feedback are presented as preliminary results. In concluding section, we provide an outlook for the next steps in the study.

2 Related Work

The concepts of value chain and business model are discussed from different viewpoints in recent studies, however, often with the main focus on value creation and capture [1]. While many studies focus on the organization's interactions with other entities in the value network [13] others have value as the conceptual focus [14]. In this paper we consider value chain as the basis of any business model [15] and introduce our understanding of these two concepts, particularly for audio industry, as follows.

Value chain is defined as a series of activities creating and delivering value by an organization [16]. Activities are categorized as primary, such as operations, logistics, marketing, sale and services, and supportive activities such as human resource management, technology and procurement [16]. With the emergence of new technologies and digitalization the value chain of the audio industry has undergone a drastic transformation, while digitalization saves costs of production, distribution and support, defining new interactions between different players of the audio industry [17]. More importantly, driven by the advancement of technologies, many players in this context have shifted their positions from being supplier of products and services to facilitator of innovations and collaborations in the digital economy [18]. Likewise, customers are not passive stakeholders anymore and become more co-creators of value [19]. Investigating these alterations in the process of value creation, the literature emphasizes the examination of relevant features of overarching business models [14] in the context of digital transformation [20].

In this paper, we use Osterwalder's definition of business model focusing on the value as the core component as well as considering further aspects such as channels, key partners and resources [14, 21]. We see this in most alignment with the idea of new value chain for the audio industry with a focus on the impact of digital technology. Following this definition, the literature shows the profound impact of digital technology on different components of (digital) business model particularly on channels (e.g., digital distribution and sales channels), customers (e.g., consumer behavior and relationship, innovative customer services and offers, etc.), strategic responses (e.g., digital transformation strategy) as well as structural and organizational changes [20]. New forms of technology can enhance and transform the business model into a digital one [22]. A digital business model is characterized as a business model which is changed fundamentally by changes of the digital technologies [23, 24]. The intangible nature [25] and business's core value [26] as well as three elements of platform, content and experience form the central elements of the digital business's value proposition [27]. Additionally, digital technologies are highly interconnected and can transform the way a business is done by enhancing the capacity for information processes [26].

3   Deriving the Value Chain

Considering the high relevance and current state of research on the value chain and the impact of digital technology in the audio industry, we used an explorative approach consisting in a review of related works with a qualitative content analysis. With the qualitative research design we identify the status-quo and derive a literature-based recent value chain draft for the audio industry.

We conducted a literature review on value chain for the audio industry in March-April 2020 and updated it in March 2021. Given the sparse literature on recent value chain for the audio industry, we extended the scope of search by using the keywords "value chain" and "business model" which were then specified in combination with further keywords "audio industry" and "digital transformation" as well as "digital business model". Following the guidelines of Vom Brocke et al. [28], we searched through a 21-year period (2000 to 2021) in eight leading IS journals (senior basket of 8), four major and other IS conferences, as well as journals of relevant fields such as innovation studies, entertainment, and finally industry reports, mainly in databases of AIS Electronic Library, WILEY Online Library and Google Scholar to cover a wide range of sources which contribute to relevance and rigor of research in the field of IS. The chosen timeframe is relevant as in 2000 the rise of digital technologies in terms of interactive websites (platforms), social media and smartphones (customer relationships) began. The search terms of our literature review were developed based on the PICO criteria (Population, Intervention, Comparison and Outcomes) to provide a convenient systematic review in the context of IS [29]. The literature search in the titles, abstracts and keywords from journals, conference proceedings and databases resulted in 62 papers. After an additional full-text screening, we excluded 28 articles with a narrow focus on one country, a very specific sector or only one player in audio industry. This step was done, at first by each author individually, then, modified through discussion and final selection. Finally, 34 articles were selected; including articles published in English, in peer reviewed conferences, and leading journals from IS and other disciplines relevant to the audio industry.

Based on the literature review, we identified core activities of the value chain in the audio industry and recognized non-linear interactions between different players of this industry. We decide to capture this under market structure in alignment with our chosen definition of value chain and business model [14] considering key partners and customers. A value chain as well as a market structure capturing the market players and their interactions were developed which provided a basis for the next step. The grey boxes in Fig. 1 illustrate the current – literature derived – market structure for entertainment industry with a focus on audio. All major parties are interconnected and form the market network: one company can hold several roles at the same time (e.g., one company can be the brand owner as well as the producer for the same audio product). The players and interactions in the initial literature-derived model are presented in grey.

4   Value Chain Validation

4.1   Focus Group Workshops

First, we presented and discussed the literature-derived artefacts in two focus group workshops with experts from a main player firm in the children entertainment industry with the focus on audio. This firm was selected based on two main criteria: (1) being one of the leading players in the sector for more than 40 years, the company has been experiencing, managing and growing on disruptive technologies in audio industry from the very beginning; and (2) considering the activities and resources of the company, it represents different roles such as producer, brand owner and distributer in the market. Therefore, experts from different departments contribute to the focus group workshops from the most various viewpoints. Moving along the literature derived value chain as the point of orientation, experts representing different activities and steps were invited randomly to the focus group workshops.

Focus group workshops are appropriate to further challenge the findings from literature, as an opportunity to consider and value feedback and positions [30]. Thus, the literature-derived value chain was presented as the starting point followed by a moderated discussion about whether and how the suggested activities and their relations are perceived in an individual firm setup as well as the industry. Following the steps outlined by Stewart and Shamdasani (2014), the two-hour workshop was performed with three scholars and two focus groups with four experts each from different business divisions of this firm, such as e-commerce, marketing, licensing, executive board, distribution and production. During the discussion, participants added a new player, emphasized an existing one (brand owner and platform – presented in dark blue Fig. 1) and created seven new interactions in the market structure (blue lines Fig. 1). The platform was included in the initial market structure. However, it's interactions as a new player were emphasized especially, impacting the whole market structure in a significant manner. Furthermore, a differentiation between buyer and consumer was considered regarding the audio products in children entertainment industry where underage consumers use the products bought by their parents.

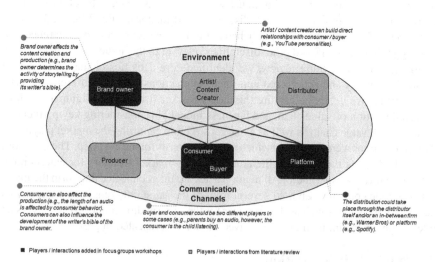

Fig. 1. Market structure: entertainment industry - focus on audio

The value chain for entertainment industry with a focus on audio consists of four primary activities which have a direct contribution to the value creation, i.e., creating an audio product (Fig. 2). The start of value creation often reflects changes in long-term customer behavior. In line with the market structure (i.e., network), several parties are involved with different activities (Fig. 1). Examples are provided in the descriptions below. The four primary activities are accompanied by two support activities, such as technology forecasts, which do not add a direct value, but are of high importance to create value. Additional classical support activities (e.g., HR management, IT service) are not shown for simplicity reasons.

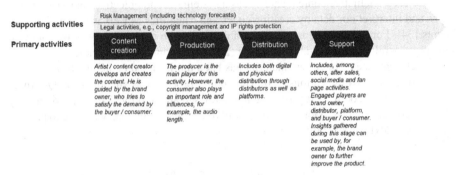

Fig. 2. Value chain: entertainment industry – focus on audio

The value chain as well was further developed on detailed descriptions and clear differentiation between primary and supportive activities as a result of the focus groups. A non-linear value chain has proven itself as a confusing attempt to capture the reality, as a new form of value chain in the workshop. However, the consideration of the market structure and the value chain as a whole provides a more realistic picture of the interactions between the main players as well as the value creation in the market.

4.2 Interviews

The modified market structure and value chain from the focus group workshops were subject to review in several semi-structured interviews. The main advantage of semi-structured interview is that while it provides a general structure to gain reliable and comparable qualitative data [31], it also enables the researcher to gain a more in-depth understanding of the phenomenon under investigation by further discussion and development of the ideas, opinions and views conveyed by interviewees [32]. Experts from the audio industry evaluated the model and its accuracy based on their experience of the current reality. The interviews with practitioners from different fields and companies in the audio industry were conducted to test for the plausibility and practical value of the revised artefacts from the focus group workshops. A set of open-ended questions were used that covered the value creation and capturing, the impact of digital technology and its challenges as well as opportunities in the audio industry. The semi-structured format allowed interviewees to approach the main topics from different points of view, enriching the research [33].

In total, we conducted thirteen interviews via video calls, lasting between 30–60 min from June 2020 onwards. We applied a purposeful sampling strategy to recruit interview partners with a broad variety of expertise, making use of several professional contacts and referrals. The experts were all male, with tenure of two to twenty years in the audio industry, and represented aspects of different market players such as brand owners, artists, producers, platforms, labels and studios (Table 1). Considering the special characteristics of the audio industry and the much specified topic of our study, the saturation was achieved at this point.

We used qualitative content analysis as a systematic and objective approach to analyze and interpret our data by creating codes and categories as well as developing concepts [34]. For a comprehensive and reliable qualitative content analysis we followed the procedural model posited by Mayring (2014) for inductive categories.

Each sentence of interview material has been unitized and coded to abstract codes presenting similar implications [35]. The coding process was supported by QCAmap software and the coding category system was revised and improved after approximately 50% of content analysis. Double coding by two scholars of our team was used to provide a greater analytical reliability [36].

Table 1. Overview: interview partners

Interviewee	Position	Type of company
IP 1	Head of Performance Management & Development	Major Label
IP 2	Co-Founder and Executive Manger	Voice Assistant Applications
IP 3	Artist, Composer, Studio Owner	Audio Play and Narratives
IP 4	Expert in Brand and Communication	Academy and Consultancy
IP 5	Software Developer	Business Process Consultancy
IP 6	Head of Marketing and Digital Business	Brand Owner and Producer
IP 7	Licensing Sales Manager	Brand Owner and Producer
IP 8	Director of Distribution	Brand Owner and Producer
IP 9	Business Intelligence Manager	Major Label
IP 10	Key Account Manager	Major Label
IP 11	Operations Administrator	Business Analytic Consultancy
IP 12	EVP Group Strategy and M&A	Music Publisher
IP 13	Recording Manager	Producer, Localization

In order to analyze the data from the interviews in more detail, we thereafter used the Gioia methodology and organized the identified codes into 1st-order concepts which were then infused into 2nd- order themes and then finally into aggregate dimensions [37]. We carefully developed the 1st-order concepts along the interviewee's terms. Proceeding to the themes and aggregate dimensions we became more abstract and used wording from the existing literature. Figure 3 demonstrates the link between category induction and data, illustrating the concepts, themes and aggregate dimensions.

In addition to more general interpretative method, we applied Gioia methodology to ensure quality rigor [37] in our inductive research and pave the ground for further validation of the value chain in a quantitative setting. With a focus on the value chain, the developed aggregate dimensions via Gioia deliver a great validation of the artefacts as well as clear path for the proceeding study. Each of aggregate dimensions may be examined explicitly in next steps of this research.

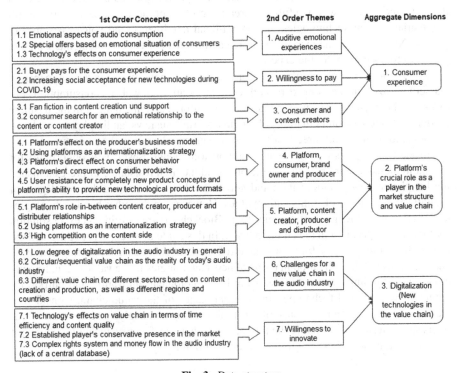

Fig. 3. Data structure

5 Preliminary Results and Discussion

As a first result we can summarize that all the experts generally agreed on the presented value chain as well as the market structure.

Aside from this generally confirming assessment, some remarks and comments on the developed artefacts have been formulated, as well. In this context, it must be noted that the experts represent different aspects and roles of the audio industry. For example, one interviewee (IP 2) highlighted the often overlapping roles, for example regarding artist, author, and brand. More detailed, in the current music market, many artists are the brand itself but may perform songs written by someone else. Consequently, we will dive deeper into this phenomenon in the following steps of our research (cf. also Next Steps) to better understand how the roles can be distinguished properly, or if there are even "new" roles (e.g., combining different "older" roles) to be added.

Focusing on the value chain, the interviewees emphasized that today's value chain in the audio industry is rather a cycle in which consumers play a more active role compared to the "traditional" audio market. Today's consumer experience is an important factor determined as an auditive emotional perception (e.g., emotional situation of audio consumption), as a valuable source to create new content (e.g., fan fiction, reviews, social media posts, etc.) or even as a general acceptance towards new technologies in the audio industry. However, a fully co-creating process or individualized offers are still a potential for new technologies such as artificial intelligence and voice assistance to initiate. Nevertheless, the market structure captures the correct complementary picture of the sector, according to the experts.

Furthermore, the crucial role of platform as the next "new" player in the audio market was emphasized in the context of both content creation as well as consumption. For example, the payment system of a platform can enforce certain changes in the business models of content creators in terms of length or form (music vs. audio play vs. podcast) of the audio product and directly affect the consumer behavior at the same time.

In addition, experts see digitalization as both a challenge as well as an opportunity for the audio industry. For example, on the one hand the high resistance of pre-established market players towards innovation and new technologies is causing the low degree of digitalization in terms of rights and loyalties. However, on the other hand technologies such as distributed ledger technologies (e.g., Blockchain) are offering an exact solution for this current problem in the audio industry. In this context, all experts highlighted the importance of technology forecast – captured in value chain as a supporting activity – and the impact of digitalization in terms of new technologies in the value chain. Experts emphasized the impact of openness towards technological innovation and purposeful applications of digital technology in different stages of the value chain. Considering the high importance and relevance of this topic, coding and analysis of first part of our interview material will structure the further research with a focus on technology forecast and examining the technology trends for the audio industry.

6 Conclusion and Next Steps

The findings of this research contribute to a greater understanding of new ways of value creation facilitated by digital technologies in the audio industry. The audio industry acts as a prominent exponent of industries which have been experiencing digital transformation in the last decades. Based on a structured literature review, a new value chain along with the market structure for the audio industry has been developed. These artefacts have been validated first in two focus group workshops where new players and interactions have been identified. Second, thirteen representatives (different backgrounds and expertise) of audio industry were interviewed in addition, by offering their insights and outlining the impact of digital technologies on the current value chain of the audio industry. At this point, the Gioia analysis approved the results from the focus group workshops and ensured the quality rigor of this study. Furthermore, the Gioia data structure and developed aggregate dimensions shed light on the impact of digital technology on value creation in the audio industry from three new aspects of customer experience, the crucial role of platforms and new technologies in the value chain. First, digitalization generates new forms of products, players and interactions which redefine the whole market structure in the audio industry. Second, today's value chain of the audio industry is rather a cycle with the consumer experience at the center which serves as a valuable source to create content. And finally, the pervasive use of digital technologies in the processes of production and distribution, along with the strongly increasing importance of customer experience, pushes the audio industry to accept more disruption in other areas of the value chain, such as application of distributed ledger technologies in supporting activities. Each of these aspects delivers a starting point for our future research in addition to the basis provided for further analysis in a quantitative setting.

Based on the preliminary findings presented, our main objective for the future is (1) to develop the current value chain of audio industry, including the recent insights generated based on the expert interviews and (2) to investigate if and how recent technology trends (e.g., Big Data, Artificial Intelligence, Blockchain, Voice Assistants, etc.) could affect our artefacts. Personalized music playlists, songs created by artificial intelligence applications, song titles that are formulated in a way that voice assistants are able to "understand" the correct title, or discussions about how Blockchain could improve the whole money flows between the parties are only some of the interesting and related topics in this context.

References

1. Tongur, S., Engwall, M.: The business model dilemma of technology shifts. Technovation **34**, 525–535 (2014)
2. Li, F.: The digital transformation of business models in the creative industries: a holistic framework and emerging trends. Technovation **92**, 102012 (2020)
3. Herbert, D., Lotz, A.D., Marshall, L.: Approaching media industries comparatively: a case study of streaming. Int. J. Cult. Stud. **22**, 349–366 (2019)
4. Hirt, M., Willmott, P.: Strategic Principles for Competing in the Digital Age. McKinsey Quarterly (2014)
5. Bockstedt, J.C., Kauffman, R.J., Riggins, F.J.: The move to artist-led on-line music distribution: a theory-based assessment and prospects for structural changes in the digital music market. Int. J. Electron. Commer. **10**, 7–38 (2006)
6. Essling, C., Koenen, J., Peukert, C.: Competition for attention in the digital age: the case of single releases in the recorded music industry. Inf. Econ. Policy **40**, 26–40 (2017)
7. Negus, K.: From creator to data: the post-record music industry and the digital conglomerates. Media Cult. Soc. **41**, 367–384 (2019)
8. Brennen, J.S., Kreiss, D.: Digitalization. In: The International Encyclopedia of Communication Theory and Philosophy, pp. 1–11 (2016)
9. Yoo, Y., Henfridsson, O., Lyytinen, K.: Research commentary—the new organizing logic of digital innovation: an agenda for information systems research. Inf. Syst. Res. **21**, 724–735 (2010)
10. Lyytinen, K., Yoo, Y., Boland, R.J., Jr.: Digital product innovation within four classes of innovation networks. Inf. Syst. J. **26**, 47–75 (2016)
11. Lusch, R.F., Nambisan, S.: Service innovation: a service-dominant logic perspective. MIS Q. **39**, 155–176 (2015)

12. Tidhar, R., Eisenhardt, K.M.: Get rich or die trying… finding revenue model fit using machine learning and multiple cases. Strateg. Manag. J. **41**, 1245–1273 (2020)
13. Weill, P., Vitale, M.: Place to Space: Migrating to eBusiness Models. Harvard Business Press, Harvard (2001)
14. Osterwalder, A., Pigneur, Y.: Business Model Generation: A Handbook for Visionaries, Game Changers, and Challengers. Wiley, Hoboken (2010)
15. Strakova, J., Simberova, I., Partlova, P., Vachal, J., Zich, R.: The value chain as the basis of business model design. J. Comp. **13**, 135–151 (2021)
16. Porter, M.E., Kramer, M.R.: Advantage. Creating and Sustaining Superior Performance, Simons (1985)
17. Berman, S.J.: Digital transformation: opportunities to create new business models. Strategy & Leadership (2012)
18. Rayna, T., Striukova, L.: Open innovation 2.0: is co-creation the ultimate challenge? Int. J. Technol. Manag. **69**, 38–53 (2015)
19. Setzke, D.S., Riasanow, T., Böhm, M., Krcmar, H.: Pathways to digital service innovation: the role of digital transformation strategies in established organizations. Inf. Syst. Front. 1–21 (2021). https://doi.org/10.1007/s10796-021-10112-0
20. Vial, G.: Understanding digital transformation: a review and a research agenda. J. Strateg. Inf. Syst. **28**, 118–144 (2019)
21. Osterwalder, A., Pigneur, Y., Tucci, C.L.: Clarifying business models: Origins, present, and future of the concept. Commun. Assoc. Inf. Syst. **16**, 1 (2005)
22. Rachinger, M., Rauter, R., Müller, C., Vorraber, W., Schirgi, E.: Digitalization and its influence on business model innovation. J. Manuf. Technol. Manag. (2019)
23. Planing, P.: Will digital boost circular? Evaluating the impact of the digital transformation on the shift towards a circular economy. Int. J. Manag. Cases **19**, 22–31 (2017)
24. Veit, D.: Business Models Business & Information Systems Engineering. Springer, Heidelberg (2014)
25. Yoo, Y.: The tables have turned: How can the information systems field contribute to technology and innovation management research? J. Assoc. Inf. Syst. **14**, 4 (2012)
26. Bican, P.M., Brem, A.: Digital business model, digital transformation, digital entrepreneurship: is there a sustainable, "digital"? Sustainability **12**, 5239 (2020)
27. Weill, P., Woerner, S.L.: Optimizing your digital business model. MIT Sloan Manag. Rev. **54**, 71 (2013)
28. Vom Brocke, J., et al.: Reconstructing the giant: On the importance of rigour in documenting the literature search process (2009)
29. Kitchenham, B., Charters, S.: Guidelines for performing systematic literature reviews in software engineering (2007)
30. Stewart, D.W., Shamdasani, P.N.: Focus Groups: Theory and Practice. Sage publications, Thousand Oaks (2014)
31. Bryman, A.: Social Research Methods. Oxford University Press, Oxford (2016)
32. Mojtahed, R., Nunes, M.B., Martins, J.T., Peng, A.: Equipping the constructivist researcher: the combined use of semi-structured interviews and decision-making maps. Electron. J. Bus. Res. Methods **12**, 87–95 (2014)
33. Mason, J.: Mixing methods in a qualitatively driven way. Qual. Res. **6**, 9–25 (2006)
34. Schreier, M.: Qualitative Content Analysis in Practice. Sage publications, Thousand Oaks (2012)
35. Ryan, G.W., Bernard, H.R.: Techniques to identify themes. Field Methods **15**, 85–109 (2003)
36. Mayring, P.: Qualitative content analysis: theoretical foundation, basic procedures and software solution (2014)
37. Gioia, D.A., Corley, K.G., Hamilton, A.L.: Seeking qualitative rigor in inductive research: Notes on the Gioia methodology. Organ. Res. Methods **16**, 15–31 (2013)

Knowledge Management Significance in Agile Organization in Lights of COVID-19 Pandemic Changes

Patryk Morawiec(✉) ⓘ and Anna Sołtysik-Piorunkiewicz ⓘ

University of Economics in Katowice, 1 Maja 50, 40-287 Katowice, Poland
patryk.morawiec@edu.uekat.pl,
anna.soltysik-piorunkiewicz@uekat.pl

Abstract. The paper discuss how organizational agility can affect the knowledge management processes in organization, especially in case of ongoing COVID-19 pandemics changes. The research problems are to show a link between knowledge management and agility in organization and to examine a COVID-19 pandemics impact on both knowledge management in organization and organizational agility. We carefully examined a literature from knowledge management-related, recognized scientific journals. We searched journal articles from 1994–2021 and divided the results into 3 time periods to show the historic view on knowledge management in agility, the current view in 2015–2019 and latest time period (2020–2021) to show the impact of COVID-19 pandemics on knowledge management and organizational agility. The study shows the relation of knowledge management and organizational agility with some diversity of research scopes related with COVID-19 pandemics. The insights of our research may be useful for organizations in transforming their knowledge management processes in dynamically changing environment.

Keywords: Organizational agility · Knowledge management · Knowledge processes · COVID-19

1 Theoretical Background

For some decades there has been a wide consensus among economists on the role played by non-material resources in economic growth. Knowledge has been especially pinpointed as the main discriminating element in economic performance. In the globalizing economy, even regional competitiveness – and consequently regional growth – is no longer dependent on the traditional production resource endowment, capital and labor. The hyper-mobility that nowadays characterizes these factors reduces their geographical concentration, and shifts the elements on which competitiveness rests from the availability of material resources to the presence of immobile local resources like local culture, competence, innovative capacity; in general knowledge.

The considerations about organizational models in knowledge-based economy should be began with defining the concept itself. The knowledge economy is the use of

© Springer Nature Switzerland AG 2022
M. Themistocleous and M. Papadaki (Eds.): EMCIS 2021, LNBIP 437, pp. 705–722, 2022.
https://doi.org/10.1007/978-3-030-95947-0_50

knowledge to create goods and services. It refers to a high portion of skilled employees and the idea that most jobs require specialized skills. In particular, the main personal capital of knowledge workers is knowledge, and many knowledge worker jobs require a lot of thinking and manipulating information as opposed to moving or crafting physical objects.

Knowledge economy emphasizes the importance of skills in a service economy, the third phase of economic development, also called a post-industrial economy. It is related to the terms: information economy, which emphasizes the importance of information as non-physical capital and digital economy, which emphasize the degree to which information technology facilitates trade. For companies, intellectual property such as trade secrets, copyrighted material, and patented processes become more valuable in a knowledge economy than in earlier eras. The transition from farming or industrial economy to knowledge economy can be also identified as entering the "Information Age" and creating an information society. In such an economy we can distinguish following types of organizations: knowledge-based organization, virtual organization, mobile organization, and agile organization.

1.1 Knowledge and Knowledge Management in Organization

Knowledge is defined in Cambridge Dictionary as understanding of or information about something, which person gets by experience or study [7]. Many literature sources mention various aspects related to knowledge and knowledge management e.g. human foundation of knowledge management [16], knowledge management as a socio-technological combination [18, 20]. Organizational view of knowledge in society is described in [26] and some of latest publications refers to new paradigms of management based on knowledge such as autopoiesis [49].

Knowledge in literature is usually described in three categories: knowledge as a general abilities and information of individuals; knowledge as a resource; knowledge as a process [15]. Knowledge in organization influences the achievement of competitive advantage [31], it also provides sustainable character of advantage due to increasing returns and continuing advantage of unlimited potential of knowledge growth [13]. Above comparisons allows to present knowledge as a resource in organization and like any other resources in organization also knowledge is manageable. Davenport & Prusak defines knowledge as a fluid mix of framed experience, values, contextual information and expert insights that provides a framework for evaluating and incorporating new experiences and information [13]. Nonaka & Takeuchi proposed "Japanese approach" to knowledge management, divides knowledge into tacit knowledge – personal, uncategorized, often not formal, not easily visible and shareable; and explicit knowledge – formal, stored in databases or documents, easily processed by electronic forms of communication [32].

Figure 1 presents a relations between tacit and explicit knowledge in Japanese knowledge management model.

Nowadays organizations are becoming more knowledge-based. Most of them are facing many different issues related with data e. g. necessity to find solutions to store, process and analyze increasing amount of data. There is revealed the process nature of knowledge management. Knowledge management can be understood as performing

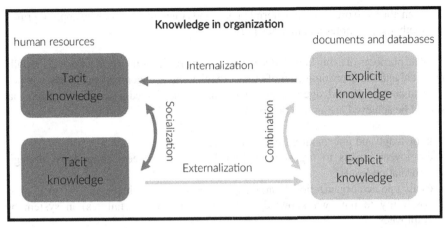

Fig. 1. Tacit & explicit knowledge relations. **Source:** Own elaboration of [17, 42]

the activities involved in discovering, capturing, sharing and applying knowledge so as to enhance in a cost-effective fashion, the impact of knowledge on unit goal achievement [6]. Processes of knowledge management in organization in literature are widely discussed, usually portrayed in five main categories [48]:

1. **Knowledge identifying** – is the process of finding internal and external sources of knowledge and ensure of data, information and skills transparency [28]. This process in literature is also mentioned as knowledge discovery, where is defined as the development of new knowledge (tacit or explicit) from data and information or from synthesis of prior (existing) knowledge [6].
2. **Knowledge gaining/ creating** – organizations can formulate their knowledge base in three ways: by acquisition knowledge from diverse resources, retention of acquired knowledge for short and long terms and modification of retained knowledge to be compatible with changing working context [44]. The key elements in creating new knowledge in organization are creativity, problem solving skills and innovation [37].
3. **Knowledge storing** – depending on the knowledge type, different media can be used to store the knowledge. Explicit knowledge is usually formal and codified in documents and databases while tacit knowledge is owned by each individual in organization.
4. **Knowledge sharing** – the technocratic approach is focused on creating repositories and knowledge bases to share the codified knowledge while behavioral approach is more focused on creating networks, communities and organizing work to promote the exchange of knowledge [14]. The problems that may occur during knowledge transfer are [30]: distributed nature of knowledge (not everyone has the same level of knowledge about process), ambiguous knowledge (to be transferable knowledge has to be commonly understandable), disruptive character of some knowledge (sharing some parts of knowledge may meet with resistance of knowledge holders).
5. **Knowledge applying** – the final step, when gained, stored and shared knowledge is actually used in organization. According to Bloom taxonomy knowledge application

is an ability to use learned material in new and concrete situations by applying rules, methods, principles and theories [12].

The purposes of using knowledge management processes in organizations are usually practical and the overriding goal of every organization is to generate profit and competitive advantage. Knowledge management is an action oriented process, and effects that should be achieved are among others [15]:

- knowledge and information freely exchange,
- employees access to organization knowledge base (except proprietary strategic information level),
- easily updated organizational knowledge base by each employee,
- possibility to put own knowledge (successes as well as failures) in system by employees.

In project-oriented organizations management of knowledge is perceived in three levels [27]:

- normative knowledge management,
- operational knowledge management,
- strategic knowledge management.

Project, due to its uniqueness creates particular knowledge, which combined with project team tacit knowledge leads to create organizational knowledge base [27].

In a literature, a little is known about knowledge management in pandemics. Ammirato et al. identifies 5 main themes related to knowledge management in pandemic crisis i.e. modeling and simulation to support decision making, community resilience, system preparedness for crisis, mitigation and containment measures in population, knowledge integration in healthcare [4].

1.2   Types of Intelligent Organization

In literature is observed the development of concepts related to some forms of intelligent organization since 90's. The following types of organizations can be distinguished:

- learning organization,
- network organization,
- open organization,
- virtual organization,
- mobile organization,
- agile organization – described in more detail in Sect. 1.3.

A concept of learning organization appeared first. This term was used in Peter Senge's book "The fifth Discipline" in 1990. Learning organization unlike traditional organization based on authoritative control methods is able to master some disciplines. Senge lists five of them which all have significant influence on each other, i.e. [40]:

1. **Systems thinking** – understood as perceiving connections between business activities and external factors instead of focusing on single aspect of organization "isolated part of the system".
2. **Personal mastery** – continually clarifying and deepening personal knowledge, vision and objectivism of single individual as an essence of organizational learning. People should be focused on self-development, have sense of their work and involvement.
3. **Mental models** – stereotypes, generalizations and assumptions which have signifi cant impact of perception of the environment and decision making. Learning organization can surface and challenge mental models starting from discover and rigorously analyze own mental models.
4. **Shared vision** – leaders should have common vision, consistent with organization goals, rather than personal visions which rarely translated onto shared vision.
5. **Team learning** – coordinated effect of collective learning as a whole team can give better results than individual learning of each team member. The key factor of successful team learning starts with dialogue, ability to suspend assumptions and focus on thinking as a group.

1.3 Organizational Agility

The term agility is commonly associated with project management methodologies and with created in 2001 Agile Manifesto. The purposes behind agile methodologies introduction were as follows [50]: to satisfy customer's needs, being more requirement change-oriented, frequently deliver added value, working with self-organized teams.

According to Sołtysik-Piorunkiewicz [42] modern organization, to meet highly unpredictable market demands have to became more elastic and flexible due to necessity to adapt their activities to situations generated by the market.

In context of organization management agility is associated with such terms as flexibility, elasticity, quickness and responsiveness [24]. Organizational agility can be defined as an ability to proactively detect signals in environment to sense and evaluate it as cues and opportunities, and the formulate adequate response [10]. Paterek & Panasiewicz proved significant impact of knowledge management processes on organizational activity [33]. Cegarra-Navarro et al. developed a model connecting organizational agility with search and retrieval knowledge in organization, which affects on company performance. Organizational agility is mediating the relationship between knowledge application and company performance in one complementary process [9].

The important element of organizational agility is change management and willingness to adapt to changing environment. Main purposes to change organizational functioning are willingness to be more customer-centric, sustainable and achieve higher performance [22]. According to Aburub, ICT adoption in organization has also positive impact on organizational agility and company performance [1] like also on organizational learning [2].

Trzcieliński notices that for agile enterprises, changes and a changing environment may become a source of opportunities and indicates that agility should be treated as a basic enterprise paradigm and necessary feature of contemporary enterprise [45].

2 Material and Methods

The research study was conducted based on literature review methods. Critical literature review method is used to identify and synthesize relevant literature to compare and contrast findings in prior domain [34]. In the study, authors carefully examined the latest and historical literature related to knowledge in organization, knowledge management, and organizational agility in recognized journals related to knowledge management i.e.:

- "Journal of Knowledge Management" by Emerald Publishing (ISSN: 1367-3270);
- "The Learning Organization" by Emerald Publishing (ISSN: 0969-6474);
- "Knowledge Management Research & Practice" by Palgrave Macmillan/Taylor & Francis Group[1] (ISSN: 1477-8238);
- "Knowledge and Process Management: The Journal of Corporate Transformation" by John Wiley & Sons (ISSN: 1099-1441);
- "International Journal of Knowledge Management Studies" by Inderscience Publishing (ISSN: 1743-8268);
- "European Journal of Information Systems" by Taylor & Francis Group (ISSN: 1476-9344);

Selection of journals was based on Serenko & Bontis ranking 2017 edition [41]. The methodology used in ranking is based on journal citation impact measure and a survey of 482 knowledge management and intellectual capital scientists.

The search queries was formulated as: "knowledge management in agile organization", "knowledge management and business agility", and "agility impact on knowledge management".

During the research process, 2 hypotheses were formulated:

- **H1 hypothesis**: Organizational agility is affecting knowledge management processes in organization.
- **H2 hypothesis**: COVID-19 pandemics has significant impact on organizational agility and knowledge management processes in organization.

Meanwhile selected journals were examined manually for knowledge management and business agility topics. The examination process covered three time periods:

- Papers published between 1994 to 2014 – since the beginnings of knowledge management discipline and first theories related to intelligent organization to current state of art.
- Papers published between 2015 to 2019 – current state of art before COVID-19 outbreak.
- Papers published in 2020 and after – current state of art during COVID-19 pandemics.

The reason for dividing searched material into three period is willingness to find how COVID pandemics influences current knowledge management methods and how is the

---

[1] Since November 2017 journal have changed publisher.

impact of the pandemics on transform traditional organizations into agile organizations. Figure 2 presents a time interval of researched articles.

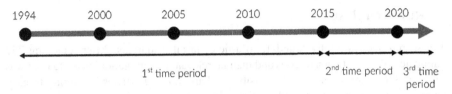

Fig. 2. Researched articles publication time interval

The research methodology is presented on Fig. 3 below.

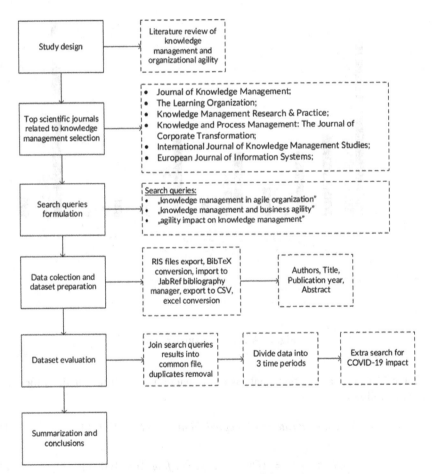

Fig. 3. Research methodology

The queries results from selected journals were exported into several RIS files as the most common format for all journals.

3   Research Results

The search queries totally found 1366 articles in all 6 journals. After removing 757 duplicate articles between queries and manual relevancy examination, to evaluation was selected 386 articles. On Fig. 4 is visible a chart showing articles belonging to each journal along with reject rate and duplicate rates between queries.

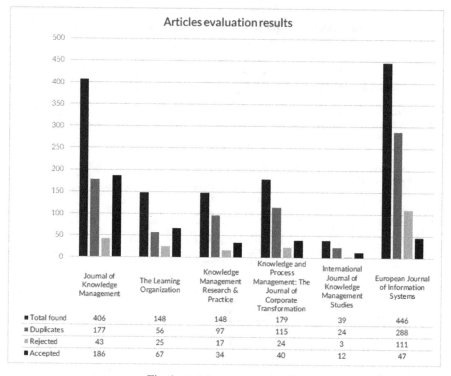

	Journal of Knowledge Management	The Learning Organization	Knowledge Management Research & Practice	Knowledge and Process Management: The Journal of Corporate Transformation	International Journal of Knowledge Management Studies	European Journal of Information Systems
Total found	406	148	148	179	39	446
Duplicates	177	56	97	115	24	288
Rejected	43	25	17	24	3	111
Accepted	186	67	34	40	12	47

Fig. 4. Articles evaluation results

Table 1 presents a statistical analysis of evaluation results. The equations for each rate are as follows:

$$Acceptance\ rate = (Accepted/Total\ found) * 100[\%] \qquad (1)$$

$$Duplicate\ rate = (Duplicates/Total\ found) * 100[\%] \qquad (2)$$

$$Rejection\ rate = z(Rejected/Total\ found) * 100[\%] \qquad (3)$$

Table 1. Statistical analysis of evaluation results

Journal	Acceptance rate [%]	Duplicate rate [%]	Rejection rate [%]
Journal of Knowledge Management	45,81	43,60	10,59
The Learning Organization	45,27	37,84	16,89
Knowledge Management Research & Practice	22,97	65,54	11,49
Knowledge and Process Management	22,35	64,25	13,41
International Journal of Knowledge Management Studies	30,77	61,54	7,69
European Journal of Information Systems	10,54	64,57	24,89

Duplicate rate is quite similar in all journals, the highest is observed in Knowledge Management Research & Practice and European Journal of Information Systems both published by Taylor & Francis, probably due to the same search algorithm. Lowest duplicate rate is observed in journals published by Emerald Group, respectively The Learning Organization and Journal of Knowledge Management. The most articles was manually rejected in European Journal of Information Systems (24,89% of articles),

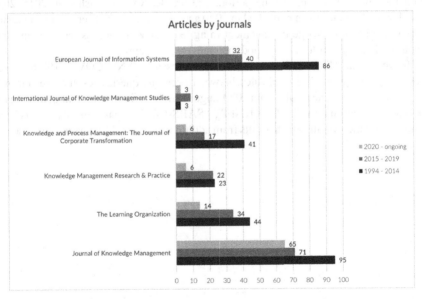

Fig. 5. Articles by time period grouped by journals

which can be result of quite different profile than other journals, not so closely related to knowledge management. The lowest rejection rate is observed in International Journal of Knowledge Management Studies (7,69%).

Figure 5 and Fig. 6 show articles division into time periods.

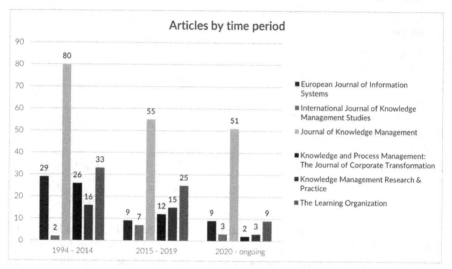

Fig. 6. Articles by journals grouped by time periods

The largest number of articles (186) comes from 1994–2014 period, which is understandable due to the longest time period, 123 articles were published in 2015–2019 period and 77 articles were published in 2020 and after. It can be observed an increasing trend related to knowledge management in agile organization in last year, taking into account relatively shorter time period than previously examined.

To verify the H2 hypothesis, additional expression "AND COVID-19" has been added to each query. The duplicates between previous queries result were removed manually. Moreover the results from 2020-ongoing time period were examined manually for phrases: "coronavirus", "COVID-19", "SARS-Cov2", "pandemics", "crisis", the results match the overall search results from additional queries. The results are presented in Table 2.

Table 2. Results of COVID-19 related queries

Journal	Author(s)	Title	Findings
Journal of Knowledge Management	Sadeghi, J. K., Struckell, E., Ojha, D., Nowicki, D.	Absorptive capacity and disaster immunity: the mediating role of information quality and change management capability	Confirmed positive relationship between absorptive capacity and organizational adaptive capability, extends these relationship on company's disaster immunity. Necessity to research multi-level impact of COVID-19 on individuals, businesses, communities and governments [39]
	Haider, S. A., Kayani, U. N.	The impact of customer knowledge management capability on project performance-mediating role of strategic agility	Customer Knowledge Management Capability (CKMC) is positively associated with project performance. Strategic agility plays a mediating role between CKMC and project performance. COVID-19 is pushing enterprises to rapidly operate in new system priorities and challenges related with decision making, efficiency and business continuity risks [19]
	Ashok, M., Al Badi Al Dhaheri, M. S. M., Madan, R., Dzandu, M. D.	How to counter organisational inertia to enable knowledge management practices adoption in public sector organisations	Specific organizational culture and bureaucratic barriers in public sector negatively affects on knowledge management practices [5]
	Chin, T., Wang, S., Rowley, C.	Polychronic knowledge creation in cross-border business models: a sea like heuristic metaphor	New idea of polychronic knowledge creating as a dynamic synthesis of space and time, Development of Nonaka's 1994 model of organiza tional knowledge creation [11]

(*continued*)

Table 2. (*continued*)

Journal	Author(s)	Title	Findings
	Raudeliuniene, J., Albats, E., Kordab, M.	Impact of information technologies and social networks on knowledge management processes in Middle Eastern audit and consulting companies	Positively confirmed impact of informative technologies and social networks on knowledge management cycle in Middle-Eastern enterprises. Global need to adopt new communication and knowledge exchange technologies aggravated by COVID-19 pandemics [36]
The Learning Organization	Welsh, R., Williams, S., Bryant, K., Berry, J.	Conceptualization and challenges: examining district and school leadership and schools as learning organizations	School as a case of learning organization under circumstances like a key aspect of collaboration and key role of organization leader in learning organization. COVID-19 pandemics makes research more difficult and plays major role in data collecting process [47]
	Haneberg, D. H.	Interorganizational learning between knowledge-based entrepreneurial ventures responding to COVID-19	Covid related adversities and enterprises reactions have influence on interorganizational learning. Four groups representing different types of behavior are developed and described [21]
	Akella, D.	A learner-centric model of learning organizations	Crucial role of learner agents in learning process in democratic learning organization and learning society. Suggested direction in organizational learning with use of learner agents [3]

(continued)

Table 2. (*continued*)

Journal	Author(s)	Title	Findings
Knowledge Management Research & Practice	Iacuzzi, S., Fedele, P., Garlatti, A.	Beyond Coronavirus: the role for knowledge management in schools responses to crisis	Coronavirus pandemics impact on tasks, methods and knowledge in Italian scholarity system. Crucial role of risk management and strategy plan for crisis [25]
Knowledge and Process Management	Van Looy, A.	How the COVID-19 pandemic can stimulate more radical business process improvements: Using the metaphor of a tree	Helpful role of business process management trees was described in context of necessity of business processes changes in organization related with COVID-19 [46]
	Rowe, F., Ngwenyama, O., Richet, J.-L.	Contact-tracing apps and alienation in the age of COVID-19	Empirical research shows covid-tracing mobile app implementation failure, three different proposals were described [38]
	Henningsson, S., Kettinger, W. J., Zhang, C., Vaidyanathan, N.	Transformative rare events: Leveraging digital affordance actualisation	A model of digital affordance as a part of rare events response [23]
European Journal of Information Systems	Carillo, K., Cachat-Rosset, G., Marsan, J., Saba, T., Klarsfeld, A.	Adjusting to epidemic induced telework: empirical insights from teleworkers in France	Teleworking crucial impact on business continuity during lockdown. Empirically evaluated adjustment to mandatory teleworking [8]
	Pee, L.G., Pan, S. L., Wang, J., Wu, J.	Designing for the future in the age of pandemics: a future ready design research (FRDR) process	The importance of new technologies in creating future post-COVID "new normal" implementation [35]
	Mandviwalla, M., Flanagan, R.	Small business digital transformation in the context of the pandemic	Digital transformation described as a "lifeline" for some of small businesses, case studies empirical analysis of small businesses handling with pandemics [29]

(*continued*)

Table 2. (*continued*)

Journal	Author(s)	Title	Findings
	Soluk, J., Kammer lander, N.	Digital transformation in family-owned Mittel stand firms: A dynamic capabilities perspective	Digital transformation process in cases of family-owned small manufacturing industry companies [43]

4   Conclusions and Limitations

The research study was based on research question concerned on knowledge management in agile organization in context of "knowledge management in agile organization", "knowledge management and business agility", and "agility impact on knowledge management". The research limitations was related with selective scope of journals, the queries limitations, and the automatization the process of searching. Further studies can take into account many other scientific sources databases, and develop the methodology of literature research review.

The final research showed the main current issues describing the knowledge management in agile organization due to current SARS-CoV-2 (or COVID-19) pandemics. There are some differences in describing the newest pandemics situation; the manuscripts were submitted during year 2020–2021. In year 2020 there were proposed to published different phrases to describe the pandemics situation: "Corona-virus", "COVID-19", "covid-19", etc. The results are showing the diversity of research findings in 16 papers along the following journals: "Journal of Knowledge Management", "The Learning Organization", "Knowledge Management Research & Practice", "Knowledge and Process Management" and "European Journal of Information Systems". Some of the papers are currently waiting for the publication and have the status "ahead-of-print". Nowadays the crucial issues are published in the following journals: "Journal of Knowledge Management" (2 papers), "Knowledge Management Research & Practice" (1 paper), "Knowledge and Process Management" (1 paper) and "European Journal of Information Systems" (6 papers).

The latest papers from "Journal of Knowledge Management" showed the two different research studies topics, the first about relationship between the customer knowledge management capability and the project performance [19], and the second one about the modern digital context of cross-cultural business models [11]. The first paper by Haider & Kayani, describes the impact of customer knowledge management capability on project performance-mediating role of strategic agility. The second paper is showing the theoretical research which complements and enriches Nonaka's theory [11]. The authors suggests a novel concept of polychronic knowledge creation mechanism from an integrative socio-cultural and philosophical perspective. The next studies in the "Journal of Knowledge Management" will be showing the complexity of interorganizational interdependencies and the need to build unique capabilities and innovative solutions, especially when confronted with man-made or natural disasters [39].

The next papers will show the public sector organizations, and how the knowledge management is associated with higher performance and innovative culture, and how can help the public sector to be fiscally lean and meet diverse stakeholders' needs [5] and the impact of information technologies and social networks on knowledge management processes in Middle Eastern audit and consulting companies [36]. There are six papers published in "European Journal of Information Systems" recently. The most important issues are concerning of COVID-19 implication on digitalization of business process in different organizations, and try to propose the future research topics in raising pandemic environment [35]. The paper by Soluk & Kammerlander is showing the adoption of digital technologies by firms in a process consisting of three stages, i.e. process digitalization, product and service digitalization, and business model digitalization, for the advancement of the digital transformation process [43]. The growing problems of the rapid digitalization in small business is described in research by Mandviwalla & Flanagan [29]. There are two papers focusing on European pandemic environment. The paper by Carillo, Cachat-Rosset, Marsan, Saba & Klarsfeld in "European Journal of Information Systems" is showing the telework model derived from the theory of Work Adjustment and the Interactional Model of Individual Adjustment due to the COVID-19 pandemic crisis based on studies conducted in France. The results demonstrate the influence of crisis-specific variables that are professional isolation, telework environment, work increase and stress. Implications for research are discussed as the recommendations for management of the organizations [8]. The second paper is published in "Knowledge Management Research & Practice". The paper is showing the Coronavirus crisis focusing the study on schools knowledge management strategies to help educational institutions deal with large-scale crises and plan the new normal life for employee after in case of Italy as a one of the most affected countries [25].

The studies showed the impact of knowledge management on agile organization with the diversity of research scopes which are conducted because of COVID-19 pandemics. The future studies should be focused on the next step of literature review of knowledge management state-of-art for describing the newest issues of agile organization model with IT tools dedicated for knowledge management in new remote business environment.

References

1. Aburub, F.: Impact of ERP systems usage on organizational agility: an empirical investigation in the banking sector. Inf. Technol. People **28**(3), 570–588 (2015). https://doi.org/10.1108/ITP-06-2014-0124
2. Aburub, F.: The influence of ERP usage on organizational learning: an empirical investigation. J. Inf. Syst. Telecommun. **6**(23), 149–156 (2018). https://doi.org/10.7508/jist.2018.03.004
3. Akella, D.: A learner-centric model of learning organizations. TLO **28**(1), 71–83 (2021). https://doi.org/10.1108/TLO-06-2020-0117
4. Ammirato, S., et al.: Knowledge management in pandemics. A critical literature review. Knowl. Manag. Res. Pract. **19**, 1–12 (2020). https://doi.org/10.1080/14778238.2020.1801364
5. Ashok, M., et al.: How to counter organisational inertia to enable knowledge management practices adoption in public sector organisations. JKM. ahead-of-print, ahead-of-print (2021). https://doi.org/10.1108/JKM-09-2020-0700
6. Becerra-Fernandez, I., Sabherwal, R.: Knowledge Management: Systems and Processes. M.E. Sharpe Inc., Armonk (2015)

7. Cambridge Dictionary: Knowledge. https://dictionary.cambridge.org/pl/dictionary/english/knowledge. Accessed 15 Feb 2021

8. Carillo, K., et al.: Adjusting to epidemic-induced telework: empirical insights from teleworkers in France. Eur. J. Inf. Syst. **30**(1), 69–88 (2021). https://doi.org/10.1080/0960085X.2020.1829512

9. Cegarra-Navarro, J.-G., et al.: Structured knowledge processes and firm performance: the role of organizational agility. J. Bus. Res. **69**(5), 1544–1549 (2016). https://doi.org/10.1016/j.jbusres.2015.10.014

10. Chatwani, N.: Organisational Agility: Exploring the Impact of Identity on Knowledge Management. Springer, Cham (2019). https://doi.org/10.1007/978-3-030-17249-7

11. Chin, T., et al.: Polychronic knowledge creation in cross-border business models: a sea-like heuristic metaphor. JKM **25**(1), 1–22 (2021). https://doi.org/10.1108/JKM-04-2020-0244

12. Dalkir, K.: Knowledge Management in Theory and Practice. Elsevier/Butterworth Heinemann, Boston (2005)

13. Davenport, T.H., Prusak, L.: Working knowledge: how organizations manage what they know. Ubiquity (2000). https://doi.org/10.1145/347634.348775

14. Dingsøyr, T.: Strategies and approaches for managing architectural knowledge. In: Ali Babar, M., et al. (eds.) Software Architecture Knowledge Management: Theory and Practice, pp. 59–68. Springer, Heidelberg (2009). https://doi.org/10.1007/978-3-642-02374-3_4

15. Flaszewska, S.: Projektowanie organizacyjne w zarządzaniu wiedzą. Polish Scientific Publishers, Warsaw (2017)

16. Gadner, J., et al. (eds.): Organising Knowledge. Palgrave, London (2004). https://doi.org/10.1057/9780230523111

17. Girard, J.P., Girard, J.L.: A Leader's Guide to Knowledge Management: Drawing on the Past to Enhance Future Performance. Business Expert Press, New York (2009). https://doi.org/10.4128/9781606490198

18. Grundstein, M.: Toward management based on knowledge. In: Wickham, M. (ed.) Current Issues in Knowledge Management. IntechOpen (2019). https://doi.org/10.5772/intechopen.86757

19. Haider, S.A., Kayani, U.N.: The impact of customer knowledge management capability on project performance-mediating role of strategic agility. JKM **25**(2), 298–312 (2021). https://doi.org/10.1108/JKM-01-2020-0026

20. Handzic, M.: Knowledge Management: Through the Technology Glass. World Scientific, New Jersey (2004)

21. Haneberg, D.H.: Interorganizational learning between knowledge-based entrepreneurial ventures responding to COVID-19. TLO **28**(2), 137–152 (2021). https://doi.org/10.1108/TLO-05-2020-0101

22. Harraf, A., et al.: Organizational agility. JABR. 31(2), 675 (2015). https://doi.org/10.19030/jabr.v31i2.9160

23. Henningsson, S., et al.: Transformative rare events: leveraging digital affordance actualisation. Eur. J. Inf. Syst. **30**(2), 137–156 (2021). https://doi.org/10.1080/0960085X.2020.1860656

24. Holbeche, L.: The Agile Organization: How to Build an Engaged, Innovative and Resilient Business. Kogan Page, New York (2018)

25. Iacuzzi, S. et al.: Beyond Coronavirus: the role for knowledge management in schools responses to crisis. Knowl. Manag. Res. Pract. 1–6 (2020). https://doi.org/10.1080/14778238.2020.1838963

26. Jasimuddin, S.M.: Knowledge in an organizational context. In: Knowledge Management: An Interdisciplinary Perspective, pp. 1–29. World Scientific, Singapore (2011)

27. Lent, B.: Cybernetic Approach to Project Management. Springer, Heidelberg (2013). https://doi.org/10.1007/978-3-642-32504-5

28. Maczuga, P.: Zarządzanie Wiedzą 2.0. https://issuu.com/piotr-maczuga/docs/km20_2015_pl. Accessed 29 Mar 2021
29. Mandviwalla, M., Flanagan, R.: Small business digital transformation in the context of the pandemic. Eur. J. Inf. Syst. 1–17 (2021). https://doi.org/10.1080/0960085X.2021.1891004
30. Newell, S.: Knowledge transfer and learning: problems of knowledge transfer associated with trying to short-circuit the learning cycle. J. Inf. Syst. Technol. Manag. 2(3), 275–289 (2005)
31. Nonaka, I.: The knowledge-creating company. In: The Economic Impact of Knowledge, pp. 175–187. Elsevier (1998). https://doi.org/10.1016/B978-0-7506-7009-8.50016-1
32. Nonaka, I., Takeuchi, H.: The Knowledge-Creating Company: How Japanese Companies Create the Dynamics of Innovation. Oxford University Press, New York (1995)
33. Paterek, P., Panasiewicz, L.: Strategia organizacji a procesy zarządzania wiedzą w zespołach projektowych wykorzystujących metodyki zwinne. Marleting i Rynek 4(2017), 294–303 (2017)
34. Paul, J., Criado, A.R.: The art of writing literature review: what do we know and what do we need to know? Int. Bus. Rev. 29(4), 1–7 (2020). https://doi.org/10.1016/j.ibusrev.2020.101717
35. Pee, L.G., et al.: Designing for the future in the age of pandemics: a future-ready design research (FRDR) process. Eur. J. Inf. Syst. 30(2), 157–175 (2021). https://doi.org/10.1080/0960085X.2020.1863751
36. Raudeliuniene, J., et al.: Impact of information technologies and social networks on knowledge management processes in Middle Eastern audit and consulting companies. JKM 25(4), 871–898 (2021). https://doi.org/10.1108/JKM-03-2020-0168
37. Rollett, H.: Knowledge Management. Springer US, Boston, MA (2003). https://doi.org/10.1007/978-1-4615-0345-3
38. Rowe, F., et al.: Contact-tracing apps and alienation in the age of COVID-19. Eur. J. Inf. Syst. 29(5), 545–562 (2020). https://doi.org/10.1080/0960085X.2020.1803155
39. Sadeghi, J.K., et al.: Absorptive capacity and disaster immunity: the mediating role of information quality and change management capability. JKM 25(4), 714–742 (2021). https://doi.org/10.1108/JKM-06-2020-0404
40. Senge, P.M.: The Fifth Discipline: The Art and Practice of the Learning Organization. Currency Doubleday, New York (1994)
41. Serenko, A., Bontis, N.: Global ranking of knowledge management and intellectual capital academic journals: 2017 update. JKM 21(3), 675–692 (2017). https://doi.org/10.1108/JKM-11-2016-0490
42. Sołtysik-Piorunkiewicz, A.: Modele oceny użyteczności i akceptacji mobilnych systemów zarządzania wiedzą o zdrowiu. University of Economics in Katowice Publishing House, Katowice(2018)
43. Soluk, J., Kammerlander, N.: Digital transformation in family-owned Mittelstand firms: a dynamic capabilities perspective. Eur. J. Inf. Syst. 1–36 (2021). https://doi.org/10.1080/0960085X.2020.1857666
44. Stein, E.W.: Organization memory: review of concepts and recommendations for management. Int. J. Inf. Manag. 15(1), 17–32 (1995). https://doi.org/10.1016/0268-4012(94)00003-C
45. Trzcielinski, S.: The influence of knowledge based economy on agility of enterprise. Procedia Manuf. 3, 6615–6623 (2015). https://doi.org/10.1016/j.promfg.2015.11.001
46. Van Looy, A.: How the COVID-19 pandemic can stimulate more radical business process improvements: using the metaphor of a tree. Knowl Process Manag. 28(2), 107–116 (2021). https://doi.org/10.1002/kpm.1659
47. Welsh, R., et al.: Conceptualization and challenges: examining district and school leadership and schools as learning organizations. TLO 28(4), 367–382 (2021). https://doi.org/10.1108/TLO-05-2020-0093

48. Young, R.: Knowledge Management Tools and Techniques Manual. Asian Productivity Organization, Tokyo (2020)
49. Żytniewski, M.: Zorientowane na procesy biznesowe oraz interakcję systemy wspomagania zarządzania firmą. University of Economics in Katowice Publishing House, Katowice(2020)
50. Principles behind the Agile Manifesto. https://agilemanifesto.org/principles.html. Accessed 20 Mar 2021

An Agile Approach for Managing Microservices-Based Software Development: Case Study in FinTech

Vu H. A. Nguyen[1,2]([✉])([iD])

[1] Banking University of Ho Chi Minh City, Ho Chi Minh City, Vietnam
vunha@buh.edu.vn
[2] LouRIM-CEMIS, Université Catholique de Louvain,
Ottignies-Louvain-la-Neuve, Belgium
vu.nguyenhuynh@uclouvain.be

Abstract. Digital transformation requires FinTech organizations to be agile and apply innovative approaches and flexible architectures that allow the delivery of new digital services to their clients, partners, and employees. To consolidate this perspective, this paper proposes an agile approach using organization modeling techniques to illustrate all management processes and disciplines in microservices-based FinTech software development. On the one hand, agile methods are development processes to drive the system life cycle in terms of incremental and iterative engineering techniques. On the other hand, microservices architecture offers nimble, scalability, and faster deployment life-cycle and the ability to provide solutions using a blend of different technologies. Typically, such methods are well-suited for implementing and adapting software processes management to cope with stakeholders' requirements and expectations immediately into the development life cycle.

Keywords: Agile · Microservices · FinTech

1 Introduction

Formerly, most FinTech applications were built based on large monolith architecture, on the basis of waterfall-inspired models for software development, which is hard to implement new features and rapid delivery to end-users [13]. Today, FinTech companies compete with traditional financial institutions by offering a set of (sub-)products and services together with using their competitive edge to fulfill customer needs and expectations and faster deliver new solutions based on the agile model. Singularly, they can be easy to develop from scratch or adjust their software products and services by using microservice architecture and agile development methods. A transition from the waterfall model towards the agile model has taken place in the last years due to changes in the competition [8]. Furthermore, the microservice architecture allows developers to independently implement and deploy services, and facilitate the adoption of agile methods [20].

© Springer Nature Switzerland AG 2022
M. Themistocleous and M. Papadaki (Eds.): EMCIS 2021, LNBIP 437, pp. 723–736, 2022.
https://doi.org/10.1007/978-3-030-95947-0_51

Consequently, FinTech companies have already started to apply or contemplate transiting to microservice architecture. It enables big players to reengineer their monolith solutions into microservices ones or integrate new microservices into a monolith system. On the subject of the software development perspective, some metrics and policies for evaluating and managing a microservices-based application are needed [4].

The purpose of this paper is to align agile model with microservices-based software development by using strategic modeling organization specifications. To this end, we propose an agile approach for managing microservices-based software development. In this approach, we use strategic modeling techniques to represent the organizational setting and management structures. Then we will discuss the use of this approach within particular processes to align agile development processes with managing microservices architecture in FinTech software.

This paper is organized as follows. Section 2 overviews the research context while Sect. 3 introduces the research approach and methodology. Section 4 proposes the meta-model for an agile approach for managing software development based on microservice architecture named AgileMS. Section 5 illustrates FinTech's case study while Sect. 6 presents the validation of this approach. Finally, Sect. 7 concludes the paper and points out future work.

2   Research Context

2.1   Agile Development

The term Agile is derived based on the idea of the *Manifesto for Agile Software Development* [5]. This manifesto is "a set of principles encapsulating the ideas underlying agile methods of software development" [19]. The Agile model [1,2,14] is an iterative and incremental development approach. Thus, it develops the system incrementally instead of building a complete solution at once. The agile system development life cycle consists of five phases (*Planning, Analysis, Design, Building,* and *Testing*) as in Fig. 1 below.

Fig. 1. The agile model from [1,2,14]

2.2 Microservice Architecture

Microservice architecture is described as "Microservice architecture is a style of engineering highly automated, evolvable software systems made up of capability-aligned microservices" [17] and "A microservice is an independently deployable component of bounded scope that supports interoperability through message-based communication" [17]. This architecture can be seen as an evolution of service-oriented architecture because its services are more fine-grained, and function independently of each other, which has recently started gaining popularity [9]. In a microservice architecture, the business logic is covered by many microservices. Some external callings of the business logic are handled by a single microservice. The more complex ones are handled by many microservices.

2.3 FinTech

Generally, FinTech is operated based on cloud computing platforms and/or mobile applications that can be consist of the technologies of data mining, blockchain, machine learning, and algorithms to offer its clients intelligent financial services automatically [10,16]. Moreover, FinTech allows its clients to communicate with a financial organization through more channels. Therefore, FinTech organizations must optimize their services through different channels to fulfill their clients' needs and expectations.

3   Research Approach and Methodology

3.1 Research Question

This section describes the research question to provide enough specifics and focus on our research. After the preliminary study based on the research context and motivation, we will ask the following research question:

> *How to align the agile model with managing microservice-based software development for business and IT alignment evaluation?*

Aligning agile model with microservices architecture management allows the software project managers to propose rules for software development processes to cope with stakeholders' requirements and expectations in terms of the IT/Business alignment perspective.

The steps of the research process are represented in the next section.

3.2 Design Science

The research process describes in this paper based on Design Science Research (DSR) methodology for Information Systems [12,18]. This determines that the initial stage of the research process is the explanation of the aims of the solution: a proper approach for managing microservices-based agile software development in alignment with stakeholders' long-term strategy. Figure 2 illustrated the acquisition architecture instantiated to our research. It is summarized as follows:

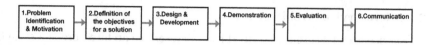

Fig. 2. Design science research methodology for information systems: acquisition architecture

- *Problem identification and motivation.* The main problem is that the inefficiency of the monolith (see Sect. 1) solution coupled with the evolution of emerging technologies. Indeed, with the ubiquitous presence of agile development, microservice architecture as well as the pressure of competition for FinTech organizations, open and flexible software systems are required for process optimization and to ensure proper IT integration;
- *Definition of the objectives for a solution.* The objectives are to propose an agile approach for managing microservice-based software development to support the business processes and to study its alignment with FinTech organizations long term strategy;
- *Design and development.* Fundamentally, we focus on an agile approach that is used to manage the microservices-based software development. In this approach, we use i* diagrams at its phases to illustrate the FinTech platform as an organization made of multiple dependent actors (microservices). This work is depicted in details in Sects. 5;
- *Demonstration.* This stage represents the ability and efficiency of managing the agile microservices-based development to support the FinTech business processes. This demonstration is illustrated in details in Sects. 5;
- *Evaluation.* The agile approach for managing microservices-based software development will be evaluated with respect to the long-term FinTech organization strategy. The evaluation is realized in Sect. 6;
- *Communication.* The main communication has been done in this paper.

3.3   Research Approach and Method

This section describes the research method by explaining how we build-up and validate the entire software development process in terms of microservices management and software engineering disciplines. Fundamentally, AgileMS extends the agile model to furnish a microservices management layer integrated with the already software engineering ones. This management layer:

- is described by strategic modeling techniques to present the organizational setting and management structures acting as guidance for practitioners;
- is aligned with the entire software development process of agile model.

4   Meta-model

This section depicts a generic meta-model for describing and formalizing of AgileMS. In this meta-model, we represent the organizational setting for the management of microservices-based agile software development. It also overviews AgileMS from both software modeling perspective and structural perspective.

4.1   AgileMS Process Elements Meta-model

Figure 3 illustrates the main meta-classes and meta-relationships of the AgileMS process. The meta-classes are:

- **Stage** represents the core stages of microservices management (*Determine, Blueprint*, and *Apply*);
- **Microservice** represents all microservices;
- **Iteration** represents all iteration plans;
- **Phase** represents the five phases of the agile software engineering process (*Planning, Analysis, Design, Building*, and *Testing*);
- **Artifact** represents all artifacts.

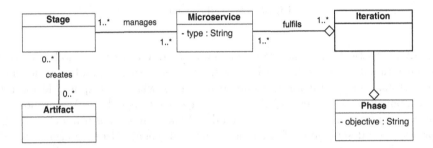

Fig. 3. AgileMS process elements meta-model.

4.2   Overview of AgileMS from a Software Modeling Perspective

This section presents an extension of the Agile model called AgileMS for aligning the management of microservices-based software development with agile principles. The purpose of this extension is to allow developing microservices-based agile software solutions to fulfill stakeholders' requirements and expectations within microservices management aspects. Figure 4 illustrates the model for AgileMS. The AgileMS model consists of three organizational decision levels: (i) strategic level; (ii) tactical level; and (iii) operational levels of decision-making in an organization.

At the strategic level, this model is presented in terms of services that are provided by actors. The objective of the AgileMS's strategic level is to determine the long-term microservices management strategy. It is useful for top managers. It considers the environment of microservices-based agile software processes management at the strategic decision level. In AgileMS, we use the Strategic Service (SS) model [21], an extension of the i* modeling framework, for representing the microservices management processes. The SS model is used to allow the stakeholders to have the most comprehensive static view of the business processes (represented in the form of services) for an adequate understanding of the system to be built.

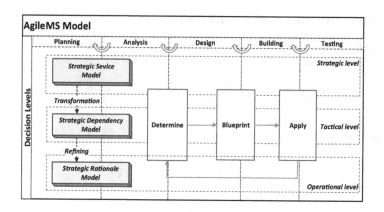

Fig. 4. The AgileMS model.

At the tactical level, each service is represented in a static method using rich organizational concepts, i.e., tasks, goals, qualities, resources, and their depending actors. It is useful for the middle managers who are responsible for the development of the objectives determined at the strategic level. We propose to use the Strategic Dependency (SD) model of the i* modeling framework [7,22] for adequate descriptions of the functional requirements of microservices-based agile software processes management at the tactical level. The SD model contains a set of actors, for instance, human or software systems, and their dependencies including Resource dependency, Task dependency, Goal dependency, and Quality dependency to represent the intentional level of a system.

At the operational level, each element needed for service realization is performed through the atomic tasks that are responsible for the achievement of the sub-processes defined at the tactical level. It is useful for first-line managers and operators. The models created at the tactical level are then mapped into a series of design models represented in this level through various points of view. We propose to use the Strategic Rationale (SR) model of the i* modeling framework [7,22] for adequate descriptions of the functional and non-functional requirements of the services. The SR model represents the rationale level of a system. It allows us to visualize the intentional elements into the boundary of an actor to refine the SD model to add reasoning ability. In the actors' boundary, the dependencies of the SD model are linked to intentional elements. The elements in the SR model are decomposed suitably to the three kinds of links: *Means-end*, *Contribution*, and *Task-decomposition*.

Figure 5 illustrates the main i* elements and their graphical representation used in the diagrams of the paper.

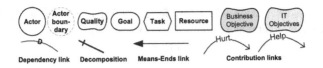

Fig. 5. i* Elements and their graphical representation.

4.3   Overview of AgileMS from a Structural Perspective

Basically, AgileMS allows determining, blueprinting, and applying microservice architecture as an add-on to the agile development method. AgileMS is organized like a classical iterative perspective based on a microservices management discipline represented in the vertical dimension and a series of phases depicted in the horizontal dimension. This discipline enables determining microservices based on requirements, blueprinting microservices, applying microservices achieved, to assure that microservice architecture fulfills stakeholders' requirements and expectations throughout the system. The microservices management discipline of AgileMS is transversal to each phase. Efforts can be spent on them during several iterations during each phase depending on the software project characteristics. Thus, this discipline can be repeated iteratively and the effort/workload spent on the discipline varies from one iteration to the other.

From a software development perspective, in order to execute the software processes from the perspective of microservices management, AgileMS redefines the **Planning, Analysis, Design, Building**, and **Testing** phases while improving those of Agile model.

In the **Planning, Analysis** and **Design** phases, this alignment assures controlling the operational environment, comprehending the stakeholders' requirements and expectations, gathering system requirements, defining the project scope, assessing an initial risk, and establishing an initial baseline for the software system architecture. It includes describing an information architecture, forming a model for technology planning, defining organization and processes, developing a microservices management plan, developing a project management model. At the end of **Analysis** phase, all microservices are identified. Then, all microservices are designed at the end of **Design** phase,

In the **Building** phase, the alignment assures implementing the software system counterparts totally the stakeholders' requirements and expectations. It consists of managing business goals and requirements continuously, designing and developing resources, validating and measuring microservices with different stakeholders based on initial prototyping results. At the end of this phase, all microservices are implemented.

In the **Testing** phase, this alignment assures delivering software system counterparts totally implementing the stakeholders' requirements and expectations.

AgileMS is represented as a generic process to be customized to specific projects for validation. The process must be refined by experiencing multiple case studies. The review of the advantages and disadvantages of developing the generic process description will be performed after each case study. Hence, the microservices management model is described herein in its current version and can be adopted as a standalone sub-process.

5   FinTech's Case Study

In this section, the AgileMS model is applied to a FinTech application called MFin. This application is an innovative FinTech solution based on microservice architecture to develop a platform that helps property agencies to manage their agents, properties, insurance, and financial departments. The architecture of MFin is separated into two levels, a domain layer, and a microservice one. The former is to illustrate the business (front-end) part the latter is to model the IT (back-end) part. Figure 6 represents the architecture of MFin.

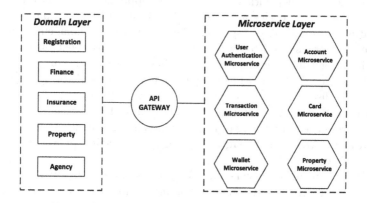

Fig. 6. MFin microservice architecture.

The microservice layer consists of several microservices as follows:

- *User Authentication*: Handles user profile creation, as well as login & logout;
- *Account*: Handles creation, management, and retrieval of a user's banking accounts;
- *Transaction*: Handles creation and retrieval of transactions made by users;
- *Card*: Handles creation, management, and retrieval of a user's cards;
- *Wallet*: Handles creation, management, and retrieval of a user's wallets;
- *Property*: Handles creation, management, and retrieval of a user's properties.

The communication between the two layers would be implemented through API Gateway. The RESTful API is the best practice for front-end communication. However, the internal API was implemented by Remote Procedure Call (RPC) based on an event-driven system to communicate between microservices, sometimes, it might be more reasonable.

We determine a strategic objective as a destination that the organization aims to achieve in long-term based on its strategies at the strategic level. Specifically, the Strategic Alignment Model (SAM) from [11] indicated two types of strategies (business strategy and the IT strategy). A graphical representation of the business objectives and IT objectives (at the strategic level) are proposed to demonstrate these strategies of the MFin application based on Non-Functional Requirements (NFR) tree [6] to refine the decomposition of the Strategic Objectives. The business strategy of the MFin is concentrated around the main objective: *Provide high-quality FinTech services*. The IT strategy of the MFin is concentrated around the main objective: *Deliver Microservice Architecture to Support FinTech services*.

MFin also divides the business logic into services for the main branches. For instance, it creates a "domain-property" service for the property branch. This service would use several microservices such as User Authentication, Account, Property, and Transaction.

The SS diagram in Fig. 7 is used to represent all microservices of "domain-property" as services at the strategic level. It briefly defines and describes the different roles played by individuals or groups of individuals in this domain and highlights the interactions between these different roles.

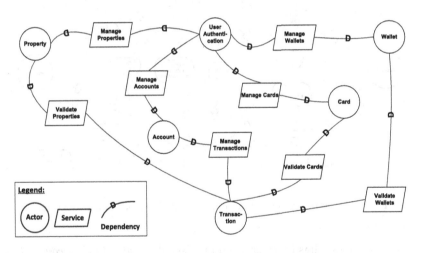

Fig. 7. Domain-property service as a strategic service diagram.

The SS diagram has six main actors (*User Authentication, Account, Transaction, Card, Wallet,* and *Property*) and eight services (*Manage Properties, Manage Accounts, Manage Cards, Manage Wallets, Manage Transactions, Validate Properties, Validate Cards,* and *Validate Wallets*). Each service represents a dependency graph summarized as follows:

- The **Manage Properties** service represents the processes that manage all properties. The **Property** is the responsible actor;

- The **Manage Accounts** service represents the processes that manage all users's accounts. The **Account** is the responsible actor;
- The **Manage Cards** service represents the processes that manage all users's cards. The **Card** is the responsible actor;
- The **Manage Wallets** service represents the processes that manage all users's wallets. The **Wallet** is the responsible actor;
- The **Manage Transactions** service represents the processes that manage all users's transactions. The **Transaction** is the responsible actor;
- The **Validate Properties** service represents the processes that validate the properties during the transactions. The **Transaction** is the responsible actor;
- The **Validate Cards** service represents the processes that validate the cards during the transactions. The **Transaction** is the responsible actor;
- The **Validate Wallets** service represents the processes that validate the wallets during the transactions. The **Transaction** is the responsible actor.

Figure 8 depicts an SD diagram applied at the tactical level of the AgileMS in "domain-property" service.

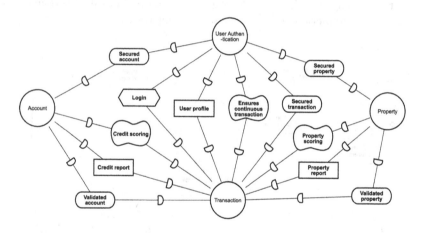

Fig. 8. Domain-property service as a strategic dependency diagram.

The SD diagram has four main actors (*User Authentication, Account, Transaction,* and *Property*), resources (*User profile, Credit report,* and *Property report*), goals (*Secured account, Validated account, Secured property, Validated property,* and *Secured transaction*), qualities (*Credit scoring, Property scoring,* and *Ensures continuous transaction*), and tasks (*Login*). These also illustrate the dependencies between actors.

In the SD diagram, the **Account** depends on the **User Authentication** to ensure the accounts is secured. The **Property** depends on the **User Authentication** to ensure the properties is secured. The **Transaction** depends on the **Account** to ensure the accounts is validated. The **Transaction** depends on the **Property** to ensure the properties is validated. The **Transaction** depends on the **User Authentication** to ensure the transactions is secured and continuous transactions quality achieved based on microservice architecture.

Figure 9 presents the SR diagram applied at the operational level of the AgileMS in "domain-property" service for the property branch. It is refined from the SD model.

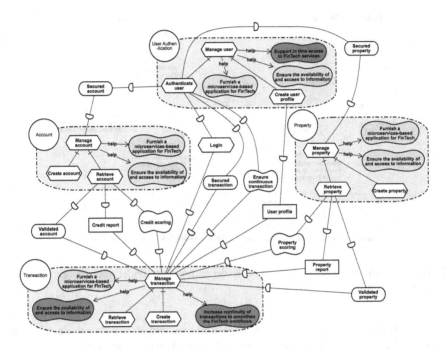

Fig. 9. Domain-property service as a strategic rationale diagram.

In the SR diagram, the **User Authentication** performs two specific tasks (*Create user profile* and *Authenticate user*) to manage users. The **Account** performs two specific tasks (*Create account* and *Retrieve account*) to manage accounts. The **Property** performs two specific tasks (*Create property* and *Retrieve property*) to manage properties. The **Transaction** performs two specific tasks (*Create transaction* and *Retrieve transaction*) to manage transactions.

The *Manage account* task depends on the *Manage user* task to secure the accounts. The *Manage property* task depends on the *Manage user* task to secure the properties. The *Manage transaction* task depends on the *Manage account* task based on *Credit report* resource to validate the account and ensure credit scoring. The *Manage transaction* task depends on the *Manage property* task based on *Property report* resource to validate the property and ensure property scoring. The *Manage transaction* task depends on the *Manage user* task based on the *Login* task and the *User profile* resource to secure the transactions and ensure continuous transactions.

6 Evaluation

Figure 10 represents the impact of the "domain-property" service onto the business and IT strategies. The same exercise can be done for each of the MFin services.

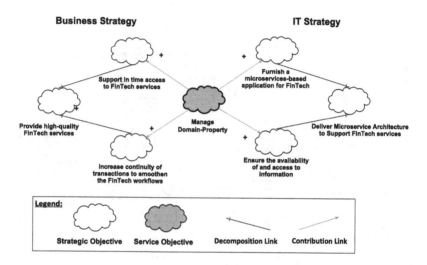

Fig. 10. IT and business strategies NFR decomposition model and domain-property service contributions

The application of the microservices management discipline along with the AgileMS' phases within the MFin project is illustrated as follows:

- During **Planning** phase, the need for the MFin application is expressed and the purpose and scope of this application system are documented. At this phase, microservices are determined based on the application's business/IT objectives (at the strategic level). The business objectives of this application are identified based on the main business objective of the MFin project's business strategy, the *Provide high-quality FinTech services.* The IT objectives of this application are also determined based on the main IT objectives of the MFin project's IT strategy, the *Deliver Microservice Architecture to Support FinTech services.*
- During **Analysis** phase, the MFin application is analysed. The identified microservices are used to support the development of the application requirements, including microservices management requirements, and microservices quality concept of operations (at the tactical level).
- During **Design** phase, the MFin application is designed. At this phase, microservices are blueprinted. The **Design** phase prototypes and further evaluates the decisions taken on microservices management through a practical mock-up. In this phase, the business/IT objectives are established. The business objectives for this application consist of the *Support in time access to*

FinTech services, and the *Increase continuity of transactions to smoothen the FinTech workflows*. The *Furnish a microservices-based application for FinTech* and the *Ensure the availability of and access to information* are the two IT objectives of this application. The microservices requirements, microservices quality expectations list, and microservices matrix are identified (at the tactical level).

– During **Building** phase, the MFin application is purchased, programmed, developed, or otherwise constructed. At this phase, microservices are applied. The **Building** phase fully implements decisions taken on microservices management. In this phase, the business/IT objectives are realized (at the tactical level). The microservices assurance, microservices requirements, quality expectations list and microservices matrix are identified (at the operational level).

– During **Testing** phase, the MFin application is deployed and operated. In this phase, the business/IT objectives are implemented and validated. The microservices requirements and microservices control are undertaken (at the operational level). The microservices is implemented and the quality achieved is delivered.

7 Conclusion

Contributions of this paper consist of a model including a meta-level specification to emphasize integration and alignment of agile methods with managing microservice architecture. Using strategic modeling organization specifications, we have proposed a development management template, called AgileMS, customized on the application of agile principles to manage microservice-based software development. The main objective of this template has been to deliver an efficient managing of development for microservice-based software that meets stakeholders' needs and expectations in terms of the IT/Business alignment perspective. The strengths of the agile model are to offer systematic structure and direction through the entire software development processes to drive the system life cycle in terms of incremental and iterative engineering techniques. However, the agile model does not point out how to establish development management rules for the microservices while the AgileMS model contains the principles of managing software development to apply in the microservice architecture, particularly, in FinTech. The AgileMS model also delivers a sequence of phases for a collaborative software development environment.

Future work points to other additional practices that need to be integrated into this model to propose a completed template taking into consideration, for instance, project management and agile practices [3,15] for managing the day-to-day activities and reacting to changing requirements and feedback. Moreover, this model should be validated on more case studies, and compared to other frameworks. In addition, a CASE tool should be developed to help to design and implement all the models defined in this paper.

References

1. Ambler, S., Nalbone, J., Vizdos, M.: Enterprise Unified Process: Extending the Rational Unified Process. Prentice Hall, Hoboken (2005)
2. Ambler, S.W.: Agile software development at scale. In: Meyer, B., Nawrocki, J.R., Walter, B. (eds.) CEE-SET 2007. LNCS, vol. 5082, pp. 1–12. Springer, Heidelberg (2008). https://doi.org/10.1007/978-3-540-85279-7_1
3. Ambler, S., Lines, M.: Disciplined Agile Delivery: A Practitioner's Guide to Agile Software Delivery in the Enterprise. IBM Press, Indianapolis (2012)
4. Asik, T., Selcuk, Y.: Policy enforcement upon software based on microservice architecture. In: IEEE 15th International Conference on Software Engineering Research, Management and Applications (SERA), pp. 283–287. IEEE (2017)
5. Beck, K., et al.: Manifesto for agile software development (2001)
6. Chung, L., et al.: Non-Functional Requirements in Software Engineering. Kluwer Academic Publishers, Dordrecht (2000)
7. Dalpiaz, F., Franch, X., Horkoff, J.: iStar 2.0 language guide. CoRR, abs/1605.07767 (2016)
8. Dingsøyr, T., Nerur, S., Balijepally, V., Moe, N.B.: A decade of agile methodologies: towards explaining agile software development. J. Syst. Softw. **85**(6), 1213–1221 (2012). Elsevier
9. Dragoni, N., et al.: Microservices: yesterday, today, and tomorrow. In: Present and Ulterior Software Engineering, pp. 195–216. Springer, Cham (2017). https://doi.org/10.1007/978-3-319-67425-4_12
10. Hendershott, T., et al.: FinTech as a game changer: overview of research frontiers. Inf. Syst. Res. **32**(1), 1–17 (2021)
11. Henderson, J.C., Venkatraman, N.: Strategic alignment: leveraging information technology for transforming organizations. IBM Syst. J. **38**(2), 472–484 (1999)
12. Hevner, A., et al.: Design science in information systems research. Manag. Inf. Syst. Q. **28**(1), 75–105 (2004)
13. Kilu, E., Milani, F., Scott, E., Pfahl, D.: Agile software process improvement by learning from financial and fintech companies: LHV bank case study. In: Winkler, D., Biffl, S., Bergsmann, J. (eds.) SWQD 2019. LNBIP, vol. 338, pp. 57–69. Springer, Cham (2019). https://doi.org/10.1007/978-3-030-05767-1_5
14. Kruchten, P.: The Rational Unified Process: An Introduction. Addison-Wesley, Boston (2004)
15. Kruchten, P.: Contextualizing agile software development. J. Softw. Evol. Process **25**(4), 351–361 (2013)
16. Lu, B., et al.: Frontiers in service science: fintech operations - an overview of recent developments and future research directions. Serv. Sci. **13**(1), 19–35 (2021)
17. Nadareishvili, I., et al.: Microservice Architecture: Aligning Principles, Practices, and Culture. O'Reilly Media, Inc., Sebastopol (2016)
18. Peffers, K., et al.: A design science research methodology for information systems research. J. Manag. Inf. Syst. **24**(3), 45–77 (2008)
19. Sommerville, I.: Software Engineering, 10th edn. Pearson Education, England (2016)
20. Taibi, D., et al.: Processes, motivations, and issues for migrating to microservices architectures: an empirical investigation. IEEE Cloud Comput. **4**(5), 22–32 (2017)
21. Wautelet, Y., Kolp, M.: Business and model-driven development of BDI multi-agent systems. Neurocomputing **182**, 304–321 (2016)
22. Yu, E., Giorgini, P., Maiden, N., Mylopoulos, J.: Social Modeling for Requirements Engineering. MIT press, Cambridge (2011)

The Continued Innovation-Decision Process – A Case Study of Continued Adoption of Robotic Process Automation

Henriika Sarilo-Kankaanranta$^{(\boxtimes)}$ and Lauri Frank

University of Jyväskylä, Jyväskylä, Finland
{henriika.sarilo,lauri.frank}@jyu.fi

Abstract. Robotic Process Automation (RPA) originally entered the field of information systems as one of those disruptive innovations that will, among other automation solutions, have a profound effect on job descriptions and work itself in near future. One of the sectors that will be revolutionized – and are in fact already changing – are financial and human resource (HR) services, such as accounting, billing, and payroll services. According to statistics, Finnish companies operating on the administrative and support services sector make little use of service robots. Companies that have initially adopted the technology do not necessary reach its full potential. We explore what factors create challenges for the continued adoption of robotic process automation by investigating two companies and using interpretive case study as our research method. The two companies are service centers. They operate on the public sector in Finland and provide financial and HR services for their owner-clients. The findings of this study include insights into the key factors that affect continued adoption of RPA, and these point towards an expanded model of Innovation-Decision Process where iterations of a new decision are triggered by new ideas on how to use the innovation.

Keywords: Robotic Process Automation · Technology adoption · Diffusion of Innovations · Adoption continuance · Information systems

1 Introduction

Workplace forecasts have for years now stressed that automation will in the very near future have a substantial effect on jobs in several industries. Accountants and auditors have been viewed as one of the professions in the non-manufacturing sector which will decline considerably due to the adoption of automation technologies, such as robotic process automation (RPA). When RPA was introduced into financial and payroll services in Finland, a common theme in the news, professional journals and seminars was that accountants and other similar professions would be replaced by robots in the near future. However, certain public sector organizations which already adopted RPA some years ago during its first hype are still actively recruiting accountants, payroll specialists etc. According to statistics, Finnish companies in the administrative and support services sector utilize service robots to a low degree [1]. Out of these observations rose

© Springer Nature Switzerland AG 2022
M. Themistocleous and M. Papadaki (Eds.): EMCIS 2021, LNBIP 437, pp. 737–755, 2022.
https://doi.org/10.1007/978-3-030-95947-0_52

the question: *How has the adoption process been continuing after the initial decision to adopt a technological innovation?* And secondly, if change has been slower than originally anticipated or the adoption rate is slower in terms of the number of the robots in production, *what factors are influencing the continued adoption of RPA?* In this paper we try to find answers to these questions and explore the main challenges the companies have been facing.

In order to find out how the adoption of RPA has been continuing after its initial adoption within accounting and HR services we visited two publicly controlled Finnish companies (service centers). While the underlying goal was to explore and understand the phenomenon, we also hoped to gather new knowledge which could deepen the theory of innovation adoption process, particularly information on the different stages of continued or discontinued adoption. This paper contains a brief discussion of earlier literature followed by an introduction to the case study and a description of the methodology used in gathering and analyzing data. The main body of the paper discusses the key findings of the thematic analysis of the interviews. Finally, we summarize the conclusions of this research and its limitations and put forward recommendations for further study.

2 Adoption of Technology and Robotic Process Automation

In this section we aim to summarize and illustrate the existing theory of the adoption of technology in a few words and discuss some recent RPA studies related to the phenomenon. Different theories on the adoption of technology and its acceptance, such as Technology Acceptance Model (TAM) [2], Theory of Reasoned Action (TRA) [3], Theory of Planned Behavior (TPB) [4], Diffusion of Innovation (DOI) [5] and its modifications [6] and Unified theory of acceptance and use of technology (UTAUT) [7] are widely used in the IS research field to explain how organizations or individuals adopt and accept technological innovations. Conceptualized factors behind the adoption can, according to these theories, be generalized as being related to a) the technology itself and its characteristics; b) the characteristics of the individual (as an adoption unit), such as demographics, norms, and innovativeness; and c) the characteristics of the organization as an adoption unit and its prior conditions. When revisited and re-evaluated, these popular theories and *a priori* study would appear to provide a good starting point for research, this one included, but nevertheless they seldom cover the continuance or discontinuance stages of the adoption of technology. Existing literature is even more limited in terms of organizational studies; hence we have explored the theoretical framework from the perspective of both individuals and organizations.

2.1 Different Elements of Adoption and Acceptance Decisions

In this study, the adoption process base framework is founded on the Innovation-Decision process of the Diffusion of Innovation. The Innovation-Decision consists of five main stages: 1. Knowledge, 2. Persuasion, 3. Decision, 4. Implementation and 5. Confirmation [5]. This process is impacted by the characteristics of an innovation. The DOI itself recognizes five key attributes for the innovation, which are *relative advantage, compatibility, complexity, trialability* and *observability*. Other studies have identified several other key elements, such as *attitudes, norms,* and *perceived behavioral control,* to explain the intention to **accept** the technology [4], or attributes such as *image, voluntariness, ease of use, visibility, trialability* and *result demonstrability* among other characteristics to be considered [6]. While *trust* and its narrower subcategories, such as *security* and *privacy* have been seen as influencing key factors in adopting such technologies as web-based shopping and internet banking [8, 9] on the consumer level, trust or *reliability* does not always affect an organization's intentions to adopt a technology [10].

The different elements mentioned earlier are related to the initial adoption of a given technology. In this case they might be relevant when our case organizations took the first decision to invest in RPA technology and put the first robot into service. Recent organizational studies emphasize somewhat different elements. One of them to be considered is *economic efficiency* [11]. In organizational motivation, *legitimacy-oriented motives* predict initial adoption and *efficiency motives* predict continued adoption [11], meaning that organizations with efficiency motives tend to adopt technologies in line with their objectives of economic efficiency. There was also a relation to be found with high *searching efforts* influencing positively on *satisfaction,* and satisfaction in turn influencing positively on continued adoption. However, the influence of *satisfaction* and *perceived usefulness* on continued adoption has also been argued to be less significant today and **organizational context factors,** such as *subjective norms,* and **environmental context factors,** such as *competitive pressure,* more significant [12].

The findings of some recent studies support the view that change within organizations needs to be managed as a continuous process instead of concentrating exclusively on the initial stage of adoption [12–14]. A behavioral approach to organizational adoption of innovations suggests that in companies involved in the development of their own technology and environment these factors (innovation characteristics in DOI) *"are not a given but emerge as a result of the company's own action"* [14]. In that case 1) *goals and technical infrastructure,* 2) *business relationships,* and 3) *key individuals* influence the continuous adoption activities and how these activities interplay and *"comprise micro-foundations of organizational innovation adoption behaviour"* [14].

When we reviewed the literature, we did not find that such factors as trust or image play a role when continued adoption progresses at a slow rate, but when it comes to the initial decision to adopt, especially when it is a question of late adoption, there is some evidence (e.g. in consumer studies) that late adoption may be related to a *negative word of mouth* [15]. If we remain on the level of individuals, *social influence* (of a more positive character) has been seen as a potential influencing factor on intentions to adopt, albeit a more potential factor with earlier than later adopters [16]. Theories which focus on organizations instead of individuals include such concepts as *mimetic behavior/isomorphism* or *institutional pressure* in the list of factors that influence the intention and the final decision to adopt an innovation. However, there was no evidence that they would have any significant influence on decisions to discontinue [18]. A survey on continued adoption conducted among purchasing managers suggests that *mimetic competitor pressures* have a negative effect on the continued adoption of a technological innovation within an organization (the firms) [11]. Among social factors, there is evidence of **technical and economic influences** in continuation inertia like *system investment* (earlier investments to other technologies) and *technical integration*, and finally research has found among forces of change such factors as *shortcomings in system performance* or *environmental changes*, which include increasing costs of system support and support being no longer available [18].

Finally, when considering whether the size of the adoption unit (organization) is related to the adoption, the literature suggested that the decision to adopt or the factors influencing the adoption are not necessarily dependent on the organization's size. This was seen in the phenomenon of adopting open-source office applications and factors influencing the adoption decision [10] as well as in the adoption rate of web services in municipalities [19]. These studies suggest that smaller organizations may be more agile, and innovativeness of individuals has a greater impact on the adoption rate in small organizations, but they often lack the necessary funds to adopt the technology.

2.2   The Adoption of RPA

There are several, if not exactly plenty of, recent articles covering general themes related to software robotics, the RPA implementation process and why RPA is initially adopted. However, the actual level of RPA usage or the stages of the process after the initial adoption do not appear to have been studied systematically. From earlier studies we can for instance find suggestions what may be success factors and risks in automation projects, including RPA [20], whereas there were very few indications on how organizations have continued adopting RPA in the years following the initial decision to adopt RPA or its implementation.

Organizations often adopt RPA with the aim to gain such benefits as operational efficiency (in terms of time, money, human resources) and to increase the quality of their services (fewer mistakes, more rule-based error checking). The Big Four accounting firms estimated in 2017–18 that between 10 to 30% of accounting processes can potentially be automated [21]. They concluded that a business process is suitable for RPA if two conditions are met: 1) it involves only structured, digital inputs, and 2) it is entirely rules-based. Studies show that reducing manual tasks and workloads can lead to significant time-saving in processes [22]. RPA is often used as an automation tool due to inadequacies in information systems and their capabilities. In accounting, RPA may be used in a wide range of tasks, from completing complex parts of processes to carrying out small automation tasks, such as running a report from an operative system. The purpose is to shift manual and standardized high volume routine tasks from humans to robots hoping to improve their accuracy and allowing experts to focus on tasks that involve interaction and problem solving [21]. The literature provides general and reasonably up-to-date information on the use of robotics in accounting and HR services [23–25], whereas scientific research articles on the topic are more scarce, but to be found such as Lacurezeanu et al. 2020 [26]. Syed et al. [22] presents a very comprehensive review of what has been written on the characteristics of tasks deemed suitable for RPA, and the paper also includes the results of different types of RPA research and identifies possible gaps in current literature on RPA.

Adopting RPA in an organization does not necessarily mean that it will meet the goals commonly associated with RPA, such as operational efficiency. Systematically composed guidelines for the benefits realization of RPA deployment are currently scarce [22]. However, an early involvement of both IT and business division in adopting technology has been found to be critical in the long-term success of RPA, as [22] posited on the basis of the literature reviewed. RPA adoption has been studied earlier in the context of service centers in Portugal [**Error! Reference source not found.**]. The study of six Portuguese shared service centers (SSC) found that important factors leading to the initial adoption of RPA included the influence of *external forces* (through a process of "normative isomorphism") and that *mimetic* ("everybody does") *isomorphism* was also a key factor. In the case referred, all the SSC's used the same consulting firms in the implementation and the same RPA technology [**Error! Reference source not found.**]. This led to the outcome that the decision to *"introduce robotization was not backed up by 'a number', such as the number of hours of human labour that could be saved, but by a normative rationality"*. The **main challenges** facing the implementation of robotics included a *lack of resources* to carry out robotization tasks and *insufficient training* to develop RPA solutions internally. Due to these challenges the SSC's had established RPA core teams that required both the necessary technological skills and a full knowledge of the processes.

We mentioned in our introduction the theme of "robots taking the jobs of accountants". This theme appears to come up often when searching for news articles and other online material. Often the theme seems to origin from a study by Oxford Martin School, which was published already in 2013 [29]. Yet accountants and HR personnel (or developers) have not been seen as a source of possible resistance towards change in the reviewed literature on RPA research. When New Zealand researchers studied the future of work and employees' views in the service sector [31], they found that automation was not seen only as a threat. Respondents of this study saw "automation as providing new opportunities, perhaps even enhancing their current jobs", which may be considered a key finding. It was quite clear that younger respondents saw automation as something that would affect their careers significantly, whereas older employees did not necessarily believe it would affect their career prospects anymore as they were able to retire soon. The study however suggested, that for older participants it would be difficult to remain competitive in work as they presumed that the adoption of new technology would not be easy, thus much work would be needed in training systems.

As will be seen later in this study, RPA is not the only automation solution for accounting and HR services. As mentioned earlier, RPA-based robots are often used to fill out the insufficient capacities of an enterprise's IT. Firms may consider other technologies as solutions and adopt several practices to digitalize and automate their processes. In general, it is not uncommon to aim to maximize the value of the current IT and to discover new technologies at the same time. Similar hybrid models have been found in other technologies, e.g. cloud computing strategies [17]. The next step after adopting RPA on a basic level is sometimes considered to be integrating AI with robotics, and, although there have been recent studies on the critical success factors and challenges related to it, e.g. [30], the focus of research is mostly placed on robots other than software-based (such as physical service robots) and on intelligent artificial systems. Searches from research databases suggest that AI is not yet an active topic in accountancy. A recent case study [27] has examined successful implementation of RPA and AI systems in accounting and auditing, including both existing RPA systems and the implementation of new ideas. However, its findings were mainly based on business and technical approaches, excluding the social factors. The study also concluded that *"the amount of identifiable challenges and risk factors are many and of various consequence"* as they also identified this domain to be relatively new [27]. Because of this, we have chosen to refrain from further examining RPA and AI adoption studies, and while the topic came up later in some of the interviews, we do not include this theme either in our theory or in our findings, since AI was not yet adopted in the case organizations.

3 Case Introduction

The case study was conducted in two publicly-controlled service centers. These were in-house companies which provide financial and HR services, such as accounting and payroll services to their customer-owners: municipalities, social and health care districts and other public utilities. While the two organizations which participated in this case study had similarities in terms of their business model, clientele, financial and payroll services and operative systems, they also had significant differences related to their other service offerings and how they had arranged their internal IT-services.

One of the events that triggered the initial decision to adopt RPA was a "Robots for Service Center" project run in 2017 and 2018 [see 32]. This was a co-operative project between seven publicly-controlled service centers, its goal to ensure their personnel's wellbeing at work in the near future when digitalization and robotics would change the nature of their work. Both companies had acquired their first robots approximately 4 years earlier, but their rates of continued adoption differed considerably. Their production models were also different: whereas in Company 1 its internal teams took care of the RPA infrastructure and the evaluation and coordination of the project, the actual design and implementation of it were outsourced. They also serviced their robots in-house, and their infrastructure and projects services included robotic projects for their owner-clients as well. Company 2 had outsourced the infrastructure but had made the decision to form an RPA team and hire both internally and externally the team members who would take care of the actual design, implementation and maintenance of the robots. Company 2 did not provide RPA as a service for their owner-clients.

Both companies had also experienced a merger some two years earlier, and this had changed their organizational structures and caused a considerable need for harmonized processes. However, neither the service processes nor the information systems of the financial and HR services were harmonized as yet.

4 Methodology

Case study was chosen as the research method with the purpose of exploring the contemporary phenomenon of inertia affecting continued RPA in accounting and HR services and to understand it in its context [33]. The data was gathered through individual interviews of 21 key members of the case organizations (see Table 1). Each interview lasted between 40 and 90 min – longer interviews encompassed more detailed discussions of the actual robots and technology. Interviews were preceded by informal discussions with contact persons from each company. We explored during these preliminary, informal and unstructured conversations the utilization rate and targets of robotization and sought to identify the key persons to interview. These conversations were noted down in brief memos, but they are not used as a base for analysis but rather as an additional reminder of the RPA targets.

Other data included process documentation from one of the companies and public news pages and press releases. The interviews were held online due to the concurrent COVID-19 situation. Semi-structured questions were used as a starting point, although the interviews were meant to follow a free course according to the interviewees' own initiative. The interviews took place between February and May 2021, one organization at a time. They were recorded and immediately written down as memos. Transcription and deeper analysis were to follow afterwards. Before each series of interviews were conducted, informal online meetings were held between the researcher and contact persons, who were later interviewed in more depth. A one-month break followed after the interviews held at Company 1. This time was used to analyze the framework of the research – namely the structure of the interviews. Results from the first data set were also analyzed during this stage.

Table 1. List of interviewees at Companies 1 and 2 of the case study

Interviews	
Company 1	Company 2
One director (financial and HR services)	Two directors of financial services (one from group and one from a subsidiary)
Three service managers (both financial and HR services and IT services)	CIO (Group)
ICT architect	Head of IT (subsidiary)
Project manager	One service manager (financial services, subsidiary)
One IT specialist	Two RPA specialists (subsidiary)
Two accountants	Three financial specialists of accounting/controller of accounts receivable (subsidiary)
Two HR and payroll experts	

The data was analyzed using thematic analysis, i.e. themes were coded from the interview memos and transcripts [34]. The process was iterative: discoveries and conclusions were organized into preliminary findings, these were then compared again with the data, and the findings were then updated. The themes that were gleaned from the interviews were also compared with the existing theory to understand what new knowledge – if any – might be drawn from these findings.

In the following chapter we present our focal observations from the analysis of the data and return to the Diffusion of Innovation theory and Innovation-Decision Process.

5 Findings

The six factors that follow below emerged from the interviews. While they may also play an important part when initial decisions are being made, they mainly manifest themselves at every new cycle of the decision-making process, and in the end they lead either to the continuation or discontinuation of the adoption. They are:

1. the role of competing technologies and compliance with Enterprise Architecture (EA)
2. the resourcing model of development
3. the incompleteness of the processes
4. interaction between IT and other teams
5. the amount of knowledge and ideas
6. resistance to change and trust

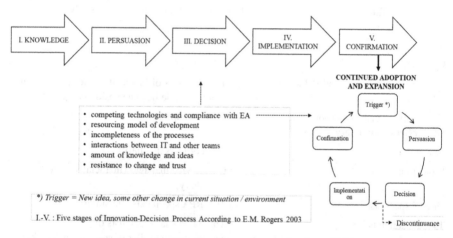

Fig. 1. Factors affecting the continued adoption of RPA

The factors affecting RPA continuation are explained in the following chapters and summarized in Appendix 1. It also explains briefly which factors have the greatest effect at each stage of the Innovation-Decision Process as well as their relations.

5.1 Competing Technologies and Compliance with EA

RPA competes with other automation solutions. It needs to be compatible with the existing information systems and match the overall enterprise architecture. At Company 1, the specialists told that as part of the evaluation they first examine the underlying need for automation or the problem to be solved and then evaluate the possible technical solutions. The technical solutions which are considered among RPA include business intelligence solutions and integration solutions. Often the specialists may even hold up the automation and request their information system supplier to develop the system itself, even if a new release takes time. The IT specialists also seem to be more familiar to the competing technologies as they use them constantly.

Company 2 had invested in an internal RPA development team, and while they considered that other automation solutions would probably play a bigger part in the future, for the time being they focused on putting new robots into service. Company 2 also hoped that their information system suppliers would develop their systems in such fashion that robots would not be needed, but they were more willing than Company 1 to develop temporary robots as a short-term solution. The key differences between the two companies is lead to assume that this was because Company 2 had its own developers with time allocated on RPA, whereas Company 1 needed to outsource all the development.

"Even though robotics is a good tool for reducing manual work and in a sense, it automates processes, it is not the only instrument for digitalization and automation." – One of the directors

"I don't know whether one of the contributing factors is that the instruments in production [for financial services] have evolved so that they have started to meet the demand. And on the other hand, how much have we been able to provide solutions with integration tools in such cases which otherwise would have been implemented with robotics. The spectrum of reasons is wide. To be honest, what is the cause and what the effect has not been investigated particularly explicitly." – One of the managers.

"As soon as we can have our software vendor implement certain things in the financial information systems, we can eliminate robots as superfluous." – One of the developers

Both companies reported problems in implementing RPA. These were caused by defects in the user interfaces of the information systems (compliance issues between RPA and the IS), and updates to these systems often made the robots malfunction. The maintenance and servicing of robots were consuming ever more hours – work hours which otherwise could have been used developing new robots. As mentioned earlier, the IS was not harmonized in the case companies and they both had more than one IS for same purpose (e.g. two systems for payroll service). Hence, they often needed more than one robot implementation to automate one task in the service process.

5.2   The Resourcing Model of the Development

Interviewees commonly spoke of change being poorly managed or about the lack of shared coordination. Company 1 had historically faced challenges trying to find the right people who would commit to managing the change and be able to find the time to do it. Establishing a cross-organizational virtual team had also taken time, and only after that progress had been made. The committed individual managers or directors did not enough time to manage the change, and their responsibilities needed to be delegated. At Company 1 the challenge was an intra-corporate one, and at Company 2 the challenge was being faced at the corporate group level, as both the senior management and the developers indicated that the development of automation needed to be managed collectively for the entire group.

> "It's just that this process, well, it does not work properly and has not worked even once. What you can say about it is that when you wait for ideas to emerge from the process, then it is very sluggish. They constantly invoke the urgency of the process as an excuse, that there is not enough time for the actual doing part of it. I don't know what the real reason is." – One of the developers [The interviewee uses term "process" both in context of a certain HR or financial service and sometimes also when referring to the actual development process from idea to implementation]

As mentioned in Sect. 5.2, Company 1 had decided to outsource its development of RPA. It seemed to be very careful with cost-benefit calculations of ideas surrounding the use of robots, although it had already invested in sufficient infrastructure and licenses. Some of the interviewees also reported issues with the outsourcing model and contracts – at least in the past. While Company 1 did not possess strong RPA competence either in the number of specialists or hours allocated for it, it had firmer knowledge of other IT services and technologies, since they were part of its core services to its clients.

The management at Company 2 had also introduced a cost-evaluation model to be employed whenever new ideas for implementation were being evaluated, but the developers did not use it. The developers tended to implement any viable idea to a robot task, because they felt they did not receive enough ideas in the first place (this will be discussed later in Sect. 5.5).

As again mentioned earlier, Company 1 seemed to be willing to wait for the new features of the operative information system to resolve automation issues, but Company 2 had chosen to build a robot while waiting for the updates, because developers had said that any change usually took longer than promised. Thus the company which relied on outsourcing did not prefer short-term, temporary robots. We assume as a conclusion that the barriers against continuing with a technology are lower when resourcing is not outsourced and that cost-benefit calculations play a relatively smaller role when the direct external costs of the technology are lower.

5.3   Incomplete Processes

The theme of incomplete processes comes up in our case organizations in two different ways: 1) robots are given only small segments of processes or single tasks in a process and 2) service processes are not mature enough and the documentation of the processes are not sufficient. In first case, automation does not cover complete service processes nor considerably large sub-processes, but tasks from here and there. The developers saw it only as a partial solution to fill the need of process automation, and they explicitly wished to have more complete processes automated. The underlying reason, they suggested, had to do with the primary business processes that were to be automated and their maturity – see number 2 above. Business/service processes were incomplete in both companies. They needed companywide harmonizing and thorough documentation. Interviewees indicated that automation would have been executed differently, had the processes been better documented, the automation implementation would have been different and the level of automation altogether higher – regardless of the automation technology used. In particular, the CIO of Company 2 brought up the need for lean thinking in process development.

> "We may robotize a section which could be completely unnecessary in the first place if we had invested in automation [elsewhere]." – CIO

While the number of robots was substantially smaller at Company 1, they had chosen to use robots to cover large or complex tasks. This, however, seemed to prolong the timescale of the project – in other words, it took several months to get a robot from design table to production. This led to other challenges, which are described in Sect. 5.5. It appears to be highly probable that the delays in projects were also due to difficulties in resourcing, as explained in Sect. 5.2.

5.4 Interaction Between Developers and Other Teams

The lack of a common language shared by the IT department or developers and the accounting and payment services and their personnel came up in the interviews conducted at both companies. This had a slowing effect on the definition and implementation stages of the development. Learning to understand each other and the jargon used by each team took time, and the learning curve may flatline if a mediator is not involved in the process. This was seen as a problem, especially when an outsourced contractor was used in an implementation project. People within the same organization found it easier and more flexible to interact and share knowledge when they could, for example, sit by the side of a substance specialist (e.g. an accountant) in an ad hoc situation and observe what they were doing. Changes within the development team slowed interaction repeatedly.

> "Often there are too many changes in personnel here, one moves out, another comes in. Work cannot go uninterrupted with the same person and in the same team. Then the procedure may change every time as well and the ideas change, and you need to start all over again. Communication might be another issue."
> -One of the developers

However, one developer at Company 2 realized that when they had introduced in the team new developers who had earlier experience in automation of accounting or other services, the design phase became gradually easier. We suggest as a conclusion that when the resourcing of technological implementation is assigned to on an organization's internal teams, it may prudent to investigate whether any personnel outside the IT department have the necessary skills and willingness to have a career change and learn the technology which is being adopted.

> *"The more one knows about the software, the easier it is to make [robots]. When you are an outsider, [In matters of financial services] a complete clot, it means that someone needs to give you hands-on guidance on how the finance side of things work."* – One of the developers

5.5   The Amount of Knowledge and Ideas

A common theme raised during the interviews held at both companies was the lack of good ideas (or any ideas whatsoever) about the use of robots. Ideas were gathered from the service teams. The interviewees thought that only those who are experts in the service process that was to be automated were expected to be able to suggest workable ideas. They also highlighted that all ideas were welcomed. This was also stressed in internal communications when ideas were being solicited.

The two companies and interviewees at all levels of hierarchy told that they did not secure as many ideas as they had hoped. At Company 2 this led to a situation where almost any technically feasible idea was developed into a robot, regardless of whether it really reduced weekly work hours or not. In contrast, IT specialists at Company 1 reported that they often had to turn down ideas because these were not feasible.

> *"I feel like our users have a somewhat incorrect notion of this thing [RPA]. And then they [the ideas] are given to the RPA team, even though they clearly should be addressed to reporting team."* – One of the ICT specialists

Lack of knowledge can also be viewed in this context as a lack of general knowledge about and knowhow of the capabilities of RPA and business processes. One key group had the necessary technical knowledge and the other key group knew the processes that could be automated, but combining this knowledge turned out to be problematic. Both those who were expected to come up with the ideas as well as those who were to evaluate and implement these ideas mentioned challenges in the past.

> *"The greatest challenge for me was to understand. I'm the kind of person who needs to know the process in depth and understand it. I still don't understand it comprehensively, so I can't utilize all my knowhow."* – One of the HR specialists

> *"If everyone could find the information easily, and if it were easier for the RPA team to gather the information, it would be easier to automate more and better robots. We in the RPA team know what a robot can do but we don't know the accounting process. An accountant knows their own processes but does not know what a robot can do."* – One of the developers

Knowledge is the initial state in the Innovation-Decision Process. However, interviewees from both companies, especially specialists, told that knowledge and knowhow – particularly when they are lacking – constantly influence the continuation of the adoption process. In Fig. 1, we have substituted the term 'knowledge' as the first stage of the adoption-continuation iterations with the term 'trigger'. The idea of a new implementation is seen as the trigger which starts a new iteration of the Innovation-Decision process. When an organization runs out of viable new ideas in such technologies as RPA, continuation of the technology is endangered.

5.6   Resistance to Change and Trust

Resistance to change came up in most of the interviews within both companies. Views varied depending on how long an interviewee had worked for the company. For example, a director at Company 2, who had been worked there for a relatively short time, was astonished by how well the personnel welcomed robotics. However, other key persons (at all levels) had seen resistance, albeit more towards the beginning. At Company 1 almost everyone mentioned it, and a few stated that this may have been the reason for the lack of ideas (an opinion shared by the ICT specialists at Company 2).

"Directors, managers, they understood the ideology of what we were doing. But let's say on staff level it is understandable that if you come and say, could you teach a robot to take your place, it may have a negative effect on motivation. And I don't know how much of an actual effect it has had on implementing automation, but I would argue that if not explicitly, at least indirectly. The level of commitment may be lower. In my opinion management in many organizations has not realized well enough this point of view, namely that people are actually afraid of losing their jobs." – One of the managers

When interviewees were asked what kind of negative memories they had or what challenges they remembered from their journey to RPA, the most common themes were constant technological challenges and resistance from the personnel. They found the resistance milder now than before, but sometimes it still raised its head within some teams or sub-teams. When resistance was more evident, it seemed generally to be mostly passive and to be expressed as dithering, for instance through delaying decision-making at all stages of the innovation-decision process.

Lack of trust (or doubt) also came up when interviewees shared their observations on the robots' capabilities. Lack of trust cam in two types: 1) a general lack of trust in the robots' capability to handle their tasks without crashing, and 2) a lack of trust in the robots' capability of handling complete and complex processes.

This is merely a suggestion that requires further study, but nevertheless lack of trust in new technology may increase the tendency to favor competing technologies. These thoughts are a conclusion drawn from the two themes that came up repeatedly in conversation with those interviewees who had a background in other automation or IT solutions: 1) the suitability of RPA over other solutions for automation and 2) the perceived number of technical issues related to RPA. The tendency to favor solutions other than RPA may also be related to the ease and comfort of continuing with old customs and habits. However, this notion needs more in-depth examination before it can be confirmed.

6 Conclusion

We explored the continued adoption of RPA in two publicly-controlled in-house service centers in Finland, and our ambition was to understand how the innovation-adoption process had continued with RPA, whether there were challenges and why. As the available literature on continued and discontinued adoption of technology is very limited, the contribution of this research is not only to add knowledge of RPA adoption but also to provide insights on how the existing theory should be expanded to explain better the stages after the initial decision to adopt a technology innovation.

We expanded the Innovation-Decision Process with iterations of the decision during the continuation phase of the adoption of technology and suggested factors which may affect the rate of continued adoption of an innovation on organizational level. The expanded model is limited by the fact that these factors are based on researching only one technology, albeit in two organizations.

In terms of continued RPA adoption, six key factors were discovered to influence the decision to continue. These factors and their effect on one another can be summarized in general terms as follows:

1. The technology under examination may be in constant competition with other technologies that the organization has adopted. These other technologies may be preferred over the examined technology, especially when:

    a. Specialists involved in decision-making and development have more knowhow on other technologies.
    b. Compatibility issues with other technologies are more easily solved by the key personnel.
    c. Instead of allocating the development to an internal core team the organization outsources it, even more so if it faces challenges with the subcontractor's delivery models.

2. Even when the desire to accelerate the change exists, the rate of adoption slows down when:

    a. The technology cannot be utilized on the desired level due to incomplete business processes and lack of knowledge.
    b. Key personnel do not share a common language and knowledge about the change process.

3. When the continued adoption of a technology depends on a constant flow of new triggers for implementation, the decision to discontinue is predicts by a depletion of ideas. Ideas run out when:

    a. There is resistance to the technology.
    b. There is a lack of trust, or the reliability of the technology is in doubt.
    c. There is not enough knowledge on how the technology could be utilized.

The first conclusion in this summary is related to 'compliance', an element of innovation in the DOI theory. It also comes close to the element of 'relative advantage' as well as 'ease of use' in TAM. The second conclusion is related to the environmental factors of the adoption unit, and the results might be different if these factors were removed. The third conclusion resonates with the element of 'attitudes' in acceptance models such as TPB and studies which highlight the need to incorporate factors arising from organizational context.

Thus it seems that a single adoption or acceptance theory alone does not explain whether the use of a technology is continued or discontinued, and DOI theory alone does not provide ready-made solutions for modeling the continuation and discontinuation stages. Also the characteristics of an innovation and adoption unit are key factors not only in the initial innovation-decision process but keep impacting the decisions to continue as well (see Fig. 1).

For the information systems managers this study highlights the importance of understanding 1) the full context and complexity of the IT environment and the underlying enterprise architecture, 2) the maturity or the organizational situation of the underlying processes and customs related to technology they are adopting, 3) the importance of solving resourcing issues at an early stage and finally 4) the importance of a shared language and early involvement of people from across the organization.

We have examined only one technology, and this has its limitations for theory building. We did not study whether these same adoption units would have similar results with other technologies. In terms of Diffusion of Innovation, this study does not take into consideration the innovativeness of an organization in general – the study did not explore the phenomenon from that point of view, and no national (or EU/ETA) statistics exist for determining the organization's position in view of the general situation of its peers. What we can depend on is how the organizations and individuals saw their current situation was related to their hopes and goals. Neither have we in this study delved deeper into the initial adoption decision made years earlier and whether for instance normative or mimetic isomorphism have played the most significant role in the initial decision and could have later influenced the decisions to continue. However, they faced external pressure from their owner-clients to search constantly for solutions bringing greater efficiency and lower costs.

Suggestions for further research include returning to a more in-depth case study or possible action research exploring business models and organizational decisions in these companies. We also suggest taking a deeper dive into the culture of an organization with the aim of understanding different rates of adoption more thoroughly through key differences in management decisions and interaction. In addition to interaction a more in-depth examination of EA is encouraged in further studies. The theory should be tested e.g. by collecting more data from other organizations, either concentrating on automation technologies or by exploring several technologies and keeping to a more general level of continuation inertia affecting the adoption of technologies.

Appendix 1

See Table 2.

Table 2. Factors influencing the continued adoption of RPA in accounting and HR

Factor	Description	Stages	Rel
A. Competing technologies and the compliance with EA	• Other automation technologies, BI, development of operative IS and investments • Familiarity of other technologies • Heterogeneity of IS and multiple implementations of one idea • Technical compliance and other technical issues with robots	Decision	→ F
B. Resourcing model of the development	*In-house production vs Outsourcing* • Cost-benefit calculation emphasized in outsourcing • Short-term, temporary robots can be made more readily if the production model is intra-corporate • Finding those who can be committed and allocated time • Completeness of the supply chain delivery model	Persuasion, Decision, Implementation	→ A, E, F
C. Incomplete processes	1) Only small segments of processes or single tasks in process are given to robots 2) The maturity of the service processes and the quality of the documentation of the processes	Knowledge, Implementation	→ E
D. Interaction between developers and other teams	Namely *Lack of shared language* between IT developers and other key personnel involved in the process of adopting the technology	Implementation	→ B

(*continued*)

Table 2. (*continued*)

Factor	Description	Stages	Rel
E. The amount of knowledge and ideas	*1) The lack of feasible ideas* or any ideas for the use of robots and *2) The lack of knowledge and knowhow* about the technical capabilities of RPA and business processes to be automated	Knowledge, Implementation	→ A
F. Resistance to change and trust	*1) Resistance to change,* mostly passive forms of resistance, such as dithering *2) Lack of trust,* as i) a general lack of trust in robots' capabilities to handle their tasks without crashing, and ii) a lack of trust in the robots' capability handling complete and complex processes	All stages	→ A, E

References

1. Official Statistics of Finland (OSF): Use of information technology in enterprises. ISSN 1797-2957 (2020). Attachment table 6 2020. Statistics Finland, Helsinki. Accessed 18 Apr 2021
2. Davis, F.D.: Perceived usefulness, perceived ease of use, and user acceptance of information technology. MIS Q. **13**(3), 319–339 (1989)
3. Fishbein, M., Ajzen, I.: Predicting and Changing Behavior: The Reasoned Action Approach. Psychology Press, New York (2010)
4. Ajzen I.: The theory of planned behavior. In: Organizational Behavior and Human Decision Processes, vol. 50, no. 2, 1991, pp.179–211. Elsevier (1991)
5. Rogers, E.M.: Diffusion of Innovations, 5th edn. Free Press, New York (2003)
6. Moore, G.C., Benbasat, I.: Development of an instrument to measure the perceptions of adopting an information technology innovation. Inf. Syst. Res. **2**(3), 192–222 (1991)
7. Venkatesh, V., Morris, M.G., Gordon, B., Davis, F.D.: User acceptance of information technology: toward a unified view. MIS Q. **27**(3), 425–478 (2003)
8. Van Slyke, C., Belanger, F., Comunale, C.L.: Factors influencing the adoption of web-based shopping: the impact of trust. Data Base Adv. Inf. Syst. **35**(1), 32–49 (2004)
9. Susanto, A., Lee, H., Zo, H., Ciganek, A.: User acceptance of Internet banking in Indonesia: initial trust formation. Inf. Dev. **29**(4), 309–322 (2013). https://doi.org/10.1177/026666691 2467449
10. Chauhan, S., Jaiswal, M., Rai, S., Motiwalla, L., Pipino, L.: Determinants of adoption for open-source office applications: a plural investigation. Inf. Syst. Manag. **35**(2), 80–97 (2018). https://doi.org/10.1080/10580530.2018.1440728

11. Obal, M.: What drives post-adoption usage? Investigating the negative and positive antecedents of disruptive technology continuous adoption intentions. Ind. Mark. Manag. **63**, 42–52 (2017). https://doi.org/10.1016/j.indmarman.2017.01.003

12. Jia, Q., Guo, Y., Barnes, S.: Enterprise 2.0 post-adoption: extending the information system continuance model based on the technology-Organization-environment framework. Comput. Human Behav. **67**, 95–105 (2017). https://doi.org/10.1016/j.chb.2016.10.022

13. Bayerl, P., Lauche, K., Axtell, C.: Revisiting group-based technology adoption as a dynamic process: the role of changing attitude-rationale configurations. MIS Q. **40**(3), 775–784 (2016). https://doi.org/10.25300/MISQ/2016/40.3.12

14. Makkonen, H., Johnston, W.J., Javalgi, R.G.: A behavioral approach to organizational innovation adoption. J. Bus. Res. **69**(7), 2480–2489 (2016). https://doi.org/10.1016/j.jbusres.2016.02.017

15. Jahanmir, S.F., Cavadas, J.: Factors affecting late adoption of digital innovations. J. Bus. Res. **88**, 337–343 (2018). https://doi.org/10.1016/j.jbusres.2018.01.058

16. Chiyangwa, T.B., Alexander (Trish), P.M: Rapidly co-evolving technology adoption and diffusion models. Telem. Inform. **33**, 56–76 (2016). https://doi.org/10.1016/j.tele.2015.05.004

17. Bian, Y., Kang, L., Zhao, J.L.: Dual decision-making with discontinuance and acceptance of information technology: the case of cloud computing. Internet Res. **30**(5), 1521–1546 (2020). https://doi.org/10.1108/INTR-05-2019-0187

18. Furneaux, B., Wade, M.: An exploration of organizational level information systems discontinuance intentions. MIS Q. **35**(3), 573–598 (2011). https://doi.org/10.2307/23042797

19. Jacobsen, D.I.: Adopting and refining e-services — the role of organization size. Public Organ. Rev. **18**(1), 111–123 (2016). https://doi.org/10.1007/s11115-016-0364-0

20. Kaushik, S.: Critical parameters for successful process automation. Softw. Qual. Prof. **20**(4), 22–32 (2018)

21. Cooper, L.A., Holderness, D.K., Sorensen, T.L., Wood, D.A.: Robotic process automation in public accounting. Account. Horiz. **33**(4), 15–35 (2019). https://doi.org/10.2308/acch-52466

22. Syed, R., et al.: Robotic Process automation: contemporary themes and challenges. Computers in Industry **115**, 103162 (2020). https://doi.org/10.1016/j.compind.2019.103162

23. Appelbaum, D., Nehmer, R.: The coming disruption of drones, robots, and bots – how will it affect CPAs and accounting practise? CPA J. **87**, 40–44 (2017)

24. Asatiani, A., Penttinen, E.: Turning robotic process automation into commercial success – case OpusCapita. J. Inf. Technol. Teach. Cases **6**(2), 67–74 (2016). https://doi.org/10.1057/jittc.2016.5

25. Tietz, W., Cainas, J.M., Miller-Nobles, T.L.: The bots are coming... to intro accounting. Strateg. Finan. **102**(2), 24–29 (2020)

26. Lacurezeanu, R., Tiron-Tudor, A., Bresfelean, V.: Robotic process automation in audit and accounting. Audit financiar, **18**(160), 752–770 (2020). https://doi.org/10.20869/AUDITF/2020/160/752

27. Gotthardt, M., Koivulaakso, D., Paksoy, O., Saramo, C., Martikainen, M., Lehner, O.: Current state and challenges in the implementation of smart robotic process automation in accounting and auditing. ACRN J. Finan. Risk Perspect. **9**(1), 90–102 (2020). https://doi.org/10.35944/jofrp.2020.9.1.007

28. Figueiredo, A.S., Pinto, L.H.: Robotizing shared service centres: key challenges and outcomes. J. Serv. Theory Pract. **31**(1), 157–178 (2020). https://doi.org/10.1108/JSTP-06-2020-0126

29. Frey C.B., M.A. Osborne, M.A.: The Future of Employment: How Susceptible are Jobs to Computerisation. https://www.oxfordmartin.ox.ac.uk/downloads/academic/The_Future_of_Employment.pdf. Accessed 17 Spet 2013

30. Mir, U.B., Sharma, S., Kar, A.K., Gupta, M.P.: Critical success factors for integrating artificial intelligence and robotics. Digit. Pol. Regul. Gov. **22**(4), 307–331 (2020). https://doi.org/10.1108/DPRG-03-2020-0032

31. Brougham, D., Haar, J.M., Tootell, B.: Service sector employee insights into the future of work and technological disruption. New Zealand J. Employ. Relat. **44**(1), 21–36 (2019)

32. University of Tampere, Työhyvinvoinnin tutkimusryhmä. Referenssit – Palvelukeskuksille robotteja, työhyvinvoinnin edistäminen (PaRot) – Digikaveri kollegaksi, miten uhka muutetaan mahdollisuudeksi (TSR) 2017–2018. https://research.tuni.fi/tyohyvinvointi/referenssit/. Accessed 5 May 2021

33. Walsham, G.: Interpretive case studies in IS research: nature and method. Eur. J. Inf. Syst. **4**(2), 74–81 (1995). https://doi.org/10.1057/ejis.1995.9

34. Meyers, M.D.: Qualitative Research in Business and Management, 3rd edn. SAGE Publications Ltd., London (2020)

The Role of Agile Pockets in Agile Transformation

Gitte Tjørnehøj[⊠]

Aarhus University, Århus, Denmark
gitj@btech.au.dk

Abstract. Agility spread from the bottom of organizations, carried by software professional acting as grassroots in promoting and integration of agility, until the practices and approaches got foothold in the organizations. This is unique in comparison with other major transformation of the industry such as that of the capability maturity model (CMM). This paper aims at understanding this agile phenomenon and the underlying informal structure and dynamics. The paper suggests to theorizes this as agile pockets of professionals playing an important role in the agile transformation. Especially four arch types of agile pockets are suggested to be crucial in pivotal situations of the transition. The theory and arguments are based in the well-known theory Communities of practice by Etienne Wenger [21, 22], but needs more development and empirical validation.

Keywords: Agile transformation · Agile pockets · Balancing agility · Software professionals · Communities of practice

1 Introduction

Since a group of knowledgeable software professionals more than 20 years ago gathered in a mountain hut to formulate some common ground for their different experiences with light-weight system development practices, [2] the agile trend and methods have been discussed and tested in practice and research.

Hundreds of papers have been published on the agile methods and the transformations that have happened in the organizations. For example, Hoada et al. [11 p.61] found "28 S(systemtic)L(iterature)R(eview)s focusing on ten different A(gile)S(systems)D(evelopment) research areas: adoption, methods, practices, human and social aspects, CMMI, usability, global software engineering, organization, embedded systems, and product line engineering" in their tertiary review of structured literature reviews within the field and Dingsøyr et al. [7] reports that five special issues on agile software development have been published from 2003 until 2011.

Early the challenge of the new agile approaches to the traditional plan-driven approaches was enroute towards a paradigm shift, but quickly settled as a discussion of home-grounds for the approaches and how to balance these to fit the complexity and risk of the organizations [3, 4]. Magdaleno et al. [14] in their structured literature review concludes that most of the literature and practice strives to reconcile the traditional

© Springer Nature Switzerland AG 2022
M. Themistocleous and M. Papadaki (Eds.): EMCIS 2021, LNBIP 437, pp. 756–766, 2022.
https://doi.org/10.1007/978-3-030-95947-0_53

approaches with agility. However it is a difficult and uncertain endeavor to transform traditional organizations towards integrating and balance agility.

Ebert and Paasivaara [9] have found "that introducing agile development means changing the culture and mind-set. It requires long-term commitment, big investments, and customization to a company's specific situation." [9 p. 103]. The challenges and success factors apparently class with CMMI [16] and other elaborate prescriptive frameworks. The discussion on agile scaling in academia has been substantial. See for example [15] and [7].

This paper study the dynamics of the dissemination of agility in large organizations in the software industry. The narrative of agility advocates that it spread from the bottom of the organizations, through software professionals acting as grassroots in promoting and integration of agility, until the practices and approaches got foothold in the organizations. Dingsøyr et al. [8 p.31] make clear that agile development "started as a bottom-up movement among software practitioners and consultants", before he address scaled agility.

This adoption journey is the total opposite to that of many other methods over the years. For example, the introduction of the CMM(I) [12, 16] just years before. The Maturity model and its prescriptive key process areas seemed to catch the attention of management in mainly large software companies. The model prescribes planned and controlled top-down improvement processes. Hansen et al. [10] sum these aspects up. Despite harsh criticism and many failed investments, the CMM(I)-wave put software quality, project planning and standardization on the agenda for good [5].

When agility came along many companies had already for a while gabbled with CMM(I) [16] with varying success. The agile manifest challenged these common software practices in organizations and the powerful actors in the market advocating standardization, statistic control and disciplined methods. Due to its simplicity and professional focus it quicky won the minds and hearts of many software engineers, making it spread bottom-up. The origin and how the agile approaches was disseminated and adopted has been exceptional.

Inspired by the history of the agile transformations I have witnessed in large software organizations in general and in one specifically I propose that agile pockets of professionals played an important role in the agile transformation as their persistent experimentation with agile approaches, their insistence that agility is plain useful and not least their results, slowly moved agility on the agenda of management. My interest is to understand the underlying informal structures and dynamics of the agile pockets and the traditional organization that these professionals worked in and their role in the overarching agile transformation of the organization. Stated as a research question it is "how can the bottom up and professional driven dissemination of agility in traditional organizations be theorized?".

There are two parts of the interest. First, how the agile pockets can be described and theorized. Section 2 suggests that agile pockets of professionals can be theorized as communities of practice of an opposing nature to the surrounding community of practice that is the traditional organization. It is a matter of creating, consolidating and not least disseminating knowledge and new practices. The agile pockets and the organizations are disconnected yet interdependent, and the dynamics of their interplay are revolving around shifting modes of action (experimenting and consolidating knowledge) and the circumstances at their bordering boundaries. Second, understanding their role in the dissemination of agility into the traditional organizations. Based in this understanding of agile pockets a framework of four archetypes of agile pockets that are especially important at pivotal times of the dissemination is developed in Sect. 3.

The theory gain solidity from being based in the well-established theory of communities of practice by Wenger [21]. Even though this is a first attempt to conceptualize the important role of the professionals in the transformations, it is not sufficient, and validation or further development through future research is needed. This is elaborated on in Sect. 4.

2 Theorizing Agile Pockets

The general definition of a pocket has proved useful to define properties of an agile pocket [6]. The nature of agile pockets as an experimenting space populated by devoted people can to a large extent be captured by the well-known theory communities of practice [21]. There are however noticeable aspects of this phenomenon that would best be captured by other theories. For example, the role of non-human actors and technology. However, for simplicity this first attempt to define and theorize agile pockets will rest on Wengers elaborate theory [21, 22].

2.1 Defining Agile Pockets

By definition in Oxford English Dictionary [6] a pocket is "A small area, population, etc., contrasted with or differing from its surroundings in some respect". Weick and Quinn [20] state in their paper on Organizational Change and Development, that "most organizations have pockets of people somewhere who are already adjusting to the new environment". These classic understandings of pockets and pockets of innovation is the base for the concept agile pocket.

The agile pocket is a small population surrounded by a traditional organization differing by their capability to sense changes in the environments and adjust in accordance.

In this case the pocket realizes the agile trend as important early and start to absorb it into their practice without mandate.

2.2 Characterizing Agile Pockets and Their Surroundings

Following most literature on balancing agile and traditional practices, traditional organizations are likely to be conservative and bureaucratic, but good at assuring quality, safety, and control [3]. The system development practices in these organizations often rest on defined processes, discipline, plan, and management-control. Principles that go well with a centralized, rather bureaucratic, and top-down managed company culture [17]. They tend to be slow to change because their complexity and size, and complacency that successful business path tend to bring [18].

Contrary to this, the employees in the pockets sense that "things speed up" outside, markets become unstable and new methods exploiting the emerging conditions evolve. Realizing this, sparks an interest in innovating own practice.

The duality of the pocket and the organization can beneficially be described as two disconnected but bordering communities of practice [22] because both has their distinct cultures and practices.

Of cause not all organizations are as petrified as described above. They can easily possess some dynamic capabilities [13] which is an important factor that influences their attitude towards the agile pocket. An organization with dynamic capabilities will presumably be less hostile than a petrified organization.

Focusing on the agile pocket alone in the light of the interpretation as a community of practice [21], I suggest that the agile pockets form around an interest or passion for in this case agility. It has a core of devotees defining the focus and providing leadership for the pocket and closer to the boundaries we find members less involved and less knowledgeable on the topic of interest. The core members of the pocket will form a group of specialized expert employees as they tend to be absorbed in their interest, agility. The members close to the rim are likely to better span the interest and outside world, which allow for another kind of learning and experiences through integration.

2.3 On Boundaries and Bridges in the Stress Zone

Communities of practices have boundaries defined by how they experience the "outside". In theorizing agile pockets, it has become clear that it is important to consider both bordering communities to understand the phenomena of agile transition. As they define themselves both by what they are and what they are not, that is what is outside the boundary, understanding the shared border as a double boundary allows better investigation of this stress zone.

Transfer across the bounding zone of knowledge, practices, funding, and other resources can be non-existing or inert. The boundaries can exist due to structures, habits, lack of knowledge, prejudice, fear, power struggles and all that can add barriers between the two. A classic example of such a boundary is ignorance or even hostility from the organization towards nonconforming employees that for example substitute given processes with agility. Facing the other way, the population in the pockets may distance themselves from the given processes and not least the management enforcing them. What is described here are two boundaries acting out, not one shared because the parties do not interact directly about the matter.

A boundary that can be permeable depending on the relationship and degree of difference between the two communities. If the community is open, the boundary is fluent if closed it is impervious. A permeable boundary will allow information and knowledge to ooze from the pocket to the surroundings and the other way. For example, the permeability will be low if the community is mainly defined by the specializing core or if the practices in the bordering communities are directly opposing. When agility first appeared, it was regarded as an opponent paradigm [1] and thus the permeability of boundaries then was likely to have been very low.

Over time bridges may develop spanning the stress zone. Bridges are any practice, event, relation, structure, or others that allow for interaction and supports funding, knowledge and practice sharing to and from the pocket. That is, any element that increases the permeability of the boundaries. One example is when the organization accepts, fund and monitor experiments with agility, that are planned controlled and carried out by professionals in the pocket. The formalization helps the management to feel in control and thus embrace the experiments, while the professionals having funding and mandate accept being monitored as the formalizations ensures their control of the experimentation and own work.

Bridges can emerge as established custom or be negotiated and agreed more formally. The members close to the borders of a community are often visiting the pocket to learn. They may be associated with both communities and are thus likely to act as boundary spanners helping bridges to develop. A member continuously belonging to both communities may well develop into an informal bridge by carrying knowledge and insights from one to the other. However, also outsiders of both communities for example external consultants may serve as boundary spanners and help bridge building.

2.4 Dynamics of Agile Pockets

In the inspiring case, the bureaucratic and inert nature of the organization was the backdrop for the innovative pockets to form. Many of the software professionals that joined the agile pockets, had felt frustrated in their work for example because of considerable time spend on overhead activities such as documentation and detailed planning and rigid architectures, technological debt and superficial compromised requirements that forced them to compromise their work standards. The distance between these professionals and the organization thus existed before the agile pockets developed. Sharing both the frustrations and the interest in agility fueled the growth of the pockets.

Individuals here and there met with or heard from colleagues from a broader professional community about agility and external consultants experienced in agility, entering the organization pushed the awareness. Sharing stories, knowledge and ideas between the interested professionals grew new informal communities exploring the new trend. Professionals in the core of the pockets explicitly experimented with agile working practices in their projects and started to accumulate knowledge and coin lessons learned and advice to share with peers.

Agile pockets are characterized by innovating own practice through experiments trying agility in different set-ups. Theoretically [20] learning processes can be described as iterations of un-freezing practice, experimentation, and re-freezing of ideas into new practices shifting between inquiry and improvisation, and rebalancing emergent changes into visible patterns and practices meaningful to the members. For this to happen the pockets need to be self-organizing, emergent, and unbound to keep the spirit of inquiry [22]. On the other hand, if they do not have critical mass and show progress, they cannot sustain sufficient learning energy [21].

2.5 Summarizing Agile Pockets

This is how I theorize the pockets of professionals that I denote "agile pockets". Figure 1 illustrates the concept. It displays an agile innovative pocket and an opposing traditional organization separated by a double boundary, that form a stress zone, and hinder transfer of knowledge, practices, and funding. Boundaries have a degree of permeability depending on the openness of the community and can be spanned by bridges of very diverse nature. The visiting members at the rim of the agile pocket are likely to play an important role as boundary spanners and bridge builders in the maturing of the agile pocket. Learning is the nature of agile pockets. Agile specialization develops in the core of the pocket while integrative activities happen at the rim.

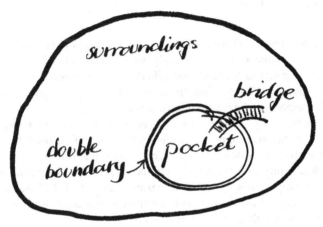

Fig. 1. This figure illustrates the concept agile pocket as summarized above. All elements are crucial to understand the nature of an agile pocket.

3 The Role of Agile Pockets in Agile Transformation

In this section a framework is developed that suggest 4 different types of agile pockets to be found during agile transformation processes and that shifts between the types of pockets can help explain the trajectory of the transformation.

3.1 Four Types of Agile Pockets

I propose that 4 types of agile pockets exist, characterized along 2 dimensions. First shifting between modes of learning (freezing and unfreezing) as part of successful practice improvement is a matter of creating, consolidating and not least disseminating knowledge and new practices. Second the relation between the agile pocket and the surrounding organization as played out in the stress zone determine the potential transfer of knowledge and new practices, that is the dissemination of agile practices. This is basically dependent on the permeability of the boundaries and the existence of bridges (Fig. 2).

	Unfreezing	Freezing
Permeable	Ephemeral Focus: Slightly twisted agility Status: Accepted Change: Exploring	Sustained Focus: Balancing agility Status: Embraced Change: Continuous change
Impervious	Emergent Focus: Agility Status: Unnoticed Change: Experimenting	Routinized Focus: Integrating agility Status: Absorbed Change: Episodic change

Fig. 2. The four types of agile pockets: emergent, ephemeral, sustained and routinized and their interest, status, and type of change.

Emergent Agile Pockets. These pockets are characterized by the loose coupled relations between professionals that have recently become aware of and interested in agility. As described before they may already individually be in opposition to their surrounding traditional organization. A core of utterly interested professional quickly form an agile pocket, while members at the rim are few or absent.

The double boundary must be characterized as impervious as the organization is ignorant of the recent and frail pocket, while the members of the pocket are not paying attention to the given processes in their fascination of original agility.

They explore agility with a strong spirit of inquiry, hardly reflecting on own practice in the light of the approaches. Here the unfreezing of the established practices takes the extreme form of neglect and their experimentation is to a large degree determined by the vivid inspirational milieu in the environments.

Under these circumstances it is unlikely that learning or funding flow between the two unless accidentally.

Ephemeral Agile Pockets. Ephemeral pockets have more members, but now with an overweight of members at the rim. This place strain on the core, as their informative and coordinating role increases leading to a drop in learning energy. Despite more members the pocket does not possess critical mass to sustain their activity.

The surrounding organization is aware of the pocket as information and ideas has started to ooze through carried or supported by the many interested visiting professionals that are still based in the traditional organization. Information, requests, and suggestions will also ooze from the organization to the pocket and may distract the core members. They or some of them may reflect on the established practice and the need of their colleagues and thus correct their explorative activities towards slightly adapted agile approaches.

The pocket is accepted in the organization as information about agility has reach management from other external sources, so they see potential in the pocket. However no or only few resources flow to the pocket. To satisfy the accepting surroundings in return for resources the agile pocket initiates freezing their gained knowledge in to lessons learned. Ephemeral pockets are vulnerable due to the lack of resources, critical mass, and the diffuse extra demands. They are at risk dying away.

Sustained Agile Pockets. The sustained agile pocket is embraced by the surrounding organization to an extent where the pockets nearly work for and is founded of the organizations.

Some of the early core members may have left the pocket and a new core may have formed as the focus and interest have shifted towards balancing of agility and traditional processes. The members of the pockets are still professionals sharing an interest in agility, but they, even the core, have closer relation to the surrounding organization, which provide high permeability of the boundaries.

They accept the goal of the innovation to be improved practice based in previously given processes and the mode of learning to be plan and controlled series of experiments providing incremental continuous change. Middle managers and change agents may now be visiting at the rim as the learning mode has shifted towards freezing activities – or in the other order.

Routinized Agile Pockets. Routinized agile pockets are absorbed by the surrounding traditional organization. The pockets are redesigned to serve the need for integration of agility as defined by the surroundings. Employees are assigned to become members of the pocket and the boundary spanners appointed to control the information flow. All or most interaction between the pocket and the surroundings go through formalized bridges such as meetings, documents and reports thus the boundaries must be characterized as impervious. An important activity in the pocket is testing of practice proposals from the surroundings. The core of pocket leaks members as many interested in agility do not thrive in the controlled settings. The agile pocket has become routinized through institutionalization allowing only for episodic and often mandatory change. Management controls the pocket; the profile of the members has changed and the modes of learning has been squeezed into a classic change patterns.

Following the four types clockwise may very well be the life cycle of an agile pocket, but not necessarily. Any of the types can easily die out if the interest in or support from the surroundings deteriorates, and new may form about other or more specialized interests. Studying practice, one would expect to see many hybrid forms. If the conceptualization turns out to be useful when validated patterns found and confirmed could spark other interesting discussions and investigations. For example: Which transformation strategies did work in agile transformation and why? And how can management and professionals navigate in such bottom-up transformation journeys? Are these transformation patterns feasible in the agile transformations of today?

4   Validation and Further Development

The validity of this theorizing comes from that it is heavily based in a well-established theory of how humans form learning communities around interests. The theory defines both the pockets and the surrounding organization as communities of practice and describe their interaction as the relations that communities of practices have to their environments. In this sense the theory is on stable ground.

However, it is not established if the concept and theory of agile pockets is at all relevant for understanding early agile transformation as part of the more than 20 years history of agility as assumed in the introduction. Neither is the usefulness of the 4 types of agile pockets in analyzing a specific agile transformation shown.

These two aspects are of cause limitations that hinder the use of the proposed explanatory theory as is. Thus, this section is dedicated sketching three future studies that can validate and develop the theory. First, a literature study will look for cases, theoretical constructs and concepts that regard the phenomenon agile bottom-up transformation. The findings will evaluate if the theory has relevance and allow for discussion and development. Second, the explanatory capability of the theory will be tested out on selected existing cases already analyzed through other theoretical lenses. Third, in case the phenomenon can still be found a more traditional case study is suggested.

As the research field of agile transformation is mature, it displays both a very broad scope of research outlets, much literature, and sliding conceptualization. For example, the slide from balancing to scaling that is so prominent. This will make carrying out a classic structured review very difficult. Also, the aim of the proposed literature study is a broad search for contributions about a specific empirical phenomenon and compile an understanding based in very differing material of that specific phenomena.

My choice is to carry out an integrative literature review in line with [19]. This kind of reviews allow for broader research question and a search approach driven by conceptualization of the field, often through adopting an analytical framework. In this case I suggest adopting the theory in question as the guiding conceptual model and develop and alter it as literature is found and integrated. The specific searches and search terms needs to be just as well-structured and documented as in the structured review, but the integrative review method allow for processing the found literature in differing ways and to over time develop the search focus and inclusion criteria. The research question that will outset this review is "What is known in the field of IS and bordering fields about bottom-up agile transformation?". The first search will address bottom-up agile transformation and synonyms. Depending on the literature found the searches may follow different leads that all contribute to the shared conceptualization. A review like this certainly set the spotlight on the proposed theory which was the goal.

While evaluating the literature found, appropriate case studies will be taken aside. That is case studies reporting from early agile transformation and that allow for characterizing the transformation process of that specific case. This means that they need to report data from the case in some detail. For all the case studies the case will be summarized and characterized and mapped to the framework of the 4 types of agile pockets. Both cases that relate to the framework and those that do not provide evidence for the evaluation of the framework. This research will confirm – or not the usefulness of the framework both for understanding the historical phenomenon, but also if it can provide guidance forthgoing.

After these two studies new versions of the theory can be suggested if it is valid. To test next generation of theorizing agile pocket, the search for an ongoing bottom-up driven agile transformation must start. When found, an in-depth single case study is proposed to add thick descriptions of how this phenomenon play out in practice. The concrete findings may be helpful for providing advice for management and professionals.

5   Conclusion

In the article a theory of agile pockets of professionals and their role in agile transformation of traditional organizations are put forward. The theory building aim at understanding the exceptional bottom-up patterns of the early adoption of the agile approaches. The theory is suggested validated and developed through an integrative literature study and an in-depth single case study of a case in which the patterns under investigation still play out.

An interesting reflection over this theme is that introducing a framework for scaled as mentioned in the introduction class with elaborate frameworks as CMMI [15] when it comes to adoption challenges [8]. An interesting question is "what happened to the agile pockets in agile transformations scaling agility?"

References

1. Baskerville, R., Pries-Heje, J., Madsen, S.: Post-agility: what follows a decade of agility? Inf. Softw. Technol. **53**(5), 543–555 (2011)
2. Beck, K., et al.: The Agile Manifesto (2001). http://agilemanifesto.org/
3. Boehm, B., Turner, R.A.: Using risk to balance agile and plan-driven methods. Computer **36**(6), 57–66 (2003). https://doi.org/10.1109/MC.2003.1204376
4. Boehm, B., Turner, R.B.: Balancing Agility and Discipline: A Guide for the Perplexed. Addison-Wesley Professional, Boston (2003)
5. Chaudhary, M., Chopra, A.: CMMI Overview. In: CMMI for Development, pp. 1–7. Apress, Berkeley, CA (2017)
6. Dictionary, O.E.: Oxford English Dictionary Online. Mount Royal College Lib., Calgary (14: Douglas, C.S. 2011) (2004)
7. Dingsøyr, T., Nerur, S., Balijepally, V., Moe, N.B.: A decade of agile methodologies: towards explaining agile software development, pp. 1213–1221 (2012)
8. Dingsøyr, T., Falessi, D., Power, K.: Agile development at scale: the next frontier. IEEE Softw. **36**(2), 30–38 (2019)
9. Ebert, C., Paasivaara, M.: Scaling agile. IEEE Softw. **34**(6), 98–103 (2017)
10. Hansen, B., Rose, J., Tjørnehøj, G.: Prescription, description, reflection: the shape of the software process improvement field. Int. J. Inf. Manag. **24**(6), 457–472 (2004)
11. Hoda, R., et al.: Systematic literature reviews in agile software development: a tertiary study. Inf. Softw. Technol. **85**, 60–70 (2017)
12. Humphrey, W.: Managing the Software Process, Addison-Wesley Publishing Company, Reading, Massachusetts (1989)
13. Lawson, B., Samson, D.: Developing innovation capability in organisations: a dynamic capabilities approach. Int. J. Innov. Manag. **5**(03), 377–400 (2001)
14. Magdaleno, A.M., Werner, C.M.L., Araujo, R.M.D.: Reconciling software development models: a quasi-systematic review. J. Syst. Softw. **85**(2), 351–369 (2012)
15. Ozkaya, I.: If it does not scale, it does not work! IEEE Softw. **36**(2), 4–7 (2019)
16. Paulk, M.C., Weber, C.V., Garcia, S.M., Chrissis, M.B., Bush, M.: Key practices of the capability maturity model, Version 1.1. CARNEGIE-MELLON UNIV PITTSBURGH PA SOFTWARE ENGINEERING INST (1993)
17. Rose, J., Aaen, I., Nielsen, P.: Managerial and organizational assumptions in the CMM'S. In: Software Processes and Knowledge: Beyond Conventional Software Process Improvement, pp. 9–28 (2008)

18. Singh, R., Mathiassen, L., Mishra, A.: Organizational path constitution in technological innovation. MIS Q. **39**(3), 643–666 (2015)
19. Torraco, R.J.: Writing integrative literature reviews: Guidelines and examples. Hum. Resour. Dev. Rev. **4**(3), 356–367 (2005)
20. Weick, K.E., Quinn, R.E.: Organizational change and development. Annu. Rev. Psychol. **50**(1), 361–386 (1999)
21. Wenger, E.: Communities of practice and social learning systems. Organization **7**(2), 225–246 (2000)
22. Wenger, E.: Communities of practice: learning as a social system. Syst. Thinker **9**(5), 2–3 (1998)

Author Index

Printed in the United States
by Baker & Taylor Publisher Services